Europe, 1780

FINLAND
(Sweden)

Gulf of Bothnia

Lake Onega

Lake Ladoga

Åbo
Vyborg
Helsingfors
St. Petersburg

Stockholm

Saaremaa

Gotland

URAL MTS.

Volkhov

Öland

Baltic Sea

Moscow

RUSSIAN EMPIRE

Volga

Dvina

Neman

Minsk

Danzig (Poland)

RUSSIA

Vistula

POLAND

Warsaw

Kiev

Don

Bug

Donets

Silesia

Oder

Vistula

Dnieper

Volga

Carpathian Mts.

Southern Bug

Galicia

HABSBURG POSSESSIONS

Dniester

Prut

Vienna

Buda
Pest

Tisza

Moldavia

Hungary

Caspian Sea

Maros (Mures)

Transylvania

Siret

Drava

Kuban'

Sava

Belgrade

Wallachia

Bucharest

Danube

CAUCASUS MTS.

Morava

Black Sea

Dinaric Alps

RAGUSA

Balkan Mts.

MONTENEGRO

Maritsa

ASIA

OTTOMAN EMPIRE

Vardar

Constantinople

Sea of Marmara

Aegean Sea

NAPLES

Ionian Sea

Athens

N

0   200   400 mi.
0   200   400 km

Crete
(Ottoman Empire)

Cyprus

SCRIBNER LIBRARY OF MODERN EUROPE

EUROPE
1789 TO 1914

AG

EDITORIAL BOARD

SCRIBNER LIBRARY OF MODERN EUROPE

EUROPE
1789 TO 1914
ENCYCLOPEDIA OF THE
AGE OF INDUSTRY AND EMPIRE

Volume 2

Colonies to Huysmans

John Merriman and Jay Winter

EDITORS IN CHIEF

CHARLES SCRIBNER'S SONS

An imprint of Thomson Gale, a part of The Thomson Corporation

Detroit • New York • San Francisco • San Diego • New Haven, Conn. • Waterville, Maine • London • Munich

Europe 1789 to 1914: Encyclopedia of the Age of Industry and Empire

John Merriman
Jay Winter
Editors in Chief

For permission to use material from this product, submit your request via Web at http://www.gale-edit.com/permissions, or you may download our Permissions Request form and submit your request by fax or mail to:

Permissions Department
Thomson Gale
27500 Drake Road
Farmington Hills, MI 48331-3535
Permissions Hotline:
248-699-8006 or 800-877-4253 ext. 8006
Fax: 248-699-8074 or 800-762-4058

LIBRARY OF CONGRESS CATALOGING-IN-PUBLICATION DATA

Europe 1789 to 1914 : encyclopedia of the age of industry and empire / edited by John Merriman and Jay Winter.
　　　　p. cm. — (Scribner library of modern Europe)
　　Includes bibliographical references and index.
　　ISBN 0-684-31359-6 (set : alk. paper) — ISBN 0-684-31360-X (v. 1 : alk. paper) — ISBN 0-684-31361-8 (v. 2 : alk. paper) — ISBN 0-684-31362-6 (v. 3 : alk. paper) — ISBN 0-684-31363-4 (v. 4 : alk. paper) — ISBN 0-684-31364-2 (v. 5 : alk. paper) — ISBN 0-684-31496-7 (ebook)
　　1. Europe–History–1789-1900–Encyclopedias. 2. Europe–History–1871-1918–Encyclopedias. 3. Europe–Civilization–19th century–Encyclopedias. 4. Europe–Civilization–20th century–Encyclopedias. I. Merriman, John M. II. Winter, J. M.
　　D299.E735 2006
　　940.2'8–dc22
　　　　　　　　　　　　　　　　　　　　　　　　　　　　　2006007335

This title is also available as an e-book and as a ten-volume set with
Europe since 1914: Encyclopedia of the Age of War and Reconstruction.
E-book ISBN 0-684-31496-7
Ten-volume set ISBN 0-684-31530-0
Contact your Gale sales representative for ordering information.

Printed in the United States of America
10 9 8 7 6 5 4 3 2 1

CONTENTS OF THIS VOLUME

CONTENTS OF OTHER VOLUMES

C

VOLUME 3

M

VOLUME 5

T

MAPS OF EUROPE, 1789 TO 1914

The maps on the following pages show the changes in European national boundaries from 1789 to 1914, including the unification of Italy and of Germany.

Europe, 1789

— International border
• City

0   100   200 mi.
0   100   200 km

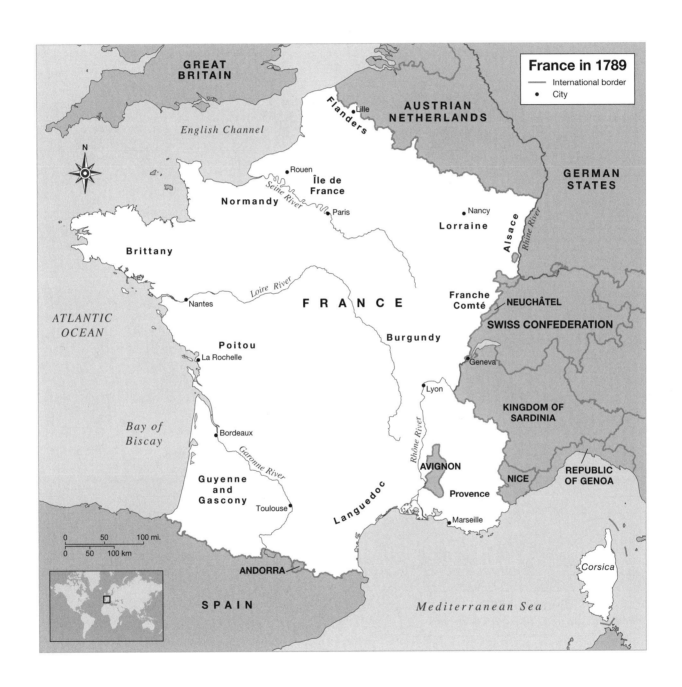

France in 1789

— International border
• City

GREAT
BRITAIN

English Channel

N

Flanders

• Lille

AUSTRIAN
NETHERLANDS

GERMAN
STATES

• Rouen

Île de
France

Seine River

Normandy

• Paris

• Nancy

Lorraine

Alsace

Rhine River

Brittany

Loire River

F R A N C E

• Nantes

*ATLANTIC
OCEAN*

Poitou

• La Rochelle

Burgundy

Franche
Comté

NEUCHÂTEL

SWISS CONFEDERATION

• Geneva

Lyon

KINGDOM OF
SARDINIA

*Bay of
Biscay*

• Bordeaux

Garonne River

Rhône River

AVIGNON

Provence

NICE

REPUBLIC
OF GENOA

Guyenne
and
Gascony

• Toulouse

Languedoc

• Marseille

0   50   100 mi.
0 50 100 km

Corsica

ANDORRA

S P A I N

Mediterranean Sea

Europe, 1815

— Boundary of the German Confederation, 1815

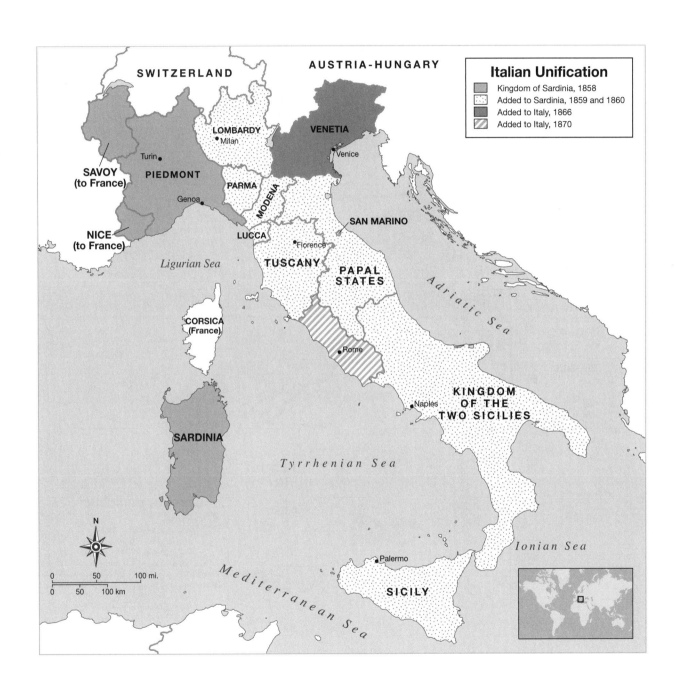

Italian Unification

- Kingdom of Sardinia, 1858
- Added to Sardinia, 1859 and 1860
- Added to Italy, 1866
- Added to Italy, 1870

SWITZERLAND

AUSTRIA-HUNGARY

LOMBARDY
Milan

VENETIA
Venice

Turin
PIEDMONT

SAVOY
(to France)

PARMA

MODENA

NICE
(to France)

Genoa

LUCCA

SAN MARINO

Ligurian Sea

TUSCANY
Florence

PAPAL
STATES

Adriatic Sea

CORSICA
(France)

Rome

KINGDOM
OF THE
TWO SICILIES

Naples

SARDINIA

Tyrrhenian Sea

Ionian Sea

N

Palermo

0   50   100 mi.
0   50   100 km

SICILY

Mediterranean Sea

German Unification
Prussia, 1865
Added to Prussia, 1866
Added to form North German Confederation, 1867
Added to form German empire, 1871
Boundary of German empire, 1871
Route of Prussian armies in Austro-Prussian War
Route of German armies in Franco-Prussian War
Battle sites
SWEDEN
DENMARK
North Sea
Baltic Sea
N
Schleswig
Holstein
Hamburg
Mecklenburg
Hanover
Pomerania
West Prussia
East Prussia
PRUSSIA
Brandenburg
Berlin
Posen
Vistula R.
NETHERLANDS
Westphalia
BELGIUM
Rhine R.
Elbe R.
Oder R.
RUSSIA
Ems
Thuringia
Saxony
Silesia
Sedan
LUX.
Frankfurt
Prague
Sadowa
To Paris
Metz
Main R.
Lorraine
Bavaria
Württemberg
AUSTRIA-HUNGARY
FRANCE
Alsace
Baden
Munich
Hohenzollern
Danube R.
Vienna
SWITZERLAND
0 50 100 mi.
0 50 100 km

Europe, 1914

International border

ICELAND

ATLANTIC OCEAN

NORWAY

SWEDEN

North Sea

Baltic Sea

DENMARK

UNITED KINGDOM

NETH.

BELG.

LUX.

GERMANY

R U S S I A

FRANCE

SWITZ.

AUSTRIA-HUNGARY

Caspian Sea

ITALY

ROMANIA

Black Sea

SERBIA

MONT.

BULGARIA

ALBANIA

PORTUGAL

ANDORRA

SPAIN

GREECE

OTTOMAN EMPIRE

PERSIA

Spanish Morocco

Tunisia (Fr.)

Mediterranean Sea

Morocco (Fr.)

Algeria (Fr.)

Libya (It.)

Egypt (Br.)

COLONIES. Colonies are, strictly speaking, settlements of people outside the borders of their home nations, usually in lands considered to be "empty" or "barbarous." These settlements remain colonies while they retain their subordinate ties with their mother countries. Once they become independent of those countries, or incorporated in them, they lose their colonial status. The word *colonies* is also used, however, in other ways. The overseas territories acquired and ruled from Europe as a result of the imperialism of the seventeenth to the twentieth centuries were generally called colonies, though the element of "settlement" here was usually minimal. This entry will cover this meaning also, though it is important to be aware of the differences between the two kinds. Lastly, the word *colonies* and its derivatives—*colonization, colonialism,* and so on—can be employed metaphorically. Thus, one reads of "colonies" of artists in famous beauty spots; or of birds; or of *barnkolonier,* holiday camps for poor children in the nineteenth-century Swedish countryside. These, however, are peripheral usages.

In the original and more correct sense of the word, all peoples have colonized. Otherwise they would not have spread. Most of this happened very early in history: original humanity pushing out from the Great Rift Valley of east Africa, for example; Stone Age man and woman colonizing the north as the last ice age receded; or Polynesians settling in present-day New Zealand around 1000 C.E. In the nineteenth century this process of contiguous colonization was still going on in many places: the Russians in Siberia, white Americans in their "west," Scandinavians in Norrland, and so on. In most of these latter cases it was at the expense of weaker indigenous inhabitants, who were either extirpated or enslaved. Even where they were treated better, the indigenes could still feel "colonized." This was because this kind of colonization invariably involved expropriation. The natives might be technically assimilated, but their cultures, polities, and property rights were not.

SETTLEMENT COLONIES

When the word *colonies* was used in the early nineteenth century, however, it nearly always referred to Europe's overseas colonies. These went back to the sixteenth century in the cases of Spain and Portugal, but were still being added to as late as the 1850s. The underlying dynamic beneath this movement was emigration, which in its turn was caused by perceived overpopulation in Europe: in the century from 1750 the population of some countries nearly doubled. Whether this really was too great for Europe to sustain on its own is doubtful; even at this time improved methods of agricultural production were enabling the population to be fed, and more people meant bigger markets, which should have kept them all employed. It may have been the organization of European societies that was at fault, causing more poverty and distress than were strictly necessary. At the time, however, an easier solution to these problems—especially for those who resisted social change—seemed to be the vast "virgin" territories that had recently been discovered and opened up across the oceans, which offered instant opportunities for new starts for millions of Europe's unfortunates. Between 1850 and 1910 (earlier figures are less reliable) a total of roughly 34 million men, women, and children emigrated out of Europe; 15 million of them from Britain, 6 million from the German-speaking countries, 6 million from Italy, 2.5 million from Spain, and nearly 2 million from Scandinavia. Most of these ended up in the United States, which by this time, of course, had long broken its formal colonial ties. But a significant number, particularly Britons, were instrumental in establishing new or sustaining older colonies overseas; of which the most significant were British North America (later Canada); the Australian colonies (federated in 1900); New Zealand; British and "Afrikaner" South Africa; and French Algeria. These—and a handful of lesser colonies—were the nineteenth century's characteristic colonies in the strict sense of the word.

The colonies sometimes posed difficult questions for contemporaries, though not usually for ethical reasons. Colonization was felt to be fundamentally different from "imperialism," which was widely felt to have an unsavory side. Colonists did not dominate or exploit other people; instead they used their own honest labor and enterprise to tame and cultivate wildernesses. That at any rate was the theory, which of course sat uneasily with the reality, in many places, of shocking treatment of the indigenes. A few European humanitarians were aware of the latter and did what they could to prevent it—under the aegis for example of the Aborigines Protection Society, founded in Britain in 1837. Generally, however, the attitude toward "natives" of this degree of "primitiveness" was that they were bound to die out in the face of the "superior civilization" of the West, sadly but naturally. Besides, to try to control the process—hold back land-hungry European emigrants—would require a greater exertion of metropolitan imperial power than was thought to be desirable from the point of view of either "economy" or "freedom." For the great virtues of colonization in this sense—the particular qualities that marked it off from imperialism—were its cheapness and its democracy. Hence the pride that many Britons, especially, felt for it. It was a means by which British liberties were

French colonial officers in Africa. Illustration by Joseph Beuzon in the *Journal des Voyages,* 4 December 1898. The French colonials literally put themselves on a higher plane than the native Africans. MARY EVANS PICTURE LIBRARY

being spread throughout the world. Most people saw these liberties culminating in colonial independence, with Canada, Australia, and the rest all going the way of the United States. It was this that justified colonization in liberal terms.

Most of the problems attaching to the British settlement colonies arose from the metropolitan government's relations with them in the meantime. An initial problem concerned restrictions on trade: the nineteenth-century colonial system (or mercantilism), which had been one of the reasons for tension with the thirteen American colonies. That however was solved as British commercial policy was progressively liberalized during the early nineteenth century, ending with the repeal of the Navigation Acts (forbidding certain colonial trades with foreign countries) in 1849. Thereafter most disputes in this area were over the colonies' wishes

TABLE 1

Growth of colonies' commodity trade with Britain (in £ millions)			
	Canada	Australia	New Zealand
Exports to Britain 1854	7.1	4.3	–
Imports from Britain 1854	6.0	11.6	0.3
Exports to Britain 1910	20.6	38.6	20.9
Imports from Britain 1910	26.2	27.7	8.7

SOURCE: Brian R. Mitchell, with the collaboration of Phyllis Deane, *Abstract of British Historical Statistics*, Cambridge, U.K., 1962, pp. 318–325.

to impose trade tariffs of their own. There were also controversies over migration to the colonies, which was resented on both sides: in Britain by those who felt themselves *forced* to emigrate by an unjust economic system at home; and in the colonies by those who suspected Britain of merely dumping its undesirables on them. This was most obvious, of course, in the case of colonies used for transporting convicts, such as New South Wales and Tasmania. (That practice stopped in 1868.) Then the colonists' treatment of the "natives" could raise concerns, either from a humanitarian viewpoint or if it provoked uprisings that the metropolitan government then had to help suppress. This was particularly serious in settlement colonies with large and relatively powerful native populations, such as New Zealand, South Africa, and (French) Algeria. Unsurprisingly, it was this kind of colony that saw most of the fiercest colonial wars of the time. Lastly, in two areas of British colonial settlement, North America and South Africa, other Europeans—French and Dutch respectively—challenged British dominance, which was then only reasserted after more damaging and expensive wars: in Canada in 1837–1840 and South Africa in 1899–1902. Otherwise, however, Britain's settlement or "white" colonies were the easiest parts of its much vaster empire to run. For the most part they ran themselves.

Their economic value to Britain was considerable, even after the end of mercantilism meant that it could not exploit that value exclusively. All furnished markets for the products of its factories—and markets of a familiar kind: customers with the same kinds of tastes as at home—as well as

(increasingly) investment opportunities. They also furnished Britain with food and raw materials, such as Canadian fur, timber, and wheat; Australian and New Zealand wool and mutton; and South African fruits and gold. Table 1 shows the growth of the colonies' commodity trade with Britain between the 1850s and the 1900s (in £ millions).

It should be emphasized that these figures never represented a majority of Britain's trade, far more of which (around 70 percent) was done with the European continent and the United States throughout this period. The same is true of emigration from Britain, which before 1904 went predominantly to the United States. The importance to Britain (and other European countries) of colonial emigration may have been its function as a social and political safety valve: forced to stay and suffer at home, people might have turned more easily to revolt. Advocates of colonization also pointed to the importance of the markets it created to the employment and living standards of those who stayed at home. These assessments, however, are still controversial. The economist John Atkinson Hobson argued that the colonial safety valve merely released employers from the necessity of paying higher wages to their domestic workers, which would have been equally stimulating for industry, and more socially beneficial.

Toward the end of the nineteenth century, under the impact of trade depression and international economic competition, many in Britain came to regard their settlement colonies more positively. Colonies were now considered assets that should not after all be allowed to "separate" naturally from Britain, but instead be encouraged to deepen their ties with Britain, for example, through a free trade area (often called a *Zollverein*, after the German) and some form of political federation that would enable them to pool their "freedoms" with Britain's. Most of the colonies' peoples of British origin were still intensely loyal to their mother country—possibly even more "imperialist" in this special sense than stay-at-home Britons were. (Empire Day, for example, came to be officially celebrated in Canada and Australia long before it was in Britain.) The main proponent of imperial federation at this time was Joseph Chamberlain, British colonial secretary from 1895 to 1903. His scheme failed, however, partly through domestic resistance, on "free trade" principles, to the discriminatory tariffs that would obviously be necessary to establish tariff preference for the colonies, and partly because even the most theoretically "loyal" of colonials were reluctant to compromise their practical independence. Nonetheless, this movement sowed the seeds of the idea that later became the (much looser) *commonwealth,* a term that originated in the 1880s.

Other European countries did not have this option to the same extent. The closest comparison is probably France's colony of Algeria, established by conquest over the local Arabs, which boasted a European population of 740,000 (about 70 percent French, most of the rest Spaniards and Italians) by 1911. Most of these immigrants were farmers, often vine cultivators, who had been granted concessions of land (seized from the locals) by the French government, in a manner similar to the American "homestead" system. Germany's main settlement colony, German Southwest Africa (present-day Namibia), was acquired in 1885 but had attracted only thirteen thousand European settlers by 1910. Most German, Scandinavian, and Italian emigrants colonized the United States instead, and so very soon became "lost," in most senses, to their mother countries. When those countries talked of establishing "colonies" from the 1880s onward, it was usually of the other, nonsettlement kind.

DEPENDENT COLONIES

Most nonsettlement, or dependent, colonies originated in the policy—or phenomenon—of "imperialism" that took hold of Europe in the later nineteenth century. They were possessions populated mainly by non-Europeans, and for both that and climatic reasons were considered unsuitable for white people to live in, except in the more temperate parts of some of them (such as—in Africa—the Kenyan and Cameroon highlands). The Europeans who lived there did so temporarily, simply in order to rule or police or proselytize or exploit the natives. They had generous leave provision (to protect their health), and almost all returned to their home countries at the ends of their careers. They numbered very few: little over two thousand British men (always men) ruling India for most of the nineteenth century, for example, lording it over a population of

something like two hundred million. It is this that distinguished these "dependent" colonies from the "settlement" ones, from the point of view both of the Europeans and of the indigenes.

One similarity was that both types of colonies were there to be exploited, in one way or another, for the benefit of Europeans. That however should not be taken entirely negatively. "Exploitation" simply means, literally, to make the best of something, and the line that enlightened people took in the nineteenth century was that the greatest benefits were mutual: that European commerce with colonial peoples, and the "development" of their resources, were bound to profit the latter too. Unfortunately things did not always work out this way. The main problem came when the freedom of labor was impaired. It was difficult to see many of the benefits of commerce, for example, trickling down to slaves. At the start of the nineteenth century most European nations with overseas colonies still practiced slavery in them, but slavery was whittled down in most colonies over the course of the next sixty-five years. Spain abolished the practice in 1811 (except in Cuba), Britain in 1833, Sweden in 1843, France in 1848 (though there had also been a brief ban during the revolutionary years), Denmark in the same year, and Holland in 1863, before the United States at last caught up in 1865. (Several contemporaries pointed out how much better off the blacks of the southern states would have been if the United States had still been part of the British Empire in 1833, which is not entirely convincing—with American support the proslavery lobby in Britain might have been able to resist emancipation longer—but illustrates the point that imperialism, as distinct from colonization, can be an agent of liberation as well as of tyranny.)

The demise of European slavery did not bring an end to adverse labor conditions in the colonies by any means. Many colonial nations retained quasi-slave systems: apprenticeship, the corvée, indentured labor, taxation to force natives to work for money wages, and so on. These systems were enough to keep the British and Foreign Anti-Slavery Society—whose motto (from the mouth of a kneeling African) was "Am I not a Man and a Brother?"—going from its creation in 1839 (on

The French Flag Hoisted at Timbuktu. Illustration from *Le Petit Journal*, 12 February 1902. The capture of the remote African trading town of Timbuktu by troops under the command of French Marechal Joseph Joffre in 1894 was deemed an important step in securing control of northern Africa. The figures in the foreground are Tuareg tribesmen, who had formerly controlled the area. PRIVATE COLLECTION/ BRIDGEMAN ART LIBRARY/ARCHIVES CHARMET

the foundation of other societies stretching back to 1787) to the twenty-first century. The Dutch colony of Java and King Leopold II of Belgium's Congo Free State (present-day Zaire) were two of the most notorious examples of exploitation of this kind. And it could be claimed that workers are never basically free under colonial or any other kind of capitalism in any case. However, the claim made by most colonial powers during the nineteenth century was that by exploiting their overseas territories, they were enriching both themselves and the natives: providing the material means by which the latter could be furnished with schools, hospitals, and so on, and ultimately—in some cases—the infrastructure for independent statehood. The British colonial governor Frederick, Lord Lugard (1858–1945),

coined the term *dual mandate* to describe this. Colonial power was legitimized by the way—or insofar as—it served both parties.

"NATIVE POLICY"

Colonies could not simply be exploited, however. They also had to be ruled. In most cases European intervention had destroyed indigenous political systems, so something needed to be put in their place. In addition, the claim to be benefiting native societies—improving the lot of the locals, and "advancing" them in "civilization"—required at least a show of a positive and constructive "native policy" to make it convincing. Colonial rulers could not be content with merely keeping the natives down, though this was how some of them—particularly the parvenu Germans—behaved. They had taken on a great responsibility here. All agreed on this (or pretended to), but not on how precisely that responsibility should be exercised.

The way this responsibility was exercised depended on two broad factors. The first was the colonists' worldview: their general perceptions of themselves and their European culture (or cultures) in relation to these "others" that they were seeking to "raise." Usually that could be described as arrogant, though we should not perhaps be too hard on the confident, "progressive" societies that composed most of Europe at that time for not being aware that material wealth, power, and even "progress" do not necessarily indicate "superiority" in any other sense. The crucial consideration was to what they attributed that superiority. If it was their race, then this could not be encouraging to those who did not share the Europeans' ethnic advantage. Racist theories were common in certain intellectual circles in Europe at this time, and unflattering racial stereotypes were even more common, in popular literature, for example. This of course is not only a characteristic of the west and in the west, it was not the whole story. There was also a strong seam of race-egalitarian thought, represented by that Anti-Slavery Society slogan, but associated more with the French, which may have grown weaker during the later nineteenth century—it certainly came more under attack—but still remained, to inspire more charitable "native policies."

An example is the government of British India prior to 1857, whose objective, according to the historian and member of the Supreme Council of India Thomas Babington, Lord Macaulay (1800–1859) was to raise up "a class of persons Indian in colour and blood, but English in tastes, in opinions, in morals, and in intellect," which would of course have been unthinkable without the assumption of equality (quoted in Stokes, p. 45). Macaulay foresaw India eventually ruling itself on parliamentary lines. French colonial policy had much the same official aim. "All the efforts of colonisation," declared a government resolution passed in 1889, "must tend to propagate amongst the natives our language, our methods of work, and gradually the spirit of our civilization" (quoted in Roberts, p. 103). When that was achieved, even the blackest of Africans would be accepted as a full-fledged Frenchman (or woman), no less. Here were two cases where the colonists' worldview augured well for their alien subjects, albeit only in theory and not without a downside.

The downside was the lack of respect for native cultures that this view implied. Because all humans were the same, they could all aspire to the same standards; and because western European standards were the most "advanced," these were what all non-Europeans were entitled to. This of course was also the missionary view, with the Christian revelation and ethic representing that peak of human enlightenment, compared with which every other religion and value system was measured, to its inevitable detriment. (Again, Christianity is not unique in this regard.) To become truly respected, therefore, and demonstrate their genuine equality with white men and women, non-Europeans needed to abandon their customary—backward, superstitious, dark, as they were usually characterized—ways.

There was an alternative, based on a different worldview that did not regard European culture as necessarily the summit, or as universally applicable, but simply as something that had grown historically out of a particular set of circumstances, just as had all other cultures in the world. This more conservative and relativist view was more likely to tolerate cultural and social differences. It is found in Britain after the Indian Mutiny (1857–1858), for example, in the criticisms that Benjamin Disraeli (1804–1881) made of the Macaulay kind of policy, on the grounds that it did not respect what

he called Indian "nationality." This is why, he claimed, the Indians—solid conservatives, just like himself—had mutinied. It is also found in a new doctrine of colonial government, called "Indirect Rule," or "rule the native on native lines," which became fashionable in British colonial circles around the turn of the twentieth century. In parts of West Africa in particular, the Colonial Office made a point of preserving indigenous forms of government and society (where they remained to be preserved)—the old emirs of northern Nigeria, for example—and encouraging political development along those traditional lines. But this doctrine had its disadvantages too. It could betray racist assumptions, if different cultures were seen as racially determined (as one of the original ideologues of indirect rule, the traveller Mary Kingsley, believed). It alienated natives who actually craved Western enlightenment and suspected indirect rule of being designed to keep them in the dark and, so, "down." And it was, in truth, more a device to excuse nondevelopment in Africa and to avoid provoking instability, in a situation in which—as we have seen—Britain could afford far too few men on the ground to be able to do much positive "good" for the natives.

In fact ideology—"worldviews" and the like—probably had less impact on "native policy" in the colonies than the sheer day-to-day circumstances faced by those who were supposed to implement those views under a myriad of pressures from (for example) the natives themselves, their kings and chiefs, European settlers, traders, capitalist "developers," missionaries, the officials' own corruptibility, and simple material factors like geography and climate. The idea that colonial practice was significantly determined by metropolitan colonial policy is mistaken in most cases. Even in France's case, where abstract theory was valued most highly—they even had an *école coloniale* to inculcate it—and where policy was supposed to be most consistent across all its colonies—with administrators being transferred between them in a way that was unusual in the British Empire—"assimilation" (into French culture) was more often a distant aspiration than an actual achievement. It had a few successes. Cochin China (the southern part of present-day Vietnam) became largely Frenchified culturally. Senegal in West Africa became so politi-

A French officer teaches farming methods to natives of Madagascar. Lithograph from the French publication *Le Petit Journal*, 7 November 1896. PRIVATE COLLECTION/BRIDGEMAN ART LIBRARY/ARCHIVES CHARMET

cally assimilated that in 1914 it furnished the French National Assembly with its first *député* of pure African descent: Blaise Diagne (1872–1934), who later rose to be undersecretary of state for the colonies. (In 1921 he resisted national independence for Senegal: "We French natives," he said, "wish to remain French, since France has given us every liberty" [quoted in Crowder, p. 22].) Elsewhere, however, the policy foundered on the rocks of local native opposition, white settler prejudice, and a gradual change of mind in the metropole in the early twentieth century in the face of these difficulties. In the case of the British colonies, the failure of ideology was less, because there was less ideology to fail (after 1857) and because what there was of it was in any case more pragmatic than France's. What Britain had done was to acknowledge the limited possibilities and capacities of any form of colonial government, and work within these. This made it difficult for it to fly high—in "raising" the natives—but unlikely that it would fall very far.

Other colonial powers never even attempted to fly, though they sometimes paid lip service to the ideal, in order to reassure more "progressive" countries like Britain and France. "For bringing civilisation to the only part of the earth which it has not yet reached, and enlightening the darkness in which whole peoples are plunged is, I venture to say, a crusade worthy of this century of progress," claimed King Leopold II of the Belgians, grandly, in 1876. "Need I say that no selfish motives impel me?" (quoted in Brunschwig, 1960, p. 35). In fact Leopold's Congo Free State was one of the most selfishly and oppressively run of all the European colonies in the 1890s—mainly by private capitalist companies with the kind of amoralism that typifies capitalism in its most unrestrained state—provoking a Europe-wide campaign against the "Congo atrocities," which led to the Belgian parliament's taking the country out of his hands completely in 1908. Portugal's older established African colonies of Portuguese West Africa (present-day Angola), Portuguese East Africa (present-day Mozambique), and São Tomé and Príncipe were run on semifeudal lines, with large estates (*prazos*) owned by colonists or their mulatto descendents, who had absolute authority over the Africans, or *colonos* (in fact Portugal was the last of the European colonial powers to outlaw even formal slavery, in 1869); until the early 1890s, when pressure from the more "progressive" European nations forced Portugal into wholesale reforms. These reforms promised to bring the benefits of a more enlightened kind of capitalism to its colonies but were never properly implemented. (They promised education for Africans, for example, but as late as 1909 only three thousand Africans and mulattos were attending primary school throughout the huge colonies of Angola and Mozambique.) In the 1900s yet another humanitarian campaign, against the cruel treatment of what were effectively slaves in the cocoa islands of São Tomé and Príncipe, made Portugal a virtual pariah among colonial nations.

CONCLUSION

The word *colony* covers a multitude of phenomena. Hence it is difficult to generalize about the significance of the actual thing. In the strict sense of the term, the colonization of countries like Canada and Australia was inevitable, the only surprising thing being that it was by people who came from so far away. This was probably a bad thing for the indigenes, with whom they shared little in common culturally; but it is by no means certain that the Aborigines of Australia, for example, would have been treated any more kindly by migrant Indonesians (their closest neighbors). What the European peopling of these parts of the world did was to spread European or "Western" institutions wider and so help strengthen their hold on the world. Whatever its importance, this kind of colony should not be confused with the other main use of the term in the nineteenth century, to describe communities of non-Europeans ruled absolutely—albeit in some cases paternalistically, at least in intention—by the European governing classes. That was a different phenomenon, raising other problems that were dealt with in widely divergent ways, according to the culture and society of the European nation that was doing the governing in any particular instance, and circumstances and pressures on the ground. Most nineteenth-century colonies of both kinds were given up during the second half of the twentieth century, though it is arguable that—rather like slavery—the thing itself survived under other names.

See also **Colonialism; Emigration; Imperialism; Missions; Race and Racism.**

BIBLIOGRAPHY

Brunschwig, Henri. *Mythes et réalités de l'impérialisme colonial français, 1871–1914.* Paris, 1960. Translated by William Granville Brown as *French Colonialism, 1871–1914: Myths and Realities.* New York, 1966.

Clarence-Smith, Gervase. *The Third Portuguese Empire, 1825–1975: A Study in Economic Imperialism.* Manchester, U.K., 1985.

Cornevin, M., and R. Cornevin. *La France et les Français outre-mer.* Paris, 1990.

Crowder, Michael. *Senegal: A Study of French Assimilation Policy.* London, 1967.

Duffy, James. *Portuguese Africa.* Cambridge, Mass., 1961.

Gann, Lewis H., and Peter Duignan. *The Rulers of German Africa, 1884–1914.* Stanford, Calif., 1977.

———. *The Rulers of British Africa, 1870–1914.* London, 1978.

Gann, Lewis H., and Peter Duignan, eds. *Colonialism in Africa, 1870–1960.* Vol 1: *The History and Politics of Colonialism, 1870–1914.* London, 1969.

Gifford, Prosser, and Wm. Roger Louis, eds. *Britain and Germany in Africa: Imperial Rivalry and Colonial Rule.* New Haven, Conn., 1967.

Hammond, Richard J. *Portugal and Africa 1815–1910: A Study in Uneconomic Imperialism.* Stanford, Calif., 1966.

Henderson, William O. *The German Colonial Empire, 1884–1919.* Portland, Ore., 1993.

Judd, Denis, and Peter Slinn. *The Evolution of the Modern Commonwealth, 1902–1980.* London, 1982.

Knoll, Arthur J., and Lewis H. Gann, eds. *Germans in the Tropics: Essays in German Colonial History.* New York, 1987.

Mansergh, Nicholas. *The Commonwealth Experience.* London, 1969. Dated, but good on the British settlement colonies.

Porter, Andrew, ed. *The Oxford History of British Empire.* Vol. 3: *The Nineteenth Century.* Oxford, U.K., 1999.

Roberts, Stephen H. *History of French Colonial Policy.* London, 1929.

Slade, Ruth. *King Leopold's Congo: Aspects of the Development of Race Relations in the Congo Independent State.* New York, 1962.

Stokes, Eric. *The English Utilitarians and India.* Oxford, U.K., 1959.

Wehler, Hans Ulrich. *The German Empire, 1871–1918.* Translated by Kim Traynor. Dover, N.H., 1985.

Woodruff, William. *Impact of Western Man: A Study of Europe's Role in the World Economy, 1750–1960.* London, 1966. Excellent for figures.

BERNARD PORTER

COMBINATION ACTS.

The Combination Acts of 1799 and 1800 struck a blow against the legal formation of trade unions in Britain. While the acts banned combinations of workers as well as employers, in practice they were used only against workers who bargained collectively for shorter hours or higher pay. The immediate cause of the 1799 act was a petition by employers frustrated by the successful combination of London millwrights. Instead of regulating just one trade, the government of William Pitt adopted the suggestion of the abolitionist member of Parliament William Wilberforce and proposed a ban on all combinations. According to the 1799 act, which became law on 12 July, workers could do none of the following: join together to demand new wages or working conditions, encourage anyone to stop working, refuse to work with others, prevent an employer from hiring, or attend meetings or collect funds for illegal purposes. As a result, trade unions were effectively declared illegal. The act also called for "summary jurisdiction" and thus targeted the often slow legal process about which employers complained. Rather than trial by jury, a magistrate would issue a ruling and could sentence convicted workers for up to three months in prison or two months of hard labor. Workers submitted petitions against the act to Parliament. The amended 1800 act, which became law on 29 July, addressed the workers' grievances, although the bulk of the 1799 act remained intact. Most notably, the 1800 act declared combinations of employers illegal (to prevent decreased wages, additional hours, or increased work); required two magistrates instead of one; and prohibited employers from acting as magistrates in cases involving their own trade.

A convenient way to understand the historical debate over the Combination Acts is to consider whether the acts marked a minor or major shift in British labor history. Arguments in favor of continuity point to several features. First, it can be argued that the acts merely rationalized and extended what had already been established in statutes and common law across the eighteenth century. Bans on combinations had long been in force in particular trades and locations through legislation that affected, for example, tailors in 1721, woolen workers in 1726, hatters in 1777, and papermakers in 1796. In fact, most anti-union prosecutions were based not on the Combination Acts but on older legal restraints like breach of contract, the 1563 Statute of Artificers punishing unfinished work, and the common law for conspiracy. The Combination Acts were thus nothing exceptional or new. Moreover, the acts did not prevent the formation of trade unions, which despite the need for secrecy continued to grow. Nor did they prevent episodes of "collective bargaining by riot," most commonly associated with the machine-breaking activity of the Luddites. Combinations survived in part because of sympathetic magistrates, aristocrats, and gentry more concerned with preventing disorder and preserving the social structure than with upholding the precise letter of the law; because of difficulties in distinguishing illegal combinations from legal self-help or friendly societies; because it was still legal for journeymen to organize for the purpose of petitioning Parliament and magistrates; and because the burden of prosecution fell on employers who risked the loss of skilled workers and income. Yet strong arguments also support the opposing view, that the Combination Acts represented a major change in British policy. Regardless of the number of prosecutions under the acts, they could nevertheless promote a climate of fear among workers and of confidence among employers. The threat of prosecuting workers was real, whether or not legal action was ever taken. The Combination Acts can also be seen as a reaction to elite fears of political sedition during the Napoleonic Wars. On this reading, the acts were an anti-Jacobin measure meant to intimidate political reformers as well as workers. And lastly, it can be argued that the acts embraced market forces at the expense of an older paternalism. Magistrates arbitrated existing contracts but no longer regulated wages, and they could also approve the hire of nonapprenticed labor. The historiographical debate outlined above demonstrates that the Combination Acts accompanied the transition from a commercial to an industrial economy. The paradox of trade unions and the Combination Acts existing side-by-side helps to explain why the acts' repeal, promoted by the well-organized efforts of Francis Place and Joseph Hume, came so easily in 1824. A subsequent outbreak of strikes resulted in an 1825 law that restricted the rights of trade unions. Consequently, unions occupied contested legal territory for much of the nineteenth century.

See also **Great Britain; Luddism; Working Class.**

BIBLIOGRAPHY

Orth, John V. "English Combination Acts of the Eighteenth Century." *Law and History Review* 5, no. 1 (1987): 175–211. A detailed description of trade-union legislation, including the 1799 and 1800 Combination Acts, with a summary of the historical debate and relevant sources.

Thompson, E. P. *The Making of the English Working Class.* New York, 1964

ELISA R. MILKES

COMMERCIAL POLICY.

Commercial policy can be defined as a set of all measures that affect directly the amount, composition, and direction of trade flows. It differs from fiscal and monetary policies, which affect trade indirectly via the effect on the exchange rate and capital flows. The set of possible measures is quite wide, but nineteenth-century governments had a pretty small range of options for their commercial policy. They resorted almost exclusively to duties on imports or (less frequently) exports. A duty is a tax that opens a wedge between domestic and world prices: a duty on imports raises the domestic price beyond "world" prices, while a duty on exports lowers it below the "world" prices.

In the nineteenth century, each sovereign country was free to set its own duties (often collected in a tariff). In some cases, these duties were intended to be permanent, but in others they were used as bargaining chips in trade negotiations with other countries. During negotiations, each country tried to lower the partner's duties on its exports and keep as much of its own duties as possible. The failure of negotiation between two states could trigger a trade war, like that between France and Italy from 1887 to 1892. Each "belligerent" state imposed higher duties on imports from its rival until one of them backed down. In contrast, a successful negotiation ended up in a trade treaty, which specified cuts in duties of each partner for a given number of years. On top of this, most treaties included the so-called MFN (most favored nation) clause—that is, the cuts on duties were automatically extended to all other countries. Thus, if successful, bilateral negotiations could yield an outcome not too dissimilar from that of the system of multilateral negotiations in the early twenty-first century (the General Agreement on Trade and Tariffs, or GATT, and its successor). However, the nineteenth century was more fragile, as the overall reduction in duties depended on the decisions of several sovereign states.

TRADE RESTRICTIONS

By 1789, European states had a long history of trade restrictions tempered only by their inability to control smuggling effectively. Some countries had mitigated the most extreme excesses of mercantilist policies in the late eighteenth century, but still protectionism prevailed throughout the whole Continent, with the notable exception of the Netherlands. The 1800s marked a potentially epochal change, with the establishment of the Continental Blockade (1806) against the imports of British manufactures. For the first time in history, most of the Continent constituted an area of free trade, clearly dominated by France. The experiment, however, did not outlast the fall of the empire, and after 1814 all European states returned to protectionist policies. The next fifty years featured a slow process of liberalization in most countries, with three major turning points. The first was the formation of the *Zollverein* (custom league) among German states around Prussia (1834), the first step toward German unification. The second was the abolition of protection to wheat (Corn Laws) in the United Kingdom (1846), which was the main barrier to free trade in agricultural goods in Europe. The third was the Cobden-Chevalier Treaty between France and the United Kingdom (1860), which strongly reduced French duties on manufactures. Many other countries followed this example in the next decade, so that the late 1860s and 1870s stand out as a period of almost wholly unfettered trade. The tide had changed already at the end of 1870s, with new tariffs on manufactures in Italy (1878), Austria (1878), Germany (1879), and France (1881). However, the key factor was the fall in prices of wheat, caused by the decline in transportation costs. This "grain invasion" triggered a protectionist backlash. In the 1880s and early 1890s, most European countries protected wheat-growing and approved comprehensive protectionist tariffs, such as the Meline tariff in France (1892). Protectionist policies allegedly prevailed all over Europe until World War I, with few exceptions, such as the United Kingdom, the Netherlands, and Denmark. The structure of tariffs differed among countries, but as a rule raw materials and coal were exempt, while duties were higher than average for three classes of goods: (a) the products of industries whose development the state wanted to foster, often for their own military interest (e.g., iron and steel industry or shipbuilding); (b) the products of industries that the state wanted to shield from foreign competition—such as wheat cultivation; and (c) goods that could not be produced at home, which the state taxed in order to raise revenue (the so-called fiscal duties).

Estimating the level of protection

The traditional narrative is mainly based on anecdotal sources (parliamentary debates, pamphlets, and so on) and on the history of legislation. The former reflect heated contemporary political debates, and thus are likely to be biased, while a list of duties and treaties is hardly sufficient to assess the nature of a trade policy. Unfortunately, to estimate the level of protection is far from easy. The simplest and most widely used measure is the average nominal protection—that is, the ratio between custom revenue and total imports. As expected, the (scarce) data for the first half of the century show a decline, from perhaps 25–35 percent in the 1820s–1830s to a trough at around 5–10 percent in the 1860s and 1870s. Average protection rose again to peak at around 20 percent for the main Continental countries in the early 1890s. The average nominal protection decreased in the 1900s, for the combined effect of new trade treaties and of the rise in prices, which reduced the impact of specific duties. European protection was lower than in the overseas countries and even at its peak, prewar protection was much lower than in the 1930s and even in the 1950s or 1960s. Indeed, only in the 1980s, after half a century of liberalization, did aggregate protection returned to the level of 1914. Thus, prima facie, the data contrast with the traditional story of fortress-like protectionist countries. But a low level of protection is consistent with the great increase in world trade during the second half of the nineteenth century.

Unfortunately, the average nominal protection may not be an accurate measure of the true level of protection. A successful protectionist policy would change the composition of trade, reducing the share of protected goods. A really successful one would block imports altogether, with paradoxical consequences: a country that prevents imports of all goods but one with prohibitive duties would appear less protectionist than another that levies a uniform 5 percent duty on all goods. This is not just a theoretical curiosity: John Vincent Nye has shown that, from the 1820s to the 1870s, average protection in "fortress" France was lower than in the United Kingdom, which raised quite heavy duties on wine and other "fiscal" goods. Thus the average duty is likely to underestimate the "true" level of protection. The bias depends on the sensitivity of imports to increases in prices (elasticity), and thus can differ between countries. Its extent can be assessed using more sophisticated measures: for instance, average nominal protection is a good proxy of "true" protection in Italy. However, computing these alternative measures is quite data-intensive and thus average duty is still widely used.

Protection and economic growth

How did trade policy affect nineteenth-century economic growth in Europe? In theory, the effects of protection are straightforward. First, it changes the structure of the economy. Duties attract factors (land, labor, capital) to the protected sector(s), which would grow, or at least not shrink, under the impact of foreign competition. Thus protection increases the share of protected import-competing goods, at the expense of the production of other imports, of exports, and of nontradable goods (such as services). This change is bound to reduce total production (GDP, gross domestic product) and income or welfare, as free trade yields the optimal allocation of factors. Second, the structural change also affects the distribution of income by factor. In fact, each sector uses a different mix of factors. Under free trade, each country would specialize in productions that use its more abundant—and thus cheaper—factor: a land-scarce, labor-abundant country would specialize in labor-intensive productions as textiles and would import land-intensive products such as wheat. In contrast, protection favors import-competing activities, which use the scarce factor more intensively. These effects are all static, as each change in duty causes a one-off reallocation of factors. But protection is likely to have long-term effects as well. On one hand, less competition from imports reduces the efficiency of domestic producers. On the other, the development of new industrial activities, although fostered with protection, might be beneficial in the long-term. These dynamic gains and losses are often invoked by supporters and adversaries of protection, but their existence is extremely difficult to prove and to measure.

Thus the historical analysis of trade policy must tackle three separate, although interrelated issues: (1) How did it affect the GDP and its overall growth? (2) How did it affect the structure of the economy? and (3) How did it affect the distribution of income? The two first questions concern the effect of trade policy on modern economic growth. For the nineteenth century, this is tantamount to asking how much the state fostered (or hindered) modern economic growth and structural change, as duties were by far the most important instrument available for microeconomic intervention. The third question is important not only for its own sake, but also because potential gains and losses determine the political process of tariff making. It is not surprising that trade policy was very controversial.

Historical debates Trade policy is quite controversial among historians as well. The debate focuses on its effects on modern economic growth, especially in the second half of the nineteenth century. The period before 1850 is somewhat neglected, partly because data are quite scarce and partly because modern economic growth had not yet started in most European countries.

Most historians tend to have quite a positive view of the effects of protection. Paul Bairoch (1976) argues that the faster growth rate in the Continental countries relative to the United Kingdom is evidence of the success of protectionist policy. This reasoning is not convincing. First, all things being equal, economic growth tends to be inversely proportional to initial income, as backward countries catch up with the more advanced ones. Thus Continental countries were bound to grow faster than the United Kingdom. Second, no matter how high the actual growth rate in GDP was, it could have been even higher with a different trade policy. More broadly, any simple post hoc propter hoc (after this, therefore because of this) inference from a visual inspection of data may be misleading. Modern economic growth is a hugely complex process, which cannot be attributed to one factor only without an in-depth analysis. Since the late twentieth century, economic historians have started to work on the issue, employing theoretically more sound approaches.

The static effect of protection of the allocation of resources can be investigated with the so-called Computable General Equilibrium (CGE) models.

They compare the actual level and composition of GDP by sector and the distribution of income with those that would have prevailed if the country had adopted free trade (or any other alternative policy). Most of these models show a substantial effect of protection on the distribution of income. For instance, according to Jeffrey Williamson, the Corn Laws increased the rents of British wheat growers by about a half, at the expense of domestic wheat consumers and of foreign consumers of British manufactures. Kevin O'Rourke estimates that the duty on wheat in the 1880s increased the returns to land by about 10 percent in France and Sweden. In contrast, the effects on the structure of the economy and on total income were not that great: the GDP of a free-trade Italy in 1911 would have been 2 to 3 percent higher than the actual one. These estimates are quite precise, but results depend on the assumptions of the model about the mobility of factors across sectors. Furthermore, by their nature, the CGE models offer only a partial view, as they measure only static effects of protection from the allocation of resources.

The dynamic effects could be captured by the other approach, the econometric estimate of the effect of protection on the growth rate of a group of countries. This approach improves on the "simple" post hoc ergo propter hoc inference, à la Bairoch, as the effect is estimated as the net of other determinants of growth, such as the level of development of the country, the amount of human and physical capital, and so on. Contrary to theoretical predictions, and to the evidence for the period after 1950, some scholars find a positive relation between tariffs and rate of growth before 1914. This positive effect seems to be much stronger for rich overseas countries than for European ones and, among these latter, for the core countries of northwestern Europe. In contrast, tariffs hampered growth in the European periphery. There are several possible explanations for these results. Perhaps tariffs on industrial goods accelerated the transfer of manpower from low productivity sectors (agriculture) to high productivity ones (manufacturing), or gave domestic producers breathing space to develop. Or perhaps the result simply reflects errors in measurement of protection using average tariffs.

Thus progress in recent times has been substantial, but the economic analysis of the effects of nineteenth-century trade policy is still far from providing a clear answer to the three questions. Much more work, for additional countries, is necessary. One can tentatively conclude that before 1913 trade policy had much smaller effects, for good or bad, on modern economic growth in European countries than has been assumed on the basis of the contemporary debate. Protection was not so high, and distortions, although substantial in some specific cases, were not huge. This conclusion is confirmed by a 2003 work by Antoni Estevadeordal, Brian Frantz, and Alan M. Taylor. They estimate that world trade would have been a third higher without tariffs in 1870 and in 1913 (note that their measure of protection does not change much between the two dates). But this conclusion is provisional. Overall, one must not forget the political consequences of protectionist propaganda. It depicted world trade as a deadly fight among countries and foreign goods as invaders that were jeopardizing the very livelihood of the population. This propaganda undoubtedly contributed to the breakdown in international relations that led to World War I.

FREE TRADE AND PROTECTIONISM

By and large, protectionist trade policies prevailed in nineteenth-century Europe, although protection was mild compared with the 1930s or the 1950s. The short interlude in the 1860s and 1870s and the free-trade policy of the United Kingdom and of other "minor" free-trade countries were exceptions that seem to confirm the rule. This practice contrasted with the almost unanimous opinion of professional economists, who regarded free trade as highly beneficial. This gap between theory and practice started to open in the eighteenth century. Until then, with very few exceptions, economists had believed that the wealth of a nation depended on its stock of gold, which had to be accumulated by running a positive trade balance, that is, by exporting more than importing. This mercantilist ideology was seriously challenged only in the 1750s and 1760s. Enlightenment thinkers such as the Italian Ferdinando Galiani (1728–1787) or the French Physiocrats advocated freedom in grain trade, and the economist Adam Smith (1723–1790) made a compelling case for overall liberalization in his *Wealth of Nations* (1776). Free trade is first and foremost a straightforward extension of the principle of the invisible hand—the market knows better than the state how to allocate resources. Furthermore, free trade increases the size of the market and hence the scope for the division of labor and specialization, which in Smith's view is the source of long-term economic growth. David Ricardo (1772–1823), in *Principles of Political Economy and Taxation* (1817), and other "classical" economists such as James Mill (1773–1836) and Sir Robert Torrens (1780–1864) sharpened Smith's argument. Specialization is not driven by absolute advantage (that is, by the comparison of costs between domestic and foreign producers) but by comparative advantage (that is, by the comparison of production costs among alternative uses of available factors). A country can gain from trade even if it could produce the imported good at a lower cost, provided that it could produce something else at even lower relative costs. Therefore, all countries have something to gain from free trade. The principle of comparative advantage is still the cornerstone of trade theory. Economists have later found some exceptions, such as Robert Torrens's (1780–1864) terms-of-trade argument for duties by large countries, Graham's external-economies argument for protection of industries with increasing returns, or James Brander's and Barbara Spencer's late-twentieth-century strategic-trade argument for export subsidies. However, these exceptions hold true only under very special circumstances: in almost all cases, free trade would deliver the optimal allocation of existing resources, given the available technology. In contrast, most arguments for protection focus on its alleged dynamic benefits. They hold that short-term losses from protection can be outweighed by long-term economic and/or geopolitical gains. The economic gains consist in the full development of the potential of the country. Alexander Hamilton (1755–1804), U.S. Secretary of the Treasury (1789–1795), and John Stuart Mill (1806–1873), the most famous British economist (and a staunch pro-trader), argued that a limited period of protection could be necessary to start potentially suitable industries (infant-industry argument). These industries need some time to acquire necessary technical and organizational capabilities, train employees, and so on, before being able to withstand foreign competition. The geopolitical argument for protection assumes that competition among states requires military capabilities, which must be obtained even at the cost of welfare losses. A great power should be able to produce all goods necessary to wage a victorious war, including, of course, its food. In this case, unlike in the infant-industry argument, protection could be permanent. This line of reasoning can be traced back to *The National System of Political Economy* (1841) by George Friedrich List (1789–1846). It was quite popular among nationalist writers in the nineteenth and early twentieth centuries. These "dynamic" arguments for protection were and still are fairly diffused among the lay public, but by and large they have failed to convince economists, who doubt that protection could ever be temporary and stress that competition from imports is a powerful stimulus for improving the efficiency of domestic producers.

THEORY VERSUS PRACTICE

How is it possible to account for the gap between theory and practice? Why has protectionism been so often adopted if it is harmful to overall welfare? One can suggest three possible answers: the need for state revenue, international relations, and the pressure from producers' lobbies.

The need for state revenue Duties can yield revenues only if imports do not fall, that is, if they are not substituted by domestic production. This is the case of duties on goods, such as wine in the United Kingdom, that cannot be produced at home. These duties were allegedly only for fiscal purposes—although they could also guarantee some protection to domestic producers of competing goods (such as beer). But also, openly protective duties could yield substantial revenue if domestic production is insufficient for the desired consumption at the prevailing price, inclusive of the duty. This fiscal motivation was particularly important in the nineteenth century, because, before the introduction of personal taxation, custom duties were in fact a major source of revenues. On the eve of World War I, they accounted for about 10–15 percent of total revenues and up to 45 percent for federal states, such as Germany. Thus, the need for revenues could be invoked to justify otherwise unpalatable increases in protection. This happened in Italy in 1894, when the duty on wheat was increased by 50 percent during

a budget crisis. In the following decade, duty on wheat provided between 3 and 4 percent of total revenues of Italy.

International relations The prevalence of protectionist policies may be associated with the lack of a "hegemonic" power, such as the United States after 1950. A "hegemonic" power would force other countries to adopt the trade policy that best fits its interests—that is, almost always, to open their markets to its own exports. In this vein, one might explain the liberalization in the first half of the nineteenth century with the rise of British political hegemony and the return to protection toward the end of the century with its decline. However, in *Bargaining on Europe* (1998), Peter Marsh strongly downplays the British role in the establishment of the network of trade treaties that was instrumental in the liberalization of the 1860s; if anything, France was in the lead in this respect. Similarly, it is difficult to attribute the return to protection since the late 1870s to the lack of a "hegemonic" power. If the system of international relations dampened the protectionist reaction via the network of trade treaties and the MFN (most favored nation) clause. Foreign policy motivations sometimes did influence negotiations for treaties, either speeding them up (Great Powers had some clout versus smaller countries) or retarding them (for instance, the breakdown of negotiations between France and Italy in 1887 was a step in a long-term realignment of Italian alliances toward Germany). However, in the overwhelming majority of cases, trade treaties were determined by demand from domestic exporters. They needed access to foreign markets, which had to be granted with reciprocal concessions with other trading partners.

Producers' lobbies The lobbying by domestic producers of import-competing goods (the political economy of tariffs) is the most frequently quoted reason for protection. Interests can organize by sector (the iron and steel industry, wheat growing) or by factor (land, labor, capital).

In the latter, most common, case, the lobby allegedly represents all employees of the sector. Lobbies are easier to organize and more effective when the number of potential members is low, as argued by Mancur Olson in his seminal book

The Logic of Collective Action (1971). Therefore organizations of consumers potentially interested in free trade have long been weak relative to producers' lobbies. Indeed there were no associations of consumers in nineteenth-century Europe, while producers' lobbies, such as the German land-owners *Bund fur Landwirtschaft* (established in 1893), were quite well organized and influential. According to a well-established tradition, in many Continental countries, some producers' lobbies dictated trade policy at the expense of consumers and of other, weaker producers. The return to protection in the 1880s in Germany and Italy, for example, was the outcome of a bargain between cereal-growing Junkers (landed aristocracy of Prussia and eastern Germany) and heavy industry. Wilhelmine Germany was called the empire of rye and iron, although small-scale livestock producers also gained from protection. France also followed this pattern, although bureaucrats there had more power in the implementation of guidelines and, most crucially, in the negotiation of treaties than in Italy or Germany.

The United Kingdom is the prime example of the alternative model of organization of interests. Parties represented factors of production, such as land (Tories), capital (Whigs), and labor (Labour), and thus trade policies were part of their agendas. Actually, the issue played a major political role on two occasions. In the early 1840s the Anti–Corn Laws League, organized and funded by Manchester cotton industrialists, waged a strong campaign against the duty on wheat. It succeeded because the Tory Party split on the issue and lost power for a long period of time. Trade policy resurfaced as a major political issue in the late 1890s, when the movement for fair trade campaigned for reciprocity (that is, to raise duties on imports from countries that taxed British imports). This proposal became the main point in the Tory manifesto for the 1906 elections, but the party was soundly defeated.

Daniel Verdier argues that these national differences in the organization of interests reflect the features of the political systems, such as the loyalty of parliamentarians to their own party and the interest of voters in trade policy. However, these characteristics, especially the latter, depend on economic features, most notably the mobility of factors among sectors. A specialized worker has little scope for changing sectors and thus is more likely to join an industry lobby than is an unskilled one. In contrast, factors that are able to move between sectors are more likely to gather in major parties.

It is thus likely that all three factors—international relations, the need for revenue, and lobbying—contributed to shape trade policy in the nineteenth century. Their relative importance changed by country and by period, but more work is need to assess how.

See also **Business Firms and Economic Growth; Economists, Classical; Industrial Revolution, First; Liberalism; Protectionism; Trade and Economic Growth.**

BIBLIOGRAPHY

Bairoch, Paul. *Commerce exterieur et développement économique.* Paris, 1976.

———. "European Trade Policy." In *The Cambridge Economic History of Europe,* edited by Peter Mathias and Sidney Pollard.Vol. 8, 1–160. Cambridge, U.K., 1989.

Brander, James, and Barbara Spencer. "Export Subsidies and International Market Share Rivalry." *Journal of International Economics* 18 (1985): 83–100.

Conybeare, John A. C. *Trade Wars: The Theory and Practice of International Commercial Rivalry.* New York, 1987.

Estevadeordal Antoni, Brian Frantz, and Alan M. Taylor. "The Rise and Fall of World Trade, 1870–1939." *Quarterly Journal of Economics* 118 (2003): 359–407.

Federico, Giovanni, and Antonio Tena. "Was Italy a Protectionist Country?" *European Review of Economic History* 2 (1998): 73–97.

Federico, Giovanni, and Kevin O'Rourke. "Much Ado about Nothing?: The Italian Trade Policy in the Nineteenth Century." In *The Mediterranean Response to Globalisation before 1950,* edited by Sevket Pamuk and Jeffrey G. Williamson, 269–296. London, 2000.

Foreman-Peck, James. *A History of the World Economy: International Economic Relations since 1850.* New York, 1995.

Lake, David. *Power, Protection and Free Trade: International Sources of U.S. Commercial Strategy, 1887–1939.* Ithaca, N.Y., 1988.

Marsh, Peter. *Bargaining on Europe: Britain and the First Common Market, 1860–1892.* New Haven, Conn., 1998.

Nye, John Vincent. "The Myth of Free-Trade Britain and Fortress France: Tariffs and Trade in the Nineteenth Century." *Journal of Economic History* 51 (1991): 23–45.

O'Rourke, Kevin. "The European Grain Invasion, 1870–1913." *Journal of Economic History* 57 (1997): 775–802.

Verdier, Daniel. *Democracy and International Trade: Britain, France, and the United States, 1860–1990.* Princeton, N.J., 1994.

Williamson, Jeffrey. "The Impact of the Corn Laws Just Prior to Repeal." *Explorations in Economic History* 27 (1990): 123–156.

GIOVANNI FEDERICO

COMMITTEE OF PUBLIC SAFETY.

The overthrow of King Louis XVI and his execution in January 1793 left the young French Republic without executive authority. Faced with a desperate military and economic crisis in the spring, the National Convention resorted to placing executive powers in the hands of a Committee of Public Safety, established by a decree of 6 April. Until 10 July Georges Danton dominated the committee. After his resignation, what became known as the "great" committee of twelve members was completed with the addition of Maximilien Robespierre on 27 July and two fellow Jacobins in September. Until the overthrow and execution of Robespierre and his associates on 9–10 Thermidor Year II (27–28 July 1794), this committee was to act as the emergency executive of the Convention, meeting in secret and with sweeping powers to pass decrees relating to the "general defense" of the republic.

The prime objective of the committee was to implement the laws and controls necessary to win the war and to strike "Terror" into the hearts of counterrevolutionaries. The Convention acquiesced in the committee's draconian measures—such as surveillance committees, preventive detention, and controls on civil liberties—seen as necessary to secure the republic to a point at which the suspension of the democratic constitution of June 1793 could be lifted. A mixture of coercion, propaganda, and the effectiveness of Jacobin officials succeeded in supplying a conscript army of nearly one million

men, an extraordinary mobilization that effectively saved the republic.

In its declaration on revolutionary government of 10 October, the Committee of Public Safety announced that the "provisional government of France is revolutionary until the peace"; all government bodies and the army were placed under the control of the committee, which had to report weekly to the Convention. Despite repeated marks of approval of the committee's work—as much by admiration as intimidation—decrees were passed by the Convention and committee that went well beyond national defense and revealed a Jacobin vision of a regenerated society worthy of the grandeur of the Enlightenment and the Revolution. This was to be created, for example, by a secular and republican education system and a national program of social welfare. It was during the period of the committee's effective rule that a new calendar was inaugurated to commemorate the first anniversary of the proclamation of the republic on 21 September 1792, with a series of new civic festivals designed to edify public spirit.

While the military threat remained, so could the existence of the Terror be justified. In Prairial Year II (20 May–18 June 1794), for example, 183 of the 608 decrees of the Committee of Public Safety concerned supply and transport matters signed by Robert Lindet; 114 related to munitions were initiated by Prieur de la Côte-d'Or; and 130 were decrees by Lazare Carnot about the army and navy. Robespierre wrote just 14 decrees, but was highly visible as the main policy link with the Convention and the Jacobin Club. By the late spring of 1794, however, the execution of popular revolutionaries to the right and left of the dominant Jacobins, and the escalation of the Terror at a time of increasing military success, alienated even the most patriotic of Jacobins and sans-culottes. Those imprisoned as suspects ranged from the Marquis de Sade to Claude-Joseph Rouget de Lisle, author of the anthem "La Marseillaise." Its victims included the country's greatest scientist, Antoine Lavoisier, and its greatest poet, André Chénier.

The turning point came with the successful battle of Fleurus (26 June), which effectively removed the threat of foreign soldiers from the soil of the republic. This exposed the new purpose for which the Terror was being used: from

March 1793 to 10 June 1794, 1,251 people were executed in Paris; following the law of 22 Prairial Year II (10 June 1794), which dramatically expanded definitions of "counterrevolutionary," 1,376 were guillotined in just six weeks. Robespierre's final speech to the Convention on 26 July (8 Thermidor Year II), with his threat to move against unnamed deputies, provided the motivation for reaction. When he was arrested the following day, his appeals for support failed to move most sans-culottes or Jacobins. The fall of Robespierre and his associates was welcomed as symbolizing the end of large-scale executions: the committee was reorganized so that one-quarter of its members had to be replaced each month. Then a decree of 24 August (7 Fructidor Year II) made it one committee among many, until in 1795 the regime of the Directory established a new executive structure altogether.

See also **Danton, Georges-Jacques; Directory; Jacobins; Reign of Terror; Robespierre, Maximilien.**

BIBLIOGRAPHY

Furet, François, and Mona Ozouf, eds. *A Critical Dictionary of the French Revolution.* Translated by Arthur Goldhammer. Cambridge, Mass., 1989.

Gross, Jean-Pierre. *Fair Shares for All: Jacobin Egalitarianism in Practice.* Cambridge, U.K., 1997.

Jones, Colin. *The Longman Companion to the French Revolution.* London, 1988.

Palmer, R. R. *Twelve Who Ruled: The Year of the Terror in the French Revolution.* 1941. Reprint, with a new preface by the author, Princeton, N.J., 1989.

PETER MCPHEE

COMMUNICATIONS. *See* **Telephones; Transportation and Communications.**

COMMUNISM. Communism as a political ideology is based on ideas that date back to Plato's great dialogue *The Republic* (c. 380–360 B.C.E.). European movements and thinkers from 1789 to 1914 thus had a long and rich tradition to draw on. The term refers to a doctrine that material

---

EXCERPT FROM *MANIFESTO OF THE EQUALS*, BY SYLVAIN MARÉCHAL

What do we need besides equality of rights?

We need not only that equality of rights transcribed in the Declaration of the Rights of Man and Citizen; we want it in our midst, under the roofs of our houses. We consent to everything for it, *to make a clean slate so that we hold to it alone.* Let all the arts perish, if need be, as long as real equality remains! . . .

The Agrarian law, or the partitioning of land, was the spontaneous demand of some unprincipled soldiers, of some towns moved more by their instinct than by reason. We reach for something more sublime and more just: *the common good* or the *community of goods!* No more individual property in land: *the land belongs to no one.* We demand, we want, the common enjoyment of the fruits of the land: *the fruits belong to all.*

We declare that we can no longer put up with the fact that the great majority work and sweat for the extreme minority.

Long enough, and for too long, less than a million individuals have disposed of that which belongs to 20 million of their like, their equals.

Let it at last end, this great scandal that our nephews will never believe existed! Disappear at last, revolting distinctions between rich and poor, great and small, masters and servants, *rulers* and *ruled.*

Let there no longer be any difference between people other than that of age and sex. Since all have the same faculties and the same needs, let there then be for them but one education, but one food. They are satisfied with one sun and one air for all: why then would the same portion and the same quality of food not suffice for each of them?

Manifesto of the Equals, by Sylvain Maréchal, translated by Mitch Abidor, available from *http://www. marxists.org/history/france/revolution/conspiracy-equals/manifesto.htm.*

---

resources are community property prior to any form of individual ownership, and that such resources are best dispersed through forms of community control.

EXCERPT FROM KARL MARX AND FRIEDRICH ENGELS, *MANIFESTO OF THE COMMUNIST PARTY* (1848)

The theoretical propositions of the communists are in no way founded on ideas or principles invented or discovered by this or that reformist crank.

They merely express in general terms the factual relations of an existing class struggle, a historical movement that is proceeding under our own eyes. The abolition of existing property relations is not distinctively communist.

All property relations have been subject to continuous historical change, to continuous historical variation.

The French revolution, for example, abolished feudal property in favour of bourgeois property.

What is distinctively communist is not the abolition of property in general but the abolition of bourgeois property.

But modern bourgeois private property is the final and most complete expression of the production and appropriation of products which rests on class conflict, on the exploitation of individuals by others.

In that sense communists can sum up their theory in a single phrase: the transformation of private property.

Karl Marx, *Later Political Writings*, translated and edited by Terrell Carver, Cambridge, U.K., p. 13.

Plato's discussion in *The Republic* raises three analytically crucial points in understanding communism. First, what is the nature of individual ownership of material resources, as opposed to prior forms of community control? Second, what level of subsistence and surplus production is appropriate to the good life in a community, and how should this be determined? Third, is a system that mixes collective control with individual ownership perhaps the most satisfactory way to organize society, or alternatively would it be inherently corrupting and dangerous? Plato argued that happiness, peace, and justice cannot rest on individual ownership of material resources; moreover, any mixed system will necessarily lead to class war and civil strife. In an attack on *The Republic,* Plato's pupil Aristotle argued in *The Politics* (c. 335–322 B.C.E.) for a general principle of individual ownership, mixed with shared use where there are mutual benefits. Since that time, communists have been correctly identified with a pure form of community control.

Thomas More's *Utopia* (1516) represents a landmark for the later communist tradition in two respects. First, it updated the critique of individualized ownership of material resources to the period of early modern commercialism, in which traditional rights of community use (say, in fields and forests) were being terminated through the assertion of private property rights by landowners. Second, his alternative communist society marks a sharp contrast with commercial societies, because of its asceticism and abolition of money, albeit an imaginary one (he coined the word *utopia,* meaning "nowhere").

MODERN MOVEMENTS

The French Revolution represents a watershed for communist theory and practice in two important ways. It created a conception of popularly driven change, not just of rulers or even of political structures, but of social values and goals toward the ultimate realization of ideals. In 1796 the *Manifesto of the Equals,* written by Sylvain Maréchal (1750–1803) and published as part of the notorious "Conspiracy," demanded forms of equality beyond those envisaged by other revolutionaries, in that the use of material resources was to be strictly controlled in order to prevent class distinctions. The goal was that there should be neither rich nor poor. François-Noël "Gracchus" Babeuf (1760–1797) was guillotined for his part in the planned uprising, and "Baboeuvism" became iconic for armed intervention to achieve mass equalization of material circumstances. After that it was easy for conservatives and reactionaries to tar anyone favoring democratization of political authority, or economic intervention by the state, with the brush of communism. But as a matter of doctrine there is a sharp line between communists, with their uncompromising hostility to mixed systems of individual and collective economic management, and socialists or "left-liberals," with their advocacy of precisely that.

In the post-Napoleonic period of reaction and authoritarianism throughout Europe (1815–1830), during which representative democracy and constitutional government were attacked and reversed in many places, it is not surprising that communist thought and action—chiefly in the form of (necessarily) secret societies—took hold, evoking figures such as Babeouf and his successors, Philippe Michel Buonarotti (1761–1837) and Louis-Auguste Blanqui (1805–1881). The 1830s also produced a flowering of communist literature, sometimes termed socialist, but identifiable as communist through its use of the utopian genre derived from More and its resolutely anticommercial approach to social reorganization. Étienne Cabet's (1788–1856) *Travels in Icaria* (1839) was widely read and became the basis for actual experiments in communal living. Working in the 1840s, Cabet effectively created a communist tradition by linking his ideas to the recent French revolutionary events of 1830 and back to the period from 1789 to 1795 in a popular history, and continuing the genre of the inspirational manifesto by publishing pamphlets on *Why I Am a Communist* and *My Communist Credo*.

Influenced by German followers of Cabet and enthused with the democratic ideals of the French revolutionary tradition, Karl Marx (1818–1883) and Friedrich Engels (1820–1895) involved themselves separately in radical journalism, pushing liberals toward an engagement with the condition of the urban and rural poor, and advocating collective economic management outside a framework of private charity. By late 1844 they were working together, and for the next forty years they pursued a remarkably consistent campaign on three fronts. One was against utopians for their small-scale and sometimes fanciful or religious visions of communism, which they dismissed as childish nonsense. Another was against socialists and reformers of all kinds, who favored "mixed" economic regimes, dismissed by Marx and Engels as dangerous and as no solution. And a third was against anarchists, with their extreme suspicion of authority and collective decision-making, which Marx and Engels dismissed as irresponsible. Working in the 1840s for the Communist League, itself a Europe-wide, umbrella organization for national secret societies, and itself a descendant of rather more shadowy

groups of the 1830s, such as the League of the Just, the two produced the *Manifesto of the Communist Party* (1848).

This work drew on pan-European and ultimately global perspectives of radical action. In uncompromising tones the *Manifesto* criticizes the economic and social institutions of commercial (termed "bourgeois") society, yet gives it a crucial role in human history. This was the development of industrial productivity to a remarkable and dizzying degree. Beyond the horrors of class-divided society lay the future institutions of communism, in which productive effort would be in harmony with individual abilities, and the distribution of material goods would correspond to individual needs. Marx and Engels's work contributed substantially to the development of communism in three distinct ways. First, it focused on the industrial working class (or "proletariat") as the crucial agent for democratizing social relations in modern societies. Second, it undermined the claims of individualistic philosophies and economic theories by identifying them as mere episodes in the development of civilization. Third, it advocated a politics of change midway between anarchistic associationism (in which the individual is sovereign) and conspiratorial collectivism (in which a small group acts in the name of individuals en masse).

Marx was among the founders of the International Workingmen's Association in 1864 (later known as the "First International"), a reincarnation of the publicity committees of the 1840s and a venue for communists wanting to push socialists toward uncompromising opposition to capitalist society. The 1860s and 1870s were an era in Europe when socialist parties were legally founded and trade union activity was increasingly permitted. While much of this activity necessitated violence and was sometimes reversed (notably in Germany during the period of the "antisocialist law" from 1878 to 1890), communists found themselves increasingly isolated from socialist advocacy of "mixed" economies and positive engagement with semidemocratic systems. After 1872 the First International fizzled out owing to internecine disputes involving anarchists, but the format was revived in 1889 with the founding of the Socialist (or Second) International, a body representing socialist engagement within, and on behalf of, democratic mixed economies. These goals were supported even by Marxists, albeit as a stage on the way to an increasingly distant communist future, where control over resources would be collective and the money economy would be abolished. This organization collapsed during World War I, after many members supported their nationalist governments in contradiction to their principles of international cooperation on behalf of the working classes of all countries.

Communists as such were thus an underground, most notably in authoritarian countries such as tsarist Russia. Ironically the most successful self-identified Russian communists were those engaged with industrial workers in urban areas, a tiny fraction of the population. In a then obscure but later celebrated work, *What Is to Be Done?* (1905), Vladimir Lenin (Vladimir Ilyich Ulyanov; 1870–1924) argued for a tightly organized party to lead the workers, make them revolutionary, and utilize political power directly. The revolutionary events of 1917 were pursued by liberals and socialists, but only the Leninist faction of the Russian Social Democratic Labor Party took advantage of popular urban support for withdrawing from World War I and for radical democratization of the government.

REVIEW AND POSTSCRIPT

While communism has a rich and diverse tradition, it has been closely identified with Marx and Engels and Marxism since the late nineteenth century. The utopian and ascetic strands of thought have given way to an embrace of urbanity and mechanization, projected forward to a system of collective control to manage production and distribution according to the principle: "From each according to his abilities, to each according to his needs" (Marx, *The Critique of the Gotha Program,* 1875). Whether communists should seize power (even in nonindustrialized agrarian countries) and create authoritarian structures to effect social change (rather than proceed through democratic gradualism) have been issues that have served to divide self-styled communists (particularly Soviet ideologues and leaders) from socialists. Communism has been truer to its ideals in its theoretical and utopian forms than in its practical manifestations, particularly

those that developed after the Russian Revolution (1917–1921) and the Soviet occupation of Eastern Europe (1945–1989).

See also **Anarchism; Engels, Friedrich; First International; Fourier, Charles; Labor Movements; Marx, Karl; Second International; Socialism.**

BIBLIOGRAPHY

Freeden, Michael. *Ideologies and Political Theory: A Conceptual Approach.* Oxford, U.K., 1998.

Heywood, Andrew. *Political Theory: An Introduction.* 3rd ed. Basingstoke, U.K., 2004.

Johnson, Christopher H. *Utopian Communism in France: Cabet and the Icarians, 1839–1851.* Ithaca, N.Y., 1974.

Lichtheim, George. *The Origins of Socialism.* New York, 1968.

TERRELL CARVER

COMTE, AUGUSTE (1798–1857), founder of sociology and positivism.

Although desirous to distinguish himself from the French revolutionaries and Napoleon, who had wreaked havoc in his youth, Auguste Comte shared their desire to launch a new era in European history. He envisioned a new global order based on secular republicanism and marked by an intellectual and emotional consensus.

Born in Montpellier, France, on 19 January 1798, Comte rebelled as a boy against the royalism and Catholicism of his parents. A brilliant mathematician, he marveled at the power of the sciences and studied at the École polytechnique, the prestigious engineering school in Paris. After being expelled for insubordination in 1816, he began in 1817 to work for Henri de Saint-Simon, a prominent social reformer. Comte later tried to deny Saint-Simon's influence after their rupture in 1824. Nevertheless, Saint-Simon showed him that the nascent industrial society had to be based on a scientific system of knowledge—a "positive philosophy"—that had to include the study of society. Having read Montesquieu (Charles-Louis de Secondat; 1689–1755), Condorcet (Marie-Jean de Caritat; 1743–1794), and the idéologues (liberal social theorists), Comte realized the significance of Saint-Simon's scattered insights. In 1826 he made his first attempt to bring knowledge together in a public course, but after a few lectures, he went mad. When he emerged from his asylum months later, he contributed articles to a journal run by the Saint-Simonians, yet he refused to join their cult. In the 1830s, he procured a position as a tutor and administrator at the École polytechnique, where he tried repeatedly and unsuccessfully to obtain a chair. He was eventually fired. Living off of his disciples' contributions, he died on 5 September 1857.

Comte's masterpiece is the six-volume *Cours de philosophie positive* (Course of Positive Philosophy), published between 1830 and 1842. It introduced his intellectual synthesis, called *positivism*. According to Comte's law of three stages, the main branches of knowledge and indeed all societies, which reflect the prevailing system of ideas, go through three stages. During the theological stage, people explain events by attributing them to a god or several gods. (There are three substages: fetishism, polytheism, and monotheism.) Priests and kings run society. During the metaphysical stage, personified nonsupernatural abstractions like Nature are said to cause occurrences. Philosophers and lawyers dominate society. During the positive stage, people stop looking for first causes and seek scientific laws that describe how, not why, phenomena function. Knowledge is considered valid only if it is based on the "positive" or scientific method and is limited to what can be observed. According to Comte's classification of the sciences, the six main sciences arrived at the positive stage in the following order, which was determined by the simplicity of their subject matter and their distance from humans: mathematics, astronomy, physics, chemistry, biology, and the study of society. The *Cours* discussed the development of each of these branches of knowledge, thus inaugurating the history of science.

Referring to the findings of the phrenologist Franz Gall (1758–1828), Comte maintained that because biology now was a positive science, it was time for the study of society to be wrested from the theologians and metaphysicians and to become a science. He called this new science *sociology* in 1839. It contained two parts: social dynamics, the study of progress (whose main historical law was

the law of three stages), and social statics, the study of order. Once he established sociology as the keystone of positivism, he assumed that an intellectual revolution would commence. It would lead to a moral revolution, which would usher in a new social and political order, doing away with the anarchy from the Revolution of 1789. The government of the new positive era would comprise a temporal power composed of industrialists and a spiritual power made up of positive philosophers. Administered by these separate powers, a new secular "Occidental Republic" would work for the betterment of all in a spirit of consensus. Comte's ambitious scheme of renewal, based on a grand view of history and the creation of an organic community, appealed to leading intellectuals such as John Stuart Mill and Maximilien-Paul-Émile Littré.

The more controversial part of Comte's life is his so-called second career, when he launched a new religion. Some scholars attribute this religion to Comte's midlife crisis. In 1845, three years after he separated from his wife, Caroline Massin, Comte fell in love with a budding novelist, who was seventeen years younger than he. Clotilde de Vaux rejected his amorous advances but grew close to him before she died of tuberculosis a year later. Crushed, Comte considered her responsible for a dramatic shift in his philosophy. Yet before meeting her, Comte had been interested in the moral reform of society. Living during the period of Romanticism, attracted to Catholic conservative thinkers such as Joseph de Maistre (1753–1821), and eager to gather the support of workers, whose marginality reminded him of his own, he never presented ideas alone as the principal motivators of people; it was important to address their feelings. In addition, as the women's movement became prominent, he tried to attract female supporters by referring to the importance of the emotions and countering the influence of the Catholic Church. In the late 1840s, thanks in part to his excitement about the Revolution of 1848, he launched a new secular religion, the Religion of Humanity, which flowed logically from positivism. People were to make society, or Humanity, not only the focus of their scientific studies but also the object of their love and activities. To encourage this new cult and the growth of sociability, or *altruism*, a word he coined, Comte devised prayers, a new calendar, and sacraments, many of which were derived from Catholicism. Around the same time, he came out in favor of a dictatorial state, especially as he placed his hopes on the new government of Napoleon III (r. 1852–1871), who, however, soon disappointed him. Comte discussed his religion and his plan for a new global order that would comprise five hundred republics in his four-volume *Système de politique positive* (1851–1854; *System of Positive Polity*, 1875–1877). It appealed to individuals who rejected God but felt uncomfortable with atheism. Some disciples, however, accused him of betraying his scientific agenda.

Comte's doctrine influenced philosophy, sociology, the history of science, and historiography. Because its assault on the church and monarchism appealed to the left and its defense of order and authority made it attractive to the right, positivism had diverse followers throughout Europe and Latin America. The Brazilian flag displays Comte's motto "Order and Progress."

See also **France; Gall, Franz Joseph; Positivism; Saint-Simon, Henri de; Sociology.**

BIBLIOGRAPHY

Primary Sources

Martineau, Harriet, ed. and trans. *The Positive Philosophy of Auguste Comte.* 2 vols. London, 1853.

Secondary Sources

Pickering, Mary. *Auguste Comte: An Intellectual Biography.* Vol. 1. Cambridge, U.K., 1993.

Wernick, Andrew. *Auguste Comte and the Religion of Humanity: The Post-Theistic Program of French Social Theory.* Cambridge, U.K., 2001.

MARY PICKERING

CONCERT OF EUROPE.

The legal basis of the Concert of Europe was established in the Second Treaty of Paris. Concluded on 20 November 1815 in the aftermath of Napoleon I's return from exile and the Waterloo campaign, that document established a twenty-year alliance of Austria, Russia, Prussia, and Britain against any renewal of French aggression. In turn Article 6 of the alliance provided for future meetings of the European powers to promote domestic tranquility, international peace, and general prosperity.

EUROPE'S NEW ORDER

In the context of European relations since the Renaissance, Article 6 was little more than a pious exhortation—certainly a slender thread on which to weave a century's diplomacy. The Concert of Europe, however, was as much a state of mind as a formal organization. It reflected a collective acceptance of restrained policies in pursuit of limited objectives. This was a sharp contrast to the eighteenth century in particular, when the ambitions of Europe's powers were constrained primarily by the means available to achieve them. The Concert of Europe differed as well from the generally accepted definition of a balance of power system: a more or less stable equilibrium maintained by states combining to check attempts by other states or alliances to dominate the international system. The concert paradigm primarily reflected the experiences of the revolutionary/Napoleonic era, when ideology and bureaucracy had combined to increase exponentially the political, economic, and above all military power available to governments.

Napoleon was not merely the embodied consequence of this development. He was also a stalking horse and a scapegoat for the mutual anxieties of his former enemies. Not only did they not trust each other—they did not trust themselves to use effectively the tools potentially lying in their hands. The real challenge facing the Great Powers in 1814 and 1815 had not been restoring an order disrupted beginning in 1789. It was creating an order from the chaos produced by the French Empire's challenge to the Continent. Inevitably the redrawn map of Europe was an artificial construction whose legitimacy was open to challenge on a broad variety of grounds, and a comprehensive compromise in which none of the principals emerged entirely satisfied.

In these contexts the four signatories of the Second Treaty of Paris were able to agree that their interests were best served in the foreseeable future by maintaining the status quo created in 1815—a perspective accepted as well by Bourbon France, for both principled and pragmatic reasons. That consensus in turn inspired a second one: that a rough equality existed among Europe's five major powers. This was not so much a positive equality based on respective strength, actual and potential, but a negative equality reflecting the capacity (most recently demonstrated at the Congress of Vienna) of any of the five to disrupt any general agreement by some combination of force or guile.

This concept of mutual equality in turn put paid to any notions of a great-power consortium exercising hegemony over the rest. Instead the Concert of Europe accepted the idea of intermediary bodies—smaller states and buffer zones—arguably including the whole of Germany and Italy, designed to cushion great-power interaction, and with their legitimacy correspondingly guaranteed. The result was a situation best expressed by the name of a lake in Massachusetts that is forty-nine letters long. Translated from the original Nipmuc, it means roughly "you fish on your side; I fish on my side; nobody fishes in the middle."

Restraint, limitation, cooperation—these were the watchwords of European diplomacy in the decade after 1815. Not every government and every statesman was happy with the process or its results. In particular George Canning, British foreign secretary from 1822 to 1827, favored a return to the individualist, competitive international relations of the eighteenth century: "every nation for itself and God for us all." The concert nevertheless not only endured but grew stronger.

In good part this increased strength reflected the increasingly specific definition of a geographic area within which the concert functioned. Austrian intervention in Naples and French intervention in Spain against local revolutionary movements during the early 1820s were processed as acts in the concert's general interest—a policy facilitated by the care the principal actors took to avoid directly aggrandizing themselves. When in contrast Britain took a hand in supporting the wars of independence in Spanish America in the same period, the concert concerned itself primarily—and successfully—with limiting the European consequences of the rebels' success. Similarly, tensions over Greek and Egyptian revolts against Ottoman rule in the 1820s, and a resulting war between Russia and the Ottoman Empire (1828–1829) strained concert relations but led to a tacit acceptance of the Near East as outside the sphere of concert interest.

The Near East crisis nevertheless indicated that the concert's original commitment to the status quo of 1815 could not be sustained indefinitely. In 1830, as part of a general revolutionary movement that also brought a new dynasty to the throne of France, Belgium declared its independence from the Netherlands and secured French support. A series of international agreements solved the issue—in Belgium's favor—by redefining the parameters of stability. In future, it was agreed, no changes in the newly modified arrangements could occur without the approval of the five Great Powers. That meant none of them could act unilaterally—but it also allowed for negotiation and compromise.

Order continued to prevail over revolution, ambition, and entropy in the revolutions of 1848. The system established at Vienna survived, essentially because the Great Powers withstood the temptation to fish in their neighbors' troubled waters. The best example was tsarist Russia's massive commitment of its armies to restore the Habsburg order in an Austrian Empire shaken to its foundations. Less obvious but no less significant was Britain's functioning as a mediator of disputes.

The Restoration of 1849 to 1850 could not remove the major changes occurring in the European system. The Eastern Question, the fate of the Ottoman Empire and its subject peoples, continued to strain the concert's structure. An ambitious adventurer, Louis Napoleon, assumed power in France, with visions of a new empire brought into being by French manipulations of the forces of nationalism and liberalism. The Crimean War (1853–1856), the first great-power conflict in forty years, was nevertheless as much a failure (and in some cases a rejection) of crisis management by individual states as a manifestation of general concert breakdown. The conduct of the war itself pitilessly exposed the military shortcomings of all the participants. The settlement reached at the Congress of Paris in 1856 was a concert outcome in a negative sense—all the participants were dissatisfied; none obviously profited from their respective adventures in high-risk diplomacy. The Concert of Europe was undermined and weakened. It nevertheless remained something more than a convenient fable on which states could agree to camouflage their individual ambitions.

EUROPE'S REORGANIZATION

This fact was manifested over the next decade in the Wars of German Unification. Prussia's Otto von Bismarck, emerging as a ruthless and effective player of Europe's power game, sought in the final analysis to structure his initiatives in a concert context. He negotiated no more than temporary, instrumental coalitions with other states, while simultaneously working to convince Europe's foreign offices that Prussian aggrandizement within the concert system would ultimately prove a force for stability. Prussia's wars were designed to be short and sharp, with objectives limited and obvious enough to be permanently negotiable. Bismarck successfully ascribed the failure of that formula in the Franco-Prussian War (1870–1871) to the intransigence of the radical leaders of the revolutionary French Republic to recognize their defeat.

In the succeeding decade Bismarck strove mightily to establish himself and the new German empire as the "honest broker" of Europe—or at least Europe's croupier, recognized as playing a straight game. When the Eastern Question again flared into war between Russia and Turkey in 1877, Bismarck kept the conflict isolated until Russia, again disabled by military and economic weakness, sought negotiations. The Congress of Berlin in 1878, like its Paris predecessor, succeeded in balancing discontents. This time, however, the antagonisms ran deeper and endured longer than the reconciliations.

Bismarck's concert was weakened by three tectonic flaws. One was Bismarck's assumption after 1871 of an insurmountable Franco-German antagonism, which led him to seek France's permanent marginalization. The second was the growing imbalance of power between Russia and Austria-Hungary. Initially Bismarck sought to maintain comity by fine-tuning their relations through the Three Emperors' Leagues of 1872 and 1881. Increasingly he found himself constrained to behave in ways construed as taking sides—usually in Austria's favor, at the expense of Germany's Russian relationship. The third structural defect of Bismarck's Europe involved Britain's withdrawal—or by some interpretations its drifting away—from a continent where its growing relative military weakness prevented effective exercise of direct influence.

Bismarck struggled with all his considerable skill to prevent reversion to a balance of power system he considered little more than a preliminary to inevitable war. During the 1880s he turned to a system of limited-commitment, defensive alliances that eventually culminated in the Mediterranean Agreements of 1887 and the accompanying Reinsurance Treaty with Russia. This loose network of treaties brought all the powers of Europe except France into a network in which any aggressor would, in theory, confront in isolation an overwhelmingly powerful defensive coalition of the other powers. One might describe it as the Concert of Europe, with formal agreements replacing the underlying commonality of purpose that informed the original.

RISE OF THE ALLIANCE SYSTEM

The weaknesses of Bismarck's system were obvious to his contemporaries. Its complexity required a manager who stood higher above the tensions and conflicts of the powers than even Bismarck could be trusted to do. It depended as well on a common commitment to the status quo that in an age of nationalism, imperialism, and economic rivalry was scarcely to be depended upon. In the aftermath of Bismarck's dismissal in 1890, alliances proliferated. The Franco-Russian Alliance of 1894 was a classic "marriage of convenience" between states feeling themselves isolated by Bismarck's web. The Austro-German-Italian Triple Alliance, which had evolved in the 1880s as a symbol and a deterrent, took on a cutting edge. Periodic efforts around the turn of the century to negotiate an Anglo-German alliance foundered on the simple ground that the two states had nothing to bring them together. In contrast, particularly after the experience of the South African Boer War (1899–1902), Britain had strong grounds for settling its extra-European disputes with its direct rivals. Britain gave up its long-standing policy of "splendid isolation" in 1902, when a naval treaty with Japan enabled the Royal Navy to begin concentrating against Germany. In 1904 the Entente Cordiale with France signaled Britain's return to direct involvement in Continental politics. Germany, increasingly perceiving itself "encircled," responded with a series of clumsy initiatives that not only brought Britain and France closer but also led in 1907 to an Anglo-Russian agreement as well.

If these regroupings of power had a common result, it was that they contributed to diplomatic insecurity rather than alleviating it. Specifically Germany's sense of isolation increased exponentially as its Italian connection frayed, and Austria, torn by ethnically based domestic crises, began declining from a European to a regional power. A long-standing arms race that escalated after the First Moroccan Crisis of 1905 tended to increase reliance on armed force as opposed to diplomacy as an instrument of first recourse in settling disputes. Ironically, the insecurity contributed significantly to reviving the Concert of Europe, at least as a concept, in the years before World War I. The alliance systems that had ostensibly replaced it had too many loopholes, too many escape clauses, for any of their respective members to feel certain of support in a crisis. The projected devastation of a high-tech, great-power war was another encouragement to resolve disputes peacefully—especially disputes originating outside the Continent.

The Concert of Europe successfully oversaw the partition of Africa in the last quarter of the nineteenth century. In the first decade of the twentieth it took up the even more delicate Eastern Question. While not able to prevent Italy's annexation of the Ottoman province of Libya or the two Balkan Wars that followed in 1912 and 1913, the powers were able to act in concert to prevent a general war. Germany checked Austria; Britain held back Russia; the overall balance among the Great Powers was sustained. What was fading was the concept of collective interest. To be effective the Concert of Europe required participants to think broadly and trust others to do so as well. It required internal calibration of behavior, so that states not seem excessively threatening to others. The Concert of Europe, in short, depended on levels of perspective and wisdom conspicuously absent from the European stage by 1914. In part the concert was taken for granted; in part it was dismissed as obsolete. Certainly the Sarajevo crisis and its apocalyptic aftermath showed that while all the Great Powers were ready enough to profit from the Concert of Europe, none of them were willing to take risks or make sacrifices to sustain the system that had maintained peace and stability for a century.

See also **Alliance System; Congress of Berlin; Holy Alliance.**

BIBLIOGRAPHY

Crampton, R. J. *The Hollow Détente: Anglo-German Relations in the Balkans, 1911–1914.* London, 1979.

Jervis, Robert. "A Political Science Perspective on the Balance of Power and the Concert." *American Historical Review* 97, no. 3 (1992): 716–724.

Langhorne, Richard. *The Collapse of the Concert of Europe: International Politics, 1890–1914.* New York, 1981.

Medlicott, W. N. *Bismarck, Gladstone, and the Concert of Europe.* London, 1956.

Schroeder, Paul W. *Austria, Great Britain, and the Crimean War: The Destruction of the European Concert.* Ithaca, N.Y., 1972.

———. "Did the Vienna Settlement Rest on a Balance of Power?" *American Historical Review* 97, no. 3 (1992): 683–706.

———. *The Transformation of European Politics, 1763–1848.* Oxford, U.K., 1994.

DENNIS SHOWALTER

CONCORDAT OF 1801. The two men responsible for the Concordat of 1801 were motivated by practical and religious considerations. Napoleon Bonaparte, first consul of France by the end of 1799, saw the need to mend the religious conflict with Catholicism unleashed by the Civil Constitution of the Clergy (1790), which attempted to place the French church under government control. As Napoleon consolidated his power in France, the bishop of Imola, Barnaba Gregorio Chiaramonti, was elected pope as Pius VII in mid-March 1800. Having preached that revolutionary ideas need not be in conflict with Catholicism, he extended an olive branch to the French. Napoleon, sensing that the French had wearied of the religious conflict, sought a settlement with Rome. Motivated by the prospect of restoring millions of souls to the church, Pius VII concurred.

Serious negotiations commenced in November 1800, on Napoleon's three basic conditions: the reinstitution of the church with a new episcopacy, the state assumption of the clergy's salaries, and the clerical renunciation of former church properties. The parties aimed to end the schism in France by reconciling the Roman religion and the Revolution, with both sides willing to ignore the thorny question of temporal power,

The Re-establishment of a Cult: A Te deum at Notre-Dame de Paris, 18 April 1802. Color lithograph by Victor Adam depicting the ceremony held to celebrate the completion of the Concordat. Bibliothèque Nationale, Paris, France/Bridgeman Art Library/Lauros/Giraudon

which the French had truncated. There were stumbling blocks, including Rome's desire to have Catholicism established as the religion of state and the French reluctance to make this concession. Napoleon dispatched emissaries to Rome in March 1801, instructing them to treat the pontiff as if he had two hundred thousand bayonets at his disposal. On 15 July 1801, an agreement consisting of two declarations and seventeen articles was approved.

In the first of the declarations that formed a crucial preamble, the republic recognized Catholicism as the faith of the great majority of the French. The second promised that this religion could expect the greatest good from the restoration of public worship and from its profession by the consuls of the republic—although Article 17 provided for the eventuality of a first consul who might not be of the faith. The articles arranged for the reorganization of the church, with 60 dioceses

in place of the 135 under the *ancien régime.* Provision was made for the resignation of all the present archbishops and bishops; their replacements were to be named by the first consul, but their canonical institution was reserved to the pope. The bishops were to appoint parish priests from a list approved by the government. In turn, the papacy specified it would not dispute the church property confiscated by the republic, nor trouble the conscience of those who had purchased it. In exchange, the state promised to return the religious edifices it retained, while providing salaries for the clergy. The Roman faith was to enjoy full freedom of public worship, and its adherents were permitted to provide foundations in land or money on its behalf.

On 15 August 1801 Pius VII ratified the Concordat, issuing two encyclicals to the bishops of France. In the first, he related the rationale for the agreement, outlining its principal clauses. In the second, he required the resignation of the entire French hierarchy, so that new appointments might be made in accordance with Article 5 of the Concordat. This extraordinary exercise of papal power represented a deathblow to Gallicanism (the traditional resistance to papal authority within French Catholicism). Skirting the issue of the temporal dominions, the accord secured for the pope the right not only to invest bishops, which he had previously possessed, but also under certain conditions to depose them, which in France represented an innovation.

Neither Paris nor Rome appeared totally satisfied with the agreement, although both drew substantial benefits. Pius appreciated the reestablishment of the Catholic hierarchy in France, the restoration of Catholic worship, and the abandonment of the religious innovations of the revolutionaries. The centralization it sanctioned in the French church clearly reinforced the position of the papacy. Napoleon, for his part, inherited the prerogatives of the monarchy vis-à-vis the church and the clergy. Furthermore, he achieved the laicization of sovereign power while depriving the royalist opposition to his regime of the most potent weapon in its arsenal.

In April 1802 the French legislature approved the Concordat, along with the Organic Articles for its implementation. Most of the measures in this lengthy appendix dealt with the relationship of the state to the Catholic Church, seeking to establish control of the former over the latter, while restricting the rights of the Holy See in France. Papal bulls, briefs, decrees, and even legates could not be received in France without governmental approval. Under its terms bishops were forbidden to leave their dioceses while obliging them to submit to state authorities the rules of their seminaries. These rules had to include adherence to the four Gallican Articles of 1682, which curtailed the powers of the French church while limiting the power of the pope therein. Additional articles stressed the primacy of civil matrimony and determined the holy days to be publicly celebrated. In his allocution of 24 May 1802, announcing the implementation of the Concordat, Pius praised the efforts of Napoleon in achieving the religious rapprochement, but deplored the Organic Articles and called for their modification.

Napoleon, likewise, had reservations about the accord and unsuccessfully sought to replace it with the coerced "Concordat of Fontainebleau" of January 1813. The 1801 Concordat survived Napoleon's downfall in 1815 and was recognized by the restored monarchy. It guided church-state relations in France throughout the nineteenth century and was repudiated only in 1905, when the Third Republic introduced a complete separation of church and state.

See also **Catholicism; French Revolution; Napoleonic Empire; Separation of Church and State (France, 1905).**

BIBLIOGRAPHY

Primary Sources

Boulay de la Meurthe, Alfred, ed. *Documents sur la négociation du Concordat et sur les autres rapports de la France avec le Saint-Siège en 1800 et 1801.* 6 vols. Paris, 1891–1905.

"Convention between the French Government and His Holiness Pius VII." In *Controversial Concordats: The Vatican's Relations with Napoleon, Mussolini, and Hitler,* edited by Frank J. Coppa, 191–193. Washington, D.C., 1999.

Secondary Sources

O'Dwyer, Margaret M. *The Papacy in the Age of Napoleon and the Restoration: Pius VII, 1800–1823.* Lanham, Md., 1985.

Roberts, William. "Napoleon, the Concordat of 1801, and Its Consequences." In *Controversial Concordats: The Vatican's Relations with Napoleon, Mussolini, and Hitler,* edited by Frank J. Coppa, 34–80. Washington, D.C., 1999.

Walsh, Henry H. *The Concordat of 1801: A Study of the Problem of Nationalism in the Relations of Church and State.* New York, 1933. Reprint, New York, 1967.

FRANK J. COPPA

CONGRESS OF BERLIN. The Congress of Berlin took place from 13 June to 13 July 1878. Its general purpose was to create a new peace settlement between the Ottoman Empire and Russia after the Russian victory in the Russo-Turkish War (1877–1878). The specific goals of the congress included a revision of the Treaty of San Stefano, which the Russian government had imposed on Turkey earlier that year: Turkey hoped for better peace conditions. The Austro-Hungarians and the

British considered the Treaty of San Stefano a violation—directed against their own interests—of previous arrangements with the Russian government. They especially opposed the establishment of a "Greater Bulgaria," fearing it would be used by the Russians as a puppet state aiding in their domination of the Balkans. In spring 1878 the Russian government concluded that their opponents, especially Great Britain, were ready to go to war, if necessary, in order to revise the Treaty of San Stefano. The British sent a fleet toward Istanbul, a gesture that looked like a possible repeat of the Crimean War (1853–1856) to the Russians. Russian leaders were aware that they were unable for military and political reasons to risk such a war against Great Britain, not to mention possibly Austria-Hungary. This was particularly so because the Russian army was weakened by disease, and thus the Russians agreed to an attempt at a compromise.

The involved powers agreed to settle the conflict through a conference. German Chancellor Otto von Bismarck, who had declared several times that Germany had no interests in this particular crisis except to preserve European peace, offered his services as an "honest broker" (*ehrlicher Makler*) in a speech made to the German parliament in January 1878. With this congress agreed to, the powers involved attempted a peaceful way to avoid war. The high-ranking participants involved made the Congress of Berlin one of the most important political events in nineteenth-century Europe. Among the participants were such prominent figures of European politics as Bismarck, Benjamin Disraeli (of Great Britain), Count Gyula Andrássy (Austria- Hungary), Alexander Gorchakov (Russia), William Henry Waddington (France), and Count Luigi Corti (Italy). Alexander Karatheodori headed the Ottoman delegation. The Balkan nations sent delegates to the conference, but they could report on the positions of their countries' leaders only upon request.

One of the most important points of issue in the discussions was determining the size of the new state of Bulgaria. The border of Bulgaria, according to the Treaty of San Stefano, was drawn according to what were considered in these times "ethnic" borders among Bulgarian populations. The leaders of Great Britain and Austria-Hungary objected to this "Greater Bulgaria," because they feared it would come to be under Russian domination, with the entirety of the Balkans and Istanbul to follow.

The agreements reached in the difficult negotiations greatly altered the Treaty of San Stefano. The Greater Bulgaria that existed in that treaty was divided into three regions: Bulgaria was made a principality under nominal Ottoman suzerainty; Eastern Rumelia (Bulgaria south of the Balkan Mountains) was to be governed, with certain autonomous rights, by a Christian appointee of the Ottoman emperor; and Macedonia was to remain under unrestricted Ottoman sovereignty. Bosnia-Herzegovina was assigned to Austria-Hungary for administration and military occupation for thirty years to follow. Austria also occupied the sanjak (Turkish district) of Novi Pazar. Montenegro, Serbia, and Romania got full independence from the Ottoman Empire and made some territorial gains, and so did Greece, which got a border rectification in Thessaly. Russia got Ardahan, Batum (now Batumi), and Kars from the Ottomans and Bessarabia from Romania, in return for the Dobruja. In a separate agreement with the Ottoman government, which was kept secret during the conference, Great Britain acquired control over Cyprus. Crete was promised its own constitutional government. Other provisions of the Congress of Berlin included the protection of religious minorities in Turkey.

Considering the diplomatic culture of the period, the Congress of Berlin was a remarkable event. Disraeli was the first European statesman to use English instead of French on such an occasion. Bismarck directed the congress efficiently and speedily but came down hard on the Turkish delegation, allowing little room for maneuvering.

The most important results of this congress were the shaping of the future of Bulgaria and the weakening of the Ottoman Empire. The Congress of Berlin preserved European peace for years to come, but did not find a permanent solution to the position of the Balkan region between the status quo and questions of nationality. The establishment of a Greater Bulgaria, according to the Treaty of San Stefano, would have been a clearer solution and would have given the history of the

Balkans and consequently the history of Europe a different outcome.

See also **Bismarck, Otto von; Bulgaria; Germany; Russo-Turkish War; San Stefano, Treaty of.**

BIBLIOGRAPHY

Langer, William L. *European Alliances and Alignments, 1871–1890.* 2nd ed. New York, 1950.

Medlicott, W. N. *The Congress of Berlin and After: A Diplomatic History of the Near Eastern Settlement, 1878–1880.* 2nd ed. Hamden, Conn., 1963.

Melville, Ralph, and Hans-Jürgen Schröder, eds. *Der Berliner Kongress von 1878: Die Politik der Grossmächte und die Probleme der Modernisierung in Südosteuropa in der zweiten Hälfte des 19. Jahrhunderts.* Wiesbaden, Germany, 1982.

Taylor, A. J. P. *The Struggle for Mastery in Europe, 1848–1918.* Oxford, U.K., 1954.

HOLGER AFFLERBACH

CONGRESS OF TROPPAU. The principles of reaction established after 1815 by the conservative powers of Austria, Russia, and Prussia and manifested in the Holy Alliance worked temporarily to suppress revolutionary movements and activities. In 1820, however, revolutions in Portugal, Spain, and Naples compelled the respective monarchs to accept constitutional governments. The creation of constitutional monarchies was clearly the product of revolutionary contagion, yet the legitimate monarchs of the three states remained on their thrones.

The situation presented particularly ominous and complex problems for Clemens von Metternich, the Austrian foreign minister, and Alexander I, the Russian tsar. Before 1819, Alexander had encouraged liberal movements in Italy and Germany, and this presented Metternich with both ideological and political dilemmas. Russia's diplomatic influence in Europe was substantial and often ran counter to Austrian interests. In 1819 Alexander experienced a significant transformation in which he fundamentally rejected liberalism and embraced reaction. The tsar's reversal was triggered by the assassination that year of his favorite conservative writer, August Kotzebue, in Germany. Although Metternich capitalized on this event to suppress revolutionary

movements in Germany, he was less inclined to encourage the tsar when it came to matters in Italy.

Metternich was far more concerned about Italian events than what was occurring in the Iberian Peninsula. Austria had held Lombardy-Venetia since 1814 as part of the emperor's new patrimony. The Habsburgs' extended family occupied the thrones of Modena, Parma, and Tuscany. In 1815 in Naples, Austrian forces restored Ferdinand IV to his throne (as Ferdinand I, king of the Two Sicilies). When Alexander reacted to the Neapolitan revolution of 1820 by threatening to send troops to restore Ferdinand as an absolute monarch, Metternich was compelled to act quickly to discourage Russian intervention in Italy.

Thus, Metternich convened a meeting of the Quintuple Alliance on 25 October 1820 at Troppau, in Silesia (modern-day Opava, Czech Republic). This was the first serious test of the Holy Alliance, and at the same time it illustrated the differences between those states and the other members of the Quintuple Alliance. Great Britain, a vital part of the latter alliance, was not sympathetic to Austrian and Russian concerns; the British recused themselves from the affair and sent only their ambassador in Vienna to observe the proceedings. Britain did not perceive constitutionalism as a threat to its national interests, and relations between Naples and London had been quite good since the late eighteenth century. France as well did not participate, but sent only an observer. Frederick William III, the Prussian king, agreed to participate, and dispatched Baron Karl von Hardenberg, his foreign minister, to Troppau, although the king had little interest in encouraging Russia and Austria to expand their influence in Europe.

Metternich sought to establish a principle of intervention that would preclude Alexander from using military force, but permit Austria to represent the Holy Alliance and the Concert of Europe and to act against revolutionary movements when necessary. To this end Metternich and Alexander hammered out a statement of intent to be broadcast to the revolutionary governments. The Troppau Protocol, of 19 November 1820, proclaimed that governments that arose as a consequence of revolution were illegitimate and could be declared outside the European concert. Such states would face sanctions that could include armed intervention in order to restore the legitimate monarchy to full power.

Metternich made no immediate decision to dispatch troops to Italy, as the Austrian army in Lombardy-Venetia was not prepared for military operations. Metternich and Alexander, however, agreed to meet again in several months at Laibach to discuss the specifics of armed intervention in Italy. The Troppau Protocol gave Metternich the right of intervention, specifically because Ferdinand requested it, but also because the threat of revolution was very real throughout the peninsula. The protocol further provided Metternich with a means of limiting Alexander's options in Italy and Germany. Yet, at the moment of his victory at Troppau, Metternich alienated Great Britain, which essentially withdrew from the alliance, although it remained an interested observer in Continental affairs.

See also **Alexander I; Concert of Europe; Congress of Vienna; Holy Alliance; Metternich, Clemens von.**

BIBLIOGRAPHY

Artz, Frederick B. *Reaction and Revolution, 1814–1832.* New York, 1934. Reprint, New York, 1963.

Reinerman, Alan J. "Metternich, Alexander I, and the Russian Challenge in Italy, 1815–1820." *Journal of Modern History* 46, no. 2 (1974): 262–276.

Schroeder, Paul W. *The Transformation of European Politics, 1763–1848.* Oxford, U.K., 1994.

FREDERICK C. SCHNEID

CONGRESS OF VIENNA.

The Congress of Vienna, which met officially from September 1814 through June 1815, was the most significant diplomatic conference since the Peace of Westphalia in 1648. The doctrine established by the participating powers was—in most cases—far more important than the specific redistribution of territories that the diplomats discussed and determined in detail. The congress accepted the principle of a European balance of power enforced by collective action. The use of territorial compensation as a means of maintaining a general balance became the method of preventing any immediate or future hostilities among European powers. At the conclusion of the conference, the conservative powers of Austria, Russia, and Prussia also moved to suppress future revolutionary movements and to uphold the legitimacy of monarchical powers.

The congress worked out and reaffirmed the articles of the Treaty of Paris (March 1814), which concluded the Napoleonic Wars. Austria, Prussia, Russia, and Great Britain temporarily put aside their differences and geopolitical interests to defeat Napoleon. With victory imminent, the allied powers moved quickly to secure territory and guarantees for their specific interests in Europe. Article XXXII of the Peace of Paris called on the signatories to discuss these issues—and implied that all Europe was invited to the conference for similar purpose. Representatives from all causes and corners of Europe arrived in the autumn of 1814 to press their respective claims.

The architect of the congress was Prince Clemens von Metternich, the Austrian foreign minister. His diplomatic skill made him the dominant figure at the talks, challenged only by Prince Charles-Maurice de Talleyrand-Périgord, the French foreign minister. Baron Karl August von Hardenberg represented Prussia, and Tsar Alexander I, Russia. Robert Stewart, Lord Castlereagh, the British foreign secretary, stood for England. Before the meeting, the allied powers were determined to make the ultimate decisions. Talleyrand and Pedro Gómez Labrador, the Spanish representative, vehemently opposed this plan. Talleyrand argued that the restoration of the Bourbons necessitated the acceptance of France as an equal among the major powers. Spain, Portugal, and Sweden similarly demanded a seat at the table, as they had been members of the anti-French coalition that had defeated Napoleon. The congress was postponed until November, when the former allied powers admitted France to the decision-making process to the exclusion of the others.

Although the members of the European alliance had temporarily put aside their respective differences, specific territorial interests and particular concerns for the future geopolitical structure of Europe were foremost on their minds. The most pressing issue was the Polish-Saxon question. Tsar Alexander demanded compensation for Russia's military contributions with the annexation of the Grand Duchy of Warsaw to Russia's new kingdom of Poland. Frederick William III, king of Prussia (r. 1797–1840), however, was unwilling to support the absorption of former Prussian territory without fair compensation. To this end he was determined to annex the kingdom of Saxony. Metternich and Talleyrand were unwilling to accede to Alexander's and Frederick William's desires, as that would enlarge Russian and Prussian borders to the detriment of Austria, and run counter to French sympathies for the Poles. Castlereagh too, was not inclined to encourage Russian expansion or the close relationship between that empire and the Prussians, which had developed during the war.

Metternich and Castlereagh became appropriately concerned about Russian power at the moment France ceased to be the central threat to European peace. The Polish-Saxon question was hotly debated even before the opening of the congress in November. This critical problem was resolved by January 1815, when all parties grudgingly agreed to a middle course. Russia received two-thirds of the grand duchy, while Prussia annexed a third of Saxony and gained significant expansion of its territories on the Rhine. This compromise satiated Alexander and Frederick William III, gave Metternich and Austria a sense of "equilibrium" in central Europe, and kept France at bay by strengthening Prussia in the west.

Great Britain's interests were not limited to central and eastern Europe. The Revolutionary and Napoleonic Wars also illustrated the danger of French occupation of Belgium and Holland. Castlereagh therefore desired the establishment of a strong state in the Low Countries that would prohibit French expansion. He successfully negotiated an enlarged Kingdom of the Netherlands, which included Belgium. In Germany, he gained the restoration of Hanover to the British royal family, and thereby wrested it from the Prussians, who had possessed it since 1806. Castlereagh also pressed for the removal of Napoleon's sister, Queen Caroline, and brother in law, King Joachim Murat, from the Neapolitan throne. Ferdinand IV, the Bourbon king of Naples (r. 1759–1806, 1815–1825) and of the Two Sicilies as Ferdinand I (r. 1816–1825), had fled his capital in 1806 for the protection of the British in Sicily. In 1814, Murat and Caroline defected to the allied coalition

in exchange for their thrones. Metternich brokered this agreement without English consent. Castlereagh's desire to revise this arrangement came to naught until the spring of 1815, when Napoleon escaped from exile and Murat went to war with Austria. Murat's defeat in May 1815 led to Ferdinand's return to Naples, courtesy of Great Britain.

The fate of Italy and Germany were foremost on Metternich's mind, too. Napoleon had removed all vestiges of Habsburg influence in Germany and elevated and enlarged many of the German principalities. Metternich desired to restore some semblance of Habsburg authority to counter Prussia. Hence, he proposed a German Confederation with Austria acting as the presiding power. He was ultimately successful in this, as many of the middling German states found Prussia's enhanced strength and size a threat to their relative independence. They accepted Metternich's proposal of a German Confederation playing Austria off of Prussia. Although Austria presided over this new Germany, Habsburg influence remained a shadow of its former importance.

Italy provided a particular dilemma for Metternich and the other statesmen. The peninsula was under French control for almost two decades. The House of Savoy that ruled Piedmont-Sardinia had been in exile since 1802. Furthermore, Napoleon excluded the Bourbon and Habsburg dynasties from the peninsula. Many of the Italian states were absorbed into his kingdom of Italy or the Italian departments of imperial France. Metternich wanted Austria to be compensated for its wartime efforts by the annexation of Lombardy and Venetia to the empire. In return, he accepted Russian expansion in Poland and Prussian acquisitions in Germany. Metternich also placed extended members of the Habsburg dynasty in Modena, Parma, and Tuscany. This arrangement worked to balance a potentially pro-British Naples, as well as an independently minded Piedmont-Sardinia, which had traditionally been a thorn in Austria's side.

The congress completed much of its work by the spring of 1815; however, Napoleon's escape from Elba and return to the French throne led to the temporary postponement of the final act. Talleyrand had initially secured France's position as an equal among its former enemies. He retained

Le Congrès. French cartoon c. 1815. The negotiations of the congress are depicted as a complicated dance. Shown left to right are: Metternich (who seems to observe the proceedings with calm amusement), Lord Castlereagh of England, Francis I of Austria, Alexander I of Russia, Frederick William II of Prussia, Frederick Augustus I of Saxony (attempting to keep hold of his crown), and Talleyrand. Musée de la Ville de Paris, Musée Carnavalet, Paris, France/Bridgeman Art Library/Lauros/Giraudon

French borders as of 1792, including Nice and Savoy and territory taken from the west bank of the Rhine. The Hundred Days (March–June 1815)—Napoleon's return—seriously undermined what Talleyrand had achieved the previous year. The allied powers took the opportunity to strip France of captured lands, accepting only those borders of 1789. Furthermore, France had to suffer allied occupation until it paid an indemnity of 700 million francs to the coalition.

The final treaty, reached in March, was not signed until June 1815. It included 110 articles that embodied both the grand and the petty interests of the participating powers. Austria, Great Britain, France, Russia, Prussia, Spain, Portugal, and Sweden were the primary signatories. Their accession to the treaty presented the other states with a fait accompli. At the conclusion of the congress, Tsar Alexander proposed to Frederick William III and Francis I of Austria (r. 1804–1835) a "Holy Alliance" of sorts, which he based on the conservative principles of the three Christian monarchs. Concomitantly, the major powers—to the exclusion of France—agreed to monitor events in Europe in order to preserve the newly established "equilibrium."

The Congress of Vienna produced a relatively viable and lasting peace in Europe for the next century. Although the doctrine of revolutionary suppression did not last beyond midcentury, the concept of diplomatic negotiation and territorial compensation to limit state expansion was quite successful in restraining European conflicts and mitigating their consequences. What made the congress unique, however, was that its participants agreed to this new system of international relations as a principle and did not define it solely by their immediate desires.

See also **Alexander I; Castlereagh, Viscount (Robert Stewart); Concert of Europe; French Revolutionary Wars and Napoleonic Wars; Hardenberg, Karl August von; Holy Alliance; Metternich, Clemens von; Napoleon.**

BIBLIOGRAPHY

Kissinger, Henry. *A World Restored: Metternich, Castlereagh, and the Problems of Peace, 1812–1822*. Boston, 1973.

Nicolson, Harold. *The Congress of Vienna: A Study in Allied Unity, 1812–1822*. Reprint. New York, 1974.

Schroeder, Paul. *The Transformation of European Politics, 1763–1848*. Oxford, U.K., 1994.

Webster, Charles. *The Congress of Vienna, 1814–1815*. London, 1963.

FREDERICK C. SCHNEID

CONRAD, JOSEPH (1857–1924), Polish-born English writer.

Joseph Conrad was born as Józef Teodor Konrad Korzeniowski on 3 December 1857 at Berdichev, which was then part of Ruthenia but later became part of Ukraine. His family was part of the Polish gentry but at the time of his birth Poland was partitioned between Prussia, Russia, and Austria. It did not exist as a geographical entity but survived as a culture, a language, a literature, and a fervent patriotic force. Conrad's father, Apollo Korzeniowski, and his mother, Ewa Bobrowska, were leaders of the Polish patriotic resistance in 1863, and for this they were imprisoned by the Russians and died as a result of ill-treatment. Their only child led his father's funeral procession through the streets of Krakow as part of a major public expression of patriotic Polish feeling.

By the age of eleven, the orphaned Joseph Conrad was the ward of his uncle, Tadeusz Bobrowski. The contrast between Conrad's father, who was romantic, impulsive, and altruistic, and his uncle, who was prudent, self-interested, cautious, and circumspect, profoundly influenced the models of masculinity that occur in the mature Conrad's novels; typically, his male heroes are suffering, divided, and self-doubting.

Between 1876 and 1893, Conrad was a sailor, serving first in the French and then in the British merchant marine. Although known as a great English novelist, Conrad wrote in his third language, Polish and French being his first and second. To the end of his life, he spoke English with a heavy Polish accent, and in his early texts he habitually used French and Polish constructions (some of which were corrected by his English wife, Jessie, who typed his manuscripts).

Conrad would not have become an English novelist at all had the French and the Russians not signed a treaty in which France recognized Russia's right to hold its male citizens liable for twenty-five years of military service. It was to avoid service that Conrad joined the British merchant marine in 1878 as an ordinary seaman on the *Skimmer of the Sea,* a ship that carried coal between Newcastle upon Tyne and Lowestoft. His introduction to English was through the often difficult to understand dialect called Geordie, spoken in northeast England.

During his years at sea, Conrad read Gustave Flaubert, Guy de Maupassant, Russians such as Fyodor Dostoyevsky and Ivan Turgenev, the classic English authors (Conrad's father had translated Charles Dickens and William Shakespeare into Polish), and his great contemporary Henry James. By 1890 he had written his first novel and he carried the manuscript with him when he took a job in the Belgian Congo, an experience that transformed his art and by extension the whole of English literature, since it led to the writing of *Heart of Darkness* (published in serial form between 1899 and 1900). In 1894, after some twenty years at sea, he married and settled in the southeast of England. His first novel, *Almayer's Folly,* was published in 1895 and was followed in quick succession by *An Outcast of the Islands* (1896) and *The Nigger of the Narcissus* (1897). With the publication of *Lord Jim* in 1900, Conrad had in effect invented the modern novel.

Heart of Darkness and *Lord Jim* take narrative themes familiar to the late Victorians—exploration in Africa and the Far East—and use radical narrative to transform the traditional material of the action story into an exhaustive moral and psychological exploration of the human condition. He also used a

Polish narrative tradition, the *gaweda,* or told-tale: both *Heart of Darkness* and *Lord Jim* use a frame narrator, who presents an inner narrator, Marlow, who tells the story of an elusive, enigmatic (and now dead) figure, Kurtz and Jim respectively. The narrative device forces the reader into a collaborative rather than a passive relationship with the text, attending at every point to the way the tale is being told.

These novels of personal crisis and moral tragedy lead into the next group of narratives, the political novels *Nostromo* (1904), *The Secret Agent* (1907), and *Under Western Eyes* (1911), set in South America, London, and Russia, respectively. In these, inquiry into individual predicaments coexists with the investigation of whole societies. Conrad's complex relationship with political power, already visible in *Heart of Darkness*'s treatment of European imperialism, recurs in his South American and Russian novels; in the latter, his personal loathing of Russia takes center stage. His London novel treats the institutions and attitudes of his adopted country with withering and corrosive irony. In the same period, Conrad wrote short stories of rich psychological complexity, the most powerful of which, "The Secret Sharer," can serve as a supplement to the study of tensions within the self that was extensively explored in the Dostoyevskian figure of Razumov in *Under Western Eyes.*

After his major phase, which closes with *Under Western Eyes,* novels such as *Chance* (1914), *Victory* (1915), and *The Rover* (1923) were less innovative, although *The Shadow-Line* (1917) is a late masterpiece that fully recovers his earlier subtlety and complexity. On his death in 1924, he was the acknowledged master of the English novel.

See also **Dostoyevsky, Fyodor; Great Britain; Imperialism; Poland; Turgenev, Ivan.**

BIBLIOGRAPHY

Batchelor, John. *The Life of Joseph Conrad: A Critical Biography.* Oxford, U.K., 1994.

Berthoud, Jacques. *Joseph Conrad: The Major Phase.* New York, 1978.

Conrad, Borys. *My Father: Joseph Conrad.* New York, 1970.

Daphna, Erdinast-Vulcan. *Joseph Conrad and the Modern Temper.* New York, 1991.

Hervouet, Yves. *The French Face of Joseph Conrad.* New York, 1990.

Najder, Zdzislaw. *Joseph Conrad: A Chronicle.* Translated by Halina Carroll-Najder. New York, 1983.

Thorburn, David. *Conrad's Romanticism.* New Haven, Conn., 1974.

Watt, Ian. *Conrad in the Nineteenth Century.* Berkeley, Calif., 1979.

JOHN BATCHELOR

CONSERVATISM. Conservatism, by definition, is a relative word. Derived from the Latin *conservare,* it refers in the broadest sense to the effort to safeguard or "conserve" elements of a culture, society, or political regime in the face of threatening or sudden change. It follows from this description that those describing themselves, or who are described, as "conservatives" will vary tremendously in accordance with what it is they seek to protect. When elements of the Soviet establishment sought to resist the changes proposed by Mikhail Gorbachev in the 1980s, they were characterized in the popular press as "hardliners" or "conservatives," despite the fact that they were attempting to preserve a system—communism—that is otherwise associated with more radical tendencies. By contrast, self-described "conservatives" or "neoconservatives" in the early-twenty-first-century United States frequently uphold views that are radical in certain contexts. It may well be conservative to defend democracy and free-market capitalism in America, where the two are long established. But to aim to bring them to parts of the world that have never known them—even, if necessary, by force—is anything but.

Scholars of conservatism have attempted to take into account this semantic instability since at least the 1920s, when the Hungarian-born sociologist Karl Mannheim (1893–1947) undertook a still-valuable study of the concept. Mannheim defined conservatism as an ideology "oriented to meanings that contain different objective contents in different epochs." More recently, the political scientist Samuel Huntington has described conservatism as a "positional ideology," always relative to time and circumstance. In Huntington's view, it makes little sense to speak of conservatism as an enduring political, intellectual, or ideological phenomenon.

If one treats conservatism as a transhistorical category, then Huntington undoubtedly has a point. Yet if conservatism is considered as a European intellectual and political tradition that took shape in the eighteenth and nineteenth centuries, then it is possible to speak of the phenomenon as an abiding set of general beliefs that, although varying considerably according to time and circumstance, nonetheless do cohere into something more specific than a mere positional ideology. Seen in this light, conservatism is, as the scholar Jerry Muller has observed, a set of enduring "assumptions, themes, and images." As such, it takes its place alongside the other great "isms" central to nineteenth-century European history: republicanism, socialism, and liberalism.

THE ORIGINS OF CONSERVATISM

It is revealing that the earliest uses of the terms *conservatism* and *conservative* occur in France and England. For it was in these two countries that conservatism assumed its earliest coherence as a political disposition. In France, the word *conservateur* was in use from at least 1794 to refer to one who advocated "conserving" various elements of the *ancien régime,* then under attack by the forces of the French Revolution. By 1815 the liberal theorist Benjamin Constant (1767–1830) was making reference to a "conservative spirit" (*esprit conservateur*) everywhere apparent in France following the defeat of Napoleon. In the subsequent decade, usage of this kind was increasingly common—witnessed, most strikingly, by the establishment of a leading French weekly, *Le Conservateur,* in 1818. Boasting the direct participation of François-René de Chateaubriand (1768–1848) and Louis de Bonald (1754–1840), among others, the journal vowed in its inaugural issue to uphold "religion, the King, liberty . . . and respectable people" in an effort to preserve traditional values and institutions from revolutionary attacks.

In England, the word *conservative* was first employed in a self-consciously political sense as early as 1816, when the *Anti-Jacobin Review* saw fit to write "of those conservative principles which all good men ought not passively to foster and cherish, but actually promote." As in France, uses

of the term multiplied in the succeeding decade, culminating in the first reference to the Tory Party as the "Conservative party" in an essay by John Miller of Lincoln's Inn in the *Quarterly Review* in January 1830. Although it would take the Tories some time to officially adopt that title, their spokesmen readily assumed the mantle informally, presenting themselves as the defenders of "conservative principles."

Conservative and *conservatives,* then, are predominantly nineteenth-century terms. Yet it would be shortsighted to assume that the principles of those who adopted these labels were no older than the words themselves. In fact, much of the intellectual capital on which later conservatives drew was developed in the eighteenth century in response to three great movements of change: state centralization, the Enlightenment, and the French Revolution.

The first of these movements involved the usurpation of powers and prerogatives formerly in the hands of corporate bodies, towns, landed aristocrats, and local elites. As centralizing governments in the eighteenth century developed state bureaucracies and other institutions (armies, courts, police) capable of extending their dominion over ever-larger segments of the population, they threatened to displace the traditional authorities and aristocratic families that for centuries had administered justice and mediated power in local arenas. The result was not only bitterness but also the elaboration of a rhetoric that defended the importance of preserving established authorities and privileges as a means to defend against the lurking despotism of the state. As the French aristocrat and jurist Charles-Louis de Secondat, baron de Montesquieu (1689–1755) observed in his 1748 classic *The Spirit of the Laws,* "all experience proves that every man with power is led to abuse it." Consequently, "to prevent the abuse of power, things must be so ordered that power checks power."

The *Spirit of the Laws* was the most articulate eighteenth-century attempt to think through such an ordering. And although Montesquieu's arguments on behalf of what he called "intermediary powers" would also prove appealing to American revolutionaries and nineteenth-century liberals—most famously Alexis de Tocqueville (1805–1859)—they provided a powerful rationale to contemporary conservatives who sought to protect vested interests from the creeping encroachments of the state. Repeated widely, they inspired spirited defenses from many other across Europe, most notably the Westphalian civil servant Justus Möser (1720–1794).

This eighteenth-century response to state centralization thus formed one fertile source of early conservative rhetoric. Of equal importance in terms of mobilizing conservative opinion was the Enlightenment. A multifaceted movement, replete with rival currents and national variations, the Enlightenment was by no means a universally radical phenomenon, and in fact produced conservative spokesmen of its own. Yet it was above all the radical thrust of Enlightenment culture that brought into being the most virulent response. Especially in the Catholic countries, the Enlightenment's attacks on what it deemed the "fanaticism" of the church provoked a broad-based "Counter-Enlightenment" response. Asserting the centrality of religious orthodoxy to social and political stability, this response put forth the necessity of hierarchy and authority to rein in fallen human beings predisposed to sin. It produced arguments on behalf of sentiment, emotion, and inherited norms (prejudice) as sources of knowledge as valid as reason. It greeted Enlightenment calls for greater sexual freedom with defenses of moral rectitude and the sanctity of the family. And it met the stilted claims of Enlightenment partisans to serve as torchbearers for an age of darkness with arguments on behalf of the wisdom of tradition. According to this perspective, the general tendency of the Enlightenment's abstract theorists was destructive. The duty of its opponents was clear: to conserve.

Well before the French Revolution, then, Europeans had generated a considerable body of conservative thought, even if they never used the term itself. Neither, for that matter, did their greatest heir, the British statesman Edmund Burke (1729–1797). And yet in his *Reflections on the Revolution in France* (1790), Burke offered the definitive statement of conservative philosophy for centuries to come.

The immediate purpose of the *Reflections* was itself profoundly conservative: to protect England and English institutions from the revolutionary conflagration in France. But in serving this immediate end, Burke fashioned a number of timeless principles that were applicable to a great variety of situations. Not surprisingly, many of them echoed the earlier sentiments of European conservatives *avant la lettre.* Burke stressed the need, for example, voiced by Montesquieu and others, for intermediary authorities—"opposed and conflicting interests"— to "interpose a salutary check to all precipitate resolution." Like Counter-Enlightenment polemicists, he lambasted "men of theory" and "intriguing philosophers" for their "political metaphysics," emphasizing the "fallible and feeble contrivance" of human reason, and man's propensity to "pride, ambition, avarice, revenge, lust, [and] sedition." He argued the necessity of hierarchy and a church to rein in human passions, and he highlighted the supreme importance of moral values to provide a "decent drapery" to cover over and contain our many human failings. Finally, and most famously, Burke presented culture and government as the product of the "collected reason of ages." Given that natural failings are many, and private allotment of reason small, human beings should treat with respect the legacy that had been granted to them by their ancestors, appreciating that there was a "latent wisdom" that prevailed in established customs, practices, and prejudices.

Which is not to say that Burke was opposed to innovation or improvement. Throughout the *Reflections,* he reiterated the necessity of a "slow, well-sustained progress," arguing that a government "without the means of some change is without the means of its conservation." The twin tasks of statecraft, as he saw it, were "at once to preserve and to reform."

And yet there was another, somewhat darker, side to Burke's rhetoric in the *Reflections.* His allusions to the mob run rampant—"a swinish multitude"—ever-ready to trample its social betters under foot; his regrettable readiness to associate "jew-brokers" and "jew-[stock]jobbers" with both the "monied interest" and political intrigue; and finally his invocation of the language of conspiracy, warning of the "confederacies" and "cabal" of philosophers and Masons, who had formed a plot, a "regular plan" for the destruction of thrones and altars across Europe—all this found a receptive audience of people with whom Burke would otherwise have been ill at ease. Whereas his thought bequeathed a fund of principles that could be drawn upon by self-professed liberals and conservatives of a moderate cast, it also was embraced by men and women farther to the right who wanted no truck with parliaments, or tolerance, or well-sustained progress at all.

NINETEENTH-CENTURY CONSERVATISM

Historians sometimes distinguish between conservatism and "reaction" to characterize the often blurry line that separated those who followed the more moderate Burkean course from those, especially on the Continent, who believed that politics could never be a matter of compromise when it came to fighting the noxious influences of the Enlightenment and the French Revolution. What Counter-Enlightenment polemicists had seen as the cosmic, world-historical battle between Enlightenment philosophy, on the one hand, and Christianity and divinely ordained kingship, on the other, was carried over into the postrevolutionary period and presented as an epic struggle between good and evil. As the Savoyard nobleman Joseph de Maistre (1753–1821) declared, the struggle between Christianity and philosophy was a "war to the death" waged between God and his enemies. In a war of this kind, there could be no middle ground.

Insofar as figures of this ilk advocated policies aimed explicitly at restoring the status quo ante—recovering privileges or rebuilding institutions destroyed by the Revolution or Napoleon (r. 1804–1814/15)—the terms *reaction* or *reactionary* are useful. Upholding a firm alliance between throne and altar, right-wing reactionaries sought the restitution of properties seized during the Revolution and the Napoleonic regimes and pressed for the recovery of other lost privileges and institutions of the *ancien régime*. Above all, they avowed allegiance to the "legitimate" monarchs who had ruled prior to the Revolutionary and Napoleonic upheavals.

The heyday of such reaction was the period of the Restoration following the defeat of Napoleon in 1815. But this heyday was short-lived, brought to a close not only by revolution and revolt but also by these forces' own intransigence. In France, ultraroyalist reactionaries soon found themselves at odds with the restored Bourbon ruler Louis XVIII (r. 1814–1815, 1815–1824), disillusioned by his apparent willingness to accommodate various aspects of the revolutionary heritage. Elsewhere in Europe, one can trace a similar phenomenon. It is evident in the response of Prussian Junkers to the practical reform efforts of Frederick William III (r. 1797–1840); in the response of the Amicizia Cattolica, an association of pious aristocrats, to that group's dissolution by Charles Felix (r. 1821–1831), king of Piedmont-Savoy, in 1828; in the politics of the Zelanti, the reactionary cardinals of the Papal States who fought all concession to the legacy of the Enlightenment and the Revolution; and most dramatically, in the opposition to the limited, constitutional monarchy of Spain by the "Carlists," men more royalist than the king, who were willing to defend their convictions by taking up arms against the state.

Uncompromising, militant, inflexible, the politics of throne and altar was thus reactionary in its increasingly unrealistic desire for the restoration of a vanished Old Regime. But that same lack of realism—the visionary, even revolutionary insistence on taking Europe back to an idealized past that had never really existed—should prevent the free application of the term *reactionary*. For in certain respects, the Manichean politics of the early "right"—a term that had come into use during the French Revolution to designate the seating preferences of delegates to the National Assembly—was more indicative of the future than of the past. In the vision of a Maistre—at total odds with the pluralism, individualism, and secularism of modernity, obsessed with social cohesion, and quick to contemplate violence in the service of its preservation—one glimpses an early foretaste of the radical right-wing movements of the late nineteenth and twentieth centuries. Although it is far too sweeping to suggest, as Isaiah Berlin (1909–1997) once did in a famous essay, that in Maistre one finds a precursor of European fascism, it is nonetheless undeniable that his thought, like that of other early right-wing prophets resonated with later, more combustible figures of the radical right, who were all too ready to mix nationalism, racism, and the politics of mass mobilization in terrible and explosive concoctions.

Between these forces, on the one side, and liberals, republicans, and (by the second half of the nineteenth century) socialists and communists, on the other, stood conservatives. In their common aversion to revolution, conservatives were perfectly ready at times to make common cause with reactionaries and those farther to the right, as they did during the European-wide revolutions of 1848 and in other cases thereafter. Yet they were also prepared to pursue their wider goals through practical accommodation with established governments, whether these be dynastic, parliamentary, or imperial. As the German conservative Friedrich von Gentz (1764–1832) explained, a conservative is someone "who seeks, within reasonable limits, to maintain the old ways and to guide the tide of history, when he is unable or unwilling to stem it, along controllable channels." In order to guide the tide of history, that is, it was easier to labor along channels already dug.

This, in fact, is the central story of nineteenth-century conservatism from the outset, when Prince Clemens von Metternich (1883–1859) and other leading statesmen established the Concert of Europe to preserve the inviolability of regimes after the fall of Napoleon. Working from within to ensure order and prevent the recurrence of further social upheaval, conservatives found their place in practical, pragmatic accommodation with extant powers.

That general pattern holds true even after the events of 1830 and 1848 proved the limitations of this policy, and spelled the demise of the Metternichian system. Whether as officials in the Prussian or Habsburg civil service; proponents of the French *juste-milieu* that ruled France under Louis-Philippe (r. 1830–1848); supporters of the Napoleonic legacy as embodied in his nephew, Napoleon III (r. 1852–1871); or representatives of the British Tory or Spanish Conservative parties, which for much of the second half of the nineteenth century shared power with their Whig and Liberal opponents—conservatives and conservatism continued to operate pragmatically to guarantee order and the rule of law. They sought to protect property rights and backed the established churches, pushing for a central role for religion in evolving national education programs. They upheld principles of hierarchy and social order, acting in support of notables and the aristocracy. And they worked to promote the love of country and the love of place, defending local interests while lending their support to evolving national patriotism.

Without question, conservatism's predilection for power often translated into cozy relationships with those in positions of wealth and authority in finance and industry, the army and the church, the aristocracy and the rural gentry. Moreover, conservative fears of disorder meant, in practice, the adoption of paternal or repressive policies designed to ensure that the "mob" did not take to the streets. To the extent that the machinery of the state could be harnessed in service of this task, conservatives displayed a proclivity for what the historian Michael Broers has called, borrowing a term from Marc Raeff, the "well-ordered police state," administered in defense of their own interests and general moral order. That proclivity coexisted, however, in uneasy tension with the older conservative distrust of central authority.

Yet the story of nineteenth-century conservatism is far more complicated than a simple opposition to disorder, change, modernity, or progress. It is undeniable, for example, that conservatives played a major role in breaking up the guilds, customs barriers, and other feudal atavisms that continued to impede freedom of trade and profession in the liberal nineteenth century. It was Sir Robert Peel (1788–1850), a man who has been described as the founder of the Conservative Party in England, who finally repealed the Corn Laws at the expense of the great landed families, opening England's markets to foreign grain. And it was only with the aid of key conservatives that the Zollverein, the free-trade customs union of the German states, established in 1834, became a reality. In the French liberal François Guizot's (1787–1874) famous dictum *"enrichissez-vous"* ("get rich"), many conservatives also found a long-term answer to the problem of poverty, and they worked to create the conditions—in finance, banking, manufacturing, and industry—so that more and more could do just that.

It was a conservative, Benjamin Disraeli (1804–1881), who greatly expanded the English suffrage, enfranchising many working-class males in the Second Reform Act of 1867. And it was a conservative, Otto von Bismarck (1815–1898), who pushed through significant social legislation in the 1880s, initiating state-sponsored accident and old-age insurance as well an early form of subsidized medicine. It may be argued in both cases that the motives were cynical, and that is undoubtedly partly true.

Yet the legislation was passed regardless, largely in the realization of that pragmatic conservative truth that in order to preserve, one must also reform.

CONSERVATISM AND THE NEW RIGHT

That same willingness to make compromises and concessions, however, entering into agreements with political opponents, could also prove a double-edged sword. This was especially the case on the Continent, and ironically, only after conservatives there had begun to learn that the "people" was not necessarily their enemy. Whereas at the beginning of the century conservatives had generally sought to restrict the suffrage, defending high property requirements for voting, the experience of Napoleon III and then the examples of Bismarck and Disraeli demonstrated that the "people" could be quite conservatively disposed. This was most clear in the realm of religion, where the second half of the nineteenth century witnessed the mass mobilization of Catholics and other religious groups in defiance of the anticlerical policies favored by liberals, republicans, and socialists. A transnational phenomenon, Christian and especially Catholic mobilization involved the effective use of the means of mass politics, employing demonstrations and public protests, mass-circulation media, voluntary associations, and political parties to defend Catholic and conservative values. By opposing civil marriage or divorce, or fighting to defend and extend religious education to deprived social groups, conservative politicians could draw on considerable mass support.

And yet to do so in the arena of parliamentary regimes meant entering into compacts and compromises with the opposition. In Spain, for example, in a system that was known informally as the *turno*, conservatives and liberals of the Restoration monarchy (1875–1923) rotated regularly in power. Seen from the outside, and from the perspective of extraparliamentary extremes, Spanish liberals and conservatives could seem virtually indistinguishable. The danger for both parties was that they risked being tainted by the sins of their opponents, implicated in a larger regime that by the turn of the century was coming to be seen (and not without reason) as narrow and corrupt.

With parliamentary governments throughout Europe marred by scandals at the end of the nineteenth century, observers outside of Spain noted similar phenomena. The French socialist Jules Guesde (1845–1922), for example, remarked ruefully that members of the moderately republican Radical Party distinguished themselves from conservatives only by their hypocrisy. Meanwhile, conservative Catholics in France might wonder how much their alleged supporters really differed from their left-wing colleagues across the aisle. Speaking in November 1874, the erstwhile Orléanist Adolphe Thiers (1797–1877) could maintain that "the Republic, if it is to exist at all, cannot but be conservative," and for some time it was, prompting many Catholics to heed Pope Leo XIII's (r. 1878–1903) call to "rally" to the republic in the early 1890s. Already by this point, however, the confederation of French conservatives known as the "Union des Droites" that had acted with some success in parliament in the 1880s was losing its influence. By the beginning of the twentieth century it was helpless to prevent a succession of blows to the church in France that culminated in the expulsion of the religious orders and the formal separation of church and state in 1905.

In the eyes of growing numbers on the right, such developments demonstrated both the incapacity of parliamentary conservatives to further their interests and the essential insolvency of the republic. As early as 1890 the extreme right-wing polemicist Charles Maurras (1868–1952) could write to a colleague that "there are two conservative parties in France, the living one and the other." "The first," he specified, "was with [Édouard] Drumont," the author of a virulently anti-Semitic tract of 1886, *La France Juive*. The second, the "other," was bound up with the moribund republic, antiquated, compromised, and complicit in a decadent regime.

Maurras's distinction between living conservatives and dead conservatives, between conservatives old and new, was overstated, but telling. For although he himself advocated an idiosyncratic form of neoroyalism, his methods and outlook pointed forward to something disturbingly new. In the year before Maurras's letter, the tremendous interest generated by the French general Georges Boulanger (1837–1891), who flirted openly with the prospect of a royalist coup, had highlighted the demagogic possibilities of a strongman willing to threaten direct action against the republic. And in the years following, during the heat of the Dreyfus affair, the political potential of anti-Semitism and populist national chauvinism peddled by the likes of Drumont was already clear. By blending these explosive forces with the means of modern mass communication, Maurras and the early leaders of the protofascist Action Française, founded in 1898, concocted a new politics and a "new right" that was largely without precedent, even if it did at times recall—in its Manicheanism and penchant for conspiracy theories, its rhetorical violence and its rejection of individualism, pluralism, and the values of the French Revolution—the language of earlier figures like Maistre.

Notwithstanding these similarities, the Action Française unquestionably represented a new development, one that with its street gangs and pseudobiological racism, its anticapitalism and populist mass mobilization, had parallels throughout Europe, above all in Germany. There, as in France, the period between the 1890s and World War I witnessed an explosive growth in groups brandishing the ideological weaponry of the new right, or what the historian Zeev Sternhell has identified as a "revolutionary right," the ideological forefather of fascism. Attacking the ravages of industrial capitalism, they invoked sinister conspiracies of Jews and international financiers. They praised the racial superiority of the German *volk* and preached militant nationalism and the supremacy of German values and German soil. Radical, even revolutionary, they aimed to transform the allegedly decadent society they knew and detested through mass mobilization, direct action, and the "purifying" clarity of violence.

Volkish, anti-Semitic, populist, these early ideologists of the new right ceased, as the scholar Hans-Jurgen Puhle has observed, "to be conservative in any reasonable sense of the term." They were, on the contrary, revolutionaries, who rejected the central impulse toward preservation that had governed European conservatism since its inception in the eighteenth century. When eventually they came to power throughout Europe in the 1930s and 1940s, they would show themselves adept only at destruction, leaving to others—conservatives and radicals alike—the task of piecing together the shards of European civilization that war and human malice had not obliterated entirely.

See also **Action Française; Bismarck, Otto von; Burke, Edmund; Carlism; Catholicism, Political; Chateaubriand, François-René; Concert of Europe; Disraeli, Benjamin; Dreyfus Affair; Liberalism; Maistre, Joseph de; Maurras, Charles; Metternich, Clemens von; Nicholas I; Restoration.**

BIBLIOGRAPHY

Berdahl, Robert M. *The Politics of the Prussian Nobility: The Development of a Conservative Ideology: 1770–1848.* Princeton, N.J., 1988.

Berlin, Isaiah. "Joseph de Maistre and the Origins of Fascism," *New York Review of Books* 37, no. 14 (September 27, 1990): 57–64.

Broers, Michael. *Europe After Napoleon: Revolution, Reaction, and Romanticism, 1814–1848.* Manchester, U.K., 1996.

Clark, Christopher, and Wolfram Kaiser, eds. *Culture Wars: Secular-Catholic Conflict in Nineteenth-Century Europe.* Cambridge, U.K., and New York, 2003.

Clark, J. C. D. *English Society, 1688–1832: Ideology, Social Structure, and Political Practice during the Ancien Regime.* Cambridge, U.K., and New York, 1985.

Epstein, Klaus. *The Genesis of German Conservatism.* Princeton, N.J., 1966.

Hirschman, Albert O. *The Rhetoric of Reaction: Perversity, Futility, Jeopardy.* Cambridge, Mass., 1991.

Huntington, Samuel. "Conservatism as an Ideology," *American Political Science Review* 51, no. 2 (June 1957): 454–473.

Jenkins, T. A. *Disraeli and Victorian Conservatism.* Houndsmills, U.K., and New York, 1996.

Jones, Larry Eugene, and James Retallack, eds. *Between Reform, Reaction and Resistance: Studies in the History of German Conservatism from 1789 to 1945.* Providence, R.I., 1993.

Journal of Contemporary History 13, no. 4 (October 1978). A Century of Conservatism, Part 1.

Journal of Contemporary History 14, no. 4 (October 1979). A Century of Conservatism, Part 2.

Kirk, Russell, ed. *The Portable Conservative Reader.* New York, 1982.

Mannheim, Karl. *Conservatism: A Contribution to the Sociology of Knowledge.* 1925. Edited by David Kettler, Volker Meja, and Nico Stehr and translated by David Kettler and Volker Meja. London and New York, 1986.

McMahon, Darrin M. *Enemies of the Enlightenment: The French Counter-Enlightenment and the Making of Modernity.* Oxford, U.K., and New York, 2001.

Muller, Jerry Z. *Conservatism: An Anthology of Social and Political Thought from David Hume to the Present.* Princeton, N.J., 1997.

Rémond, René. *The Right Wing in France from 1815 to De Gaulle.* Trans. James M. Laux. Philadelphia, 1966.

Sack, James J. *From Jacobite to Conservative: Reaction and Orthodoxy in Britain c. 1760–1832.* Cambridge, U.K., and New York, 1993.

Sirinelli, Jean-François. *Histoire des droites en France.* 3 vols. Paris, 1992.

Sternhell, Zeev. *La droite révolutionnaire, 1885–1914.* Paris, 1997.

Suvanto, Pekka. *Conservatism from the French Revolution to the 1990s.* Translated by Roederick Fletcher. New York, 1997.

Velema, Wyger R. E. *Enlightenment and Conservatism in the Dutch Republic: The Political Thought of Elie Luzac.* Assen, the Netherlands, 1993.

Winock, Michel. *Nationalism, Anti-Semitism, and Fascism in France.* Translated by Jane Marie Todd. Stanford, Calif., 1998.

DARRIN M. MCMAHON

CONSTABLE, JOHN (1776–1837), English painter.

Along with J. M. W. Turner (1775–1851), the most celebrated landscape painter of his day, John Constable came of age at the turn of the eighteenth century, when William Wordsworth (1770–1850) and Samuel Taylor Coleridge (1772–1834) were launching a revolution in poetry that came to be known as English Romanticism. Just as Wordsworth proclaimed—in the preface to the second edition of *Lyrical Ballads* (1800)—that poetry should speak "the real language of men in a state of vivid sensation" and celebrate man's emotional bond to nature in "humble and rustic life," Constable affirmed the value of a "natural painture"—a natural style in painting— and dedicated himself to achieving "a pure and un-affected manner" of painting rural scenes. Like Wordsworth, he represented rustic life as an alternative to urban life when the Industrial Revolution was drawing thousands into English cities. Unlike Turner, who painted railway trains and coal furnaces as well nature in all its glory, Constable strove to capture the simplicity of rural life and labor just as industrial displacement was radically transforming both.

Constable achieved his distinctive style much more slowly than Turner did, and not till the age of fifty-two did he gain full membership in the Royal Academy, the professional association of British artists. His long quest for recognition was partly impeded by his subject matter. Born and raised in the village of East Bergholt, Suffolk, in the valley of the River Stour, where his father owned several water mills and considerable property, Constable grew so attached to the scenery of his birthplace that it came to dominate his canvases. "I should paint my own places best," he wrote. "Painting is but another word for feeling. I associate my 'care-less boyhood' to all that lies on the banks of the *Stour.* They made me a painter (& I am gratefull)" (*Correspondence*, vol. 6, p. 78). Though rural scenery now holds a distinguished place in the history of British art, it had to fight for that place. In 1799, when Constable began studying at the academy, landscape painting was still considered inferior to "history painting"—the representation of Biblical and historical events. But landscape had long since begun to rival and challenge history. Activated and authorized by what had already become a tra-dition of landscape painting, Constable's work reflects both nature and artistic nurture. Beginning with *Dedham Vale* (1802), his paintings spring not only from his scrutiny of trees, clouds, and streams but also from his study of landscape in the works of Claude Lorrain and Titian (Tiziano Vecelli), of seventeenth-century Dutch masters such as Rembrandt and Jacob van Ruisdael, and of English painters such as Thomas Gainsborough, who like-wise depicted the scenery of his native Suffolk.

Constable seldom painted portraits and scar-cely presents a face in any of his paintings, but human beings play distinctive roles in them, for his landscapes typically represent men and women at work. In *The Hay Wain* (1821), probably his best-known painting, two men drive a hay wagon across the River Stour toward a distant field where several others—mere spots of white—are gathering hay. In *The Lock* (1824), Constable depicts a brawny-armed, red-vested workman straining to open the shutter of a lock gate so as to release the water in a basin where a barge is waiting to make its way down the river to the sea. Because the view-point is low and the lock operator occupies the midpoint of the painting, he becomes—in every sense—its central figure.

Dedham Lock and Mill. Painting by John Constable, 1820. PRIVATE COLLECTION/BRIDGEMAN ART LIBRARY

Besides challenging the supremacy of history painting by making a place for rural scenery and for nameless figures in his art, Constable also rejected the notion that landscape paintings should look burnished, should always wear the golden brown hue of an old fiddle. He displeased some connoisseurs because they thought he used too much green, and when he strove to catch the sparkling iridescence of nature by means of white highlights, they thought his work "unfinished." But Constable gradually taught his public how to see. In the spring of 1824, when *The Lock* made a decided hit at the Royal Academy exhibition, he triumphantly declared: "My picture is liked at the Academy. Indeed it forms a decided feature and its light cannot be put out because it is the light of nature. ... My execution annoys most of them and all the scholastic ones—perhaps the sacrifices I make for *lightness* and *brightness* is [*sic*] too much, but these things are the essence of land-scape" (*Correspondence,* vol. 6, p. 157). Later in the same year, *The Hay Wain* and *View on the Stour near Dedham* (1822) won a gold medal in Paris at the Salon, the official exhibition held each year by the French Royal Academy of Painting and Sculpture. The winning pictures, which to one observer made the ground look "covered with dew," powerfully influenced the great French Romantic painter Eugène Delacroix (1798–1863). Though Constable left no English succes-sors, he may—through Delacroix—have led the way to impressionism.

See also **Impressionism; Romanticism; Turner, J. M. W.**

BIBLIOGRAPHY

Primary Sources

John Constable's Correspondence, edited by R. S. Beckett. 6 vols. London, 1962–1966.

Leslie, Charles Robert, ed. *Memoirs of the Life of John Con-stable.* Rev. ed., edited by Jonathan Mayne. London, 1951.

Secondary Sources

Reynolds, Graham. *The Later Paintings and Drawings of John Constable.* 2 vols. New Haven, Conn., 1984.

Rosenthal, Michael. *Constable: The Painter and His Landscape.* New Haven, Conn., 1983.

JAMES A. W. HEFFERNAN

CONSTANT, BENJAMIN (1767–1830), French politician, writer, and theorist.

Benjamin Constant de Rebecque was best known in his lifetime as a politician and political journalist and later as a novelist. With the resurgence of interest in liberal ideas in France in the 1980s, however, his importance as a political theorist has come to be appreciated. Previously he was dismissed as a political adventurer, but since the late twentieth century scholars have found a deeper theoretical consistency in Constant's writings, and he is increasingly regarded as one of the outstanding theorists of nineteenth-century liberalism.

Constant was born in Lausanne in 1767. His mother, who died shortly after giving birth, came from an old French Protestant family; his father was a colonel in a Swiss regiment in the service of Holland. Constant was educated at the Universities of Erlangen (Bavaria) and Edinburgh, where he came into contact with the central ideas of Scottish political economy, which would have a profound impact on his political thought. From 1788 to 1794 he served at the court of Brunswick, where in 1789 he married the Baroness Wilhelmina von Cramm. The failure of that marriage led him to return to Switzerland where he met and fell in love with Germaine de Staël, whom he accompanied to Paris in May 1795. His relationship with the brilliant but manipulative Staël was to endure, intermittently, for a decade and a half.

In France, Constant was elected to the Tribunate in January 1800, but his advocacy of freedom of speech antagonized Napoleon Bonaparte (r. 1804–1814/15), who dismissed him in 1802. He spent the years from 1802 to 1814 in exile with Staël, whom Bonaparte had expelled from France. In 1808 he married Charlotte von Hardenberg, with whom he had had a prolonged if irregular relationship since their first meeting in 1793. From 1814 he lived predominantly in France, where he served as a deputy from 1819 to 1822 and from 1824 to 1830, and championed such causes as the freedom of the press, the abolition of the slave trade, and Greek independence. He died in December 1830.

Constant was the author of a short novel, *Adolphe* (1816), which has come to be recognized as something of a classic, not least for its innovative introspective narrative style. Along with a posthumous novel, *Cécile* (1951), and his autobiographical works also published posthumously from manuscripts, *Adolphe* articulates a powerful sense of the importance of personal independence. He also engaged in a lifelong study of the history of religion. This remained incomplete at his death, although at the end of his life he published a five-volume study, *De la religion* (1826–1831). It was initially intended as a sophisticated defense of the radical Enlightenment proposition that ancient polytheism had been more conducive to religious toleration than had Christianity. But the final work reversed this position, for Constant came to see ancient toleration as a consequence of indifference. Modern toleration, by contrast, rested on a sense of the radical importance of religious belief to personal identity, and hence on a profound respect for individual belief.

As a political writer Constant is often viewed as a thinker of the Restoration, since it was during this last period that he published most; but in fact his political views had taken a more or less definitive form by 1806. However, they remained in manuscript form at his death: notably his *Principes de politique,* which was completed in draft in 1806, and *Fragmens d'un ouvrage abandonné sur la possibilité d'une constitution républicaine dans un grand pays,* which was composed between 1795 and 1807. Constant drew on these manuscripts for a number of shorter pieces, including his celebrated speech on ancient and modern liberty.

Constant was criticized, in his lifetime and after, for his political inconsistency: a republican under the Directory, he rallied to Napoleon during his Hundred Days and then, during the Restoration, defended the superiority of constitutional monarchy. But Constant always believed that the contest between hereditary monarchy and republic meant little in comparison with the need to establish constitutional guarantees for individual freedom. He was among the first to articulate the postrevolutionary liberal critique of the French Revolution: he saw that the transfer of a formally unlimited sovereignty from king to people offered little guarantee of individual freedom. The principle that all legitimate power must belong to the body of citizens does not imply that they may use that power however they wish, for oppression is not made legitimate by the size of the majority that commits it. Here Constant anticipated nineteenth-century liberalism's quest to limit the scope of the public authority.

Constant's most enduring contribution to political theory was his distinction between the liberty of the ancients and the liberty of the moderns. This was expounded in a speech of 1819, but he and Staël had first formulated the essential distinction as early as 1798. Constant argued that ancient liberty consisted in active participation in the public affairs of the state, whereas the distinctive characteristic of the modern concept of liberty was its emphasis on negative rights against the state. However, he was no straightforward advocate of a negative concept of liberty. His central point was the historical one that it was impossible for the moderns to recapture the ancient concept of liberty in its integrity, for the growth in the size of modern states, the growth of commerce, and the demise of slavery had combined to undermine the social foundations of ancient liberty. Even so, Constant did not give up on political participation. When he first formulated his ideas on liberty in 1798, he was preoccupied with the dangers of the pursuit of civic virtue untrammelled by any regard for privacy. But by 1819 the Napoleonic experience had demonstrated the converse dangers of a retreat to the private sphere, and the threat from the intransigent Ultras on the right revived Constant's older republican enthusiasm. He now felt profoundly that there was something noble about active citizenship, and self-development mattered as much as the maximization of happiness.

See also **France; Liberalism; Staël, Germaine de.**

BIBLIOGRAPHY

Constant, Benjamin. *Political Writings.* Edited and translated by Biancamaria Fontana. Cambridge, U.K., and New York, 1988.

Fontana, Biancamaria. *Benjamin Constant and the Post-Revolutionary Mind.* New Haven, Conn., and London, 1991.

Holmes, Stephen. *Benjamin Constant and the Making of Modern Liberalism.* New Haven, Conn., 1984.

Pitt, Alan. "The Religion of the Moderns: Freedom and Authenticity in Constant's *De la Religion.*" *History of Political Thought* 21 (2000): 67–87.

Wood, Dennis. *Benjamin Constant: A Biography.* London and New York, 1993.

H. S. JONES

CONSUMERISM.

"Since our Wealth has increas'd, and our Navigation has been extended, we have ransack'd all the Parts of the Globe to bring together its whole Stock of Materials for *Riot, Luxury,* and to provoke *Excess.*" So wrote a Scottish doctor, George Cheyne (1761–1743), in 1733, explaining what he considered to be the "nervous disorders" of his time. Such worries about excess consumption drew from deep wells: Christian teaching about the sins of greed, unrestrained appetite, and envy; humanist views that private wealth undermined public virtue; and an economic paradigm in which to consume meant to waste. The same concerns infused this characteristic rhetoric, from an aristocratic proponent of sumptuary laws who demanded the "immediate suppression of bare-fac'd Luxury, the spreading Contagion of which is the greatest Corrupter of Publick Manners and the greatest Extinguisher of *Public Spirit.*"

The economic and cultural changes that brought very different views of consumption to the fore were among the most far-reaching of modern European history. The birth of consumerism, the deliberate promoting of consumer demand, and the response to it, involved not only more goods and new practices in everyday life but also overhauling assumptions about the economy and redefining "needs" and therefore entitlements—all processes with political as well as social and cultural implications.

Pinpointing a single "consumer revolution" has proved impossible. Such a "revolution" has been qualified and backdated so often that most historians shy away from the term. How, then, does the nineteenth century fit into the long history of consumption? Revolutionary changes in productivity, the legal, political, and social fracturing of a society of orders, and Europe's expanding global and imperial networks did more than produce more goods, less expensively, from ever larger territories for more people. Dismantling systems that had traditionally regulated manufacture and commerce ushered in entirely new forms of distribution and retailing. The enterprise of selling (or retailing), indeed, became an ever more specialized, separate, and valued economic activity—the domain of stores, shopping districts of cities, lavish display, magazines, advertising, and, eventually, social science. This process is the heart of *consumerism*, and it first took shape in the nineteenth century, aimed at and practiced by a new middle class.

If the spectacular expansion of bourgeois consumerism was one side of the coin, the other was creakingly slow and uneven change in popular consumption. To be sure, agricultural productivity rose in the late eighteenth through the nineteenth century. Networks of food distribution became much more efficient. Grain riots, previously the preeminent form of popular politics, faded away throughout most of Europe by 1850. But nineteenth-century consumption was embedded in a deeply hierarchical society. Only toward the 1880s did Europe, primarily France and England, begin to see the more democratized consumption, cutting across class boundaries, that is associated with mass consumption.

EIGHTEENTH-CENTURY CONSUMPTION

Some historians insist that the eighteenth-century British Empire saw a "consumer revolution." Much ink has been spilled in dissent. What has been established is a long, slow rise in consumer demand, driven by factors including falling prices for many basic goods for purchase (especially food); intensified labor (particularly of women and children); the production and importation of a vast array of new goods, and, in the middle classes, new codes of genteel behavior, new standards of cleanliness, and, perhaps, an early

Romantic cultivation of aesthetic sensitivities. Middle-class families spent more on everything from furniture to china and pottery, mirrors and pictures, linens, carriages, and books.

Further down the social scale, people contented themselves with buying smaller items: soap, candles, and, less expensive printed fabrics. The poor made do with very little. A poor family in eighteenth-century England, for instance, would have owned, perhaps, one chair, battered pottery that had been passed down for two generations, and some spoons to eat with, but few knives, no forks, and no table linens.

Still, historians have charted rising consumption of tea, coffee, chocolate, sugar, and tobacco among a remarkably broad sector of society. They estimate that 25 percent of the population used one of these products once a day, to the distress of doctors (who denounced the traffic in stimulants and drugs) and to the delight of café and tavern proprietors. Such a genuinely broad pattern of consumption was inextricable from the new patterns of eighteenth-century sociability, including the rising readership of books and newspapers.

The First Industrial Revolution (from the mid-eighteenth through the early nineteenth centuries) brought innovations through the entire circuit of production, distribution, and consumption. The china manufacturer Josiah Wedgwood (1730–1795) did not owe his spectacular success to production-side innovations—experiments with factory labor and the techniques of glaze and design—alone. Wedgwood's business benefited from improved roads and canals; from the quickening trade in tea, coffee, and chocolate; and from population growth and rising incomes. On the consumerist side, Wedgwood lavished attention on design, fashion, and his product line, transferring the cachet of his tea services to snuffboxes and knife handles. He priced different lines of pottery and china strategically, aiming at different markets. He was extremely attentive to publicity, orchestrating newspaper articles that showcased his wares and famous customers. Matthew Boulton (1728–1809), the famous improver of the steam engine, was no less an innovator in promoting consumption in the "button trade," which included buttons, buckles, watch chains, candlesticks, and other ornaments.

Wedgwood, Boulton, and others pursued both modern commercial techniques and traditional state and courtly patronage. In this as in other respects, their careers reflected a period of transition. To become the queen's potter was a mark of Wedgwood's success; Boulton needed and sought connections to the king's architect, clockmaker, and so on. Court sponsorship played an even more central role in the circuit of production, distribution, and consumption across the channel. Sumptuary laws, which had attempted to limit consumption of luxury goods by status (for instance, granting only some people the right to buy and wear gold, silver, or silk), had fallen away by the end of the eighteenth century. But the states of continental Europe regulated the production of and commerce in almost all goods, from grain to clothing and furniture.

INDUSTRIALIZATION AND NEW FORMS OF COMMERCE

In the early nineteenth century the processes already under way grew stronger. Productive capacities multiplied; transportation quickened; cities, with fashionable arcades and sprawling open-air markets alike, grew. The century also saw the dismantling of traditional regulation of commerce and production, first in France and in different stages across the Continent. Clothing, for instance, was already more freely bought and sold than other consumer goods, and in prerevolutionary France (as in eighteenth-century England), the clothing trade expanded as elites bought more, more expensive, and different kinds of clothes in what the historian Daniel Roche calls a new "culture of appearances." The French Revolution, however, abolished the laws that had carefully distinguished between those granted the privilege to sell fabrics and those allowed to make clothing. This new legal regime, combined with a revolution in textile and clothing production, ushered in fundamental changes in how commerce and retail could operate. The 1820s and 1830s brought stores selling what they produced: rudimentary ready-made in the form of shawls, cloaks, and children's clothing. Later, in women's clothing, couture houses began to sell fabric, clothing, and design—and to call the combination fashion.

With a second generation of stores in the 1850s and 1860s, a new urban consumerism came into its own. Already in the 1780s, shops with large glass windows on streets brightened at night by new gas street lanterns had dazzled wealthy visitors to London. But in the mid-nineteenth century the combination of economic development; political stability; rapid urban growth; massive investments in urban infrastructure in Paris, Vienna, London, and elsewhere; and the confidence of a new social elite made London's West End into a swank shopping district and ensured the success of the *grands magasins* in Paris: the Bon Marché (1852), Printemps (1865), and the Samaritaine (1869).

The *grands magasins* pioneered not only new modes of retailing but also new forms of sociability and leisure. They are a case study in how simple *consumption* could be transformed into *consumerism*, or the systematic cultivation of consumer demand—and of how the provisioning of needs became shopping, a fashionable, sought-after ritual. The new stores displayed fabrics, gloves, umbrellas, fans, and shoes in plate-glass cases rather than tucking them behind counters and in arrangements aimed to seduce with their sumptuousness and impress with their abundance and modernity. They offered calendars of special events such as fashion shows and concerts, hair salons, reading rooms, and displays organized around themes to draw customers in and to entertain them while in the store. In Émile Zola's (1840–1902) *Au Bonheur des Dames* (1883), the century's classic evocation of the cultural magnetism of department stores (based on the history of the Bon Marché and the Grands Magasins du Louvre), the fictional owner fills the central hall and stairway with umbrellas to create the image of "large Venetian lanterns, illuminated for some colossal festival." "Free entry" encouraged potential customers to browse and enjoy the experiences. Fixed, posted prices freed customers from negotiations with salespeople. Consumption did not require an interaction with a producer, or even a merchant; it was an activity enjoyed with other shoppers.

The department stores illustrate a larger structural trend: the emergence of retail and consumption as increasingly autonomous and specialized economic activities. The new stores came to anchor distinctive shopping districts, removed from the smells and sounds of production in artisanal neighborhoods;

cities were segregated by economic function as well as class. Although most nineteenth-century stores continued to make the goods they sold, and had custom shops for dresses, suits, or furnishings, the department stores, by definition, did not specialize. Their broad range of prices and goods underscored that the stores' expertise lay in choosing what to sell, how to make goods desirable, and how to make customers happy, rather than focusing on processes of production.

BOURGEOIS CONSUMPTION/MIDDLE-CLASS CONSUMERISM

The clientele for these stores was decidedly middle class and female. Zola's portrait of women made delirious in department stores was a caricature, though one based on preconceptions common in his time. Since at least the eighteenth century, production (and technology) had been seen as male, and consumption, associated with hedonism, waste, and temptation, female. Still, retailers' appeals to women, women's responsibility for many purchases, and the centrality of goods to middle-class female identity were among the distinguishing features of nineteenth-century consumerism. Much of that consumerism focused on assiduously cultivating the home. Studies of budgets show that even in hard times, middle-class families tried to maintain spending on either housing or servants, both of which were benchmarks of middle-class status and dignity. Over the course of the century middle-class homes grew larger, with more rooms for specific functions: studies, sewing rooms, salons. Wealth was displayed in more plentiful and specialized furniture, upholstered in fine fabrics, or worked with exotic woods from the reaches of Europe's expanding empires, and by thick curtains, works of art on the walls, gilded chandeliers and clocks, jewelry and silver, pianos, and so on.

Some historians argue that specific middle-class tastes had a direct economic impact, giving small industries and high-quality artisans a remarkable resilience. There is no doubt of the power of possessions to shape identity and self-presentation, spelled out in countless etiquette manuals and furniture catalogs. Portraits and furnishings could provide links to a family's past; an elaborately decorated sewing machine could pay tribute to womanly virtue. Educated, tasteful consumption, preserving (or, if possible, raising) the family's status, balancing the household's books: these were tasks that fell to middle-class women across Europe. For middle-class men, too, identity and status were constructed with careful purchases: different suits and hats for business, family events, or weekends in the country; ostentatious watches; and other emblems of distinction.

POPULAR CONSUMPTION

What of patterns of consumption among the common people? This topic used to be framed as the history of the "standard of living" during industrialization, about which historians disagreed, often fiercely. They found it hard to measure wages and prices, however, and general conclusions remained elusive. More recent historical research has focused on more qualitative aspects of popular consumption. Peasant and working-class households were not self-sufficient, or isolated from consumption and the market, but they followed distinct, class-specific patterns of consumption, and those patterns were shaped by the cultural meanings attached to different goods.

For working people, food was the primary expense and priority. Bread took less of a household's food budget, which meant increased spending on more varied foods. An 1872 French study of one hundred working-class families, for instance, found that thirty-nine ate meat daily, forty-four frequently, and seventeen rarely, significantly higher than a century earlier. As industrialization spread across Europe, drinking coffee, wine, rum, and other alcoholic beverages—already on the rise since the eighteenth century—continued to become more popular. Food and drink provided the core of social life. They were also barometers of hard times. Even at the end of the nineteenth century, European workers had to spend more to feed their families than did their counterparts in the United States. A European family with three or more children rarely ate meat at dinner and bought only inexpensive dark bread.

Clothing came second in popular budgets. The falling price of fabric in the 1860s enabled working people to wear lighter, warmer, and more comfortable clothing. But working people spent little on everyday garb. In a stratified culture, where one's dress on the street instantly flagged one's status and class, Sunday clothes were more important, for they provided an accessible form of social mobility, escape, and celebration.

Decent housing was expensive and in short supply everywhere in Europe; it was virtually beyond the common people's reach. Even in good times, working people had to settle for crowded, dark, and barely ventilated places. This, indeed, was one of the most significant lines that divided classes. Even when lower-middle-class families earned only a little more than their working-class counterparts, they spent their money very differently, often putting off marriage and children until they could afford to spend more on rent and properly bourgeois furnishings.

In the last few decades of the nineteenth century, however, the rise of consumerism was beginning to reach the common people, largely through the expansion of credit. As far as historians can determine, peasants were more likely than workers to save, largely because they hoped to acquire more land. But working-class life ran on regular infusions of short-term credit from bakers, grocers, and wine merchants in their neighborhoods, which drove up the price of food. Workers regularly resorted to pawnshops, getting loans at 5 or 6 percent interest against mattresses, linens, jewelry, and the occasional piece of family silver. From the 1860s onward, large-scale commerce began to adapt to the popular habit of buying on credit. In the 1880s the *grands magasins* Dufayel opened its doors in Barbès, a working-class neighborhood in Paris. Dufayel deliberately echoed the presentations of elite department stores, and it offered necessities and furnishings, from furniture and clocks to coal stoves, all on credit. By 1907 almost half of the working-class families of Paris had "subscribed," via door-to-door salesmen, to Dufayel's credit payment plans, and other merchants, attuned to the possibilities of a larger buying public, adopted credit plans as well.

MASS CONSUMERISM

The last quarter of the century ushered in the Second Industrial Revolution, and, as one contemporary remarked, credit and advertising were as much a part of that revolution as electricity and oil. Forms of advertising multiplied in the last decades of the century, from handbills distributed on street corners to lavishly illustrated mail-order catalogs to posters. On this front, Paris was again a pioneer; tourists flocking to the world's fairs of 1889 and 1900 and innovations in graphic arts helped to turn the city into one of the largest advertising markets in the world. The same enterprises that extended credit, already experts in the new commercial world of the late nineteenth century, also turned their hand to publicity. Dufayel, for instance, proclaimed advertising to be "the soul of commerce" and sold advertising space in the city's kiosks, urinals, trams, railroad stations, at the centennial celebration of the French Revolution and world's fairs, and in new dance halls like the Folies Bergères and the Moulin Rouge.

Advertising quickly transformed the visual landscapes of late-nineteenth-century Moscow, St. Petersburg, Vienna, Berlin, and London. The combination of advertising's demand for experimental hard-hitting imagery and the marvelous spectrum of colors made possible by lithography attracted some of the preeminent artists and artistic schools of the period: Jules Cherét (1836–1932), Henri Toulouse-Lautrec (1864–1901), the Jugendstil artists in central Europe, the Munich Secession of 1893, and Russian futurist painters. While only the largest companies could afford advertising on this scale, changes in consumption made the prewar period in important respects the apogee of European commercial culture and a forcing ground of modernism.

Advertising illustrates the structural trend underscored earlier: the increasing investment in commerce and distribution as separate and value-enhancing economic activities. During the eighteenth century, advertising had been an afterthought; producers simply listed themselves in guides to business and even pioneers like Wedgwood sought to establish their reputation by word of mouth and court patronage. One hundred years later, advertising had its own enterprises, personnel, and trade journals that cast a critical eye on graphic artists' techniques and advertisers' strategies. As one of those journals declared, advertising had outgrown simple "empiricism," "it has become a true science, whose precise laws need to be discovered."

Advertising poster for Michelin bicycle tires, 1913. The use of specially created characters such as the Michelin Man to promote brand identification was a feature of print advertising almost from its inception. His placard reads: "The best and least expensive." © SWIM INK/CORBIS

The late nineteenth century quickened the pace of consumerism across Europe. By the 1890s department stores could be found in many of Germany's provincial cities. Germany's most successful retailers included the Tietz family and Adolf Jandorf (1870–1932), who opened his most elegant and elaborate store, the Kaufhaus des Westens in Berlin, in 1907, marking the beginning of the Kurfürstendamm as Berlin's retail and entertainment center, in the same mold as London's West End. Selfridge's debuted in London in 1909, the child of Harry Gordon Selfridge (c. 1864–1947) from Marshall Field's in Chicago, whose elaborate merchandising was widely acclaimed. Selfridge's advertising proclaimed that the store changed shopping from "merely part of the day's work" to "pleasure, a time of profit, recreation and enjoyment." Moreover, recreation proper—or entertainment—also opened up as a new field for consumerism. Novel

kinds of journalism fed sensationalized news to a wider reading public. World's fairs, music halls, spectator sports, circuses, dioramas and panoramas, and, by the late 1890s, movies were all pieces of a new entertainment industry that beckoned to new consumer-spectators. Within a decade of their start in 1894, the Pathé brothers (Charles [1863–1957] and Emile [1860–1937]) reached an international market for their short films at nickelodeons and had begun to open movie halls. There were ten such halls in Paris in 1907 and more than 150 in 1914. Still largely segregated by class, gender, and age, commercialized leisure was nonetheless robustly adaptable. Russian intellectuals might deplore the absence of middle-class political institutions, but modern middle-class commercial entertainment and consumerism thrived.

A CONSUMERIST ECONOMICS/SOCIAL SCIENCE

It was at the end of the nineteenth century, too, that consumption itself began to command more sharply focused attention from economists and social scientists and to occupy a different place in the discursive structure of economics. Since the rise of political economy in the eighteenth century, consumption, if no longer necessarily conceived as an evil, had remained a distinctly minor issue. Bernard Mandeville's (1670–1733) *Fable of the Bees* (1714) satirized orthodoxies of economic restraint and the association of luxury with desire, or appetite, disorder, and disobedience. Mandeville and others argued that the "vice" of consuming luxuries actually promoted the nation's wealth. Adam Smith (1723–1790) saw consumption as one of the self-improving impulses of humanity that promoted economic development and enhanced the public good, contrary to the teachings of classical republicanism and in defiance of views such as those cited at the beginning of this article. Smith declared consumption to be "the sole end and purpose of all production." But there the subject stayed, a distinctly minor concern, while economists trained their gaze on production, wages, and value. Nineteenth-century critics of political economy worked in the same paradigms; Karl Marx's (1818–1883) brilliant passages on commodity fetishism depicted consumption as a realm of reification, mystification, and non-value.

These views began to change in the 1870s. One set of revisions came with the theory of marginal utility, whose proponents disagreed with classical political economy's (and socialism's) emphasis on labor as the source of value. All goods, they argued, had more or less (marginal) value depending on factors like the quantity of goods on the market and consumer preferences. Not production but pricing and the marginal utility of goods (established by rational, market-calculating individuals) were the keys to understanding value and to explaining the allocation of economic resources. Other intellectuals, many of them critics of the marginalists' abstract approach, zeroed in on social psychology and on the "cultural situations" in which consumption was embedded. The American Thorstein Veblen's (1857–1929) *Theory of the Leisure Class* appeared in 1899; in Europe, Gabriel Tarde (1843–1904) wrote on emulation, the German statistician Ernst Engel (1821–1896) and the French sociologist Maurice Halbwachs (1877–1945) studied social patterns of consumption, Engel in search of laws that governed consumer expenditures and Halbwachs demonstrating that the weight of class and culture shaped people's expectations and "levels of living," disproving Engel's laws.

Europe in 1914 was still far removed from a society or culture of mass consumerism. Consumption remained deeply stratified by class until well after World War I. This was not a culture in which it made sense to speak of a "standard of living"; that term suggests norms, entitlements, and government commitments to maintaining or even democratizing consumption that only came later. The development of consumerism in late-nineteenth- and early-twentieth-century Europe paled by comparison with its growth in the United States, where a large domestic market, larger and more efficient networks of distribution, rising incomes (or the higher wages–mass consumption vision associated with Henry Ford), and less stratification converged to make the "American standard of living" the yardstick for the twentieth century. European intellectuals at the turn of the century worried about developments across the Atlantic, on the American horizon, about the "economic convulsions" of the present, and socialists fretted that mass consumerism and culture would sow political apathy. Right-wing thinkers warned the "more intimate mingling of the classes" would undermine social hierarchies and traditional values, and they mobilized nationalist and anti-Semitic rhetoric against "Jewish" retailers or "cosmopolitan" department stores. Contemporary concerns notwithstanding, on the eve of World War I consumer markets were small and local. Across Europe 90 percent of sales went through small shopkeepers. Europe remained a world of bourgeois consumerism, in which popular purchasing power was weak, class distinctions were plainly demarcated, and middle-class individuals' conceptions of taste were firmly yoked to their cultural influence and political power.

See also **Cities and Towns; Industrial Revolution, First; Industrial Revolution, Second; Paris; Sewing Machine; Trade and Economic Growth.**

BIBLIOGRAPHY

Auslander, Leora. *Taste and Power: Furnishing Modern France.* Berkeley, Calif., 1996.

Brewer, John, and Roy Porter, eds. *Consumption and the World of Goods.* London and New York, 1993.

Coffin, Judith G. "A 'Standard' of Living? European Perspectives on Class and Consumption in the Early Twentieth Century." *International Labor and Working-Class History* 55 (spring 1999): 6–26.

De Grazia, Victoria. *Irresistible Empire: America's Advance through Twentieth-Century Europe.* Cambridge, Mass., 2005.

De Grazia, Victoria, ed., with Ellen Furlough. *The Sex of Things: Gender and Consumption in Historical Perspective.* Berkeley, Calif., 1996.

McKendrick, Neil, John Brewer, and J. H. Plumb. *The Birth of a Consumer Society: The Commercialization of Eighteenth-Century England.* Bloomington, Ind., 1982.

McReynolds, Louise. *Russia at Play: Leisure Activities at the End of the Tsarist Era.* Ithaca, N.Y., 2003.

Perrot, Michelle. *Les ouvriers en grève: France, 1871–1890.* Paris, 1974.

Rappaport, Erika Diane. *Shopping for Pleasure: Women in the Making of London's West End.* Princeton, N.J., 2000.

Strasser, Susan, Charles McGovern, and Matthias Judt, eds. *Getting and Spending: European and American Consumer Societies in the Twentieth Century.* Cambridge, U.K., and New York, 1998.

Walton, Whitney. *France at the Crystal Palace: Bourgeois Taste and Artisan Manufacture in the Nineteenth Century.* Berkeley, Calif., 1992.

Williams, Rosalind H. *Dream Worlds: Mass Consumption in Late Nineteenth-Century France.* Berkeley, Calif., 1982.

JUDY COFFIN

CONTINENTAL SYSTEM.

CONTINENTAL SYSTEM. The term *Continental System* was used during the Napoleonic Empire to denote the French commercial war on Great Britain (1806–1813), and also more loosely to describe the economic policy of France toward its subject states in mainland Europe. The Continental System (*Système continental*), or Continental Blockade (*Blocus continental*) as it was also called, was officially proclaimed by Napoleon's Berlin Decree of 21 November 1806. This declared the British Isles in a state of blockade, forbade all communication with them, and sanctioned the seizure of British ships and goods as lawful prize. Similar measures had been adopted during the French Revolution, most notably the Directory's stiff embargoes of 31 October 1796 and 18 January 1798 on British trade, with their accompanying unfavorable implications for neutral shipping. Other elements of the system had also been anticipated by Napoleon's earlier "coast system," especially as from 1803, and as codified in the comprehensive customs tariff of 30 April 1806. Yet the Berlin Decree was a more immediate reaction to the British order in council of 16 May 1806, which imposed a naval blockade along the coastline of France and its satellites between Brest and the estuary of the Elbe. New orders in council were issued in February and November 1807, extending and strengthening that blockade, and also requiring neutral ships to call at a British port for inspection and to pay duties and seek licenses there for trade with enemy ports. Napoleon responded with the Milan Decrees of 23 November and 17 December 1807, by which all neutral vessels complying with those orders were in effect assimilated to British shipping and so made liable to capture.

From an early stage, the Continental System was thus much more than an economic war on Britain; it soon became enmeshed with Napoleon's foreign and military policies toward other states, whether belligerent or neutral. As from 1807, its enforcement was imposed, officially at least, on his satellite states in Italy, Germany, Holland, Switzerland, Poland, and Spain, and it was also a factor in his later imperial annexations in Italy (1809–1810), in the "Illyrian Provinces" of the Adriatic hinterland (1809), and in Holland and northwestern Germany (1810–1811). Even his Russian campaign of 1812 was partly driven by a determination to stamp out breaches of the system in the Baltic region after the rupture of the Treaties of Tilsit (1807).

THE SYSTEM'S EFFECTIVENESS

How far the Continental System achieved its aims was largely determined by two factors. First, it was most effective during periods of relative peace on the Continent, when imperial troops could be deployed in customs surveillance, and least effective when Napoleon needed his armies on campaign: 1809, in particular, was a bonanza year for smuggling and also the high-water mark of British exports in the period. Second, the system had its maximum impact on the British economy when periods of comparatively tight customs control on the Continent coincided with a rupture in Anglo-American relations, because it was then that British traders most needed alternative markets across the Atlantic. Such conditions applied from July 1807 to July 1808 and again during the years 1811 and 1812, culminating in the American declaration of war on Britain in June 1812.

In crucial respects, however, Napoleon weakened the system by his own inconsistency in applying the embargoes. He was often willing to grant special licenses for trade with Britain—at different times, for instance, to overstocked wine merchants in Bordeaux and grain dealers in the west country of France. Although he intensified the war on British manufactured goods by his Fontainebleau Decree of 18 October 1810, thereby unleashing two years of "customs terror" in the North Sea and Baltic ports, he relaxed the embargoes on other commodities at the same time. The Trianon Tariffs of 5 August and 17 September 1810 allowed the import of many formerly prohibited colonial goods, subject however to exorbitant duties. Indeed, the fiscal motives behind the tariffs had already become clear in the Saint-Cloud Decree of 3 July 1810, which institutionalized a "new system" of licenses on a grander scale, soon matched by similar "permits" for American shipping. During 1813, as Napoleon's need for cash became more pressing, he greatly multiplied issues of the licenses, fatally undermining the system from within several months before the military structures that underpinned it themselves finally collapsed.

IMMEDIATE AND WIDER IMPACT

As a historical episode, the Continental System was the climax of a much longer commercial conflict between France and Britain in their pursuit of global markets and sources of supply. In the longer term, Britain's naval supremacy and commercial and technological superiority actually increased during the maritime wars of 1793 to 1815. As a short-term instrument of war, the system did not cripple Britain's economy; nor did it force Britain to sue for peace or reduce its capacity to finance military coalitions against France. Moreover, because the French then lacked the naval power to enforce it directly on the seas, following their heavy defeat at Trafalgar (1805), the system was not a blockade properly so called, but rather a self-blockade, or a boycott of British goods. As such, it provided conditions for economic expansion on the Continental mainland, chiefly in the Rhenish and Belgian departments of the empire, especially in the years from 1807 to 1810, as the major trade routes shifted from the beleaguered coastline toward the inland regions. Its wider orbit of protected markets gave a particular boost to the production of cottons, woolens, and silk stuffs, to the war industries, and to secondary metallurgy. Such growth, however, was liable to disruption during recurrent hostilities; and the economic crisis of 1810 to 1811 affected France no less than Britain, embarrassing established merchant houses as well as parvenu speculators. Manufacturers of textiles in those parts of Italy, Germany, and Switzerland that lay beyond the imperial customs frontiers had good cause to complain about their official exclusion from the enlarged French home market, even if the cotton entrepreneurs of Saxony somehow managed to flourish independently of it. The smuggling of contraband goods was more or less ubiquitous, often with the connivance of imperial customs officers, notwithstanding the very harsh penalties. During the "customs terror" of 1810 to 1812 an agricultural depression spread across several of the subject states of France, especially along the Baltic, as surpluses that could not be legally exported through British shipping were also denied outlets in France, and this in turn reduced their capacity to absorb French exports.

CONCLUSION

On the whole, the Continental System has had a bad press from historians. Most have criticized the naive simplicity of Napoleon's mercantilist reasoning, including not least the self-defeating consequences of his declared priority of "France first." Some have cited it as a prime example of the futility of economic blockades in general. But these critics have not always appreciated that Napoleon had inherited a recent legacy of French colonial losses and maritime disruption, and that his harbor-bound navy could not challenge Britain effectively at sea. His Continental System could thus be seen as a last resort, a function of his essentially landlocked power, an extraordinary contrivance of particular wartime circumstances over which he had only limited control. Although its ultimate failure both as a war machine against Britain and as a French market design to engross the resources of the Continental mainland seems clear, its more positive industrial and commercial results should be recognized. Indeed, its most enduring effect was to reinforce a long-term shift in the center of gravity of the French economy from the Atlantic littoral toward France's northeastern regions during the maritime wars of 1793 to 1815.

See also **French Revolutionary Wars and Napoleonic Wars; Napoleonic Empire.**

BIBLIOGRAPHY

Bergeron, Louis. *Banquiers, négociants et manufacturiers parisiens du Directoire à l'Empire.* Paris, 1978. Magisterial study of the Parisian financial and industrial elite.

Crouzet, François. "Wars, Blockade, and Economic Change in Europe, 1792–1815." *Journal of Economic History* 24, no. 4 (1964): 567–588. Seminal article offering a global overview.

———. *L'économie britannique et le blocus continental.* 2nd ed. Paris, 1987. The most authoritative statement on the British aspect of the subject.

Ellis, Geoffrey. *Napoleon's Continental Blockade: The Case of Alsace.* Oxford, U.K., 1981. Concentrates on the inland aspects of the subject.

Heckscher, Eli F. *The Continental System: An Economic Interpretation.* Edited by Harald Westergaard. Reprint, Gloucester, Mass., 1964. Classic liberal economic interpretation that was for many years the standard text after its first publication in English in 1922.

GEOFFREY ELLIS

COOPERATIVE MOVEMENTS.

As industrial capitalism spread across Europe during the nineteenth century, working people adopted various associational forms to defend their interests. One of the earliest and most important of these associations was the cooperative society, symptomatic of the search for new sources of community life in the context of increasing social fragmentation and individualism. Workers were exploited as consumers as well as producers, and early factory masters frequently established truck shops that invariably sold overpriced and adulterated food and also led to widespread debt and dependency. Cooperative initiatives of various kinds were designed to check such abuses and encourage working-class self-help or independence. By the late nineteenth century cooperatives had become a fundamentally important feature of the European labor movement. The history of national cooperative movements is complex, however, as cooperatives have been bent to various, often competing, visions of class, gender, religion, and nation.

Not surprisingly, Britain acted as a pacesetter for cooperative development from the late eighteenth century. Some of the earliest forms were flour societies and cooperative corn mills, designed to provide good quality, affordable bread. Founded in 1795, the Hull Anti-Mill Society, for instance, operated successfully for more than a century and has been regarded as an attempt to assert the moral economy of the laboring poor against an encroaching market society. This ethical dimension can be found more explicitly in the cooperatives founded from the 1820s by followers of the pioneer socialist Robert Owen, who linked storekeeping with the desire to construct utopian, anticapitalist communities.

Cooperatives were also taken up by the Chartist reform movement, especially its female supporters, who regarded them as a vital economic weapon in the struggle for working-class political power. Although most of these early societies did not survive the crisis of 1848, this phase provided many of the leaders of the later movement.

THE ROCHDALE MODEL AND CLASS COLLABORATION

After midcentury, British cooperators took the society founded in the Lancashire mill town of Rochdale in 1844 as their inspiration. The Rochdale Society of Equitable Pioneers was highly successful at a time when many societies collapsed, and consequently its rules and practices seemed to furnish an ideal model. It divided trade surplus among members in proportion to their purchases (the dividend); strongly condemned the practice of credit trading; insisted that each member could only have one vote in running the affairs of the society, regardless of the number of shares held; and favored religious and political neutrality. Propagandists such as the ex-Owenite missionary G. J. Holyoake vigorously publicized the "Rochdale model" of consumer cooperation, and its fame spread throughout Britain and the Continent. The support of middle-class Christian Socialists, who were keen on profit-sharing cooperative workshops as an antidote for class struggle and socialism, was also important during this period, especially in achieving legal recognition. The consumer movement was considerably strengthened by the establishment of the English and Scottish Cooperative Wholesale Societies (CWS) in 1863 and 1868, whose leaders regarded consumption as the basis of economic, social, and cultural change. After decades of bitter conflict within the movement between profit sharers and those who prioritized the consumer, the latter finally won out by the early 1890s.

In France, cooperative ideas can be traced back to Charles Fourier's associationism, but there was little practical experiment before midcentury. State-sponsored cooperative production was advocated by the republican socialist Louis Blanc, before and during the 1848 revolution, but real growth came much later. The Rochdale model of consumer cooperation was supported enthusiastically by the political economist Charles Gide, and a national organization was founded in 1885 to coordinate the activities of a burgeoning movement; there were more than two thousand cooperatives by 1906, though these tended to be much smaller on the whole than their British counterparts. Once again, bourgeois support was in evidence during this phase, as cooperation was seen by many intellectuals to represent a "third way" between classical political economy and socialism and was also intimately bound up with the influential theory of solidarism, which stressed the importance of class conciliation and peaceful change.

Similar class dynamics were apparent in other national contexts. Middle-class liberal intellectuals, for instance, sponsored cooperatives in both Italy and Sweden after midcentury. The distinctive German contribution to cooperative development took the form of credit societies, designed specifically to provide capital for the lower middle class or *Mittlestand,* a social group threatened by capitalist industry that played an important ideological role within liberalism. The key figure here was the jurist and progressive deputy Hermann Schultz-Delitzsch, who championed credit cooperatives in particular from the 1860s. By 1867 there were 1,122 credit cooperatives and 250 consumer cooperatives in Germany, many of which affiliated to a federation, the *Allgemeine Verband.* The leaders of the German movement typically regarded these forms as productive of moral qualities such as thrift, respectability, and self-reliance among the artisanate.

If the class origins and affiliations of cooperatives were often complex, so too were religious particularities. Catholic cooperatives were an important, if subordinate, presence in Germany, Italy, and Belgium during the second half of the nineteenth century, though they did not seem to undermine the progress of socialist cooperatives, in Belgium at least.

TOWARD THE COOPERATIVE COMMONWEALTH?

Indeed, from the late nineteenth century through to World War I, the largest cooperative movements in Europe shifted to the left and became more avowedly proletarian and combative in character. In Britain the hegemony of the Wholesale Societies did not lead to the demise of the vision of a "cooperative commonwealth" as earlier

scholars suggested—just the opposite, in fact. The German movement split in 1902 when supporters of the Schulze-Delitzsch artisanal cooperatives managed to expel working-class consumer cooperatives from the *Allgemeine Verband.* Links between the majority German movement and the Social Democratic Party strengthened during the following decade. A similar transformation occurred in Scandinavian movements, but without splitting the ranks of cooperators. In France alternatives were increasingly polarized after the formation of the *Bourse des coopératives socialistes* in 1895. This body affirmed the class struggle and had been inspired by striking glass workers in Carmaux and the ambitious Belgium cooperative movement, which was regarded as quintessentially socialist in character: the Maison du Peuple at Brussels and the Vooruit at Ghent seemed literally to embody the coming worker's utopia. Gide was disingenuous when he told the French movement that it should not "expect to teach many new ideas to our English comrades because it is from them that we have received almost everything" (Gide, p. ix), as there had been a traffic of ideas and practices across the channel throughout the nineteenth century; French, Belgium, and other cooperators regularly visited their comrades in England, who were themselves keenly interested in Continental developments.

This fascination was hardly surprising, for by World War I socialist cooperatives were the most dynamic aspect of what was now a truly European movement. This led French socialist leaders such as Jean Jaurès to describe cooperation as one of the "three pillars of socialism," a phrase that was quickly taken up by other national leaders. Both in Britain and Belgium cooperators far outnumbered members of labor and socialist parties and trade unions; there were more than three million members of cooperative societies in Britain in 1914, and the English CWS alone boasted an annual net sales of nearly thirty-five million pounds, making it one of the largest enterprises of its kind in the world at this time. The movement generated a distinctive culture that sought to provide members with education and fellowship as well as honest goods and that represented an alternative to mass consumer capitalism. Especially in France, Belgium, and Britain, cooperative movements controlled a substantial part of retail trade, though capitalist competition in the sphere of consumption was rapidly increasing as department and chain stores continued to proliferate. Modern scholarship has stressed that such changes in the structure of capitalism, combined with internal gender antagonism and hostile government intervention, undermined the long-term stability of cooperative movements. The strength and vitality of the European movement on the eve of total war throws the subsequent decline of cooperation into vivid relief.

See also **Associations, Voluntary; Civil Society; Labor Movements; Socialism.**

BIBLIOGRAPHY

Primary Sources

Gide, Charles. *Consumers' Cooperative Societies.* London, 1921.

Holyoake, George Jacob. *Self-Help by the People: History of Co-operation in Rochdale.* London, 1858.

Potter, Beatrice. *The Co-operative Movement in Great Britain.* London, 1891.

Secondary Sources

Backstrom, Philip N. *Christian Socialism and Co-operation in Victorian England.* London, 1974.

Cole, G. D. H. *A Century of Co-operation.* London, 1944.

Earle, John. *The Italian Cooperative Movement: A Portrait of the Lega Nazionale delle Cooperative e Mutue.* London, 1986.

Fay, C. R. *Co-operation at Home and Abroad.* 2 vols. New York, 1908.

Furlough, Ellen. *Consumer Co-operation in France: The Politics of Consumption, 1834–1930.* Ithaca, N.Y., 1991.

Furlough, Ellen, and Strickwerda, Carl, eds. *Consumers against Capitalism? Consumer Cooperation in Europe, North America, and Japan, 1840–1990.* Lanham, Md., 1999.

Gaumont, Jean. *Histoire générale de la coopération en France.* 2 vols. Paris, 1924.

Gurney, Peter. *Cooperative Culture and the Politics of Consumption in England, 1870–1930.* Manchester, U.K., 1996.

Hasselman, Erwin. *Consumers' Co-operation in Germany.* 3rd ed. Hamburg, 1961.

Redfern, Percy. *The New History of the C.W.S.* London, 1938.

Scott, Gillian. *Feminism and the Politics of Working Women: The Women's Cooperative Guild, 1880s to the Second World War.* London, 1998.

PETER J. GURNEY

CORN LAWS, REPEAL OF. Regulations on the import and export of grain can be dated in England to as early as the twelfth century, but the best known of the corn laws was passed in 1815, when Parliament had to address the profound economic slump that followed the end of the Napoleonic Wars. A number of arguments weighed in favor of protecting the agricultural sector. Protection would stimulate domestic agriculture, preventing famine and guaranteeing national independence in wartime. It would also promote a smooth transition to peacetime by reducing the impact of falling demand. And agriculture was a vital component of the nation's overall economic health because it influenced other sectors of the economy, such as labor and domestic manufacture. While economic arguments in favor of the Corn Law entered the political debate, there was a class interest at work as well because many aristocrats were large landowners who would benefit from special protection. To protect British agriculture, the 1815 Corn Law banned foreign imports of grain into British markets as long as the domestic prices per quarter (twenty-eight pounds or eight bushels) fell below a certain level: twenty-seven shillings for oats; forty for barley and beer; fifty-three for rye, peas, and beans; and eighty for wheat. The last was the most bitterly resented because during the nineteenth century wheaten bread was the staple of the average Briton's diet. Loaves made with other grains were considered inferior.

No one was especially pleased with the results of the 1815 law. Landlords and farmers never saw the high prices they expected while consumers (especially urban laborers and manufacturers) saw no benefit from cheaper grains marketed elsewhere in Europe. Modifications to the 1815 law came in 1822, 1828, and 1842. In 1828, for example, sliding scales of duties replaced the total ban on grain imports below the set price. As the price of domestic grains went up, the duty paid on foreign grains went down. Overall, the Corn Laws were damaging to consumers. Historians have calculated that without the special protection for British agriculture, wheat would have cost between 17 and 33 percent less during the first half of the nineteenth century. Moreover, merchants learned how to maximize profits by withholding foreign wheat from the market until the highest price, and thus the lowest duty, applied. The market worked differently for foreign barley and oats, which farmers used to feed cattle and horses and which tended to be released onto the market sooner. Consequently, as one historian has observed, animals did somewhat better than people.

CAMPAIGN FOR REPEAL

What made the Corn Laws so remarkable was not the fact of their existence but the manner in which they were eventually repealed in 1846. Before then, there had been sporadic opposition to the laws. But they soon became a rallying point for a new middle-class form of politics. Effective and sustained opposition to the Corn Laws began with the establishment of the London Anti–Corn Law Association in 1836, the Manchester Anti–Corn Law Association in 1838, and finally the Anti–Corn Law League, into which a number of associations were organized, in 1839. The League was headquartered in Manchester, signaling a shift in political momentum away from London and the landed elite and toward a new moneyed elite based in the urban manufacturing centers of the north. The best known of the League's leaders were Richard Cobden (1804–1865) and John Bright (1811–1889), both of whom were elected to Parliament (Cobden in 1841, Bright in 1843), where they pushed for repeal.

Why did the Corn Laws become the focus of middle-class attacks? First, a single-issue campaign was politically prudent; resources could be concentrated to chip away at the nation's landed, vested interests. Second, many reformers saw repeal as beneficial for the entire nation: with the Corn Laws repealed, bread prices would drop, which in turn would lower labor costs, encourage domestic manufacturing, decrease unemployment, and boost international trade. Third, the 1840s saw deep economic distress, including the Irish potato famine, which intensified cries for

economic reform. And lastly, the refrain of "Free Trade" attracted many reformers who embraced Adam Smith's (1723–1790) economics. Arguments like these gained support especially among the middle classes who believed that the sacrifices of British manufacturers and workers benefited only the aristocracy, whose economic relevance in an industrializing economy was seen as increasingly marginal. Significant support for repeal could also be found among dissenters, who equated attacks on the Corn Laws with attacks on the established church, yet another bastion of elite interests. Irish nationalists, too, appropriated the language of repeal in their efforts to promote independence.

Despite the enfranchisement of the middle classes in the 1832 Reform Act, their votes were not enough to secure repeal of the Corn Laws, which many had come to believe were harming Britain's economic, social, and moral well-being. Other means were required. The tactics employed by the Anti–Corn Law League established a successful and influential model for future extraparliamentary campaigns. Funds were collected, mass meetings organized. The League sent traveling lecturers, assisted by an expanding railroad network, into local communities. Women supporters sponsored tea parties and bazaars. The League churned out publications of every description—pamphlets, periodicals, petitions, circulars, addresses, handbills, almanacs, newspapers (the *Anti–Bread Tax Circular*, succeeded by *The League*, first appeared in 1841)—to educate, pressure, and persuade. Other proponents of free trade increased the flow of ink, like James Wilson (1805–1860), a Scottish hat manufacturer, who in 1843 founded *The Economist*.

The anti–Corn Law campaign was heavily tinged with a religious fervor and drew on a well-worn rhetoric of religious freedom. If Protestantism had rightly crushed religious monopolies, why then were economic monopolies allowed to stand? Hundreds of ministers converged on Manchester in 1841 and Scotland in 1842 to support repeal while Anglican clergymen numbered among its most prominent opponents. The League also developed an electoral strategy that achieved mixed but sometimes impressive results with its emphasis on voter registration, by-elections, and county elections. All of the League's

A bread riot, London, 1815. Angry citizens storm the entrance to the House of Commons to protest enactment of the Corn Laws. ©BETTMANN/CORBIS

techniques shared a strong rejection of violent protest (although Cobden proposed acts, never carried out, of civil disobedience) because Leaguers wanted to distance themselves from those working-class and Chartist activists who favored physical force. Chartists, who campaigned for political reforms that would open the electorate to the working classes, in turn often opposed repeal, which they viewed as a disguised attempt to lower workers' wages.

RESULTS OF REPEAL

The League's connection to formal party politics was complex. Although supporters of repeal tended to support Whigs, there was good reason to keep repeal a nonpartisan issue. After all, protectionists and free traders could be found among the ranks of both Whig and Conservative members of Parliament. The Whig leader, John Russell (1792–1878), eventually embraced the immediate and total repeal of the Corn Laws, while the

Conservative prime minister, Robert Peel (1788–1850), who had drastically reduced duties on foods and raw materials, resigned from office in 1845 when his cabinet proved unwilling to support some version of repeal. When Russell failed to form a new government, Peel returned to office committed to repealing the Corn Laws. Immediately after repeal was achieved in June 1846, Peel resigned again and the Conservatives split, unable to mount a serious challenge to the Liberals until Benjamin Disraeli (1804–1881) reversed his party's fortunes. Peel thus enjoyed the reputation of having sacrificed political ambition as well as partisan advantage for the greater good of the nation.

The repeal of the Corn Laws can be assessed in a number of ways. It was undoubtedly a political triumph for the League and for middle-class interests, but it did not destroy the political power of the British aristocracy. In fact, it can be argued that repeal helped to preserve its power; the next major electoral reform came only in 1867, the Church of England remained an established institution, and the House of Lords stayed intact for the rest of the nineteenth century. Nor did repeal bring a dramatic drop in grain prices, although it did blunt the price rise that Britain would have witnessed because of increased demand. The repeal that Leaguers secured was neither immediate nor total. Under Peel's plan, repeal would be gradually implemented over three years, and even then, a small duty of one shilling per quarter on foreign grain was retained. Some scholars have suggested that repeal would have occurred even if the League had never formed. Others have questioned to what extent the campaign for repeal should be described in class terms. The League attracted members from across the social spectrum, aristocrats as well as handloom weavers, whereas among opponents of repeal, agricultural interests may have trumped purely aristocratic ones.

Despite these important claims, the Anti–Corn Law League had a profound effect on British politics. The League inspired subsequent political movements and also secured an iconic status for free trade within the expanding British electorate. For many, a vote against free trade came to be seen as a vote against democracy itself.

See also **Capitalism; Industrial Revolution, First; Protectionism; Trade and Economic Growth.**

BIBLIOGRAPHY

Primary Sources

Kadish, Alon, ed. *The Corn Laws. The Formation of Popular Economics in Britain.* 6 vols. London, 1996. A documentary collection of reprints.

Schonhardt-Bailey, Cheryl, ed. *The Rise of Free Trade.* 4 vols. London, 1997. The first two volumes are the most relevant.

Secondary Sources

McCord, Norman. *The Anti–Corn Law League, 1838–1846.* 2nd ed. London, 1968. Still the best narrative account of the League's institutional history.

Pickering Paul A., and Alex Tyrrell. *The People's Bread: A History of the Anti–Corn Law League.* London and New York, 2000. A social and cultural history of the League.

Prest, John. "A Large Amount or a Small? Revenue and the Nineteenth-Century Corn Laws." *The Historical Journal* 39 (1996): 467–478. A detailed account of how the Corn Laws operated.

ELISA R. MILKES

COROT, JEAN-BAPTISTE-CAMILLE
(1796–1875), French painter.

Jean-Baptiste-Camille Corot was born in Paris and apprenticed to a cloth merchant at age nineteen, in spite of his desire to become an artist. It was not until seven years later that his parents agreed to pay him a small yearly allowance that would enable him to pursue his calling. Opting against an academic training, Corot did not enroll in the École des Beaux-Arts but studied briefly with Achille-Etna Michallon (1796–1822) and upon the latter's death entered the studio of Jean-Victor Bertin (1767–1842), a well-known painter of historical landscapes.

Historical landscape painting (*paysage historique*) was the most highly rated form of landscape painting in early-nineteenth-century France. It called for landscapes to serve as settings for scenes from history, literature, mythology, or the Bible. It also was the only kind of landscape painting that was encouraged by the Academy, which each year awarded a travel grant to enable a young, aspiring landscape painter to study in Rome. Study in Italy was extremely important for anyone who wanted to become a historical landscape painter, since the Italian scenery, with its mountains, rivers, and Roman ruins, was considered eminently appropriate for *paysage historique* and for its important subgenre, the *paysage classique* or classical landscape (historical landscapes with scenes from ancient history and mythology).

Though not a student at the École des Beaux-Arts, Corot followed the academic tradition and left for Italy in 1825. Headquartered in Rome, he traveled around Italy, making plein-air oil sketches of landscape, scenery, and monuments. Such sketches were important to artists, since they served them as aides-mémoire for large landscape compositions, which invariably were done from

Souvenir of Castel Gandolfo. Painting by Jean-Baptiste-Camille Corot. Louvre, Paris, France/Bridgeman Art Library/Giraudon

memory and imagination inside the studio. Sketching in oils had become a popular practice in the early nineteenth century, after the academic landscape painter Pierre-Henri de Valenciennes (1750–1819) had promoted it in his *Eléméns de perspective pratique à l'usage des artistes* (1799–1800). Previously, artists had confined their outdoor sketching to pencil and watercolor. The advantage of the oil sketch was that it enabled artists better to retain the immediacy of the sketch in the finished composition.

Corot stayed in Italy for four years, then returned to France and settled in Paris. However, he continued to travel incessantly, both in France and abroad. Corot's first Salon submissions were paintings of Italian scenery but without the obligatory historical characters. He was apparently less

interested in receiving academic accolades than in appealing to middle-class collectors who preferred "pure" landscape scenery to the traditional historical landscapes. His *View at Narni* and *The Roman Campagna* or *La Cervara,* exhibited at the Salon of 1827, both presented panoramic views of Italian landscapes with contemporary Italian peasants. Although both landscapes were clearly done in the studio and composed with the help of one or more sketches done outdoors, they are remarkable for the artist's convincing suggestion of light and atmosphere.

In 1835 Corot exhibited his first historical landscape, *Hagar in the Desert,* which was highly acclaimed and established his reputation. After this, his production alternated between historical landscapes, topographic landscapes (landscapes depicting specific scenery in France or abroad), and idyllic landscapes (imaginary landscapes populated with nymphs, fauns, and other mythical creatures). Corot also developed a class of landscapes all his own, which he called "*souvenirs.*" Paintings such as *Souvenir de Mortefontaine* (1864) and *Souvenir des environs du lac de Nemi* (Souvenir of the Lake Nemi region) present existing landscapes in poeticized form, as if seen in one's mind eye or in a dream. In addition to landscapes, after 1865 Corot painted a series of beguiling figure paintings, full-length or half-length views of single women reading, contemplating an art work in a painter's studio, or daydreaming. Their mood of reverie resonates with the dreamlike quality of the souvenirs.

Although Corot often worked in the Fontainebleau Forest, he never became a full-fledged member of the Barbizon school of landscape painting; however, he was acquainted with its most important representatives, Théodore Rousseau (1812–1867) and Jean-François Millet (1814–1875), whose works he did not like. Indeed, he never became part of any group or coterie, although he was supportive of his colleagues, using both his influence and his money to help them. Corot's works, especially his landscape paintings of French sites, which often retain the freshness of the original oil sketch (for example, *A Village Near Beauvais,* 1850–1855) were an important source of inspiration for the early impressionists, such as Camille Pissarro and Claude Monet, who admired Corot's ability to capture effects of light, weather, and season.

See also **Barbizon Painters; France; Impressionism; Painting.**

BIBLIOGRAPHY

Galassi, Peter. *Corot in Italy: Open-Air Painting and the Classical Landscape Tradition.* New Haven, Conn., 1991.

Musée du Louvre. *Figures de Corot.* Paris, June–September 1962.

Robaut, Alfred. *L'Oeuvre de Corot: Catalogue raisonné et illustré.* 4 vols. Paris, 1905; supplements compiled by A. Schoeller and J. Dieterle. 3 vols. Paris, 1948–1974.

Tinterow, Gary, Michael Pantazzi, and Vincent Pomarède. *Corot.* New York, 1996.

PETRA TEN-DOESSCHATE CHU

COSSACKS. The Cossacks emerged as distinct communities in the sixteenth century on the Don and Dnieper Rivers in present-day Russia and Ukraine. These communities were self-governing and considered themselves autonomous from the Polish-Lithuanian Commonwealth and Muscovy (and later the Russian Empire). In the following centuries, many more Cossack hosts came into being: some by independent action of the Cossacks themselves such as the Terek and Yaik Cossacks in the sixteenth century and some by direct government action like the Orenburg Cossacks in the eighteenth century or the Ussuri and Amur Cossacks in the nineteenth century. The hosts consisted of the entire Cossack community including women and children who were an integral part of the community. Originally Cossacks supported themselves through a mixture of hunting and fishing, but in the nineteenth century they turned increasingly to farming. However, it was for their military skills that Cossacks were famed. They provided invaluable service guarding the borders of Muscovy and the Polish-Lithuanian Commonwealth against attacks by the Crimean Tatars. Later, Cossack hosts were used by the Russian Empire to protect its southern and eastern borders from attacks by indigenous nomadic peoples.

The early Cossack communities were entirely autonomous in their internal affairs and possessed considerable autonomy in external relations. A democratic assembly consisting of all Cossacks exercised authority in the hosts. This assembly elected leaders, either atamans or hetmans depending on the host, and a small number of officials to provide assistance. The constituent parts of the Cossack host—the stanitsas—replicated this democratic organization. Cossacks lived according to their own law and acknowledged the authority of the Polish king or Muscovite tsar in a very limited way.

From the very first appearance of organized Cossack communities, the Polish-Lithuanian and Muscovite governments sought to integrate the Cossacks into their armed forces, preserving their military abilities, but stripping them of their autonomy. The Cossacks violently resisted these attempts, successfully defeating the attempts of the Polish Lithuanian Commonwealth but eventually succumbing to imperial Russia. The imperial government relied on a strategy of incorporating local or indigenous elites into the imperial ruling class in return for unswerving loyalty to the empire. By the end of the eighteenth century, the government had successfully incorporated Cossack elites into the empire and, as part of this process, had abolished the democratic assemblies that had dominated Cossack life.

Until the nineteenth century the government had very little interest in the lower orders as long as they paid their taxes, did their military service, and obeyed their elites. Cossack democracy survived in the stanitsas, where communities continued to administer themselves through their assemblies (*sbory*), their elected atamans, and their own norms of justice. After the Napoleonic Wars, the government began to take a much greater interest in the lives of ordinary Cossacks and was no longer content to leave them under the somewhat distant control of their own elite. Four major legislative measures over the course of the century in 1835, 1870, 1875, and 1890 expanded government control over Cossack life. Elected atamans now had to be confirmed in office, rules were established for the competence and conduct of local assemblies, and Cossack military service was integrated more closely into the regular army. Most importantly, the government progressively restricted the competence of Cossack courts until by the end of the century they were reduced to hearing very trivial cases. Many contemporaries believed that Cossack autonomy had all but disappeared by the end of the century.

In reality, however, government control was less than it first appeared. The government's ambitions were severely limited by the absence of any bureaucratic presence in all but a few designated administrative centers. It had to rely on local people and institutions, which in effect left their autonomy substantially intact even if there was rather more government oversight than before. Cossack military service likewise remained separate and distinct from the regular army. In addition, the last two tsars, Alexander III (r. 1881–1894) and Nicholas II (r. 1894–1917), strenuously resisted attempts by the bureaucracy to reduce Cossack autonomy further, believing it to be an expression of their autocratic power, which the bureaucracy was eroding. By the twentieth century the process

A Cossack prevents starving peasants from leaving their village near Kazan, Russia. Engraving by R. Caton Woodville for the *Illustrated London News*, 16 January 1892. During the 1891 famine in Russia, Cossack troops actually contributed to the suffering of the poor by enforcing wrongheaded government policies. MARY EVANS PICTURE LIBRARY

of integration had began to unravel as the Cossacks distanced themselves psychologically from the regime due to the rising costs of military service, caused in part by the military reforms of the 1870s, and the increasing use of the Cossacks for internal repression. During the Revolution of 1905 substantial numbers of Cossack military units mutinied and unrest in Cossack territories was widespread. By 1914 the tsarist government had exhausted its credibility among the Cossacks no less than among others peoples of the empire.

The integration of the Cossacks into imperial Russia was a facet of the expansion of the state in the nineteenth century. Until the end of the eighteenth century, the state had concerned itself only with elites, but in the nineteenth century the state sought to extend its control over the mass of people who made up the empire's population. The integration of the Cossacks was part of this wider trend, but, as with so much else in imperial Russia, it remained incomplete and subject to contradictory pressures. By World War I the process of integration had ground to a halt and had even gone into reverse.

See also **Armies; Russia; Ukraine.**

BIBLIOGRAPHY

Barrett, Thomas M. *At the Edge of Empire: The Terek Cossacks and the North Caucasus Frontier, 1700–1869.* Boulder, Colo., 1999.

Longworth, Philip. *The Cossacks.* London, 1969.

McNeal, Robert. *Tsar and Cossack, 1855–1914.* London, 1987.

O'Rourke, Shane. *Warriors and Peasants: The Don Cossacks in Late Imperial Russia.* London, 2000.

SHANE O'ROURKE

COUNTERREVOLUTION. Shortly after the fall of the Bastille, in July 1789, the term *revolution* came to assume its modern meaning, and with this its antithesis came into common usage as well. As soon as the brothers of Louis XVI (r. 1774–1792), and then his aunts, fled France, they were suspected of conspiring against the new constitutional regime being shaped by the deputies of the Constituent Assembly, and fear of counterrevolution became a salient feature of the political landscape of revolutionary France. Throughout the late months of 1789, and on into 1790, increasing numbers of émigré nobles gathered in Koblenz and Turin, just across the French border. Patriots suspected the émigrés of corresponding with networks of counterrevolutionaries within France, and violent incidents in Lyon seemed to confirm those fears. The *bagarre de Nîmes,* the first serious incident of counterrevolutionary violence, claimed between two hundred and three hundred lives in a clash that pitted Protestants against Catholics, a distant echo of the hostilities of the Wars of Religion in southeastern France. Two months later nearly twenty-five thousand peasants, led by local nobles, gathered in a camp on the plain of Jalès, in Ardèche, north of

Nîmes. No violence followed, but a loosely organized leadership did emerge, and Jalès became synonymous with counterrevolution in southern France for the next three years. Camps gathered at Jalès at least twice thereafter, and a military engagement in the summer of 1792 resulted in the deaths of several hundred rebels.

In Paris the fear of counterrevolution following the military defeat at Verdun in late August 1792 triggered the September Massacres in the prisons, claiming nearly two thousand lives, many of them clergy, and in spring 1793 the introduction of military conscription led to rebellion in the Vendée, the first widespread counterrevolutionary upheaval in France. The Vendée, a region along the Atlantic seaboard just to the south of Nantes, was a predominantly rural area, with no major cities. The textile economy in towns such as Cholet had suffered in the last years of the Old Regime, and few of the local peasantry had benefited from the sale of *biens nationaux* (confiscated church lands) in the early years of the Revolution. Indeed, the peasants of the Vendée were intensely loyal to their priests, most of whom had been recruited locally, and most of whom refused to swear the civil oath of the clergy in accordance with a law passed by the Constituent Assembly in July 1790. Military recruitment, a slumping local economy, and resentment over the Civil Constitution of the Clergy thus brought together a coalition of disaffected peasants, refractory clergy, and royalist aristocrats in the most serious counterrevolutionary movement of the entire French Revolution.

Scattered uprisings quickly grew into something much larger, and the rebels formed what they called the Royal and Catholic Army. They took the city of Saumur in early June 1793, and by the end of the month Nantes was under siege. Republican volunteers rushed to the Vendée to combat the uprising, not only from Paris but also from throughout western France, including cities such as Caen and Bordeaux that were themselves resisting the National Convention at that time. The main rebel army was defeated in December 1793, with atrocities committed on both sides. In January 1794 General Louis-Marie Turreau unleashed his *colonnes infernales* to carry out a scorched-earth policy against the remnants of the rebel forces and their rural supporters. In Nantes, Jean-Baptiste

Carrier oversaw the execution of approximately three thousand people, most of them accused of having participated in the Vendée rebellion.

While the severe repression may have shattered the capability of the rebels to mount a serious military challenge in the Vendée region, it also inspired widespread resentment and perpetuated scattered resistance for years to come. A formal treaty was signed in February 1795, ostensibly ending the rebellion, but a failed landing of émigré forces (supported by the British) at Quiberon in June 1795 triggered renewed unrest, and it was not until the signing of the Concordat under Napoleon Bonaparte in 1801 that peace returned permanently to the region. The cost to the west of France was enormous, with the countryside laid waste and as much as one-third of the population killed in the fighting and the Terror that followed.

After the fall of Maximilien Robespierre on 9 Thermidor (27 July 1794), the *jeunesse dorée*, or gilded youth, grew increasingly bold in their expression of counterrevolutionary sentiments and their attacks on republican officials. The violence of the Terror now gave way to a White Terror, particularly in regions of southern France and along the Rhone Valley, and the two-thirds decree passed by the National Convention in 1795, aimed at ensuring continuity in the national government, produced an upsurge of counterrevolutionary activity in and around Paris quelled only by military action in Vendémiaire 1795—Napoleon's famous "whiff of grapeshot." The fear of counterrevolution did not entirely subside until Napoleon seized power in 1799, but the political opposition between left and right, between revolution and counterrevolution, would persist long into the nineteenth century.

CONGRESS OF VIENNA

While the regime of Napoleon Bonaparte (later Napoleon I, 1804–1814/15) suppressed republican politics within France, his imperial armies carried revolutionary ideas and ideals with them as they marched across Europe. After Napoleon's defeat, first in 1814 following the disastrous Russian campaign, and then definitively in 1815 following Waterloo, the monarchies of Europe sent their delegates to Vienna to craft a settlement that would both contain France and stem the revolutionary tide in Europe. Many European countries were represented at the Congress of Vienna, but the dominant players were Austria, Prussia, Russia, and Great Britain. The two most influential delegates at the table were Prince Clemens von Metternich (1773–1859), in charge of Austrian foreign affairs since 1809, and Robert Stewart, Viscount Castlereagh, representing Great Britain. Tsar Alexander I (r. 1801–1825) represented Russia himself, and while France was initially denied representation, Prince Charles-Maurice de Talleyrand-Périgord eventually traveled to Vienna to join the talks and defend French interests.

The treaty that emerged reduced French borders to an area just slightly larger than its 1789 boundaries. The treaty also sought to restore the balance of power in Europe by reestablishing traditional institutions and returning legitimate rulers to power. To preserve the peace and the balance of power moving forward, the five great powers came together in what was called the Concert of Europe, whereby Great Britain, France, Austria, Prussia, and Russia agreed to bring their disputes to the negotiating table rather than going to war. This informal agreement did indeed prevent the outbreak of a Continental war until 1914.

Tsar Alexander I hoped that the great powers would more formally affirm the religious basis of legitimate monarchical rule by signing a document that he wrote as the basis for a Holy Alliance. France was not invited to sign, and Castlereagh refused to commit Great Britain to this project, but Prussia, Austria, and Russia did sign, pledging to uphold Christian principles of charity and peace and to provide mutual assistance in the face of challenges from revolution or liberalism. In the decades following the Congress of Vienna the Holy Alliance had several opportunities to defend its principles. In 1820, a weak and corrupt government in Naples collapsed, and revolutionaries succeeded in instituting a new regime and constitution. Metternich, citing the principle that constitutions could only legitimately be granted by sovereigns, not forced by revolutionaries, called on the Holy Alliance to intervene, which it did, sending Austrian troops into Naples to restore Ferdinand IV (king of Naples as Ferdinand IV, r. 1759–1806, 1815–1825; king of the Two Sicilies as Ferdinand I, r. 1816–1825) to the throne. Thousands of liberals and revolutionaries fled

Naples, many of them finding their way to Spain, which was already facing unrest in its South and Central American colonies. While the European powers were unwilling to prop up Spanish monarchical rule in its colonies, the Holy Alliance did send two hundred thousand troops to Spain in 1823, easily routing opposition to the crown and forcing advocates of liberal revolution into exile or prison. Metternich and Tsar Alexander also intervened in the early 1820s to bolster Ottoman rule in Greece, though Greek nationalists did ultimately achieve Greek independence in 1829.

INTELLECTUAL UNDERPINNINGS

The diplomatic and political forces of counterrevolution were underpinned in the early nineteenth century by several important intellectual advocates of monarchical authority and political conservatism. First among these was Edmund Burke, whose *Reflections on the Revolution in France* appeared in 1790. Burke, an Irishman by birth and member of the British House of Commons, condemned the French Revolution as a blind incarnation of the abstract philosophy of the Enlightenment and its assertion of human universals. He argued that the events of 1789 in France represented a repudiation of the organic social order of France and a rejection of its historic tradition, and predicted that the Revolution would lead inevitably to atheism and military dictatorship. Burke's critique was recognized immediately and for many years thereafter as an eloquent expression of the ideology of counterrevolution.

Joining Burke in his repudiation of Enlightenment reason were two Frenchmen, Louis de Bonald (1754–1840) and Joseph de Maistre (1753–1821), both of whom emigrated from France during the Revolution. De Bonald argued that monarchy and Christianity, more particularly the Catholic Church, were the twin pillars necessary for the preservation of social order. He championed an organic vision of society in which the papacy and divine monarchs were the natural protectors of God's order on earth. De Maistre, too, believed that sovereignty flowed from God, not from the people, and rejected the Enlightenment concept of natural rights in favor of the natural order that had prevailed in Europe for centuries. For the conservatives who rallied to de Bonald and de Maistre,

God and history (or tradition) were the only legitimate sources of political authority. And that authority, they argued, must be sustained by force. As de Maistre wrote, "the first servant of the crown should be the executioner."

Conservatives, then, rejected the universalism of the Enlightenment and the French Revolution, insisting that the only legitimate rights were those granted by monarchs to their people. But they could not deny the powerful force, the enormous energy, unleashed by French nationalism during the 1790s, and the advocates of counterrevolution sought a way to tap that energy without unleashing the forces of liberalism and radical reform. Some found inspiration in the writings of Johann Gottfried von Herder (1744–1803), a Prussian Romantic who argued that national identity was rooted in a common history and culture, most profoundly expressed through language and folk literature. In Herder's ideas those who opposed popular sovereignty and individual liberties found an expression of a conservative nationalism that would serve the forces of counterrevolution well through the first half of the nineteenth century, and that would eventually lead to the unification of Germany in 1870.

REVOLUTIONS OF 1830 AND OF 1848

The revolutions of 1830, however, marked an end to the ability of the Holy Alliance to hold back political change across Europe. The most important of these occurred in France. When Charles X (r. 1824–1830) came to power in 1824, succeeding Louis XVIII (r. 1814–1815, 1815–1824), he attempted to reassert elements of traditional monarchical power and restrict political freedom. This led to a wave of protest and political agitation, culminating in popular uprisings in July 1830 that toppled the Bourbon crown and brought the more liberal Orléanist wing of the royal family to power. Louis-Philippe, the "citizen king," would govern France until 1848.

The change of regime in Paris inspired Belgian patriots to demand more autonomy from the Dutch king. Tsar Nicholas I (r. 1825–1855) wished to intervene in support of the Dutch, but troubles in Poland prevented a Russian mobilization. The Belgian revolution succeeded, with Belgium gaining complete independence. Great Britain and France then stepped in to negotiate an agreement whereby all five great powers pledged to recognize and guarantee Belgian neutrality in perpetuity. In Poland, by contrast, the Russian tsar acted with force to repress middle-class revolutionaries in 1831, and Poland was effectively annexed to Russia.

For the next two decades most Europeans saw the political landscape as one pitting proponents of revolution against the forces of counterrevolution. Metternich and his allies did all that they could to hold back the tide of parliamentary liberalism, to ward off the threat of social disorder and godless radicalism, but in the end they were fighting a losing battle. Liberal revolutionaries agitated all across Europe in the 1830s and 1840s, both openly and clandestinely, and as industrialization spread in western Europe and Great Britain, the advocates of liberal parliamentarianism were soon pressured from below by working people demanding universal manhood suffrage and socialist policies. When revolution did erupt in 1848, with major upheavals occurring almost simultaneously across the Continent, the first instinct of monarchs in France, Germany, Austria, Hungary, and Italy was to step back in fear and grant concessions for reform.

In France, relatively peaceful protests in Paris in February 1848 brought an end to the Orléanist monarchy, with King Louis-Philippe (r. 1830–1848) fleeing to London, and revolutionaries declaring a second French Republic. Widespread demonstrations in the German states, prompted by news from France and reports of upheaval in Vienna, led the Prussian king Frederick William IV (r. 1840–1861) to convene a United Diet of German states, to meet in Frankfurt in May with the purpose of drafting a constitution. Troubles in Austria began with an independence movement in Hungary, the news of which triggered protests among students and artisans in Vienna. Metternich quickly resigned his post, and Emperor Ferdinand I (r. 1835–1848) promised a liberal constitution and the granting of civil liberties. In northern Italy, advocates of liberal reform joined those eager to see Italian unification and independence from Austria.

CONCLUSION

Despite these initial successes, however, the forces of counterrevolution would ultimately prevail in nearly every case. Divisions among the revolutionaries themselves, and the strengthened resolve of the ruling houses, doomed the revolutions to failure. Much more rapidly than in 1789 or 1830, divisions emerged between the propertied bourgeoisie and the lower classes, both workers and peasants. Fearful of unrest and the "socialist" threat, the middle classes were willing to compromise some of their liberal ideals so that stability and order might be reestablished. In France this meant the election of Louis-Napoleon Bonaparte, nephew of Napoleon I, as president in December 1848. Although he campaigned as a populist, he soon introduced an authoritarian regime, sent French troops in 1849 to support the pope against republican rebels in Italy, and in December 1851 declared himself emperor as Napoleon III (r. 1852–1871). Austria joined France and the papacy in sending troops against the Italian revolutionaries, who were easily defeated. At home, Francis Joseph I (r. 1848–1916) succeeded his uncle, Ferdinand, as Austro-Hungarian emperor in spring 1848, and the Habsburg government employed a military siege to suppress the revolutionary movement in Vienna, killing nearly three thousand rebels in the process. Austria required the assistance of Russian troops in the summer of 1849 to finally quell the Hungarian independence movement. In Germany, Frederick William IV dissolved an assembly meeting in Berlin in November 1848 and sent royal troops to occupy the city. The diet meeting in Frankfurt, composed largely of moderate liberals, could not agree on whether a unified Germany should include Austria, or be centered on the kingdom of Prussia. When they finally opted for the latter, and approached Frederick William to accept the new throne, he refused to accept "a crown from the gutter." The Prussian king now moved to dissolve the Frankfurt assembly and sent troops against the last flickers of revolt in the smaller German states.

In the end, then, counterrevolution prevailed and monarchies survived the revolutions of 1848. The unification of Italy and of Germany would eventually come, in 1870, but on much more authoritarian terms than the liberal revolutionaries of 1848 had envisaged. Otto von Bismarck's triumph in Germany did bring an end to the Second Empire in France, but the return of a republican government in Paris did little to shake the foundations of monarchy in the rest of Europe. Not until the convergence of World War I and the Bolshevik Revolution would emperors finally be toppled from their thrones in Berlin, Moscow, and Vienna.

See also **French Revolution; Revolutions of 1830; Revolutions of 1848.**

BIBLIOGRAPHY

Hamerow, Theodore S. *Restoration, Revolution, Reaction: Economics and Politics in Germany, 1815–1871.* Princeton, N.J., 1958.

Kissinger, Henry. *A World Restored: Metternich, Castlereagh, and the Problems of Peace, 1812–1822.* Boston, 1957.

Lively, Jack, ed. *The Works of Joseph de Maistre.* New York, 1965.

Mayer, Arno J. *The Persistence of the Old Regime: Europe to the Great War.* New York, 1981.

Merriman, John M. *The Agony of the Republic: The Repression of the Left in Revolutionary France, 1848–51.* New Haven, Conn., 1987.

Talmon, Jacob Leib. *Romanticism and Revolt: Europe, 1815–1848.* London, 1967.

Weiss, John. *Conservatism in Europe, 1770–1945: Traditionalism, Reaction, and Counterrevolution.* New York, 1977.

PAUL R. HANSON

COURBET, GUSTAVE (1819–1877), French painter.

Born in Ornans, a small village in the Jura Mountains of France, Jean Desiré Gustave Courbet took his first drawing lessons at the Collège Royal de Besançon. At age twenty, he moved to Paris, where he studied briefly with the successful portraitist Charles de Steuben (1788–1856). Then, deciding to pursue his art studies independently, he copied old-master paintings in the Louvre and drew after live models in an open studio. In 1842 he started to submit works to the annual Paris Salon but although he submitted two works every year for the next six years, the jury accepted only three and none brought him critical acclaim.

Courbet's breakthrough as an artist had much to do with the Revolution of 1848, which spelled the end, if only temporarily, to the rigid jury system of the Salon. To the unjuried Salon of that year, he sent no fewer than ten works. More important for his future, however, was the 1849 Salon, juried by a committee democratically elected by all artists, where he exhibited six paintings and received a medal. This meant that henceforth he was *hors concours*: his works no longer had to pass by the jury to be admitted. This new status allowed him to make an important statement at the combined Salon of 1850/51, where he exhibited nine paintings, including the *Stonebreakers* and the *Burial at Ornans*, two paintings that received much critical attention. Both works were related to the ideology and the events of the Revolution and the short-lived Second Republic that followed it (1848–1851). The first, showing two men engaged in the meanest form of contemporary labor—the manual breaking of fieldstones to create gravel for roads—dealt with poverty, a hot-button issue during the Second Republic. The second, a monumental group portrait of rural bourgeois and well-to-do peasants, alluded to the new sense of civic equality that had been created by the introduction, in 1848, of universal suffrage. On an artistic level, it also called into question the traditional hierarchy of genres. Courbet had painted an ordinary scene of contemporary life on a canvas the size of a monumental history painting. Maintaining that the *Burial*, in fact, was a history painting, he claimed that, contrary to traditional history paintings, which reimagined the past for the public of the present, his work offered an accurate record of the present for the viewers of the future. This new concept of history painting was an important aspect of Courbet's artistic program, which he referred to as realism.

Courbet continued to send several controversial works to the Salons of the next few years. These paintings included *Young Ladies of the Village* (1852), *The Bathers* (1853), and the *Grain Sifters* (1855). Although these works often got negative press, the sheer amount of publicity made Courbet exceedingly well known in Paris and eventually brought him some patrons. The eccentric collector Alfred Bruyas (1821–1876) bought Courbet's notorious *Bathers* in 1853 and commissioned the artist to paint his portrait. Encouraged by this commercial success, Courbet painted a huge self-referential painting for the art exhibition to be held at the International Exhibition of 1855: *The Atelier*

The Stonebreakers. Painting by Jean Désiré Gustave Courbet, 1849; destroyed in the bombing of Dresden, 1945.
GEMAELDEGALERIE ALTE MEISTER, DRESDEN, GERMANY/BRIDGEMAN ART LIBRARY/ STAATLICHE KUNSTSAMMLUNGEN DRESDEN

of the Artist or Real Allegory of Seven Years of My Artistic Life. When the organizing committee of that exhibition refused to hang the work, Courbet managed to organize a private exhibition, held in a specially built pavilion (Le Pavillon du Réalisme) on the very grounds of the fair. This was a revolutionary step that would set an example for the next generation of French artists, especially Édouard Manet (1832–1883) and the impressionists.

His reputation made, Courbet, after 1855, began to concentrate on sales. As landscape paintings were especially salable at the time, he began to specialize in this genre, which he had practiced since the beginning of his career but on a modest scale. He now began to paint larger landscapes, for the most part representing the rugged scenery of the Jura Mountains. Some of these he exhibited at the Salon, and their success brought him numerous commissions from dealers and collectors for copies, replicas, or smaller versions. Along with landscapes, he also painted portraits and produced floral still lifes, another popular genre among collectors.

Always a fierce opponent of the Second Empire, Courbet applauded Napoleon III's (1808–1873) defeat by the Prussians in the Battle of Sedan in 1870. In 1871 Courbet joined the Paris Commune and played an important role in the demolition of the Vendôme Column, that much-hated French imperialist monument. For his role in the Commune he spent six months in prison. The demolition of the Vendôme Column cost him more dearly. Threatened with the sequestration of all his possessions in 1873, he went into exile in Switzerland to save at least some of his assets. There he died, severely alcoholic, in 1877.

See also **France; Impressionism; Manet, Édouard; Painting; Paris Commune; Realism and Naturalism; Revolutions of 1848.**

BIBLIOGRAPHY

Primary Sources

Chu, Petra ten-Doesschate, ed. and trans. *Letters of Gustave Courbet.* Chicago, 1992.

Secondary Sources

Chu, Petra ten-Doesschate. *The Most Arrogant Man in France: Gustave Courbet and the Nineteenth-Century Media Culture.* Princeton, N.J., forthcoming.

Faunce, Sarah, and Linda Nochlin. *Courbet Reconsidered.* Brooklyn, N.Y., and New Haven, Conn., 1988.

Fried, Michael. *Courbet's Realism.* Chicago, 1990.

Nochlin, Linda. *Gustave Courbet: A Study of Style and Society.* New York, 1976.

Rubin, James H. *Courbet.* London, 1997.

PETRA TEN-DOESSCHATE CHU

CRIME. It is always difficult to measure the incidence of crime, and given the different legal definitions of offenses, it is equally difficult to draw clear contrasts or similarities between criminal activities in different states and regions. Nevertheless, the development of criminal statistics in the early nineteenth century enabled some significant assessments to be made of patterns and parallels. Across Europe as a whole the spread of the nation-state and of its powers of repression appears to have had some impact on crime. Changing ideas about how humankind had developed and functioned led to new and different emphases in the way people understood the causes of criminal offending; so too did anxieties about the burgeoning industrial cities and towns. Finally, the expansion of the popular press during the nineteenth century fed off and fed into people's perceptions of crime.

THE PATTERN OF CRIME

In the early nineteenth century European governments and intellectuals put tremendous faith in the ability of statistics to reveal the moral facts about a society and to enable rational, improved, and improving policies to be developed. The statistics of crime figured significantly in this faith. The British government began collecting statistics of this kind in the first decade of the century hoping that these would contribute usefully to debates about punishment and especially to debates about the death penalty. The French had begun collecting various forms of crime statistics toward the end of the Old Regime. During the Revolution such collection

became more systematic, in part at least to enable checks to be made on the extent to which magistrates were doing what was expected of them. The most significant step forward, however, came in the 1820s with the annual publication of the *Compte générale de l'administration de la justice criminelle* (General account of the administration of criminal justice). By the end of the 1830s the *Compte* was providing a detailed breakdown of offenders by age, sex, place of birth, level of education, trade, and whether their residence was rural or urban. It provided a model for similar statistical collections in other countries.

The development of the *Compte* encouraged social thinkers to draw conclusions about patterns of criminality. The most important of the early analysts was the Belgian academic Adolphe Quetelet (1796–1894). Using the French statistics and such as he could glean from elsewhere, Quetelet made a series of deductions, some of which reflected the evolving opinions of his contemporaries about, for example, racial types, but others of which have stood the test of time. The statistics showed that, overwhelmingly, principal offenders were young men. They also suggested that the same number of crimes in roughly the same geographical regions were being committed year after year. But Quetelet was shrewd enough to appreciate that there were problems with the statistics. In particular he recognized the difficulty created by offenses that were never reported and hence never listed. Modern criminologists use the term *the dark figure* to describe the unknown number between the crimes reported and listed and the crimes that were actually committed. This makes any estimate of the actual level of crime impossible, though it did not discourage many nineteenth- and early-twentieth-century criminologists and has not discouraged attempts by historians to gauge the changing patterns of crime across the period.

In very general terms the figures show property crime represented a much greater overall percentage of the total than violent crime. This can be seen as a continuation and perhaps even culmination of an overall shift in offending from violence to theft that historians have detected as developing from the late medieval and early modern periods. During the nineteenth century violent crime was more apparent in southern Europe than in the north. This was especially the case in those regions such as Corsica, Greece, the south of Italy, and Sicily, where vendetta and honor killing were still practiced and where the state struggled to establish its authority. But throughout the century violent crime, particularly murder and rape—those crimes that most frightened and shocked people—constituted only a small proportion of the offenses in the statistics. The greatest proportion of offenses involved property crime, and the overwhelming majority of thefts were small. Often the stolen goods were taken to a pawnbroker's shop for a few coins. In very general terms too the statistics suggest a gradual increase in crime in the first half of the century with a general leveling out and, in some instances, even a decline in the second.

Early on some of the individuals working with the crime figures began to suggest a close link between economic downturns and criminality. Most significant here was Georg von Mayr (1841–1925), who, in the mid-1860s as a member of the Bavarian Statistical Bureau, produced two important statistical surveys. The first concerned beggars and vagrants while the second showed a correlation between a rise in the price of grain and a rise in the figures for theft. But the possible link between poverty and crime was not always one that many commentators were keen to stress.

ECONOMY AND GEOGRAPHY

Changes in economic structure and the power of the state appear to have generated changes in the pattern of crime across the nineteenth century. The assumption was made by some of the earliest serious academic historians of crime that industrialization, the capitalization of industry, and an increasing sanctity surrounding private property fostered crime as a form of protest among the growing and increasingly self-conscious working classes. Evidence for such a change has, however, been difficult to come by. On the other hand, the growth of financial institutions and of capitalist investment provided unscrupulous but outwardly respectable gentlemen with considerable opportunities to profit, sometimes criminally, at the expense of gullible investors.

The wars at the end of the eighteenth and beginning of the nineteenth centuries disrupted economies and left large numbers of draft dodgers, deserters, and army stragglers over much of continental Europe. Many of these men slipped in and out of banditry. At the same time there were sparsely populated districts, often spanning state frontiers, where banditry and smuggling throve among the poor peasantry. During the Revolutionary and Napoleonic Wars some of these bandits began to acquire the aura of anti-French Robin Hoods and guerrilla fighters. Johannes Bückler, known as Schinderhannes, was one such in the Rhineland, and Michele Pezza in Calabria, known as Fra Diavolo, was another. Several of the Spanish guerrilla gangs that claimed to be fighting Napoleon's armies were often bandits masquerading under more respectable colors. The romantic image surrounding such figures was also often something that developed after the wars; the bandits themselves were usually cruel, violent, and as much a threat to the local peasantry and anyone else who crossed their path as they were to the French. The growth and greater effectiveness of the state's means of control and repression during the nineteenth century—the spread of gendarmerie corps in rural areas, for example—meant that the number of remote regions in which banditry could flourish became fewer and fewer.

By the second half of the century banditry was largely restricted to the south of Europe and to the vast expanses of the east where police were particularly thin on the ground. In Spain and Sicily, however, the bandit problem was aggravated by influential local landowners who recruited strong-arm men to discipline their workforces and to defend their properties. These strong-arm men slipped in and out of banditry but were protected by the landowners. Moreover, "bandit" and "brigand" are indeterminate labels present largely in the eye of a beholder. The draconian Pica Law of 1863 gave the army and the carabinieri a virtual free hand in suppressing peasant resistance in the south of the newly unified Italy. Under the directives issued to the forces of order in the south of Italy, even a small group of laborers carrying agricultural implements might be considered as "brigands."

Yet while there could be danger in the countryside, it was the towns and cities that during the nineteenth century were the principal focus of fears about crime and criminals. A variety of commentators worried that the wealth of expanding

Spanish Contrabandista. Lithograph after a painting by Richard Ansdell, 1861. Smuggling goods across poorly defended borders was a common criminal activity in Europe throughout the nineteenth century. BIBLIOTHÈQUE DES ARTS DECORATIFS, PARIS, FRANCE/BRIDGEMAN ART LIBRARY/ARCHIVES CHARMET

towns and cities provided a temptation for thieves and that the anonymity of the urban world provided easy escape and plenty of hiding places for offenders. In the early nineteenth century particularly such fears became enmeshed with concerns about revolution and the assumption that the courts and tenements of towns and cities were infested with a dangerous, criminal class eager for revolutionary outbreaks that would furnish opportunities for mayhem, murder, and plunder.

CLASS AND HEREDITY

In 1840 a French police administrator, Honoré Frégier (1789–1860), published *Des classes dangereuses de la population dans les grands villes et des moyens de les rendre meilleurs* (On the dangerous classes of the population in large cities and the means to make them better). Frégier was aware

that corrupt and depraved individuals could be found in all social classes, but, he warned, when a poor man yielded to wicked passions and ceased to work seeking to exist by other means, then he became a dangerous enemy of society. In this he was echoing the kinds of comments made by his contemporaries elsewhere. In Britain, for example, in the Report of the Royal Commission on a Rural Constabulary, the Benthamite reformer Edwin Chadwick (1800–1890) argued that criminals were motivated by a general indolence and by a desire for excitement. According to Chadwick and his like-minded commissioners, men made a rational choice to follow a criminal career in the belief that the profits would be easier, quicker, and greater than those acquired by honest, respectable labor. What such commentators were doing was labeling as the cause of crime that behavior among the working class of which they most disapproved. This behavior included, most notably, drinking and gambling and also any leisure taken in the streets that looked like idleness. They ignored the fact that much labor in the first half of the nineteenth century remained seasonal, and consequently people were often on the move looking for work or on the streets passing time as a result of underemployment or simply unemployment.

Frégier's formulation "the dangerous classes" was employed in Britain and in Italy (*classi pericolose*), while the Germans preferred their traditional word *Gauner* to describe tricky, indolent, but always mobile working-class offenders. The assumption was that this was a kind of countersociety with its own hierarchy and language. Several of the commentators who described criminals wrote page after page on criminal argot and provided long lists of their words and phrases. At times the offenders could be described almost as a different race, and Friedrich Avé-Lallement (1809–1892), a German police official who wrote a massive four volumes on the German *Gauner* in the middle of the century, stressed the influence of Gypsies and Jews among them. Analyses of this sort also gendered the criminal classes: the men were thieves and murderers; the women were prostitutes. This kind of literature often warned that prostitutes led their clients to alleyways or rooms where their menfolk attacked and robbed them. It would be wrong to argue that

Female convicts at work in Brixton prison, 1860.
Illustration from the book *The Criminal Prisons of London and Scenes of Prison Life* by Henry Mayhew and John Binny. Victorian moral attitudes resulted in a disproportionate incarceration rate among poor and working-class women.
PRIVATE COLLECTION/BRIDGEMAN ART LIBRARY/THE STAPLETON COLLECTION

this never happened, though the evidence of the courts does not suggest that it happened with the frequency described in the popular accounts.

Criminal children also figured in the depictions of the criminal classes. There was an assumption that child offenders began their criminal careers as pickpockets and progressed from this to more serious crimes. Such offenders were sometimes portrayed as the offspring of criminals and thus bred to their careers, or else as the children of feckless or alcoholic parents who abandoned them on the streets. But again the evidence from the courts does not bear this out. A very few children and juveniles stole because they were put up to it by professional receivers such as Charles Dickens's Fagin. Some stole through need, but opportunism,

peer pressure, and stealing or doing damage for fun all seem to have been at least as important. Moreover, the evidence does not suggest that these offenders were invariably the children of men and women who were known criminals or of drunken or otherwise bad parents. Often the parents appear to have been struggling for respectability and were distraught by the behavior of their offspring. Indeed, it was known for the police to be called upon by parents to discipline their difficult children.

In the last third of the century assumptions about a criminal class were given a significant scientific underpinning. Cesare Lombroso (1835–1909) claimed that it was while he was serving as a doctor with the Italian army that he was presented with the head of a notorious brigand and that this inspired him to develop his theory of the born criminal. Over the following decade Lombroso combined his empirical study of the skulls of "inferior" and "primitive" peoples with the theoretical work of men such as Auguste Comte and Ernst Haeckel. Then, in 1876, he published the first edition of *L'uomo delinquente* (The delinquent man). Over the next twenty years the book went through five editions and increased eightfold in size to two thousand pages. At the same time his ideas shifted from the notion of criminal man carrying the atavistic tendencies of ancient and savage peoples and publicly demonstrating these through his facial and physical characteristics, to a much broader perception of criminality. While he continued to insist that some criminals were born, Lombroso's later work also pointed to other offenders formed through alcoholism, malnutrition, venereal disease, and other forms of degeneracy.

Lombroso rapidly acquired a school in Italy; indeed, it was one of his disciples, Enrico Ferri, rather than Lombroso himself, who coined the term *born criminal.* But during the 1880s, at a series of international congresses on what began to be called criminal anthropology, Lombroso and his Italian followers clashed heatedly with French experts. The French attacked Lombroso's use of ill-defined words as well as the idea of primitive anatomical characteristics being an indication of criminal propensities. At the same time they put much greater emphases on environment and nurture. The key figure here was Gabriel Tarde

C. LOMBROSO — L'homme criminel.   Pl. XXXVII.

FOUS CRIMINELS.

Monomaniaques: N. 32, 33, 38, 41, 49 type. — Maniaques: N. 31, 34, 46 type. — Lipé-
maniaques: N. 47, 48. — Déments: N. 35 type, 36 type, 42, 45. — Imbéciles: N. 26, 28,
30, 39 type, 40 type, 41 type, 43 type. — Idiots: N. 27, 37. — Folie circulaire: N. 29, 50.

**A page from a French edition of Cesare Lombroso's
L'uomo delinquente shows the facial characteristics
of people deemed to be criminal types.** MARY EVANS
PICTURE LIBRARY

(1843–1904), who had begun his working life as a
provincial magistrate, went on to head up the
Bureau of Statistics in the Ministry of Justice, and
concluded his career as professor of sociology at
the Collège de France. Tarde's *La criminalité
comparée* (Criminality compared, 1886) and *La
philosophie pénale* (Penal philosophy, 1890)
rejected the idea of the born criminal, stressing
environment and individual choice in the making
of a criminal offender. But he was also wedded to
the notion of the criminal career beginning with an
apprenticeship in small offending and progressing
to more serious crimes.

While one set of experts argued over the relative importance of heredity and milieu as causes of
crime, another group focused their attention on
gender and sexuality. From early on in the century
there were some members of the new science of
psychiatry who described some forms of theft as
the result of a kind of madness. The idea of kleptomania became particularly popular in the last
quarter of the century to explain why some bourgeois women, who appeared to want for nothing,
were found stealing from the new retail phenomenon the department store. While there were
some men who suffered from the same "disease,"
kleptomania was rapidly linked to assumptions
about female weakness, the impact of the men-
strual cycle, a difficult pregnancy, menopause, or
becoming a widow.

Taking the nineteenth century as a whole, a
broad shift can be detected in the way that criminal
behavior was understood. In the first half of century
the assumption was that committing a crime was a
matter of choice by an individual. By the end of the
century, however, the arguments of medical men and
of exponents of the new science of criminal anthropology or criminology suggested that offenders were
damaged individuals whose behavior was dictated by
heredity, by nurture and environment, or by some
combination of these. This shift in thinking led to
shifts in arguments about how convicted offenders
should be treated. Thus, at the beginning of the
century there were attempts to establish equality of
punishment and essentially to make punishments fit
crimes. By the end of the century, encouraged by the
arguments of criminologists and medical men,
judges across Europe began to think increasingly in
terms of passing sentences that involved a punishment designed to fit the individual criminal.

WRITING ABOUT CRIME

Few people experience crime on a regular basis.
What most people know about crime is what they
have learned from the media. This can have a
distorting effect on the way that the population
as a whole understands crime. Sensational and
thrilling stories sell books and newspapers. Petty,
opportunist theft does not attract an audience;
major thefts and murders do. It was the same in
the nineteenth century.

The eighteenth century witnessed the beginning
of the gradual demise of the chapbook and the
broadside that recounted the tale of a brigand, a

highwayman, or a murderer and reported his farewell speech from the scaffold. These accounts of last words were usually coupled with a warning not to follow in the offender's footsteps and to avoid strong drink and loose women. By the middle years of the century this kind of literature had largely been replaced, at least in much of central and western Europe, with sensational novels and a few books written by former police officers and even by criminals. The books by policemen and criminals had an aura of authority even though they usually embroidered the truth. Indeed, François-Eugène Vidocq (1775–1857), the former convict who subsequently became head of the Paris police detective squad, was so outraged by the way in which a ghostwriter embellished his story that he refused to sign off the fourth volume of his memoirs. Pierre-François Lacenaire, a thief and multiple murderer, in turn was keen to portray himself as a poet of crime, and in the France of Louis-Philippe there were sufficient woolly headed romantics to encourage him and to romanticize his memory long after he had been guillotined.

Novelists of the 1830s and 1840s built on the image of the dangerous, criminal classes described by Frégier. Dickens's *Oliver Twist* (1837–1839)— with its evil receiver, Fagin, directing a gang of trained juvenile pickpockets and in league with a brutal burglar-murderer, Bill Sikes, who in turn lives with a young prostitute, Nancy—is simply the best known and arguably the best written of many. In the early 1840s the French novelist Eugène Sue published *Les Mystères de Paris* and set a trend of a variety of similar "mysteries" fancifully describing the criminal underworlds of cities all over Europe. More than thirty such appeared in Germany in 1844, and in the following year the Chartist G. W. M. Reynolds commenced publishing the weekly installments of *The Mysteries of London*, a popular underworld saga that continued until 1848.

The cheap popular press that began to appear in the middle of the century recognized from the start that sensational crime sold newspapers. It was the London newspaper press that, during the series of brutal murders of prostitutes in Whitechapel in the fall of 1888, popularized the murderer with the name Jack the Ripper. At the same time, the press pushed back the frontiers of decency in detailing the wounds inflicted by the Ripper on his victims.

Some twenty years later the world's largest-selling newspaper of the time, *Le Petit Parisien,* which had always devoted a large amount of space to sensational crimes, launched a "Great Referendum" on capital punishment. The referendum was accompanied by an increase in the column space devoted to crime and was carefully constructed both to sell more copies of the newspaper and to generate a resounding "no" to proposals for the abolition of the death penalty.

Crime may have been leveling out according to the statistics, but that was not how the press chose to see the problem. In addition to the opportunities provided by such exceptional killings as those of Jack the Ripper, of Jean-Baptiste Troppmann on the edge of Haussmann's Paris, of Imre Balentics in Budapest and so on, the press also chose to construct threats from gangs and to link various forms of offending with the concerns for racial purity and preservation that influenced many politicians and commentators at the turn of the century. In the 1890s the British press made much of the threat from the youth gangs that acquired the new name of "hooligans." Youth gangs existed; they wore distinctive clothes and they fought ferocious battles with each other over territory and girlfriends. Yet while some of their members committed other offenses, the gangs were organized to fight each other rather than to assault and rob ordinary members of the public. In Paris an arguably greater panic focused on the so-called apaches. The French bourgeoisie's fascination with Native Americans went back at least to the July Monarchy and to translations of the novels of James Fenimore Cooper. During Napoleon III's Mexican adventure, stories had come back about the alleged cold cruelty of the Apache, and when, at the end of the century, a name was felt necessary for young, violent street thieves, the French press looked no further.

Finally, it is worth emphasizing that, on occasions even as late as the turn of the century, when dreadful crimes were committed old scapegoats were pointed at anew. There were suggestions that Jack the Ripper was a Jew and that his butchery was linked with a myth that Orthodox Jewish men were required ritually to murder any gentile woman with whom they had been sexually intimate. In several parts of Europe the discovery of a murdered child

THE WHITEHALL MYSTERY.

DISCOVERING THE MUTILATED TRUNK.

The Whitehall Mystery: Discovering the Mutilated trunk. An English engraving c. 1888 is typical of the lurid newspaper and magazine illustrations inspired by the murders committed by the killer known as Jack the Ripper. PRIVATE COLLECTION/BRIDGEMAN ART LIBRARY

or juvenile ignited the old panic about ritual murder by Jews. In such instances there were all too often vicious anti-Semites, sometimes in clerical robes, prepared to fan the flames or even to provoke the disorder by fabricating the rumors themselves. In the 1890s there was a series of such outbreaks, most notably in the Austro-Hungarian Empire and Prussia. Among the best researched is that which occurred in the small West Prussian town of Konitz in March 1900. A high school student, Ernst Winter, disappeared. When parts of his dismembered body began to be found, rumors spread that he was the victim of a ritual murder. Several weeks of sporadic anti-Semitic violence ensued, and the only individuals to be prosecuted in the whole affair were the young men arrested for their part in the rioting.

By the beginning of the twentieth century it was possible to look back on a cluster of distinct changes that had taken place over the previous hundred years. The press continued to delight in

bandit gangs when there was an opportunity, but except in remote areas such as the Russian steppes or parts of the Mediterranean where state power had yet to exert control, the old-style bandits and highwaymen had disappeared. Picking pockets remained possible, and the development of the bustle as part of women's fashion facilitated theft from pockets and purses that were carried in this new accoutrement. Goods remained exposed in markets and in front of shops, but they were also exposed in the new department stores, providing new opportunities for the shoplifter. Automobiles and trains were said to enable major offenders to make fast getaways. But motor transport and trains also made it difficult for thieves to jump onboard a freight vehicle and pull things from the back while it was moving. The telegraph made it possible to pass on a suspect's description before a train or boat arrived at its destination. At the same time, the photograph and the fingerprint, together with Alphonse Bertillon's system of physical recognition by measuring certain parts of the body, made the apprehension of the recidivist a little easier.

See also **Cities and Towns; Class and Social Relations; Degeneration; Lombroso, Cesare; Quetelet, Lambert Adolphe Jacques; Statistics; Working Class.**

BIBLIOGRAPHY

Becker, Peter. *Verderbnis und Entartung: Eine Geschichte der Kriminologie des 19. Jahrhunderts als Diskurs und Praxis.* Göttingen, Germany, 2002.

Chevalier, Louis. *Labouring Classes and Dangerous Classes in Paris during the First Half of the Nineteenth Century.* Translated by Frank Jellinek. London, 1973.

Emsley, Clive. *Crime and Society in England 1750–1900.* 3rd ed. London, 2004.

———. *Crime, State and Society in Europe 1750–1940.* Oxford, U.K., 2007.

Emsley, Clive, and Louis A. Knafla, eds. *Crime Histories and Histories of Crime: Studies in the Historiography of Crime and Criminal Justice in Modern History.* Westport, Conn., 1996.

Evans, Richard J. *Tales from the German Underworld: Crime and Punishment in the Nineteenth Century.* New Haven, Conn., 1998.

Gibson, Mary. *Born to Crime: Cesare Lombroso and the Origins of Biological Criminality.* Westport, Conn., 2002.

Nye, Robert A. *Crime, Madness, and Politics in Modern France: The Medical Concept of National Decline.* Princeton, N.J., 1984.

CLIVE EMSLEY

CRIMEAN WAR.

The Crimean War (1853–1856) concluded a period of forty years in which Russian expansion and Ottoman Turkish weakness had created a major problem for the European state system. If the Ottoman Empire collapsed, who should profit, and how could the balance of power be preserved if Russia, Britain, France or Austria were to acquire more resources than their rivals? Hitherto Anglo-Russian consensus on the need to preserve Turkey had staved off the threat of a major war, although Turkey had surrendered Greece and part of the Balkans. Only when Bonapartist France interfered in 1851 did the system fail.

While the spark for war came from a dispute among France, and Russia, and Turkey over the Christian shrines in Palestine, the cause was Russian ambition to control the Dardanelles and Bosphorus, to exclude the strategic threat of British sea power, and ensure the free passage of Russian exports. Britain joined France in diplomatic attempts to avert war, but by the time Tsar Nicholas I (r. 1825–1855) realized Britain was serious he was too deeply committed to back down. The war began in October 1853, when Turkey declared war on Russia and attacked across the Danube. On 30 November a Turkish flotilla heading for the Circassian coast was annihilated at Sinope by a Russian fleet. Britain persuaded France to adopt a global strategy based on command of the sea, for campaigns in the Baltic, the Black Sea, the White Sea, and the Pacific. Britain and France declared war respectively on 27 and 28 March 1854. They planned an amphibious attack on Sevastopol, after the destruction of a Russian battle squadron at Reval (Tallinn) in the Baltic.

A fifty-thousand-man joint expeditionary force was sent to secure European Turkey, led by Field Marshal Lord Raglan (1788–1855), who had been for many years the Duke of Wellington's (Arthur Wellesley, 1769–1852) Military Secretary, and Marshal Armand-Jacques Saint Arnaud (1798–1854), one of the leading architects of Napoleon III's (r. 1852–1871) coup d'etat. The two armies had rifled small arms, but still used Napoleonic tactics. British long-service regulars were well trained for combat, but ill prepared for the harsh realities of campaigning. The French combined volunteers hardened in the Algerian war with conscript units that proved fragile in battle. The Russian army, the largest in Europe, had no rifles, and did not trouble recruits with aiming. None of the belligerents had a modern administration.

The Baltic campaign of 1854 began with the discovery that Reval was empty, but produced the first major Allied success, the capture of the fortified Aland Islands in August. The British also imposed an effective economic blockade that crippled Russian finances.

In the Black Sea neutral Austria demanded that Russia evacuate the Danubian Principalities (modern Romania) or face war. Russia complied, leaving the allied army at Varna on the Bulgarian coast with no role. The British Government decided to attack

A British cavalry camp during the Crimean War. Photograph by Roger Fenton, 1855. ©CORBIS

Sevastopol, expecting a grand raid of no more than a month to seize the city, destroy the Russian Black Sea fleet, and demolish the naval base. The French agreed. In mid-September 1854 the Allies landed in the Crimea almost sixty thousand strong. They marched south toward Sevastopol, encountering the Russian army under Prince Menshikov (1787–1869) well dug in on the banks of the River Alma on 20 September. The French used a coastal path to turn the Russian flank while the British drove through the Russian center. The Russians retreated in disorder, unable to withstand British infantry firepower. After a delay caused by Saint Arnaud's terminal illness the Allies marched round Sevastopol harbor to begin a conventional siege from the south, based on the ports of Balaklava and Kamiesch Bay. An attempt to storm the city failed on 17 October,

allowing Menshikov to stage a flank attack on Balaklava on 25 October.

After holding off the Russians with slender resources a misunderstanding led the British Light Cavalry Brigade, some 650 troopers, to charge a strong position, which they cleared, and then drove off several times their number of Russian horsemen. Usually portrayed as a disaster, the charge was highly effective, with casualties no heavier than those incurred at the Alma. It broke the morale of the Russians, who would never again face British cavalry. However, British political agitation calling for domestic political reform used the Charge as a metaphor for aristocratic mismanagement and created the myth of disaster.

The other great myth of the war had the same purpose. Florence Nightingale (1820–1910) was lionized as the "Lady with the Lamp" who nursed sick and wounded troops. In reality Nightingale was a hospital manager, the nursing was done by male orderlies. The "nurses" cooked and cleaned. Nightingale's status reflected the fact that she was the only noteworthy middle-class figure in the conflict. The new universal heroism was reflected in the Victoria Cross, a conspicuous gallantry award for all ranks.

On 5 November another Russian attack, on the Inkermann Heights, came close to driving the Allies into the sea. The massive Russian attack columns became separated in the fog, allowing small British units to hold them off until reinforcements and two siege guns arrived to turn the tide of battle. Nine days later a hurricane demolished the Allied camp, and they had to prepare for a winter in trenches before Sevastopol. The Allies survived, despite appalling hardships, because they had uncontested command of the sea, steam shipping to bring in supplies and reinforcements, and ultimately a railway to mechanize the siege.

Over the winter Britain and France reconsidered their strategy. The Grand Raid on Sevastopol had failed, and they had been drawn into a prolonged battle of attrition around the city between three armies, all well dug in and well supplied with heavy (largely naval) artillery. The French, with far larger military resources, gradually took control. Napoleon III favored assembling a large field army to pursue and destroy the Russian army, but his local commanders preferred the steady attrition of local trench attacks. The British still employed a maritime strategy, sending a joint expedition to seize the Straits of Kertch and take control of the Sea of Azov in May 1855. When Marshal Canrobert (1809–1895) had to withdraw his troops from the operation under orders from Paris he resigned the high command, exchanging positions with one of his divisional generals. Marshal Pélissier (1794–1864) carried out the Azov operation, enabling British steam gunboats to cut the Russian logistics link with the River Don, crippling the field army, and limiting supplies to Sevastopol. Raglan and Pélissier stepped up their attacks, and despite the occasional failure, and Raglan's

death on 28 June, the vital Malakhov bastion fell to French troops on 9 September. The Russians abandoned Sevastopol, burning the last remnants of their fleet.

This success had come at a heavy cost, but it produced little strategic or political impact. Tsar Nicholas I had died in early 1855, but Alexander II (r. 1855–1881) was not going to make peace because a small dockyard town had been taken. Russia was bankrupt and with its economy in ruins it needed peace. France was weary of war now that it had harvested a full measure of *la gloire* by taking Sevastopol, so Napoleon III sought peace. Neutral Austria had been bankrupted by the costs of keeping its army mobilized.

Franco-Austrian diplomatic maneuvers limited Russian humiliation and tried to keep the British out of the peace process. The British, aware of the drift of events in Paris, quickly shifted their Baltic strategy to a full-scale assault on Cronstadt, the fortress protecting St. Petersburg. By late 1855 the British were building a massive armada for this operation, and ensured the Russians knew they were ready to use it.

Over the winter of 1855–1856 the diplomats patched up a peace, but Britain kept up its naval mobilization to ensure that both its enemy and its ally recognized British claims. The Peace of Paris was signed in March, but on 23 April 1856 the British celebrated their victory by showing in a demonstration bombardment of Southsea Castle what their Baltic fleet would have done to Cronstadt. This form of coercive diplomacy served Britain well—it did not fight another major war until 1914.

The Crimean War was at once the last preindustrial war and the first modern conflict. It occurred in a period of rapid transformation in the conduct of war at all levels. British strategic thinking, developed from the Napoleonic era, combined economic warfare, global power projection, intelligence-gathering, and new technology into a winning combination. However, while the war moved by steam, military logistics were still working to the rhythm of the oxcart. The small peacetime army simply did not have the capability to mobilize fresh troops. Under pressure from the powerful news media, administrative

British and French soldiers hold a party in camp during the Crimean War. Photograph by Roger Fenton, 1855. ©Corbis

reform was inevitable. That said, the British were the first to employ mass-produced rifles; build tactical railways; and employ rifled cannon, intercontinental cable communications, and photography. The French pioneered armored warships, the Russians submarine mines. Although the political aims were limited, the Crimea was a global conflict between the two leading powers of the era, Russia and Britain, with France anxious to improve its status. The war preserved Ottoman Turkey for another half-century, while Russia was forced to reconstruct the very foundations of the state before modernizing its military institutions wholesale. However, the main beneficiary was Prussia. Freed from Russian dominance Berlin had created a unified Germany by 1870, over the wreckage of Louis-Napoleon's Imperial France. It was not the

least of the ironies of this war was that while it preserved the balance of power in eastern Europe it created ideal conditions for an altogether more dangerous altercation in the west.

See also **Black Sea; Nightingale, Florence; Nurses; Ottoman Empire; Red Cross; Russia; Russo-Turkish War.**

BIBLIOGRAPHY

Goldfrank, David M. *The Origins of the Crimean War.* London, 1994.

Lambert, Andrew D. *The Crimean War: British Grand Strategy, 1853–56.* Manchester, U.K., and New York, 1990.

ANDREW LAMBERT

CRISPI, FRANCESCO (1818–1901), Italian politician, a leader in the movement for Italian unification.

Francesco Crispi was born on 4 October 1818 into a Greek Orthodox family of minor landowners, businessmen, and priests in Ribera, a small agricultural community in the southwest of Sicily. Sicily, which had been under British occupation for much of the Napoleonic period, then formed part of the Kingdom of the Two Sicilies and was ruled from Naples. As an eldest son, Crispi carried the burden of family ambitions, and after receiving an excellent education at the Greek Orthodox seminary in Palermo, he enrolled as a law student at Palermo University. There he became a prominent figure in the local intellectual community, founding his own newspaper, *L'Oreteo,* and championing the cause of literary Romanticism and moderate reforms. He moved to Naples in the mid-1840s to practice as a lawyer and became active in radical political circles, conspiring in the second half of 1847 to launch a revolution in Sicily.

In the course of the Sicilian revolution of 1848–1849, Crispi served as a deputy in the Palermo parliament, and was employed as an official in the ministry of war, where he honed his considerable administrative talents. Like most of his fellow revolutionaries, Crispi aspired to an autonomous Sicily within a federal Italy, but the failure of the moderate leadership to mobilize popular resistance and defend the revolution against the advancing Neapolitan forces pushed him toward more extreme democratic views. In exile after 1849, in Turin, Malta, London, and Paris, Crispi moved in democratic circles, and under the influence of Nicola Fabrizi (1804–1885) in Malta and above all Giuseppe Mazzini (1805–1872) in London, he came to believe strongly in the need for a unitary Italian state.

When, through the instigation of the Piedmontese prime minister, Count Cavour (Camillo Benso, 1810–1861), war broke out in northern Italy in the summer of 1859, Crispi conspired to trigger a democratic insurrection in Sicily. When this failed, he joined other leading democrats in persuading the charismatic soldier Giuseppe Garibaldi (1807–1882) to head a small army of volunteers to Sicily in the spring of 1860. During the famous Expedition of the Thousand, which ended in the unification of most of Italy, Crispi served as Garibaldi's secretary of state and played an important part in ensuring the political success of the revolution in Sicily and in enabling Garibaldi to cross to the mainland and march on Naples. However, he was bitter at the way in which Cavour then hijacked the revolution and prevented Garibaldi from reaching Rome, and in 1861 he entered the new Italian parliament as a spokesman for the far left, deeply critical of the government.

DEPUTY OF THE LEFT

In the course of the 1860s, Crispi became one of the leading figures of the left in parliament. He also established himself as among the most successful and best-paid lawyers in the country, and his wealth enabled him to sit almost uninterruptedly in parliament until his death in 1901, and also, from 1867, to fund a major national newspaper, *La Riforma.* Politically in the early 1860s Crispi was still quite close to Mazzini, but he broke with him acrimoniously in the years 1864 and 1865 over the issue of the monarchy, with Crispi insisting that in a country of widespread illiteracy, strong municipal and regional loyalties, and limited national sentiment, the crown was vital to the maintenance of unity. As he said in parliament, in what became the most famous political phrase of his career, "the monarchy unites us, a republic would divide us." Thereafter Crispi was seen as a constitutionalist, and he played an important part in helping to steer sections of the disaffected revolutionary left into constitutional channels.

Political power still eluded him, however, and after the capture in 1870 of Rome—the main objective of the left in the 1860s—he became unsure of his future. His domestic life also began to unravel. In exile during the 1850s, he had married a Savoyard washerwoman, Rosalie Montmasson, but the relationship broke down in the early 1870s, and in 1875 the couple separated with Crispi claiming, speciously, that the original wedding had been technically invalid. When the left came to power in 1876, Crispi was appointed speaker of the Chamber of Deputies, and then at the end of 1877, minister of the interior in the second government of the Piedmontese politician Agostino Depretis

Caricature of Francesco Crispi. This lithograph by Henri Meyer, which appeared on the cover of the French publication *Le Petit Journal* on 9 February 1896, lampoons the Italian defeat at Adwa, Ethiopia. PRIVATE COLLECTION/BRIDGEMAN ART LIBRARY/GIRAUDON

socialist, and militant Catholic ideas among the working classes. As a result, he felt, personal freedom might at times have to be sacrificed to safeguard the nation from political subversion.

Part of the reason for Crispi's changing views was the international situation and his feeling, especially after the French occupation of Tunisia in 1881, that Italy was being "suffocated" in the Mediterranean. He claimed that France had aggressive designs on Italy, and he called in the 1880s for increased spending on the army and navy to prepare Italy for what he maintained was an inevitable European war. In parliament Crispi lacked a significant following, and his attempts to remedy this in 1883 by forming an opposition party of the left, the Pentarchy, met with limited success. In the country as a whole, however, Crispi's calls for a more assertive foreign policy and his denunciations of the "anemia" of parliament and the "inertia" of the government led by the sick and elderly Depretis struck a chord. When, early in 1887, a column of Italian troops was massacred at Dogali in east Africa, there was a public clamoring for Crispi to come to power. Crispi was appointed minister of the interior in Depretis's last government, and became prime minister when Depretis died in July 1887.

PRIME MINISTER

Crispi was the first southerner to be appointed prime minister of Italy, and his administration from 1887 to 1891 was one of the most remarkable in the country's history. Domestically it was marked by a vigorous program of reforms. A new public health law and a law giving the government greater control over charitable bodies (*opere pie*) laid the foundations for a modern welfare state, while an extension of the local government suffrage marked a significant advance in democracy. A new and more liberal penal code was introduced, and there were other important reforms in public security, policing, and prisons. A major law was also passed to deal with abuses committed by public officials. Crispi was determined with his reforms to show that the Italian state could tackle the country's mounting social and political problems effectively, and the spirit of the new laws was for the most part liberal. However, Crispi was well aware of the risks faced by taking such measures as the extension of

(1813–1887). Crispi's tenure of office was brief, however: early in 1878 he married a Sicilian woman some years his junior, Lina Barbagallo, and shortly afterwards found himself accused by political enemies of bigamy. Though acquitted by the courts, Crispi was forced to resign, and for a time it seemed as if his career was over.

Crispi's political ideas underwent an important evolution from the late 1870s. Though as a man of the left he remained committed to democratic reforms, such as a broadening of the suffrage, more equitable taxation, greater accountability of public officials, and improvements in welfare, education, and health provision, he became increasingly concerned by the gap between the mass of the population and the state and by the lack of what he called the "political education" of Italians. In the past he had favored a weak state and administrative devolution in order to maximize liberty, but he now came to believe that a strong state was required so as to complete the country's "moral unification" and counter the spread of anarchist, local democracy, and the government's agents in the provinces, the prefects, received extensive new powers to control those administrations that returned "subversive" councilors.

Crispi was the foreign minister as well as prime minister and minister of the interior from 1897 to 1891, and it was foreign policy that consumed most of his time and energy. Crispi hoped to turn the Triple Alliance (of which Italy had been a member with Germany and Austria since 1882) from a defensive into an offensive alliance. He seemed genuinely to believe that France was incorrigible in its hatred of Italy and Germany, and with General Boulanger inciting national sentiment in France, there seemed a real likelihood of a conflict. In Crispi's eyes a successful war against France would give the Italian state the prestige that it lacked, guarantee Italy's position as the dominant Mediterranean power, and promote the formation of a "national consciousness." On becoming prime minister, he signed a secret military convention with Germany, greatly increased spending on the army and navy, and attempted to lure France into a rash act of aggression during 1888 and 1889. The idea of a preventive war against France and Russia enjoyed considerable support in German military circles at this time, but it was Otto von Bismarck's (1815–1898) policy of peace that prevailed.

Crispi fell from power in January 1891, but he returned as prime minister in December 1893 at a moment of acute crisis. A major banking scandal was rocking the political establishment (and threatened the monarchy); the state faced bankruptcy; and Sicily seemed in danger of being engulfed by socialist-led rioting. Crispi declared martial law in Sicily and suppressed the socialist movement there ruthlessly. He also took firm and effective measures to sort out the public finances. But he faced growing opposition in parliament; at the end of 1894, he was in danger of himself being sucked into the banking scandal. His response was high-handed: he prorogued parliament and looked to a war in Africa to divert attention from the country's (and his own) plight. Italy had been developing a colony on the shores of the Red Sea since the mid-1880s, but in the course of 1895 it got drawn into a full-scale war with the Ethiopian emperor, Menelik II (r. 1883–1913). Crispi seriously underestimated the strength of the enemy and injudiciously pressed the Italian commander onto the offensive. The result was a disastrous defeat at the Battle of Adwa on 1 March 1896. Crispi was forced to resign, and he died on 11 August 1901, deeply disillusioned and pessimistic about Italy's future.

Crispi was the most high-profile and best-known Italian politician in Europe between Cavour and Benito Mussolini (1883–1945). He was greatly admired in Germany, not least by his friend Bismarck; he was feared in France, and understandably so; and in Britain he was seen as a troublesome but necessary ally. Although his important contribution to the movement for national unification before 1860 has not been questioned, Crispi remains a controversial figure in Italy. The Fascist regime celebrated him as an exponent of nationalism and authoritarianism, and he was often referred to as the "precursor" of Mussolini. Largely as a reaction to this, he was widely dismissed after World War II as a maverick and a liberal renegade. In the 1970s, however, he attracted attention from historians for the light he appeared to shed on the roots of fascism. At the turn of the twenty-first century, his progressive reform program, his attempts to modernize the Italian state, and his concern with the civic education and nationalization of Italians have made him the subject of considerable renewed debate.

See also **Bismarck, Otto von; Cavour, Count (Camillo Benso); Italy; Mazzini, Giuseppe; Sicily; Tunisia.**

BIBLIOGRAPHY

Adorni, Daniela. *Francesco Crispi: Un progetto di governo.* Florence, 1999.

Chabod, Federico. *Italian Foreign Policy: The Statecraft of the Founders.* Princeton, N.J., 1996.

Duggan, Christopher. *Francesco Crispi: From Nation to Nationalism.* Oxford, U.K., 2002.

CHRISTOPHER DUGGAN

CROCE, BENEDETTO (1866–1952),
Italian historian, philosopher, critic.

Benedetto Croce was the central figure in a distinctive intellectual tradition, based on a radical recasting of historicism and philosophical idealism, that emerged around 1900 and came to dominate Italian intellectual life for almost half a century thereafter. First with Giovanni Gentile (1875–1944) as his junior partner, Croce sought to show how Western culture might overcome the hesitations and confusions that seemed to accompany the erosion of its longstanding religious and philosophical foundations. By pushing through to conceive the world without transcendence, or in terms of radical immanence, he thought it possible to give new meaning to morality and truth, freedom and creativity, and thereby to enable us to proceed responsibly, heading off irrationalism, skepticism, and relativism.

In seeking to conceive the human situation without transcendence, Croce learned especially from Giambattista Vico (1668–1744), whose thinking seemed to suggest that the human world is forever built up in some particular way as human beings respond creatively, in language, to a succession of novel situations. Engagement with Vico, but also with German Romanticism, informed Croce's *Estetica come scienza dell' espressione e linguistica generale* (1902; *Aesthetic as Science of Expression and General Linguistic*), which brought him to international attention. While treating imagination, expression, and cognition, this work offered a conception of creativity in language with grandiose implications for the place of the human being in an ever-new world.

By 1903 Croce had developed the confidence to launch his own bimonthly review *La Critica*, which would appear regularly until the mid-1940s. Independently wealthy, unencumbered by teaching duties, he continued to develop his cultural program from his base in Naples for almost a half century thereafter. Although he made numerous enemies, by 1914 he had become Italy's most influential intellectual, and he was becoming one of the best known in the world.

His early encounters led Croce to a life-long engagement with Georg Wilhelm Friedrich Hegel (1770–1831), whom he first treated systematically in an essay published in 1907. As Croce saw it, Hegel had been on the right track in conceiving the world as historical, and even as a totality. But he had confused distincts with opposites and thus had assumed that art, for example, might be overcome dialectically in philosophy, or absolute knowledge. In presupposing an a priori frame and telos, with spirit becoming aware of its own free-dom, Hegel was positing too much as given a priori, to be discovered, or to come to human consciousness, through historical experience. For Croce, the future is more radically open to creative human response.

Encounter with Hegel helped Croce build from the *Aesthetic* to a quasi-systematic philosophy, especially in the twin works of 1908–1909, *Logica come scienza del concetto puro* (*Logic as the Science of the Pure Concept*), on the cognitive or theoretical side of human activity, and *Filosofia della pratica: Economia ed etica* (*Philosophy of the Practical: Economic and Ethic*) on the practical side, which encompassed both the ethical and the useful. Partly to establish the irreducibility of truth and morality in the face of utilitarianism, pragmatism, and Marxism, Croce insisted on distinctions among the basic modes of human activity. But though the autonomy of each was essential, so was the circular relationship among them. Most basically, knowing serves action, which then creates a new moment, even a new world to be known.

Croce was seeking not to confine reality in a closed system but just the opposite—to establish openness, the endless provisionality of the world. Because there can be no dialectical overcoming, there is no telos, no goal or end. Art is not resolved into philosophy but continues to well up as human beings respond to an ever-new world, thereby helping to make it new yet again. Although the world continues without a goal, a particular history results because of free, creative human response along the way.

To show what truth and knowing mean in a world of radical immanence, Croce sought to address the uses and limits of both philosophy and science, for it was partly overblown claims on behalf of each that bred skepticism, irrationalism, and mysticism. His most immediate target was positivism, bound up with what seemed the overselling of science by the beginning of the twentieth century. In a flattened-out, purely historical world, genuine knowledge stems from "individual judgment," grasping the place of this or that individual instance not in terms of some stable scientific class, category, or law, but in the becoming of our particular world through history. Useful, even essential though they are, the law-like generalizations of science are merely convenient tools, not genuine knowledge. Only the illusion of some transcendent sphere leads us to take the abstractions from particular instances as "higher," truer.

In treating philosophy, too, Croce insisted on the primacy of history, and thus the historicity of any genuine philosophy, which always emerges from concrete practical problems. Because the world, through history, is constantly changing, we must periodically redo our philosophical categories in order to come to terms with the novel circumstances that history generates. Croce claimed that he himself had offered not some definitive, systematic philosophy but simply the ad hoc clarifications necessary to enable us to get on with the ongoing work of the world, writing poetry or history, responding morally, acting politically.

Having taken the measure of what seemed the best ideas from abroad, Croce came to believe, by the eve of World War I, that the new Italian current had moved to the forefront of modern thought. But by this point he and Gentile had began to diverge, as certain philosophical differences became public in 1913, adumbrating the dramatic split that ensued after World War I. Gentile was on his way to the explicitly totalitarian vision he offered as a fascist; Croce, in contrast, was articulating the sense of limits, the need for humility and pluralism, that would make him a bitter enemy of totalitarian pretenses—and arguably the world's most notable antifascist. Although the seeds of Croce's later thinking were surely evident by 1914, the meaning and import of his intellectual program would come into focus only gradually thereafter.

See also **Hegel, Georg Wilhelm Friedrich; History; Marx, Karl; Positivism.**

BIBLIOGRAPHY

D'Amico, Jack, Dain A. Trafton, and Massimo Verdicchio, eds. *The Legacy of Benedetto Croce: Contemporary Critical Views.* Toronto, 1999.

Moss, M. E. *Benedetto Croce Reconsidered: Truth and Error in Theories of Art, Literature, and History.* Hanover, N.H., 1987.

Roberts, David D. *Benedetto Croce and the Uses of Historicism.* Berkeley, Calif., 1987.

DAVID D. ROBERTS

CRUIKSHANK, GEORGE (1792–1878), English artist.

George Cruikshank is now remembered, if at all, for his work as illustrator of two early works by Charles Dickens, *Sketches by Boz* (1836) and *Oliver Twist* (1837–1838). Cruikshank, by the time of those collaborations well known as a caricaturist and illustrator of classic and contemporary literature, saw his own role in the production of such texts devalued as Dickens's reputation soared, and he felt compelled, especially in the last years of his life and after Dickens's death in 1870, to spend much of his time campaigning for the respect and honor he believed were his due. By the 1870s, however, the notion that the creators of the verbal and visual elements of a text should be considered collaborators rather than superior and subordinate was only rarely accepted.

Cruikshank's father, Isaac (1764–1811), and his older brother, Isaac Robert (1789–1856; often known simply as Robert), were also artists. The father, an increasingly popular caricaturist who never quite gave up on a career in more respected art genres such as watercolor and oil, died from the consequences of a drinking match and left George the principal breadwinner in the family before he turned twenty. The brother, for a time considered to be George's peer, became from about 1840 a virtual unknown.

Cruikshank's caricatures of King George IV's dissolute life, both during the period when he was prince regent (1810–1820) and after his assumption of the throne at George III's death on 29 January 1820, were disturbing enough to warrant attempts by emissaries from the royals to buy up those works that were most disturbing and also in June 1820 to bribe the artist with a payment of £100 to desist from any further productions that depicted the new king in "any immoral situation." The caricatures, however, continued to appear, especially in reference to the king's fight to prevent his estranged wife, Princess Caroline of Brunswick, from becoming queen after her arrival in England in June 1820. The new king initiated divorce proceedings, and a flood of caricatures and pamphlets appeared, weighing in on the matter. Cruikshank, working with the publisher William Hone, produced

Mayhew's Great Exhibition of 1851: The First Shilling Day, Going In. Etching by George Cruikshank, 1851. Cruikshank depicts the crowds of poorer Londoners who took advantage of reduced entry fees to attend the exhibition at the Crystal Palace. ©YALE CENTER FOR BRITISH ART, PAUL MELLON FUND, USA/BRIDGEMAN ART LIBRARY

some of the most devastating to the king's side of the dispute, notably *The Queen's Matrimonial Ladder,* but he also produced at least one powerful image damaging to the queen's cause. Cruikshank's images from 1810 to 1830 mocking Napoleon, the Duke of Wellington, and a vast array of hypocritical and pretentious behaviors and fashions often deserved the term the artist's brother Robert used to describe the woodcuts done with Hone on this occasion, "Gunpowder in Boxwood."

From the mid-1820s Cruikshank's energies went mainly to book illustration. Many significant figures in the literary and critical world such as the novelist William Makepeace Thackeray would later remember vividly how their first experiences of many influential texts were emphatically shaped by their association with Cruikshank's illustrations. The art critic John Ruskin remembered Cruikshank's copperplate etchings for an English translation of the brothers Grimm's fairy tale collection as

"the finest things, next to Rembrandt's" since the invention of the art.

Although Cruikshank never left the British Isles for more than a day trip, Continental audiences were familiar with his work, and it was not unusual for critics throughout Europe to refer to an artist from their own land as the Cruikshank of their own country or region. Henry Monnier, Honoré Daumier, Gustave Doré, and Paul Gavarni were some of the French artists mentioned in this way, or who themselves acknowledged Cruikshank's influence. Cruikshank's own vanity prevented him from acknowledging the undeniable ways in which his style derived in some cases from these same artists.

From 1847 on, Cruikshank, publicly renouncing the signature drunken rowdiness of his first fifty years, worked hard in the temperance cause. Two suites of powerful plates, *The Bottle* (1847) and *The Drunkard's Children* (1848), depicted the gradual destruction of a happy family through the insidious progress of alcoholism from a convivial hearthside drink to a deadly domestic quarrel for the parents and short lives as dissolute criminals for the children. The artist also produced in the 1860s a series of adapted fairy tales, in which all bad characters and misfortunes arose from alcohol abuse. Dickens, though quite capable of appropriating fairy tales to his own purposes, attacked Cruikshank for perpetrating "Frauds on the Fairies." For the last decades of the artist's life, he was increasingly preoccupied with the completion and display of an enormous temperance propaganda oil painting, *The Worship of Bacchus* (1862) and the marketing of prints from the painting. None of these later projects was financially rewarding, and Cruikshank died virtually insolvent, leaving the artistic work that survived him to the mistress by whom he had fathered ten children, and whom he had maintained in a separate secret household around the corner from his official address for many years. At the time of his death, comparatively few remembered how much impact the images of Cruikshank's art once had on English society and its behavior.

See also **Daumier, Honoré; Dickens, Charles; Doré, Gustave.**

BIBLIOGRAPHY

Buchanan-Brown, John. *The Book Illustrations of George Cruikshank.* London and Rutland, Vt., 1980. A gathering of 250 illustrations with an introductory essay and extensive notes.

Patten, Robert L. *George Cruikshank's Life, Times, and Art.* 2 vols. New Brunswick, N.J., 1992 and 1996. The definitive biography: the only work to treat all of Cruikshank's artistic endeavors thoroughly, and the only work based on an exhaustive collection and review of the artist's correspondence and papers.

Wardroper, John. *The Caricatures of George Cruikshank.* London, 1977. An insightful account of Cruikshank's genius in this genre, with reproductions of the most notable caricatures.

LOGAN DELANO BROWNING

CRYSTAL PALACE. Generally regarded as the first modern building, the Crystal Palace was designed by Sir Joseph Paxton (1801–1865) for the Great Exhibition of the Works of Industry of All Nations, the first world's fair, held in Hyde Park, London, during the summer of 1851. Featuring modular, prefabricated, iron and glass construction, the Crystal Palace stretched 1,848 feet long, 72 feet wide, and 64 feet high, with a barrel-vaulted transept rising to 104 feet. It was built from start to finish in just seven months, at a cost of £170,000.

The Great Exhibition was organized by Prince Albert (1819–1861) and the Royal Society of Arts to improve the quality of industrial design in Britain and to demonstrate the advantages of British manufactures by putting them in competition with goods from around the world. It was opened by Queen Victoria (r. 1837–1901) on May Day 1851, and closed six months later on 11 October. In between, there were more than six million paid entrances, or approximately one-fifth of the British population, allowing for multiple visits and visitors from abroad. Men and women from all social classes mingled inside the Crystal Palace, a remarkable occurrence in a society still reeling from Chartism and the revolutions of 1848.

The Crystal Palace, which received its nickname from Douglas William Jerrold (1803–1857) of *Punch* magazine, was unique at the time for its size and transparent qualities. So large as to be virtually boundless—the Crystal Palace covered some nineteen acres—the interior was defined only by the three-dimensional grid of coordinates that the regularly spaced iron stanchions and girders provided. Inside, it was impossible for visitors to discern the size of the building, and the Crystal Palace was in all likelihood the first building in which a person, standing at one end, could not see the opposite end. Moreover, the glass walls and roof provided a maximum of daylight and a minimum of enclosure, prompting many visitors to describe the building as a "fairy palace."

Inside, the Crystal Palace divided the world into two groups. To the west of the transept were the products of Britain and its colonies; to the east were those of the rest of the world. In the British half, the exhibits were arranged in four main groups: raw materials, machinery, manufactures, and the fine arts. The ordering of the exhibits, therefore, replicated the industrial manufacturing

The south entrance to the Crystal Palace. Engraving c. 1851 by P. Brannon and T. Picken. GUILDHALL LIBRARY, CORPORATION OF LONDON. UK/BRIDGEMAN ART LIBRARY

process, as raw materials—lumps of coal, bales of cotton—were taken by heavy machinery—steam engines, hydraulic presses, power looms—to manufacture works of industry such as mirrors, tables, cloth, anything one might find in the home. The fine arts, such as statues and stained glass, were included to demonstrate beauty, so that manufacturers might be inspired to apply good design principles to their manufactured goods. The organizers were concerned that the reigning aesthetic style in furniture and the fine arts was leading to large, dark, heavy, ornate objects, now commonly referred to as "Victorian."

New and important inventions that were exhibited in 1851 included the electric telegraph, the Singer sewing machine, Goodyear rubber, the Colt revolver, and Schweppes soft drinks such as ginger ale. The Great Exhibition, however, also encouraged the useless and the preposterous along with the inventive and the ingenious. There was a kite-drawn carriage for traveling without horses on windy days; a corset that opened upon impact during a train accident to allow the female victim to

breathe instantly; and a silent alarm clock, which instead of ringing at the designated time, turned the bed on its side and dumped its occupant into a tub of cold water.

After the exhibition closed, turning a profit of £186,000 (which would eventually be used to purchase land in South Kensington where the Victoria and Albert Museum would be built), the Crystal Palace was relocated to the London suburb of Sydenham in 1854 and rebuilt on an even larger scale. The new Crystal Palace added a vaulted roof along the length of the nave, as well as vaulted side wings (one of which burned down in 1866). It also featured extensively landscaped grounds with hundreds of fountains, along with the first life-sized models of dinosaurs.

Inside the Sydenham Crystal Palace, the organizers constructed a number of courts, each to illustrate the art and architecture of various periods in history. The most spectacular of these was the Egyptian court, with full-size copies of the Sphinx and the famous Abu Simbel statues of Ramses II. There was also a natural history department illustrating the development of the human race, and in the nave Paxton arranged a display of vegetation that included the Victoria Regia, the giant water lily from South America that inspired his original glasshouse design.

The Sydenham Crystal Palace took on a very different meaning than its Hyde Park predecessor. Whereas the rhetoric surrounding the original Crystal Palace had focused on international peace and understanding, the Sydenham Crystal Palace had a more jingoistic undercurrent, embodied in an 1872 speech there by Benjamin Disraeli (1804–1881) in which he asserted the empire's centrality to Britain and to the Conservative Party. The building's apogee as an imperial site came with the Colonial and Indian Exhibition (1886) and the Festival of Empire (1911). The latter, designed to demonstrate to the British public the significance of the empire and to encourage consumption of imperial goods, featured a train journey through the empire that took visitors past replicas and scale models of a Jamaican sugar plantation, a Malay village, and an Indian palace.

Additionally, whereas the Great Exhibition had been organized primarily to educate British men and women about industrialization and tasteful consumption, the Sydenham building was designed to entertain and to amuse, with fireworks displays, balloon flights, and dog shows. Especially popular were the musical festivals, as the Crystal Palace became the most important venue for public music-making in the United Kingdom. Weekly concerts there introduced thousands of British men and women to classical music and stimulated the composition of English music, and the large-scale performances of Handel's oratorios transformed the performance of choral music for a century.

Finally, whereas the Hyde Park building had symbolized the mixing of the classes and the masses, the Sydenham site was clearly for the latter, a point made by George Gissing's novel *The Nether World* (1888), in which workers celebrate their August bank holiday at the Crystal Palace, enjoying its circus-like games and refreshments but suffering from the heat and dust inside the glass building.

Despite the popularity of the events held there, the Crystal Palace began experiencing financial

Interior of Crystal Palace at Sydenham Opened by Her Majesty, June 10, 1854. Engraving by Thomas Hosmer Shepherd. ©STAPLETON COLLECTION/CORBIS

problems as early as the 1870s, and saving it took the intervention of Lord Plymouth, who in 1911 put up £230,000 to preserve the site, which was subsequently used as a naval supply depot during World War I. There was one final attempt to refurbish the building after the war, when the Imperial War Museum opened there in 1920, but the building had become run-down beyond repair. Late in the evening on 30 November 1936, a fire of unknown origin broke out in the building, and by morning there was little left but molten glass, twisted iron, and a pile of ash and rubble.

Both the Great Exhibition and the Crystal Palace have proved to be enormously influential. A succession of world's fairs and expositions followed in the wake of the 1851 London event, including Vienna (1873), Philadelphia (1876), Paris (1889, 1900, 1937), Chicago (1893), St. Louis (1904), and New York (1939, 1964). The Crystal Palace building prompted the design of derivative structures in New York (1853),

Dublin (1853), Munich (1853–1854), Manchester (1857), and Madrid (1873), and the Paddington railway station in London designed by Isambard Kingdom Brunel (1806–1859) contains a "Paxton roof." The Crystal Palace can also be seen as the forerunner of the Centre Pompidou in Paris, and insofar as there was a proposal after the exhibition closed to convert the Crystal Palace into a 1,000-foot-high tower with elevators, all modern skyscrapers owe their origin to the Crystal Palace.

Perhaps most importantly, the Crystal Palace has become one of the foremost symbols of modernity itself. In *Notes from Underground* (1864), Fyodor Dostoevsky (1821–1881) complained that the mathematical exactitude and rationality of the Crystal Palace left nothing to doubt, that it was the last word and the ultimate truth. It has also been seen as giving form to Karl Marx's (1818–1883) dictum that "all that is solid melts into air." Admired by Charles-Edouard Jeanneret (1887–1965, known as Le Corbusier) and Émile Zola (1840–1902), vilified by Charles Dickens (1812–1870) and John Ruskin (1819–1900), the Crystal Palace, both in Hyde Park and in Sydenham, remains a projection screen for public opinion about industrial capitalism.

See also **Civilization, Concept of; Imperialism; Leisure; Victoria, Queen; World's Fairs.**

BIBLIOGRAPHY

Auerbach, Jeffrey A. *The Great Exhibition of 1851: A Nation on Display.* New Haven, Conn., 1999.

Greenhalgh, Paul. *Ephemeral Vistas: The Expositions Universelles, Great Exhibitions and World's Fairs, 1851–1939.* Manchester, U.K., 1988.

Hoffenberg, Peter H. *An Empire on Display: English, Indian, and Australian Exhibitions from the Crystal Palace to the Great War.* Berkeley, Calif., 2001.

McKean, John. *Crystal Palace: Joseph Paxton and Charles Fox.* London, 1994.

Musgrave, Michael. *The Musical Life of the Crystal Palace.* Cambridge, U.K., 1995.

Piggott, Jan R. *Palace of the People: The Crystal Palace at Sydenham 1854–1936.* London, 2004.

Walton, Whitney. *France at the Crystal Palace: Bourgeois Taste and Artisan Manufacture in the Nineteenth Century.* Berkeley, Calif., 1992.

JEFFREY A. AUERBACH

CUBISM. Cubism is the name given to one of the seminal movements in modern art in the early twentieth century. There were two groups of cubists who interacted in various ways. The Spaniard Pablo Picasso (1881–1973), French artist Georges Braque (1882–1963), and their circle—including the poets/art critics Guillaume Apollinaire (1880–1918) and André Salmon (1881–1969)—congregated in the Bateau Lavoir (Washboat), a building on the slopes of Montmartre where Salmon, Picasso, and the Spanish artist Juan Gris (1887–1927) had their studios. The second cubist group frequently met in Puteaux, a town on the outskirts of Paris where other key figures lived, including French artist Albert Gleizes (1881–1953) and the Duchamp-Villon brothers: Gaston Duchamp (pseudonym Jacques Villon, 1875–1963), Raymond Duchamp-Villon (1876–1918), and Marcel Duchamp (1887–1968). The French painter Jean Metzinger (1883–1956) moved between these two circles. Metzinger lived in Montmartre from 1906 to 1912, and from 1907 on he frequented Picasso's studio and befriended Braque, poet Max Jacob (1876–1944), Salmon, and Apollinaire. In December 1908, Metzinger exhibited paintings alongside those of Braque and Picasso at Wilhelm Uhde's small Notre-Dame-des-Champs gallery.

These two groups differed in their exhibition practices and their choice of subject matter. The Puteaux group regularly exhibited paintings of epic and sometimes allegorical subjects in Paris's large public venues, such as the spring Salon des Indépendants and the fall Salon d'Automne. They became the public face of the cubist movement and are frequently referred to as the salon cubists. The critic Roger Allard identified Henri Le Fauconnier (1881–1946), Gleizes, and Metzinger as the progenitors of a new movement in his review of the 1910 Salon d'Automne. At the 1911 Salon des Indépendants, these artists proclaimed their allegiance to cubism by exhibiting together, with the addition of French painters Robert Delaunay (1885–1941), Marie Laurencin (1885–1956), and Fernand Léger (1881–1955). Typical works by these cubists include Delaunay's *Eiffel Tower* (1911), Gleizes's *Chartres Cathedral* (1912), Léger's *The Wedding* (1911), and Le Fauconnier's *Abundance* (1910–1911). Paintings by the salon cubists were frequently monumental in scale and

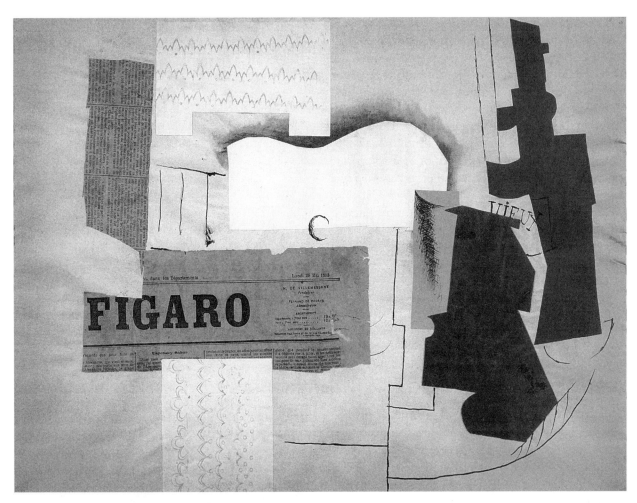

Bottle of Vieux Marc, Glass, Guitar, and Newspaper. Collage by Pablo Picasso, 1913. TATE GALLERY, LONDON/ART RESOURCE, NY. ©2006 ESTATE OF PABLO PICASSO/ARTISTS RIGHTS SOCIETY (ARS), NEW YORK

depicted public events or well-known edifices identified with modern Paris or the history of France. These subjects sometimes had a political inflection: for instance, Gleizes's paintings of Gothic cathedrals in 1912–1913 registered his allegiance to the French Celtic League, while Le Fauconnier's *Abundance* is an allegorical symbol not only of France but of French Catholicism.

In the heyday of cubism, Picasso, Braque, and Gris used a private dealer, Daniel-Henry Kahnweiler (1884–1979). From 1909 to 1913, Braque and Picasso developed their version of cubism in close collaboration, with small-scale still lifes and intimate half-length portraits as their preferred motifs. By 1912 Kahnweiler had signed exclusive contracts with these artists, restricting them from exhibiting anywhere in Paris other than their studios or his gallery. Kahnweiler also campaigned to exhibit his

artists' work outside of Paris, where it was shown together with many of the salon cubists, for instance in exhibitions before 1914 in Lyons, Amsterdam, Munich, Budapest, Moscow, London, New York, Chicago, and Boston. Before 1912, the work of Picasso and Braque was also visible at Uhde's gallery, where Picasso had a show in May 1910; another Picasso exhibition appeared at Ambroise Vollard's gallery in December 1910–February 1911. Additionally, Braque until spring 1909 and Gris until 1912 exhibited their emerging cubism at the public salons.

A "second wave" of foreign artists joined the movement after 1911, including painters Louis Marcoussis (1883–1941), Alice Halicka (1895–1975), Francis Picabia (1879–1953), and sculptors Alexander Archipenko (1887–1964), Henri Laurens (1885–1954), and Jacques Lipchitz

(1891–1973). In 1912 Braque and Picasso took cubism in a new direction with their invention of collage. They now used glue to paste the detritus of everyday life, including newsprint, advertisements, cheap wallpaper, and other cut items into their cubist still lifes. Among their peers the Italian futurists took up the practice in late 1912, followed by Gris in early 1914. Scholars have also debated the political significance of Picasso's usage of collage, differing over whether the newspaper clippings in works like his *Glass and Bottle of Suze* (November 1912) indicate his anti-militarist opposition to the threat of war and the anarchist import of Picasso's avant-gardism, or his assimilation of such reportage into an artistic medium devoid of ideological punch.

What united the cubists was a revolt against the conventions of academic illusionism. Braque's *Violin and Palette* (1909) is exemplary of such cubist deconstruction. This painting shows a table with sheet music on a small music stand and a violin resting on a green cloth; behind this, a green curtain hangs on the right and an artist's palette hangs from a nail. Yet Braque makes no attempt to paint a naturalist rendition of the subject. The table itself is not viewed in perspectival recession, but has been tilted up nearly parallel to the picture plane. The edges of the violin are distorted and discontinuous with each other; one of the shoulders of the violin is rounded, the other quite cubic. The sound-holes appear as free-floating transitions between the disjunct upper and lower halves, while, even more obviously, the strings break in the middle over the bridge. And whereas these different areas seem generally to be seen from above, the neck and scroll of the violin are viewed at a more radical angle, twisting into an expressive arabesque at the top. Myriad details of light and shade contradict each other, with shadows cast for example onto the left side of the violin's neck, the right side of the lower right section, and none cast at all by the strings. Light is treated as arbitrarily as form, and chiaroscuro—the use of shadow and light to describe volume—no longer serves to help define the three dimensionality of the objects or their location in space. At the top of the canvas the highly legible nail and its cast shadow underscore by way of contrast Braque's bold departure from the painterly methods associated with the naturalist tradition.

Violin and Palette. Painting by Georges Braque, 1 September 1909. Oil on canvas, 36 1/8 x 16 7/8 inches (91.7 x 42.8 cm). Solomon R. Guggenheim Museum, New York, 54.1412. © 2005 Artists Rights Society (ARS), New York/ADAGP, Paris.

The salon cubists worked in a comparable manner, but they alone justified their technique in terms of non-Euclidean geometry and the fourth dimension, and related theories of human cognition and subjectivity, most notably the conventionalism of mathematician Jules-Henri Poincaré (1854–1912), and notions of psychological time developed by the French philosopher Henri-Louis Bergson (1859–1941) and American Pragmatist William James (1842–1910). Interest in these thinkers emerged before 1910 among those artists and writers who attended the weekly soirées of the American writer and collector Gertrude Stein (1874–1946). Concurrently, poets and critics associated with the salon cubists openly articulated their debt to Bergson. Beginning in 1910 the salon cubists and their literary allies publicized these precepts, a practice that culminated in the first book on cubism, Gleizes and Metzinger's *Du Cubisme* (1912). *Du Cubisme* proved to be highly influential and was translated into English and Russian in 1913. Picasso and Braque did not articulate these concerns but were certainly aware of them, as evidenced by Picasso's close friendship with Stein, and their frequent interaction with Metzinger. The degree to which Braque and Picasso shared in these theoretical interests is subject to debate. Many scholars argue that their cubism was initially a purely empirical response to the aesthetic innovations of French artist Paul Cézanne (1839–1906), as evidenced in Braque's *Houses at L'Estaque* (1908), and their exposure to African sculpture, which partially inspired Picasso's *Les Demoiselles d'Avignon* (1906–1907). Others have interpreted their manipulation of visual and verbal conventions, especially in the guise of collage, in light of the structuralism of Ferdinand de Saussure (1857–1913), arguing that this theoretical orientation was qualitatively distinct from the philosophical preoccupations of the salon cubists. More recently scholars have argued for a middle ground, noting that any interest Braque and Picasso may have had in semiotics needs to be historicized before their motivations can be properly compared to those of their cubist peers.

The existence of a coherent cubist movement ended in August 1914 due to the geopolitical fragmentation of the international avant-garde caused by World War I. During the war cubism came under attack from cultural conservatives, and although Gleizes and art dealer Léonce Rosenberg (1879–1947) attempted to revive the cubist movement after 1919, it was a spent force. However, cubist precepts continued to have an impact long after the movement's decline: Marcel Duchamp's conceptual approach to art during World War I was a studied reaction to cubist theory, and in subsequent years collage would have a profound impact on movements as diverse as Russian constructivism, Dada, surrealism, and American pop art. In addition, the development of montage techniques in film and photography in interwar Europe owed much to cubist experimentation.

See also **France; Painting; Picasso, Pablo.**

BIBLIOGRAPHY

Primary Sources

Antliff, Mark, and Patricia Leighten, eds. *A Cubism Reader: Documents and Criticism, 1906–1914.* Chicago, 2007.

Secondary Sources

Adams, Bruce. *Rustic Cubism: Anne Dangar and the Art Colony at Moly-Sabata.* Chicago, 2004.

Antliff, Mark. *Inventing Bergson: Cultural Politics and the Parisian Avant-Garde.* Princeton, N.J., 1993.

Antliff, Mark, and Patricia Leighten. *Cubism and Culture.* London, 2001.

Cottington, David. *Cubism in the Shadow of War: The Avant-Garde and Politics in Paris, 1905–1914.* New Haven, Conn., 1998.

Green, Christopher. *Cubism and Its Enemies: Modern Movements and Reaction in French Art, 1916–1928.* New Haven, Conn., 1987.

———. *Art in France, 1900–1940.* New Haven, Conn., 2000.

Henderson, Linda Dalrymple. *The Fourth Dimension and Non-Euclidean Geometry in Modern Art.* Princeton, N.J., 1983.

———. *Duchamp in Context: Science and Technology in the Large Glass and Related Works.* Princeton, N.J., 1998.

Herbert, Robert L. *From Millet to Léger: Essays in Social Art History.* New Haven, Conn., 2002.

Karmel, Pepe. *Picasso and the Invention of Cubism.* New Haven, Conn., 2003.

Krauss, Rosalind. "Re-presenting Picasso." *Art in America* 68, no. 10 (1980), 90–96.

Leighten, Patricia. *Re-Ordering the Universe: Picasso and Anarchim, 1897–1914.* Princeton, N.J., 1989.

Poggi, Christine. *In Defiance of Painting: Cubism, Futurism, and the Invention of Collage.* New Haven, Conn., 1992.

Rubin, William. *Picasso and Braque: Pioneering Cubism.* New York, 1989.

Silver, Kenneth. *Esprit de Corps: The Art of the Parisian Avant-Garde and the First World War, 1914–1925.* Princeton, N.J., 1989.

Zelevansky, Lynn, ed. *Picasso and Braque: A Symposium.* New York, 1992.

MARK ANTLIFF

CULTURE. *See* **Popular and Elite Culture.**

CURIE, MARIE (1867–1934), Polish physicist and chemist.

Maria Sklodowska was born in Warsaw, Poland, the youngest of six children. Maria's father taught mathematics and physics and her mother ran a private girls' school. Although Maria was obviously a brilliant student, advanced studies were not accessible to women in Poland, then a part of the Russian Empire. Knowing that their family could not afford to send them to study abroad, Maria and her sister Bronya agreed that Maria would work as a governess so that Bronya could study medicine in Paris. When Bronya graduated, Maria would join her and enroll at the Sorbonne.

In 1891, Maria Sklodowska moved to Paris to study mathematics and physics. While a student at the Sorbonne, she adopted the French form of her name. Within three years she had earned master's degrees in physics and mathematics, placing first among the candidates in physics and second in mathematics. Before meeting French physicist Pierre Curie (1859–1906), Sklodowska planned to earn a teaching certificate and return to Poland. One year later, in July 1895, Marie and Pierre Curie were married in a simple civil ceremony. Marie Curie gave birth to Irène in 1897 and Ève in 1904.

THE DISCOVERY OF RADIOACTIVITY, POLONIUM, AND RADIUM

In 1896, when French physicist Antoine Henri Becquerel (1852–1908) attempted to determine whether X-rays, which had been discovered the previous year by the German physicist Wilhelm Conrad Roentgen (1845–1923), were related to

Marie Curie in her laboratory. Undated photograph. AP/ WORLDWIDE PHOTOS

the phenomenon known as luminescence, he discovered a new type of radiation emitted by uranium salts. Although Becquerel's discovery attracted little attention at first, Marie Curie decided that a systematic investigation of "Becquerel rays" would be a suitable topic for her doctoral research. After investigating the radiation released by uranium compounds, Curie systematically tested other materials to see which elements might give off similar radiation. Only thorium and uranium produced spontaneous radioactivity, but certain natural ores, including pitchblende and chalcolite, seemed to give off more radiation than predicted by measurements of their uranium and thorium content. Curie concluded that these ores must contain unknown elements that were intrinsically more radioactive than uranium and thorium.

From her initial studies of uranium and thorium, Marie Curie arrived at a remarkable theoretical insight, one that challenged long-held beliefs about the nature of the atom. Curie realized that the strength of radiation was a function of the amount of uranium or thorium in a sample, and it was independent of the specific chemical compound being studied. Ordinarily, an element exhibits very different chemical and physical properties when it combines with other elements to form chemical compounds. Curie concluded that the release of radioactivity was an intrinsic property of the interior of the atom, rather than a function of the arrangement of atoms in a molecule. It was Marie Curie who introduced the term *radioactivity* ("ray action").

In 1898, the Curies announced the existence of two new radioactive elements, which they called *polonium* and *radium*. These elements were orders of magnitude stronger sources of radioactivity than uranium and thorium, but they were present in crude ores in very minute amounts. In order to isolate sufficient quantities of the new elements for the determination of their chemical properties and atomic weights, the Curies needed tons of pitchblende. (A ton of uranium ore contains about one ounce of radium.) Marie Curie's isolation of minute quantities of radium took years of extremely arduous labors under difficult conditions.

While processing tons of pitchblende, the Curies worked in a large, unoccupied shed. Friedrich Wilhelm Ostwald (1853–1932), an eminent German chemist, described it as more like a stable or a potato shed than a laboratory. Marie Curie later said that the years she and Pierre spent in that unheated, drafty, leaky, malodorous shed were the best and happiest of their lives. She also treasured memories of coming back to the shed at night and seeing their partially purified preparations glowing in the dark with a lovely pale blue light. Nevertheless, the four years of drudgery involved in the isolation of radium left both of the Curies perpetually ill and fatigued from what was later called radiation sickness. Marie Curie presented her findings as a doctoral dissertation in June 1903. Members of her thesis committee commended her discoveries and theoretical insights as probably the most significant scientific contributions ever made in a doctoral dissertation. For her work on radium, Marie Curie, the first woman in Europe to receive a doctorate in science, was awarded the degree of Doctor of Science "with great distinction."

The potential uses of radium, especially in medicine, were quickly recognized and entrepreneurs built factories for large-scale production. The Curies generously supplied samples of radium to fellow researchers and gave advice about its preparation to industrialists. Because they believed that scientific knowledge should be shared with the world at large, the Curies did not patent their discoveries. During the last decades of her life, Marie Curie apparently had some regrets about this decision. Years of arduous fund-raising activities forced her to realize how much her work would have been expedited by a reliable source of funding. She actively supported a resolution developed by the Commission on Intellectual Cooperation of the League of Nations to protect the intellectual property rights of scientists and inventors.

In 1903 the Academy of Sciences debated nominating Becquerel and Pierre Curie for the Nobel prize in Physics. Warned about these proceedings by a colleague, Pierre Curie made it clear that a Nobel prize for research in radioactivity that failed to acknowledge Marie would be a travesty. Although both Curies shared the 1903 Nobel prize in Physics with Becquerel, they were too ill from radiation sickness to attend the award ceremony. Despite their poor health and constant fatigue, the Curies did not believe that radiation could have a detrimental effect on human health. Researchers at the time handled radioactive substances without any precautions. In 1905, the Curies made the trip to Stockholm, where Pierre delivered the Nobel Lecture. The Nobel Institution was pleased by the universal interest in the romantic story of the Curies, but Marie was intensely disturbed by the media attention and invasion of privacy.

In 1904, Pierre Curie was finally granted an appointment to a professorship at the Sorbonne, and Marie was given the title Chief of the Laboratory, as well as a small salary. When university officials offered to nominate Pierre for the prestigious Legion of Honor, he refused the award and said he would rather have a laboratory. Tragically, Pierre died before the laboratory was completed. On 19 April 1906, he was struck and killed by a horse-drawn cart while crossing the street. Marie Curie was devastated, but when she was offered a pension she refused it, insisting that she wanted to work. Marie Curie took over Pierre's courses, thus becoming the first woman to teach at the Sorbonne. Nevertheless, it took two years for the university to officially appoint her as Professor. She also became Director of the Curie Laboratory in the Radium Institute of the University of Paris.

THE NOBEL PRIZE IN CHEMISTRY

When Marie Curie won the 1911 Nobel prize in Chemistry for the discovery of radium and polonium, and the isolation and characterization of pure radium, she became the first person to receive two Nobel prizes. In her Nobel Lecture, Curie clearly enunciated her own ideas and discoveries, as well as her unique collaboration with Pierre Curie. Despite her remarkable scientific achievements, the year in which Curie received her second Nobel prize was one of great distress. She was attacked in the right-wing French press for becoming a candidate for the Academy of Sciences and her relationship to Paul Langevin (1872–1946), a French physicist, who was married and the father of four children. The medical work carried out by Curie and her daughter Irène during World War I was significant in restoring her place as a much-loved icon in French history. Curie worked ceaselessly to equip vehicles that acted as mobile field hospitals, as well as X-ray installations near the battlefront. She also trained people to use diagnostic X-ray technology.

After the end of World War I in 1918, Curie's Radium Institute became France's premier research laboratory, but Curie had to devote a lot of time and energy to the task of raising funds for the Institute. Tours of the United States in 1921 and 1929, supported by the Federation of American Women's Clubs, raised enough money to purchase radium for Marie Curie's Institute in France and for a Radium Institute in Warsaw. Marie Curie was the author or co-author of many scientific articles and books including *Investigations on Radioactive Substances* (1904), *Treatise on Radioactivity* (1910), *Radioactivity and the War* (1921), *Pierre Curie* (including autobiographical notes by Marie Curie, 1923), *Radioactivity* (1935), and a collection of Pierre's work (1908).

Marie Curie died of leukemia on 4 July 1934. In keeping with her desire for privacy, she was buried next to Pierre Curie in a simple private ceremony. Albert Einstein (1879–1955) paid tribute to Marie Curie as "the only person to be uncorrupted by fame." On 20 April 1995, the bodies of Marie and Pierre Curie were ceremoniously transferred to the Panthéon in Paris. French President François Mitterrand (1916–1996) sponsored this honor as a way of acknowledging the equality of women and men. Marie Curie was the first woman to receive this honor on her own merit.

See also **Chemistry; France; Science and Technology.**

BIBLIOGRAPHY

Primary Sources

Curie, Marie. *Recherches sur les Substances Radioactives.* Paris, 1903. Marie Curie's doctoral dissertation, presented at the Sorbonne in 1903.

———. *Pierre Curie.* Translated by Charlotte and Vernon Kellogg. New York, 1923. Only the American edition received Marie Curie's permission to include her autobiographical notes.

———. *Oeuvres de Marie Sklodowska Curie.* Edited by Irène Joliot-Curie. Warsaw, 1954.

Secondary Sources

Brush, Stephen G. "Women in Physical Science: From Drudges to Discoverers." *The Physics Teacher* 23 (January 1985): 11–19. This classic article explores the "Marie Curie Syndrome" and the negative effects caused by stereotypical descriptions of female scientists.

Curie, Eve. *Madame Curie, A Biography.* Translated by Vincent Sheean. New York, 1937. Intensely personal, moving biography, published by her daughter only three years after Curie's death. A new edition, with a preface by Mitchell Wilson, was published in London, 1968.

Giroud, Françoise. *Marie Curie, a Life.* Translated by Lydia Davis. New York, 1986. Not intended as a scholarly biography but as a way of presenting Giroud's own interpretation of Curie's personality and her role in the history of science and France.

Goldsmith, Barbara. *Obsessive Genius: The Inner World of Marie Curie.* New York, 2005. A biography that emphasizes personal relationships rather than science.

McGrayne, Sharon Bertsch. *Nobel Prize Women in Science: Their Lives, Struggles, and Momentous Discoveries.* Secaucus, N.J., 1993. Allows readers to compare the work and world of Marie Curie with other women who became Nobel Laureates.

Pflaum, Rosalynd. *Grand Obsession: Madame Curie and Her World.* New York, 1989. Emphasizes the exhausting and laborious nature of the work conducted by Marie and Pierre Curie, as well as their daughter Irène and son-in-law Frédéric Joliot. Also explains the technical aspects of their work in clear and accessible terms.

Quinn, Susan. *Marie Curie: A Life.* London, 1995. Uses newly available archival material to provide new insights into the emotional life of the legendary scientist.

Reid, Robert. *Marie Curie.* London, 1974. This comprehensive and well-documented biography was the basis for the BBC five-part miniseries *Marie Curie* (1978).

LOIS N. MAGNER

CURZON, GEORGE (1859–1925), British statesman.

George Nathaniel Curzon, Marquess Curzon of Kedleston, was born in 1859 into an aristocratic family of Norman origin and raised in his family's distinguished Derbyshire estate, Kedleston Hall. Schooled at Eton, he went on to study at Balliol College, Oxford, which was becoming a training-ground for the political and imperial elite. Curzon dedicatedly pursued a prepolitical career, serving as president of the Oxford Union. He was known for his eloquent debating skills, Tory sentiments, and social connections, but also for his apparent sense of superiority. This provoked an uncharitable verse that would dog him for life:

> My name is George Nathaniel Curzon,
> I am a most superior person.
> My cheek is pink, my hair is sleek,
> I dine at Blenheim once a week.

After winning a prestigious fellowship at All Souls College, Oxford, Curzon was elected to Parliament as a Conservative member of Parliament (MP) in 1886. Inspired in part by a lecture he had heard as an Eton schoolboy, he decided to cultivate an expertise in Asian affairs. His preferred method of doing so involved traveling as much as possible. In 1887 he set off on a trip around the world; over the next seven years Curzon traveled to Russia, Persia, Afghanistan, central Asia, and east Asia, writing up his experiences in a series of multivolume books. In 1891 Curzon's specialist knowledge earned him a position as undersecretary of state for Indian affairs. From 1895 to 1898 he served as undersecretary of state in the foreign office and acted as the government's chief spokesman on foreign affairs in the House of Commons. In 1895 Curzon also concluded a period of romancing high-society women by marrying Mary Victoria Leiter, the daughter of a Chicago millionaire.

Curzon's ambitions directed him toward the position of viceroy of India, to which he was appointed in 1898. He arrived in India just forty years old, determined to reform the entire structure of British administration in the country and to assume a quasi-royal role. It was happy coincidence that Calcutta's Government House, built nearly a century before, had been modeled on Kedleston Hall. Curzon promoted an emphatically paternalistic vision of British imperial government. He believed in the alliance of power with spectacle and staged what many scholars see as the defining celebration of the British Empire at its peak: the Coronation Durbar of 1903, held in Delhi in honor of the coronation of King Edward VII (r. 1901–1910). Curzon's aristocratic paternalism also manifested itself in the 1904 Ancient Monuments Bill, designed to protect Indian architectural and archaeological heritage. He considered one of his greatest accomplishments to be the restoration of the Taj Mahal.

But not all Curzon's interventions were successful. He discounted the emerging Indian National Congress as an actor in India's political future. Most controversially, Curzon decided in 1905 to partition Bengal into two regions, one Hindu-majority and the other Muslim-majority. This was interpreted by Indian nationalists as an effort to "divide and rule" and was actively opposed in what is now seen as a defining moment in the Indian independence struggle. Curzon also invited criticism by sending Sir Francis Edward Younghusband (1863–1942) on a mission to Tibet that forcibly opened the region to British influence. But the viceroy was ultimately undone by a dispute with Lord Kitchener (Horatio Herbert Kitchener; 1850–1916), a war hero and commander-in-chief of the Indian army, over military restructuring. Confrontation between the two men led to Curzon's resignation in August 1905.

Curzon left India in disfavor and did not seek elected office. He also suffered the death of his beloved wife, Mary, in 1906. But he soon rebounded. In 1907 Curzon became chancellor of Oxford University and the following year took a seat in the House of Lords, where he opposed then chancellor of the Exchequer David Lloyd George's radical "People's Budget" of 1909 but helped broker a solution to the political impasse that followed. Curzon's career revived during World War I. He sat in the coalition cabinet of 1915 and spearheaded the effort, in December 1916, to replace the apparently ineffectual prime minister Herbert Henry Asquith with Lloyd George. Curzon served on Lloyd George's war cabinet for the remainder of the war. In 1917 he also ended an eight-year affair with the novelist Elinor Glyn (1864–1943) and married an American widow nearly twenty years his junior.

During the 1919 peace negotiations, Curzon was appointed foreign secretary. He opposed Jewish settlement in Palestine and advocated the creation of Arab states under British supervision. While dedicated to the preservation of empire, he also acknowledged the need for strategic withdrawal, notably in Egypt. Curzon and Lloyd George parted ways on the question of peace with Turkey. Unlike the feud with Kitchener, however, Curzon prevailed, leading successful negotiations with Turkey after the Conservatives regained power in 1922. He narrowly missed being asked to become prime minister when Andrew Bonar Law resigned in 1923. But this was to be the last of Curzon's perceived failures. After a life plagued by health problems, he died in 1925 at the age of sixty-six.

Curzon is known as the last great Victorian proconsul and as an Edwardian statesman forced to grapple with the legacies of World War I. But his cultural stature, in Britain as in India, was at least as significant. He was a trustee of the National Gallery, president of the Royal Geographical Society, and an active architectural preservationist, restoring several stately homes and presenting them to the nation. Another accomplishment was to orchestrate the peace and remembrance day ceremonies commemorating World War I. For these services and his political work he was made an earl (1911), a knight of the garter (1916), and a marquess (1921).

See also **Great Britain; Imperialism; India.**

BIBLIOGRAPHY

Fisher, John. *Curzon and British Imperialism in the Middle East, 1916–1919.* London, 1999.

Gilmour, David. *Curzon.* London, 1994.

Goradia, Nayana. *Lord Curzon: The Last of the British Moghuls.* Delhi, 1993.

Moore, Robin J. "Curzon and Indian Reform." *Modern Asian Studies* 27, no. 4 (1993): 719–740.

MAYA JASANOFF

CUVIER, GEORGES (1769–1832), French naturalist, paleontologist, zoologist.

Georges Cuvier was born in the French-speaking, largely Lutheran principality of Montbéliard, part of the Duchy of Württemburg. He was educated in Stuttgart at the Karlsschule, an academy designed to train future ducal civil servants. When, upon graduation in 1788, he was not offered a government job, he took a position as a tutor to an aristocratic Protestant family in Normandy. He lived in Normandy through the most violent years of the French Revolution. There, in the countryside and especially at the seashore, he found abundant opportunities to develop his interests in natural history.

Cuvier went to Paris in 1795, hoping to make a career as a naturalist. Skilled in dissecting animals, he brought his knowledge of comparative anatomy to bear on questions of zoological taxonomy. Key to his thinking was the principle of the "subordination of characters," the idea that the parts or characters of an organism most essential to its conditions of existence should be weighed more heavily than other parts in determining the organism's taxonomic relations. He used this principle to propose a reformation of mammalian class-ification and, more fundamentally, to divide the large, inchoate Linnaean class of "worms" into five new classes based on their internal structures. Cuvier proved adept at negotiating patronage relations within a community just recovering from the Reign of Terror. He was chosen to fill in for J.-C. Mertrud, the enfeebled professor of animal anatomy at the newly constituted National Museum of Natural History. He was also elected to the First Class of the Institut de France, the successor to the abolished Académie des Sciences.

In addition to his classificatory work, Cuvier established the foundations for the science of vertebrate paleontology. In a paper of 1796 he argued not only that Asian and African elephants constitute distinct species but also that other elephant species, no longer living, once roamed the earth. At a time when the question of extinction remained in doubt, Cuvier's careful comparison of fossil and living vertebrate forms demonstrated convincingly the reality of broadscale species extinction. He proposed that geological catastrophes of global proportions were responsible for the destruction.

Offered the opportunity to join Napoleon's expedition to Egypt in 1798, Cuvier chose to remain instead in Paris, estimating that continuing to work with the natural history collections there was the best way to advance his career. His calculations proved correct: upon Mertrud's death in 1802, Cuvier was chosen professor of comparative anatomy at the museum. The following year he was elected Permanent Secretary of the First Class of the Institut de France. Other distinctions and honors followed, including his appointments as Inspector-General of the Imperial University and Vice Rector of the Faculty of Sciences. If his place of birth, his German education, and his Protestant background made him something of a social outsider in France, they also enhanced his self-identification as an objective man of science prepared to serve the state dispassionately and effectively.

Cuvier was the dominant figure in French paleontology, geology, and zoology through the first third of the nineteenth century. His most authoritative work in paleontology and geology was his 1812 *Recherches sur les ossemens fossiles* (Research on fossil bones). There he explained how fossil remains could be understood as evidence of catastrophic "revolutions" in the earth's history. His major classificatory work was his 1817 *Le règne animal* (The animal kingdom). In this broad, systematic work he promoted the idea that the animal kingdom is represented by four wholly distinct plans of organization (or "branches")—the vertebrates, the mollusks, the articulates, and the radiates.

Cuvier was a staunch opponent of the idea of organic evolution, promoted primarily by his colleague at the Museum of Natural History, Jean-Baptiste Lamarck. As Cuvier saw it, the func-

tional integrity and "correlation of parts" of every organism were such that a significant change in any part would render the animal unable to live. He also argued against the idea of species mutability by citing the lack of transitional forms in the fossil record and the similar lack of transitions between the four major types of animal organization. Cuvier likewise opposed Étienne Geoffroy Saint-Hilaire's idea that all animals are based on but a single plan. Their disagreement on this score erupted in a famous public debate in 1830.

Cuvier died in 1832. Although he is often cast in the role of a scientific conservative, his contributions to comparative anatomy and paleontology were crucial in developing a scientific understanding of the history of life on earth.

See also **Evolution; Lamarck, Jean-Baptiste; Science and Technology.**

BIBLIOGRAPHY

Coleman, William. *Georges Cuvier, Zoologist: A Study in the History of Evolution Theory.* Cambridge, Mass., 1964.

Outram, Dorinda. *Georges Cuvier: Vocation, Science and Authority in Post-Revolutionary France.* Manchester, U.K., 1984.

Rudwick, Martin J. S. *Georges Cuvier, Fossil Bones, and Geological Catastrophes.* Chicago, 1997.

RICHARD W. BURKHARDT JR.

CYCLING. Cycling emerged as a spectator sport and recreational activity in 1868, shortly after the pioneer firm Michaux of Paris introduced a novel pedal-powered two-wheeled vehicle known as a "vélocipède" (from the Latin for "fast feet"). This basic bicycle, later dubbed a "boneshaker" on account of its harsh ride, was both costly and crude. Its pedals were attached directly to the front hub, its wheels were wooden, and its frame was solid iron. Typically weighing about seventy pounds, it could barely achieve ten miles an hour. Nevertheless, it was an encouraging breakthrough in the ancient quest for a practical "mechanical horse."

Amid general excitement, velocipede racing soon proved a popular attraction. The first well-publicized contests, covering barely a mile, took place in the Parisian suburb of Saint Cloud on 31 May 1868. A year later, bicycle construction had improved appreciably, and outdoor races had become commonplace throughout France. Often linked to popular festivals, programs typically featured colorful jockey attire, women's races, obstacle races, and "slow" races (the winner being the last to cross the finish line without having fallen). The first major city-to-city race took place on 7 November 1869, between Paris and Rouen. The winner, James Moore, covered about eighty miles in the impressive time of ten and one-half hours.

In the same period, recreational cycling began to attract scores of athletic, well-to-do males. As early as January 1868 Albert Laumaillé of Chatêau-Gontier ordered from Michaux an especially robust bicycle with which he intended to tour Brittany. By mid-1869 more than a dozen velocipede clubs operated across France, conducting regular jaunts into the countryside. The trade periodical *Le Vélocipède Illustré* reported race results and kept enthusiasts abreast of the latest technical developments. About a hundred French firms were producing bicycles by this time, and their collective output is believed to have reached tens of thousands.

Despite the evident technical limitations of the velocipede and its prohibitive cost, many enthusiasts fully expected it to evolve into a practical and affordable vehicle, possibly even supplanting travel by horse. The Société Pratique des Véloci-pèdes, founded in Paris in December 1868, offered prizes to mechanics who found ways to improve bicycle construction or lower its cost. The outbreak of the Franco-Prussian War in mid-1870, however, derailed the French bicycle industry before it could realize a "people's nag." Fortunately, several other countries had already adopted the bicycle. The American industry met an early demise, plagued by exorbitant royalty demands stemming from the Lallement patent. Filed in New Haven, Connecticut, by the French mechanic Pierre Lallement, this unique patent defining the basic bicycle was granted on 20 November 1866. Calvin Witty, a carriage and velocipede maker in Brooklyn, acquired the patent in early 1869 and immediately issued steep royalty demands on his competitors,

causing considerable consternation in the nascent industry. However, the primitive vehicle found especially fertile territory for development in England. Even as popular interest there faded by the end of 1869, the budding sport had established a devoted community of racers, tourists, and mechanics.

THE HIGH-WHEEL ERA, 1870S AND 1880S

In the early 1870s a new bicycle profile began to take shape in England, having an enlarged front wheel for improved gearing and a correspondingly reduced trailer. By the middle of that decade, the "high bicycle" (sometimes referred to by historians as a high-wheeler or penny farthing) had emerged as the dominant cycle. This trumpeted "modern bicycle" weighed only about forty pounds and could approach twenty miles per hour, thanks to such key innovations as wire wheels, solid rubber tires, and a tubular frame. Its joints also became smoother, with ball bearings coming into general use by 1880. The cyclist sat almost directly over the pedals, allowing application of his or her full force. The large elastic wheel also coped reasonably well with the poor roads of the day, allowing daily journeys in excess of one hundred miles and generally keeping the rider above the road dust.

The daunting new bicycle was nonetheless of limited popular appeal. It was manifestly impractical for everyday errands, and was widely perceived as a purely recreational vehicle for the amusement of affluent and physically fit young men. That market was nonetheless a significant one, and the British bicycle industry, based largely in Coventry, enjoyed prosperity in the late 1870s. Britain hosted dozens of cycling clubs and about one hundred thousand bicycles and tricycles. Cycling also spread throughout continental Europe, North America, and the entire British Empire, despite widespread complaints that "silent steeds" frightened horses and provoked accidents. To ensure access to the roads, and to improve their construction, cyclists formed lobbying groups such as the Bicycle Union in Britain and the League of American Wheelmen in the United States. Other organizations, such as Britain's Cyclists' Touring Club (established in 1878) catered to recreational riders, offering members maps and discounts at hotels and pubs.

Despite the public's misgivings about the high mount on the road, it continued to favor bicycle racing. The sport became especially prominent in Britain, where races on outdoor tracks, typically covering between one and twenty-five miles, regularly drew thousands of spectators. By the mid-1870s the country had produced a number of well-known amateur racers such as Ion Keith-Falconer, a towering Scottish aristocrat who became a noted Arab scholar and Christian missionary. John Keen, a maker in Surbiton, was among the most accomplished professionals. Endurance riding on tracks, covering hundreds of miles over periods of up to six days, also became a popular attraction. Meanwhile, the bicycle continued to prove itself on the road. The press regularly reported cycling exploits such as record-setting rides from Land's End to John O'Groats, the two most distant points in Great Britain. Thomas Stevens's celebrated round-the-world adventure, initiated in 1884, helped to project a romantic image of bicycle touring. Parades featuring club members in uniforms also regaled the public.

The technical success of the high bicycle, and its evident recreational benefits, prompted growing demands among the well-to-do for safer varieties of cycles. By the mid-1880s tricycles had gained a strong following on both sides of the Atlantic, notably among society women. Growing numbers of men, wary of being pitched from the precarious high mount (an indignity popularly known as a "header"), also favored the more stable three-wheeler. Alternative bicycle configurations designed to minimize the risk of injury, such as the British Kangaroo and the American Star, likewise achieved a degree of commercial success. For the most part, however, cycling remained an expensive and elitist pursuit.

THE BICYCLE BOOM, 1890S

The cycling scene changed dramatically in the 1890s, following the introduction of a new-style low mount popularly known as the safety bicycle. As early as 1885 James K. Starley of Coventry, England, presented his Rover bicycle, which used a chain and sprocket to achieve favorable gearing without the need for an oversize driving wheel. At first, few anticipated that this comparatively complicated design would claim a significant market share, much less supplant the conventional high bicycle. But as the new design gradually improved, and more makers began to offer variations, its advantages became increasingly apparent. The timely introduction of the inflatable or pneumatic tire, presented by the Scottish veterinarian John Dunlop in 1888, sealed the fate of the high wheeler, or Ordinary, as it came to be called. The safety bicycle with pneumatic tires proved not only the safer alternative, but also the faster machine. The inviting low-mount also appealed to women, who had been largely excluded from the sport.

By the early 1890s demand for safety bicycles surged on both sides of the Atlantic. Dozens of firms rushed into the trade and soon produced a variety of models and millions of machines. Some reactionaries protested that cycling encouraged immodest dress and even promiscuity among women, as well as reckless riding among men. Others warned that excessive cycling would lead to permanent health problems such as a stooped posture. But the general consensus held that moderate cycling was a healthy and desirable activity for both sexes, regardless of age.

With so many people identifying with the new-style bicycle, cycling as a spectator sport reached new heights of popularity. Thousands flocked to indoor and outdoor rinks known as velodromes to watch celebrated champions such as the American A. A. Zimmerman compete for lucrative prizes. Road racing also excited the popular imagination, especially in Europe. One memorable race in 1893, from Vienna to Berlin, introduced millions of central Europeans to the sport. Road races also proved an effective way for cycle manufacturers to market their products to the broad public. An early example was the 1891 race from Paris to Brest and back, won by the veteran Charles Terront, who showcased the latest Michelin clincher tires.

Although bicycles remained relatively expensive during the boom, costing perhaps several months' worth of wages, the pastime was already cutting across class lines. The sheer prominence of cyclists, the pervasive press coverage of all things cycle-related, and the increasing willingness of dealers to extend credit, as well as the burgeoning secondhand market, all helped to popularize the sport. Moreover, shortly after the boom subsided in 1897 the price of a bicycle plummeted from about seventy-five dollars to twenty-five dollars. Even as the upper classes and the leading bicycle makers began to turn their attention to the emerging automobile, the bicycle was already well established as an article of necessity. It was widely appreciated, especially in Europe, not only as a racing machine but also as a cheap and efficient vehicle for everyday commuting and weekend touring.

EARLY TWENTIETH CENTURY

Although the American bicycle industry all but collapsed after the boom, its European counterpart readjusted and thrived in the years leading up to World War I, a time when automobiles were still prohibitively expensive. Raleigh Cycle Company of Nottingham, England, became the world's leading bicycle maker and exporter, thanks to ever more efficient production lines. Germany and France were also major producers of bicycles and cycling accessories. Sturdier models with such practical concessions as freewheels, caliper brakes, soft seats, upright handlebars, and fenders helped to sustain a popular demand for utilitarian bicycles. Hub gears, originating in Britain, came on the market about 1903, followed by derailleur systems, developed primarily in France. The availability of multiple gears to handle diverse terrain enhanced the appeal of bicycle touring, especially among the middle classes.

The public, meanwhile, continued to follow competitive cycling. Velodromes continued to flourish in numerous European and American cities, hosting such popular events as the celebrated Six-Day race. Sprinters such as the African American Marshall "Major" Taylor enjoyed international fame. Road racing also became increasingly prevalent in Europe. The year 1903 marks the first Tour de France, sponsored by the journal *Vélo-Auto*. Originally it was composed of six stages, run day and night. The contest was later confined to daylight hours, but the format was extended to include multiple stages spanning two or three weeks and covering the most diverse terrain. The French public adored homegrown champions such as Lucien Petit-Breton, who in 1908 became the first to win a second title. But the Tour quickly assumed an international flavor as well, with several early champions hailing from Belgium and Luxembourg. Italy was also quick to adopt road racing, launching its own version of the Tour in 1909 called the Giro d'Italia, and establishing its own prewar heroes such as Costante Giradengo, a perennial national champion.

See also **Popular and Elite Culture; Sports.**

BIBLIOGRAPHY

Herlihy, David V. *Bicycle: The History*. New Haven, Conn., 2004.

Lloyd-Jones, Roger, and M. J. Lewis, with the assistance of Mark Eason. *Raleigh and the British Bicycle Industry: An Economic and Business History, 1870–1960*. Aldershot, Hants, U.K., and Brookfield, Vt., 2000.

McGurn, James. *On Your Bicycle: An Illustrated History of Cycling*. New York, 1987.

Startt, James. *Tour de France, Tour de Force: A Visual History of the World's Greatest Bicycle Race*. Updated and revised edition. San Francisco, 2003.

Vant, André. *L'industrie du cycle dans la région stéphanoise*. Lyon, 1993.

DAVID V. HERLIHY

CZARTORYSKI, ADAM (1770–1861), Polish general and statesman.

Prince Adam Jerzy Czartoryski came from a distinguished family of Polish aristocrats. His grandfather August (1697 1782) and his father, Adam Kazimierz (1734–1823), were both leading politicians in eighteenth-century Poland, and the Czartoryski family estate in the town of Puławy served as the informal headquarters for a cultural and political reform movement devoted to the spread of Enlightenment ideals. The last king of Poland, Stanisław II August Poniatowski (1732–1798), was affiliated with the Czartoryski clan, and during his reign they were probably the most influential family in the country. This came to an abrupt end with the conquest and partition of Poland in 1795, which left the Czartoryskis in a very precarious position. In an attempt to demonstrate loyalty to the new ruler and thus preserve the family's property and social standing, Adam and his brother Konstanty were sent in 1795 to serve at the court of Catherine II in St. Petersburg.

Because of his family's wealth and prestige, Czartoryski was able to gain entry into Petersburg's aristocratic high society, and within a year he had established a close personal friendship with Catherine's grandson, the Grand Duke Alexander. He also became quite fond of Alexander's wife, Elizabeth, with whom he had an affair that led to the birth of a daughter in 1799. Faced with the ensuing scandal, Tsar Paul I (who had succeeded his mother in 1796) got Czartoryski out of the country by sending him on a spurious mission to the king of Sardinia. Curiously, the episode did not weaken Czartoryski's bond with Alexander, and when the latter rose to the Russian throne in 1801, he welcomed the Polish prince back to Petersburg with honors.

In those years Czartoryski was part of a tight circle of the young tsar's friends committed to the systemic reform of the Russian state along constitutional lines. Czartoryski believed that a new Russia was about to be born, and that the interests of Poland could best be served within a reconstituted empire. He has often been described as a "conservative liberal," similar to such thinkers as Edmund Burke or Alexis de Tocqueville. He had an Enlightenment faith in universal reason, a moderate anticlericalism (he was a lifelong Freemason), and a belief that society was equally threatened by the stagnation of entrenched despotism and the chaos of unchecked revolution. The ideal state, for Czartoryski, would be respectful of tradition and legitimacy but governed by a constitutional order and the rule of law. He supported legal and economic reforms that would take Poland beyond the serf-based system that seemed to be holding back the country's development, but only if such changes could be introduced without seriously upsetting the existing social order. His commitment to the Polish cause was framed (his critics would say constrained) by this quest for an ideological golden mean.

In 1803 Czartoryski was placed in charge of the newly created Wilno (Vilnius) educational district encompassing most of the territory recently taken from Poland by Russia, and in this capacity he built a network of Polish primary schools (in a region that had experienced only very limited Polonization under the old Polish-Lithuanian republic). He also supervised the creation of the University of Wilno, which flourished in the first decades of the nineteenth century as a leading center of Polish culture. Czartoryski's growing importance at the Russian court was demonstrated in 1804, when he was named minister of foreign affairs, and a year later with his appointment to the Senate and the Council of State. But as quickly as he had risen to prominence, he fell again with the start of the War of the Third Coalition (1805–1807), which he had opposed. He was dismissed as Foreign Minister in 1806, and he fell into deeper disfavor after the creation of the Grand Duchy of Warsaw a year later. Although Czartoryski himself continued to advocate the restoration of Polish independence alongside or within the Russian Empire, the fact that the overwhelming majority of Poles (including many members of Czartoryski's own family) were enthusiastically supporting the French-sponsored duchy made the prince suspect in Petersburg. This situation became even worse in 1812, when Polish troops joined Napoleon's Grand Army in the invasion of Russia.

The defeat of Napoleon brought Czartoryski back into Tsar Alexander's inner circle, as the prince became Russia's chief negotiator at the Congress of Vienna (1814–1815). The dream Czartoryski had cultivated for so long was finally realized: an autonomous, constitutional "Polish Kingdom" was created, and linked to Russia in a dynastic union. Czartoryski himself played a leading role in writing a constitution for the kingdom, but after the new state was established he was once again marginalized. Alexander was already turning away from the more liberal ideals of his youth, and in any case he preferred to surround himself with aides who would be more subservient than the strong-willed Czartoryski. For the final decade of Alexander's reign, the prince withdrew to his private estate in Puławy.

The political climate in the kingdom deteriorated steadily after Alexander's death in 1825 and the elevation to the throne of the more authoritarian Nicholas I (1796–1855). As long as Alexander was alive, Czartoryski's personal loyalties kept him from engaging in any open opposition, but he felt no such constraints with Nicholas as tsar.

Moreover, under Alexander there had been hope that Poland's constitutional regime would gradually spread to the entire Russian Empire; under Nicholas it quickly became evident that, instead, the empire's autocratic politics would tightly limit Poland's parliamentary system. In the late 1820s Czartoryski became a leading voice for the moderate opposition in the Polish Senate, and for the first time in his life he enjoyed widespread respect and authority among his compatriots.

In November 1830, a group of young radicals in Warsaw launched a rebellion against Russian rule, much to the surprise and displeasure of Czartoryski. Tsarist troops were withdrawn momentarily from the Polish capital, and a group of (mostly conservative) politicians formed a provisional government, led by Czartoryski, to negotiate an end to the crisis. The Russians, however, had no interest in any compromise resolution, and in early 1831 the Polish parliament formally dethroned Nicholas and named Czartoryski the president of a new five-man governing council. Militarily, the revolt was a disaster, and within a year the Poles had been utterly defeated. All of Czartoryski's property was confiscated, and he was sentenced to death—a fate he avoided only by escaping abroad. He would remain an émigré the rest of his life.

Settling in Paris, Czartoryski purchased a residence known as the Hôtel Lambert, which would serve as the informal headquarters for more conservative Polish émigrés during the coming decades. The Hôtel Lambert was in part a cultural center: the Polish Library that Czartoryski opened there still functions today, and the Hôtel's salons and concerts made it a prestigious address for artists, musicians, and poets. But the primary function of the Hôtel Lambert was political

and diplomatic. From this base, Czartoryski dispatched agents to all the courts and governments of Europe in an attempt to persuade Great Britain, France, and other states to use their influence on behalf of the Polish cause. He understandably abandoned his previous support for Russia, but his belief in the efficacy of traditional institutions of power and influence remained. Thanks to the prince's reputation, his aristocratic lineage, and his many years of diplomatic service, he was able to win audiences for his emissaries and thus keep the "Polish question" alive among diplomats throughout the mid-nineteenth century. Indeed, he came to be known as the "Uncrowned King of Poland" because of his ability to sustain a Polish presence in the halls of power across the Continent. On the other hand, Czartoryski never received anything more than token rhetorical support from the governments of Europe. When he died in 1861, public demonstrations and conspiratorial activities were again stirring unrest in Poland, but the Hôtel Lambert had little influence over the course of events to come.

See also **Alexander I; French Revolutionary Wars and Napoleonic Wars; Nationalism; Poland; Revolutions of 1830.**

BIBLIOGRAPHY

Czartoryski, Adam. *Memoirs of Prince Adam Czartoryski.* Edited by Adam Gielgud. London, 1888. Reprint, New York, 1971.

Skowronek, Jerzy. *Adam Jerzy Czartoryski, 1770–1861.* Warsaw, 1994.

Zawadzki, W. H. *A Man of Honour: Adam Czartoryski as a Statesman of Russia and Poland, 1795–1831.* Oxford, U.K., 1993.

BRIAN PORTER

DAGUERRE, LOUIS (1787–1851), French artist and inventor of the daguerreotype.

Louis-Jacques-Mandé Daguerre was born 18 November 1787 in Cormeilles-en-Parisis, France, and attended public school in Orléans before moving to Paris around 1803. In 1808, he appears in the official records of the painting studio of the Opera, where he held various posts through 1816, when he was named the chief decorator of the Ambigu-Comique theater. He returned briefly to the Opera studio as co-chief painter with Pierre-Luc Ciceri from 1820 to 1822.

Simultaneous with his work as a stage painter, Daguerre also exhibited in the official Parisian Salon, where he made his debut in 1814. His early works share much in common with the troubadour style, a kind of medieval revival in painting, as exemplified by the historical genre scenes by Pierre Révoil and Fleury-François Richard, as well as the gothic interiors popularized by François-Marius Granet. Daguerre was also among the first French artists to experiment with lithography, producing prints for two important illustrated works, Count Auguste de Forbin's *Voyage dans le Levant* (1819) and several volumes of Charles Nodier and the baron Isidore-Justin-Séverin Taylor's *Voyages pittoresques et romantiques dans l'ancienne France* (1820–1878).

Daguerre was also the entrepreneur of the popular spectacle known as the Diorama, which he organized as a limited stock company in 1821 with his partner, the painter Charles-Marie Bouton. The Diorama was a building designed by Daguerre that housed two large, semitransparent paintings illuminated by natural light. Daguerre and Bouton employed blinds and colored screens to represent natural effects of time, light, and movement in painted interior and exterior views. The public, seated in a central auditorium, was transported from one scene to the next by means of a rotating viewing platform. Daguerre's talent for lighting effects and illusionism, along with his solid understanding of printmaking techniques, led him to the invention of the daguerreotype (first publicly announced in 1839), which became the first commercially successful photographic process.

The daguerreotype is a photographic image with a mirrorlike surface on a silver or silver-coated copper plate. Unlike most paper photographs, the daguerreotype is not produced from a negative, and the final image has the ability to appear either positive or negative depending on the angle of reflected light. Daguerreotypes are remarkably luminous and capable of producing subtle gradation of tone and extraordinary detail. These qualities are evident in Daguerre's own daguerreotypes of architectural scenes and still-lifes of plaster casts. The daguerreotype process eventually was used primarily for portraiture, but Daguerre's own early interest in and production of portraits is still a debated topic, as is his business relationship with Joseph-Nicéphore Niépce, who had invented an earlier photographic process distinct from the daguerreotype.

Le boulevard du Temple. Photograph by Louis Daguerre, c. 1838. This early example was taken from Daguerre's studio window. BAYERISCHES NATIONAL MUSEUM, MUNICH

By January 1826, when Daguerre wrote to Niépce about the possibility of fixing the images of a camera obscura, the latter had already worked out the fundamentals of his photographic process, which he called *heliography.* Niépce had begun experimenting with photochemical processes as early as 1816, achieved notable results by 1824, and produced the world's earliest extant stabilized camera image sometime in 1826–1827. Niépce eventually visited Daguerre at the Diorama in August 1827, and the two men formed a company on 14 December 1829 in order to exploit both Niépce's invention, based on the photosensitvity of bitumen of Judea, an asphaltic residue used in etching, and Daguerre's improvements to the camera obscura. After Niépce's death (5 July 1833), Daguerre signed a new contract on 9 May 1835 with Niépce's son, Isidore. The new contract changed the name of the partnership from "Niépce-Daguerre" to "Daguerre and Isidore Niépce," in light of Daguerre's recognition of the chemical bases of the daguerreotype—iodine and mercury. A final contract was signed on 13 June 1837, naming Daguerre as the sole inventor of the new process, which François Arago, the politician and scientist, announced on 7 January 1839. Arago formally divulged the process to a joint meeting of the Academy of Science and Academy of Fine Arts on 19 August 1839, after the purchase of the process by the French government. Following Arago's announcement, Daguerre sent daguerreotypes to Louis I of Bavaria, Ferdinand I of Austria, Nicholas I of Russia, Frederick William III of Prussia, the Austrian chancellor Clemens von Metternich, and the Austrian ambassador to France A. G. Apponyi. Daguerre also offered daguerreotypes to Arago and to Alphonse de Cailleux, the curator of antiquities at the Louvre.

In 1840 Daguerre retired to the village of Bry-sur-Marne, outside of Paris. While he continued to work on the daguerreotype, periodically sending news of improvements to Arago, photography was no longer his affair. He painted his last diorama for the church of St. Gervais–St. Protais at Bry in 1842. In 1848 he constructed a natural grotto in the park at Bry, returning to the source of his original inspiration, the landscape. He died on 10 July 1851, the same year he was planning another religious diorama painting, a cavalry, for the church at Perreux, in the neighboring town of Nogent-sur-Marne.

See also **France; Nadar, Félix; Photography.**

BIBLIOGRAPHY

The Dawn of Photography: French Daguerreotypes, 1839–1855. Exhibition catalog. On CD-ROM. New York and New Haven, Conn., 2003.

Gernsheim, Alison, and Helmut Gernsheim. *L. J. M. Daguerre: The History of the Diorama and the Daguerreotype.* 2nd rev. ed. New York, 1968.

Gunthert, André. "L'affaire tournesol." *Études photographiques* 13 (July 2003): 2–5.

Paris et le daguerréotype. Exhibition catalog. Paris, 1989.

Pinson, Stephen C. "Daguerre: Expérimentateur du visuel." *Études photographiques* 13 (July 2003): 110–135.

———. *Speculating Daguerre: Art and Enterprise in the Work of L. J. M. Daguerre.* Chicago, in press.

Potonniée, Georges. *Daguerre: Peintre et décorateur.* Paris, 1935.

STEPHEN C. PINSON

DANISH-GERMAN WAR.

The origins of the Danish-German War of 1864 lay in an issue whose complexity is best illustrated by an aphorism attributed to Britain's Lord Palmerston. He declared that only three men ever truly understood the Schleswig-Holstein question: a Danish politician who was dead, a German professor who went mad, and Palmerston himself—who had forgotten it.

Essentially the provinces were legally joined together under the personal rule of the Danish crown. Holstein was also part of the German Confederation created in 1815. When in 1848 Denmark proposed to integrate Schleswig into its administrative structure, the confederation resisted. The resulting compromise steadily eroded until in 1863 Denmark announced a new constitution including Schleswig.

German nationalists accused Denmark of plotting the annexation of Schleswig in defiance of international law. The German Confederation voted armed sanctions with ruffles and flourishes. And Otto von Bismarck, the Prussian minister-president (prime minister), saw an opportunity to propel his state into a position of leadership in Germany. He began by persuading Austria to cooperate in taking the military initiative against Denmark. Each state dispatched an army corps, and in January 1864 the newly minted allies crossed into Holstein.

Most of the 35,000 to 40,000 Danes called to arms for the crisis were reservists, including married men in their thirties and volunteers with neither training nor experience. The bulk of them were deployed in Schleswig, manning improvised fieldworks they had no chance of holding for long against the forces of two Great Powers. But withdrawing without even token resistance was to concede the war.

While the Prussians were slow off the mark, a series of dashing Austrian attacks compelled the Danes to evacuate Schleswig, retreating into Jutland and to the permanent fortifications at Düppel (Dybbøl in Danish). Prussia and Austria faced the simultaneous challenges of convincing the other powers that further military action was not aimed at the territorial and political integrity of Denmark, and of overcoming Düppel's formidable landward defenses, which offered few possibilities for anything but a time-consuming formal siege.

Helmuth von Moltke, the Prussian chief of the general staff, argued that stalemate in the field was the best guarantee of great-power intervention. The bulk of the Prussian contingent remained around Düppel. The Austrians advanced toward Denmark proper as Bismarck convinced their dubious government they were in too deep to withdraw. The allies approved a plan based on capturing Düppel and Alsen (or Als) Island, lying immediately behind it, and mounting a full-scale advance into Jutland for the purpose of screening those operations against a Danish counteroffensive.

Danish troops in position during the Danish-German War, 1864. ©HULTON-DEUTSCH COLLECTION/CORBIS

Austria's agreement freed Bismarck to respond positively to increasingly uncompromising British and Russian demands for an international conference on the question of the duchies. That, however, was only one of the cards Bismarck was playing. Simultaneously, he began to prepare public, political, and royal opinion for the direct annexation of Schleswig and Holstein to Prussia.

Both initiatives depended on a Prussian victory. As men and equipment moved into position to begin the slow-motion ballet of a siege, Bismarck put increasing pressure on his generals to finish off Düppel by assault. As an alternative to a lengthy siege and a costly storm, a junior staff officer proposed an amphibious operation—a surprise attack in force on Alsen Island to bypass the Danes' defenses and force them into the open. Moltke regarded the risks as too high. For six weeks the Prussians brought up guns and dug trenches. For two weeks more they bombarded the Danish fortifications. On 18 April the assault finally went in. At the cost of a thousand casualties the defenses were overrun.

The Danes responded by evacuating their last mainland fortress of Fredericia. Moltke saw that as a sign that Denmark no longer had any intention of undertaking large-scale land operations. Despite Austrian reluctance, he oversaw the overrunning of the Jutland peninsula as representatives of the Great Powers met in London, seeking to resolve the Schleswig-Holstein question in an international context. Bismarck took full advantage of continuing Danish refusal to compromise, rejecting even Franco-British initiatives for dividing the duchies and British proposals for arbitrating Denmark's new frontier.

On 29 June Moltke supervised the crossing of the Alsen Fjord by 25,000 Prussians. They encountered no significant resistance from an army by now demoralized by three months of inactivity. Alsen marked the end of the serious fighting. As Moltke busied himself with plans for an attack on Fünen (Fyn in Danish) and an invasion of Zeeland, Denmark's King Christian IX (r. 1863–1906) decided further resistance was impossible. Denmark's French and British patrons had no leverage remaining. On 1 August Christian ceded all rights to the duchies to Prussia and Austria.

See also **Bismarck, Otto von; Moltke, Helmuth von.**

BIBLIOGRAPHY

Bucholz, Arden. *Moltke and the German Wars, 1864–1871.* Basingstoke, U.K., 2001. Contains the best account of the military operations.

Carr, William. *Schleswig-Holstein, 1815–1848.* Manchester, U.K., 1963. The best English-language source on the background of the duchies' status.

Showalter, Dennis. *The Wars of German Unification.* London, 2004. Covers the diplomacy as well as the campaign.

DENNIS SHOWALTER

D'ANNUNZIO, GABRIELE (1863–1938), Italy's most important playwright and poet from the 1880s to World War I.

At age sixteen Gabriele D'Annunzio published his first book of poems, *Primo vere* (In early spring). Initially, he was influenced by Giosuè Carducci, but his reading of Friedrich Nietzsche responded to a self-image of tragic heroism, a cult of oneself, and the cultivation of basic passions. The D'Annunzian hero was a superior being who dominated the mass of humanity. Starting in the 1890s D'Annunzio published a series of dramas (*Dead City, The Flame, The Daughter of Jorio, The Ship, Glory, Beyond Love,* and *Fedre*) that confirmed his status as Italy's major playwright. The poet also gained equal fame for his scandalous love affairs with leading actresses, most notably Eleonore Duse.

D'Annunzio entered politics during the turbulent decade of the 1890s. These years were marked by banking scandals, Italy's defeat in Ethiopia in 1896, and protest against the rising cost of living followed by the imposition of martial law in May 1898. Elected initially as a right-wing deputy to Parliament in 1897, D'Annunzio proclaimed a new kind of aesthetic politics: "The fortune of Italy is inseparable from the destinies of Beauty, of which she is the mother. . . . The Latin spirit cannot reestablish its hegemony in the world without reestablishing the cult of One Will" (Witt, p. 36). In March 1900 D'Annunzio, dubbed the "deputy of beauty," confirmed his reputation for theatrical politics by walking from the benches of the extreme right to the far left with the explanation, "I go toward life." His experience among the Socialists was relatively brief. By the end of the decade he took up positions close to the far right imperialist Italian Nationalist Association and published a collection of poems, *Canzoni della gesta d'oltremare* (Song of deeds beyond the sea), justifying Italian expansion. In 1910 D'Annunzio fled his creditors in Italy and took up residence in Paris, where he staged *The Martyrdom of Saint Sebastian,* with music by Claude Debussy.

D'Annunzio's blend of aesthetics and politics appealed to those who were impatient with the mundane struggle to build the infrastructure of the new Italian state. He encouraged the belief that politics was an act of will by which a superior individual could shortcut the path to greatness and world power. The notion that politics could be reduced to style over substance, to rhetoric over achievement, proved alluring to young intellectuals who chafed at the seemingly base political deals and cautious foreign policy that marked the many governments of Giovanni Giolitti from 1903 to 1914. The poet moved center stage in April and May 1915, when he returned from France to lead the mass demonstrations to bring Italy into the war on the side of the Entente powers (Britain, France, and Russia). Arrayed against him in favor of continued neutrality in the Great War were the parliamentary majority, controlled by the former prime minister Giovanni Giolitti, the Catholic Church, and the Italian Socialist Party. Italy's entry into the war in May 1915 against the will of these powerful institutions confirmed the notion that determined elites could overcome the passive majority.

D'Annunzio volunteered for service in World War I. With a flair certain to capture the popular imagination he undertook several aerial missions over enemy territory, the most notable in August 1918, when he dropped leaflets urging surrender over Vienna. His romantic stature was enhanced by the loss of an eye on one of these flights. In 1919 D'Annunzio, at the head of a group of veterans, right-wing nationalists, and some revolutionary syndicalists, seized the disputed city of Fiume, which both Italy and the new Yugoslav state had claimed at the Paris Peace Conference. With this rag-tag army D'Annunzio held Fiume from September 1919 to December 1920, when a resolute government headed by Giovanni Giolitti finally ousted him from the city. Briefly, in 1919 and 1920, it seemed that D'Annunzio, not Benito Mussolini, would lead the movement to overthrow the Italian parliamentary state, but it soon became clear that D'Annunzio was incapable of the kind of sustained leadership that could mount a successful coup.

With the advent of Mussolini's government D'Annunzio retired from political life, accepted a gilded exile in a villa at Gardone di Riviera, and in 1924 was nominated to the Italian Senate.

See also **Italy.**

BIBLIOGRAPHY

Becker, Jared M. *Nationalism and Culture: Gabriele D'Annunzio and Italy after the Risorgimento.* New York, 1994.

Drake, Richard. *Byzantium for Rome: The Politics of Nostalgia in Umbertian Italy, 1878–1900.* Chapel Hill, N.C., 1980.

Witt, Mary Ann Frese. *The Search for Modern Tragedy: Aesthetic Fascism in Italy and France.* Ithaca, N.Y., 2001.

ALEXANDER DE GRAND

DANTON, GEORGES-JACQUES
(1759–1794), French lawyer and revolutionary.

An unknown and thoroughly respectable young lawyer in Paris at the outset of the French Revolution, Georges-Jacques Danton quickly achieved celebrity as a neighborhood militant spearheading a grass-roots challenge to the constitutional monarchists who had come to power in July 1789. Having thereby acquired his revolutionary bona fides as a tribune of the Parisian popular movement, he rode a powerful wave of revolutionary radicalization to a

position of ever-increasing prominence on the national political stage until emerging as the most influential member of the provisional government established after the fall of the monarchy on 10 August 1792. Over the next year, as a leading figure in the National Convention (which proclaimed the First French Republic on 20 September 1792) and a key member of that body's first Committee of Public Safety, a pragmatic and conciliatory strain within his temperament came to the fore as he grappled with the responsibilities of power and sought to moderate and defuse an increasingly venomous struggle between the factions known to history as "Jacobins" and "Girondins." After the June 1793 purge of the Girondins, however, revolutionary power gravitated toward the more consistently radical and more ostentatiously virtuous Maximilien-Francois-Marie Isidore de Robespierre (1758–1794), and Danton passed into the ranks of the political opposition. Targeted by Robespierre and his allies on the second Committee of Public Safety as the leader of a faction of "Indulgents" who aimed to dismantle the Reign of Terror then raging, Danton was arrested on 31 March 1794. After a perfunctory trial over which the governing Committee exerted almost total control, he was guillotined on 5 April 1794.

Immortalized in statue form at the Odéon Métro stop entrance in Paris, Danton is universally regarded as one of the "giants of the French Revolution," a status which largely rests on the central role that he played in rallying French resistance to Prussian invaders who, in September 1792, seemed to be on the verge of crushing the Revolution. Indeed, as a figure that calls up associations to the patriotic fervor that accompanied the Revolution and to its efforts to forge a new sense of national unity, Danton can be seen as a worthy candidate for such immortalization. As a revolutionary politician, however, Danton's approach to politics was oddly antithetical to what might be thought of as the "spirit of the Revolution." For in contrast to the insistence of any number of historians that the fundamental driving force of the French Revolution was an attempt to remake the world according to a preconceived ideological blueprint, Danton, unlike his nemesis Robespierre, made his mark in history as more of a political wheeler and dealer than an ideological visionary, as more of a working democratic politician than an embodiment of abstract democratic values.

First attracting attention as the leader of the Cordeliers district on Paris's Left Bank, the affable and gregarious Danton owed his early political clout to the building of what amounted to a highly effective urban political machine through which favors were dispensed to and loyalty secured from a tight network of friends and associates, a number of whom (most notably Camille Desmoulins [1760–1794] and Philippe-Francois-Nazaire Fabre d'Eglantine [1750–1794]) stayed with him until the day they mounted the scaffold together. Moreover, further demonstrating his intuitive grasp of the way working democratic politicians tend to operate, Danton quickly developed what historian Norman Hampson calls the "habit of conforming to revolutionary extremism in public while pursuing limited and realistic objectives in private" (p. 30). Thus, while continuing to employ radical rhetoric to sustain his revolutionary credibility, even as he ascended to the corridors of power, his approach to the art of governing seemed to revolve around a deeply ingrained inclination to accommodate and conciliate as wide a spectrum of political opinion as possible.

But however viable such an approach might be for a politician seeking to govern under normal political conditions, one wonders just how realistic it may actually have been in the boiling caldron that was the French Revolution. In any event, Danton was unable to sustain the delicate balancing act through which he sought to rein in the Revolution while simultaneously attempting to retain the support of "advanced patriots." More specifically, with respect to the attempt to reassure moderate and conservative elements, his attempts to reach a negotiated settlement with the invading Prussians and Austrians ended in failure and his schemes to save Louis XVI (1754–1793) and Marie Antoinette (1755–1793) all came to naught. At the same time, however ferocious a tone he may have sounded in his legendary oratory, he was always subject to being "outbid" by the new waves of revolutionary militancy that were continually emerging in the neighborhoods of the capital. Like a series of other would-be guides of the Revolution (Jacques Necker [1732–1804], Marie Joseph Paul Lafayette

Georges-Jacques Danton. Portrait by Pierre Alexander Wille, 1794. ©GIANNI DAGLI ORTI/CORBIS

[1757–1834], comte de Mirabeau [1749–1791], Antione-Pierre-Joseph-Marie Barnave [1761–1793], and Jacques-Pierre Brissot de Warville [1754–1793]) whose revolutionary credentials were ground to dust through their efforts to construct some kind of broad governing coalition, Danton, too, found that he could not "ride the revolutionary tiger." Indeed, it can be said that the Dantonist phase of the French Revolution came to an end on 10 July 1793, when the Convention, rendering what amounted to a parliamentary vote of no confidence, removed him from the Committee of Public Safety; a new government was put in place two weeks later when Robespierre was added to the Committee.

Apparently subject throughout the years of the Revolution to severe mood swings, which might today be diagnosed as a form of bipolar disorder, Danton largely withdrew from political life in the months following this reorganization of the Committee of Public Safety. Claiming illness, he received permission from the Convention in early October 1793 to retire to his native town of Arcis-sur-Aube in Champagne. In mid-November, however, he returned to the fray and, though operating largely behind the scenes, seems to have been deeply involved in maneuvers to overturn the Robespierrist Committee. In any event, whatever actual role he and his fellow Indulgents might have played in attempting, through their campaign against the Terror, to undermine the rule of the Committee, it is clear that the Committee regarded Danton as, at the very least, a serious potential threat to its continued dominance. In the lethal atmosphere of 1793–1794, there was, in fact, no space for legitimate opposition; no middle ground, that is, between providing unwavering support for the government and being seen as conspiring against it.

Temperamentally inclined toward compromise and flexibility and also rather easygoing when it came to standards of personal probity (put bluntly, he was apparently not at all adverse to having his palms greased), the pleasure-loving Danton served for generations in many Marxist and Jacobin histories of the French Revolution as a corrupt foil to the austere and ideologically pure Robespierre. In the late twentieth century, with the advent of global "neo-liberalism" in the post–Cold War world, the same constellation of traits won him praise for personifying a heroic resistance to alleged Robespierrist proto-totalitarianism. Yet, however valid it may be to think of Danton as either, in abstract terms, a corrupt or heroic embodiment of "anti-Robespierrism" or "anti-Jacobinism," it should also be recalled that Danton and Robespierre worked in tandem through the early years of the Revolution and that Danton played a significant role in establishing the Jacobin institutions that he would later turn against. In particular, it should be noted that, in his efforts to appease the Parisian popular movement ("let us," he said, "be terrible to dispense the people from the need to be terrible themselves"), it was Danton who spearheaded the Convention's creation of the infamous Revolutionary Tribunal on 10 March 1793.

With this in mind, it might be worth looking more closely at one especially crucial moment in Danton's short life: his decision to return to the political fray in November 1793. Surely this astute political player knew that he would be putting himself in harm's way, that he would have a far better chance of avoiding being engulfed by the dynamics of revolutionary repression that had already overtaken the constitutional monarchists and the Girondins if he quietly remained in Champagne. As something of an adventurer and a gambler, Danton may possibly have had an exaggerated idea of his own ability to influence events and may even have thought that he had a decent chance of regaining power. Or it may be that he was partially impelled by a strong sense of loyalty to friends and associates still politically active in Paris. One wonders, however, whether some sense of responsibility and/or guilt for his own role in nurturing the dynamics of repression may have had something to do with his decision to return: whether, that is, his participation in the campaign for indulgence was to at least some degree motivated by a desire to undo some of the damage that he himself had done. In any event, whatever factors may have led him to this choice, the return to Paris was a return to what Danton knew was a deadly political game, a game from which there would be no further opportunities for escape.

See also **Committee of Public Safety; French Revolution; Girondins; Jacobins; Reign of Terror.**

BIBLIOGRAPHY

Primary Sources

Danton, Georges-Jacques. *Discours de Danton.* Edited by André Fribourg. Paris, 1910.

Secondary Sources

Hampson, Norman. *Danton.* New York, 1978.

Howell, Michael W. "Danton and the First Republic." Ph.D. diss., University of North Carolina, 1982.

Mathiez, Albert. *Autour de Danton.* Paris, 1926.

Mirkine-Guetzévitch, Boris. "Le parlementarisme sous la Convention nationale." *Revue du droit public et de la science politique en France et à l'étranger* (1935): 671–700.

Ozouf, Mona. "Danton." In *A Critical Dictionary of the French Revolution,* edited by François Furet and Mona Ozouf, translated by Arthur Goldhammer, 213–223. Cambridge, Mass., 1989.

BARRY M. SHAPIRO

DARWIN, CHARLES (1809–1882), English naturalist.

Born in Shrewsbury, England, on 12 February 1809, Charles Darwin was the grandson of a physician, Erasmus Darwin (1731–1802). His father, Robert Waring Darwin, was also a physician; his mother, Susannah Wedgwood Darwin, was a member of the noted English pottery family. From 1818 to 1825, Darwin attended boarding school but was not a top-notch student. In 1825 Darwin was sent to Edinburgh University, which featured the best medical school in Britain. When Darwin recoiled from the idea of surgery and rejected becoming a physician, his father arranged for extra tutoring to prepare him for study at Cambridge University. Darwin enrolled at Christ's College at Cambridge in 1828. Darwin's father hoped that he would study theology at Cambridge and prepare for a comfortable life as a country parson. Instead, Darwin spent much of his time gambling and riding horses, and his father complained that he was interested only in "shooting, dogs, and rat catching." Yet Darwin eventually proved to be a successful student at Cambridge, ranking tenth out of 178 students on the final bachelor's examination and impressing his teachers, including the botantist Robert Henslow.

VOYAGE OF THE *BEAGLE*

When the Cambridge University faculty was asked to recommend a student to serve as ship's naturalist aboard a British surveying ship, Henslow recommended Darwin. The ship, the H.M.S. *Beagle*, was scheduled to make a five-year voyage through the South Pacific and along the coast of South America. Paying the deference to his father that was expected from sons in upper-class Victorian families, the twenty-two-year-old Darwin asked his father's permission to apply for the job. Although his father thought the work "useless" and initially rejected the idea, permission was granted after an uncle intervened.

The voyage, which lasted from 1831 through 1836, proved to be the most formative event in Darwin's professional career. Darwin was haunted by his discoveries during the voyage. He returned to Britain with a large collection of fossils and

DARWIN ON NATURAL SELECTION AND HUMAN ORIGINS

In his *On the Origin of Species* and *The Descent of Man,* Darwin made an effort to take the most optimistic view possible of natural selection, which most of his contemporaries feared was a "blind" process whose future outcome was uncertain and unpredictable.

Judging from the past, we may safely infer that not one living species will transmit its unaltered likeness to a distant futurity ... it will be the common and widely-spread species, belonging to the larger and dominant groups, which will ultimately prevail and procreate new and dominant species. ... Hence we may look with some confidence to a secure future of equally inappreciable length. And as natural selection works solely by and for the good of each being, all corporeal and mental endowments will tend to progress toward perfection. (*Origin of Species,* 1st ed., p. 489)

In regard to bodily size or strength, we do not know whether man is descended from some small species, like the chimpanzee, or from one as powerful as the gorilla; and therefore, we cannot say whether man has become larger or stronger, or smaller and weaker, than his ancestors ... an animal possessing great size, strength, and ferocity ... like the gorilla, could defend itself from all enemies, [and] would not have perhaps become social; and this would most effectually have checked the acquirement of the higher mental qualities such as sympathy and the love of his fellows. Hence it might have been an immense advantage to man to have sprung from some comparatively weak creature. (*The Descent of Man,* p. 65)

animal and plant specimens, many of which he distributed to universities and scientific institutions. The fossils that he collected appeared to show that a large number of species had become extinct, but they did not answer the central question of why that had happened. The voyage of the *Beagle* also impressed on Darwin how geography had influenced species. He was struck by the similarities, as well as the differences, between species from nearby islands, particularly in the chain of Galápagos Islands. Reasoning that plants and animals had developed somewhat differently at different geographical locales, Darwin, by the end of the voyage, was willing to conclude that species were not "immutable." When his diary aboard the *Beagle* was published as *Journals and*

THE OXFORD DEBATE

Darwin's defenders frequently framed the issue of evolution as the search for scientific truth. In 1860, the year after the publication of the *Origin,* Darwin's friend Thomas Henry Huxley publicly debated the merits of the book with a bishop of the Church of England, Samuel Wilberforce. The occasion was a meeting of the British Association for the Advancement of Science at Oxford University. It pitted one of the most talented speakers among the English bishops—whose nickname was "soapy Sam"—against Darwin's most spirited defender—whose nickname would become "Darwin's bulldog." The bishop, speaking first, diverged from his scheduled topic to ask whether Darwin claimed ancestry through an ape grandfather or an ape grandmother. Huxley felt compelled to respond. After all, Darwin had written that the details of human origins were uncertain, but he had added that apes and human beings probably shared a common ancestor. While there are a number of accounts of what Huxley said, they are generally similar.

An Oxford undergraduate who was present wrote a friend that Huxley had replied:

> I asserted—and I repeat—that a man has no reason to be ashamed of having an ape for his grandfather. If there were an ancestor whom I should feel shame in recalling it would rather be a man—a man of restless and versatile intellect—who, not content with an equivocal success in his own sphere of activity, plunges into scientific questions with which he has no real acquaintance, only to obscure them by an aimless rhetoric, and distract the attention of his hearers from the real point at issue by eloquent digressions and skilled appeals to religious prejudice.

An instructor at Oxford wrote this account to Huxley's son:

> The Bishop had rallied your father as to the descent from a monkey, asking as a sort of joke how recent this had been, whether it was his grandfather, or further back. Your father . . . then went to this effect—'But if this question is treated, not as a matter of calm investigation of science, but as a matter of sentiment, and if I am asked whether I would choose to be descended from the poor animal of low intelligence and stooping gait, who grins and chatters as we pass, or for man, endowed with great ability and splendid position, who should use these gifts (here, as the point became clear, there was a great outburst of applause, which mostly drowned out the end of the sentence) to discredit and crush humble seekers after truth, I hesitate what answer to make.'

A third person who was present added:

> No one doubted his meaning, and the effect was tremendous. One lady fainted, and had to be carried out; I, for one, jumped out of my seat. (*Life and Letters of Thomas Henry Huxley,* edited by Leonard Huxley [New York, 1901], p. 199)

Remarks, 1832–1836 (1839), it did not raise the issue of "transmutation," the term used at the time to describe species change. Yet his "Red Notebook," done during the last months of his *Beagle* voyage, and his "B" notebook, began after his return, did discuss transmutation. Darwin had begun the voyage believing in the "permanence of the species," but he ended it with "vague doubts."

PROBLEMS FOR EVOLUTION

Yet it was twenty-three years from the time that the *Beagle* returned to Britain until the appearance of Darwin's famous book that proposed his version of evolution, *On the Origin of Species* (1859). Why did it take him so long? Why did he not rush to publication? The answer appears to be that he was acutely aware that his theories on evolution would jar the Victorian world and risked making him a social outcast and a religious pariah. Since the late twentieth century increasing attention has been given (by Adrian Desmond and James Moore, among others) to the mysterious illness that afflicted Darwin for many years after the voyage of the *Beagle,* leaving him with frequent bouts of fatigue and a "nervous stomach." One explanation is that he was aware that his work might not only alienate him from some of his friends but also reopen what one contemporary termed "the warfare between science and religion."

While Darwin worried about the impact of his theories of evolution, he was also wrestling with serious scientific problems for his ideas. Darwin and his colleagues did not take seriously the Biblical account of the earth's creation in six days, and they also dismissed the ideas of the Irish bishop James Ussher (1581–1656), who had totaled the number of generations represented in the Bible and had announced, on the basis of such calculations, that the creation of the universe began on 23 October 4004 B.C.E. Much more respect was given to the work of the noted British mathematician and physicist Lord Kelvin. Assuming that the earth began as a fiery ball, Kelvin had used the laws of thermodynamics to determine that the age of the earth did not exceed some 200 million years. That was not sufficient time for a true evolution.

The necessary long time frame for the history of the earth was furnished by geology. Until the early nineteenth century, most geologists were "catastrophists," who believed that the earth's surface had been shaped by periodic cataclysms such as floods. "Catastrophism" fit with the Biblical story of a great flood. It also allowed writers to explain fossils without resorting to evolution. The doctrine of "Special Creation" held that God re-created life on Earth following periodic catastrophes; fossils were seen as evidence of what life was like before the previous Creation.

By the 1820s, however, a new school of geology, uniformitarianism, emerged. Uniformitarians held that the laws of nature operated "uniformly" in time throughout the earth—great mountains, for example, were produced by forces operating gradually, in processes such as erosion. The new theory argued that the same slow forces seen shaping the earth today had also operated in the past. During the voyage of the *Beagle,* the ship's captain (and Darwin's closest friend during the voyage), Robert FitzRoy, gave him a copy of the first volume of a major uniformitarian book—Charles Lyell's *Principles of Geology* (1830–1833). Because Lyell and other uniformitarians assumed a much longer time span for the history of the earth than previously believed, Darwin later commented that his own evolutionary book *On the Origin of Species* "half came out of Lyell's brain."

What was lacking, until Darwin, was a plausible explanation of the mechanism of evolution—the "how" of the process that drove and shaped species change. There had been previous attempts, none of which was considered successful, to explain "transmutation." The most significant evolutionary theory before Darwin came from the French naturalist Jean-Baptiste Lamarck, who speculated that animals might deliberately acquire characteristics or organs that they needed in order to survive in their environment. These new characteristics—a fish forced to live on land coming to acquire lungs, for example—might then be passed down to following generations. How this might occur remained a puzzle, since the science of genetics would not emerge until the late nineteenth and early twentieth centuries.

Larmarck's theory, called the theory of the "inheritance of acquired characteristics," received less attention among scientists on the European continent after fellow French naturalist Georges Cuvier ridiculed the idea at a scientific conference in 1830. For much of the first half of the nineteenth century, evolution became the province of philosophy, as the German philosophers Lorenz Oken and Friedrich von Schelling promoted the idea that an inner force or "vital spirit" drove all living matter to self-improvement. Their evolutionary philosophy, named *Naturphilosophie* (nature philosophy), gained little acceptance among scientists outside of Germany.

THE INFLUENCE OF MALTHUS AND SPENCER

In September 1838, Darwin read the *Essay on the Principle of Population* (1798) by the English economist Thomas Malthus. Malthus held that human population was growing faster than the supply of available food, with the result that there would always be competition among human beings for the "means of subsistence." Darwin had come to believe that new traits or "variations" constantly appeared among plants and animals. Some traits or "variations" condemned an animal to a short life; others might be more "favorable," allowing the animal to live a longer life. Darwin concluded that what Malthus called the "struggle for existence" might be used to explain how, in evolution, "favorable variations" would tend to be preserved and "unfavorables ones" destroyed.

Darwin also would eventually accept a phrase from the philosopher Herbert Spencer, a nonscientist who was the most popular writer on evolution

The *Beagle* sailing around Cape Horn. Undated engraving. ©BETTMANN/CORBIS

in mid-nineteenth-century Britain. Darwin and his friends held little respect for Spencer's system of evolution—which Spencer said proceeded from the simple to the complex, or from the "homogeneous" to the "heterogeneous"—since it was based on philosophic speculation rather than science. When Spencer treated Darwin rather arrogantly at their first meeting, Darwin's friend Thomas Henry Huxley retaliated by quipping that Spencer's idea of tragedy was "a deduction killed by fact." Yet Darwin eventually came to accept a phrase used by Spencer after Darwin's own theories were published—"survival of the fittest"—to describe evolution.

THE SLOW PATH TO THE *ORIGIN*

Darwin did not prepare to publish his theories until he received a letter in 1858 from a biologist with similar ideas, but he had long been at work producing a number of unpublished writings on the subject. By the 1840s, he was writing that "I am almost convinced . . . that species are not . . . immutable," adding that "it is almost like confessing a murder." In 1842 he produced a thirty-five-page description of what he termed "natural selection" to explain evolution, and in February of 1844, he gave his wife a 231-page manuscript on evolution, with instruc-

tions that it be published after his death. Darwin began writing his groundbreaking book, *On the Origin of Species,* in May 1856. At first he intended to write for scientists alone. By now he had abandoned the idea that evolution occurred only when conditions, or the environment that an animal lived in, changed. Now he favored the idea that nature was a place of constant struggle, with new "variations" continually appearing.

Alfred Wallace, a less accomplished biologist, forced Darwin to make his ideas public. Wallace wrote to Darwin in June 1858, proposing, from his own travels and from also reading Malthus, that changes in species were driven by competition and overpopulation. Typically generous, Darwin refused to try to deny recognition to Wallace (even considering, for a time, allowing Wallace to garner much of the initial credit). In July 1858, at a time when Darwin was too ill to appear, two colleagues in the scientific community, Huxley and Joseph Hooker, presented Darwin's 1844 essay, along with a paper by Wallace, to the Linnean Society; both were later published together.

When Darwin's book *On the Origin of Species* appeared in 1859, it demonstrated the influence of Malthus and the impact of the voyage of the H.M.S.

Beagle. The book's distinctive idea of "natural selection" was based on the belief that as plants and animals overproduced, the resulting struggle for resources tested which plants and animals best "fit" in their environment. In "natural selection," nature selected from variations that regularly appeared. The survivors lived longer, founded new species, and produced the most offspring. The *Origin* proved to be Darwin's most celebrated book, one that was translated into at least thirty-six languages in his lifetime and is still read widely.

Since the late twentieth century writers such as Dov Ospovat have traced Darwin's efforts to achieve a more optimistic view of the "struggle for existence" than Malthus had presented. Darwin first proposed that animals, in responding to changes in their environment, would create a new "stable" relationship with the environment and that the "struggle for existence" would cease. He later changed his mind, however, deciding that struggle was a constant part of nature. Another assessment of Darwin, by the writer Robert Young, concludes that Darwin attempted to prove that evolution represented "progress" by reasoning that natural selection led to greater "complexity" in nature, which Darwin considered desirable.

The last chapter of the *Origin* drew much attention, since it included the statement that "light" would soon be thrown on "human origins." Darwin fulfilled that promise in 1871, when he published *The Descent of Man.* The *Descent* made human beings part of the process of natural selection, arguing that early humans were hairy beings with large ears and that human beings, monkeys, and apes probably shared a common ancestor. In the *Descent* Darwin wrote that human mental and moral abilities differed from those of animals only by degrees. The implication was that the moral standards of human society were patterns of behavior that human beings had utilized, in evolution, in order to survive.

Darwin's book *The Expression of Emotion in Animals* (1872) extended the argument, attempting to establish connections between the emotional and intellectual life of human beings and animals. During the last twenty years of his life Darwin also worked to explain how natural selection operated in the plant world. Scholars have recently paid much more attention to his writings on this subject, since

Illustration of palm trees from *The Voyage of the Beagle*, 1845. SNARK/ART RESOURCE, NY

Darwin appeared to believe that his readers were more likely to accept the concept of natural selection if it was applied to plants rather than to animals.

Wealthy from investments and from inheritances, Darwin and his wife, his first cousin Emma Wedgwood (whom he married in 1839), were able to live a comfortable life. Eventually they had ten children. Because of Darwin's frequent fits of nervousness, his wife often protected him from uninvited visitors to his home in Down, England, sometimes claiming that she could not locate her husband. Some honors were bestowed on Darwin, although far fewer than might be expected from a man considered one of the scientific greats of the nineteenth century. When he died on 19 April 1882, however, his friends, including Huxley, were able to arrange for burial in Westminster Abbey, close to a monument to another scientific giant, Isaac Newton.

POPULAR AND SCIENTIFIC RECEPTION

Outside of the scientific community, much of the early reaction to the *Origin* and the *Descent* focused on the issue of human origins. The British humor magazine *Punch* published a famous cartoon showing monkeys discussing their human relatives. The playwright George Bernard Shaw declared that no decent-minded person could believe Darwin's theories. Behind public debates over Darwinism lay deeper fears among the Victorians, who were repulsed by the idea of nature as a battleground between individuals that was filled with misery and suffering. Late-twentieth and early-twenty-first-century writers on Darwin such as Michael Ruse have pointed out that "Darwinism" raised major philosophic questions. Many of Darwin's contemporaries worried that there were no standards of conduct or accountablity for individual actions in an evolutionary world.

The American writer Henry Adams was not quite accurate when he said that "evolution pleases everyone—except curates and bishops"—but his words underlined the degree to which "Darwinism" became a cause in itself, since it raised the possibility that Nature operated on its own, without divine guidance. Ernst Mayr, a twentieth-century biologist, has argued that until about 1940, "Darwinism" meant the idea that the world might be explained only through natural processes (and that only after that time did Darwinism signify "natural selection"). The poet Alfred, Lord Tennyson wrote that if Darwin's version of Nature was God's creation, God had to be "disease, murder, and rapine." Even Darwin's wife worried that her husband's work "puts God further off." Nevertheless, when Tennyson said to Darwin, "Your theory of evolution does not make against Christianity," Darwin replied, "No, certainly not." Some liberal Protestant clergy in Darwin's time, such as Charles Kingsley, would come to accept evolution in general (although not necessarily natural selection), with Kingsley approving the concept that "God created primeval forms capable of self government." Darwin himself seemed to encourage such views, conceding that the idea that "this grand and wondrous universe could not have arisen through chance" was the "chief argument for the existence of God."

Even within the scientific community, religious and philosophic issues played a role in determining whether Darwin's ideas were accepted or rejected. A major opponent was the director of the Kensington Natural History Museum, Richard Owen, who insisted that Nature Philosophy was correct in describing evolution as the operation of a "vital force" in organisms. In the United States, the Harvard geologist Louis Agassiz insisted that species, once created by God, are fixed and unchangeable, although another prominent American biologist in the late nineteenth century, Asa Gray, defended the *Origin*. In general, scientists in Darwin's time were more likely to accept the idea of evolution than the concept of natural selection. Huxley himself accepted evolution but said that natural selection remained unproved.

Darwin's theories of evolution were generally accepted within the scientific community in the early decades of the twentieth century, but with major modifications. The "Neo-Darwinians" of the first half of the century combined natural selection with newer genetic theories. The work of the Dutch geneticist Hugo De Vries provided an explanation for the cause of Darwin's important "variations"—continual genetic mutations in organisms. Not every aspect of Darwin's ideas has been accepted, however. The biologist Stephen Jay Gould has been one of the advocates of the theory of "punctuated equilibrium," which holds that species, rather than undergoing the very gradual changes described by Darwin, actually undergo rapid genetic alterations or "genetic jumps," followed by long periods of little or no change.

THE SOCIAL DARWINIANS

The Social Darwinians, largely nonscientists, were social and political commentators who cited Darwin to buttress their own preconceived ideas. Darwin had provided little guidance regarding the meaning of his system of evolution for political or social issues. One exception was the theory of laissez-faire, the name of the nineteenth-century economic belief that governments should not interfere in the operations of the business world. Darwin favored the concept of laissez-faire, opposing a proposal by British trade unions that factory workers should be paid by the hour rather than by the piece. He wrote that it meant "excluding competition," which, in turn, would be a "great evil for the future progress of mankind." Such comments led Karl Marx to describe the *Origin* as an example of "British greed morality."

Charles Darwin, c. 1880. The Granger Collection

The majority of Social Darwinians claimed to see in natural selection a justification for laissez-faire, nationalistic beliefs, or theories of racial superiority. To the American writer William Graham Sumner, life was a constant struggle, and humanitarian efforts to eliminate poverty were "ill conceived." On the continent of Europe, the German historian Heinrich von Treitschke saw war as a Darwinian testing ground that led to the "utter annihilation of puny man," separating the "wheat" from the "chaff." As European nations came to dominate large areas of Asia and Africa in the late nineteenth century, some Social Darwinians sought to justify these colonial adventures by asserting white racial superiority.

A smaller group of Social Darwinians thought that the struggle for existence, instead of being a struggle between individuals, was a struggle of whole groups of animals against their environment. The most prominent member of this school of thought was the Russian writer Peter Kropotkin. Using his own observations of the behavior of animals in the harsh winters of Siberia, Kropotkin

insisted that the "struggle for survival" was a joint struggle of animals against their own environment; the "fittest" animals were those who supported each other through what he termed "mutual aid."

Social Darwinism took a fateful turn in the twentieth century with the emergence of the eugenics and "racial hygiene" movements. Darwin's cousin Francis Galton had coined the term *eugenics* to describe "selective efforts at human improvement." Although Darwin did not endorse his cousin's ideas, Darwin's theories were cited during the early twentieth century by members of eugenics societies in Europe and the United States. Some of these societies promoted the forced sterilization of the "feeble-minded," the insane, the criminal, and the deaf.

During the 1930s and early 1940s the German dictator Adolf Hitler and his National Socialist movement used a crude Social Darwinism to justify their racial policies and glorify war. The ultimate result of Nazi "racial hygiene" was the death of eleven million people in concentration camps. No "racial hygienist" was an internationally respected scientist, however, and Darwin had consistently rejected prowar analogies drawn from his theories. Darwin argued, in fact, that the earliest human beings emerged in Africa rather than in Europe or North America. Modern anthropologists tend to agree.

See also **Agassiz, Louis; Eugenics; Evolution; Great Britain; Haeckel, Ernst Heinrich; Humboldt, Alexander and Wilhelm von; Lamarck, Jean-Baptiste; Mendel, Gregor; Science and Technology; Wallace, Alfred Russel.**

BIBLIOGRAPHY

Primary Sources

Burkhardt, Frederick, and Sydney Smith. *The Correspondence of Charles Darwin* Cambridge, U.K., 1985–. This, the most complete publication of Darwin's letters, will fill an anticipated thirty-two volumes and supersedes *The Life and Letters of Charles Darwin* (3 vols., 1887) and *More Letters of Charles Darwin* (2 vols., 1903), edited by Darwin's son Francis.

Darwin, Charles. *On the Origin of Species by Means of Natural Selection, or the Preservation of Favoured Races in the Struggle for Life.* London, 1859. Numerous reprintings.

———. *The Descent of Man and Selection in Relation to Sex.* 2 vols. London, 1871. Numerous reprintings.

————. *Autobiography*. Edited by Nora Barlow. London and New York, 1958. Reprint, 1993. This edition of Darwin's autobiography restored passages, omitted from an earlier edition by Darwin's wife, in which Darwin wrote that the existence of God might be neither proved nor disproved, a position known as agnosticism.

————. *Diary of the Voyage of the H.M.S. Beagle*. Edited by Richard Darwin Keynes. Cambridge, U.K., and New York, 1988. Reprint, 2001.

Secondary Sources

Aydon, Cyril. *Charles Darwin: The Naturalist Who Started a Scientific Revolution*. London and New York, 2002. Darwin's life and theories explained for the general reader.

Bowler, Peter J. *Evolution: The History of an Idea*. Berkeley, Calif., 1989. 3rd ed., 2003. Authoritative in its description of the development of various evolutionary theories.

Browne, Janet. *Charles Darwin: Voyaging* and *Charles Darwin: The Power of Place*. Princeton, N.J., 1996, and New York, 2002. This two-volume biography uses new material from family archives.

Desmond, Adrian, James Moore, and James R. Moore. *Darwin: The Life of a Tormented Evolutionist*. London and New York, 1992. Reprint, 1994. Part of this book deals with Darwin's fears that the *Origin* would engender so much controversy that its scientific merit would be ignored.

Eiseley, Loren. *Darwin's Century: Evolution and Men who Discovered It*. New York, 1958. Reprint, 1961. This book, by an anthropologist, treats Darwinism as the central event in the history of evolutionary theories, and makes other figures, such as Buffon and the Swedish botanist Carl Linnaeus, into "precursors" of Darwin.

Glick, Thomas F., ed. *The Comparative Reception of Darwinism*. Chicago, 1988. Reprint, 2003. Glick's book covers not only Europe and the United States but also areas such as Mexico and the Islamic world.

Gould, Stephen Jay. *The Structure of Evolutionary Theory*. Cambridge, Mass., 2002. Evolution presented by a biologist who was a major twentieth-century dissenter from some of Darwin's theories.

Greene, John C. *The Death of Adam: Evolution and Its Impact on Western Thought*. Ames, Iowa, 1959. Reprint, 1961, 1996. Focuses on Darwinism as a materialist threat to the older view of nature as a tool of God.

Himmelfarb, Gertrude. *Darwin and the Darwinian Revolution*. London and Garden City, New York, 1959. Reprint, 1996. Distinctive among Darwin biographies for its critical tone toward both Darwin's personality and scientific work.

Hull, David. *Darwin and His Critics: The Reception of Darwin's Theory of Evolution by the Scientific Community*. Cambridge, Mass., 1973. Reprint, 1993. Contrasts with the Glick book by focusing more on the debates over the scientific merits of Darwin's theories.

Kohn, David, ed. *The Darwinian Heritage: Including Proceedings of the Charles Darwin Centenary Conference*. Princeton, N.J., 1985. Reprint, 1988. Thirty-two leading scholars assess the social and cultural impact of Darwin.

Mayr, Ernst. *One Long Argument: Charles Darwin and the Genesis of Modern Evolutionary Thought*. Cambridge, Mass., 1991. Reprint, 1993. A modern view of Darwin by a major twentieth-century biologist.

Ospovat, Dov. *The Development of Darwin's Theory: Natural History, Natural Theology, and Natural Selection, 1838–1859*. Cambridge, U.K., and New York, 1981. An influential book that concentrates on the period when Darwin was formulating his theory of natural selection.

Rogers, James Allen. "Darwinism and Social Darwinism." *Journal of the History of Ideas* 33 (1972): 265–280. A groundbreaking article which argues that the Social Darwinians, by using "unnecessary concepts," which Darwin borrowed from Malthus and Spencer, distorted the essence of Darwin's theories

Ruse, Michael. *The Darwinian Revolution: Science Red in Tooth and Claw*. Chicago, 1979. Reprint, 1981, 1999. Ruse's book concludes that while many scientists came to accept "evolution," many did not accept "natural selection."

Russett, Cynthia Eagle. *Darwin in America: The Intellectual Response, 1865–1912*. San Francisco, 1976. An important book that focuses on the reaction to Darwin's theories by major American thinkers of his time.

Young, Robert M. *Darwin's Metaphor: Nature's Place in Victorian Culture*. Cambridge, U.K., and New York, 1985. Examines the implications of, and the debate over, the significance of Darwin's work for the place of human beings in nature at large.

NILES R. HOLT

DAUMIER, HONORÉ

DAUMIER, HONORÉ (1808–1879), the leading French caricaturist from 1830 to 1872.

Honoré Daumier's nearly 4,000 satirical lithographs appeared up to thrice weekly in the illustrated Parisian press and provided a running critical commentary on politics and society. Daumier's work includes 991 book illustrations, some 281 paintings, 826 drawings and watercolors, as well as sculpture.

Born in Marseilles in 1808, the son of a glazier and aspiring poet and playwright, Daumier came with his family to Paris in 1816. By 1832 he was their sole support, working as a messenger boy for a bailiff at the law courts, assisting in a bookshop, and then working with a publisher of lithographic portraits. Daumier reportedly studied with Alexandre Lenoir (1761–1839), founder of the Museum of French Monuments, and intermittently attended life class at the Académie Suisse.

EARLY POLITICAL CARICATURE

Daumier's lithographs were first published in *La Silhouette* in 1829 and in *La Caricature* in 1830. *Gargantua* (December 1831) depicted Louis Philippe (r. 1830–1848), king of France, enthroned, being fed bribes and defecating honors. Daumier was given a six-month suspended sentence for offense to the king, subsequently imposed. Further caricatures of Louis Philippe were banned but censorship led to subterfuge. Together with his editor Charles Philipon (1800–1862), Daumier devised the symbol of the pear, *le poire*, also meaning fat-head, a pun for the pear-shaped bourgeois king.

Le Ventre législatif (The legislative paunch) was published in January 1834 by the monthly subscription print club established to avoid censorship and offset the fines to *Le Charivari*, which succeed *La Caricature*. Daumier drew analogies between the political and anatomical body of the glutinous deputies. Numerous *portraits-chargés* (charged portraits) appeared beginning in 1832, inspired by *Célébrités du juste milieu* (1832–1835; Celebrities of the mediocre majority), some thirty-six clay busts commissioned by Philipon. With the September Laws of 1835, the censors halted all political caricature.

SOCIAL CARICATURE

After the censorship laws were put into effect, Daumier turned to social types and situations, often with political overtones. Robert Macaire, the quintessential con man, was depicted in different professional guises in the 101 *Caricaturana* (1836–1838) with captions by Philipon. Daumier's ignoble lawyers, often implying political complicity, appear frequently. *Les gens de justice* (1845–1848; The people of the courts), with thirty-eight plates, was particularly successful. He grasped the professional structure—doctors, teachers, landlords—of the expanding bourgeoisie. Independent ambitious women were treated critically. Daumier also caricatured the Parisian population by avocation and diversion and by class and character, in daily situations and social disjunctions, with an acute grasp of physiognomy, bearing, and gesture.

SECOND REPUBLIC

With the Second Republic (1848–1852) and the lifting of censorship laws, Daumier resumed political caricature, most notably with the sculpture and thirty lithographs of *Ratapoil*, an agent provocateur. Daumier's painting submitted to the competition for a representation of the Republic was among eleven finalists. He also painted and drew themes from mythology, religion, history, literature, as well as lawyers and street life: two paintings were in the Salons of 1850–1852. The motif of fugitives or emigrants appears in Daumier's plaster reliefs, paintings, and drawings.

LATER WORK

When Napoleon III was declared emperor in December 1852, Daumier returned exclusively to social caricature, featuring the spectator motif and the Haussmannization of Paris, the massive urban redesign and development, with its inconveniences and obstructions, new boulevards and transportation. He drew twelve hundred lithographs on contemporary life during this period.

In 1860 *Charivari* fired Daumier, claiming viewer dissatisfaction and police complaints. Daumier subsisted on sales of his watercolors, including a series on railway passengers. There are also paintings of *The Third Class Carriage,* c. 1862–1864, as well as washerwomen, lawyers, actors, audiences, art connoisseurs, and themes from Jean de La Fontaine, Molière, and Miguel de Cervantes's Don Quixote and Sancho Panza, arguably his alter egos, whom he painted thirty times from 1849–1873.

In 1863 *Charivari* rehired Daumier, who then drew Paris diversions and country excursions. Daumier returned to political caricature exclusively in 1866 when censorship was lifted and

The Legislative Paunch. Lithograph by Honoré Daumier, 1834. BIBLIOTHÈQUE NATIONALE, PARIS, FRANCE/BRIDGEMAN ART LIBRARY

shifted from national to international politics using symbolic figures: Prussia as obese, Diplomacy as an old hag, and France as Prometheus. The threat of war predominates, then the disastrous Franco-Prussian War (1870–1871), and the defeat of Napoleon III. The recurring figure of the jester with a pen as witness and chronicler is emblematic of Daumier's own role.

Daumier's last caricatures in *Le Charivari* were published in September 1872. His late drawings include drinkers at cafés (prefiguring the impressionists), poignant street performers, tragic clowns, and sideshows. Charles Baudelaire (1821–1867) compared the quality of his drawing to the old masters. Among his last paintings (1873–1875) are images of the artist before his easel. Daumier died in Valmondois (near Barbizon), where he lived his last years, poor and nearly blind.

Daumier expanded the definitions of art to include popular imagery, influencing Édouard Manet, Edgar Degas, Henri de Toulouse-Lautrec, Georges Rouault, Pablo Picasso, and the cartoonist TIM (the name Louis Mitelberg used in signing his caricatures). He set the standard for caricature.

See also **France; Louis-Philippe; Napoleon III; Painting; Revolutions of 1848.**

BIBLIOGRAPHY

Baudelaire, Charles. "Quelques caricaturistes français." In *The Painter of Modern Life and Other Essays,* translated and edited by Jonathan Mayne. London, 1986. Early, highly perceptive section on Daumier.

Bouvy, Eugène. *Daumier: l'Oeuvre gravé du maître.* Paris, 1933.

Clark, T. J. *The Absolute Bourgeois, Artists and Politics in France, 1848–1851.* London, 1973. Chapter on Daumier in political context.

Daumier, 1808–1879. Paris, 1999. Catalog of 1999 exhibition, detailed chronology.

Delteil, Loÿs. *Honoré Daumier.* Paris, 1925–1930. Available from http://www.daumier-register.org.

The Third Class Carriage. Painting by Honoré Daumier, c. 1862–1864. METROPOLITAN MUSEUM OF ART, NEW YORK, USA/BRIDGEMAN ART LIBRARY

Ives, Colta, Margret Stuffmann, and Martin Sonnabend, eds. *Daumier Drawings*. New York, 1992. Reevaluation of the drawings.

Laughton, Bruce. *Honoré Daumier*. New Haven, Conn., 1996.

Maison, K. E. *Honoré Daumier: Catalogue Raisonné of the Paintings, Watercolours, and Drawings*. 2 vols. London, 1968.

Prevost, Louis. *Honoré Daumier: A Thematic Guide to the Oeuvre*. Edited by Elizabeth C. Childs. New York, 1989.

Wasserman, Jeanne L. *Daumier Sculpture*. Greenwich, Conn., 1969.

Wechsler, Judith. *A Human Comedy: Physiognomy and Caricature in 19th Century Paris*. London, 1983. Chapters on Daumier and the press in the context of urban change.

JUDITH WECHSLER

DAVID, JACQUES-LOUIS (1748–1825), French painter.

Between 1785 and 1815 Jacques-Louis David was the most important and influential painter in Europe. David's working life spanned the Enlightenment, the French Revolution, the Napoleonic era, and the Bourbon Restoration.

Born in Paris to a merchant family, he was the pupil of Joseph-Marie Vien (1716–1809). In 1774 David won the Prix de Rome contest at the Académie Royale and spent October 1775 to July 1780 in Rome. During the 1780s, David created dramatic and didactic paintings on morally elevating subjects such as the *Oath of the Horatii* (1785), a painting about patriotism and the sacrifice of the individual for the good of the nation. Its severe and

Napoleon Crossing the Alps. Painting c. 1801 by Jacques-Louis David, who made the transition from artist of the revolution to iconographer of Napoleon. ©ARCHIVO ICONOGRAFICO, S.A./CORBIS

spare style based on precise draftsmanship and hard-edged subdued colors was later termed neoclassicism. In 1789, shortly after the storming of the Bastille, he exhibited *The Lictors Bringing Brutus the Bodies of His Sons;* the republican nature of Brutus (who rid Rome of the last of its kings, the Tarquins) meant that in following years the painting acquired a political significance that David did not originally intend.

As a liberal David welcomed the promise of social change that the Revolution offered, and from September 1790, when he joined the Jacobin club, he became directly involved in politics. David opposed the privileges and elitism of the Académie Royale and was instrumental in its abolition in 1793. Elected a deputy of the Convention in September 1792, he allied himself closely with the "Mountain" group of Maximilien Robespierre (1758–1794). In 1793 David voted for the death of Louis XVI (r. 1774–1792) and served a term as president of the Convention in January 1794. Most importantly, David devoted his brush to the revo-

lutionary cause and produced paintings that glorified three Republican martyrs, most notably the moving and iconic *Marat at His Last Breath* (1793). Here the radical journalist, assassinated by the moderate Charlotte Corday (1768–1793), was transformed into a saint to inspire revolutionary fervor and patriotism. David also designed and organized great Revolutionary festivals that worked as powerful propaganda instruments to unify the new Republic in celebrations of brotherhood and liberty.

At Robespierre's fall in 1794, David narrowly avoided the guillotine and spent a total of six months in prison, painting a *Self-Portrait* (1794), almost as a defense plea that he was a painter, not a politician. In prison he also started an ambitious history painting *The Intervention of the Sabine Women* (completed 1799), an image of reconciliation as the Sabine women separate the warring factions of their men folk and the Roman soldiers who have come to reclaim their abducted females. The picture also demonstrated a change in painting style from the muscular Roman bodies of the *Horatii* to smoother and more sculptural forms.

After release from prison, David vowed that he would no longer follow men but principles, but quickly came under the spell of Napoleon I (r. 1804–1814/15) whom he first painted early in 1798. Only the head was completed in a three-hour sitting. After Napoleon's coup of Brumaire (10 November 1799), David then painted *Napoleon Crossing the Alps* (1801), "calm on a stormy horse," as a commission from Charles IV of Spain (r. 1788–1808).

After Napoleon's coronation as Emperor of the French in December 1804, David was appointed his First Painter and charged with commemorating the events of the coronation. *The Coronation of Napoleon and Josephine* (also known as *Le Sacre,* 1805–1808) shows Napoleon crowning a kneeling Josephine in Notre Dame and is a glittering panorama of the new imperial court. To capture the splendor of the event, David moved away from his austere neoclassicism and worked in rich and sumptuous colors.

But David was a clumsy imperial courtier and asked for inflated prices for his work, which resulted in commissions being passed to less expensive artists.

His last portrait of Napoleon (1812) was actually commissioned by the Englishman Alexander Douglas (later 10th Duke of Hamilton, 1767–1852). This life-size portrait showed the emperor as both soldier and lawgiver working for the people of France into the early hours of the morning.

After Napoleon's defeat and exile, all regicides were banished and although the restored Bourbon regime offered to let him stay in France, David moved to a frustrating exile in Brussels in 1816. His last large-scale painting, *Mars Disarmed by Venus and the Three Graces* (1824) reveals the unsettling combination of the real and the ideal and the overall effect bordered on parody. At his death in December 1824, David was denied burial in France and an impressive funeral was arranged for him by the Belgian government.

See also **French Revolution; Jacobins; Napoleon; Painting.**

BIBLIOGRAPHY

Bordes, Philippe. *Empire to Exile.* London, 2005.

Brookner, Anita. *Jacques-Louis David.* London, 1980.

Crow, Thomas E. *Painters and Public Life in Eighteenth-Century Paris.* New Haven, Conn., 1985.

David, Jean-Louis Jules. *Le Peintre Louis David, 1748–1825: Souvenirs et documents inédits.* Paris, 1880.

Delécluze, Etienne-Jean. *Louis David, son école et son temps.* Paris, 1855. Reprint, with introduction and notes by Jean-Pierre Mouilleseaux. Paris, 1983.

Lee, Simon. *David.* London, 1999.

Schnapper, Antoine. *David.* Translated by Helga Harrison. New York, 1982.

Schnapper, Antoine, and Arlette Sérullaz. *David 1748–1825.* Paris, 1989. Exhibition catalog.

Vaughan, William, and Helen Weston, eds. *Jacques-Louis David's The Death of Marat.* Cambridge, U.K., 2000.

SIMON LEE

DAVIES, EMILY (1830–1921), English educator.

Any account of nineteenth-century British feminism must place Emily Davies squarely in the center at of it, even though, paradoxically, her political beliefs and social conservatism often put her at odds with much of its agenda. Born into a professional upper-middle-class family, Davies felt acutely her father's refusal to provide her with any of the educational opportunities he afforded her brothers. While they attended elite public schools and Cambridge University, she was refused even the most basic instruction; her strenuous and persistent efforts to open higher education to women, culminating in the founding of Girton College in 1869, derived their inspiration and sustenance from her personal experience of discrimination. She spent the entirety of her adult life campaigning against the societal beliefs and strictures that justified inequality for women on the basis of the so-called natural differences of the sexes, arguing that what society regarded as innate qualities of femininity were no more than mere conventional expectations.

But what we might see as a fairly radical philosophical stance was complicated and constrained by a profound belief in conservative principles: Davies might demand extensive educational and legal reforms for women, but, unlike her coworkers in the struggle for women's rights, she had no wish to transform the society in which she, they, and future generations lived. So strong were her conservative and Conservative principles that when the campaign for votes for women became identified with the Radical wing of the Liberal Party, she removed herself from the London Society for Women's Suffrage. When she rejoined the movement in the 1880s, she dissented from its aims to enfranchise women on the same terms as men; rather, she sought the vote only for single women who met a substantial property qualification. Again, in the early years of the twentieth-century, when the National Union of Women's Suffrage Societies decided upon an affiliation with the Labour Party in order to elect members of Parliament who favored votes for women, Davies resigned from the women's suffrage movement.

Although known primarily for her work to obtain educational opportunities for women, Davies was involved in virtually every aspect of the women's movement from its inception in the 1860s. She became a member of the pioneering Langham Place group in 1862 and took over the editorship of its *English Woman's Journal*; she was a founding member and secretary of the London Women's Suffrage Society; and she spearheaded the effort to gain a medical degree for Elizabeth Garrett Anderson (1836–1917), sister of activist Millicent Garrett Fawcett (1847–1929). Indeed, one biographer argues that Davies *was* the women's movement of the nineteenth century, so central was she to the activities and survival of so many individual organizations. She worked tirelessly behind the scenes, corresponding with people she believed would further the interests of the association she represented, but disavowing any public action or affiliation with any individuals that she feared would bring the causes she supported into disrepute. Here again is the paradox of her politics: involved in a variety of reform efforts that as a whole sought to dramatically change British society, Davies regarded each one as a discrete entity with a particular concrete goal, eschewing any possibility of a larger social or political intent. And, in seeking out prominent people she believed would be influential in furthering her causes, she necessarily found herself dealing with advocates who sought far less extensive reforms than she envisaged. When she sought the support of the Dean of Canterbury, for instance, in gaining admission for girls to the Cambridge Local Examinations, he responded that, though he warmly wished for the expansion of women's education, he could not sign on to an effort that would introduce "anything like *competition* or personal public *designation* into the characteristic of female society in England—believing that any personal eminence would be dearly bought at the sacrifice of that unobtrusiveness, which is at the same time the *charm* and the *strength*, of our English women" (Caine, p. 101).

Such talk was calculated to incense Davies, but she was unable to bring herself to enlist the support of sympathetic people who had any connection with radical or unconventional causes.

Davies's own radical and unconventional belief that the "natural" distinctions drawn between men and women were artificial contrivances informed her most significant achievement—the founding, with Barbara Leigh Bodichon (1827–1891), of Girton College at Cambridge. Davies insisted that the women attending Girton study a curriculum identical to that of the men's colleges; anything less, she believed, would pander to societal notions of weak femininity. She demanded "a fair field and no favor" for women students; the fact that the classical curricula of Cambridge and Oxford were, at that time, under attack by educational reformers swayed her not a bit: no matter how misguided it might be for men, it must be the same for women. Davies sought in an equality of education for women the means by which men and women could act as intellectual and political equals of one another, engage in discussion as equals, learn from and enrich one another as equals. She refused the prescriptions of femininity that painted women as maternal, intrinsically nurturing, unable to withstand the rigors of learning. At the same time, she embraced the conventions that assigned to them particular social roles, insisting that her students behave with decorum in every aspect of their lives, in accordance with the strictures of her class. In this as in so many other ways, her deep-seated conservatism did battle with her radical inclinations, making her a person her coworkers found difficult to work with and a figure historians have found difficult to understand. For all of her centrality to the nineteenth-century women's movement, for all her efforts to make pronounced and profound changes for the way women might conduct their lives, her express unwillingness to advocate for a new world for women and men has left her but a shadow lurking in the recesses of the pantheon of British feminists.

See also **Fawcett, Millicent Garrett; Feminism; Suffragism.**

BIBLIOGRAPHY

Bennett, Daphne. *Emily Davies and the Liberation of Women.* London, 1990.

Bradbrook, Muriel. *"That Infidel Place": A Short History of Girton College.* London, 1969.

Caine, Barbara. *Victorian Feminists.* Oxford, U.K., 1992.

Davies, Emily. *The Higher Education of Women.* London, 1866. Reprint, London, 1988.

Fletcher, Sheila. *Feminists and Bureaucrats: A Study in the Development of Girls' Education in the Nineteenth Century.* Cambridge, U.K., 1980.

Stephen, Barbara. *Emily Davies and Girton College.* London, 1927.

SUSAN KINGSLEY KENT

DEÁK, FERENC

DEÁK, FERENC (also known as Francis Deák; 1803–1876), Hungarian politician and statesman, referred to as the Sage of the Fatherland.

Ferenc Deák was born a Catholic on 17 October 1803 in Söjtör, Zala County, in southwestern Hungary. Members of the medium nobility, his family owned a manor house in neighboring Kehida, where Deák later loved to stay. Having lost his father as a small child, he grew up as a ward of his brother and sister, to both of whom he remained deeply attached. He never married and nothing is known of his private life and passions. He was admired for being patient, kind, charming, witty, cultivated, and exceedingly generous, yet he suffered from bouts of deep depression, which caused him to flee public life periodically. This might explain why he was unable to match the brilliant political success of his contemporary the Hungarian patriot and statesman Lajos Kossuth, at least in revolutionary times.

Deák followed the traditional career of the wealthier rural nobility by studying and practicing law as well as by occupying varying posts in the county administration. His election to the National Diet in 1833 brought him into contact with the political greats, who were often also Hungary's foremost poets, writers, and linguistic innovators. His specialty in those feverish times became judicial reform, indispensable if this semifeudal country was to enter the modern world. In 1842 Deák emancipated his serfs; a year later he withdrew from politics in disgust over a violent and rigged election campaign. Still, he was seen as the leading liberal, and when a bloodless revolution broke out in March 1848, he rejoined his fellow politicians at Pozsony (today Bratislava in Slovakia) where the diet was in session.

Having entered Hungary's first modern constitutional government, appointed by the Habsburg emperor-king on 7 April, Minister of Justice Deák was greatly responsible for the redrawing of the country's laws and for renegotiating Hungary's relations with the dynasty. New Hungary was to be a sovereign state in personal union with the rest of the Habsburg possessions, a proposition that was only temporarily acceptable to the besieged dynasty and the new Austrian liberal government. Also, Hungary's ethnic minorities, who together formed an absolute majority, now demanded the same political rights that Hungarians had achieved in that year. The result was civil war and, in the late fall, war between Austria and Hungary. By year's end, Kossuth was virtual dictator and Deák had withdrawn to his estate.

The defeat of the war of independence in August 1849 caused Kossuth and thousands of others to flee abroad; more than a hundred were executed at home. Deák, however, was not prosecuted and could thus become the unofficial leader of the passive resistance against Austrian absolutism. He reentered politics in 1860 after the emperor-king Francis Joseph (r. 1848–1916) issued the so-called October Diploma, which offered limited constitutional rule to the peoples of the monarchy. Having at first insisted that Hungary be given back the constitution of April 1848, Deák now slowly moved toward a solution that would allow the foreign and the military affairs of the monarchy to be handled by common ministries. But not until after the defeat of the Austrian army by the Prussians in 1866 did the ruler come around to accepting the famous Compromise Agreement of 1867 and the creation of what came to be commonly called Austria-Hungary. In these negotiations, Deák was powerfully assisted by the empress-queen Elizabeth (r. 1854–1898), who was his admirer. The new state, which was founded on the principles of Western-style liberalism, brought emancipation to all religious groups, including the Jews. It was Deák's crowning achievement. He declined to become prime minister and continued to live simply in a Budapest hotel.

The Compromise Agreement and the reform laws of 1868 allowed Hungary to progress economically at a phenomenal pace, but they did not solve the problem either of the landless in a country of vast aristocratic estates or that of relations with the nationalities. For the Slavs and Romanians in the monarchy, the division of powers between Austro-Germans and Hungarians seemed to be directed against them. Lajos Kossuth in exile also strongly condemned the agreement, which, in his prophetic view, tied Hungary's fate to Austria, and through Austria to the German Reich. For others, the ruling "Deák Party" was not sufficiently nationalistic. Disillusioned by parliamentary quarrels, Deák gradually withdrew from politics, dying in Budapest on 28

January 1876. His name stands for the idea of wise compromise with superior powers, be it Germany of World War II, or the Soviet Union following the defeat of the 1956 revolution in Hungary.

See also **Austria-Hungary; Kossuth, Lajos.**

BIBLIOGRAPHY

Deák, Ferenc. *Deák Ferencz: beszédei.* 6 vols. Edited by Manó Kónyi. Budapest, 1903.

———. *Válogatott politikai írások és beszédek.* Edited by András Molnár and Ágnes Deák. Budapest, 2001.

Ferenczi, Zoltán. *Deák élete.* 3 vols. Budapest, 1904.

Király, Béla K. *Ferenc Deák.* Boston, 1975.

ISTVÁN DEÁK

DEATH AND BURIAL. The period from 1789 to 1914 began and ended in experiences of mass death. Deaths took on political significance in a century marked by the expansion of citizenship and movements of national mobilization. The public nature of mass death encouraged the expression of new meanings of death, but demographic, social, and cultural developments throughout the century prompted the emergence of modern ways of dying and dealing with the deaths of others.

Foundational events in the French Revolution were often accompanied by deadly violence, and the experience of the Terror and international warfare in the Revolutionary and Napoleonic eras gave meaning to large numbers of deaths. The coming of World War I brought on another era of political and international bloodletting, but the hundred years' peace between those cataclysmic events saw changes in mortality, in causes of death, in ways of disposing of the dead, and in ways of representing and understanding death.

A fall in European mortality contributed to the demographic transition. Europe-wide figures indicate the general retreat of death, but different age groups, regions, and social classes experienced the transition on different schedules. The biggest changes occurred in infancy and childhood, but even those rates fell differently in different geographic settings. In the 1870s, the worst urban slums had death rates six times worse than those that obtained in the healthiest rural regions. Breastfed infants fared better than the bottle-fed. Industrialization increased working-class mortality rates for a generation or two. Attention to drinking water and sewage resulted in eventual improvements in urban life expectancy. The smallpox vaccine had an impact on childhood mortality in the first half of the nineteenth century; the Pasteurian revolution of the 1870s and 1880s redirected medical attention. Mortality retreated earlier in western and central Europe than in the east and south.

Historians of disease refer to an epidemiological and sanitary transition, as infectious diseases gave way to cardiovascular illnesses and cancer as primary causes of death. The cholera epidemic of the 1830s traumatized urban populations, but public health measures proved effective, and the late experience of Hamburg (which had a final epidemic in 1892) was the exception that proved the rule. Industrial neighborhoods experienced high rates of tuberculosis, but state institutions learned to deal with workplace hazards.

Already in the decades preceding the French Revolution, physicians and urban administrators began paying attention to problems of disposing of the dead. They encouraged the removal of burial grounds from city centers, and in the early nineteenth century, new suburban cemeteries began appearing. Urban growth, including annexation of inner suburbs, eventually incorporated those burial grounds within the city limits, but the result was still the creation of specialized zones for burial and commemoration. Dissenting cemetery companies in England had an impact on burial reform, but Père Lachaise in Paris offered the dominant model. Cemeteries became virtual cities, complete with numbers and addresses for particular plots. The visit to the cemetery became part of the culture of nineteenth-century families.

In some ways it was the general triumph of life over death that gave mortality a new cultural meaning—better prevention may well have made deaths harder to accept—but different historians emphasize different tendencies. Philippe Ariès's overview identifies the passing of the loved one as the great theme of the period. For Ariès, changes in the culture of death indicated the triumph of private life. His remarks concerning the eroticization of death paved the way for more specialized cultural

Death as Victor. Woodcut by Alfred Rethel from *Another Dance of Death*, 1849. Rethel's volume of woodcuts was inspired by the dramatic political turmoil and violence that swept Europe in 1848. The Dance of Death genre in art had developed in the late medieval period and served most often as a comment upon the inevitability of death. Rethel uses the genre here to suggest that whatever the outcome of the political unrest, death was the only true victor. Private Collection/Bridgeman Art Library

studies. Michel Vovelle's work reveals a continuation of eighteenth-century secularization and the emergence of a space for alternative afterlives. Vovelle also reminds us that different populations experienced changes in attitudes toward death at different rhythms, but he still sees the big shift running from religious mentalities and ceremonies to more secular ones. One strand of the historical literature privileges elite culture, such as Romantic fascination with death or fin-de-siècle decadence. Another looks at changes in everyday practices such as mourning rituals, but elite and popular spheres were hardly distinct, as technologies of mass reproduction allowed easy transmission of ideas about death, and consumer culture encouraged the development of the Victorian macabre.

The coming of World War I meant another experience of mass mobilization and politicized death, but deaths in smaller conflicts, such as the Crimean War and the Franco-Prussian War, encouraged democratization of patriotic and public death, and notable deaths throughout the nineteenth century played a role in the development of national identities. Late-nineteenth- and early-twentieth-century concern for suicide and euthanasia also anticipated themes that would emerge in the aftermath of the Great War.

See also **Childhood and Children; Demography; Disease; Old Age; Public Health; Statistics.**

BIBLIOGRAPHY

Anderson, Olive. *Suicide in Victorian and Edwardian England.* Oxford, U.K., 1987.

Ariès, Philippe. *The Hour of Our Death.* Translated by Helen Weaver. New York, 1981.

Bardet, Jean-Pierre, Patrice Bourdelais, Pierre Guillaume, et al. *Peurs et terreurs face à la contagion: Choléra, tuberculose, syphilis: XIXe–XXe siècles.* Paris, 1988.

Bardet, Jean-Pierre, and Jacques Dupâquier, eds. *Histoire des populations de l'Europe.* Vol. 2: *La révolution démographique 1750–1914.* Paris, 1998.

Binion, Rudolph. *Love Beyond Death: The Anatomy of a Myth in the Arts.* New York, 1993.

Burleigh, Michael. *Death and Deliverance: "Euthanasia" in Germany c. 1900–1945.* Cambridge, U.K., 1994.

Evans, Richard J. *Death in Hamburg: Society and Politics in the Cholera Years, 1830–1910.* Oxford, U.K., 1987.

Jalland, Patricia. *Death in the Victorian Family.* New York, 1996.

Jupp, Peter C., and Clare Gittings, eds. *Death in England: An Illustrated History.* Manchester, U.K., 1999.

Jupp, Peter C., and Glennys Howarth, eds. *The Changing Face of Death: Historical Accounts of Death and Disposal.* New York, 1997.

Kselman, Thomas A. *Death and the Afterlife in Modern France.* Princeton, N.J., 1993.

Schofield, Roger, David Reher, and Alain Bideau, eds. *The Decline of Mortality in Europe.* Oxford, U.K., 1991.

Troyansky, David G. "Death." In *Encyclopedia of European Social History*, vol. 2, edited by Peter N. Stearns, 219–233. New York, 2001.

Vovelle, Michel. *La mort et l'Occident: De 1300 à nos jours.* Paris, 1983.

Wolffe, John. *Great Deaths: Grieving, Religion, and Nationhood in Victorian and Edwardian Britain.* Oxford, U.K., 2000.

DAVID G. TROYANSKY

DEBUSSY, CLAUDE (1862–1918), French composer.

Achille-Claude Debussy is widely regarded as the leading proponent of the impressionist movement in music. His novel musical style challenged existing conventions, and his compositions, among them works for solo piano, orchestra, solo voice, and voice with orchestra, evoked the literary and artistic landscapes of fin-de-siècle France.

Debussy entered the Paris Conservatory in 1873 where he studied piano, solfège (a system for sightreading music using syllables [do, re, mi ...]), and, later, composition. A precocious and inquisitive student, Debussy distinguished himself in the classroom and obtained the institution's coveted prizes for his performance in all of his classes. Nevertheless, Debussy quickly established a reputation as an unorthodox pupil who rejected and later renounced pedestrian, textbook rules. His attitude toward traditional teaching marked him as a maverick, one whose revolutionary ideas confounded his fellow students and angered the conservatory's conservative teachers. Debussy became known for his tirades against accepted rules for harmony, and his own novel harmonies. In particular, his use of parallel fifths and octaves, and chords of the seventh and ninth resolved "incorrectly" or not at all, bewildered his colleagues. It was astonishing that this young, rogue composer won the Prix de Rome, the most sought-after prize in composition in France, in 1884. Debussy's first-prize–winning cantata, *L'enfant prodigue*, was the clear favorite among Prix de Rome judges. Critics extolled Debussy as a young musician of talent and pointed to the outstanding individuality of his work. Debussy, on the other hand, was unmoved by his achievement and came to resent the popular success of this composition. In later years Debussy repudiated the entire Prix de Rome competition, writing that "it is a purely arbitrary affair, without any significance as regards the future" (Vallas, 1973, p. 29).

Debussy's disdain of the Prix de Rome was emblematic of his contempt for all competition as well as his refusal to align himself with any one school of compositional thought. He believed that musicians must be detached from every school, since the "enthusiasm of a circle spoils an artist" (Vallas, 1967, p. 18). This belief—that an artist must have free rein over his ideas and a distinctive style—were the hallmarks of Debussy's conception of musical artistry. Debussy voiced his "no rules" credo repeatedly in his writing, affirming it vehemently to distinguish his thinking from that of the pedants and intelligentsia. He wrote: "To some people, rules are of primary importance. I love music passionately, and because I love it, I try to free it from barren traditions that stifle it. It must never be shut in and become an academic art" (Vallas, 1967, p. 10). This refusal to adhere to rules was the guiding light for his mature compositional style and for the innovations for which he was noted throughout the early twentieth century.

Debussy was a prolific composer who wrote in a variety of musical styles. He is widely known for his orchestral work and compositions for solo piano. They contain the understatement characteristic of the leading symbolist writers of the late nineteenth and early twentieth centuries, among them Stéphane Mallarmé and Maurice Maeterlinck. Although Debussy's designation as an "impressionist composer" is the subject of some debate, most of his mature work, that dating from the early 1900s, is marked by atmospheric suggestion and was intended to sound improvisatory. Indeed, the names of some of his compositions are directly inspired from the world of art, including *Images* and *Estampes*. These mature compositions feature the musical characteristics for which Debussy is best known: whole-tone scales, parallel fifths, unprepared and unresolved seventh and ninth chords, and, above all, an extraordinary mastery of orchestral color.

Debussy's first important orchestral work, *Prélude à l'après-midi d'un faune* (1894; *Prelude to the Afternoon of a Faun*), captures the words and imagery of Mallarmé's poem *L'après-midi d'un faune* as it evokes, according to Debussy, the successive scenes of the faun's desires and dreams on a steamy afternoon. In this work, the traditional symmetry of classical symphonies gives way to fragmentary treatment of the thematic material, introduced by the flute and other woodwinds, and the instrumentation showcases the various and unique colors, or timbres, of the orchestral families. Debussy's opera *Pelléas et Mélisande* (1902) broke new ground in its treatment of form, melody, and harmony. It also resulted in endless debate between opposing schools of compositional thought, foremost among which were the "d'Indyists," whose sensibilities lay with French composer Vincent d'Indy and his Schola Cantorum, and the "Debussyists," who championed the ideology of the composer who, ironically, rejected ideological factions and discourse. In *La mer*, three orchestral sketches completed in 1905, Debussy gave full rein to the timbral palette of the orchestra. Critics either lauded Debussy for his inventiveness and master-

ful use of "shimmering" color or they assailed the work for not being a felicitous representation of the sea.

See also **France; Impressionism; Music.**

BIBLIOGRAPHY

Primary Sources

Debussy, Claude. *Debussy on Music: The Critical Writings of the Great French Composer Claude Debussy.* Collected and introduced by François Lesure. Translated and edited by Richard Langham Smith. New York, 1977.

Secondary Sources

Fulcher, Jane F., ed. *Debussy and His World.* Princeton, N.J., 2001.

Nichols, Roger. *The Life of Debussy.* Cambridge, U.K., 1998.

Vallas, Léon. *The Theories of Claude Debussy, musicien français.* Translated by Maire O'Brien. New York, 1967.

———. *Claude Debussy: His Life and Works.* Translated by Maire and Grace O'Brien. New York, 1973.

GAIL HILSON WOLDU

DECADENCE. *Decadence* was an artistic current that flourished in Europe at the turn of the century, primarily in France and Britain; it was most often expressed in prose, but also influenced poetry and the visual arts. As the name suggests, Decadent art of the 1880s and 1890s was associated with the discourse of cultural pessimism that had been developing among European intellectuals since the late eighteenth century and that had only become intensified by the more specific discourse of "Degeneration" during the fin de siècle. Cultural pessimists of the early to mid-nineteenth century had identified many sources of political, social, cultural, and spiritual decline in European civilization. These ranged from the assault on nature by the Industrial Revolution, the threat to traditional forms of society represented by the French Revolution, the challenge to the concept of a rational and autonomous human agency adumbrated by the philosophy of Arthur Schopenhauer (1788–1860), the rebuke to the Enlightenment idea of progress embodied by the Second Law of Thermodynamics, and the undermining of revealed religion and the anthropocentric cosmos heralded by the theory of evolution advanced by Charles Darwin (1809–1882).

By the late nineteenth century, the idea that modernity signified a decline rather than an advance had been given memorable expression by the German journalist Max Nordau (1849–1923) in his widely translated *Entartung* (1892; Degeneration). Nordau specifically targeted modern artists as emblematically degenerate figures, physically damaged from the enervating effects of urban life and mentally deranged by the excessive introspection encouraged by a psychologizing age. Artists themselves addressed the themes of decline and degeneration: as early as the 1830s, French Aesthetes advocated a turn away from life to "art for art's sake," whereas the naturalists of the fin de siècle dispassionately charted the stunted lives of those afflicted adversely by their heredity and environment.

The Decadent artists of the 1880s and 1890s combined the Aesthetes' preference for art over life with the naturalists' unstinting depictions of decline, disgrace, and desolation. But they did not just reflect the discourse of degeneration in their works: they also responded to it by celebrating the perverse. They turned the idea of decadence into a productive aesthetic sensibility, one that paradoxically became more vivid and alive as it embraced decay and death. Their works often chronicled the hypertrophy of the senses experienced by the truly perceptive in the face of modern flux and change; as well as the ennui suffered by the gifted trapped in a bourgeois world that extolled soulless productivity. The Decadents also accepted willingly their allotted role as afflicted martyrs in the service of art, gleefully describing the heterodox practices and aristocratic prejudices that set the artist apart from the leveling tendencies of the age. Decadent works often celebrated deviant sexualities and amoral behaviors as deliberate affronts to middle-class morality and looked back nostalgically to periods in which aristocratic taste and refined pleasures were not overshadowed by populist prejudices.

Like the early Romantics, Decadent artists turned to art as a source of transcendence in a secularizing age, but unlike the Romantics they did not believe that art expressed some underlying spiritual force that could reconcile the human mind with external nature. For such "late romantics" as the Decadents, nature as revealed by contemporary science was as ugly and bereft of spiritual significance as modern civilization; transcendence could only be found through the deliberate artifice represented by art. In consequence, Decadent literature privileged a finely wrought and ironic style, one that flaunted its artificiality and was tailored to express exquisite perceptions that would transport the reader out of the ordinary world into a baroque world of the imagination. With few exceptions, Decadent artists tended to be male, and Decadent works tended to be misogynistic: women were often depicted as prisoners of organic nature, alluring "femme fatales" who could not resist their instinct to reduce men to their fallen level. Conversely, the "unnatural" in all its guises—art, homosexuality, supernatural or scientific creations, altered states of consciousness—was a dominant concern in Decadent works.

Decadence as a literary current emerged in its most characteristic form in France. There were a host of factors that prompted public discussion of degeneration, including France's humiliating defeat in the Franco-Prussian War of 1870–1871; statistics revealing that birthrates were declining and suicides increasing; an upsurge of labor unrest and feminist agitation; lurid media depictions of the spread of syphilis and the recourse to crime, drugs, alcohol, prostitution, and homosexuality. Writers such as Gustave Flaubert (1821–1880), Charles Baudelaire (1821–1867), and Arthur Rimbaud (1854–1891) had demonstrated that such insalubrious facts could be both transmuted and transcended by making them the subject of art, and in 1886 Anatole Baju (1861–?) provided a label for this literary trend by publishing *Le Déca-dent,* a literary journal that continued through 1889. The public image of Decadence was given its most forceful expression in *À Rebours* (1884) by Joris-Karl Huysmans (1848–1907), which the contemporary English critic Arthur Symons (1865–1945) called "the breviary of Decadence" and Oscar Wilde (1854–1900) chose as the book that contributed to the corruption of Dorian Gray. Its aristocratic protagonist, Des Esseintes, repudiates the natural and social worlds by retreating into a self-created world of the most refined sensory pleasures. Among other notable artists deemed

"Decadent" by themselves or by others were Jean Lorraine (1855–1906, the pseudonym of Paul Duval), Jules-Amedee Barbey d'Aurevilly (1808–1889), Rachilde (1860–1953, the pseudonym of Marguerite Eymery Vallette, one of the few women identified with the Decadents), Joséphin Péladan (1858–1918), Jean Moréas (1856–1910; the pseudonym of Yannis Papadiamantopoulos), Villiers de l'Isle-Adam (1838–1889), and Octave Mirbeau (1850–1917).

The Decadent current in Britain was influenced by France—Wilde was a frequent visitor to Paris and served as an important intermediary—but it tended to be more conservative than its French counterpart. British artists, unlike the French, found it hard to separate the values of art and society: the aestheticism of the Pre-Raphaelites, for example, was associated with a medieval moral and spiritual order, and Walter Pater (1839–1894) came to regret his famous aestheticist injunction "To burn always with this hard, gem-like flame" because he feared misleading impressionable readers. Wilde's own decadent aperçus were paradoxical expressions delivered with such irony that they did not really threaten, and in his essay "The Soul of Man under Socialism" he continued to link art with social policies. Wilde's most "decadent" work, the play *Salomé* (1894), had a negligible impact in England, partly because he originally wrote it in French, and partly because it was banned from the London stage by the Lord Chancellor. Decadence in England tended toward the risqué rather than the perverse, although it did approach the latter in the sinuously erotic drawings of Aubrey Beardsley (1872–1898) for the Decadent periodical *Yellow Book*, published between 1894 and 1897. It was only when Wilde was convicted of homosexuality in 1895 that *Decadence* in England rapidly moved in public perception from the risqué to the perverse—and, as a matter of policy, the suppressed. Many jettisoned the term that Wilde's conviction had brought into opprobrium, embracing the term *symbolism* in its place: most notably when Symons's 1899 survey of recent artistic trends was retitled from *The Decadent Movement in Literature* to *The Symbolist Movement in Literature*. Nevertheless, there were English writers whose Decadent works approximated that of their French peers, among them Count Eric Stenbock (1859–1895), R. Murray Gilchrist (1868–1917), and M. P. Shiel (1865–1947).

While France and Britain were the most visible founts of the Decadent current, other European nations served as tributaries. In Russia, Vsevolod Garshin (1855–1888) and Leonid Andreyev (1871–1919) produced works classified as Decadent, as did Gabriele D'Annunzio (1863–1938) in Italy, and Frank Wedekind (1864–1918) and Hans Heinz Ewers (1871–1943) in Germany. Decadence was a symptomatic expression of the concerns of the fin de siècle, and dissipated in the early decades of the new century. But its preoccupations with the beauty of the perverse and the autonomy of imaginary worlds continued to influence cultural expressions through the twentieth century.

See also **Baudelaire, Charles; Beardsley, Aubrey; Degeneration; Homosexuality and Lesbianism; Huysmans, Joris-Karl; Prostitution; Wilde, Oscar.**

BIBLIOGRAPHY

Hustvedt, Asti, ed. *The Decadent Reader: Fiction, Fantasy, and Perversion from Fin-de-siècle France*. New York, 1998.

Pierrot, Jean. *The Decadent Imagination 1880–1900*. Translated by Derek Coltman. Chicago, 1981.

Showalter, Elaine, ed. *Daughters of Decadence: Women Writers of the Fin-de-siècle*. New Brunswick, N.J., 1993.

Weir, David. *Decadence and the Making of Modernism*. Amherst, Mass., 1995.

MICHAEL SALER

DEGAS, EDGAR (1834–1917), French painter, sculptor, and printmaker.

Hilaire-Germain-Edgar Degas is probably best known for images of ballet dancers and the multimedia sculpture, *The Little Dancer Aged Fourteen* (1879–1881). This popular image, however, overlooks the formidable output of an artist who worked in multiple media, ranging from oils to prints to photographs, and who had an active career from the 1860s to 1912. An examination of Degas's paintings, drawings, prints, photographs, and sculptures reveals favorite themes and subjects—ballet dancers, portraits of contemporaries, washerwomen, women bathing, female nudes, café scenes, and equestrian pictures, particularly images of jockeys and horse races. Degas was born and remained a Parisian, and his art reflected the vibrant life of his Parisian milieu.

Edgar Degas was born in Paris on 19 July 1834 into a comfortable and cultured family. He attended the prestigious Lycée Louis-le-Grand and received a classical education. To study painting, he enrolled in the École des Beaux-Arts (1855–1856), where he studied with Louis Lamothe (1822–1869), once a pupil of Jean-Auguste-Dominique Ingres (1780–1867), whom Degas met and greatly admired. In French painting of the first half of the nineteenth century, Ingres was considered the champion of drawing and the line, whereas Eugène Delacroix (1798–1863), whom Degas equally regarded, was viewed as the master of color. After a year of schooling, Degas departed for a three-year sojourn in Italy, where he had relatives. Living and traveling in Naples, Rome, Florence, and other Italian locales, he studied and copied the Italian masters, including Giotto (1266/1267 or 1276–1337), Michelangelo (1475–1564), and Leonardo da Vinci (1452–1519), among others. Degas's training in art was thus rooted in the traditions of the old masters.

Back in Paris in 1859, Degas sought to establish himself as an artist by exhibiting at the official Salon. He exhibited twice, showing, for example, *The Steeplechase* in 1866, but found himself dissatisfied with his efforts at producing the type of grand historical paintings favored by the Salon's judges. Nevertheless, he produced a number of such works, including *Young Spartans Exercising* (c. 1860). During the 1860s, Degas gradually shifted the subjects of his art to contemporary Parisian scenes, and he painted horse racing, portraits of contemporaries, and ballet dancers. His circle of friends and acquaintances included realists, like the novelist and art critic Émile Zola (1840–1902), and independent artists associated with the Café Guerbois, like Édouard Manet (1832–1883), Pierre-Auguste Renoir (1841–1919), Camille Pissarro (1830–1903), and others. Despite his association with these future impressionists, with whom he would also exhibit, Degas preferred to work in the studio using drawings, and not out of doors.

After serving in the National Guard during the Paris Commune, Degas traveled to New Orleans, where he painted the celebrated *Cotton Market at New Orleans* (1873). Back in Paris, Degas showed ten works at the first Impressionist Exhibition (1874), including *Carriage at the Races* (c. 1872). He later exhibited at all of the Impressionist Exhibitions, except the seventh (1882). His celebrated and controversial *The Little Dancer Aged Fourteen* was shown at the sixth Exhibition (1881) and the female nudes shown at the Eighth Exhibition sparked adverse comments. Unlike the works of most of the impressionists, Degas's paintings and drawings, often images of contemporary Parisian life, became popular and they sold.

Two themes dominate Degas's life in the 1880s. His paintings, prints, and drawings tend to focus more on women, particularly ballet dancers, cabaret singers, and working women. There are also numerous views of nude or seminude women bathing or at the toilette, in which the focus is the human form, often depicted from unusual angles. Second, Degas expanded his own collection of art, which ultimately included not only his own works but also works by old masters like El Greco (Doménikos Theotokópoulos; 1541–1614) and contemporaries like Manet and Paul Gauguin (1848–1903). He also collected works by Ingres and Delacroix. Degas's works continued to sell, and he patronized noted dealers like Paul Durand-Ruel (1831–1922) and Ambroise Vollard (1865–1939).

Changes in Degas's style became evident during the last of his working years. His use of color became bolder and his figures less realistic, as is evident in *Fallen Jockey* (c. 1896–1898). Some historians attribute this shift to Degas's failing eyesight, while others point to the influence of Gauguin and other artists. Furthermore, the Dreyfus affair had an impact on Degas's life. Because he took a position against Dreyfus, he lost many friends, especially those who were Jewish, and the size of his social world declined. In 1912, because of continued problems with his eyesight and failing health, he ceased working. He died on 27 September 1917 in Paris and is buried in Montmartre Cemetery in Paris.

Degas's reputation has fluctuated. At the height of his career in the 1870s and 1880s, he

Three Dancers in a Diagonal Line on the Stage. Pastel by Edgar Degas c. 1882. Private Collection/Bridgeman Art Library/
Lefevre Fine Art Ltd., London

was considered a realist or naturalist, one who successfully depicted the essence of contemporary Parisian life. Some, however, objected to his female nudes and complained that the models were unattractive. Nonetheless, works by Degas were sold to collectors and museums, and he avoided the poverty endured by many of his contemporary impressionists. At his death, the Parisian art world was amazed at the size and richness of his art collection. The late twentieth century brought renewed interest in Degas. Catalogs of his works have appeared, his letters and notebooks have been published, and several major exhibitions have taken place. A considerable body of scholarship has focused on his representations of women, and his overall career has been undergoing a major reassessment by scholars such as Richard Kendall.

See also **Dreyfus Affair; Impressionism; Manet, Édouard; Monet, Claude; Pissarro, Camille; Renoir, Pierre-Auguste; Zola, Émile.**

BIBLIOGRAPHY

Primary Sources

Degas, Edgar. *Degas by Himself: Drawings, Prints, Paintings, Writings.* Edited by Richard Kendall. Boston, 1987. Lavishly illustrated selection of writings by Degas and his contemporaries.

Secondary Sources

Boggs, Jean Sutherland, et al. *Degas.* New York and Ottawa, 1988. Exhibition catalog, with chronologies and a bibliography.

Kendall, Richard. *Degas: Beyond Impressionism.* London and New Haven, Conn., 1996. Well-illustrated study of Degas's later years.

McMullen, Roy. *Degas: His Life, Times, and Work.* London, 1985. A comprehensive biography.

ROBERT W. BROWN

DEGENERATION. During the later nineteenth century, the term *degenerate* became an influential medicopsychiatric and criminological description that was often applied to inmates of prisons and mental asylums. *Degeneration* also came to be inflated into a general cultural epithet that was, in turn, adopted (more or less seriously) by a plethora of "naturalist" and "decadent" writers, artists, and critics. Juxtaposed with concepts of regeneration, purification, fitness, and so forth, the language of degeneration entered significantly into racial thought (most notoriously into anti-Semitism), and was also assimilated to varying degrees across the range of the human sciences. Sometimes the label *degenerate* was used with anti-aristocratic innuendo, but most importantly it was taken to refer to specific subgroups among the socially disadvantaged, the casual poor, or new immigrants, the "residuum" and "outcast" of the cities (or sometimes remote "uncivilized" rural hinterlands), the white or black "trash" so often conjured in American hereditarian thought.

The cluster of distinguishable but interconnected beliefs now referred to under headings such as "the new scientific racism," "eugenics," "social Darwinism," and "degenerationism" provided new positivist rationalizations of much older social anxieties, hatreds, prejudices, and hierarchies. But Victorian theories of evolution and degeneration also reshaped in powerful ways the understanding of the self and society, international relations, laws, and institutions. Increasingly the notion of "degeneration" became enmeshed with the great English naturalist Charles Darwin's famous account of how evolution occurred through natural selection. Many alarmist writings appeared during the final Victorian years to describe the reversal of evolutionary "improvement" and to predict imminent social and political collapse. Biological and social concerns converged, for instance, in a book by an English zoologist, Edwin Ray Lankester, *Degeneration: A Chapter in Darwinism* (1880). Here, the problem of thriving "parasites" was taken to be a significant sociopolitical *and* scientific concern. Titles such as *Degeneration amongst Londoners* (1885) or *Evolution by Atrophy in Biology and Sociology* (1899) typified significant intellectual tendencies across fin-de-siècle Europe. Labels and diagnoses of "dégénérescence" multiplied still further in Charles Samson Féré's series of works on criminality, pathological emotions, and neuropathic families, and in the Viennese physician Richard von Krafft-Ebing's frequently reissued *Psychopathia Sexualis* (1886).

In this extensive literature, the source of fear fluctuated: degeneration might be glimpsed in imperial overreach or excessive political timidity, in war or in peace, in population increase or decline (depending on the national context or cultural moment). Meanwhile the shadowy figure of the brute or overly sophisticated "degenerate" flitted back and forth between the peripheries of empire and the heart of the metropolis. The widely regarded founding text of degenerationism—the French doctor Bénédict Augustin Morel's *Traité des dégénérescences physiques, intellectuelles, et morales de l'espèce humaine* (Treatise on physical, intellectual, and moral degeneracy in the human species)—appeared in 1857, prior to, and independently of, Darwin's own landmark publication, *The Origin of Species* (1859). Nonetheless, many readers of Darwin's work feared that he had been overoptimistic in assuming that fecundity was tantamount to fitness. This was the issue that increasingly exercised Darwin's cousin, Francis Galton, who coined the term *eugenics* in 1883 to describe a potential science of selective breeding that would produce an improvement of "the race." Galton urged the necessity of a series of "positive" and "negative" measures to shape future human reproduction—encouraging "the fit" to have babies and discouraging or preventing "the unfit" from doing so. As Galton had contemplated the differential birthrate between the working and middle classes in Britain, he foresaw a growing biological and political crisis. Darwin considered Galton's early work on heredity "admirable," but one can only speculate on whether he would have considered equally praiseworthy Galton's successful endeavor to establishing a eugenics movement in Edwardian Britain.

KEY TEXTS

While the theme of degeneration had already found expression in ancient times and arguments for racial "decline and fall" are also culturally widespread, the specific ensemble of scientific ideas at stake in the present discussion was decisively formulated and developed in and beyond the 1850s. It is true that Enlightenment naturalists such as Georges-Louis Leclerc de Buffon had used the term *degeneration* in the eighteenth century to describe the effect upon the body of migration to distant lands and to account for racial variations, but Morel's endeavor added quite new connotations of anxiety to Buffon's relatively cool description and gave the debate an intense urgency. Morel's theory can partly be understood as an attempt to bolster the

status of an emerging subspecialty of medicine—psychiatry—at a time when its authority and funding were seriously in question during the Second Empire (1852–1870) of Napoleon III. But the *Traité* was far more than a manifesto to promote the interests of a professional "vested interest." Rather, it pulled together into a compelling narrative diverse fears about madness, crime, political upheaval, inheritance, and death.

Morel's thesis was broadly Lamarckian in flavor—it assumed the inheritance of acquired characteristics. Importantly, Morel sought to demonstrate how a certain tendency to pathology might be transmitted through the family line: illnesses hitherto considered discrete were now linked together, understood as different forms of the same underlying disorder. Morel believed that degenerate families became sterile in a few generations, but some significant later commentators took issue with his reassuring expectation of extinction within degenerate lines. During the period of the Third Republic (1870–1940), the celebrated French psychiatrist Valentin Magnan further developed Morel's pioneering work, elaborating the technical vocabulary and removing the most conspicuous traces of Morel's Catholicism in which degeneration was seen in terms of sin and "the fall."

No single degenerationist text, Morel's included, produced shock waves—or a clash with orthodox religion—quite on the scale of Darwin's *Origin,* but the argument and themes of the *Traité* certainly did have enduring importance within social and scientific thought for the remainder of the century, and beyond. Ideas about degeneracy powerfully informed a new tradition of thought on crime and punishment, which challenged assumptions about free will and thus brought it into conflict with the traditional views of human responsibility deployed by lawyers and churchmen. What came to be known in the later nineteenth century as "positivist" criminology involved a rejection of so-called classical penology. The latter approach—developed by the influential Italian philosopher Cesare Beccaria (author of a famous treatise on crimes and punishments of 1764) and the great early-nineteenth-century English "utilitarian" systematizer Jeremy Bentham—was committed to viewing each subject as a potentially reasonable being, who could calculate right and wrong and the personal price to be paid in the event of social transgression.

In the work of the important Italian doctor and psychiatrist Cesare Lombroso, it seemed obvious that at least some criminals were functioning at a far lower stage of evolution and had no real understanding of their actions. Lombroso became the best-known pioneer of the new "positivist" approach, which he also described as "criminal anthropology." He referred to criminals as "atavistic" (from *atavus*, Latin for ancestor) and doubted that such creatures could calculate rationally for themselves; they had either regressed from, or not fully evolved to, the standards and mental capacities of the civilized and should thus be segregated or even eliminated altogether for the sake of progress in the newly unified Italian nation. If Lombroso's brigands and other assorted villains were cast as spectacularly monstrous (with handle-shaped ears, hairy faces, thick skins, etc.), others feared less visible forms of social morbidity, suspecting the presence of mutations and lesions inside the offender's body. Lombroso's works, such as *L'uomo delinquente* (1876; *Criminal Man*, 1911), were always controversial but lay at the center of international debate about the nature of the criminal for several decades. At major international congresses held in European capitals in and beyond the 1880s, the so-called Italian School and its swelling band of critics engaged in fierce and animated discussion concerning the balance of "nature and nurture" (to borrow Galton's phrase), the sources of recidivism, and the consequences of the pathological milieu.

In psychiatry, criminology, and, later, sexology, degeneration always implied a condition of attenuated will, if not total moral helplessness: degenerates were more or less enslaved by their organic state, the "tyranny of their organisation," as one specialist, the Victorian doctor Henry Maudsley, memorably declared. Not all commentators favored interpretations as pessimistic as those expressed in the later work of Maudsley (from *Body and Will* [1883] to *Organic to Human* [1916]), nor solutions to crime problems as draconian as Lombroso's, but these basic ideas and models were extensively developed on both sides of the Atlantic. Detailed genealogical case studies of families in the United States—*"The Jukes": A Study in Crime, Pauperism,*

Disease, and Heredity (1877) was the best known—appeared to confirm the inherited nature of anti-social behavior. Readers of Émile Zola's contemporaneous cycle of novels on the degeneration of the Rougon-Macquart family would not have been surprised by such gloomy American conclusions.

Degeneration was used to comprehend a bewildering range of physical, mental, and sexual conditions. Not infrequently, medical certificates of this period would begin "dégénérescence mentale avec ..." (mental degeneracy with ...). But solemn claims for the scientific validity of the word sat uneasily with its actual variability of use. It was, however, this very plasticity that had made it so durable a concept, albeit one subject to an increasingly powerful critique by the 1890s. If it first implied a "falling away from an ideal type" (however defined), it quickly came to cover a multitude of inherited ailments and sins, and had the potential to implicate the loftiest prince as well as the most downtrodden pauper.

Precisely because of its discursive ambiguity, it could be deployed as a term by scientists, artists, and novelists of varying political sympathies. Excessive appetite for literature on degeneration itself sometimes led to diagnoses of moral morbidity. In criticism of the so-called Decadent literary mood of the fin de siècle, Max Nordau, the physician and Hungarian émigré to Paris (better known perhaps as a key figure in the early history of Zionism), caused a stir in 1892 by publishing his outrageous compendium, *Entartung* (Degeneration), in which many illustrious writers were severely condemned.

Some of Nordau's critics flippantly accused him of being degenerate himself, but the arcane nomenclature showed no sign of abating. The stories of, among others, Guy de Maupassant, Joris-Karl Huysmans, Zola, and Joseph Conrad; the paintings of James Ensor; the racial commentaries and grand musical ambitions of Richard Wagner; the dramas of Henrik Ibsen; the philosophy of William James and Friedrich Nietzsche—all these works cannot be explained away through "degenerationism," but they were nonetheless powerfully informed by these concerns, as were many of the works of early-twentieth-century modernism.

The pioneer of psychoanalysis, Sigmund Freud, was also deeply intrigued by—and increasingly skeptical of—such hereditarian models, particularly as associated with the "Napoleon of the Neuroses" who had initially so inspired him, the great French neurologist Jean-Martin Charcot. But perhaps no fin-de-siècle appropriation of degenerationist classifications has more poignancy than Oscar Wilde's reference to the theme in a letter to the English home secretary. Jailed in England in 1895 as a homosexual, under the Criminal Law Amendment Act of the previous decade, Wilde sought clemency on the declared grounds that he was indeed a degenerate and therefore worthy of treatment rather than punishment. He cited Nordau's and Lombroso's views of "the petitioner" himself and remarked of his own sexual behavior: "Such offences are forms of sexual madness."

More important than the sheer quantity of degenerationist jeremiads was their shared acceptance of natural scientific authority. In this approach, the fate of the individual and/or the ups and downs of Western society at large were no longer discussed primarily as religious, philosophical, or ethical problems, but as the precise outcome of physical conditions and organic processes.

INFLUENCE IN THE POST–WORLD WAR I ERA
During World War I (1914–1918), propagandists on each side of the conflict accused the other nation of suffering from racial degeneracy. The theme of degeneration can be traced beyond 1918, not only with regard to psychiatric and cultural diagnosis but also in terms of national self-definitions and the concern with eugenic purity. The Nazi sterilization laws of the 1930s were in part shaped by much earlier debates in German eugenics, but also, crucially, reflected and grotesquely extended broader European thought on race and degeneration, not to mention specific legislation introduced in various American states during the early decades of the twentieth century. Nowhere was the inseparability of such cant medicomoral terminology more ominously portrayed in the twentieth century than in Nazi cultural political rhetoric itself, even before the full horrors of Nazi racial policy had emerged. The "Degenerate Art" exhibition in Munich in 1937 was, among other things, a gruesome legacy of the form of cultural criticism pioneered in different circumstances at the fin de siècle. The display was paralleled by an exhibition of approved German work. Although the history of the Third Reich and the "final solution" inevitably shadows one's reading of the nineteenth-century literature, it is important to recognize the quite different contexts in which degenerationist thought had originally been formulated, as well as the political and scientific ambiguity of this field of investigation, at least until World War I and well into the 1930s. It is only in the light of the Holocaust that the language of degeneration and eugenics has come to be so widely excoriated in Western culture, and exorcised from mainstream political discourse, although not so completely even then, as has sometimes been supposed. To assume that it is extinct, or that it has always been a function of an exclusively German tradition, would involve a powerful and dangerous cultural amnesia.

See also **Body; Civilization, Concept of; Eugenics; Imperialism; Public Health.**

BIBLIOGRAPHY

Ascheim, Steven E. "Max Nordau, Friedrich Nietzsche, and Degeneration." *Journal of Contemporary History* 28, no. 4 (1993): 643–657.

Barron, Stephanie, ed. *Degenerate Art: The Fate of the Avant-Garde in Nazi Germany.* Los Angeles and New York, 1991.

Chamberlin, J. Edward, and Sander L. Gilman, eds. *Degeneration: The Dark Side of Progress.* New York, 1985.

Childs, Donald J. *Modernism and Eugenics: Woolf, Eliot, Yeats, and the Culture of Degeneration.* Cambridge, U.K., 2001.

Greenslade, William. *Degeneration, Culture, and the Novel, 1880–1940.* Cambridge, U.K., 1994.

Hurley, Kelly. *The Gothic Body, Sexuality, Materialism, and Degeneration at the Fin de Siècle.* Cambridge, U.K., 1996.

Kevles, Daniel. *In the Name of Eugenics: Genetics and the Uses of Human Heredity.* New York, 1985.

Neve, Michael R. "The Influence of Degenerationist Categories in Nineteenth-Century Psychiatry, with Special Reference to Great Britain." In *The History of Psychiatric Diagnoses: Proceedings of the 16th International Symposium on the Comparative History of Medicine—East and West,* edited by Yosio Kawakita, Shizu Sakai, and Yasuo Otsuka. Tokyo, 1997.

Nordau, Max. *Degeneration.* 1895. Reprint, translated from the second edition of the German work, with an introduction by George L. Mosse. Lincoln, Nebr., 1993.

Pick, Daniel. *Faces of Degeneration: A European Disorder, c. 1848–c. 1918*. Cambridge, U.K., 1989.

Traverso, Enzo. *The Origins of Nazi Violence*. Translated by Janet Lloyd. New York, 2003. Translation of *La violence nazie: Une généalogie européene*.

DANIEL PICK

DELACROIX, EUGÈNE (1798–1863), French painter.

Ferdinand-Eugène-Victor Delacroix was a leader of the Romantic movement in the visual arts and, by the second half of the nineteenth century, its quintessential embodiment. Despite his reputation as an iconoclastic modern artist, Delacroix grew increasingly disillusioned with modernity and saw himself as a continuator of the great tradition of history painting begun in the Renaissance. In his later life he was widely perceived as an opponent of tradition and classicism, and an antagonist to Jean-Auguste-Dominique Ingres, but in fact he was the last great monumental French painter working in the grand manner.

Delacroix was the son of Charles Delacroix, a government administrator, and Victoire Oeben, the daughter of a successful cabinetmaker. It was rumored that his biological father was the prominent statesman Charles-Maurice de Talleyrand, whom Delacroix strongly resembled. Delacroix distinguished himself as a student at the prominent Lycée imperial (now Louis le Grand) before entering the studio of Pierre-Narcisse Guérin to train as a painter. There he was particularly influenced by Théodore Géricault. While still a student he produced a number of prints that reveal his early attraction to Liberal politics.

Delacroix was a great admirer of literature and exhibited a precocious taste for Romantic writers (Goethe, Byron, and Sir Walter Scott) and those literary figures of the past whom they admired (especially Shakespeare and Dante). His first submission to the Salon, the major biennial art exhibition in Paris, was *Dante's Barque* (1822), which combined these newly fashionable literary tastes with an eclectic mix of sources from classical sculpture, Michelangelo, Antoine-Jean Gros, and Géricault, and won the artist considerable acclaim when it was purchased by the government.

For the next two Salons, Delacroix submitted paintings treating the Greek War of Independence (1821–1832). The Greek cause was championed by Liberals and other parties opposed to the Restoration government of Charles X, who favored the Ottoman Turks in the struggle. While Delacroix's paintings protested the suffering of the Greeks at the hands of the Turks, they also revealed a morbid fascination with cruelty, rape, and miscegenation. In the 1820s he painted numerous pictures of violent subjects drawn from Romantic literature and France's medieval past. His penchant for images of gratuitous death and destruction found full expression in *The Death of Sardanapalus* (1827), which depicted the last Assyrian king immolating himself, his concubines, chattel, and riches on an enormous pyre, rather than let them pass to the conquering Medes. The painting's dynamic composition, rich palette of reds and gold, and painterly bravura, combined with the outrageous subject, placed Delacroix at the center of the Romantic rebellion against official art.

The Revolution of 1830 renewed Delacroix's overt engagement with domestic politics and inspired his most famous work, *Liberty Guiding the People* (1830). Delacroix pictured the violent insurrection that brought down Charles X through the image of a group of revolutionaries rushing across a barricade near the Pont d'Arcole in Paris. The revolutionaries, who rise up so heroically underneath the tricolor flag, include workers and street urchins, but also a bourgeois and members of both sexes, suggesting broad support for the July Revolution. In approaching the work, Delacroix was torn between, on the one hand, the high moral purpose and universality conveyed through classical nude figures and, on the other, the drama and specificity of a realistic portrayal of contemporary events. The central woman ingeniously combines idealized, allegorical elements (nudity and Phrygian cap) with the unidealized dress of a working-class woman. Her profiled head and raised arm have the flatness and simplicity of an emblem, while the sculptural form of the rest of her body joins her to the real world of historical events. The painting was well received, and the new government purchased the picture and awarded Delacroix the Legion of Honor.

Self-portrait by Eugène Delacroix, 1840. ALINARI/ART RESOURCE, NY

In 1832 Delacroix traveled with a diplomatic mission to convince the sultan of Morocco to acquiesce to the French occupation of Algeria. The voyage was a revelation to the artist. In a variation of the myth of the noble savage, he claimed to have found a living antiquity in contemporary North African society, every bit as beautiful as classical Greece or Rome and far more inspiring for his artistic pursuits than the traditional trip to Italy. He filled seven sketchbooks with brilliant drawings and watercolors recording his experience. Throughout the rest of his career he created paintings from his sketches, notes, and remembrances. These mix ethnographic observation and orientalist fantasy in complex ways, though toward the end of his life they increasingly provided an escape from modern society into the more elemental world he believed North Africa to be.

Throughout his visit to North Africa, Delacroix tried to gain entrance into a harem, a prime locus of fantasy for European men. Only on his return voyage, during a brief visit to Algiers, was he able to do so, though some scholars doubt a visit to a harem ever took place. Upon returning to France,

he completed his *Women of Algiers in Their Apartment* (1834), in which three women sit indolently around a hookah while their servant draws back a curtain. Nineteenth-century viewers reveled in the purported accuracy of the picture, which allowed them to penetrate the space of the harem. The true brilliance of the picture lies in the rich colors, sensuous brushwork, and lambent atmosphere, all of which answered to the European desires surrounding the subject.

During the latter half of his career Delacroix continued to pursue literary and historical subjects associated with Romanticism, and many of his major works evince a continuing fascination with troubled heroes and the barbaric underside of civilization. At the same time, he became increasingly concerned to emulate the grand manner and traditional subject matter of such past masters as Rubens and Veronese. He received major commissions from the July Monarchy for mural decorations for the Salon of the King (1833) and the library of the Chamber of Deputies (begun 1838) in the Bourbon Palace (now the National Assembly), and the library of the Senate in Luxembourg Palace (1840). Other major monumental commissions include the Chapel of Holy Angels in St. Sulpice (1949), the ceiling of the Gallery of Apollo in the Louvre (1850), and the Salon of Peace in the Hôtel de Ville (1851).

Delacroix's literary output was considerable. As a young man he considered a career as a writer and completed an unpublished play and novella. During the course of his career he published important essays on Michelangelo, Raphael, Nicolas Poussin, Antoine-Jean Gros, and Pierre-Paul Prud'hon. He kept a private journal, remarkable for its candor and clarity of expression, from 1822 to 1824, and again from 1847 to the end of his life. His journal and letters were published posthumously and have become major sources for understanding nineteenth-century aesthetic thought.

Official recognition was slow to come to Delacroix. In 1855, at the Universal Exhibition in Paris, he was honored with a retrospective exhibition as one of the four most prominent living artists in France, but only in 1857, on his eighth attempt, was he admitted to the Academy of Fine Arts. His influence was enormous. Cézanne, the impressionists, and many of the postimpressionists, among others, found direct inspiration in his imaginative imagery, technical innovations, brilliant color, and lively brushwork. Today he is considered one of the greatest French painters of all time.

See also **France; Géricault, Théodore; Painting; Revolutions of 1830; Romanticism.**

BIBLIOGRAPHY

Primary Sources

Delacroix, Eugène. *Correspondance générale d'Eugène Delacroix.* 5 vols. Paris, 1936–1938.

——. *Ecrits sur l'art.* Paris, 1988.

——. *Journal, 1822–1863.* Paris, 1996. Originally published 1950.

Secondary Sources

Fraser, Elisabeth A. *Delacroix, Art and Patrimony in Post-Revolutionary France.* Cambridge, U.K., and New York, 2004. Relates Delacroix's art from the Bourbon Restoration to politics, constructions of the family, and practices of collecting and art criticism.

Hannoosh, Michele. *Painting and the* Journal *of Eugène Delacroix.* Princeton, N.J., 1995.

Jobert, Barthélémy. *Delacroix.* Princeton, N.J., 1998. A comprehensive survey of Delacroix's career.

Johnson, Lee. *The Paintings of Eugène Delacroix: A Critical Catalogue, 1816–1831.* 6 vols. Oxford, U.K., 1981–1989. Catalogue raisonné with commentary.

Wright, Beth S., ed. *The Cambridge Companion to Delacroix.* Cambridge, U.K., and New York, 2000. Collection of critical essays on various aspects of Delacroix's art and career.

DAVID O'BRIEN

DELCASSÉ, THÉOPHILE (1852–1923),
foreign minister of France (1898–1905 and 1914) and architect of the Anglo-French Entente Cordiale of 1904.

Théophile Delcassé was born in southwestern France, the son of a minor court official (*huissier*) in Pamiers (Ariège), on the edge of the Pyrenees. After studies at the University of Toulouse, Delcassé followed the route of ambitious young men to Paris, where an introduction to Léon Gambetta (1838–1882), the leading Radical politician of the early Third Republic, led to a career in journalism. Writing for Gambetta's newspaper,

La République française, Delcassé soon became involved in politics, and at age twenty-five he inherited the paper's column on colonial and foreign affairs.

Delcassé's articles made him one of the Radical Party's leading voices on foreign affairs, and Gambetta encouraged him to stand for office but died in 1882 before securing the election of his protégé. Delcassé became a strong supporter of Jules Ferry (1832–1893) in the mid-1880s when Ferry launched his controversial policy of colonial expansion. Delcassé backed Ferry in *La République française,* although others denounced him for the expansionism or for colonial cooperation with Germany. When Georges Clemenceau (1841–1929), the most passionate voice of the Radical Party after the death of Gambetta, attacked Ferry in parliament in 1885, leading to the overthrow of the Ferry government, Delcassé was a member of the inner circle who met with Ferry.

DELCASSÉ IN THE CHAMBER OF DEPUTIES
His close ties to Gambetta and Ferry and his growing reputation as an authority on international relations earned Delcassé the support needed for a successful parliamentary campaign, and he was elected to the Chamber of Deputies from Ariège in 1889, a seat he would hold until 1919. In his first major speech, in November 1890, Delcassé attacked the government of Charles de Freycinet (1828–1923, a former rival of Gambetta) for following a weak foreign policy and for backing down to the English in Egypt. Delcassé became a leading voice on French colonial affairs, resulting in his appointment as undersecretary for the colonies in 1893–1894 and then minister of the colonies in 1894–1895. In these posts he advocated cautious expansionism, based on a realistic appraisal of national interests rather than expansion for expansion's sake.

Delcassé used his prominent position in the Radical Party to support the Franco-Russian Alliance as it evolved in the 1890s at a time when many Radicals feared that collaboration with autocratic Russia compromised the liberal-democratic principles of the party. When Henri Brisson (1835–1912) formed a cabinet including several Radicals in 1898, Delcassé was considered the logical choice to be foreign minister.

DELCASSÉ AND THE DIPLOMATIC REVOLUTION

Delcassé came to office in June 1898, at the height of the Fashoda Crisis, in which Britain and France confronted each other over control of Egypt and the Sudan. He extracted France from a vulnerable position by withdrawing a small exploratory mission (the Marchand mission) from the banks of the Nile (where they confronted a large British army), and won praise for his resolution of the crisis, but Delcassé realized that the Fashoda affair had exposed French vulnerability. He consequently negotiated two protocols strengthening the Franco-Russian Alliance (1899 and 1901) and then contemplated the need for France to resolve its differences with either Britain (in colonial affairs) or Germany (in continental affairs). The latter possibility remains the most controversial issue in the scholarly interpretation of Delcassé's career.

Delcassé briefly considered a Franco-German détente—the idea that had destroyed Ferry's career but later won a Nobel Peace Prize for Aristide Briand (1862–1932) and later still made the European Union possible—but he found negotiations much easier with the British. Delcassé thus became the central architect of the Anglo-French treaty of 1904, known as the Entente Cordiale. By this agreement, Britain and France settled centuries of lingering colonial disputes. France recognized the British position in Egypt, and Britain recognized the French position in Morocco.

The Entente Cordiale was not a military alliance analogous to the Franco-Russian Alliance or Germany's Triple Alliance, although it evolved into military collaboration. Combined with the Russian alliance, it represented one of the greatest diplomatic revolutions in modern European history, ending the isolation of France and counter-balancing the German alliances.

When Germany precipitated a crisis in 1905 to test the Entente Cordiale, a nervous Chamber of Deputies drove Delcassé from office. He remained a leading voice in international affairs and returned to serve as minister of the navy in 1911–1913. When World War I began in 1914 and the French formed a coalition ministry of all talents (the "sacred union"), Delcassé returned to the Foreign Ministry, where he stayed until 1915.

See also **Clemenceau, Georges; Ferry, Jules; France; Gambetta, Léon-Michel.**

BIBLIOGRAPHY

Andrew, Christopher M. *Théophile Delcassé and the Making of the Entente Cordiale.* London, 1968.

Neton, Albéric. *Delcassé, 1852–1923.* Paris, 1927.

Porter, Charles W. *The Career of Théophile Delcassé.* Philadelphia, 1936. Reprint, Westport, Conn., 1975.

Renouvin, Pierre. *La Politique extérieure de Théophile Delcassé, 1898–1905.* Paris, 1962.

Zorgbibe, Charles. *Théophile Delcassé, 1852–1923: Le Grand ministre des Affaires étrangères de la Troisième République.* Paris, 2001.

STEVEN C. HAUSE

DEMOGRAPHY. In the course of the nineteenth century, European governments began to organize their national statistical systems. The data, although imperfect, reveal some decline of mortality, the onset of family limitation within marriage, and an accelerating natural population increase (the difference between the birthrate and the death rate) that resulted in large growth; this was tempered by large emigration streams. As a result of demographic changes, the population grew at a different pace in the various regions and countries of Europe. Table 1 shows the population of the Continent and of the largest countries in 1800 and 1913, the factor by which their numbers were multiplied between the two dates, and the rate of growth at the beginning and end of the period.

MORTALITY

Existing statistical series for England and France show an increase of the mean duration of life or life expectancy at birth, from around thirty-five years about 1800 to close to fifty years on the eve of World War I. In these two countries, the social consequences of rapid industrialization and urbanization resulted in relative stagnation in the improvements at midcentury. The statistics suggest that the decline of mortality was more sustained in the rural Scandinavian countries, although mortality was very high in large cities like Stockholm. At the beginning of World War I Denmark had the highest life expectancy at birth, at 57.5 years. At

TABLE 1

Population growth between 1800 and 1913 in selected European countries

Country	Population (1000)		Ratio	Annual growth (%)	
	1800	1913	1913/1800	1800–1850	1900–1913
Austria-Hungary	24,000	52,578	2.2	6.1	8.4
France	26,900	59,853	1.5	5.2	1.7
Germany	24,500	67,362	2.7	7.4	13.7
Italy	18,124	35,531	2.0	5.5	6.9
Russia	39,000	132,610	3.4	8.6	14.6
Spain	10,745	20,357	1.9	6.3	6.9
United Kingdom	10,284	41,440	3.8	13.2	8.0
Europe	187,693	457,515	2.4	6.9	10.2

SOURCE: Massimo Livi-Bacci, *The Population of Europe: A History.* Translated by Cynthia De Nardi Ipsen and Carl Ipsen. Oxford, U.K., 1999.

that time, however, the figure remained quite low in southern and eastern Europe (37.5 in Hungary for example), and it is likely that little improvement had occurred in these regions before the end of the nineteenth century. The mortality of cities was everywhere higher than that of the countryside. Children and infants were especially vulnerable, and only during the last decades of the nineteenth century was a spectacular decline of infant mortality notable throughout Europe.

There has been a great deal of speculation about the factors behind the decline of mortality. The deaths that resulted from the Napoleonic Wars have been estimated at several million men for France alone, but compared to previous centuries the nineteenth was relatively free of wars. The drop in the death rate reflected to some extent the less frequent visitation of epidemics and food shortages, although there were still some major mortalities, including several subsistence crises and deadly epidemics of cholera. Most notable was the famine that ravaged Ireland and several regions of Europe in the 1840s when a potato blight destroyed what had become the main food crop in these regions. What characterized the decline of mortality, however, was not so much the disappearance of exceptional flares but rather the prolonged decline of the background level. This corresponded to what has been termed the epidemiologic transition, a progressive change in the main causes of deaths from acute infectious diseases affecting people mostly at a young age to chronic, degenerative conditions such as cardiovascular diseases and cancers prevalent among older people.

The course of mortality during the period was influenced in opposite ways by the conflicting effects of economic and social change. On the one hand, an increasing part of the population resided in cities where high population density and poor living conditions encouraged the spread of infections (notably tuberculosis and diarrheas). The widespread use of child and female labor in industry and the poor hygienic conditions for working-class mothers were also factors. On the other hand, improvements of economic opportunities affected living standards and the development of transportation and markets may have resulted in better nutrition. The rapid diffusion of vaccination from the beginning of the century practically eradicated smallpox, a disease that may have accounted for up to a tenth of all deaths in earlier times. The technologies of sanitation made slow progress toward the provision of clean water and the construction of sewage systems. The discoveries of the French chemist and microbiologist Louis Pasteur (1822–1895) and the German physician Robert Koch (1843–1910) changed the theories of disease causation by showing that many diseases could be attributed to specific external causes such as bacteria, viruses, and parasites. Physicians became more aware of the need for antiseptic procedures, particularly in obstetrics and surgery. Most of all, the stage was set for more focused public-health efforts to control disease by improving sanitation and by educating the public on child nutrition and care. However, although public-health messages advocated maternal breast-feeding, the main improvement in infant health may well have resulted from the more hygienic use of bottle feeding, pasteurization of milk, and the sterilization of bottles and rubber nipples. These efforts, in turn, probably accounted for the steep drop of infant and child mortality at the end of the period under consideration.

FERTILITY

For most of Europe until the end of the nineteenth century the proportion of the population that was married remained an essential determinant of fertility. In eastern Europe, early and almost universal marriage resulted in a large number of births per woman. For example, total fertility in Russia reached seven children per woman. In contrast, western Europe was characterized by low intensity of marriage, a pattern that is accounted for by the requirement of individual access to the means of supporting a family before a young man could contract a marriage. A substantial proportion of the population never married; in Ireland, for example, close to 30 percent of women were still single on their fiftieth birthdays at the end of the century. Because of late marriage, the total fertility of those who married was also limited, typically to an average of four to five children. Illegitimate fertility accounted for only a small number of births in most regions of Europe. Nuptiality, in the demographic regime prevailing at the beginning of the nineteenth century, thus provided a mechanism linking reproduction to economic resources. This situation changed at a different pace in various parts of the continent.

In England a decline in age at marriage and an increase in the proportions ever-married resulted in higher overall fertility starting toward the middle of the eighteenth century, and reaching its peak around 1820; after that, a decline in nuptiality, combined with sustained marital fertility, led to a decline in the birthrate. France, however, followed a different model: an early decline of marital fertility, perceptible at the national level since the beginning of the nineteenth century, was accompanied by a progressive relaxation of the preventive check of marriage. In most countries of Europe, however, there was little change either in the frequency of marriage or in marital fertility before the end of the century. The decline in the fertility of

TABLE 2

Reproductive strategies in France, Ireland, and Russia c. 1900

Country	I$_g$ Marital fertility	I$_m$ Proportions married	I$_f$ Overall fertility
France	38	54	24
Ireland	71	33	24
Russia	77	69	55

marriages, due to the increasing adoption of birth control, was noteworthy after 1870 in most of Europe. Between 1880 and 1914 a majority of the province-sized administrative units of Europe had undergone the onset of a steady decline in marital fertility. There were laggards, but principally in rural areas remote from the center of the continent.

Table 2 illustrates the differences in the determinants of fertility about 1900. The indices in the table are those used in a large project on the decline of fertility in Europe conducted at Princeton University between 1963 and 1986. I$_g$ is an index of the fertility of married women, expressed as a percentage of the very high fertility of a standard population, the Hutterites of North America, whose religious beliefs prohibited the use of birth control. I$_f$, overall fertility, is computed in the same way, but this time without distinction of marital status, while I$_m$ is the proportion of married women weighted by their potential fertility. In the absence of illegitimate births, the product of I$_g$ and I$_m$ would equal I$_f$. In other terms, the indices show the extent to which overall fertility is determined by the level of marital fertility and by marriage. In Russia and Ireland, the levels of marital fertility are about the same, and probably unaffected by voluntary birth control, but the check on marriages in Ireland reduces overall fertility to the level reached by France, where the adoption of family limitation was paralleled by younger and more universal marriage than earlier in the century.

Factors causing the decline of marital fertility involved both a change in the demand for children and the development and spread of methods of birth control and their acceptability. The transition occurred before the widespread use of sophisticated techniques and implements, but that does not mean that there was no cultural diffusion of contraceptive practices and of the small-family ideal. The increase in demand was linked to many factors, including a growing concern for the health and welfare implications of large families; it occurred in the face of opposition by religious and civil authorities. The states were concerned by the military implications of differential national growth.

MIGRATION

The growth of population would have been considerably higher in most European countries if the outlet of international migration had not been available. The statistics are not precise, particularly in the beginning of the period, but it can be estimated that close to fifty million Europeans emigrated during the period (not counting upward of five million Russians moving to Siberia, that is, from the European part of the country to its Asian provinces). Three-quarters of the international migrants went to the United States. The demographic effect on growth includes not only the migrants, but also their own natural increase. Migration released demographic pressure, particularly on the land, at the time when increases in productivity, the decline of cottage industry, and consolidations of tenure led to growth of landlessness and rural poverty in Europe. Mass migration occurred primarily in search of employment.

Agricultural crises pushed workers and their families off the land. In particular the potato blight in 1846 and 1847 for Ireland and southwestern Germany resulted in the large emigration. More than one million Germans and an even larger number of the Irish departed between 1844 and 1854. The improvement of transportation, particularly by seafaring ships (the shift from sail to steam had occurred by 1870) and railroad facilitated mass migration. Legal and administrative obstacles to migration were progressively removed, and it was often encouraged and assisted by the authorities. Emigrants were particularly numerous from the British Isles, Germany, and Scandinavia before the 1870s, largely in the direction of the United States. After 1880 and until 1914, however, migration from southern, central, and eastern Europe accounted for more than 70 percent of the total. The list of countries of destination expanded, too,

with large streams of migration from Europe to Australia, New Zealand, Canada, Brazil, and Argentina, all countries where abundant land and an expanding capitalist economy promoted the growth of agriculture and industry.

Taken together, the changes in mortality, fertility, nuptiality, and migration that took place during the long nineteenth century amounted to a profound transformation of the demographic system. They accompanied many economic, social, and technological changes occurring during the century, at the same time making them possible and made possible by them. It would be wrong to say that the mortality decline caused the decline of fertility, or that these two declines were closely determined by economic and social changes. Medical technologies and the ideology of birth control were widely diffused. In the space of one century, Europe was well on its way from a situation of high to one of low mortality and fertility. The peaks of population growth and migration witnessed by the long nineteenth century would not be encountered again.

See also **Emigration; Immigration and Internal Migration; Marriage and Family; Public Health; Transportation and Communications.**

BIBLIOGRAPHY

Bardet, Jean-Pierre, and Jacques Dupâquier, eds. *Histoire des populations de l'Europe.* Vol. 2: *La révolution démographique, 1750–1914.* Paris, 1998. Extensive discussion by European experts, with chapters on components of demographic change and on individual countries.

Coale, Ansley J., and Susan Cotts Watkins, eds. *The Decline of Fertility in Europe.* Princeton, N.J., 1986. The result of a large research project based on data on some seven hundred province-size units.

Hatton, Timothy J., and Jeffrey G. Williamson. *The Age of Mass Migration: Causes and Economic Impact.* Oxford, U.K., 1998.

Livi-Bacci, Massimo. *The Population of Europe: A History.* Translated by Cynthia De Nardi Ipsen and Carl Ipsen. Oxford, U.K., 1999. A compact summary insisting on mechanisms.

Schofield, Roger S., David Sven Reher, and A. Bideau, eds. *The Decline of Mortality in Europe.* Oxford, U.K., 1991. A collection of essays discussing facts and theories.

ETIENNE VAN DE WALLE

DENMARK. All but a quarter of Denmark was under cultivation in the nineteenth century. The country's principal crops were oat, barley, rye, wheat, and sugar beets. Agriculture improved over time through more effective ploughing and irrigation. In addition, the Danes practiced dairy, pig, and poultry farming with considerable government support. They exported butter, bacon, and eggs, and imported timber, coal, minerals, and metals, mainly from Germany and Britain. Except on Iceland, Greenland, and the Faeroe Islands, where fishing ruled, Denmark was essentially a country of peasants.

AGRARIAN AND INDUSTRIAL CHANGE

In the eighteenth century large noble estates worked by serfs were the norm. New laws enacted in the period from 1786 to 1788 abolished serfdom, so that by 1800, peasants could live independently, free from feudal restraints. Denmark increasingly became a country of small ("freehold") farmers. Over half of them owned their own land by 1825, but because their numbers were multiplying, many suffered meager subsistence on very small plots—trying to make ends meet through cooperatives.

In nineteenth-century Denmark artisans and merchants far outnumbered factory hands. The only miners were in Greenland, for criolite and coppers. Old, water-powered factories producing linen or paper for domestic markets were small shops. But the first steam engine began operation in 1829, and the first railroad—between the capital and Roskilde—commenced service in 1847. New, steam-powered, mechanized cotton spinning and weaving mills, employing mostly young women, soon went into production. Despite waves of emigration to the United States of America and Canada, in 1901 the population of Denmark had reached two and a half million people, about two and a half times that of a century earlier. Even so it Denmark's population remained more rural than urban (62 to 38 percent).

ROYAL COPENHAGEN

Denmark's homelands—Jutland, the promontory connecting it to Germany, and its satellite islands, notably Zealand and Funen—lacked coal and metal, but certainly not clay. The chemist Frantz Heinrich Müller had taken advantage of this bounty in 1772, founding a porcelain factory on Bornholm. The establishment set the pace internationally both in manufacture and design. Such was its success that the monarchy turned it into a royally funded monopoly, "Royal Copenhagen." A law of 1790 forbade the importation of "china." The company's signature achievement, however heavy and ornate, is arguably the "Flora Danica" service of 1790–1802. Rivaling anything ever produced in Dresden and Sèvres, this gift to Empress Catherine II (r. 1762–1796) of Russia numbered thousands of pieces, featuring imagery of typical Danish flora (certified for accuracy by the botanist Theodor Holmskjold). In time, especially under the direction of Philip Schou and his master of design, Arnold Krog, the enterprise favored subtler, simpler forms and patterns. Their work was recognized as uniquely trendsetting at the International Paris Exposition of 1889.

This transition in aesthetic—from grandiose to modest—also marked the development of sculpture and painting. The sculptor Bertel Thorvaldsen (1768 or 1770–1844; born in Copenhagen to Icelandic parents who were woodcarvers) paid skilled and beautiful homage to the Hellenic-Roman heritage. It was on the Mediterranean that he found inspiration for his statues of Adonis and Bacchus, and for his tribute to Emperor Napoleon I (r. 1804–1814/15), invoking Alexander the Great's conquest of Babylon.

And like Thorvaldsen, his students and admirers delighted in travels to Italy. But if neoclassicism pleased Danes in the first half of the nineteenth century, the next generation increasingly appreciated realism, such as Peder Severin Krøyer's imagery of contemporary, gentrified Paris. The painters Johan Lundbye, Godtfred Rump, and Jørgen Sonne, who captured everyday life in Denmark, including flora and fauna, likewise enjoyed popularity. The art historian Niels Lauritz Høyen promoted their celebratory national oeuvres.

LIBERALISM

The abolition of serfdom and the rise of industrialization and urbanization gradually prompted Denmark to adopt progressive laws. In 1798 Jews were granted the right to marry Christians and given access to both primary and secondary education. As of 1814 education was made compulsory and free for every child between the age of seven and fourteen. By then a system of poor relief had also been instituted, funded by a tax. In 1834 King Frederick VI (r. 1808–1839) began taking counsel from advisory bodies of leading citizens. And in 1837 the crown agreed to the establishment of town councils; indeed by 1841 counties and parishes could also make recommendations to the monarchy. Based on the ownership of property, admission to these forums was limited. But the promise of representative government had been introduced: previously closed debates on taxes and the military's expenditures and rules of conscription turned public. To keep his power and maintain calm, an astute, conciliatory King Frederick VII (r. 1848–1863) in 1848 declared Denmark a constitutional monarchy.

The king, in part, hoped to end what had become virtually a civil war in the contiguous Danish territories of Schleswig and Holstein between Danish-speakers in the former and German-speakers in the latter, each a majority in its duchy. Buffering the Danes from the "Germans," Schleswig and Holstein were not only graced by fertile lands, but also contained vital waterways and harbors to the North and Baltic Seas. They moreover offered strategic, military, and commercial entry into Europe.

When in 1848 Denmark sought to incorporate Schleswig into its kingdom, fighting broke out. Prussia, which also claimed title to the duchy, sent an army representing the German Confederation (of 1815) to oppose Denmark there and to defend its own claim on Holstein, where a provisional revolutionary government had been established. The Armistice of Malmö (1848) and the London Protocol of 1852—achieved with international support based on fear of political radicalism—restored the status quo. But in 1863 the king of Denmark, willing to negotiate Holstein, proclaimed a new constitution for Schleswig that would join it to his monarchy. Prussia, supported by Austria, demanded he repeal this plan or it would forcefully interfere. When the king refused this ultimatum, Prussia and Austria declared war on Denmark and won easily. In 1864 the Treaty of Vienna gave Schleswig and Holstein to Prussia and Austria jointly. Both duchies came under Prussian rule following the Austro-Prussian War of 1866 and became part of united Germany in 1871.

The Danish Constitution of 5 June 1849, revised in 1863 and 1866, introduced a national, legislative parliament (*Rigsdag*) divided between a lower and an upper house, a *Folke-* and *Landsting*, the former controlled by the latter—that is, by the king, his administrative elite, and men of landed wealth. This constitution also guaranteed freedom of religion and of the press and it forbade monopolies on industry and trade, although it would not enforce the order until 1856 to 1857. Thanks to the movement led by the schoolteacher Frede Bojsen, in 1891–1892 Danes gained the benefits of health insurance subsidies and old-age pensions. In 1899, due to the actions of labor unions led by Jens Jensen, workers gained the formal rights to organize, strike, and go to arbitration. In 1901 Denmark established a full parliamentary system, by which (under the nominal king) the majority party in the *Folkesting* would form a government. Soon the nation would undergo a general property assessment and turn to a system of progressive taxation.

RELIGION AND SCIENCE

This new liberal Denmark did not impress every Dane. Its lack of interest in Protestantism and the church disturbed many. Increasingly ignored by most in everyday life, religion served mainly for the celebration of christenings, confirmations, weddings, and funerals; only at Christmas and Easter could it be said that people flocked to the cross. The spread of atheism, pregnancy out of wedlock, and divorce evoked more than one complaint from the philosopher Søren Kierkegaard. In *Either/Or* (1843) and *Training in Christianity* (1850) he promotes an engaged Christian life, urging vigilance against complacency or easy indulgence of the material world. The fables of Hans Christian Andersen, the son of cobblers in Odense, arguably also meant to cure, by satire rather than logic, what the author perceived as an epidemic of vanity and competition. From 1835, his works, aimed not exclusively at children, include "The Ugly Duckling," "The Little Matchgirl," and "The Little Mermaid," as well as "The Emperor's New Clothes," based on a tale from the 1300s.

But regarding Denmark's future there was reason for optimism. The accomplishments of the scientists Niels Ryberg Finsen (1860–1904), Hans Christian Ørsted (1777–1851), and Valdemar Poulsen (1869–1942) inspired confidence in the possibility of continuous individual and social improvement: the first originated a method of light therapy for the cure of lupus; the second discovered electromagnetism (and established Copenhagen's Polytechnic University); the third devised the arc and wave system of radio-telegraphy. Denmark also took heart in Joachim Frederik Schouw (1789–1852), a botanist and the author of an *Atlas of Plant Geography*.

See also **Danish-German War; Finland and the Baltic Provinces; Sweden and Norway**

BIBLIOGRAPHY

Begtrup, Holger. *Det danske folks historie i det nittende aarhundrede.* Copenhagen, 1909–1914.

Christensen, Lars K. "The Textile Industry and the Forming of Modern Industrial Relations in Denmark [2004]." Available at http://iisg.nl/research/denmark.doc.

Harvey, William J., and Christian Reppien. *Denmark and the Danes: A Survey of Danish Life, Institutions, and Culture.* London, 1915.

Jones, W. Glyn. *Denmark.* London, 1970.

Oakley, Stewart. *A Short History of Denmark.* New York, 1972.

JOHAN ÅHR

DERAISMES, MARIA (1828–1894), French feminist.

Maria Deraismes deployed an excellent education, wealth inherited from her liberal republican father, formidable speaking and writing talent, and organizational skills to become one of the most influential women in nineteenth-century France. Fully engaged in the struggles that engulfed the Second Empire (1852–1870) and the early Third Republic (1870–1940), Deraismes devoted her life to causes such as liberal republicanism, freethinking, and women's rights.

As a political activist determined to advance the ideals of liberal republicanism as well as the careers of individual politicians, Deraismes hosted a republican salon in Paris, authored republican tracts such as *France et progrès* (1873), and, in the early 1880s, published the journal *Le Républicain de Seine-et-Oise*. These efforts proved effective when her home department of Seine-et-Oise elected its first republican deputy during the Seize Mai crisis of 1877, followed by the victory of a full slate of handpicked republican candidates in 1885. Four years later, Deraismes transformed her salon on the rue Cardinet into a republican command post to help thwart the prospective coup d'état of General Georges-Ernest-Jean-Marie Boulanger (1837–1891).

Deraismes's commitment to freethinking reflected her conviction that the Roman Catholic Church represented a threat to both republicanism and feminism. Again, her activism took the form of writing tracts, such as her *Lettre au clergé français* (1879), and organizing like-minded partisans. In 1881 she served as vice-president of France's first Congrès anticlerical, and in 1885 she assumed the presidency of the Fédération des groupes de la libre pensée de Seine-et-Oise. She also fought to secure women's equality within the ranks of French Freemasonry, a bulwark of republicanism and anticlericalism. Expelled in 1882 from a local lodge, she joined in 1893 with Senator Georges Martin (1845–1916) to found the Grande Loge symbolique écossais de France: Le Droit Humain, which extended membership to women and men as equals.

Deraismes's campaign for women's rights began in the last years of the Second French Empire when she lent backing in 1869 to Léon Richer's journal *Le Droit des Femmes* (1869–1891), and then, a year later, joined him in founding the Société pour l'amélioration du sort de la femme. In 1878, she and Richer hosted the first French Congrès international du droit des femmes, a collaboration they repeated in 1889 with the second Congrès français et international du droit des femmes. Deraismes's feminism helped to produce such practical reforms as greater educational opportunities for women, the reenactment in 1884 of a law permitting divorce, and the right of businesswomen to vote for judges of Commerce Tribunals. Her feminist writings included *Eve contre Dumas fils* (1872) and *Eve dans l'humanité* (1891).

Like the majority of her contemporary liberal French feminists, Deraismes subscribed to the *politique de la brèche,* a strategy that called for the piecemeal "breaching" of the wall of masculine privilege and domination. This strategy placed Deraismes in opposition to the other wing of the emerging liberal French feminist movement, the wing led by suffragist Hubertine Auclert (1848–1914) and marked by the *politique de l'assaut,* a strategy that called for "assaulting" the wall all at once through securing women's right to vote. The "breach" strategy enabled Deraismes to present herself as a moderate and to pursue specific reforms of benefit to women, but it also left her awkwardly dependent on republicans, whose fear of clerical conservatism and the "priest-ridden" minds of women resulted in women remaining without the right to vote until the end of World War II. Deraismes also found herself awkwardly at odds with other feminists and reformers on the issue of protective legislation for women, opposing it as a violation of the liberal commitment to the ideal of equal rights for women—and men—as individuals.

Other causes to which Deraismes lent her influence included support in France for the crusade against legal prostitution led by Josephine Butler (1828–1906), an English woman; condemnation of decadent novelists, such as Émile Zola (1840–1902); and concern for the mistreatment of animals, especially the practice of vivisection. Critics abounded during Deraismes's lifetime. Some Freemasons viewed her as a "kind of monster." Workers resented her class background; the bourgeoisie scoffed at her passion for women's emancipation. Other feminists complained that she had not only tried to impose her personal stamp on the movement but had also confused women's rights with anticlericalism and liberal republicanism. Shortly after her death, the Paris municipal council renamed a street in her honor, and in 1898 her friends erected a statue to her in the Square des Epinettes. Only the pedestal remains today.

See also **Auclert, Hubertine; Butler, Josephine; Feminism; Richer, Léon; Suffragism.**

BIBLIOGRAPHY

Bidelman, Patrick Kay. *Pariahs Stand Up! The Founding of the Liberal Feminist Movement in France, 1858–1889.* Westport, Conn., 1982.

Hause, Steven C., with Anne R. Kenney. *Women's Suffrage and Social Politics in the French Third Republic.* Princeton, N.J., 1984.

Klejman, Laurence, and Florence Rochefort. *L'Égalité en marche: le féminisme sous la Troisième République.* Paris, 1989.

Krakovitch, Odile. *Maria Deraismes.* Paris, 1980.

PATRICK KAY BIDELMAN

DEROIN, JEANNE (1805–1894), French feminist socialist.

Jeanne Deroin was a French feminist socialist who in 1848 became the first to demand votes for women. A virtually self-educated needleworker, she was introduced to the Saint-Simonians in 1831. Deroin applauded their mission to liberate women and workers, but deplored their leader's doctrine of free love as likely to enslave, rather than free, women. She joined a small group of former Saint-Simonian working women in running a women's newspaper, *Femme libre* (1832–1834). One of her contributions, "The Woman of the Future," hoped "The time is arrived when woman shall find *her* place, her acknowledged, her useful and *dignified* place upon [earth]. . . . This . . . we can effect, both on condition of forming ourselves into *one solid union.* Let us no longer form two camps—that of the women of the people, and that of the women of the privileged class. . . ." The Owenite Anna Wheeler translated and published the article in 1833 in the Owenite paper, *The Crisis.* Subsequently in the years to 1848 Deroin focused on rearing her three children, one of whom was severely handicapped with hydrocephalus, and helping take care of fellow feminist Flora Tristan's family when Tristan died in 1844. With the help of her local priest, Deroin gained the *brévet* to qualify as a primary school teacher and ran a tiny school for daughters of workers.

In March 1848 Deroin joined other former Saint-Simonian women, including Eugénie Niboyet (1797–1883) and Pauline Roland (1805–1852), to publish *La voix des femmes,* a newspaper and a club for women. They argued as earlier for fairer wages and better education for women, nurseries and workers' associations, and the restoration of the divorce law, which had been abolished in 1816.

Women Carrying Jeanne Deroin in Triumph. Illustration from *Les femmes célèbres*, 1848. Bibliothèque Marguerite Durand, Paris, France/Bridgeman Art Library/Archives Charmet

In addition, given that the republicans introduced universal male suffrage, Deroin took the lead in demanding votes for women. When their club and paper were forced to close in the repression that followed the June Days (a revolt by workers in Paris), she edited the short-lived *Politique des femmes* (August 1848), followed by *L'opinion des femmes* (1848–1849). This was forced to close in August 1849, when the government raised the caution money (a fee paid by newspapers to the French government). Deroin tried to stand as a candidate in the Parisian artisan district of Saint-Antoine in the legislative elections in 1849. Radical socialist voters listened to her and fifteen voted for her. *The Times* of London reported this with some enthusiasm for both her speech and her candidature. However the Fourierists' leader, Victor Considérant (1808–1893), was one of few socialists who supported her. The French novelist George Sand (Amandine Dudevant; 1804–1876) commented that it was too soon to give women the vote.

Deroin and Roland made valiant efforts to organize associations of workers, both for teachers and needleworkers. Their most ambitious project was an association of associations that linked together over a hundred mutual aid groups. However, after the June Days the right of association was regarded as a dangerous threat by the increasingly conservative government of Louis-Napoleon Bonaparte (later Napoleon III, r. 1852–1871). In May 1850 the association's offices were closed down and its officers tried and imprisoned. In 1851 Deroin was jailed for six months, struggling abortively to defend the individual's right to petition the parliament while herself in prison. On her release, Deroin was constantly aware of the threat of rearrest, and this persuaded her to flee into exile with her children in 1852. Her husband died of typhoid fever before he could join them.

Deroin spent the rest of her life in Shepherd's Bush, west London. Fellow exiles helped her find work as an embroiderer. She ran a small girls' school, but this foundered because she charged such low fees. Deroin edited three almanacs for women, one of which was published in English. She continued to demand women's rights to equality. Women, she argued, had a particular spiritual role, both as mothers and in mutual aid groups. Deroin kept in touch with Léon Richer (1824–1911), a feminist activist for the revision of the Civil Code in France. Later she corresponded with the much younger feminist, Hubertine Auclert (1848–1914).

Deroin struggled to provide for her family and could never afford subscriptions to radical French papers. When the Third Republic was established, former exiles organized a small pension for her. In her eighties, she joined William Morris's *Socialist League*. Morris lived not far from her and gave the oration at her funeral.

Jeanne Deroin was a passionate feminist socialist, who expressed her ideas in an uncompromising, somewhat abrasive fashion. Léon Richer said that when Deroin spoke at a meeting, one could imagine that she was waving a rifle. In fact her socialism was never revolutionary, and her admiration for what she came to describe as "social solidarity" became increasingly spiritual.

See also **Auclert, Hubertine; Feminism; Richer, Léon; Roland, Pauline; Suffragism; Tristan, Flora.**

BIBLIOGRAPHY

Gordon, Felicia, and Máire Cross. *Early French Feminisms, 1830–1940.* Brookfield, Vt., 1996.

Pilbeam, Pamela. *French Socialists before Marx: Workers, Women, and the Social Question in France.* Teddington, U.K., 2000.

———. "Jeanne Deroin: Feminist, Socialist Exile." In *Exiles from European Revolutions: Refugees in Mid-Victorian England,* edited by Sabine Freitag, 275–294. New York, 2003.

PAMELA PILBEAM

DE VRIES, HUGO (1848–1935), Dutch botanist.

Hugo Marie de Vries was one of the leading scientists of the Netherlands around 1900, the year in which he and three other plant biologists independently rediscovered Gregor Mendel's whole-number ratios in the distribution of inherited characteristics.

Born in Haarlem on 16 February 1848, de Vries trained in medicine at Heidelberg and Leiden and became a full professor of plant physiology, a new branch of botany, at the new University of Amsterdam in 1881. He belonged to the generation of European scientists most affected by the late-nineteenth-century fascination with statistics, aware of the basic mathematics pioneered in Ludwig Boltzmann's thermodynamics and Francis Galton's studies of human variation. Some, like Galton himself, went on to research in human breeding ("eugenics"), but de Vries was among the majority who confined its application to breeding plants and animals.

GALTON CURVE AND OSMOSIS

De Vries published, as contemporary Dutch scientists had to, in at least four languages. His first major paper on the biological use of the "Galton curve" (the name he gave to the so-called normal, bell, or Gaussian curve used in statistics to sort out data) appeared in German in 1894. To de Vries, a "half-Galton curve" result indicated discontinuous variation and a double-peaked curve showed the presence of two characteristics or races, which further selective breeding could isolate from each other.

At the time this paper was published, de Vries's major scientific contributions had been to the understanding of the fluid pressure and fluid exchange in plant tissues—plasmolysis and osmosis. His early papers on these subjects appeared in German and French in 1888.

Four years before however, in 1884, de Vries had told his Dutch colleague Jacobus Hendricus van't Hoff (1852–1911) about experiments by the German botanist Wilhelm Pfeffer showing that osmotic pressure across semipermeable (ferrocyanide) membranes was proportional to the concentration of solutes. Van't Hoff suggested an explanation that followed the entropy law of thermodynamics based on the assumption of molecules, and his research in this vein led to a Nobel prize in chemistry in 1901.

PLANT BREEDING AND GENETICS

For de Vries, this line of research petered out around 1890, and he returned to botany. In the year that Mendel died, 1884, de Vries began publishing on the subject of plant breeding, starting with the first of a three-year series called "Thoughts on the Improvement of the Races of Our Cultivated Plants." In 1885 he began breeding *Dipsacus sylvestris,* the common teasel or thistle, and later *Oenothera lamarckiana,* or evening primrose. His goal became the elucidation of the true submicroscopic mechanism of heredity, something that Charles Darwin had attempted in 1868 with his ultimately unsatisfactory "gemmule" theory. In 1889 de Vries published *Intracellular Pangenesis,* in which he maintained that hereditary qualities were independent units. These "pangenes," as he called them, were multiple, one for each trait, and they divided in their own cells and propagated to daughter cells. Some entered the cell's cytoplasm and thus had an effect, whereas others stayed in the cell's nucleus and did nothing. By changing occasionally, they might spontaneously cause mutations and new species. The idea excited great interest but seemed essentially unproven, either by observational or by statistical methods.

DISCONTINUOUS INHERITANCE, MENDEL, AND THE GENE

Continuing his long-term breeding experiments in 1896, de Vries crossed two varieties of the opium poppy, *Papaver somniferum,* "Mephisto" and "Danebrog," which yielded 1,095 with a black petal base and 358 with a white petal base in the third generation after the first cross, or "F3." De Vries presented these results to his advanced students as a demonstration of a law of "segregation of characteristics," segregation that could be teased from the raw data using statistics and Galton (normal) curves. De Vries had in fact arrived at the Mendelian genetic law but refrained from publishing it until 1900.

By then it was almost too late. Four plant biologists were zeroing in on the same law of segregation or discreteness of heritable characteristics—the "gene" or atomic idea of heredity—in the spring of 1900. On 17 January, in Vienna, the Austrian botanist Erich Tschermak von Seysenegg defended his doctoral thesis ("On Crossbreeding in Peas"), which was published later in the year in Austria; it mentioned Mendel but underplayed the idea. De Vries's own paper came second, but the word *law* was in its title ("The Law of Segregation of Hybrids"); it was received on 14 March by the leading German-language journal, *Berichte der deutschen botanischen Gesellschaft* (Reports of the German Botanical Association). Twelve days later de Vries was presenting it in French at the Paris Académie des sciences. In May it was the turn of William Bateson, whom de Vries had met in England in 1899; Bateson's lecture called "Problems of Heredity as a Subject for Horticultural Investigation" appeared in the *Journal of the Royal Horticultural Society.* In retrospect, however, it was the paper by the German botanist Carl Correns, received by the *Berichte* in April, whose title ("Mendel's Law concerning the Behavior of Progeny of Varietal Hybrids") best revealed the event. The "law" was in fact not de Vries's; it was the discovery of a substitute high school physics teacher named Gregor Mendel, whose two-year experiment in crossbreeding peas had been published by his local scientific society in 1866 and ignored for thirty-four years, until the times became more receptive to discontinuitarian explanations. De Vries's paper, like the other two, acknowledged Mendel's priority. In a letter to H. F. Roberts in 1924, de Vries wrote that he had found the 1866 result in the bibliography of a pamphlet appended by the American horticulturist Liberty Hyde Bailey to later editions of his 1895 book (*Plant-Breeding*), though Theo J. Stomps argued in 1954 that de Vries had gotten the news in a letter from his colleague Martinus Willem Beijerinck in Delft in 1900. De Vries had nevertheless secured his research and reputation, if not his priority, and in 1909 a colleague, Wilhelm Johannsen, discussing de Vries's work in a book, coined the word *gene* by dropping the "pan" from de Vries's term *pangene,* from 1889.

After 1900 de Vries returned to his 1886 discovery of a new form of evening primrose in a field in Hilversum, and he became identified with the evolutionary mechanism he called "mutation," by which new species might arise with saltatory (discontinuous) suddenness amid the continuous, almost imperceptible change implied by Darwin's natural selection. He published a book on this topic, *Die Mutationstheorie* (1901–1903; The mutation theory), and more than thirty papers. In 1904 he went to the United States, opening the Cold Spring Harbor Laboratory's Station for Experimental Evolution on Long Island, lecturing at the University of California, Berkeley, and giving a paper at the scientific congress of the St. Louis World's Fair. He returned to the United States in 1906 and 1912, remaining on the lookout for any new mutations in his research plant, the evening primrose, though in the end the mutations all turned out to be hybrids.

De Vries's work was fundamental and timely but not quite original enough to win him one of the first Nobel prizes, like those won by his Dutch colleagues, van't Hoff in chemistry in 1901 and Hendrik Antoon Lorentz (1853–1928) in physics in 1902. De Vries died near Amsterdam on 21 May 1935, a scientific statesman.

See also **Darwin, Charles; Evolution; Galton, Francis; Science and Technology.**

BIBLIOGRAPHY

Allen, Garland E. "Hugo De Vries and the Reception of the 'Mutation Theory.'" *Journal of the History of Biology* 2 (1969): 55–87.

Darden, Lindley. "Reasoning in Scientific Change: Charles Darwin, Hugo de Vries, and the Discovery of

Segregation." *Studies in History of Philosophy and Science* 7 (1976): 127–169.

Mayr, Ernst. *The Growth of Biological Thought: Diversity, Evolution, and Inheritance.* Cambridge, Mass., 1982.

Olby, Robert C. *Origins of Mendelism.* 2nd ed. Chicago, 1985.

Stomps, Theo J. "On the Rediscovery of Mendel's Work by Hugo De Vries." *Journal of Heredity* 45, no. 6 (1954): 293–294.

WILLIAM EVERDELL

Costume design by Leon Bakst for Diaghilev's 1911 production of *Narcisse*. MUSÉE NATIONAL D'ART MODERNE, CENTRE POMPIDOU, PARIS, FRANCE, LAUROS/GIRAUDON/BRIDGEMAN ART LIBRARY

DIAGHILEV, SERGEI (1872–1929), Russian art critic and ballet impresario.

Born in Novgorod Province of an aristocratic family, Sergei Pavlovich Diaghilev became—like many other Russian provincials (Peter Tchaikovsky and Anton Chekhov, for example)—one of the great figures in the history of Russian culture. Unlike them, he had no notable talent in any of the arts, but possessed an unquenchable love for them, impeccable taste, and savvy business skills. Diaghilev studied law in St. Petersburg at the alma mater of Tchaikovsky, Vladimir Stasov, and Vladimir Lenin, and staggered his legal lessons with study at the Conservatory of Music, which had been founded a decade before his birth. Possessing broad and deep aesthetic erudition, Diaghilev was consumed by art history, music, and theater and managed to publish an able volume on eighteenth-century Russian portraiture in 1902. But it was the public and international face of art—particularly contemporary art—not scholarship that came to fill his life.

With the artist Alexander Benois, Diaghilev coedited a sumptuously illustrated journal, *The World of Art* (1898–1904). In an effort to make Russian graphic art known to Europe, already under the thrall of Fyodor Dostoyevsky and Leo Tolstoy, Diaghilev organized shows in Berlin, Paris, Monte Carlo, and Venice in 1906 and 1907. From 1907, he brought the "Historical Russian Concerts" to Europe, with the participation of the composers Nikolai Rimsky-Korsakov, Sergei Rachmaninov, and Alexander Glazunov; the singer Fyodor Chaliapin; the pianist Josef Hofmann; and the conductor Arthur Nikisch. In St. Petersburg, *The World of Art* sponsored

"Evenings of Contemporary Music" from 1902, featuring the works of Gustav Mahler, Claude Debussy, Arnold Schoenberg, Max Reger, Alexander Scriabin, and Rachmaninov. At one of these, Diaghilev met Igor Stravinsky whom he persuaded to compose the music for *Petrushka* (*Petrouchka*). Thus Diaghilev paved a two-way street between the cultures of Europe and Russia, old and new.

In 1908 began the "Seasons of Russian Opera" in Paris, which included Modest Mussorgsky's *Boris Godunov,* Rimsky-Korsakov's *The Maid of Pskov,* and a handful of excerpts. Diaghilev's biggest triumph, the ballet seasons, introduced the European public to Stravinsky's three early masterpieces: *Firebird* (1910), *Petrushka* (1911), and *The Rite of Spring* (1913). The modernity of the latter set off a well-known scandal at its Paris premiere that catapulted Diaghilev's name into world renown. Driven by the Wagnerian dream of a total work of art, Diaghilev fused original dance forms, music, and decor into fantastic spectacles that thrilled audiences in Europe and later in the United States and Latin America. A master at harnessing (and manipulating) talented people, he pressed into service Stravinsky, Sergei Prokofiev, and a whole string of French composers; the set designers Benois, Nicholas Roerich, Léon Bakst, and Pablo Picasso; the choreographer Michel Fokine and others; and the legendary dancers Anna Pavlova, Tamara Karsavina, and Vaslav Nijinsky.

The outbreak of World War I in 1914 and the Russian Revolution of 1917 cut Diaghilev off from his native land and he could no longer draw new dancing talent from the great Imperial theaters—the Maryinsky in St. Petersburg (Petrograd after 1914) and the Bolshoi in Moscow. In exile, the impresario traveled the globe with his Diaghilev Ballet, which had premiered in 1913. In the 1920s, his thirst for innovation pushed him further into modernism and avant-garde forms, including the use of acrobatic tricks. Contrary to received opinion, Diaghilev did not remain wholly alien to Soviet culture. In 1927 he staged in Paris and London, with Léonide Massine as director, Prokofiev's little-known ballet, *Pas d'acier* (The steel step), a wildly modern and experimental constructivist work set in a factory, with a clear "proletarian" plot. Soon after, however, the Diaghilev tradition and the emerging Soviet style under Joseph Stalin parted company. In many ways, Soviet ballet defined itself as a negation of Diaghilev and opted for lengthy narrative works, often done up in an academic manner. Diaghilev's 1921 London staging of Tchaikovsky's *Sleeping Beauty,* first choreographed by the masterful Marius Petipa, failed to recapture the magic of the older version. Diaghilev died in Venice in 1929, but his ballet company, under varying names, most famously the Ballets russes de Monte Carlo, carried on long after his death.

The controversies surrounding the life of the stormy impresario fall into the personal and the artistic. The former—all too familiar in the world of theater—involved Diaghilev's titanic ego, explosive temper, and alleged sexual misuse of his male dancers, Nijinsky in particular. Diaghilev's cruel streak was captured brilliantly by Anton Walbrook in the 1948 film *The Red Shoes.* Far more interesting was Diaghilev's contribution to the world of theater arts. Even Soviet scholars—who routinely accused Diaghilev of promoting "reactionary bourgeois modernism"—conceded readily that his and his colleagues' earlier work had contributed in a major way to the reanimation of ballet in Europe and to the establishment of national and private ballet companies around the world.

See also **Avant-Garde; Dostoyevsky, Fyodor; Nijinsky, Vaslav; Paris; Stravinsky, Igor.**

BIBLIOGRAPHY

Buckle, Richard. *Diaghilev.* London, 1979.

Dyagilev i ego epokha. St. Petersburg, 2001.

Eksteins, Modris. *The Rites of Spring: The Great War and the Birth of the Modern Age.* Toronto, 1989.

Garafola, Lynn. *Diaghilev's Ballets russes.* New York, 1989.

Rosenfeld, Alla. *Defining Russian Graphic Arts: From Diaghilev to Stalin, 1898–1934.* New Brunswick, N.J., 1999.

Scholl, Tim. *From Petipa to Balanchine: Classical Revival and the Modernization of Ballet.* London, 1994.

RICHARD STITES

DICKENS, CHARLES (1812–1870), English novelist.

Charles John Huffam Dickens was born near Portsmouth, England, on 7 February 1812, to Elizabeth Barrow and John Dickens. The happiest years of his early childhood were spent between 1817 and 1823 in Chatham, Kent, where he attended school and was first introduced to the world of literature and drama. In 1823, John Dickens moved his family to London, and the eleven-year-old Charles found himself suddenly catapulted into the excitement of big-city life and the trauma of financial hardship. In 1824, Dickens's father was arrested for debt and incarcerated in Marshalsea Debtors Prison. For the months that John Dickens and his family lived in a single, cramped room in the Marshalsea, Charles lived alone in lodgings and worked at Warren's Blacking Factory, where he spent ten hours a day pasting labels on bottles of shoe polish. The six shillings (less than a third of a pound) that Dickens earned weekly had to both pay for his keep and help support his family.

Dickens's time at the blacking factory importantly shaped his outlook as a writer and social critic. A great many of his novelistic images and themes—prisons, degraded conditions of labor, children lost in the city, the importance of education, the dangers of unstable capital in industrialized urban culture—grew out of this traumatic childhood experience. The Warren's factory experience can also be seen reflected specifically in Dickens's later writing: several chapters of the semi-autobiographical *David Copperfield* (1850) illustrate the misery of his time at the factory, and it was at Warren's that Dickens met the boy on whom he would base the infamous Artful Dodger of *Oliver Twist* (1837–1839).

Dickens was able to leave Warren's and return to school after a legacy improved his family's financial situation. He attended the Wellington House Academy during the years 1824 to 1827, and, at fifteen, entered the adult world as a solicitor's clerk. In his spare time, he studied shorthand at Doctors' Commons, which led to work as a parliamentary reporter and a position as a staff reporter for the *Morning Chronicle*. By 1833, Dickens had contributed his first sketches of urban life to the *Monthly Magazine* and other periodicals. These pieces were soon collected in his first book, *Sketches by Boz* (1836). Shortly after publishing this first book, Dickens married Catherine Hogarth.

In 1836, at the age of twenty-four, Dickens began the weekly serial publication of *The Posthumous Papers of the Pickwick Club* (1836–1837), which grew to become a sensational success and solidified Dickens's literary fame and reputation. In 1837 Dickens began his next novel, *Oliver Twist,* edited *Bentley's Miscellany,* and celebrated the birth of his first child. The joys of this active time were dampened, however, by the death of Catherine's sister Mary, to whom both Catherine and Charles were deeply attached. Dickens's idealization of Mary can be seen in his many portraits of saintly, diminutive female characters, including Little Nell and Little Dorrit. Continuing the pattern of prolific industriousness that would typify his entire career, Dickens began to produce *Nicholas Nickleby* in 1838, and between 1840 and 1841 he published both *The Old Curiousity Shop* and his first historical novel, *Barnaby Rudge,* in the weekly periodical *Master Humphrey's Clock.*

Charles Dickens. © BETTMANN/CORBIS

In 1842, Dickens took America by storm. His six-month trip—during which he met such American literary lions as Washington Irving (1783–1859), Henry Wadsworth Longfellow (1807–1882), and Edgar Allan Poe (1809–1849)—bore subsequent literary fruit: the controversial *American Notes* (1842) and the slyly devastating American episode in *Martin Chuzzlewit* (1843–1844). *A Christmas Carol,* the first of five widely popular Christmas books, was published in December 1843. The mid- to late-1840s saw the publication of *Pictures from Italy* (1846), *Dombey and Son* (1848), and Dickens's "favorite child," *David Copperfield* (1850). During these years Dickens's marriage became increasingly troubled, while the ever-increasing Dickens family—by 1852, Catherine and Charles had ten children—lived in Italy, Switzerland, and Paris, as well as maintaining residence in London. Despite his family difficulties, extensive travel, and grueling writing schedule, Dickens also found time during this period to help establish and support such philanthropic causes as Miss Coutts's Home for Homeless Women.

The 1850s marked both increasing attention to social problems and a return to journalism. In 1850 Dickens launched the periodical *Household Words,* which was eventually incorporated into *All the Year Round* (1859–1893). *Household Words* combined informative journalism with fiction and published important contemporary novelists such as Elizabeth Gaskell (1810–1865) and Wilkie Collins (1824–1889). *Bleak House,* a frontal attack on urban poverty and the foggy and wasteful English legal system, was serialized between 1852 and 1853, and was followed immediately by *Hard Times* (1854) and *Little Dorrit* (1855–1857), novels that derided exploitative industrialism and rapacious greed. All this social criticism had the effect of pushing Dickens firmly toward the top of the social ladder: In 1856 Dickens found himself finally able to purchase the gentleman's residence he had once fantasized owning, Gad's Hill Place in Kent. The end of the decade saw both the publication of his second and final foray into historical fiction, *A Tale of Two Cities* (1859), and his permanent separation from Catherine.

In 1858, Dickens both made the acquaintance of the actress Ellen Ternan, with whom he maintained a close relationship until his death, and began his immensely popular public readings. The stress and strain of these performances, which he toured in both England and the United States, led to a breakdown in 1869. The 1860s saw the publication of *The Uncommercial Traveller* (1860), a collection of journalistic essays, and the serializations of *Great Expectations* (1860–1861) and *Our Mutual Friend* (1864–1865). After a farewell season of public readings early in 1870, Dickens began *The Mystery of Edwin Drood.* His poor health, however, would not relent, and Dickens died on 9 June 1870, leaving *Edwin Drood* uncompleted. Dickens was buried in the Poets' Corner of Westminster Abbey.

Dickens is well known for his humor, his social criticism, and his popularity. He was a comic master whose extravagant characters neatly eviscerated aristocratic snobbery, social stratification, and human fallibility. He is also renowned for his atten-tion to social issues and his sympathy for the poor and underprivileged in the rapidly changing landscape of the industrialized nineteenth century. His impact spanned continents: his novel *Bleak House* was so widely embraced as a powerful indictment of social injustice that Frederick Douglass (1817–1895) saw fit to publish its serial installments in his American abolitionist paper. Dickens also contributed mightily to the development of the novel form. He significantly helped "reinvent" serial fiction, drawing on earlier eighteenth-century experiments in serialization for his publication of *The Pickwick Papers* and using the serial format for all subsequent novels. In addition to reaching back into the eighteenth century, Dickens responded in sensitive and nuanced ways to contemporary genre developments in narrative. Elements of the popular working-class "urban mysteries" novel, the protest novel, the detective novel, and the city novel inform his writing. Finally, Dickens's work was important to nineteenth-century theatrical development, and he is increasingly seen as a proto-modernist writer (T. S. Eliot [1888–1965], for instance, originally named his famous modernist poem *The Waste Land* after a line from *Our Mutual Friend,* "He Do The Police in Different Voices"). From the publication of *The Pickwick Papers* to the twenty-first century, Dickens has not only had great impact on literary history but has also enjoyed an almost unprecedented and enduring literary fame.

See also **Childhood and Children; Gaskell, Elizabeth; Great Britain; London; Realism and Naturalism.**

BIBLIOGRAPHY

Ackroyd, Peter. *Dickens: Public Life and Private Passion.* London, 2002.

Chesterton, G. K. *Appreciations and Criticisms of the Works of Charles Dickens.* London, 1911.

Forster, John. *The Life of Charles Dickens.* London, 1872–1874.

Glavin, John. *After Dickens: Reading, Adaptation and Performance.* Cambridge, U.K., 1999.

Houston, Gail Turley. *Consuming Fictions: Gender, Class, and Hunger in Dickens's Novels.* Carbondale, Ill., 1994.

Johnson, Edgar. *Charles Dickens: His Tragedy and Triumph.* 2 vols. New York, 1952.

Jordan, John O., ed. *The Cambridge Companion to Charles Dickens.* Cambridge, U.K., 2001.

Kaplan, Fred. *Dickens: A Biography*. New York, 1988.

Schor, Hilary M. *Dickens and the Daughter of the House*. Cambridge, U.K., 1999.

Stewart, Garrett. *Dickens and the Trials of Imagination*. Cambridge, Mass., 1974.

Vlock, Deborah. *Dickens, Novel Reading, and the Victorian Popular Theatre*. Cambridge, U.K., 1998.

Welsh, Alexander. *The City of Dickens*. Oxford, U.K., 1971.

SARA HACKENBERG

DIET AND NUTRITION. Although the European diet had been expanded by the new plants and animals discovered during and after Columbus's late-fifteenth-century voyages to the Americas, many Europeans still faced undernutrition and starvation throughout the period from 1789 to 1914.

STARVATION, SUBSISTENCE, AND DISEASE

War, bad weather, and plant and animal diseases are obvious causes of food peril. These obvious causes are often exacerbated by political and social factors. For example, the Great Irish Famine of the mid-nineteenth century was caused by a complex combination of factors: bad social policies and reliance on a single crop. Irish peasants had become so dependent on the potato that when blight rendered the potatoes inedible, most peasants had nothing to eat. The series of repeated poor harvests, no seed potatoes left to plant, disease, and ineffective poor relief led to more than two million people starving and emigrating between 1845 and 1855.

Even without war and bad harvests, food could be scarce. Obviously, diet depended on social class, with different diets for the upper class, the urban middle-class workers, the farm workers, and the unskilled urban wage laborers. In 1789, the beginning of the French Revolution, women in Paris demonstrated against the price of bread: a four-pound loaf cost 14.2 sous, which was almost the total daily wage of a laborer (18 sous). Since bread was the mainstay of the diet, the price of bread was important. In about 1850, a German worker's family might spend 50 to 70 percent of its income on food. In 1972, a German worker's family might spend 35 percent of its income on food.

No matter what the social class, a carbohydrate product was the basis of the European diet in 1789: bread, other grain products, or potatoes constituted about 75 percent of the diet. The laboring class ate dark breads, but dreamed of white loaves. In the mid-nineteenth century, when British workers could finally afford light-colored bread, they were actually worsening their nutrition, since white bread has been stripped of many nutritious vitamins, minerals, and fiber. And some unscrupulous bakers would add adulterants to make their bread more attractive; for example, in 1830, French and Belgian bakers began using small amounts of toxic alum and highly toxic copper sulfate to whiten the bread.

Clean water was a precious commodity in many European cities. Water sources faced a variety of contaminates, from garbage, to excrement, to waste from slaughterhouses, to chemicals from tanneries and factories, to seepage from cemeteries. Diseases such as cholera were spread by water pollution. These conditions were not new to the nineteenth century, but were exacerbated by industrialization and urbanization. People continued to drink light beer and light wine as a safe alternative, but increasingly new and caffeinated beverages (tea and coffee) were drunk.

INDUSTRIALIZATION

Industrialization caused a change in meals, since workers could no longer go home to eat with the family. Often the entire family worked in the factory, so there was no one at home to cook the meal. Of course, a family of factory workers usually had no time or land to grow domestic crops, so most foodstuffs would have to be purchased, unlike in earlier days. While this allowed some choice in foods, it was also more expensive, generally less nutritious, and afforded less time with the family group. In Northern England, poor workers might eat a bit of bacon and potatoes. Poorer workers would not have the bacon, only potatoes, bread, cheese, and porridge. By 1830, a British writer lamented the state of English peasant cookery, believing that the English peasants had forgotten domestic baking and brewing skills because they bought meals already cooked. Middle- and upper-class families had much more variation in their diet.

As more people ate food that was produced or cooked by strangers, concerns about food adulteration (such as the chemical whitening of bread mentioned above) heightened. These concerns led to the first British adulteration of foods law in 1860. However, adulterated foods became so prevalent that many people came to prefer the contaminated version. Thus, in 1891 British grocers felt forced, despite pure-food laws, to sell adulterated pepper to common folk; for example, consumers had become so used to adulterated pepper that some customers returned pure pepper to stores because it was too dark or too strong.

TECHNOLOGICAL ADVANCES

Industrialization also produced changes in the food itself, as new methods of preparing and preserving foods were invented. For example, the use of antiseptic methods, freezing techniques, and heating in a vacuum were all new in the nineteenth century. Infants, and foundlings in particular, had the most to gain from the work of Louis Pasteur (1822–1895), who demonstrated the existence of microorganisms and developed pasteurization in the 1860s. When mothers do not breast-feed infants, not only an alternative food but an alternative method of administering that food is required. Thus, before sterilization techniques were widespread, non-breast-fed infants were dying from the bacteria that grew in the unsterilized cloths or bottles that were used to feed them.

Merchant fleets, navies, and the military encouraged methods of food preservation. Bouillon broth was dried, formed into bars, and used as ships rations. In the early nineteenth century, Nicolas-François Appert (1750–1841), a French confectioner, developed canning as a method of preserving meats for Napolean's armies. Initially, canned goods were expensive because the cans were individually made and packed by hand, so it was not until industrial methods were developed near the end of the century that canned goods were used regularly by the general public.

Much of the worry over preservation focused on meat. The rival to canning was freezing, and refrigeration techniques allowed sea fish to be taken inland for sale. These new methods of preservation were popular because they eliminated the need for so much curing, and frozen or canned meats had less salt. Ironically, even as new preservation techniques were developed for meat, the need for those techniques was diminishing: with the advent of rail service, dressed meat could be shipped in quickly before it spoiled. However, these techniques would pave the way for cheaper meat from the Americas and from Australia and New Zealand. The first successful transatlantic shipment occurred in 1878: a ship sailed from Buenos Aires, Argentina, with five thousand carcasses of frozen mutton and arrived in Le Havre, France, with the mutton intact.

Of course, changes in transportation also affect the availability and diversity of food. In 1844, milk reached Manchester, England, by rail for the first time, and shipments soon began to London; rail transport lowered British food prices and made fresh eggs, green vegetables, fresh fish, and country-killed meat available more quickly.

Europeans also had an increasing desire for sugar, which by the nineteenth century was usually provided by slave labor in the colonies in the West Indies and Americas. However, when Britain's naval blockade impeded importation of sugar to France, Napoleon announced a prize for finding an alternative solution. In 1801 the first sugar-beet factory was built. As Europeans became less dependent on their colonies or other countries for sugar, sugar became more and more important in the European diet.

See also **Alcohol and Temperance; Coffee, Tea, Chocolate; Demography; Wine.**

BIBLIOGRAPHY

Shephard, Sue. *Pickled, Potted, and Canned: How the Art and Science of Food Preserving Changed the World.* New York, 2001.

Tannahill, Reay. *Food in History.* New York, 1973.

Teuteberg, Hans J. "The General Relationship between Diet and Industrialization." In *European Diet from Pre-Industrial to Modern Times,* edited by Elborg Forster and Robert Forster. New York, 1975.

Thorne, Stuart. *The History of Food Preservation.* Totowa, N.J., 1986.

Woodham Smith, Cecil. *The Great Hunger: Ireland, 1845–1849.* London, 1962.

KATHRYN A. WALTERSCHEID

DILTHEY, WILHELM (1833–1911), German philosopher.

Wilhelm Dilthey was born in Biebrich, near Wiesbaden, in 1833 and died in Siusi am Schlern, in the South Tyrol, in 1911. He studied in Berlin under the philosopher Friedrich Adolf Trendelenburg (1802–1872) and the leaders of the "Historical School." After giving up early theological studies, he turned to a wide-ranging examination of the culture of the age of Johann Wolfgang von Goethe (1749–1832), as seen also through the prism of the life and work of Friedrich Schleiermacher (1768–1834). The result was a colossal but never completed *Life of Schleiermacher,* of which only a first volume (1870) appeared in Dilthey's lifetime.

After teaching in Basel, Kiel, and Breslau, Dilthey returned to Berlin in 1882 and stayed there until the end of his life. In 1883 he published an *Introduction to the Human Sciences,* which presented the theoretical and methodological results of his philosophical reflections and historical research. The work was conceived as the first part of a "critique of historical reason" whose foundation was the principle of anthropological unity and the conception of temporality as the historical dimension of reason. In this volume Dilthey deployed both the analysis of inner experience and the investigation of historicocultural reality in support of the idea that the knowledge characteristic of the "human sciences" was a knowledge founded not on explanation but on understanding. His essays of the 1880s and 1890s, dealing with issues still outstanding, including the theory of knowledge, logic, methodology, and so on, effectively rounded out and articulated the entire project. Thus in "Poetics" (1887), the analysis of artistic creativity helped explain the metamorphic character of experience.

An essay on reality published in 1890 stressed that the origin of belief in the external world lay in will and sentiment rather than in representation; and two psychological papers (1894–1895) evoked a method of investigation that rejected the methods of explanation and association derived from empiricism and sought instead to apprehend what is typical and historical in individuals. The general outline of Dilthey's thought is discernible in several manuscripts of the same period that also propose the development of a not formal logic that would reveal the immanent structures—or "categories"—of life. These years also produced fruitful correspondence between Dilthey and Count Paul Yorck von Wartenburg.

From 1896 on, Dilthey delved more deeply into important aspects of the "history of the German spirit," exploring the origins of anthropological knowledge, before Goethe, and producing monographic studies such as that on the young Georg Wilhelm Friedrich Hegel (1770–1831) or those of a historicoliterary nature collected in *Lived Experience and Poetry* (1906). At the same time he reviewed the general principles of his philosophical orientation, finding fresh avenues to explore not only in the history of hermeneutics but also in the incipient phenomenology of Edmund Husserl (1859–1938). In his writings after 1905, these avenues converged into a new phenomenological and hermeneutic project, a "construction of the historical world," centered on the relationships between lived experience, expression, and understanding, that was integral to Dilthey's morphological comparison of the ways in which life and world are conceived of by different Weltanschauungen.

The last year of Dilthey's life was marked by his polemic with Husserl, who in an essay had accused him of vitalism and relativism. As the correspondence between the two philosophers makes clear, Dilthey looked on this polemic as evidence of the same sort of inattentive reading and misunderstanding that had underlain criticisms leveled at his work at the time of his psychological studies of 1894–1895. On the other hand, it needs to be borne in mind that much of the historical reception of Dilthey's thought has been dominated by the application of preconceived notions. In fact many early interpreters described Dilthey's thinking in terms of antithetical phases, and sought to supply continuity by speaking of a psychological phase and a hermeneutic one, or a Kantian moment and a Hegelian one, thus failing to grasp its radical unity. Matters were not improved later, when twentieth-century hermeneutics, notably that of Hans-Georg Gadamer (1900–2002), merely reinforced the image of a Dilthey imbued with the Romantic spirit but at the same time caught in the toils of positivism, as though his entire work were exclusively concerned with methodological problems. No less destructive were interpretations of Dilthey from the camp of Marxist cultural criticism, which often stressed the supposedly antirationalist aspects of his philosophy of life.

Research in the 1970s based on important, hitherto unpublished manuscripts threw serious doubt on such readings. The upshot has been a new sense of the unity of a Diltheyan thought engaged in rich and fruitful dialogue with crucial aspects of phenomenology. This has in turn helped illuminate the strong relevance that Dilthey's philosophy had in the 1920s not only for Husserl but also for Martin Heidegger (1889–1976); it has likewise facilitated the reassessment of developments in Diltheyan thought attributable to the philosopher's principal followers (notably Georg Misch, 1889–1965).

See also **Goethe, Johann Wolfgang von; Hegel, Georg Wilhelm Friedrich; History; Husserl, Edmund; Ranke, Leopold von; Schleiermacher, Friedrich.**

BIBLIOGRAPHY

Primary Sources

Dilthey, Wilhelm. *Selected Works.* Edited by Rudolf A. Makkreel and Frithjof Rodi. 5 vols. Princeton, N.J., 1985–2003.

Secondary Sources

Hodges, Herbert Arthur. *The Philosophy of Wilhelm Dilthey.* London, 1952.

Makkreel, Rudolf A. *Dilthey, Philosopher of the Human Studies.* Princeton, N.J., 1975.

Rodi, Frithjof. *Das strukturierte Ganze: Studien zum Werk von Wilhelm Dilthey.* Weilerswist, Germany, 2003.

GIOVANNI MATTEUCCI

DIPLOMACY.

Since the fifteenth century, the European international system had been composed of sovereign states, among which five Great Powers had attained ascendancy by 1750: France, Great Britain, Russia, Prussia, and Austria. Each sovereign state recognized no higher law or authority than itself. The inevitable result was unrestrained competition for power and survival, which reached its climax in the late eighteenth century with the Partitions of Poland (1772, 1793, and 1795), which its perpetrators did not even try to justify by any law. The only restraint was the idea of the "balance of power": if one state became so strong as to threaten imperial domination over all, the others would unite to prevent it.

REVOLUTION AND NAPOLEON

This international anarchy became still more ruthless after the French Revolution (1789), whose revolutionary ideals provided both a rationalization for aggression and a new means to sustain it: the nation in arms. A generation of war, lasting from 1792 to 1815, was the result, brought to its climax by the insatiable ambition and military genius of Napoleon. During these years, European diplomacy consisted of little more than efforts, unsuccessful until 1813, to form a coalition that could defeat him.

THE CONGRESS OF VIENNA

When after Napoleon's fall Europe's statesmen met at the Congress of Vienna (1814–1815), they came convinced that Europe could not afford another generation of war. Simply reviving the balance of power and taking precautions against renewed French aggression would not suffice. A new diplomatic order for Europe had to be constructed, one that would avoid the flaws not merely of the revolutionary era, but of the age of iron power politics that had preceded and paved the way for it. Their solution was the "Concert of Europe," a concept based on the realization that war was a threat to all, and so all must cooperate to prevent it. The Great Powers, following a novel policy of restraint and limited aims, would work together to settle disputes by consensus rather than confrontation. This policy was successfully applied at the congress: although many disputes arose, involving major national interests that in earlier times would probably have led to war, all were settled peacefully.

To carry on this policy after the congress, in 1815 Britain, Russia, Austria, and Prussia signed the Quadruple Alliance. It was directed against further French aggression, but its true importance was that it also provided that the signatories would hold periodic meetings to settle problems that might threaten the peace. This was the foundation for the system of conferences that was largely responsible for the relative peace Europe would enjoy until 1914.

THE CONCERT IN OPERATION

For forty years after 1815, conferences met to deal with any threat to peace. One threat came from liberal-nationalist revolutions against the existing order, which were often in areas where the interests of the Great Powers clashed. For example, in 1820 revolution broke out in Italy. Austria, the predominant power there, was determined to suppress it, but met with opposition from France and Russia, which had their own Italian ambitions. A serious quarrel arose, but in the end, the spirit of the concert prevailed and a peaceful settlement was reached. A greater threat to peace came with the Belgian revolt against Dutch rule in 1830. Belgium had long been a flashpoint, where the colliding interests of the powers had often led to war. But the powers met in conference, and a question that in earlier times would surely have led to war, was settled peacefully by mutual agreement that Belgium would become independent and neutral. Even in the great revolutionary wave of 1848 to 1849, covering the entire continent west of Russia, conference diplomacy prevented any war among the powers. Another danger lay in the "Eastern Question." The Ottoman Empire was in terminal decline, threatened by revolt among its Christian subjects in the Balkans and the territorial ambitions of Russia—ambitions the other Great Powers opposed, because, if gratified, they would upset the balance of power. Several crises resulted, but all were settled peacefully.

DECLINE OF THE CONCERT

But in the 1850s the Concert of Europe began to decline. The basic cause was the passing of the generation of statesmen who had endured the Napoleonic Wars and their replacement by new leaders who, lacking those traumatic memories, were more willing to go to war to achieve their ambitions. Chief among them was Emperor Napoleon III (r. 1852–1871) of France. He aimed to make France once again the leading power, by acting as the champion of the European nationalist movement. Since the conservative powers, especially Russia, opposed this aim, he deliberately broke with the concert, and engineered a war intended to weaken Russia. For the first time in forty years, the Great Powers went to war—the Crimean War (1853–1856), Russia versus France, Britain, and Turkey. Russia was badly defeated, and for the next decade withdrew from international affairs.

The field was now free for Napoleon III to act. His first target was Italy, where a growing nationalist movement sought to end Austrian domination and create a unified state. In 1858 he negotiated a secret agreement with Count Camillo Cavour, leader of Piedmont-Sardinia, the strongest and most ambitious Italian state: they would provoke the Austrians into war, drive them out, and set up an Italian confederation, in which France was to have a dominant role. Attempts by the other powers to mediate were brushed aside, and once again, war was deliberately provoked, ending in Austrian defeat and Italian unification.

Napoleon's policy had seriously weakened the concert, but Otto von Bismarck of Prussia provided the final blow. Though Bismarck used German nationalism to win popular support, his true aim was to strengthen Prussia by expanding its control over all Germany. Because this aim could be attained only by war, he too rejected the concert. With great skill and unscrupulousness, he provoked a war in 1866 with Austria that led to Prussian control of northern Germany. France opposed any further Prussian advance as a threat to its security, so Bismarck maneuvered France into the Franco-Prussian War (1870–1871). Victory allowed him to complete German unification, at the cost of lasting French hostility.

By 1871 irretrievable damage had been done to the Concert of Europe. Leaders had defied it, rejected its efforts at mediation, and benefited by deliberately provoking wars. Their success was fatal to the spirit of the concert. Conferences were still held in times of crisis, but not, as in the past, to settle problems in a spirit of consensus, but as tests of power between rival states.

EUROPE WITHOUT THE CONCERT

Europe thus entered upon a new and dangerous era. The Eastern Question reemerged, as revolts by the Christian peoples of the Balkans against Turkish rule multiplied, reviving Russian ambitions, to the alarm of the other powers. Serious crises resulted in 1875 and 1884. Another source of tension was the rise of the "new imperialism" in the 1880s. Unlike earlier European imperialism, which had sought economically valuable colonies such as India, the new imperialism was largely driven by irrational factors, as a means to demonstrate national greatness. The most spectacular example was the "scramble for Africa," in which virtually that entire continent was seized by one power or another. Here too, fierce competition among the powers for colonies lead to several crises, notably the Fashoda Affair in 1898, when British and French expeditionary forces stumbled into each other in southern Sudan, and war between France and Britain seemed briefly possible.

That these crises did not lead to war among the Great Powers was not because the concert revived, but because in each crisis the strength of one side or the other was so clearly superior that its rival did not dare risk war. Another factor making for peace was, ironically, Bismarck. Since he saw his new German Empire threatened by the usual tendency of the powers to unite against any state that seemed to threaten the balance of power, he ostentatiously followed a policy of restraint. Fearing that Germany would be dragged into any European war, he used all his skill to settle crises peacefully. He arranged alliances with most of the other powers, partly to isolate France, but also as a means of influencing his allies to keep the peace.

THE ROAD TO WORLD WAR I

Deterioration began when the new German emperor, William II, dismissed Bismarck in 1890. Though the emperor did not have the plans for European domination often ascribed to him, he had little grasp of the realities of international affairs or of Germany's true interests. Moreover, he was tactless and given to rhetorical outbursts about Germany's rightful place in the world. He soon managed to alienate most of Germany's allies and to arouse growing suspicion of his ultimate objectives.

By 1907, Russia and France were allies, and Britain had come to an understanding with them for cooperation. Germany's only remaining ally was Austria.

The stage was now set for the crises that paved the way for World War I. Two crises, in 1905 and 1911, arose from French efforts to annex Morocco, violating German interests there guaranteed by earlier agreements. Germany had cause for complaint, but the threatening way in which it demanded compensation alienated the other powers, which backed France. In both crises Germany retreated, because the question clearly was not worth war, but remained resentful.

The two Balkan crises were far more dangerous, for they involved the vital interests of a Great Power. Since 1903, Serbia had sought by agitation and terrorism to force the multinational Austrian Empire to yield its southern Slavic lands. Austria was determined to resist, fearing that if after the loss of Italy and Germany, its Slavic provinces too were lost, it would mean the end of the empire. Austria could have easily subdued Serbia, but the latter was supported by Russia and its allies France and Britain, while Germany felt compelled to support Austria, its only remaining ally, or face isolation. Thus, Austro-Serb quarrels led to crises that threatened war, in 1908 to 1909 and 1912 to 1913. In both, Austrian policy was essentially defensive, facing an aggressive Serbia backed by Russia. Each side appealed to its allies, and soon Austria and Germany faced Russia, France, and Britain in a crisis that threatened war. On both occasions, Britain and France refused to go to war over Balkan issues, forcing Russia to retreat. Peace was preserved, but the international situation remained very dangerous. Russia, bitterly resentful, was resolved to accept no more defeats, while France and Britain feared that another failure to support Russia would lose its alliance. Austria found its victories did it little good, for Serbia, more hostile than ever, escalated its agitation and terrorism.

THE 1914 CRISIS

On 28 June 1914 Serbian-backed terrorists assassinated Francis Ferdinand, heir to the Austrian throne. This convinced the enraged Austrians that since diplomatic victories had failed to end Serbian terrorism, only military action would suffice. Austria sent Serbia an ultimatum designed to be rejected and so give a pretext for invasion. Austria wanted only a limited war, hoping that strong German support would force Russia to back down once again. William II promised support, giving Austria-Hungary the infamous "blank check," although he too hoped that a firm stand would prevent a general war. But Russia after two previous humiliations was in no mood to retreat: it promised Serbia full support and mobilized its army. The other powers responded with their own mobilizations. France, afraid to lose Russia's alliance, promised it full support. Last-minute efforts by Britain and Germany to avert war failed—no power was willing to accept another diplomatic defeat, and none realized how disastrous modern war would be: all expected a quick, relatively bloodless conflict, not the four-year-long bloodbath that lay ahead. On 31 August Germany demanded that Russia and France end mobilization, and after their refusal, declared war.

World War I was the logical consequence of Europe's gradual return to international anarchy after 1850. In 1815 statesmen horrified by the disasters of the Napoleonic Wars had created the Concert of Europe in the hope of establishing the basis for lasting peace. Their great effort had been undermined by leaders whose determination to achieve their ambitions had led them to forget the lesson the statesmen of 1815 had learned from bitter experience—that war was the common enemy of all. Europe would now have to learn that lesson again, in an even greater war.

See also **Bismarck, Otto von; Cavour, Count (Camillo Benso); Concert of Europe; Congress of Vienna; Eastern Question; Fashoda Affair; Francis Ferdinand; Napoleon III; William II.**

BIBLIOGRAPHY

Primary Sources

German Diplomatic Documents, 1871–1914. Selected and translated by E. T. S. Dugdale. 4 vols. London, 1928–1931.

Metternich, Clemens von. *Memoirs of Prince Metternich.* Edited by Richard von Metternich-Winneburg. Translated by Mrs. Alexander Napier. 5 vols. London, 1880–1882.

Secondary Sources

Anderson, M. S. *The Eastern Question, 1774–1923: A Study in International Relations.* London, 1966.

Bridge, F. R. *The Habsburg Monarchy among the Great Powers, 1815–1918.* New York, 1990.

Gulick, Edward Vose. *Europe's Classical Balance of Power: A Case History of the Theory and Practice of One of the Great Concepts of European Statecraft.* Ithaca, N.Y., 1955. Reprint, Westport, Conn., 1982.

Jelavich, Barbara. *A Century of Russian Foreign Policy, 1814–1914.* Philadelphia, 1964.

Pflanze, Otto. *Bismarck and the Development of Germany.* 2nd ed. 3 vols. Princeton, N.J., 1990.

Schroeder, Paul W. *The Transformation of European Politics, 1763–1848.* Oxford, U.K., 1994.

Taylor, A. J. P. *The Struggle for Mastery in Europe, 1848–1918.* Oxford, U.K., 1954.

ALAN J. REINERMAN

DIRECTORY. The Directory, the name given to the form of executive power adopted in France from August 1795 to November 1799, has not been much favored by historians. For too long it was cast to one side, treated as an unwanted codicil by a generation whose main focus was on the Jacobin Republic and who showed little interest in a regime that preferred stability to radical change and sought to impose order at almost any price. Its limited constitution—seen as a reversal of the move toward wider participation that had marked the early years of the republic—was dismissed as timid or bourgeois, a step backward from democracy that reflected the natural caution of leaders whose respect for order was matched only by their contempt for the ordinary people of Paris. Its executive of five directors was derided for the supposed mediocrity of its members—in the first instance Paul de Barras, Louis-Marie de La Révellière-Lépeaux, Jean-François Reubell, Louis-Honoré Letourneur, and Lazare Carnot. France, it was alleged, was bored—a claim that is supported in the falling away of political activity, the closure of clubs, and the slow, lingering death of a once vibrant political press. For many the Directory seemed a period of drab decline, a staging post along the road to the military coup d'état of 18 Brumaire (9 November 1799) that brought Napoleon to power.

But it is questionable whether the Directory represented a real break in the continuity of the

Revolution. In Georges Lefebvre's words, "the Thermidorians abandoned power and right away took it back again under cover of the Constitution of the Year III" (p. 1). The same deputies continued in office, with an essentially unchanged agenda. And the new constitution struggled with the same problem, that of finding a workable balance between executive and legislative power, a problem endemic since the end of the constitutional monarchy, when the revolutionaries enshrined all sovereign authority in a single body, the Convention. The new constitution was intended to correct the errors of the Jacobins, to create responsible and durable institutions for the republic. It did not betray the principles of the republic, but rewrote them in a way that supported the owners of property, the defenders of the social order. The words of the Declaration of the Rights of Man were still inscribed above the text, as they had been in every constitution since 1791, giving them the power of constitutional law; but, in contrast to previous constitutions, these words were now accompanied by others, defining the obligations incumbent on citizens, the duties that came with the fundamental rights. What had changed was simply the balance of responsibility between the individual and the collectivity; and yet this was a quite fundamental change. Gone was the dream of universal male suffrage. A French citizen was defined as "every man fully twenty-one years of age, born and residing in France, who has had himself enrolled on the civil register of his canton, has lived thereafter on the territory of the Republic, and pays a direct land tax or personal property tax"; soldiers who had fought for the republic were given citizenship without this qualification. Gone, too, was the notion that citizens should vote directly for their legislators; the new electoral system was indirect, with electors choosing the deputies, while the legislature itself was reconstituted in two chambers, the Conseil des Cinq-Cents (Council of the Five Hundred) and the Conseil des Anciens (Council of the Ancients), whose members were older, at least thirty and forty, respectively. At every turn the Directory sought to guarantee maturity and stability.

REPUBLICAN CREDENTIALS

The new regime shared with the Thermidorians a fear of neo-Jacobinism and popular violence. But its republican credentials should not be questioned. The creation of a five-man executive did not contradict any political law of republicanism—after all, the Jacobins had passed executive power to a much more authoritarian body, the Committee of Public Safety—while legislative answerability was assured by instituting annual elections. In fact, the turnout in these elections was often poor, especially in rural areas, and there was considerable uncertainty about who had the right to vote. The Directory never succeeded in persuading the electorate to give it their enthusiastic support, and the apparent self-interest shown by the deputies in passing the Two-Thirds Law, which attempted to guarantee their retention of office, was seen by many as a blatant attempt to subvert the will of the people. Besides, having to hold elections every year was itself a source of public disorder in many parts of the country, and the Directory had to use military force to make the constitution work: there were serious coups, from either the Left or the Right, every year from 1797 to 1800. In response the government appeared to swing like a pendulum from one year to the next, aligning itself opportunistically against the perceived danger of the moment—be it François-Noël Babeuf's Conspiracy of the Equals in 1796 or a serious threat of royalist insurrection in 1797. The recurrent hustings only provided an excuse for electoral violence, violence that bred upon the bitterly divided polity that the Directory inherited from the Jacobins and their tormentors. The elections also threatened the very stability that the Directors sought to ensure, and when the voting threatened to produce a majority that was too extreme—most notably with the neo-Jacobin resurgence in Year VI (1798)—the government did not hesitate to overturn the results and order a purge of the legislature. The appearance of weakness was hard to conceal, and this was only increased by stumbling attempts to counter the financial instability that the Directory had inherited. By 1795 the assignat was wholly discredited, rendered worthless by a mixture of public distrust and uncontrolled inflation. The government therefore abandoned it in order to avert financial chaos, turning first to another form of paper, the *mandats territoriaux* (a system of government bonds backed by national lands), before reverting to metal currency and setting off a spiral of deflation and misery. It was only in 1798 that measures to balance the budget and consolidate the national debt began to rebuild confidence and establish fragile economic stability.

POLICY UNDER THE DIRECTORY

If the political order was built within the republican tradition, so were the Directory's priorities in policymaking. Bourgeois it may have been, and charges of corruption against its leaders were certainly sustainable. But there was no attempt to subvert the republic; the directors' stated aim was to strengthen republican values by avoiding the excesses of radical egalitarianism and political factionalism. They praised the value of republican symbolism, enforcing the use of the new calendar and introducing a panoply of revolutionary festivals to mark everything from the seasons of the year to the phases of human life. They opposed royalism in all its forms, whether in cliques within the army or in the return from emigration of some of the nobles and monarchists who had sought refuge abroad. They also remained true to the anticlericalism of the Jacobins, making no attempt to reinstate the clergy or to reinstitute religious worship in France. The most that the Directory would do for Catholic opinion was to permit individual communities to reopen their churches and hold Catholic services—but there was no official encouragement to do so; it remained a concession made in response to local demand, often from vocal groups of local women who had not acclimatized to the faithless world of dechristianization. Elsewhere, churches remained closed, and after the royalist coup of 18 Fructidor Year V (4 September 1797), the government insisted that all practicing clergy should swear an oath of hatred to kings. In areas such as the West, the religious wounds opened by the Civil Constitution of the Clergy (1790) remained raw, and by 1799 the Directory faced renewed violence in the Catholic heartlands of the Vendée.

The measures taken by the Directory in other spheres contributed to the maintenance of a secular regime. Educational reforms promoted institutions of higher learning—notably the École normale supérieure and the École polytechnique, in Paris—while Joseph Lakanal urged greater interest in public schooling at the primary level, again without proposing any role for the church. If laws and decrees suggested greater investment than actually occurred, it is as much a reflection on the state of the economy as on the difficulties experienced in finding and training schoolteachers in the small towns and villages of the provinces. Increasingly, indeed, state policy was thwarted by financial restraints—at a time when the country's energy was increasingly channeled into foreign war and imperial acquisition. The Directory aimed to increase French influence across Europe—the wars after 1795 were conducted entirely on foreign soil—and the electorate at home followed the campaigns of generals such as Louis-Lazare Hoche and Napoleon Bonaparte with enthusiasm. The contrast between foreign glory and domestic malaise was only too glaring, as the French created sister republics in Holland and Switzerland, and divided Belgium, the Rhineland, and northern Italy into departments on the French model. They claimed to be bringing the benefits of liberty to the peoples of Europe. But they also pillaged the lands they conquered, seizing money and art treasures in Italy and sequestrating one-third of the grain produced in Belgium. This invited resentment, proving that liberty cannot easily be imposed at the point of a bayonet.

See also **French Revolution; Jacobins; Reign of Terror; Sister Republics.**

BIBLIOGRAPHY

Cobb, Richard. *Reactions to the French Revolution.* London, 1972.

Crook, Malcolm. *Elections in the French Revolution: An Apprenticeship in Democracy, 1789–1799.* Cambridge, U.K., 1996.

Dupuy, Roger, and Marcel Morabito, eds. *1795: Pour une République sans Révolution.* Rennes, France, 1996.

Godechot, Jacques. *La grande nation: L'expansion révolutionnaire de la France dans le monde de 1789 à 1799.* 2nd ed. Paris, 1983.

Lefebvre, Georges. *The Directory.* Translated by Robert Baldick. London, 1965.

Lyons, Martyn. *France under the Directory.* Cambridge, U.K., 1975.

ALAN FORREST

DISEASE. An epidemic is a sudden disastrous event in the same way as a hurricane, an earthquake, or a flood. Such events reveal many facets of the societies in which they occur. The stress they cause tests social stability and cohesion. Epidemics, however, have their own characteristics, one of which is that while they cause social upheaval they are also caused by it. The massive dislocation brought about by the transformation of agrarian into industrial societies from the end of the eighteenth century in Western states produced its own patterns of epidemic invasions.

DISEASE AND DISASTER: EPIDEMICS AND SOCIETY IN THE NINETEENTH CENTURY

In Britain, for example, up to the late seventeenth century the population grew gradually. The early modern period witnessed new surges in population growth in a society with an exponentially expanding economic base. In the nineteenth century epidemic diseases caused massive levels of mortality in the first industrial society, and yet population growth soared. Toward the end of the nineteenth century Britain began to see a dramatic decline in premature mortality and an increased length of average life. In other Western industrializing societies similar patterns recurred. Changing patterns of economic development were a major factor in bringing about demographic change from the early modern to the modern period, allowing earlier marriage and rising standards of living, which led to increased fertility and less hunger. But can the modern rise of population be accounted for purely by the reduction in famine and malnutrition and improved overall levels of nutritional status? Or has intervention in the spread of infectious disease played an equally important role?

Studying the epidemic streets of nineteenth-century industrializing societies provides one insight into these questions. The sprawling urban world of high-density masses took the lives of innocents more than anything else. Infant death was responsible for a huge proportion of preventable mortality in the nineteenth-century industrial city. Among the most economically deprived who had least access to the facilities that would provide a hygienic environment for infant life, millions of infants died. They succumbed to measles, whooping cough, smallpox, and, above all, diarrhea. Children and young adults died of diphtheria and tuberculosis. Everyone from all age groups caught fever—

typhoid and typhus—and the great grim reaper, cholera, brought periodic devastation. Urban proletariats, however, were largely well fed enough throughout the nineteenth century to remain above the level of malnutrition that would effect immunity to these diseases, so what accounts for declining mortality from them as the century wore on? How can this be explained if improved nutrition does not provide the whole answer?

Taking the British case as an example a bit further, the prevention of infantile diarrhea depended upon a clean water supply for washing utensils and maintaining sufficient levels of domestic hygiene. This gradually became available in Britain starting in the late nineteenth century and coincided with the period of mortality decline. Diphtheria, by contrast, needed the temporary isolation of the disease from the school population in order to prevent the disease from spreading. Starting in the 1870s, local health officers in Britain had the power to close schools and isolate victims and their siblings. At this time a number of factors began to converge that increasingly provided a protective environment for all against infectious disease. Newer levels of social stability created the opportunity for masses of the population to settle and control their immediate environments as the pace of industrial growth and urbanization slowed and its infrastructural developments became fixed and functional. Direct interventions to halt the routes of infection had also been operating for a continuous period by this time, namely, the environmental and preventive medical reforms of the sanitary and state medical movements. In Britain the preventive idea had been proselytized by new bearers of a professionalized hygienic ideology, medical officers of health, and by the turn of the century this began to have an effect on domestic consciousness, reducing the apathy toward infectious disease and encouraging new practices within the home. Above all a society that had experienced a century of massive economic, social, and technological transition was beginning to solidify and learn to cope with the penalties of expansion. Displaced populations were beginning to settle, social dislocation was reduced, public health intervention had begun to take effect, and infectious disease began to decline.

Two epidemic diseases of the nineteenth century illustrate this process more than any other and have come to characterize the costs of the level of urbanization that accompanied industrialization. Typhus is a disease that flourishes among populations who live under the circumstances of refugees without access to stable, hygienic shelter, clean water, and enough food. It became a persistent feature of poverty among inner-city populations, especially among the migrant and itinerant poor. Typhus is transmitted to humans through the vector of body lice. It attacks people who live in dirty conditions without access to clean surroundings and clothes. It was traditionally associated with jail inmates, armies, and famine victims, all of whom lived under such conditions. In the nineteenth century it was the migrant urban populations who suffered from typhus most. Migration became a defining demographic characteristic of early industrial societies. Agricultural laborers migrated to become industrial workers and members of the industrial proletariat, and *Lumpenproletariat* often moved more than once during a lifetime to follow the geography of the business cycle. But the populations that migrated to look for work became the poorest and most deprived in the urban environment. They were last in line and had least access to the facilities the city could offer—a stable roof over their heads, clean water, regular employment, and a sufficient income to provide them with an adequate subsistence. They were dirty, hungry, and, in the winter, cold. They became louse-ridden. They were attacked by typhus in droves.

Typhus became a disease that the migrant poor always had with them, but among epidemic disasters of the nineteenth century cholera was king. Asiatic cholera swept through Europe from India like an avenging angel. Caused by waterborne fecal germs, cholera revealed its own story about the social, political, and economic relations of industrial societies. It demonstrated the dysfunction of mass aggregation in the urban environment and the tenuous stability of class relations. Over the course of the century, it stimulated governments into creating policies to improve the environmental conditions that had facilitated its massive pandemic spread. Cholera killed with shocking speed and vicious regularity. At its peak it could wipe out communities in a week. The social-psychological effect of cholera on the nineteenth-century mentality was devastating. It became the symbol of the human costs of exponential industrial and economic growth.

Understanding epidemic disease in industrial society and how to control it required nineteenth-century state and civic authorities to rethink their approaches. Following traditional patterns of quarantine and isolation employed in the control of plague proved inadequate. For one thing, cholera seemed to defy the contagionist theory of disease. It bypassed quarantine procedures and isolation measures, cutting across all traditional barriers erected to protect the community. Miasmatic etiology seemed to offer a more plausible explanation. It could explain cholera's transmission across cordon sanitaires and suggested the answer might be to clean up the environment rather than issue quarantines, which stopped the economic lifeblood of free-market trading societies. As cholera raged among urban communities until late in the nineteenth century, politicians, doctors, and disease theorists fought over how it was caused and how it could be eliminated.

DISEASE, DISLOCATION, AND SOCIAL ORDER

Epidemic disease took the question of population health to a high point on the political agenda of the nineteenth century. Disease became the definitive symbol of the dislocations experienced by industrializing societies.

Numerous scholars who have looked at disease in history, such as William H. McNeill and Alfred W. Crosby, have discovered how it has frequently precipitated widespread social disruption and upheaval and has been a factor in bringing about revolutionary changes. Disease has subsequently been examined as a test of social cohesion at different periods. Much of the scholarly work on nineteenth-century cholera, for example, has set out to demonstrate the link between pandemic waves and revolutionary uprisings. Other scholars have suggested that cholera was the spur to the development of public health administration throughout Europe. More recent studies, however, have challenged this view and have demonstrated how a much broader set of events combined with epidemic episodes to stimulate the growth of public health administrations.

Did disease precipitate social disruption or was it precipitated by it? Certainly cholera pandemics coincided with times of severe disorder and unrest in nineteenth-century Europe. The first European epidemic of 1831 to 1832 followed the tail end of the revolutions on the European continent in 1830 and took place during the most violent period of civil disorder resulting from political agitation for parliamentary reform in Britain in 1832. The second pandemic of 1848 to 1849 began in the year of revolutions in Germany and France, and the 1854 epidemic followed the outbreak of the Crimean War (1853–1856). The 1866 epidemic occurred as the German federation was demolished after Otto von Bismarck's war with Austria, and the Second Empire fell in France as cholera spread during 1871. At the time of the last wave of cholera in 1892, there were major disturbances in Russia and Poland.

Cholera created violence and rioting, especially during the epidemic of 1831 to 1832. In Russia the peasant masses rioted against their feudal lords in the belief that there was a deliberate campaign to poison the water as part of a Malthusian conspiracy to kill off the poor and relieve the state of the financial burden of poverty. Riots occurred in Paris against medical officials for similar reasons. In England the cholera riots of 1832 were directed at doctors, this time in the belief that the medical profession was encouraging the spread of cholera to obtain bodies for anatomical dissection.

It is easy to understand why cholera should have created such unrest if one considers how European authorities generally responded to it. Most authorities when faced with the prospect of the epidemic in 1831 simply employed the old quarantine procedures used in feudal times against the plague. That is, they set cordon sanitaires with military enforcement, closed down public meeting places, and sealed off cities and towns. But these measures, which were passively accepted by the masses living under absolute states in the seventeenth and eighteenth centuries, were not so easily imposed upon a generation that had witnessed the rise of radical democratic popular movements, following the lead of the American and French Revolutions. The coincidence of inexplicable mass mortality and the sudden appearance of government officials, medical officers, and military troops aroused popular suspicion and unrest. The bourgeois authorities became the object of conspiracy theories among the poor and were attacked as the

agents of a class war. The homes of noblemen and the offices of health authorities were ransacked throughout Prussia, and officials were murdered in Paris. In Britain doctors were attacked in Bristol, not for being agents of the state, but as the result of the popular conceptions about their sinister, macabre trade in dead flesh.

Cholera, however, spread though Europe largely as an effect of social disorder rather than being the cause of it. It did follow dearth and famine, but there is only limited evidence that malnutrition lowers the stomach acid level and weakens resistance. Much more significantly it followed the movements of troops and the disruption of war. Cholera was first transmitted from its original home in India by the military campaign fought by the Marquis of Hastings against the Marathas in 1817. In 1831 the Russian war against Poland spread the disease from Asia to Europe. British troops spread it to Portugal, and in 1866 cholera was spread by the war between Austria and Italy. In 1854 French troops transferred the disease again eastward when they landed in Gallipoli during the Crimean War. It is easy to understand why troop movements spread the disease. War produces mass movements of refugee populations who abandon their homes only to end up living in appalling, unsanitary encampments. Troops themselves are cramped and confined in grossly unsanitary camps that rapidly spread disease to the nearest civilian settlement. Demobilized soldiers carry disease back to their civilian homes. Above all, overcrowded prisoner-of-war camps became fever hubs.

Apart from war, the increasing mobility of populations through the expansion of trade during the nineteenth century was the most important vehicle for the spread of cholera. The waterborne disease followed canal routes and rivers and was carried by sailors, traders, and shipping workers. Service occupations involving water, such as cleaning and washing and innkeeping, were always the first groups to succumb.

Cholera was also spread by social dislocation and subsequently exacerbated it. This pattern of social dislocation and epidemic spread is equally demonstrated for another acute infection characteristic of the times, typhus. Typhus has a long history of being associated with war and famine, frequently flourishing in military encampments and jails. Typhus, however, became almost endemic among some urban populations during the nineteenth century. Again, this reflected the social dislocation occurring in the everyday life of towns and cities that were undergoing rapid, large-scale economic and social change based on incessant population migration. The precise relationship of cause and effect between typhus and industrialization is, nevertheless, complex and difficult to untangle.

Taking the example of one city, the patterns of typhus epidemics in Victorian London are not immediately easy to explain. A steady decline of the disease occurred without any apparent correlation to hygiene or nutrition. There is no nutritional basis to immunity to typhus, although hunger is connected with it indirectly, and it followed periods of dearth and famine in the eighteenth century. Urban typhus, however, did not follow the slumps of the business cycle in Victorian Britain, and therefore different circumstances must account for its unpredictable pattern. Typhus epidemics in Victorian London were precipitated by the much more complex phenomenon of urban crisis rather than nutritional crisis. Urban crisis describes the combination of a number of features of deprivation, including hardship from political and economic conflicts, such as strikes and lockouts, and homelessness and overcrowding resulting from slum clearance and demolition for the construction of railways. Such forces can produce urban stress that a disease such as typhus can exploit.

Continuing outbreaks of typhus in London occurred between 1861 and 1869. Throughout the late 1850s the workers in the building trades in London had been locked out by their masters for refusing to not join a union. The industrial unrest caused widespread hardship and malnutrition. It coincided with a massive program of housing clearance for the construction of the railways. Certain areas of London were, by the 1860s, filled with families living in grossly overcrowded conditions—up to twelve people in one room—hungry and without a clean or regular water supply.

Typhus is a rickettsia disease that is spread by the human body louse. The rickettsias multiply in the body of the louse and are ejected in its feces. Humans contract it from scratching and breaking the surface of the skin. The disease can remain active in the feces dust of the louse for a long period and therefore can be breathed in from house dust in a dwelling that has not been disinfected. Hungry people feel the cold more and in the middle of winter are less likely to change their linen or wash their clothes. In these conditions they are much more likely to harbor lice and increase the opportunity for infection (leading to the flourishing of typhus in the winter months).

It was in the areas of great overcrowding where typhus became epidemic in the 1860s and then suddenly and dramatically declined after 1870. What accounted for the decline? First, the demolition program of the railways ceased, and municipal building programs began distributing the slum populations to new housing. The fever-nest slums were subsequently demolished. Second, a clean and constant water supply became available beginning at the end of the 1860s, which enhanced the chances of improved personal and domestic hygiene. Third, London's economy stabilized, and the laboring poor experienced a comparative period of minimum prosperity. Typhus clearly followed the social dislocation that resulted from urban crisis in Victorian London. The pattern of infection among Irish immigrants demonstrates this relationship most clearly. Contemporary moralists and medical investigators presumed that typhus was indigenous to the Irish and referred to it as Irish fever. But the epidemics occurred in London before they occurred in Dublin. The fact that many Irish immigrants lived in infected localities reflects the way that this group more than any other suffered the deprivations of urban crisis and were the most vulnerable to its ravages.

FRAMING HISTORY

Nineteenth-century typhus and cholera epidemics reveal how disease framed and is framed by history. Its biological existence was directly determined by social, economic, and political conditions, and it in turn brought about historical changes in those relationships. Epidemic diseases characterized the downside to economic and urban growth. They also revealed some of the intricate social changes taking place in industrial society.

Epidemic infections declined toward the end of the nineteenth century, creating the conditions for the demographic transformation of the increasingly aging and chronically sick populations that characterized advanced industrial societies by the middle of the twentieth century. The interventions of the state into the means by which epidemic infections were transmitted among mass urban populations and impoverished rural populations played a crucial role in their decline. Furthermore, the role of the state in providing for the public health altered the profile of disease.

See also **Chadwick, Edwin; Cholera; Cities and Towns; Economic Growth and Industrialism; London; Nightingale, Florence; Nurses; Paris; Revolutions of 1848; Smallpox; Syphilis; Tuberculosis.**

BIBLIOGRAPHY

Aisenberg, Andrew R. *Contagion: Disease, Government, and the "Social Question" in Nineteenth-Century France.* Stanford, Calif., 1999.

Coleman, William. *Death Is a Social Disease: Public Health and Political Economy in Early Industrial France.* Madison, Wis., 1982.

Cooter, Roger. "Anticontagionism and History's Medical Record." In *The Problem of Medical Knowledge,* edited by Peter Wright and Andrew Treacher, 87–108. Edinburgh, 1982.

Crosby, Alfred W. *Ecological Imperialism: The Biological Expansion of Europe, 900–1900.* 2nd ed. Cambridge, U.K., 2004.

Delaporte, François. *Disease and Civilization: The Cholera in Paris, 1832.* Translated by Arthur Goldhammer. Cambridge, Mass., 1986.

Durey, Michael. *The Return of the Plague: British Society and the Cholera, 1831–1832.* Dublin, 1979.

Evans, Richard J. *Death in Hamburg: Society and Politics in the Cholera Years, 1830–1910.* Oxford, U.K., 1987.

———. "Epidemics and Revolutions: Cholera in Nineteenth-Century Europe." *Past and Present* 120, no. 1 (1988): 123–146.

Farley, John. *The Spontaneous Generation Controversy from Descartes to Oparin.* Baltimore, Md., 1977.

Foster, W. D. *A History of Medical Bacteriology and Immunology.* London, 1970.

Hardy, Anne. *The Epidemic Streets: Infectious Disease and the Rise of Preventive Medicine, 1856–1900.* Oxford, U.K., 1993.

Howard-Jones, Norman. "Cholera Therapy in the Nineteenth Century." *Journal of the History of Medicine and Allied Sciences* 27, no. 4 (1972): 373–395.

Hudson, Robert P. *Disease and Its Control: The Shaping of Modern Thought.* Westport, Conn., 1983.

Kiple, Kenneth F., ed. *The Cambridge World History of Human Disease.* Cambridge, U.K., 1993.

Latour, Bruno. *The Pasteurization of France.* Translated by Alan Sheridan and John Law. Cambridge, Mass., 1988. Translation of *Les microbes.*

Longmate, Norman. *King Cholera: The Biography of a Disease.* London, 1966.

McGrew, Roderick E. *Russia and the Cholera, 1823–1832.* Madison, Wis., 1965.

McNeill, William H. *Plagues and Peoples.* Garden City, N.Y., 1976. Reprint, New York, 1989.

Morris, R. J. *Cholera, 1832: The Social Response to an Epidemic.* London, 1976.

Pelling, Margaret. *Cholera, Fever, and English Medicine, 1825–1865.* Oxford, U.K., 1978.

Porter, Dorothy. "Stratification and Its Discontents: Professionalisation and the English Public Health Service, 1848–1914." In *A History of Education in Public Health: Health that Mocks the Doctors' Rules,* edited by Elizabeth Fee and Roy M. Acheson, 83–113. Oxford, U.K., 1991.

Ranger, Terrance, and Paul Slack, eds. *Epidemics and Ideas: Essays on the Historical Perceptions of Pestilence.* Cambridge, U.K., 1992.

Reid, Robert. *Microbes and Men.* London, 1974.

Richardson, Ruth. *Death, Dissection, and the Destitute.* 2nd ed. London, 2001.

Rosenberg, Charles E. *Explaining Epidemics and Other Studies in the History of Medicine.* Cambridge, U.K., 1992.

Shryock, Richard H. "Germ Theories in Medicine Prior to 1870: Further Comments on Continuity in Science." *Clio Medica* 7, no. 1 (1972): 81–109.

Snowden, Frank M. *Naples in the Time of Cholera, 1884–1911.* Cambridge, U.K., 1995.

Spink, Wesley W. *Infectious Diseases: Prevention and Treatment in the Nineteenth and Twentieth Centuries.* Minneapolis, Minn., 1978.

Winter, Jay M. "The Decline of Mortality in Britain, 1870–1950." In *Population and Society in Britain, 1850–1980,* edited by Theo Barker and Michael Drake, 100–120. London, 1982.

Wohl, Anthony S. *Endangered Lives: Public Health in Victorian Britain.* London, 1983.

Woods, Robert, and John Woodward, eds. *Urban Disease and Mortality in Nineteenth Century England.* New York, 1984.

Zinsser, Hans. *Rats, Lice, and History.* Boston, 1935. Reprint, New York, 1996.

DOROTHY PORTER

DISRAELI, BENJAMIN (1804–1881),
British writer and statesman.

Benjamin Disraeli was born in London on 21 December 1804, the son of a dilettante antiquarian. His grandfather's death removed his father's last tie with the Jewish religion, and Benjamin was baptized into the Church of England in July 1817. Between 1821 and 1824 he was articled to a solicitor's firm, and later he briefly trained as a barrister. However his enthusiasm for Byron and Romanticism drove him to seek literary fame instead. But his attempt to establish his financial independence by speculating on South American mines ended in disaster, leaving him seriously indebted until the late 1840s. His first novel, *Vivian Grey* (1826), was also a failure, and its satire of London society damaged his reputation. In reaction to these setbacks, Disraeli suffered a nervous breakdown in the late 1820s. But his confidence returned after a trip to the east—particularly Athens, Constantinople, and Jerusalem—in 1830–1831. This helped to fashion his emerging identity as a cosmopolitan figure whose awareness of Eastern racial and religious culture allowed him to see more deeply into the nature and problems of the west. In this way, Disraeli began to come to terms with, and exploit, his Jewishness. Two novels, *Contarini Fleming* (1832) and *The Wondrous Tale of Alroy* (1833), reflect his growing interest in these themes and in the problem of how men of genius could reconcile their need for artistic creativity with their quest for political power.

PARLIAMENT

Stimulated by the political crisis of 1830–1832, Disraeli decided to seek a seat in Parliament, which would also protect him from imprisonment for debt. He stood unsuccessfully four times, at first as an independent radical, but latterly as a Tory, the label under which he was finally elected as member of Parliament (MP) for Maidstone in 1837. After his comember died, Disraeli married his widow, Mary Anne Lewis, in 1839; she settled many of his financial obligations.

Disraeli made a name for himself during the government of Sir Robert Peel, in 1841–1846. He did so first by associating loosely and briefly with a group of romantic backbenchers who came to be known as "Young England" for their idealistic reinterpretation of traditional ideas of social and religious obligation. In 1844 and 1845 he also produced his two best-known novels, *Coningsby* and *Sybil*, and criticized Peel for his lack of fidelity to Tory principles in a series of bold independent speeches that demonstrated his self-confidence. Peel's decision to abandon agricultural protection by repealing the Corn Laws then gave him a cause, and his deadly invective against the prime minister in 1846 undoubtedly contributed to the coherence of the protectionist movement and to the party's fatal split in June. Disraeli's main argument for a protection system was its importance for Britain's international power and standing. Beyond that, his assault on Peel's mode of governing reflected his desire for fame but also his anxiety about the unheroic quality of political leadership and the triumph of low commercial ideals in 1840s Britain. *Coningsby, Sybil,* and his subsequent novel, *Tancred* (1847), are all concerned to attack the class divisions and materialistic excesses of the decade by improving the vigor and tone of the governing classes. They project a love of English history and an insistence that the aristocracy and the church can, with effort, regain an inspirational presence in society, but, especially in *Tancred,* they marry this with a more exotic argument that the defense of religion, property, and political leadership would benefit from the assistance of philosophical men who understand Judaism and "the great Asian mystery." Though Disraeli's political importance or prospects should not be exaggerated at this time, the novels can be read as a way of justifying both to himself and to others his desired role as a Conservative Party prophet.

After the defection of the Peelites from the Conservative Party, the protectionists who remained lacked debating talent. Lord George Bentinck (1802–1848), their leader, promoted Disraeli to the front opposition bench in 1847. Helped by Bentinck's influence and family money, he became MP for Buckinghamshire in 1847 and bought the small estate of Hughenden Manor, near High Wycombe, in 1848. This was a major step because it allowed him to see himself as an English country gentleman defending the long continuum of national history. Bentinck died suddenly in 1848; Disraeli later produced an admiring biography of him. No other Conservative MP could match Disraeli's oratorical talents or industriousness in parliamentary maneuver. Though snobbery and decorum prevented him being accepted as leader for some years, his dominance in the Commons was undeniable by the time the Conservative Party was invited to form a minority government in February 1852, with Lord Derby, Edward George Geoffrey Smith Stanley (1799–1869), as prime minister. Disraeli became chancellor of the Exchequer and leader of the House of Commons, but the government lasted only ten months.

With the exception of another fourteen-month spell as chancellor in the minority government of 1858–1859, Disraeli spent the next fourteen years leading the Conservative opposition in the Commons. He took an interest in reforming party organization and tried to build up support for the party in the press. He tried some intriguing political strategies: for example, he blamed the Mutiny of 1857 on the excessively Westernizing policy pursued in India since the 1840s. In the early 1860s he sought to build a coalition of Anglican and Irish Catholic MPs in opposition to the Liberals' anticlerical tendencies at home, in Italy, and elsewhere in Europe. In these years Disraeli envisaged an impending clash of philosophies in Europe, between the forces of religion and authority and those of republicanism and unbelief, a theme developed in his last complete novel, *Lothair* (1870).

Derby came to power as prime minister of a minority Conservative government for the third time in 1866, with Disraeli again chancellor. In order to stay in power, they needed to settle the question of parliamentary reform. They did so by accepting the principle of household franchise in the boroughs (the principle for which radical Liberals cared most), while limiting the significance of this by various restrictions, and defending the Conservatives' interests by making few changes in seat distribution or the county franchise. During the bill's passage through the Commons, the major restrictions were removed by MPs, substantially increasing the borough electorate, but the other conservative elements of the bill mostly survived, and Disraeli won a series of personal tactical victories over his rival William Ewart Gladstone

Cartoon of Queen Victoria crowning Disraeli. This 1878 cartoon lampoons the royal patronage Disraeli earned with his expansion of British imperial power during his tenure as prime minister. ©BETTMANN/CORBIS

(1809–1898). The Reform Bill dominated the 1867 session, adding to Disraeli's reputation for intrigue, shoring up the government, and making it almost inevitable that, when Derby retired through ill health in February 1868, Disraeli would succeed him as prime minister.

PRIME MINISTER

He had little room to maneuver during his first premiership. Unsurprisingly, he failed to realize his idea of an Anglican-Catholic alliance on the Irish question. Then, as expected, his party lost office after the election of November 1868. Once more he faced a long period in opposition, and the death of his wife in 1872 left him desolate as well as tired. Despite a couple of well-publicized speeches, Disraeli contributed little to the powerful middle-class, Anglican, and propertied reaction of the early 1870s against Gladstone's Liberal government. Still, it swept him back into power in February 1874, this time with a majority, the first one enjoyed by the Conservatives since 1841.

As prime minister, Disraeli enjoyed his warm relations with the queen (though privately he sometimes found her "very mad") and liked dispensing patronage. In the relative calm of the 1870s—so different from the atmosphere of the 1840s—there was little urgency in domestic affairs. However he encouraged the emphasis on relatively uncontentious social reform measures proposed by ministers Richard Assheton, first Viscount Cross (1823–1914) and Lord Derby (Edward Henry Smith Stanley, 1826–1893), because it added to the government's reputation for constructive competence and kept Parliament occupied. Nonetheless, the efficiency of his conduct of Commons business was increasingly criticized, and, beset by ill health, he took a peerage in August 1876 as Earl of Beaconsfield, allowing him to lead the ministry from the Lords.

Disraeli's main interest was in foreign policy, where he soon found a mission in asserting British power as his eighteenth-century heroes had done. He saw this as necessary both strategically, in order to check German and Russian domination of Europe, and in terms of raising the tone of domestic politics by counteracting the baleful influence of low-spending commercial isolationist sentiment in the Liberal Party. These goals drove his overseas policy, not the pursuit of imperial territory as such, which he regarded as a secondary concern, to be avoided if it threatened financial or diplomatic difficulties.

His policy proceeded partly by grand gestures of national assertiveness, such as the purchase of a large stake in the Suez Canal Company in 1875, and the bestowal of the title of Empress of India on the queen in 1876. During the Eastern crisis of 1876–1878 he sought to ensure that Britain's views and interests were not ignored by the other powers, though this required a degree of support for Turkey that offended many humanitarians at home. He then urged the cabinet to take a firm anti-Russian line in 1877–1878, even at the risk of war. This approach won the approval of the queen and some popular sentiment, but was extremely controversial, because of anti-Turkish opinion and fear that war in the east would overstretch the navy. On the other hand, many argued that his firm stance made possible a successful international settlement at Berlin in 1878, which was certainly popular at home. However the other powers had also wanted a settlement; moreover, new British commitments to the defense of Turkey sparked fresh domestic criticism, particularly when followed by an expensive and difficult war against Afghanistan, for which the enthusiasm of Disraeli's Indian viceroy Lord Lytton (Edward Robert Bulwer-Lytton; 1831–1891) was mainly responsible. In Afghanistan, and in a similarly fraught war in South Africa, Disraeli seemed unable to control the expansionist pressures encouraged by his own rhetoric. The result was heavy military costs and great Liberal criticism of his "imperialism," by which was meant the perceived similarity of his regime to that of Napoleon III (r. 1852–1871) in foreign policy and in its disregard for constitutional liberties and fiscal restraint. Income tax tripled from 1874 to 1880, and the Conservatives lost the 1880 election, which was fought in a bad economic depression.

Disraeli died on 19 April 1881, within a year of leaving office. A Disraeli myth soon emerged, the result of the failure of the Liberals' imperial policy after 1880 and the need of the Conservative Party to appeal to the much-enlarged post-1885 electorate. Disraeli's commitment to vigor abroad was naturally one element of this powerful posthumous reinvention, while his attack on laissez-faire in the 1840s and his minor social reforms of the 1870s were also pressed into service to underline the party's willingness to address working-men's interests and to create "One Nation." Disraeli himself is probably best understood by focusing on his Romantic desire for national recognition, his struggles with his Jewish inheritance, the great social crisis of the 1840s, and his perception of the destiny of his generation to respond to that crisis by rebuilding confidence at home and tackling the legacy of insular commercialism in overseas affairs.

See also **Gladstone, William; Great Britain; Imperialism; Romanticism; Tories.**

BIBLIOGRAPHY

Blake, Robert. *Disraeli*. London, 1966.

Parry, J. P. "Disraeli and England." *Historical Journal* 43 (2000): 699–728.

Shannon, Richard. *The Age of Disraeli, 1868–1881: The Rise of Tory Democracy*. London, 1992.

Smith, Paul. *Disraeli: A Brief Life*. Cambridge, U.K., 1996.

Stewart, Robert. *The Foundation of the Conservative Party, 1830–1867*. London, 1978.

Swartz, Helen M., and Marvin Swartz, eds. *Disraeli's Reminiscences*. New York, 1975.

JONATHAN PARRY

DOHM, HEDWIG (1831–1919), author and early German feminist.

Hedwig Dohm was born in Berlin on 20 September 1831 as the fourth child and first daughter of a large bourgeois family. Although she was one of eighteen children, she had a lonely childhood. Her father, a baptized Jew who had changed his name from Schlesinger to Schleh, owned a tobacco factory and was distant from the children. He and Hedwig's mother presided over a strict and hierarchical family. Hedwig felt unloved and later wrote about complicated mother-daughter relationships.

After witnessing the revolutionary upheaval in Berlin in 1848, Hedwig convinced her parents to let her enroll in a teacher-training school, which disappointed her because it did not satisfy her desire for an educational challenge. In 1852 she met Ernst Dohm (1819–1883), the onetime revolutionary and editor of the satirical Berlin magazine *Kladderadatsch,* who was ten years her senior, and they were married in 1853. Little is known about her marriage to Dohm, with whom she had five children. Her eldest child and only son died young; she sought to be a good mother to her daughters. (Her eldest daughter would be the mother of Katia Mann.)

The Dohms ran a salon in Berlin, which was a meeting place for writers, artists, politicians and other members of Berlin's intellectual elite—a social context very different from the confines of her parents' home. She quickly learned about the opportunities and shortcomings of bourgeois society, especially its sexual double standard. Her first independent publication about Spanish literature appeared during this time in 1867.

In 1869–1870, the family encountered serious financial difficulties that led to the temporary dissolution of their household. Ernst and their daughters stayed with friends and relatives while Hedwig lived with her sister, a painter, in Rome. Here Dohm experienced a new kind of freedom and, after her return to Berlin, she began to write more assertive, satirical texts about discrimination against women based on their supposed biological inferiority to men. Dohm believed that women's lives were artificially and unfairly limited by the patriarchal structure of society. She demanded women's emancipation, by which she meant complete equality (social, political, educational, etc.) and women's suffrage, an issue that nobody had seriously raised in Germany at this point. Her particular targets for attack and ridicule included pastors, who argued that it was spiritually and physiologically important to limit women's opportunities ("Was die Pastoren von den Frauen denken" [What pastors think of women], 1872). She also attacked bourgeois women, especially antifeminists, who fulfilled their roles as housewives and mothers without questioning them ("Der Jesuitismus im Hausstande" [Jesuitism in the home], 1873; "Die Antifeministen" [The Antifeminists], 1902; and "Die Mütter" [Mothers], 1903). In addition, she disparaged doctors and other professionals who wanted to bar women from advanced education, because—she argued—they feared the competition and loss of authority ("Die wissenschaftliche Emanzipation der Frau" [The scientific emancipation of women], 1874), and the misogynism of leading philosophers of the time ("Der Frau Natur und Recht" [Women's nature and rights], 1876).

Although Bohm was timid and shy in her social interactions, her writings were clear and peppered with piercing satire. Dohm used the written word as her weapon; she joined few organizations and rarely spoke publicly, but many feminist activists by the 1890s knew her and drew on her writings for inspiration. In fact, the demands she issued in her texts were far more radical and far-reaching than those of other early women's activists who hoped to improve women's positions incrementally and many of whom believed in the fundamental difference between men and women. Dohm, however, always operated in the context of bourgeois society, not least because she perceived the Socialists to be concerned exclusively with men's issues.

After her husband's death in 1883 Dohm turned increasingly to writing fiction, although she never gave up her polemical pamphlet literature. She now published novels, poetry, comedies and serious plays, and short stories about women in various social contexts and situations that were sometimes autobiographical. Her fictional work was less biting and satirical than her pamphlets. Nevertheless, Dohm continued even here to expose the hypocrisy of contemporary bourgeois society as she saw it, especially regarding the position of women. In widowhood and increasing old age, her home remained an important meeting place, especially for leading women's activists. In her writing she continued to be one of the most radical voices for women's suffrage, emancipation, and equality.

When the war started in 1914, Dohm became a pacifist. Hedwig Dohm died on 1 June 1919 in Berlin, just before her eighty-eighth birthday.

See also **Augspurg, Anita; Feminism; Suffragism.**

BIBLIOGRAPHY

Brandt, Heike. *"Die Menschenrechte haben kein Geschlecht." Die Lebensgeschichte der Hedwig Dohm.* Weinheim, Germany, 1989.

Duelli-Klein, Renate. "Hedwig Dohm: Passionate Theorist (1833–1919)." In *Feminist Theorists: Three Centuries of Key Women Thinkers,* edited by Dale Spender. New York, 1983.

Meissner, Julia. *Mehr Stolz, Ihr Frauen! Hedwig Dohm— eine Biographie.* Düsseldorf, Germany, 1987.

Müller, Nikola. *Hedwig Dohm (1831–1919); Eine kommentierte Bibliografie.* Berlin, 2000.

Singer, Sandra L. *Free Soul, Free Woman?: A Study of Selected Fictional Works by Hedwig Dohm, Isolde Kurz, and Helene Böhlau.* New York, 1995.

JULIA BRUGGEMANN

DORÉ, GUSTAVE (1832–1883), French artist. Gustave Doré was a major force in nineteenth-century European art. The French fine arts establishment ignored his paintings (some said he was colorblind), so Doré appealed directly to the public. Creating his own genre, the Doré literary folio, Doré elevated popular art to the level of fine art, appealing to French, English, Spanish, Italian, and German sentiments through each country's literary classics. Critics said Doré was too popular, too talented, too prolific, too dramatic. Known as

"the last of the romantics," he embodied the basic artistic conflicts of raw talent versus instruction, illustration versus painting, black and white versus color, religious versus secular, realist versus Romanticist. In the early twenty-first century most viewers recognize the style and otherworldly quality of his art but not his name. The legacy of his largely monochromatic art is to be rediscovered by succeeding generations and reinterpreted through colorization.

Born in Strasbourg on the German border, Doré's artistic talent was apparent early in drawings from the age of four. By age twelve, he was carving his own lithographs into stone. He was fifteen when his family visited Paris, where Doré marched into the office of publisher Charles Philipon (1800–1862) with original drawings that would lead to a contract, making Doré the highest paid illustrator in France. The "boy genius" became the toast of Paris. During his teen years, he produced thousands of caricatures for periodicals before turning to more serious literary art, with engravings for the works of François Rabelais, Honoré de Balzac, Alexandre Dumas, Victor Hugo, William Shakespeare, and Charles Dickens.

Both success and failure made Doré restless for new artistic media. Perceiving a cold shoulder from the Paris Salon, he conceived a series of literary folios (often 13" x 17" and weighing twenty to forty pounds) with his large dramatic engravings (referred to as black and white paintings). At his own expense, he published his 1861 Dante's *Inferno,* which won him the Legion of Honour. Other folios followed: *Baron Munchausen, Fairy Tales, Don Quixote,* and in 1865 what became the most popular set of illustrations ever made, 230 folio engravings for *The Doré Bible,* so famous that Mark Twain (1835–1910) casually mentioned it in *Tom Sawyer.* Doré's growing fame benefited from a timely new invention, the electrotype, a zinc molding plate allowing unlimited engraving reproduction with no quality loss.

The popularity of Doré's folios spread throughout Europe and the world: *Milton: Paradise Lost, Tennyson: Idylls of the King, LaFontaine: Fables, Ariosto: Orlando Furioso, Chateaubriand: Atala, Coleridge: Rime of the Ancient Mariner, Poe: The Raven,* a historical work *Michaud: History*

Homeless Family Sleeping on a Bridge. Engraving by Gustave Doré c. 1871, from a series depicting the problems of industrialized England. SNARK/ART RESOURCE, NY

of the Crusades, and his masterpiece social commentary *Jerrold: London, a Pilgrimage* (only Doré could so dramatically visually contrast the pampered life of the wealthy with the squalor of poor beggars). Many of his powerful engravings are etched into our collective memory. But Doré still longed for respect in the fine arts. With the British lauding those paintings the French had ignored, a gallery of Doré paintings opened in London. He then turned to watercolor landscapes and works of sculpture. But he basically worked himself to death by the age of fifty-one, from his frenzied pace of artistic output. As late as the 1890s, an exhibition of his paintings toured the United States, breaking many attendance records.

Doré was the most prolific and popular illustrator ever, with more than ten thousand engravings of all types, and many thousands of book editions reprinting his engravings. But he also produced more than four hundred oil paintings, some twenty by thirty feet, such as his religious canvases *Christ Leaving the Praetorium*, *Christ's Entry into Jerusalem*, and *The Dream of Pilate's Wife*. His highest selling paintings have been literary nudes; his

Andromeda and *Paolo & Francesca* each sold for more than $500,000. In addition, Doré painted several hundred watercolor landscapes, produced thousands of mixed media sketches, and chiseled nearly a hundred works of sculpture, such as *The Doré Vase* (an enormous wine bottle with hundreds of mythological creatures), *The Human Pyramid*, and his Paris monument to Alexandre Dumas (1802–1870). At the end of the twentieth century he finally gained fine arts recognition, even in France. Major exhibition books of Doré fine art displays in England, France, Germany, and the United States have revealed the full scope of Doré the artist.

But his literary folio engravings are the pinnacle of his artistic oeuvre. It did not take long for them to be colorized in hundreds of watercolors, chromolithographs, hand-painted magic lantern slides, and oil paintings by artists such as Vincent van Gogh (1853–1890) and Pablo Picasso (1881–1973). Doré's name faded after 1900, but his influence on theater, music, literature, and film never diminished. Films influenced by his art include *King Kong* (1933), *Snow White* (1937), *Great Expectations* (1946), *The Ten*

Commandments (1956), Star Wars (1977), Amistad (1997), and Shrek 2 (2004). By the early twenty-first century Doré's art had been adapted into more than 130 pop culture formats.

See also Daumier, Honoré; France; Painting; Romanticism.

BIBLIOGRAPHY

Malan, Dan. Gustave Doré: Adrift on Dreams of Splendor. St. Louis, Mo., 1995.

Malan, Dan. Gustave Doré: A Biography. St. Louis, Mo., 1996.

Zafran, Eric, with Robert Rosenblum and Lisa Small. Fantasy & Faith: The Art of Gustave Doré. New Haven, Conn., 2005.

DAN MALAN

DOSTOYEVSKY, FYODOR (1821–1881), Russian novelist.

Fyodor Mikhailovich Dostoyevsky, the creator of the modern psychological novel and arguably the most important influence on the twentieth-century novel, was born on 11 November (30 October, old style) 1821 in Moscow's Hospital for the Poor. His father, Mikhail Andreyevich, was an ill-tempered physician and his mother, Maria Fyodorovna, was a loving woman who liked to play music and read poetry. Fyodor had seven siblings but became close only to his older brother Mikhail with whom he was sent to a boarding school in St. Petersburg at the age of sixteen, one year before their mother's death. Although he was studying engineering, Fyodor was able to become acquainted with classic Russian and European writers such as Alexander Pushkin, E. T. A. Hoffmann, Johann Wolfgang von Goethe, Friedrich von Schiller, Honoré de Balzac, Victor Hugo, and Nikolai Gogol. During his stay at the boarding school, Dostoyevsky learned that his father was killed by his own serfs because he treated them cruelly. Fyodor was shocked and began to experience periodic fits of epilepsy. After graduation from the St. Petersburg Military Engineering School in 1843, Fyodor entered civil service, which he soon left to become a full-time writer.

After finishing a translation of Balzac's Eugénie Grandet, Dostoyevsky began writing Poor Folk (Bednye lyudi, 1846), which, like most of his novels, was published serially by the well-known critic and author Nikolai Nekrasov; it brought him instant fame. His second novel, The Double (Dvoynik, 1846), was less successful. In 1847 Dostoyevsky joined the Petrashevsky Circle, a utopian socialist discussion group whose members were arrested by the tsarist police in 1849. The author was imprisoned in the Peter and Paul Fortress and after a two-week trial sentenced to death. Dostoyevsky's sentence, however, was soon commuted to four years of hard labor and four years in the army in Siberia. In 1857 the author married Maria Dmitrievna Isaeva, in 1858 he was released from the army, and in 1859 he was allowed to return to St. Petersburg. There he published with his brother Mikhail the journal Time (Vremya, 1861–1863), which tried to find a compromise between the liberal "Westerners" views and those of conservative "Slavophiles." Nevertheless, the Siberian experience, which he described best in Memoirs from the House of the Dead (Zapiski iz myortogo doma, 1862), a great study of prison life, caused Dostoyevsky to become a political and social conservative and a fervent Russian Orthodox believer.

With the publication of Notes from the Underground (Zapiski iz podpolya) in 1864, Dostoyevsky started his great period, which is characterized by a perceptive psychological analysis of characters as well as a deep discussion of philosophical, moral, and social problems. In 1867, three years after the death of his first wife from tuberculosis, he married his secretary, Anna Grigorievna Snitkina, an understanding and tolerant woman twenty-five years his junior. They had a daughter and a son, both of whom died young. Where in Notes from the Underground Dostoyevsky described an alienated, neurotic intellectual with no solution for his unhappy predicament, with Crime and Punishment (Prestupleniye i nakazaniye, 1866) the author created a complete novel that is considered to be one of the greatest novels ever written. By psychologically dissecting the poor student Raskolnikov, the author discussed the nature of good and evil and reached a religious conclusion that salvation can be found only through suffering. In 1868 Dostoyevsky published two more novels, The Gambler (Igrok) and The Idiot (Idiot). The former reflected his own passion, while the latter was a portrait of a truly beautiful, pure person, Prince Myshkin, who is driven to insanity by the corrupt society. In 1872 he published *The Devils* (*Besy,* often translated as *The Possessed*), a story of political intrigue, which was followed several years later by perhaps his finest—albeit incomplete—creation, *The Brothers Karamazov* (*Bratya Karamazovy,* 1879–1880). This is a novel of patricide with each of the four sons representing different aspects of human life. The three legitimate sons are allegorical figures but strikingly real. A planned sequel to the novel never materialized because of the author's death on 9 February (28 January, old style) 1881 in St. Petersburg. Just before his death, Dostoyevsky delivered a famous speech at the second Russian Literary Society meeting in which he praised Pushkin as the greatest Russian writer and his spiritual teacher. At his funeral, thousands of admirers followed the coffin to its grave at St. Petersburg's Alexander Nevsky Monastery.

Dostoyevsky is one of the most widely read Russian writers, and he contributed greatly to the nineteenth-century Russian literary golden age. Most of the characters found in Dostoyevsky's novels reflect the author himself. They have complicated, contradictory, dual personalities, believing in God and proudly rejecting God, showing vitality and zest for life or suffering from epilepsy and generally being in poor health. The author's own ability to empathize with his protagonists who are constantly torn between opposite poles make them real and believable. Sigmund Freud on several occasions expressed his admiration for Dostoyevsky's brilliant psychological insights, and many critics view the author's ability to portray the psychology of his characters as unsurpassed in world literature. Many world-renowned twentieth-century writers, such as Thomas Mann, André Gide, and Franz Kafka, have publicly acknowledged their indebtedness to the great Russian author.

See also **Pushkin, Alexander; Russia; Slavophiles; Tolstoy, Leo; Turgenev, Ivan; Westernizers.**

BIBLIOGRAPHY

Frank, Joseph. *Dostoevsky: The Seeds of Revolt, 1821–1849.* Princeton, N.J., 1976.

———. *Dostoevsky: The Years of Ordeal, 1850–1859.* Princeton, N.J., 1983.

———. *Dostoevsky: The Stir of Liberation, 1860–1865.* Princeton, N.J., 1986.

———. *Dostoevsky: The Miraculous Years, 1865–1871.* Princeton, N.J., 1995.

———. *Dostoevsky: The Mantle of the Prophet, 1871–1881.* Princeton, N.J., 2002.

Grossman, Leonid. *Dostoevsky: A Biography.* Translated by Mary Mackler. London, 1974.

Hingley, Ronald. *Dostoyevsky: His Life and Work.* London, 1978.

Jackson, Robert Louis. *Dostoevsky's Quest for Form.* New Haven, Conn., 1966.

Lavrin, Janko. *Dostoevsky: A Study.* London, 1943. Reprint, New York, 1969.

Magarshack, David. *Dostoevsky.* London, 1962.

Mochulsky, Konstantin. *Dostoevsky: His Life and Work.* Translated by Michael A. Minihan. Princeton, N.J., 1967.

Payne, Robert. *Dostoyevsky: A Human Portrait.* New York, 1961.

Scanlan, James P. *Dostoevsky the Thinker.* Ithaca, N.Y., 2002.

Wasiolek, Edward. *Dostoevsky: The Major Fiction.* Cambridge, Mass., 1964.

RADO PRIBIC

DOYLE, ARTHUR CONAN (1859–1930), British writer.

Sir Arthur Conan Doyle, one of the most widely known writers in the world, was born in Edinburgh, Scotland, on 22 May 1859. Doyle was a man of three nations: Irish by descent, Scottish by birth, and English by allegiance.

Beginning in 1870, Doyle was educated at the Roman Catholic school Stonyhurst. In 1875, Doyle went to a Jesuit school at Feldkirch in Austria. Having decided to become a doctor, the following year in 1876 Doyle enrolled at Edinburgh University, from which he received his Bachelor of Medicine degree in 1881. In 1882, he announced to his family that he had abandoned Catholicism. An adventurer, Doyle traveled to the Arctic in 1880 and to West Africa in 1881. In 1885 he was awarded his doctoral degree from Edinburgh University, having written his dissertation about syphilis.

During the time he was launching his medical career, Doyle began writing. An early story was published in the prestigious *Cornhill Magazine* in 1883. By 1891, Doyle had decided to leave medicine and devote himself full time to writing.

Doyle's achievements as a writer are marked by the range of forms in which he wrote. These include detective novels and stories, stories of medical life, histories, poems, historical novels, science fiction novels, writings about spiritualism, tales of terror and horror, and texts about contemporary events. In addition, he published an autobiography, *Memories and Adventures,* in 1924.

Doyle is renowned for his creation of the detective Sherlock Holmes. Doyle modeled Holmes on one of his professors at Edinburgh University, Joseph Bell. Doyle was fascinated by the way Bell exercised logical observation to deduce the illnesses and diseases of his patients. Ultimately, Doyle wrote fifty-six short stories and four novels about the exploits of Sherlock Holmes, most of them narrated by his friend Dr. John H. Watson, with whom he shared rooms at the immortal address 221B Baker Street.

These writings about Sherlock Holmes span the late Victorian, Edwardian, and Georgian periods. Holmes first appears in the novel *A Study in Scarlet* in 1887 in *Beeton's Christmas Annual.* The three other novels about Holmes are *The Sign of Four* (1890), *The Hound of the Baskervilles* (1902), and *The Valley of Fear* (1915). The short stories about Holmes begin with "A Scandal in Bohemia" in the *Strand Magazine* in July 1891. Holmes's decadent qualities, such as his cocaine use, become muted in the middle-class *Strand.* These *Strand* short stories were collected in five volumes: *The Adventures of Sherlock Holmes* (1892), *The Memoirs of Sherlock Holmes* (1894), *The Return of Sherlock Holmes* (1905), *His Last Bow* (1917), and *The Case-Book of Sherlock Holmes* (1927).

Although many of these stories focus on crime (murder, theft, blackmail, terrorism, espionage, counterfeiting), not all these narratives do involve overt criminality. Rather, they concern transgressive behavior, which may or may not be strictly illegal or criminal, albeit amoral or immoral. For example, in "The Man with the Twisted Lip" (December 1891), Neville St. Clair impersonates a beggar even though he lives in the suburbs with his family, impelled because he is attracted by the transgression itself.

While engrossing, these tales are not escapist. Through them, Conan Doyle addresses many cultural agendas. Because Holmes is not part of the official police force but rather a private consulting detective, his methods may involve procedures that are illegal. The stories imply that law and justice are not mutually compatible. Holmes bests men such as Lestrade from Scotland Yard, raising the question of the ability of the official force to maintain order.

Multiple cultural situations are probed in these narratives. For example, the issue of gender relations is very prominent. Often, nefarious men as in "The Speckled Band" or "The Copper Beeches" try to cheat women out of their income or property, resorting to imprisoning or murdering women. Doyle questions privileged male authority at a time when women were securing educational, legal, and marital reforms.

Hence, many of these stories police masculinity and male behavior, as in "The Three Students." The damaged male body in many of these stories, such as "The Boscombe Valley Mystery," "The Crooked Man," *The Sign of Four,* or Watson's own shifting wound, symbolically reveals Doyle's concern with masculinity in crisis. This crisis had repercussions for the British Empire. Although Doyle supported British imperial campaigns such as the Boer War (1899–1902), it is noteworthy that criminality often originates in a colonized region only to devolve to England, as in *The Sign of Four.*

In many of these narratives, England is menaced by foreign nations and nationals. The threat of international espionage, a major concern as British imperial power waned, appears in many stories, such as "The Naval Treaty," "The Second Stain," or "The Bruce-Partington Plans." Fear of Germany is evident in "The Engineer's Thumb." Organized crime or global terrorist societies are a focus in such tales as "The Five Orange Pips," "The Red Circle," or *The Valley of Fear.* Despite Doyle's assertions of admiration for America, Americans are deceiving or deadly in several stories, including "The Yellow Face," "The Noble Bachelor," "The Dancing Men," and *A Study in Scarlet*. As "The Dancing Men" demonstrates, Holmes does not always succeed.

Doyle's other writings comprise a variety of literary forms. He strongly aspired to be an historical novelist in the vein of Sir Walter Scott and Charles Kingsley. Some of these efforts include *The White Company* (1891), set in the fourteenth century; its prequel *Sir Nigel* (1906); and *Micah Clarke* (1889), about the attempt by the Duke of Monmouth to seize the English throne in 1685. Despite Doyle's belief in these novels, they do not endure as do the Sherlock Holmes texts.

In another literary form, Doyle wrote adventure tales verging on science fiction, such as *The Lost World* (1912), *The Poison Belt* (1913), and *The Land of Mist* (1926). Doyle dealt with the Napoleonic era in *The Exploits of Brigadier Gerard* (1896) and *The Adventures of Gerard* (1903). He authored dazzling short stories of terror and horror, collected in such volumes as *Round the Fire Stories* (1908) and *Danger! And Other Stories* (1918). Doyle's tales about medicine in *Round the Red Lamp* (1894) are exceptional. *The Great Boer War* (1900) shows Doyle's engagement with contemporary issues. His *Collected Poems* appeared in 1922. As a committed spiritualist, Doyle wrote a number of volumes about the movement, such as *The New Revelation* (1918), *The Coming of the Fairies* (1922), and *The History of Spiritualism* (1926).

Doyle was knighted in 1902 for his services as a doctor during the Boer War (not for authoring the Sherlock Holmes stories). Illustrious and rich, Doyle died on 7 July 1930. While he is famous for the Sherlock Holmes narratives, Doyle's achievements in so many different literary forms render him one of the most important writers of his age.

See also **Crime; Great Britain.**

BIBLIOGRAPHY

Primary Sources

Doyle, Sir Arthur Conan. *Uncollected Stories: The Unknown Conan Doyle.* Edited by John Michael Gibson and Richard Lancelyn Green. London, 1982.

————. "Filmed Interview" (c. 1929). *Sherlock Holmes: The Great Detective.* (A&E Biography). New York, 1985.

————. *Memories and Adventures.* Edited by Richard Lancelyn Green. London, 1988.

————. *Round the Fire Stories.* San Francisco, 1991.

————. *Sir Arthur Conan Doyle: Interviews and Recollections.* Edited by Harold Orel. New York, 1991.

————. *The Horror of the Heights and Other Tales of Suspense.* San Francisco, 1992.

————. *The Oxford Sherlock Holmes.* Edited by Owen Dudley Edwards, Richard Lancelyn Green, W. W. Robson, and Christopher Roden. 9 vols. Oxford, U.K., 1993.

Secondary Sources

Barnes, Alan. *Sherlock Holmes on Screen.* Richmond, Surrey, U.K., 2002.

Cox, Don Richard. *Arthur Conan Doyle.* New York, 1985.

Green, Richard Lancelyn, and John M. Gibson. *A Bibliography of A. Conan Doyle.* Oxford, U.K., and New York, 1983.

Jaffe, Jacqueline A. *Arthur Conan Doyle.* Boston, 1987.

Kestner, Joseph A. *Sherlock's Men: Masculinity, Conan Doyle, and Cultural History.* Aldershot, U.K., and Brookfield, Vt., 1997.

Stashower, Daniel. *Teller of Tales: The Life of Arthur Conan Doyle.* New York, 1999.

JOSEPH A. KESTNER

DREADNOUGHT. When the Royal Navy commissioned HMS *Dreadnought* in December 1906, Britain's fleet gained an immediate technological advantage over any potential adversary at sea. This revolutionary battleship, displacing 17,900 tons, intensified the naval building race with imperial Germany and reset the standard by which all navies measured themselves.

The generation of battleships preceding the dreadnoughts were powerful warships but possessed two major disadvantages. The typical battleship of the 1890s, expecting to fight at relatively close ranges, mounted a mixed battery of four twelve-inch guns (in two turrets) and numerous intermediate-size guns. Major drawbacks of this arrangement included the difficulties of spotting and adjusting fire for mixed batteries, and of maintaining sets of spare parts for different types of guns. Pre-dreadnought battleships also were powered by reciprocating steam engines, whose operation at high speed (fifteen to eighteen knots)

HMS *Dreadnought*, photographed off the coast of England in 1909. ©Hulton-Deutsch Collection/Corbis

caused extreme stress to the machinery, requiring frequent overhauls and forcing commanders to limit speeds to fourteen knots or less in order to avoid breakdowns.

HMS *Dreadnought* was a revolutionary design because it incorporated a number of innovations in a single hull. The first innovation was an all-big-gun armament, a concept considered by British, Italian, and American naval architects for a number of years. An Admiralty design board, chaired by First Sea Lord Admiral Sir John Arbuthnot Fisher (1841–1920), decided to arm the new ship with ten twelve-inch guns arranged in five twin turrets. With one turret on the bow, one on each wing, and two astern, the gun arrangement allowed *Dreadnought* to fire eight heavy guns in each broadside—giving her the equivalent long-range fire of two pre-dreadnought battleships. Fisher eliminated the intermediate-caliber guns and saved only a few light quick-firing guns to repel close-in torpedo boat attacks.

Moreover, *Dreadnought* was the first battleship to employ turbine engines, a new propulsion system employing fewer moving parts, requiring less space in the hull and accounting for less weight. The new turbines would give *Dreadnought* a design speed of almost twenty-one knots, a sustainable three-knot advantage over most potential enemies. Superior speed was seen as enabling battleships to close with a retreating enemy and control the range of an engagement. Fast battleships could maintain a range short enough for their own heavy twelve-inch guns to be effective but long enough to neutralize the shorter-range intermediate armament of the enemy. Fast battleships would also be able to stay out of range of a new threat to their command of the sea—torpedoes launched from swift torpedo boats and submarines.

Construction began on 2 October 1905 at Portsmouth Dockyard and was extraordinarily brief. Due to the prefabrication of many subsystems and an increased pace of construction by the already efficient dockyard staff, HMS *Dreadnought* was launched on 10 February 1906. By September 1906 her first captain, Reginald Bacon, began a systematic set of machinery, engine, steering, and armament trials. On 2 December, *Dreadnought* completed her acceptance trials and was commissioned to full complement on 11 December 1906.

Although contemporaries and historians alike have criticized Fisher for making all non-dreadnought designs obsolete, and hence negating Britain's already considerable battleship superiority, it was only a matter of time before other naval powers fielded such a design. In essence, Fisher stole the lead on all other navies. British yards, vastly superior in efficiency and capacity to most others in the world, would be able to build dreadnoughts at an unmatched rate. Germany, Britain's chief rival at sea by this time, began its own dreadnought program in 1909, and the competition led to further increases in ship size, caliber and number of heavy guns, and speed. Fisher also initiated another type of dreadnought called the battle cruiser, a warship with the light armor and high speed of a cruiser but possessing the size and heavy armament of a dreadnought battleship. In May 1916, thirty-seven British dreadnought battleships and battle cruisers met twenty-one German dreadnoughts at the Battle of Jutland.

It is ironic that the ship universally known for providing her name to the final generation of battleships never fired her main guns in anger. During World War I she served in home waters and on 18 March 1915 earned the recognition of being the only battleship to sink (by ramming a U-29) a German submarine. While her consorts faced the German High Seas Fleet at Jutland, she was refitting at Rosyth. After the war, she joined the Reserve Fleet but soon joined a growing list of ships sold for scrap.

See also **Germany; Great Britain; Naval Rivalry (Anglo-German).**

BIBLIOGRAPHY

Marder, Arthur J. *From the Dreadnought to Scapa Flow: The Royal Navy in the Fisher Era, 1904–1919.* 5 vols. London, 1961–1970.

Massie, Robert K. *Dreadnought: Britain, Germany and the Coming of the Great War.* New York, 1991.

Roberts, John. *The Battleship Dreadnought.* Annapolis, Md., 1992.

Sumida, Jon T. *In Defense of Naval Supremacy.* Boston, Mass., 1989.

JOHN J. ABBATIELLO

DREYFUS AFFAIR.

DREYFUS AFFAIR. Alfred Dreyfus (1859–1935) was a French army officer tried as a German spy in 1894. Largely because he was Jewish, his case became an affair. "Dreyfusards" fought for individual rights, equality, citizenship, and other values associated with the French Revolution (which had given citizenship to Jews). "Anti-Dreyfusards" fought for national security, hierarchy, "blood" as the marker of Frenchness, and other values associated with the monarchy.

THE CASE (1894)

The affair began when the French intelligence service—the "Statistics Section"—discovered a *bordereau,* a list enumerating secret documents sent to the Germans. The Section wrongly assumed that only an officer-in-training could have gotten all the documents. That limited the field. Dreyfus's name soon came to the fore. That he was a Jew—the first Jew to rise so high in the army—did not directly influence investigators, but was a factor in negative reports that drew the investigators' attention: among aristocrats in the army, he was an outsider.

Dreyfus was arrested on 15 October 1894, but the case faltered. Dreyfus was independently wealthy and had no need for additional income. He was a devoted family man and deeply patriotic: his family had, at considerable cost, left their Alsatian home in 1871 rather than become German citizens. Investigators were considering dropping the case, when, on 28 October, the anti-Semitic daily newspaper, *La libre parole* (The free word), got a leak and ran a huge story: the Jewish Lobby was maneuvering to get charges dropped against a Jew arrested for high treason.

Fearing to appear soft on spies and Jews, the army set Dreyfus's court-martial for 22 December 1894. Three of five handwriting experts now refused to identify Dreyfus as the writer of the *bordereau.* There was no other evidence. The Statistics Section, however, found in their archives a letter referring to "that scoundrel [*canaille*] D." To implicate Dreyfus as "D," someone in the Section, either its head or Major Hubert Henry, constructed another letter, implicating Dreyfus. This forgery—the "Guénée forgery"—and the "scoundrel" letter were presented to the military judges without the defense counsel's knowledge, in a "secret dossier."

To this dossier prosecutors added forty-seven love letters—some very explicit—between the German and Italian military attachés, who were having a hot affair. It had nothing to do with Dreyfus, who was a faithful husband, but prosecutors assumed that mud would stick. Conservatives were preoccupied with "degeneration," the decline of the European race, which they perceived in the apparent emergence of Jews, homosexuals, and effete males, all of whom they attacked as effeminate and untrustworthy. As Nicolas Dobelbower has pointed out, the judges could be expected to experience general disgust about Jews and homosexuals, whom conservative discourse already linked.

Dreyfus was found guilty and formally degraded: while a crowd howled "Down with the Jew," his insignia were stripped off and his sword broken. He was imprisoned on Devil's Island, a rocky outcrop off the coast of French Guiana.

FROM CASE TO AFFAIR (1894–1897)

Initial reactions supported Dreyfus's conviction: a traitor had been punished. Jean Jaurès, the great socialist leader (soon one of Dreyfus's leading partisans) used the case as an example of injustice: a private from the poorer classes could be sentenced to death for a momentary act of insubordination, but even for treason an officer received only a life sentence.

Doubts were soon raised. On 18 September 1896 Dreyfus's wife, Lucie, published an open letter. This was followed in November 1896 by Bernard Lazare's pamphlet, *Une erreur judicaire: La vérité sur l'affaire Dreyfus* (Judicial error: The truth about the Dreyfus case), which had to be privately printed in Brussels but was quickly taken up by a French publisher. And the spying continued! Lieutenant Colonel Georges Picquart investigated and correctly fingered Major Ferdinand Esterhazy as the spy, but the minister of war ordered a search for more evidence. Major Henry forged another document. He found a letter from the Italian military attaché to his German lover inviting him to dinner with "three friends from my embassy, including one Jew." Henry cut the letter apart and added similar paper, on which he himself wrote words incriminating Dreyfus as "that Jew." Picquart was banished to the provinces to prevent the truth from leaking out. By June 1897, fearing for his life, Picquart revealed all to his lawyer, who enlisted Auguste Scheurer-Kestner, vice president of the Senate. Scheurer-Kestner threw his weight behind efforts to reopen the case. It became a national affair, fought out in the emerging mass media.

THE CULMINATION (1897–1899)

The army put Esterhazy on trial in December 1897, but he was acquitted. Émile Zola, France's most famous living writer, wrote an open letter to the president of the republic, accusing the army of deliberately concealing the truth. Georges Clemenceau, a leading republican politician, gave it the title by which it is known—"J'accuse" (I accuse)—and published it in his newspaper on 13 January 1898. It sold a record three hundred thousand copies.

In response, the Catholic daily *La croix* (The cross) and other Catholic organs went into orgies of anti-Semitism and hatred of the republic, ensuring that republicans continued to view the church as

their major opponent. And the army prosecuted Zola for libel in February 1898. Zola's fame made the affair an international issue. Faced with appeals to faith in the army, Zola was convicted. Also in February, leading pro-Dreyfusard intellectuals founded the Ligue des droits de l'homme et du citoyen (League of the rights of man and of the citizens), better known as the Ligue des droits de l'homme, still the guardian of French republican liberties. Convicted on appeal in July, Zola fled to England to prevent the verdict's being officially served on him and to keep the case open, adding more drama to the affair.

A new war minister, Eugène Godefroy Cavaignac, made a major speech on 7 July 1898. Aiming to restore faith in the army, he detailed all the proofs against Dreyfus. Jaurès responded with a series of articles called "The Proofs" (10–24 August 1898), demonstrating by textual analysis that the "proofs" must be forgeries. Cavaignac interrogated Major Henry, who confessed. The next day, using a razor provided by fellow officers, he committed suicide in his prison cell. Anti-Dreyfusards made him a hero: he had created "le faux patriotique" (the patriotic forgery) "for the public good" (Bredin, p. 337). *La libre parole* collected 131,000 francs for this "martyr for patriotism"; many donors added vicious anti-Semitic comments (Weber, pp. 32–33). The royalist Charles Maurras also defended Henry. Maurras hated "Hebraic thought and all the dreams of justice, of happiness and of equality it drags in its wake." Major Henry had, Maurras wrote, defended France against the Jew "for the good and the honor of all" (Weber, p. 8). Maurras joined other anti-Dreyfusards in founding the Comité d'Action Française (Committee of French Action); he soon emerged as its leader.

Following Henry's suicide, Cavaignac resigned and Major Esterhazy fled to Belgium (then to England), but the president of the republic, Félix Faure, still resisted reopening the case. Faure died in February 1899 and was succeeded by Émile Loubet. A retrial was granted on 3 June 1899. The next day, at the Longchamps races, a furious young aristocrat smashed Loubet's top hat with his cane. The socialist parties called a massive counterdemonstration for 11 June 1899, and other republicans joined in, beginning a tradition of

Cinq Cen...

L'AURORE
Littéraire, Artistique, Sociale

J'Accuse...
E AU PRÉSIDENT DE LA RÉP
Par ÉMILE ZOLA

The headline of Émile Zola's article in *L'Aurore*. © BEMBARON JEREMY/CORBIS SYGMA

rallying for the republic when it was threatened. The next day, the socialist deputy Édouard Vaillant moved no confidence, and the ministry fell.

Loubet called on René Waldeck-Rousseau to form a government committed to ending the affair. Dreyfus was brought back for a second trial; the judges found him "guilty but with extenuating circumstances," hoping to make possible a light sentence and defuse the affair. Waldeck-Rousseau immediately arranged for Dreyfus to be pardoned on 19 September 1899.

FROM PARDON TO INNOCENCE (1900–1998)
In 1904 Dreyfus's case was reopened, and in July 1906 he was formally cleared, given the Legion of Honor, and reinstated in the army with the rank of major, a rung below the level he would have expected to reach. Picquart was reinstated with the rank of brigadier general. Dreyfus soon retired, but returned to the army to fight in World War I. On 13 January 1998, the centenary of "J'accuse,"

President Jacques Chirac formally apologized to Dreyfus's and Zola's descendants.

The Dreyfus affair consolidated the republic and led to the separation of church and state in 1905. Zola's intervention set a precedent for intellectuals to take a special role in politics, both in France and worldwide. The affair led many Jewish observers to strive for a Jewish homeland rather than to count on assimilation. Foremost among these was Theodor Herzl, who organized the 1897 congress that founded the World Zionist Organization and became its president, after observing the affair as Paris correspondent of the Viennese newspaper, *Neue Freie Presse*.

The affair also catalyzed the formation of a new extreme right, fusing anti-Semitism and nationalism with populist resentment against the new economic order and opposition to parliamentary democracy. In 1908 Action Française, the core of this new right, founded a daily to foster a nationalist monarchism based on hatred of foreigners and Jews. Ernst Nolte, a well-known right-wing historian later involved in much controversy, wrote in his pioneering *Three Faces of Facism* that Action Française was the "missing link" between the nineteenth century and fascism. Few historians in the early twenty-first century go so far, but most agree that Action Française kept alive values on which later extreme right movements were based.

See also **Action Française; Anticlericalism; Anti-Semitism; Boulanger Affair; Clemenceau, Georges; France; Maurras, Charles; Nationalism.**

BIBLIOGRAPHY

Bredin, Jean-Denis. *The Affair: The Case of Alfred Dreyfus.* Translated by Jeffrey Mehlman. New York, 1986.

Burns, Michael. *Rural Society and French Politics: Boulangism and the Dreyfus Affair, 1886–1900.* Princeton, N.J., 1984.

———. *Dreyfus: A Family Affair, 1789–1945.* New York, 1991.

Cahm, Eric. *The Dreyfus Affair in French Society and Politics.* London, 1996.

Forth, Christopher E. *The Dreyfus Affair and the Crisis of French Manhood.* Baltimore, Md., 2004.

Griffiths, Richard. *The Use of Abuse: The Polemics of the Dreyfus Affair and Its Aftermath.* Oxford, U.K., 1991.

Kleeblatt, Norman L., ed. *The Dreyfus Affair: Art, Truth, and Justice.* Berkeley, Calif., 1987.

Lazare, Bernard. *Une erreur judiciaire: L'affaire Dreyfus.* 2nd ed. Paris, 1897. Reprint, arranged by Philippe Oriol. Paris, 1993.

Weber, Eugen. *Action Française: Royalism and Reaction in Twentieth-Century France.* Stanford, Calif., 1962.

Zola, Émile. *Truth.* Translated by Ernest A. Vizetelly. New York, 1903. Reprint, Amherst, N.Y., 2001.

———. *The Dreyfus Affair: "J'accuse" and Other Writings.* Edited by Alain Pagès. Translated by Eleanor Levieux. New Haven, Conn., 1996.

CHARLES SOWERWINE

DRUGS. From the Middle Ages, *drugs* referred to medicinal substances employed by chemists, pharmacists, and apothecaries. The word did not take on its modern associations with narcotics in particular until the mid-nineteenth century, with the increased recognition of opiate addiction. Once concepts and terminology evolved to address phenomena involving opiates, they transferred easily to substances such as cannabis and cocaine. Hallucinogens, however, were not widely acknowledged until the mid-twentieth century.

OPIATES

For centuries, opium (the congealed juice of poppy seed pods) was used in folk remedies and patent medicines to treat many common afflictions. It was cheaper than liquor, a fact often blamed for its popularity as a Saturday night recreation for English Midland factory hands and fenland farm workers in the 1830s and 1840s. As early as 1700, a few treatises on opium noted effects such as tolerance (the necessity for ever greater dosages to produce the original effect) and withdrawal (the onset of uncomfortable symptoms when dosages of the substance are decreased or halted), but these phenomena were little discussed until the mid-nineteenth century. *Confessions of an English Opium-Eater* (1821) by Thomas De Quincey (1785–1859) built upon a pattern hinted at in the 1816 poem "Kubla Khan" by Samuel Taylor Coleridge (1772–1834), establishing opium in the European popular imagination as both an exotic Oriental hallucinogen and the object of a shameful thralldom. Both writers also associated opium with visionary artistry, a connection cemented by other prominent artists who addressed opium in their works or were notorious users themselves, including English writers Percy Bysshe Shelley (1792–1822), Lord Byron (1788–1824), and Charles Dickens (1812–1870), American writer Edgar Allan Poe (1809–1849), French writer Charles Baudelaire (1821–1867), and French composer Hector Berlioz (1803–1869).

One reason opium's addictive tendencies went largely unremarked until midcentury was that raw opium is much less addictive than its alkaloid, morphine, which was first isolated in 1803 by the German pharmacist Friedrich Sertürner (1783–1841) and made popular throughout the developed world by the advent of the hypodermic syringe in the 1850s. By the 1870s, European medical professionals led by the Austrian Heinrich Obersteiner (1847–1922) and the German Eduard Levinstein (1831–1882) had defined a new disease known as "morphinism" or "morphinomania," characterized by a compulsion to use morphine. Linked closely to the treatment and legal control of alcoholism, the treatment of opiate addiction emerged as a new medical specialty.

Opium was also inextricably linked in the nineteenth-century with "the Orient," in part because popular traveler's tales often featured exotic Orientals eating or smoking opium, and the majority of the drug in European domestic use came from Turkey, Persia, and Egypt. Furthermore, the British East India Company's smuggling activities precipitated two so-called Opium Wars with China (1839–1842 and 1856–1860), prompting anti-opium crusaders to warn that Britain would someday suffer retribution. Such fears spread in the latter half of the nineteenth century. They figured prominently in published accounts of Oriental and English smokers in supposedly innumerable Chinese opium dens in London's East End, despite evidence that there were only a few modest establishments with any claim to the title at the time.

HASHISH

Oriental exoticism also pervaded the infamous Club des Haschischins, a group of Parisian intellectuals fascinated with the "Assassins" (Haschischins), legendary Islamic militants who reputedly smoked hashish (the resin secreted by flowers of the hemp plant) to see visions of paradise, be thereby inspired to murder their religious enemies, and so gain entrance to paradise. Members of the Club des Haschischins included Baudelaire, Gérard de Nerval (1808–1855), Alexandre Dumas (1802–1870), and Théophile Gautier (1811–1872). According to Gautier's 1846 account in *Revue des Deux Mondes,* members met in a secret Paris location where the drug was administered by an eminent doctor, often assumed to have been the psychologist Jacques-Joseph Moreau de Tours (1804–1884), who reported his self-experimentation with hashish in *Du Haschisch et de l'Aliénation Mentale* (1845; Hashish and mental illness). Baudelaire later recorded his own impressions of hashish and published them along with loosely translated excerpts from De Quincey's *Confessions* as *Les paradis artificiels* (1860; Artificial paradises). Gautier's and Baudelaire's descriptions of hashish were faintly echoed in Britain in a smattering of anonymous magazine articles and in the reference by Oscar Wilde (1854–1900) to an Oriental "green paste"

East End Opium Den. Engraving by Gustave Doré, 1870. Regarded as a wonder drug early in the nineteenth century, opium had become associated with poverty and licentiousness by the 1860s. Doré included this engraving in his series exploring the problems of poverty in London. MARY EVANS PICTURE LIBRARY

associated with the title character's debauchery in *The Picture of Dorian Gray* (1891). Interest in the United States was evident in such publications as Fitz Hugh Ludlow's *The Hasheesh Eater* (1857) and H. H. Kane's subsequently famous "A Hashish-House in New York" in *Harper's Monthly* (1883).

COCAINE

Workers in Peru, Bolivia, and Ecuador, where the coca plant grows wild, had long chewed coca leaves to limit fatigue and provide pleasure. The plant's potential was not widely noted in Europe, however, until the active alkaloid was isolated and named in 1860 by a graduate student, Albert Niemann (1834–1861), working with the chemistry professor Friedrich Wöhler (1800–1882) at the University of Göttingen. The same decade saw the advent of Vin Mariani, a Bordeaux wine steeped with coca leaves. First manufactured in 1863 by the French chemist

Angelo Mariani (1832–1914), this coca wine became popular with drinkers throughout Europe, including Queen Victoria (r. 1837–1901) and Popes Leo XIII (r. 1878–1903) and Pius X (r. 1903–1914). It spawned imitations, most notably Coca-Cola, a preparation of coca leaves and cola nuts first marketed as a tonic in the United States in 1886. In 1883, German army physician Theodor Aschenbrandt published his findings that cocaine improved the endurance of soldiers. Sigmund Freud (1856–1939) read Aschenbrandt's article and experimented with cocaine on himself and others. He published a glowing account in 1884, making him one of the most visible representatives of a class of medical professionals who were initially enthusiastic about cocaine, as some others had been about morphine. As the danger of addiction and psychotic symptoms became clearer, however, recriminative counterarguments followed and Freud's professional reputation suffered.

See also **Alcohol and Temperance; Baudelaire, Charles; Coleridge, Samuel Taylor; Decadence; Opium Wars; Popular and Elite Culture; Shelley, Percy Bysshe; Tobacco; Wilde, Oscar; Wine.**

BIBLIOGRAPHY

Primary Sources

Jay, Mike, ed. *Artificial Paradises: A Drugs Reader.* London, 1999.

Secondary Sources

Berridge, Virginia, and Griffith Edwards. *Opium and the People: Opiate Use in Nineteenth-Century England.* London, 1981.

Davenport-Hines, R. P. T. *Pursuit of Oblivion: A Global History of Narcotics, 1500–2000.* London, 2001.

Lewin, Louis. *Phantastica, Narcotic and Stimulating Drugs: Their Use and Abuse.* Translated by P. H. A. Wirth. London, 1931.

BARRY MILLIGAN

DRUMONT, ÉDOUARD (1844–1917),
French publicist and anti-Semitic activist.

Few cases of notoriety are as puzzling as the strange case of Édouard Drumont. Drumont, a French publicist, emerged suddenly in 1886 to become one of Europe's leading anti-Semitic activists. Sprung from the humblest of provincial beginnings—his father was a ne'er-do-well who ended his days in an insane asylum—Drumont abandoned his mother and sister to their fates and made his way to Paris. Through the 1860s, 1870s, and well into the 1880s, the scrivener made a sort of life for himself as a minor journalist, moving from newspaper to newspaper, most of them right wing, often Bonapartist.

LA FRANCE JUIVE

Then, in the spring of 1886, Drumont published a two-volume work entitled *La France juive*—or *Jewish France*. The book sat in the stores for a month, then received some important (if critical or mixed) reviews in the press, after which it suddenly took off, becoming France's largest bestseller since Joseph-Ernest Renan's *La vie de Jésus* (1863; *Life of Jesus*).

Jewish France is a sprawling pastiche, a confection of hoary religio-cultural notions and newfangled socioeconomic and "scientific" (racist) ideas that had been floating in the Zeitgeist (general cultural climate) for the previous few decades. The highly repetitive and factually faulty work displays a complete absence of rigor or system, and even of the force and energy that drive certain other, equally repellent, writings (such as Adolf Hitler's *Mein Kampf* of 1925–1927, which cites Drumont approvingly).

Drumont loudly denies he has anything against Judaism as a religion; rather, he claims to demonstrate that the Jews as "a people" are arrogant, anti-Catholic, rich, and controlling. "Foreigners everywhere," they are "unpatriotic cosmopolites" in every nation they inhabit. "France," Drumont writes, "is for the French." Herein lies a contradiction—if France is "Jewish," then how can the French Jews not be French? He adds, the Jews are "capitalists by nature" but also, curiously, "revolutionaries"—another contradiction. And a third: Drumont borrowed a large sum from a leading Jewish banker of the day, a man whom he was vilifying in the press.

Drumont wrote other books—*Le testament d'un antisémite* (1891; *Testament of an Antisemite*), *La fin d'un monde: Étude psychologique et sociale* (1889; The world we have lost), *Le secret de Fourmies* (1892; The secret of Fourmies), and so forth—none nearly as famous as his first. In all of them, he often uses the word *race,* though what he generally means by it is not so much a set of physical and genetic traits (though he does occasionally speak of such) but rather the characteristics of group solidarity and aggression that are associated with *nationalism.*

The gravamen of his charges turned on two issues: the Jews' alleged financial control of the French economy and, correspondingly, their political influence in the Third Republic. Together with a handful of Protestants who held high office in the regime ("every Protestant is half a Jew"), the Jews, he averred, constituted the activist core of France's governing classes and therefore were singularly responsible for the anticlerical legislation of the 1880s (and after) against the Catholic Church.

In short, the "new" French anti-Semitism of the 1880s and after consisted of a politico-religious kernel lying within a socioeconomic husk. This should not be surprising. In a nominally Catholic nation such as France, the Church of Rome keenly felt the "rude blows" raining down on it from a secular regime intent on creating republican citizens. Catholics might normally have responded by launching a political party of their own, as they did in Germany and Austria, yet they did not do so in France.

A number of contentious newcomers therefore entered the French political world. Drumont's anti-Semites, as also the monarchists and the nationalists, took as their model of opposition Hippolyte-Adolphe Taine's attack on the French Revolution and the Third Republic, only reoutfitted as an attack on "Jewish France," rather than "the Jacobin Republic." But their appeals and styles were new; for Drumont, like some of his more intuitive right-wing rivals, had an opportunistic finger on society's pulse, and in the 1890s they managed to enlist a number of anarchists, socialists, and workers. This ceased by the end of the decade, when the far left turned against organized anti-Semitism; yet French socialism never entirely overcame its occasional tendency to inveigh against "Jewish finance."

EFFECTIVENESS AND INEFFECTIVENESS

Drumont's new "ism" thus had its moments— small triumphs that battened on the great political

"affairs" that shook the regime through the turn of the century: Boulanger, Panama, Dreyfus. This last crisis saw anti-Semitic riots break out in provincial France. Drumont's National Anti-Semitic League of France amounted to nothing, although it, and a successor league, gave the impression of huge size. Drumont's daily newspaper, *La libre parole* (Free Speech), however, boasted well over a hundred thousand readers on most days. Drumont accepted prison and exile on behalf of his convictions, and he frequently risked his neck in duels with many of the leading figures of the day (including the Radical statesman Georges Clemenceau). In 1898 he was elected on an anti-Semitic platform from Algeria for a term to the Chamber of Deputies, where he sat with a couple of dozen other anti-Semitic representatives. But formal anti-Semitism was by 1902 largely a thing of the past, its organizations and leadership diminished, and certainly nothing remotely akin to the mighty parties, numerous newspapers, or powerful parliamentary delegations that anti-Semitism fielded in Germany, Austria, or Russia.

Then, too, Édouard Drumont was anything but a Karl Lueger or a Georg von Schoenerer, to name the two most famous German-speaking anti-Semites. Lacking entirely their organizational capabilities, he was an introvert, preferring his study to the street. This was perhaps just as well, for he also lacked these leaders' charisma and their apparent civic-mindedness. Instead, Drumont was misanthropic, a man of fathomless querulousness who broke with every ally he ever had, and made enemies where he did not need to. Thus, the Vatican, for example, which quietly supported the Austro-German Catholic parties, nearly condemned Drumont for his invective against the pope and the bishops. Drumont's own confessor, Father du Lac—a renowned Jesuit who had aided the publication of *La France juive*—wrote to him a few years later, "Almost nobody believes you any more. . . . Almost no one takes you seriously."

Finally, perhaps relatedly, Drumont's ideas remained narrow and negative—too obviously the acting out of his tortured psyche and emotional conflicts. He never learned how to associate his anti-Semitism with other, more positive, political and cultural stances and ideas, as Karl Lueger managed to do when he became mayor of Vienna. "I feel my heart more capable of hatred than of love," Drumont wrote Father du Lac, in what was, for once, not only a sincere but also an accurate statement.

Drumont's historical fame results from his nationality, his being French. Simply because *La France juive* appeared in the home of the democratic Revolution of 1789—the only major European power to be a republic—it provoked international astonishment and won its author some degree of reknown. But the "movement" that he sought to create from his book's reception proved stillborn, as the French anti-Semitism of this era remained a porous entity with transparent borders, not a formal ideology or organized party. Though anti-Jewish ideas infected the Zeitgeist, they proved a difficult doctrinal sell in postrevolutionary culture. When anti-Semitism showed itself in prewar France, it was commonly as an accompaniment of other doctrines, a momentary revitalizer of failed causes, such as Boulangism.

See also **Anti-Semitism; Boulangism; Dreyfus Affair; Jews and Judaism.**

BIBLIOGRAPHY

Primary Sources

Beau de Loménie, Emmanuel. *Édouard Drumont; ou, L'anticapitalisme national: Choix de textes.* Paris, 1968.

Drumont, Édouard. *La France juive devant l'opinion.* 2 vols. Paris, 1886.

Secondary Sources

Busi, Frederick. *Pope of Antisemitism: The Career and Legacy of Edouard-Adolphe Drumont.* Lanham, Md., 1986.

Byrnes, Robert F. *Antisemitism in Modern France.* Vol. 1: *The Prologue to the Dreyfus Affair.* New Brunswick, N.J., 1950.

Poliakov, Leon. *Histoire de l'antisémitisme.* Paris, 1968.

Wilson, Stephen. *Ideology and Experience: Antisemitism in France at the Time of the Dreyfus Affair.* London, 1982.

STEVEN ENGLUND

DUBLIN. At the end of the eighteenth century, Dublin was the second largest city in the British Isles and the tenth largest in Europe, with a population of 182,000. An era of rapid expansion was coming to an end; indeed, the population of Dublin city and county combined fell between 1821 and 1831. The city's population reached 258,000 in 1851, falling to 245,000 by 1891. Suburban growth more than compensated for the decline in the city, although after a brisk expansion in midcentury, it tailed off during the 1880s. City and suburbs entered another phase of expansion during the 1890s, which continued up to the eve of World War I. In 1911 Dublin and its suburbs had a population of 400,000, but Belfast, with a population of only 20,000 in 1800, was Ireland's largest city.

POPULATION

A commercial and administrative city, offering limited industrial employment, Dublin failed to attract significant immigrants from rural Ireland; in 1841 just over one-quarter of the population was born outside Dublin city and county; by 1911 the comparable figure (in an enlarged city) was under 30 percent. Non-Dubliners were best represented among the professional and middle classes and domestic servants; general laborers were overwhelmingly Dublin born. Many skilled and unskilled Dublin workers migrated to Britain, some settling permanently. Jewish immigrants from eastern Europe began arriving in Dublin in the 1880s; the only other significant non-Irish group in the city were the garrisons of British soldiers.

Epidemics of fever, smallpox, and cholera were a regular feature of Dublin life until the 1870s, but despite their disappearance, Dublin's death rate declined at a much slower pace than other cities in the United Kingdom; until the 1880s, deaths regularly exceeded births. Infant mortality, which was below the average for U.K. cities until 1890, was 20 percent above that average by 1914. The death rate among adults was significantly higher than in British cities, with tuberculosis and respiratory disease the major killers. Tuberculosis peaked in Dublin several decades later than in Belfast or in British cities; poverty, overcrowding, and poor hygiene were significant factors. By 1911 completed family size in Dublin was slightly below the Irish average, and there is evidence that some Protestant families were controlling fertility.

INDUSTRY

Many of the industries found in late-eighteenth-century Dublin had catered to the landed gentry; during the nineteenth century, these trades tended to stagnate or disappear because landed incomes were less buoyant, and the Act of Union of 1800 (which abolished the Irish parliament) lessened the attractions of the Dublin Season. Guinness's Brewery, which claimed to be the largest brewery in the world by the 1880s, employed fewer than two thousand workers; the distillation of Irish whiskey employed less than five hundred. General laborers, many in casual employment, accounted for between 20 and 25 percent of the workforce. Most women were engaged in laundry work, dressmaking, and domestic service; there were few openings for young boys or girls. The coming of the railways resulted in a major expansion in Dublin port. By 1875 Dublin was Ireland's largest port and the fifth largest in the United Kingdom, but the growth in port activity tailed off sharply during the 1880s, as did investment in the port. By 1907 Dublin ranked twelfth among U.K. ports; Belfast was ninth.

Because of a surplus of general laborers, the gap between skilled and unskilled wages was higher than in British cities, and casual employment was common. In 1908 James Larkin (1876–1947), a fiery and charismatic labor leader who had previously worked as a union organizer in Liverpool and Belfast, began to enroll Dublin laborers and dock workers in his Irish Transport and General Workers' Union. Larkin's militant tactics initially achieved some gains for the workers, but in 1913 Dublin employers decided to face Larkin down by dismissing all workers who failed to sign an undertaking not to join the union; the 1913 Lock-Out lasted for several months and ended in defeat for the workers.

SOCIAL GEOGRAPHY

By the close of the eighteenth century, the Wide Streets Commissioners had laid out the modern Dublin streetscape. The opening of the magnificent Custom House (1791) and Carlisle Bridge (1791–1794) by the architect James Gandon (1742–1823) shifted the axis of the city to the east, away from its Viking and medieval roots. Port development migrated to the north banks of the river Liffey, and this together with the growing trade in live cattle (who walked to the port) spelled doom for the formerly fashionable north city streets and squares. They were converted into tenement housing for dock laborers, casual workers, and prostitutes—their habitués have been well captured in the plays of Sean O'Casey (1880–1964), and the "Night-town" scene in *Ulysses* by James Joyce (1882–1941). Fashionable Dublin retreated to the southeast of the city and the adjoining suburban townships of Pembroke and Rathmines. Suburbia offered an escape from disease and poverty, from higher local taxes, and from a city that was increasingly being taken over by Catholics and nationalists.

CITY POLITICS

In 1840 Dublin Corporation was transformed from a closed corporation, dominated by a small and largely self-perpetuating body of freemen, to one elected by property owners. Daniel O'Connell (1775–1847), member of parliament (MP), became the first Catholic lord mayor since the Protestant Reformation and immediately used the office to launch a campaign to restore the Irish parliament. O'Connell went to some effort to retain a Protestant presence in Dublin Corporation—inaugurating an informal arrangement where the office of lord mayor was held alternatively by a Catholic/liberal and a Protestant/conservative, but this pact broke down during the 1860s as tensions rose over Italian unification, disestablishment of the Church of Ireland, and the refusal of a government charter to Dublin's Catholic university. The city's Protestant population fell by ten thousand (19 percent) between 1861 and 1871. During the 1880s, the triumphant Home Rule party further eroded Protestant/unionist representation in city politics through a strong campaign for voter registration and militant tactics, such as refusing an address of welcome to the visiting Prince of Wales. The 1898 Local Government Act (Ireland's equivalent to Britain's 1888 Act) increased the electorate from eight thousand to thirty-eight thousand, resulting in a modest labor representation. However, Dublin Corporation continued to be dominated by supporters of the Irish Nationalist Party; labor and the newly emerging Sinn Féin Party failed to establish a significant presence.

View of College Green and the Bank of Ireland, Dublin, c. 1900. A statue of Irish nationalist politician Henry Grattan stands in the foreground. ©BETTMANN/CORBIS

The post-1840 Dublin Corporation was frequently accused of corruption. However, some of the criticism reflects Protestant resentment at losing power. Between the 1840s and the 1860s, the membership of Dublin Corporation included a significant number of the city's business elite—brewers, distillers, railway directors, and prominent merchants—but by the 1880s it was increasingly dominated by the city's publicans, many of them also tenement landlords. During the 1860s, Dublin Corporation successfully carried out a major water scheme, but a main drainage scheme was not completed until 1906, and for many years the river Liffey acted as the city's main sewer. The delay was mainly due to financial difficulties—the city's income was substantially reduced in 1854 and did not return to the 1850 level until the mid-1880s. Dublin Corporation attempted to revolve this problem by extending city boundaries to include the adjoining suburban townships, but the latter proved adept at resisting their efforts. In 1900 the city absorbed the poorer suburbs to the north and west, but the prosperous southside townships of Rathmines and Pembroke remained independent until 1930, largely thanks to the support of the Irish Unionist MP Baron Edward Henry Carson (1854–1935), whose father had been a property developer in both townships.

By 1914 Dublin Corporation had provided housing for 7,500 persons, 2.5 percent of the population, a proportion that they claimed was greater than in any other city in the United Kingdom; local authority and philanthropic housing combined accounted for almost 20 percent of the city's housing stock, yet in that year twenty thousand people were living in one-room tenements, and an official inquiry estimated that fourteen thousand new houses were urgently needed. The relocation of working class families in the suburbs did not begin until the 1920s.

CULTURE

Dublin's National Library, National Gallery, and National Museum are nineteenth-century foundations. In 1815 the Royal Dublin Society (RDS, founded in 1731) purchased Leinster House, the former townhouse of the Duke of Leinster, which became the society's library and museum. In 1853 the RDS organized the Dublin Industrial Exhibition with the financial assistance of railway magnate William Dargan (1799–1867). In 1857 the society erected a Natural History Museum on its grounds with government assistance; thirty thousand books from the RDS's library formed the nucleus of the National Library that opened in 1890.

During the first half of the nineteenth century, Ireland's leading learned society, the Royal Irish Academy (founded 1785) accumulated an impressive collection of Irish antiquities and manuscripts, and in 1852 they moved to new premises in Dawson Street that included a dedicated museum and library. When the Science and Art Department at South Kensington opened a museum in Dublin in 1890, the Royal Irish Academy's collection became the nucleus of the antiquities collection. The museum was renamed the National Museum in 1908.

Theater and music formed part of Dublin's cultural fabric, but they were not represented in any buildings of significance; the Abbey Theatre, founded in 1904 in Dublin's down-at-the-heels north city, achieved its reputation for pioneering contemporary Irish drama despite precarious finances and modest premises.

In 1800 Dublin had one university, Dublin University, founded in the sixteenth century, and its single college, Trinity College. During the nineteenth century, Dublin University followed a pattern similar to many other universities, opening professional schools in law and medicine and expanding its curriculum to include natural sciences, history, and economics. Catholics were admitted in 1793, but they were precluded from becoming scholars or fellows for many decades. In 1854 John Henry Newman (1801–1890) opened the Catholic University in the hope that it would

become "A Catholic Oxford in Ireland," but although the foundation stone for university buildings was laid in the northern suburb of Drumcondra in 1861, lack of funds meant that it was not constructed. The Catholic University, renamed University College Dublin, survived as a small college with a liberal arts program and a medical school until 1908, when it became a constituent college of the new National University of Ireland.

RELIGIOUS INSTITUTIONS

Catholics constituted a majority of Dublin's population from the early eighteenth century, but the penal laws meant that all prominent religious buildings were the property of the established church. The two Church of Ireland cathedrals, Christ Church and St. Patrick's, date from medieval times and were extensively renovated and partly remodeled in the second half of the nineteenth century. The Catholic pro-cathedral (1816) reflected the pre-Catholic Emancipation era: it was erected on a minor street in the north city. Most of the early Catholic churches were erected in poorer quarters; later constructions were more ostentatious befitting a growing Catholic assertiveness. John Henry Newman remarked that the (unfashionable) north side was "the specially Catholic side of Dublin"; the northern suburb of Drumcondra became the home to Catholic seminaries and the residence of the archbishop. Religious institutions catering to all denominations flourished during this period: schools, universities, hospitals, orphanages, and charities were all denominationally based, as was recruitment by many private employers. One Dubliner recalled that "From childhood I was aware that there were two separate and immiscible kinds of citizens: the Catholics of whom I was one, and the Protestants who were as remote and different from us as if they had been blacks and we whites" (Andrews, p. 9).

By 1914 Dublin was anticipating the return of devolved government with the establishment of a Home Rule parliament, but these plans were overtaken by World War I and the 1916 Easter Rising. Between 1916 and 1923, large areas of central Dublin were destroyed by rebellion and civil war. The new state inherited a capital city that was very different from the city of the Irish parliament of the late eighteenth century: more Catholic, more nationalist, somewhat down-at-the-heels—a city that is best captured by Joyce's *Dubliners* or *Ulysses*.

See also **Cities and Towns; Great Britain; Ireland; London.**

BIBLIOGRAPHY

Andrews, C. S. *Dublin Made Me: An Autobiography.* Dublin, 1979.

Craig, Maurice. *Dublin 1660–1860.* London, 1992.

Daly, Mary E. *Dublin: The Deposed Capital, 1860–1914.* Cork, 1985.

Hill, Jacqueline. *From Patriots to Unionists: Dublin Civic Politics and Irish Protestant Patriotism, 1660–1840.* Oxford, U.K., 1997.

McParland, Edward. "Strategy in the Planning of Dublin 1750–1800." In *Cities and Merchants: French and Irish Perspectives on Urban Development, 1500–1900.* Edited by Pierre Butel and L. M. Cullen, 97–108. Dublin, 1986.

Vaughan, W. J. *Ireland under the Union, I: 1801–1870.* Vol. 5 of *A New History of Ireland.* Oxford, U.K., 1989.

———. *Ireland under the Union, II: 1870–1921.* Vol. 6 of *A New History of Ireland.* Oxford, U.K., 1996.

Whelan, Yvonne. *Reinventing Modern Dublin: Streetscape, 1900–1966.* Dublin, 1999.

MARY E. DALY

DUELING. During the nineteenth century, dueling was still practiced widely on the European continent. Although many contemporaries had predicted and called for its abolishment, it survived well into the twentieth century. But the duel changed its face: it embraced different people, it was fought over different issues, and it was fought with different weapons and different consequences. Dueling modernized, so to speak, and adapted to the exigencies and challenges of the modern world.

THE DISCURSIVE BATTLEGROUND

A vital element of noble culture during the *ancien régime,* dueling was heavily criticized during the Enlightenment. It was supposed to be irrational, since it did not respond to an attack in an appropriate way; it was held to be immoral since it inter- fered with man's right to live; and it was illegal. In addition, it was seen as a symbol of aristocratic and military privilege that excluded civilians and looked down on middle-class men. But there were also defendants of the dueling principle, among them as enlightened a man as the British physician Bernard Mandeville (1670–1733) and the German writer Johann Wolfgang von Goethe (1749–1832). They praised the civilizing consequences of the point of honor holding back the worst assaults of violence. They cherished dueling not as an instru- ment of vengeance but as a medium of reconcili- ation that transformed an enemy into a friend. They even went so far as to suggest that dueling guaranteed personal integrity and individuality, that it strengthened social equality, and that it protected masculinity against feminizing influence.

Those arguments marked the discursive battle- field on which the campaigns for and against dueling were waged throughout the long nineteenth cen- tury. They involved a large number of participants, both in theoretical and in practical terms. Every duel that was fought and went public incited fierce debates on its pros and cons. Duelists thus could not help but feel embattled, often torn between contradictory claims. The law clearly forbade what they did; lawyers and judges, though, were among those who tenaciously clung to the habit of defend- ing their honor by standing up to the attacker. Other academics like doctors and professors joined them, as did journalists and higher civil servants. For members of the aristocracy and the military, dueling was a must, in any case. The unwritten rules of their class and profession simply demanded it, regardless of public opinion or legal provisions. To evade a duel would have meant social death; only if the challenger was a person of bad reputation or lower social class could a duel be refused.

HONOR

What made men of the upper-middle classes and the aristocracy so anxious about their honor? Why did they not sue the offender instead of putting their lives at high risk? Most men actually did use the services of the judiciary system, and the number of lawsuits filed because of insults rose dramatically during the nineteenth century. This was mainly due to the increasing frequency and density of communication, which produced a multitude of

A Tragic Duel: The Death of Monsieur Harry Alis. Engraving by Oswaldo Tofani from *Le Petit Journal*, 17 March 1895. Harry Alis was the pseudonym of the French writer Jean-Hippolyte Percher, who was killed in a duel in Paris on 2 March 1895. PRIVATE COLLECTION/BRIDGEMAN ART LIBRARY/GIRAUDON

potential conflicts, particularly in the realm of politics, commerce, and journalism. Still, among certain groups of men and for special offenses like adultery, seduction, or physical assault, no other way seemed possible than to challenge the culprit to a deadly fight. In this respect, duelists did not compromise: the weapons that were used—swords or pistols—had to have potentially fatal results. Not every duel ended fatally, though; among those that are known of (because they were reported to the police and followed by a court case), only every third or fourth did.

The possibility of death was thought to be necessary in order to turn the duel into a serious event. Duelists firing into the air or trying to avoid injury were castigated by those who were eager to protect the custom from descending into the realm of ridicule, leniency, and free riding. German

duelists reproached their French counterparts with just that, while the French accused the Germans (especially after 1871) of exceptional brutality and ruse. National rivalries and differences notwithstanding, European dueling culture displayed a remarkable degree of conformity. What was perceived as a gentleman's point of honor transcended national borders. Russian, Polish, French, Spanish, Italian, Austrian-Hungarian, and German duelists basically spoke the same language and observed the same rules of conduct.

Up to the middle of the nineteenth century, this language had also been understood by British gentlemen. Since then, they gradually backed down from the code that had compelled them to take up arms in order to defend their honor. The reasons are manifold: the relative social openness of the elites that could do without additional means of integration is one of them. Another is the burgeoning colonial office that procured ample opportunity to prove manly virtues on a larger and more patriotic scale. The invisibility of the military, which in continental Europe served as a stronghold of dueling, further helped to uproot traditional habits. Conversely, the growing importance and size of the German army in the wake of national unification gave a big thrust to dueling. In France, the military defeat of 1870–1871 did just the same, elevating dueling to a republican virtue that counteracted national humiliation and emasculation. Italy, too, witnessed a veritable dueling craze after unification, which can be largely attributed to the insecurities of the emerging political culture.

In most European countries, then, dueling not only shook off the criticism of enlightened discourse but also gained more and more adherents among the rising middle classes. While some men might have just been imitating aristocratic and military habits, others tended to breathe their own values into the practice, praising its fairness, discipline, and restraint. All participants, though, were equally keen on safeguarding its elitist aura. Even in republican France, they set clear limits to further democratization, and neither women nor men of lower social origin were considered fit to give or take satisfaction. The duel thus survived as a class and gender privilege and upheld its prestige by its very exclusiveness.

This lasted until World War I, which dealt a heavy blow to the European dueling culture. Although the practice did not stop altogether thereafter, its spell was definitely broken. As much as the gigantic bloodshed of 1914–1918 had shattered former concepts of wars perceived as honorable duels, the idea of individual combat seemed anachronistic when set against the unforeseen mass killing and destruction. Changing gender relations and class structures further contributed to its final decline and delegitimization.

See also **Class and Social Relations.**

BIBLIOGRAPHY

Frevert, Ute. *Men of Honour: A Social and Cultural History of the Duel.* Cambridge, U.K., 1995.

Kiernan, Victor G. *The Duel in European History: Honour and the Reign of Aristocracy.* Oxford, U.K., 1988.

Nye, Robert A. *Masculinity and Male Codes of Honor in Modern France.* Oxford, U.K., 1993.

Spierenburg, Pieter, ed. *Men and Violence: Gender, Honor, and Rituals in Modern Europe and America.* Columbus, Ohio, 1998.

UTE FREVERT

DURAND, MARGUERITE (1864–1936), leading French feminist and "new woman" of the belle epoque era.

Born the illegitimate daughter of a royalist general, Marguerite Durand was raised in a respectable bourgeois family by her grandparents and convent-educated. Rebelling against her background, however, she went off to study acting at the Conservatoire and in no time achieved fame as a star actress at the Comédie Française. In 1885 she quit the stage to marry the Radical deputy George Laguerre, an ally of Georges Clemenceau (1841–1929) and an ardent supporter of the populist General Georges-Ernest-Jean-Marie Boulanger (1837–1891). Durand shared her husband's enthusiasm for Boulanger and served to publicize his cause in Laguerre's newspaper *La Presse* as well as exploiting her talents as a salon hostess to win over support. She divorced Laguerre after Boulangism collapsed in 1889, but remained in journalism, joining the staff of *Le Figaro* and becoming the lover of its editor, Antonin Périvier (1847–1924), by whom she had a son.

Following her conversion to feminism in 1896, she founded a daily newspaper, modeled on the heavyweight bourgeois press, which would be written and produced entirely by women. The result was *La Fronde*, launched in 1897, which though neither exclusively devoted to feminism nor aligned with any particular feminist group provided a platform for the burgeoning feminist cause. For several years, with a heightened feminist accent after 1900, Durand turned out a product of remarkably high quality and numbered among her collaborators some of the greatest female talents of the day, including Clémence Royer (1830–1902), the translator of Darwin; Séverine (1855–1929), the combative reporter who covered the Dreyfus affair; Jeanne Chauvin (1862–1926), a pioneering female barrister; and the children's education expert Pauline Kergomard (1838–1925). The paper always struggled financially, however, and eventually folded in 1905.

Despite the immense boost that *La Fronde* gave to the feminist cause, Durand remained an isolated and controversial figure in the movement on account of her *mondaine* lifestyle and reputed sexual liaisons. She herself liked to claim that "feminism owes a great deal to my blonde hair," by which she meant that not only was her stunning personal beauty a refutation of the stock antifeminist charge that feminists were ugly harridans with a grudge against men but that in addition she was able to use her charms to influence the attitudes of her male lovers (who included the leading politician René Viviani [1863–1925]) and even to get them to contribute to the feminist coffers. Other feminist leaders were scandalized by her allure of the demimonde and thought of her as little more than a courtesan. The militant suffragette Hubertine Auclert (1848–1914) called her a "cocotte" and also took issue with Durand's initial lack of enthusiasm for female suffrage based on her belief, widely entertained and propagated by her male friends in the Radical-Socialist party, that women in France were still too subject to clerical influence to be entrusted with the right to vote.

Nor was Durand popular with the world of the French labor movement. Although initially dismissed as an irrelevance by male trade unionists, feminism posed issues with which they were forced to grapple. Because of Durand's all-women policy for the production of *La Fronde*, she founded a female printers' union that was refused recognition by the militantly masculinist Fédération du Livre. In 1901, during a printers' strike at Nancy, Durand volunteered twelve of her women workers as scab labor. The problem of women's work was one in which Durand maintained a passionate interest, and in 1907 she organized a conference to lobby the Ministry of Public Works to set up a special department to tackle gender-specific issues in the workplace. In 1912, Durand championed Emma Couriau, who was refused admission to the printers' union at Lyon, and her husband Louis, who was expelled from the union for failing to use his marital authority to make his wife give up her job.

By 1910, like other moderate republican feminists, Durand had become convinced of the necessity of creating the female citizen and advocated the right of women not only to vote but also to stand as candidates. In the parliamentary elections of 1910, she and three other women presented themselves as candidates in Parisian constituencies, and although all polled badly their campaign helped to raise the profile of the women's movement still further. The vote remained the focus of Durand's feminist endeavors in the years immediately prior to the outbreak of World War I, when she became a member of the Ligue Nationale pour le Vote des Femmes, a new and more militant suffrage group.

Like most bourgeois feminists, Durand placed patriotism ahead of feminism in wartime and briefly revived *La Fronde* as a means of doing something for the war effort. The attempt lasted only a few weeks, however, and a later postwar relaunch of *La Fronde* in 1926 with a number of her old collaborators such as Séverine and the novelist Marcelle Tinayre (1872–1948)—as well as some new, male staff—likewise quickly foundered. Durand's heyday was the belle epoque, but perhaps her most durable legacy is her archives and papers, donated to the Municipality of Paris and preserved in the Bibliothèque Marguerite Durand.

See also **Auclert, Hubertine; Boulanger Affair; Feminism; Suffragism.**

BIBLIOGRAPHY

Hause, Steven C., with Anne R. Kenney. *Women's Suffrage and Social Politics in the French Third Republic.* Princeton, N.J., 1984.

Klejman, Laurence, and Florence Rochefort. *L'Égalité en marche: Le féminisme sous la Troisiènne République.* Paris, 1989.

McMillan, James F. *France and Women, 1789–1914: Gender, Society, and Politics.* London, 2000.

Roberts, Mary Louise. *Disruptive Acts: The New Woman in Fin-de-Siécle France.* Chicago, 2002.

JAMES F. McMILLAN

DURKHEIM, ÉMILE (1858–1917), French sociologist.

Although he built on the work of others, Émile Durkheim is arguably the most influential, and thus important, sociologist to have ever lived. Not only did he establish the discipline of sociology as a field of academic study in France, he also provided the concepts that continue to inspire sociological thought and research everywhere. The reason for his continuing influence lies in both the scientific pertinence of his work and its ideological applications. Although other "classical" social thinkers—such as Karl Marx, Auguste Comte, and Max Weber—are equally important to the evolution of modern social thought, it was Durkheim who laid the foundations of sociology.

LIFE AND CAREER

David-Émile Durkheim was born on 15 April 1858 in Épinal, in the French province of Lorraine. The Prussian occupation of Lorraine in 1870 undoubtedly contributed to the intense nationalist sentiments Durkheim manifested throughout his life. He was the son of a prominent rabbi, and Durkheim's Jewish origins are also important in that they reinforced a preoccupation with social cohesion and national integration that must be considered a major source of his social thought.

A French patriot throughout his adult life, Durkheim was nevertheless strongly influenced by German philosophical and even political thinking. Educated in prestigious French schools, such as the Lycée Louis-le-Grand and the École Normale Supérieure in Paris, he also spent the academic year of 1885 to 1886 in the German universities of Marburg, Leipzig, and Berlin. During the next several years he taught philosophy in Troyes (1886–1887) and then social science and pedagogy at the University of Bordeaux. In 1893 he completed his doctoral dissertation, published as *The Division of Labor in Society*. In 1902 he was given a position at the Sorbonne in Paris, and in 1906 he became full professor there.

Throughout his career, Durkheim endeavored to accomplish two related goals. First, his scholarly production was designed to establish the conceptual and methodological foundations of sociology. Second, he waged a permanent campaign to obtain official recognition and formal academic acceptance of sociology as a professional and scientific discipline within the French system of national education.

Because he was concerned to establish sociology institutionally as much as scientifically, Durkheim actively collaborated with the Radical Republican and Radical-Socialist Party, which, contrary to what its name might imply to non-Europeans, was a moderate social reform party. His appointment to the Sorbonne immediately followed the victory of this political party in the national elections of 1902. The institutional acceptance of sociology was accomplished in stages. In 1913 his chair at the Sorbonne was renamed that of "Science of Education and Sociology." Sociology did not, however, become a separate degree program until the early 1960s.

THE FUNDAMENTAL IDEAS

Strongly influenced by the ideas and social conceptualization he encountered during his residence in German universities as a student, Durkheim built upon them and, ultimately, adapted them to French social and political conditions. In his doctoral dissertation, *The Division of Labor in Society*, he introduced the distinction between "mechanical" and "organic" social organization. This binary typology constituted, in effect, a theoretical framework for the study of all societies.

Durkheim maintained that all societies and "social structures" must be understood in terms of how essential tasks are allocated and performed by their populations. "Mechanical" societies are those in which the division of labor is rudimentary, most people carrying out the same economic functions. In these relatively simple collectivities (which anthropologists and others might call "primitive," "traditional," or "preindustrial" societies), culture and social bonds are based on the similarity and relative simplicity of the tasks performed. Modern societies, in contrast, are those in which the division of labor is complex and the tasks performed demand specialized skills. The interdependence characterizing such complex forms of economic and social interaction produces a culture that is more integrated, which is why Durkheim calls it "organic."

The importance of Durkheim's conceptual dichotomy is best understood by comparing it to that which he wished to discredit. Durkheim's work was an attempt to refute the ideas of the German sociologist Ferdinand Tönnies as expressed in the latter's *Gemeinschaft und Gesellschaft* (1887; *Community and Society*), which argued that modern society was essentially destructive of human relationships because capitalism and industrialism progressively shatter communal bonds and rituals. Tönnies, seeing his work as continuing the conceptualization established by Karl Marx, focused on what he considered the characteristics of the new type of social collectivity created by capitalist production. Human contact was dramatically different in the environment created by what he called *bürgerliche Gesellschaft* (bourgeois society) because money relations condition all aspects of life and mentality. The disintegrating effects of capitalism meant that the very idea of *Gesellschaft* (society) presented a paradox in that a cohesive social entity had become impossible. *Gesellschaft* was thus only an idea of association; it was a speculative fiction. But at the same time the collectivity existed. There was an association of individuals in which each performed some task demanded by the capitalist system of production, but this very system subverted social cohesion.

By suggesting that modern societies were *more* "organic" than preindustrial societies, and not less, Durkheim reversed the paradigm established by Tönnies and provided contemporary sociology with a conceptual system that has been used consistently to discredit Marx's idea of an essentially unstable and conflictual society in which different forms of alienation predominate.

For Durkheim, society was becoming more cohesive, not less. The increasingly complex division of labor and greater population density created relations of greater mutual dependence and, in addition, a common culture or consciousness he called the "conscience collective." What was often understood to be evidence of social disintegration—socialist ideas, working-class organization and strikes, anarchist terror, and so on—were only temporary symptoms of the transition to a more cohesive social organism. Durkheim's work was an attempt to create a new idea of society, one in which industrial capitalism provided an integrative dynamic that showed Marx's ideas to be false. Much, if not most, sociological thought and practice in the twentieth century was based on these Durkheimian ideas.

In order to establish the new paradigm, Durkheim had shown that it resulted from a strict application of scientific method. In *The Rules of Sociological Method* (1895), he maintained that the scientific study of society involved a strict focus on what he called "social facts," as opposed to isolated, individual phenomena. The object of study must be collective institutions, their functional existence, and mass behavior, rather than historical development, political events, or economic processes. In this way, he asserted that a certain kind of "objectivity" is integral to the new discipline of sociology, in contrast to other disciplines purporting to explain social conditions.

Durkheim's most well-known and, perhaps, most successful application of his paradigm is found in *Suicide* (1897). In this work, he used statistical evidence to show that the incidence of suicide can be considered a measure of social disintegration taking the form of a feeling of estrangement from society and other individuals. He called this feeling "anomie," a psychological state resulting from the cultural confusion caused by industrialization and urbanization. *Suicide* was, and is, an extremely important study in the history of academic sociology because it represented the concrete application of the "rules of sociological method" elucidated in the book of that title published two years previously. It was a highly focused examination of one "social fact," an empirical study founded upon statistical evidence and offering a typology of suicide ("egotistical," "altruistic," and "anomic") that clarified social processes and historical development. Although it purported to be a strictly scientific study, Durkheim's analysis of suicide as a social phenomenon also responded to immediate preoccupations in France. A combination of labor agitation, the rise of socialist parties, and anarchist terrorism, he said, were other symptoms of "anomic" pathology occurring during a painful transition to modern society.

This combination of apparent scientific method and a tendency to respond to contemporary social questions was characteristic of Durkheim's work. This tendency can be seen, for example, in his *The Elementary Forms of the Religious Life* (published in 1912, but elaborated early in the century as a series of lectures), considered to be a pioneering study of aboriginal religious practices. As in *Suicide,* Durkheim further developed and applied the paradigm that gave his work undoubted originality and a conceptual thrust that has informed social scientists since. However, coming at a time of controversy over church and state, *The Elementary Forms of the Religious Life* was also a commentary on the religious mentality in general that strengthened a certain critique of religious schools during the imposition of a secular state-directed national education system. In spite of its scientific attributes and contributions, Durkheim's sociology consistently interpreted his social world in a way that was congruent with particular political objectives.

See also **France; Positivism; Sociology; Weber, Max.**

BIBLIOGRAPHY

Primary Sources

Durkheim, Émile. *The Elementary Forms of the Religious Life: A Study in Religious Sociology.* Translated by Joseph Ward Swain. London, 1915.

———. *The Rules of Sociological Method.* 8th ed. Translated by Sarah A. Solovay and John H. Mueller. Chicago, 1938.

———. *Suicide: A Study in Sociology.* Translated by John A. Spaulding and George Simpson. Glencoe, Ill., 1951.

———. *The Division of Labor in Society.* Translated by George Simpson. Glencoe, Ill., 1964.

Secondary Sources

Lukes, Steven. *Émile Durkheim, His Life and Work: A Historical and Critical Study.* New York, 1972.

Nisbet, Robert A. *Émile Durkheim.* Englewood Cliffs, N.J., 1965. Reprint, Westport, Conn., 1976.

Parkin, Frank. *Durkheim.* Oxford, U.K., 1992.

Pickering, W. S. F. *Durkheim's Sociology of Religion.* London, 1984.

LARRY PORTIS

DVOŘÁK, ANTONÍN (1841–1904), Bohemian composer.

A popular postcard sold in tourist shops in Prague pictures caricatures of "The Czech Quartet," the most important representatives of four generations of composers in the second half of the nineteenth and the beginning of the twentieth centuries: Bedřich Smetana (1824–1884), Antonín Dvořák, Leoš Janáček (1854–1928), and Bohuslav Martinů (1890–1959). The legacy bequeathed to Martinů by his three predecessors was considerable. Cultivating a nationalist agenda initiated by Smetana, Dvořák established himself as the most important spokesperson in music for a Czech-speaking populace that, at the time, was ruled from Vienna by the German-speaking Habsburgs. During the 1860s, Dvořák played viola in the the orchestra of the Provisional National Theater—from 1866 conducted by Smetana—and the two composers appreciated each other's works while maintaining cordial, if rather distant, relations. Dvořák and the younger Janáček first became acquainted in 1875, when Janáček left Brno in Moravia to study at the Prague Organ School (from which Dvořák had graduated in 1859), and they remained close friends right up to Dvořák's death in 1904.

Dvořák seems to have been determined already at an early age to pursue a career in music. The myth that he initially followed his father into the butcher's trade is still being circulated in the early twenty-first century, even though the certificate of apprenticeship that often is presented as documentary proof was shown to be a forgery by the preeminent Dvořák scholar Jarmil Burghauser in 1987. At the time of Antonín's birth in 1841, his father, František (1814–1894), operated a butcher shop while concurrently serving as proprietor of a tavern and small dance hall in Nelahozeves. The village, situated about fourteen miles north and slightly west of Prague, was not a particularly thriving county seat. Besides working as a tradesman, František was an accomplished zither player who, later in life, devoted almost all of his time teaching zither and playing in local folk and dance groups. Thus, he—as also his wife, Anna (née Zdeněk, 1820–1882), whose father was a farm and livestock foreman—quickly recognized and nurtured the young boy's talent for music.

During his formative years, Antonín Dvořák never received anything more than a basic, elementary education, and whatever erudition he demonstrated later in life was the result of knowledge learned on his own. He was a kind, sensitive person, a strict but dedicated teacher, an animal lover, and a good family man to his wife, Anna (née Čermák, 1854–1931), and their five children who grew into adulthood (three others died in infancy). Brought up in the Roman Catholic Church, he remained devoutly religious and frequently wrote on the last pages of musical manuscripts phrases such as *Zaplať pán Bůh!* or *Bohu díky!* (Thanks to the Lord!). He was cautious in personal relationships at first, but steadfast in his devotion to his many trusted friends, who came from all walks of life, all classes of society. Michael Beckerman's proposal that he suffered from agoraphobia has generated considerable debate. In any case, Dvořák certainly preferred country environs to the hustle and bustle of urban centers; yet he was fascinated by modern technological developments, most especially steamships and railway locomotives, and the sociological changes they engendered.

Before moving to Prague at the age of sixteen, Dvořák was blessed with the opportunity of studying music with his father and with local *Musikanten Nelahozeves*, Zlonice, and Česká Kamenice, and of developing his skills as a practical performing musician in church and with various folk groups and dance bands (principally on violin and organ). As he began to develop as a composer, the music of Wagner was a powerful early influence, as was also that of Ludwig van Beethoven, Felix Mendelssohn, Bedřich Smetana, Franz Schubert and, less obviously, Anton Bruckner. Recognition as a composer came slowly at first, more rapidly once his works became known outside of Bohemia, namely in Vienna and the principal cities of Germany. Johannes Brahms played a major role in his early rise to fame by recommending to his own publisher, Fritz Simrock of Berlin, such works as the *Slavonic Dances* (first series in piano duet and orchestral versions published 1878, second series 1887) and the first set of *Moravian Duets* for two voices (1879). On the strength of the quality and craftsmanship of his compositions, Dvořák's fame spread rapidly to England and America. Between the years 1884 and 1891, he made eight trips to England for the purpose of personally conducting recently completed works at prestigious choral festivals in London and Worcester (*Stabat Mater*, 1884; Edward Elgar played in the orchestra for the performance at Worcester), Birmingham (*The Spectre's Bride*, 1885; *Requiem*, commissioned by the festival's organizers, 1891), and Leeds (*Saint Ludmila*, commissioned 1886), and also at concerts

of the Philharmonic Society (the Seventh Symphony was commissioned by the Society in 1885).

Dvořák's large-scale choral works are especially popular in England, but elsewhere his instrumental music is generally better known. He cultivated both in nearly equal measure. Americans are familiar with his Symphony no. 9 in E minor, subtitled *Z nového světa* (From the New World), and Cello Concerto in B minor, both of which he composed in New York City during his tenure from 1892–1895 as director of the National Conservatory of America, and they may also have heard the two great chamber works he wrote during the summer of 1893 in Spillville, Iowa, the String Quartet in F major, op. 96, and the String Quintet in E-flat major, op. 97. But the *Biblical Songs*, also composed in America, are unjustly overlooked, as are the several other major contributions to the genre of song cycle he produced during the course of his career, most significantly the *Gypsy Songs* (1881) and *Love Songs* (1888). Since the mid-1980s, several of his eleven operas have been successfully mounted on stages outside of the Czech Republic: these include *Vanda* (1875, rev. 1880, 1883, 1901), *Dimitrij* (1882, rev. 1883, 1885, 1895), *The Jacobin* (1888, rev. 1897), *Kate and the Devil* (1899), and *Rusalka* (1900). Dvořák cultivated nearly every type of musical composition, and within each genre there are many gems.

See also **Music; Nationalism; Prague.**

BIBLIOGRAPHY

Beckerman, Michael. *New Worlds of Dvořák: Searching in America for the Composer's Inner Life.* New York, 2003.

Clapham, John. *Dvořák.* New York, 1979.

Dvořák, Antonín. *Antonín Dvořák: Letters and Reminiscences.* Edited by Otakar Šourek. Translated by Roberta Finlayson Samsour. Prague, 1954. Reprint, New York, 1985.

Hurwitz, David. *Dvořák: Romantic Music's Most Versatile Genius.* Pompton Plains, N.J., 2005.

ALAN HOUTCHENS

EASTERN QUESTION. In the last decades of the nineteenth century the *Eastern Question* was a popular term used to describe the impact of the power vacuum that would occur should the Ottoman Empire lose control of its Balkan provinces. This, in turn, would force inevitable confrontations between Austria-Hungary and Russia over Ottoman territory, and Russian and Great Britain over Russian access to the Mediterranean. After 1879, these disputes threatened to bring in the allies of the principals as well. The term entered the popular vocabulary in 1876 with the publication in Britain of William Gladstone's pamphlet titled *The Bulgarian Horrors and the Question of the East*. Britain, in particular, was concerned about Russian aspirations to acquire the Turkish straits (the Bosphorus and the Dardanelles) should the Turkish hold on the Balkans dissolve. In effect, the Eastern Question constantly threatened to bring the Great Powers of Europe into conflict.

Beginning in the early 1700s the inability of the Ottoman Empire to control the ethnic minorities in the Balkans led to the independence of Hungary, Greece, Serbia, and Romania. In 1875 and 1876 uprisings in Turkish-held Bosnia and Herzegovina and Bulgaria resulted in a war between the Serbs and Turks, and precipitated the Eastern Crisis (1875–1878). Turkish atrocities and battlefield successes against the Christian Slavs led the Russians to consider direct intervention. In conferences in July 1876 (the Reichstadt Agreement) and January 1877 (the Treaty of Budapest),

the Russians reached agreement with Austria-Hungary for a partial dismemberment of Ottoman Bosnia and Herzegovina. The agreements also gave Russia the green light to invade Ottoman Bulgaria, which it did that April.

The central dilemma at the heart of the Eastern Question was its effect on the relationships between the Great Powers of Europe. The Russo-Turkish War of 1877 to 1878 resulted in massive Russian victories in the Caucasus and in Bulgaria. But it was the catastrophic Treaty of San Stefano, imposed by Russia on the Turks in March 1878, that illuminated the reality of the Eastern Question itself. The treaty was unduly harsh and ruined the Ottoman strategic position in the Balkans. In particular, the Treaty of San Stefano created a Russian-dominated Greater Bulgaria (with access to the Aegean Sea) on the doorstep of the Turkish straits. This result was so destabilizing to British and Austrian interests that it almost led to war between them and the Russians. Such a war threatened to destroy German Chancellor Otto von Bismarck's carefully constructed Dreikaiserbund (Three Emperors' League), which dated from 1873, by pitting Austria-Hungary against Russia and forcing Germany to choose between them. The looming crisis energized Bismarck to convene the Congress of Berlin in July 1878.

THE CONGRESS OF BERLIN

The Congress of Berlin was a fateful turning point in European diplomacy that led directly to the destabilization of the Concert of Europe and to the creation of a new alignment of great-power relationships. Bismarck, working to satisfy British and Austrian interests and prevent Russian hegemony, reversed the Treaty of San Stefano. Stillborn Greater Bulgaria was dismembered, ending the Russian threat to the Turkish straits. Austria-Hungary was allowed to administer Bosnia-Herzegovina. Britain got Cyprus, and the Serbs gained some land as well. The Ottoman Empire survived. Russia was left with small territorial gains in Europe and the Caucasus but little else. It was a massive diplomatic humiliation for the tsar.

Above all, the Congress of Berlin ended the strong relationship between Germany and Russia and contributed to the introduction of Russian military improvements aimed at Germany. Moreover, the demonstrated weakness of the Turks served to inflame Balkan nationalism and encouraged the Austrians to become players in Balkan politics. In 1879 Bismarck moved to solidify the new alignment of power by engineering an alliance between Germany and Austria-Hungary. Bismarck nevertheless still needed to resolve the unanswered Balkan questions as well as appease the Russians, and in June 1881 he orchestrated a second Three Emperors' League (Austria-Hungary, Germany, and Russia). This convention and its separate protocol annex committed the three signatory nations to maintaining the status quo of the Balkan provinces of the Ottoman Empire (Turkey in Europe). Other clauses closed the Turkish straits to warships, settled the Eastern Rumelian question (thus paving the way for a medium-sized Bulgaria), and granted the Austrians the future right to annex Bosnia-Herzegovina. This convention restored friendly relations between the three empires and appeared to settle the Eastern Question. In fact, the Balkans remained a tinderbox of local nationalism and great-power rivalries.

THE BOSNIAN CRISIS

In 1897 Austria-Hungary and Russia finally began cooperating (via the Goluchowski-Muraviev agreement) in order to defuse tensions involving ethnic minorities in the Balkans. Further cooperation ended the Macedonian crisis by establishing the Mürzsteg Program in 1903, which put a European-led gendarmerie in place to monitor the Ottomans. British concerns over

the straits also diminished in August 1907 with the signing of a convention between Britain and Russia, which although concerning Asia became the third leg of the Triple Entente. The Young Turk revolution of July 1908 further satisfied Britain that the Balkans were tending toward stability.

Relationships took a turn for the worse when an aggressive Austria-Hungary forged a secret oral agreement with Russia at Buchlau in October 1908. The agreement traded the annexation of Bosnia-Herzegovina for support of Russia's free use of the Dardanelles. Premature annexation by Austria soured the deal, and the angry tsar began to mobilize his army against the Austrians. This led to a war crisis in March 1909, in which Germany backed Austria-Hungary by giving a démarche to the Russians. Russia, still weak from its disastrous defeat in the Russo-Japanese War (1904–1905) and unsupported by Britain and France, was forced to back down. The consequences of this crisis were significant. The Russians, humiliated once again, emerged with a determination to be ready the next time. The Austrians emerged with a sense of confidence that its German ally would unconditionally support its Balkan policies.

THE BALKAN WARS

In the Balkans, rebellions by ethnic minorities in Albania and Macedonia continued to plague the Ottoman Empire. Pan-Slavic support of Serbia and Bulgaria by Russia fed the fires of nationalism, and in 1912 Serbia, Montenegro, Greece, and Bulgaria formed a Balkan Pact against the Turks. The Christian states attacked the Ottoman Balkan provinces in October 1912 and enjoyed astonishing success, taking Salonika (Thessaloníki) and driving the Turks to the gates of Istanbul. Faced with the de facto breakup of Turkey in Europe, the Great Powers brokered an armistice and convened the London Conferences in December 1912. Hosted by Edward Grey, the British secretary of state for foreign affairs, the purpose of the conferences was to use the reality of the Ottoman defeat to manage a mutually agreeable solution to the Eastern Question. By this time, the Eastern Question had matured into a deeply complex problem involving Albanian independence, Serbian and Bulgarian access to the Mediterranean Sea, the sanjak (Turkish district) of Novi Pazar, the Romanian border, the straits question, the Aegean islands, and the protection of minority rights. Ultimately, negotiations collapsed as the warring parties renewed the fighting in February 1913. The First Balkan War ended in April 1913 with Bulgaria in possession of Adrianople (now Edirne) and the Aegean coast. Fighting resumed, however, when the Bulgarians attacked their erstwhile allies in an attempt to seize Macedonia. The Second Balkan War (June–August 1913) resulted in a devastating defeat for Bulgaria in which it lost almost all of its gains. One important outcome of this war was that Russia was forced to choose between supporting Serbia or Bulgaria. The tsar chose to support the Serbs, which ended Russia's strong relationship with Bulgaria and replaced it with strong ties to Serbia.

THE FIRST WORLD WAR

It seemed that the Eastern Question was now resolved. Instead the effects of Buchlau and the 1909 crisis, and the outcome of the Balkan Wars, combined to ignite the Balkan powder keg once more. Serbian nationalists, encouraged by success and with Russian backing, began a terrorist campaign (under the infamous name, the Black Hand) in Austrian-held Bosnia-Herzegovina. On 28 June 1914 Serb nationalists assassinated the Austrian Archduke Francis Ferdinand in Sarajevo. The enraged Austrians again turned to Germany for support. Austria-Hungary sought and received the famous "blank check" from their German allies, which encouraged them to issue an ultimatum to Serbia on 23 July. The Serb refusal and mobilization two days later forced a partial Austrian mobilization. This fully alarmed the Russians, who were determined to avoid the humiliation of 1909. Although not wanting a war, the Russians desperately sought a way to support its Serb client state. Unfortunately, lacking a workable partial mobilization plan, the Russians declared full mobilization on 30 July 1914. The next day Germany declared war on Russia, setting in train the events leading to World War I.

Postwar settlements in 1919 and 1920 appeared to settle the Eastern Question concerning Turkey in Europe, while the Treaty of Lausanne in 1923 appeared to settle the problems of Turkey in Asia. Unfortunately, these treaties favored the interests of the Great Powers and ignored the self-determination of ethnic minorities. As the twentieth century closed, renewed ethnic conflicts enveloped the former Ottoman provinces in the Balkans, Caucasia, and in the Middle East. It is now clear that the incomplete resolution of the Eastern Question continues to haunt the troubled successor states of the former Ottoman Empire and their European and Middle Eastern neighbors.

See also **Bulgaria; Ottoman Empire; Serbia.**

BIBLIOGRAPHY

Anderson, M. S. *The Eastern Question, 1774–1923: A Study in International Relations.* London, 1966.

Erickson, Edward J. *Defeat in Detail: The Ottoman Army in the Balkans, 1912–1913.* Westport, Conn., 2003.

Shaw, Stanford J., and Ezel Kural Shaw. *History of the Ottoman Empire and Modern Turkey.* Vol. 2: *Reform, Revolution, and Republic: The Rise of Modern Turkey, 1808–1975.* Cambridge, U.K., 1977.

Taylor, A. J. P. *The Struggle for Mastery in Europe, 1848–1918.* Oxford, U.K., 1954.

EDWARD J. ERICKSON

EAST INDIA COMPANY. The East India Company began as a joint-stock enterprise incorporated by royal charter; established a trading monopoly with East Asia, Southeast Asia, and India; and became progressively involved in both domestic and international politics. It played a vital role in securing Britain's hegemony over maritime shipping and was instrumental in the foundation of the British Empire in India. With settlements in the Indian coastal cities of Bombay, Surat, Calcutta, and Madras, the Company exported cotton and silk piece goods, indigo, saltpeter, and spices in exchange for bullion, eventually expanding its trade to the Persian Gulf, parts of Southeast Asia, and East Asia, including China, in the nineteenth century. Merging in 1708 with its main competitor to form an exclusive monopoly, the Company was run by twenty-four directors elected annually by a

Court of Proprietors, who also exerted powerful influence in the British Parliament.

In India the Company obtained a Mughal charter of duty-free trade (1717), and invested heavily in local manufacture, especially textiles, operating from Fort William, Calcutta, and Fort Saint George, Madras, on the eastern seaboard. Company servants became involved in lucrative internal and coastal trade for their own private investments, leading to friction with local authorities. In Bengal, private trade in salt, betel nut, tobacco, and saltpeter; the fortification of Calcutta; and connections with indigenous traders ill-disposed toward the Nawab (Siraj-ud-Dawlah, c. 1729–1757) resulted in conflict, Robert Clive's (1725–1774) victory at the Battle of Plassey (1757), and the installation of "puppet" rulers. One of them, Mir Kasim, (r. 1760–1763) protested the flagrant abuse of trading privileges by Company servants, which led to the decisive Battle of Baksar (1764) in which Kasim, the Nawab of Awadh, and the Mughal emperor Shah Alam II (r. 1759–1806) joined forces, only to be routed by the Company's superior Bengal Native Army. The Mughal emperor, in exchange for a yearly tribute, made the Company the collector (Diwan) of revenues of Bengal, Bihar, and Orissa, an annual gain of approximately £6 million, which solved its investment and currency problems. However, revenue collection proved difficult and administrative negligence coupled with drought led to crop failure and the famine of 1770, in which millions perished.

In southern India the East India Company was involved in a protracted military and diplomatic contest with the Marathas, the Nizam's dominion of Hyderabad, kingdom of Mysore ruled by Hyder Ali (1722–1782), and the French. The Company was successful in stalling the French, who were led by François Dupleix (1697–1763), but the conflict escalated during the Seven Years' War (1756–1763) leading eventually to an end of the French challenge at Wandiwash (1760). Soon after, both Arcot and Tanjore came under indirect British rule. Mysore provided stiff resistance until the defeat of Tippu Sultan (1749–1799) in 1799. The Marathas, divided into various ruling houses, their forces depleted by the confrontation with the Afghans (1761), finally succumbed to the British after 1803. The Sikhs of Punjab were humbled in the 1840s and other princely states accepted the suzerainty of the Company, which had emerged as the most formidable fiscal-military state in the subcontinent.

Company affairs, especially mismanagement in Bengal, led to parliamentary inquiry into Indian affairs. Through the Regulating Act (1773) and Pitt's India Act (1784) a Board of Control responsible to Parliament was established, ending the undue influence of shareholders in Indian policy. Warren Hastings (1732–1818), the first governor-general of India (1772–1785), sought to restructure the fiscal and military affairs of the Company, but was charged with corruption by Parliament (led by Edmund Burke [1729–1797]), impeached (1788), and much later acquitted. Significant changes took place in British India by the early nineteenth century: the revenue system was restructured with new property rights vested in land; marketplaces, custom, and police were overhauled; an extensive cartographic survey of India was initiated; a new civil service trained at Haileybury College was put in place; strict limits were placed on all concourse between Britons and Indians; English education was gradually promoted; and modern technologies, including railways, steamships, and the telegraph, were selectively introduced.

In the aftermath of the loss of the American colonies, India under Company rule had emerged as a cornerstone of imperial Britain, although as a dependency and not a settler colony, a fact that possibly restricted the direct impact of the Indian imperial venture on British domestic politics. Under the Company Raj, Indian manufacturers declined in the nineteenth century, making way for a vast, largely dependent market for Britain's industrial output. In 1813 the Company forfeited its commercial monopoly, although it remained as the administrative agent in India till the Sepoy Mutiny and popular uprisings of 1857: a brief debacle for British rule in India that set the stage for direct Crown Rule.

See also **Colonialism; Colonies; Great Britain; Imperialism; India; Sepoy Mutiny; Trade and Economic Growth.**

BIBLIOGRAPHY

Chaudhuri, K. N. *The Trading World of Asia and the English East India Company, 1660–1760.* Cambridge, U.K., and New York, 1978.

Furber, Holden. *Rival Empires of Trade in the Orient, 1600–1800.* Minneapolis, Minn., 1976.

Keay, John. *The Honourable Company: A History of the English East India Company.* London, 1991.

Lawson, Philip. *The East India Company: A History.* London and New York, 1993.

Marshall, P. J. *East Indian Fortunes: The British in Bengal in the Eighteenth Century.* Oxford, U.K., 1976.

SUDIPTA SEN

ECONOMIC GROWTH AND INDUSTRIALISM.

Since the mid-nineteenth century, neoclassical economists, Marxists, and institutionalists have debated the role of markets, popular movements, and institutions (including states, cultural milieux, and corporations) in nineteenth-century European economic growth and industrialism. A review of major works by scholars of these persuasions identifies underlying issues that remain relevant.

THE DEBATE BEGINS

Neoclassical economics traces its origins to Adam Smith (1723–1790) and argues that once the dead hand of state coercion is lifted, economic affairs will follow the laws of supply and demand and an informed rationality that seeks to maximize utility (in the case of individuals) or profits (in the case of firms). Prominent neoclassical economists include Alfred Marshall (1842–1924), William Stanley Jevons (1835–1882), and Milton Friedman (b. 1912). Marxists accept the central role of the free market—the play of supply and demand—in the development of nineteenth-century capitalism, but stress capitalism's susceptibility to economic crises and the role of popular collective movements in challenging the capitalist order. Prominent Marxists include Rosa Luxembourg (1870–1919), Vladimir Lenin (1870–1924), and Ernest Mandel (1923–1995). Institutionalists emphasize the role of institutions in both sustaining markets and correcting their faults. They tend toward pluralistic explanations and see political ideologies as important elements in reform. Prominent institutionalists include John Rogers Commons (1862–1945), Karl Polanyi (1886–1964), and Douglas North (b. 1920).

Neoclassicism During the first two-thirds of the nineteenth century, neoclassical thought was still in formation, but its early progenitors generally followed Smith in advocating laissez-faire—the idea that the state should not intervene in economic matters. In Britain during this period a remarkable series of popularizers incorporated the tenets of laissez-faire into the common intellectual heritage of the Anglo-American world. Despite periods of disfavor these principles have ever remained close to the popular consciousness.

The devoted follower of Adam Smith and advocate of laissez-faire Richard Cobden (1804–1865) became famous for his leadership of the struggle to repeal the Corn Laws, laws designed to protect British farmers by limiting the import of corn when prices fell below a fixed point. Cobden fought for free trade—defined as trade among countries with minimal tariffs and no trade barriers. Like many early free traders, Cobden sought to slash state budgets to the bone and was aggressively antimilitaristic. He contrasted the voluntary, interest-oriented principles of free trade with the coercive practices of states. He feared that Britain's economic supremacy was threatened by the costs of imperial hegemony and tried to severely cut the British armed forces, including the navy. Cobden believed that taxes spent on the fleet increased production costs, rendering British goods less competitive than those produced in the United States, which at that time spent practically nothing on the military.

Marxism Writing in late 1847, Karl Marx (1818–1883) agreed that market expansion and the reorganization of production were the dynamic forces in capitalist expansion but believed that capitalism's days were numbered. Like Cobden, the young Marx identified industrial capitalism with free trade. As a critic of capitalism, Marx wanted to expose the elements of economic compulsion hidden behind the libertarian, antistatist rhetoric of laissez-faire economics. He believed that his world was hurtling toward a homogeneous, bourgeois-dominated world of child labor, fourteen-hour working days, starvation wages, and periodic crises. Bourgeois-controlled states could never fundamentally reform capitalism. Reform movements were basically training grounds for keeping workers in shape for the final conflict. In the end, general immiseration would produce socialist revolution.

Institutionalism In contrast to both Cobden and Marx, the German civil servant and publicist Georg Friedrich List (1789–1846) believed that state power and national communities were central to the creation of competitive capitalist economies. List, the father of dependency theory, feared that British doctrines of laissez-faire served to prevent other countries from successfully industrializing and so competing with Britain. For List, laissez-faire was a British ideology designed to devastate Continental Europe's fragile "infant industries" by opening them to full-blown British competition. List emphasized that industrializing countries must not neglect the state. In his view, Adam Smith "ignores the very nature of nationalities, seeks almost entirely to exclude politics and the power of the State, presupposes the existence of a state of perpetual peace and of universal union, underrates the value of a national manufacturing power, and the means of obtaining it, and demands absolute freedom of trade" (quoted in Szporluk, p. 136).

MAJOR TWENTIETH-CENTURY CONTRIBUTIONS

The quarrels of Cobden, Marx, and List were taken up by succeeding generations. In the course of the debate different theorists expanded their theories in new directions and modified or amended the arguments of their intellectual predecessors. Neoclassicists showed a new interest in history, Marxists recognized that states possess considerable autonomy, and institutionalists broadened their understanding of economic structure.

Neoclassicism Generally uninterested in history, late-twentieth-century neoclassical economists were nonetheless attracted by a nineteenth-century European case in which an extraordinary and unprecedented mobility of labor and capital produced sustained economic growth. In *Child Labor and the Industrial Revolution* (1990), the neoclassical economist Clark Nardinelli takes a positive view of child labor in the cotton factories—long considered one of the horrors of the English Industrial Revolution. Nardinelli reminds us that most young working-class children were expected to work and argues that factory laborers received a better wage than those employed at home. According to Nardinelli, child labor in the factory was a choice made by parents to increase family income, something that ultimately benefited the children themselves. From Nardinelli's perspective, legislation restricting child labor was an attack on working-class households and it only occurred when child labor was already in decline.

While Nardinelli performs a helpful task in pushing historians to question easy assumptions about child labor, his argument is hardly uncontested. Some scholars argue that he underestimates the degree to which child labor was not a product of choice but of compulsion—many child laborers were drafted from orphanages, and some parents sent their children to work under the pressure of local welfare authorities. Some question the assumption that parents making the decision to send children to work in the factories did so for the good of the family. Finally, some argue that the advance of child labor produced a decline in the demand for adult labor, reducing adult wages and ultimately undermining family income.

Marxism Twentieth-century Marxist historians offered some insight into the origins of the Industrial Revolution, although their explanations involve amendments to rather than literal interpretations of Marx's text. From his earliest writings, Karl Marx identified the capitalists' coercive hold over wage labor, but later Marxists stressed the influence of imperial conquest. For example, the work of Eric Williams (1911–1981), a Marxist from Trinidad, still influences debates over the origins of the English industrial revolution. In *Capitalism and Slavery* (1944) Williams argues that Caribbean unfree labor was used to subsidize the growth of British wage labor. He presents the British prohibition of the slave trade in 1807 as part of an effort to protect the declining profitability of its West Indian colonies. This effort was vital to the British economy, where super profits from the colonies played an instrumental role in the financing of early factories. Particularly interesting is Williams's implicit abandonment of Marxist stage theories of development. Williams saw Caribbean slavery not as a backward form of production but as one of the major paths of capitalist advance in the eighteenth-century Atlantic world.

Scholars have cast doubt on many of the concrete linkages between West Indian planters and the birth of the factory proposed by Williams, but his powerful idea that Caribbean slavery fueled the English industrial revolution still commands support. By 1820 there was already a mass consumer demand for coffee, sugar, and tobacco in Europe. In the Caribbean there was also a mass market for the cotton goods and hardware produced by English factories. Slaves needed cotton clothes, and planters required ironware. England's monopoly on these markets during the Revolutionary Wars provided cotton masters and hardware producers with an extensive and secure market. The willingness of the British state to intervene to secure Caribbean markets and the Caribbean's central importance to British economic development suggest some problems in Cobden's devaluation of British naval power.

Institutionalism Institutionalists too offered insight into capitalist origins. The Hungarian Karl Polanyi (1886–1964) roundly criticized neoclassical accounts of economic growth and industrialization for their lack of realism. Like Marx, Polanyi also argued that the supposed voluntarism of trade and commerce was undergirded by force. Polanyi portrayed men like Richard Cobden as zealots who ignored the human consequences of subjecting society to self-regulating markets. To illustrate his case, Polanyi analyzed the 1795 Speenhamland Act—an effort by English magistrates to supplement wages of poor workers based on the price of bread and family size. In the Speenhamland area farmers responded to the magistrates' subsidies by lowering wages, reducing all laborers to impoverished and degraded pauperism. Thus, mistaken social policy influenced by free market principles, not the desire for self improvement, drove laborers to the factory gates.

Looking at the spread of the gold standard—the use of gold as the currency of international trade—as a prime example of efforts to create a self-regulating market, Polanyi discerned a "double movement" in which societies that adopted market principles simultaneously implemented social reforms to protect sensitive populations from market exposure. Whatever their ostensible political principles, no elected legislature in Britain, France, or Germany would tolerate a laissez-faire that produced crippled children or public starvation. Polanyi saw laissez-faire as an impossible ideal but feared that fanatical efforts to implement it could produce dramatic responses, from communism to fascism.

Polanyi was a passionate advocate, truly horrified by the premises of neoclassical economics, but his own response was often intemperate and one-sided. He seriously exaggerated the effects of Speenhamland legislation and differentiated it too sharply from earlier English welfare provisions. Polanyi emphasized the importance of culture in organizing distribution in premodern societies; markets were only one way to organize distribution, cultural forces based on reciprocal exchange or ceremonial redistribution had played a much more important role in the human past. His work encouraged anthropologists and economists to emphasize the constructed character of markets, but Polanyi's own adamant refusal to recognize markets in the ancient past weakened his case. Polanyi's concern about the ecological damage produced by unchecked capitalist development in nineteenth century Europe were unusual for his time.

Strongly influenced by institutionalism, the economic historian David Landes's work gave a new centrality to technological innovation. His 1969 masterwork, *The Unbound Prometheus,* traces out the series of innovations that transformed nineteenth-century Europe. He distinguished a "First Industrial Revolution," a British-led wave of innovation in the late eighteenth and the first half of the nineteenth centuries, and a "Second Industrial Revolution," a more broadly shared wave of technologies in the last quarter of the nineteenth century. His division of economic growth into an age of cotton, iron, and steam and an age of steel, chemicals, and electricity has proved enduring.

While Landes presented important insights into the character of European nineteenth-century growth, his work remained somewhat short on explanation. Why Europe? Why the nineteenth century? To explain economic growth, neoclassical authors drew on Adam Smith, who claimed that humans had a natural propensity to truck and barter and that markets had an inherent tendency to grow and expand. Faced with a world in which capitalist expansion seemed largely confined to the Western world and Japan, Landes, like Polanyi, turned to culture. Smithian individualism, it turned out, was less a feature of universal human nature than a product of Western and Japanese cultures of individualism, rationalist in means and activist in ends. While Landes's explanation was intriguing it was also poorly specified. Did cultural explanations explain why, over four centuries, Western economic leadership passed from Venice to Amsterdam to London? The dynamic expansion of Islamic merchants toward Southeast Asia in the same period as the West's expansion across the Atlantic seemed kindred developments. Did cultural factors explain Islamic mercantile abilities in Asia but not in Europe?

THE DEBATE CONTINUES

Debates among neoclassicists, Marxists, and institutionalists continue, although some elements of common ground have emerged and there is an increased sense that the old moorings are giving way. States, institutions, and popular movements generally play a more important role in accounts, by all schools, of nineteenth-century economic growth and development.

Neoclassicism Since the late twentieth century, work in economic history strongly influenced by neoclassical approaches has shown a new attention to the political dangers of unrestrained markets and even recalls Karl Polanyi. For example, Timothy J. Hatton and Jeffrey G. Williamson's *Age of Mass Migration* (1998), a study of transatlantic migration between 1850 and 1914, largely validates the predictions of neoclassicists. The remuneration of unskilled workers in low-wage economies such as those of Ireland and Sweden rose as laborers moved across the Atlantic, and income inequality within these nations decreased. Meanwhile, the relatively higher wages in industrialized portions of the Americas declined with a resultant increase in inequality. But Hatton and Williamson note that continued long-term decline in wages and increasing inequality in American nations led to the rise of popular protectionist movements that eventually closed American labor markets to European migrants. The implicit lesson is that state intervention to moderate the workings of markets may be necessary to preserve their operation.

Marxism In *The Great Divergence* (2000) Kenneth Pomeranz presents 1800 as a key dividing point in the evolution of European economic growth and development. Pomeranz echoes Eric Williams in arguing that imperial conquest was one decisive element in British success. Arguing persuasively that efforts to compare the huge Chinese empire and a relatively small nation in a tiny continent are unwieldly at best and unfair at worst, Pomeranz instead compares England and a highly commercialized portion of the Chinese empire, the lower Yangtze, a comparison that challenges many longstanding assumptions about non-European economies. In the seventeenth and eighteenth centuries, living standards, agrarian productivity, birth rates, market development, energy consumption, and enforceable property rights in the lower Yangtze were similar to those in England.

Pomeranz argues that both regions were approaching the limits of growth in 1800 and were facing strained resources and falling productivity. England was saved by its coal resources and the windfall profits of imperial conquest. The conquest of the Americas was especially important because American resources were complementary to those of England and Europe. The apparently limitless American acreage produced saleable commodities that would have placed impossible demands on the extremely limited European acreage had it been diverted to supply these growing markets. For example, sugar, cotton, tobacco, timber, and coffee were much in demand in Europe, but could not be produced, or at least produced efficiently, on the Continent.

Pomeranz is generally suspicious of cultural explanations and instead emphasizes the capitalism-coercion nexus. Whereas Western governments mobilized military power to defend their economic interests, the Chinese government was focused on the military threat from Eurasia and its efforts to extend its influence into Southeast Asia. Defending mercantile interests was a much lower priority than for the Portuguese, the Dutch, and the English.

The Pomeranz argument has introduced important new elements into our understanding of European growth and industrialization. Much debate has focused on his assertion that English production was facing diminishing returns and falling prices in 1800. Regardless of whether this argument is accepted, the great merit of Pomeranz's study is to have encouraged scholars to reexamine their beliefs about the institutional structure of premodern Asian economies. Broad, slapdash comparisons of Asia and Europe are clearly outmoded, and an era of more focused comparison with more attention to institutional characteristics seems the wave of the future. Along the way, historians' appreciation of the role of armed force in capitalist advance is likely to increase.

Institutionalism The late twentieth century also witnessed a resurgence of institutionalism in economics, political science, and sociology. *Scale and Scope* (1990), Alfred Chandler's comparative study of business organization in England, Germany, and the United States, pioneered this development. In it, Chandler argues that history matters a great deal in the formation of business organization. Chandler shows that the "Second Industrial Revolution" was a more complex and differentiated process than David Landes had suggested. Differences in the organization of corporate enterprise were an important factor in each nation's adoption of the new technologies. Chandler shows that British entrepreneurs had developed in an era of swashbuckling individual competition focused on productivity. British entrepreneurs were much less willing than Americans or Germans to develop impersonal business structures or to attend to distribution and research as well as production. But the industrial giants of the era, Germany and the United States, developed their own different patterns. The German banking structure encouraged cooperation among large corporations in which powerful banks had a common interest, leading to a "cooperative managerial capitalism" in contrast to the American "competitive managerial capitalism." American institutionalists have suggested that many of these differences in national corporate organization remain and have profoundly influenced corporate development; hence they explain the very significant differences in industrial organization and industrial relations in these different countries. Thus, increasingly institutionalists emphasize the importance of contingency (possibility) and historicity (historical actuality) in analyses of economic growth and development. Much recent work suggests that industry and industrial relations can be organized in a variety of ways, each of which can sustain international economic competition.

CONCLUSION

This brief survey of debates over European economic growth and industrialization reveals the enduring presence of competing neoclassical, Marxist, and institutionalist interpretations. These debates originated in the earliest days of European economic growth and industrialization and continue up to the present day. They have contributed powerfully to our understanding of the nineteenth-century European economy, especially as the three schools of thought have moved toward one another in important ways. Since the 1850s both neoclassicists and Marxists have increased their appreciation of the role of institutions. Neoclassicists have begun to consider the effects of mass movements, Marxists of state coercion and warmaking, and institutionalists of culture, contingency, and historicity.

See also **Industrial Revolution, First; Industrial Revolution, Second; Protectionism; Trade and Economic Growth.**

BIBLIOGRAPHY

Primary Sources

Cobden, Richard. "America." In *The Political Writings of Richard Cobden*, 97–153. London, 1867.

Marx, Karl. *The Communist Manifesto.* 1847. New York, 1998.

Polanyi, Karl. *The Great Transformation.* New York, 1944.

Williams, Eric. *Capitalism and Slavery.* 1944. Chapel Hill, N.C., 1994.

Secondary Sources

Chandler, Alfred. *Scale and Scope: The Dynamics of Industrial Capitalism.* Cambridge, Mass., 1990.

Duchesne, Ricardo. "On the Rise of the West: Researching Kenneth Pomeranz's *Great Divergence.*" *Review of Radical Political Economists* 36, no. 1 (winter 2004): 52–81.

Hatton, Timothy J., and Jeffrey G. Williamson. *The Age of Mass Migration: Causes and Economic Impact.* Oxford, U.K., 1998.

Hejeebu, Santhi, and Deirdre McCloskey. "The Reproving of Karl Polanyi." *Critical Review* 13, nos. 3–4 (1999): 285–314.

Humphries, Jane. "Cliometrics, Child Labor, and the Industrial Revolution." *Critical Review* 13, nos. 3–4 (1999): 269–283.

Landes, David. *The Unbound Prometheus: Technological Change and Industrial Development in Western Europe from 1750 to the Present.* London, 1969.

Nardinelli, Clark. *Child Labor and the Industrial Revolution.* Bloomington, Ind., 1990.

Pomeranz, Kenneth. *The Great Divergence: China, Europe, and the Making of the Modern World Economy.* Princeton, N.J., 2000.

Polanyi-Levitt, Karl, ed. *The Life and Work of Karl Polanyi: A Celebration.* New York, 1999.

Solow, Barbara L., and Stanley L. Engerman, eds. *British Capitalism and Caribbean Slavery: The Legacy of Eric Williams.* Cambridge, U.K., 1987.

Szporluk, Roman. *Communism and Nationalism: Karl Marx versus Friedrich List.* Oxford, U.K., 1988.

Tilly, Charles, and Chris Tilly. *Work under Capitalism.* Boulder, Colo., 1998.

MICHAEL HANAGAN

ECONOMISTS, CLASSICAL.

There is no precise definition of classical economics, but the term is generally applied to British economists from Adam Smith (1723–1790) to John Stuart Mill (1806–1873). They were concerned with the production, distribution, and consumption of wealth, wealth being understood as commodities produced by human activity.

ADAM SMITH

Adam Smith's *Inquiry into the Nature and Causes of the Wealth of Nations,* published in 1776, is best understood as a theory of growth based on capital accumulation and increasing the productivity of labor. Smith also made the radical proposal that the well-being of society could be maximized by allowing decisions about consumption and investment to be made by individuals acting in their own self-interest. Smith's proposal was based on his belief that self-interested behavior could be made to promote the public well-being through competition in the marketplace.

In passages in both *The Theory of Moral Sentiments* (1759) and *The Wealth of Nations,* Smith introduces the metaphor of the "invisible hand" to illustrate how selfish and even apparently antisocial behavior can have the result of promoting the public interest. In *The Wealth of Nations,* Smith writes:

> As every individual, therefore, endeavours as much as he can both to employ his capital in the support of domestic industry, and so to direct that industry that its produce may be of the greatest value; every individual necessarily labours to render the annual revenue of the society as great as he can. He generally, indeed, neither intends to promote the public interest, nor knows how much he is promoting it. ... [He] intends only his own gain, and he is in this, as in many other cases, led by an invisible hand to promote an end which was no part of his own intention. Nor is it always the worse for society that it was no part of it. By pursuing his own interest he frequently promotes that of the society more effectually than when he really intends to promote it. I have never known much good done by those who affected to trade for the public good.

The Wealth of Nations is an explanation of how "cheapness and plenty" can be brought about, thus assuring greater wealth for the main bulk of the population. It is essential to the argument that the marketplace be a competitive arena, and equally essential is a political framework that ensures the security of property. As Smith puts it in book 5: "That security which the laws of Great Britain give to every man that he shall enjoy the fruits of his labour, is alone sufficient to make any country flourish ... and this security was perfected by the revolution." The revolution to which Smith refers was the liberal revolution of the seventeenth century.

What is to be consumed must first be produced and distributed. Production is dependent on the amount of work done and the efficiency with which that work is carried out. Accordingly, book 1 of *The Wealth of Nations* is concerned with the productivity of labor. The key concept is the division of labor. Book 1 also explains how the product will be distributed to "the different ranks of the People." The level of production, or total output, will depend on both the productivity of the producers and the number of people at work, and in book 2, Smith examines the question of what determines the total number of productive workers. The answer is that the number of productive workers depends on the accumulation of capital.

Chapter 1 of book 1 introduces the celebrated pin factory with the explanation of the means by which the division of labor enhances total output of the given labor force, that is, increases its productivity. The essential reasons for this increase in productivity are that individual skill and dexterity is increased, that less time is wasted in moving from task to task, and only thirdly, though this was to become a major factor in industrialization, that the dividing up and simplifying of aspects of the production increases the likelihood of the invention of tools and machines that will increase the productivity of the worker.

Book 1 contains a theory of prices that is at the same time a theory of income distribution. Smith's economic world contains three social categories. Entrepreneurs (called "undertakers" by Smith) have "stock," or capital, or can if necessary borrow funds to use as capital. The entrepreneurs pay wages to the laborers they require and also pay rent to landlords. Given then that stock has accumulated and become necessary to production and that land is privately owned, the price or value of any commodity contains an allocation for profit, wages, and rent. These three categories constitute the value added in the production process and determine the long-run, competitive market price of any product. Smith explains in book 1, chapter 7, that there is "in every society or neighbourhood an ordinary or average rate both of wages and profit in every different employment of labour and stock." The rate is regulated by the "general circumstances" of the society. These circumstances include the wealth or poverty of the society and also the rates of growth or decline of the society. Similarly, there is an average rate of rent, regulated by the general circumstances of the society. The resolution of price into the three categories of wages, profit, and rent at the same time produces a distribution of revenues that enables the product to be divided up among the potential consumers. All incomes are derived from one of these three original categories of income.

Smith recognizes that short-run fluctuations in supply and demand can cause actual prices to deviate from this, but the long-run market price reflects the actual cost of producing a product. The wealth of a society can be increased by pushing down the cost of producing an item. The latter can be done by increasing the productivity of the work involved in the production process by means of the division of labor.

The division of labor can progress only as "stock is previously more and more accumulated." The storing up of stock requires a degree of personal wealth, but turning "stock" into "capital" also requires a specific social attitude:

> When the stock which a man possesses is no more than sufficient to maintain him for a few days or a few weeks, he seldom thinks of deriving any revenue from it. He consumes it as sparingly as he can, and endeavours by his labour to acquire something which may supply its place before it be consumed altogether. His revenue is, in this case, derived from his labour only. This is the state of the greater part of the labouring poor in all countries.
>
> But when he possesses stock sufficient to maintain him for months or years, he naturally endeavors to derive a revenue from the greater part of it; reserving only so much for his immediate consumption as may maintain him till this revenue begins to come in. His whole stock, therefore, is distinguished into two parts. That part which, he expects, is to afford him this revenue, is called his capital.

Capital is characterized by the fact that it produces a revenue, and it produces this revenue by "maintaining labour," or more precisely by putting to work "productive labourers." Only by increasing capital in relation to revenue could industry, and thus wealth and future consumption, be stimulated: "Wherever capital predominates, industry prevails: wherever revenue, idleness." Happily, the "private frugality and good conduct of individuals," driven by "the uniform, constant, and uninterrupted effort of every man to better his condition," is capable of increasing capital. Private, self-interested behavior is sufficient to bring about investment and thus future production.

In book 4, Smith defines political economy as a "branch of the science of a statesman." As such political economy was concerned with "plentiful revenue for the people" and supplying a "revenue sufficient for public services" to the state or commonwealth. Smith undertook as part of the plan of *The Wealth of Nations* an examination of the errors, as he saw them, of various misguided approaches to public policy, such as the "mercantile system," which is the subject of a large part of book 4. The mercantile system aimed at promoting the wealth of the state, and undoubtedly lined the pockets of the friends of the government who influenced the restraints on trade, but a sound political economy should "enrich both the people and the sovereign" and could do so by maintaining "that order of things which nature pointed out."

Thus the "simple system of natural liberty" did not imply an absence of government. Government was necessary for justice and security. The sovereign clearly had a duty to protect the people from violence and invasion and to protect "every man from injustice or oppression." Smith allowed that "erecting and maintaining public works" was an obligation of the sovereign, especially because they might not be privately provided, but might "frequently do much more than repay [their expenses] to a great society." And in book 5, chapter 1, Smith recognizes that the government must have an interest to offset the deleterious effects of the division of labor. Yet, in the end, in Smith's view, it is competition in the market that will best serve the interests of the majority of the people, as "every man," as long as he observes the rules of justice, pursues his own interest in his own way.

The difficulty, as Smith's followers found, was in maintaining the connection between "private" and "public and national" opulence. A new challenge for the followers of Smith was the question of democracy. While there was a "democratic" aspect to Smith's promotion of "cheapness and plenty" for the whole population, there was no question in his time of a political movement for democracy. The radical democracy that had surfaced at the time of the English revolution had been suppressed. It was to return to England in the wake of revolution in France. *The Wealth of Nations* provided an essential document for use in the battle for liberalism. The concept of the "natural progress of society," central to liberalism and a key component of Enlightenment thought, gave Smith's followers a metaphor for social prescription that was far more effective on the body politic than any argument from historical fact and also frequently immune to any mere recital of statistical evidence of inequality.

A GENERATION OF POLITICAL DEBATE AND NEW ECONOMIC THEORIES

The economic historian C. R. Fay wrote that "it is a truism to say that Adam Smith dominated the fiscal policy of nineteenth-century Britain. But [David] Ricardo and [Thomas Robert] Malthus, the one with his Iron Law of Wages, the

other with the *Essay on Population,* dominated—unhappily—the social thinking of their age." In fact, it was the German socialist Ferdinand Lassalle who later coined the term "Iron Law of Wages," but Ricardo and Malthus, with the help of Harriet Martineau and others, made political economy the "dismal science."

In 1795 the British Parliament was considering a bill to enable justices of the peace to regulate the wages of rural workers, in effect subsidizing them from the poor rates. The framework for this policy was the Elizabethan Poor Laws, under which the parish was responsible for levying "poor rates" and providing for the relief of the sick, aged, and unemployed who had a claim by virtue of residence and good conduct within the parish. In the 1790s, the growth of population and high food prices intensified the systemic rural poverty. The bill reflected the concerns of many magistrates who were ultimately attempting to maintain the peace while keeping a lid on the rising poor rates. This situation was the cause of a major social debate in which, for the first time, arguments derived from political economy played a decisive role in a confrontation with traditional political concerns with obligation and maintaining order.

The best-known outcome of the 1790s debate on the Poor Laws was the work of Malthus (1766–1834). In the first edition of his *Essay on the Principle of Population* (1798), Malthus explained why "laws of nature" posed "unconquerable difficulties in the way to perfectability": "the power of population is indefinitely greater than the power in the earth to produce subsistence for man." Malthus added a mathematical formulation: population when "unchecked" increases in a geometrical ratio, while subsistence increases only in an arithmetical ratio. Given these assumptions, it was not hard to arrive at pessimistic conclusions. But Malthus's purpose was to arrive at more specific conclusions: Although in principle there are two potential "checks" to population, "preventative" (reduced births) and "positive" (starvation), the number of those who constitute the "lowest orders of society" is ultimately kept in check by starvation. Furthermore, any attempt to share resources, as with the Poor Laws, simply encourages the poor to marry and thus increases population without increasing food supply: "thus in reality it is the poor laws that create the poor." Malthus joined his demonstration that inequality was "natural" with the market perspective of political economy as suggested by Smith: abolition of parish laws, creation of a free labor market, an end to "corporations" and apprenticeship. Lastly—and here Malthus outlined the principle that, when it was enshrined in the new Poor Law of 1834, would make him infamous—the final refuge for those in extreme distress should be the workhouse: "The fare should be hard, and those that were able obliged to work. It would be desirable that they should not be considered as comfortable asylums in all difficulties."

Given the lead by Malthus, the political economists drummed the message that it was the Poor Laws that were creating poverty. Prosperity could be achieved only by the creation of a free labor market and enhanced labor mobility. With the new Poor Law of 1834, the British government entered on a fundamentally new social policy. Accepting the principle that every "necessitous person" had a right to relief, the law imposed new conditions for eligibility: "outdoor relief" was abolished and relief was to be given only in the workhouse, where conditions were to be made harsher than outside, by among other things, separating families, and where only the "deserving poor" would avail themselves of help on such terms.

Malthus was active in other economic controversies of the time, especially in the form of a continuing debate with Ricardo (1772–1823), a financier, political economist, and member of Parliament, on the topic of underconsumption and overproduction. Following Smith, Ricardo and most classical economists believed that production created its own demand either for consumption or for investment goods, but Malthus thought inadequate demand could be a problem. In contrast to Smith, however, Ricardo shared the opinion of Malthus that wages would of necessity be at a social minimum. For Ricardo this was because a predetermined wage-fund available for hiring labor would have to be shared among a workforce that would multiply to the maximum point consistent with subsistence levels. Ricardo also showed that, in the short run at least, labor could be displaced by machinery, given that a predetermined fund was available for both hiring labor and purchasing machinery.

Like Smith, Ricardo was concerned with economic growth, and like Smith, he identified investment as the key. In *Observations on Parliamentary Reform*, Ricardo delivered the short and, for the political economists, essential point:

> The quantity of employment in the country must depend not only on the quantity of capital but upon its advantageous distribution and above all, the conviction of each capitalist that he will be allowed to enjoy unmolested the fruits of his capital, his skill and his enterprise. To take from him this conviction is at once to annihilate half the productive industry of this country and would be more fatal to the poor labourer than to the rich capitalist himself.

Ricardo placed his economic theories in the center of another intense political debate. The British government's Corn Laws provided for duties on the import of wheat, adjusting the amount of duty according to the scarcity or plenty of British harvests. Ricardo's argument showed that with an increase in population and an accumulation of capital, more land would have to be cultivated, and lower quality land would have to be brought into production, thus increasing the marginal cost of production, and thus raising the price of food. This argument was sharply political because such an outcome would not be in the interests of wage earners or of manufacturers, who would have to pay higher wages to keep the level up to subsistence. The outcome would favor landlords, who would collect a higher share of the national income in rent.

The political edge was made even sharper by the additional conclusion that the higher cost of food could be offset by lower-priced imports, if the Corn Laws were to be repealed. The supporters of the Corn Laws were those same landlords in their role as Parliamentarians, who were thus a barrier to the economic policy of industrial growth. The Anti–Corn Law League attempted to rally political support by showing a common interest between workers and manufacturers. Tory landowners, on the other hand, lost no opportunity to argue that manufacturers wanted to repeal the Corn Laws only in order to bring in cheap food and then drive down wages in order to increase profits. Ricardo's economics was of course already made the object of attention by its connection of the "wage fund" to Malthusian population theory, but the acrimonious debate over the interests of industry and agriculture and their connection with income distribution further shaped the context in which political economy was made known to the general public.

The Corn Laws were repealed in 1846, and Britain moved decisively toward a "free trade" policy. This appeared to be a vindication of Smith's liberal perspective that all trade should be "natural" and mutually beneficial. With trade the division of labor is not hindered by the "narrowness of the home market," but can be carried to the "highest perfection," as Smith argued. Ricardo had advanced the theoretical case for free trade with his "theory of comparative advantage." Ricardo's trade model demonstrated the advantages of the extension of the market by foreign trade, showing that, in trade between two countries, both countries could benefit by exporting the products they could produce most productively.

Political debate was also shaped by events outside of Britain. In 1848 France and other European countries experienced a new outbreak of revolutions. Nassau Senior (1790–1864), an economist who had played a major role in the formation of the new Poor Law when he had been an advisor to the British government of the time, saw the "unhappy" events in France as the result of the widespread acceptance of views that he called "disguised socialism." The rapid growth of the national workshops and the concept of "the right to work" demanded by the Paris workers, Senior suggested, had been the result of the unfortunate theory that it was "in the power of the State to correct the inequalities of fortune." While the error was "a plausible one" to those untrained in economics, it was necessary, Senior argued, to show that capital accumulation was a fragile growth that could be stunted by ill-considered actions of the state. Accepting a "right to work," Senior argued, meant that either the state would have to become an employer, soon ending up as the greatest employer, and private property would become an encumbrance, or the right to work will lead to the need to ensure work by preventing "stagnation" through the retarding or accelerating of production, which would require management and regulation and the organization of industry. The consequences were either communism or socialism. It was, Senior concluded, necessary to distinguish between the right to relief and the right to employment.

The ideological battlefield of political economy was a major sphere of operations, but decisive victories in the class war required a change in the realities of the "condition of England," a change that was still beyond the horizon. In the summer of 1849 an outbreak of cholera reminded the country of some uncomfortable facts of life in the new industrial world. Within a period of three months there were some thirteen thousand deaths in London alone. While the precise reasons for the spread of the disease were still unknown, the fact that it was most deadly in the poorest districts was inescapable.

In September 1849 a remarkable report appeared in a national newspaper. It was a description of the journalist Henry Mayhew's visit to one of the poorest areas of London. Shortly after publishing the article, the *Morning Chronicle* commented in an editorial:

> The primary cause of the pestilence is to be found in the filth and squalor of the poor. ... We, the richest nation on the face of the earth, have allowed our fellow-creatures to "fust" in styes, reeking with filth, such as farmers, now-a-days, know that swine would pine and dwindle in. We have allowed them ... to quench their thirst and cook their food with water poisoned with their own excretions.

Mayhew, commissioned by the same newspaper, went on to write a series of articles on the laboring poor in London. He observed the very great difference in working and living conditions that separated the skilled artisans from the unskilled. One of the conclusions he drew concerned the poverty that resulted from the aggressive competition and unregulated conditions in the needle trades. In December 1849 Mayhew drew the fire of *The Economist*. The articles, it said:

> have given occasion to throw discredit on free trade, to cast a slur on commercial greatness, to beget doubts of the advantages of civilisation, to bring reproach upon cheapness and excite a strong communist feeling against competition. ... The people can only help themselves. Only they can put restrictions on their numbers, and keep population on a level with capital. ... [The] rich are no more responsible for their condition than they are responsible for the condition of the rich.

The *Morning Chronicle* replied with an opposing argument. Reform, it said, was the only way to avoid "communism."

JOHN STUART MILL

The doctrines of political economy had been popularized by the immensely successful publication of monthly stories illustrating the truths of political economy, written by Harriet Martineau (1802–1876) between 1832 and 1834. Each month more than ten thousand copies were sold, and the entire series was reprinted. The publisher estimated that there were 140,000 readers. The tales drew from Smith, there was a central place for Malthus, and the most frequent source was James Mill's text *Elements of Political Economy* (1821). Martineau was a Unitarian who believed that the improvement of society could be achieved by self-mastery through education. Chartism and socialism were symptoms of distress, but society could be saved by the recognition by the rich of their obligations and by inducing the poor to learn the limits to help from others. Political economy set a negative limit; positive action could come from an active morality.

In an essay written in 1834 titled "Miss Martineau's Summary of Political Economy," John Stuart Mill objected to treatises on political economy that "presuppose in every one of them that the produce of industry is shared among three classes altogether distinct from one another, namely labourers, capitalists and landlords." Not being able to imagine any other form of society might produce an opposition to all reform:

> And we think there is some danger of a similar result in the case of the English political economists. They revolve in their eternal circle of landlords, capitalists, and labourers, until they seem to think of the distinction of society into those three classes as if it were one of God's ordinances, not man's, and as little under human control as the division of day and night.

Unfortunately, Mill had to agree, it was not yet time for "ulterior enquiries" to come into contact with practice: "society has many incumbrances to throw off before it can start fair on [a] new journey."

If Mill thought that Martineau had reduced the laissez-faire system to an absurdity, he was equally troubled by those who pressed the "claims of labour." In 1845, reviewing a book with that title, Mill returned to what was becoming his keynote theme: "society cannot with safety, in one of its gravest concerns, pass at once from selfish supineness to restless activity. It has a long and difficult apprenticeship yet to serve."

Mill believed that the deductive, conceptual study of political economy that had been evolved from Smith's *Wealth of Nations,* by virtue of the contributions of Bentham, Malthus, James Mill and Ricardo, contained some essential truths concerning "mankind as occupied solely in acquiring and consuming wealth." Political economy had achieved a status as an "abstract science" that was not yet available to any other branch of "social science," Mill concluded in his *System of Logic* (1843). It was essential, Mill thought, that an understanding of the "science" of political economy be applied to the urgent political issues of the day. The main thrust of the changes since Smith's time, in Mill's opinion, was the consequence of two contradictory forces: on the one hand, the new industrial organization of production had created a far more active "spirit of accumulation" that even offered the prospect of a "surplus" of capital; on the other hand, the conditions of life and work for the majority of the population remained unacceptably wretched. This latter situation was largely, though not exclusively, in Mill's opinion, a consequence of the poverty perpetuated by the accompanying excessive population growth. The opportunity to move to an "improved" state of society, beyond the narrow confines of the "cash nexus," contrasted with the danger that the demand for democracy would undermine the circumstances that made improvement possible. A central message from Mill was that it would be folly to "subvert" the "system of individual property," but equally irresponsible not to improve it.

Mill's political economy rested on the traditional liberal claim that property was the consequence of labor and frugality, but at the same time he recognized the strength of the claim that "in the present state of society" it was "manifestly chimerical" to believe that there was "any proportionality between success and merit, or between success and exertion." The socialists were able to make, Mill conceded, "a frightful case." Where the socialists were wrong, however, in Mill's opinion, was first in claiming that wages were falling. However low, Mill concluded, they were on the whole gradually increasing and would increase more when the connection with population growth was understood by the majority. Second, the socialists were wrong to condemn competition. Competition might encourage a "gambling spirit" and even some profitable fraud, but competition was essential to progress and an inherent part of "liberty." The less attractive aspects of competition could, Mill suggested, be overcome with the slow progress of cooperation as mankind reached a more improved state, but some element of competition would be necessary.

In the third edition of his *Principles of Political Economy*, published in 1852, Mill explicitly states that socialism might be regarded as the ultimate aim of human progress, unacceptable though it was in the present "unprepared state of mankind in general, and of the labouring classes in particular." The real issue for Mill, however, was that "the principle of private property has never yet had a fair trial in any country," and political economy showed the means by which society could acquire both liberty and prosperity.

Mill was skeptical of the power of unions, but he maintained that allowing unions to exist legally would serve an important educational function: "experience of strikes has been the best teacher of the labouring classes on the subject of the relation between wages and the demand and supply of labor: and it is most important that this course of instruction should not be disturbed." By the later editions of his *Principles*, Mill had added a section in which he recognized that the market rate of wages was the result of bargaining, as Smith had said. Unions, then, Mill concluded, were a "necessary instrumentality of the free market ... the indispensable means of enabling the sellers of labour to take due care of their own interests under a system of competition." But, Mill added, combinations must be voluntary: moral compulsion alone should be used to enforce solidarity.

Mill's *Principles* investigated many of the possible boundaries between private and collective action. With respect to the "laissez-faire or non-interference principle," Mill argued that laissez-faire should be the general practice: "every departure, unless required by some great good, is a certain evil." But there was a considerable list of cases to be made for government intervention. Children, for example, needed protection from the "freedom of contract," which was another way of saying "freedom of coercion." There could be no contracts in perpetuity, because there was no possibility of adequate future knowledge. There were important public services, including the creation of "a learned class," which no private interest would produce. At some time, Mill allowed, the list would be longer. There were both necessary functions for the government and optional functions, but the role of government would never be limited to mere protection against "force and fraud." With respect to payment for government services, Mill concluded that taxation should be regulated by Smith's "classical" maxims of proportionality and certainty, and that a "permanent" national debt would be "pernicious," though he added the interesting caveat that this might not be true if there was a surplus of funds, so that the debt did not raise the rate of interest.

Mill also made a celebrated distinction between the "laws of production" and the "laws of distribution" of wealth. While the laws of the production of wealth "partake of the character of physical truth," the distribution of wealth is "a matter of human institution solely." While this distinction appeared to open up considerable flexibility for the "system of private property," it also introduced considerable confusion. Changes in distribution have political consequences, and Mill was certainly aware that not all proposals for distribution would have a benign effect on production. His fulminations on the Poor Laws made that point clear.

Mill looked forward to better days than those in which he lived. It would eventually be possible to go beyond the "inordinate importance attached to the mere increase of production": it would be possible to escape from the eternal conception of society as a set of "classes" with competing interests, and society could become an association of equal individuals, without the "delusive unanimity" produced by "the prostration of all individual opinions." But there were some points of political economy on which unanimity was required. Some of the unanimity could be achieved by experience; some might require the imposition of authority. Mill clearly regarded democracy as a desirable goal, and he can be seen as one of the founders of liberal democracy, but he thought that there must be limits to democracy, and even to liberalism, in his time.

See also Malthus, Thomas Robert; Martineau, Harriet; Mill, James; Mill, John Stuart.

BIBLIOGRAPHY

Hollander, Samuel. *Classical Economics.* Oxford, U.K., 1987.

Macpherson, C. B. *The Life and Times of Liberal Democracy.* Oxford, U.K., 1977.

North, Douglass C. *Institutions, Institutional Change, and Economic Performance.* Cambridge, U.K., 1990.

O'Brien, D. P. *The Classical Economists Revisited.* Princeton, N.J., 2004.

Schumpeter, Joseph A. *History of Economic Analysis.* New York, 1954. Reprint, with a new introduction by Mark Perlman, New York, 1994.

JOHN HUTCHESON

EDUCATION. At the beginning of the long nineteenth century in Europe, few statesmen, reformers, or local worthies considered mass, universal schooling desirable, useful, or feasible. A third or more of the population was under fifteen years of age; in many regions, life expectancy was forty years or less. Most children were workers rather than pupils; if they attended school, it was before they were of much use anywhere else, or else when weather interrupted work in the fields. Whatever their ambitions, families, communes, churches, and states had only a fraction of the resources needed to build, staff, and supervise schools for all of the poor. In some countries, many villages, townships, or congregations had an elementary school of sorts, but learning how to become a member of one's church and obey parents and masters, or else sew, spin, or make lace, were seen as more important than learning to read and write. Even more frequently than boys did, girls learned all the useful skills considered necessary in the home. When they did attend school, it was for a shorter period than their brothers, often leaving before writing was tackled. Later in life, about twice as many men as women could sign their name. Many of those who did learn to read had not done so at school. Even formal educational arrangements rarely dealt with a specified age group, used standardized tools, or taught children

in groups rather than individually. For purposes of state, it did not yet matter much what languages working people spoke; in any case, few of the vernaculars used by Europeans had a fixed written form. Sons of the wealthy were far more likely to receive prolonged and systematic instruction. But even here, childhoods dominated by schools, and schools organized into systems, lay in the future.

By the end of the long nineteenth century, this future became clearly visible. Money remained chronically scarce, but a sizable portion of much larger state budgets was allocated to schools. Not all ten-year-olds in a much more numerous age group were under instruction, but literacy and enrollment statistics became accepted measures of a civilized nation. Disagreements persisted about how to run and organize schools, and perfection was nowhere in sight, but reformers and educators began to agree on what a modern education system should look like. Teachers should be trained, classes graded, school days divided into lessons of equal length and distinct content, schools held in purpose-built buildings fitted with special furniture. All children, regardless of the way they spoke at home, should learn to read and write the national language. They should be sorted into classes by age and individual attainment, follow a standardized sequence of lessons, use specially designed textbooks to prepare for standardized exams, and become expert at obeying school orders, using school tools, and participating in school rituals. State authorities should use regular inspections and examinations to stamp their will on the conduct of teachers and pupils, provide most of school funding, and collect and publish educational statistics. Parents should no longer be allowed to fetch children from school when they were needed at home. Whatever else their duties, boys' and girls' key occupation, each school day over six or more years, should be schoolwork.

Among the explanations for this far-reaching change, concerns with social order appear particularly pressing. As the peoples of Europe multiplied, older forms of authority no longer seemed adequate to render them docile, pious, and industrious. In regions of central and eastern Europe, late-eighteenth-century reformers became convinced that peasants became so lazy, stupid, and stubborn that serfdom was now a fetter on economic progress. In parts of northwestern Europe, literate wage workers were plentiful enough, but were also prone to insolence and strikes. Nuisance, crime, and seditious ideas, it appeared, could at any moment turn to riot and insurrection. Even protoindustrial artisans, in spite of their dependence on the market, showed little capitalist rationality. Finally, nothing seemed able to stop the poor from forming their own households and having children. And yet, wealthy commentators believed, most laboring men made appalling household heads and their wives were unfit to be mothers. Just as new machines and ways of organizing production augmented the productivity of one pair of hands, so mastery could be made less laborious and more effective through molding desirable dispositions at school. Obscurantism—the desire to keep the poor ignorant—increasingly appeared as irresponsible folly. For their part, radicals became convinced that knowledge was power and began struggling for appropriate educational media to bring enlightenment to their brothers and sisters.

As states and rulers developed an interest in shaping the content of humble subjects' minds, they typically instructed communes to tax themselves in order to build a school and pay a teacher. But many localities and households were too poor or had quite other priorities. Even where schools existed, what precisely they produced seemed to be a matter of chance. The way such issues were confronted and strategic choices made depended on a myriad of local and regional factors. Everywhere, the building of education systems became an inseparable part of building states and their capacity to visualize, comprehend, and govern the populations inside of their borders. In this process, periods of close cooperation between church and state could alternate with decades of competition, intransigence, and combative animosity.

REGIONS WITH MANY CITIES

In regions with many cities, established municipal organizations, widespread commercial and market activity, and extensive wage labor (as in England, Scotland, the Netherlands, France, Belgium, Switzerland, and parts of Germany and Austria), widespread literacy, and a dense network of complementary, competing, and overlapping educational institutions long predated nineteenth-century campaigns to enforce compulsory schooling. Farmers, petty producers, mechanics, craftsmen, and traders frequently needed literacy to carry on important parts of their day-to-day work. Early industrialization drew on the accumulated wisdom of such communities but, initially at least, depressed levels of literacy and disrupted school attendance. Here, the first tasks included locating establishments where teaching took place, finding effective means of influencing what went on inside those deemed to be schools, and working out how to close down the rest.

England   Around 1750, 60 percent of males and 35 percent of females in England were literate. Over the following 150 years, the population of England and Wales grew from six to thirty-two million. The English navy helped consolidate the increasingly powerful empire's overseas holdings, and English cottons and steam engines began conquering the world of trade and industry. For some decades, English technologies of instruction began transforming the world of the school. Monitorial schools, invented around 1800 for the charitable instruction of poor children, were conducted by a single paid master assisted by unpaid senior pupils. Up to a thousand children were divided into groups of ten pupils of equal attainment in particular skills, each group seated at a separate desk and allocated a monitor who taught them the task at hand, having earlier in the morning received instruction from the master himself. Soon, monitorialism spread to Greece, Switzerland, Italy, Spain, Russia, France, Sweden, and Denmark.

Yet while English economic and political power grew, the provisions made for instructing the country's swelling crowds of children were increasingly condemned as inadequate and unsystematic. In ideal conditions, monitorial schools held miraculous promise. In practice, increasing numbers of reformers concluded, they failed to deliver what they set out to do—mass produce meek, biddable, well-instructed children. More importantly, the majority of girls and boys attended no school at all, or else learned to read in disorderly neighborhood dame schools. It was at the height of Chartist agitation in the 1830, in response to the threat posed by an increasingly literate and articulate subaltern public, that the first public grants to assist voluntary charitable school organizations were made, and the first central government educational authority established. Four decades later, the government began to assert a measure of direct local control. The 1870 Elementary Education Act provided for the setting up of elected local school boards, and empowered them to enforce local attendance provisions and build new schools where they were needed. The school leaving age was raised to twelve in 1889, although, as in most other countries, pupils were not required to attend each day that schools were opened. Free elementary education was granted in 1893 but was fully implemented only after 1918. The employers had long ceased to advocate keeping the poor in ignorance, but remained sceptical of the practical benefits of school expenditure. Even advanced technical training, they believed, was better provided on the shop floor rather than from books: the latest equipment could be used and trade secrets less easily stolen. Between 1870 and the early 1880s, the proportion of the group aged five to fifteen enrolled in "inspected schools" rose from a quarter to a half. In many localities, transient, unofficial schools persisted, but since they were not inspected, those who made use of them were not counted as "under instruction."

France In France, the sinews of state power were far more visible, and periods of revolutionary turmoil more sharply drawn. Dramatic reversals of power between Catholic monarchists and secular republicans, combined with profound ambiguity regarding the civil status of women, at times made *laïcité*, or secularism, one of the core themes of political and educational discourse. Although their blueprints for instructing children of the people differed, republicans and royalists alike were hampered by scarce resources and limited knowledge of local conditions; both admired the "simultaneous method" of instruction developed by Brothers of the Christian Schools, whose complex system of signs and signals enabled a single teacher, in theory at least, to control classes of up to 150 pupils. When in 1816 Louis XVIII decreed that all school teachers be authorized by the reconstituted *Université*, royal officials had no idea how many schools there were or where they were located. Many of the provincial notables entrusted with mapping existing educational provisions failed to carry out their

new role, and others could not agree what constituted a school. The Guizot law of 1833 required each commune in France to have a primary school. Yet much of the apparent growth in provision, after a permanent, full-time school inspectorate was established in 1835, resulted from counting, for the first time, girls' educational institutions, which were previously not thought to be schools. It was during the Second Empire (1852–1870), which facilitated cooperation between secular and Catholic authorities, that schools were finally built in all communes. Enrollments increased from over three million in 1850 to over five million by the late 1870s; almost the total cohort of school-age children was on the books of officially recognized institutions several years before legislation making attendance compulsory was passed. Catholic schools accounted for all but a fifth of this growth. In 1876 four-fifths of the half million French children in nursery schools, over half of elementary school girls, and nearly a quarter of boys were in the care of religious congregations. In some regions, the proportions were much higher: in the diocese of Lyon in 1863, 72 percent of boys and 86 percent of girls in the department of the Loire attended congregational schools. Since school funding was the responsibility of local councils, the success of many Catholic schools, with their bequests, cheap staff, and church subsidies, was less a reflection of the religiosity of the population than the stinginess of municipal councillors. Conversely, becoming a nun was an attractive option in an age when the state showed little interest in training female teachers, and there were few nonmanual jobs for the many women who needed to work. Two hundred thousand women joined some four hundred religious orders, most dedicated to teaching and some enjoying a considerable degree of semiprofessional autonomy, between 1800 and 1880.

The Third Republic, proclaimed in 1875, inherited what amounted to two systems of elementary schooling: a secular one, staffed mainly by men, that dealt with most boys and less than half of the girls in the population and a Catholic one, staffed mainly by women, that catered predominantly to girls and infants. By now, what used to be a convenient compromise, similar to that achieved in other Catholic countries, began to appear as a source of social discord. Heightened class conflict, falling fertility, and high infant mortality, bourgeois reformers argued,

The Reverend Thomas Guthrie teaches a class at his school in Edinburgh c. 1850. Guthrie was a prominent advocate of free public education for the poor, and his concept of schools for poor children—called ragged schools—was eventually adopted throughout Great Britain. After the 1870 Education Act, the ragged schools were gradually absorbed into the British school system. ©Hulton-Deutsch Collection/Corbis could all be alleviated if working-class women tamed their husbands' radicalism and brought up healthy and industrious republican children. For their part, labor leaders worried that women, captive to the church, would betray working-class movements. Men from opposite sides of the republican spectrum shared fears that spiritual divorce between themselves and, as Jules Michelet wrote, "wives and daughters brought up and governed by our enemies" would shatter their own domestic tranquillity (quoted in Price, p. 319). The French government increased funding of municipal elementary schools, greatly expanded provisions for the training of lay women teachers, and opened the first state-funded high schools for girls. Within three decades, all parts of an increasingly unified and stratified education system were secularized.

REGIONS WITH FEW CITIES

In regions with few cities, agricultural predominance and relatively uncommercialized economies, the dynamics of school building differed again. Here, direct coercion tended to play a major part in production, and rulers typically created ponderous fiscal machines to extract the means of war out of local populations. In the eighteenth century, in absolutist Prussia, Austria, Russia, and Spain, costly territorial wars, followed by decades of sharpening exploitation, precipitated widespread famines and left whole regions simmering with discontent. Tightening feudal obligations any further, reformers began to argue, had no chance of increasing landlords' returns. At best it would lead to debilitating poverty, more likely it would spark off murderous uprisings. The only way out, it seemed, was to free the serfs, break up the estates, and commute labor services to rents. But first, it was necessary to educate the poor into new forms of thinking and feeling. In some parts of Prussia and Austria such educational projects drew on long traditions of schooling and popular literacy and achieved considerable success. Elsewhere, they faced formidable obstacles. In the Habsburg Empire, Maria Theresa signed the General School Ordinance, mandating school attendance of all children between six and twelve, in 1774—three years before a voluntary patent for the commutation of labor services was issued. In the province of Bohemia, two-thirds of all school-age children were enrolled in school by 1790. An Austrian census taken in 1900 showed that for those born in the 1850s, 96 percent of Czech speakers and 93 percent of Germans could read, compared to 17 and 11 percent respectively of those speaking Serbo-Croatian and Ruthenian (Ukrainian).

Prussia In Prussia, Frederick the Great's school edict of 1763 reasserted the compulsory attendance provisions of earlier legislation and applied them to the entire monarchy. In theory at least, country schools came under full state jurisdiction, with Protestant and Catholic clergy delegated the task of inspection and supervision. All instruction, hours, curricula, schedules, and texts were regulated by law. The legislation, which for many decades was only unevenly enforced, provided for free education for the poor, specific qualifications for teachers, graded classes, and uniform schoolbooks. In 1808 a ministry of education was established to supervise all public instruction. In 1817 it merged with the department overseeing church matters to become the Ministry of Education and Religious Affairs. By 1826 all schoolteachers were required to be certified through a state examination; many were taught, and a number tried to practice, inquiry-based approaches to classroom instruction that are still respected today. Many *Volksschule,* historians warn, were not nearly as good as enthusiastic visitors, keen to shame their own governments into action, reported. Still, in a period when British industry and political institutions were admired and Prussian regimentation and backwardness condemned, Prussian common schools were held up as a model of enlightened educational practice, and English ones decried as uncivilized and inefficient.

The emperor's own enthusiasm for educational innovation cooled during the revolutionary 1840s. Direct state contribution to schooling remained small: in 1867 it amounted to only 4 percent of the total, growing to 12 percent in 1878. In 1852 there were on average ninety pupils per teacher in Prussian elementary schools, and many country teachers struggled with ungraded classes of a hundred or even a hundred and fifty students. Yet, the fact remains that nine out of ten Prussian army recruits were able to read in 1841; and in 1880 female illiteracy in Prussia was, at 6 percent, a third of that in England. In the early 1870s seven out of ten five- to fourteen-year-olds were enrolled in school in Prussia, twice the number attending "inspected schools" in England and Wales. In reminiscing about their childhood, many German working-class people wrote bitterly about the harsh necessity to complete their share of remunerative labor before and after mandatory attendance at school. British and French autobiographers, in contrast, frequently noted that family necessity compelled them to miss out on going to school. In many rural regions of Spain and Italy, there were simply no classes to go to.

Italy and Spain In Italy, laws requiring communes to provide two to four years of free, compulsory schooling, passed in the Kingdom of Sardinia in 1851, were extended to all regions of unified Italy in 1877, and expanded over the following decades. Yet only 43 percent of five- to fifteen-year-olds were enrolled in school by 1907. In the rural south in particular, local elites vetoed new taxes and refused to allocate funds for schools or night classes and enforce attendance as required by law. "Money for schooling" they argued, "is often harmful: obligatory education is useless and dangerous, serving only to create socialists and anarchists who are the ruin of Italy" (quoted in Reeder, p. 101). As long as no better life seemed possible, most agricultural laborers themselves saw little point in attending adult education classes or sending children to school. According to the 1901 census, 65 percent of Sicilian males and 77 percent of females over the age of six were illiterate. But this does not mean that all were trapped in a timeless, traditional society. Thousands of southern Italian men helped build the trappings of modernity in the four corners of the globe before they learned to read. They paved city streets in Buenos Aires, constructed tunnels and railroads in Canada, and built skyscrapers in New York. The hope and savings they sent home inspired their wives and neighbors to see literacy as a useful and attainable goal. In Spain too, local authorities charged with implementing the 1857 school legislation frequently chose to ignore it. In the 1890s school spending was less than a quarter of that in France, over two-thirds of children did not attend school, and half of Spanish men and three-quarters of women were illiterate. The powerful socialist and anarchist movements that emerged during this period educated and organized the masses through radical newspapers written so they could be read out aloud to illiterate comrades. For their part, the powerful tended to see popular literacy as a source of sedition and schools for the poor as unwarranted expense rather than a "fountain of prosperity," and preferred to meet the challenge of radical movements with force.

EDUCATING THE COMMON PEOPLE

Throughout Europe it was seen as desirable, though often not possible, to prepare boys and girls for their differently subordinate station in life in separate schools. Less clear was the pattern of authority teachers could emulate. Should classrooms resemble a monastery, an army regiment, a factory, or a well-run household? Should teachers embody the virtues of a sergeant, a mother made conscious, a wise patriarch, a nun, or a bureaucrat? Could not such preferences be amended to utilize women keen to teach for half or less of male rates of pay? One indication of the differently gendered answers to such questions is the proportion of men and women trained and employed as elementary schoolteachers in various regions of Europe. In Italy, almost three-quarters of trainees were women in 1870 and 93 percent in 1900. In 1837, two of every three French elementary schoolteachers were men; by 1863, more than half were women. The first Prussian teacher training institution for women opened in 1832, but in 1897 only 6 percent of trainees were women. The city of Berlin hired its first female elementary teachers in 1863; but in 1900 only a quarter of city teachers and 9 percent of those in the countryside were women. When the city of Zurich hired the first women teachers in 1874, the majority of elementary school instructors in England were female. In most of Europe, women teachers were paid around half of what men earned; in Austria they received equal pay from the 1870s.

One of the main reasons for sending all children to school was to teach them the national language. This helped create a sense of national unity and pride. It provided a vehicle for transmitting and inculcating (often recently invented) national traditions. It simplified the issuing of orders and regulations, and made army recruits easier to train and bureaucracies easier to staff and manage. As families who spoke one of the nondominant verna-

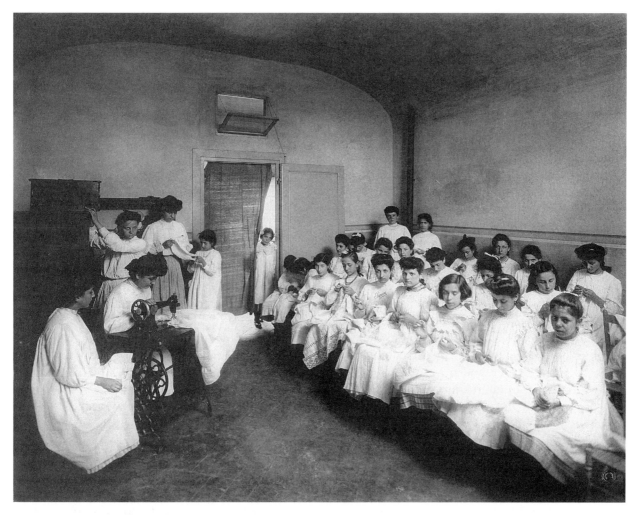

A sewing class for girls, Florence, Italy, c. 1907. Although the idea of universal public education had become widely accepted by the end of the nineteenth century, female students often learned primarily domestic skills in school. © ALINARI ARCHIVES/CORBIS

culars knew only too well, one needed to be fluent in the official language of state to deal with government bureaucrats, trade with strangers, become a teacher, or secure even the lowliest uniformed job in the post office or the railways. The problem was that the peoples of nineteenth-century Europe spoke many more languages than there could ever be viable states. In the Prussian, Austrian, Russian, and Ottoman empires, German, Polish and Czech; Hungarian, Slovak, Ukrainian, Romanian, Italian, Slovenian, and Yiddish; Albanian, Greek, Serb, and Turkish; Russian, Polish, Finish, and German villages existed side by side. In newly unified Italy, less than one in twenty inhabitants actually spoke the Italian language for ordinary purposes of life;

in France at the end of the eighteenth century, six or more languages and thirty dialects were spoken, and six million people relied on a language other than the French in which "national" works of literature—and school textbooks—were written.

In multiethnic empires, the language question was multifaceted and complicated: Should a plurality of languages be tolerated, if necessary provided with a written form, and taught at school? Would this not give rise to undesirable separatist tendencies? Alternately, would not the determined pursuit of linguistic nationalism inflame counter-nationalism among those whose mother tongue became a mere dialect, or else a foreign language, in the locality where they lived? Should religious precepts be written down and explained to children in the vernacular they spoke and understood, even if it delayed the teaching of the national language to all inhabitants of an empire? Were some faiths naturally associated with particular ethnolinguistic groups? For example, could the Muslims among Albanian speakers be automatically reckoned Turks, Orthodox Christians, Greeks, or Russians, and Roman Catholics Latins or Slavs? And should all Muslims then learn to read and write the language of the Prophet, whether or not they spoke any Arabic? And if, as eventually happened, they decided against overwhelming odds to read and write Albanian, which alphabet should they use?

Many of the regions where the language question was the hardest to resolve—the Breton, Provençal, Catalan, Basque, Sicilian, and Balkan hinterlands—came to be reckoned educationally backward. Elsewhere, as in parts of central and eastern Europe, opposition to imperial domination turned peasant women and men into clandestine teachers, and schoolchildren into patriots. In Prussian provinces of partitioned Poland, government prohibition on the use of Polish for religious instruction—and children's refusal to say prayers in German at school—sparked off widespread school strikes and helped create an unlikely oppositional alliance between the Roman Catholic Church, peasants, and nationalist gentry and intellectuals.

EDUCATION OF THE ELITE

The elementary schooling of common people was one thing, the education of their betters quite another. Common schools taught basic skills and the duties of everyday life. The wealthy learned to read and write at home; their formal education tended to begin where that of the poor ended, it revolved around genteel attributes and arcane knowledge that ordinary people lacked and that their schools did not furnish. Elementary schools served a third, half, or more of a given age group; advanced schools and universities combined might serve one or two in a hundred. Rather than patronize different levels of one education system, the rich and the poor received quite different instruction in separate institutions. Elementary schoolteachers were trained in higher elementary rather than secondary schools; advanced schools and even universities had their own preparatory classes. Schools for

the people were regulated and inspected by central authorities but financed mostly by fees and local taxes; universities and boys' classical schools were often funded by the state. Since only (some) men but no women could become professionals, vote, or hold government office, females (together with people of the wrong faith) were for most of the nineteenth century excluded from public examinations and the universities.

But questions remained about how to articulate a powerful tradition of classical studies with professional forms of apprenticeship and with "modern" areas of learning, and how to instruct young ladies. The education of English and German barristers illustrates the different ways such issues could be tackled. The English common law is based on interpretations and adaptations of ancient custom by legal practitioners. Associations of such practitioners, the Inns of Court, organized informal apprenticeship provisions for aspiring barristers and controlled their admission to practice. Oxford and Cambridge universities provided some lectures on jurisprudence and legal history, but not on current practice. There were no examinations for entry to the civil service before the 1870s; until after World War II, university education was neither a prerequisite nor even the most common preparation for admission to the bar. A disproportionate number of top professionals were educated in the eight most influential English public schools, but these, despite their name, were free of government control.

In much of continental Europe, in contrast, laws were systematized by royal officials; since the late eighteenth century, university training was considered an integral part of preparation for senior ranks of government service. In Prussia, six years of rigorous study in a classical *Gymnasium* (closely regulated by state authorities since the 1770s), assured boys' grasp of examinable facets of Greek and Roman culture—and secured them exemption from army conscription. Two more years prepared them for the *Abitur* examination, without which one could not enter university. Successful university study culminated in a state examination and a junior post in the bureaucracy. After several years of such work, candidates could sit a final qualifying state examination. Despite vast differences in legal systems, government structures and professional

Interior View of the Women's Section of the St. Petersburg Drawing School. Painting by Ekaterina Nikolaevna Khilkova. Although education was not considered necessary or desirable for women throughout much of the nineteenth century, the study of music and painting was considered desirable for the wives and daughters of the wealthy. ©THE STATE RUSSIAN MUSEUM/CORBIS

training, English and German authorities both insisted that only men could become barristers. Although a handful of women did complete legal studies and apprenticeships, they did not win admission to the bar until after World War I.

Latin and the rarefied mysteries of classical learning constituted the common currency of cultured distinction, formed the subject matter of the most prestigious exams—and gave young men the confidence to despise "practical hacks" who merely learned science. Those without the money—or desire—to become cultivated, gentlemanly amateurs patronized less prestigious but often highly inno-

vative middle-class schools. Teaching "modern" and utilitarian studies such as science, geography, surveying, modern languages, and shipbuilding, many of these schools trained excellent merchants, technicians, and businessmen. Not least because such occupations were considered vulgar by the elite, modern schools and technological institutes struggled to gain parity with those built around classical culture. Eventually, most faced one of two difficult options: accept an intermediate rank on an emerging educational pyramid, or recast the subjects they taught to resemble the unworldly, examinable curriculum of grammar schools, *Gymnasien,* and *lycées.*

For decades, young women from privileged backgrounds had no direct access to either world of learning. Ladies' academies and convents, intricately differentiated by the status of their clients, provided individualized, home-like instruction in a universally recognized set of female accomplishments. For middle-class women compelled to earn their own living, teaching these skills provided one of the few avenues of genteel employment. It was concern about expanding employment opportunities for such women that played a key role in opening of the first academic schools for young women, and in turn created a demand for female secondary teachers. Initially, girls' academic schools were of little interest to the state; most were established by local associations and financed by fees. In the 1890s, for example, 272 of 568 Prussian secondary schools for boys, but only 4 of 128 girls' schools, were supported by the state. It took years of struggle before women were allowed to sit the same academic examinations as their brothers, enroll in universities, and practice professions. Women were admitted to university schools of medicine in Zurich from 1864, Paris from 1867, and Italy in the 1870s; separate women's medical colleges were set up in Russia in 1872 and in Britain in 1874. By 1901 women constituted 3.3 percent of all university students in France, 4.8 percent in the Netherlands, 5.1 percent in Switzerland, and 2.9 in Sweden. Prussian universities did not admit women until 1908. The eventual victories, significant as they were, came at a cost. Women played little part in the making of the (masculine) public sphere, and their strengths, preoccupations, and insights were marginalized as they, too, adopted an education built around competitive academic knowledge.

"The sons of noble persons, councillors, and clerks," an Austrian edict of 1776 decreed, "are to be admitted [to the classical *Gymnasia*] even if they possess only mediocre talent and little proficiency in the necessary subjects. Children from the lower orders, however, are to be admitted only if they possess exceptional talent." Few statesmen were so blunt. Yet, by the end of the nineteenth century, the education systems they helped establish embodied—more or less perfectly—just such principles.

Gentry and aristocracy accounted for up to half of total enrollments in the eight most influential English public schools. In the second half of the nineteenth century, these supplied over four-fifths of Oxford and Cambridge university students. As late as 1881, 47 percent of Russian Gymnasium students came from the nobility. Between 1864 and 1907, around half of the fathers of German *Gymnasium* students, but between 60 and 80 percent of French academic *lycée* students came from upper-middle-class backgrounds. At one of the most elite French university schools, the École Polytechnique, the total share of the upper-middle class advanced from 70 percent just after 1815 to almost 90 percent before 1880. Until the 1870s, almost two-thirds of those who reached German universities came from the 5 percent of the work force in government, the professions, and the services. Between 1860 and 1910, only 1 percent of students in Prussian universities were the children of laborers, in Vienna and Prague universities, 6 to 7 percent.

The technologies of instruction, conceptual tools, and institutional frameworks with which we think of education today were taken up, recast, and sometimes invented in the course of the nineteenth century. They helped crystallize gendered social inequality and set the parameters of childhood and adolescence. They helped constitute notions of measurable intelligence and ideas of appropriate family size. They allow us to distinguish between work and education, current and future usefulness, social dependency, and the pursuit of knowledge. For all these reasons, history of education remains relevant today.

See also **Childhood and Children; Ferry, Jules; Literacy; Professions; Secularization.**

BIBLIOGRAPHY

Albisetti, James. "Female Education in German-Speaking Austria, Germany, and Switzerland, 1866–1914." In *Austrian Women in the Nineteenth and Twentieth Centuries*, edited by David Good, Margarete Grandner, and Mary Jo Maynes, 39–57. Providence, R. I., and Oxford, U.K., 1996.

Cohen, Gary. *Education and Middle-Class Society in Imperial Austria, 1848–1918.* West Lafayette, Ind., 1996. Combines institutional history with material on students' experiences; includes detailed comparative statistics.

Eklof, Ben. *Russian Peasant Schools: Officialdom, Village Culture, and Popular Pedagogy, 1864–1914.* Berkeley, Calif., 1986. Influential contribution to debates about peasant attitudes to schools.

Flora, Peter. *State, Economy, and Society in Western Europe, 1815–1975: A Data Handbook in Two Volumes.* Chicago, 1983. An outstanding collection of key dates and statistics.

Gemie, Sharif. "What Is a School?: Defining and Controlling Primary Schooling in Early Nineteenth-Century France." *History of Education* 21, no. 2 (1992): 129–147.

Gosden, P. H. J. H., ed. *How They Were Taught: An Anthology of Contemporary Accounts of Learning and Teaching in England, 1800–1950.* Oxford, U.K., 1969. A well-chosen collection of documents.

Grew, Raymond, and Patrick Harrigan. *School, State, and Society: The Growth of Elementary Schooling in Nineteenth-Century France: A Quantitative Analysis.* Ann Arbor, Mich., 1991. A key text, which corrects for reliance on what reformers said by careful statistical analysis.

Hurt, John. *Elementary Schooling and the Working Classes, 1860–1918.* London, 1979. Insightful and detailed social history.

Lamberti, Marjorie. *State, Society, and the Elementary School in Imperial Germany.* New York, 1989. Insightful social history.

Maynes, Mary Jo. *Schooling in Western Europe: A Social History.* Albany, N.Y., 1985. Still an excellent overview of themes and debates.

Melton, James Van Horn. *Absolutism and the Eighteenth-Century Origins of Compulsory Schooling in Prussia and Austria.* Cambridge, U.K., 1988. An influential interpretation of the rise of compulsory schooling.

Miller, Pavla. *Transformations of Patriarchy in the West, 1500–1900.* Bloomington, Ind., 1998. Links rise of mass schooling to contested changes in patriarchal governance.

Ortiz, David, Jr. "Redefining Public Education: Contestation, the Press, and Education in Regency Spain, 1885–1902." *Journal of Social History* 35, no. 1 (2001): 73–94. On the way the popular radical press addressed an illiterate audience.

Price, Roger. *A Social History of Nineteenth-Century France.* New York, 1987.

Purvis, June. *A History of Women's Education in England.* Milton Keynes, U.K., and Philadelphia, 1991. An accessible overview.

Reeder, Linda. "Women in the Classroom: Mass Migration, Literacy, and the Nationalization of Sicilian Women at the Turn of the Century." *Journal of Social History* 32, no. 1 (1998): 101–125.

Ringer, Fritz. *Education and Society in Modern Europe.* Bloomington, Ind., 1979. Influential comparative study of education and social stratification in Germany, France and England.

Stone, Judith. "The Republican Brotherhood: Gender and Ideology." In *Gender and the Politics of Social Reform in France, 1870–1914,* edited by Elinor Accampo, Rachel Fuchs, and Mary Lynn Stewart, 28–58. Baltimore, Md., and London, 1995. Important recasting of debates on *laïcité* and republicanism.

Tomiak, Janusz, in collaboration with Knut Eriksen, Andreas Kazamias, and Robin Okey, eds. *Schooling, Educational Policy, and Ethnic Identity.* New York and Aldershot, U.K., 1991. First volume of comparative studies on governments and nondominant ethnic groups in Europe between 1850 and 1940.

PAVLA MILLER

EDWARD VII (1841–1910; ruled 1901–1910), king of Great Britain and Ireland.

Edward VII spent most of his life waiting. Born on 9 November 1841, he was the son of an extraordinarily long-lived mother, Queen Victoria. Edward lived for decades as the heir to the throne, and this shaped what he would become and defined his behavior, position, and rectitude in relation to his mother.

He arrived early in the reign of Queen Victoria, child to her and Prince Albert of Saxe-Coburg-Gotha. Christened Albert Edward, he did not please his parents. He was not much of a student, did not particularly like hard work, and frequently bullied his playmates. In a family where duty and hard work were watchwords, these traits were not well received. When his father died in 1861, shortly after journeying to Cambridge to get Edward out of a scrape, Queen Victoria blamed him, at least partly, for Albert's death. That chill eased somewhat when, in 1863, Edward married Princess Alexandra of Denmark, a solid match for the heir to the throne, and someone for whom Queen Victoria developed a fondness. Edward was not a particularly attentive husband, preferring instead the company of his friends and of a succession of mistresses. Alexandra could do little but accept the situation. They produced the required children—Albert Victor, George, Louise, Victoria, and Maud—and settled into something of a domestic life.

Edward VII, photographed in 1889. ©UNDERWOOD & UNDERWOOD/CORBIS

W. & D. DOWNEY
PHOTOGRAPHERS

57 & 61, EBURY STREET
LONDON, S.W.

choice, Albert Edward decided to ascend the throne as Edward VII and not Albert I, as his mother had wished. He was fifty-nine years old when he was crowned on 22 January 1901. As king, he largely continued in the way he had before reaching the throne. He was a public monarch and proud of it, living a riotous life out in the open. His horses won the Derby; his mistresses were public figures; he gloried in the ceremony of the throne. Edward pioneered the figure of the public monarch, whose daily life became the grist for a new mass media. The public accepted and even enjoyed his decadent lifestyle, and he was a signally popular king.

But even as the king became a central figure on the public stage, the monarchy's political powers continued their slow decline. His mother through force of personality and long endurance had sustained a measure of influence and respect. Edward lacked the interest or ability to do the same. Neither the Tories nor the Liberals paid him much more than surface attention. The sole exception to this was in the military, and Edward's support for both Richard Burdon Haldane at the War Office and John Fisher at the Admiralty helped ensure that Britain had a modern and modernizing military. Edward also had the good judgment to include his second son, George—heir after the death of Albert Victor in 1893—in the workings of the monarchy, helping prepare him for his stint on the throne.

Given his lack of influence, it is thus something of an irony that Edward presided over one of the more serious constitutional crises in twentieth-century British history. When open political warfare broke out in 1909 between the Liberal government and the House of Lords over the aggressive role the upper house had playing in nullifying the government's reforming agenda, Prime Minister Herbert Henry Asquith turned to the king for help. The Liberals, in Asquith's plan, would introduce a parliamentary bill sharply reducing the power of the Lords. If the House of Lords did not go along with this, Edward would elevate enough Liberal politicians to the peerage to overwhelm the Conservative majority in that house. It was a drastic threat, and Edward, whose sympathies were largely with the Lords and who, in any case, was not eager to be responsible for such a drastic action, was reluctant. He asked Asquith to hold a general election, the

But the distance from his mother never wholly abated. The queen did not trust Edward to keep a secret, and thus did not include him in the daily business of the monarchy, refusing him access to state papers. Yet he became, in the 1860s and 1870s, something of the public face of the monarchy. Queen Victoria had retreated after the death of her husband into years of mourning, and Edward took her place in the popular eye. Edward seemed to stand for everything that Queen Victoria was not. She was stern and moral and the living embodiment of upright British values. He played cards, gambled, ran with a fast crowd, and was named several times in divorce suits, most particularly the Mordaunt case of 1870.

Edward's lengthy wait for the throne ended in 1901 when Victoria died. In a particularly telling second such election in 1910, to show that the country was behind such an action. Asquith agreed to do so, but fate and years of smoking and good eating intervened. King Edward VII had a series of heart attacks in April 1910, and expired on 6 May. As Edward lay dying, news arrived that one of his horses had galloped home to win a race at Kempton Park.

See also **Aristocracy; Great Britain; Victoria, Queen.**

BIBLIOGRAPHY

Hibbert, Christopher. *Edward VII: A Portrait.* London, 1976.

DAVID SILBEY

EGYPT. A province of the Ottoman Empire since 1517, Egypt had been dominated since the early eighteenth century by a cluster of largely autonomous Mamluk beys (provincial governors in the Ottoman Empire). The Mamluks were members of a politically powerful military class in Egypt. In 1786 the Ottomans sought to reassert their authority by installing a new governor. The attempt failed, and the Mamluks Murad Bey (1750–1801) and Ibrahim Bey (1735–1817) took power instead. In European eyes, late-eighteenth-century Egypt appeared to be beset by internal political disorder, and the Ottoman Empire seemed to be in decline, following a major defeat by Russia in 1774.

THE FRENCH INVASION AND THE REIGN OF MEHMET ALI PASHA

These factors encouraged European powers, especially France, to contemplate invading and colonizing Egypt. On 2 July 1798, a French army commanded by Napoleon Bonaparte landed at Alexandria, with the twofold intent of making Egypt a French colony and threatening British interests in South Asia. The French quickly captured Alexandria and marched south toward Cairo, defeating the Mamluks at the Battle of the Pyramids on 21 July. Ten days later, however, the British navy under Admiral Horatio Nelson (1758–1805) demolished the French fleet, in what became known as the Battle of the Nile. Now marooned in Egypt, Bonaparte attempted to save face by cultivating fraternal relations with the Egyptian Arab elite and by marching into Syria. Turned back at the walls of Acre, Bonaparte abandoned his army and left for France in August 1799. French occupation of Egypt continued under the command of General Jean-Baptiste Kléber (1753–1800), who was assassinated in June 1800, and followed by General Jacques-François de Menou (1750–1810), a widely unpopular figure and a convert to Islam. In early 1801 a joint British-Ottoman force launched a counterinvasion of Egypt, capturing Cairo; the French surrendered in September, and by mid-1803 all French and British forces had withdrawn.

Bonaparte had failed to establish an enduring French colony in Egypt, but he had managed to topple definitively the old Mamluk establishment. In the ensuing power vacuum, an Albanian-born general named Mehmet Ali (1769–1849), who had come to Egypt with the Ottoman army, skillfully outmaneuvered a series of rivals to assume power himself. He was appointed pasha, or governor, of Egypt by the Ottoman sultan in 1805. He secured his authority in part by weakening the landed elite, through revisions to the tax system and expropriation of land. In 1811 he dealt a deadly blow to his Mamluk rivals, luring them to a ceremony at the Cairo Citadel and having them murdered to a man.

Neither Britain nor France had abandoned their imperial interests in the region. Convinced that Mehmet Ali was a pawn of the French, Britain attempted a misbegotten invasion of Egypt in 1807—an episode that underscored the key place that Egypt now occupied in European imperial politics. Mehmet Ali Pasha shrewdly played British and French interests off each other to pursue a series of reforms and modernizing schemes. Notably, he built up his army using European military advisers and technology. Long-staple Jumel cotton was introduced in the early 1820s, and power looms were imported for industrial textile production. Mehmet Ali also pursued educational reforms, creating professional schools and sending Egyptian students to France to study. He paid for British and French aid partly by granting rights to excavate and export Egyptian antiquities, which had become all the rage following the publication of the twenty-four-volume *Description de l'Égypte*

European powers. This became sharply evident during the Greek War of Independence, when the pasha sent Egyptian forces to help the Ottomans suppress the Greeks. British and French sympathies sided strongly with the Greeks, however, and in 1827 a joint Anglo-French squadron sailed into the bay of Navarino and destroyed the Egyptian navy.

Of larger concern was the fact that Mehmet Ali's conquests in Syria and elsewhere threatened to upset the stability of the Ottoman Empire as a whole, and with it the European balance of power. European diplomats, concerned to protect Ottoman integrity, met in London in 1840 to find a way of scaling back Mehmet Ali's territory. Working in the face of French opposition, the British foreign secretary Lord Palmerston (Henry John Temple, 3rd Viscount Palmerston; 1784–1865) hammered out a treaty that granted Mehmet Ali hereditary title to Egypt but deprived him of all his conquests except Sudan and curtailed the size of his army. Palmerston then forced the pasha into submission in 1841 using his preferred tactic of gunboat diplomacy. Egypt would never be an empire; nor, for the rest of the century, would it be truly independent.

THE KHEDIVES AND BRITISH OCCUPATION

Mehmet Ali Pasha died in 1849 and was succeeded by his relatively pro-British son Abbas I (1813–1854), who granted Britain a concession to build a railroad linking Alexandria, Cairo, and Suez. With the accession of Said Pasha (1822–1863) in 1854, the pendulum swung in favor of France. Said Pasha's childhood friend Ferdinand-Marie de Lesseps (1805–1894) successfully won permission to build a canal across the Isthmus of Suez. When the Compagnie Universelle du Canal Maritime de Suez went public in 1858, 44 percent of the shares were foisted on the pasha himself, who could ill afford the liability. This marked the start of Egypt's rapid slide into insolvency. Construction on the Suez Canal began in 1859, initially using forced corvée labor (unpaid labor often in lieu of taxes).

During the early 1860s, Egypt enjoyed an economic boom thanks to the skyrocketing price of cotton brought on by the American Civil War. Said Pasha's nephew Ismail (1830–1895) ascended the throne in 1863 and poured money into transforming Cairo and Alexandria into European-style

A woman carries water in a vessel on her head in the Valley of the Tombs of the Kings, Egypt, c. 1870s.
©MICHAEL MASLAN HISTORIC PHOTOGRAPHS/CORBIS

(1809–1828), compiled by the savants who had accompanied Bonaparte's army.

In addition to "modernizing" Egypt, Mehmet Ali Pasha's ambitions included ensuring dynastic power in Egypt and building an empire beyond it. Using his European-style army, Mehmet Ali helped the sultan suppress the Wahhabi rebellion in the Hijaz (1811–1813). In 1820–1822 he conquered northern Sudan, where he briefly tried to form an army of Sudanese askaris (native soldiers); and in 1831 his son Ibrahim (1789–1848) invaded Syria and Anatolia, in hopes of securing Egyptian rule over Syria. But Mehmet Ali's intervention in wider Ottoman affairs brought him into conflict with

A section of Cairo photographed c. 1900. ©MICHAEL MASLAN HISTORIC PHOTOGRAPHS/CORBIS

cities, with gaslit boulevards, parks, public buildings, trams, and railways. The opening ceremonies for the Suez Canal, in 1869, were marked by exceptional opulence: Ismail Pasha built a lavish palace replicating the Tuileries for the French empress Eugénie and commissioned the opera *Aïda* from Giuseppe Verdi (1813–1901) to inaugurate the new Cairo Opera House. Unfortunately his expenditures vastly outran his revenue. Cotton prices plunged after 1865, while both Ismail's debts to European creditors and his tributary obligations to the Ottoman sultan mounted. By 1875 Egypt's national debt had multiplied thirtyfold.

Ismail attempted to stave off bankruptcy by selling off his Suez Canal shares in 1875. The British prime minister Benjamin Disraeli, who recognized the enormous significance of Suez to

British imperial interests, pounced on the opportunity. With a loan from Lord Lionel de Rothschild (Lionel Nathan Rothschild; 1808–1879), the British government bought Ismail's controlling stake in the canal for a bargain £4 million. But the sale did not prevent Egypt from going bankrupt. In 1876 the international Caisse de la Dette Publique was established to oversee the repayment of debts. Egyptian finances were further regulated by a system of dual control, with a British agent to administer Egyptian revenue and a French agent to supervise Egyptian expenditure.

Ismail (who had earned the title *khedive* in 1867) resisted European-imposed changes, only to be forcibly deposed by the Ottoman sultan in 1879 and replaced by his nephew Muhammed Tawfiq Pasha (1852–1892). But a more serious opposition to European administration was fomenting in the Egyptian army, under Colonel Ahmad Urabi (1839–1911), an Egyptian of modest *fellah* (peasant) origins. Angered by European manipulation and khedival mismanagement, Urabi and his supporters set about forming a nationalist ministry. Faced with Urabi's rapidly increasing success, Tawfiq asked for British and French military support. In June 1882 Urabist riots broke out in Alexandria under the slogan "Egypt for the Egyptians." Britain responded by bombarding Alexandria in July; British forces landed in the Suez Canal zone, defeated the Urabists at Tel el Kebir in September, and occupied Cairo. Urabi was court-martialed and exiled to Ceylon.

British military occupation of Egypt was meant to be temporary; many Britons opposed taking on new imperial commitments. But Britain would not withdraw until its strategic and financial interests were secured. Events in Sudan soon provoked deeper entanglement. In 1881 a rebellion had broken out against Egyptian rule, organized by a messianic leader known as the Mahdi (Muhammad Ahmad; 1844–1885). In 1883 an Egyptian army commanded by the British officer William Hicks tried to put down the uprising, only to be slaughtered by the Mahdists at El Obeid. Bowing to public pressure, Prime Minister William Gladstone sent General Charles Gordon (1833–1885) to Sudan to restore order. Gordon, a zealous Christian and imperial hero, proved insubordinate and intemperate; yet, besieged in Khartoum, his plight attracted wide sympathy in Britain. Again submitting to public opinion, Gladstone dispatched a mission to rescue Gordon. Chugging up the Nile on tourist steamers, the expeditionary force reached Khartoum on 28 January 1885, only to find that the Mahdists had stormed the city two days earlier. Gordon's body was never found. The Mahdists would control Sudan until their defeat by the British at Omdurman in 1898.

Britain's "temporary" occupation became what has been termed a "veiled protectorate." From 1883 to 1907 it was steered almost single-handedly by the consul-general Evelyn Baring, Lord Cromer (1841–1917). Cromer endeavored to clean up Egypt's finances, promoted railway and canal construction, and reformed agricultural practice: whipping of *fellahin* and corvée labor were abolished. He also, however, epitomized "Orientalist" superiority, insisting on Egypt's need for paternalistic British stewardship. Meanwhile, nationalist sentiment coalesced around the young, anti-British khedive Abbas Hilmi (1892–1914) and found voice through intellectuals such as Mustafa Kamil (1874–1908), the founder of the influential newspaper *al-Liwa*.

In 1906 anti-British feeling was further galvanized by the Dinshaway incident, when five British officers on a pigeon-shooting trip in the village of Dinshaway accidentally wounded a local woman. In the resulting fray two officers were wounded, one mortally. British authorities tried fifty-two villagers for premeditated murder; four were hanged. This disproportionate show of force outraged Egyptians and contributed to Cromer's resignation in 1907. With the outbreak of World War I, Britain ended its ambiguous position in Egypt to declare it a protectorate outright. But as the formal structure of British imperial rule hardened, Egyptian nationalism had already gained shape.

See also **French Revolutionary Wars and Napoleonic Wars; Great Britain; Ottoman Empire; Suez Canal.**

BIBLIOGRAPHY

Cole, Juan R. I. *Colonialism and Revolution in the Middle East: Social and Cultural Origins of Egypt's 'Urabi Revolt.* Princeton, N.J., 1993.

Fahmy, Khaled. *All the Pasha's Men: Mehmed Ali, His Army, and the Making of Modern Egypt.* Cambridge, U.K., 1997.

Landes, David. *Bankers and Pashas: International Finance and Economic Imperialism in Egypt.* 2nd ed. Cambridge, Mass., 1979.

Marsot, Afaf Lutfi al-Sayyid. *Egypt in the Reign of Muhammad Ali.* Cambridge, U.K., 1984.

Mitchell, Timothy. *Colonising Egypt.* Cambridge, U.K., 1988.

Owen, Roger. *Lord Cromer: Victorian Imperialist, Edwardian Proconsul.* Oxford, U.K., 2004.

MAYA JASANOFF

EHRLICH, PAUL (1854–1915), German bacteriologist.

Paul Ehrlich was born on 14 March 1854 in Strehlen in Upper Silesia, the son of well-to-do

Jewish citizens, and died on 20 August 1915 in Bad Homburg. He attended grammar school in Breslau, completing his entrance requirement for university education in 1872. He then studied in Breslau as well as Strasbourg, whence he had followed the anatomist Wilhelm Waldeyer, who familiarized him with microscope technology. Already in Strasbourg a catchy phrase came into existence, which punned on a German proverb and his last name. The proverb, "Ehrlich währt am längsten" (literally, "honest lasts longest," that is, honesty is the best policy), was rendered "Ehrlich färbt am längsten" ("Ehrlich stains the longest"); this phrase accompanied him all his life. His dissertation at Leipzig University was entitled "Contributions to Theory and Practice of Histological Staining."

In 1878 the internist Friedrich Theodor von Frerichs asked Ehrlich to come to Berlin's Charité Hospital. There Ehrlich succeeded in introducing dyes into living cells. By means of this technique he managed to differentiate between leukocytes (white blood cells) and lymphocytes (typical cellular elements of lymph) and shortly afterward to classify them even further according to their stainability.

Ehrlich married Hedwig Pinkus, the daughter of a Jewish textile manufacturer from Silesia (1883). He received the title of professor (1884) two years before actually qualifying as a university teacher. His 1885 monograph entitled *The Requirement of Oxygen for the Organism* was accepted as a qualification to become university lecturer. After recovering completely from an encounter with tuberculosis, which had forced him to spend two years in Egypt, he returned to Berlin in 1889 and equipped a laboratory of his own.

In 1891 the Prussian government set up the Institute for Infectious Diseases with Robert Koch as director, and Paul Ehrlich moved his laboratory to the institute in that same year. At this time Emil Adolf von Behring and Shibasaburo Kitasato were reporting about their research on diphtheria and tetanus immunity. However, production of an immune serum turned out to be extremely difficult, and serum quality was inadequate. Robert Koch intervened and brought Behring together with Ehrlich.

Ehrlich had demonstrated that feeding small, steadily increasing amounts of poison to laboratory animals rendered them immune against an otherwise lethal dose. Owing to these studies he had developed the basic notions of active and passive immunity. The collaboration between Ehrlich and Behring resulted in the production of substantial amounts of a standardized serum used in German children's hospitals. The 1895 German Internists' Congress recommended the new medication unanimously, praising it as the best method of treatment hitherto offered. At last, a therapeutic concept had been discovered that would be used for years to come.

In order to ensure the standardization of the serums more effectively, a separate testing department was initially founded at the Institute for Infectious Diseases; not long after, it was reorganized as the Institute for Serum Research and Testing (1896). The institute was set up in an old bakery, and Ehrlich quipped that in order to conduct his research he needed only the most rudimentary equipment, like test tubes, a flame, and blotting paper. Yet in later years he struck a different note: "The guarantee of good results consists of the four Ps: proficiency, patience, providence, and pennies."

The year 1899 saw the opening in Frankfurt am Main of the Royal Institute for Experimental Therapy; Ehrlich was appointed director of the facility. Using funds from an endowment by the Frankfurt banker's widow Franziska Speyer, the Georg-Speyer House began operations in 1906 right next door to the institute, managed by Ehrlich at the same time.

During the period from 1890 to 1900 Ehrlich worked on his immunity and side-chain theories. In Ehrlich's view, apart from a performing nucleus there had to be side chains situated in the protoplasm; these side chains must have specific characteristics allowing them to bind certain toxins into the shape of receptors. Secreted into the circulation, these receptors acted as antitoxins or antibodies. Hypothetically, these second-order receptors would include, in addition to the haptophoric group (capable of combining), a zymphoric group (carrying enzymes) conducting the agglutinating, or binding activity of the antibodies. In postulating this idea of the lock-and-key reaction, Ehrlich had supplied the crucial theory for understanding immune response, even though in detail his concepts did not prove correct.

The side-chain theory also led Ehrlich in the direction of the *therapia magna sterilisans,* the search for the magic bullet. He was envisaging control of pathogens and toxins in the human body by means of a chemical substance that, just like the side chains, would have a special affinity to the disease-causing agent, yet would be effective in concentrations not harming the body.

Taking as a starting point atoxyl, which he had studied together with Kiyoshi Shiga, Ehrlich developed the notion of the development of pathogenic "drug resistance," conducted trials with arsenic compounds, and from May 1909 intensified the search in collaboration with his Japanese assistant Sukehachiro Hata. Preparation number 606 spelled success. In the summer of 1909 the Hoechst Company applied for a patent on arsphenamine, later known as salvarsan, used in the treatment of syphilis. In 1908 Paul Ehrlich received jointly with Élie Metchnikoff the Nobel prize for his work in immunology. This award—given to the main proponents of the humoral and, respectively, the cellular principles of antibody development—inadvertently showed the direction in which immunology was to evolve over the next one hundred years.

See also **Koch, Robert; Public Health; Syphilis.**

BIBLIOGRAPHY

Ehrlich, Paul. *Collected Papers.* Edited by Fred Himmelweit with Martha Marquardt, under the direction of Henry Dale. London and New York, 1956–1960.

Silverstein, Arthur M. *Paul Ehrlich's Receptor Immunology: The Magnificent Obsession.* San Diego, Calif., 2002.

Winau, Florian, Otto Westphal, and Rolf Winau. "Paul Ehrlich: In Search of the Magic Bullet." *Microbes and Infection* 6 (2004): 786–789.

ROLF WINAU

EIFFEL TOWER. Measuring 300.5 meters (986 feet) in height and weighing in at 6,300 metric tons (7,000 tons), the Eiffel Tower is the most famous landmark in France. It was constructed during the period from 1887 to 1889 by the French civil engineer Gustave Eiffel (1832–1923), whose name the monument has always borne. The tower was originally intended to serve as the gigantic entrance gate for the 1889 Exposition Universelle, but it quickly took on a life of its own. It is built on a large open field known as the Champ-de-Mars located in the seventh arrondissement in Paris. In shape, the tower consists of a base of about 10,300 square meters (2.54 acres) at ground level and a tapered vertical column. It is constructed entirely of perforated steel and cast iron, which gives it a vast, scaffold-like appearance. To soften its harsh metallic effect, Eiffel selectively adorned his creation with ornamental latticework in the French manner. The tower has three levels, each accessible by elevator. The first level includes a rectangular promenade with restaurants and souvenir shops, and the second originally housed editorial offices of the well-known newspaper *Le Figaro.* The third level contains Eiffel's private apartment and a tiny observation deck.

CONSTRUCTION AND DESIGN

The Eiffel family owned one of the most successful iron-building companies in France. Since the 1860s, Gustave Eiffel had a career designing and constructing metal bridges, viaducts, and railroad stations in France and elsewhere. He is also remembered for his construction of the interior metal scaffolding of the Statue of Liberty in New York City. The Eiffel Tower—or Eiffel's Tower, as it was first known—is now widely regarded as a masterpiece of modern design and construction. In sheer technical terms, Eiffel's achievement was astonishing: no structure of its kind had ever been attempted, and all calculations had to be accurate to one-tenth of a millimeter. Several prominent scientists maintained at the time that it was technically impossible to build such a tall structure. Likewise, construction workers had never worked at this height. Upon completion, the nearly 1,000-foot tower became the tallest building in the world, a distinction it retained for nearly forty years. (It was topped only in 1930 by the Chrysler Building in New York City.)

Contemporaries regarded the Eiffel Tower as above all "modern." It was constructed of metal, a human-made material associated with the Industrial Revolution, rather than wood or stone. Its impressive verticality overcame space and gravity. Unlike the Gothic cathedrals and Egyptian pyramids it was inevitably compared with, the tower was built quickly, in just two years, rather than over generations. It was designed not by an architect but a civil engineer. Unlike certain other major modern engineering projects—for example, the Panama Canal and Brooklyn Bridge—only a single worker lost his life in the Eiffel Tower's construction. Its observation deck, located a quarter mile up in the sky, provided an unprecedented bird's-eye view down onto the French capital, which had recently been extensively modernized by Baron Georges Haussmann, the powerful prefect of the Seine during the 1850s and 1860s. The tower also boasted a number of modern scientific and technological appurtenances, including elevators, a weather station, and, later, a radio antenna from which the first overseas broadcast from Paris was beamed to Casablanca, Morocco, in 1907. Not least of all, visitors to the exposition in 1889 were dazzled by powerful electric lights that radiated down from the tower and illuminated the fair and the city. At the end of the nineteenth century, the tower seemed the perfect spectacle of modernity.

CONTROVERSIES DURING PLANNING AND CONSTRUCTION

Although now a beloved symbol of French national identity, the Eiffel Tower was conceived and constructed in a controversial ideological context. During the last third of the nineteenth century, French governments mounted a major international exhibition every eleven years. The 1889 fair was special, however, in that it also celebrated the centennial of the 1789 Revolution. The Third Republic, France's first stable and sustained exercise in parliamentary democracy, was eighteen years old at the time. The Republic traced its historical and ideological lineage back to the First French Republic of the 1790s. Royalists and Bonapartists on the political Right were not enthusiastic about the exposition and its most prominent building. The revolutionary tricolor flag flew from the tower's summit. Unlike other Parisian landmarks, such as Notre-Dame Cathedral, the Louvre Palace, and the Arc de Triomphe, the tower did not incarnate the ideologies of Catholicism, or monarchy, or national military greatness. Rather,

The Eiffel Tower. Engraving, 1889. ©GIANNI DAGLI ORTI/CORBIS

it celebrated the spirit of science and technology, a spirit that underpinned the secular positivism of the Third Republic. In the French culture wars of the fin de siècle, it was often contrasted to the Sacré-Coeur basilica, which overlooked the city from the neighborhood of Montmartre and had been constructed a decade earlier by Catholic conservatives to atone for alleged national sins.

In the planning stages, there was also outspoken opposition to the tower on artistic grounds. Eiffel's bold and brilliant creation represented an entirely new aesthetic. "A tall, skinny pyramid of iron ladders," "this giant and disgraceful skeleton," "a hollow chandelier," and "a vertiginously ridiculous tower dominating Paris like a black, gigantic, factory chimney"—these were among the descriptions used to denigrate the architectural plan. Other critics bemoaned the tower as pointless and nonutilitarian.

Local inhabitants feared that it would collapse. Still others wondered if visitors would be able to breathe the rarefied atmosphere at the summit. The controversy hardened into formal opposition with the organization of the Committee of Three Hundred. Signatories of a petition to block construction included artistic personalities such as the architect Charles Garnier, the painter J.-L.-E. Meissonier, the poet Sully Prudhomme, and the novelist Alexandre Dumas. Most interesting was the charge that Eiffel's industrial style was "un-French," which seemed to mean that it did not draw on the national heritages of classical, Gothic, or baroque architecture. Many critics sincerely believed that the tower's construction would be an ugly commercial desecration of their beloved city.

SUBSEQUENT POPULAR SUCCESS

Despite public protests, Eiffel's vision was realized; inevitably it quickly became and remained a great popular success. The tower was the principal attraction at the 1889 exposition. Admirers labeled it "the eighth wonder of the world." Many viewers quickly came to see the tower as a monument to a great French tradition of structural engineering, which had been launched by Napoleon I at the beginning of the century with the founding of the École Polytechnique. Like his contemporaries Louis Pasteur and Marie Curie, Eiffel himself became a cultural hero of science. During the 1890s, new debates ensued: Could a great work of architecture be constructed in metal? Should the tower be regarded as a work of art or science or both? Ought the building to be preserved or dismantled after the exposition, as was originally intended? Ironically, by the early twentieth century, the tower was being memorialized tenderly by avant-garde painters, such as Georges Seurat, Henri Rousseau, and Robert Delaunay. "Eiffelomania" set in, and all manner of memorabilia were marketed.

By the 1920s, the Eiffel Tower was being dwarfed by American skyscrapers as the preeminent symbol of architectural modernism. The tower, however, was in fact a significant inspiration for these later constructions: it was after all the first high-rise steel-frame structure, and developers and architects quickly conceived the idea of building horizontal floors on such a vertical structural frame. Eiffel's "symphony in iron" remains the symbol of the French capital across the world. During the 2000 millennium celebrations, the French government chose a fireworks display at the tower as the national image to broadcast around the world, and in the wake of the New York City terrorist attacks on 11 September 2001, the tower was the first nongovernmental building to be secured in France.

See also **Fin de Siècle; France; Haussmann, Georges-Eugène; Napoleon III; Paris.**

BIBLIOGRAPHY

Barthes, Roland. "The Eiffel Tower." In his *The Eiffel Tower and Other Mythologies,* 3–17. Translated by Richard Howard. New York, 1979.

Evenson, Norma. *Paris: A Century of Change, 1878–1978.* New Haven, Conn., 1979.

Harriss, Joseph. *The Tallest Tower: Eiffel and the Belle Epoque.* Boston, 1975.

Hervé, Lucien. *The Eiffel Tower.* New York, 2003. Includes photographs by Hervé, with an introduction by Barry Bergdoll.

Levin, Miriam R. *When the Eiffel Tower Was New: French Visions of Progress at the Centennial of the Revolution.* South Hadley, Mass., 1989.

Loyrette, Henri. *Gustave Eiffel.* Translated by Rachel and Susan Gomme. New York, 1985.

———. "The Eiffel Tower." In *Realms of Memory: The Construction of the French Past.* Vol. 3, 349–371. Edited by Pierre Nora. English-language edition edited by Lawrence D. Kritzman and translated by Arthur Goldhammer. New York, 1998.

Sagan, Françoise, and Winnie Denker. *The Eiffel Tower: A Centenary Celebration, 1889–1989.* New York, 1989.

MARK S. MICALE

EINSTEIN, ALBERT (1879–1955), German-born physicist.

Albert Einstein, the only son of Hermann and Pauline (Koch) Einstein, was born on 14 March 1879 in Ulm, Germany. In the summer of 1880 the family moved to Munich where Hermann and his youngest brother became partners in running an electrochemical factory, and where, in 1881, Albert's sister, Maria ("Maja"), was born. Albert, who was slow in learning to speak, nevertheless manifested, as a young child, a prescient interest in magnetism, mathematics, and the electrical devices in his father's shop. At the age of six he began attending a nearby school, the Catholic Peterschule, where he was the only Jew among over seventy classmates. Four years later he was accepted by Luitpold Gymnasium, and the school's principal later claimed, contrary to a popular myth, that Albert was actually a good student. Einstein's own recollections were that he was fond of some teachers and subjects, especially geometry, but he disliked this secondary school's regimented learning.

In the summer of 1894 Hermann, whose business failed because of lost contracts to large firms, moved his family to Pavia in northern Italy where he and his brother began another company, but Albert was left in Munich to complete his gymnasium education. Lonely and unhappy, he convinced authorities that he was suffering from "neurasthenic exhaustion," dropped out of school, and joined his family in Italy. After a period of recuperation he took and failed the entrance examination for the Federal Institute of Technology (or Polytechnic) in Zurich, Switzerland, necessitating a remedial program at a cantonal school in Aarau. In 1896, after passing the entrance examination, he began a four-year program in physics and mathematics during which he did well in courses that he liked and poorly in courses he disliked. He befriended Marcel Grossmann, whose excellent course notes permitted Einstein to pursue private studies of the works of such scientists as James Clerk Maxwell and Ernst Mach. He also met and fell in love with Mileva Marič, an Orthodox Christian Serb who was preparing, like Albert, to become a physics teacher. After Einstein received his Polytechnic diploma in 1900, he was unable to get a job as a physicist and made do with temporary teaching positions. His situation was complicated by Mileva's pregnancy. She returned to her parents' home in Hungary where their daughter Lieserl was born (her subsequent fate remains a mystery). When Marcel Grossmann's father helped Einstein obtain a position as an examiner at the Patent Office in Bern, he was able to marry Mileva on 6 January 1903.

CAREER AND ACHIEVEMENTS

During his tenure as a patent clerk, Einstein, in his spare time, made discoveries that would lead scho-

Albert Einstein. ©CORBIS

lars to rank him with such revolutionary figures as Isaac Newton and Charles Darwin because, like them, he transformed our basic conceptions of the world. He began publishing papers in which he offered insightful interpretations of the scientific observations of others, and in 1905, the year he received his doctorate from the University of Zurich, he published significant papers on Brownian motion, the photoelectric effect, and special relativity.

The Scottish botanist Robert Brown had observed the random zigzagging of pollen grains in water, but Einstein was able to explain these apparently chaotic motions in terms of the fluctuations of the water molecules hitting these particles. His mathematical analysis, which allowed him to determine the number of water molecules in a specific volume, helped convince skeptical physicists of the reality of the atom.

Physicists had earlier found that when light hit a metal plate, electrons were ejected (the photoelectric effect), and the speed of these electrons did not depend on the brightness of the incident beam. Einstein explained this photoelectric effect, which was inexplicable in terms of the wave theory of light, by expanding Max Planck's quantum theory to include light falling on the metal as packets (or quanta) of radiation (later called photons). Einstein would receive the 1921 Nobel prize in physics for this explanation.

The two papers on the special theory of relativity that Einstein wrote in 1905, his "wonderful year," presented a new view of matter, motion, time, and the universe that revolutionized physics. He called this theory "special" because it dealt only with uniformly moving systems in which he assumed that all physical laws are invariant and the speed of light is a constant. He then proved that two widely separated observers assign different times to the same event (the relativity of simultaneity), that a rapidly moving clock runs slow, and that an object's inertial mass increases with speed—leading to the century's most famous equation, $E = mc^2$, which related energy (E), mass (m), and and the speed of light (c).

Einstein went on to extend his ideas to non-uniformly moving systems (the general theory of relativity). This task, based on the equivalence of gravitational and inertial mass, was much more difficult than the special theory, but during the second decade of the twentieth century he explained how matter influences the curvature of space, leading to his prediction that a light ray from a distant star would follow a curved path near the sun. When, after the end of World War I, this prediction was tested in 1919, it was confirmed by observations made during a solar eclipse, an event that captured the public imagination and turned Einstein into a symbol of the scientific genius of the twentieth century.

While Einstein was working on the special and general theories, he and Mileva had two sons, but the marriage was troubled by his adulteries and his increasing emotional separation from his wife. The success of his theories had led to his leaving the patent office and to a series of academic positions, principally in Switzerland, but in 1917 he became the prestigious director of the Kaiser Wilhelm Institute of the University of Berlin, an event that resulted in his permanent separation from Mileva, who retained custody of their boys, and to their divorce in February of 1919. Four months later he married his cousin, Elsa Einstein Löwenthal, a

widow with two daughters. During the 1920s and for the rest of his life Einstein worked to generalize his theory of gravity so that it would include electromagnetic phenomena (the unified field theory), but unlike the special and general theories, he failed in his many efforts to effect this unification.

Now internationally famous, he traveled around the world, and it was in 1933, during one of his trips, that the Nazis, who had assumed political power, deprived Einstein of his German citizenship and confiscated his property. He emigrated to the United States and took up residence in Princeton, New Jersey, where he had an appointment to the Institute of Advanced Study. Eventually his stepdaughter Margot and his sister Maja joined him and Elsa. Concerned about the growing military power of Nazi Germany, Einstein signed a letter to President Franklin D. Roosevelt in the summer of 1939, which played an important role in the origin of the "Manhattan Project" to develop an atomic bomb. Einstein became an American citizen in 1940 and served as an adviser to the U.S. Navy during World War II. In the postwar period he campaigned against nuclear weapons, championed world government, and refused an offer to become president of Israel. Elsa had died in 1936, and his sister's death in 1951 left him emotionally distraught. A ruptured aortic aneurysm caused his own death on 18 April 1955 in a Princeton hospital. His passing did not mean the end of his influence, and physicists around the world continue to pursue "Einstein's dream" of the unification of the basic forces of the universe.

See also **Mach, Ernst; Maxwell, James Clerk; Physics; Planck, Max.**

BIBLIOGRAPHY

Primary Sources

Einstein, Albert. *Autobiographical Notes: A Centennial Edition.* LaSalle, Ill., 1979. This brief autobiography was first published in *Albert Einstein: Philosopher-Scientist,* edited by Paul Arthur Schilpp (Evanston, Ill., 1949).

———. *The Collected Papers of Albert Einstein.* 9 vols to date. Princeton, N.J., 1987–. This massive project, now under the general editorship of Diana Kormos Buchwald, aims to provide as complete an account as possible of Einstein's public and private writings. Introductions and scholarly apparatus are in English, and every document appears in its original language, but each volume is also supplemented by English translations of the non-English materials.

Secondary Sources

Fölsing, Albrecht. *Albert Einstein: A Biography.* Translated by Ewald Osers. New York, 1997. Originally published in German in 1993, this biography has been called the best general treatment of Einstein's life.

Pais, Abraham. *"Subtle Is the Lord—": The Science and the Life of Albert Einstein.* Oxford, U.K., and New York, 1982. An excellent scientific biography written by a physicist who knew Einstein and had complete access to his archives.

ROBERT J. PARADOWSKI

ELECTRICITY. During the last decades of the nineteenth century, electricity brought Europeans a wide variety of innovations that ultimately improved the lives of most people. Among other things, electricity made possible the undersea cable, the electromagnetic telegraph, and the telephone. It gradually transformed industry, transportation, and for many people, home life.

Although some awareness of electricity had existed as far back in time as classical Greece and the Renaissance, in the eighteenth century observations and discoveries, including those of Benjamin Franklin, became more systematic. In 1820 Hans Oersted (1777–1851), a Danish physicist, noted that a strong current moving through a wire could cause a compass to move, and that currents were mutually attractive if they moved in the same direction but had the opposite effect if they moved in different directions. Oersted's English colleague Michael Faraday (1791–1867) investigated the effects of electromagnetism, discoveries that later influenced the development of electric generators and transformers. In 1866 Werner von Siemens (1816–1892), a German, invented the first dynamo, which made possible the production of great amounts of electrical energy. In 1879 the American Thomas Edison (1847–1931) invented the incandescent electric lamp. Soon after, the development of electric alternators and transformers and improvements in cable and insulation made it possible for electric power to be generated and diffused. The first electrical power stations started up in 1881. By the end of the century, electric streetlights made it easier to find one's way around town at night, and electric tramways could be found in a number of cities. Still, in much of Europe electricity remained a luxury identified with grand hotels, department stores, and wealthy neighborhoods.

European economic growth and particularly industry benefited from electricity during the last two decades of the nineteenth century, in part because electric power could be carried quite easily, replacing water power, coal, and gas in many industries, including textiles, steel, and construction. German industries in particular benefited early on from the transformation effected by electricity. Gradually in many European countries, particularly in western Europe, electric sewing machines, refrigerators, fans, and vacuum cleaners were available to those who could afford them.

The first electric lights were not always located in cities: often the pioneers in the field were factories, as was the case with the Finlayson factory in Tampare, Finland, in 1882 and in Resita, Romania, in a metallurgical factory that same year. As a rule, the new lighting system was first tried out in the smaller factories before bids were extended to large cities. One of the first initiatives of the kind occurred in Hungary. Following the successful modernization of corn mills, in 1878 a young engineer, Károly Zipernowsky, was hired by the Ganz company in Budapest to carry out research with a view toward laying the foundations of an electrotechnological industry in central Europe. However, as occurred in many cities, the Budapest municipality initially rejected the idea of switching from gas to electric lights, reluctant to allocate public money to a technological innovation that remained rather mysterious. The Ganz company nevertheless managed to take the market of public lighting, prevailing over Edison's company (all the more so, as Zipernowsky and his colleagues had made the technological choice of alternating current, which guaranteed more efficient transport). Thanks to its system Ganz eventually served Vienna, Innsbruck, Milan, Turin, Cologne, Lucerne, Sofia, Belgrade, and Stockholm as well as Budapest. In 1906, 44 percent of the electric power produced in Hungary was used for lighting, with Budapest accounting for 60 percent of the electric power produced. In Bohemia, Prague had the largest thermo-electric power plant in the country (coal was very cheap). Setting aside these two countries, use of electric power to provide lighting was not as prevalent in central European nations as it was in western Europe. However, one must consider that a plant providing a city with power used essentially for lighting is in fact underused (it runs at only 10 to 20 percent of its full capacity); to make electric power profitable, providers either had to serve only those areas with high purchasing power or find new markets, such as industry or public transports.

Clearly in these early years electric power was more costly than gas, but in 1882 its Russian advocates promoted it by pointing out that it burned regularly, gave off less heat, did not pollute the air, and did not emit a whizzing sound. All these arguments were used in European cities, especially with regard to gas-powered lights (or those burning kerosene or oil, two other fuels used to provide light in urban areas). In public places such as theaters, which were flooded with light, the heat and smell from lights were as a rule considered a nuisance. Thus with the spread of electric power came an enhanced sense of urban glamour, particularly in capital cities. When world exhibitions were held (for example, in Paris in 1889 and 1900), electricity demonstrated that the capital was a modern city. When Romania became an independent country after the Russo-Turkish War of 1877–1878, Bucharest did its best to show that it had achieved the status of European capital. In this case authorities strongly supported the first attempts to provide the city with electric lighting, and in 1882 the city accepted a proposal made by the Austrian subsidiary of an English company. However, the most prestigious installation in Europe undeniably was the illumination of Berlin, in particular that of Unter den Linden, together with that of other major thoroughfares in the city. The management of the BEW electric company (a subsidiary of the powerful industrial firm AEG) noticed the public's preference for electric lights, conducive to a livelier nightlife. And in England, the new technology was used to create a lavish show of electrical effects: for Queen Victoria's Golden Jubilee in 1887, electric candelabra reproducing the colors of the rainbow and electric crowns placed on the tops of buildings lined London's streets.

Major cities provided opportunities for comparing the various lighting systems (gas versus electric power, or contrasting electric systems with one another). For example, electric arc lamps and incandescent lamps were compared. The first device made it possible to illuminate large spaces such as public gardens, parks, and squares, but its main drawback was that it was very unpleasant to the eye and could not be divided into smaller lighting units. Conversely, incandescent lamps made the new light much easier to use. At first, when cities put up arc lamps, as was done in Vienna in 1882, the nearby streets that were still lit by gas lamps seemed quite dark by comparison. Arc lights were so powerful that some proposed projects involved lighting a whole city with one single source of light. Many city councils tested gas and electrical systems in nearby streets, as was done in Paris in the 1880s. Some cities chose one system over the other, while other cities allowed the two systems to exist side by side; arc lamps and gas lamps coexisted harmoniously, for example, in Berlin. In St. Petersburg in 1914, 47 percent of street lamps burned gas, 37 percent burned kerosene, and 16 percent worked on electric power. In Russia electric power faced competition from kerosene lamps rather than from gas because the country produced cheap oil in large quantities. Before the Bolshevik Revolution, most electrically powered installations were located in Moscow and St. Petersburg but also in Baku, which is surprising unless one considers the rapid expansion of this oil-producing city at the close of the nineteenth century. Finally, it must be noted that all the European capitals boomed with the "war of systems," opposing the proponents of continuous electric current (Edison, to name one), who argued that it was safe, and proponents of alternating electric current (Westinghouse and Ganz), which might have resulted in city dwellers running major risks (comparable to those of lightning). The controversy died out when electric power no longer was produced inside towns but farther and farther afield, in which case alternating current became a necessity, and more particularly three-phase current.

Throughout the nineteenth century, the urban consumer had become more demanding, believing that the city must become more and more pleasant and the streets more and more illuminated. Electricity answered this desire by providing a form of lighting that was both easy to use and hygienic, and by the early twentieth century not only lights but also other electric-powered conveniences were passing from the status of a luxury to that of a basic need.

See also **Cities and Towns; Industrial Revolution, Second; Science and Technology; Transportation and Communications.**

BIBLIOGRAPHY

Beltran, Alain, and Patrice A. Carré. *La fée et la servante: La société française face à l'électricité XIX–Xxème siècle.* Paris, 1991.

Canby, Edward Tatnall. *History of Electricity.* New York, 1963.

Coopersmith, Jonathan. *The Electrification of Russia 1880–1926.* Ithaca, N.Y., 1992.

Hannah, Leslie. *Electricity before Nationalisation: A Study of the Development of the Electricity Supply Industry in Britain to 1948.* London, 1979.

Hughes, Thomas P. *Networks of Power: Electrification in Western Society 1880–1930.* Baltimore, Md., and London, 1988.

Marvin, Carolyn. *When Old Technologies Were New: Thinking about Electric Communication in the Nineteenth Century.* Oxford, U.K., 1988.

Mori, Giorgio, ed. *Storia dell'industria elettrica in Italia.* Vol. 1: *Le origini (1882–1914).* Rome, 1992.

Morus, Iwan Rhys. *Frankenstein's Children: Electricity, Exhibition, and Experiment in Early-Nineteenth-Century London.* Princeton, N.J., 1998.

———. *Michael Faraday and the Electrical Century.* Cambridge, U.K., 2004.

Myllyntaus, Timo. *Electrifying Finland: The Transfer of a New Technology into a Late Industrialising Economy.* Houndmills, U.K., and Helsinki, 1991.

Paquier, Serge. *Histoire de l'électricité en Suisse.* Vol. 1: *La dynamique d'un petit pays européen 1875–1939.* Geneva, 1998.

ALAIN BELTRAN

ELIOT, GEORGE (Mary Anne Evans; 1819–1880), English novelist.

Born Mary Anne Evans in 1819, George Eliot lived the first thirty years of her life in rural Warwickshire, England, part of the English Midlands that later became the setting for her novels. The youngest of five children, she took over the duties of housekeeping soon after her mother, Christiana Pearson, died in 1835, when Mary Anne was still in her teens. Her father, Robert Evans, managed Newdigate Estate, and when he retired to the nearby provincial center of Coventry in 1841, she went along, caring for him until his death in 1849. During that time, she worked on her fluency in foreign languages—which included Latin, Greek, German, Italian, French, and Hebrew—studied literature, and began reading German higher criticism of the Bible. She was encouraged in this self-imposed intellectual regimen by Charles and Caroline Bray, the centers of the local circle of intellectuals. Through them, she was introduced to the much larger community of London intellectuals who visited the Brays. In 1851 she changed her name to the less provincial sounding "Marian Evans," and moved to London, where she would reside until her death. She wrote for and, beginning in 1852, became the anonymous editor of the influential *Westminster Review,* a position that brought her into contact with new developments in European philosophy, science, and literature.

The following year, at age thirty-four, the fledgling writer fell in love with George Henry Lewes (1817–1878), then editor of a radical London weekly, the *Leader.* A protégé of the philosopher John Stuart Mill (1806–1873) and an important popularizer of Auguste Comte's (1798–1857) philosophy of positivism; he became well known for his *Life and Works of Goethe* (1855) and published widely as a critic, scientist, and philosopher. Unfortunately Lewes was married, and though separated from Agnes Lewes, divorce was an impossibility. After 1854, he and Eliot lived openly together in a companionship that scandalized English society. As a result Marian Evans Lewes (as she now signed her name) was largely excluded from polite society, although later in life her reputation as a writer of considerable wisdom gave her a renewed social acceptability. Their life together was characterized by annual trips to the Continent, with visits to Germany, France, Spain, and Italy until Lewes's death in 1878. Two years later Eliot caused another scandal when she married the much younger John Cross (1840–1924), who later wrote her first biography. She died less than a year after the wedding, on 22 December 1880, and is buried next to Lewes in London's Highgate Cemetery.

EARLY WORKS

Her first published volume was not fiction but a translation of the German philosopher David Friedrich Strauss's *Das Leben Jesu, kritisch bearbeitet* (1846; *The Life of Jesus, Critically Examined*). Eliot was much interested in higher criticism, which appealed to her realist values by historicizing the Bible, and in 1854 she published a translation of Ludwig Feuerbach's *Das Wesen des Christenthums* (*The Essence of Christianity*). Intermittently, she translated from Latin the works of Baruch de Spinoza (1632–1677), the Renaissance philosopher and forerunner of higher criticism. Her version of his *Ethics* went unpublished until 1981.

Eliot developed her own views on realism and fiction in her writing for the *Westminster Review* during the 1850s, before her relatively late appearance as a novelist toward the end of the decade, at age thirty-seven. "We want to be taught to feel, not for the heroic artisan or the sentimental peasant, but for the peasant in all his coarse apathy, and the artisan in all his suspicious selfishness," she wrote in 1856, expressing an insistence on factual accuracy that became a key element in her realism (1963, p. 271). She began writing fiction that same year and three stories in *Blackwood's Magazine* signed "George Eliot" were the immediate result, soon republished as *Scenes from Clerical Life* (1858). The pseudonym was in part a tribute to her partner, but the choice of a male pen name is thought to be a pragmatic response to the practices of reviewers at the time, who rarely took works by women seriously, a problem she discussed in an important *Westminster Review* article in 1856, "Silly Novels by Lady Novelists." Her stories were praised as the voice of a major new writer, and because of their success the identity of the author (along with her unsanctioned marriage) was soon unmasked.

NOVELS

She cemented her critical reputation with her first two novels. Set in the English Midlands, *Adam Bede* (1859) focuses on a rural carpenter who is hopelessly in love with a local farm girl. Beautiful, shallow, and none too smart, Hetty Sorrel is the first of a female type that reappears throughout Eliot's fiction. The character nonetheless receives a compassionate treatment, and the narrator's sympathy for Hetty as she commits infanticide illustrates a hallmark of Eliot's style as a realist. In *The Mill on the Floss* (1859), Eliot adds a historical dimension to rural life that was absent from *Adam Bede*. The action illustrates the broader pattern of social change caused by England's transition from an agricultural to a commercial society. The novel's "spitfire" heroine, Maggie Tulliver, is Eliot's first extensive engagement with the limited possibilities available to women and a model for subsequent Eliot heroines.

Her two middle novels distance themselves in different ways from the English Midlands. *Silas Marner: The Weaver of Raveloe* (1861) injects a dose of lyrical fantasy into the story of a rural outcast who finds a new home in another village. *Romola* (1862–1863) is a historical fiction of a young woman's disastrous marriage set in fifteenth-century Italy.

The late novels see a return to the familiar Midlands setting. *Felix Holt: The Radical* (1866) thematizes the effects of the electoral reform bill of 1832 on a working-class community, but emotionally it centers on the tragic and rich portrait of Mrs. Transome. *Middlemarch: A Story of Provincial Life* (1872) revisits the same historical setting, but employs a larger canvas to paint Victorian social issues, particularly that of the Woman Question, a more extreme problem in England than on the Continent. *Middlemarch* was also a technical breakthrough for the writer, who successfully masters the intricacies of a double-plotted novel, in which two independent stories intersect to convey a broader sense of community than either could do alone. The strategy reappears in her last novel *Daniel Deronda* (1876). Together with *Middlemarch*, this work marks the high point of the Victorian realist novel. While partially set in the Midlands, this last novel is also her first to use London, a city she knew well, as a setting. Deronda is a young man of unknown birth who slowly discovers and then embraces his Jewish heritage. Gwendolyn Harleth is a beautiful, headstrong, and spoiled young woman whose family loses its fortune; her choice to marry for money, rather than love, proves unbearable.

In addition to novels, essays, and reviews, Eliot also published poetry; her novel-length *The Spanish Gypsy: A Poem* (1868) has thematic similarities to *Daniel Deronda* as an exploration of Victorian racial theory. Few know how to classify her final work, *Impressions of Theophrastus Such* (1879), a fascinating series of character sketches that can readily be seen as her most innovative work of fiction.

See also **Dickens, Charles; Gaskell, Elizabeth; Mill, John Stuart.**

BIBLIOGRAPHY

Primary Sources

Eliot, George. *Essays.* Edited by Thomas Pinney. New York, 1963. The standard collection of her essays and reviews.

———. *The Journals of George Eliot.* Edited by Margaret Harris and Judith Johnston. Cambridge, U.K., 1998. The first complete edition of the journals she maintained from 1854 to her death.

Secondary Sources

Ashton, Rosemary. *George Eliot: A Life.* London, 1996. An authoritative critical biography in which Eliot emerges as more independent and strong-willed than in earlier biographies.

Beer, Gillian. *George Eliot.* Bloomington, Ind., 1986. A thoughtful examination of Eliot's major novels as the products of a woman writer.

Bodenheimer, Rosemarie. *The Real Life of Mary Ann Evans: George Eliot, Her Letters and Fiction.* Ithaca, N.Y., 1994. An important study that finds her novels more revealing of her emotional life than her letters.

Levine, George, ed. *The Cambridge Companion to George Eliot.* Cambridge, U.K., 2001. An informative series of essays by prominent Eliot scholars on her novels and ideas about science, religion, politics, philosophy, and gender.

Rignall, John, ed. *Oxford Reader's Companion to George Eliot.* Oxford, U.K., 2001. A fact-filled encyclopedia of biographical, historical, and critical information.

PETER MELVILLE LOGAN

ELLIS, HAVELOCK

ELLIS, HAVELOCK (1858–1939), British author of the seven-volume *Studies in the Psychology of Sex.*

Henry Havelock Ellis was a major figure in the development of sexology and the popularization of a new vision of sexuality. The son of a sea captain, he traveled widely with his father in his youth, and spent some time in Australia as a schoolteacher in the outback. There he had a mystic revelation that led him to devote his life to the elucidation of the mysteries of sex. He returned to London to study medicine as a necessary preliminary, though once qualified he practiced very little, supporting himself instead by literary journalism and editing. He was involved with radical and progressive circles in London, and though a shy and retiring man had an extensive and international community of friends and colleagues.

He was already planning his massive study, and was shortly to publish the "proem" *Man and Woman* (1894), surveying current understanding of the differences between sexes, when in 1892 he was approached by the writer and critic John Addington Symonds about including a study of homosexuality in the Contemporary Science Series that he was editing. Ellis's own thoughts had already been independently turned to this question by the discovery that his wife, Edith Lees Ellis (1861–1916), whom he had married in 1891, was predominantly lesbian, as well as through his association with Edward Carpenter, the early advocate of the rights of homosexuals. However, before the collaborative volume, *Sexual Inversion,* was completed, Symonds died. British publishers were reluctant to be associated with the venture, although a German edition appeared in 1896, until a shady character calling himself de Villiers produced an English edition through his Watford University Press, early in 1897. Family pressures led Symonds's executor, Horatio Brown, to buy up and destroy the entire first printing, and to persuade Ellis to remove all traces of Symonds's involvement. This revised version appeared in November 1897 under Ellis's name. A police detective purchased a copy (only the third one sold) from George Bedborough, who was under police surveillance due to suspected anarchist associations; then applied for a warrant for Bedborough's arrest for selling of "a certain lewd wicked bawdy scandalous and obscene libel." Although a defense committee was formed, Bedborough struck a deal, and the question of whether or not *Sexual Inversion* was obscene was never addressed. Ellis was thus unable to argue in its defense: devastated by this outcome, he became more cautious, even reclusive.

He was not deterred from his monumental task, turning out a further five substantial volumes by 1910: indeed he initially saw the publication of *Sex in Relation to Society* in that year as the culmination of his efforts, though a further volume of additional studies and observations appeared in 1927. His formidable erudition was evident in the massive accumulation of data from the literature covering a wide range of disciplines and in many languages contained in this work. Although volume two of the *Studies* appeared under de Villiers's aegis, subsequent volumes and later editions were published by a reputable American publisher, the F. A. Davis Company of Philadelphia. The seven volumes of *Studies in the Psychology of Sex* have never all been published in the United Kingdom. Although copies of the U.S. edition did circulate, booksellers were cautious about selling it directly to members of the public, rather than to doctors or lawyers, and its expense also limited sales. More accessible versions of Ellis's ideas were disseminated through his extensive journalism in periodicals and newspapers on both sides of the Atlantic and numerous volumes of essays.

Ellis's work was characterized by a broad tolerance for diversity: he perceived variations in sexual practices and orientation as existing along a spectrum rather than being clearly divided. He was strongly committed to an agenda of education and enlightenment, rather than any form of compulsion or legislation. After the revelation of his wife's same-sex desires, both partners pursued relationships outside the marriage. Ellis had intimate friendships, often lasting many years, with a number of women, several of them distinguished writers or social reformers, in spite, or perhaps because, of the reportedly unassertive quality of his sexuality and his interest in urolagnia (women urinating).

In 1938 he received the distinction of being awarded the Fellowship of the Royal College of Physicians under a special regulation, a medical honor seldom accorded to those with medical qualifications as humble as his. By the time of his death in 1939 he was a recognized and respected figure, one of the icons of modernity, whose name features as a signifier of the modern and enlightened in a number of literary works and memoirs of the period. He remains a figure of considerable historical interest both for the development of sexology in England and on the international scene. The extent and nature of his influence is a continued topic of debate. It has been plausibly suggested that in the United Kingdom his theories of homosexuality remained more powerful than Freudian concepts well into the post–World War II era, and played an important role in the debates on decriminalization that affected the final report of the Wolfenden Committee and thus led, ultimately, to the Act of 1967 embodying the Committee's recommendations.

See also **Freud, Sigmund; Homosexuality and Lesbianism; Krafft-Ebing, Richard von; Sexuality.**

BIBLIOGRAPHY

Grosskurth, Phyllis. *Havelock Ellis: A Biography.* London, 1980.

Nottingham, Chris. *The Pursuit of Serenity: Havelock Ellis and the New Politics.* Amsterdam, 1999.

Rowbotham, Sheila, and Jeffrey Weeks. *Socialism and the New Life: The Personal and Sexual Politics of Edward Carpenter and Havelock Ellis.* London, 1977.

LESLEY A. HALL

EMANCIPATION OF THE SERFS.
See Serfs, Emancipation of.

EMIGRATION.

International migration was a major feature of the history of Europe in the long nineteenth century. More than 50 million people left Europe for overseas destinations and another 10 million left European Russia for Siberia. Similar numbers left other continents. The effect of this movement was a major redistribution of the European population. In 1815, for example, only about 4 percent of people of European origin lived outside Europe (or Siberia). By 1914, that number had

TABLE 1

European emigration, 1830–1914	
Countries of origin (1914 boundaries)	Number (in millions)
Britain	11.5
Italy	10.0
Ireland	7.0
Germany	5.0
Spain/Portugal	4.5
All Europe	52.0

The small amount of emigration before 1830 was rarely recorded.

SOURCE: Baines, *Emigration from Europe*, p. 3, adapted from Wilcox and Ferenczi, *International Migrations*, pp. 230–231.

TABLE 2

European overseas emigration, 1830–1914	
Destination countries	Number (in millions)
United States	33
Argentina	5
Canada	5
Brazil	5
Australia	4
Total	54

The discrepancy between numbers for individual countries and the total is due to variations in the definition of "immigrants" in the available data.

SOURCE: Baines, *Emigration from Europe*, p. 2, adapted from Wilcox and Ferenczi, *International Migrations*, pp. 230–231; Mitchell, *European Historical Statistics*, pp. 139–147.

increased to 21 percent, and it continued to rise through the next century. There were also as many emigrants from the rest of the world, and in some respects emigration rates in this period were higher than those of the early twenty-first century. For example, in 1914 a larger proportion of the world's population lived in a different country than the one in which they were born than is the case in 2005. (This is partly because of the growth of restrictions.)

There are many reasons why emigrants left Europe. Some of these—for example, German sects or British Mormons—left because of religious persecution and often established religious communities in the New World. Some left to escape military service, for example in the Austro-Hungarian army. Some—for example, Jews in Russian Poland—left to escape deadly persecution. Some were resettled by landlords anxious to develop their land, as in the case of the Scottish Highlanders. Some were transported criminals, especially to Australia. And finally, some left to escape famine, of which the Irish Potato Famine of 1846–1848 was by far the most important.

The main reason, however, why international migration was so high was economic—what is now called globalization. Emigration rates were relatively low in the early nineteenth century but increased in the second half as transport costs fell and as international trade and capital mobility increased. The key effect of globalization on emigration was that it linked Europe with economies that were resource abundant and labor scarce. Earnings in these countries were much higher than in Europe, which, in comparison, was labor abundant and resource scarce. Hence both labor (emigrants) and capital (investment) flowed to the so-called regions of recent settlement—the United States, Canada, Australia, and Argentina.

DIMENSIONS AND CHARACTER OF EUROPEAN EMIGRATION

There are some data problems, particularly those concerning the definition of "emigrant," but the main dimensions of European emigration are clear. Table 1 shows that about 52 million people left Europe for overseas destinations between 1830, when sufficient data are available, and 1914. More than half of these emigrants came from only three countries: 22 percent (11.5 million) from Britain, 19 percent (10 million) from Italy, and 13 percent (7 million) from Ireland.

The emigrants went to a relatively limited number of destinations. Table 2 shows that virtually all the European emigrants went to only five countries: 61 percent (33 million) to the United States; nearly 10 percent (5 million) went to each of Canada, Argentina, and Brazil; and 7 percent (4 million) went to Australia. Only a tiny number of European emigrants went to the nonwhite colonies.

Finally, table 3 shows which European countries produced proportionately the greatest number of emigrants. It is based on the mean emigration rates of the highest four decades. This is a little arbitrary because the eastern European countries had very high emigration rates but only at the end of the period, when emigration was curtailed by World War I. Table 3 shows that Ireland had the highest emigration rate, followed by Norway, Italy, Britain, Sweden, Spain, and Portugal. The Netherlands, Belgium, and France had very low emigration rates.

Why was emigration low from many poor countries and high from several rich countries? This is best explained by considering the way an emigration stream developed. Most emigration was governed by the economic benefits of migration and the costs of achieving them. Initially, most people were too poor to emigrate. The cost of travel and the income forgone before they found employment in another country was too high. Moreover, by definition, there were few previous emigrants to help them. (This is why the Finnish famine of 1816 led to little emigration compared with the Irish famine thirty years later.) But as the European economies grew, potential emigrants were richer; transport became cheaper, and crucially, information became more abundant. (Because growth was related to urbanization, one consequence was that more emigrants came from urban areas.) Unsurprisingly, European emigration spread from west to east. In the early nineteenth century, Britain and Ireland experienced large-scale emigration. Emigration then spread to Germany (i.e., the German states), Scandinavia, and Italy. By the early twentieth century it had spread to Hungary, Poland, and the Balkans. There was a relationship between the onset of large-scale emigration and the extent to which an economy was integrated into the international economy. (This was not a sufficient condition, however. Several developed western European countries had little emigration.)

The majority of emigrants traveled individually or as part of a family. Group emigration was largely confined to the early years. And relatively few traveled with a subsidy. Hence a decision to emigrate may be characterized as an individual (or family) decision that compares future income (widely defined) if he or she stayed at home with future income if he or she migrated, taking account of the costs of moving. Annual emigration rates from several countries have been related to economic variables (such as employment and wage differences), which confirm that economic motives dominated the decision to emigrate.

The "relative income" explanation has to be modified in two important respects. The first is that

TABLE 3

Emigration rates per year per thousand population (1914 boundaries)

Highest incidence

Ireland	12.0
Norway	7.0
Italy	6.0
Britain	5.0
Sweden	5.0
Portugal	5.0
Spain	5.0

Lowest incidence

Netherlands	0.7
Belgium	0.5
France	0.2

SOURCE: Baines, *Emigration from Europe*, p. 4, adapted from Wilcox and Ferenczi, *International Migrations*, pp. 200–201; Mitchell, *European Historical Statistics*, pp. 150–153.

it does not account for the very large fluctuations in annual emigration rates. Obviously the long-run benefits of emigration were much the same if an emigrant decided to leave in one year rather than another. But annual emigration rates could fluctuate by plus- or minus-50 percent—in other words, much more than could be predicted by differences in the emigrant's expected lifetime income. This was mainly because emigrants could not afford to be out of the labor market for very long. The emigrant had to get to the port, find a passage, and crucially, find employment once he or she arrived. Overall this could take three months or even more when emigrants traveled by sail. If job prospects were poor, emigration would be too risky. An important observation follows: the fluctuations in annual emigration rates were common to all countries experiencing emigration at the time, and they conform to economic conditions in the destination countries. The key peaks were in 1854, 1873, 1883, 1907, and 1913. This means that information about economic conditions in the destination countries must have been available to most potential emigrants.

The second problem is that emigration rates from different European regions varied considerably. Emigration rates from the Italian regions of Calabria, the Abruzzi, and Sicily, for example, were eight to ten times those from Emilia-Romagna and Sardinia. Other famous emigration regions

The Old World and the New. A political cartoon from 1854 reflects Irish disillusionment with emigration. In the panel on the left, a man contemplates sailing for the United States; on the right, he considers returning to Ireland. ©BETTMANN/CORBIS

include Cornwall (England), Berslagen (Norway), Galicia (Spain), Vaasa (Finland), and Galicia and the Bukovina (Austria-Hungary). A common explanation is *path dependency*. The fluctuations reveal that most potential emigrants must have been in possession of good-quality information. The two most important sources were emigrant letters to relatives and the experience of emigrants who had returned. Another important implication follows: in the main, the letter writers and the returned emigrants cannot have been emigrants who had "failed," since their experience would have had a negative influence on potential emigrants, which clearly it did not.

Remittances from earlier emigrants were helpful, although there is not enough data to say precisely how important these monies were. Remittances were used to help maintain family members left in Europe, thus creating communities that depended on emigration. Some were used to finance the emigration of family members, sometimes by sending prepaid tickets. Hence the cost of travel was often paid out of money that was earned overseas where wages were higher than in Europe.

Emigration from particular regions was partly path dependent. It is impossible to calculate precisely how far information and remittances determined the migration flow because it is impossible to measure the information flow independently of the emigration itself. Emigration in one year makes emigration in the following year easier. This means, of course, that those explanations of emigration rates that depend on the amount of information flowing back to Europe are essentially circular.

EMIGRATION TO THE NEW WORLD: "OLD" VERSUS "NEW" IMMIGRANTS

The character of European emigration underwent major changes in the last quarter of the nineteenth century. An increasing proportion of European emigrants came from southern and eastern Europe. At the same time, there was a marked increase in the rate of return. By the early twentieth century, 40 to 50 percent of Italian and 30 to 40 percent of Polish, Portuguese, and Hungarian emigrants were returning permanently to Europe. (The average for all countries for the whole period was 33 percent, mainly after 1870. It was only 10 percent before 1870.)

The increase in returns was largely because transport became cheaper, safer, and more comfortable. After the mid-1870s virtually all emigrants traveled by rail and steamship, and eventually it became possible to purchase through-tickets from inland Europe to New World destinations. Better transport changed the nature of the emigration decision. Because it became easier to return, the decision to leave became less final, reducing the psychological cost. Most important, cheaper transport made it possible to emigrate for a limited period. In other words, cheaper transport increased the number of "target earners," some of whom emigrated more than once.

This led to an important political issue, particularly in the United States. By the late nineteenth century the main source of immigrants had shifted from western and northern Europe, particularly Britain, Ireland, Germany, and Scandinavia, to southern and eastern Europe, particularly Italy, Russian Poland, Croatia, and Hungary. The former were called "old" immigrants and the latter "new" immigrants. A commission of the U.S. Senate (1907–1911) examined the differences between old and new and concluded that the latter had been of less economic value to the economy than the former. Based on this assessment, immigration in the 1920s from southern and eastern Europe was restricted far more than immigration from western and northern Europe. In effect, the argument was about assimilation. The old immigrants (described as "settlers") were likely to have arrived as part of a family group. Many had become farmers. The later new immigrants (described, pejoratively, as "labor migrants") were likely to have arrived as young single adults and were at least three times more likely to return to Europe than the earlier immigrants. U.S. society at the time was seen as a melting pot where all immigrants ultimately became homogeneous "Americans." (Some immigrants were invisible, however. For example, the British in the United States and Australia were not normally thought of as immigrants.) But the new immigrants, who were concentrated in ethnic ghettos, were very visible and less assimilated.

The differentiation between relatively desirable old and relatively undesirable new immigrants does not bear economic scrutiny. The contribution of the new immigrants reflected changes in the U.S. economy. When the old immigrants arrived in the first half of the century, return to Europe (by sailing ship) was difficult. Hence most emigrants were settlers. Moreover, cheap or even free land was available. By the later nineteenth century, western expansion was over. The demand for labor was in industry and urban services, which created an entry for a new kind of immigrant. In other words, labor migrants were exactly what the U.S. economy needed, although not everybody appreciated this at the time. The importance of assimilation was also misunderstood. For example, the ethnic ghetto was seen as an extension of Europe, which the immigrants had to leave before they could make a major contribution to the economy. In fact, it was a socially heterogeneous and economically vibrant community that was led by immigrant entrepreneurs.

In the main, the new immigrants were assumed to be unskilled and the old immigrants to have been skilled. The former is true but the latter is not. For example, most emigrants to the United States from Britain and Ireland were unskilled. Emigrants were usually a sample of the population. Hence a large proportion of British emigrants were unskilled (urban) workers, and a large proportion of Italian emigrants were peasants.

It has already been noted that emigration rates from southern and eastern Europe in the late nineteenth and twentieth centuries were exceptionally high. This turns out not to be because southern and eastern Europeans were more prone to emigration than northerners but because they would emigrate even when the economic benefit was relatively low. It was simply that wages in southern and eastern Europe were so low and returns to emigration were so high. Real wages in Italy in 1870 were only 23 percent of those in the United States, for example, and the gap did not significantly narrow before 1914.

It is likely that the only way emigrants were systematically selected was with respect to their age. For example, it is frequently stated that emigrants were relatively more "enterprising" than nonmigrants. But this cannot be tested because, for example, the opportunity to become a successful entrepreneur in a resource-rich open economy, such as the United States in the nineteenth century, was particularly high. Hence the success of immigrant entrepreneurs does not tell us if the immigrants were the more "enterprising" people in the European populations from which they were drawn.

The Emigrants. Engraving by Elizabeth Walker after a painting by W. Alsworth, c. 1850. This engraving depicts the wealthy Scottish farmer James Mackay and his family, who emigrated to New Zealand in 1845. NATIONAL LIBRARY OF AUSTRALIA, CANBERRA, AUSTRALIA/BRIDGEMAN ART LIBRARY

The effect of age selection was important, however. Emigrants were typically young adults because emigration involved an investment decision. The benefits were higher the longer the future lifetime. In addition, emigration took place at key moments in the life cycle—for example, when a young person decided to leave home. The point was that young adult immigrants were a free gift of capital. They entered the labor market at the peak of their earning power and when their education and upbringing had been borne by the European economy. Moreover, if they returned home, the immigrants reduced the dependent population. For example, 76 percent of the immigrants into the U.S. economy (1860–1910) were in the prime age

groups (15–40), compared with only 36 percent of the American-born. This increased the proportion of young adults in the U.S. population from 36 percent to 42 percent.

The stylized facts about the effect of immigration on New World labor markets before World War I is that, on average, immigrant earnings were initially less than native, holding skills constant, but that they caught up with native earnings within a lifetime. One reason that immigrant earnings were initially lower was that immigrant qualifications were relatively undervalued. This included informal qualifications and, of course, ability in the native language.

TABLE 4

Real earnings of various European countries as a percentage of U.S. real earnings, 1870–1910		
	1870	1910
Britain	60	62
Germany	50	51
Ireland	43	54
Italy	23	29

SOURCE: Adapted from Hatton and Williamson, *Age of Mass Migration*, p. 221.

ECONOMIC IMPACTS

In the fifty years before World War I there were few restrictions on the movement of capital, goods, and labor—that is, few restrictions as long as the immigrants were white. In the 1920s two Swedish economists, Eli Filip Heckscher and Bertil Ohlin, produced a simple formulation of the effect of European emigration. The New World had relatively abundant resources and relatively scarce labor, which is true by definition. Europe had the opposite. Hence labor flowed to the high-wage, labor-scarce economy. But this should also have meant that capital (overseas investment) flowed to the low-wage economy because investment was more profitable. The implication of the Heckscher-Ohlin model is that the gap between earnings in Europe and earnings in the immigration countries should have narrowed. Table 4 shows real earnings according to the main migration flows: the first line shows that British real earnings were 60 percent of U.S. real earnings in 1870 and 62 percent in 1910, the second that real earnings in Germany were 50 percent of U.S. real earnings in 1870 and 51 percent in 1910. In other words, despite forty years of heavy emigration, no wage convergence had occurred between Britain and the United States and Canada, nor between Germany and Italy and the United States. It is not surprising that high rates of emigration continued for such a long time.

The reason why the earnings gap did not fall was that both earnings and the returns on investment were higher in the New World. Capital and labor were moving in the same, not opposite, directions. This was partly because the cost of resources, particularly in the United States, was very low compared with that in Europe. Access to raw materials was a major factor in production costs at the time, in contrast to the early twenty-first century when transport costs are much lower.

Most important, the United States had developed resource-intensive technologies (in steel and chemicals, for example) that could not be transferred to Europe. Hence the profitability of investment remained higher in the United States than in Europe. (Further, the United States had developed the management techniques to operate these large-scale "business corporations.") Real wages in the United States and other destinations remained higher than in Europe. Rather than falling, emigration rates from Europe increased in the early twentieth century. They only fell because of World War I, which was followed by serious restrictions on European immigration into many countries and the collapse of the international economy, which confirms the connection between trade, capital movements, and emigration.

See also **Colonies; Immigration.**

BIBLIOGRAPHY

Baines, Dudley. *Emigration from Europe, 1815–1930.* Cambridge, U.K., and New York, 1995.

Bodnar, John E. *The Transplanted: A History of Immigration in Urban America.* Bloomington, Ind., 1985.

Hatton, Timothy J., and Jeffrey G. Williamson. *The Age of Mass Migration: Causes and Economic Impact.* New York, 1998.

Mitchell, B. R. *European Historical Statistics, 1750–1975.* 2nd rev. ed. London, 1980.

Wilcox, Walter F., and Imre Ferenczi. *International Migrations.* Edited on behalf of the National Bureau of Economic Research. New York, 1929.

DUDLEY BAINES

ENDECJA. The National Democratic Movement (commonly called the Endecja [pronounced en–DE–tsya], a term formed by pronouncing the initials *N. D.* in Polish) was the leading right-wing nationalist group in early-twentieth-century Poland. Its origins can be traced to a small conspiratorial organization called the National League, which was founded in 1893 by Roman Dmowski, Jan Ludwik Popławski, and Zygmunt Balicki. The League (the existence of which remained secret until 1899) served as the institutional core for a wide range of larger, more public groups. Among these were the Democratic National Party (founded 1897), the Union of Polish Youth (first created in 1887, but reconstituted and absorbed into the structure of the League in 1898), the Society for National Education (an organization dedicated to spreading national identity among the peasantry, created in 1899), and the National Workers' Union (1905).

The Endecja constituted a dramatic break with nineteenth-century traditions of Polish patriotism. Since the country's partition by Russia, Prussia, and Austria at the end of the eighteenth century, national activists had staged periodic uprisings in a futile attempt to regain independence. The Poles who participated in the nineteenth century's many conspiracies and revolts represented a wide range of political ideologies, but broadly speaking they were united by a romantic, idealist notion of their cause. A slogan coined in 1830 but repeated incessantly afterward was "For Your Freedom and Ours," which activists deployed to suggest an ideological linkage between the quest for Polish independence and a universal struggle for liberation from both national and social oppression. Because of this legacy, the young national activists of the 1880s and 1890s were easily drawn to those varieties of socialism and populism that could be customized to include national liberation alongside the cause of social justice.

Dmowski, in a sharp repudiation of this tradition, challenged any universal, transnational vision of social or political change. He appropriated the "scientific" rhetoric of late-nineteenth-century positivism, and claimed to offer a more "realistic" approach to the national question. The cause of Polish liberation was not justified by any appeal to universal rights or any abstract notions of justice, Dmowski argued. Instead, he described the nation as a social "organism," locked with other nations in an unending struggle for survival. In that eternal battle, all means were appropriate if they contributed to the nation's objectives. For all their purported "realism," however, the early National Democrats spoke of the nation in idealistic terms. Virtually any objective standard for measuring national identity was inadequate for them, be it language, historical traditions, geography, religion,

or self-identification. All these measures, Dmowski and his colleagues believed, led to an overly rigid definition of the nation. Instead, they preferred to speak of a national "essence" or "soul" that manifest itself within an ever-changing social body. Linguistic and cultural homogeneity were extremely important, but they were the results of nation building, not the standards by which a nation was delineated. As a nation expanded, it could use education or assimilation to increase its size, and national boundaries could be set according to strategic interests rather than ethnographic studies or plebiscites.

Among the Endecja's many opponents, two stood out. The socialists were seen by the National Democrats as far too cosmopolitan to be genuinely committed to the national cause. Emphasizing social exploitation could only plant seeds of dissent and disunity within the nation, Dmowski and his colleagues thought, and the use of universal standards of justice could hinder the nation in its struggle for existence. Less central to the Endecja's ideology at the beginning, but increasingly important after the turn of the century, was anti-Semitism. The National Democrats were opposed to every national and ethnic group in northeastern Europe, but the Jews played a special role in their imagination. In the social Darwinist scheme advanced by Dmowski and his colleagues, the Jews had no obvious place, unless one accepted the conspiracy theories already circulating elsewhere in Europe about Jewish plots to dominate the world. During the first decade of the twentieth century the Endecja emerged as the primary vehicle for spreading modern anti-Semitism in Poland.

The Russian Revolution of 1905 was a turning point for the Endecja, because during the unrest its adherents emerged for the first time as a mass political organization. Afterward, they moved from the world of underground activism to open political life, campaigning for parliamentary seats in all three partitions (though their base was strongest in the Russian Empire). When World War I broke out in 1914, Dmowski allied his organization with the tsars—not because of any Russophilia, but because he was convinced that Germany was a far greater danger to Poland. By the time Poland finally regained its independence in 1918, the National Democrats were one of the most important political forces in the country, and although they never held power during the interwar years, they remained a force in public life and helped shape the political and cultural landscape of twentieth-century Poland.

See also **Anti-Semitism; Nationalism; Poland; Revolution of 1905 (Russia); Russia.**

BIBLIOGRAPHY

Kozicki, Stanisław. *Historia Ligi Narodowej: Okres, 1887–1907.* London, 1964.

Porter, Brian. *When Nationalism Began to Hate: Imagining Modern Politics in Nineteenth-Century Poland.* New York, 2000.

Wapiński, Roman. *Narodowa Demokracja, 1893–1939.* Wrocław, Poland, 1980.

BRIAN PORTER

ENGELS, FRIEDRICH (1820–1895), German political theorist.

Friedrich Engels is chiefly known as the sometime collaborator, political associate, lifelong friend, and literary executor of Karl Marx (1818–1883). However, by the time that he and Marx agreed to work together in late 1844, Engels was already a widely published journalist, pamphleteer, and social critic. Before joining Marx in Brussels the following spring, Engels completed work on *The Condition of the Working Class in England* (1845), a notable and still widely read exposé of the bad housing, poor sanitation, and appalling nutrition to which industrial workers were subjected. His career then took a turn, and for the rest of his life he supported Marx as best he could, not least financially. This included a vast output of reviews, introductions, and popularizing pamphlets, extending to posthumous editions of Marx's works and manuscripts.

EARLY YEARS

Engels was born not far from what is now Wuppertal in the Ruhr district of Prussia. For some generations his family had been mill-owning entrepreneurs, eventually running textile enterprises as far afield as Manchester. They were staunch fundamentalist Protestants, rather hostile to undue learning. After an unremarkable education, Engels was put into the family firm at sixteen. Finding commercial life rather undemanding, he was by seventeen a published poet and at eighteen the author of the scandalous, and fortunately pseudonymous, "Letters from Wuppertal" (1839), which appeared in the Hamburg press. Drawing on his own eyes and ears, he wrote of industrial pollution, moralizing hypocrisy, and wretched working conditions in his twin hometowns, Elberfeld and Barmen. While working in Bremen he also read the radically skeptical *Life of Jesus* (1835–1836) by D. F. Strauss (1808–1874) and embraced the liberal nationalism of "Young Germany."

In Berlin in 1841–1842, ostensibly to do military service, Engels attended lectures at the university and became a "Young Hegelian" pamphleteer, championing the atheism implicit in Ludwig Feuerbach's (1804–1872) *Essence of Christianity* (1841). In the repressive climate of the time agitation for liberalizing and democratizing measures necessarily took place in a somewhat coded, philosophical form. This was an argument that the vast works of G. W. F. Hegel (1770–1831) could be read as a call for further historical change in order to realize human freedom more adequately.

In late 1842 Engels visited the offices of the liberal paper *Rheinische Zeitung* in Cologne, where he encountered Moses Hess (1812–1875), and swiftly declared himself a communist. At that time socialism and communism were used somewhat interchangeably, and these largely French ideas looked beyond the formal institutions of representative democracy to a classless society where poverty and exploitation would be resolved. Engels was on his way to work in Manchester, where in that more liberal political climate he embraced the cause of Chartism, a mass movement for liberal reform within which many socialists participated.

Writing for both English and German-language papers, Engels promoted the cause of democratization, working-class political participation, shorter working hours in industry, and protection from poverty and unemployment. During 1843 he wrote a long article, *Outlines of a Critique of Political Economy* (1844), and sent it for publication in a German émigré periodical edited in Brussels (by Marx, among others). This tightly argued piece, imbued with both a knowledge of political economy (the economic theory of the day) and a businessman's knowledge of the trade and employment cycles, greatly impressed Marx and was undoubtedly the reason why Engels was warmly received by him in Paris in August 1844. Engels's conclusions were just what he wanted to hear: capitalism was a system based on wild swings in supply and demand that brought misery and ruin to the very people who produced the wealth.

IN PARTNERSHIP WITH MARX

Engels and Marx then embarked on various schemes of joint publication, beginning with *The Holy Family* (1845), a little-read polemic against certain German socialists whom the two considered too intellectual and too remote from working-class politics. While Engels had some misgivings about Marx's polemical efforts against further German (and eventually French) socialists of the time, he acted as collaborator and amanuensis on *The German Ideology* (written 1845–1846), a large, occasionally undecipherable manuscript soon abandoned by the authors, and first published only in the 1930s. While Part One of this work is considered today to be of profound philosophical importance, there are insoluble problems with the ordering of the text, who-wrote-what, and exactly what arguments it makes.

Nonetheless *The German Ideology* clearly outlines a new conception of human history. This is rooted in the practical activities of subsistence and luxury production, the structural features of legal systems and class divisions, and a rejection of any explanations or theories of historical development in terms of ideas alone, whether religious, moral, or philosophical. Calling this a new materialism (to distinguish it from the philosophical idealism that they were criticizing), the two linked this demystification of historical change to the socialist movement and working-class politics. After all, workers were engaged in the quintessential human activity but denied adequate subsistence, yet others—who merely owned property—were guaranteed a life of leisure. For Marx and Engels capitalist production presented this glaring contrast, yet industrialization held out the promise of

Friedrich Engels. ©HULTON-DEUTSCH COLLECTION/CORBIS

adequate levels of consumption for everyone. This was the socialist vision they promoted all their lives.

Working with both liberals and socialists, Marx and Engels associated themselves with international "correspondence committees," among which was the Communist League. The two were commissioned to write a unifying document, and Engels drafted two: a communist confession of faith, and a more declaratory set of principles. At the London conference in November 1847 the two were charged with preparing a final version, published there in February 1848. Though Marx was the final hand on the document, the narrative historical sweep and withering scorn for middle-class morality are characteristically Engelsian. This work was soon lost in the revolutionary events of 1848 as they swept across Continental Europe, and its major influence came much later in the 1870s when the *Communist Manifesto* was used to promote a "Marxist" tendency in international socialism.

During the revolutionary events Engels joined Marx successively in Paris and Cologne, engaging in radical journalism and local agitation. He also found time to take a walking tour of Burgundy during the late autumn of 1848, and then rather more excitingly he joined the revolutionary troops in Elberfeld the following May. He led an armed raid on a Prussian arsenal, but eventually beat a final retreat into Switzerland. He re-established contact with Marx and other exiles in London in late 1849 on his way to work once again for the family firm in Manchester.

EXILE AND MARXISM

In a role that he later characterized as "junior partner," Engels reviewed Marx's *A Contribution to the Critique of Political Economy* (1859). While little read at the time, this review contains all the most important elements of his "framing" of his mentor, and in effect signals the founding of Marxism with these defining concepts: dialectic, materialism, determinism, metaphysics, idealism, interaction, contradiction, and reflection. These were later presented somewhat more systematically in works such as *Anti-Dühring* (1878), *Socialism: Utopian and Scientific* (1880), *Ludwig Feuerbach and the End of Classical German Philosophy* (1886), and the posthumously published *Dialectics of Nature* (1927). Engels presented Marx as a "materialist" Hegel, formulating a unified theory of nature, history, and thought, and using a method summarized in three dialectical laws: interpenetration of opposites, transformation of quantity into quality, and negation of the negation. Moreover in *The Origin of the Family, Private Property and the State* (1884), he attempted to merge Marx's work with that of Darwin, by incorporating biological reproduction and sexual selection into their account of human social structure and long-term political change.

While Marx's works show little of this drive for such a comprehensive quasi-Hegelian philosophical synthesis, Engels's thus appeared supplementary, rather than contradictory, to most Marxists. Engels, of course, was Marx's earliest intellectual biographer, and the biographer of their relationship, which he portrayed as seamless. Early-twenty-first-century scholarship is making this account increasingly untenable, and also putting Engels's

editing of Marx's manuscripts for *Capital*, volumes 2 (1885) and 3 (1894), under rigorous scrutiny.

LATER YEARS

In 1869 Engels (at the age of forty-nine) retired from his duties with the family firm and set up house in London (and also settled some money on Marx). He had for some years maintained a discreet domestic relationship, first with Mary Burns (c. 1823–1863), and then with her sister Lydia ("Mrs Lizzie") (1827–1878), both Irish working-class in origin and mill-girls by trade. It is likely that neither attained real literacy, and neither was ever received by the Engels family back home. Cross-class marriage was unthinkable at the time, and inheritance was clearly an issue: Engels married Lizzie on *her* deathbed. Whether this was a socialist arrangement flouting bourgeois convention, or an all too bourgeois form of masculine exploitation, is up to one's own judgment. Both views were current at the time.

Engels was a considerable personal influence on international socialism as it gained ground, particularly in Germany, during the 1880s when it was illegal and then in the 1890s after liberalization. He attended the 1893 congress of the Socialist International in Zurich as a "grand old man" and honorary president. He died of cancer of the throat in London, and both the German Social Democratic Workers' Party and the Marx family benefited from his will.

See also **Communism; Marx, Karl; Second International; Socialism.**

BIBLIOGRAPHY

Primary Sources

Marx, Karl, and Friedrich Engels. *Collected Works.* 50 vols. London, 1975–2004.

Secondary Sources

Carver, Terrell. *Friedrich Engels: His Life and Thought.* Basingstoke, London, and New York, 1989.

Henderson, W. O. *The Life of Friedrich Engels.* 2 vols. London and Portland, Oreg., 1976.

Rigby, S. H. *Engels and the Formation of Marxism: History, Dialectics and Revolution.* Manchester, U.K., and New York, 1992.

TERRELL CARVER

ENGINEERS. In the late eighteenth century a diverse collection of technically proficient men emerged as leading figures of the early industrial age. French architects and state engineers, German mechanics, Dutch hydraulic engineers, Scottish inventors, and British agronomists all contributed to the emerging profession of engineering in the nineteenth century. Collectively, these technically inclined men came to shape the emerging industrial face of every nation in Europe. Engineers based their claim to expertise on elite training acquired through apprenticeships or mentors in the late eighteenth century and from elite engineering schools in the nineteenth century. They sought to apply scientific principles and technical analysis to promote innovative designs for civil and mechanical engineering problems. Civil engineers built elaborate road, canal, and rail networks, while mechanical and industrial engineers helped create the machinery that powered production in mines, textile mills, and factories. Over time engineers increasingly set themselves apart as technical experts, as political advisors, and as managers of natural resources such as water and rivers, as well as of the built environment they constructed. Engineering priorities began with an intense focus on water usage, agriculture, and canals in the early nineteenth century and gradually expanded to include roads, railways, factories, and urban infrastructure.

The emergence of the engineering profession was not without struggle and owed much to eighteenth-century patronage and royal tradition. As royal projects became increasingly ambitious, governments increasingly favored designers who could claim technical training, skill, and accomplishments over those with architectural training that emphasized aesthetic and classical concerns. French projects such as the ambitious Canal du Midi across southern France demanded technical skill that favored engineers rather than architects. This tension between elegance and function played out differently in England, where a strong tradition of classical liberalism led parliamentary commissions to award projects to individuals rather than state-organized corps of engineers. Consequently, a wider variety of architects, engineers, and self-taught experts emerged in England, where prominent architects such as Christopher Wren

(1632–1723) had earlier established a strong tradition of individual design in England. Consequently, some of the most notable triumphs of nineteenth-century British civil and industrial engineering were the product of private enterprise and rugged independent thinkers and tinkerers.

By contrast, France, Belgium, and Spain developed strong traditions of state planning by prestigious corps of state-trained civil engineers. In France by the time of the French Revolution the civil engineers of the Royal Corps des Ponts et Chaussées (Bridges and Roads) had wrested control of state projects from competing architects of the beaux arts tradition. State-sponsored engineering corps were populated by graduates of the elite École Polytechnique, which prepared students for both civil and military engineering careers.

In the opening decades of the nineteenth century large-scale civil engineering projects focused on agricultural improvements and water usage. Dutch and English engineers continued eighteenth-century trends toward scientific farming, crop rotation, and enclosure by bringing irrigation, land drainage, pumps, and dikes to bear on their regions' age-old preoccupations with land recovery and productive farming. Nineteenth-century agricultural engineers deployed a remarkable array of new farming machinery, including improved versions of Jethro Tull's (1674–1741) seed drill and Andrew Meikle's (1719–1811) threshing machine as well as steam-powered tractors. British equipment designed for producing irrigation and drainage tiles quickly found its way to the Continent, where French engineers under Napoleon III (r. 1852–1871) sought to implement a nationwide campaign to drain swamps and increase the amount of land under cultivation.

Canals constituted a second eighteenth-century initiative that flourished through the 1820s and 1830s as coal, ore, and textile entrepreneurs demanded ready access to waterpower and transportation of heavy goods. A network of more than thirty-five hundred miles of canals linked existing rivers and ports as diverse as London and Bristol with cities like Manchester, Leeds, and Birmingham. The even-more-ambitious plan by Louis Becquey (1760–1849) to link all major French rivers with canals had its political origins in the 1820s but only became a reality when state engineers completed

Construction of London sewers, 1862. Workers construct the brick tunnels, designed by engineer Joseph Bazalgette, that will carry London's sewage beneath the city's streets. ©HULTON-DEUTSCH COLLECTION/CORBIS

canals through Burgundy and between the Rhine and Rhône Rivers by the 1850s. Unlike its counterpart in England, much of the French network was planned to stimulate industry and trade, rather than as a response to existing shipping demands. While some early British canals were extremely profitable, as were selected segments of the French network, both systems found themselves eclipsed by the speed and flexibility offered by railways by the 1840s and 1850s. In Prussia centralized planning by industrialists and engineers transformed the river networks of the Ruhr valley and surrounding areas feeding the Rhine into a tightly regulated network of dams and canals designed to support urban, industrial, and shipping demands at the expense of natural environmental conditions.

In the United Kingdom engineers boasted varied backgrounds and uneven educational training, yet came to be seen as pioneers in the development of steam power, railway engineering, and early uses of iron and steel. Scottish and English engineers, including James Watt (1736–1819), built reputations based on hands-on experience and apprenticeship with other engineers, rather than through formal university or technical school training. These informal personal and family networks influenced many engineers, including John Rennie (1761–1821), a Scottish engineer who began his career with Andrew Meikle and worked for Matthew Boulton (1728–1809) and Watt before moving into civil engineering. Rennie's firm executed his designs for numerous canals, bridges, and ports, including dockyards for the Royal Navy. Continuing the family tradition, upon Rennie's death in 1821 his design for London Bridge was supervised by his youngest son. Reputation and personal connections led both Rennie's sons to work for George Stephenson (1781–1848) in the construction of the Liverpool and Manchester Railway. The Institution of

Garabit viaduct, Cantal, France. Designed by Gustave Eiffel and built in 1884, the railroad viaduct bridging the Truyère River at the Garabit Valley was innovative in its use of lightweight wrought-iron trusses. ©ARTHUR THÉVENART/CORBIS

Civil Engineers, founded in 1818 and promoted extensively by Thomas Telford (1757–1834), served as a nexus where members developed personal connections as the profession expanded.

In France the state played a central role in the training and employment of civil and mining engineers. The state fostered a public engineering culture through examination-based admission and training at the École Polytechnique. Graduates entered the military and the state's most prestigious engineering corps: the Corps des Ponts et Chaussées (Bridges and Roads) and the Corps des Mines. These corps fostered an internal culture of state service that combined family connections with an ethos of elitism and professional national service. Demand for industrial engineers led to the creation of other of technical schools, including regional Écoles d'Arts et Métiers and the École Centrale, whose graduates tuned machines, designed factory equipment, and operated factories. Social connections and political power allowed state civil engineers to preserve a dominant position politically and in the public eye, even as engineers in other domains gained importance.

German models of engineering training were more varied, but evolved into a tiered system by 1914. At the highest levels, roughly a dozen elite technical schools operated with similar status to universities and offered advanced training that emphasized civil projects and industrial applications. Workers and foremen attended vocational schools, most of which did not require a high school diploma. Between these two systems emerged a wide array of technical schools that required apprenticeship or experience, rather than a high school diploma, as a prerequisite for admission. As engineering practice diversified after the 1870s to include specialists in electricity, chemistry, dyes, armaments, and naval architecture, the German educational model allowed tight collaboration between technical schools and emerging industrial firms.

Construction of the Eiffel Tower, 1887. The 300-meter all-steel tower was built for the Paris Centennial Exposition of 1889. © BETTMANN/CORBIS

Nineteenth-century engineers shared an unusual transnational culture based on the exchange of techniques and elegant solutions to complex problems. French engineering students made regular study tours of England and Prussia to report on the design of railway depots, advances in road construction, ports, and other current projects. Belgian city planners actively solicited advice from Henri Darcy (1803–1858), a French engineer, on how to copy the water-supply system he had designed for the city of Dijon. The Scotsman John McAdam's (1756–1836) paving solutions were quickly adopted across the Continent, where they were adapted to existing road construction techniques. Overseas, European engineers exported both the machinery and technical knowledge of national rail and canal construction to the Americas, Russia, Greece, and Turkey and to their colonies in Africa, India, and Asia. In the United States Robert Fulton's (1765–1815) experiments with steamboats were directly inspired by his French training and by British successes with Watt & Boulton engines.

Engineers across Europe shared the common language of technique and construction challenges, but their projects also bolstered national pride for nations engaged in intense competition in the decades before 1914. British engineers such as George Stephenson, whose locomotive *The Rocket* propelled him to prominence, and his sometime rival Isambard Kingdom Brunel (1806–1859), the architect of the Great Western Railroad, established England as a leader in the design of railway bridges, tunnels, and viaducts. Overseas, French engineers could point triumphantly to the Suez Canal or, closer to home, to Gustave Eiffel's (1832–1923) elegant use of iron in the elegant Garabit Viaduct in Cantal, France (1884), and his three-hundred-meter tower in Paris (1889). An alpine rail tunnel in Mount Cenis between France and Italy and the St. Gotthard tunnel connecting Germany to Italy via Switzerland, showcased the engineering prowess of French and Swiss engineers while at the same time opening an era of international cooperation and rapid rail communication to Italy and the Mediterranean.

Engineers occupied a vital position in nineteenth-century society. They used their technocratic expertise to balance natural resources, plan for industrial and urban growth, and mediate between diverse constituencies. This monumental task of "mastering" nature in the service of modern society brought the world closer together and created enduring symbols of national pride.

See also **Brunel, Isambard Kingdom; Industrial Revolution, First; Industrial Revolution, Second; Professions.**

BIBLIOGRAPHY

Ahlström, Göran. *Engineers and Industrial Growth: Higher Technical Education and the Engineering Profession during the Nineteenth and Early Twentieth Centuries: France, Germany, Sweden, and England.* London, 1982.

Alder, Ken. *Engineering the Revolution: Arms and Enlightenment in France, 1763–1815.* Princeton, N.J., 1997.

Bailey, Michael R., ed. *Robert Stephenson—the Eminent Engineer.* Aldershot, Hants, U.K., and Burlington, Vt., 2003.

Buchanan, R. Angus. *Brunel: The Life and Times of Isambard Kingdom Brunel.* London and New York, 2002.

Cioc, Mark. *The Rhine: An Eco-biography, 1815–2000.* Seattle, Wash., 2002.

Day, Charles R. *Education for the Industrial World : The Écoles d'Arts et Métiers and the Rise of French Industrial Engineering.* Cambridge, Mass., 1987.

Evans, Richard J. *Death in Hamburg: Society and Politics in the Cholera Years, 1830–1910.* Oxford, U.K., and New York, 1987.

Gispen, Kees. *New Profession, Old Order: Engineers and German Society, 1815–1914.* Cambridge, U.K., and New York, 1989.

Kranakis, Eda. *Constructing a Bridge: An Exploration of Engineering Culture, Design, and Research in Nineteenth-Century France and America.* Cambridge, Mass., 1997.

Peters, Tom F. *Building the Nineteenth Century.* Cambridge, Mass., 1996.

Thomas, Donald E., Jr. *Diesel: Technology and Society in Industrial Germany.* Tuscaloosa, Ala., 1987.

Weiss, John Hubbel. *The Making of Technological Man: The Social Origins of French Engineering Education.* Cambridge, Mass., 1982.

DANIEL RINGROSE

ENVIRONMENT. Human history is embedded in its natural environments. Space and topographical variations encourage or restrict historical development. Industrialization in Great Britain, for example, benefited from low transportation costs made possible by Britain's extensive waterways and long coast. In many countries, the existence of raw materials such as coal or iron ore enabled certain regions to develop as industrial centers (for example, coal mines in the Ruhr Basin). Climate is also a factor in history. Up to the middle of the nineteenth century, bad weather frequently caused crop failures and often resulted in famine, which could trigger upheavals such as those that took place on the eve of the French Revolution. The Irish potato famine of 1845 through 1850 was the result of an agricultural blight and caused hundreds of thousands of deaths by starvation and disease, along with massive emigration, changing the social and cultural structure of Ireland. Unfavorable environmental conditions frequently encouraged people to improve their environment through innovation. The Dutch seventeenth-century land reclamation project using dikes and polders not only protected the land from storm tides but was also accompanied by modern, capital-intensive, highly specialized, export-oriented agriculture, which created sustainable economic growth.

THE NINETEENTH CENTURY IN ENVIRONMENTAL HISTORY

In general, the influence of nature on human life, economy, consumption, and politics was much more important in early modern times than it has been since the twentieth century. Thus the nineteenth century represents a transition period in the relationship of humankind to its environment. The most important factors influencing this transformation were industrialization, the modernization of agriculture, and urban growth. In early modern times, Europeans were limited by the amount of food they could produce. During the nineteenth century, however, and particularly during its second half, they learned to mobilize natural resources and manipulate their environment to an unprecedented extent. By the beginning of the twentieth century, the manipulation of nature became the subject of systematic planning. Europeans disconnected their living conditions gradually from the vagaries of nature—and suffered more and more from pollution.

Some environmental historians argue that industrialization caused the transition from a sustainable to an unsustainable economy. Modern societies, they say, severely damage the environment and rely on nonrenewable resources, especially fossil fuel. Others, however, argue that not even agricultural societies are sustainable, pointing to soil degradation and forest overexploitation in early modern times.

Few dimensions of historical inquiry are as diverse as environmental history. As a general rule, only a regional, and often only a local, approach can produce results of any value. The information contained in this article refers primarily to the industrializing regions of west and central Europe because they pointed the way for Europe's development.

AGRICULTURE

The European population more than doubled between 1800 and 1914. Death rates fell, for example, from twenty-seven per thousand in Germany in 1850 to seventeen per thousand in the early twentieth century. This was mainly due to the increased stability of agrarian production and to improved sanitary conditions in the big cities. Since the eighteenth century, agricultural reformers inspired by the Enlightenment had tried to increase the productivity of farming, proposing more efficient variations on traditional methods. During the nineteenth century, agriculture combined traditional elements, such as crop rotation and the use of human and animal labor, with innovations such as limited mechanization, capital investment, and imported fertilizers (guano, for example) or chemical products (for example, nitrogen-based fertilizers promoted by the German chemist Justus von Liebig beginning in the middle of the century).

Before midcentury, agriculture in certain regions began to specialize and large landowners extended monoculture. In Germany, beginning in the 1860s the regions of Magdeburg and the lower Rhineland were dominated by the intense cultivation of sugar beets, which replaced imported sugar cane. Entrepreneurs opened sugar refineries in the

vicinity. The German sugar regions provide a good example of the dependence of commercial monoculture on technical improvement, capital investment, and proximity to infrastructure. In the south of France, Languedoc became a vast monoculture of vineyards. The ecological fragility of monocultures was demonstrated by the phylloxera blight in the late nineteenth century, which devastated French wine production.

THE TRANSFORMATION OF LANDSCAPES

Agrarian modernization had an important impact on the European landscape. The growing influence of agronomics (i.e., the scientific research for the improvement of rural economy) made agriculture increasingly uniform. Local biodiversity was reduced by monocultures and general biodiversity was reduced by selection of the most productive cultivated plants. On the other hand, the agricultural use of non-European species (such as the potato) and the importation of ornamental plants from overseas increased the number of species populating the European countryside and both urban and rural gardens. Since the late eighteenth century, the draining of wetlands had been a central goal of agrarian policy. In England, for example, the enclosures of the late eighteenth century, transforming common ground into privately owned land, encouraged private investment in drainage. Since the Napoleonic era, the French government had supported the draining of marshes by private and public landholders. The most significant wetland drainage and construction of irrigation canals had been carried out by 1860 and nearly all of France's shallow marshes had disappeared. The amount of arable land had been expanded and severe diseases such as malaria had become less of a threat.

Many of the big central European rivers were altered in order to reclaim fertile land for agriculture, reduce flooding, and improve transportation. One of the most significant of these projects was the alteration of the Rhine between 1809 and 1876, which reduced by one-fourth the distance ships had to travel between Basel and Bingen and also accelerated the river's flow, lowering the water table. In the late nineteenth century, floods on the lower Rhine were commonly attributed to these measures. In the early twentieth century, in the

Sheffield, England, c. 1800. Engraving after a drawing by J. M. W. Turner presents a bucolic view of Sheffield at the beginning of the nineteenth century. MARY EVANS PICTURE LIBRARY

most industrialized regions of Europe, several rivers were turned into mere canals, used for shipping and to absorb waste water.

Modern forestry also changed European landscapes. In the early modern period, forests were used in ways that often conflicted. These uses included pasturing, hunting, berry picking, producing charcoal, gathering firewood, and cutting timber for building. In general, forest use was regulated to at least some extent by common law. Beginning in the eighteenth century, authorities began to transform forests into public or private property. German foresters developed the idea of sustainable use (*nachhaltige Nutzung*), in which cutting had to be planned carefully and balanced by new plantings. They considered the production of timber the main goal of forestry, banning other uses from the woodlands. As a result, forests often were turned into rationally designed plantations

of rectangular monocultures, uniform in both species and age. Where scientific forestry dominated, the result was a forest vulnerable to disease, insect predation, and storm. In many regions, the wooded areas expanded, and foresters often favored conifers over other trees. Landes, near Bordeaux, which had been one of the biggest swamplands in Europe, was transformed into an immense woodland under Emperor Napoleon III when millions of stone pines were planted. The German Black Forest, which had been deciduous woodland, was replanted with pine trees and firs.

Industrialization also altered the notion of space during the nineteenth century, when the mobility of persons and goods increased. In Great Britain, 2,500 miles of canals were built between 1750 and 1815; they constituted 95 percent of the canals in use in 1900. Nevertheless, railways dominated nineteenth-century traffic. The age of the railway started in 1825, when the first public line opened between Stockton and Darlington, in England. By 1850 the French railway network comprised approximately 1,900 miles. In 1885 118,000 miles of railroad were built in Europe, including 25,000 in Germany, 19,000 each in England and France, 6,000 in Italy, 2,500 in Belgium, and 100 in Greece. Railroad building itself constituted an important interference with the environment and also allowed Europeans to move natural resources far from their sources.

ENERGY SYSTEMS

Industrialization was accompanied by a revolution in the use of energy. The wooden or solar era ended when coal was introduced for industrial use. The early modern economy had relied on renewable energy sources such as wood, charcoal, water, wind, and human or animal labor. Whereas these sources of energy were based on the short-term input of solar energy, fossil fuel is solar energy captured over millions of years. By the end of the nineteenth century, fossil fuel had enabled Europeans to overcome the energy shortage that had hindered economic growth in the eighteenth century. Coal-fired engines empowered humankind to mobilize natural resources seemingly without limit. Since then, human impact on the environment has continued to grow. In the early twentieth century, petroleum and natural gas joined coal as energy sources, and the introduction of electricity required the construction of large power plants. However, these new sources of energy caused problems. First, the use of nonrenewable resources is, in the long run, not sustainable. Second, the burning of coal caused air pollution from smoke, dust, and chemical compounds such as carbon monoxide. The new (and old) manufacturing processes tended to produce artificial substances that disturbed the environment, causing problems for humans, flora, and fauna. The immense increase in production and the concentration of consumption in the cities also caused perpetual problems with garbage.

INDUSTRIAL POLLUTION

Air pollution was not a new phenomenon, but during the nineteenth century it became more and more serious. One important source was the coal-fired engine. Additionally, the smelting of ore released large amounts of sulfur, which harmed plants, animals, and people. In some places, this problem dated back to the preindustrial era. Technicians and health experts looked for ways to reduce the harmful effects of pollutants. With respect to industrial air pollution, the common solution all over Europe was dilution. Factories built high chimneys so that the smoke could drift away. The tallest one (approximately 450 feet) was built in Freiberg, in Saxony, in 1889. Even then, some experts argued that the emissions did not disappear when diluted, but high chimneys lowered the concentration of toxins and made it difficult to identify any specific source of pollution. Other solutions were suggested, including filters, but they proved less efficient and too expensive.

Industry was not the only source of air pollution. The coal stoves used in many households emitted high levels of dust, sulfur dioxides, and particulates. The famous London fog, for example, was in large part the result of individual heating.

Industry produced other forms of pollution. It frequently used fresh water as a resource and dumped waste water into the rivers. The manufacture of sugar from beets required between 247 and 953 cubic feet of water per ton of beets. The nineteenth-century chemical industry produced acids, alkalis, fertilizers, and dyes, and it produced new noxious substances, including formaldehyde, formic acid, phenol, and acetone. Although the dangers posed by these toxins were known, safety precautions were minimal and the chemical industry often poisoned rivers and ground water. In some places, the smell and the color of the rivers depended on the production process of the local industry. Not surprisingly, one of the most striking phenomena of nineteenth-century river pollution was the frequency of large-scale fish kills. Fishermen and hygiene experts were often the most important groups to fight river pollution. One of the few examples of improvement was the production of alkali, which became cleaner as the century progressed. In 1863 England passed the Alkali Acts, forcing soda factories to reduce their emissions of hydrochloric acid.

Agriculture also contributed to water pollution. The runoff of fertilizers added nutrients to

SHEFFIELD SMOKE.
From a Drawing by A. MORROW.

Sheffield Smoke. An 1885 engraving from the *English Illustrated Magazine* depicts air pollution in Sheffield that resulted from industrial development in the town during the nineteenth century. MARY EVANS PICTURE LIBRARY

the water, dissolving the oxygen and leading to eutrophication.

CITIES AND POLLUTION

Urban growth was an important element of everyday life in nineteenth-century Europe. London grew from about 1 million inhabitants in 1800 to 2.3 million by 1850. This increasing concentration caused considerable problems involving hygiene and health. Some twenty thousand Parisians died in the great cholera epidemic of 1832,

which was caused by water pollution. It was common for mud containing organic garbage and human and animal manure to be discharged into the streets and the rivers. Eventually, public authorities had to react. Whereas few cities possessed an adequate sewage system in the middle of the nineteenth century, by 1900 nearly all major cities in northern Europe had facilities to ensure the distribution of clean water, and these were separated from the evacuation of waste water. Sewers contributed significantly to a reduction in epidemics of cholera and typhoid, and in some places urban manure was put to use. In 1870 Paris established an area of several hundred hectares on the outskirts of the city that was fertilized by sewage water; it was used by farmers who grew vegetables for the capital and constituted a new model for symbiotic urban-rural relations, including consumption, evacuation, and recycling/production. Many cities copied the Parisian example. But the big rivers suffered severely from urban pollution. Although by around 1900 several cities had established their first sewage plants, the cleansing of rivers remained an unsolved problem, not least because it was expensive.

During the nineteenth century, pollution remained regional. Highly industrialized areas and urban centers suffered immensely, but other regions were left nearly untouched by chemicals, smoke, and organic waste.

ATTITUDES TOWARD NATURE AND THE ENVIRONMENT

In general, nineteenth-century European political and economic thought celebrated technical progress and human liberation from the constraints of nature, and most Europeans welcomed the control of nature. Life expectancy and the quality of life both improved during the nineteenth century.

The Romantics identified what they called "pristine nature" as an inspiring counterpart to modern humanity. Later, agrarian Romanticism developed as a cultural and political ideology, and after 1900 urban reform and health movements called their members "back to nature." At the same time, powerful political movements developed to protect animals and nature itself. Whereas bourgeois landscape protection concentrated on aesthetic issues, pollution control was largely debated among experts and technical specialists. Far from neglecting the harmful effects of pollution, they tried to work out practical solutions. The driving forces behind pollution control were public administrators. In spite of the existence of global environmental protection strategies, authorities tried to solve local problems individually. So the British Public Health Act (1875) contained a smoke abatement section in order to reduce the health problems caused by domestic heating and industrial emissions. As long as damages to the population's health were difficult to prove scientifically, however, the only way for individuals to defend their interests against the big polluters was through lawsuits by claiming economic losses.

The two sides of nineteenth-century attitudes toward nature are exemplified by the human relationship with animals. On the one hand, animals were integrated into the increasingly complex structures of urban, agricultural, and industrial life. Public transportation in the cities relied on horses until the end of the century, as did coal mining. The newly established slaughterhouses ensured the total, efficient, and hygienic processing of livestock. On the other hand, among the middle classes, the keeping of pets resulted in a new vision of the animal as a companion to humans, highly esteemed and even loved. Large predators such as bears and wolves, however, were nearly exterminated when they disturbed farmers. Species that served industrial production were exploited like other natural resources. Whaling, for example, grew into a bloody industry based on explosive harpoons and factory ships. By contrast, birds were greeted as the feathered friends of humankind. In northern Europe, at least, songbirds were excluded from menus and the use of their plumes was a subject of heated debate by 1900.

See also **Cities and Towns; Industrial Revolution, First; Industrial Revolution, Second.**

BIBLIOGRAPHY

Brüggemeier, Franz-Josef. *Tschernobyl, 26 April 1986: Die ökologische Herausforderung.* Munich, 1998. Outlines major environmental problems from 1800 to the present.

Cioc, Mark. *The Rhine: An Eco-Biography 1815–2000.* Seattle, Wash., 2002. Ecological transformations of one of the largest rivers in Europe.

Delort, Robert, and François Walter. *Histoire de l'environnement européen.* Paris, 2001. First comprehensive European environmental history.

Hughes, J. Donald. *The Mediterranean: An Environmental History.* Santa Barbara, Calif., 2005.

Luckin, Bill, Geneviève Massard-Guilbaud, and Dieter Schott, eds. *Urban Environment: Resources—Perceptions—Uses.* London, 2005. Collection of essays on the urban environment.

Radkau, Joachim. *Natur und Macht: Eine Weltgeschichte der Umwelt.* Munich, 2000. English translation forthcoming. World environmental history from the beginnings to the twentieth century, with special focus on agriculture.

Sieferle, Rolf Peter. *The Subterranean Forest: Energy Systems and the Industrial Revolution.* Cambridge, U.K., 2001.

Simmons, Ian G. *An Environmental History of Great Britain: From 10000 Years Ago to the Present.* Edinburgh, 2001.

Whited, Tamara, et al. *Northern Europe: An Environmental History.* Santa Barbara, Calif., 2005.

JENS IVO ENGELS

■

ESTATES-GENERAL. The convening of the Estates-General in May 1789 is generally thought of as the opening act of the French Revolution. The Estates-General was the Old Regime assembly of delegates from the three estates of the kingdom: the clergy, or First Estate; the aristocracy, or Second Estate; and the commoners, or Third Estate. Over the course of the seventeenth and eighteenth centuries, however, the French monarchy had grown increasingly absolute in its powers, and the Estates-General did not meet between 1614 and 1789. After so lengthy a hiatus, it is not surprising that the decision to convene them in August 1788 was akin to opening Pandora's box.

THE FISCAL CRISIS OF THE OLD REGIME

A fiscal crisis brought on that fateful decision. In the late 1770s the French monarchy sent both financial and material aid to the American colonies in their struggle for independence from the British crown. King Louis XVI's finance minister, Jacques Necker, paid for this aid by levying a temporary tax in 1776, and by contracting a number of short-term loans, scheduled to fall due in the late 1780s and 1790s. When Necker resigned his post in 1781 he published an accounting of the royal budget, which showed a modest surplus in the treasury. Either Necker misread the situation or he misrepresented it intentionally, because just five years later it became clear to a new finance minister, Charles-Alexandre de Calonne, that the royal treasury was in serious trouble. For 1787 Calonne projected that interest on the debt would absorb 50 percent of taxes collected, and that 50 percent of the anticipated tax revenue had already been spent in advance.

The crown could not easily impose additional taxes, because France was not presently at war, nor was additional borrowing in European financial markets an option. Faced with a looming crisis, Calonne convinced Louis XVI to convoke an Assembly of Notables in February 1787. The Assembly of Notables was a carefully selected group of 144 men, including 7 princes of the blood, 14 bishops, 36 titled noblemen, 12 intendants and councillors of state, 38 magistrates from the parlements, 12 representatives from the *pays d'état* (the relatively privileged provinces of the kingdom), and 25 mayors. Calonne presented to this distinguished group an ambitious program, calling for tax reform, the abolition of internal tariffs, and creation of provincial assemblies. When the notables balked at these proposals, Calonne appealed to the public for support, which infuriated the assembly. Courtly intrigue led to Calonne's dismissal and his replacement by Étienne-Charles de Loménie de Brienne, who had led resistance among the notables. Loménie was no more successful than Calonne, however, in persuading the Assembly of Notables to endorse either structural reform or new taxes. They insisted that only the Estates-General could authorize such extraordinary measures.

CONVENING AT VERSAILLES

Faced with this impasse, Louis XVI recalled Jacques Necker to office. In August 1788 Necker persuaded the king to convene the Estates-General, and a second Assembly of Notables was called to rule on its composition. In the midst of spirited public debate and discussion, this second assembly of privileged elites issued a very traditional ruling, calling for equal representation for each of the three estates, separate meeting quarters for each estate, and voting by estate rather than by head. The ruling aroused considerable public protest, particularly in Paris, and a flurry of published pamphlets, most notable among them Emmanuel-Joseph Sieyès's *What Is the Third Estate?* Two questions in particular became quite contentious: Should the Third Estate be granted additional delegates, to reflect their greater proportion of the population, as some argued? And how should the delegates vote, by head or by order? At the urging of Necker, the king in December 1788 ordered a "doubling of the Third," but the question of how the delegates would vote remained unresolved until after the Estates-General convened at Versailles in May 1789.

On 5 May 1789 the Estates-General met at Versailles. The delegates, numbering 1,139, half from the Third Estate, filed ceremoniously past the king to their seats in the meeting hall, the clergy and nobility dressed in their finery and the delegates of the Third Estate dressed drably in black. The delegates brought with them the *cahiers de doléances,* or grievance lists, that voters had drawn up in electoral assemblies throughout France at the request of the king. The nature of the elections—multistage and indirect in the case of the Third Estate—meant that the *cahiers* were relatively moderate, but they reflected consensus on a number of issues. They called for equitable taxation, judicial reform, and reform of the seignorial system. The *cahiers* of the clergy and nobility, while frequently expressing a willingness to pay their share of taxes, also asserted the legitimacy of traditional privilege. The most significant thing about the *cahiers* is that they had, in a sense, politicized the country—for several weeks people had given serious consideration to the problems confronting the country and had offered advice to the king. All eyes were now focused on Versailles to see what the king and the Estates-General together would do.

EVOLUTION INTO NATIONAL ASSEMBLY

Louis XVI received the *cahiers,* greeted the delegates, and ordered the three estates to reassemble in their separate meeting halls for the verification of credentials. Neither the king nor his ministers offered a program for reform. No strong leadership was evident; no clear direction was marked out. Nothing was said about the method of voting, but the separate meeting halls suggested that voting would be by order, not head. Alarmed at that suggestion, and disturbed by the lackluster opening of the assembly, the delegates of the Third Estate refused to verify credentials until the issue of voting was resolved. Six weeks passed with no apparent progress. Delegates sent pessimistic reports home to their constituents, and the mood grew increasingly restive. Led by the comte de Mirabeau, a fiery orator, and the political tactician Emmanuel-Joseph Sieyès, the Third Estate called for a written constitution, and on 10 June invited the other two estates to meet together with it. A number of parish priests, resentful of the power and affluent lifestyle of the upper clergy, rallied to the Third Estate. On 17 June, heartened by that support, the Third Estate adopted the program set out earlier in Sieyès's pamphlet and declared itself the National Assembly.

Liberal aristocrats and a number of clergy now joined the Third Estate, and when the king ordered their meeting hall locked on 20 June, 576 deputies swore the Tennis Court Oath. Wherever they met there was the nation, they declared, and they would not adjourn until France had been given a new constitution. Louis XVI attempted to thwart that initiative on 23 June, by ordering the three estates to resume their separate deliberations, but in the face of determined resistance he accepted unified deliberation and voting by head on 27 June. On 9 July 1789 the delegates to the Estates-General declared themselves the National Constituent Assembly. A handful of delegates, conservative clergy or nobility, now resigned their seats and returned home, asserting that their constituents had not elected them to a National Assembly. But the vast majority set immediately to work and within months had drafted the Declaration of the Rights of Man and of the Citizen, issued decrees abolishing seignorial dues and other privileges, redrew the administrative map of France, abolished noble titles, and confiscated the properties of the church to pay off the national debt. All of this was not accomplished without royal resistance, nor without popular uprising, especially in Paris. But before they adjourned, in the fall of 1791, the deputies of the Constituent Assembly had adopted a new constitution, creating a constitutional monarchy.

See also **French Revolution; Louis XVI.**

BIBLIOGRAPHY

Applewhite, Harriet B. *Political Alignment in the French National Assembly, 1789–1791.* Baton Rouge, La., 1993.

Fitzsimmons, Michael P. *The Remaking of France: The National Assembly and the Constitution of 1791.* Cambridge, U.K., 1994.

———. *The Night the Old Regime Ended: August 4, 1789, and the French Revolution.* University Park, Pa., 2003.

Hampson, Norman. *Prelude to Terror: The Constituent Assembly and the Failure of Consensus, 1789–1791.* Oxford, U.K., 1988.

Lefebvre, Georges. *The Coming of the French Revolution.* Translated by R. R. Palmer. 1947. Reprint, with a new preface by R. R. Palmer, Princeton, N.J., 1989. Translation of *Quatre-vingt-neuf.*

Tackett, Timothy. *Becoming a Revolutionary: The Deputies of the French National Assembly and the Emergence of a Revolutionary Culture, 1789–1790.* Princeton, N.J., 1996.

PAUL R. HANSON

ETIQUETTE. *See* **Manners and Formality.**

EUGENICS. Eugenics was defined in 1904 by Sir Francis Galton (1822–1911), who coined the word, as "the science which deals with all the influences that improve and develop the inborn qualities for a race" (*Nature* [1904] 70:82). From this innocuous beginning, the eugenics movement gave support to some of the twentieth century's most frightening decisions about population, including many thousands of forced sterilizations in the United States and Nazi Germany, and the deaths of thousands of persons deemed too inferior to be allowed to live. At the height of its influence in the period between the two world wars, it had few enemies: official Catholicism and the extreme left were almost alone in their opposition. The movement lost its political support after World War II; sterilization legislation was repealed in the 1960s and 1970s. However, a shadow of the old eugenics still persists in the early twenty-first century in the form of genetic counseling of individuals at risk and also in efforts at population control in underdeveloped countries.

The eugenics movement proper began in the early twentieth century with the founding of eugenics societies in various countries. But for decades before that, there had been a pervasive feeling that humanity and human society were degenerating. In art and literature as well as science, degeneration was the focus of discussion. In Germany Max Nordau (1849–1923) argued that all modern art was a product of disease, and in Italy Cesare Lombroso (1835–1909) claimed to recognize criminal types by their degenerate physiognomy. From the mid-nineteenth century on, "meliorist" groups seeking to improve society—in Britain, the Social Science Association (1857), Charity Organisation Society (1869), the Society for the Study and Cure of Inebriety (1884), The National Association for the Care of the Feeble-Minded (1896), and the Moral Education League (1898)—concerned themselves with the minds and bodies of the urban poor and the influence of poisons such as city life, syphilis, and alcoholism. All but the Society for the Study and Cure of Inebriety had many women members.

In the last decades of the century, birthrates began to fall: steeply among the upper classes, but far less steeply among the so-called residuum, the slum-dwellers of the industrial cities. As early as 1865 Sir Francis Galton (1822–1911), a cousin of Charles Darwin (1809–1882), had suggested that talent and character were hereditary; in 1869 his *Hereditary Genius: An Inquiry into Its Laws and Consequences* appeared. If talent was hereditary, and the talented were failing to reproduce, society was doomed. The addition of Mendelian theory around 1900 gave scientific support to the fears of the upper classes that social value was hereditary and could die out.

The first eugenics society, the German Racial Hygiene Society, was founded in 1905, and the Eugenics Education Society of Britain in 1907. In the United States, legislation to permit sterilization of "undesirables" antedated the eugenics movement. The American Breeders Association began in 1903 and included a section on eugenics. The Eugenics Record Office was founded the same year. The French Eugenics Society was set up in 1912. These four represent a cross-section of the early movement, with a basic program in common, and each with some national elements. Other groups came to be set up later, but these formed the backbone of the movement. All looked to Galton as their inspiration, used his new word *eugenics,* and subscribed to his definition.

The German Racial Hygiene Society incorporated Aryanism, with its racist mythology, and social hygiene, in the persons of Wilhelm Ploetz (1860–1940), a physician and journalist, the organizer of the group, and his friends Ernst Rüdin (1874–1952), a psychiatrist; Richard Thurnwald (1869–1954), an anthropologist; and Anastasius Nordenholz (1862–1953), a social scientist. The original Berlin group sponsored subgroups in Munich, Freiburg, Dresden, and Stuttgart. By 1913 there were 425 members: physicians, university teachers, and biologists, very few of them women. The German attitude to genetic theory was very sophisticated: Wilhelm Weinberg's (1862–1937) mathematical Mendelism was available by 1908, and he himself was a member of the Stuttgart chapter. Mendelism explained the inheritance of such conditions as schizophrenia, as Rüdin claimed to have demonstrated in 1916, but in 1920 he and his colleagues in Munich abandoned Mendelism for "empirical prognosis," a theory-less collection of family data that accorded better with the group's plans for sterilization of mental patients and the "socially worthless."

The Eugenics Education Society in London, with Galton as its figurehead, had 1,047 members by the outbreak of World War I, at least a third of them women, many of them also members of the activist social societies out of which it was formed. Its original organizer was Sybil Gotto (later Sybil Neville-Rolfe), a youthful social activist inspired by Galton's books, and a lawyer friend of Galton's named Montague Crackanthorpe (1832–1913), its second president, later succeeded by Leonard Darwin (1850–1943), a son of Charles Darwin. Local groups formed elsewhere, for example in Cambridge. Most of the membership belonged to the educated middle class: they spoke on its behalf, with an aggressively outspoken class-consciousness. The Society's focus was particularly on the defective heredity of the "pauper class," those who were dependent on relief. Pauperism was seen as having many causes—inebrity, venereal disease, and feeblemindedness—but the Society's project of collecting pedigrees of pauper families underlined its insistence that the root of social failure was bad heredity. Pedigrees linking several families showing an interbreeding pauper class, studded with alcoholics, syphilitics, and the feebleminded, were prepared for the Society by Eric J. Lidbetter, a Poor Law Relieving Officer. The differential fertility of classes suggested that soon most of society would be replaced by descendents of the prolific paupers.

Proposed remedies mirrored those of the Association for the Care of the Feeble-Minded, with its segregated farm schools and institutions, where the feebleminded could be interned for life. The Society began a campaign to legalize voluntary sterilization in 1930; it was unsuccessful.

Not all eugenists belonged to the Society: the statistician Karl Pearson (1857–1936), an admirer of Galton, despised the amateurishness of the Society's science and its reliance on drawing-room talks. His group was actively hostile to Mendelism and preferred Galtonian statistics—the new techniques of frequency and standard deviation, the so-called bell curve, regression, and correlation. The Society itself used simple pedigrees, with no emphasis on any particular scientific method.

The American eugenists were Mendelian to the core. The American Breeders' Association was mainly concerned with the breeding of animals and plants for agriculture, but it had a section devoted to eugenics. In 1910 its Secretary was the biologist Charles Davenport (1866–1944), head of the Carnegie Institute's Station for Experimental Evolution at Cold Stream Harbor, set up in 1904. The Association's journal published articles explaining Mendelism to agricultural breeders, who were rather unreceptive. The eugenics committee, however, was very active, and keenly interested in racial degeneration under the chairmanship of David Starr Jordan (1851–1931) of Stanford University. Harry H. Laughlin (1880–1943), who was doing breeding experiments with poultry at the Experiment Station, made contact with Davenport, and in 1910, joined him in setting up the Eugenics Record Office, also at Cold Stream Harbor. It was funded by a private donor, Mary Williamson Averell Harriman (1851–1932), who was interested in horse breeding.

Laughlin and Davenport worked together to train teams of field workers who would go out, armed with a "Trait Book," and collect human pedigrees. Their standardized pedigree diagrams were soon adopted by other eugenists. Beginning with brachydactyly (a harmless condition producing very short fingers and toes) and albinism, clear examples of Mendelian inheritance, they went on to include pedigrees showing insanity, alcoholism, criminality, and feeblemindedness. The workers visited state institutions, hospitals, and inbred rural communities in search of material. Davenport showed the way in *Eugenics: The Science of Human Improvement by Better Breeding* (1910). The Eugenics Records Office's pedigrees appeared in his *Heredity in Relation to Eugenics* (1911), but thousands more were archived at the Eugenics Record Office. Laughlin wrote on the legal aspects of sterilization. Speaking to the First National Conference on Race Betterment in 1914, he estimated that about 10 percent of the population was defective, and that their numbers would increase to a level that would destroy society. Therefore, he thought, these individuals must be institutionalized and sterilized. Laughlin was later to concern himself actively with immigration control on racial grounds.

Legislation enabling involuntary sterilization on hereditarian grounds of the insane, feebleminded, and "moral imbeciles"—often single mothers—was already being enacted in the United States before this work appeared. The Indiana law of 1907, a model law often copied elsewhere, authorized the sterilization of inmates of state institutions. The California Act came in 1909. Between 1905 and 1918 seventeen states voted on sterilization bills, and by 1920, 3,233 persons had been sterilized in the United States. When the laws were repealed in the 1960s, 63,678 had been sterilized, many after 1930, mainly of the feebleminded and mentally ill. These laws provided a template for the Nazi sterilization law of 1933.

The First International Congress of Eugenics was held in London in 1912. The seven hundred participants represented a progressive elite, optimistically advocating a mixture of new science, politics, and social reform, their movement dedicated to the raising of the human race to new levels of beauty and productivity, while weeding out its supposed defectives. Women supported it as a scientific validation of their authority in the reproductive sphere. The French sent a delegation to the Congress; after the meeting, they went home to start their own society. The differential birthrate was not a focus in France. The famous pediatrician Adolphe Pinard (1844–1934) led the way with pronatalism, a drive to reverse the fall of the French birthrate, and his *puériculture,* a new insistence on careful management and feeding of both infants and pregnant mothers. These two elements formed the core of French eugenics. Neither had anything to do with heredity, although the discussion of genetic defect more usual in other countries was later to appear in France as well.

By 1914 the founding societies were well established. The series of International Congresses, continued in the United States after World War I, bound the movement together and enabled concepts produced in one country to take root in others. The eugenics movement swept up some of the most influential thinkers of the time; so far, there had been very little opposition.

See also **Darwin, Charles; Degeneration; Galton, Francis; Lombroso, Cesare; Marriage and Family; Mendel, Gregor; Population, Control of; Race and Racism; Science and Technology.**

BIBLIOGRAPHY

Allen, Garland E. "The Eugenics Record Office at Cold Spring Harbor, 1910–1940: An Essay in Institutional History." *Osiris* (1986) 2:225–264.

Kimmelman, Barbara A. "The American Breeders' Association: Genetics and Eugenics in an Agricultural Context, 1903–13." *Social Studies of Science* (1983) 13:163–204.

Mazumdar, Pauline M. H. *Eugenics, Human Genetics, and Human Failings: The Eugenics Society, Its Sources and its Critics in Britain.* London, 1991.

Reilly, Philip R. *The Surgical Solution: A History of Involuntary Sterilization in the United States.* Baltimore, Md., and London, 1991.

Schneider, William H. *Quality and Quantity: The Quest for Biological Regeneration in Twentieth-Century France.* Cambridge, U.K., 1990.

Thomson, Mathew. *The Problem of Mental Deficiency: Eugenics, Democracy and Social Policy in Britain, c. 1870–1959.* Oxford, U.K., 1998.

Weindling, Paul. *Health, Race and German Politics between National Unification and Nazism, 1870–1945.* Cambridge, U.K., 1989.

PAULINE M. H. MAZUMDAR

EURASIANISM.

Eurasianism is a complex doctrine according to which Russia belongs to neither Europe nor Asia, but forms a unique entity defined by the historical, anthropological, linguistic, ethnographic, economic, and political interactions of the various genetically unrelated peoples who once constituted the Russian Empire. The doctrine's formulators believed that Russia-Eurasia's rare and unique geography creates an indivisible ethnocultural and geopolitical unity with a singular destiny: to emancipate humankind from the hegemony of European civilization.

Eurasianism emerged in the 1920s as young Russian émigré intellectuals reacted to the Russian Revolution of 1917, the collapse of the Russian Empire, and the postwar crisis in Europe. In seeking new sources of legitimacy for Russian imperial space and a new role for non-European peoples in the modern world, they developed a doctrine that departed sharply from the conventional vision of Russia. Nevertheless, Eurasianism had nineteenth- and early-twentieth-century precursors.

CONSTRUCTING THE ORIENT

Pre-Eurasian ideas stemmed from discussions of Russia's encounter with Asia. Many nineteenth-century intellectuals saw Russia's location between Europe and Asia as a metaphor for its distinctive spirit and destiny. A key question inevitably arose: was Russia an agent of European civilization vis-à-vis the Orient, or, on the contrary, had Russia's mentality itself been shaped by its often traumatic relations with Asia, especially by the so-called Tatar yoke (that is, the Mongol invasion and rule over Russia in the thirteenth through fifteenth centuries)? Moreover, if contact with the Orient did play a formative role in Russian identity, how was that role to be evaluated?

Peter Chaadayev (1794–1856), one of the first philosophers of Russian history, contended that Orthodoxy, inherited from Byzantium, had isolated Russia from Western Christendom, doomed it to destructive Eastern influences, and led to its disappearance from world history. He opened his first *Philosophical Letter* (written from 1827 to 1831, published in 1836), with the startling assertion, "We are neither of the West nor of the East." Russian intellectuals responded to this provocative statement throughout the nineteenth century.

The Westernizers, who took Russia's European identity for granted, defined the Orient as Europe's "other"—a realm of despotism, stagnation,

religious fanaticism, and stifled individuality. Although the Slavophiles fostered anti-European sentiments and defined Russian national identity through Byzantine Orthodoxy and Slavic culture, they also embraced the conventional assumption of Russia's superiority over the East. The striking consensus of these two rival intellectual groups went unchallenged until 1836, when a Russian Schellingist made one of the first attempts to articulate proto-Eurasian ideas. Vladimir Titov, the Russian envoy to Istanbul and a member of the society Lovers of Wisdom (followers of the German philosopher Friedrich Wilhelm Joseph von Schelling), added a new perspective to the question of Russia and the Orient. Titov praised Oriental cultures for the power of their religious conviction, their governments' paternal relationship to their subjects, and, finally, their preference for subtle pleasures (*keif*) over Western "creature comforts." Like the Slavophiles, Titov condemned government-sponsored Westernization as a tragic turn in Russian history, but unlike them, he identified Russia's "abandoned" past with its Asiatic roots. According to Titov, Russia's return to its Asiatic legacy would stimulate the country's development and confirm its unique destiny "to serve as a link between East and West." Using the Romantic philosophy of organic unity as the epistemological basis for their ideas, the Eurasians later developed this approach into a systematic doctrine.

"RUSSIAN SOCIALISM" AND ASIAN BARBARISM

A dramatic reinterpretation of Russia's encounter with Asia and its role in shaping the nation's destiny arose out of revolutionary ideology, another important source of Eurasianism. The brilliant émigré writer Alexander Herzen (1812–1870), who had observed the revolutionary wave of 1848 in Italy and France, concluded that social revolution could not take place in the West, where bourgeois values had corrupted the ideologues of socialism. In the 1850s, Herzen predicted that the Slavic countries—and above all Russia—would become the homeland of social revolution. He credited Russia's isolation from the West with preserving the village commune, a traditional institution of rural Russia, which he idealized as the kernel of communist society. Herzen thus reinterpreted the traumatic experiences that had divorced Russia from Europe—above all, the Tatar yoke—as a cultural advantage.

Although Herzen attributed conventional negative characteristics to Asia, he argued that the Tatar yoke had saved Russia from Europe by preserving its authentic cultural patterns and keeping its "young energies" undefiled by bourgeois corruption. Unlike most intellectuals, he praised the theory of Russia's Turanian origins—that is, the cultural, racial, and anthropological blending of Russians with Finno-Ugric and Asiatic populations, a theory that arose as part of anti-Russian propaganda spread by Polish revolutionary émigrés. Comparing western Europe to Rome in its decline, Herzen saw Russians as the new barbaric tribes, fated to destroy the old civilization and breathe new life into it by realizing the socialist project. Purged of its Westernizing spirit, Herzen's construct would later pave the way for the Eurasians' startling redefinition of Russia as the sole inheritor of Genghis Khan's empire and the leader of the non-European peoples' revolt against the Western world.

A PRECURSOR OF EURASIANISM

The founders of Eurasianism credited Konstantin Leontiev (1831–1891)—conservative philosopher, diplomat, journalist, novelist, and literary critic— with preparing the conceptual groundwork for their doctrine. Following Herzen, Leontiev saw Russians' "Turanian nature" as a counterweight to a "dying" Europe, but, unlike his predecessor, Leontiev rejected European civilization entirely and justified Asiatic despotism and theocracy. As the basic criterion for a nation's viability, Leontiev proposed an "aesthetics of living," that is, a concept embracing cultural diversity. He believed that multiple customs could thrive only where an external force—such as political despotism, religious discipline, or communist compulsion—held interacting traditions in check. Leontiev called this state of society the "flowering of complexity," which he contrasted with the aesthetic monotony and consequent decay resulting from the triumph of bourgeois and egalitarian ideals in the West. Leontiev found such an aesthetics of living in the contemporary Orient but only partially in Russia. Consequently, he thought that Turkey or "a renewed China or awakened India" was fated to change the world.

Russia could play a role in world history only by developing forms of despotism that would "freeze" its authentic cultural patterns, as well as its unique blending of Asiatic and Slavic traditions.

In his *Byzantinism and Slavdom* (1875), Leontiev positioned himself as a disciple of Nikolai Danilevsky (1822–1865), the author of *Russia and Europe* (1869), a tract that served as another source of Eurasianism. Danilevsky's scheme, which identified several successive "cultural types" in world history and prophesied the collapse of the currently dominant "Romano-Germanic cultural type," inspired Leontiev to reevaluate the Orient. Instead of condemning Oriental characteristics—such as stagnation, indolence, contemplation, religious fanaticism, and stifled individuality—as ridiculous (the conventional view), he saw them as proof of the life force and creative energies of Eastern civilization. Yet unlike Danilevsky, Leontiev harshly criticized Pan-Slavism (rejected later by the Eurasians) and even justified the Ottoman Empire's rule over southern Slavs as a way to protect them from Europe's damaging influences. He condemned ethnic (in his terminology, tribal) nationalism both as a revolutionary ideology that mimicked European national movements and as an egalitarian doctrine that concealed Europe's homogenizing impact.

SOLOVIEV'S ORIENT

Although marginal in the nineteenth century, Leontiev's ideas began to take hold among the cultural elite in the early twentieth century, when his legacy was mainly passed along through the poetry and religious philosophy of Vladimir Soloviev (1853–1900). In *The Philosophical Principles of Integral Knowledge* (1877), Soloviev outlined three stages of human evolution. The Eastern world represented the initial stage—a phase of primitive, undifferentiated organic unity in which religion defined all spheres of human activity. Soloviev held the Muslim East superior to the next evolutionary phase, Western civilization, in which egotism, anarchy, and atomization reigned supreme. Although Soloviev, unlike Leontiev, criticized Oriental despotism, he nevertheless found positive traits in the East that were to be embodied anew in a final phase of human development represented by the Slavs (above all, Russians) who would reconcile Eastern and Western values.

Soloviev's ideas evolved over time, but he always considered East and West as complements. According to his later views, it was Christianity (not the Russian nation) that would successfully reunite West and East. In his poem "Light from the East" (*"Ex Oriente Lux,"* 1890), Soloviev identifies Russia with the East, yet poses a fundamental question unresolved in the poem: will Russia be the East of slavery and despotism or the East of Christianity, freedom, and love? In his final years, Soloviev became pessimistic about mankind's future and wrote the *Tale of the Antichrist* (1900), which anticipates Europe's invasion by a yellow-skinned race, the imposition of a new Mongol yoke, and the Antichrist's subsequent, but temporary triumph (a prelude to the Second Coming).

PROTO-EURASIAN IDEAS IN THE EARLY TWENTIETH CENTURY

The first two decades of the twentieth century witnessed a striking upsurge in Oriental motifs in Russian literature. Proceeding from the Romantic conviction that "primitive" cultures were superior to European civilization, the symbolist poets sought in Asia a "forgotten" incarnation of Russia's true self. Greatly influenced by Soloviev's philosophy, "Silver Age" poets found his theme of the Asian menace a source of anxiety and inspiration. Defeat in the Russo-Japanese War (1904–1905) intensified their fear but did not diminish their admiration for the might and creative potential of the Eastern world.

The Eurasians recognized Alexander Blok (1880–1921) as their nearest precursor among the symbolists. In his cycle "On Kulikovo Field" (1908), devoted to the Russians' triumph over the Golden Horde in 1380, Blok develops two interconnected themes: the "eternal struggle" between Russians and Asiatic nomads and their intertwined historical fates. In "Scythians" (1918), these ideas became a metaphorical expression of Russians' double identity—Asiatic and European. The poem's concluding verses raise the threat of Russia's union with the "barbarous" East, a union predicted to prove fatal for the West.

The symbolist Andrei Bely (1880–1934) saw the image of "a new Kulikovo" as the emblem of an apocalyptic struggle between Pan-Mongolism and the European world. Following the 1905 revolution, he planned an "East-West" trilogy, but completed only two novels. In the first, *The Silver Dove* (1910), a confrontation between the occult East and the rational, atheist West leads to a tragic denouement. In his famous second novel, *Petersburg* (published serially 1913–1914), Bely contrasts the Russia of St. Petersburg, shorn of its national roots, to the "real," organic Russia, which he defines as partially Asiatic.

The Eurasians also identified their ideas in the works of the futurist Velimir Khlebnikov (1885–1922), a connoisseur of Eastern cultures. In his 1912 poem "Khadzhi-Tarkhan" (the Turkic name of Astrakhan), Khlebnikov portrayed the Volga's lower reaches as a place where the Slavic and Eastern worlds meet. In his 1918 manifestoes "An Indo-Russian Union" and "Azosoyuz," Khlebnikov dreamed of young Asia as a "single mega-island" (which included Russia) engulfed by revolution. Such projects resonated with the Eurasians' dream of emancipating the colonized peoples of Asia under Russian leadership.

Like Khlebnikov, the visual artist Nikolai Roerich (1874–1947) used proto-Eurasian motifs. For Sergei Diaghilev's "Seasons of Russia Opera" in Paris (1908–1913), Roerich portrayed Russian culture as a synthesis of Slavic and Asian traditions in the set designs and costumes he created for Alexander Borodin's opera *Prince Igor*, Nikolai Rimsky-Korsakov's opera *The Snow Maiden*, and Igor Stravinsky's ballet *The Rite of Spring*. Stravinsky, who developed a "Turanian musical style" must have affected proto-Eurasian motifs in various forms of cultural production.

The ideologues of Eurasianism insisted that the strong focus of Russian philosophy and science on teleological (as opposed to causal) aspects of evolution distinguished the Russian from the Western intellectual traditions and thus paved the way to comprehending Eurasia as an indivisible geopolitical, cultural, and social entity. The Eurasians clearly drew upon Western intellectual achievements—including the Romantic thought of Schelling and the naturalist Alexander von Humboldt, Oswald Spengler's prophecy of Europe's decline, Friedrich Ratzel's concept of "ethnological territories," Wilhelm Schmidt's theory of "cultural areas," Franz Boas's and Alfred Louis Kroeber's concepts of cultural relativism in anthropology, and Johannes Schmidt's and August Leskien's studies of linguistic of the geochemist Vladimir Vernadsky, who studied the convergence of the elements contained within biospheres (closed systems with autonomous properties). All these theories profoundly influenced the Eurasians' definition of culture as a product of natural conditions and their vision of the former Russian Empire as an autarkic territory.

THE EURASIAN MOVEMENT

Eurasianism as a movement dates from the 1920s, when Prince Nikolai Trubetskoy, a linguist, published his treatise "Europe and Mankind" (1920). This was followed by a collective volume, *Exodus to the East* (1921).

According to the Eurasians, World War I and the Russian Revolution marked the beginning of a new period of history, one characterized by the decline of the West and the concomitant rise of the East. The Eurasians transmuted the gospel of humanity's emancipation from "Romano-Germanic" domination, dating back to Danilevsky and Leontiev, into a vision of Russia-Eurasia leading an uprising of Asia's colonized peoples against the Old World.

After flourishing during the 1920s and 1930s, the Eurasian movement, which had provided a conceptual framework capable of absorbing a wide variety of ideas, foundered because of internal dissent and the dispersal of its members. The most visible rupture came when some members proposed cooperation with the Soviet regime, thereby incurring the condemnation of others. Born out of war, revolution, and the specific experience of a group of young intellectuals in exile searching for their lost homeland, Eurasianism gradually disappeared in the emigration, but was revived again in Russia at the end of the twentieth century.

See also **Bely, Andrei; Blok, Alexander; Chaadayev, Peter; Herzen, Alexander; Slavophiles; Soloviev, Vladimir; Westernizers.**

BIBLIOGRAPHY

Primary Sources

Savitskii, Petr, Petr Suvchinskii, Nikolai Trubetskoi, and Georgii Florovskii. *Exodus to the East: Forebodings and Events; An Affirmation of the Eurasians.* Translated by Ilya Vinkovetsky, Catherine Boyle, and

Costume of a Russian peasant girl. Design by Nikolai Roerich for Igor Stravinsky's ballet *The Rite of Spring,* 1913. Roerich's design clearly reflects the influence of Asian art and culture. ERICH LESSING/ART RESOURCE, NY

innovations across genetic boundaries. Yet Eurasianism's founders insisted that "Russian science" served as their immediate source of inspiration. They modified certain patterns and paradigms developed by Russian naturalists, critics of Darwinism, who emphasized goal-oriented evolutionary mechanisms. They fastened onto the syncretic theory of natural zones, formulated by the geoscientist Vasily Dokuchayev, because of its focus on the multifaceted interactions between various elements and agents within a single zone. The ideas of the zoologist Lev Berg, who emphasized boundary unity within certain landscapes, allowed them to argue for the commonality of the genetically unrelated peoples of Eurasia. They also referred frequently to the works

Kenneth Brostrom. Edited by Ilya Vinkovetsky and Charles Schlacks Jr. Idyllwild, Calif., 1996.

Trubetzkoy, Nikolai Sergeevich. *The Legacy of Chingis Khan and Other Essays on Russia's Identity.* Edited by Anatoly Liberman. Ann Arbor, Mich., 1991.

Secondary Sources

Becker, Seymour. "Russia between East and West: The Intelligentsia, Russian National Identity, and the Asian Borderlands." *Central Asian Survey* 10, no. 4 (1991): 47–64.

Riasanovsky, Nicholas V. "The Emergence of Eurasianism." *California Slavic Studies* 4 (1967): 39–72.

Sériot, Patrick. *Structure et totalité: Les origines intellectuelles du structuralisme en Europe centrale et orientale.* Paris, 1999.

Taruskin, Richard. *Stravinsky and the Russian Traditions: A Biography of the Works through Mavra.* 2 vols. Berkeley, Calif., 1996.

OLGA MAIOROVA

EVOLUTION. The idea of evolution came to dominate many aspects of Western thought in the late nineteenth century. Although associated primarily with the theory of the evolution of life on earth presented by Charles Darwin (1809–1882), the general idea of a natural development through time was also applied in many other areas, including the history of the universe, of the earth, and of human society and culture. Evolution was generally assumed to be progressive: that is, to advance toward higher levels of organization, with the human species—and modern Western culture—as the goals toward which it was driven.

Evolutionism was controversial because it challenged the Biblical story of creation and implied that humans were merely improved animals, thereby threatening the traditional belief that humans are the direct creations of God, possessing immortal souls that will be judged by eternal moral values. Darwin's theory of natural selection drove home the destructive implications of this challenge by showing how the appearance of new species could come about through the interaction of apparently unplanned and essentially haphazard natural processes. It also implied that struggle and competition were natural and indeed necessary

aspects of nature's activities. Late-twentieth-century studies of the "Darwinian revolution" suggest, however, that the radical implications that modern thinkers find in Darwin's theory were largely subverted at the time. Evolution became popular because it was seen as the motor of progress, and natural selection merely weeded out the system's less efficient products. The human race was still the goal of creation, but produced by the purposeful laws of nature rather than supernatural divine action.

EVOLUTION BEFORE DARWIN

Although Darwin's *Origin of Species,* published in 1859, is credited with converting the scientific world to evolutionism and sparking a major public debate on the topic, the idea had been in circulation for at least a century. Although at first seen as a radical theory, modern historians have shown that by the 1850s the idea was being transformed into something that the middle classes could find acceptable. Darwin merely precipitated a transformation that had already been building up behind the scenes.

In the early eighteenth century, it was still widely believed that the earth was created only a few thousand years prior, with Noah's flood being the only agent of geological change. But by the later decades of the century, geologists had begun to show that the earth had an extensive history far beyond that of the human race. In the early nineteenth century, anatomists such as Georges Cuvier (1769–1832) began to reconstruct the fossil bones of extinct species and developed the concept of a sequence of geological periods each with its own inhabitants. Initially, conservative naturalists interpreted this evidence in terms of a modified version of the old idea of divine creation. Instead of a single creation in the Garden of Eden, God formed a new collection of species at the beginning of each epoch of earth history.

Highly speculative theories of the natural origin of species had already been postulated in the late eighteenth century. In his *Des époques de la nature* (Epochs of nature) of 1778, the Comte de Buffon (1707–1788) had argued that related species had gradually diverged from a single prototype as separate populations adapted to new environments. But he thought that the original types had been formed by a process of spontaneous generation at certain points in the earth's history, a view shared by materialist philosophers. Something resembling the modern idea of evolution emerged in the writings of Erasmus Darwin (1731–1802, Charles Darwin's grandfather), whose *Zoonomia* of 1791–1794 contained a chapter expounding the view that the laws of nature have led to the progressive development of life from the simplest organisms to humanity over a vast period of time. Such ideas were developed further in France by Jean-Baptiste-Pierre-Antoine de Monet de Lamarck (1744–1829), who also stressed a particular mechanism of transformation that would later be known as *Lamarckism*. This was the inheritance of acquired characters: the ancestral giraffes reached up to eat the leaves of trees, and the longer necks they thus acquired were transmitted to their offspring.

Although conservative scientists scorned Lamarck, modern research has shown that there was a strong current of radical thought in the 1820s that took his ideas seriously. In 1844, an attempt was made to adapt the idea of progressive transmutation to middle class attitudes in the anonymously published *Vestiges of the Natural History of Creation* (written by Robert Chambers [1802–1871]). Chambers presented evolution as the unfolding of a divinely ordained plan, and he explicitly included the human species as the end-product of the trend. Although *Vestiges* attracted much criticism, it gained the idea of evolution a hearing and thus shaped the way public opinion would respond to Darwin.

DARWIN AND DARWINISM

Charles Darwin had gained wide experience as a naturalist, especially on his voyage around the world on HMS *Beagle* (1831–1836). Soon after his return to England, he began looking for a natural explanation of how isolated populations would adapt to their environment, eventually producing new species. His theory of natural selection postulated a struggle for existence driven by shortage of resources, as outlined in the theory of population pressure advanced by Thomas Robert Malthus (1766–1834). Since individual animals have slightly varying characters, the best adapted would survive and breed, while maladapted individuals would be weeded out. This is the process that philosopher Herbert Spencer (1820–1903) would call the "survival of the fittest"—which encouraged many of Darwin's readers to assume that the "fittest" were the highest on a scale of progressive development, although Darwin had really focused on varying degrees of adaptation to the local environment.

When the *Origin of Species* was eventually published in 1859, there was renewed debate. Natural selection did not seem like the kind of mechanism a benevolent God would employ. Darwin published his views on human origins in his *Descent of Man* (1871) and it became clear that he saw the human mind very much as a product of natural evolution, with huge implications for the traditional view of morality. Darwin's supporters, including the young naturalist Thomas Henry Huxley (1825–1895), ensured that his theory survived the attacks of religious conservatives, and by the 1870s the majority of scientists and educated people had begun to accept the basic idea of evolution. The enthusiasm was so great that the idea of progressive evolution was soon being applied to social issues, generating the movement known as "social Darwinism." Spencer was the philosopher of the evolutionary movement, applying the idea to the whole development of life and of human society and culture. Spencer stressed the role of progress, and for him natural selection was a negative process that merely weeded out the less successful products of progressive evolution. Spencer invoked Lamarckism to explain how new characters were formed, as did the leading German Darwinist, Ernst Heinrich Philipp August Haeckel (1834–1919).

LATER DEVELOPMENTS

Spencer linked Darwinism to the competitive ethos of free-enterprise capitalism, which made his views especially attractive in America. Haeckel preferred to concentrate on competition between nations and races, not between individuals, and by the end of the century this model was widely incorporated into the rhetoric of imperialism. Evolutionism thus became the foundation for a variety of radical and liberal ideologies in various countries. But precisely because evolutionism was identified with progress, liberal religious thinkers were also able to accommodate the theory by seeing progress toward humanity as the unfolding of a divine purpose.

MR. BERGH TO THE RESCUE.

THE DEFRAUDED GORILLA. "That *Man* wants to claim my Pedigree. He says he is one of my Descendants."

MR. BERGH. "Now, Mr. DARWIN, how could you insult him so?"

Thomas Nast cartoon about evolution, c. 1871. Henry Bergh, founder of the American Society for the Prevention of Cruelty to Animals, is shown chiding Charles Darwin for insulting the gorilla by arguing that humans are descended from apes. ©CORBIS

Although various forms of social Darwinism remained popular, among scientists there was growing distrust of natural selection, leading to an "eclipse of Darwinism" in which Lamarckism and other non-Darwinian mechanisms were preferred. In the early twentieth century, the philosopher Henri-Louis Bergson's (1859–1941) idea of "creative evolution" became a popular alternative to Darwinian materialism, although in fact Bergson's image of nature struggling blindly upward was more in tune with the open-ended, haphazard model of evolution implied in Darwin's work. There was no preordained goal toward which na-

ture was being drawn, as in the older forms of progressionism.

Bergson's ideas influenced many biologists and thus helped to encourage a less teleological image of evolution. But natural selection remained suspect, and in biology, the most powerful alternative to Darwinism was genetics, popularized after the "rediscovery" of the work of Gregor Johann Mendel (1822–1884) on heredity in 1900. Genetics postulated clearly defined unit-characters transmitted from parent to offspring and ruled out any Lamarckian influence from the environment. Such rigid models of heredity played an important role in providing scientific plausibility for Sir Francis Galton (1822–1911) and the eugenics movement's calls for the sterilization of the "unfit" members of society. Artificial selection would thus replace the survival of the fittest as the means by which the human race would be perfected.

Geneticists initially rejected natural selection, believing that new characters produced by sudden "mutations" could establish new species instantaneously. But their theory had undermined the plausibility of Lamarckism, and Darwinism itself stressed the determining role of heredity. By 1914 a few biologists were beginning to realize that natural selection might act to weed out the less well-adapted mutations within the population. The stage was set for the reconciliation of genetics and selectionism that would create modern Darwinism in the interwar years.

See also **Bergson, Henri; Darwin, Charles; Galton, Francis; Haeckel, Ernst Heinrich; Huxley, Thomas Henry; Lamarck, Jean-Baptiste; Mendel, Gregor; Spencer, Herbert.**

BIBLIOGRAPHY

Bannister, Robert C. *Social Darwinism: Science and Myth in Anglo-American Social Thought.* Philadelphia, 1979.

Bowler, Peter J. *Evolution: The History of an Idea.* 3rd ed. Berkeley, Calif., 2003.

Browne, E. Janet. *Charles Darwin: Voyaging.* London, 1995.

———. *Charles Darwin: The Power of Place.* London, 2002.

Desmond, Adrian J. *The Politics of Evolution: Morphology, Medicine and Reform in Radical London.* Chicago, 1989.

Moore, James R. *The Post-Darwinian Controversies: A Study of the Protestant Struggle to Come to Terms with Darwin in Britain and America, 1870–1900.* Cambridge, U.K., 1979.

Secord, James A. *Victorian Sensation: The Extraordinary Publication, Reception, and Secret Authorship of Vestiges of the Natural History of Creation.* Chicago, 2000.

PETER J. BOWLER

EXILE, PENAL. Exile and banishment are some of the earliest forms of penal punishments. Although terminology differs and *exile* has generally been used to describe both these punishments, in a strict sense *banishment* is the exclusion or expulsion of an individual from a particular territory, while *exile* is a specific form of banishment in which the location of exile is specified. Criminals are banished *from* the homeland but exiled *to* a specific location. Exile was more difficult and costly to organize because it presumed some form of mechanism to ensure that the exile was restricted to the exile zone, and that the exile zone was to some extent under the control of the home country. It could be an island such as St. Helena, where the British exiled Napoleon in 1815; it could be a distant fortified city like Accra, where the Ottoman Empire exiled the popular Iranian religious leader Baha Allah in 1868. But these were privileged exiles who were treated with respect and not forced to engage in penal work.

Penal exile is a subcategory of exile that requires some additional penal sanction in the exile zone. In practice there was little difference between penal exile and exile for the poor. In order for the poor to survive in their place of exile they had to find work, and if the only available work was that organized by the authorities, the penal exiles had to accept the work on the conditions that it was offered in order to survive. For wealthier, more privileged exiles there clearly was a difference. In most cases the financial situation within the penal establishments was such that exiles who had money were given privileges that exempted them from having to engage in the harsh penal work of the poor. If the state wanted to punish the wealthy it would execute or imprison them rather than send them to penal exile.

Some of the earliest examples of modern colonial penal exile developed out of galley slavery, as in the early Spanish penal exile of about 220 *forzados* (convicts) to the mercury mines of Almaden in Mexico from the 1550s. In other cases penal exile arose from the need to find employment for those imprisoned in castles, especially in places of colonial expansion. In the Spanish case this applied to the presidios of North Africa or the Caribbean where *desterrados* (exiles) served out their banishment.

BRITISH PENAL EXILE: TRANSPORTATION TO THE COLONIES

British penal exile, in the form of transportation to the American colonies, had been used in the seventeenth and eighteenth centuries as a substitute for the death penalty, particularly for those claiming benefit of clergy (meaning the right not to be executed on the grounds that they could read). The numbers of criminals transported to America rose from about 4 per year at the beginning of the seventeenth century to about 180 per year at the beginning of the eighteenth century and peaked at about 1,000 per year in 1770. The American Revolution put a sudden end to this form of punishment just as its numbers were becoming significant. For a while the British reverted to putting dangerous prisoners to work in the docks and on naval installation and lodging them in decommissioned vessels known as "the hulks." Attempts were made to find other possible locations for transportation or penal exile, including Canada, Gibraltar, or the Gambia and Senegal Rivers in Africa, before the decision eventually was made to set up a penal colony at Botany Bay in Australia.

The initial attempts to establish Australia as a penal colony were disturbed by the Napoleonic Wars. The first fleet of 1788 contained 759 convicts, the second fleet in 1790 contained over 1,250, and the third fleet of 1791 over 2,000. But numbers then fell dramatically during wartime and only resumed a level of over 1,000 per year in 1814. By 1818 more than 3,000 convicts were being sent out per year and over 4,000 in 1820. Figures probably peaked at 6,500 per year in 1833 but fell sharply in 1840 when transportation to New South Wales ceased. Transportation to Van Diemen's Land (Tasmania) continued until 1852 and to Western Australia, on a smaller scale, to 1867. Altogether about 187,000 convicts were sent to Australia from 1788 to 1867, and they provided the basis upon which the colony was to develop.

Unlike in America, where convicts had been sold to private contractors who employed them as they wished, the employment of convicts in the Australian colonies was under much more direct government control. Initially convicts were used for many kinds of productive work, but as the colony developed the tasks became more restricted to labor such as road building, timber production, and construction.

The punishment of penal exile in Australia had appeared very severe at first, when mortality rates were high and the fate of the colony seemed unsure. But as the colony prospered and the transportation conditions eased, the sentence began to loose some of its dread. The discovery of gold in the colony and massive improvements in local wealth quickly led authorities to seek alternative punishments. Port Arthur in Van Diemen's Land developed as a center for secondary punishment.

FRENCH PENAL EXILE

Although there was much debate among British penologists about the failures of the penal colony, the French were eager to emulate it. Following the decommissioning of the French galleys in the middle of the eighteenth century the French had sent their hard-labor prisoners to a series of naval dockyards (*bagnes*), mainly in Toulon, Brest, Rochefort, and Lorient. On the eve of the French Revolution the *bagnes* contained about 5,400 hard-labor prisoners.

The Revolution transformed the legal system and introduced a form of penal exile that entailed deportation for life. This was designed as a punishment of hard labor for second offenders, but only after they had served their second sentence in France. This initiated a search for possible locations for penal exile. Some political offenders were sent to French Guinea in the 1790s, but this was a disaster, with many dying. In 1801 Napoleon expressed his support for the transportation of 6,000 common criminals who at the time were filling the prisons. However, no location was found and by 1810 the *bagnes* are estimated to have contained about 16,000 *forçats* (convicts). The Revolution of 1848 resulted in the arrest of 15,000 insurgents, which greatly added to the problem of penal overpopulation. Eventually many of these prisoners were sent to penal exile in Algeria. Following the 1851 coup d'état of Louis-Napoleon Bonaparte, 27,000 opponents of the regime were arrested. About half of these were sentenced by special courts to penal exile in Algeria, and 239 of the most dangerous were sent to a newly created penal colony in French Guiana. In addition, about 3,000 *forçats* in the *bagnes* were cajoled into volunteering to go into penal exile in French Guiana rather than remain in France. This again turned into a disaster with an extremely high death rate. In 1863 New Caledonia was declared an alternative site for penal exile from France. From 1867 until its closure in 1896, New Caledonia operated as the only site for exile from France, while Guiana continued to be used for exiles from the French colonies, only ceasing operations in 1938. Altogether it is estimated that 104,000 prisoners served time in these two exile colonies over these years.

RUSSIAN PENAL EXILE

The nature of Russian penal exile was somewhat different from that in Britain or France and more similar to the earlier Spanish experience. The Russian word *katorga* derives from the Greek word for galley slave and was introduced in Russia at the beginning of the eighteenth century by Peter the Great, on the advice of his friend Ambassador Andrei Vinius. Under Peter and his successors the death penalty was virtually abolished for civil offenses, and many of those who would have received the death penalty in Britain or France were sentenced to *katorga* instead.

The *katorzhniki* built much of the new capital, St. Petersburg. They later labored on the great canal structures linking it with Moscow. Eventually the *katorzhniki* were moved farther east into increasingly remote locations and began to take on the nature of forced exiles, where they worked in the mines of Yekaterinburg and Nerchinsk, in timber cutting or on construction sites.

Apart from the legal category of *katorzhnik*, the Russian penal system included a number of categories of offenders who were sent into exile as an administrative measure and were able to escape the penal aspects of this punishment. This applied to revolutionaries such as Vladimir Lenin, who were provided with food and money by their friends and relatives and could spend their time writing or hunting. Although political offenders are often the best known of the Siberian exiles, they are quite untypical of the mass of penal exiles whose lives were very hard indeed. Less privileged groups included those who were exiled by their local village communities. This included former criminals, who were not accepted back into their village communities and who automatically faced exile, but also other groups that had earned for some reason the disfavor of their local communities. At the central level, apart from wealthy and well-known political leaders, local troublemakers and youths charged with hooliganism could find themselves in these categories. Prior to 1871 many of these groups would have been forced into the army, but military reforms of that year did away with this kind of punishment.

Following the abolition of corporal punishment for civil society in 1845 and the legal reforms of the 1860s, the situation may have improved somewhat, although corporal punishment continued to be applied in penal establishments. Exile was formally abolished as a form of punishment in 1901. However, from 1905 there was much resort to extrajudicial punishments and the continuation of something that looked very similar to the former exile system, even though it was supposed to have been abolished.

Because of these changes in categories and the poor accounting of exiles once they were in Siberia, it is difficult to assess precisely the numbers of penal exiles in Russia. The numbers transported to Siberia appear to have grown from about 2,000 per year in the early nineteenth century to about 7,000 per year at midcentury and 17,000 per year at the end of the century.

CONCLUSION

Penal exile was a significant form of punishment in a number of European countries in the nineteenth century that had access to colonies or large underpopulated areas. It provided an alternative punishment to the death sentence for serious crimes when the widespread use of the death sentence seemed inappropriate. In many of these countries penal exile was used to assist colonial expansion and development of poorly populated areas, but as colonial development proceeded the scope for continuing to send exiles was reduced.

See also **Class and Social Relations; Colonies; Crime; Police and Policing.**

BIBLIOGRAPHY

Adams, Bruce F. *The Politics of Punishment: Prison Reform in Russia, 1863–1917.* De Kalb, Ill., 1996.

Evans, Richard J. *The German Underworld: Deviants and Outcasts in German History.* New York, 1988.

Forster, Colin. *France and Botany Bay: The Lure of a Penal Colony.* Melbourne, Australia, 1996.

Hughes, Robert. *The Fatal Shore: A History of the Transportation of Convicts to Australia, 1787–1868.* London, 1996.

Morris, Norval, and David J. Rothman, eds. *The Oxford History of the Prison: The Practice of Punishment in Western Society.* New York, 1998.

Pike, Ruth. *Penal Servitude in Early Modern Spain.* Madison, Wis., 1983.

Rusche, Georg, and Otto Kirchheimer. *Punishment and Social Structure.* New York, 1939.

Shaw, A. G. L. *Convicts and the Colonies: A Study of Penal Transportation from Great Britain and Ireland to Australia and Other Parts of the British Empire.* Melbourne, 1978.

Wheatcroft, S. G. "The Crisis in the Late Tsarist Penal System." In *Challenging Traditional Views of Russian History,* edited by S. G. Wheatcroft, 27–54. Houndmills, U.K., 2002.

STEPHEN G. WHEATCROFT

EXPLORERS. During the nineteenth century technological advances, nationalist fervor, and commercial development spurred European interest in opening up uncharted regions of the globe. Through a combination of public and private initiatives, nations sponsored extensive programs of scientific and geographical exploration. Explorers, primarily men but also a few women, became international celebrities whose stories and adventures stirred the imagination of the public.

OVERVIEW

During the late eighteenth and early nineteenth centuries exploration of the South Pacific continued following the voyages of the British captain James Cook (1728–1779) and the French Comte de la Pérouse (1741–c. 1788). Between 1795 and 1803 Matthew Flinders (1774–1814) circumnavigated and mapped the coastline of Australia for the Royal Navy, and Nicolas-Thomas Baudin (1754–1803) mapped the Australian coastline for France. The establishment of Britain's permanent settlements in Australia opened up the interior of the continent to many explorers over the next several decades. Edward John Eyre (1815–1901) was the first European to walk across southern Australia, in 1840, and Edmund Kennedy (1818–1848) explored the interior of Queensland and New South Wales later in that decade. Robert Burke (1820–1861) and William Wills (1834–1861) were the first Europeans to cross the continent from south to north in 1860–1861, and died attempting to make the return trip.

The primary focal point of nineteenth-century exploration, however, was Africa. Before the late eighteenth century, the difficulties presented by disease and terrain meant that Europeans knew very little of Africa's interior. Technological and medicinal advances during the first half of the century, such as the development of the steamboat and the discovery of quinine's antimalarial properties by Europeans, made the African interior increasingly accessible to European explorers.

The Scotsman Mungo Park's (1771–1806) explorations of the Niger River between 1795 and 1805, popularized in his 1799 work *Travels in the Interior of Africa,* not only confirmed the course of the river but also stoked popular interest in the mysteries of the continent's interior. Other adventurers soon followed in his wake. In 1828, lured by the ten thousand–franc reward put up by the French Geographical Society, René-Auguste Caillié (1799–1838) became the first European to travel to Timbuktu and return safely. Much more information about the interior of northern Africa came about as a result of the journeys made by the German Heinrich Barth (1821–1865) between 1849 and 1855. Traveling alone for much of the time, Barth immersed himself more deeply into African societies and cultures than did many nineteenth-century explorers. His *Travels and Discoveries in Northern and Central Africa,* published in 1857–1858, remains one of the most detailed accounts of the peoples of Northern Nigeria and the Western Sudan.

The most famous midcentury explorer was the missionary-turned-explorer David Livingstone (1813–1873). He began his African career in the service of the London Missionary Society in 1841, and throughout the 1840s explored much of southern Africa beyond the Orange River. By the 1850s, however, Livingstone had given up on the life of a settled missionary and turned his attention toward the interior of sub-Saharan Africa. Between 1853 and 1856 he crossed Africa from the Atlantic coast to the Indian Ocean, along the way becoming the first European to see Victoria Falls. Livingstone's best-selling account of his travels, *Missionary Travels and Researches in South Africa* (1857), engaged the public with tales of his adventures, excited evangelical Christians with accounts of unknown peoples introduced to the gospel, interested merchants

French lieutenant Mizon on his 1892 mission of exploration of the River Benue area in Nigeria. Illustration from *Le Petit Journal,* July 1892. During the late nineteenth century, British, French, and German explorers attempted to secure hegemony over the Niger and Benue Rivers. Mizon's efforts resulted in a short-lived treaty with the Emir of Muri. PRIVATE COLLECTION/BRIDGEMAN ART LIBRARY/GIRAUDON

with the prospects of trade in the African interior, and impressed the scientific community with its geographic observations. Livingstone made his third and final series of journeys, in East Africa, between 1866 and 1873. During this time he attempted to open trade routes on the Zambezi River, established the ill-fated Universities Mission in Nyasaland, and sought further information on the debate over the source of the Nile. Livingstone died in Africa in 1873, and his remains were returned to England, where he received a hero's funeral and burial in Westminster Abbey.

Livingstone's name is now forever linked with that of Henry Morton Stanley (1841–1904), the journalist and adventurer sent in 1871 by the *New York Herald* to find Livingstone in the African interior. Stanley made several other significant journeys of exploration during the subsequent decades. Crossing the continent from east to west between 1874 and 1877, he confirmed Lake Victoria as the source of the Nile. He assisted King Leopold II

(r. 1865–1909) of Belgium in the establishment of the Congo Free State. In 1887 he led the expedition to rescue the German-born governor of Equatoria, Emin Pasha (born Eduard Schnitzer) (1840–1892), who had been isolated in the interior because of the Mahdist rebellion in the Sudan.

Richard Burton (1821–1890) and John Hanning Speke (1827–1864) played the central roles in discovering the source of the Nile, the greatest geographical mystery of the century. In 1856 the Foreign Office and the Royal Geographical Society commissioned Burton, already famous for his journeys to Mecca and Medina, to lead an expedition in search of the source of the great river. Burton invited Speke, an officer in the British Indian army who had traveled with Burton through Somalia in 1854. The expedition set off from Zanzibar in 1857 in search of the great lakes of the interior of eastern Africa, reaching Lake Tanganyika in early 1858. When Burton fell ill Speke continued on to a second, larger lake, to which he gave the name Lake Victoria. Upon their return the two engaged in a well-publicized dispute, Burton claiming that Lake Tanganyika was the ultimate source of the Nile and Speke insisting it was Lake Victoria. Subsequent explorations by Speke, Livingstone, and Stanley ultimately confirmed that Lake Victoria was the source.

Although men dominated the field of exploration, by the end of the century women explorers became more common. Mary Kingsley (1862–1900), the daughter of the physician and travel author George Henry Kingsley (1827–1892), made two journeys to West Africa in 1893–1894. Kingsley was the first European to visit certain remote parts of Gabon and the French Congo. Her 1897 book, *Travels in West Africa,* was controversial for its sympathetic portrayal of indigenous Africans and its critique of certain European imperialist policies. The Swiss-born Isabelle Eberhardt (1877–1904) frequently disguised herself as a man during her travels in North Africa. Eberhardt's accounts of her travels, and of the secret Sufi brotherhood, the Qadiriya, were published in books and numerous French newspapers.

During the first decades of the twentieth century the attention of explorers and the public turned to polar exploration. The American Robert Peary (1856–1920) led the first successful expedition to the North Pole in 1909. Included in his team was Matthew Henson (1866–1955), one of very few African American explorers. More dramatic was the race to the South Pole between the Englishman Robert F. Scott (1868–1912) and the Norwegian Roald Amundson (1872–1928). During his second Antarctic expedition, Scott set off for the pole from Ross Island in November 1911. However, traveling a shorter distance across the Ross Ice Shelf with a smaller team, Amundson reached the pole first on 14 December. Scott arrived about a month later, discovering to his disappointment a Norwegian flag and a letter from Amundson. Polar exploration was especially hazardous, taking the lives of many explorers, including Scott, whose entire team perished attempting to return from the pole, and Amundson, who died in an Arctic plane crash in 1928.

MOTIVATION

A variety of factors motivated both explorers and the organizations or individuals that supported them. The growth of nineteenth-century European exploration occurred as a direct result of the development of scientific, industrial, financial, and organizational resources that could be directed toward the systematic study of unknown areas of the globe. Expeditions occurred primarily as a result of assistance from government or private interests. National geographic societies, established in Paris in 1821, Berlin in 1828, and London in 1830, provided both logistical and financial support for most major expeditions of the nineteenth century. Missionary societies also sometimes facilitated exploration, as in the early career of David Livingstone.

The general interest in adventure and knowledge of faraway places drove popular support for exploration, while commercial and imperial concerns impelled government involvement. Most explorers and expeditions emphasized their scientific objectives, but some journeys, such as Jean-Baptiste Marchand's (1863–1934) 1895 march to Fashoda, were entirely imperial from their conception. Even the early twentieth-century polar explorations, the most ostensibly scientific given the nature of the regions being explored, were not immune to nationalist sentiment, as is evident in Amundson and Scott's race to the South Pole.

On a personal level most explorers were driven by a combination of a desire for adventure, the pursuit of scientific knowledge, and the lure of popular adulation. Although some, such as Burton, produced vividly written accounts of the societies and cultures they encountered, most explorers showed a general hostility toward all things indigenous. Burton's descriptions of East Africa were colorful, but also contained ample evidence of his lack of respect for the people and cultures he was describing. Stanley was infamous, even during his own era, for the violence and brutality of his dealings with Africans. Nineteenth-century explorers were men of adventure, and often men of science, but were rarely ever humanitarians. Livingstone was the primary exception. He conceived of his exploration as part of the divine calling to end the slave trade and bring Christianity, commerce, and civilization to the African interior. To what extent ordinary Africans desired or welcomed the benefits of Livingstone's humanitarian cause remains open to debate. He was, nevertheless the only of the well-known explorers to clearly articulate a vision of exploration that promised Africans a form of future progress and advancement.

IMPACT

Assessing the impact of the nineteenth-century era of exploration is complicated. Explorers clearly facilitated the process of cross-cultural exchange, bringing indigenous peoples into contact with Europeans and European culture. They played an instrumental role in transmitting information about the geography and the peoples of the globe to European audiences, although it is important to also recognize that many of the "discoveries" made by European explorers were often little more than the affirmation of things already known to indigenous populations. Clearly the opening up of the interiors of Africa or Australia to European involvement had profound long-term negative consequences for the indigenous societies of those continents. Even though the largest expeditions numbered in the hundreds, it is not at all clear that they had much direct contemporary impact. The vast majority of Africans went about their lives completely unaware of the explorers in their midst and of the longer term consequences of their presence. While exploration was inextricably linked with the expansion of nineteenth-century European imperialism, it should be seen as only one of several factors. Livingstone's humanitarian and moral arguments likely played a far more significant role in encouraging European involvement in Africa than his scientific and geographical discoveries. Explorers were as important to the history of nineteenth-century Europe for their role in circulating information about then-unknown parts of the globe as they were for their role as agents of imperialism.

See also **Africa; Civilization, Concept of; Imperialism; Missions; Oceanic Exploration.**

BIBLIOGRAPHY

Baker, J. N. L. *History of Geographic Discovery and Exploration.* 1937. Reprint, New York, 1967.

Bell, Morag, Robin Butlin, and Michael Heffernan, eds. *Geography and Imperialism, 1820–1940.* Manchester, U.K., and New York, 1995.

Keay, John, ed. *The Royal Geographical Society History of World Exploration.* London, 1991.

Rotberg, Robert I., ed. *Africa and Its Explorers: Motives, Methods, and Impact.* Cambridge, Mass., 1970.

Stafford, Robert A. "Scientific Exploration and Empire." In *The Oxford History of the British Empire: Vol. III, The Nineteenth Century,* edited by Andrew Porter. Oxford, U.K., and New York, 1999.

Van Orman, Richard A. *The Explorers: Nineteenth Century Expeditions in Africa and the American West.* Albuquerque, N.M., 1984.

MICHAEL A. RUTZ

FABIANS. The Fabian Society, Britain's most durable socialist organization, an offshoot of the utopian Fellowship of the New Life, was launched by Edward Reynolds Pease (1857–1955) and Frank Podmore (1856–1910) in January 1884. Its name is an allusion to the Roman general Quintus Fabius Maximus Cunctator (d. 203 B.C.E.), who purportedly defeated Hannibal through a strategy of cautiously waiting for the right moment and then striking hard. Less a manifestation of the socialist revival of the 1880s than of alienation from the certainties of Christianity and Victorian capitalism, the Fabian Society, its several hundred members drawn from among intellectuals and the salaried middle class, had few ties to organized labor or to such rival socialist bodies as the Social Democratic Federation of Henry Mayers Hyndman (1842–1921). Its intellectual roots showed a stronger affinity to the ideas of John Stuart Mill (1806–1873) than to those of Karl Marx (1818–1883), and its earliest political links were to London radicals seeking to implement collectivist municipal reforms.

Despite some initial flirtations with revolutionary doctrines, by 1886 the Society declared itself unequivocally in favor of constitutionalism, of working through parliamentary action. Given their skepticism about the prospects for a working-class party in the foreseeable future, Fabians believed that their best hope for implementing programs was by persuading the existing political parties to adopt socialist measures. All members of the Society were obliged to subscribe to the set of innocuous doctrines known as the Fabian "basis," but it was not until George Bernard Shaw (1856–1950) and Sidney James Webb (1859–1947) became intellectually dominant that the Fabians began to formulate a distinctive ideological perspective. In the *Fabian Essays* (1889), Shaw, Webb, and four other members offered a reasoned exposition of socialism that would provide an alternative to a revolutionary program. While anticipating the eventual elimination of private property, the essayists postulated a gradual evolution based on the extension of democracy and forms of public control that had already been initiated. The essays asserted that progress toward socialism was inevitable, but that it must be pursued gradually in order to suit the inclinations of the British. While they hoped to transform the economic structure, they believed that socialism could be accommodated within existing British political institutions.

During its first decades, the Fabian Society was preoccupied with research into economic and social problems, the dissemination of ideas through lectures and tracts, and permeation of political parties by experts. In contrast to most radicals, Fabians largely ignored foreign affairs and the threat of armed conflict. Indeed, during the Boer War, they generally supported the British military effort and the civilizing mission of imperialism. After 1905, the old guard—especially Shaw—resisted a scheme advanced by author H. G. Wells (1866–1946) to transform the Fabian Society into a militant mass organization, but it was soon reenergized in various ways. In 1895, Sidney and Beatrice Potter Webb had used a bequest to the Society to found the London School of Economics, and in the decade before 1914, the Fabian Nursery (for younger members), the first Fabian summer school, the Fabian Women's Group, the Fabian Research Department, and the *New Statesman* were all launched. Although the Society remained aloof from the embryonic Labour Party, its influence in political circles continued to grow.

See also **Marx, Karl; Mill, John Stuart; Shaw, George Bernard; Socialism; Webb, Beatrice Potter; Wells, H. G.**

BIBLIOGRAPHY

Cole, Margaret. *The Story of Fabian Socialism.* Stanford, Calif., 1961.

McBriar, A. M. *Fabian Socialism and English Politics 1884–1918.* Cambridge, U.K., 1962.

Shaw, George Bernard, ed. *Fabian Essays.* London, 1889.

FRED M. LEVENTHAL

FACTORIES. The rise of factory production is a major theme in discussions on European industrialization. Associated particularly with mechanization in the textile industries from the late eighteenth century, the factory is seen to have symbolized the emergence of "modern" or "revolutionary" forms of production, which not only vastly improved labor productivity (output per head) but which also brought fundamental changes in the way families lived and worked.

In considering the theme, several key matters need to be addressed. The most obvious, perhaps, is how factory production can best be defined. While premises using powered machines to process textiles are usually regarded as factories, what of premises using powered equipment in other branches of industrial activity? And must the use of power-driven equipment be seen as a necessary characteristic of a factory, or might premises in which sole reliance is made on handicraft techniques also be included? Furthermore, irrespective of whether or not powered machinery is used, how far does the size of premises enter into the account,

either in terms of the numbers employed or the amount of capital expended in establishing them?

A further matter is how important factory production actually became in European economies. Certainly the factory system was extensively adopted during the nineteenth century, but even so, much economic activity continued to take place outside the factory environment, including that in the expanding service sector. Moreover, even with regard to manufacturing activity, domestic premises, along with workshops located in nondomestic premises, provided other locations than the factory in which production could take place. While in proportionate terms the contribution the non-factory sector made to European manufacturing output may have declined markedly during the nineteenth century, it was by no means negligible and did not necessarily signify the use of outdated or inefficient modes of production.

Other questions relate to the ways in which factory production grew in importance and its impact on working practices. Rising labor productivity was undoubtedly a major consideration, but how it was achieved and with what impact needs further study, as do the ways in which working practices and conditions changed for those who worked as factory operatives and the contemporary debates about their well-being.

DEFINING THE FACTORY

Nineteenth-century British legislation to regulate industrial working conditions offers some useful insights into how a factory might be defined. At first, regulation was restricted to establishments where textiles were spun or woven by means of powered machinery. From the 1860s, however, regulation was extended to a range of non-textile industries, while broader distinction was drawn between workshop and factory, the former relying on manual power and the latter on mechanical power. Yet the categories were not precise because some types of factory were included as manually powered establishments while factories were, for a time, defined as premises in which fifty or more people were employed in any type of manufacturing activity.

Drawing a distinction between factories and workshops solely on the basis of the type of power used produced some rather curious results. Listing

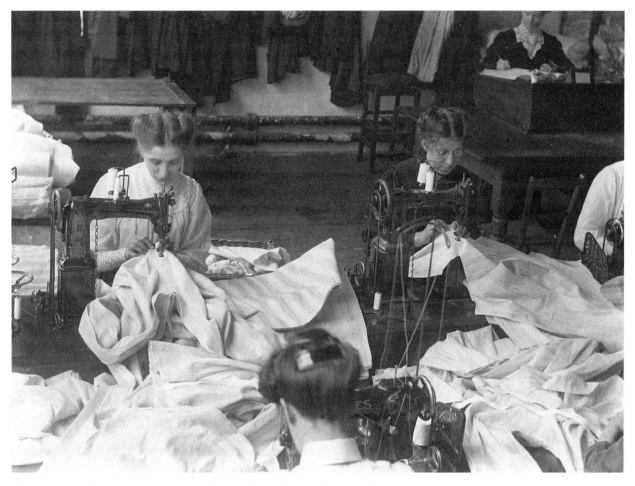

Shirt factory, Manchester, England, 1909. ©Hulton-Deutsch Collection/Corbis

small, water-powered iron forges or windmills used to grind corn as examples of factories does not seem to be particularly appropriate given the limited number of people they employed and the uncertainty as to how regular a work regime they imposed. Equally, manufacturing premises that were designed to house, say, a hundred or more hand looms and associated winding equipment might well be thought of as factories rather than workshops, especially if their proprietors sought to impose rigid work regimes; perhaps the term *manufactory* defines them better. The issue is complicated further because the growing use of gas engines and electric motors from the later decades of the nineteenth century provided power sources that could be used for a wide range of small-scale workshop manufacturing. It is clear, therefore, that both the type of technology employed and the size of the establishment need to be borne in mind when distinguishing between factory and work-

shop, a point that evidently exercised the minds of Britain's nineteenth-century factory legislators.

It is also important to distinguish between workshop and domestic production. This is particularly so where sizable workshops were attached to manufacturers' houses, the labor required being drawn mainly, if not solely, from nonfamily sources, like the two-story "frame shops" attached to hosiers' dwellings in Leicestershire, England. Yet production based on family groups working at home, whether it took place in rooms that doubled up as, say, workshop and bedroom or in rooms specially designed as workshops, was a major feature of European industrialization. Such forms of production are commonly described as being dispersed in order to distinguish them from centralized forms of production associated with factory and workshop activity, which take workers away from home.

When it comes to distinguishing between different modes of production, both during and before the nineteenth century, factory, workshop, and domestic forms were all to be found in European economies. Factory production became increasing important, especially from the late eighteenth century, but it would be wrong to assume that it superseded workshop and domestic forms of production. Nor should it be supposed that factory production was rarely to be found prior to this period. There was a marked shift in production modes, but each type offered opportunities for innovation to take place—not least regarding product development—in response to changing market circumstances, and the factory was not always best placed to respond to these changes.

CENTRALIZED PRODUCTION: EIGHTEENTH-CENTURY PRECURSORS

Although centralized forms of production became such a notable feature of the European economies from the late eighteenth century, they were by no means absent in earlier times. For example, water-powered silk-throwing mills were constructed in the Po Valley of northern Italy from the end of the seventeenth century. Production was not always continuous, but it did take place for several months each year. The mills were evidently small-scale concerns, but examples of sizable centralized enterprises for manufacturing textiles emerged too. Among them is the famous silk-throwing mill opened at Derby, England, in 1721 by John and Thomas Lombe. The mill consisted of several buildings, the largest being the five-story, water-powered throwing mill, which was 110 feet long and $55\frac{1}{2}$ feet wide. In 1732 the mill employed 300 people. Sizable concentrations of activity also occurred in handicraft production, such as the cloth manufactory established in 1715 by Count Johann von Waldstein at the small Bohemian village of Horni Litvinov. Accommodated in several buildings and employing skilled craftsmen from England and the Netherlands, the manufactory produced light woolen cloths (new draperies). By 1731 it employed no fewer than 401 workers, of whom 54 were weavers and 169 were spinners, in addition to numerous domestic outworkers.

The use of water-powered equipment gave rise to centralized production in a varied range of industrial activity in early modern Europe. As part of the finishing processes in wool manufacturing, for example, water-powered fulling stocks—essentially large, cam-driven mallets made from wood—were used to thicken and cleanse the cloth. In iron smelting, blast-furnace bellows were driven by water power, while water-powered forge hammers were used to refine pig iron (the product of the blast furnace) into wrought iron bars. Water-powered machinery was also used in corn mills, paper works, sawmills, and ore-crushing plants. Because of site availability, the use of water power favored the growth of centralized production in rural locations, a development that helped to loosen the restrictive influence of urban guilds.

As the case of the von Waldstein enterprise illustrates, the relatively large capital expenditure needed to establish centralized forms of production was sometimes met by the nobility. But merchants and monarchs were also involved. For example, in an attempt to free himself from dependency on foreign countries for weapons, Frederick William I of Prussia financed the construction of small arms factories at Potsdam and Spandau during the early 1720s. Workers from Liège who were experienced in arms manufacture were employed, and at the Spandau site musket barrels, bayonets, and ramrods were produced using water-powered forging, boring, grinding, and polishing equipment. Other parts of the muskets were manufactured at Potsdam, where they were also assembled.

FACTORY PRODUCTION FROM THE 1780S TO 1850

From the closing decades of the eighteenth century, as European industrialization intensified, centralized forms of production came to have far greater significance than hitherto. They emerged with varying pace and to a differing extent, at first showing the quickest early growth in Britain's manufacturing districts. By the second quarter of the nineteenth century, however, they had become a familiar sight in industrial regions on the European mainland as well, often drawing strongly on British equipment and expertise. The data are far from accurate, but the figures on factory production of cotton textiles in Britain and France give an indication of the advances made. There were over 2,300 cotton factories in Britain in the late 1830s, compared to about 700 in France a decade later. In both countries, as elsewhere in Europe, water power was widely adopted, giving rise to numerous factory colonies in rural locations. Steam power was also being widely used, although, again, emerging at differing speeds from one country to another. While around a third of the French cotton factories were steam powered, the figures for Britain had reached 70 percent.

Centralized production enabled employers to achieve better control over the quality of production than was the case with outwork, as well as making savings by avoiding outworkers' embezzlement of the materials their employers distributed to them. Additionally, productivity could be improved through the division of labor, as workers specialized in a particular part of the production process; by imposing more regular working hours than was possible under the domestic system of production; and by using powered equipment. In the cotton textile industry, the dramatic advances in productivity that could be achieved with powered machines have been illustrated by applying the concept of operative hours to process: whereas an Indian hand spinner took more than 50,000 hours to process 100 pounds of cotton, power-assisted mules could achieve the same end in just 135 hours.

The adoption of steam power, along with the development of more powerful and efficient steam engines, resulted in larger factories, although even in Britain most remained small or medium-size. Additionally, steam power helped to overcome the stoppages that could occur periodically, and for lengthy periods, where water-powered equipment was used. This was the case, for example, with the iron forges at Liessies and Consolver in northern France, which, according to a report published in 1848, had to be closed down for five to six months each year owing to water shortages. The switch to steam power concentrated factories in coalfield locations to reduce fuel transportation costs and on town outskirts to ease labor-supply and transportation problems. During the closing decades of the nineteenth century, electricity also emerged as an important source of industrial power, though by no means replacing steam. The fact that almost half of Berlin's engineering factories were powered by electricity in 1907 gives some idea of the progress made, though the general pace of advance was far slower, and steam engines, which were still being improved, continued to be installed.

The rise of centralized production reflected the continuing expansion of established industries, such as metal smelting and refining, in which it had traditionally occurred. But new industries also emerged, including various branches of engineering, that were based on centralized production from the outset and in some cases produced on an impressive scale, such as the famous Cockerill works at Seraing in Belgium. The founder of the enterprise, William Cockerill, moved from England to Belgium in 1798, establishing textile machinery works at Verviers and Liège. In 1817 his son John transferred the enterprise to Seraing, where steam engines as well as textile-spinning machinery were produced. In 1819 the works employed no fewer than 3,000 people and utilized steam engines with a combined capacity of 900 horsepower.

Centralized production also expanded as traditional industries switched from domestic production, textiles providing the major example. From the late eighteenth century cotton, wool, and linen spinning became increasingly factory based, the transformation in Britain taking place within a generation but more slowly on the European mainland. Cotton printing also became a factory industry in the same period. However, textile weaving became mechanized and hence moved to factory production at a much slower pace. In Britain the decisive shift in coarse cotton production occurred during the 1840s, as the development of much-improved power looms coincided with a major investment boom in the economy associated with railway building. But in Britain and other countries, the transition was much slower in the manufacture of finer and fancier cottons and in other branches of textile production. For example, at Krefeld, the most progressive of the German silk-producing towns, only 5,400 power looms had been installed by 1890, with 22,500 hand looms still in use.

LATER NINETEENTH CENTURY AND THE GROWTH OF INDUSTRIAL ZONES

The rise of factory production in Europe's main industrial districts during the latter half of the nineteenth century dwarfed that of the preceding half-century, a point that is well demonstrated in case of France. According to French government statistics, the number of industrial establishments using one or more steam engines grew from 6,500 in 1852 to as many as 63,000 in 1912. To obtain a more accurate measure of factory growth from these data, premises using other forms of power than steam would need to be added to them, while those for mines would need to be removed. Yet such adjustments would not alter the conclusion that remarkable change occurred. That is even more evident when the tendency for factories to become larger is taken into account. Variation in size remained marked, with small and medium-size units predominating. But economies of scale arising from using larger and more sophisticated pieces of equipment and the integration of successive stages of production on a single site created numerous works across a range of industries that occupied extensive sites and employed sizable labor forces. In France, an industrial census taken in 1906 counted 574 establishments, including mines, that employed more than 500 people. In the case of manufacturing, the large-scale factories were to be found mainly in textiles (200) and metal production (163) but were also well represented in chemicals (21), glass (20), and papermaking (20). In the larger European factories, employees were numbered in the thousands. For instance, the Singer sewing machine factory in Scotland employed 7,000 people in 1900.

As factories and factory sites increased in size, and because they were often built in close proximity to one another, they created industrial zones that became a major feature of European urban growth. These zones might be located alongside lines of communication, which not only facilitated transport needs but, in the case of canals, also provided water supplies for steam raising and condensing. The steel and engineering works located in the lower Don Valley, to the northeast of Sheffield, provide a striking example. Built alongside both sides of the North Midland line, which was opened in 1838, the zone developed into a major concentration of manufacturing activity in the middle decades of the nineteenth century. Several steelworks of an unprecedented size were constructed, including that of John Brown. By the early 1860s, his Atlas Works, comprising an extensive range of iron and steel furnaces, rolling mills, and tilt-hammer forges, covered some sixteen acres and gave employment to between three thousand and four thousand people.

The rise of centralized production in workshops and factories did not entirely supersede domestic production, however, not least as far as the manufacturing of clothing was concerned. In England and Wales, about a third of the 591,000 tailors and dressmakers recorded in the 1911 census worked at home, the majority on their own account. In the French clothing industry, a million domestic workers were still employed in 1896, including 220,000 in shoe manufacturing. From the employers' perspective, the continued use of domestic workers saved on the cost of investing in premises and equipment and enabled employment of non-unionized labor. Moreover, when downturns in demand occurred, labor could be laid off without the costs of idle machinery still having to be met. Short production runs might anyway prove costly if undertaken by machine. From the employees' perspective, staying at home enabled more flexible patterns of work to be undertaken, a matter of particular importance to married women, given the domestic responsibilities they were expected to assume. Indeed, married women formed only a small proportion of the European factory labor force even in such industries as textiles, which made considerable use of female workers.

SOCIAL IMPACT AND LEGISLATION

The threat that centralized production brought to flexible forms of working was a matter that critics of the factory system were keen to emphasize. Drawing on graphic accounts of appalling conditions that at least some factory workers endured, along with the rigid discipline that factory working rules sought to impose, they denounced the long hours that factory work could bring, especially for children; the dangers to life and limb associated with using powered machinery; and the moral lapses they thought could arise when young people of both sexes congregated together. Supporters of the factory system maintained that such concerns were greatly exaggerated, however. They argued that working with powered machinery required less effort than with hand technology, and they opposed calls for state regulation of factory work on the grounds that the liberty of the individual would be threatened: the employer would not be free to deploy labor to the best advantage nor parents to send their children to work in factories as they thought fit.

Paint shop in the Daimler Motor Company, Unterturkheim, Germany, 1904. ©Austrian Archives/Corbis

Yet at times that varied from country to country, and with periodic revisions, factory legislation was introduced that was especially concerned with controlling the age at which children could begin work and the number of hours they could work each day. Educational clauses were also incorporated. In Britain the 1833 Factory Act, which applied to the textile industry, had particular significance because a paid inspectorate was established to help enforce its provisions. How effective the inspectorate proved has been debated, but many thousands of prosecutions were brought against both parents and employers. Paid inspectors were gradually introduced in other countries. For example, a factory inspectorate was established in Prussia in 1853, when the Child Labor Law of 1839 was revised to raise the minimum age for factory work from nine years to twelve and to reduce the working day for those age twelve to fourteen to six hours.

Factory workers might also benefit from the paternalism of their employers, which could be manifested in various ways, such as providing good quality housing; social facilities, including schools; and treating at festivals or other occasions. The paternalistic dimension of the entrepreneur's role has been seen as being stronger on the European mainland than in Britain, helping to promote the goodwill of workers and hence their efficiency. However, following the 1848 revolutions in Europe, paternalism is seen to have taken a more defensive turn, with the aim of diverting workers from participation in the labor movement. Thus Friedrich Alfred Krupp, who provided subsidized housing for his employees as well as a range of welfare facilities, urged his employees in 1877 to concern themselves, after the working day was over, with house and home rather than with politics.

See also **Industrial Revolution, First; Industrial Revolution, Second; Working Class.**

BIBLIOGRAPHY

Berg, Maxine. *The Age of Manufactures 1700–1820: Industry, Innovation, and Work in Britain.* 2nd ed. London, 1994.

Caron, François. *An Economic History of Modern France.* New York, 1979.

Clapham, J. H. *The Economic Development of France and Germany 1815–1914.* 4th ed. Cambridge, U.K., 1945.

Daunton, M. J. *Progress and Poverty: An Economic and Social History of Britain 1700–1850.* Oxford, U.K., 1995.

Goodman, Jordan, and Katrina Honeyman. *Gainful Pursuits: The Making of Industrial Europe 1600–1914.* London, 1988.

Habakkuk, H. J., and M. M. Postan, eds. *The Cambridge Economic History of Europe.* Vol. 6: *Incomes, Population, and Technological Change. The Industrial Revolutions and After.* Cambridge, U.K., 1965

King, Steven, and Geoffrey Timmins. *Making Sense of the Industrial Revolution: English Economy and Society 1700–1850.* Manchester, U.K., 2001.

Milward, Alan S., and S. B. Saul. *The Development of the Economies of Continental Europe 1850–1914.* London, 1977.

Ogilvie, Sheilagh C., and Markus Cerman, eds. *European Proto-Industrialization.* Cambridge, U.K., 1996.

Perrot, Michelle. "The Three Ages of Industrial Discipline in Nineteenth-Century France." In *Consciousness and Class Experience in Nineteenth-Century Europe,* edited by John M. Merriman, 149–168. New York, 1979.

Pollard, Sidney. *Peaceful Conquest: The Industrialization of Europe 1760–1970.* Oxford, U.K., 1981.

JOHN GEOFFREY TIMMINS

FAMILY. *See* **Marriage and Family.**

FASHION. *See* **Clothing, Dress, and Fashion.**

FASHODA AFFAIR. The Fashoda Affair of September 1898 was a product of long-standing tensions between Britain and France over their relative influence in Egypt. Since the reign of Louis XIV (1643–1715) France had harbored ambitions of building a canal through the Suez isthmus, linking the Mediterranean with the Red Sea and dramatically shortening trade routes between Europe and Asia. Thus, in 1858, French commercial interests, backed by the French government, formed the Suez Canal Company. Owned jointly by the French and the Khedive of Egypt, the company completed the canal in 1869. Initially, the British government attempted to thwart the massive project. As the Egyptian government incurred growing debts in the 1860s and 1870s, however, Britain began purchasing Egyptian shares in the Suez Canal Company, thereby enhancing British authority in the country. With Egypt increasingly unable to pay the interest on its outstanding loans by the mid-1870s, the country's finances were placed under Anglo-French control. When this growing European suzerainty led to violent nationalist uprisings in 1882, Britain intervened militarily. A divided French government declined to participate. In consequence, the British established themselves as de facto rulers of Egypt, incurring the resentment of many French political leaders.

For the next fifteen years, Britain maintained its authority in Egypt while struggling to suppress Islamic fundamentalist dervishes further south in the Sudan. The threat emanating from this area became particularly acute in March 1896, when Ethiopian forces, assisted by French and Russian advisors, defeated an Italian army at Adowa. This raised the prospect of French and Russian intrusion into British territories in East Africa, as well as an alliance between Ethiopia and fundamentalist Muslim elements in the Sudan. The British government despatched Major-General Sir Horatio Herbert Kitchener (1850–1916; later Earl Kitchener of Khartoum) with an expeditionary force that defeated the dervishes at Omdurman on 2 September 1898. After learning of the presence of a French force further up the Nile, Lord Kitchener proceeded upriver, meeting the smaller French detachment at Fashoda on 19 September. This force, under Captain Jean-Baptiste Marchand, had been despatched to the headwaters of the Nile to find a suitable location for a dam that would divert the river and undermine British control of Egypt. A standoff ensued, as the French and British governments refused to budge. Public opinion in both countries became increasingly agitated. War, however, was never a likely outcome of the confrontation. Outnumbered on the ground in the Sudan and outgunned by the royal navy at sea, France had little choice but to back down and order the withdrawal of Marchand's force on 3 November 1898.

Fashoda represented a low point in Anglo-French relations in the late nineteenth century. Nonetheless, it encouraged the two European powers to defuse their rivalries in Africa and sign the Entente Cordiale of 1904. Théophile Delcassé, the French foreign minister from 1898 to 1905, recognized that France could not risk a direct confrontation with Britain in East Africa, especially when France's principal ally, Russia, was not prepared to provide assistance. Thus, in March 1899 France signed a convention that effectively renounced its claims to the upper Nile. According to the document, the British and French spheres of influence in the region would be marked by the watersheds of the Nile and the Congo, respectively. The willingness of France to concede Britain's influence on the Nile encouraged the British to support French claims elsewhere in Africa.

Growing concerns over aggressive German foreign policy and the expansion of the German navy reinforced Britain's desire to iron out disputes with the French, particularly as France could also facilitate better relations between Britain and Russia. Britain gradually abandoned its policy of encouraging the independence of Morocco. On 8 April 1904, the two countries signed a series of agreements in which France recognized British influence over Egypt. Since Egypt's financial affairs remained under the management of an international committee that included a French representative, this concession was crucial in enabling Britain to consolidate its control over the country. The British reciprocated by acknowledging French influence over Morocco. The Entente Cordiale, as the agreements were known, removed ambiguities in the two principal areas of Africa where European influence was still disputed. In the process, it helped end the "scramble for Africa" that had prevailed among the European powers since the Berlin Conference of 1884–1885. Thus, many historians see the Fashoda Affair as a turning point in Anglo-French relations. The standoff in the Sudan brought the Anglo-French rivalry in Africa into focus, allowing Britain and France to negotiate solutions to specific disputes and develop closer relations in the process.

See also **Berlin Conference; Delcassé, Théophile; Egypt; France; Great Britain; Imperialism; Kitchener, Horatio Herbert.**

BIBLIOGRAPHY

Bates, Darrell. *The Fashoda Incident of 1898: Encounter on the Nile.* New York: 1983. An account of the Fashoda Affair and the tensions it produced between Britain and France.

Judd, Denis. *Empire: The British Imperial Experience from 1765 to the Present.* London, 1996. An episodic survey of the history of the British Empire, with several chapters devoted to the British role in the "scramble for Africa."

Otte, Thomas. "The Elusive Balance: British Foreign Policy and the French Entente before the First World War." In *Anglo-French Relations in the Twentieth Century: Rivalry and Cooperation,* edited by Alan Sharp and Glyn Stone. New York, 2000. An analysis of the specific factors that contributed to the Anglo-French Entente of 1904.

NIKOLAS GARDNER

FAUVISM. Although most commentators and art historians describe fauvism as an early-twentieth-century movement of French painters, it was never a truly independent movement with its own style or its own theory. The *-ism* designates merely a new approach to painting, full of color and energy but beyond that difficult to define. This loose meaning of the term *fauvism* is bound up with its coining by the art critic Louis Vauxcelles, who used it, in his review for the periodical *Gil Blas* of the third autumn salon (1905), as a label for the paintings of Charles Camoin, André Derain, Henri-Charles Manguin, Albert Marquet, and Henri Matisse. Fauvism implied a conscious attempt to abandon the impressionist approach, and it built on the chromatic and technical innovations of Georges Seurat, Paul Signac, Vincent van Gogh, and Paul Gauguin. Fauvist works were typified by the use of vivid and saturated colors, emphasized by means of violent contrasts.

The beginnings of the fauves date back to the years 1894 to 1897, when Manguin, Marquet, Camoin, and Matisse were fellow students in Gustave Moreau's studio at the École des Beaux-Arts in

Paris. To their names should be added those of such artists as Georges Braque; André Derain, who met Matisse at Eugène Carrière's academy; Raoul Dufy; Othon Friesz; Kees van Dongen; Jean Puy; Georges Rouault; Louis Valtat; and Maurice de Vlaminck.

Apart from its use of color, fauvism proposed a new conception of light and perspective. A canvas such as Matisse's *Fenêtre ouverte, Collioure* (1905; The Open Window, Collioure) abolished the distinction between foreground and background. In this way, Matisse combined the contributions of Seurat and Gauguin. In his *Sieste* (Siesta), painted in the same year, the separation between interior and exterior tended to give way to an overall vision of the painted surface. Matisse's approach to painting was echoed by Derain's.

The years 1904 and 1905 were a time of great innovation and collaboration for the fauves. Derain and Vlaminck worked together in Chatou, and Derain and Matisse a little later in Collioure. Among the resulting works were three portraits— Matisse's of Derain (1905), Derain's of Matisse (1905), and Vlaminck's of Derain—along with numerous landscapes attesting to the evolution of fauvism and to the way in which these three artists strove to incorporate and transcend the contributions of their predecessors.

Derain's *Pont de Westminster* (1905; Westminster Bridge) demonstrates his preoccupation with the solid assembly of the elements of a painting. Like Matisse and Vlaminck, Derain removed color from its traditional role in the description of reality and assigned it an expressive function instead. Consider the newly wrought vision of London embodied in *Le pont de Charing Cross* (Charing Cross Bridge) and *Hyde Park*, both done in 1906. Derain works out two fresh ways of expressing themes on the canvas, one based on a broader brush, the other on construction by means of masses of color. The outcome is a fauve London where figures may stroll along pink paths in Hyde Park; the artist transforms the city by means of colors and light that are quite arbitrary if considered relative to nature.

As for Vlaminck, he ensured his position as the most audacious of the fauves with *La Cuisine* (Kitchen) of 1904 and *Le Pont de Chatou* (The bridge of Chatou) of 1906, paintings in which he

André Derain. Portrait by Henri Matisse, 1905. TATE GALLERY, LONDON/ART RESOURCE, NY/© 2006 SUCCESSION H. MATISSE, PARIS/ ARTISTS RIGHTS SOCIETY (ARS), NEW YORK

worked with a very tight focus. His radicalism is manifest, for example, in *Paysage aux arbre rouge* (1906–1907; Landscape with red tree), which obliges the eye to get past a grid of color before reaching a second plane. Vlaminck deployed the entire chromatic range of red in this work, in which schematic houses can be discerned beyond five colored tree trunks. A truly original approach is likewise displayed by Marquet in, for example, his *La fête foraine au Havre* (Traveling fair at Le Havre) or *Le Pont-Neuf au soleil* (The Pont-Neuf in the sunshine), both painted in 1906. These pictures enshrine a dynamic that is set in motion by color and heightened by a plunging point of view. The year 1906 was surely the high point of the movement, for it was then that all these painters embraced an intense and expressive use of color and in so doing created the moment of fauvism.

The fauves imposed no restrictions on subject matter: Dufy depicted a *14 juillet au Havre* (*14 July in Le Havre*) in 1906, while Marquet took

Les affiches à Trouville (1906; Posters at Trouville) for his subject and Braque brought his attention to bear on *Le Viaduc de L'Estaque* (1907–1908; The viaduct at L'Estaque). But all clung to their own particular characteristics and techniques: Vlaminck was given to dabbing brushwork whereas Matisse and Derain worked with flat areas of color.

It is, therefore, not useful to study fauvism in terms of thematic resemblances; rather, its practitioners should be compared on the basis of differences in technique and the duration of their obsession with contrasting colors. For Braque or Friesz, for instance, fauvism was simply a step along the way—in Braque's case to cubism and in Friez's to expressionism. Fauvism was also closely related to the painting of Wassily Kandinsky (1866–1944) or of Alexei von Jawlensky (1864–1941). It might further be likened to the work of the German group Die Brücke, and to that extent it qualifies as an international movement.

Despite fauvism's brief life span, attributable to the rise of cubism on the one hand and to the diverging routes taken by its exponents on the other, the group produced many major works, among them (to mention only works by the movement's senior member, Matisse) *Luxe, Calme, et Volupté* (1904–1905; Luxury, calm, and pleasure) and *Femme avec un chapeau* (1905; Woman with a hat).

See also **Cubism; Matisse, Henri; Modernism; Seurat, Georges.**

BIBLIOGRAPHY

Clement, Russel T. *Les Fauves: A Sourcebook.* Westport, Conn., 1994.

Dagen, Phillipe. *Le Fauvisme: Textes de peintres, d'écrivains et de journalistes.* Paris, 1991.

Ferrier, Jean-Louis. *Les Fauves: Le règne de la couleur: Matisse, Derain, Vlaminck, Marquet, Camoin, Manguin, Van Dongen, Friesz, Braque, Dufy.* Paris, 1992. Translated as *The Fauves: The Reign of Color: Matisse, Derain, Vlaminck, Marquet, Camoin, Manguin, Van Dongen, Friesz, Braque, Dufy.* New York, 1995.

Freeman, Judi. *The Fauve Landscape.* New York, 1990.

Giry, Marcel. *Le Fauvism: Ses origines, son évolution.* Neuchâtel, Switzerland, 1981.

Leymarie, Jean. *Fauves and Fauvism.* New York, 1997.

Pernoud, Emmanuel. *L'estampe des fauves: Une esthétique du contraste.* Paris, 1994.

Paris Musées. *Le fauvisme ou L'épreuve du feu: Éruption de la modernité en Europe.* Paris, 1999.

CYRIL THOMAS

FAWCETT, MILLICENT GARRETT

(1847–1929), leader in the British women's suffrage movement.

Born into a comfortable middle-class British family of liberal political leanings, Millicent Garrett Fawcett became active in a number of movements aimed at increasing women's rights starting in the 1860s. Efforts to secure property rights and higher education, and to open the medical profession to women, as well as campaigns to end the double standard of morality for men and women as it was exemplified in divorce and matrimonial law, occupied the first generation of British feminists. The campaign for the vote, these pioneers recognized, was by far the most radical of the reforms they sought, and it was to Fawcett that they entrusted the "Cause."

Best known for her leadership of the constitutional wing of the women's suffrage movement, Fawcett worked tirelessly throughout the late nineteenth and early twentieth centuries to gain votes for women. As head of the National Union of Women's Suffrage Societies (NUWSS), which brought numerous discrete women's suffrage societies into a single umbrella organization in 1897, she directed a sustained, if unsuccessful, campaign to persuade politicians to extend the franchise to women on the same terms as it was or would be granted to men. On the face of it a conservative demand, because the property qualifications required for possession of the vote excluded a significant portion of working-class men from wielding it, suffragists meant for the vote to be the means by which they would dramatically alter the lives of women and men in all realms of life—social, economic, and personal as well as legal and political. As a symbol of civic personhood, they believed that votes for women would help to counteract notions about the natural differences between men and women that justified inequality and the sexual oppression of women. As a pragmatic instrument of power, they sought the vote to

Millicent Fawcett c. 1895–1905. ©HULTON-DEUTSCH
COLLECTION/CORBIS

eliminate laws that enshrined women's inequality and sexual vulnerability to men in the constitution.

Fawcett was careful to keep any taint of scandal from attaching to the campaign for women's suffrage, but she supported the efforts of reformers like Josephine Butler (1828–1906) and William Thomas Stead (1849–1912) to end the sexual exploitation of women and girls. In one instance, she acted to expose the behavior of member of Parliament (MP) Henry Cust (1861–1917, who had deserted a woman he had impregnated, and prevent him from standing for reelection. In response to the assertion of Conservative Party leader Arthur James Balfour (1848–1930) that Cust's private behavior was "of no public concern," Fawcett declared that it was precisely this acceptance of the double standard of morality for men that enabled exploitation of women to take place. She vowed that the enfranchisement of women would establish a "healthy 'coercion' of law and public opinion" that would prevent men like Cust from behaving as they did.

Overshadowed by the spectacular agitation of the militant Women's Social and Political Union (WSPU) headed by Emmeline Pankhurst (1858–1928) and Christabel Pankhurst (1880–1958), which brought the cause of women's suffrage to public notice in 1906, the NUWSS under Fawcett conducted its campaign through law-abiding activities of petitioning MPs, holding public meetings, and sponsoring marches and public demonstrations. In contrast to the Pankhursts, who led the members of the WSPU with an authoritarian control that would brook no dissent, Fawcett presided over an inclusive, democratic organization. She did not agree with the convictions and strategies of some of her colleagues who sought to ally with the Labour Party in order to advance the cause of women's enfranchisement, but she worked to ensure that the NUWSS presented a unified public face. With the outbreak of war in 1914, both the WSPU and the NUWSS suspended their suffrage activities in order to support the prosecution of the war. Unlike the WSPU, however, the NUWSS maintained its organizational structure throughout the war; when it became clear to the government in 1917 that a new franchise would be required if men of the armed forces were to be allowed to vote when they returned from the war, Fawcett mobilized her NUWSS colleagues to demand that women be included in any new bill.

Over a period of months, Fawcett negotiated with parliamentary officials to reach an agreement. The 1918 Representation of the People Act granted universal suffrage to men over the age of twenty-one but it restricted the vote to women over the age of thirty, seeking thereby to ensure that women would not enjoy a majority over men, whose numbers had been so dramatically reduced by the carnage of World War I. Fawcett's acceptance of the bill constituted an abandonment of the long-held principle of sex equality; she and other NUWSS leaders explained to their discontented Labour followers, most of whom would not be admitted to the franchise because they were under age, that they did not wish to jeopardize their chances for partial success by holding out for more. Fawcett resigned as president of the NUWSS in 1918, but she steadily continued to work for complete women's suffrage until it was granted in 1928. Until the 1980s, scholars tended to overlook her and the constitutional movement she led,

THE FRENCH REVOLUTION & THE NAPOLEONIC ERA

LEFT: Louis XVI. Portrait by Antoine-François Callet, 1788. The king is shown in his coronation robes in this official portrait, painted on the eve of the revolution. ERICH LESSING/ART RESOURCE, NY

BELOW: Marie Antoinette with her children. Painting by Elizabeth Vigée-Lebrun, 1787. A sympathetic portrait of the queen intended to improve her reputation among her subjects. THE ART ARCHIVE/MUSÉE DU CHATEAU DE VERSAILLES /DAGLI ORTI (A)

Ludewig den XVI.^{des} Konge af Frankerige Henrettelse den 21. Januari 1793.

RIGHT: *The Death of Marat.* Painting by Jacques-Louis David, 1793. The acknowledged master of French painting during the revolutionary period, David was sympathetic to the aims of the revolution, as revealed in this homage to Jean Marat, who was assassinated in 1793. THE ART ARCHIVE/DAGLI ORTI

INSET BELOW: *The Night of the 9th to 10th Thermidor, Year II.* Engraving by Jean Joseph François Tassaert, c. 1794. After ordering the execution of thousands of French citizens suspected of counterrevolutionary acts or sentiments, members of the Committee of Public Safety were overthrown in a coup on the evening of 27 July 1794. The most prominent member, Maximilien Robespierre, was shot in the face during the coup and guillotined the following day. MUSÉE DE LA VILLE DE PARIS, MUSÉE CARNAVALET, PARIS, FRANCE/BRIDGEMAN ART LIBRARY

BOTTOM: *The Festival of the Supreme Being at the Champ-de-Mars, 20 Prairial, An II.* Painting by Pierre-Antoine Demachy, c. 1794. The Festival of the Supreme Being was organized by Maximilien Robespierre in an attempt to gain support for his leadership and was held on 8 June 1794. RÉUNION DES MUSÉES NATIONAUX/ART RESOURCE, NY

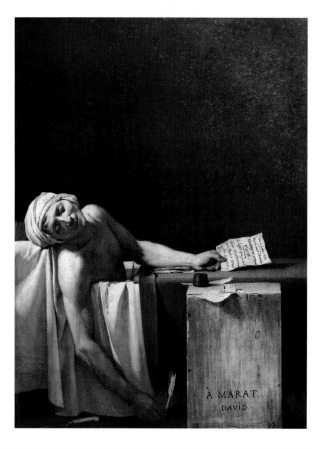

RIGHT: *General Napoleon Bonaparte at the Bridge of Arcola, 17 November 1796.* Painting by Antoine-Jean Gros, 1796. A pupil of Jacques-Louis David, Gros became acquainted with Joséphine de Beauharnais in Genoa and was subsequently appointed Napoleon's official battle painter in 1793. His romantic depictions contributed significantly to the growing aura of heroism surrounding the young general. Réunion des Musées Nationaux/Art Resource, NY

BELOW: *Entry of the National Guard into Paris through the Barrière de Pantin.* Painting by Nicholas Antoine Taunay, 1807. The soldiers of Napoleon's elite Imperial Guard were greeted by cheering crowds upon their return to Paris after their triumphant 1807 campaign against the forces of Tsar Alexander I of Russia. Erich Lessing/Art Resource, NY

OPPOSITE PAGE: *Napoleon on His Imperial Throne.* Painting by Jean-Auguste-Dominique Ingres, 1806. Two years after the coronation, Ingres painted the emperor in a manner intended to solidify his position as the legitimate sovereign. Erich Lessing/Art Resource, NY

AN ENGLISH BULL DOG and a CORSICAN BLOODHOUND

RIGHT: *In the Year 1812.* Painting by Illarion Mikhailovich Pryanishnikov, 1873. Napoleon's troops are shown on the retreat from Moscow. ODESSA FINE ARTS MUSEUM, UKRAINE/BRIDGEMAN ART LIBRARY

BELOW: *The Battle of Waterloo.* Illustration from the London *Sunday Times,* 18 June 1815. © ARCHIVO ICONOGRAFICO, S.A. /CORBIS

devoting their attention to the more visible and exciting militant campaign led by the charismatic Pankhursts. Since then, however, historians have given Fawcett her due, recognizing the central role played by the NUWSS in championing and ultimately winning women's suffrage, and crediting Fawcett's steady, quiet, conciliatory leadership with its success.

See also **Butler, Josephine; Feminism; Pankhurst, Emmeline, Christabel, and Sylvia; Suffragism.**

BIBLIOGRAPHY

Primary Sources

Fawcett, Millicent Garrett. *What I Remember.* London, 1924.

Secondary Sources

Caine, Barbara. *Victorian Feminists.* London, 1992.

Holton, Sandra Stanley. *Feminism and Democracy: Women's Suffrage and Reform Politics in Britain, 1900–1918.* Cambridge, U.K., 1986.

Hume, Leslie Parker. *The National Union of Women's Suffrage Societies, 1897–1914.* New York, 1982.

Kent, Susan Kingsley. *Sex and Suffrage in Britain, 1860–1914.* Princeton, N.J., 1987.

Oakley, Ann. "Millicent Garrett Fawcett: Duty and Determination." In *Feminist Theorists: Three Centuries of Women's Intellectual Traditions,* edited by Dale Spender. London, 1983.

Rubenstein, David. *A Different World for Women: The Life of Millicent Garrett Fawcett.* New York, 1991.

Strachey, Ray. *Millicent Garrett Fawcett.* London, 1931.

SUSAN KINGSLEY KENT

FEDERALIST REVOLT. The federalist revolt occurred in the summer of 1793, at a pivotal moment in the French Revolution. The name itself suggests a decentralizing movement, a reaction to the strong central government emerging at that time under Jacobin leadership in Paris. But while the revolt was based in provincial cities, the rebels did not seek a federated republic. Rather the federalists protested against what they took to be a violation of the unity and integrity of the national assembly.

The national assembly at that moment in the course of the Revolution was known as the National Convention, elected in the fall of 1792 after Louis XVI had been toppled from power by a Parisian uprising. Almost from its first meeting, the National Convention was hopelessly divided between two rival factions: the moderate Girondin deputies and the radical Montagnards. The first point of contention was the September Massacres, which claimed the lives of more than one thousand alleged counterrevolutionaries in the prisons of Paris. The Girondin leadership soon denounced the killings as the inevitable consequence of public anarchy, and accused leading Montagnards of having incited the violence. The Montagnards, many of them the champions of the Paris crowd, defended the massacres as a regrettable, but necessary, instance of popular justice. This polarity carried over into the trial of Louis XVI, the stalemate over the constitution of 1793, the trial of Jean-Paul Marat, and the ongoing debate about the legitimacy of popular politics and the influence of the Paris crowd on national politics. This bitter division within the National Convention, decried both by Parisians and by many citizens of the provinces, came to an end following the uprising of 31 May to 2 June 1793, when Parisian militants forced the proscription of twenty-nine Girondin deputies. Nearly fifty departmental administrations protested that action by letter, and some thirteen departments engaged in prolonged resistance to the Montagnard Convention in what has come to be known as the federalist revolt.

The revolt centered around four provincial cities—Bordeaux, Caen, Lyon, and Marseille—and in each instance it was departmental administrators who took the leading role. Typically the rebels constituted a new popular assembly to lead the resistance, in order to claim the mandate of the people for their actions, and probably to deflect charges of treason from official administrative councils. In addition to sending delegations or letters of protest to Paris, they declared themselves in a state of resistance to oppression, withdrew their recognition of the National Convention and all legislation issued since 31 May, and called on their constituents to take up arms and march to the capital to restore the proscribed deputies to office. In Caen and Marseille the rebels arrested representatives on mission (national deputies) in the early stages of the revolt, taking them as hostages, in a sense, against the safety of the proscribed Girondins.

Seven Breton and Norman departments sent delegates to the Central Committee of Resistance to Oppression, meeting in Caen. That assembly issued a manifesto, the closest thing that exists to a federalist program. In mid-July a small force left Caen for Paris, but there was little popular support for the revolt in Normandy or elsewhere and the call for a march on Paris failed to mount a serious threat to the capital. The Norman force dispersed after a single, farcical battle near Vernon, and none of the other rebel forces even left the limits of their own departments. Coupled with the peasant rebellions in the Vendée, however, the federalist revolt confronted the young French Republic with the very real danger of civil war, and the Montagnards responded forcefully to that threat. First they presented a defense of the 31 May uprising and the proscription of the Girondin deputies, which they circulated to the provinces via special envoys. Then they moved quickly to complete a new constitution, adopted in the Convention and presented to the nation in late June. In July the Montagnards prepared an indictment of the proscribed deputies, though they would not be brought to trial until October. Finally, the Committee of Public Safety sent armed forces to suppress the rebellion in those areas that continued to resist.

The federalist revolt collapsed quickly in Caen, and Robert Lindet oversaw a remarkably mild repression in the late summer months, dismissing rebel officials from office, placing many under arrest, but ordering no executions. In Bordeaux and Marseille, where resistance to Paris endured until the final days of summer, the revolt came to an end without violent resistance, but the repression that followed sent roughly three hundred rebels to the guillotine in each city. In Lyon, however, the federalist rebels executed the leading Jacobin in the city, Joseph Chalier, and the city capitulated only after a two-month siege. In October the National Convention decreed that "Lyon is no more," renamed it "Ville-Affranchie" (Freed City), and sent the representatives on mission, Georges Couthon, Jean-Marie Collet d'Herbois, and Joseph Fouché, to oversee the repression. They ordered the execution of more than nineteen hundred rebels, making Lyon one of the bloodiest sites of the Terror.

Although the federalist revolt was nominally a reaction to the proscription of the Girondin deputies, the causes of the revolt ran much deeper. Political elites in the provinces had grown wary of the militant activism of the Parisian sans-culottes, and often felt threatened by the mobilization of popular politics in their own towns. They resented what they considered the excessive influence of Paris on national politics and the interference of representatives on mission in local affairs. In the federalist revolt, then, national and local politics came together, as the French revolutionaries struggled to define sovereignty and how it should be exercised.

See also **French Revolution; Girondins; Jacobins; Louis XVI; Reign of Terror; Robespierre, Maximilien.**

BIBLIOGRAPHY

Edmonds, W. D. *Jacobinism and the Revolt of Lyon, 1789–1793.* Oxford, U.K., 1990.

Forrest, Alan. *Society and Politics in Revolutionary Bordeaux.* London, 1975.

———. *The Revolution in Provincial France: Acquitaine, 1789–1799.* Oxford, U.K., 1996.

Hanson, Paul R. *Provincial Politics in the French Revolution: Caen and Limoges, 1789–1794.* Baton Rouge, La., 1989.

———. *The Jacobin Republic under Fire: The Federalist Revolt in the French Revolution.* University Park, Pa., 2003.

Scott, William. *Terror and Repression in Revolutionary Marseilles.* London, 1973.

PAUL R. HANSON

FEMINISM

FEMINISM. The word *feminism*, which originated in France during the nineteenth century, was not used in reference to female emancipation until the 1890s; even into the twentieth century some movements for women's emancipation did not use the word. There is, moreover, no single, specific definition for the term. This article uses the term *feminism* synonymously with *women's emancipation*—unorganized and organized efforts to improve women's status and oppose their systematic subordination. Critical responses to women's subordination appeared in Europe as early as the fifteenth century, but the eighteenth-century Enlightenment philosophy, with its emphasis on reason, education, progress, individual self-fulfillment, and natural law as a source of knowledge, redefined what it meant to be human, and thus raised issues about women's humanity. The role of women, and in particular, their legal civil status and their education, played a large role in Enlightenment discourse.

Karen Offen and other historians of feminism have detected two feminist currents evolving in the nineteenth century that were based on different representations of women. The "individualist," or egalitarian current derived from the assumption that women and men share a common human identity and therefore should also have equality in the public, political realm. Access to knowledge, education, and work would allow women to pursue self-fulfillment as individuals, just as men pursued their constitutionally guaranteed right to "happiness." The other current emphasized the difference between men and women, and particularly women's physical, emotional, psychical, and social capacities in motherhood and other relational—rather than individualistic—roles. Women's special cultural and social contributions as self-sacrificing nurturers formed the basis for advocating an improvement in their status and in their right to have a public role. It is important to keep in mind, however, that these two categories are a means for historians to understand and analyze the many faces of feminism, and that contemporaries did not necessarily perceive these distinctions in categorical terms. Feminists lived lives, espoused ideologies, and participated in movements that combined both currents. At the same time feminism emerged within specific national contexts and national identities, as well as in relation to other reform movements, philosophies, or nonconformist religions—all of which gave it multifaceted characteristics. But issues raised in one national context often inspired political movements across borders, and by the second half of the nineteenth century international organizations began forming, which, in turn, reinforced national movements.

THE FRENCH REVOLUTION AND ITS INFLUENCE

In the efforts to implement Enlightenment principles, the French Revolution gave birth to modern feminism. That is not to say, however, that European feminism had only one moment of birth, or that the Revolution gave rise to a feminist "movement"—but it created a ripe occasion for intensified philosophical debate and political action. When Louis XVI (r. 1774–1792) called for the Estates-General to meet and invited his subjects to submit their grievances, women demanded economic and political justice for their sex. A few women immediately denounced male privilege, especially in the legal realm. In abolishing the estate system, eliminating feudal privileges, and producing the Declaration of the Rights of Man and of the Citizen, claiming that "Men are born and remain free and equal in rights," the National Assembly of 1789 sought to implement "universal" principles about human rights that immediately and deliberately excluded women, who were viewed as incapable of reason and unable to act as morally independent individuals. One staunch advocate of political rights, the marquis de Condorcet (Marie-Jean de Caritat; 1743–1794), argued that women should be granted citizenship; he eloquently stated that differences between men and women stemmed from education, not nature. He further unveiled the contingency of "natural" determination when, for example, he queried, "Why should beings exposed to pregnancies and to passing indispositions not be able to exercise rights that no one ever imagined taking away from people who have gout every winter or who easily catch colds?" (quoted in Hunt, p. 120).

A small group of women formed a *cercle social* (social circle) in 1790–1791 to campaign for women's rights, especially civil equality in marriage, divorce, property ownership, and education. In 1791 the playwright and essayist Olympe de Gouges published the "Declaration of the Rights of Women," in which she offered a poignant critique of female exclusion from the "Declaration of the Rights of Man." She stated that "woman is born free and remains equal to man in rights" and therefore should partake in all "public dignities, offices and employments." But none of the national assemblies ever seriously considered legislation that would grant women political rights, and the constitutions of 1791, 1793, and 1795 deliberately excluded them.

Nonetheless women engaged in street politics that, in their own minds, conferred citizenship. The Society of Revolutionary Republican Women, for example, had as its main purpose combating counter-revolution and defending, at a time of war, invasion of the Republic by foreign enemies. The group sought to expand women's political and even military participation. Their fate exemplifies the need to redefine and even rigidify gender roles in the revolutionary context. The group's confrontational activities in support of the Republic led the government to ban all women's clubs and societies in 1793. Lawmakers proclaimed that nature determined only men should take on public and political roles. The ultrarevolutionary journalist Pierre-Gaspard Chaumette (1763–1794) complained that women were making themselves into men, and pointedly noted that nature had not given men breasts to feed children. The Revolution created a more intense need to emphasize men's and women's natural biological differences and to determine their social roles accordingly. That same year Olympe de Gouges met her fate at the guillotine, denounced as an "unnatural" woman, and convicted as a counterrevolutionary. In reaction to the revolutionary chaos, the Napoleonic Code of 1804 codified women's subjugation by stipulating that married women had to obey their husbands in return for their protection and that they could not make legal contracts, control their own property or wages, or engage in business without their husband's permission; in short, the code placed women in the same status as children, criminals, and the mentally deficient.

More important than the explicit feminist activity during the French Revolution was the philosophical debate about women's civil and political rights that it provoked well beyond France. Condorcet's *Plea for the Citizenship of Women* became well known throughout Europe, as did Olympe de Gouges's "Declaration." The Englishwoman Mary Wollstonecraft caused a stir with her *Vindication of the Rights of Woman* (1792), in which she argued eloquently, like Condorcet, for women's inherent capacity to reason and for their need of much better education. Demands for women's rights were made in Belgium, the Dutch Republic, and in some German and Italian states and principalities. But there too advocates faced a backlash as well as the legal subordination of women as the Napoleonic Code was adopted throughout Europe.

RESTORATION, REACTION, AND THE PERSISTENCE OF A "FEMINIST" CRITIQUE

The Restoration of monarchical and religious authority throughout Europe after 1815 reinforced

Caricature of feminists. By Robert Sigl for the cover of the French satirical journal *L'Assiette au Beurre,* 18 September 1909. The popular masculine view of feminists as embittered women is manifested with particular venom in this illustration. MARY EVANS PICTURE LIBRARY

women's legal subjugation. Science and philosophical conceptions of knowledge—such as positivism—reinforced women's physiological inferiority and their natural incapacity for any public function. Even in this conservative climate, however, social criticism of women's position persisted. The field for thinking about women changed dramatically in the contexts of increased female literacy, industrialization, urbanization, national independence movements, evolving nation-states, and the rise of socialism. A "literary feminism" emerged in tracts and novels such as Marion Kirkland Reid's *A Plea for Women* (1843), and Charlotte Brontë's novels *Jane Eyre* (1847) and *Shirley* (1849). Germaine de Staël's *Delphine* (1802) and *Corinne* (1807), and George Sand's *Indiana* (1832) and *Lélia* (1833) caused considerable controversy. These works implicitly or explicitly criticized marriage and stirred their readers with imaginative alternatives. Writers in Denmark,

Spain, Germany, Bohemia, Russia, and Scandinavia produced similarly influential novels. The genre empowered women as writers and influenced the consciousness of readers.

The question of women's status gained more poignancy with the emergence of French and British utopian socialist movements between 1820 and 1840. In reaction to the visible impoverishment of the working classes, whose living conditions were worsened by industrialization and urbanization, utopian socialists turned their attention to the family. In particular, they attacked marriage as an institution that economically and sexually subjugated women. Followers of Henri de Saint-Simon (1760–1825), particularly Marthélemy-Prosper Enfantin (1796–1864), promoted a romantic vision of feminism that emphasized harmony between the sexes based on the complementary nature of their differences. While Enfantin encouraged women's emancipation, he also advocated free love, a move that caused dissension among his followers and eventually brought government prosecution. However some of Enfantin's followers began a newspaper that stressed the importance of women's economic independence and their right to work. The focus on sexual difference also led Saint-Simonian women to stress motherhood itself as a basis for equality, particularly in the role of childhood education.

Saint-Simonianism failed as an emancipatory movement for women in part because men in the movement would not share real power. Many of these feminists then turned to the ideas and followers of Charles Fourier, whose 1808 tract *Théorie des quatre mouvements* claimed that human progress as a whole required the emancipation of women. Another group of feminist men and women clustered around the newspaper *Gazette des femmes;* they circulated petitions demanding the suppression of article 213 in the Napoleonic Code, which required a wife's obedience to her husband. They also made explicit demands for equal parenting rights and for the right to work, to vote, to sit on juries, to attend universities, and particularly to study and practice law and medicine.

Anne Wheeler advocated Saint-Simonian ideas in Britain, where she wrote with the political theorist William Thompson *Appeal on Behalf of Women* (1825), in which she argued that the economy should be restructured to reduce competition. In the 1830s the utopian socialist Robert Owen criticized the family and women's sexual oppression within it. Antislavery and nonconformist religious movements also inspired advocates of women's emancipation in Britain. Meanwhile, in the German Confederation, reform Jews called for greater equity between men and women. In industrialized Saxony, Louise Otto sought improved conditions among working-class women, and campaigned for educational reform for middle-class women. In Italy, the Risorgimento gave female proponents of national unity considerable political voice. Among the most influential were Clara Maffei in Milan and Christina Trivulzio Belgioioso; Belgioioso had been inspired by Fourier.

THE REVOLUTIONS OF 1848 AND THEIR AFTERMATH

The revolutions of 1848 that erupted throughout Europe everywhere brought women into the political arena alongside men, and created new opportunities and new reasons to criticize their legal status. When the French monarchy was overthrown and a Republic established, feminist clubs and newspapers proliferated as they never had before. Various clubs advocated different types or degrees of female emancipation, ranging from complete equality in both private and public spheres to specific demands for the right to work. Most feminists at this time were not concerned with autonomy from men, children, and the family, but instead focused on motherhood as the reason for greater access to education and the right to participate in civil and political life. The concept of mother-educator not only became a source of dignity for women, but a key strategy in French feminism for justifying public involvement despite formal exclusion from politics.

The 1848 revolutions in central, eastern, and southeastern Europe also gave women political experience and to various degrees promoted an emancipatory consciousness among them. Women founded associations in German principalities and in parts of the Habsburg Empire to support political demands, such as education for the lower classes and the abolition of serfdom. Some of them sought change in the status of women. German feminists, for example, like the French, emphasized their distinctive contributions as women; but in the drive toward national unification, they also stressed their role in nation-building. Louise Otto founded the *Frauen-Zeitung* (Women's newspaper), in which she insisted that those who advocated emancipation should also embody a "true womanliness." The revolutions produced a long list of eloquent feminists throughout Europe who made various demands through their newspapers, magazines, and in their political participation. But just as had happened from 1793 on in France, revolutionary governments eventually excluded women from politics, censored their newspapers, and disbanded their clubs. Then the forces of counterrevolution throughout Europe further silenced feminists and the social movements that had supported them. The Habsburg Empire was so fearful of the power women had exhibited in this era of upheaval, it passed a law in 1849 that prohibited female participation in any political activity. In 1850, the Prussian king denied women the rights of assembly and association.

Untouched by the cycle of revolution and reaction, England produced the first sustained female emancipation movement in the second half of the century. Its solid liberal foundation and stable parliamentary system could more easily tolerate the feminist challenge than could the emerging nation-states of Continental Europe. British activists had been inspired by earlier French feminism. But they also learned from the successful organizational efforts of American women in the 1840s antislavery movement that then led to the first Women's Rights Convention in Seneca Falls, New York, in July 1848. British activists protested the marriage law that subordinated married women more completely than in any other European country; they demanded reform of the divorce law; and they criticized the moral double standard in the Contagious Diseases Acts of 1864, 1866, and 1869, which subjected female prostitutes (and women of the working classes wrongly suspected of prostitution) to medical examinations in order to prevent the spread of venereal disease. Josephine Butler spearheaded a loud campaign to repeal the acts, and her efforts spawned movements in France and Italy that opposed regulated prostitution.

Meanwhile, the social critic Harriet Taylor Mill, also inspired by American women, exerted tremendous influence on her husband, the well-known political theorist and parliamentarian John Stuart Mill. In 1869 he published *The Subjection of Women*, a scathing and eloquent critique that compared women's status to that of slaves: "I am far from pretending that wives are in general no better treated than slaves; but no slave is a slave to the same lengths, and in so full a sense of the word, as a wife is. Hardly any slave . . . is a slave at all hours and all minutes. . . . Above all, a female slave . . . is considered under a moral obligation to refuse to her master the last familiarity. Not so the wife: however brutal a tyrant she may unfortunately be chained to" (p. 41). Mill also stressed the injustice of a system that deprived women of their own property and even their own earnings, and claimed "the *power* of earning is essential to the dignity of a woman" (p. 60). Mill's tract was immediately translated into French, German, Swedish, Danish, Russian, Dutch, and Italian; before the end of the century, it was also translated into Polish, Spanish, and Japanese. In many countries it became the philosophical foundation for women's rights and the direct inspiration for organized movements.

THE PEAK OF PRE–WORLD WAR I FEMINISM

Organized movements for women's emancipation developed throughout Europe by the end of the nineteenth century. Extended male suffrage, new concepts of citizenship, the rise of the mass press, improved education for girls, and organized socialist movements were among the factors that inspired or facilitated the demands for improved legal status, higher education, more employment opportunities, equal pay, and compensation for the work of mothers. In Italy, national unification required the codification of laws that varied across provinces, and thus raised questions about women's legal and civic status. In France, Léon Richer and Maria Deraismes demanded change in the French marriage law, particularly with regard to women's property rights. National tensions and military build-up throughout Europe gave added meaning to citizenship. Conscription into the military meant that men earned citizenship through the "blood tax" of national service; women argued that they too paid a blood tax by risking their lives in childbirth and raising their children to be good citizens. Their emphasis on the social functions of motherhood had strategic importance as governments increasingly viewed their populations as a national resource—just at a time when birth rates began to fall precipitously.

With the help of a burgeoning feminist press, the movement peaked between 1890 and 1910. Feminists continued to demand change in the realms of both the private (marriage law, property, divorce, custody of children) and the public (obtaining the vote, higher education, equal pay, access to professional work). The movement's peak coincided with movements for women's access to female forms of birth control that arose throughout Europe and that raised issues regarding female reproductive and sexual freedom. The kind of philosophy espoused by John Stuart Mill and others led women to think about possession over their own bodies and the concept of "voluntary motherhood"—which suggested the limitation of pregnancies through abstinence or through the use of female contraceptive devices such as sponges and pessaries. For the most part, however, organized feminism shunned birth control movements; while many women privately supported family limitation, they also feared that separating sexuality from reproduction would turn women into objects denuded of any dignity. Although some radicals attempted to make birth control a feminist issue—such as Nelly Roussel (1878–1922) in France—it would take another half century, and a revolution in consciousness, for reproductive freedom to assume a central role in the feminist agenda.

As feminism grew, so did the issues that divided its adherents. Socialism became one such wedge. The ideological marriage of female emancipation with the plight of the working poor and the vision of restructuring or overthrowing capitalism in the first half of the century was torn asunder in the second half with the legalization of labor unions, the International Workingmen's Association, and the birth of socialist parties. Because women worked for lower pay, most labor unions demanded a "family wage" for men, which would make it unnecessary for women to work outside the home, and this demand was articulated during the debate about the "woman question" at the 1866–1867 congress of the First International. Feminists responded with a renewed demand for the right to work at equal pay with men. Karl Marx, Friedrich Engels, and other socialist theorists including Clara Zetkin further articulated the notion that women could not possibly be emancipated until after a socialist revolution. Capitalism, not "masculinism," was the true enemy. In the 1880s the Second International further articulated this position, which became the official ideology of socialism. Most socialists viewed feminists—the vast majority of whom were bourgeois—as misled counterrevolutionaries who undermined the socialist-revolutionary project of overthrowing the bourgeoisie. Socialist feminists such as Clara Zetkin refused to work with "bourgeois" feminists, some of whom also opposed capitalism, but given the remote possibility of revolution, sought to improve women's status within the existing system. Religion further divided feminists; Christian women rose to the cause of female emancipation, but within a conservative framework: they sought social services and charity to make marriage and motherhood easier for women, and renounced the individualism and political demands of their sisters.

Initially, nineteenth-century advocates of women's rights did not seek political equality through the vote. But as demands for universal male suffrage grew louder in the 1860s, the first group advocating the vote for women formed in England. In 1904 suffragists formed the International Alliance for Women's Suffrage in Berlin, which helped advance the cause throughout Europe. The movement in Britain became the most vociferous and violent. Members of the Women's Social and Political Union, founded by Emmeline and Christabel Pankhurst in 1903, resorted to violent civil disobedience; as the Parliament refused even to discuss the vote for women, the WSPU disrupted political meetings. By 1909 "suffragettes"—the term distinguished the radicals from the more moderate "suffragists"—were regularly breaking windows of official buildings. Suffragettes' demonstrations soon became riots, and organizers were arrested. The prisoners went on hunger strikes to further publicize their cause. They were then subjected to the brutal torture of force-feeding. By 1913 suffragettes resorted to placing bombs in public places and destroying museum paintings. That same year Emily Wilding

Suffragist gathering, 1913. A group of British suffragists proclaim themselves to be law-abiding, in contrast to others such as Emmeline Pankhurst who engaged in acts of civil disobedience. ©HULTON-DEUTSCH COLLECTION/CORBIS

Davidson sacrificed her life to the cause of female suffrage when, before thousands of spectators at the Derby, she threw herself in front of the king's horse. These acts of violence and tragedy drew condemnation, but they also created a good deal of publicity that brought worldwide attention—and ultimately support—to the cause of votes for women.

CONCLUSION

The historiography of feminism remains relatively new, and much research remains to be done. "Second wave" feminists—those of the 1970s—rediscovered the forgotten experience of women's emancipatory efforts in the nineteenth century. They understandably labeled their findings as the "first wave" of feminism that ended when women in most European countries were granted

the vote after World War I. Karen Offen has more recently suggested a different metaphor—that of volcanic eruptions, the molten lava of which is never inert, and which continually pushes through fissures of established patriarchal power structures. This metaphor indeed helps promote an understanding of different national experiences and a better appreciation of the ongoing efforts of all sorts that persisted between the so-called waves. The French Revolution produced the most radical questioning of gender roles, which in turn led to a severe repression of women's voices, a pattern replicated in subsequent nineteenth-century periods of revolution and reaction. Countries less touched by revolution, diverse as they were—such as Britain, Russia, and the United States (whose feminism so influenced Europe)—could more easily afford to tolerate women's organizations. But everywhere World War I silenced the feminist voice, as the vast majority of women put aside demands specific to their sex and loyally devoted themselves to their respective nationalist causes and war efforts.

See also **Butler, Josephine; Engels, Friedrich; Fourier, Charles; Gender; Gouges, Olympe de; Marx, Karl; Mill, Harriet Taylor; Revolutions of 1848; Roussel, Nelly; Saint-Simon, Henri de; Sand, George; Suffragism; Utopian Socialism.**

BIBLIOGRAPHY

Primary Sources

Bell, Susan Groag, and Karen M. Offen, eds. *Women, the Family, and Freedom: The Debate in Documents, 1750–1950.* 2 vols. Stanford, Calif., 1983.

Hunt, Lynn, ed. and trans. *The French Revolution and Human Rights: A Brief Documentary History.* Boston, 1996.

Mill, John Stuart. *The Subjection of Women.* Toronto, 2000.

Waelti-Walters, Jennifer, and Steven C. Hause, eds. *Feminisms of the Belle Epoque: A Historical and Literary Anthology.* Texts translated by Jette Kjaer, Lydia Willis, and Jennifer Waelti-Walters. Lincoln, Neb., 1994.

Wollstonecraft, Mary. *A Vindication of the Rights of Woman.* New York, 1988.

Secondary Sources

Allen, Ann Taylor. *Feminism and Motherhood in Germany, 1800–1914.* New Brunswick, N.J., 1991.

Moses, Claire Goldberg. *French Feminism in the Nineteenth Century.* Albany, N.Y., 1984.

Offen, Karen. *European Feminisms, 1700–1950.* Stanford, Calif., 2000.

Paletschek, Sylvia, and Bianka Pietrow-Ennker, eds. *Women's Emancipation Movements in the Nineteenth Century: A European Perspective.* Stanford, Calif., 2004.

Rendall, Jane. *The Origins of Modern Feminism: Women in Britain, France, and the United States, 1780–1860.* London, 1985.

Stites, Richard. *The Women's Liberation Movement in Russia: Feminism, Nihilism, and Bolshevism, 1860–1930.* Princeton, N.J., 1991.

Taylor, Barbara. *Eve and the New Jerusalem: Socialism and Feminism in the Nineteenth Century.* Cambridge, Mass., 1993.

ELINOR ACCAMPO

FERDINAND I (1793–1875), emperor of Austria (1835–1848).

Ferdinand I was born 19 April 1793 in Vienna and died 29 June 1875 in Prague. Ferdinand's significance consists largely of the effect that his poor physical and mental condition (he developed epilepsy early in life) had on the legitimist, divine-right absolutist system by which the Habsburg dynasty and its advisers sought to rule the Austrian Empire. While the principle of legitimacy persuaded Francis I (emperor of Austria, 1804–1835) to designate Ferdinand, his eldest son, as his crown prince and heir, the consequences of Ferdinand's incapacity after his succession in March 1835 were deleterious to the proper functioning of the absolutist regime, and the disarray caused in the Habsburg authorities' ranks played a major role in the initial success of the 1848 revolutions. It was the perceived failure of Ferdinand to resist, or adequately cope with, the revolutionary demands in that year that led to his forced abdication on 2 December 1848, in favor of his nephew, Francis Joseph (r. 1848–1916).

Evident soon after his birth, Ferdinand's medical condition made him a constant embarrassment and problem for a dynasty based on the legitimacy of birthright. Ferdinand was evidently much brighter as a child than his relatives and their advisors gave him credit for. He learned to speak four languages and showed a great interest in the natural sciences. The inadequate contemporary understanding of his ailments, however, led him to receive an education that was inappropriately coercive and hence in many respects unsuccessful. Once Ferdinand had reached his majority, his father, Francis I, still kept him at arm's length from the exercise of power. After 1818 Ferdinand undertook some representative duties, but only in 1829, at the age of thirty-six, was he allowed to sit on the state council.

Married to Maria Anna of Piedmont-Sardinia in 1831, Ferdinand succeeded to his father's empire in 1835, but he never was allowed to exercise the power that his position as absolute monarch suggested. Instead, based on his father's will, Ferdinand's power was in reality wielded by a Privy State Conference that first met in December 1836. Ferdinand was officially president of this body and was occasionally present, but in practice it was headed by Archduke Louis, Ferdinand's brother, and the other permanent members—Archduke Francis Charles (another brother and the father of Francis Joseph), Count Clemens Metternich, and

Count Franz Anton Kolowrat-Liebsteinsky—were the major deciders of policy. The rivalry between Metternich and Kolowrat, however, meant that many vital policy decisions were not made, and Austrian policy stagnated, leading to the period of societal unrest known as *Vormärz* (Before March), to which the authorities reacted with most unimaginative, and inefficient, repression.

Economic distress in the mid-1840s exacerbated unrest in the rural and urban lower classes, and the unwillingness of the authorities to co-opt into the political system the growing numbers in the educated middle-classes led to unrest there as well. The nationalist revolt of the Galician Polish nobility in 1846 was suppressed successfully, with the aid of a revolt by the peasantry against their lords. However the revolts in March 1848, in Vienna and Budapest and elsewhere, saw lower and middle classes in temporary solidarity. The collapse of the Habsburg family's willpower in the face of these revolts transformed them into revolutions. On 13 March 1848, Metternich was sacked on the advice of the most liberal Habsburg, Archduke John, and in the turmoil that followed Ferdinand was forced to accede to many of the demands of the revolutionaries. In April he even acceded to the flying of the German black-red-gold national flag over the Hofburg.

Ferdinand was at all times during the events of 1848 the official embodiment of the Habsburg cause, and his concessions made him a popular figure among the more moderate revolutionaries. Yet he was hardly ever actually in charge of Habsburg decision making, and as over the summer the more reactionary course of Prince Alfred Windischgrätz took hold, Habsburg policymakers came to oppose, and regret, the concessions made in Ferdinand's name. After October, therefore, once the revolution in Vienna was crushed, and the Hungarian revolutionary forces put on the defensive, the Habsburg family and its advisors decided that Ferdinand would have to go. Although he initially resisted, Ferdinand eventually abdicated on 2 December 1848 in favor of his nephew, Francis Joseph.

Ferdinand spent the rest of his life in the Hradschin Palace in Prague.

See also **Congress of Vienna; French Revolutionary Wars and Napoleonic Wars; Metternich, Clemens von; Napoleonic Empire; Prussia; Restoration.**

BIBLIOGRAPHY

Holler, Gerd. *Gerechtigkeit für Ferdinand.* Vienna and Munich, 1986.

Okey, Robin. *The Habsburg Monarchy: From Enlightenment to Eclipse.* New York, 2001.

Sked, Alan. *The Decline and Fall of the Habsburg Empire, 1815–1918.* London and New York, 1989

STEVEN BELLER

FERDINAND VII (1784–1833), king of Spain (ruled March–May 1808, 1814–1833).

Ferdinand VII has the reputation of being the worst monarch in Spanish history. In some respects this is unfair. So great were the problems faced by Spain during his reign that even the greatest of rulers would have been hard put to cope with them. That said, however, Ferdinand was hardly an admirable figure. Deeply hurt by the hold that the favorite, Manuel de Godoy, possessed over his parents, Charles IV (r. 1788–1808) and María Luisa, he emerged as a cowardly, narrow-minded, unintelligent, suspicious, and highly vindictive young man whose chief characteristic was a violent hatred for king, queen, and favorite alike.

Ferdinand was both extremely foolish and easily malleable, and from 1800 on he fell prey to an aristocratic faction eager to reverse the inroads that Bourbon enlightened absolutism had made on the privileges of the nobility. This faction saw him as a puppet whom they would be able to manipulate at will once the aging Charles IV had died. Terrified of retribution, these conspirators encouraged Ferdinand to seek Napoleon's protection, while also popularizing him as a "prince charming" who was going to initiate a new golden age.

The result was a serious crisis at court, considerable popular agitation, and, in the end, French intervention in Spain and the overthrow of the Bourbon monarchy. Exiled to France by Napoleon, Ferdinand spent most of the war that followed in comfortable imprisonment. Back in Spain, patriot propaganda conjured up visions of Ferdinand bravely defying Napoleon, but, in reality, he not only made no attempt at resistance but wrote frequent letters to Napoleon congratulating him on his victories.

Released by the emperor in 1814 in a desperate bid to end the Peninsular War, Ferdinand in May of that year overthrew the constitution of 1812—a highly progressive document elaborated in the so-called *cortes* of Cádiz by a group who became known as the *liberales* and thereby provided posterity with the modern term *liberal*—with the aid of a faction of the officer corps that had been alienated by the reforms of the constitution's progenitors and their handling of the war effort. In fairness, Ferdinand did not simply turn the clock back to 1808. Recognizing that some of the changes introduced in the course of the Peninsular War were actually long-standing goals of Bourbon enlightened absolutism, he adopted a surprisingly pragmatic attitude: the abolition of feudalism, for example, was never reversed, while 1817 saw the de facto reintroduction of the system of taxation introduced at Cádiz. Yet the liberals remained unreconciled. More worryingly, trouble also quickly developed in the military. A minority of officers had always been loyal to the constitution and this group was now joined by a number of other malcontents (typically generals who had not been given the rewards they hoped for and lower-ranking figures who had been placed on half-pay in the wake of the army's demobilization).

From 1814 onward, then, Spain witnessed a series of conspiracies in favor of the constitution of 1812, though it was not until March 1820 that Ferdinand's opponents succeeded in overthrowing the regime. There followed the "liberal triennio" of 1820–1823. A new *cortes* was assembled in Madrid while Ferdinand was reduced to playing the role of a constitutional monarch. Yet the constitution of 1812 brought no more happiness than it had eight years before. Split into increasingly antagonistic factions, the liberals had inherited a bitter war in South America, Ferdinand having strained every nerve to put down the rebellions that had broken out against Spanish rule from 1810 onward. No more willing to give up Spain's empire than the king had been, they sought to build up their forces by imposing conscription. Allied with desperate economic conditions, this provoked serious unrest in the countryside and enabled traditionalist opponents of the liberals to whip up widespread popular rebellion.

An attempt to restore absolutism on the part of the royal guard miscarried in July 1822, but the growing chaos provided a pretext for foreign intervention and in the summer of 1823 a French army crossed the frontier to restore order. Effectively a prisoner, Ferdinand was carried off to Cádiz by the fugitive Spanish government, but resistance collapsed and he was quickly liberated. Absolutism then returned but, a brief period of intense repression notwithstanding, Ferdinand refused to go along with his more extreme supporters and continued to operate in the bureaucratic traditions of his predecessors, Charles III (r. 1759–1788) and Charles IV. In response, his more traditionalist backers themselves rose in revolt in 1827. Defeated in a brief civil war, they then began to coalesce around the figurehead provided by the king's disaffected younger brother, Charles.

Until this point Ferdinand had been childless, but in October 1830 his fourth wife, Maria Cristina of Naples, presented him with a baby daughter. This situation presented many complications. According to the law as it was generally understood, women were excluded from the royal succession, but in 1789 this proscription, which dated from only 1713, had been lifted. Ferdinand could therefore legitimately claim that he now had an heir, but Charles and his supporters could just as legitimately maintain that the change in the law was null and void (for reasons that remain a mystery, it had, in fact, never been published).

In any case, the cause of traditionalism was now in serious trouble, for in his last years Ferdinand's commitment to bureaucratic absolutism was such that he had started to restore to favor many of the reformist thinkers and bureaucrats who had backed the French in the Peninsular War. Civil war therefore loomed yet again, and no sooner had Ferdinand died on 29 September 1833 than the first of three terrible "Carlist" wars broke out. To conclude, then, Ferdinand VII was never a pleasant individual—his ministers, for example, found him cold and ungrateful—and he was often very foolish, particularly in his handling of the army. Underlying his defects, however, was a certain canniness, and this in the end ensured that he was never quite the figure of black reaction of legend.

See also **Carlism; Napoleonic Empire; Peninsular War; Restoration; Revolutions of 1820; Spain.**

BIBLIOGRAPHY

Carr, Raymond. *Spain, 1808–1975.* Oxford, U.K., 1982.

Esdaile, Charles J. *Spain in the Liberal Age: From Constitution to Civil War, 1808–1939.* Oxford, U.K., 2000.

CHARLES J. ESDAILE

FERRY, JULES (1832–1893), prime minister of France and principal founder of the French secular school system.

Jules Ferry was the son of a prosperous bourgeois family of Lorraine, the grandson of a textile manufacturer, son of a lawyer, and brother of a banker. He practiced law in Paris, but his wealth allowed Ferry to devote himself to politics, and he became a public figure as a journalist critical of the Second Empire.

Ferry worked for the republican opposition during the parliamentary elections of 1863, resulting in his arrest and conviction in the notorious "trial of the thirteen" (republicans). He received a hefty fine, but he continued to criticize the imperial government in the Parisian press. His most important work appeared in *Le Temps,* whose editor, Auguste Nefftzer (1820–1876), introduced Ferry to another part of the republican opposition, drawn from the Protestant elite.

Ferry became an acknowledged leader of French republicanism with the publication in *Le Temps* of a series of articles entitled *Les comptes fantastiques d'Haussmann* (Haussmann's fantastic account books), an exposé of the expenses, profits, and corruption of the rebuilding of Paris under the prefect, Baron Georges-Eugene Haussmann (1809–1891). The fame of these articles, republished as a pamphlet, earned Ferry his own editorship at *L'Electeur* (The voter), where another series of hard-hitting articles, attacking the system of official electoral candidates, led to his second conviction and a larger fine. This made Ferry a prominent figure at the republican Congress of Nancy in 1865, which drafted a program of democratic opposition to the empire. His celebrity then led to his being elected in 1869 to join the opposition in the Corps Législatif. In his short term in the imperial parliament, Ferry distinguished himself by calling for reforms that the "liberal empire" of the 1860s had overlooked: municipal self-government, freedom of the press, freedom of association and assembly, freedom of education from church control, separation of church and state, and the democratic election of the legislature.

THE GOVERNMENT OF NATIONAL DEFENSE AND THE NATIONAL ASSEMBLY

Despite his long opposition to the Second Empire, Ferry supported the imperial government by voting for war credits in July 1870, during the crisis leading to the Franco-Prussian War. When Parisian republicans reacted to news of the defeat of France at the Battle of Sedan (2 September 1870) by occupying the town hall and proclaiming a republic (4 September 1870), Ferry led one of the columns that converged on the town hall. He was immediately named to membership in the republican provisional government, the Government of National Defense.

Ferry's outspokenness about the administration of the city of Paris resulted in his being named prefect of the Seine, the post that Haussmann had held. Ferry consequently served as mayor of Paris during the Prussian siege of the city, staying behind when Leon-Michel Gambetta (1838–1882) and other members of the National Defense escaped by hot air balloon. Ferry distinguished himself by organizing the National Guard of Paris, by work on the fortifications of Paris, and by the strict but fair system of bread rationing that he established. (Nonetheless, the nickname "famine Ferry" stuck with him in some circles.)

Ferry resigned as mayor of Paris in early 1871 to return to Lorraine as a candidate for the National Assembly, the body that would decide upon peace with Germany, and later upon the Constitution of the Third Republic. He was thus absent when the Commune of 1871 was proclaimed, sitting in Versailles as deputy from the Vosges. His presence there was an embarrassment to the monarchist majority at Versailles, due to his long association with the idea of self-government for Paris. Conservatives solved this problem by naming Ferry ambassador to Greece, thus removing him from domestic politics.

ARCHITECT OF THE SECULAR REPUBLIC

Ferry was elected to the first Chamber of Deputies of the Third Republic in 1876, representing his hometown, Saint-Dié (Vosges), and he immediately assumed one of the most important roles in shaping

JULES FERRY SPEECH ON SECULARISM, 1876

"I pronounce the words *secular state* without any trepidation, even though, for some of our honorable colleagues they would seem to have a certain radical, anarchist, or revolutionary flavor. Yet I am not saying anything new, revolutionary or anarchist when I maintain that the state must be secular, that the totality of society is necessarily represented by secular organizations.

"What, exactly, is this principle? It is a doctrine that [the church] prides itself on having introduced to the world: the doctrine of the separation of temporal and spiritual power. Yes, Christianity introduced the doctrine of the separation of these two domains. ... However, there is one reproach we could make against the church in this matter. After taking four or five centuries to introduce this doctrine, the church has then spent seven or eight centuries attacking it. (*Applause on the left.*)

"Gentlemen, what was the key accomplishment, the major concern, the great passion and service of the French Revolution? To have built this secular state, to have succeeded in making the social organisms of society exclusively secular, to have taken away from the clergy its political organization and role as a cadre within the state—that, precisely, is the French Revolution in its full reality. Well, now, we do not presume to convert the honorable members seated on this side of the Chamber [the monarchists, seated on the right] to the doctrines of the revolution. We only wish it to be understood that we do not deviate from these doctrines. Convinced that the first concern, the first duty of a democratic government is to maintain incessant, powerful, vigilant and efficient control over public education, we insist that this control belong to no other authority than the state. We cannot admit, we will never admit, and this country of France will never admit that the State can be anything but a secular one." ("*Very Good!*" shouts from left and center.)

Source: *Journal official de la République française,* 3 June 1876, as translated in Jan Goldstein and John W. Boyer, eds., *Nineteenth-Century Europe: Liberalism and Its Critics* (Chicago, 1988), p. 358.

---

the democratic and secular institutions of the republic. In that same year he married Eugénie Risler, a Protestant heiress whose family shared Ferry's background in textiles and republicanism (her grandfather was a member of the Constituent Assembly of 1848). By this alliance, Ferry became the in-law of five other members of parliament, including both Charles-Thomas Floquet (1828–1896, a leading voice of radical republicanism) and Auguste Scheurer-Kestner (1833–1899, a leading voice of Alsatian émigrés).

Ferry's long-time advocacy of universal, secular education resulted in his first appointment to the cabinet, as minister of education in 1879. He retained this position under three consecutive cabinets and chose to keep the portfolio for public instruction when he became prime minister himself in 1880. He later returned for two more terms as minister of education and one long term as prime minister. This exceptional tenure in office allowed him to achieve a long series of laws (often collec-

tively called the Ferry Laws) between 1879 and 1885, and in an equally long and important series of administrative decisions, legislation that created the French public school system. These laws (chiefly the Ferry Law of 1882) made education universal, mandatory (for ages six through thirteen), free, and secular. They included significant progress at creating equal education for girls (especially the Camille Sée Law of 1880 for the secondary education of girls) but did not remove all barriers (especially in matters of curriculum and in higher education). They also included steps to create a national educational infrastructure, such as the Paul Bert Law of 1879 that required a teacher training school (*École normale*) for men, and another for women, to serve every department in France.

The first fully republican government of the Third Republic (the William Henry Waddington [1826–1894] ministry of 1879) had been in office barely one month when Ferry deposited two bills that began this process. The first dramatically changed the *Conseil supérieure de l'instruction publique* (the council of educational experts that oversaw school questions) by removing it from control of the Catholic clergy and permitting the minister to name the experts who sat on the council. The second established state regulation of private schools of higher education (*Écoles libres*) and closed them to members of any nonauthorized religious order.

Through his power of appointment, Ferry drew into government service a team of educational experts who were dedicated to his vision of secular (the French often prefer to say "laic") public education, a group who joined him in founding the public school system. Many of these administrators were drawn from the Protestant minority in France, a subculture that had long protested against sending their children to schools run by Catholic clerics and backed the idea of secular public schools. This group of Protestant educational administrators included Ferdinand-Edouard Buisson (1841–1932, later to win the Nobel Peace Prize) as the national director of primary education and Pauline Kergomard (1838–1925), the first woman appointed to *Conseil supérieure*. Ferry himself had been born Catholic, left the faith, and joined the Freemasons in 1875.

The role of Protestants in creating the public school system did not mean a new theology. Instead, the laic school removed all religious teaching from the classroom, leaving it to church and family. Instead of religion, the schools taught a "civic morality" (*morale laïque*) developed by Buisson and others. When conservatives, led by Jules Simon (1814–1896), proposed that the schools should teach "duties toward God and the fatherland," the Chamber rejected the motion.

Catholic protests against losing control of the school system led to redoubled anticlericalism, and many of the laic laws of the period from 1879 to 1885 were shaped by this as much as by educational philosophy. A noteworthy example occurred in 1879, when the Senate blocked Ferry's plan for state regulation of *Écoles libres*. The Chamber responded by vigorous action against nonauthorized religious orders, which led to the expulsion of the Jesuits from France in June and July 1880, who were sometimes removed from their houses by force.

Although Ferry in the 1880s advocated a more moderate republicanism ("opportunism") than the radical republicanism he had supported in his early career, Ferry's governments achieved many of the fundamental legislative goals that defined republicanism: laws granted freedom of the press (1881), the right to form trade unions (the Waldeck-Rousseau Law of 1884), and the right of divorce (the Naquet Law of 1884).

THE NEW IMPERIALISM

Ferry was detested in many conservative and Catholic circles for his laic laws, but the controversy that drove him from office and ended his career was entirely different: the "new imperialism" under which France rapidly expanded its colonial empire in the late nineteenth century. As prime minister in 1880, Ferry chose to be minister of foreign affairs, and this led him to the conclusion that France should rebuild its colonial empire, recovering some of the prestige lost in the Franco-Prussian War, and expanding both French culture and the French economy on a global basis.

Ferry launched his program of imperial expansion in 1881 by sending an expeditionary force to Tunisia, and the success of French arms there led him to colonial ventures in Africa and Asia. Ferry's new imperialism included the French occupation of Senegal, Guinea, Dahomey, the Ivory Coast, and Gabon in sub-Saharan Africa; expanded roles in many islands, especially Madagascar and Tahiti; and the consolidation of the French protectorate in Indochina in the years 1883 to 1885.

The diplomacy of imperialism made Ferry as many enemies as his secularism had. French expansion benefited from the encouragement of Otto von Bismarck (1815–1898) of Germany, who generally opposed German imperialism and who reasoned that a reawakened French imperialism would lead to Anglo-French confrontations over empire. At international congresses of 1878 and 1884, Bismarck encouraged French ventures, and his support made the conquest of Tunisia possible. Ferry, who already faced the anger of anti-imperialist radicals, now faced the anger of anti-German nationalists who denounced his détente with Germany as treasonous and branded him "Bismarck's valet."

Opposition to Ferry's imperialism produced a strange coalition of the left (led by Georges Clemenceau [1841–1929]) and the right that drove Ferry from office in 1885, following the news of a military reverse outside Hanoi. The nadir came in 1887 when Ferry was seriously wounded in an assassination attempt. The man who had perhaps been the most important single founder of the Third Republic's institutions remained in politics until his death in 1893, but he was rejected for the presidency of France and never returned to high office.

See also Clemenceau, Georges; Education; France; Imperialism; Separation of Church and State (France, 1905).

BIBLIOGRAPHY

Acomb, Evelyn Martha. The French Laic Laws, 1879–1889. New York, 1941. Reprint, New York, 1967.

Gaillard, Jean-Michel. Jules Ferry. Paris, 1989.

Guilhaume, Philippe. Jules Ferry. Paris, 1980.

Pisani-Ferry, Fresnette. Jules Ferry et le partage du monde. Paris, 1962.

Power, Thomas Francis, Jr. Jules Ferry and the Renaissance of French Imperialism. New York, 1944. Reprint, New York, 1966.

STEVEN C. HAUSE

FICHTE, JOHANN GOTTLIEB
(1762–1814), German philosopher.

Johann Gottlieb Fichte is best known for his lifelong effort to develop a comprehensive system of transcendental idealism under the general name Wissenschaftslehre or "Theory of Scientific Knowledge," which would be true to the "spirit" if not to the letter of Kantianism. Fichte is also known for his popular lectures and writings on philosophy of history, education, and religion, including his controversial Addresses to the German Nation.

Fichte was born in very humble circumstances in Saxony and educated in Jena and Leipzig. His first encounter with Immanuel Kant's Critiques was enough to persuade him to devote the rest of his life, first of all, to popularizing the salubrious consequences of transcendental idealism, and secondly to the systematic reformulation of the same upon a more secure foundation. His first book, Attempt at a Critique of All Revelation (1792), which appeared without his name and was mistakenly attributed to

Kant, immediately established his reputation, on the basis of which he obtained a professorship at the University of Jena (1794–1799). His public defense of the principles of the French Revolution earned him a reputation as a political radical.

In Jena, Fichte set out the basic principles of his new "System of Human Freedom" in his lectures and books, Foundations of the Entire Wissenschaftslehre (1794–1795) and Outline of Distinctive Character of the Wissenschaftslehre with Respect to the Theoretical Faculty (1795). In this "foundational" portion of his system, he showed how "theoretical" consciousness of the I and its objects presupposes and is made possible by "practical" striving and willing, thereby installing at the heart of his new system "the primacy of the practical." This was accomplished by limiting the realm of transcendental philosophy to that of analyzing the structure of pure subjectivity itself, the realm of the autonomous or "absolutely self-positing" I.

During this period Fichte also developed, in his Foundations of Natural Right (1796–1797), a highly original political theory or philosophy of law, stressing the independence of the latter from morality and including a "deduction" of intersubjectivity as a condition for self-consciousness. His most accomplished work during the Jena period was his System of Ethics (1798), in which he reformulated the foundations of his system and tried to replace Kant's merely "formal" ethics with a real or material theory of morals, which stresses the constitutive role of moral consciousness ("conscience") as a condition for self-consciousness as such.

In 1799 Fichte was charged with atheism on the basis of his apparent identification of God with the "moral world order" (in his essay "On the Basis of our Belief in Divine Governance of the World" [1798]) and subsequently lost his position at Jena. He then moved to Berlin, where he spent most of the rest of his life. At first he supported himself as a freelance author and lecturer. In works such as The Vocation of Man (1800), Characteristics of the Present Age (1806), The Way toward the Blessed Life (1806), and Addresses to the German Nation (1808) he tried to present the standpoint of the Wissenschaftslehre in a broadly "popular" and accessible manner and to apply the same to the pressing historical, moral, educational, and political needs of his own time—including the immediate need for spiritual rejuvenation and heightened self-awareness on the part of the "German nation" that had been humiliated by Napoleon. When the University of Berlin was established in 1810, Fichte became dean of the philosophy faculty and then rector of the university, as well as professor of philosophy.

At the same time Fichte was trying to engage with the events and needs of his era, he was also busy developing and revising the theoretical foundations of his *Wissenschaftslehre*—a process he began in Jena, with his lectures on *Wissenschaftslehre nova methodo* (1796–1799) and continued in Berlin and elsewhere. In all, he produced at least fifteen radically different presentations of the *Wissenschaftslehre,* only the first of which was published during his own lifetime. Some of the later versions were included in the edition of Fichte's *Works* published by his son in the mid-nineteenth century, but it is only in recent decades that some of the later versions of the *Wissenschaftslehre* have become available in the new critical edition of his *Works* published under the auspices of the Bavarian Academy of the Sciences.

Fichte's influence during his own lifetime was immense and was not limited to his well-known philosophical influence upon Friedrich von Schelling and Friedrich Hegel. They both learned from his philosophy (from, for example, his pioneering development of the "dialectical method") and ultimately rejected the same as "subjective idealism." He also had a direct influence upon the first generation of German Romantic authors, including Friedrich Schlegel and Novalis, and his *Addresses* played a controversial role in the subsequent development of German nationalism. Since the later versions of his system were not published until long after his death, the "reception" of Fichte's philosophy is a process that continues into the early twenty-first century.

See also **Hegel, Georg Wilhelm Friedrich; Novalis (Hardenberg, Friedrich von); Schelling, Friedrich von.**

BIBLIOGRAPHY

Breazeale, Daniel, ed. and trans. *Fichte: Early Philosophical Writings.* Ithaca, N.Y., 1988.

———. *Foundations of Transcendental Philosophy (Wissenschaftslehre) nova methodo (1796/99).* Ithaca, N.Y., 1992.

———. *Introductions to the Wissenschaftslehre and Other Writings, 1797–1800.* Indianapolis, 1994.

———. *The Popular Works of Johann Gottlieb Fichte.* 2 vols. Bristol, U.K., 1999.

Breazeale, Daniel, and Günter Zöller, eds. and trans. *System of Ethics.* Cambridge, U.K., 2005.

Heath, Peter, and John Lachs. *Science of Knowledge.* Cambridge, U.K., 1982.

Neuhouser, Frederick, ed. *Foundations of Natural Right: According to the Principles of Wissenschaftslehre.* Translated by Michael Baur. Cambridge, U.K., 2005.

Wright, Walter E., ed. and trans. *The Science of Knowing: J. G. Fichte's 1804 Lectures on the Wissenschaftslehre.* Albany, N.Y., 2005.

DANIEL BREAZEALE

FILM. *See* **Cinema.**

FIN DE SIÈCLE. The phrase *fin de siècle* began showing up in French writing in 1886, reflecting emergent interest in the nineteenth century's closing years (particularly its final decade) as a distinct historical period. In the 1890s "fin de siècle" became a popular catchphrase in France that spread to Britain, the United States, and to German-speaking countries. It designated either the modernity of that period or its identity as an autumnal phase of decline. It meant either up-to-date and fashionable or decadent and worn-out.

The fin de siècle brought an outpouring of historical assessments of the century. Paeans to "progress" were favorites of state officials and spokespersons for the middle and upper echelons of society. Buoyed by Darwinian theories of evolution, they focused on various evidence of civilization's movement to "higher" levels. For example, common people across Europe were enjoying more reliable and abundant food supplies, better home heating and lighting than ever before, and access to primary education. The last great European crises—the Franco-Prussian War of 1870–1871 and the Paris Commune—were decades in the past. Scientists were making great strides forward, gathering observable "facts" and "discovering" "natural laws," according to advocates of the scientific philosophy known as "positivism." "Progress" was perhaps most clearly demonstrable in the era's cascade of technological innovations—from the telephone to the automobile. Millions of Europeans saw such progress in profusion at the Paris Universal Expositions of 1889 and 1900, where they beheld dazzling displays of electric lighting, the latest armaments and powerful machines, a moving sidewalk, the world's largest Ferris wheel (*La Grande Roue*), and examples of the recently invented motion picture. Fairgoers also saw a gathered world of colonial pavilions, testaments to the unprecedented reach of European power. From that vantage point, the century was ending on a triumphant note.

But outside the mainstream, a host of hard-to-ignore voices—from Bohemian artists to early social scientists—took a pessimistic view. Among them were some of the most important and influential figures of that time. The German philosopher Friedrich Nietzsche (1844–1900), the Norwegian playwright Henrik Ibsen (1828–1906), the Irish writer Oscar Wilde (1854–1900), and the English illustrator Aubrey Beardsley (1872–1898), to name only a few, assailed the repressive conventions and hypocrisy of middle-class societies. Other critical observers poured their anxieties and fears into jeremiads about the decline of almost everything—nation and empire, race, religion, morality, the family, women, and the arts. A sense of crisis was heightened in the 1890s by international anarchist attacks on modern civilization, using dynamite and guns to assassinate presidents and kings and to sow terror, all in the hope of bringing down the corrupt old order and ushering in a communitarian world of justice and equality.

CULTURAL MODERNITIES

The sense of decline was particularly strong in two capital cities that were cultural crucibles of the first order: Paris and Vienna. In both cities an old sense of primacy was being eroded by the new importance of Germany's power since its unification in 1871—military and economic power together with

a huge population. At the same time bold newcomers and outsiders with extraordinary originality and talent were challenging the established cultural and political leaders and elites. In the Austrian capital, mounting political and social tensions were straining the fabric of a crazy-quilt empire led by an aging emperor, backward-looking nobles, and self-regarding bourgeois men. In the 1890s a younger generation rebelled creatively against the old order of religious and imperial dogmatism, moralistic and rationalist middle classes, and the cautious aesthetics of academies and official patrons. Gustav Klimt (1862–1918) gave graphic form to instinct, sexuality, and an uneasy sense of flux in his paintings for several university buildings in Vienna, outraging the upholders of tradition. In Paris in the 1890s a stream of artists and writers sharing a bohemian lifestyle brought wave after wave of artistic shocks to upholders of conventional taste and morality (Alfred Jarry in theater, Henri de Toulouse-Lautrec in painting, and Erik Satie in music, for example).

One of the emblematic aesthetic expressions of the 1890s was the style called Modern Style in Great Britain and France, where it was also known as Art Nouveau. Reviving rococo decorative motifs, French producers of the "new art" worked flowing, organic lines into architecture, ceramics, jewelry, posters, and furniture. The style's sinuous forms also appeared in the plantlike iron entryways for Paris's earliest subway stations (1900), designed by Hector-Germain Guimard (1867–1942). In Vienna, Berlin, Munich, and Prague, too, the new art found brilliant champions (Klimt among them), young talents who produced *Jugendstil* (youth style) masterpieces in opposition to the conventions favored by their elders. In Austria and France this movement of innovators, unlike others, received state support, because their program of reviving traditional arts and crafts in an industrial age seemed reassuring and socially unifying to those in power.

PERCEIVED DANGERS AND CRISES—
AND DANGEROUS FANTASIES

The view of the era as decadent came readily to old elites, whose political, moral, and cultural authority was under attack from artistic rebels, anarchists, socialists, trade unionists, champions of democracy, and advocates of women's rights. To them the century's close was bringing the barbarian masses to power and swamping the cultural scene with vulgar and immoral works pandering to the tastes of the vulgar plebians. Fears of "the lower orders" and the "other" in myriad guises were rampant among the middle and upper classes in the fin de siècle.

Pioneering scholars in the new social sciences lent weighty support to worries about waxing dangers and looming crises. Experts in psychology, sexology, eugenics, and sociology defined and described the pathological and the abnormal expansively, overlaying old moralism with a new scientific authority. The German psychiatrist Richard von Krafft-Ebing (1840–1902), who was famous in the 1890s (when Sigmund Freud was not), graphically described a plethora of "psychopathological" behaviors or "perversions" (homosexuality, masturbation, sadism, masochism, fetishism, among others) in his tome *Psychopathia Sexualis* (1886). His alarming conclusion was that sexual crimes were widespread and on the increase. The Viennese physician Max Nordau (1849–1923) made an even more sweeping diagnosis of the era in his influential book *Degeneration* (published in German in 1893, English trans. in 1895). He highlighted not only the alarming increase of mental and physical degeneration, crime and suicide, but also the rise of "degenerate" "tendencies and fashions" in the arts (Nietzsche, Ibsen, Émile Zola, Richard Wagner, and others).

In the pessimistic commentaries, the growth of big cities loomed large as a cause of the ills of modern society. Fast-paced, hyper-stimulating urban life reputedly wore people out, and the constant nervous strain resulted in an epidemic of mental diseases (especially neurasthenia and the catchall diagnosis "hysteria"). Further, the urban "masses" were irrational and dangerous: they erupted all too frequently as mad, destructive "crowds" (the thesis of Gustave Le Bon's *La psychologie des foules*, published in 1895). Cities generated syphilis, prostitution, alcoholism, suicide, and crime. They were also hotbeds of a burgeoning, demoralizing mass culture—tasteless tabloids, detective stories, spy novels, science fiction, and mindless films.

Caught in the maelstrom of transformations, most fin-de-siècle men were on the defensive, fearing loss of control at every turn—in the home, workplace, marketplace, politics, and culture. Among the multiple menaces to tradition were women who pressed for greater economic and educational opportunities, rejecting the ideal of feminine domesticity and patriarchy. Their demands for rights and the small-but-important advances for women (for example, laws allowing them control of property, and the entry of an early few into higher education and the medical profession) were enough to stir an antifeminist reaction—denunciations of women who dared go against "nature." Women prostitutes represented another direct challenge to conventional gender codes as well as a threat to bourgeois morality, public health, and society's control of women's sexuality, especially as it became clear that the state systems of medical exams and licensed brothels were not effective or satisfactory to anyone. Fears and misogyny also manifested themselves in a surge of "fantasies of feminine evil," expressed in innumerable paintings of castrating, murderous *femmes fatales* (works by Edvard Munch and a host of others). Homosexuals, increasingly visible and vocal, also aroused fears of the feminine and anxiety about the stability of masculine identity, for they were widely viewed as unmanly and feminized (or "inverted"). Along with "dangerous" women and sexual "inverts," Jews were prime targets for those disturbed by economic and social changes. Anti-Semitism found a new support in cobbled-together racist theories about "Aryans" and the (allegedly inferior) other "races," and it took new form as a mass-political program in demagogic electioneering in Vienna (Karl Lueger, mayor of Vienna, 1895–1910), Paris (the anti-Dreyfusards), and Germany.

SHIFTING HISTORICAL PERSPECTIVES

In the late 1890s a debate raged (as it did in 1999) about exactly when the old century ended. Some, including Germany's emperor, opted for the turn of the calendar to 1900, but most people celebrated the turn to 1901. Historians have taken more liberty, choosing symbolic events such as the conviction (1895) or death (1900) of Oscar Wilde, the death of Queen Victoria (1901), or the military defeat suffered by the tsar's empire in the Russo-Japanese war (1904–1905).

The period called "fin de siècle" was not followed by an analogous one called "beginning of the century": no historical term for the early 1900s emerged. After World War I with its unexpected carnage and postwar hardships, Europeans began to look back on the years around 1900 not as a century's end, but as the era before the war—a vanished time of peace and economic stability. The period labels "l'avant-guerre" (before the war), "1900" (as an era), and "turn of the century" entered the vernacular. During and after World War II, the last decades of the nineteenth century and the prewar years became known in France as the "belle époque" (the beautiful period), a phrase that eclipsed the label "fin de siècle" for several decades, especially in popular usage. But in the twentieth century's last years, as the approach of the new century and new millennium stirred anticipation and anxiety, the phrase "fin de siècle" returned in force as a subject of historical reflection in scholarly studies and the media.

See also **Art Nouveau; Decadence; Eiffel Tower; LeBon, Gustave; Nietzsche, Friedrich; Paris; Vienna; Wagner, Richard.**

BIBLIOGRAPHY

Dijkstra, Bram. *Idols of Perversity: Fantasies of Feminine Evil in Fin-de-siècle Culture.* New York, 1986.

Pick, Daniel. *Faces of Degeneration: A European Disorder, c. 1848–c. 1918.* Cambridge, U.K., and New York, 1989.

Rearick, Charles. *Pleasures of the Belle Epoque: Entertainment and Festivity in Turn-of-the-Century France.* New Haven, Conn., 1985.

Schorske, Carl E. *Fin de siècle Vienna: Politics and Culture.* 1979. New York, 1981.

Schwartz, Hillel. *Century's End: A Cultural History of the Fin de siècle—from the 990s through the 1990s.* New York, 1990.

Seigel, Jerrold E. *Bohemian Paris: Culture, Politics, and the Boundaries of Bourgeois Life, 1830–1930.* New York, 1986.

Silverman, Debora L. *Art Nouveau in Fin-de-siècle France: Politics, Psychology, and Style.* Berkeley, Calif., 1989.

Weber, Eugen. *France, Fin de siècle.* Cambridge, Mass., 1986.

CHARLES REARICK

FINLAND AND THE BALTIC PROVINCES.

For the peoples of the tsarist Russian territories of the Grand Duchy of Finland and the three Baltic provinces of Estonia, Livonia (Livland), and Courland (Kurland), the nineteenth and early twentieth centuries witnessed the development of the modern Finnish, Estonian, and Latvian nations, which in the late eighteenth century seemed unlikely candidates for nationhood. This corner of northeast Europe was overwhelmingly agrarian in the late eighteenth century, with small urban populations. By the early twentieth century, however, the societies of the Baltic were undergoing industrialization and urbanization, and the region included one of the largest metropolises in the Russian Empire, the important port city of Riga.

The constitutional position of the Baltic provinces on the one hand, and Finland on the other, differed significantly. The formerly Swedish-held provinces of Estonia and Livonia, annexed by the Russian Empire in 1710 in the course of the Great Northern War (1700–1721) between Sweden and Russia, and the Polish-held Duchy of Courland, part of the Russian state after the Third Partition of Poland in 1795, were all made provinces of the Russian state. The Baltic German rural and urban corporative elites never saw themselves as "Russian"; rather, they held to the understanding that the traditional rights and privileges of the corporations of nobility and the urban magistrates were confirmed in exchange for their loyalty to the ruling Romanov dynasty.

The idea of Finnish independence from Sweden germinated among a group of rebellious Swedish officers from Finland in the 1780s, who were inclined to cooperate with Russia to attain their goal. In 1808 Russian troops attacked the Swedish crown by invading Finland, in fulfillment of the terms of the 1807 Treaties of Tilsit between France and Russia. Thus, in 1809, Finland came under Russian control. That year, the Russian tsar, Alexander I (r. 1801–1825), convened the Diet of the Estates, where he made Finland an autonomous grand duchy within the empire, giving the country separate administrative status for the first time in its history. In 1812 the Russian state attached to the grand duchy a borderland strip in southern and western Karelia ("Old Finland"). Finland kept these geographical boundaries until 1944.

In the Baltic provinces, a Russian-appointed governor was the highest local authority (a single governor-general administered the Baltic provinces from 1775 to 1876); he oversaw the activities of the central tsarist ministries, whose personnel were often themselves Baltic Germans, and later in the nineteenth century, Estonians and Latvians. Administration of local affairs was controlled by Baltic German elites—the corporations of nobility in the countryside and magistrates in urban areas.

Though a constituent part of the Russian Empire, Finland was not subject to central tsarist administration, but had its own council of government (soon renamed the Senate), which was composed of privileged, Swedish-speaking Finns. A governor-general, always a Russian military officer, with a staff primarily from Russia, was the highest local representative of the tsarist state and formally was chairman of the Senate. These separate lines of authority resulted in a degree of administrative dualism, although attempts to limit Finland's autonomy came only late in the century. Contributing to Finland's distinctive status within the empire was the creation of the position of state secretary of Finland, located in St. Petersburg, and occupied generally by a Finn; directives of the Russian state had to clear this office before they could be enacted in Finland.

There were, however, similarities in the relationship of the Baltic provinces and Finland with the tsarist state. On both sides of the Gulf of Finland the Russian state left local elites in place, granting them control of local administrative and judicial matters. In Finland, these were for the most part Swedish speakers, in the Baltic provinces, Baltic Germans. The tsarist state never intended to alter significantly the composition of Baltic and Finnish societies or to absorb them into the broader Russian population. Rather, it was more interested in these lands as buffer zones between Russia proper and western Europe.

ETHNICITY AND NATIONALISM

Self-consciously national Finnish, Estonian, and Latvian cultures were formed in the nineteenth century under Russian rule. On the whole, the Russian state was favorably disposed to this development, and often even encouraged it, seeing these cultures as counterbalances to the power of the Baltic German elites in the Baltic provinces and the Swedish-speaking elites in Finland.

As throughout much of central and eastern Europe, ethnolinguistic differences in the Baltic region paralleled differences in social and economic status. The peasants of Estonia and northern Livonia were Estonians, whereas the countryside of southern Livonia and Courland was Latvian-dominated. Latvian areas were somewhat more urbanized than Estonian ones; in 1862 nearly 15 percent of the residents of southern Livonia and Courland lived in towns and cities, whereas under 9 percent of the population in northern Livonia and Estonia were urban. Baltic Germans formed a majority, if not a plurality, in all towns and cities in the eighteenth century. By the mid-nineteenth century, Estonians began displacing them as the numerically dominant group in Estonia and northern Livonia; however, urbanization of Latvians in southern Livonia and Courland proceeded somewhat more slowly. Estonians made up a majority of the population of Tallinn by 1871. In Riga, however, Latvians never held a majority in the tsarist period; by 1897 Latvians made up a plurality, though not a majority, of the city's population at 41.6 percent. Russians formed a significant urban minority, composed largely of old merchant families from pre-tsarist times, military officers, and, later in the century, Russian bureaucrats. In Riga and in the towns of Courland, Jews also had a notable presence. A small number of Swedes were found on islands off the west coast of Estonia. And the coast of the Gulf of Riga was home to a few surviving Livs, a people related to the Finns and Estonians.

In Finland, the correlation between ethnicity and native language on the one hand, and socioeconomic status on the other, was strong, though not as striking as it was in the Baltic provinces. Finnish speakers, who made up the bulk of the population, tended to be farmers and laborers. Swedish speakers, nearly 14 percent of the population in 1865, composed the majority of the urban and intellectual elite, but Swedish speakers also formed the bulk of the population in the coastal areas of southern and western Finland. Small Russian and German minorities could be found in several cities.

In the Baltic provinces, noble elites dominated in both town and countryside for most of the nineteenth century. These nobles were German speakers, descendants of medieval crusaders and traders, along with some more recent immigrants from German lands, most prominently, schoolteachers

Riga, Latvia, c. 1890–1900. The Library of Congress

and clergy. Finland's nobles—Swedish speaking (including some Swedicized Finns)—were much less powerful in relative terms than their Baltic German counterparts. Many Baltic Germans rose to positions of great prominence in the Russian military and civil service, including Field Marshal Prince Mikhail (or Michael) Barclay de Tolly (1761–1818); Alexander von Benckendorff (1781–1844), secret police chief under Nicholas I (r. 1825–1855); explorer Baron Ferdinand Wrangel (1796–1870); Finance Minister Count Mikhail Reitern (Michael Reutern; 1820–1890); and Justice Minister Konstantin von der Pahlen (1830–1912). State service was also attractive to Finns, and by midcentury over a fifth of the country's small nobility was in Russian state service, both in Finland and Russia proper. The most prominent figure in Finland in the twentieth century, Swedish-speaking nobleman Carl Gustaf Mannerheim (1867–1951),

began his career in the Russian cavalry, becoming a lieutenant general and corps commander before the collapse of the tsarist regime.

Though serfdom was ended in the Baltic provinces in the second decade of the nineteenth century (1816 in Estonia, 1817 in Courland, and 1819 in Livonia), Baltic German landowners maintained control of the land and thus, to a great degree, over the lives of the peasants. Municipal power remained in the hands of the Baltic German and Swedish-speaking elites, and wealthy merchants dominated city life. Finland did not experience serfdom, but Finnish-speaking Finns, overwhelmingly peasants, had little input into government. Upwardly mobile urban Estonians, Latvians, and Finns, such as skilled artisans and the occasional professional, experienced near universal Germanization or, in Finland, Swedization. Despite the growth of nationalist movements in the second half of the century, this trend was not halted until the early twentieth century.

The consolidation of a Finnish, Estonian, and Latvian national identity began in the late eighteenth century and continued in the first half of the nineteenth century with the work of folklorists, ethnographers, and philologists, who studied the culture and language of the Finnish, Estonian, and Latvian common people. Inspired by Enlightenment ideals and Herderian notions of the primordial nature and ontological separateness of each nation (*Volk*), these German- and Swedish-speaking scholars published works that helped define the contours of the Finnish, Estonian, and Latvian national culture. By the 1840s, individual educated Estonians, Latvians, and Finns began to identify themselves publicly by these national appellations— commonly regarded in educated circles as synonyms for "peasants"—despite their primary fluency in German or Swedish. These intellectuals also cultivated the idea of a golden age of cultural and spiritual purity supposed to have existed before the arrival of Western crusaders and conquerors to the Baltic region in the twelfth and early thirteenth centuries.

In Finland, the spread of national sentiment at midcentury centered on the issue of language. Members of the "Fennoman" movement, led by Johan Wilhelm Snellman (1806–1881), advocated that Finnish replace Swedish in public life. Beginning in the 1840s, some educated, Swedish-speaking Finns abandoned their accustomed language for what they held to be their true mother tongue— Finnish. By the 1860s, the language conflict became heated. The majority within the educated class, however, championed the "Svecoman" view set out by the philologist Axel Olof Freudenthal (1836–1911), favoring a language-based Swedish nationality in Finland.

Published works that combined the worlds of scholarship and belles lettres contributed to the emergence of nationalism both in Finland and the Baltic provinces. Most important is the Finnish epic *Kalevala* (1835, enlarged in 1849) compiled by the physician-folklorist Elias Lönnrot (1802–1884) from oral poetry he collected among Finns living in Russia's Kola Peninsula. Inspired by Lönnrot's achievement, the Estonian folklorist and physician

Friedrich Reinhold Kreutzwald (1803–1882) used elements of Estonian folk poetry to create his *Kalevipoeg* (The son of Kalevi; 1857–1861). Latvians' rich folk songs, first collected systematically in the 1880s, provided the impetus, if not the actual material, contained in the Latvian epic *Lāčplēsis* (The bear slayer), published by Andrejs Pumpurs in 1888.

Nationalist sentiment began to spread to wider sections of the population in the Baltic provinces in the 1860s. There was no single movement nor unified ideological or cultural program among those who began openly to espouse a self-consciously Latvian or Estonian identity. This was largely attributable to a lack of agreement on views toward the growing confrontation between the Russian state and the Baltic Germans. Among the small number of Estonian intellectuals and professionals, the journalist Johann Voldemar Jannsen (1819–1890) and the philologist-clergyman Jakob Hurt (1839–1907) held a moderate view toward the Baltic Germans. The more radical Estonian activists, who sought help from the Russian state in strengthening Estonian identity, were led by the journalist Carl Robert Jakobson (1841–1882). The foremost Latvian national activists of the 1860s, Krišjānis Valdemārs (1825–1891) and Krišjānis Barons (1835–1923), edited a Latvian-language newspaper in St. Petersburg. Also Russophiles, they criticized the dominance of the Baltic German nobility and called for Latvians and the Latvian language to play a greater public role. The wider propagation of Estonian- and Latvian-language newspapers beginning in the 1860s was crucial in the spread of nationalist feeling and the creation of Estonian and Latvian public opinion.

Voluntary associations were important in the consolidation and development of Estonian, Latvian, and Finnish nations. Associational activity in the Baltic provinces was strongest among the Baltic Germans, who formed scholarly societies in the early decades of the nineteenth century, but associational life was particularly crucial to the spread of national identity to wider numbers of Estonians and Latvians, who formed their own societies beginning in the 1860s. Music, agricultural, and temperance societies were especially popular. The most influential society among Latvians was the Riga Latvian Association, founded in 1868. Key

Estonian brass band, nineteenth century. Music societies played an important role in forging an Estonian national identity.
ESTONIAN CULTURAL HISTORY ARCHIVES AT ESTONIAN LITERARY MUSEUM

for the Estonians were the Vanemuine Society in Tartu and the Estonia Society in Tallinn, both founded in 1865. These two Estonian music associations and the Riga Latvian Association organized a number of Estonian and Latvian song festivals throughout the remainder of the tsarist period, which were important in the development of Estonian and Latvian self-expression and group identity. In Finland, voluntary associations also helped Finnish speakers create a modern society out of a socially unorganized peasant society.

RUSSIFICATION AND THE TSARIST STATE
The tsarist state undertook a series of reforms in the Baltic provinces beginning in the mid-1860s aimed at reducing Baltic particularism in local governance and administration. Most Baltic Germans opposed the measures, which entailed the weakening of Baltic German influence upon the peasant

townships, the replacement of Baltic German estate-based city magistrates with elected city councils, and the replacement of Baltic German police and judicial institutions with Russian ones. Educational reform beginning in the mid-1880s introduced Russian as the sole language of instruction in primary schools. The state also intensified proselytism of Orthodoxy among the Estonians and Latvians, who were mostly Lutheran. Tensions eased some with the death of the Russian nationalist emperor Alexander III in 1894, who was succeeded by his son, the less confrontational Nicholas II.

When Finland refrained from any sympathy protest in reaction to unrest in Poland in 1863, a grateful Alexander II responded with the first convening of the Finnish Diet since 1809 (which thereafter met regularly) and the granting of a promise to abide by constitutional principles in matters regarding the grand duchy. The reactivated

Diet, elected on a restricted franchise, developed a wide-ranging legislative program. Finland acquired its own monetary system in 1865, and the legal framework for a Finnish army was passed in 1878. Much energy, however, was spent on a renewed battle on the language issue. A significant victim in the struggle was the Liberal Party, which in its emphasis on constitutional rights instead of language difference had attempted to find a path between the nationalist Finnish (Fennoman) and Swedish (Svecoman) parties.

In the 1880s and 1890s, some in the Baltic provinces and Finland began to see social problems, not the linguistic and national struggle, as the central concern facing their societies. In Finland, the Young Finnish Party emerged in opposition to the socially conservative Finnish Party; by the turn of the century its energies were subsumed into the Finnish labor movement. Among Latvians, the members of the New Current voiced cultural discontents with the older nationalist generation and were Marxist in orientation. The Young Estonia movement that emerged after 1905, socialist though not Marxist in political orientation, was aimed primarily at founding a modern Estonian culture based in urban, not rural, culture.

Confidence had grown in Finland beginning in the 1860s that the relationship with Russia was fundamentally constitutional, not imperial, in nature and that Finland had developed from being a Swedish province to a state only allied with Russia. While deep social and class differences remained in Finland into the twentieth century, a shared Finnish political self-awareness spread widely; speakers of Finnish and Swedish alike saw themselves as Finns. Few recognized the seriousness of the pressure in the 1890s from nationalists and pan-Slavists within the Russian government and from Russian public opinion for the diminution of Finland's special status within the empire. Like the Baltic Germans, Finns emphasized their relationship with the Russian sovereign as protector of their special rights. But on 15 February (3 February, old style) 1899, Russian Emperor Nicholas II asserted in a public manifesto the right to bypass the Finnish Diet in enacting laws he felt were in the interest of the Russian state. Though the conservative Finnish nationalist leaders counseled acquiescence, nearly half of Finland's adult population signed petitions opposing the move. When conscription of Finnish soldiers into the tsar's army was announced in 1901, resistance was widespread, and in 1904 the governor-general, Nikolai Bobrikov, was assassinated in Helsinki.

In the Baltic provinces, Latvians and Estonians were more concerned with ending political and economic domination by Baltic Germans and continued to see the Russian state as an ally. On the whole, Baltic Germans maintained their loyalty to the house of the Romanovs, even though Baltic German claims to a constitutional relationship between the tsarist state and Baltic German corporate elites—and thus, they claimed, to the entire Baltic region—became untenable after the reforms of the 1870s and 1880s. After 1905, some Baltic German leaders were increasingly attracted to the German Reich as a source of economic, and, potentially, political support, but nothing came of this. Latvian and Estonian leaders also called for autonomy for the Baltic region. Because Baltic German opposition to reform continued to be near universal, cooperation between them and Latvians and Estonians never developed. Thus unlike the Finns, residents of the Baltic provinces never developed a shared political identity.

THE REVOLUTION OF 1905 AND ITS AFTERMATH

The Russian Revolution of 1905 was a central event on both sides of the Gulf of Finland. The events of this year wrought a political awakening among large numbers of Estonians, Latvians, and Finns who previously had not been involved in the public discussion of political and social issues. By the early twentieth century, all three groups had a property-owning middle class, strong in number if not in wealth, and a growing urban intelligentsia. Cities in the region had become increasingly industrialized in the last decades of the nineteenth century, with large numbers of Finnish, Estonian, and Latvian peasants arriving to work in factories. Mass revolutionary action and violence marked all three Baltic provinces in 1905, particularly areas of Latvian settlement. In urban areas of Livonia, workers went on strike on average nearly five times in 1905, the highest frequency rate in the tsarist empire. Peasants wrecked and burned Baltic German manor houses throughout the region. In southern Livonia and Courland, some 38 percent of manor houses (412 total) were completely or partially destroyed. The revolution also offered opportunities for the emergence of open political debate and the formation of legal political parties in the Baltic provinces, and Latvian and Estonian leaders called for political and cultural autonomy within the framework of a democratic Russian state. Violence and illegal political activity (the banned Social Democrats were particularly strong in Latvian areas) was halted in December 1905 and early 1906 by punitive expeditions of tsarist troops combined with private Baltic German forces, which together killed at least one thousand people and by some estimates, many more.

When the general strike in St. Petersburg in mid-October 1905 coerced Nicholas II into granting Russia civil rights and a legislative assembly, Finns responded with their own weeklong national strike in late October and early November. The Russian state responded with the granting of a new unicameral parliament (the Eduskunta), with equal and universal suffrage. In the first elections, held in 1907, the Social Democrats, not banned in Finland and strengthened by political mobilization of the impoverished rural poor of southern Finland, received the largest number of votes. The Russian state, however, soon prevented the parliament from functioning as a real legislature, and Finnish affairs were decided by the tsarist government in St. Petersburg. Unlike the Balts, the Finns refused to elect representatives to the all-Russian parliament, or Duma, in St. Petersburg.

The lack of meaningful public political life either in Finland or the Baltic provinces in the last ten years of tsarist rule made it impossible for residents to come to an agreement on the principles by which they could amicably share the lands they all called home. On the one hand there was a great deal of peaceful, productive development, and features of civil society began to take shape. Estonians, Latvians, and Finns continued to develop modern cultures, associational life flourished, and economies continued to grow. On the other hand, new pressures were developing in the Baltic provinces. While the old estate structure of society was crumbling, divisions along national lines were proving tenacious, and new tensions of a class nature, which crossed national lines, were forming. Baltic Germans, a minority declining in numbers, faced perhaps the greatest political chal-

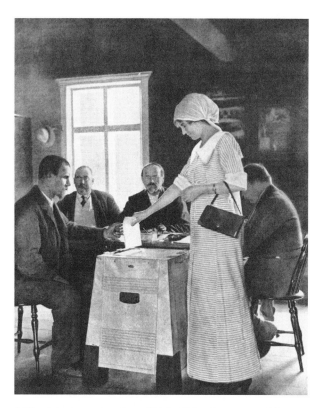

A Finnish woman votes, 1906. Finland was one of the first European nations to extend the franchise to women. ©BETTMANN/CORBIS

lenge as neither democratic reforms nor cooperation with an increasingly nationalist Russian state offered the political and social prominence they now felt slipping away. In Finland, the socialists rejected the principles upon which constitutionalists envisioned Finland's development. With the added chaos of World War I and the collapse of tsarist power in 1917, these unresolved tensions would break out in civil conflict, with particularly devastating vehemence in Finland and Latvia.

See also **Revolution of 1905 (Russia); Russia; Sweden and Norway.**

BIBLIOGRAPHY

Engman, Max, and David Kirby, eds. *Finland: People, Nation, State.* London, 1989.

Hirschhausen, Ulrike von. "Die Wahrnehmung des Wandels: Migration, soziale Mobilität, und Mentalitäten in Riga, 1867–1914." *Zeitschrift für Ostmitteleuropa-Forschung* 48, no. 4 (1999): 475–523.

Jansen, Ea. "Die Verwandlung der Sozialstruktur und der Beginn der nationalen Bewegung der Esten." In

Entwicklung der Nationalbewegungen in Europa, 1850–1914, edited by Heiner Timmermann, 497–503. Berlin, 1998.

Jussila, Osmo, Seppo Hentilä, and Jukka Nevakivi. *From Grand Duchy to a Modern State: A Political History of Finland since 1809.* Translated by David and Eva-Kaisa Arter. London, 1999.

Jutikkala, Eino, and Kauko Pirinen. *A History of Finland.* 5th ed. Translated by Paul Sjöblom. Porvoo, Finland, 1996.

Kirby, David. *The Baltic World, 1772–1993: Europe's Northern Periphery in an Age of Change.* London, 1995.

Oberländer, Erwin, and Kristine Wohlfart, eds. *Riga: Portrait einer Vielvölkerstadt am Rande des Zarenreiches, 1857–1914.* Paderborn, Germany, 2004.

Pistohlkors, Gert von. "Die Ostseeprovinzen unter russischer Herrschaft (1710/95–1914)." In *Baltische Länder,* edited by Gert von Pistohlkors, 266–450. Berlin, 1994.

Plakans, Andrejs. *The Latvians: A Short History.* Stanford, Calif., 1995.

Raun, Toivo U. *Estonia and the Estonians.* 2nd ed. Stanford, Calif., 2001.

Thaden, Edward C., ed. *Russification in the Baltic Provinces and Finland, 1855–1914.* Princeton, N.J., 1981.

Whelan, Heide W. *Adapting to Modernity: Family, Caste, and Capitalism among the Baltic German Nobility.* Cologne, Germany, 1999.

BRADLEY D. WOODWORTH

FIRST INTERNATIONAL.

The International Workingmen's Association, now called the First International, was the first successful attempt to organize labor at the local, national, and international levels. It emerged after the great outpouring of socialist ideology, primarily French, prior to the 1860s and before the rooting out of labor unions and socialist parties in the latter part of the nineteenth century. The entity through which social ideologies were reformulated and refined, the First International was also the conduit through which they were passed on to later generations of socialists. Moreover, it encouraged and aided the creation of unions and socialist parties. These involvements made it a battleground for four major nineteenth-century ideologies—Proudhonism, anarchism as expressed by Mikhail Bakunin (1814–1876), Blanquism, and Marxism.

ORIGINS

The International was an Anglo-French creation, with France the bulwark of the organization's strength as well as the source of most of its ideological direction. It was founded in London on 28 September 1864 under the direction of a weak and impoverished central committee called the General Council, based in London and comprised mainly of English labor leaders. At this time Karl Marx (1818–1883) sought quietly to guide the International to his analysis of economics and society. Each year in September the International held a conference or congress to which the local branches sent delegates and where the major issues facing the organization were debated. There were meetings in London (1865), Geneva (1866), Lausanne (1867), Brussels (1868), Basel (1869) (the Paris conference for 1870 was canceled because of the Franco-Prussian War), London (1871), and Geneva (1872).

Although the organization was open to all labor, it appealed primarily to traditional artisan trades—bronze engraving, shoemaking, bookbinding, carpentry, jewelry-making, and others. Even among these, the elite of the nineteenth-century labor force, the inclination to join the International was limited, so the number of individual memberships was always small. Trade union adhesion to the International did swell the ranks, but it is indeterminable how much union members subscribed to the program of the organization. Industrial labor—except for a scattering of machinists, few miners, and a miners' union—was almost absent. The membership of the International regarded itself as a self-selected elite of labor, and though few in number they were confident of "their holy cause," as a French labor leader put it, and saw themselves as the advance guard of social regeneration. The self-assurance of the members was rooted in the assumption that the International would transform society according to the laws of social science, which in turn reflected the nineteenth-century worship of science. Though the International was rich in ideology drawn from nineteenth-century socialism, it was poor in membership and finances, and the organization itself was extremely fragile.

At the Basel Congress the International endorsed collectivism, by which it meant the end of private ownership of agricultural land and, usually, the common ownership of mines and rail-ways. Through debates in the International the boundaries of socialist ideology in Europe were drawn and the fundamentals of the socialist program were established. The animators of the International probably contributed to the dramatic growth of trade unions and the use of strikes as a union weapon. The International's Geneva Congress was the first socialist body in Europe to endorse the eight-hour workday, a cause that would animate labor for the rest of the nineteenth century

The International declared itself to be pacifis-tic, just as socialists and socialist organizations in succeeding decades would do. War, it held, was caused by rulers, governments, and the bourgeoi-sie, while workers only wanted peace with their fellow workingmen. To stop war, the Brussels Congress declared, the workers would "cease all work in the case where a war has broken out in their respective countries." This was the same for-mula the Second International adopted prior to World War I, and it proved to be equally ineffective in stopping war.

DECLINE

The Franco-Prussian War (1870–1871) and the subsequent formation of Parisian and provincial communes simultaneously both destabilized and stimulated the International in France and Europe. The suppression of the Left in the spring of 1871, however, brought the French International down with it and the Dufaure Law of 14 March 1872, making membership in the International illegal, only confirmed the demise that had taken place ten months before. Nearly every government in Europe castigated it and persecuted its members (England, Belgium, Switzerland, and the Nether-lands being the notable exceptions).

Following the Paris Commune, many of the conflicts that had existed within the International in Paris and across France were transported across the Channel to the General Council. They were borne abroad by the French political refugees who made their way to London, many of whom were eager to regroup. Marx was determined not to let the organization fall into the hands of either of his rivals, the followers of Auguste Blanqui (1805–1881) or of the anarchist Bakunin, so at

the last congress in 1872 he effectively put the International out of their grasp by having the seat of the General Council transferred to the United States. The Congress voted the expulsion of Bakunin and his supporters.

Marx and the founders of the International emphasized the International's place at the cross-roads of two diametrically opposed approaches to politics. On the one hand, there was the secret, conspiratorial, revolutionary grouping of a self-selected elite that was the prevalent form of radical opposition groups in the period between the end of Napoleon's domination of Europe and the revolutions of 1848. The other approach, which appeared later, particularly in the last three de-cades of the nineteenth century, was the emergence of mass political groupings, especially socialist parties, labor unions, and a multiplicity of interest groups.

See also **Bakunin, Mikhail; Marx, Karl; Proudhon, Pierre-Joseph; Second International; Socialism.**

BIBLIOGRAPHY

Archer, Julian P. W. *The First International in France, 1864–1872: Its Origins, Theories, and Impact.* Lanham, Md., 1997.

Braunthal, Julius. *History of the International.* Translated by Henry Collins and Kenneth Mitchell. New York, 1967.

Morgan, Roger. *The German Social Democrats and the First International, 1864–1872.* Cambridge, U.K., 1965.

JULIAN ARCHER

FLÂNEUR. The simplest literal translation of the French world *flâneur* is an idler. One of the first people to write at length about it insisted that the verb *flâner*'s core meaning was "to do noth-ing," and that the glory of the *flâneur* lay in just that. Such nothing was done in a particular place, however, namely the modernizing city that was a center of vibrant activity, ever-shifting spectacle, and sometimes-violent conflict and change. It was out of this contrast between the evident energy and busy animation of modern urban life and the pos-sibility it offered some inhabitants for leisured and tranquil contemplation and reverie that the idea of the *flâneur* emerged. Paris was its birthplace, perhaps partly by chance (because no one denied there were *flâneurs* elsewhere), but also because, more than any other great city, it was its nation's undisputed center of political, social, and cultural life, the site where a highly self-conscious (and often conflict-ridden) people displayed the sociability, wit, and style many thought to be their hallmark. But much about the *flâneur* remains difficult to pin down; we do not know who originally coined the term, or how many people it properly fit (or may still fit) in any given time and place. If the *flâneur* remains famous today, it is largely because the figure was celebrated by some great writers, especially the French poet Charles Baudelaire in the 1850s and the German critic Walter Benjamin in the 1920s and 1930s; but they built on a broader interest in the phenomenon articulated by less-eminent people.

HUART'S EARLY PHYSIOLOGY

One of these less-eminent people was Louis Huart, a little-known journalist who portrayed contemporary *flâneurs* in terms at once serious and humorous in a little book of 1841. Huart distinguished the *flâneur* (and later writers would follow him) from its cousin the *badaud* (the gawker or rubberneck), driven by curiosity or the rage to see great sights or occasions. By contrast the *flâneur* was the observer who took in whatever scenes his aimless wanderings brought before him (it was not thought proper for women to engage in such unsupervised moving about), and made something of them.

> The *flâneur* frames a whole novel out of nothing more than the simple sighting of a little woman with a lowered veil on an omnibus—then the next instant he gives himself up to the most exalted philosophical, social, and humanitarian considerations as he admires all the wonders that education can work on simple scarab beetles that fight duels like real St. Georges. (Huart, pp. 55–56)

Unlike the *badaud* the *flâneur* never covets the things displayed in city shops and he is never bored: "He suffices to himself, and finds nourishment for his intelligence in everything he encounters" (p. 124).

BAUDELAIRE'S "THE PAINTER OF MODERN LIFE"

When, fifteen or so years later, Baudelaire saw the *flâneur* incarnate in the journalist and illustrator Constantin Guys, whom he immortalized as "The Painter of Modern Life," he infused these qualities with meanings born from his sense that the city, with its crowds, its anonymity, its unpredictable encounters, was the consummate place to experience the modernity he famously defined as "the ephemeral, the fugitive, the contingent." Inserting himself into this ever-changing scene, the *flâneur* distilled an essence from it, as bees with flowers.

> For the perfect *flâneur,* for the passionate spectator, it is an immense joy to set up house in the heart of the multitude, amid the ebb and flow of movement in the midst of the fugitive and the infinite. . . . The lover of universal life enters into the crowd as though it were an immense reservoir of electrical energy. Or we might liken him to a mirror as vast as the crowd itself; or to a kaleidoscope gifted with consciousness. . . . He is an 'I' with an insatiable appetite for the 'non-I,' . . . rendering and explaining it in pictures more living than life itself. (Baudelaire, p. 9)

The *flâneur* knew the possibilities urban modernity offered for an expanded personal existence, a life charged up with the imagined content of other lives, finding in the world of ordinary experience the promise of entry into another, higher, and more poetic world. And yet, that promise was never fulfilled. Other realities overcame it, ugliness, poverty, loneliness (Huart had noted more prosaic ones, such as getting splashed with mud in the foul Paris streets)—the dark side of things that the Baudelairean urban wanderer experienced as *spleen*.

BENJAMIN'S "ARCADES PROJECT"

One element in this seesaw between hope and despair was revolution, whose highs and lows Baudelaire experienced in 1848, and the imagination of revolution would continue to color the image of the *flâneur* cherished by Benjamin, its greatest twentieth-century cultivator. In the 1920s and 1930s Benjamin gathered much material about *flâneurs* in the notebooks he filled for his never-completed "Arcades Project" (published after his death in the fragmentary form in which he left it), his evocation of Paris as "the capital of the nineteenth century." Viewing Baudelaire's city through a heady glass concocted out of mystical messianism, Marxist hope for a postcapitalist social order, and a mix of Freudian and surrealist belief in the transformative power of desire, Benjamin projected a *flâneur* who embodied the dreaming state of absorption, wishfulness, and anxiety out of which humanity would awake to a more fulfilled existence. Among the animating features of his *flâneur* were intoxication, a state Baudelaire had also prized for its ability to give wings to imagination, and simultaneity, the quality of combining the disparate moments and the separated sites of experience into a mode of consciousness that dissolved the bounds of ordinary time and place. Like Baudelaire's, Benjamin's *flâneur* drew energy from the city's streets and crowds, but it was an energy rooted in mythical images of primitive humanity, and in desires aroused by what the city at once offered and withheld, both material well-being and the ennobling equality that rose like a mirage at the horizon of modern life. To Benjamin, writing at a time when the Soviet experiment could still seem a beacon of hope to liberals and progressives, in the shadow of the fight against fascism, Baudelaire's image of the *flâneur* bore "prophetic value," forecasting a redeemed future. That prophecy has lost much of its persuasive power since Benjamin's day, but the image of the *flâneur* still beguiles, bearing with it the mix of hopes and fears that modern city life calls forth.

See also **Paris.**

BIBLIOGRAPHY

Aragon, Louis. *Paris Peasant.* Translated by Simon Watson Taylor. London, 1971. Reprint, Boston, 1994.

Baudelaire, Charles. "The Painter of Modern Life." In *The Painter of Modern Life and Other Essays,* translated and edited by Jonathan Mayne. London, 1964.

Benjamin, Walter. *The Arcades Project.* Translated by Howard Eiland and Kevin McLaughlin, based on the German volume edited by Rolf Tiedemann. Cambridge, Mass., 1999.

Huart, Louis. *Physiologie du flâneur.* Paris, 1841.

White, Edmund. *The Flâneur: A Stroll through the Paradoxes of Paris.* New York, 2001.

JERROLD SEIGEL

FLAUBERT, GUSTAVE (1821–1880),

French novelist. If the nineteenth century is known in France for prolific writers such as Honoré de Balzac, Victor Hugo, and Émile Zola, Gustave Flaubert is a notable exception. His reputation as one of the century's greatest novelists is based on a handful of works, in particular *Madame Bovary* (1857), *Sentimental Education* (1869), and a collection of stories, *Three Tales* (1877). Through these and his other books—*Salammbô* (1862), *The Temptation of Saint Anthony* (1874), and the posthumous *Bouvard and Pécuchet* (1881)—Flaubert prefigured many of the key aesthetic and ethical issues of twentieth-century literature. He left a legacy of formal perfectionism to which many subsequent writers have turned for inspiration.

Flaubert was born in December 1821 into a prosperous middle-class family in Rouen; his father and older brother were both doctors. Flaubert was a law school dropout who essentially lived off his family's wealth, making relatively little money even from his successful books. In his twenties he took a formative trip to the Orient (1849–1851) that provided the impetus for several of his fictional works, and in 1857 he traveled for inspiration to Tunis, the site of his historical novel, *Salammbô.* He spent his later life in his family's country house in Croisset, near Rouen, with annual stays of up to a few months in Paris.

Although Flaubert composed several prose works in his youth, he did not gain recognition until the 1857 publication of *Madame Bovary,* a tale of a doctor's wife's adulterous affairs in a small Normandy town. The novel, considered by many to be the greatest ever written in French, was accused of immorality, and Flaubert suffered the indignity of a law trial but was acquitted in February 1857.

Madame Bovary, along with *Sentimental Education,* "A Simple Heart" (*Three Tales*), and *Bouvard and Pécuchet,* represents one of the two currents that characterized Flaubert's writings, that dealing with settings familiar to his readers. *Sentimental Education,* poorly received in 1869 but now considered by many a masterpiece equal to or greater than *Madame Bovary,* uses the Revolution of 1848 as the backdrop for a love story between a young man and an older, married woman, a character based on Flaubert's lifelong infatuation with Elise Schlésinger. In "A Simple Heart," the servant Félicité devotes herself first to an undeserving mistress, then to her beloved pet parrot, Loulou. *Bouvard and Pécuchet,* published in an incomplete form after Flaubert's death, tells of two middle-aged

Parisian clerks who retire to the Normandy countryside and explore various aspects of human endeavor in the arts and the sciences, an enterprise that fails miserably.

The other, more exotic current of Flaubert's work involves historical and mythological materials. *Salammbô*, a historical novel set in ancient Carthage, is a mystical love story between the virginal Salammbô and the Libyan mercenary Mathô. *The Temptation of Saint Anthony*, a project Flaubert first conceived in 1845 when he saw Breughel's painting, is a loosely structured work presenting a series of mysterious, dreamlike tableaux, while "Saint Julian Hospitator" and "Hérodias" (*Three Tales*) are also based on Christian legends.

Flaubert focused on the subjectivity of his characters, believing that writers, like God, should remain invisible even though their presence is felt everywhere in their works. Preoccupied with style and precision, he was criticized for creating unsympathetic characters, including his most famous heroine, Emma Bovary. Flaubert was an extremely hard worker but a notoriously slow one, researching his projects for years and reading hundreds of books before starting to write. He was an obsessive reviser and could spend sixteen hours producing less than a single usable page. He read his texts aloud to himself as he composed them, and later to friends and fellow writers.

Flaubert never married nor had children but he had many lovers, most notably the writer Louise Colet, with whom he had a stormy liaison that lasted for seven years, yielding a lengthy correspondence. He helped raise his niece, Caroline Hamard (later Commanville), after his beloved sister died shortly after childbirth, and he remained a devoted uncle even when Caroline's husband created enormous financial hardships for Flaubert in his later years. Most of Flaubert's friends, including George Sand and Ivan Turgenev, were writers. He was often ill, subject to epileptic fits in early adulthood and later to various ailments exacerbated by overwork and unhealthy living. He died unexpectedly, probably of a stroke, in May 1880. His was a life of great solitude and suffering, and to the end he remained a confirmed pessimist who believed that literature was the only thing of lasting value.

See also **Balzac, Honoré de; Egypt; Realism and Naturalism; Revolutions of 1848; Zola, Émile.**

BIBLIOGRAPHY

Lottman, Herbert. *Flaubert: A Biography.* Boston, 1989.

Starkie, Enid. *Flaubert the Master: A Critical and Biographical Study (1856–1880).* New York, 1971.

Wall, Geoffrey. *Flaubert: A Life.* London, 2001.

RICHARD E. GOODKIN

FONTANE, THEODOR (1819–1898), German novelist.

Theodor Fontane was born in Neuruppin (just northwest of Berlin) on 30 December 1819, and he died in Berlin on 20 September 1898. Best known for his novels *Frau Jenny Treibel* and *Effi Briest*, Fontane is considered by many as the greatest German novelist of the nineteenth century, even as the leading novelist writing in German between the death of Goethe and advent of Thomas Mann. In addition to novels and novellas, Fontane published poetry, war reportage, travel literature, and drama criticism.

Initially trained like his father as an apothecary, Fontane practiced pharmacy for only a few years. From an early age he knew he wanted to be a professional writer. An adherent of liberalism, Fontane found it difficult to support himself and his family after the Revolution of 1848. He left his family to become a correspondent for the Prussian Central Press Agency in London, remaining in England through most of the1850s. Returning to Berlin in 1859, Fontane continued his career as a correspondent, covering firsthand the wars of German unification.

Although previously having published only several short stories and poems, Fontane produced his first major literary work, *Gedichte* (Poems), in 1851 and a collection of ballads, *Männer und Helden* (Men and heroes), which drew heavily on English and Scottish folk poetry in 1860. He also wrote travel literature at this time, which included his sojourns through the small towns and countryside of his native Brandenburg, the best-known of which is the four-volume *Wanderungen durch die*

Mack Brandenburg (Journey through the Mark Brandenburg), published over the course of the 1860s and 1880s. Only when he achieved some financial security as a drama critic did Fontane devote himself entirely to literature.

Fontane did not write his first novel until he was fifty-eight. *Vor dem Sturm* (1879; Before the storm), considered a classic of historical fiction, presents a panorama of the years of German liberation from Napoleon. In all his later novels, he turned away from stories set in the past for the depiction of contemporary Prussian, and specifically Berlin, society. The decades of the 1880s and 1890s were very productive; Fontane turned out the novels for which he will always be remembered: *L'Adutera* (1882), *Schach von Wuthenow* (1883; *Man of Honor*), *Irrungen, Wirrungen* (1888), *Stine* (1890), *Unwiederbringlich* (1891), *Frau Jenny Treibel* (1893), *Effi Briest* (1895), and *Der Stechlin* (1898).

Fontane belongs to that broadly defined tradition of nineteenth-century realism, which aimed at the depiction of individuals of identifiable social origins within a specific time and place. In general Fontane's subject matter evolved from the portrayal of personal conflict of his early novels to the depiction of social milieux. His best novels combine the two. In *Effi Briest,* for instance, the setting emerges before the main action takes place. The conflict among individual characters is thus understood as the realization of more inclusive political, social, and ideological tensions. The distinctive nature of Fontane's realism is the result of interplay between foreground conflicts and background tensions.

As a novelist Fontane will always be remembered as the memorialist of nineteenth-century Berlin and Brandenburg. He exhibited a particular fondness for portraying the social code of the declining Prussian Junker class, with its mixture of horror, pride, and arrogance. Fontane most often set the Prussian aristocracy against the new, aggressive, but still insecure middle class that emerged as a result of the economic miracle of the early years of the new Reich. He did not simply pillory the vulgarity of the middle class; rather, he showed the inner conflicts within it, most often between the vulgar bourgeoisie of money and the vain bourgeoisie of education, between the *Besitzbürgertum* (the middle class by wealth) and the *Bildungsbürgertum* (the middle class by education—professionals). Yet, even this social opposition is not absolute. His educated middle class yearns after wealth just as the uneducated. Fontane's ability to integrate personal characteristics within social groups comes forth most clearly in his depiction of a wide range of minor characters, which are skillfully interlaced into the structure of his mature novels.

Once he found his subject matter and his genre, Fontane quickly developed a style all his own. Based on powers of observation and a deeply ingrained historical sense, this style is founded upon the anonymity of its author and his refusal to pass judgment on his characters and their actions. Fontane therefore is never moralizing or sarcastic and only rarely sentimental. In addition, he is not an omniscient author. He does not intrude into inner thoughts and motivations of his characters but lets them appear on their own and within their familiar and social situations. In this way, he allows his readers to come to their own judgments.

This style has been characterized as "perspectival" because it lets personalities emerge, not directly through the author's evaluative statements, but through multiple viewpoints and especially through dialogue. Characters are revealed through what they do, through what others say of them, and most tellingly through what they say and how they say it. Fontane in fact became a master of dialogue. For him dialogue is the most direct way to depict the intersection of character and circumstance. This use of dialogue gives a great depth to his characters. As a result Fontane's version of realism is created by a sense of overhearing ongoing conversations that reveal individual characters but also social and generational contrasts. In *Effi Briest,* for instance, Fontane presents the complex life of the seemingly simple Baltic seaport and resort town of Kessin. His readers can judge small town life with all its characters and personal and social conflicts on their own. In his Berlin cycle as well, Fontane invites his readers to get to know the city not through description of its various quarters and highly mixed population (German, Slavic, Jewish, Swiss, Flemish, and Huguenot) but through hearing the famous Berlin irony and archness of speech.

Most of the literary criticism on Fontane hovers around the question of the power of his realism. It inevitably results in comparisons with the established masters of this novelistic form. Earlier critics emphasized the blandness of Fontane's realism, compared with that of Stendhal or Honoré de Balzac; the weakness of his social criticism, compared to that of Émile Zola or even Charles Dickens; and his characters' general lack of psychological depth, compared to those of Gustave Flaubert or Fyodor Dostoyevsky. Georg Lukács, for instance, pointed to his failure to develop a strong critical voice. All such evaluations, however, miss the point. Although suggestive, these comparisons overlook many of the subtleties of Fontane's type of characterization and his sensitive ear for dialogue. In addition, Fontane never assumed the role of reformist in his novels, and in fact his tone most often evokes nostalgia for the fading world of old Prussia. He could be ironic but this irony was more loving than biting. Later criticism appreciates his more subtle, less opinionated realism. In other words there has been a growing appreciation of Fontane's powers of observation and his artistry in conveying these observations through his unique stylistic qualities. In fact, Fontane is now often favorably compared to the masters of European realism, Stendhal, Balzac, Flaubert, Turgenev, and Dostoyevsky.

See also **Dickens, Charles; Germany; Prussia; Realism and Naturalism; Zola, Émile.**

BIBLIOGRAPHY

Denmetz, Peter. *Formen des Realismus: Theodor Fontane.* Munich, 1964.

Minder, Robert. *Kultur und Literatur in Deutschland and Frankreich.* Frankfurt am Main, 1962.

Müller-Seidel, Walter. *Theodor Fontane: Soziale Romankunst in Deutschland.* Stuttgart, 1975.

Ohff, Heinz. *Theodor Fontane: Leben und Werk.* Munich, 1995.

Reuter, Hans-Heinrich. *Fontane.* 2 vols. Berlin, 1968.

Scholz, Hans. *Theodor Fontane.* Munich, 1978.

Ziegler, Edda, and Gotthard Erler. *Theodor Fontane, Lebensraum und Phantasiewelt. Eine Biography.* Berlin, 1996.

BENJAMIN C. SAX

FOOTBALL (SOCCER).

Various forms of "football" were being codified throughout the Anglo-Saxon world starting in the 1860s, a reflection of the advanced economies of these countries and two general desires: first, young middle-class men wanted to create a game that they could continue to play at university by agreeing on a common set of rules from those they had played at school; and second, young professional men wanted to make a more civilized game out of the various school football games, which tended to feature rough-and-tumble violence.

ASSOCIATION FOOTBALL IN THE UNITED KINGDOM

First among these was the creation of the rules of the Football Association (FA), drawn up at Freemasons' Tavern, London, in October 1863. From this came association football, known as "soccer" from about the turn of the century in those Anglo-Saxon countries outside of the United Kingdom where other codes of football were played. Of these codes, Rugby Football Union (RFU), a running game in contrast to a dribbling game, was founded in 1871, ironically by a group who had objected to the banning of hacking (kicking an opponent's shins) in 1863, claiming that it robbed the game of its manliness; the RFU's rules of 1871 also banned hacking. In Australia in 1866 and in the United States starting in 1869, distinctive codes of football were developed. Rugby League came from a split with the RFU in 1895, and Gaelic football was codified in Ireland in 1885. Of these the association game, under the auspices of the Football Association, would go on to conquer the world as the "people's game," by far the most popular sport in nearly every country in the world with the notable exceptions of the former British colonies.

Football originally referred to ball games played on foot as distinct from the more aristocratic equestrian sports: as such it has always had a plebeian appeal and reputation. Forms of football have been played in most societies since records were first kept, but by the time of the French Revolution in Europe village games were played regularly according to custom, the seasons, and special "holy" days. These were violent affairs, often village against village with virtually no rules, and in England in particular, often served as a front for political purposes, to tear down enclosures and other modernizing innovations that interfered with the rights of the commoners. Football was played in the prisons during the Terror of the French Revolution, as indicated in a painting by Hubert Robert, showing a game with about half a dozen on each side and a couple of hundred watching. Oliver Cromwell is said to have been a ferocious exponent of the game, and Sir Walter Scott famously claimed that he would sooner his son carry the colors of his team in the "match at Carterhaugh" (in the Scottish border country) than attain the highest honors in the "first university in Europe."

It is often stated that football in Great Britain was dying out in the first part of the nineteenth century, when the dark, satanic mills of the Industrial Revolution spread out into the countryside. This indicates more a lack of research than a reality and is reflected in the speed with which the ordinary folks adapted to the game codified by their "betters" and made it their own. Moreover, before 1863, and not just in the public schools, rules had been drawn up to govern local competitions, most notably in Sheffield, a close rival to London for what became the dribbling and non-handling game.

The first teams often formed around cricket clubs, public houses, the workplace, and church organizations: many of these are still in existence in the early twenty-first century. By the 1880s football in Britain was being taken up by workers in the various industries in the north of England and central Scotland, helped by the gradual adoption of the Saturday afternoon holiday. The social changes in the game were dramatically demonstrated in 1883, when Blackburn Olympic beat Old Etonians in the final of the FA Cup, and the balance of power swung to the north of England and stayed there for the next few decades. Suspicions held by the southern amateurs that the "mechanics and artisans" who made up the teams from the north were being paid to ply their wares on the football field were well justified.

The men of the FA, for the most part tied to the old school ethos, were faced with the reality that spectators prepared to pay to watch their local heroes were also pleased to see these players rewarded for the pleasure they gave. These spectators, like the men playing the game, came largely from the working class. The owners of the teams often represented the new wealth of the cotton and other industries, and soon tired of the hypocrisy of "under-the-table" payments to players. This difference in attitude was said, with some truth and a great deal of snobbery, to be a clash between the morality of the "public schools" and that of the "public houses." But the men of the south—unlike the rugby people—wisely bowed before reality, and in 1885 the FA recognized professionalism, albeit with various caveats, most of which were soon overlooked.

Three years later the Birmingham-based Scottish businessman William McGregor introduced the Football League, to keep the professionals active when there were no cup competitions or "friendlies" to be played. Openly claimed to be a "league of the selfish," it controlled the professional game, but left all other aspects of the game to the amateurs of the FA. The Football League was not called the English League because it was hoped the Scottish clubs would join, but amateurism prevailed north of the border until 1893, three years after the institution of the Scottish League, deliberately created to pave the way for professionalism. The game may have been becoming increasingly commercialized, but it was not run on capitalist lines: indeed the players who signed professional contracts found themselves bound to a form of "wage slavery" that would last until the 1960s when the maximum wage and the "retain and transfer" system were abolished.

The game had become a veritable passion throughout industrial Scotland in the 1880s, and its best players were tempted to move south ostensibly for work but just as often to receive illegal payments for playing football. These Scottish professors adopted a style of play that they would take with them wherever they went, which was just about everywhere, as Scots contributed out of all proportion in the spread of the British Empire and capitalism around the world: as engineers, workers, professional men, and clerks, as well as in the service of God or the military.

The progress of the game was assisted in the last decade of the nineteenth century by technological advances in transport and communications, above all in the electric-powered trams crisscrossing the expanding cities, which aided the growth of "local derbies," and the telephone, which allowed

An English soccer club. Engraving from the *Illustrated Sporting and Dramatic News*, February 1875. Mary Evans Picture Library

rapid reporting of matches that were then transferred to the newspaper where readers could digest in the evening reports of games played that afternoon. Some men of the cloth were not always sure about the "progress" of the game, and expressed their horror at the swearing, drinking, gambling, and violence that they believed the game encouraged. Others saw the benefits of the game, not just as a "muscular" means of spreading Christianity, but as a source of joy that kept the young out of the devil's reach in their otherwise "idle" time.

By the turn of the century the organization of association football in the United Kingdom was far in advance of any other sports organization anywhere in the world. Central to this success was the FA Challenge Cup, founded by Charles William Alcock in 1871, a knockout competition open to every team that was a member of the FA. Scotland followed when the Scottish Football Association, founded in 1873, set up its own competition in that year. In addition to these were various local and county cup competitions. The game's popularity was further advanced with the league system adopted in England and Scotland, especially when second, third, and other divisions were introduced to accommodate the increasing number of teams and when promotion and relegation added to the excitement of the competition. The other competition that established the popularity of association football was the regular Home International Championship inaugurated in 1883. The Welsh Football Association was founded in 1876, the Irish Football Association four years later, and in 1882 the International Football Association Board was created to agree on the rules and enable regular annual competitions between the four "nations" of the United Kingdom. The Welsh, and to a lesser extent the Irish, would find in rugby a more rewarding source of national pride, but the Scotland versus England internationals, first played officially in 1872, became the longest-standing annual international competition in sport, ending only in 1988.

Shortly after the turn of the century crowds of over one hundred thousand were recorded at some Cup finals in England; in Scotland the annual international against England attracted fifty thousand in 1896, while matches between the Rangers (founded 1872) and Celtic (founded 1887) in Scotland, increasingly based on the sectarian antagonisms of the Irish-Catholic Celtic and the Protestant (and increasingly anti-Catholic) Rangers, were regularly sold out. The Old Firm of Rangers and Celtic supplanted the supremacy of Queen's Park (founded 1867), a club that has achieved the remarkable feat of remaining in regular competition in the professional Scottish leagues through the early twenty-first century. Even more remarkable, in 1903 Queen's Park constructed Hampden Park, a stadium that was the largest in the world and would remain such until the construction of the Maracana in Brazil in 1950.

In addition to the professional game, association football in Great Britain boasted an immense network of amateur competitions with their own league and cup competitions: church organizations, schoolboy and other youth groups, as well as competitions for adults. These were based at the municipal, county, and ultimately the national level. The English Schools Football Association introduced a national cup competition in 1904. A separate Amateur Football Association (AFA) was founded as a split from the FA in 1907, but the FA itself adequately catered to the amateurs, and the AFA returned to the fold just before the outbreak of war in 1914.

ON THE CONTINENT

It is not surprising, then, that the progress of soccer on the continent of Europe was largely ignored in Britain. The progress being made in Europe, too, was very much under the guidance or example of Britons abroad, whether on business or pleasure or by expatriates: as elsewhere in the world where British commercial and industrial expertise was transported, football was said (according to an official FA history) to be Britain's "most enduring export." It was, however, an unintended consequence, as the rulers of the game in Great Britain showed a sovereign indifference to its spread beyond their own islands.

The game in continental Europe followed the path of those countries that had close business,

moral, or educational ties to Britain. Before the 1880s references to "football" did not necessarily mean the association game, so Switzerland's claim to have played it in the 1860s is somewhat stretched, although the "little England" colonies no doubt helped establish the game. Belgium and the Netherlands were soon active participants in the British game, and Denmark placed second to Great Britain in the Olympic Games of 1908 and 1912. Other Scandinavian countries soon adopted the FA rules, especially through the seaports—as well as in the embassies. In Germany the followers of "British games" faced stern opposition from the more nationalistic German gymnastics (*Turnen*), and although this intensified as war threats grew, there were enough British coaches and players interned in Germany in 1914 to constitute a successful football competition in the years of captivity at the Ruhleben internment camp in Berlin—competitions that are said to have won over their captors to the game. In France, rugby at first held its own before soccer took over about 1905, while in Italy, the foremost football nation of the 1930s, the talents of Vittorio Pozzo had to wait for the Fascist regime before his methods bore fruit. So too in Spain it was not until after World War I that football began to rival bullfighting as the national passion. In the Balkans, as in Russia and the Ottoman Empire, football was seen as a potentially revolutionary force, especially when played by ethnic minorities, and was often banned. It was in central Europe that soccer blossomed most fully in the prewar period and in the years just after: competition in and between teams from the capital cities of Vienna, Prague, and Budapest were the talk of the coffeehouses that represented a way of life brutally interrupted in 1914.

In all of these countries there was usually a British connection, often with businessmen or educationalists who had spent some time in Britain: in Switzerland, Swiss pupils in British schools; in the Netherlands, Lancashire spinners in the new factories; and in Sweden, Scottish riveters in Göteborg and then sailors in the other Swedish ports. Famously in Austria, the Baron Rothschild's Scottish gardeners set up the First Vienna Football Club. Pozzo learned all about football while a language teacher in England. The "father" of German football was Walter Bensemann, an Anglophile and English teacher who founded *Kicker* magazine in 1920. With Ivo Schricker, Bensemann helped finance visits by many British clubs starting in the 1880s. The first president of the German Football Association (Deutscher Fussballbund) in 1900 was Ferdinand Hueppe, who had championed the English "games" at the Moravian Boys' School in Neuwied on the Rhine. In Russia soccer was said to have been played by British sailors at the Black Sea port of Odessa in the 1860s, but the organized beginnings of the game there are inevitably associated with Harry Charnock, the British manager of a mill outside Moscow, who hoped that healthy sport would provide an alternative to vodka to occupy the minds of his workers.

Before 1914, and for some time to come after that, the most eagerly anticipated games on the Continent were those involving a team from England or Scotland, usually on an end-of-season trip, and often treated by them as a holiday. An even bigger attraction was when two touring British clubs agreed to play each other, as in Budapest in 1914, when twenty thousand are said to have turned up to watch Celtic play Burnley. In addition to the professionals came crusading amateur teams such as the Middlesex Wanderers and Corinthians. At first these teams expected to have easy victories, and they blamed the occasional defeat on lighter balls, bumpy playing fields, and incompetent refereeing. This changed as the competition from leading clubs in Prague and Vienna in particular showed they could hold their own with the British tourists. On the eve of conflict in 1914 this was already apparent, and in the years immediately after the war crowds would multiply and the visitors from Britain would find that their former pupils now had a few lessons to give their one-time masters.

In Paris in 1904 came the founding of the body that would—albeit much later—take over from the London FA as the ultimate arbiter in the control and administration of association football: the Fédération Internationale de Football Association, always known by its acronym, FIFA. Even before the turn of the century the idea of an international body to regulate games between national teams had been raised by the Belgians in the 1890s and then by the Dutch banker C. A. W. Hirschman. But as so often in international sport, it was a Frenchman, Robert Guérin, an engineer and journalist, who organized the meetings that led to the formation of FIFA.

International football on the Continent before 1914 was more often a game between the major cities, and many of the nations of the later twentieth and early twenty-first centuries did not exist before the breakup of the Prussian, Russian, Austro-Hungarian, and Ottoman empires after World War I. Claims to national status, in soccer as in the Olympic Games, by Bohemia or Finland, for example, could be seen as a political as much as a sporting claim in the days of the old world empires. The first "international," however, between Austria and Hungary in 1902, became a regular annual event. Another problem was that in some countries, most notably France, there was more than one sporting body claiming to represent football. Despite such setbacks, the meeting of the delegates representing seven countries took place in Paris in May 1904 to found an organization that a century later would be compared to the United Nations in regard to its international significance.

Present at that meeting were representatives from France, Belgium, the Netherlands, Denmark, and Switzerland, while Sweden and Spain were represented by proxy. Germany sent its support by telegram. These European nations were represented in a body that did not add a geographical qualifier, despite the absence of representatives from the South American countries, Argentina, Uruguay, and to a lesser extent Chile, that were already passionate followers of the game. Absent but fervently wanted, were the British associations. The English FA consented to join in 1905, and Daniel Burley Woolfall was made president the following year on the resignation of Guérin. The Scottish and Welsh associations followed in 1910 and Ireland in 1911, in violation of the FIFA rule that there be only one national team for each sovereign nation. This anomaly has remained into the twenty-first century, and for most of its existence before 1946 when it had few English-speaking members, English was the ultimate language for cases in dispute, while the British International Football Association Board, with only token non-British membership, was the ultimate appeal in regard to the rules. The first non-European country to join FIFA was South Africa in 1910, followed by Argentina, Chile, and the United States. By 1914 there were twenty European members.

In 1914 soccer in Europe outside of Great Britain was largely a middle-class game played by amateur players, with top crowds attracting no more than about fifteen thousand spectators. This would change dramatically in the years after the war, which itself contributed to the success of the game, but even before then it was apparent that Europe had caught the football bug and would never lose it.

See also **Body; Education; Gender; Leisure; Popular and Elite Culture; Sports.**

BIBLIOGRAPHY

Holt, Richard. *Sport and Society in Modern France.* London, 1981.

———. *Sport and the British: A Modern History.* Oxford, U.K., 1989.

Lanfranchi, Pierre, Christiane Eisenberg, Tony Mason, and Alfred Wahl. *100 Years of Football: The FIFA Centennial Book.* London, 2004.

Mason, Tony. *Association Football and English Society, 1863–1915.* Sussex, U.K., 1980.

Murray, Bill. *Football: A History of the World Game.* Aldershot, U.K., 1994.

———. *The World's Game: A History of Soccer.* Urbana, Ill., 1996.

BILL MURRAY

FORSTER, E. M. (1879–1970), English novelist, biographer, and critic.

E. M. Forster was one of the most influential European writers of the twentieth century, and a tireless defender of humane values. Although he lived until 1970, in some ways he always remained an Edwardian liberal.

Forster was born in London on New Year's Day 1879. His father, Edward Morgan, a promising architect, died less than a year later. He was raised by his mother, Alice Whichelo Forster, and his aunt, Marianne Thornton, who would leave him a legacy that enabled him to attend King's College, Cambridge.

After a period of unhappiness at Tonbridge School, he flourished at Cambridge, where he became a member of the Apostles, the university's most prestigious discussion group. Forster's membership in the Apostles not only helped shape his philosophical and aesthetic points of view, but it also led to close ties with friends such as Lytton Strachey (1880–1932), John Maynard Keynes (1883–1946), and Roger Fry (1866–1934). These men were later to be associated with the Bloomsbury Group, which was a kind of London extension of the Apostles, with the addition of the talented Stephen sisters, Vanessa Bell (1879–1961) and Virginia Woolf (1882–1941).

At Cambridge, Forster acknowledged his agnosticism and his homosexuality. The latter is a crucial aspect of his personality and art, as is his antipathy for Christianity. In terms of his early work, perhaps even more significant than Forster's sexual orientation was his sexual frustration, which manifested itself in the emphasis in the Edwardian novels on the need for sexual fulfillment.

After graduating from King's College in 1901, Forster traveled in Italy and Greece and then began drafting two novels. In the early years of the new century, Forster's distinctive voice suddenly matured: confidential, relaxed, gentle, and nearly always tinged with sadness, even when lyrical or ironic.

Forster's first novel, *Where Angels Fear to Tread*, appeared in 1905, followed by *The Longest Journey* in 1907, and *A Room with a View* in 1908. These novels are passionate protests against sexual repression and English hypocrisy. While *Where Angels Fear to Tread* is a strangely sad ironic comedy, *The Longest Journey* a fierce tragedy, and *A Room with a View* a fascinating composite of social comedy and prophetic utterance, these early works gain unity by virtue of their celebration of the natural and the instinctual.

Forster's first three novels made him a minor literary celebrity; with the publication of his fourth, *Howards End*, in 1910, he became a major one. Ranking among the most important English novels produced in the period between the death of Queen Victoria and World War I, *Howards End* concretely embodies the tensions and conflicts of that superficially placid age. Characteristically, the liberal humanism espoused by the novel has metaphysical as well as political dimensions.

A social comedy and an unusual love story, *Howards End* also articulates a comprehensive social vision, focused particularly on the role of the individual in a rapidly changing society. While the novel vindicates Forster's liberalism, it nevertheless acknowledges its inner weaknesses and contradictions. The author's awareness of the vulnerability of his most cherished values contributes to the book's urgency and integrity.

Although Forster published a collection of short stories in 1911, the success of *Howards End* induced a painful writer's block. After beginning and abandoning several projects, in 1913 he finally undertook a novel of homosexual love that he knew was not publishable at the time. *Maurice,* which would not be issued until the year after Forster's death, has been derided as thin and sentimental, but it is actually a significant achievement, a political novel that is also a book of haunting beauty.

While serving in Alexandria with the Red Cross during World War I, Forster fell in love with an Egyptian tram conductor Mohammed el Adl, with whom he enjoyed his first fully satisfying sexual affair. His experiences in Alexandria, coupled with his service as secretary to the Maharajah of Dewas Senior in India in 1921 and 1922, brought Forster face to face with the East, and helped shape his masterpiece, *A Passage to India.*

Although the novel did not appear until 1924, *A Passage to India* reflects the spiritual and political crises inspired by World War I. The novel established Forster as a major voice in English fiction and as a discerning critic of imperialism. But while it is rooted in the complex realities of India at a particular moment, the novel also transcends the specifics of time and place to question the nature of meaning itself. A profoundly spiritual novel, *A Passage to India* explores the limitations of human consciousness and the loneliness of the human condition. It is a brooding and unflinching exploration of the twentieth-century spiritual wasteland.

For the last forty-six years of Forster's long life, he published no more novels. He did continue to write short stories and he produced a distinguished body of nonfiction, including criticism, essays, and biographies. During this period he attempted to adapt the best tenets of Edwardian liberalism to the various heartening or frightening challenges posed by the twentieth-century cultural and political revolutions. In the process, he became England's foremost exponent of liberal humanism in a world increasingly threatened by the clash of totalitarian ideologies.

Forster died in Coventry, England, on 7 June 1970. His suppressed novel *Maurice* was published in 1971 and *The Life to Come and Other Stories* in 1972.

Forster's reputation declined severely after his death and the revelation of his homosexuality, but it stabilized in the last decades of the twentieth century. The question of his relationship to modernism, the tenability and coherence of his liberalism (including his anti-imperialism), and his sexuality have been the dominant issues in late-twentieth- and early twenty-first-century criticism.

See also **Great Britain; Homosexuality and Lesbianism; Imperialism; Liberalism.**

BIBLIOGRAPHY

Primary Sources

Forster, E. M. *The Abinger Edition of E. M. Forster.* Edited by Oliver Stallybrass. London, 1972–1998.

Secondary Sources

Martin, Robert K., and George Piggford, eds. *Queer Forster.* Chicago, 1997.

Summers, Claude J. *E. M. Forster.* New York, 1983.

Tambling, Jeremy, ed. *E. M. Forster: Contemporary Critical Essays.* New York, 1995.

Wilde, Alan, ed. *Critical Essays on E. M. Forster.* Boston, 1985.

CLAUDE J. SUMMERS

■

FOUCHÉ, JOSEPH (1759?–1820), French politician, best known for being Napoleon's chief of police and for his central role in the Hundred Days and bringing about the Second Restoration.

The son of a merchant sea captain, Joseph Fouché was educated in the Oratorian school in his hometown of Nantes, then in the Oratorian College in Paris. He was never fully ordained as a priest, but taught in several Oratorian schools in the west of France before moving to Arras, where he became acquainted with Maximilien Robespierre.

In 1790 he returned to Nantes as a college principal, and two years later he was elected as a deputy to the National Convention. Initially he linked himself with the Girondin faction, but early in 1793 he voted for the king's death, and over the following months, as a representative on mission in the provinces, he acquired a reputation for being a vigorous de-Christianizer and Jacobin terrorist. Returning to Paris he came into conflict with Robespierre and was involved in the Thermidorian coup (July 1794). He spent the next few years in obscurity, reemerging after the coup of Fructidor (September 1797) to hold diplomatic posts in Italy and the Netherlands. In August 1799 he was appointed minister of police under the Directory, the revolutionary government. As such he played a passive role in the coup of Brumaire (November 1799) that established the Consulate, which replaced the Directory. Bonaparte kept him in that post until September 1802, when, believing the internal situation to have settled down, he abolished the Police Ministry and passed its duties to the Ministry of Justice. Twenty-two months later, however, following a succession of plots and rumors, the ministry was revived and Fouché, once again, was put at its head.

Shortly after the Brumaire coup Fouché presented the first consul, Bonaparte, with a memorandum for reorganizing the Police Ministry that would have put it on a par with the Ministry of the Interior. Every official with policing responsibilities, including prefects and mayors, as well as every organization with policing tasks, would have been subordinated in some measure to the ministry. While Bonaparte favored centralized control, he was not prepared to contemplate such a powerful police minister, and the system that was established fell some way short of Fouché's plan. There was never a single police organization in Napoleonic France, and there were sharp rivalries between police institutions and their directors, not least between Fouché and General (later Marshal) Moncey, the inspector general of the Gendarmerie. Nevertheless, the Police Ministry that was established in the summer of 1804 was a formidable institution and, while under Fouché, a very efficient and effective one. The ministry divided the empire into four districts: the north, west, and part of the east of France; the rest of the east and the south; the

Italian departments; and Paris. Each district was under a state counselor; for Paris this was the prefect of police. Regular reports were received from the districts, and these were distilled into a daily bulletin for Napoleon advising him of serious crimes, public order problems, and the state of public opinion. The print media and the theaters were controlled. In the context of the time this was, indeed, a police state. But even though Fouché countenanced and ordered the use of preventive detention for suspects, there were no show trials and few executions. He believed that it was counterproductive to get too concerned about, and to take serious punitive measures against, every utterance of seditious words and the occasional scurrilous printed comment about the emperor and the regime.

Napoleon never entirely trusted Fouché. In May 1810 he dismissed him for negotiating with the British. Yet, though he was banished from Paris, Fouché kept his title, Duke of Otranto (bestowed in 1809), and his other honors and posts. In 1813 he was made governor of the Illyrian provinces.

On Napoleon's first abdication in 1814 Fouché spoke up for the returning Bourbons in the senate. This did not prevent him accepting the post of minister of police from Napoleon on his return to France early in 1815. He maintained contact with the powers ranged against Napoleon throughout the Hundred Days, and following Napoleon's defeat at Waterloo, Fouché contributed significantly to ensuring the emperor's second abdication and to establishing the provisional government that welcomed back Louis XVIII. Continuing as minister of police, he was required to list those who should not be considered for amnesty by the new regime; he helped many of these to leave the country. In spite of his assistance to the Bourbons, as a regicide and minister during the Hundred Days, Fouché himself was forced into exile in 1816. He died in Trieste in 1820.

See also **Hundred Days; Napoleon; Police and Policing.**

BIBLIOGRAPHY

Arnold, Eric A. *Fouché, Napoleon, and the General Police.* Washington, D.C., 1979.

Fouché, Joseph. *Les mémoires de Fouché*. Edited by Louis Madelin. Paris, 1945. This scholarly edition of Fouché's memoirs was made by one of his biographers.

Tulard, Jean. *Joseph Fouché*. Paris, 1998. A biography by the leading figure in Napoleonic studies in modern France.

CLIVE EMSLEY

FOURIER, CHARLES (1772–1837), French social theorist.

Charles Fourier can best be described as the nineteenth century's complete utopian. A social critic who advocated "absolute deviation" from existing philosophies and institutions, he surpassed Jean-Jacques Rousseau (1712–1778) in the intransigence of his rejection of his own society. A psychologist who celebrated the passions as agents of human happiness, he carried to its ultimate conclusion the utopian denial of original sin. A social prophet who designed work schedules, dinner menus, and nursery furniture for his utopia, he was obsessively concerned with giving precise definition to his conception of the good society.

Central to Fourier's thinking was the belief that in a rightly ordered world there would be no disparity between our desires and our ability to satisfy them. All basic human drives were meant to be expressed, he argued, and most social ills were the result of instinctual repression. Fourier's utopia was an attempt to spell out precisely the kind of society that would have to exist to make possible the economic, social, psychic, and sexual liberation of humanity.

The key institution in Fourier's utopia was the Phalanx, a community of 1,620 men and women of varied tastes, inclinations, ages, and social backgrounds. Within this community, work and play would be organized in small groups (and "series" of groups); children would be raised collectively; and all activities would be organized according to the "dictates" of the passions, those innate drives that Fourier regarded as the basic forces in the social universe.

Fourier was an autodidact who spent much of his life working as a traveling salesman and clerk for silk merchants in the city of Lyon. His utopian ideas first took shape in the 1790s as part of a larger "theory of the destinies" that he began to formulate in the hope of filling the intellectual and moral vacuum created by the French Revolution. His first book, the *Théorie des quatre mouvements* (1808) was ignored, and a second book, the *Traité de l'association domestique-agricole* (1822) was ridiculed in the Paris press. Still, in 1816 Fourier acquired a disciple, a functionary at the Besançon prefecture named Just Muiron.

With Muiron's encouragement and financial assistance Fourier moved to Paris in 1822, and he spent the rest of his life seeking the support of a wealthy patron who would subsidize the creation of an experimental community or "trial Phalanx," which would demonstrate to the world at large the merit of his theory. The patron never appeared, but by 1832 Fourier did manage to attract a group of disciples committed to spreading his ideas and applying them in a model community.

After Fourier's death in 1837 the leadership of the Fourierist movement was assumed by Victor Considerant (1808–1893), who popularized Fourier's theory and established a daily newspaper. Considerant's great accomplishment was to create an audience for Fourier's ideas and to bring them within the orbit of the existing socialist movement. In the process, however, Considerant and his colleagues transformed Fourier's doctrine, weeding out the "extravagant" sexual and cosmological speculations and shifting the emphasis from instinctual liberation to the organization of work.

Only one practical application of Fourier's ideas had much success in France. This was the *Familistère* or stove factory created by Jean-Baptiste Godin (1817–1888) at Guise, which survived into the twentieth century. In America, however, some twenty-five Fourierist phalanxes were established in the 1840s and a few more later. The most famous, Brook Farm, attracted numerous writers and intellectuals, one of whom, Nathaniel Hawthorne (1804–1864), left a wry portrait of the community in his *Blithedale Romance*.

FOURIER'S LEGACY

For more than a hundred years after Fourier's death, scholars focused on the question of his socialism. Was he a socialist, they asked, given the fact that he called for the payment of interest on invested capital and the retention of some forms of private property? And what was the relation of his thought to the "scientific socialism" of Karl Marx (1818–1883) and Friedrich Engels (1820–1895)? More recently attention has been given to Fourier's psychological writings and notably his analysis of love and repression. He has been seen as a precursor not of Marx but of Sigmund Freud (1856–1939)—or at least of the radical Freud recovered in the 1950s and 1960s by Herbert Marcuse and Norman O. Brown.

Fourier has also rightly been seen as an early male feminist. His writings include vigorous pleas for the emancipation of women, and his insistence that "the extension of the privileges of women is the fundamental cause of all social progress" became a battle cry of early radical feminism.

Although Fourier was long viewed primarily as a "precursor," his reflections on attractive labor, female emancipation, and instinctual liberation are now recognized as original contributions to social theory in their own right; and he is seen as a thinker who probed deeply and imaginatively into the problem of the relationship between the human instincts and human society.

See also **Communism; Owen, Robert; Socialism; Utopian Socialism.**

BIBLIOGRAPHY

Beecher, Jonathan. *Charles Fourier: The Visionary and His World.* Berkeley, Calif., 1986.

Beecher, Jonathan, and Richard Bienvenu, eds. and trans. *The Utopian Vision of Charles Fourier: Selected Texts on Work, Love, and Passionate Attraction.* Boston, 1971.

Fourier, Charles. *The Theory of the Four Movements.* Edited by Gareth Stedman Jones and Ian Patterson. Cambridge,U.K., 1996.

Guarneri, Carl J. *The Utopian Alternative: Fourierism in Nineteenth-Century America.* Ithaca, N.Y., 1991.

JONATHAN BEECHER

FOX, CHARLES JAMES (1749–1806), English politician.

Charles James Fox led the main political opposition connection in Britain from 1784 until his death in September 1806. Born on 24 January 1749, he was educated at Eton and Oxford, and was elected to Parliament on 10 May 1768 for the borough of Midhurst. He briefly held minor offices at the Admiralty Board and at the Treasury Board between 1770 and 1774 under Lord North's (Frederick North, prime minister, 1770–1782) administration. From this point on, Fox became an unyielding critic of the influence of the crown and a fierce opponent of North and his policy toward the American colonists, arguing for the recognition of American independence. He also adopted other more liberal causes than he had previously supported, such as moderate parliamentary reform and the repeal of the Test and Corporation Acts (which discriminated against non-Anglicans).

After the fall of North in March 1782, Fox became foreign secretary under Charles Watson-Wentworth, the Marquis of Rockingham, but he resigned in June 1782 after Rockingham's death because he was unable to agree with the home secretary, William Petty, Earl of Shelburne, over the American peace terms. He then, to the surprise of many, allied himself and the Rockingham Whigs with North, with whom he defeated Shelburne in the House of Commons, and then forced the king to yield the government, in February 1783. The Fox-North coalition lasted in power only until December 1783, when George III (r. 1760–1820) dismissed them—having secured the defeat of their East India Bill in the House of Lords—and replaced them with the administration of William Pitt the Younger, who was able to keep Fox out of office until February 1806. Fox believed that this maneuvering by the king was an unconstitutional intervention and a monumental injustice, and it determined his politics for the rest of his life.

Foiled in his hopes of political advancement by the king's recovery from serious illness in 1788 and 1789, Fox's attitude to the French Revolution was shaped partly by his response to events in France but also by his resolve to establish and maintain a permanent party of opposition in Parliament. He had long been an ardent francophile, and he associated the early events of the revolution in France with those of the Glorious Revolution in England in 1688 and with the American Revolution. While some of the old Rockingham connection, under William Henry

Cavendish Bentinck, the Duke of Portland, gradually changed sides between 1791 and 1794 to support Pitt over the issue of the war against France, Fox and a rump of some sixty-six members of Parliament continued to view George III and Pitt as greater enemies to British liberties than armed French revolutionaries. To Fox, the British war against France was not provoked by any serious threat to national security. Rather, it was another evidence of corruption in high places within Britain. The later violence of the Terror dismayed him deeply, although in public the Foxites excused it on the grounds of the long reign of absolutist oppression, which had created a pent-up flood of frustration and fury to be unleashed by the revolution.

Fox divided Parliament over the war even when he had no chance of defeating Pitt in a vote, partly to record opposition to government policy and partly to maintain a sense of party within his own ranks. From October 1797 until 1801, however, he seceded from Parliament in an attempt to impress on the country how little notice was taken of argument and reason in the House of Commons. Historians disagree over how far Fox and his followers in Parliament supported radicals outside Parliament in the 1790s. It is clear that they dabbled in popular politics, associated with provincial radicals, supported them at their trials for treason and made some inflammatory speeches outside Parliament. However, most scholars also emphasize their more conservative tendencies. Certainly Fox himself never explicitly supported universal manhood suffrage, even if he toasted popular sovereignty in 1798, when government repression was at its height and he was anxious to rouse a show of public hostility to the government.

After Pitt's death in January 1806, George III reluctantly accepted Fox as foreign secretary in the administration of William Grenville, better known as the "Ministry of All the Talents" (1806–1807). Fox tried to negotiate peace with France during his brief tenure of office, but he was already in poor health by the time he entered government, and he died on 13 September 1806. A brilliant parliamentary speaker and a man of considerable personal charm, he nevertheless failed to achieve much in tangible political terms other than the basis of a legitimate party of opposition.

See also **French Revolution; Great Britain; Tories; Whigs.**

BIBLIOGRAPHY

Graham, Jenny. *The Nation, the Law, and the King: Reform Politics in England, 1789–1799.* Lanham, Md., and Oxford, U.K., 2000. Argues that Fox and his followers were much more sympathetic to and supportive of the radicals outside Parliament than most historians allow.

Mitchell, Leslie. *Charles James Fox.* Oxford, U.K., 1992.

O'Gorman, Frank. *The Whig Party and the French Revolution.* London, 1967.

EMMA VINCENT MACLEOD

FRANCE. The French Revolution (1789–1799) effectively challenged monarchical absolutism on behalf of popular sovereignty in France and in Europe. The destruction of the monarchy and the establishment of a republic would have long-term consequences in European political life. And so would the continued centralization of the French state, as well as the popular violence that accompanied the French Revolution.

ORIGINS OF THE REVOLUTION

The Revolution should be seen in the context of hard economic times in the decades that preceded it. High prices, compounded by periodic harvest failures (notably those of 1775, but also 1787 and 1788), and low wages brought considerable hardship, while reducing the taxes that reached the coffers of the state. This meant that nobles received less in payments (including seignorial dues) and other obligations from the peasants who worked their land, making it more difficult for some to continue to "live nobly." Some of them put the squeeze on their peasants, the so-called seignorial reaction that generated considerable anger, indeed resistance, among the rural poor in parts of France. Nobles hired collectors and enforcers, and enforced with increasing care remaining rights of justice over the peasants, including the seignorial courts used to enforce noble rights over forests, lakes, and streams.

The social lines dividing nobles from bourgeois had become considerably less clear in the late eighteenth century. The French monarchy was locked in a deep financial crisis. Assistance to the American colonies rebelling against Great Britain had compounded the financial plight of the monarchy. King Louis XVI (r. 1774–1792) sold noble titles to raise cash, ennobling about 2,500 families during the fifteen years that preceded 1789. Long-entrenched noble families saw the newcomers as crass parvenus. At the same time, commoners resented the exoneration of nobles from taxes. The king created more offices in order to sell them to anyone who would buy them—there were about fifty thousand offices in France at the time of the Revolution. This eroded public confidence in the monarchy as it swam in an enormous pool of debt.

France remained a society of overlapping and often confusing layers of privilege, rights, traditions, and jurisdictions. Enlightenment discourse emphasizing freedom in the face of entrenched economic, social, and political privilege helped mobilize opposition to the policies of the king and to many existing privileges. The language of the philosophes emphasized equality before the law, and distinguished between absolute and despotic rule, while appealing to the tribunal of public opinion.

Yet virtually no one envisioned an alternate regime to monarchy. Queen Marie-Antoinette (1755–1793), the daughter of the Habsburg queen Maria Theresa, was vilified for being an outsider, but also because her notorious infidelities further increased the image of Louis XVI as powerless in the grip of an imposing female, thus weakening the French throne.

Assembly of Notables What was the king to do? The parlements (the sovereign law courts) were suspicious of any reforms and wanted to avoid any increase in the tax on land. Charles-Alexandre de Calonne, controller general of finance, asked Louis XVI to convoke an Assembly of Notables, which would be made up of representatives selected from the three estates (clergy, nobles, and everybody else—the Third Estate). This would allow the monarchy to avoid the troublesome parlements. The king would propose reforms, imposing a land tax that would strike nobles as well as everyone else. More than this, Calonne, denouncing "the dominance of custom," proposed a reorganization of the entire financial system. In particular he wanted to reorganize the system of tax collection, which was both notoriously inefficient (particularly compared to the system in Britain) and counter-

productive (collectors retained a good part of the taxes they collected). However, the Assembly of Notables (1787) rejected the proposed reform, defending the exemption of nobles and clergy from most taxation. Nobles convinced the king to dismiss Calonne in April 1788. But when his successor, Étienne-Charles de Loménie de Brienne, asked the parlements to register, and in doing so approve, several royal edicts aimed at reform, namely a new tax on land and a stamp tax, the Parlement of Paris refused to do so. This plunged the monarchy into crisis.

Not all members of the Assembly of Notables opposed reform and refused all new taxes. But they wanted to guarantee their privileges. They wanted Louis to convoke the Estates-General, which had not met since 1614. This put the king in a difficult position. He needed to reduce the privileges of the nobles, but did not want to risk accusations of tyranny by doing so without their approval. But if he exchanged new taxes for acquiescing to the demands of the First and Second Estates (the clergy and the nobility), he risked compromising his absolute authority, implicitly suggesting that he was subject to the approval of the nobility, if not the nation.

Louis sought compromise, withdrawing the new taxes in exchange for maintaining the tax on income (the *vingtième*), which had been assessed in the 1750s to finance the Seven Years War (1756–1763). Loménie de Brienne made clear that the crown would have to pay its debts with paper money, however. Louis ordered that new loan edicts be registered without regard to the parlements' response. To an objection from his cousin, the duc d'Orléans, the king replied, "That is of no importance to me . . . it is legal because I will it."

Louis then suspended the parlements, creating new courts to replace them and a new plenary court that would register royal edicts. The "revolt of the nobles" spread against what the nobles considered to be the abuse of the rights and privileges of the nobles by the monarchy, which they accused of acting despotically. Resistance followed, first from the Assembly of the Clergy, which was to decide on its annual gift to the monarchy, and then from ordinary people, who rioted in several cities. The king announced on 5 July 1788 that he would convoke the Estates-General on 1 May 1789, assuming that it would agree to new taxes.

Estates-General But would the Estates-General vote by estate, which would give an advantage to the First and Second Estates, or by head, which would give an advantage to the Third Estate? The Parlement of Paris, which had been reinstated, supported the king's insistence that voting be by estate. But calls could be heard from political writers who saluted the Third Estate as representing the "nation"—a significant term that had come to be used with increasing frequency during previous crises in the 1770s, namely the attempts of the administrator and economist Anne-Robert-Jacques Turgot (1727–1781) to liberalize the economy. The "nation" thus potentially represented an alternate, not complementary, form of allegiance, particularly as the king appeared to be behaving despotically. A "Patriot" party emerged, a coalition of bourgeois and liberal nobles who wanted change. It included the marquis Marie Joseph Paul de Lafayette (1757–1834). And in January 1789, Abbé Emmanuel-Joseph Sieyès reflected this shift in public opinion with his "What Is the Third Estate?" He contrasted the "nation" against royal absolutism and noble prerogatives, demanding a prominent role for the Third Estate in French political life.

Before the Estates-General was to convene, the king asked local electoral assemblies and the first two estates to draw up lists of grievances, which the Estates-General would discuss. These *cahiers de doléances* criticized royal absolutism and the seigneurs, asked for a fairer tax structure, and, among other things, called for the establishment of a new representative body. While they never actually reached the king, they reflected a growing public awareness of the dimensions of the crisis.

When the Estates-General first met on 5 May 1789 (nearly one thousand strong, 578 of whom were in the Third Estate) the question of voting had not yet been decided. The deputies of the Third Estate, already irritated when the king kept them waiting, and furious when it became apparent that voting would be by Estate, met on 17 June and declared themselves the "National Assembly," representing national sovereignty, an authority parallel, if not superior, to that of the king. When the First Estate voted to join the Third, the Third Estate found itself on 20 June locked out of its meeting hall. Moved to a nearby tennis court, the Third Estate voted not to leave "until the constitution

of the kingdom is established and consolidated on solid foundations." Louis then proclaimed the Third Estate's deliberations null and void. But he announced some reforms, including the periodic convocation of the Estates-General, the abolition of the *taille* (the tax on land that weighed heavily on the peasants) and the *corvée* (labor tax), and to eliminate the troublesome varied tolls and tariffs that struck the transport of goods. Henceforth, the Third Estate would indeed vote by head, but only when the matter at hand did not concern "the ancient and constitutional rights of the third orders." Five days later, after threatening to dissolve the Estates-General by force, Louis reversed himself and ordered the first two estates to join the third.

REVOLUTION OF 1789

In the meantime, in Paris, where food shortages and high prices were causing considerable discontent, rumor had the king, under the advice of his most reactionary noble advisors, planning to dissolve the National Assembly by armed force. Demonstrators attacked the customs barriers at the gates of Paris, tearing down toll booths. On the morning of 14 July, thousands of people stormed into the Invalides (a veterans hospital) to seize weapons, and then headed toward the Bastille, an imposing fortress on the eastern edge of Paris, believing guns and powder to be stored there, as well as political prisoners. The Bastille had emerged as a symbol of royal despotism, as some of its prisoners had been sent there by virtue of *lettres de cachet*, orders signed by the king or on his behalf. The crowd forced the surrender of the Bastille. The king recognized a newly elected municipal government of "the Commune of Paris," as well as a national guard commanded by Lafayette. On 17 July he came to Paris from Versailles, putting on an emblem of three colors, red and blue for the city of Paris, and white for the Bourbons. The tricolor would become the flag of the French Revolution.

In many parts of rural France the news from Paris brought expectations of reform and perhaps even better times. In some places peasants attacked the châteaus of seigneurs and burned title deeds and lists of obligations they owed. The peasant rebellions helped bring about "the Great Fear," sparked by rumors of an aristocratic "famine plot" to starve out the poor, or burn them out, with the help of brigands. National guard units formed in an atmosphere of panic that spread rapidly through large parts of France. Gradually, the establishment of new town governments helped restore order. But the rural violence and the Great Fear led the National Assembly on the night of 4 August to abolish formally the "feudal regime," including seignorial rights, although the sanctity of property was maintained and compensation promised. Thus the National Assembly renounced privilege, which had been arguably the fundamental organizational principle of the *ancien régime.* Other privileges held by certain provinces and cities were also soon abolished.

These remarkable events had destroyed French absolutism. On 26 August, the Assembly then promulgated the Declaration of the Rights of Man and of the Citizen, which would serve as a preamble to a Constitution. Article 1 proclaimed that "Men are born and remain free and equal in rights." They would be equal before the law and no one could be persecuted for religious beliefs. The Declaration placed sovereignty in the nation, although social distinctions would remain.

Louis XVI, who remained at Versailles, rejected the decrees of 4 August as well as the Assembly's offer on 11 September of a "suspending," or delaying veto over legislation. Popular anger in Paris mounted, as ordinary people were convinced that he remained in the clutches of conservative, aristocratic advisors (which was indeed the case). "Patriots" increasingly demanded that the king reside in Paris. And on 5 October, when women from modest neighborhoods near the Bastille found the market poorly provisioned, they began a march to Versailles that eventually brought together about ten thousand people. The next morning, when a crowd tried to force its way into the royal palace, the guards shot someone dead, and the crowd then killed two guards. Louis announced that he accepted the August decrees of the Assembly and agreed to go to Paris with his family.

The National Assembly, which had moved its deliberations to Paris, now proclaimed Louis "king of the French," instead of "king of France," implying that he now embodied the sovereignty of the people. Some frightened nobles began to leave France, including the king's brother Charles-Philippe,

comte d'Artois (later Charles X), soon followed by about twenty thousand émigrés. In November the Assembly declared the property of the church "national property" and put about 10 percent of church lands up for sale at auctions; the land was purchased by urban bourgeois and wealthy peasants. The Assembly then made the remaining church lands the collateral for paper money called *assignats.* In February 1790 the Assembly abolished religious orders and on 12 July passed the Civil Constitution of the French Clergy, creating a national church and making the clergy dependent on salaries paid by the state. Soon all priests had to swear an oath of loyalty to the Revolution. More than half of priests refused to do so, and the Assembly decreed that these "nonjuring" clergy would be forbidden from administering the sacraments. This divided France regionally (with the clergy of the west and Alsace, in particular, refusing the oath), but also split many parishes. The Assembly also rationalized the administrative structure of France by eliminating the old provinces (thus undercutting some noble influence) and creating *départements,* named after prominent geographic characteristics, particularly the names of rivers.

From monarchy to republic The Constitution of 1791 substituted a constitutional monarchy for the absolute rule of the king. The king would retain only a suspending veto, but would continue to dictate foreign policy and command the army, even if acts of war required the Assembly's approval. Although all citizens were to be equal before the law, the Assembly differentiated between "active citizens," who paid the equivalent of three days wages in direct taxes, and "passive citizens," the very poor. The National Assembly granted citizenship and civil rights to Protestants and Jews (1790); ended the monopoly of the guilds over the production and distribution of goods; and in 1791 passed the Le Chapelier Law, forbidding workmen from joining together to refuse work to a master, a victory for free trade. The Assembly also established proceedings for obtaining a divorce, established civil marriage, ended primogeniture, and abolished slavery in France, but not in the colonies. It ignored the calls of Olympe de Gouges (1745–1793) for equal rights for women.

Opposition to the Revolution had already begun in parts of the south and west of the country, as well as in Alsace. In Paris, political clubs began to play a greater role in mobilizing popular opinion for the Revolution, pushing it to the left. The Jacobin Club and the Cordeliers Club brought together radicals, including the artisans and other ordinary people, the "sans-culottes" who believed in the Revolution. The Jacobins soon had many clubs in the provinces. Increasingly fearful for his future and wishing to reverse the Revolution itself, Louis XVI decided to flee Paris. In June 1791 he and his family left the Tuileries, Paris, in disguise in the middle of the night, but were recognized in the eastern town of Varennes, not too far from the Belgian border, and returned to Paris. This increased calls for his destitution and the creation of a republic. The king's formal acceptance of the constitutional limits of his reign on 14 September could not stem ever increasing popular support for a republic, including within the newly elected National Assembly, where the radicals of the "left," so called because of the location of their seats in the assembly, dominated.

In the Assembly, the faction that became known as the "Girondins" (several of whom were from the *département* of the Gironde, of which Bordeaux was the capital), called for a revolutionary war to free Europe from the tyranny of monarchs and nobles. In April 1792 France declared war on Austria. The war, coming at a time of higher prices in Paris and fears that émigrés were organizing a campaign against the Revolution, brought early defeats on the northern frontier. In June, a crowd pushed its way into the Tuileries, calling for the destitution of the king. On 11 July the Assembly declared the nation to be "in danger." Austria and Prussia issued the Brunswick Manifesto, warning the French that they faced harsh punishment if the royal family were harmed. The neighborhood "sections" of Paris demanded that the king be deposed. A radical committee took over the city council. On 10 August sans-culottes invaded the Tuileries, killing six hundred of the Swiss Guards and servants. The Assembly declared the end to the monarchy. However, military defeats accentuated the panic in Paris, leading to the massacre of prisoners in September. Yet, on 20 September 1792, the army of conscripts defeated the Prussian and Austrian armies at Valmy, near Châlon-sur-Marne. The next day (although news of the battle was not yet known), the Assembly proclaimed the French Republic. French troops pushed across the Rhine, and the National Convention (as the Assembly was now called) declared the annexation of Savoy and of the town of Nice. The king went on trial for treason, accused of conspiring with the Revolution's enemies. Louis XVI was tried and guillotined in January 1793.

THE FIRST REPUBLIC

Full-scale counterrevolution within France began in the west in March 1793. The Vendée, as the insurgency is called after the *département* of the same name, was waged by peasants who still respected nobles and clergy and resisted conscription. Facing foreign armies and internal civil war (not only in the west, but now also including "federalist" revolts in Lyon, Marseille, Bordeaux, and Caen against Jacobin authority centralized in Paris), France lapsed into the Terror.

The Terror The Convention turned authority over to the Committee of Public Safety, whose most prominent members included Maximilien Robespierre and Louis-Antoine-Léon de Saint-Just. After expelling the Girondins in June, the Committee restricted civil rights (notably through the Law of Suspects in September 1793) and began guillotining those considered enemies of the Revolution. Ultimately, well more than ten thousand people perished in the Terror, the majority in regions affected by warfare against the Revolution. The Committee of Public Safety struck against its enemies on the left, notably the *enragés* who demanded even stricter measures, as well as moderates who wanted the Terror reined in. The Jacobins abolished the old calendar of twelve months, initiating a revolutionary calendar based on cycles of ten days. Radical revolutionaries launched an ambitious campaign of "dechristianization" against symbols of the church. Robespierre sought (without much success) to initiate and popularize a secularized "Cult of the Supreme Being," to replace the church as the embodiment of moral authority.

The Directory Moderates (potentially those next in line to be executed) plotted against Robespierre and his colleagues, arresting him on the night of 9 Thermidor—under the revolutionary calendar (27 July 1794). He and Saint-Just were

Committee of the Year Two. Engraving by J. B. Huet c. 1793. The Committee of Public Safety is shown questioning a man in aristocratic dress who attempts to prove his good citizenship with a previously issued certificate. Robespierre is depicted at the far right. ©CORBIS

tried in haste and quickly guillotined. The victors of "Thermidor" dismantled the Paris Commune, reducing the authority of the Committee of Public Safety. They proclaimed a new constitution, two assemblies, and an executive authority of five directors. The subsequent period is known as "the Directory." People of property benefited from the "Thermidorian Reaction." The number of those eligible to vote was reduced. The poor suffered hard economic times, particularly the awful winter of 1795, as the wars against the Revolution's enemies went on. That spring, troops put down two demonstrations in Paris. The Directory nipped in the bud an insurrection organized by François-Noël "Gracchus" Babeuf, who espoused a society

of equals, and confronted continued mobilization by Royalists who wanted a monarchical restoration. The Directory simply annulled an election in 1797, because it would have brought to the Council of Five Hundred (one of the representative bodies) a considerable number of Royalists. A coup d'état on 4 September 1797 cast aside two of the directors.

The Consulat In 1799 Abbé Sieyès, one of the directors, began to plot another coup in order to put an end to a troubled, rather chaotic period. He turned to the young Napoleon Bonaparte, whose military victories in Italy had made him the talk of Paris. Following the coup d'état of 18 Brumaire (9 November 1799), the victorious plotters established a new government, the Consulat, with three consuls, including Napoleon, replacing the five directors. A new constitution was quickly promulgated, approved by 99 percent of voters in a plebiscite. The Consulat provided political stability, with Napoleon as first consul (he named the other two). He began to ruthlessly suppress potential opposition, and made peace with the Catholic Church, signing a Concordat in 1801 with the papacy. Protestants and Jews would receive the protection of the state.

In 1802 Napoleon took the title "consul for life," which another plebiscite approved overwhelmingly. He used a conspiracy allegedly organized against him by Royalists to strike out at them, and then moved to establish himself as emperor, snatching the crown from Pope Pius VII (r. 1829–1830) to crown himself during the ceremony on 2 December 1804.

FIRST EMPIRE

Napoleon I (r. 1804–1814/15), who could never live with peace, lured Britain into another war. In 1805 Britain, Austria, and Russia formed a coalition (the third) against France. The French navy suffered a disastrous defeat at Trafalgar in October of that year, but did better on land, defeating the Austrians at Ulm and the Russians at Austerlitz. A year later, Napoleon's troops defeated the Prussians at Jena, occupying Berlin, and then the Russians again at the Battle of Friedland in June 1807, a defeat that led to the Treaty of Tilsit the next month. Britain alone was left to challenge Napoleon's empire, particularly after another Austrian defeat at Wagram two years later.

When he was not waging war on Europe, Napoleon established some of the most essential foundations of modern France. He honed the centralization of the state bureaucracy, making the prefects (the chief administrative authorities in each *département*) even more important, while the senate, legislative body, and tribunate, institutions that had come with the Consulat, were left with only ceremonial functions. The council of state's influence was reduced. Napoleon established the Bank of France in 1800 and organized education into regional academies. The Napoleonic Code (1804) he considered the centerpiece of the empire. More than two thousand articles long, it proclaimed the equality of all people in France before the law

(although women were less free than men) and the freedom of religion, and reaffirmed the ban on associations of workers or employers. With the army and the bureaucracy standing as the two pillars of the empire, Napoleon created a new hierarchy, topped by an elite of "notables" whose status came from their service to the state. And he created innumerable titles and decorations, including the Legion of Honor (1802).

However, the tide began to turn against Napoleon, as French rule brought resistance in many countries. The "Continental System," essentially a blockade that aimed at strangling the British economy by cutting off its trade with the continent, failed, despite the War of 1812, which pitted Britain against the United States. Rebellion in Spain turned into the Peninsular War (1808–1814), with guerrilla attacks on French troops taking their toll. The "Spanish ulcer" cost Napoleon dearly. Military reforms in Prussia and Austria led to stronger armies to challenge Napoleon. The emperor's decision to invade Russia in 1812 proved to be catastrophic. The "Grand Army," half of which consisted of conscripts from conquered countries, found the devastating Russian winter arguably its biggest enemy. The bitter cold and Russian forces killed off the bulk of the largest army that had ever marched; only some forty thousand of six hundred thousand ever returned to France.

The Russian debacle encouraged the other powers, and French victories in 1813 only forestalled Napoleon's almost inevitable defeat in 1814, as Prussian and Austrian armies marched into Paris. Napoleon abdicated, going into exile on the island of Elba. The comte de Paris assumed the throne as King Louis XVIII (r. 1814–1815, 1815–1824), claiming that he was in the seventeenth year of his reign, which he dated from the death of his nephew, the son of Louis XVI (1785–1795), in a Paris prison in 1795. The new king signed a constitutional "Charter," against the wishes of most nobles, which served to recognize that much had changed since 1789. The Restoration would have a Chamber of Deputies, to be elected on the basis of a very restricted electoral franchise that gave the vote essentially to wealthy landowners.

Then the seemingly impossible happened. Napoleon escaped Elba and returned to France, marching to Paris from the south of France, as Louis

XVIII left the country. But this Napoleonic adventure lasted but one hundred days, as the allies gathered their forces, defeating Napoleon's hurriedly organized army at Waterloo in the Austrian Netherlands (Belgium) on 16 June 1815. This time the exile would be permanent, to the tiny island of St. Helena in the South Atlantic, a thousand miles from any mainland. The great adventure was over.

RESTORATION

The election of the first parliament of the regime, to be known as the *Chambre introuvable,* took place in an atmosphere of political terror in August 1815. Some 50,900 electors selected 402 deputies. Of these 78 percent were clearly very conservative and among them 52 percent were *ancien régime* nobles. Of the others, most were not opposed to the regime, but only to the demands of its more extreme adherents, the so-called *ultras.* Louis XVIII was unwilling to risk the politically divisive measures demanded by the *ultras.* He dissolved the Chamber in September 1816 and, partly through the use of government influence, was able to secure the election of a far more moderate majority. Among its achievements was to be the electoral law of 1817, which by means of a three hundred franc tax qualification restricted the electorate to one hundred thousand, primarily made up of landowners. The requirement that candidates for election should be at least forty years old and pay one thousand francs in direct taxation, ensured that only around 1,650 were eligible. The government also purged *ultras* from the administration and allowed the return of political exiles. Reconciliation could go only so far however. In 1820 the assassination of Louis XVIII's nephew the duc de Berri, the heir to the throne and the last in the direct line of Bourbons until the posthumous birth of his son, precipitated a major crisis. Together with the uncovering of Bonapartist plots in the army it appeared to justify exceptional repression, including detention without trial for three months, tighter censorship, and yet more restrictive electoral legislation.

The accession, in September 1824, of Charles X (r. 1824–1830), signified the effective end of efforts to broaden the base of support for the regime. The new king had a conception of his rights hardly compatible with constitutional monarchy. Initially, a ministry led by Joseph Villèle and an *ultra*-dominated Chamber, elected in the aftermath of the assassination crisis, supported the king. Three-fifths of the deputies were nobles and one-half former émigrés. This majority was to be characterized by bitter divisions, however, between the proponents of an aristocratic and clerical monarchy and constitutional monarchists. The compensation of former émigres whose land had been confiscated during the Revolution, was described by liberals as a fine on the nation imposed by a self-seeking noble majority. Concern about the regime's intentions was increased by its close alliance with a church intent on restoring "moral order."

The government continued to manipulate the electoral system, reducing the number of voters from one hundred thousand to eighty-nine thousand between 1817 and 1827. Together with the preferential treatment of nobles within the army and administration, and the pressure for restitution exerted by parish priests on purchasers of former church property, government policies created an increasingly widespread belief that a return to the *ancien régime* was planned. The regime's critics were essentially liberals committed to constitutional monarchy, including lawyers or merchants or displaced members of the former imperial service élite and army officers retired prematurely on half-pay.

Liberal successes in the 1827 elections persuaded the king to replace Villèle with the more liberal Jean-Baptiste-Sylvère Gay, vicomte de Martignac, a move that seemed only to stimulate further opposition. In August 1829 he appointed his old friend the comte Auguste-Jules-Armand-Marie de Polignac, a religious mystic, to head a ministry, a move that was widely taken to symbolize defeat, national humiliation, and the White Terror of 1815. The liberal association *Aide-toi le ciel t'aidera* (Heaven helps those who help themselves), originally formed to encourage the registration of voters, called for a nationwide refusal to pay taxes, led by moderate and legalistic figures such as François Guizot. Poor harvests, high food prices, unemployment, and misery added to the sense of crisis. Two successive elections in 1830 returned majorities hostile to the government. In the second, and in spite of government pressure, 270 liberals were returned and only 145 government supporters. Charles X invoked the emergency decree powers he possessed under the terms of the Charter and in July introduced ordinances that tightened censorship, dissolved the newly elected Chamber before it even met, revised election procedures to increase administrative influence, and reduced the electorate to its wealthiest quarter, made up of twenty-three thousand mainly noble landowners. This brought the crisis to a head.

Revolution of 1830   The liberals gave the signal for resistance with a poster calling for protest. The call to defend "liberty" mobilized a disparate coalition drawn from the middle and working classes of the capital city. Around midday on 27 July, the first clash occurred between demonstrators and *gendarmerie* units attempting to disperse crowds. In the afternoon, exasperated troops seem to have fired without orders. This was followed by the construction of barricades and bitter street fighting. The armed crowds, which had taken over the streets, frightened the liberals, as did the shouts of "Vive Napoléon II" and "Vive la République." Therefore once again they vested Lafayette, the aging hero of 1789, with command of a National Guard and established a municipal commission to restore order. On 30 July they offered the throne to the duc d'Orléans, a prince with a liberal reputation, on condition that he agree to respect the principles of constitutional monarchy. The following day, the new king Louis-Philippe (r. 1830–1848) appointed a government and convened a meeting of the Chamber of Deputies. On 8 August the Chamber voted in favor of a revision of the constitution that significantly altered the balance of power between king and parliament. A substantial purge of the administration, together with the withdrawal of many nobles from public life, confirmed the defeat of aristocratic reaction.

THE JULY MONARCHY

Most liberals were satisfied. The new electoral law, which brought the tax qualification for voting down from three hundred francs to two hundred, significantly reduced the weight of nobles within the electorate while enfranchising mainly landowners (about 56 percent of voters in 1846), officials (about 8 percent), professionals (about 10 percent), and businessmen (about 26 percent). They would consistently provide the regime with solid parliamentary support. The vast majority of

Liberty Leading the People, 28 July 1830. Eugène Delacroix's renowned painting celebrates the republican spirit that inspired the July Revolution. The personification of liberty, wearing the red cap adopted by opponents of the monarchy during the French Revolution, leads figures from various levels of society as they overrun soldiers symbolizing monarchical power. ©ARCHIVO ICONOGRAFICO, S.A./CORBIS

lower-middle-class, peasant, and worker citizens remained unenfranchised, although growing prosperity would enlarge the electorate gradually from 166,000 to 241,000 by 1846. The 1831 municipal election law gave the vote to some three million. In the aftermath of revolution, however, "liberté" had diverse meanings, freely discussed at meetings and in newspapers. In Paris, workers took to the streets to demand the trial of Charles X's ministers, higher wages, a shorter working day, and the banning of employment-threatening machinery. They assumed that a regime that they had created should recognize the basic human right to a living wage, but received little sympathy from a government committed to "the freedom of industry." The brief seizure of control over the city of Lyon by armed silk workers in November 1831 and their slogan "Live working or die fighting!" caused a great stir. Small groups of middle-class republicans began to look outside the narrow electorate for support, and attempted to politicize discontented workers through organizations such as the "Society for the Rights of Man." This agitation would, however, largely be terminated by a law banning political meetings—introduced in April 1834, following a second insurrection by Lyonnais silkworkers—and by increasingly brutal repression. In an effort to safeguard "social order" in the longer term, a major law on primary education (1833) required each commune to have a school (although this would not be the case for some time in parts of rural France), sought to "moralize" the lower orders through religious instruction, to encourage the use of French in place of regional languages, and to enhance the sense of national identity.

The political peace of the following years was due to firm government, but additionally to support from the narrow electorate for a regime that through parliament allowed them to represent their own particular interests. Louis-Philippe made full use of his powers and insisted that ministers sympathize with his objectives; opposition both within and outside parliament was weak and divided. It ranged from the supporters of another Bourbon restoration, the legitimists on the right, to the republicans on the left. However, its most numerous and vocal critics were drawn from the ranks of the so-called dynastic opposition, made up of politicians excluded from office who sought to improve their prospects by enlarging the electorate, not in order to enfranchise the masses, but to secure the wider representation of the property-owning middle classes.

Certainly, the position of the regime was not as secure as it appeared. Its foreign policy appeared to be subservient to British interests. It also suffered from continuous opposition criticism of electoral corruption and the use of patronage to control deputies, and especially from the severe economic crisis beginning in 1845–1846, which shattered the image of prosperity it had assiduously cultivated. The "banquet" campaign, its form a means of circumventing the laws against political meetings, was initiated by members of the dynastic opposition. However, these moderates, who wanted a modest expansion of the electoral franchise, rapidly lost the initiative to republicans such as Alexandre-Auguste Ledru-Rollin, who at Lille in November 1847 demanded manhood suffrage and (unspecified) reforms to end the people's suffering.

Revolution of 1848   The campaign was planned to culminate in a mass banquet in Paris. Afraid of disorder, the government banned this gathering, a move that was accepted with relief by liberal and moderate republican politicians. More radical figures called for protest however. On 22 February 1848 crowds of students and workers gathered on the Place de la Concorde, and sporadic violence occurred as the police attempted to disperse them. On the following day elements of the solidly middle-class National Guard rejected orders from a government that seemed to represent the interests solely of the upper classes. This seems to have persuaded the king and his advisors of the wisdom of reform. The intransigent Guizot was replaced with the more liberal Louis-Mathieu Molé. However, a murderous fusillade, fired at around 10 P.M. without orders, by nervous troops guarding the foreign ministry, led an enraged population to construct hundreds of barricades in the narrow streets of the old city. Louis-Philippe was encouraged to abdicate, and members of the dynastic opposition vainly attempted to establish a regency for his grandson. At the same time, republican leaders at the offices of the newspapers *National* and *Réforme* were beginning to realize that a more radical outcome was possible. In the late afternoon, a provisional government made up of well-known republican politicians and journalists was proclaimed by the crowds at the Hôtel-de-Ville.

THE SECOND REPUBLIC

The members of this provisional government were divided socially, personally, and politically. A majority of moderates, led by the aristocratic poet and historian Alphonse-Marie-Louis de Prat de Lamartine, saw their role as essentially one of preserving order and administrative continuity until the election of a constituent assembly. Nevertheless, the sense of expectancy in Paris forced them to recognize manhood suffrage—it being widely assumed that women lacked the intellectual capacity to make political judgements; the "right to work"; democratization of the National Guard; and freedom of the press and of assembly.

Great enthusiasm was expressed in the host of new newspapers, political clubs, and workers' associations for what appeared to be the dawning of a new era. The establishment of the Luxembourg Commission—composed of representatives of government, employers, and workers—to inquire into

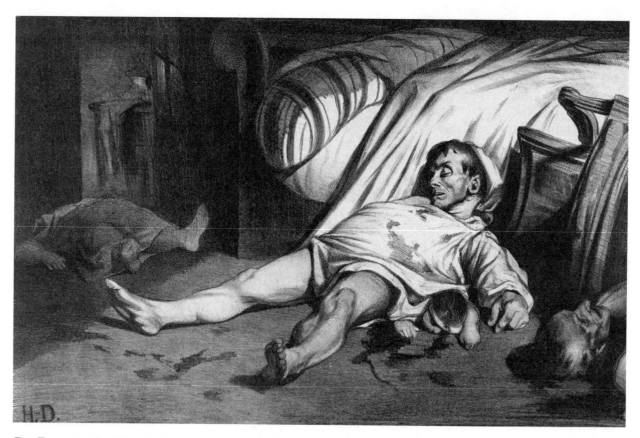

Rue Transnonain, 15 April 1834. A Murdered Family. Daumier's 1834 lithograph appeared in the publication *L' Association mensuelle,* depicting a poor family wantonly slain by Louis-Philippe's soldiers. The king attempted to have all copies of the publication confiscated. ERICH LESSING/ART RESOURCE, NY

working conditions reinforced the belief that major changes were imminent. "National Workshops" were established in Paris and most other urban centers to provide immediate relief for the unemployed. The creation of producers' cooperatives to replace capitalist exploitation was eagerly anticipated. Mass demonstrations were organized to maintain pressure on the government. In practice the main concern of ministers was to reestablish business confidence, which required the preservation of public order and avoidance of "socialistic" measures. The introduction of a 45 percent supplement to the land tax to pay for the National Workshops largely destroyed support for the new regime among the rural population.

For conservatives the prospect of a "universal" vote on Easter Day 1848 was a nightmare, the likely first step toward a thoroughgoing social revolution. In practice, however, in the absence of organized parties, the selection of candidates, especially in rural constituencies, remained dependent

on the activities of politically experienced notables. Faced with a plethora of candidates, many voters turned to those whose wealth, education, or functions gave them status, including the clergy. Republicans had little time to counter this. A large majority of the successful candidates were to be former monarchists, even if, reflecting a continuing crisis of confidence, they adopted the republican label. Indeed when they met as a Constituent Assembly they elected an executive commission made up of the more moderate members of the previous provisional government.

The election results inevitably caused great dissatisfaction among radicals. A major demonstration in Paris on 15 May culminated in the chaotic invasion of the Assembly's meeting place and a call for the establishment of a committee of public safety and the levying of a wealth tax to finance the creation of producers' cooperatives. On 22 June the closure of the National Workshops was announced. The next day, barricades again went up throughout the poor eastern *quartiers* of the city. A substantial number of men and women (perhaps twenty to thirty thousand) were willing to risk their lives in the struggle for "justice." The forces of "order" included National Guards from the wealthier western *quartiers,* but about one-fifth of them were workers. Moreover, the mobile guards recruited from young, unemployed workers, together with the regular army, became in the eyes of the propertied classes the "saviors of civilization." The war minister General Jean-Baptiste Cavaignac concentrated his forces and smashed the insurrection in three days of vicious street fighting. Contemporaries saw this conflict as one between *bourgeois* and *peuple,* as a form of class struggle. Subsequently, political activity was severely restricted. The new constitution promulgated on 4 November 1848 provided for the election of a president with strong executive authority. The successful candidate on 10 December was Louis-Napoleon Bonaparte, with 74 percent of the vote, compared with Cavaignac's 19 percent. The emperor's nephew was able to take advantage of the messianic cult of the great leader created by the outpouring of books, pamphlets, lithographs, and objects of devotion over the previous thirty years.

Bonaparte's appointment of a ministry made up mainly of figures associated with the Orléanist monarchy seemed to confirm his commitment to the so-called party of order. Its members aware of their growing political isolation, the Constituent Assembly voted its own dissolution on 29 January. In the elections that followed on 13 May a clear right-left division emerged between a reactionary conservatism and a radical republicanism with the center, the moderate republicans, squeezed in between. The *démocrate-socialiste* or *Montagnard* movement, which might be seen as the first attempt to create a modern national party, incorporated both democrats and socialists determined to defend the republic and work for social reform. In May some two hundred *Montagnards* were elected, and although this compared badly with the five hundred conservatives the latter were alarmed by such an unexpected radical success. In spite of constant repression, in some areas *démocrate-socialiste* organization and propaganda in the form of newspapers, pamphlets, almanacs, engravings, and songs, managed to survive. It promised that the establishment of a *République démocra-*

tique et sociale would secure cheap credit to satisfy peasant land hunger, free and secular education, a guaranteed right to work, and state support for the establishment of producer and consumer cooperatives. These measures were to be financed by taxation of the "rich" and nationalization of the railways, canals, mines, and insurance companies.

In response, a new electoral law introduced stricter residential qualifications, removing around one-third of the poorest voters from the rolls, and ever more intense action was directed at left-wing newspapers and organizations, driving many of them underground. In an effort to safeguard the future, another law on primary education (*loi Falloux*) in 1850 reinforced the religious and socially conservative message delivered in the schools. As the 1852 legislative and presidential elections came closer, rumors of socialist plots abounded. Although the constitution debarred him from a second term of office, Bonaparte was determined not to hand over power with what he believed to be his historical mission, the regeneration of France, unachieved.

As head of the executive branch, Bonaparte was well placed to mount a coup d'état on 2 December 1851. Although directed against both the monarchist groups represented in the National Assembly and the radical republicans, the fact that only the latter offered resistance gave it an essentially antirepublican character. In Paris and other cities only very limited conflict occurred, thanks to preventative arrests and obvious military preparedness. Few workers were willing to defend the rights of monarchist deputies against a president who promised to restore "universal" suffrage. However, in some nine hundred communities, mainly in the southeast, around one hundred thousand men were mobilized by clandestine secret societies that had begun to spring up, particularly in the south, in 1850 and 1851, organizations to defend the *République démocratique et sociale.* The columns of troops that moved into the countryside easily crushed these movements. A settling of accounts with the Left followed, with more than twenty-six thousand arrests. Conservatives gave thanks to God for their deliverance. On 20 December a plebiscite was held to sanction the extension of the prince-president's authority. The result was predictable: 7,500,000 voted "yes," 640,000 "no," and

1,500,000 abstained, with opposition concentrated in the major cities. For the second time, supported by the army, a Bonaparte had destroyed a republic. Following another carefully orchestrated campaign, a second plebiscite (on 21–22 November 1852) approved the reestablishment of the hereditary empire.

THE SECOND EMPIRE

The intentions of the new emperor, Napoleon III (r. 1852–1871) were clear: to establish a strong and stable executive power capable of promoting economic and social modernization. The tradition of ministerial responsibility to parliament gradually built up since 1814 was effectively annulled, and the *Corps législatif* rendered largely quiescent. In the first decade political repression and close cooperation with reactionary and clerical forces characterized the regime. Elections were carefully managed. The new regime remained inescapably dependent on the aristocratic and *grands bourgeois* servants of previous governments. The majority of ministers were conservative former Orléanists. There were remarkably few genuine Bonapartists, despite the fact that Napoleon III appears to have assumed that the notables would rally to his government.

Political stability, accompanied by economic prosperity, certainly enhanced the regime's status. Substantial investment in the transport infrastructure and in the construction of a "modern" capital city provided a major stimulus to the economy. Much of the rural population on whose electoral support he depended saw Napoleon as "their emperor" offering protection both against a restoration of the *ancien régime* and revolutionary chaos. The regime brought benefits in the shape of railways and roads, and offered subsidies for the construction of churches and schools. Many workers were also attracted by the Napoleonic legend and the emperor's show of sympathy for the poor. Thus the Second Empire enjoyed a broader consensus of support than had its predecessors. Election results suggest that this reached its peak in 1857. Subsequently, with order apparently restored, notables would press for the reestablishment of a parliamentary system. The growing number of critics therefore ranged from those who had initially welcomed the coup but no longer saw any need for authoritarian rule, to republicans, the victims of the coup who entirely rejected the empire.

The context for political activity was to change. Anxious to create a constitutional regime less dependent on his own survival, by a decree of 24 November 1860 the emperor conceded to the *Corps législatif* the right to discuss the address from the throne at the beginning of each parliamentary session, and further agreed to nominate ministers without portfolio to explain and defend government policy. Debates could now be reproduced in full in the press. In December 1861 Napoleon responded to anxiety about the growth of the national debt and Georges-Eugène Haussmann's unorthodox arrangements for financing the reconstruction of Paris by allowing increased parliamentary control over the budget. Throughout the decade too, although repressive legislation remained intact, much greater tolerance was displayed toward the press.

Initially, the policy of liberalization represented confidence in the stability of the regime. However, a series of measures—including an amnesty for republicans; alliance with Piedmont against Austria and in support of a "Europe of the nationalities"; a loosening of the alliance between church and state; the 1860 commercial treaty with Britain designed to force the pace of modernization; the enhanced role of parliament; and the legalization of strikes—had complex and often contradictory effects. The realization that the regime was unlikely to resort to brute force against its opponents encouraged criticism. Among the most vocal were clericals anxious about the threat posed by Italian nationalism to the papacy's temporal power and political liberals concerned about the economic dislocation that might result from "free trade." They demanded further liberalization to facilitate greater parliamentary control over government policy and to restore the influence of established social elites.

The vitality of this opposition made it clear that the regime had failed to engineer a national reconciliation. However, unlike his predecessors, Napoleon III was prepared to adapt. Further liberalization thus represented concessions to the growing pressure clearly evident in the gradual collapse of the system of official candidature; the number of opposition candidates increased, as did their success. The May 1863 elections thus saw the reconstitution of an extremely heterogeneous, but increasingly effective parliamentary opposition, which included legitimists determined to defend the interests of the church, irreconcilable Orléanist notables, and independent liberals and republicans. Although only thirty-two outright opponents were successful they combined with some of the regime's more liberal adherents to constitute a Third Party. Further concessions were made: most notably the liberties accorded in 1868 to public meetings and the press. Again, the political context was changed decisively. There was a spectacular revival of newspapers and political meetings. The circulation of Parisian newspapers, which had been around fifty thousand in 1830, rose to more than seven hundred thousand in 1869, reflecting rising literacy and falling production and distribution costs as well as the renewal of interest in politics. Moreover the campaign was marked by the emergence of Léon-Michel Gambetta as the leading figure on the left. His espousal of a program that included vague promises of social reform, was accompanied by large antiregime demonstrations in Paris. The outcome of the 1869 elections was a severe blow to the regime, with 4,438,000 votes cast for government candidates, 3,355,000 for opponents, and 2,291,000 abstentions.

Seventy-eight opposition deputies were elected, forty-nine of them liberals and twenty-nine republicans—essentially moderates determined to employ strictly legal forms of political action. Even the "radical" Gambetta was committed to "progress without revolution," afraid that, as in 1848, socialist agitation would frighten the mass of small property owners and provoke repression. In addition, however, at least ninety-eight erstwhile government supporters were liberals whose views differed little from those of opposition deputies. There was an immediate demand for a government responsible to the *Corps legislative,* closer parliamentary control over both ministers and the budget, and the formation of a government likely to enjoy both the confidence of the emperor and majority support in the Chamber. This culminated in the appointment on 2 January 1870 of a ministry headed by a former moderate republican, Émile Ollivier. Although liberals remained dissatisfied because of the emperor's retention of considerable personal power, most deputies were prepared to accept this as necessary for the preservation of order in a situation of growing political unrest.

The early measures of the new government reinforced this conservative support. They included the final abandonment of the system of official candidature; the dismissal of Haussmann, in order to satisfy orthodox financial interests, and of the secularist education minister Victor Duruy to pacify clericals; the announcement of an inquiry into customs legislation, which was seen as the prelude to a return to economic protectionism; and determined action against strikers in major industrial centers such as Le Creusot and republican demonstrators in Paris. Indeed for many liberals liberalization had gone far enough. There seemed to be no alternative to supporting the regime as the most effective guarantor of social order and Christian civilization, a point repeatedly made in official propaganda.

On 8 May 1870 a plebiscite was held. The electorate was asked to decide whether it "approves the liberal reforms introduced since 1860." The results were an overwhelming success for the regime: 7,350,000 voters registered their approval, 1,538,000 voted "no," and a further 1,900,000 abstained. To one senior official it represented "a new baptism of the Napoleonic dynasty." Although opposition remained strong in the cities, it generally appeared to be waning.

The empire's sudden collapse resulted from the incompetent management of foreign affairs. The Prussian triumph over Austria in 1866 had altered the European balance of power, and ever since many commentators had believed in the inevitability of war. When it came in 1870 however it was due to errors by a government under pressure from a hysterical right-wing reaction to the news of a Hohenzollern candidature for the Spanish throne. Although both the emperor and Ollivier might have accepted a simple withdrawal of this candidature, conservative deputies demanded guarantees, which—in the infamous Ems telegram—the Prussian minister-president Otto von Bismarck refused in deliberately insulting terms. Although aware that the military preparations were seriously defective, Napoleon succumbed to pressure from the empress and other authoritarian Bonapartists, hoping that victory would further consolidate the regime.

Even more republicans rallied to the national cause. The first defeats brought panic however. The emperor's response was to replace the Ollivier

The Execution of Emperor Maximilian of Mexico, 19 June 1867. Painting by Edouard Manet, 1867. The Austrian archduke Ferdinand Maximilian was installed as emperor of Mexico in 1864 by an agreement between Napoleon III and conservatives in Mexico. The idea was a dismal failure; after three years of opposition from Mexicans loyal to former president Benito Juárez, Maximilan was captured and executed. ERICH LESSING/ART RESOURCE, NY

government with one made up of authoritarian Bonapartists. This could not alter the fact that the army was better prepared for dealing with internal security problems than for waging a major European war. Its mobilization had been chaotic. It lacked adequate trained reserves and its maneuvers in the field suffered from a lack of effective coordination. The capitulation at Sedan of an army led by the emperor represented governmental failure on a scale sufficient to destroy the regime's legitimacy. On 4 September crowds invaded the Palais Bourbon and drove out the imperial *Corps législatif.* In an uncertain political situation the troops and police responsible for the assembly's security were unwilling to use their weapons. A group of Parisian deputies proclaimed the republic, and established a provisional government of national defense. In the provinces there appeared to be no immediate alternative to acceptance of the Parisian initiative.

THE THIRD REPUBLIC

Once the republic had been proclaimed, its survival seemed to depend on a successful outcome to the war. The shortages of trained troops and equipment made this unlikely. Moreover, conservatives questioned the wisdom of fighting a lost war particularly because they feared that this would lead to political radicalization, just as in 1792. In this desperate situation, with Paris under siege, the government was obliged to request an armistice and in February 1871 held elections essentially on the issue of whether or not to continue the war. The discrediting of both the Bonapartist and republican advocates of war resulted in a massive majority, especially in rural areas, for the mainly monarchist notables who stood as peace candidates. However, in the capital, besieged by the Prussians from 19 September 1870 to 28 January 1871, many of the men who had been incorporated into a National Guard to defend the city felt betrayed by the government's acceptance of a "humiliating" peace.

There was also concern that the newly elected National Assembly, meeting in Bordeaux on 12 February, would destroy the republic and all hope of democratic and social reform. Certainly the nomination of a government made up of the most moderate republicans and led by Louis-Adolphe Thiers did little to calm these fears. Indeed, the crisis deepened because of the government's decision to end payment of National Guards and require the immediate payment of rents and commercial debts; measures that threatened widespread destitution. Nevertheless the revolt, which began on 18 March, was largely unpremeditated. Initially it involved popular resistance to an incompetent effort to seize National Guard cannon parked on the heights of Montmartre. Thiers ordered a withdrawal to Versailles to await reinforcements. The resulting power vacuum undoubtedly stimulated the wider insurrection he had feared.

The Commune Two rival political authorities came into existence, with the central committee of the federation of National Guard battalions in the city and the national government at Versailles each controlling its own armed force. On 26 March, following the failure of confused negotiations, insurrection turned into revolution with the election in Paris of the Commune. Fighting between the two bodies began on 2 April. Enjoying little provincial support and isolated by a military *cordon sanitaire*, the Parisian movement was doomed. It was suppressed with extreme brutality by the troops of the imperial army, largely freed from German prison camps for the purpose. In fierce street fighting the army lost four hundred

men. Estimates of insurgent casualties vary between ten and thirty thousand (twenty-five thousand seems to be the most accurate figure); most of them were summarily executed after surrendering. Subsequently more than thirty-eight thousand others were arrested. For moderate republican ministers, monarchist deputies, and generals this was another opportunity to settle accounts with those they accused of plotting to destroy "civilized society." On the other side of the political divide the Commune created a socialist myth of revolutionary heroism. More significantly, however, this was to be the last of the great nineteenth-century revolutions.

New regime The precise character of the new regime remained to be settled. The elections held in February 1871 had returned an assembly, a majority of whose members (about 400 of 645) favored the establishment of some kind of monarchy. In May 1873 Thiers, whose government had crushed the Commune and secured the withdrawal of German occupying forces through payment of a five billion franc indemnity, as well as beginning to reorganize the army, was replaced by more committed Royalists, with the marshal Marie-Edme-Patrice-Maurice de MacMahon as president and the duc Jacques-Victor-Albert de Broglie as prime minister.

The obvious candidate for the throne, Charles X's grandson, Henri-Charles-Ferdinand-Marie Dieudonné d'Artois, the comte de Chambord, in exile in Austria, continued to insist on the replacement of the tricolor, "the emblem of revolution" by the white flag and fleur-de-lis of the old monarchy. His refusal to compromise was supported in the National Assembly by around one hundred legitimist deputies, but opposed by the two hundred Orléanists, uncomfortable with legitimist devotion to throne and altar. Monarchist leaders decided to wait until the death of the childless Chambord, when the succession would legitimately pass to the House of Orléans, securing the natural fusion of the warring monarchist groups. In the meantime, with the assistance of the church, they were determined to establish a regime devoted to reestablishing moral order. Increasingly, it was the defense of religion that supplied a sense of purpose to conservatives during these early years of the Third Republic.

In contrast, for many of the 150 republicans elected in 1871, together with their fundamental determination to defend the republic, anticlericalism provided a basic sense of unity. Republican spokesmen made every effort to dissociate the republic from revolution, insisting that it was the monarchists who threatened the status quo. These policies were to enjoy growing electoral success. By-elections meant that the composition of the Assembly changed quite rapidly. As early as July 1871, a further one hundred republicans were elected, indicating how peculiar the circumstances of the February elections had been. By January 1875 a conservative Catholic, Henri-Alexandre Wallon, was able to obtain sufficient support for a constitutional amendment in favor of the definitive establishment of the republic. The constitution of that year sought to avoid the mistake of 1848 by ensuring that the president was elected by parliament and denied the authority accorded by a popular vote. In the aftermath of the Commune the president was certainly granted substantial executive power, but in practice the Chamber of Deputies, increasingly dominated by republicans, would insist on its own predominance. The key role in government would be assumed by the *président du conseil* (prime minister) dependent on parliament. The 1876 general elections brought 340 republicans, elected especially in the east and southeast, into the Chamber of Deputies, alongside 155 monarchists, mainly from rural areas of the west and northwest. Around half of these were Bonapartists, elected mainly in the southwest and representing a revival that would end with the futile death of the prince imperial Eugene Bonaparte (1856–1879) in 1879. In these circumstances a final showdown between the increasingly confident republican deputies and the monarchist president of the republic could be postponed no longer. In May 1877, following a vote of no confidence, MacMahon dissolved the Chamber. The following October, and in spite of a return to a Bonapartist system of administrative pressure, the electorate returned 321 republican and only 208 monarchist deputies. MacMahon was obliged to invite the moderate republican Armand Dufaure to form a government. Cohabitation was to fail, however, and when in January 1879 the delegates of the communes elected a republican majority in the senate, MacMahon finally accepted that his position was untenable.

This triumphant republican victory cannot be explained in simple sociological terms. Ideological divisions cut across those of class. Certainly, it represented a defeat for a traditional social elite made up primarily of noble and non-noble landowners, but which had also come to include many wealthy business and professional men. Nevertheless a substantial portion of the economic elite had come to favor a conservative republic. So too had the much larger numbers of business and professional men with local standing and influence, in relatively close touch with a mass electorate that had attained a significant level of political consciousness and that had increasingly come to believe that its material and social aspirations would best be served by a republic.

Conservative republican rule The resignation of MacMahon was followed by a long period of conservative republican rule, lasting until 1898. Rapidly shifting parliamentary alliances and repeated ministerial crises should not be allowed to obscure this basic reality. In the absence of a modern party organization, unity and a sense of purpose were conferred on moderate republicans by informal networks, electoral committees, and newspapers that associated the republic with indefinite progress toward liberty and material well-being. At the outset, a program designed to firmly establish a liberal-democratic political system was introduced, representing, whatever its shortcomings, a major affirmation of individual liberty. Restrictions on the press and public meetings and on the right to create associations, including trade unions, were eased (laws of 29 January, 30 June 1881, and 28 March 1884 respectively) and less repressive policies adopted toward strikes. For Jules Ferry the law of 28 March 1882 establishing free and obligatory primary education and removing religious instruction from the curriculum provided the means of securing the republic against its clerical and monarchist enemies. Additional legislation in 1886 provided for the gradual replacement of clerics by lay personnel in all public schools. Furthermore, instruction in civic responsibility, patriotism, and respect for the law, property, and the established social order was intended to reduce the revolutionary sentiment. In response to the onset of economic depression in the late 1870s, Charles-Louis Freycinet

A May Day march in the main square of Fourmies, France, 1891. Engraving from *Le Monde Illustré,* 9 May 1891. Soldiers fired on the striking workers, resulting in nine dead, including two children. A Catholic priest seeks to intervene. PRIVATE COLLECTION/ BRIDGEMAN ART LIBRARY/ARCHIVES CHARMET

introduced a major program to construct branch railway lines and local roads. Criticized for its cost, it proved very attractive to the host of rural and small town voters. The reintroduction of protective customs tariffs by Félix-Jules Méline between 1881 and 1892 similarly consolidated support for a republic that promised progress and well-being.

Criticism grew nevertheless. Many middle-class and conservative republicans, having ousted the traditional élites, now sought to defend their own privileged positions. Younger men such as Raymond Poincaré, Jean-Louis Barthou, and Théophile Delcassé, with fewer emotional attachments to the past, were more concerned about the rise of socialism than with continuing the struggle against the clericals. The rash of anarchist attacks in the

early 1890s, which included the assassination of President Sadi Carnot, encouraged this outlook. In the event, and in spite of the electoral success of these moderate "Opportunists" in 1893, the hoped-for realignment was not to occur. The 1898 elections suggested that an alliance with the right was unacceptable to too many voters. Moreover, suspicion of the extreme right was intensified by the Dreyfus affair, and in February 1899 by Paul Déroulède's farcical attempt to persuade soldiers to participate in a coup, as well as by the hostile crowd that in June insulted the president of the republic, Émile-François Loubet, at the Auteuil races. Together with the evident moderation of many so-called Radicals, these developments promoted instead a realignment toward the center-left and in defense of the republic, which resulted in the formation of the *bloc des gauches* for the 1902 elections including conservative republicans such as Poincaré and René Waldeck-Rousseau, together with Radicals and even reformist socialists such as Alexandre Millerand.

The absence of disciplined parties meant that the deputy's first loyalty was to his constituents. His primary responsibility was to obtain a fair share of new roads, schools, and jobs. The boundaries between "parties" were always fluid, and ministerial instability was the inevitable result. The Radical Party had thus remained a *parti des cadres* based on informal groupings of professional politicians and local notables who, rather than a mass party, created autonomous power bases by dispensing patronage. Its deputies had posed as the protagonists of the *petits* (the ordinary folk) against the *gros* (the wealthy classes). They had condemned the *opportunistes* for their cautious religious policies and for their close links with big business. Additionally, during periods of crisis such as that precipitated by the neo-Bonapartism of General Georges Ernest Jean-Marie Boulanger, who seemed on the verge of overthrowing the republic in 1889, or when, following the first ballot in the 1895 elections, a victory for clerical conservatives seemed possible, Radicals were prepared to cooperate with more conservative republicans and to respect *discipline républicaine*. In similar circumstances they participated in the Waldeck-Rousseau government of *défense républicaine* in June 1899. Their role was thus essentially a secondary, supportive one, except when Léon-Victor-Auguste Bourgeois was able to form a government in October 1895, only to lose parliamentary support the following April as a result of his rather modest income tax proposals.

However, these limited successes did suggest that an effort to improve Radical organization might pay a handsome political dividend. As a result, something akin to a modern party electoral organization was created and contributed to the election of 233 Radical deputies in 1902, a victory that inaugurated the great period of Radical administration. This survived until 1909 with governments led successively by Émile Combes, Ferdinand Sarrien, and Georges Clemenceau. It saw the first timid efforts to introduce old-age pensions, but was above all characterized by a further assault on the church, in large part in response to the Dreyfus affair and the renewed threat to the republic from the extreme right.

The Dreyfus affair had been caused by the court-martial of a Jewish staff officer for spying. It had become a cause célèbre in 1898 when the great novelist Émile Zola challenged the verdict in an open letter to the president of the republic. The evidence against Alfred Dreyfus was dubious, but for many conservatives upholding it came to be synonymous with defending the honor of the army. Regarding themselves as the only true patriots, they were hostile toward all those "bad" French who questioned their chauvinism, and in particular socialists, trade unionists, Jews, and Radicals such as Joseph-Marie-Auguste Caillaux, who presented horrifying proposals for an income tax to finance social reform. The intellectual leaders of the extreme right, Paul Déroulède, Maurice Barrès, and especially Charles Maurras, rejected the egalitarian values of the republic in favor of a mystical Catholicism and a glorification of violence and war. This new right created a more potent political force than conservatism had known since the 1870s, one that was fundamentally antidemocratic and antiparliamentarian in its demands for a strong executive power to overcome political and social "factionalism."

Separation of church and state The response on the left was once again to denounce clericalism as the enemy, and to attack its roots, the Catholic schools, whose particularistic teaching was seen as a threat to national unity and republican institutions. Thus a series of measures was introduced, culminating in July 1904 in the suppression of the Catholic teaching orders and the closure of their schools, and in December 1905 in the disestablishment of the church. Official inventories of church property the next year stimulated an intense but short-lived resistance. Once the Radicals had achieved their "final" victory over the *ancien régime,* however, their main preoccupation became the growth of unrest both among industrial workers and peasants in wine-producing areas in the south, who between 1905 and 1907 protested about the collapse in prices induced by overproduction. Clemenceau, who as minister of the interior had already inaugurated a repressive response, became *président du conseil* in 1906. His coercive policy represented a fundamental commitment to the ethos and institutions of a bourgeois property-owning society and to social order.

How real was this social threat that so exercised both Radicals and more obvious conservatives? The socialists had taken some time to recover from the repression that had followed the Paris Commune. They remained ambivalent about a republic that promised social reform and then deployed troops against strikers. Nevertheless the election of a socialist deputy in Marseilles in 1881 had been followed by steady growth in support and in 1914 socialist candidates would obtain 1,413,000 votes. Conservative fears were exaggerated nonetheless. Bitter sectarian squabbling constantly weakened the socialist movement. In April 1905, the creation of a unified socialist party—the *Parti socialiste unifié* known as the SFIO after its idealistic subtitle *Section française de l'Internationale ouvrière* (French section of the Workers' International), could not resolve the many ideological and tactical differences within the movement.

Even more decisive in the realignment of internal politics than the supposed rise of socialism was the impact of deteriorating relationships with an increasingly assertive imperial Germany. International affairs took pride of place among politicians' concerns, and resulted in the nomination of the conservative republican Poincaré as head of government in January 1912 and to the presidency in May. His efforts to form a "national" government foundered on Radical hostility to the proposed presence in government of conservatives like Méline or of Catholic spokesmen. Subject to the baneful influence of intensely Germanophobic foreign ministry officials, and with support from the Right, Poincaré nevertheless continued to prepare for a war he believed to be inevitable. Abroad, this involved efforts to reinforce links with Britain and Russia, and at home measures designed to increase both the status and strength of the army and to develop a greater sense of national unity. The colonial empire, acquired as a result of the ruthless expansionism favored by an alliance of military, commercial, and missionary interests, had also become a token of the nation's great-power status as well as its civilizing mission. In case of war, its myriad peoples would compensate for the shortage of military manpower in the *metropole*. The conservative press and mass circulation dailies such as *Le petit Parisien* contributed to the creation of an increasingly chauvinistic mood. The socialists and many Radicals continued to resist this nationalistic xenophobia, which threatened to restore the right to power, and made up the minority of 204 deputies who in August 1913 opposed the extension of military service from two to three years. However, the 358 deputies who made up the majority were determined that France should make an effort to match German military strength.

The April–May 1914 elections were fought on this conscription issue as well as the question of how to finance the growing military budget. The electoral victory of the left with 342 successful candidates, including 102 socialists, many of whom had stressed the need to mobilize international working-class opposition to an imperialist war, was evidence of the strength of hostility to extended military service. In the last resort however the new government headed by the independent socialist René Viviani, but dominated by Radicals, would prove unwilling to risk weakening the army by repealing the three-year law. Significantly, during the international crisis in July 1914, on an official visit to Russia, President Poincaré did little to encourage caution. His essential concern was to ensure united action against Germany. General mobilization was ordered on 1 August, and Germany declared war two days later. The population seems to have reacted more from a sense of resigned acceptance rather than with any great enthusiasm. The critics of the republican regime both to the right and left rallied to the cause of defending the French Republic against an autocratic and aggressive German Empire. A genuine *union sacrée* developed, a truce from which the various political and social groups would seek to gain the maximum possible advantage.

See also **Algeria; Alsace-Lorraine; Boulanger Affair; Boulangism; Caribbean; Colonialism; Colonies; Counterrevolution; Dreyfus Affair; Eiffel Tower; Fashoda Affair; Fin de Siècle; Franco-Austrian War; Franco-Prussian War; French Revolution; French Revolutionary Wars and Napoleonic Wars; Haiti; Imperialism; Indochina; Napoleon; Napoleonic Empire; Paris; Revolutions of 1830; Revolutions of 1848; Separation of Church and State (France, 1905).**

BIBLIOGRAPHY

Agulhon, Maurice. *The Republican Experiment, 1848–1851.* Translated by Janet Lloyd. New York, 1983.

Crook, Malcolm, ed. *Revolutionary France: 1788–1880.* Oxford, U.K., 2002.

Englund, Steven. *Napoleon: A Political Life.* New York, 2004.

Forrest, Alan I. *Soldiers of the French Revolution*. Durham, N.C., 1990.

Hunt, Lynn A. *Politics, Culture, and Class in the French Revolution*. Berkeley, Calif., 1984.

Jones, Peter M. *The Peasantry in the French Revolution*. Cambridge, U.K., 1988.

Lequin, Yves, ed. *Mosaique France: Histoire des étrangers et de l'immigration*. Paris, 1988.

Margadant, Ted W. *French Peasants in Revolt: The Insurrection of 1851*. Princeton, N.J., 1979.

McMillan, James F. *Napoleon III*. New York, 1991.

McPhee, Peter. *Social History of France, 1780–1880*. New York, 1992.

———. *The French Revolution, 1789–1799*. Oxford, U.K., 2002.

Merriman, John M. *The Agony of the Republic: The Repression of the Left in Revolutionary France, 1848–51*. New Haven, Conn., 1978.

Merriman, John M., ed. *1830 in France*. New York, 1975.

Perrot, Michelle. *Workers on Strike: France, 1871–1890*. Translated from the French by Chris Turner; with the assistance of Erica Carter and Claire Laudet. New York, 1987.

Pilbeam, Pamela. *The Constitutional Monarchy in France, 1814–48*. Harlow, U.K., 1999.

Pinkney, David H. *The French Revolution of 1830*. Princeton, N.J., 1972.

Price, Roger. *The French Second Republic: A Social History*. Ithaca, N.Y., 1972.

———. *The French Second Empire: An Anatomy of Political Power*. Cambridge, U.K., 2001.

Sowerwine, Charles. *France since 1870: Culture, Politics, and Society*. New York, 2001.

Tackett, Timothy. *Religion, Revolution, and Regional Culture in Eighteenth-Century France: The Ecclesiastical Oath of 1791*. Princeton, N.J., 1986.

Tombs, Robert. *France, 1814–1914*. Harlow, U.K., 1996.

———. *The Paris Commune, 1871*. Harlow, U.K., 1999.

Weber, Eugen. *France, fin de siècle*. Cambridge, Mass., 1986.

JOHN MERRIMAN, ROGER PRICE

FRANCIS I

FRANCIS I (1768–1835), last Holy Roman Emperor as Francis II (1792–1806) and first emperor of Austria (1804–1835).

Francis I was born 12 February 1768 in Florence and died 2 March 1835 in Vienna. As his dual title suggests, Francis was a transitional figure from the eighteenth century to the nineteenth century. Unfortunately for him and his Austrian Empire, he himself failed to keep up with that transition.

Francis was the son of Leopold I, grand duke of Tuscany (1765–1790), and the nephew of Holy Roman Emperor Joseph II (r. 1765–1790). He was brought to Vienna in 1784 and given the education of an enlightened absolutist. Following Joseph II's premature death in 1790, Francis's father became Emperor Leopold II; his death on 1 March 1792 resulted in Francis's succession to the Habsburg patrimony, and coronation as Emperor Francis II on 14 July 1792.

The declaration of war by revolutionary France on Austria and Prussia on 20 April 1792 had already unleashed the forces of revolution and war that were to consume, among others, Francis's aunt, Marie-Antoinette, and then most of the European *ancien régime*. Defeat of Austria in the First Coalition War (1792–1797) and the Second Coalition War (1799–1801) resulted in the humiliating Treaty of Lunéville of 1801 and, eventually, the reorganization of the Holy Roman Empire in 1803. After further defeat in the Third Coalition War (1805) and the creation of the Confederation of the Rhine in July 1806, Francis abdicated as Holy Roman Emperor on 6 August 1806, declaring the empire dissolved. He had, however, already declared himself first "hereditary Emperor of Austria" on 11 August 1804, in response to Napoleon's becoming emperor of the French earlier that year. Hence Emperor Francis II became Emperor Francis I.

Francis met the minor threat of revolution in Austria with the brutal suppression of domestic opposition, as in the execution of the "Austrian Jacobins" in 1794. The traumatic military losses to the French, however, compelled him to embrace in 1806 the "nationalist" reform program of Count Johann Philipp Stadion-Warthausen. The military was modernized by Francis's brother, Charles (1771–1847). Reform was cut short, however, by the premature declaration of war in February 1809. Coordinated with a rebellion against Bavarian rule in Tyrol, the new war led to even more disaster. Charles handed Napoleon his first defeat in battle at Aspern-Essling, but the war was lost and the Treaty of Schönbrunn of

14 October 1809 reduced Austria to a French satellite. Abandoning reform, Francis appointed Count Clemens Metternich as foreign minister in 1809. Initially Metternich followed a pro-French line, arranging the marriage of Francis's eldest daughter, Marie Louise, to Napoleon and having Austria participate in the invasion of Russia in 1812. Once the tide had turned, however, Metternich adeptly changed sides and returned Austria to the anti-French coalition, which finally conquered the French in 1814. Francis I thus ended the French wars as the victorious host of the Vienna Congress (1814–1815), the nine-month-long conference at which Europe was "restored."

Austria emerged from the French Wars territorially larger and more integrated; Metternich, promoted to state chancellor by Francis in 1821, was regarded as the doyen of diplomacy and the "coachman of Europe." Through the Holy Alliance of 1815 and a series of Congresses (Aix-la-Chapelle, 1818; Troppau, 1821; Laibach, 1821; and Verona, 1822), Metternich imposed his "system," and hence an apparent Austrian hegemony, over Continental European affairs. The appearance of Austrian power was illusory. Austria had been severely damaged economically and financially by decades of war, with a state bankruptcy in 1811, and its economic recovery after 1815 lagged behind that of other European states. Austria, therefore, could never really afford its new responsibilities in Metternich's system.

Francis I himself was so traumatized by the experience of "revolution" and its consequences that his response after 1815 was to stop all political change wherever possible. Hence Austria was involved in suppressing national and liberal movements in Italy, Germany (notably in the Carlsbad Decrees of 1819), and elsewhere, which earned it the reputation of being the chief oppressor of the European peoples. At home as well, Francis backed a policy that valued loyalty and obedience above all else. He even refused to act on cosmetic reform measures that Metternich himself proposed. Although not averse to economic change, as shown by his favorable attitude to entrepreneurs, including Jewish financiers such as the Rothschilds, Francis rigidly opposed all political change and persisted in his bureaucratic but highly inefficient and procrastinating, absolutist practice.

The relative peace and prosperity of the "Biedermeier" period after 1815 meant that Francis I, with his reputed love of middle-class domesticity, enjoyed a quite good relationship with most of his subjects up to his death in 1835. Yet he was hated by the liberal and nationalist intelligentsias of his empire and of Europe, and his reactionary approach is usually seen as being a major cause of Austria's problems at midcentury.

See also **Congress of Vienna; French Revolutionary Wars and Napoleonic Wars; Metternich, Clemens von; Napoleonic Empire; Prussia; Restoration.**

BIBLIOGRAPHY

Rumpler, Helmut, *Eine Chance für Mitteleuropa.* Vienna, 1997.

Sked, Alan. *The Decline and Fall of the Habsburg Empire, 1815–1918.* London and New York, 1989.

Tritsch, Walther. *Metternich und sein Monarch.* Darmstadt, 1952.

Wheatcroft, Andrew. *The Habsburgs: Embodying Empire.* Harmondsworth, U.K., 1995.

Ziegler, Walter. "Franz I. von Österreich (1806–1835)." In *Die Kaiser der Neuzeit, 1519–1918,* edited by Ziegler and Anton Schindling, 309–328. Munich, 1990.

STEVEN BELLER

FRANCIS FERDINAND (1863–1914), archduke of Austria.

Francis Ferdinand was born 18 December 1863 in Graz. His assassination in Sarajevo on 28 June 1914 led to World War I.

Francis Ferdinand received a strict, Catholic, and conservative upbringing and pursued a career in the military. He unexpectedly became heir apparent to the Habsburg Monarchy on the death of his cousin, Crown Prince Rudolf, in 1889. After a world trip in 1892 and 1893, Francis Ferdinand was laid low for several years by tuberculosis, from which he recovered only in 1898. In the same year he was made deputy in military affairs to his uncle, Emperor Francis Joseph I (r. 1848–1916).

Relations between the emperor and his heir apparent were never all that good, however, and they worsened exponentially over Francis Ferdinand's determination to marry Countess

Sophie Chotek. Chotek, though a noblewoman, was not regarded by Francis Joseph as of sufficiently high status to be an appropriate spouse for a future Austrian emperor. A compromise was reached whereby on 28 June 1900 Francis Ferdinand formally renounced the rights of any children from the prospective, morganatic marriage. On 1 July he married Chotek.

From 1906 Francis Ferdinand was allowed to play a role in the politics of the Monarchy. His advisors, grouped around his military chancery in the Belvedere Palace, and known collectively as the Belvedere Circle, achieved a level of influence over Habsburg policy. They usually only did so, however, once they had become the emperor's ministers, and this often meant opposing the wishes of their former patron. Max Vladimir Beck, for instance, became Austrian prime minister and achieved passage of the electoral reform of 1907. Yet his policies came to be opposed by Francis Ferdinand, and the heir apparent intrigued to arrange Beck's dismissal in 1908. Francis Ferdinand had allies within the regime, such as the chief of the general staff, Franz Conrad von Hötzendorf, but his attempts to increase his influence over policy were persistently resisted by Francis Joseph.

This may have been just as well. Francis Ferdinand was ideologically a radical conservative and shared the authoritarian sentiments of William II (emperor of Germany and king of Prussia; r. 1888–1918) and Tsar Nicholas II of Russia (r. 1894–1917). An archconservative Catholic, he held anti-Semitic views and combined contempt for the Magyars with a general dislike for liberalism. His plan for the Monarchy was to reduce Hungarian autonomy and counter Magyar power in Hungary by increasing the rights of the minority nationalities in the kingdom. This approach brought him the sympathy of many minority nationalists, who supported some form of federalism, or, in the South Slav case, trialism (the uniting of the South Slav provinces in the Austrian and Hungarian halves of the Monarchy, as well as Bosnia, in a new, third South Slav "kingdom" under the Habsburg monarch). Francis Ferdinand's reputed sympathy for trialism made him hated by many Serb nationalists, for trialism threatened the dream of an independent Greater Serbia. Ironically, Francis Ferdinand had little time for real trialism (at most he wanted to reorganize the South Slav lands to reduce Hungarian power), nor was he for federalism. Instead, he envisaged recentralizing power in Vienna and subordinating all of the Monarchy's peoples once more to the emperor's rule. His succession was looked on by trepidation by many in the German and Magyar middle classes and the liberal intelligentsia, and especially by Habsburg Jews.

He was seen, moreover, due to his military involvements and his links with Conrad von Hötzendorf as a militarist and warmonger. Public opinion was quite wrong in this. Francis Ferdinand was a believer in authoritarianism, but this also made him a supporter of peace between the Habsburg Monarchy, Germany, and Russia, as a guarantor of authoritarian conservatism. He was hence against an aggressive policy in the Balkans, and constantly counseled staying out of the Balkan Wars of 1912–1913. Nevertheless, as the representative of the Habsburg military, especially after his appointment as general inspector of the army in 1913, with his reputation as a warmonger and with his supposed support of anti-Serb trialism, Francis Ferdinand became a target for Bosnian Serb nationalist terrorists. On 28 June 1914, while on a trip to inspect the military maneuvers, he and his wife were gunned down in their car in Sarajevo by Gavrilo Princip. The assassination of the heir apparent was then used by Francis Joseph and his advisors as the excuse for launching a "preventive" war against Serbia, exactly what Francis Ferdinand had counseled against, that in days led to World War I and eventually the collapse of the Monarchy.

See also **Austria-Hungary; Francis Joseph; Nationalism.**

BIBLIOGRAPHY

Hoffmann, Robert. *Erzherzog Franz Ferdinand und der Fortschritt.* Vienna, 1994.

Kann, Robert A. *Erzherzog Franz Ferdinand Studien.* Vienna, 1976.

Okey, Robin. *The Habsburg Monarchy: From Enlightenment to Eclipse.* New York, 2001.

Weissensteiner, Friedrich. *Franz Ferdinand: Der verhinderte Herrscher.* Vienna, 1983.

STEVEN BELLER

FRANCIS JOSEPH (1830–1916), emperor of Austria (1848–1916) and king of Hungary (1867–1916).

Francis Joseph was born 18 August 1830 in Vienna and died 21 November 1916 in Vienna. Emperor of Austria from 2 December 1848 until his death in 1916, Francis Joseph was one of the longest-reigning monarchs of nineteenth-century Europe. His reign saw great changes in the Austrian Empire, including a profound change in the structure and character of that state, into the Dual Monarchy of Austria-Hungary in 1867. While he presided over large-scale modernization of his Monarchy's economy and society, and tolerated its political modernization, acting in his later decades as a quasi-constitutional monarch, Francis Joseph was unable to overcome the shortcomings of the Habsburg Monarchy in handling its ethnic, national diversity. One of these shortcomings was Francis Joseph's own refusal to cede real power over the Monarchy's foreign policy and military, or indeed over crucial aspects of domestic political life. His hold on power, even in his "constitutional" phase, means that an account of his career is inseparable from the political history of the Monarchy as a whole. Tellingly, his personal fate and that of his Monarchy came to be so inextricably tied together in the Austro-Hungarian public's mind that many predicted that his death would see the collapse of the Monarchy. Yet it was while he was still alive that Francis Joseph effectively signed Austria-Hungary's death warrant by declaring war on Serbia in 1914, hence starting World War I.

Francis Joseph's career falls into three main parts: the era of reaction and neo-absolutism; the large middle period of his reign, of constitutionalism and Austro-Hungarian dualism; and the final couple of decades marked by crises at home and abroad stoked by nationalism and imperialism (not primarily Austrian).

NEO-ABSOLUTISM

Francis Joseph was made emperor of Austria on 2 December 1848, after the forced abdication of his uncle Ferdinand I (r. 1835–1848), as a response by the Habsburg family and its advisors to the 1848 revolutions. Raised by his mother, Sophie of Bavaria (1805–1872), to be a champion of divine-right absolutism in the spirit of his grandfather, Francis I (last Holy Roman emperor as Francis II [1768–1806] and emperor of Austria [1804–1835]), and without being bound by promises to the revolutionaries as was his uncle, Ferdinand I, Francis Joseph was seen by the Habsburg family and its advisors as the person who could use his youthful vigor and willpower to restore Habsburg fortunes, but in a new, more dynamic way. Under the tutelage of his prime minister, Felix zu Schwarzenberg, Francis Joseph did achieve an apparent restitution of the Habsburg position, in reasserting control in Germany and Italy, as well as, eventually and with Russian help, crushing the Hungarian rebellion in 1849. In domestic politics, he initially went along with the constitutionalism introduced by the revolution, but soon (against Schwarzenberg's advice) reverted to the absolutism of his upbringing, abolishing the constitution of March 1849 (that he had himself decreed) and restoring his absolute rule by the Sylvester Patent of 31 December 1851.

Francis Joseph was determined to rule henceforth as a modern absolute monarch. His conservative religious faith led to a cession of power to the papacy in the Concordat of 1855, but, otherwise, the ensuing period of "neo-absolutism" saw widespread reform in education, administration, and the economy, intended to modernize Austria from above and hence enhance Habsburg power within international affairs. His marriage for love to the beautiful Elizabeth of Bavaria in 1854 was also symbolic of a youthful breaking with past convention.

The partial success of neo-absolutism in modernizing Austria was heavily outweighed by the catastrophic failures in military and foreign policy, for which Francis Joseph was, after the death of Schwarzenberg in April 1852, ultimately responsible. Austrian ambivalence in the Crimean War (1854–1856) left Austria isolated, and this led to defeat by France in the Franco-Austrian War of 1859. Francis Joseph made himself Austrian commander-in-chief in the decisive battle of Solferino and was hence directly responsible for this defeat. The resulting loss of Lombardy and of all confidence in Austria's shaky finances led to the collapse of neo-absolutism.

DUALIST CONSTITUTIONALISM

From 1860 Francis Joseph was forced to undertake a complete overhaul of the governing structures of his monarchy, which meant a return to a form of the constitutionalism that he had proudly abolished in 1851. At first a conservative-federalist structure (October Manifesto of 1860) was tried, then a liberal-centralist one (February Patent of 1861). Then the failed attempt to reassert hegemony in the Germanic Confederation led to the Austro-Prussian War of 1866, in which the Austrians suffered a resounding defeat at the battle of Königgrätz (Sadowa), with the result being their ejection from German affairs and the loss of Venetia to Italy (Prussia's ally). In the aftermath of this further disaster, Francis Joseph was forced to make peace with the Magyar leadership, led by Ferenc Deák, on their terms. The result was the *Ausgleich* (Compromise) of 1867, which effectively split the Austrian Empire into two states, the kingdom of Hungary and the rest, which came to be known as Cisleithania but continued to be informally known as Austria. Francis Joseph was to attempt to change the basis of at least the Austrian half of his monarchy in 1871, when the Fundamental Articles were proposed as a means to give the Czechs more autonomy. This was not successful, however, and it was thus the *Ausgleich*, and the two constitutional systems set up in Hungary and Austria in its wake, that remained the basis of what was known as the Dual Monarchy, or Austria-Hungary, until its end.

Despite the fact that he had struggled against becoming one, Francis Joseph proved quite an adept constitutional monarch, or at least quasi-constitutional monarch. (In both halves of his monarchy he retained large prerogatives, especially veto power, and military and foreign policy remained his prerogative alone.) As king of Hungary he was prepared to allow the Magyar liberal nationalists, led after 1875 by Kálmán Tisza, full rein, as long as they remained compliant with his foreign policy goals. In Austria as well he tolerated German Liberal hegemony in politics and their progressive agenda, despite much Slav opposition to this and his own personal distaste for many aspects of the Liberals' ideology and praxis, especially their anticlericalism. Partly from his own conviction, he went along with the rescinding of the Concordat in the wake of the declaration of papal infallibility in 1870. When, however, the

Emperor Francis Joseph I with his grandchildren (from left) Franz Carl, Hubert, and Elizabeth. ©AUSTRIAN ARCHIVES/CORBIS

German Liberal leadership challenged his prerogative over foreign policy by opposing the annexation, or at least occupation, of Bosnia-Herzegovina in 1878–1879, his response was to concentrate all his efforts on unseating them from power. He achieved this through the electoral success of Count Eduard von Taaffe, whose "Iron Ring" coalition of Slavs, conservatives, and federalists dominated Austrian politics in the 1880s, furthering a culturally conservative (but socially quite progressive) agenda and diminishing German hegemony within the state apparatus. At the same time, Francis Joseph fully approved of the Dual Alliance that Gyula Andrássy, his foreign minister, negotiated in 1879 with Otto von Bismarck, the chancellor of the German Empire.

NATIONALISM AND (GERMAN) IMPERIALISM

Francis Joseph's relative success in the 1880s did not last. The death of his only son, Crown Prince Rudolf, in the legendarily murky murder-suicide at Mayerling on 30 January 1889, was not only a major state crisis and a personal tragedy for the emperor, but also ushered in a period that saw the collapse of the political status quo in both halves of the Monarchy. The failure of the Bohemian Compromise of 1890 led to prolonged political turmoil and national conflict between Czechs and Germans, which saw the collapse of Taaffe's ministry and reached a crescendo in the near-revolutionary events surrounding German protests at the Badeni language ordinances of 1897. The assassination of his wife Empress Elizabeth, "Sisi," in 1898 added a personal dimension to a catalogue of political woes that were only partially resolved by the skills of the Austrian prime minister from 1900 to 1904, Ernst Körber. Meanwhile in Hungary, the build-up of nationalist pressures eventually erupted in 1903 in a major crisis over the status of German as the language of command in the joint Habsburg army, with the Magyars directly challenging one of Francis Joseph's most cherished prerogatives.

Once again, Francis Joseph responded with vehemence to a threat to his powers. In 1905 he threatened to expand the franchise to include the Magyar lower classes and the other nationalities of the kingdom, hence ending the political hegemony of the Magyar gentry ruling class, and he withdrew this threat only when the Magyar leadership surrendered. With his powers maintained, Francis Joseph reverted to his relatively acquiescent style as king of Hungary, especially once István Tisza became Hungary's de facto leader in 1910.

While Francis Joseph had used franchise reform as a threat in Hungary, he was instrumental in the introduction of actual universal suffrage in Austria in 1906. He appears to have thought that this was a way to reduce the power of the nationalist parties in the *Reichsrat* (Austrian parliament) and hence was prepared to pursue radical reform, and even be in effect an ally of the socialists, but all in order to achieve a more compliant assembly that would better fund his military and foreign policy goals. The new parliament proved, however, no more manageable than the old, and the various national conflicts continued unabated. Partly to distract from these internal woes, and to provide some focus of unity, Francis Joseph fully supported the plans of his foreign minister, Baron Alois Lexa von Aehrenthal, to practice a more aggressive foreign policy, culminating in the annexation of Bosnia-Herzegovina in October 1908. This proved in the short term an effective boost to Habsburg prestige, but was in the long term a disaster, riling South Slav

dissent in Serbia as well as within the Monarchy, where Magyar nationalist policies and the refusal of the Austrian emperor to intervene with the king of Hungary (both Francis Joseph) had severely alienated Serb and Croat opinion in both halves. Consciousness of this internal South Slav unrest, coupled with fear of a hostile and ever larger and more successful Serbia as a result of the First (1912–1913) and Second (1913) Balkan Wars, had led by 1914 to Austrian foreign policy, still overseen by Francis Joseph, being focused on stopping Serbia at all costs. The assassination of his nephew, the heir apparent Francis Ferdinand, in Sarajevo on 28 June 1914 thus led eventually to the declaration of war against Serbia on 28 July, despite the fact that Francis Joseph had never much liked his heir and despised him for his marriage to a mere noblewoman.

Having started World War I, Francis Joseph then lost any further control over events. The Austro-Hungarian military campaign was run not by the emperor but by Conrad von Hötzendorf, the chief of the general staff, and the poor performance of the Habsburg army had led by September 1916 to an Austro-German Joint High Command being instituted, with Austria-Hungary very much the junior partner to its overbearing German ally. The emperor appears to have realized the tragic course events were taking and made efforts at peace abroad and liberalization at home, but it was too little too late. He died on 21 November 1916 with his state already on the way to being subordinated to Hohenzollern Germany and eventual dismemberment.

See also **Adler, Victor; Alliance System; Aristocracy; Austria-Hungary; Deák, Ferenc; Lueger, Karl; Revolutions of 1848.**

BIBLIOGRAPHY

Beller, Steven. *Francis Joseph.* London and New York, 1996.

Corti, Egon C. *Vom Kind zum Kaiser.* Graz, Austria, 1950.

———. *Mensch und Herrscher.* Graz, Austria, 1952.

———. *Der alte Kaiser.* Written with Hans Sokol. Graz, Austria, 1955. Comprehensive three-volume biography.

Sked, Alan. *The Decline and Fall of the Habsburg Empire, 1815–1918.* London, 1989.

Steed, Henry Wickham. *The Habsburg Monarchy.* New York, 1969. Reprint of the 1914 2nd edition.

Steinitz, Eduard von, ed. *Erinnerungen an Franz Joseph I.* Berlin, 1931.

Redlich, Joseph. *Emperor Francis Joseph of Austria: A Biography.* New York, 1929.

STEVEN BELLER

FRANCO-AUSTRIAN WAR.

The Franco-Austrian War of 1859, which pitted France and the Kingdom of Sardinia-Piedmont against Austria, was not exactly a surprise. After the revolutions of 1848 the Austrian Empire had based its foreign policy on seeking a central position as Europe's mediator. First applied during the Crimean War (1853–1856), the new course left Russia nursing a sense of betrayal without securing Austria either gratitude or respect from England and France.

ORIGINS

Austria's Italian position had been ostensibly restored by the suppression of the revolutionary/nationalist movement in 1849 and 1850. Lombardy and Venetia had benefited since the 1840s from a state-driven industrial revolution designed to integrate their peoples into the empire. By 1855 Italy was providing a full quarter of Austria's tax revenues. Geographically and diplomatically, however, the provinces remained vulnerable.

An assertive Piedmont under Camillo Benso, Count Cavour, had been increasingly overt both in fostering anti-Habsburg sentiments throughout Italy and in soliciting French support for its position. Every artifice, from sending Piedmontese troops to fight alongside France in the Crimean War to procuring the Piedmontese king's fifteen-year-old daughter as a bride for the cousin of Napoleon III, the French emperor, foundered on Napoleon's unwillingness to be the first to break the Continent's peace. The Austrian emperor, Francis Joseph I (r. 1848–1916), was no less cautious. Not until Piedmont opened its borders to Lombardians allegedly fleeing the rigors of Habsburg conscription, and then replied to Vienna's protests by summoning its own reserves, did Francis Joseph order mobilization.

The Austrian army in the 1850s did not suffer from financial stringencies. A government that had no doubt of just how much its support rested on bayonets was by Metternichian standards unprecedentedly generous. Over two billion florins were devoted to military spending in the first decade of Francis Joseph's reign. How that money was spent was another story. Apart from the pensions, the sinecures, and the parallel appointments, procurement and administration remained swamps of embezzlement, bribery, and outright theft. Not until the eve of war did the army decide to replace its smoothbore muskets with up-to-date rifles.

The movement of reservists and reinforcements into Lombardy in the spring of 1859 highlighted everything wrong with Habsburg military administration. The single-track line connecting Vienna with Milan was incomplete when war broke out. No institutions existed to integrate the rest of the empire's still-developing rail network into mobilization plans that were themselves largely the product of improvisation. Nevertheless a hundred thousand men were on the Piedmontese frontier by early April, ready to implement Francis Joseph's initial strategy of a first-strike punitive expedition designed to crush Piedmont's pretensions by forcing demobilization before France could intervene effectively. Against Piedmont's unmotivated conscript army, badly trained and worse officered, the plan had promise. Instead the Austrian commanders hesitated for three weeks as French reinforcements poured into northern Italy by land and sea.

France, like Austria, aspired to a role as the fulcrum of Europe—a position that required an army able to break from a standing start and win. The French soldier, whether volunteer, long-term conscript, or hired substitute, was expected to be a go-anywhere, do-anything fighting man, a work tool in the hands of his officers, at the government's disposal for "policy wars" anywhere in Europe or the world. He benefited as well from what a later generation would call "combat multipliers." The French army was quick to introduce rifled small arms. The artillery adopted rifled cannon in the early 1850s. The infantry supplemented what was believed to be the French soldier's natural courage and daring with extensive training in skirmishing and marksmanship.

COURSE

The Austrians, by contrast, were preoccupied with finding shoes that fit, securing their next meal, and learning how to load their rifles. Once operations began they were chivied across eastern Piedmont in a fashion, with often contradictory and poorly executed orders rendered nearly aimless. Straggling and desertion in the ranks and confrontational arguments at command levels were the first consequences. In limited encounters at Montebello and Palestro, the Austrians suffered defeat at the hands not only of the French but of the long-despised Piedmontese as well. At Magenta on 4 June, they stood on the defensive, to be outmaneuvered and outfought by a French army that itself reached the field a corps at a time, then attacked in a disorganized, piecemeal fashion.

In the aftermath of defeat Francis Joseph assumed command in an effort to impose control on his squabbling generals. When he sought to resume the offensive, orders and counterorders generated disorder exacerbated by administrative collapse. When on 24 June the Austrians again stood to arms near the village of Solferino, there had been no systematic distribution of bread for three days. Some regiments had eaten nothing for twenty-four hours. Francis Joseph ordered a double ration of "brandy"—raw distillate whose effects were compounded by empty stomachs and taut nerves. By the time the French and Piedmontese finally attacked around noon, a significant number of Austrian infantrymen were sufficiently impaired that their best chance of hitting anything with their new rifles involved guessing which of the blurred multiple images they saw was the real target.

Faced with a static enemy, French infantry, well supported by artillery boldly handled in battery strength, thrust forward into the gaps in the Austrian line—in what, to a degree, was a form of "forward flight." For all their defective training, Austrian riflemen initially inflicted significant damage on French formations. Once the French were on the move, too many Austrians forgot to reset their sights. Instead of suffering their heaviest casualties as they approached their objective, French losses dropped as the range closed. Austrian battalions were overrun or—far more frequently—broke and ran as much from their sense of isolation as from the actual effect of cold French steel.

At the end of the day over twenty thousand Austrians were dead, wounded, or missing. Another ten thousand had been knocked loose from their units to spread panic in already disorganized rear areas. The Austrian emperor, shocked by the carnage, decided to seek peace with Napoleon, equally disconcerted by the war's economic and human costs. Austria surrendered Lombardy to Piedmont but retained Venetia, to the indignation of nationalists throughout Italy. An arguably greater consequence was the postwar founding of the Red Cross by another shocked eyewitness, the Swiss humanitarian Jean-Henri Dunant.

See also **Cavour, Count (Camillo Benso); Francis Joseph; Military Tactics; Red Cross.**

BIBLIOGRAPHY

Showalter, Dennis. *The Wars of German Unification.* London, 2004.

Turnbull, Patrick. *Solferino: The Birth of a Nation.* New York, 1985. Good history of the war for general readers.

Wylly, H. C. *The Campaign of Magenta and Solferino, 1859.* London, 1907. Conceptually outdated and operationally focused, but useful for the military aspects.

DENNIS SHOWALTER

FRANCO-PRUSSIAN WAR. The Franco-Prussian War, in reality a war pitting the French Second Empire against Prussia and its south German allies, completed the process of German unification and fundamentally altered the balance of power in Europe. Its immediate roots lay in the Austro-Prussian War of 1866, whose rapid ending denied French Emperor Napoleon III the territorial and diplomatic concessions he considered the Second Empire's due as Europe's primary power. As he vainly sought compensation from Otto von Bismarck, the Prussian minister-president (prime minister), Bismarck pursued with equal futility a closer political and military relationship with the south German states of Baden, Württemberg, and Bavaria.

ORIGINS

Success in the latter endeavor would change European power relationships in ways France could hardly be expected to ignore. Contemporary opinion in fact laid primary responsibility for the events of 1870 at the door of Napoleon III, who allegedly forced a conflict to shore up his unstable regime. Beginning in the 1890s, responsibility was increasingly shifted to a Bismarck described as provoking war in the interests of German hegemony: "blood and iron" in a European setting. Late-twentieth-century scholarship emphasizes Bismarck's desire to keep as many options as possible open for as long as possible. He prided himself on being able to step into a situation and stir things up, confident that he could respond to confusion exponentially better than his associates and opponents. In the spring of 1870 he had his chance.

Bismarck's primary objective was resolving the German question in Prussia's favor. The argument that Bismarck's initial approval of Spain's offer of its vacant crown to Prince Leopold of Hohenzollern-Sigmaringen (a branch of the ruling house of Prussia) was intended to provoke a war overstates Bismarck's belligerence while underrating his self-confidence. The Hohenzollern candidacy was designed to provoke a crisis with France. But it was so managed that at each stage the final initiative, the final choice, remained with Paris. Bismarck recognized that war was an extremely likely outcome of the situation. At the same time he was testing the intentions of the emperor and of France itself.

An international incident is what one of the parties involved wishes to define as an international incident. Negotiating room remained in the first days of July, particularly after Leopold withdrew his candidacy in the face of French hostility. But a French government enjoying its triumph overplayed its hand by demanding that Prussia guarantee the candidacy would not be renewed. Bismarck's negative reply was interpreted in Paris as a justification for a war Bismarck by now also believed inevitable. On 15 July the North German Confederation issued its mobilization orders.

COURSE

Neither party had a significant advantage in mobilization. The Franco-Prussian War was a classic "come-as-you-are" collision and as such its initial advantages rested with the French. War from a standing start was the kind of con-

Inflating a hot-air balloon during the seige, 1870. The French were eventually able to break the Prussian blockade of Paris with hot-air balloons, which had previously been used primarily for entertainment. The first launch took place on 23 September, when a pilot transported important messages to the nearby town of Evreux. A few weeks later, French Minister of the Interior Leon Gambetta escaped Paris by balloon to organize French resistance to the Prussians in the countryside. ©HULTON-DEUTSCH COLLECTION/CORBIS

flict around which France's military system had been developed and refined since Waterloo (1815). The Prussians compensated with speed and system. Helmuth von Moltke, the chief of the general staff, saw the war's true objective as the French army. Decisively defeating it was the best way to convince other powers, Austria in particular, to let half-drawn swords return to the scabbards. And the best way to engage the army was to advance on Paris. The heart of France and of the Second Empire, Paris could not be sacrificed in a strategic withdrawal that in any case was foreign to the French way of war.

Moltke faced two diametrically opposed strategic prospects. The French army might cross the Rhine and hit the Prussians while they were still unloading their troop trains. Or the French might assume the natural defensive positions in which the frontier region abounded, meet the Prussian

Prussian troops parade on the Champs Elysées after their occupation of Paris, January 1871. ©Hulton-Deutsch Collection/CORBIS

advance in a series of encounter battles, then counterattack a weakened, confused enemy. Moltke's response represented a major contribution to the development of what has been called "operational art," the shadowy level between strategy and tactics. He planned to concentrate in the Rhineland/ Palatinate area of Prussia, swing his main force south of the French fortress complex at Metz, then advance northwest toward the Moselle and force a major battle before reaching the river.

What the Prussian military strategist Carl von Clausewitz called "fog and friction" affected the Prussians at every turn. Nevertheless, facilitated by a culpably disorganized French mobilization and concentration, the Prussians won a series of initial victories on the frontier and pushed steadily forward. This time it was the French who had a superior infantry rifle, and the chassepot easily stopped German frontal attacks with heavy losses. What decided battle after battle was the ability of the Prussians, and the south Germans who had joined Prussia in the face of what seemed French aggression, to envelop enemy flanks as superior Prussian artillery held the French in place.

By mid-August the main French army had retreated in confusion to Metz. The Prussians got behind it and in a series of battles fought between 16 and 18 August drove the French into the fortress and besieged it. The passivity of French commanders at all levels is indicated by the fact that the Germans were fighting in the wrong direction: facing toward Germany, with their own flanks and rear completely exposed.

Napoleon III, who had escaped encirclement at Metz, organized a relief force from the troops remaining to him. That army was in turn surrounded at Sedan on 1 September and forced to surrender the following day in one of the nineteenth century's most decisive tactical victories. With Napoleon a prisoner, the Second Empire collapsed. The newly created Third Republic of France, determined to continue the war, stamped mass armies out of the ground as another revolutionary government had done in 1793 and set them to relieving Paris, besieged by a Prussian/German army that was unable to develop any other plan for ending the war. These civilian levies proved no match for the Germans in battle. Nor did a burgeoning partisan movement develop any more than a nuisance value. The French maneuvers nevertheless combined to prolong the war to a point at which, despite the favorable terms Germany received, specifically French surrender of the frontier provinces of Alsace and Lorraine, Bismarck and Moltke were desperate to conclude peace and determined to avoid a similar situation in the future.

Once the guns fell silent, Europe rushed to copy the military methods that seemed to have brought Prussia victory. France brooded over its wrongs and losses. A new German empire sought to consolidate its achievements. In less than half a century these consequences would combine in an immeasurably more destructive conflict.

See also **Austro-Prussian War; Bismarck, Otto von; France; Germany; Military Tactics; Moltke, Helmuth von; Napoleon III.**

BIBLIOGRAPHY

Bucholz, Arden. *Moltke and the German Wars, 1864–1871.* Basingstoke, U.K., 2001.

Howard, Michael. *The Franco-Prussian War: The German Invasion of France, 1870–1871.* 2nd ed. London, 2001. Still the standard work, by a master of the craft.

Showalter, Dennis. *The Wars of German Unification.* London, 2004.

Wawro, Geoffrey. *The Franco-Prussian War: The German Conquest of France in 1870–1871.* Cambridge, U.K., 2003. Excellent on operational matters.

DENNIS SHOWALTER

FRANKFURT PARLIAMENT.

The German Revolution of 1848 received its popular energy from aggrieved peasants, artisans, and workers; its political program, however, from the liberalism of the educated upper middle class. The liberal aim was constitutional government both in the separate German states and in a new national state.

In March 1848, under the pressure of revolutionary turmoil, the Confederation Diet called for a National Parliament (*Nationalversammlung*) to meet in Frankfurt and draft a national constitution. The Frankfurt Parliament, created to establish a united German state, also became its symbol.

POLITICAL AND SOCIAL DIVISIONS

The Revolution subsequently failed, and the Parliament was unable to secure support for its constitution, in part due to liberal politicians' alienation of their popular base; even the May 1848 parliamentary election seems to portend this. The Diet had appeared to endorse manhood suffrage, but in fact suffrage varied by locale, often to the exclusion of poor men. Likewise, the elected members, who met in Frankfurt on 18 May, tended to be middle class, the majority having a university degree, many with careers in state administration.

St. Paul's Church (*Paulskirche*) was the setting for the Frankfurt Parliament's deliberations, which were marked by bitter ideological division. No party system gave coherence to the debate, but historians categorize the parliamentarians by certain broad views of governmental form. A small radical group on the left sought a republic with full democracy—one man, one vote. The great majority sought to balance monarchy with popular representation. The liberal position was to concede considerable authority to the monarch and limit suffrage by property or education. On the right, based on conservative ideology, some delegates favored as much power for the monarch, and as much autonomy for the separate states, as possible.

THE NATIONAL QUESTION

Nationalism colored every discussion of German identity or interest, but ideas about "the nation" varied. Of Prussia and Austria, the dominant states, should one play the leading national role? Religion influenced this debate, Protestants tending to favor the Prussian Hohenzollern dynasty, Catholics the Austrian Habsburg. Also controversial was the issue of national boundaries. Another question was the treatment of non-German minorities and German-speaking Jews.

Foreign policy came to the fore as "Germany" opposed Denmark in the crisis over Schleswig-Holstein. The Prussian king, Frederick William IV, sent troops to assert the German claim to these duchies, a move applauded by German nationalists, including those in the Frankfurt Parliament. International pressure and the threat of the Danish navy convinced Prussia to sign an armistice at Malmö on 26 August 1848. Amid nationalist outcry, Frankfurt, by a slim majority, condemned this agreement, but then reversed itself in recognition that it lacked the power to compel Prussia against her will.

Frederick William's withdrawal from Schleswig-Holstein was a sign not only of Prussian indifference to the Parliament, but also of the recovery of initiative by conservative, monarchical forces.

THE FAILED CONSTITUTION

In the meantime, the Parliament made slow progress in drafting the constitution. In final form, in March 1849, it merged monarchy and democracy. Its national conception centered Germany around Prussia. Even after Malmö, Protestant members from north Germany sought the Prussian and not the Austrian solution, *Kleindeutschland* (smaller Germany) rather than *Großdeutschland* (greater Germany). And as the Austrian monarchy grew more conservative, so did the movement to exclude it from a more liberal, predominantly Protestant nation. That had the advantage, too, of excluding Austria's non-German lands. Germany would be an "empire," its throne occupied by the Prussian king. This vision, favored by Frankfurt's Minister President and leading liberal spokesman Heinrich von Gagern, failed at first to win a parliamentary majority. The liberals' recourse was to secure votes on the democratic left, thus broadening the franchise and limiting the Emperor's power.

The constitution addressed the catalog of liberal rights, although not without controversy. Freedom of speech and religion was affirmed, while the traditional right of noble privilege was abolished. However, on the removal of feudal tenure from peasant land, the door was left open to peasant indemnification of landlords in return for ownership. On the issue of free residency the Parliament bowed to pressure from towns fearing an influx of new residents. About the "right to work," demanded by many workers, the constitution included nothing, and in general tended to affirm political and civil rights while leaving lower-class economic grievances unaddressed.

It is often emphasized that Frankfurt favored German over other national claims and interests. Schleswig-Holstein is one example; another is the decision to draw German boundaries to include many Poles in the Prussian province of Posen.

Frederick William IV rejected the Imperial crown, and the German constitution came to naught. By April 1849 the German political tide was so conservative that liberal initiatives almost everywhere were stymied. The Parliament, remote from the populace and powerless to halt counterrevolution in the states, fell apart.

PERSPECTIVES

The classic account is the 1968 study by Frank Eyck, *The Frankfurt Parliament*. Eyck's condemnation of the parliamentary left attracts little interest in the early twenty-first century. The real shift in historiography has come from work that portrays Frankfurt against the background of an economy moving from a traditional to a market structure, with society unsettled by this change. Wolfram Siemann, in an important 1985 study of the Revolution, cites writers in the nineteenth century dealing with social demands that the Parliament failed to meet. One such writer was Friedrich Engels, the collaborator of Karl Marx. Siemann's point is not to reinforce the Marxist view of Frankfurt as the forum of an economic bourgeoisie, but to underline concern with the popular uprising. Siemann's own tendency is to cast German social unrest as a "modernization" crisis.

In the early 2000s, the historian Brian Vick countered the view that Frankfurt liberals were fierce nationalists, showing that their nationalism permitted moderation—for example, in addressing minority rights and in drawing German borders.

Conservatism, shocked but not destroyed in March 1848, returned and brought down the

Parliament. The divided Germany of the Confederation, also, had too many centers from which this solitary national institution was undermined and attacked.

But the Frankfurt Parliament was a boost to German liberals in the long term, by representing the value of parliamentary government and by its political divisions, which later reappeared as parties. It continued as a symbol of the national claim to self-determination, not yet achieved.

See also **Frederick William IV; Germany; Nationalism; Revolutions of 1848.**

BIBLIOGRAPHY

Primary Sources

Engels, Frederick. *Germany: Revolution and Counter-Revolution*, edited by Eleanor Marx. New York, 1969. Written by Engels, but originally appeared under the name of Karl Marx as articles in the *New York Daily Tribune*, 1851–1852.

Secondary Sources

Eyck, Frank. *The Frankfurt Parliament.* New York, 1968.

Siemann, Wolfram, *The German Revolution of 1848–49.* Translated by Christiane Banerji. New York, 1998. Translation of *Die deutsche Revolution von 1848/49* (1985).

Vick, Brian E. *Defining Germany: The 1848 Frankfurt Parliamentarians and National Identity.* Cambridge, Mass., 2002.

ROBERT E. SACKETT

FRAZER, JAMES (1854–1941), Scottish anthropologist and historian.

Death alone stilled the magisterial prose of James Frazer. Nothing else deterred his ever-expanding efforts in anthropology, classics, folklore, and the history of religions: neither a decade's blindness nor a generational shift in academic anthropology away from comparative surveys to functionalist ethnography. Never resting on his laurels (a knighthood, many prizes, world renown), Frazer cultivated an international reading public, aided by Lady Lilly Frazer, his wife and canny manager of a virtual cottage industry producing her husband's and her own books and translations, particularly in her native France.

Born in Glasgow in 1854, Frazer excelled there and at Cambridge in classics; he was directed to anthropological topics by the Scottish theologian William Robertson Smith (1846–1894). Frazer's abundant works include *Totemism and Exogamy* (4 vols., 1910), *Pausanias's Description of Greece* (6 vols., 1898; translation and commentary); *Folklore in the Old Testament* (1918); and of course *The Golden Bough,* that Victorian-Edwardian cornucopia of ethnological, historical, and literary depictions of sacrificial and sacramental forms that Frazer felt lay beneath and behind human reason—and possibly even in its future. Ambiguous prognosis characterizes its gargantuan third edition (12 vols., 1907–1915, plus 1936 *Aftermath*). "Magic, religion, and science," Frazer intones,

> are nothing but theories of thought; and as science has supplanted its predecessors, so it may hereafter be itself superseded by some more perfect hypothesis. . . . Brighter stars will rise on some voyager of the future—some great Ulysses of the realms of thought—than shine on us. The dreams of magic may one day be the waking realities of science.

This unsettling prospect resonates with *Psyche's Task* (1909), where Frazer argues that superstition remained the underpinning of civilization's highest achievements: crown and mitre, marriage, and private property.

The evolutionary or maturational sequence—magic, religion, science—described in the earlier editions of *The Golden Bough* (2 vols., 1890; 3 vols., 1900) is somewhat diluted in the third edition's vastness. Frazer also modulated his aggressive anticlericalism of 1900, when he had provocatively set Purim and Christ in the company of his key themes: dying gods and vegetal rites; legends of cyclically assassinated priest-kings; all manner of baffling primitive festivals, classical myths, and peasant lore. Readers of Frazer have long debated his stance toward rationalism and religiosity. The literary scholar Stanley Hyman, concluding that he oscillated inconclusively, puts Frazer in the company of Charles Darwin, Karl Marx, and Sigmund Freud. Frazer's biographer Robert Ackerman rightly places Frazer high in the ranks of figures who have expanded the modern idea of humanity's mysterious past.

Frazer briefly held (at Liverpool) Britain's first official chair in "social anthropology." Not a fieldworker, he nevertheless marshaled resources for intensive ethnography by others in Melanesia, Australia, and Africa. Contrary to his "armchair" reputation, Frazer made arduous travels in Greece for his translations and archaeological surveys. That authoritative Frazerian tone can sound imperious (and imperialist); his sonorous expansiveness may strike today's readers as consonant with colonialism "on which the sun never set." But Frazer's vivid and informed compilation of ostensibly bizarre rites possibly undermined more than buttressed supposedly self-confident Victorian values. Just how much subsequent approaches in anthropology—from Bronislaw Kasper Malinowski (1884–1942) to contemporary cultural critique—owe to Sir James remains a subject of contention.

Frazer's immense learning—in Greek, Latin, Hebrew, and world ethnology—surpassed German rivals; his translations of *Apollodorus* (1921) and of Ovid's *Fasti* (1929) remain influential. His more general impact has outlasted that of Edward Burnett Tylor (1832–1917), Ernest Renan (1823–1892), Andrew Lang (1844–1912), and sundry scholars of his era. Frazer too retailed sensational metaphors of "survivals": primitive Aryans among us today, peasants still savage at heart. Ultimately, however, his work conveys no moral of Aryan superiority or Christian preferability. Those hoping to understand Frazer must reckon with his attraction to the "romantic irony" of Friedrich von Schlegel (1772–1829), Heinrich Heine (1797–1856), and Jean Paul (Jean Paul Friedrich Richter; 1763–1825). The philosopher Ludwig Wittgenstein (1889–1951), in his own striking "remarks on Frazer," might have made more of this dimension of Frazer's vision.

Recent revaluations stress the durability of Frazer's controversial tomes and their relevance to travel writing, narratives of remembrance, discursive eloquence, and critical issues of cultural fragmentariness. His captivating evocations of sacrifice and scapegoats have reverberated in popular culture as well (e.g., the filmmaker Francis Ford Coppola and the musician Jim Morrison). Frazer's interdisciplinary salience is manifest whenever anthropologists, historians of religions, classicists, and scholars of cultural and literary studies resume a comparative mission.

See also **Imperialism; Primitivism; Science and Technology.**

BIBLIOGRAPHY

Ackerman, Robert. *J. G. Frazer: His Life and Work.* Cambridge, U.K. , 1987.

Fraser, Robert. *The Making of The Golden Bough: The Origins and Growth of an Argument.* London, 1990.

Hyman, Stanley Edgar. *The Tangled Bank: Darwin, Marx, Frazer, and Freud as Imaginative Writers.* New York, 1962.

Manganaro, Marc, ed. *Modernist Anthropology: From Fieldwork to Text.* Princeton, N.J., 1990.

Stocking, George. *After Tylor: British Social Anthropology, 1888–1951.* Madison, Wis., 1995.

Vickery, John B. *The Literary Impact of* The Golden Bough. Princeton, N.J., 1973.

JAMES A. BOON

FREDERICK III (1831–1888), prince of Prussia (1831–1888), German crown prince (1871–1888), and German emperor (1888).

When asked to comment on the death of Emperor Frederick III in 1888, Liberal British Prime Minister William Gladstone called him a powerful defender of German liberalism. Although this claim was somewhat exaggerated, Frederick was the only German emperor who genuinely supported liberal reform. Tragically, he came to the throne when he was mortally ill with cancer and never had the chance to implement reforms during his ninety-nine-day reign.

Liberalism was not always a part of Frederick's life. As a young man, he rejected the views of his reform-minded mother, Princess Augusta of Prussia, and favored the policies of the conservative court in Berlin. This changed after Augusta arranged for her son to marry Princess Victoria (1840–1901), the eldest daughter of Queen Victoria of England and her consort, Prince Albert. Though she was only seventeen years old at the time of her marriage, Princess Victoria was intelligent, well educated, and determined to convert her husband to British-style liberalism.

By most accounts, the marriage was a success. The couple had six children, the eldest of whom later reigned as Emperor William II. In the realm of politics, Frederick appeared to follow his wife's lead: he fostered ties with prominent liberals and rejected the domestic and foreign policies of his father's chief adviser, the conservative Otto von Bismarck. In 1863 Frederick made a speech in Danzig opposing Bismarck's edict against the liberal press. Frederick's father, King William I of Prussia, was incensed by the incident and considered throwing his insubordinate son into jail until calmer counsels prevailed. The incident and the ensuing estrangement between father and son led to speculation that Frederick accepted his wife's views and was firmly in the liberal camp.

Though Frederick rejected Bismarck's domestic policies, he, like many Prussian liberals, was attracted to Bismarck's vision of a united Germany under Prussian leadership. He and his wife hoped that unification could be achieved via peaceful means. To their chagrin, Bismarck's policy of unification by force prevailed. But although Frederick found Bismarck's methods distasteful, Frederick distinguished himself in the wars of unification against Austria and France. In the Austro-Prussian War of 1866, he led the Second Army to victory at the decisive battle of Königgrätz (now Hradec Králové, Czech Republic; also called the battle of Sadowa). In the Franco-Prussian War four years later, he led the Third Army to victories at Wörth and Weissenburg, France.

At the time of the victory over France and the subsequent unification of Germany in 1871, Frederick's father, the newly proclaimed Emperor William I, was seventy-three years old. It was expected that Frederick's reign was imminent, and that he would pursue a liberal program under the guidance of his wife, Victoria. These assumptions were incorrect. William reigned as emperor for seventeen years, despite advanced age and two attempts on his life. The expectation that Victoria would design policy for her husband when he came to the throne was also misguided. The unpublished correspondence of the royal couple shows that politically, Frederick and Victoria were often very much at odds with each other. Frederick firmly resisted Victoria's attempts to persuade him to support British-style reforms, such as increasing the powers of parliament at the expense of the monarchy. Frederick was first and foremost a constitutional liberal. What this meant was that while he was willing to fight for the preservation of the constitution, he did not want it to be replaced by a more liberal charter. In the end, he favored adoption of liberal reforms only within the framework of the constitutional status quo. Nor did the royal couple see eye-to-eye where Bismarck was concerned; the correspondence shows that on several occasions, Frederick and Bismarck were in agreement on several issues, much to Victoria's dismay.

Frederick's hopes for a liberal Germany were dashed by Bismarck's shift from cooperation with liberals to an alliance with antiliberal forces in 1879. Frederick became subject to fits of depression and feelings of hopelessness. Nonetheless, he warned Bismarck that he would not work with a chancellor who subverted the constitution during his coming reign.

In 1887 Frederick was diagnosed with cancer of the larynx. German physicians insisted that without surgery to remove the larynx, the prognosis was fatal. But because surgery itself had a high mortality rate, Bismarck recommended that other physicians be consulted. A British physician, Morrell Mackenzie, insisted that the growth was not cancerous and that Frederick could be cured. The royal couple embraced the diagnosis, but in the months that followed, it became clear that the initial diagnosis was correct. In March 1888 Emperor William I died. By that time, his son could barely speak. During his brief reign, he dismissed the conservative minister of the interior and bestowed decorations on prominent liberals, but was incapable of doing more. He died in Potsdam on 15 June 1888.

Victoria's grief over the loss of her beloved husband was compounded by her anger at the way in which her eldest son, now Emperor William II, utterly rejected the liberalism of his parents. In her letters and correspondence after her husband's death, Victoria sharply criticized her son's rule and insisted that her husband would have ruled Germany according to her liberal views. In so doing, she made the late emperor the progressive liberal he never was in life. Her agitation on behalf of her husband's alleged liberal views fostered the legend of Frederick III. The legend, in the end, ultimately obscured Frederick's contributions as a constitutional liberal.

See also **Austro-Prussian War; Bismarck, Otto von; Franco-Prussian War; Germany; William I; William II.**

BIBLIOGRAPHY

Dorpalen, Andreas. "Emperor Frederick III and the German Liberal Movement." *American Historical Review* 54, no. 1 (1948): 1–31.

Frederick III. *The War Diary of the Emperor Frederick III, 1870–1871.* Translated and edited by A. R. Allinson. London, 1927.

Kollander, Patricia. *Frederick III: Germany's Liberal Emperor.* Westport, Conn., 1995.

Nichols, J. Alden. *The Year of the Three Kaisers: Bismarck and the German Succession, 1887–1888.* Urbana, Ill., 1987.

Röhl, John C. G. *Young Wilhelm: The Kaiser's Early Life, 1859–1888.* Translated by Jeremy Gaines and Rebecca Wallach. Cambridge, U.K., 1998.

PATRICIA KOLLANDER

FREDERICK WILLIAM III (1770–1840; r. 1797–1840), king of Prussia.

Frederick William III presided over his kingdom during dynamic times: the shocking wars of the French Revolution and Napoleon I (r. 1804–1814/15), the crushing loss to the French in 1806, the time of reform that this debacle necessitated, the Wars of Liberation and final defeat of Napoleon at Waterloo, the reactionary era of Restoration after 1815, and the age of early industrialization that spanned the decades he ruled. Frederick William III suffered from melancholia, preferred to withdraw from politics into family life, and usually dreaded having to make decisions, but his sense of duty compelled him to struggle against his nature and shape Prussian and German history in significant ways. He was definitely not the nonentity that traditional historical scholarship has depicted.

During his first decade on the throne, Frederick William III became increasingly involved in the delicate game of negotiating deals with France that allowed Prussia to make territorial gains at the expense of smaller German states as the Holy Roman Empire entered its death throes. By 1806 most of Germany north of the Main River had either fallen to Prussia or under Prussian influence. Having unwisely remained neutral while Napoleon defeated the Austrians and Russians at Austerlitz in 1805, however, Prussia's king faced Napoleon alone in 1806. After the twin battles of Jena and Auerstedt, the French emperor occupied Berlin and Frederick William fled to East Prussia, not to return until 1809.

Prior to 1806 the Prussian monarch considered many ambitious reforms, including peasant emancipation. Educated by tutors who introduced him to enlightened principles, Frederick William appreciated the need to stay abreast of the zeitgeist, but he also possessed a pragmatic nature that made him wary of "phrase-makers," which, together with his reserved nature, produced inaction, especially in these early years. Conservative noblemen also opposed his reform ideas. Thus Prussia entered its disastrous war with Napoleon largely unreformed from the Old Regime that characterized central and eastern Europe. Defeat, however, advanced a new set of advisers who counseled radical change to gird Prussia for survival in the modern world of revolutionary France. The king approved most of their recommendations: a start to peasant emancipation, opening the officer corps to middle-class talent, abolition of guild privileges, establishment of autonomous city governments, and the promise of a constitution. After Napoleon's defeat in Russia in 1812, Frederick William joined Russia and Austria in the campaigns that led to victory at the Battle of Nations outside Leipzig in 1813, the march on Paris in 1814, and the terminating victory over Napoleon at Waterloo in 1815.

The coming of peace saw central Europe transformed from the long-standing Holy Roman Empire of hundreds of German states to a German Confederation of thirty-nine states dominated from Vienna and Berlin. The Confederation, it was clear, would facilitate military cooperation against the threat of French aggression, but the question of political reforms within the Confederation remained uncertain. Austria stood steadfastly against parliaments, but by 1819 four German states had introduced constitutions. Frederick William now had to decide whether to fulfill his promise of liberal parliamentary institutions. The radical student demonstration at Wartburg in 1817, coupled with the assassination of conservative poet August Friedrich Ferdinand von Kotzebue in 1819, convinced the Prussian king that parliamentary reforms, however justified in principle, were imprudent in practice. "No representative constitution will help in the least," he would later write, against "the crazy drive to topple everything which exists." The "most complete proof of this" was supplied by parliamentary countries in the west, where "things were really the worst." Thus, "even if one could come to say heartfelt things about adopting the same institutions for here, that which really happens in the world fully suffices to bring one back away from this" (Brose, p. 94). Limited parliamentary reforms waited for the reign of his son, Frederick William IV (r. 1840–1861), who fulfilled the promise in 1848–1849.

That Prussia was Germany's most rapidly industrializing state by 1840 also owed a lot to its king of forty-three years. The kingdom's free enterprise legislation of 1811, the rejection of conservative advice to rescind these laws in 1824, the opening of the Customs Union in 1834—also over conservative objections—and the decision to move forward with stalled railroad construction in 1838—also against conservative counsels—were tough decisions Frederick William III made somewhat more easily than during his first insecure decades as king. Although it was not his intention—he wanted no German crown—both the Customs Union and the railroads contributed to eventual German unification in 1871.

See also **Congress of Vienna; French Revolutionary Wars and Napoleonic Wars; Germany; Napoleonic Empire; Prussia; Restoration.**

BIBLIOGRAPHY

Brose, Eric Dorn. *The Politics of Technological Change in Prussia: Out of the Shadow of Antiquity 1809–1848.* Princeton, N.J., 1993.

Stamm-Kuhlmann, Thomas. *König in Preussens grosser Zeit: Friedrich Wilhelm III: Der Melancholiker auf dem Thron.* Berlin, 1992.

ERIC DORN BROSE

FREDERICK WILLIAM IV (in German, Friedrich Wilhelm IV; 1795–1861; ruled 1840–1861), king of Prussia.

One of the most mercurial and controversial monarchs in nineteenth-century Europe, Frederick William IV was also one of the more consequential.

Long a target of liberal and radical historians, he was often pilloried during his own lifetime as a hazy, dreamy "Romantic on the throne" who was utterly disconnected from the major currents of his age. In fact, though, he devoted his entire adult life to a consistent and intensely ideological struggle against the "revolution," by which he meant secular values and "French-modern" forms of constitutionalism, parliamentarism, republicanism, and centralized, bureaucratic "absolutism." He focused his efforts on a monarchical project that he conceived as a "Christian-German" alternative to secular modernity. Central to this project was an organicist vision of a society organized on the basis of historically defined estates, each suffused with its unique group energies, values, and functions. A group-based, estatist (*ständisch*) form of representation would serve as an alternative to individualist, "mechanical" parliamentarism; and all the estates of the realm would be united in harmony with a monarch who ruled quite literally by the grace of God. To carry out his anti-"revolutionary" program, Frederick William used a number of modern methods of political mobilization and propaganda. An avid supporter of railway building, he was the most widely traveled monarch in German history until that time; and, employing his considerable rhetorical gifts, he was the first to deliver public speeches to his civilian subjects on such notable occasions as his Berlin enthronement in October 1840 or the dedication of Cologne cathedral in 1842.

Born in 1795 to the future Frederick William III and the future Queen Louise, the crown prince spent an idyllic childhood, quickly demonstrating exceptional intelligence and a remarkable aptitude for art and especially architecture. The idyll was disrupted by the catastrophe of 1806–1807, when Napoleon shattered Prussia's once-vaunted armies and imposed a humiliating peace settlement at Tilsit. Frederick William served in the liberation war against France (1813–1815), and thereafter on a royal commission that in 1823 introduced provincial estates (*Provinziallandtage*) as a partial concession to demands for political representation. He also collaborated closely with Prussia's leading architects, especially Karl Friedrich Schinkel, on many projects in the vicinity of his beloved Potsdam, which he hoped to transform into an Italian-style garden paradise. These justly praised activities continued until the late 1850s. Finally, Frederick William became the focal point of the "Crown Prince's Circle," an informal gathering of so-called High Conservatives who criticized Metternichean absolutism. Among them were many of Frederick William's chief advisors, including Joseph Maria von Radowitz and the brothers Leopold and Ernst Ludwig von Gerlach.

The positive expectations that attended Frederick William's accession to the throne in 1840, especially from the diffuse ranks of German liberals hoping for change after the paralysis of the 1830s, were quickly dashed. Seeking to satisfy his father's long-delayed constitutional promises without actually resorting to a constitution, Frederick William attempted between 1842 and 1847 to introduce his estatist ideas in both politics and ecclesiastical affairs. These culminated in the United Diet of 1847, which, far from implementing the king's ideas, turned into a quasi-parliamentary forum for the discussion of political reform. By this time the economic and social crisis of the "hungry forties" had reached the boiling point, contributing to the eruption of 18–19 March 1848. Frederick William's response to the barricade battles—his lachrymose appeal "To My Dear Berliners" and the withdrawal of Prussian troops from the city—has often been criticized, but in fact he was more decisive than most others in Berlin, including his brother and heir, the later William I.

The king spent the postrevolution months in Potsdam with an informal "camarilla" (or cabal) of High Conservative advisers whose influence has been exaggerated but who did contribute to the counterrevolution in November and the compromise constitution of December 1848 (later amended and accepted by the king in February 1850). Frederick William had always embraced a vision of German national unity—he was quite modern in this respect too—but in April 1849 he rejected the imperial crown proffered by the Frankfurt National Assembly. Thereafter he supported the Prussian Union plans of his friend Radowitz, a conservative alternative to the Frankfurt ideas, but they ended with failure in November 1850.

During the decade of reaction after 1850 Frederick William reluctantly accommodated himself to Prussia's new constitution and learned how to use it to advance his own agenda, sometimes over the opposition of his High Conservative allies in the *Kreuzzeitung* party. After 1853–54 he supported a policy of neutrality in the Crimean conflict. Incapacitated by strokes after 1857, he died in 1861; his brother William had become regent in 1858.

See also **Conservatism; Germany; Prussia; Revolutions of 1848; Romanticism.**

BIBLIOGRAPHY

Barclay, David E. *Frederick William IV and the Prussian Monarchy, 1840–1861.* Oxford, U.K., 1995.

Blasius, Dirk. *Friedrich Wilhelm IV., 1795–1861: Psychopathologie und Geschichte.* Göttingen, Germany, 1992.

Büsch, Otto, ed. *Friedrich Wilhelm IV. in seiner Zeit: Beiträge eines Colloquiums.* Berlin, 1987.

Bußmann, Walter. *Zwischen Preußen und Deutschland: Friedrich Wilhelm IV.; Eine Biographie.* Berlin, 1990.

Kroll, Frank-Lothar. *Friedrich Wilhelm IV. und das Staatsdenken der deutschen Romantik.* Berlin, 1990.

Sperber, Jonathan, ed. *The Short Oxford History of Germany: Germany, 1800–1870.* Oxford, U.K., 2004.

DAVID E. BARCLAY

FREEMASONS. A selective fraternal organization based on private initiation rituals, whose symbols and customs are allegedly derived from medieval stonemasons, Freemasonry was first established in England by 1717. Masonic lodges soon appeared elsewhere in France, the Netherlands, the German and Italian states, and Russia. By 1789 perhaps as many as fifty thousand European Masons, most often from the royal courts, landed nobility, and professional middle classes, professed in their lodges the Enlightenment principles of social equality, religious toleration, and moral virtue. For the next 125 years, however, largely in response to the dramatic historical consequences of political and industrial revolution, Freemasons on the Continent especially developed substantially new versions of their initiation rituals and the organizations that regulated their authenticity; they grew in political

SOME PROMINENT FREEMASONS

Philippe-Égalité, duc d'Orléans (initiated 1771), regicide cousin of Louis XVI

Marquis de Lafayette (1775), French general and statesman, "Hero of Two Worlds"

Nikolai Novikov (1775), Russian statesman, confidant of Catherine the Great

Alexander Radishchev (c. 1780), Russian political reformer

George, Prince of Wales (1790), George IV of England

Duke of Wellington (1791), English general and statesman, victor of Waterloo

François Guizot (1804), French historian and statesman in the July Monarchy

Filippo Buonarroti (c. 1806), Italian-born French revolutionary and leader of the Carbonari

James Rothschild (1810), English banker

Alexander Pushkin (1821), Russian poet

William I (1840), king of Prussia and emperor of Germany

Franz Liszt (1841), Hungarian musician and composer of Romantic music

Giuseppe Garibaldi (1844), Italian revolutionary nationalist

Albert Edward (1869), Prince of Wales, Edward VII of England

Léon Gambetta (1875), French patriot and republican political leader

Jules Ferry (1875), French politician, architect of French public education

Rudyard Kipling (1886), English author and champion of British Empire

Annie Besant (1902), English political activist and theosophist

Louise Michel (1904), French revolutionary and Communard

Alexander Kerensky (c. 1910), prime minister, Provisional Government of Russia

MASONIC RITUALS AND ORGANIZATIONS

Fundamental to Freemasonry were its secret rituals. The initiations of new Masons took them symbolically in three discrete stages from the "profane" world to the values of brotherhood, charity, and truth. The first degree or grade, the Entered Apprentice, learned what distinguished the Mason from the non-Mason; the second degree, the Fellowcraft or Journeyman, acknowledged the transition to a new life in Masonry; and the third degree, the Master Mason, welcomed the initiate to full rights and responsibilities to vote on admission of new members and take a leadership role in their initiation. Additional degrees, such as those worked by the Knights Templar or the Scottish Rite, built on these foundational grades. In the nineteenth century, the tendency was to add many more degrees; by 1900 the rites of the Memphis-Misraïm worked up to ninety-nine of them.

Dramatizing the symbolic changes in a Mason's status, the specifics of these rituals varied considerably over time and are the main reason for Masonic secrecy: every Mason was sworn not to reveal the ritual mysteries of the craft to noninitiates. Nevertheless, the indiscretions of individual Masons, such as Leo Tolstoy's father, or the efforts of hostile profanes, such as Roman Catholic officials, led to revelations or exposés not officially sanctioned by Freemasonry. Forms and customs once tied to the medieval stonemasons increasingly gave way to mystical and esoteric rituals, even though the obediences disapproved and tried to limit these novelties in Masonic symbolism.

A product of liberal Enlightenment ideals, Masonic lodges valued their independence from centralizing authority. Yet coordination of membership among the different lodges, especially those practicing the same ritual, was desirable to foster organizational order. Accordingly, the English were the first to create a Grand Lodge in London, often called the "Moderns" (1717), but they soon encountered resistance from lodges working different rituals in York (1725) and elsewhere in London, better known as the "Antients" (1751). In December 1813 this rivalry ended in the formation of the United Grand Lodge of England (UGLE), which elected a new Grand Master (the Duke of

influence and controversy even as their social status became more diffuse and less prominent. In short, they participated actively in the troubled, uneven evolution of modern civic culture in nineteenth-century Europe.

MASONIC TERMINOLOGY AND ABBREVIATIONS

Adoption: The practice of initiating women under a special system of rituals. Adoption appeared first and most pervasively in polite society in France before 1789. After a brief vogue during the Napoleonic Empire, adoption was not revived again until 1901.

Apprentice or Entered Apprentice: The first degree in Freemasonry. Symbolically, the initiation suggests the end of the new Mason's previous life and the beginning of a new one.

Constitutions: The 1723 document by the Reverend James Anderson laying out the rules of Masonic activity, which is foundational to Freemasonry as an institution. The 1738 revision of the Constitutions provided a historical explanation of "speculative" or symbolic Masonry, much of it an elaborate mythology underlying the organization's rituals.

Grand Architect of the Universe: The Supreme Being—as Creator of Heaven and Earth—recognized by all Freemasons initiated into the rituals overseen by the United Grand Lodge of England, but not the Grand Orient of Belgium (since 1871) and the Grand Orient of France (since 1877).

GLF: Grand Lodge of France, the rival obedience to the Grand Orient of France, founded in 1895.

GOF: Grand Orient of France, the most important obedience in France.

GSLF: Grand Symbolic Lodge of France, the first obedience to consider initiating women in annual convents in the 1890s.

Journeyman or Fellowcraft: The second degree in Freemasonry. This intermediary grade between the Entered Apprentice and the Master Mason was often granted at the same time as the first.

Le Droit Humain: The International Mixed Masonic Order, established in France in 1894 by Maria Desraismes and Georges Martin, and the first and most prominent obedience for both men and women.

Lodge: The local gathering of Masons for the working of the craft or degrees.

Master Mason: The third degree in Freemasonry. The culmination of the Apprentice and Journeymen degrees, Master Masons were entitled to full participation in their lodges, including the right to vote on new members and the leading of initiation rituals.

Obedience: The organizational authority of Masonic lodges observing the same rituals, generally referred to as the "Grand Lodge" or the "Grand Orient," which grants permission to individual lodges to initiate and to work degrees or grades. The most widely recognized Masonic obediences are the United Grand Lodge of England and the Grand Orient of France.

Royal Art or the Craft: Freemasonry's universal symbolism.

Scottish Rite, Ancient and Accepted: The system of higher, or side, degrees beyond that of Master Mason. The Scottish Rite has developed thirty-three degrees, which are often associated with certain elitist, knightly, and Christian tendencies in Freemasonry outside the English context.

UGLE: United Grand Lodge of England, the largest and most widely recognized authority in European Freemasonry, founded in 1813.

Sussex), crafted a common constitution, and created a uniform philosophic framework for the first three degrees. From then onward, all subsequent Masonic activity, including the recognition of new lodges in England and Wales, was subject to the authority of the UGLE.

These efforts at centralization in England, however, were unwelcome on the Continent. The French were particularly creative in establishing another Grand Lodge (1738) and then a rival Grand Orient (1773), until 1799 when these two merged into the Grand Orient of France

Freemason's Hall, London, 1808. ©Historical Picture Archive/CORBIS

(GOF). Other obediences were obliged briefly to coordinate their activities. In 1804 the Scottish Rite entered into an agreement with the GOF, only to regain its independence a year later. Also in 1804 the Supreme Council assumed responsibility for regulating the first three degrees, including the creation of new lodges (after 1820), and in 1805 the Grand Directory of Rites, later the Grand College of Rites (1826), took charge of regulating all other degrees.

The largest proliferation of French obediences occurred after 1850. The Grand Symbolic Lodge of France (GSLF), an emanation of the Supreme Council, started under another name in 1880; the Grand Lodge of France (GLF), following the

Scottish Rite, was founded in 1895 and fused with the GSLF in 1896. The Grand Lodge of the Ancient and Primitive Rite of Memphis-Misraïm appeared in 1899. Finally, after years of interest expressed by women in participating, the International Mixed Masonic Order: Le Droit Humain was organized in 1894, and the adoptive lodges under the auspices of the GLF began in 1901. In Masonic history, France was an innovator in ritual and organization.

Freemasonry had even less central authority in the other European countries. Freemasons were regulated for less than ten years during France's First Empire (1804–1814), when the GOF was authorized to oversee Masonic activity everywhere French hegemony prevailed, in the Netherlands, many of the German and Italian states, and Spain. Immediately after the empire, European lodges worked the craft most often in secret because the reactionary Restoration regimes outlawed them as revolutionary cells. The establishment of nation-states, especially in the wake of Italian and German unification in 1870 and 1871, respectively, reinforced the decentralization of Masonic authority. In Russia Freemasonry was forbidden until 1918.

POLITICAL AND HISTORICAL ENGAGEMENTS

Under the long, stable reign of Queen Victoria (r. 1837–1901), English Freemasons enjoyed an uninterrupted detachment from politics. Princes of the realm and their relatives regularly served as Grand Masters and Provincial Grand Masters of the UGLE without controversy primarily because of a studious political disengagement in the lodges. The Masonic enthusiasm of Albert Edward, the Prince of Wales (1841–1910), enabled the UGLE to prosper before his accession to the throne (as Edward VII) in 1901. Finances from dues-paying Masons increased more than threefold during the nineteenth century. The principal concerns remained the rapid expansion of lodges in the British Empire.

Elsewhere Freemasons were often embroiled in political conflict. In 1789 Masons appeared in the tumultuous Estates-General; 103 out of 578 deputies in the revolutionary National Assembly were Freemasons. Consequently, archconservatives such as the Abbé Augustin de Barruel created the myth of a Masonic conspiracy, even though sixteen of Napoleon I's twenty-six marshals became members and lent Masonry an official legitimacy. With the Restoration in 1815, however, a comparable movement, the Carbonari, actually used its secrecy for revolutionary purposes in France and the Italian states. Individual Masons were active in much revolutionary activity in Russia (1825), in France and the Italian and German states (1830 and 1848), and again in France (1870–1871), despite the explicit policy of the main obediences not to challenge political authority, especially after unification in Italy and Germany.

Under the pontificate of Pius IX (r. 1846–1878), the Roman Catholic Church actively combated the rival religion it saw in Freemasonry. Repeated papal bulls threatened all Catholic Masons with excommunication. Church officials condemned the Masonic principles of religious tolerance, which had led many assimilated Jews to join. The GOF in 1877 dropped from its texts and rituals all references to the Grand Architect of the Universe, that is, to a Supreme Being, despite the opposition of the more traditional UGLE and its Continental affiliates. The rupture between the GOF and the UGLE continued into the twenty-first century. The basis for the sweeping Catholic condemnation of Masonry, due in part to the Vatican's struggle with recently unified Italy, seemed justified by the anticlerical politics of many GOF Masons in the French Third Republic, culminating in Émile Combes's forced separation of church and state in 1905.

Because of its selective secrecy, Freemasonry soon acquired a distinctive historical mythology. Masons borrowed the suggestions of James Anderson's 1738 imaginative history to elaborate their own lore, derived from the Bible and cultures with impressive stone monuments, to legitimize their organization and to enrich the symbolism of their rituals. Scottish Rite Masons, for example, adopted the myth of the Knights Templar, which formed the basis for their many medieval degrees. These efforts were given force by creative works such as Charles Gounod's opera *The Queen of Sheba* (1862) and Tolstoy's novel *War and Peace* (1865–1869). But they did so in the face of powerful counter-myths promoted by the church and a popular culture eager to seize on Freemasonry's deliberate mystifications. In 1892, the unscrupulous French publicist Léo Taxil took advantage of widespread fascination with the occult and of fierce anticlericalism to write a best-selling revelation of a self-professed female Mason, Miss Diana Vaughan, which turned out to be an elaborate hoax.

The controversies over Freemasonry eased with the rapid proliferation of civic culture in liberal societies on the eve of World War I. Masons probably represented more than 10 percent of the adult male population in Britain and France by 1914, and had begun to attract a growing number of women in Le Droit Humain and the new

A female Freemason giving a sign of identification. Watercolor, French School, 1805. Bibliothèque de l'Institut de France, Paris, France/Bridgeman Art Library/Archives Charmet

BIBLIOGRAPHY

Primary Sources

Anderson, James. *The Constitutions of the Free Masons.* London, 1723. Reprint, London, 1976.

Lane, John, ed. *Masonic Records, 1717–1894.* 2nd ed. London, 1895.

Tolstoy, Leo. *War and Peace.* Translated by Constance Garnett. 3 vols. New York, 1994.

Secondary Sources

Hamill, John. *The History of English Freemasonry.* Addlestone, Surrey, U.K., 1994.

Headings, Mildred J. *French Freemasonry under the Third Republic.* Baltimore, Md., 1949.

Katz, Jacob. *Jews and Freemasons in Europe, 1723–1939.* Translated by Leonard Oschry. Cambridge, Mass., 1970.

Roberts, John M. *The Mythology of Secret Societies.* London, 1972.

Smyth, Frederick, comp. *A Reference Book for Freemasons.* London, 1998.

JAMES SMITH ALLEN

lodges of adoption, which had been reconstituted in France, Spain, and Italy. Since the eighteenth century, Freemasons had included many more members of the newer, middling social groups created by a century of industrialization. Teachers, office managers, salesmen, and government functionaries joined social and political elites in the lodges, often for mixed motives such as employment networks and charitable activities, mostly in small towns. By the end of the long nineteenth century, Freemasonry had become a widely recognized if not exemplary civic organization in modern Europe.

See also **Anticlericalism; Carbonari; Pius IX.**

FREGE, GOTTLOB (1848–1925), German mathematician, logician, and philosopher.

Friedrich Ludwig Gottlob Frege devoted most of his career to a single project: the attempt to provide foundations for arithmetic. What is it to provide foundations for arithmetic? To provide foundations for a science, in Frege's sense, is to systematize it: to list its primitive truths and concepts and to show how these primitive truths and concepts figure in the justification of the truths of the science. The resulting systematization of a science is meant to exhibit the source of the knowledge of its truths. Mathematical work provided him with one model of this sort of systematization, the arithmeticization of analysis.

MATHEMATICAL BACKGROUND

Analysis originated in the seventeenth century as a response to the needs of physics and astronomy. Its proofs originally exploited techniques of geometry. In the mid-nineteenth century, however, it became apparent that many of the geometrical proofs were not as secure as they seemed. Some apparently good proofs were identified as fallacious. The difficulties were attributable, in part, to confusions about some basic notions of analysis, including those of limit and continuity. The response was to try to show that the foundations of analysis lay in arithmetic: to offer a systematization of analysis in which only terms of arithmetic were used. Arithmetic was also systematized. Julius Wilhelm Richard Dedekind (1831–1916) provided an easily surveyable list of axioms from which, it was thought, all truths of arithmetic were derivable. But Frege was not content with Dedekind's systematization. For Dedekind's axiomatization did not, according to Frege, exhibit the source of our knowledge of the truths of arithmetic. The problem was that the terms of arithmetic (for example, "0") appeared in Dedekind's axioms, and that his axioms included familiar truths of arithmetic (for example, that 0 does not equal 1). Such terms and truths are not primitive, in Frege's sense, because it is not clear what the source of knowledge about numbers is. To see why, it is necessary to look at Frege's views about the sources of knowledge.

SYSTEMATIZATION OF SCIENCE AND SOURCES OF KNOWLEDGE

Sense experience is indisputably a source of some knowledge. The empiricist view can be characterized as the view that sense experience is the source of *all* knowledge. Frege thought that the German philosopher Immanuel Kant (1724–1804) had refuted this view by showing that some knowledge, including knowledge of Euclidean geometry, does not have the senses as its source. The source of this knowledge is, rather, pure intuition—a faculty underlying perception of objects in space. But Kant erred, according to Frege, in failing to recognize that some substantive knowledge requires neither sense experience nor pure intuition for its justification. Knowledge of arithmetic, Frege believed, is more basic than that of either the special sciences or geometry. The source of this knowledge is something that underlies all knowledge: reason alone. The science of reason, the science of the general laws that underlie all correct inference, is logic. Frege was convinced that the truths of arithmetic and, indeed, of all mathematics other than Euclidean geometry were logical truths. But many truths of arithmetic (e.g., that 0 does not equal 1)

seem to be truths about particular objects, not general laws of logic. Frege thought he could show that all arithmetical truths are truths of logic by defining the numbers and the concept of number from purely logical concepts and proving the basic truths of arithmetic using only these definitions and logical laws. The result would be logical foundations for arithmetic: foundations showing that reason alone is the source of the knowledge of the truths of arithmetic.

THE HISTORY OF FREGE'S PROJECT

Although Frege was convinced that the truths of arithmetic were logical truths, he was aware that they were not derivable using the logical systems generally accepted in his time. But he was also convinced that these logical systems were inadequate. Thus he began by constructing a new logic. In the 1879 monograph, *Begriffsschrift*, he set out the first logical system adequate for the expression and evaluation of the arguments that are regarded as logically valid. His next major work, *Die Grundlagen der Arithmetik* (1884; *The Foundations of Arithmetic,* 1950), was an informal description of his project, its motivations, and Frege's strategy for accomplishing his goals. The project was to have been completed in his *Grundgesetze der Arithmetik* (*Basic Laws of Arithmetic*).The first volume of *Basic Laws* was published in 1893. In 1902, when the second volume was in press, Frege received a now-famous letter from the mathematician and philosopher Bertrand Russell (1872–1970), demonstrating that the logical system was inconsistent. Frege ultimately concluded that the project, as he had envisioned it, was doomed to failure.

FREGE'S LEGACY

Although Frege failed to accomplish the task he set himself, he made profound contributions to logic and philosophy. One of these is Frege's new logic. The inconsistency in the logic set out in *Basic Laws* is easily eliminated by omitting the two basic logical laws that were needed for the definitions of the numbers. The resulting logical system is not only more powerful than earlier logical systems, it is also formal in several important respects. In Frege's logic it is a mechanical task to determine, for any string of symbols in the logical language, whether it is a well-formed name or sentence of the language. It is also a mechanical task to determine whether a sentence is a basic law and whether or not a sentence follows immediately by one of the rules of inferences from other sentences. Thus there is a mechanical procedure for evaluating a purported gapless proof of the argument in the formal language. These formal features make it possible to regard the logical system itself as a mathematical entity. The field of mathematical logic thus has its origin in Frege's new logic.

Another important Fregean legacy comes from his approach to his philosophical problem. Frege believed that he could solve a philosophical problem about the nature of the truths of arithmetic by introducing definitions, using purely logical terms, that could replace numerals in all contexts. The justification of these definitions was provided by an analysis of how certain symbols (the numerals) are used and a demonstration that these symbols can be dispensed with by defining them from other terms. The philosophical question that Frege wanted to answer appears to have nothing in particular to do with language or meaning. Yet he answered the question by engaging in a linguistic investigation. The use of this strategy marks Frege as one of the first (perhaps the very first) to take the so-called linguistic turn that is characteristic of analytic philosophy, the dominant school in Anglo-American philosophy since the middle of the twentieth century.

Finally, many of Frege's writings on specific issues concerning language, logic, and mathematics remain immensely influential in the twenty-first century. A great deal of work in linguistics and the philosophy of language has its origin in his discussions of language. Indeed, a substantial number of early-twenty-first-century philosophers regard themselves as neo-Fregeans. Even the logicist project that Frege regarded as having been decisively refuted has been resurrected and forms an important strand of contemporary philosophical thought about arithmetic. Frege's work attracted only a small audience in his lifetime. But in the years since, his influence on contemporary philosophy, especially on thought about language and logic, has become ubiquitous.

See also **Science and Technology.**

BIBLIOGRAPHY

Primary Sources

Frege, Gottlob. *Foundations of Arithmetic: A Logico-Mathematical Enquiry into the Concept of Number.* Translated by J. L. Austin. 2nd edition. Oxford, U.K., 1980. Translation of *Die Grundlagen der Arithmetik.*

Beaney, Michael, ed. *The Frege Reader.* Oxford, U.K., 1997. Collection containing Frege's most well known articles as well as excerpts from his most important books.

Secondary Sources

Dummett, Michael. *Frege: Philosophy of Mathematics.* London, 1991. A scholarly work by one of Frege's most influential contemporary interpreters

Weiner, Joan. *Frege Explained: From Arithmetic to Analytic Philosophy.* Chicago, 2004. An introduction to Frege's works intended for nonspecialists.

JOAN WEINER

FRENCH REVOLUTION. France's involvement in the war of independence waged by Britain's North American colonies from 1775 to 1783 partially revenged the humiliations Britain had inflicted on France in India, Canada, and the Caribbean; the war, however, cost France over one billion livres, more than twice the usual annual revenue of the state. As the royal state sank into financial crisis after 1783, the costs of servicing this massive debt impelled the monarchy to seek ways of ending noble immunity from taxation and the capacity of noble-dominated high courts (parlements) to resist royal decrees to that end.

Historians agree that it was this financial crisis that erected the stage on which the French Revolution of 1789 was enacted. They do not agree, however, on whether this was only the immediate cause of a much longer and deeper crisis within French society. Were the long-term pressures of royal state-making that fueled pressures to remove the nobility's fiscal immunities paralleled by another challenge to the nobility, from a wealthier, larger, and more critical bourgeoisie and a disaffected peasantry? If this was not the case, it could be argued that there was no deep-seated, long-term crisis within this society, that the Revolution had only short-term and therefore relatively unimportant causes, and that it was therefore avoidable.

Since the early 1990s some historians have seen debates about the socioeconomic origins of the Revolution as moribund and have contested the applicability of terms such as *class* and *class-consciousness* to eighteenth-century France. Instead, they have argued that the origins and nature of the Revolution are best observed through an analysis of "political culture," especially the emerging sphere of "public opinion." Other historians have focused on the "material culture" of eighteenth-century France, that is, the material objects and practices of daily life. From this research it seems clear that a series of interrelated changes—economic, social, and cultural—was undermining the bases of social and political authority in the second half of the eighteenth century. The limited but highly visible expansion of capitalist enterprise in industry and in agriculture in the outskirts of major cities, and above all the growth of commerce, linked to the colonial trade, was generating forms of wealth and values at odds with the institutional bases of absolutism, corporate privilege, and the claims to authority of the nobility and church. The most articulate statements of these challenges to established forms of politics and religion are known as the Enlightenment. Well before 1789, a language of "citizen," "nation," "social contract," and "general will" was being articulated across French society, clashing with an older discourse of "orders," "estates," and "corporations."

The lively world of literature in the 1780s was essentially an urban phenomenon: most men and women in towns could read. There is little sign of an "Enlightenment" in the countryside. Nevertheless, rural France was in crisis in the 1780s, because of the rapid increase in rents owing to long-term increases in agricultural productivity and population, and in some areas to the collapse of the textile industry following the free trade treaty with England in 1786. While the surviving traces of the feudal regime were relatively light in some regions, resentment of seignorial prerogatives everywhere bonded rural communities together against their lords.

During 1787 and 1788 royal ministers made successive attempts to persuade meetings of the most prominent "Notables" to agree to lift the fiscal privileges of the nobility, or Second Estate. These foundered on the nobility's insistence that only a gathering of representatives of the three orders (clergy, nobility, commons) as an Estates-General could agree to such innovation. Tension between crown and nobility came to a head in August 1788, with the parlements insisting that the measures King Louis XVI's ministry sought to impose amounted to "royal despotism." In such a situation, both sides looked to an Estates-General to provide legitimacy for their claims. They were both mistaken. Instead, the calling of the Estates-General for May 1789 facilitated the expression of tensions at every level of French society. The remarkable vibrancy of debate in the months before May 1789 was facilitated by the suspension of press censorship and the publication of several thousand political pamphlets. This war of words was fueled by Louis's indecision about the procedures to be followed at Versailles. Would representatives of the three orders meet separately, as at the previous meeting in 1614, or in a single chamber? Louis's decision on 27 December to double the size of the Third Estate representation served to highlight further this crucial issue of political power, because he remained silent on how voting would occur.

In the spring of 1789, people all over France were required to elect deputies to the Estates-General and to formulate proposals for the reform of public life by compiling "lists of grievances." The drawing up of these *cahiers de doléances* in the context of subsistence crisis, political uncertainty, and fiscal chaos was the decisive moment in the mass politicization of social friction. At least on the surface, the *cahiers* of all three orders show a remarkable level of agreement: they assumed that the meeting of the Estates-General in May would be but the first of a regular cycle; and they saw the need for sweeping reform to taxation, the judiciary, the Catholic Church, and administration. On fundamental matters of social order and political power, however, entrenched divisions were to undermine the possibilities of consensual reform. Rural communities and the nobility were in sharp disagreement about seignorial dues, and bourgeois across the country challenged the nobility by advocating "careers

A pro-revolution cartoon c. 1789. A peasant woman is shown carrying a nun and an aristocrat on her back; the caption reads "Let's hope that this game ends soon." RÉUNION DES MUSÉES NATIONAUX/ART RESOURCE, NY

open to talent," equality of taxation, and the ending of privilege. Many parish priests agreed with the commons about taxation reform in particular, while insisting on the prerogatives of their own order.

THE REVOLUTION OF 1789

Some 208 of the 303 First Estate deputies were lower clergy; only 51 of the 176 bishops had been elected as delegates. Most of the 282 noble deputies were provincial men prominent in their districts. The 646 Third Estate deputies were almost all officials, professionals, and men of property. The latter body of delegates rapidly developed a common outlook, insistent on their dignity and responsibility to "the Nation"; they refused to meet in a separate chamber, and on 17 June proclaimed themselves the National

Assembly. This was the first revolutionary challenge to absolutism and privilege. Louis appeared to capitulate, ordering all deputies to meet in a common assembly, but at the same time he invested Paris, 16 kilometers (10 miles) from Versailles and a crucible of revolutionary enthusiasm, with twenty thousand mercenaries.

The National Assembly was saved from probable dissolution only by a collective action of Parisian working people, angry at an escalation in the price of bread, and certain that the assembly was under military threat. Arms and ammunition were seized from gunsmiths and the Invalides military hospital. The main target was the Bastille fortress in the Faubourg Saint-Antoine, known to have supplies of arms and gunpowder; it was also an awesome symbol of the arbitrary authority of the monarchy. The seizure of the Bastille on 14 July not only saved the National Assembly, it also strengthened the calls for change elsewhere in the country. In communities all over France, "patriots" seized control of local government. News of the storming of the Bastille reached a countryside simmering with conflict, hope, and fear: the harvest failure in 1788 had been followed by a harsh winter, and widespread hunger as crops ripened was matched by hopes invested in the Estates-General. In what became known as the Great Fear, rumors swept the countryside of nobles taking revenge in the wake of the Parisian revolution by hiring "brigands" to destroy crops. When the acts of revenge failed to materialize, armed peasant militias seized foodstuffs or compelled seigneurs or their agents to hand over feudal registers.

On the night of 4 August, panic-stricken nobles mounted the rostrum of the National Assembly to respond to the Great Fear by renouncing their privileges and abolishing feudal dues. In the succeeding week, however, they made a distinction between instances of "personal servitude," which were abolished outright, and "property rights" (especially seignorial dues payable on harvests) for which peasants would have to pay compensation before ceasing payment. This distinction was to fuel ongoing peasant revolt for the next three years.

Later, on 27 August, the National Assembly voted its Declaration of the Rights of Man and of the Citizen. Fundamental to the declaration was the assertion of the essence of liberalism, that "liberty consists of the power to do whatever is not injurious to others." The declaration guaranteed rights of free speech and association, of religion and opinion. This was to be a nation in which all were to be equal in legal status, and subject to the same public responsibilities: it was an invitation to become citizens of a nation instead of subjects of a king. The August decrees and the Declaration of the Rights of Man together marked the end of the absolutist, seignorial, and corporate structure of eighteenth-century France. They were also a revolutionary proclamation of the principles of a new golden age. But, while the declaration proclaimed the universality of rights and the civic equality of all citizens, it was ambiguous on whether the propertyless, slaves, and women would have political as well as legal equality, and was silent on how the means to exercise one's talents could be secured by those without the education or property necessary to do so.

Both the August decrees and the declaration met with refusal from Louis. The Estates-General had been summoned to offer him advice on the state of his kingdom: did his acceptance of the existence of a "National Assembly" require him to accept its decisions? Once again the standing of the National Assembly seemed in question. This time it was the market women of Paris who took the initiative, convinced that the king had to sanction the decrees and return to Paris: in this way they believed that the noble conspiracy to starve Paris would be broken. Louis did so on 6 October. Later he married the white of the Bourbon family to the blue and red of Paris to symbolize the unity of king and nation. The Revolution seemed secure and complete, but Louis's reluctant consent to change was only thinly disguised by the fiction that his obstinacy was solely due to the malign influence of his court.

Elsewhere in Europe and America, people were struck by the dramatic events of the summer. Few failed to be enthused by them, despite news of bloodshed. Among the crowned heads of Europe, only the kings of Sweden and Spain and Catherine the Great of Russia were resolutely hostile from the outset. Others may have felt a certain pleasure at seeing one of Europe's Great Powers incommoded

The Sans-Culotte. Undated French lithograph depicting a supporter of the revolution with his clogs and red Phrygian cap guarding a captive aristocrat. The term *sans-culottes* derived from the fact that members of the working and lower classes wore plain long trousers rather than the knee breeches, or culottes, favored by the wealthy. BIBLIOTHÈQUE DES ARTS DECORATIFS, PARIS, FRANCE/BRIDGEMAN ART LIBRARY/ARCHIVES CHARMET

by its own people. Among the general American and European populaces, however, support for the Revolution was widespread, and initially there were few outspoken "counterrevolutionaries" such as Edmund Burke.

The euphoria of the autumn of 1789 was tempered by awareness of the magnitude of what remained to be done. The revolutionaries' declaration of the principles of the new regime presupposed that every aspect of public life would be reshaped. The *ancien régime,* as it was now called, had been overthrown, but what was to be put in its place?

THE RECONSTRUCTION OF FRANCE, 1789–1791

Over the next two years, the deputies threw themselves into the task of reworking every dimension of public life. The reconstruction of France was based on a belief in the equal status of French citizens whatever their social or geographic origin. In every aspect of public life—administration, the judiciary, taxation, the armed forces, the church, policing—a system of corporate rights, appointment, and hierarchy gave way to civil equality, accountability, and popular sovereignty. The institutional structure of the *ancien régime* had been characterized by extraordinary provincial diversity controlled by a network of royal appointees. Now this was reversed: at every level officials were to be elected, but the institutions in which they worked were everywhere to be the same. The institutional bedrock would be the forty-one thousand new "communes," mostly based on the parishes of the *ancien régime*, the base of a hierarchy of cantons, districts, and eighty-three departments.

The complex set of royal, aristocratic, and clerical courts and their regional variants was replaced by a national system deliberately made more accessible, humane, and egalitarian. In particular, the introduction of elected justices of the peace in every canton was immensely popular for its provision of cheap and accessible justice. The number of capital offenses was sharply reduced, and the punishment for them would be a style of decapitation perfected by a deputy, the Parisian doctor Joseph Guillotin, and accepted as humane by the National Assembly. This vast project of creating a new legal framework was matched by a zeal for individual rights. By the end of 1789 full citizenship had been granted to Protestants and, by the following January, to the Sephardic Jews of Bordeaux and Avignon. The latter was passed only by 374 votes to 280, however, and the Ashkenazic Jews of the east had to wait until September 1791 for equal recognition.

From the outset the ideals of liberty and equality were compromised by pragmatic considerations of vested interests. Neither poorer men—dubbed "passive" citizens—nor women were judged capable of exercising sovereign rights. A similar hesitancy was expressed over whether the principles of 1789 should be extended to the Caribbean colonies. A bitter debate pitted the colonial lobby (the Club Massiac) against the Société des amis des Noirs (Society of the Friends of the Blacks), which included Jacques-Pierre Brissot and Maximilien

Robespierre. In May 1791 the National Assembly granted "active" citizen status to free blacks with free parents and the necessary property, but avoided the issues of slavery and the slave trade.

The National Assembly had inherited the monarchy's bankruptcy, and this pressing problem was now aggravated by popular refusal to pay taxes. Several measures were taken to meet this crisis. In November 1789 the vast church lands were nationalized and, from November 1790, sold at auction, mainly to local bourgeois and the wealthiest peasants. These sales were also used to back the issue of assignats, a paper currency that soon began to decline in real purchasing power. Fiscal exemptions were finally ended by a new system of taxation, based on the estimated value of and income from property, introduced from the beginning of 1791.

Until 1791 the Revolution was overwhelmingly popular: sweeping changes in public life occurred within a context of mass optimism and support. The Festival of the Federation, on the first anniversary of the storming of the Bastille, celebrated the unity of church, monarchy, and Revolution. Two days earlier, however, the National Assembly had voted a reform that was to shatter this unity. The widespread agreement in the *cahiers* on the need for reform guaranteed that the National Assembly had been able to push through the nationalization of church lands, the closing of contemplative orders, and the granting of religious liberty to Protestants and Jews. Mounting clerical opposition to these changes ultimately focused on the Civil Constitution of the Clergy, adopted on 12 July 1790. Many priests were materially advantaged by the new salary scale, and only the upper clergy would have regretted that bishops' stipends were dramatically reduced. Most contentious, however, was the issue of how the clergy were to be appointed in the future: in requiring the election of priests and bishops, the National Assembly crossed the line separating temporal and spiritual life. In the end, it would prove impossible to reconcile a church based on divinely revealed truth and hierarchical authority, and a certainty of one true faith, with a Revolution based on popular sovereignty, religious tolerance, and the certainty of earthly fulfillment through the application of secular reason.

The Method of Making Aristocratic Bishops and Priests Swear Allegiance to the Civil Constitution in the Presence of the Municipalities according to the Decree of the National Assembly. Undated cartoon. The reluctance of Catholic clergy to submit to the demands of the secular revolutionary state became a major concern for republican authorities, while lingering pro-religious sentiment led to divisions among the citizenry. BIBLIOTHÈQUE NATIONALE, PARIS, FRANCE/BRIDGEMAN ART LIBRARY/ LAUROS/GIRAUDON

Parish priests were required to take a civic oath in order to continue their functions, and their difficult choice—felt as one between loyalty to the Revolution and loyalty to God and the pope—was often influenced by parishioner sentiment. By mid-1791 two Frances had emerged, the pro-reform areas of the southeast, the Paris basin, and much of the center contrasting with the west and southwest, much of the north and east, and the southern Massif Central. The strength of refractory, or non-oath-taking ("non-juring"), clergy in border areas fed Parisian suspicions that peasants who could not understand French were prey to the "superstitions" of their "fanatical" priests.

Everywhere, the birth of new systems of administration within a context of popular sovereignty and hectic legislative activity was part of the creation of a revolutionary political culture. The work of the National Assembly was vast in scope and energy. The foundations of a new social order were laid, underpinned by an assumption of the national unity of a fraternity of citizens. This was a revolutionary transformation of public life. At the same time, the Assembly was walking a tightrope. On one side lay a growing hostility from nobles and the elite of the church angered by the loss of status, wealth, and privilege, and bolstered in many areas by a disillusioned parish clergy and their parishioners. On the other side, the National

Assembly was alienating itself from the popular base of the Revolution by its compromise on feudal dues, its exclusion of the "passive" citizens from the political process, and its implementation of economic liberalism.

One element of the new political culture was the many thousands of political clubs established in the early years of the Revolution, the most famous of which was the Jacobin Club of Paris, known by the name of its premises in a former convent. Many of these clubs catered to "passive" citizens. In 1791 active democrats among the *menu peuple* (common people) became widely known by a new term, *sans-culottes*, which was both a political label for a militant patriot and a social description signifying men of the people who did not wear the knee breeches and stockings of the upper classes.

Ever since July 1789 the National Assembly had had to face a double challenge: How could the Revolution be protected from its opponents? Whose Revolution was it to be? These questions came to a head in mid-1791. Louis fled Paris on 21 June, publicly repudiating the direction the Revolution had taken, especially in reforms to the church. On the evening of the next day, Louis was recognized in a village near the eastern frontier and arrested. Although he was suspended temporarily from his position as king, the National Assembly was determined to quell any popular unrest that might threaten the constitutional monarchy. On 17 July, an unarmed demonstration to demand Louis's abdication was organized on the Champ-de-Mars by the democratic Club of the Cordeliers, with some Jacobin support, at the same "altar of the homeland" on which the Festival of the Federation had been celebrated a year earlier. The marquis de Lafayette, the commander of the National Guard, was ordered to disperse the petitioners; his guardsmen killed perhaps fifty of them.

On 14 September an apparently sincere Louis promulgated the Constitution that embodied the National Assembly's work since 1789. France was to be a constitutional monarchy in which power was shared between the king, as head of the executive, and a legislative assembly elected by a restrictive property franchise. The issues of his loyalty and of whether the Revolution was over were, however, far from resolved.

It was in this highly charged context that a new Legislative Assembly was elected and convened in Paris in October 1791. At the outset most of its members sought to consolidate the state of the Revolution as expressed in the Constitution, and deserted the Jacobin Club for the Feuillants, a club similarly named after its meeting place in a former convent. Growing anxiety about the opposing threats of popular radicalism and counterrevolution, on the one hand, and bellicose posturing from European rulers, on the other, was to convince the Legislative Assembly that the Revolution and France itself were in danger.

A SECOND REVOLUTION, 1792

A key element in this unease was the rebellion of hundreds of thousands of mulattoes and slaves in Saint Domingue, beginning in August 1791. The Legislative Assembly responded in April 1792 by extending civil equality to all "free persons of color." The slave revolt in the Caribbean colonies so important to the French economy further convinced the deputies of the insidious intentions of France's rivals, England and Spain.

The Jacobin followers of Brissot argued that the Revolution would not be safe until this foreign threat was destroyed and the loyalty of French citizens to the Constitution demonstrated by a patriotic war against internal and external enemies. The war declared on 20 April against Austria exposed internal opposition, as the "Brissotins" hoped, but it was neither limited nor brief. With the Civil Constitution of the Clergy, it was to prove one of the major turning points of the revolutionary period, influencing the internal history of France until Napoleon's defeat in 1815. The French armies were initially in disarray because of the emigration of many noble officers and internal political dissension within garrisons. The vitriol of counterrevolutionary rhetoric added to the popular conviction that Louis was complicit in the defeats being suffered by the army. In response, the forty-eight neighborhood "sections" of Paris voted to form a Commune of Paris to organize insurrection and an army of twenty thousand sans-culottes from the newly democratized National Guard. After Louis took refuge in the nearby Legislative Assembly, six hundred Swiss guards, the palace's main defenders, were killed in the fighting or subsequently in bloody acts of retribution. This insurrection thereby succeeded in overthrowing the monarchy on 10 August 1792.

Among those who participated in the overthrow of the monarchy were soldiers from Marseille en route to the battlefront. They brought with them a song popular among republicans in the south—"La Marseillaise"—composed by the army officer Claude-Joseph Rouget de Lisle as the "Chant de guerre pour l'armée du Rhin" (War song of the Army of the Rhine). This song would later be adopted as the French national anthem.

The declaration of war and overthrow of the monarchy radicalized the Revolution. The political exclusion of "passive" citizens now called to defend the French nation was untenable. Moreover, by overthrowing the monarchy, the popular movement had issued the ultimate challenge to the whole of Europe. The Revolution was now armed, democratic, and republican.

On 2 September, news reached Paris that the great fortress at Verdun, just 250 kilometers (155 miles) from the capital, had fallen to the Prussians. The news generated an immediate, dramatic surge in popular fear and resolve. Convinced that "counterrevolutionaries" (whether nobles, priests, or common-law criminals) in prisons were waiting to break out and welcome the invaders once the volunteers had left for the front, hastily convened popular courts sentenced to death about 1,200 of the 2,700 prisoners brought before them, including 240 priests.

About two weeks after these "September massacres," revolutionary armies won their first great victory, at Valmy, 200 kilometers (125 miles) east of the capital. As news arrived of the victory, the new National Convention, elected by universal manhood suffrage, was convening in Paris. The men of the Convention were mostly middle class by social background. They were also democrats and republicans: immediately on convening, they abolished the monarchy and proclaimed France a republic.

The Jacobins within the Convention were somewhat closer to the popular movement, and exuded a militant republicanism. Their habit of sitting together on the upper-left-hand benches in the Convention earned them the epithet of the

An officer of the National Guard swears an oath of allegiance before the Altar of the Constitution and the Declaration of the Rights of Man. PRIVATE COLLECTION/ BRIDGEMAN ART LIBRARY/LAUROS/GIRAUDON

"Mountain." The label given to their opposition, the "Girondins," denoted men closer in sympathy to the concern for political and economic stability among the upper bourgeoisie of Bordeaux, capital of the Gironde.

The trial of Louis XVI exposed this division. Whereas the Girondins sought to placate the rest of Europe by considering a sentence of exile or mercy, the thrust of the Jacobin argument during this dramatic and eloquent debate was that to spare Louis would be to admit his special nature: for them "Louis Capet" was a citizen guilty of treason. The Convention narrowly agreed, and Louis went to the guillotine on 21 January 1793. One effect of this regicide was the expansion of the enemy coalition to include Britain and Spain.

THE REVOLUTION IN THE BALANCE, 1793–1794

As the external military crisis worsened in early 1793, most of the uncommitted deputies swung behind the Jacobins' emergency proposals. The Convention ordered a levy of 300,000 conscripts in March. In the west this provoked massive armed rebellion and civil war, known, like the region itself, as "the Vendée." Ultimately, the civil war was to claim perhaps as many as 200,000 lives on each side, as many as the external wars waged from 1793 to 1794.

The nation was in grave danger of internal collapse and external defeat. In the spring of 1793 the Convention responded by vesting emergency executive powers in a Committee of Public Safety and placing policing powers in a Committee of General Security. The military challenge was met by an extraordinary mobilization of the nation's resources and repression of opponents. The Convention appointed "deputies on mission" from its own number to supervise the war effort. It passed emergency decrees, such as those declaring émigrés "civilly dead," and placed controls on grain and bread prices.

Despite these measures, by midsummer 1793 the Revolution faced its greatest crisis, which was simultaneously military, social, and political. Enemy troops were on French soil in the northeast, southeast, and southwest and, internally, the great revolt in the Vendée absorbed a major part of the republic's army. These threats were aggravated by the hostile response of sixty departmental administrations to the purge of twenty-one leading Girondins in June.

With the appointment of Robespierre in July and two other Jacobins in September, the Committee of Public Safety had the resolve to mobilize an entire society in defense of the Revolution and to decimate its internal and external opponents. Essential to this mobilization was the creation by the Jacobin government of a rural–urban alliance through a mixture of intimidation, force, and policies aimed both at meeting popular grievances and placing the entire country on a war footing. The Convention acted to meet sans-culotte demands by decreeing the "general maximum" of 29 September, which pegged the prices of thirty-nine commodities. It also responded to the waves of rural unrest that had affected two-thirds of all departments since 1789, with the complete abolition of seignorialism. From 17 July 1793, former seigneurs were left with only nonfeudal rents on land. The feudal regime was finally dead.

The central purpose of what became known as the Terror was to institute the emergency and draconian measures deemed necessary at a time of military crisis. The Convention acquiesced in draconian measures—such as surveillance committees in neighborhoods and villages, and suspension of civil liberties—necessary to secure the republic to a point where the newly drafted democratic constitution of June 1793 could be implemented. The Law of Suspects (17 September) was designed to imprison the unpatriotic with detention, to intimidate them into inaction, or to execute them as counterrevolutionaries. In the last three months of 1793, 177 of the 395 accused before a newly instituted extraordinary criminal court, the Revolutionary Tribunal, were sentenced to death, including the Girondin leaders and Marie-Antoinette. This mixture of national mobilization and intimidation was so successful that by the end of 1793 the threat of civil war and invasion had at least been countered.

The Jacobins who now dominated the Convention and the Committee of Public Safety also sought to realize their vision of a regenerated society worthy of the grandeur of the Enlightenment and the Revolution. During the eighteen months after the overthrow of the monarchy in August 1792, a combination of radical Jacobin reforms and popular initiative created an extraordinary force for republican "regeneration." Supporters of the Revolution—"patriots," as they were most commonly known—marked their repudiation of the old world by attempting to eradicate all of its traces, giving children names drawn from nature, classical antiquity, or contemporary heroes, and purging place-names of religious or royal connotations. A new citizenry was to be created by a secular and republican education system. Most radically, in order to mark the magnitude of what had been achieved since the proclamation of the republic on 21 September 1792, the Convention introduced a new calendar that replaced the Gregorian calendar and its saints' days and religious cycles with a decimal calendar based on *décades*, periods of ten days—three *décades* comprising a month. A year thus still consisted of twelve months, the names of which were drawn from nature, plus five *sans-culottes* days named after the virtues (with one extra holiday, Revolution Day, added in leap years). The calendar began on 22 September 1793: the first day of the Year II of liberty and equality.

In the eighteen months between August 1792 and early 1794, the political participation of urban working people reached its zenith. The sans-culottes had a vision of a society of small farms and workshops created by property redistribution and underpinned by free education, purges of old elites, and direct democracy.

The achievements of this new alliance of Jacobins, sans-culottes, and some of the peasantry were dramatic by the end of 1793. By then, republican forces led by a young artillery officer, Napoleon Bonaparte, had recaptured Toulon, and foreign armies had suffered major reverses in the northeast and southeast. The Vendéan rebellion had been contained and other revolts crushed, both at a huge cost in lives. Though the "general maximum" had not been fully implemented, the economic slide had been reversed, and the purchasing power of the assignat had climbed back to 48 percent from 36 percent a few months earlier.

For the majority of the Convention, however, the goal of the Terror was the attainment of peace, and economic and political controls were but temporary constraints to that end. The regular extension of the powers of the committees was a recognition of their achievements during the continuing war crisis, but it was not a measure of support for Jacobin ideology. In late 1793 "moderate" Jacobins such as Georges Danton and Camille Desmoulins urged an end to the controls of the Terror and the implementation of the constitution of 1793. For several months Robespierre and his closest Jacobin associates were able to paint Danton and his associates as "indulgents," like the "Enragé" militants seen as guilty of undermining republican unity. Success in the war effort, especially the battle of Fleurus (26 June 1794)—which finally ended the threat of Austrian troops on French soil—exposed the divisions in the popular alliance of the Year II. The geographic incidence of executions during the Terror had been concentrated in departments where the military

A list of people to be guillotined at the Place de la Révolution in August 1792. The beheading of Louis David Collenot, whose name appears first on this list, represented the first use of the guillotine to execute a political prisoner. Such lists were sold in the streets of Paris. ©Hulton-Deutsch Collection/Corbis

threat had been greatest; but now, as the military threat receded, the number of executions for political opposition increased. Such executions included Danton and his associates, sent to the guillotine in April 1794.

A speech to the Convention by Robespierre on 26 July (8 Thermidor), with his vague threat to unnamed deputies, provided the motivation for reaction. Among those who plotted his overthrow were Joseph Fouché, Jean-Marie Collot d'Herbois, Louis Fréron, and Paul Barras, fearful that Robespierre intended to call them to account for their bloody repression of revolts in Lyon, Toulon, and Marseille.

The execution of Robespierre and his associates on 28 July marked the end of a regime that had had the twin aims of saving the Revolution and creating a new society. It had achieved the former, at great cost, but the vision of the virtuous, self-abnegating civic warrior embodying the new society had palled for most within the Convention. The expression "the system of the Terror" was first used two days later by Bertrand Barère.

The year of the Terror has always polarized historians. To those sympathetic to the goals of the Revolution and mindful of the magnitude of the counterrevolution determined to crush it, it has seemed a successful emergency military regime during which excesses were regrettable but explicable. Others have emphasized the disproportionate level of violence against the Revolution's opponents, particularly as the military crisis receded. Still others have seen in the messianic social vision of the Jacobins a precursor to the most authoritarian regimes of the twentieth century. Whatever the case, the overthrow of Robespierre was universally welcomed at the time as symbolizing the end of large-scale executions.

ENDING THE REVOLUTION, 1794–1799

The post-Thermidorian regimes were republican, but they were driven above all else by the imperative to end the Revolution, most obviously by suppressing the sources of instability represented by the Jacobins and sans-culottes. The Thermidorians were hard men, many of them former Girondins, who had lived through the Terror in quiet opposition, and were determined that the terrifying experience would not be repeated. While there was a widespread longing for a return to democratic freedoms, a bitter social reaction was unleashed by the removal of wartime restrictions.

The end of all fixed prices in December 1794 unleashed rampant inflation, and, by April 1795, the general level of prices was about 750 percent above 1790 levels. In this context of social and political reaction and economic deprivation, the sans-culottes made a final desperate attempt to regain the initiative. The risings of Germinal and Prairial Year III (April and May 1795) effectively sought a return to the promises of the autumn of 1793, the epitome of the sans-culottes' influence. The crushing of the May 1795 insurrection unleashed a wide-ranging reaction, with thousands of arrests. Prison camps were established in the Seychelles and French Guiana.

The majority in the Convention now sought a political settlement that would stabilize the Revolution and end popular upheaval. The Constitution of the Year III (August 1795) restricted participation in electoral assemblies by wealth, age, and education as well as by sex. Popular sovereignty was to be limited to the act of voting: petitions, political clubs, and even unarmed demonstrations were banned. The social rights promised in the Jacobin constitution of 1793 were removed; property ownership was again to be the basis of the social order and political power, as was the case from 1789 to 1792. Gone now was the optimism of the period 1789 to 1791, the belief that with the liberation of human creativity all could aspire to the "active" exercise of their capabilities. The constitution of 1795 now included a declaration of "duties," exhorting respect for the law, the family, and property. In this sense, the constitution can be seen to mark the end of the Revolution.

One important difference in the new constitution was the attempt to resolve religious divisions by separating church and state. On 11 Prairial Year III (30 May 1795) the regime allowed the reopening of churches closed during the Terror and allowed émigré priests to return under the decree of 7 Fructidor Year IV (24 August 1797), but only on condition of their taking a civic oath. Religious observance was to be a purely private matter: bells and outward signs of religiosity were forbidden. The church was to be sustained by the offerings of the faithful rather than direct state support.

By excluding the poor from active participation in the political process, the Directory sought to create a republican regime based on "capacity" and a stake in society. To avoid a strong executive with its Jacobin connotations, there were to be frequent partial elections to the Council of the Five

Hundred and rotation of executive authority. The rule of the committees was over. This combination of a narrow social base and internal instability caused the regime to vacillate between political alliances to the right and left to broaden its appeal and forced it to resort to draconian repression of opposition and to the use of military force.

For the better off, the regime of the Directory represented much of what they wanted: the guarantee of the major revolutionary achievements of the period 1789 to 1792 without threats from popular politics. The years of the Directory were often characterized, however, by bitter tensions occasioned by religious divisions, desertion from the army and avoidance of conscription, political abstention, and violent revenge for the deadly politics of the Year II. Underpinning all these tensions were the Directory's economic policies, which ultimately alienated the great mass of people.

As it trod its narrow path the Directory had to protect the regime against resurgent political forces on either side. The elections of 1797 returned a majority of royalists of various nuances. In response, the Directors annulled the elections of 177 deputies and called in troops on 17–18 Fructidor Year V (3–4 September 1797). A new wave of repression followed against refractory clergy, many of whom had returned in hope after the elections. Then, on 22 Floréal Year VI (11 May 1798) another coup was effected to prevent a resurgence of Jacobinism: this time 127 deputies were prevented from taking their seats.

The republican rationale for war in 1792—that this was a defensive war against tyrannical aggression that would naturally become a war of liberation joined by Europe's oppressed—had developed since 1794 into a war of territorial expansion. Peace treaties were signed with Prussia and Spain in 1795. In 1798 the Directory established "sister republics" in Switzerland and the Papal States; and the left bank of the Rhine was incorporated into the "natural boundaries" of what was increasingly referred to as "la grande nation." Conflict with Britain and Austria continued. A peace treaty with the latter was signed at Campo-Formio on 25 Vendémiaire Year VI (17 October 1797), but hostilities recommenced in Italy in 1798. This, together with the extension of war with Britain into Ireland and Egypt, convinced the Directory

that irregular army levies had to be replaced by an annual conscription of single men aged twenty to twenty-five years (the Jourdan Law, 19 Fructidor Year VI [5 September 1798]).

The Directory's military ambitions were increasingly resented by rural populations liable to conscription and requisitioning at a time of economic difficulty. Resentments climaxed in the summer of 1799 in large-scale but uncoordinated royalist risings in the west and southwest. By that time, too, the requisitioning, anticlericalism, and repression practiced by French armies was provoking discontent and insurrection in all of the "sister republics." This and the initial successes of the Second Coalition formed between Russia, Austria, and England provided a pretext for a challenge to the Directory, led by Napoleon, the army officer who had dispersed the royalist insurgents in 1795 and who now abandoned his shattered forces in Egypt. Emmanuel-Joseph Sieyès and Charles-Maurice de Talleyrand, two of the architects of revolutionary change in the period from 1789 to 1791, supported Napoleon. On 18–19 Brumaire Year VIII (9–10 November 1799), the furious members of the Five Hundred were driven out by troops and a decade of parliamentary rule was over.

Napoleon moved quickly to establish internal and external peace. On 15 July 1801 a concordat was signed with the papacy, formally celebrated at Easter mass at Notre-Dame de Paris in 1802. The treaty of Lunéville was signed with Austria on 21 Pluviôse Year IX (9 February 1801) and that of Amiens with Britain on 5 Germinal Year X (25 March 1802). The end of war offered the chance for deserters to be amnestied and for returning émigrés and priests to be reintegrated into their communities in a climate of reconciliation. The peace with Europe was, of course, to be temporary.

THE SIGNIFICANCE OF THE REVOLUTION

A revolution that had begun in 1789 with boundless hopes for a golden era of political liberty and social change had thus ended in 1799 with a military seizure of power. French people had had to endure a decade of political instability, civil war, and armed conflict with the rest of Europe. Despite this, the Revolution had permanently changed France, and these changes were to reverberate through Europe for decades to come.

View of the Elevated Mountain at the Champ de la Reunion for the Festival of the Supreme Being, 20 Prairial, Year 2 of the French Republic (8 June 1794). The Festival of the Supreme Being was instituted by French republicans to supplant traditional Catholic holidays. MUSÉE DE LA RÉVOLUTION FRANÇAISE, VIZILLE, FRANCE/BRIDGEMAN ART LIBRARY/VISUAL ARTS LIBRARY, LONDON, UK

Many of these changes were put in place from 1789 to 1791, when revolutionaries reshaped every aspect of institutional and public life according to principles of rationality, uniformity, and efficiency. The eighty-three departments (today ninety-six) were henceforth to be administered in precisely the same way; they were to have an identical structure of responsibilities, personnel, and powers. Diocesan boundaries coincided with departmental limits, and cathedrals were usually located in departmental capitals. The uniformity of administrative structures was reflected, too, in the innovation of a national system of weights, measures, and currency based on new, decimal measures. These evident benefits to business and commerce were accentuated by the abolition of tolls paid to towns and nobles and internal customs.

For the first time, the state was also understood as representing a more emotional entity, "the nation," based on citizenship. All French citizens, whatever their social background and residence, were to be judged according to a single uniform legal code and taxed by the same obligatory proportional taxes on wealth, especially landed property. This uniformity gave substance to the ideals of "fraternity" and "national unity," meanings reinforced by the new political culture of citizenship and the celebration of new national heroes drawn from antiquity or the revolutionary struggle itself.

Historians agree that French political life had been fundamentally transformed. For the first time, a large and populous country had been reformed along democratic, republican lines. Even the Restoration of the monarchy in 1814 could not reverse the revolutionary change from royal absolutism to constitutional, representative government. But twenty-five years of political upheaval and division left a legacy of memories, both bitter and sweet. In the west, in particular, memories of the Terror and of mass conscription and war were etched deep into the memories of every individual and community. The Revolution was a rich seedbed of ideologies ranging from communism and social democracy to liberal constitutionalism and authoritarian royalism, and French people were to remain divided about which political system was best able to reconcile authority, liberty, and equality.

Whatever the importance of these changes to government, political ideas, and memories, many of the essential characteristics of daily life emerged largely unchanged—especially patterns of work, the position of the poor, and social inequalities. In the colonies, too, the prerevolutionary hierarchies of race were reimposed, with one exception. In January 1802 French troops landed in Saint Domingue to reimpose colonial control; but after two years of bloody fighting the first postcolonial black nation—Haiti—was born. Elsewhere Napoleon reversed the Jacobin abolition of slavery in 1794 and in 1802 reintroduced the Code Noir of 1685, which treated slaves as the property of the slave owner. The slave trade would not be abolished until 1818, and slavery itself not until 1848.

Women emerged from the revolution with no political rights and limited legal rights, but one effect of the abolition of seignorialism may have been that rural women and their families were better nourished. In March 1790 the National Assembly abolished inheritance laws that had favored the first-born son in some regions. Although this was enacted more with a view to breaking the power of great noble patriarchs than to recognizing the rights of women, one outcome was the strengthening of the position of daughters. Another consequence of this legislation may have been a sudden drop in the national birthrate, from 39 per thousand in 1789 to 33 in 1804, as parents sought to limit family size and therefore pressures to subdivide the family's farm.

Despite the exhortations of revolutionary legislators to a peaceful, harmonious family life as the basis of the new political order, it is doubtful whether patterns of male violence changed. What did change, albeit temporarily, was the legal capacity of women to protect their rights within the household. The divorce law voted at the last session of the Legislative Assembly, on 20 September 1792, gave women remarkably broad grounds for leaving an unhappy marriage. Nationally, perhaps thirty thousand divorces were decreed under this legislation, especially in towns, and it was working-women above all who used this law, which lasted until the enactment of the Napoleonic Code in 1804.

Perhaps 20 percent of land changed hands as a result of the expropriation of the church and émigrés, and much of this was acquired by better-off peasants. Indeed, peasants who owned their own land were among the most substantial beneficiaries of the Revolution. After the abolition of feudal dues and the church tithe, both of which had normally been paid in grain, farmers were in a better position to concentrate on using the land for its most productive purposes; they were also better fed. The gains for the peasantry went beyond tangible economic benefits. The abolition of seignorialism underpinned a revolutionary change in rural social relations, voiced in political behavior after 1789. Despite the emigration and death of many nobles, most noble families retained their properties intact, but nothing could compensate them for the loss of judicial rights and power—ranging from seignorial courts to the parlements—or the incalculable loss of prestige and deference caused by the practice of legal equality.

Those who had taken the initiative in creating the new France after 1789 had been the bourgeoisie, whether professional, administrative, commercial, landowning, or manufacturing. The Revolution created economic chaos for the commercial middle classes in the great coastal towns because of the uncertainties caused by wars and blockades and the temporary abolition of slavery. Many other bourgeois benefited from the new war industries, from a stronger internal market, and from uniform economic legislation. Everywhere, however, the Revolution had opened up political life for them and changed the dominant social values necessary to recognize their importance in the life of the nation. The Revolution was their triumph.

See also **Citizenship; Committee of Public Safety; Danton, Georges-Jacques; Directory; Estates-General; France; French Revolutionary Wars and Napoleonic Wars; Girondins; Haiti; Jacobins; Lafayette, Marquis de; Louis XVI; Marat, Jean-Paul; Marie-Antoinette; Napoleon; Paris; Reign of Terror; Robespierre, Maximilien; Toussaint Louverture.**

BIBLIOGRAPHY

Agulhon, Maurice. *Marianne into Battle: Republican Imagery and Symbolism in France, 1789–1880.* Translated by Janet Lloyd. Cambridge, U.K., 1981.

Andress, David. *French Society in Revolution, 1789–1799.* Manchester, U.K., 1999.

———. *The French Revolution and the People.* London, 2004.

Aston, Nigel. *Religion and Revolution in France, 1780–1804.* Basingstoke, U.K., 2000.

Bertaud, Jean-Paul. *The Army of the French Revolution: From Citizen-Soldiers to Instrument of Power.* Translated by R. R. Palmer. Princeton, N.J., 1988.

Brown, Howard G. *War, Revolution, and the Bureaucratic State: Politics and Army Administration in France, 1791–1799.* Oxford, U.K., 1995.

Chartier, Roger. *The Cultural Origins of the French Revolution.* Translated by Lydia G. Cochrane. Durham, N.C., 1991.

Cobb, Richard. *The People's Armies.* Translated by Marianne Elliott. New Haven, Conn., 1987.

Crook, Malcolm. *Elections in the French Revolution: An Apprenticeship in Democracy, 1789–1799.* Cambridge, U.K., 1996.

———. *Napoleon Comes to Power: Democracy and Dictatorship in Revolutionary France, 1795–1804.* Cardiff, U.K., 1998.

Doyle, William. *The Oxford History of the French Revolution.* 2nd ed. Oxford, U.K., 2002.

Fick, Carolyn E. *The Making of Haiti: The Saint Domingue Revolution from Below.* Knoxville, Tenn., 1990.

Forrest, Alan. *The French Revolution and the Poor.* Oxford, U.K., 1981.

———. *The Soldiers of the French Revolution.* Durham, N.C., 1990.

Fraisse, Geneviève, and Michelle Perrot, eds. *Emerging Feminism from Revolution to World War.* Translated by Arthur Goldhammer. Vol. 4 of *A History of Women in the West,* edited by Georges Duby and Michelle Perrot. Cambridge, Mass., 1993.

Garrioch, David. *The Making of Revolutionary Paris.* Berkeley, Calif., 2002.

Godineau, Dominique. *The Women of Paris and Their French Revolution.* Translated by Katherine Streip. Berkeley, Calif., 1998.

Hesse, Carla. *Publishing and Cultural Politics in Revolutionary Paris, 1789–1810.* Berkeley, Calif., 1991.

———. *The Other Enlightenment: How French Women Became Modern.* Princeton, N.J., 2001.

Hunt, Lynn. *Politics, Culture, and Class in the French Revolution.* Berkeley, Calif., 1984.

———. *The Family Romance of the French Revolution.* Berkeley, Calif., 1992.

Jones, Colin. *The Longman Companion to the French Revolution.* London, 1988.

Jones, Colin, and Dror Wahrman, eds. *The Age of Cultural Revolutions: Britain and France, 1750–1820.* Berkeley, Calif., 2002.

Jones, P. M. *The Peasantry in the French Revolution.* Cambridge, U.K., 1988.

———. *Reform and Revolution in France: The Politics of Transition, 1774–1791.* Cambridge, U.K., 1995.

Kennedy, Emmet. *A Cultural History of the French Revolution.* New Haven, Conn., 1989.

Kennedy, Michael L. *The Jacobin Clubs in the French Revolution: The First Years.* Princeton, N.J., 1982.

———. *The Jacobin Clubs in the French Revolution: The Middle Years.* Princeton, N.J., 1988.

Lewis, Gwynne. *The French Revolution: Rethinking the Debate.* London, 1993.

Lewis, Gwynne, and Colin Lucas, eds. *Beyond the Terror: Essays in French Regional and Social History, 1794–1815.* Cambridge, U.K., 1983.

Lyons, Martyn. *France under the Directory.* Cambridge, U.K., 1975.

Markoff, John. *The Abolition of Feudalism: Peasants, Lords, and Legislators in the French Revolution.* University Park, Pa., 1996.

McPhee, Peter. *The French Revolution, 1789–1799.* Oxford, U.K., 2002.

Ozouf, Mona. *Festivals and the French Revolution.* Translated by Alan Sheridan. Cambridge, Mass., 1988.

Palmer, R. R. *Twelve Who Ruled: The Year of the Terror in the French Revolution.* 1941. Reprint, with a new preface by the author, Princeton, N.J., 1989.

Patrick, Alison. *The Men of the First French Republic: Political Alignments in the National Convention of 1792.* Baltimore, Md., 1972.

Popkin, Jeremy D. *A Short History of the French Revolution.* 3rd ed. Upper Saddle River, N.J., 2002.

Rapport, Michael. *Nationality and Citizenship in Revolutionary France: The Treatment of Foreigners, 1789–1799.* Oxford, U.K., 2000.

Rose, R. B. *The Making of the "Sans-Culottes": Democratic Ideas and Institutions in Paris, 1789–1792.* Manchester, U.K., 1983.

Rudé, George. *The Crowd in the French Revolution.* Oxford, U.K., 1959.

Schama, Simon. *Citizens: A Chronicle of the French Revolution*. London, 1989.

Soboul, Albert. *The Parisian Sans-Culottes and the French Revolution, 1793–1794*. Translated by Gwynne Lewis. Oxford, U.K., 1964.

———. *The French Revolution, 1787–1799: From the Storming of the Bastille to Napoleon*. Translated by Alan Forrest and Colin Jones. London, 1989.

Sutherland, D. M. G. *The French Revolution and Empire: The Quest for a Civic Order*. 2nd ed. Oxford, U.K., 2003.

Tackett, Timothy. *Religion, Revolution, and Regional Culture in Eighteenth-Century France: The Ecclesiastical Oath of 1791*. Princeton, N.J., 1986.

———. *Becoming a Revolutionary: The Deputies of the French National Assembly and the Emergence of a Revolutionary Culture (1789–1790)*. Princeton, N.J., 1996.

———. *When the King Took Flight*. Cambridge, Mass., 2003.

Vovelle, Michel. *The Fall of the French Monarchy, 1787–1792*. Translated by Susan Burke. Cambridge, U.K., 1984.

Woloch, Isser. *The New Regime: Transformations of the French Civic Order, 1789–1820s*. New York, 1994.

Woronoff, Denis. *The Thermidorian Regime and the Directory, 1794–1799*. Translated by Julian Jackson. Cambridge, U.K., 1984.

PETER McPHEE

FRENCH REVOLUTIONARY WARS AND NAPOLEONIC WARS.

The French Legislative Assembly declared war upon the king of Bohemia and Hungary (later the emperor of Austria, Francis I) on 20 April 1792. The conflict was not precipitated by actions of the European monarchies seeking to limit the extent of Revolutionary influence, but by the Revolutionary government wishing to divert attention emanating from domestic political, economic, and social crises by creating a foreign crisis. This act inaugurated twenty-three years of war between Revolutionary, and later Napoleonic, France and the rest of Europe. The War of the First Coalition (1792–1797) eventually placed France against an alliance of Austria, Prussia, Piedmont, Naples, Spain, England, and the Holy Roman Empire.

WAR OF THE FIRST COALITION, 1792–1797

French war aims were initially limited to traditional and historic interests, such as challenging Habsburg possession of Belgium and extending French influence along the west bank of the Rhine within the Holy Roman Empire, and to the Italian Alps. An invasion of Belgium in April 1792, however, met with disastrous results. The Duke of Brunswick also invaded France with a Prusso-German army during the summer. The defeat in Belgium, followed by the Prussian offensive, led to increased radicalization of the revolution and the overthrow of the monarchy on 10 August 1792, and the founding of the French Republic.

On 20 September 1792 the Duke of Brunswick engaged two French armies at Valmy. The battle was short, halted by Brunswick before a general advance was made. With his supply lines overextended and the French determined to stand, Brunswick withdrew to the frontier. A small French army on the Middle Rhine captured Speyer, Worms, and Mainz by mid-October, then crossed the Rhine and seized Frankfurt shortly thereafter. The French invaded Belgium once more, decisively defeating the Austrians at Jemappes on 6 November 1792.

By the opening of 1793 French armies had made significant territorial gains. The reluctant performance of Prussia following Valmy, and the apparent weakness of Austria, encouraged the republican government to expand its objectives. War was declared upon Great Britain and Holland on 1 February 1793. Not wanting to be restrained by resources or economy, the revolutionaries made war on Spain on 7 March 1793, after King Charles IV refused to entertain a French alliance.

French military exploits began to erode by the spring of 1793. France's invasion of Holland in mid-February was initially successful, but an Austrian counteroffensive into Belgium completely smashed the French army there and jeopardized the French position in Holland. At Neerwinden in mid-March the French were again defeated. A Prussian army besieged Mainz the following month, and the Spanish crossed the Pyrenees into Roussillon by the summer. The Italian front, opened in 1792 by a French invasion of Piedmont, was stalemated. Insurrection was fomenting in the

Vendée and southern France. Compound crises led to the emergence of the Committee of Public Safety as the guardian of the Revolution. Its response was the *levée en masse,* general conscription of all French males and the mobilization of French resources.

Although 1793 presented the coalition with the greatest opportunity to defeat France, it lacked coordination. Political interests and differences among the allies prevented them from pressing advantages in Belgium and southern France. French victories in Belgium at Hondschoote and Wattignies turned the tide in the north. A Prussian victory at Kaiserslautern stalled French efforts on the Lower Rhine, but there was substantial success against the Austrian and imperial forces on the Upper Rhine by the end of the year.

Perhaps the most important aspect of the French war effort in 1793 was the appointment of Lazare Carnot, former captain of engineers and current member of the Committee of Public Safety, as minister of war. France now had a singular military authority who established a clear grand strategy. He continued the main effort in Belgium and along the Rhine, while holding the Alps and containing the Spanish in Perpignan.

The war turned in 1794 with French offensives on virtually every front. At Fleurus on 26 June 1794 the Austrians were defeated, opening the way for the complete conquest of Belgium by summer's end. This was followed by an invasion of Holland in the autumn. Spanish forces already overstretched were forced back over the Pyrenees and assumed a defensive posture as the French crossed into Catalonia. The rebellious cities of Lyon, Marseille, and Toulon fell to republican armies. It was in the siege of the latter city that a young captain of artillery, Napoleon Bonaparte, first made his mark.

French victory was as much a result of the collapsing coalition as it was a consequence of the increasing size and experience of French armies. Prussia opened secret negotiations with the republic toward the end of 1794. On 5 April 1795 Prussia acceded to the first Treaty of Basel, concluding Prussian participation in the coalition. In May the Dutch surrendered to France, and by the summer Spain and Hesse-Cassel became signatories of the second Treaty of Basel. In short,

within a year of the end of the Terror, Belgium, Holland, and Germany west of the Rhine were solidly under French occupation. Only the Upper Rhine and Italian front remained active, and Carnot could dedicate substantial forces to those theaters.

The War of the First Coalition culminated in Italy in 1796 and 1797. General Napoleon Bonaparte took command of the small, ill-equipped, but highly experienced French Army of Italy at the end of February 1796. Outnumbered more than two to one by Austro-Piedmontese forces, Bonaparte broke across the Alps from Genoa, dividing the Piedmontese from the Austrians. Defeating the former at Montenotte and Dego in mid-April, he pressed on to Turin, where the Piedmontese signed an armistice at Cherasco on 28 April. Austrian attempts to push Bonaparte out of Italy through the autumn of 1796 met with defeat. In 1797 Bonaparte invaded Austria from Italy. With his army less than 240 kilometers (150 miles) from Vienna, Austria signed an armistice at Leoben in April, later formalized by the Treaty of Campo Formio in October 1797.

WAR OF THE SECOND COALITION, 1798–1801

The victory over the First Coalition was short lived, as Austria and England brought Russia into a Second Coalition by 1798. The War of the Second Coalition (1798–1801) succeeded in undoing much of what Bonaparte had done. Austrian and Russian armies overran the French in northern Italy, while the English and Russians landed expeditionary forces in Holland. The Austrians engaged the French along the Upper Rhine and were supported by a Russian offensive into Switzerland in August 1799.

The French responded by expanding the conflict, sending expeditions to Ireland and Egypt to strike at the British. Bonaparte commanded the Egyptian expedition, defeating the Mamluks at the Battle of the Pyramids in July 1798. In February 1799 Bonaparte advanced into Palestine, seizing Jerusalem and laying siege to Acre. Failing to take the city, he returned to Egypt in June. The following month he returned to France to participate in a coup against the government.

The coup d'état of 18 Brumaire (9 November) resulted in Bonaparte's assumption of power.

Fortunately for Napoleon, arguments among the coalition resulted in the withdrawal of Russian troops from central Europe. Taking command of the Army of Reserve in late spring 1800, Bonaparte crossed the Alps into Piedmont. At Marengo on 14 June, Bonaparte defeated the Austrians and turned the tide in Italy. His triumph was followed six months later by General Victor Moreau's decisive victory over the Austrians at Hohenlinden in Germany. Austria's failure led to negotiations at Lunéville, which were concluded in February 1801.

Britain was isolated. Its heavy-handed policies seeking to suppress overseas commerce with France led to the formation of the League of Armed Neutrality, sponsored by Tsar Paul I of Russia and included Prussia, Sweden, and Denmark. Fearing the League of Armed Neutrality would unite their navies, forcing the English from the Baltic, the Royal Navy raided Copenhagen decimating the Danish fleet and breaking the league's will.

Bonaparte exacted further pressure as Spain made common cause against Portugal, a British ally. He reaffirmed the Franco-Spanish alliance initially established at San Ildefenso in 1796. Negotiations, stalled through 1801, now moved with earnest as Britain sought to extricate itself. The Treaty of Amiens was concluded in March 1802 effectively ending the wars of the French Revolution.

Amiens was the product of British exigency. Few in Parliament were confident that Bonaparte would honor his agreements. Distrust between the signatories was apparent before the ink had time to dry. Within six months of the agreement war between England and France appeared imminent, and in May 1803 it broke from London. The specific issue was Britain's refusal to hand Malta to France, as required by Amiens, however the root cause was a decided lack of trust between the two states.

NAPOLEON'S CONQUEST OF EUROPE, 1805–1808

The War of the Third Coalition (1805–1807) was the product and extension of the renewed Anglo-French conflict. Spain joined France in January 1805. The specter of a French invasion of England returned, and William Pitt, the Younger, the British prime minister, attempted to cultivate a Continental alliance against France, but was initi-

ally unsuccessful. The foreign policy of the now Emperor Napoleon in Italy and Germany, however, did much to disturb Austria and Russia. Tsar Alexander I proposed an alliance to Austria and Prussia. Frederick William III rejected the overture, but Emperor Francis I eventually accepted and negotiated jointly with England. On 9 August 1805 the Third Coalition was established by treaty. Sweden and Naples joined officially in October and November respectively. The war began with an Austrian invasion of Bavaria, a French ally. Napoleon turned his Grande Armée from the Channel coast to the Rhine to meet this threat. Another army in Italy squared off against an Austrian army under the Archduke Charles. In a dramatic and decisive maneuver, Napoleon surrounded and defeated the Austrian army in Germany at Ulm, while his forces in Italy fought Charles to a draw.

At the moment Napoleon's victory in Germany was achieved, the combined Franco-Spanish fleet was destroyed at Trafalgar by Admiral Horatio Nelson's British fleet. The naval victory saved only England, as Napoleon invaded Austria in November and seized Vienna three weeks later. On 2 December 1805 he won his greatest victory, over the Russo-Austrian army at Austerlitz. The abject defeat of Austria forced Francis to accept the Treaty of Pressburg, which stripped Austria of territory in the Tyrol, Italy, and Dalmatia. Napoleon elevated his allies in Bavaria and Württemberg to the royal dignity and Baden to a grand duchy. His Kingdom of Italy was enlarged and his control of the Italian peninsula was completed with an invasion of Naples in February 1806. Prussia concluded a treaty of friendship with France in return for Hanover.

In 1806 Napoleon restructured Europe, consolidating his gains of 1805. During the summer of 1806, the Holy Roman Empire was abolished and much of Germany reconfigured into the Confederation of the Rhine, with Napoleon as its protector. In the process, Napoleon offered Hanover to England in return for peace. Prussia was made aware of this by England and declared war on France in October 1806. The campaign against Prussia was incredibly brief. On 14 October the Prussian army was destroyed in two battles at Jena and Auerstedt.

Frederick William III and the remnants of his forces retreated into Prussian Poland where they were joined by Tsar Alexander's Russian army. Napoleon moved into Poland and on 8 February 1807 won a Pyrrhic victory at Eylau. In the late spring Napoleon attacked the Russians and defeated them on 14 June 1807 at Friedland. His victory led to direct negotiations with Alexander at Tilsit, and the meeting of the two emperors in July led to an alliance.

During the course of 1806 to 1807, Napoleon issued the Milan and Berlin decrees. They established a Continental blockade of English goods from Portugal to Russia. Concomitant with his desire to block English markets, Napoleon directed an invasion of Portugal. French victory was ultimately shattered by the deployment of a British expeditionary force under General Arthur Wellesley, later the Duke of Wellington.

Spain's French alliance wore thin by 1806, and Charles IV and his prime minister, Manuel de Godoy, secretly negotiated with Britain. Napoleon became aware of Godoy's machinations and turned on his ally in the spring of 1808, committing one hundred thousand French troops to the occupation of the Iberian kingdom. The throne was given to Napoleon's elder brother Joseph.

The war in Spain became problematic for Napoleon. Although British military support was insignificant at this time, there was growing resistance from Spanish regulars and guerrillas. French troops became bogged down and even met local defeat at the hands of the Spanish. Napoleon led a second invasion in October 1808 to secure Spain. The French emperor remained in Madrid until January 1809 when he returned to Paris to meet a potential threat from Austria.

MAINTAINING THE EMPIRE, 1809–1812

With French attention focused on Spain, Austrian Emperor Francis I directed his brother, the Archduke Charles, to make war on Napoleon. He was directed to strike into Germany and Italy, to reestablish the status quo ante circa 1792. A reluctant Charles obeyed and in April 1809 launched an offensive into Bavaria, while his younger brother John invaded Italy. Napoleon's army in Germany was reduced because of his Spanish commitment, but his German allies provided substantial forces to supplement the imperial army. Napoleon success-

fully outmaneuvered Charles and defeated him at Abensberg-Eckmühl in April. Charles then retreated into Bohemia while Napoleon advanced upon Vienna. In Italy, John was initially successful, but driven back in May.

Napoleon entered Vienna in mid-May and attacked Charles across the Danube at Aspern-Essling. The battle marked Napoleon's first defeat, as he was thrown back across the river with heavy losses. Napoleon, however, called his dispersed corps to Vienna, and affected another crossing in early July. The Battle of Wagram (5 and 6 July) was the largest engagement to date of the Napoleonic Wars. This time Napoleon defeated Charles and within two weeks elicited his surrender. Austria was compelled by treaty to give up its Illyrian Provinces to France and the Trentino to the Kingdom of Italy.

By the conclusion of 1810 Napoleon's relationship with Tsar Alexander I was strained. He determined to bring Russia directly under his control and began preparations for a massive invasion of Russia. Drawing on the resources of Europe, Napoleon assembled an army of approximately five hundred thousand men, half French, the remainder from his allied and satellite armies. In June 1812 Napoleon invaded Russia. By September Napoleon's main army engaged the Russians at Borodino, 110 kilometers (70 miles) west of Moscow. The Russians were forced from the field and retreated east of the city. Napoleon established his headquarters there, but Alexander refused to negotiate. With winter approaching, and no conclusion to the conflict in sight, Napoleon withdrew from Moscow at the end of October. Alexander and his army shadowed Napoleon, only occasionally chancing military engagement. On 5 December 1812 Napoleon left the army for Paris, giving command to his brother-in-law Marshal Joachim Murat, who continued the retreat to Prussia. The cost of the campaign was enormous. No more than 160,000 troops remained, many having deserted, died of disease, become ill, or been taken prisoner.

The Russian army pursued the French into Poland with the intention of stirring Prussia into an alliance. In March 1813, the French army, now under Napoleon's stepson, Prince Eugène de Beauharnais, abandoned Berlin. Frederick William III joined

Russia in another coalition. Napoleon, however, returned to Germany in April with a new and larger army and defeated the Russo-Prussian armies at Lützen and Bautzen in May. Unable to defeat Napoleon, Alexander and Frederick William III agreed to an armistice in June, with the intention of bringing Austria into the coalition.

THE FALL OF NAPOLEON'S EMPIRE, 1813–1815

Austria did join the Fourth Coalition, which renewed the war in August 1813. The allies were joined by Sweden, whose army was led by Crown Prince Jean-Baptiste Bernadotte, one of Napoleon's former marshals. The coalition forced Napoleon's armies in central Europe into Saxony, and from 16 to 19 October the coalition soundly defeated Napoleon at Leipzig. He withdrew from Germany. The coalition offensive into Italy was not as dramatic or successful, and although there were some attempts by Austria to negotiate a settlement with France, the other allies and the French emperor did not take them seriously. As such the Prussian army under Field Marshal Gebhard von Blücher crossed the Lower Rhine and invaded France. The Austrians under Field Marshal Karl zu Schwarzenberg crossed the Upper Rhine.

Napoleon scored several astonishing victories over the allies in January and February 1814, but lacked sufficient strength to capitalize on them the way he had done in earlier years. By March the situation had changed dramatically. While Napoleon had moved to check an Austrian advance southeast of Paris, the Prussians marched on the capital and captured it. Napoleon refused to surrender, but his marshals compelled him to accept the inevitable and he abdicated the throne on 6 April 1814.

Napoleon was exiled to the island of Elba. The following February he left the island with a small contingent of his Imperial Guard and returned to France. Louis XVIII dispatched troops to intercept Napoleon, but they, and most of the French army, defected. France remained ringed by allied armies in the spring of 1815, and the coalition, whose representatives were meeting in Vienna, pledged to make common cause against Napoleon until he was defeated. An Anglo-Dutch army under the Duke of Wellington was in central Belgium, while a Prussian army under General Blücher was in eastern Belgium.

Napoleon seized the initiative and struck north into Belgium, hoping to defeat the Prussians before they could join with the British. On 16 June 1815, Napoleon attacked the Prussians at Ligny, breaking Blücher's army, sending it into full retreat. To the west a second battle was fought between the smaller French left wing under Marshal Michel Ney and the Duke of Wellington at Quatre Bras. The battle was a draw, but Wellington withdrew north toward Brussels. Despite being pursued by the French, Blücher promised Wellington he would swing his army about and join him at Mont-St.-Jean (Waterloo). On 18 June Napoleon attacked the British position. Although hard pressed, the Duke of Wellington held until the Prussian army arrived by the afternoon. The appearance of the Prussian army on Napoleon's flank was decisive. By nightfall the French army was in rout and Napoleon fled to Paris. On 22 June 1815 Napoleon abdicated for a second time. He became a British prisoner and spent the rest of his life on the island of St. Helena in the South Atlantic.

See also **Armies; Austerlitz; Borodino; Continental System; Holy Alliance; Hundred Days; Napoleon; Napoleonic Empire; Ulm, Battle of; Vienna; Waterloo; Wellington, Duke of (Arthur Wellesley).**

BIBLIOGRAPHY

Blanning, T. C. W. *The Origins of the French Revolutionary Wars.* London, 1986.

———. *The French Revolutionary Wars, 1787–1802.* London, 1996.

Esdaile, Charles J. *The Wars of Napoleon.* London, 1995.

Gates, David. *The Napoleonic Wars, 1803–1815.* London, 1997.

Rothenberg, Gunther E. *The Art of Warfare in the Age of Napoleon.* London, 1977.

———. *The Napoleonic Wars.* London, 1999.

Schneid, Frederick C. *Napoleon's Conquest of Europe: The War of the Third Coalition.* Westport, Conn., 2005.

FREDERICK C. SCHNEID

FREUD, SIGMUND (1856–1939), Austrian neurologist and founder of psychoanalysis.

Sigmund Freud was born on 6 May 1856 in the Moravian town of Freiberg, in the Austro-Hungarian

Empire (now Přibor in the Czech Republic). His father, Jacob Freud, was a small wool merchant who often barely made a living; his mother, Amalia, Jacob's third wife, was half her husband's age. Such familial constellations, which were common in Victorian culture, puzzled young Sigmund, who (to his perplexity) had two half brothers roughly the age of his mother. One of these had a son, Freud's nephew, a year older than Sigmund. The adult Freud made it his business to understand, and if possible reduce, the psychological damages imposed by such emotional hurdles.

EARLY YEARS

In 1860, the Freud family moved to Vienna, a city where Freud would spend his next seventy-eight years and which he often denounced yet regarded with some affection. His brilliance had become obvious at school and he cultivated far-reaching ambitions. Beginning in 1873 he attended the University of Vienna, initially enrolling in law, then changing to philosophy, and finally settling on natural science. Among the reasons for his choice were friendships, impressive lectures, and the much-discussed theories of Darwin, which "strongly attracted me for they held out hopes of extraordinary advances in our understanding of the world" (Freud, vol. 20, p. 8). His life would be a passionate pursuit of the knowledge of human nature.

One of the obstacles he encountered was anti-Semitism, which in the 1870s was still relatively moderate. With the accession of Emperor Francis Joseph in 1848, most of the laws that limited or excluded Jews from social and political careers had been repealed and the future of liberalism—crucial to full Jewish emancipation—seemed bright. But in 1873, the Austro-Hungarian Empire was caught in a financial catastrophe that generated hysterical outbursts by journalists and politicians, and in this period the anti-Semitic legend about Jews as financial manipulators and conspirators was born and widely accepted. But Freud, although aware that Jew-hatred was rising with unexpected fervor, remained intent on his medical research, working contentedly in the German professor Ernst Brücke's (1819–1892) physiological laboratory from 1876 to 1882. The experiments Freud undertook with Brücke looking over his shoulder and Brücke's

postivist attitude toward science won Brücke Freud's admiration and remained his ideal. Brücke was a passionate critic of mysticism and romantic vitalism. The high-flying speculations of metaphysics were, to the positivists, sheer nonsense, and Freud made this intellectual style his own.

Freud took his medical degree in 1881 because he enjoyed scientific research, but in the spring of 1882 he fell in love with Martha Bernays, who came from an upright if relatively impecunious Jewish family from northern Germany. This gave him a hard choice: giving up his fascinating research or the woman he loved. He had only one way to achieve what Victorian middle-class families believed necessary: private practice. Years of waiting ensued, broken by correspondence or occasional visits. The couple was finally married in 1886. They had six children in nine years, the last of whom, Anna, born in 1895, grew to be her father's closest associate and a productive psychoanalyst in her own right.

THE EXPLORATION OF MENTAL SUFFERING

Freud had become certain that the exploration of mental suffering, which was widely lamented but little understood, would be his destiny. In 1891 he published his first book, *On the Conception of the Aphasias: A Critical Study*, which took the novel position that aphasia was not simply a physiological expression of neurological disturbances but largely a physical reaction to mental strains. By thus identifying aphasic symptoms, Freud had introduced the mind as a cause of mental distress.

Freud was not alone in these unconventional ideas. He had developed an intimate friendship with the distinguished and imaginative Viennese physician Josef Breuer (1842–1925). And it was Breuer's patient, "Anna O.," whom Breuer had begun to treat in 1880, whose hysterical symptoms captivated Freud, and he urged Breuer to recount what became the classic case of psychoanalysis. His other intimate was the eccentric but professionally respected ear, nose, and throat specialist Wilhelm Fliess (1858–1928), from Berlin, who was receptive to new ideas and who had theories of his own linking the nose to sexuality. From the early 1890s, Freud reported to Fliess the rudiments of his new theory of the mind. He had made notes on dreams

Sigmund Freud with Martha Bernays, 1885. ©BETTMANN/
CORBIS

beginning in around 1892 and, sure of their eviden-
tial importance, had attempted to interpret them.

Then, in 1893, Freud and Breuer published a
pioneering paper, "On the Psychic Mechanism of
Hysterical Phenomena (Preliminary Communication)." Two years later, the collaborators brought
out *Studies in Hysteria*, a collection of theoretical
observations and five case histories (Breuer's "Anna
O." and the others by Freud), demonstrating his
increasing mastery of analytic techniques. But one
issue divided the two investigators and spoiled their
friendship: the place of sexuality in mental life. To
assign neuroses to sexual malfunctioning did not
shock progressive specialists; Freud's acquaintance
Rudolf Chrobak told him of a woman patient
whose neurosis he said was caused by her husband's
failures in bed and he prescribed what her husband
never could: "Penis normalis/dosim/repetatur."

SEDUCTION THEORY

Freud went further. In 1896 he argued before his
colleagues, citing thirteen cases, that only a sexual
trauma suffered in childhood and set off by a
brother, servant, or other adult could have this
result (the seduction theory). Within two years,
Freud recognized it as incredible. His self-correc-
tion was not just a humiliation; it allowed Freud to
turn that unsought discovery into a theoretical
breakthrough. His patients who reported having
been seduced were not lying but fantasizing. That
modification opened promising conduits toward
deciphering the mind at work.

In 1896, amid inner turmoil, Freud came to
terms with his father's death. He had already been
engaged in his "self-analysis," though he never
gave details about this practically unprecedented
self-examination. It was, he knew, not a full psychoanalysis but an attempt to be "completely honest" with himself, an activity he thought "good
exercise." The result, *The Interpretation of Dreams,*
appeared in November 1899, the first of the two
fundamental texts of psychoanalysis.

The genre of the *Interpretation of Dreams* is
impossible to settle. It was in part an autobiography, in part a political history of the Jews in
modern Vienna, in part an account of dream theories through the centuries, and—most conspicuously—a dream theory based on information drawn
from biology and psychoanalytic sessions. Like
nearly everything Freud published through half a
century, this monograph was written in his customary style: readable, economical, and persuasive.
He told relevant anecdotes about his childhood,
outlined his reasonable expectations in the liberal
temper of Austria in the 1860s and 1870s, and
perfected his theories.

Freud maintained that every dream is meaningful and traceable to memories, however
distorted, from childhood. Like the gibberish a psychotic speaks, a dreamer's nonsensical reports are
never simply nonsense. They can—indeed, must—
be interpreted; dream theories that attribute dream
formation to religious or metaphysical sources are
simply fictions. Despite skeptical criticisms—that
psychoanalysis is really a substitute religion—Freud
never doubted that its methods made it a kind of
science, summing up its conclusions in a simple
formula: "A dream is the (disguised) fulfillment of

a (suppressed, repressed) wish." Grasping the dreamer's meaning depends on recognizing the way the dream works to keep the wishes and anxieties too troubling for revelation from consciousness.

What conceals the hidden order of the mind is that much of it is unconscious, unavailable to direct observation. The apparent disorder of dreams, memories, or mental slips only proves the existence of unconscious processes, for the mental, like physical events, obeys laws, and the chaos that the mind presents to the world is only an appearance disguising a concealed organization. Freud never claimed to have discovered the unconscious domain; the writers of poems and prose fictions had already done that. His discovery had only clarified how the mystery of the mind had grown so mysterious.

THEORY OF SEXUALITY

Freud published *Three Essays on the Theory of Sexuality,* the second of the two founding documents of psychoanalysis, in 1905. He was no longer unknown in the psychiatric profession; even in the United States he had a few followers, and a small troop of investigators studying human sexuality, including Havelock Ellis in Britain and Richard von Krafft-Ebing in the Austro-Hungarian Empire, nourished an interest in the study of human eroticism (although they did little for Freud's theories). Still, Freud's assertions about sexuality, notably the bisexual nature of the human animal and the existence of sexual feeling in children, were still considered shocking. Between the first edition of Freud's *Three Essays* and 1939, the year of Freud's death, however, astonishing propositions to which Freud himself had to be won over became solid elements in the psychoanalytic view of the mind.

The most radical facet of Freud's *Three Essays* was its positive appraisal of the sexual impulse. Its author retained a certain hierarchy, with genital heterosexual intercourse at the top of his catalog. Freud, despite his reputation, sternly disclaimed pan-sexuality. He never believed that the sexual drive has a monopoly on creativity, and he regarded homosexual coupling as a form of love, yet when he wrote on special sexual tastes, he called them "perversions." However, his tone was neutral; he was writing like a medical researcher taking an enormous leap forward in the scientific understanding of sexuality.

BUILDING A MOVEMENT

Freud's *Interpretation of Dreams* was not a publishing success. In its first six years, it sold 351 copies, and the publisher printed a second, enlarged edition in 1909, a decade after it was first launched. Still, Freud found admiring disciples, and soon his lonely enterprise became a movement. The apparatus of collective psychoanalytic activity—Freud had coined the term *psychoanalysis* only a decade earlier, in 1896—was put into place in the following years. These led to regular meetings, international conferences, lectures (mainly to the converted), the founding of technical journals, the laying down of fundamental procedures (psychoanalysis, after all, was conceived as a treatment for neuroses as much as it was as a psychological theory), and the continual elaboration of that theory and its inescapable intellectual strains.

In these heroic years, activity was intense. In the fall of 1902, at the suggestion of Wilhelm Stekel, a Viennese physician who had been one of Freud's patients, a group of physicians and interested laypeople began to meet in Freud's apartment every Wednesday night to hear papers and discussions. Freud was always the last commentator and beyond dispute the leading spirit. In April 1908 the relatively informal Wednesday Psychological Society transformed itself into the Vienna Psychoanalytical Society. The same month saw the first international congress, at Salzburg, where Freud dazzled participants with a four-hour address on one of his most famous patients, the "Rat Man." In 1909 the case was published in the new *Yearbook for Psychoanalytic and Psychopathological Investigations;* earlier that year, Freud had brought out another case destined to achieve an immortality of its own, "Analysis of a Phobia in a Five-Year-Old Boy," the "Little Hans" case.

These case histories, now standard texts in psychoanalytic training, were not Freud's only contributions to the technical literature. His papers of these years read like a campaign to spread the relevance of his theories to new, still unexplored areas of culture. *The Psychopathology of Everyday Life* (1904) showed how analytic concepts are usable in "ordinary" life; in 1905 he enlisted Jewish humor in *Jokes and Their Relations to the Unconscious;* and in 1907 he took up one of his central themes, the irreconcilable differences between science and faith, in "Obsessive Actions and Religious Practices," the first public expression of Freud's principled atheism. To his mind, religion, including his own, was a cultural neurosis. He was proud of and never deserted his Jewish heritage, but he was, in his terse formulation, a "godless Jew." The most significant paper was Freud's essay "Leonardo da Vinci and a Memory of his Childhood" (1910), a pioneering excursion into the psychoanalytic exploration of an artist, which speaks to his affection for the Italian Renaissance and to his conviction that a close analysis of a creative figure—especially one deserving the greatest admiration—in no way denigrates a genius.

In his ambitious, evolving system, Freud also had practical matters on his mind. In an intellectual construction in which theory and therapy cooperate—in which, in fact, theory served therapy—Freud, thinking of his disciples at home and abroad, outlined the essential rules for the analyst to follow in analytic sessions. One way to disseminate these was through his case histories, which were presented in meticulous detail, also using his self-education as material to educate other psychoanalysts; another way was to sum up technical issues that confront each psychoanalyst with each analysand. Freud had written one clinical vignette, the much-disputed "Dora" case about a young hysteric, in January 1901, shortly after she left him with a fragmentary analysis lasting only eleven weeks, but he did not publish it until four years later and was quickly disparaged for bullying his analysand and imposing his interpretations on her. Other papers were more abstract and less open to criticism; those on starting the treatment and on handling the patient's emotional transference to the analyst and others like them are still useful in the early twenty-first century.

TENSIONS AND DISAGREEMENTS

It would have been unlikely that an assembly of highly educated individualists, closely linked to one another, could work together without tension. Elements of depth psychology remained obscure, virtually inviting conflicting interpretations. These tensions soon beset the Wednesday Psychological Society. The most obvious source for trouble lay in the radical Viennese physician Alfred Adler (1870–1937), to whom Freud offered considerable

respect and intellectual leeway. But Adler was obsessed with the thesis that neuroses spring from "organ inferiority" and the aggressiveness this produces. A neurosis was for Adler a failed compensation for inferiority feelings. He thus moved early childhood and its traumas in human development, which were central to Freud's theories, to the margins. Freud was not hostile to the thought that biology underlies the growing mind—his commitment to nature's share is often overlooked—but he thought Adler greatly overstated the insight, was wholly one-sided in his judgment, and therefore did damage to the psychoanalytic community.

Worse, the Viennese preoccupation with Adler as thinker and colleague, Freud believed, threatened to obstruct his plan to push forward a new, attractive group of supporters (the "Swiss," he called them), notably Carl Gustav Jung (1875–1961), a Zurich psychiatrist with whom Freud had recently formed a somewhat febrile friendship. Jung was dynamic and domineering, Freud's probably inescapable successor in whatever international organization psychoanalysts would eventually establish. Freud was keenly aware that the original Vienna group, which he had dominated since its founding, was almost exclusively Jewish, which would only make the integration of psychoanalysis into the medical community all the more problematic. Freud, aware of the increase in anti-Semitism, did not want his psychoanalysis to be known as a Jewish science.

The Freud-Jung friendship was bound to break up in acrimony. Freud was more prepared than Jung to keep it alive: he was intent on recruiting gentiles to psychoanalysis. But Jung, aggressive and impatient, was ill-suited to wait for Freud's retirement, and their correspondence records a growing alienation, with Jung becoming particularly pugnacious. Excessively sensitive to slights (real or imagined) and capable of real coarseness, Jung's character was an unfortunate combination for lasting friendship.

"ON NARCISSISM"

Meanwhile, Freud pondered the structure of psychoanalytic theory and in 1914 published "On Narcissism: An Introduction," which alerted perceptive followers like the British analyst Ernest Jones to large-scale changes ahead. The point of

"Narcissism" was deceptively innocent: an infant in its sexual evolution starts with primitive auto-eroticism and will mature to love objects. But between these phases, Freud held, is a transitional stage never wholly overcome, and that is narcissism.

This argument involved a reorientation of Freud's theory of the drives. His old theory distinguished between two classes: the ego drives, which are not libidinal, and the libidinal drives, which are not egotistic. But if, as this paper claimed, all the self can be libidinally charged—that, in short, if the infant can be in love with itself—Freud's formulation dividing non-erotic drives and erotic ones collapses. Love for oneself and love for others differ only in their object, not their nature. Furthermore, much of the libidinal energy left over with the disintegration of narcissism survives into later life converted into the "ego ideal." Freud had clearly given himself and his followers much theoretical work to do. And the coming of World War I in August 1914 presented Freud with too much time, since his colleagues, patients, and family members (including the Freuds' three sons, who all volunteered and all survived) were on active duty.

Freud, who turned sixty in the middle of the war, wrote impressive papers on the theory of psychoanalysis, and toward the end of the war he moved to solving the puzzles he had presented in "Narcissism." He had much to say about death; the irreparable catastrophe of the war had left its mark on Freud's thinking. Then, too, the death of his beloved daughter Sophie in 1920, in the influenza epidemic, generated conjectures that *Beyond the Pleasure Principle,* published in that year, was his way of mourning. His theorizing about the death drive, however, had been completed the year before and *Beyond the Pleasure Principle* was the first glimpse of an important new category, introducing the second version of Freud's picture of the mind (the so-called structural view, largely taking the place of the earlier, topographic view); it owes nearly everything to theory and virtually nothing to autobiography. Freud was so intent on demonstrating the independence of the death drive from his personal bereavement that he asked the intimates who had read his manuscript of 1919 to support his version of the story.

In postulating an instinctual combat that pervaded all of life, *Beyond the Pleasure Principle* defin-

itively set Freud off from both Adler and Jung. Adler, as Freud read him, subjected all mental activity to instinctual aggression, whereas Jung so watered down libido as to make it responsible for all destructive and constructive activities. Unlike these two, Freud saw himself as an ironclad dualist. Freud's hostility to Jung and Adler could only please his supporters, but this particular revision troubled them, especially in its extreme form, pitting a literal drive for life against one toward death; many psychoanalysts accepted a weaker form of this conflict, in which aggression faced love. One reason for this partial dissent was Freud's unaccustomed departure from empiricism: he played, and was aware that he played, with speculation in a way he generally derided.

In contrast, *The Ego and the Id* (1923) clung more closely to Freud's clinical experience. It was, he wrote in the preface, "more in the nature of a synthesis than of a speculation," and this text has been much studied. With his customary lucidity, he mapped the mind, with id, ego, and superego finding their place in the psychoanalytic scheme. He did not abandon the old topography featuring a mental event's closeness to or distance from consciousness, but in psychoanalytic thinking the origins of thoughts and emotions became more central. The brochure was well received among analysts; his tripartite division of the mind and its internal interrelations were familiar and useful to them.

Yet Freud was aging, and his health plagued him. In February 1923 he discovered a malignant growth on his palate. From then to his death, he underwent painful operations and an almost unending search for a tolerable prosthesis. He abandoned public appearances, yet his publications, written with his accustomed vigor, became popular with the educated public. In addition to semi-speculative, controversial papers on female sexuality, he published *The Future of Illusion* in 1927 and his most widely read book, *Civilization and Its Discontents,* in 1930, both of them drawing general conclusions from psychoanalytic premises.

Freud's *Future of an Illusion* returned to a favorite preoccupation: the irreparable clash between religion and science. He had, with minor distractions during his university days, advocated atheism as the only attitude worthy of respect. As a belated Enlightenment thinker additionally equipped with psychoanalytic theses, he equated religious thinking with the powerful desire to make wishes come true, something that works, in short, to support agreeable illusions. The contrast with scientific ways of thinking was, to Freud's mind, perfectly apparent. He concluded his essay with a famous declaration of faith—or, rather, unfaith: "No, our science is no illusion. But an illusion it would be to suppose that what science cannot give us we can get elsewhere" (Freud, vol. 21, p. 56).

The successor to this plea for reason, *Civilization and Its Discontents,* went deeper still. Civilization is necessary to tame potent individualistic needs, but if men find it hard to obey all the restrictions it places on human wishes, they find it impossible to live in society without them. This conflict is inherent in any social arrangement that humans can devise; even if adjustments partially appease it, they do so, at best, only partially. Many ways exist to stave off the gloom that this basic conflict produces—from the dubious pleasures of alcohol to escapes from reality through sexual adventures and other recipes—but all are doomed to failure. Productive work is the only method that receives Freud's cautious approval.

Thus Freud opened the door to the sociological investigation of personal fates; social psychology (he had written in 1921) was individual psychology writ large. Freud said so more than once: "The individual's relation to his parents and siblings, his love object, his teacher and his physician, that is to say all the relations which have so far been the principal subject of psychoanalytic research, could claim to be acknowledged as social phenomena" (Freud, vol. 18, p. 69). Neither Freud nor his followers have ever fully explored this insight; to the extent that psychoanalysis has a future, it may lie in the psychoanalysis of culture.

LEGACY

In March 1938 Nazi troops invaded Austria and forced an aged and reluctant Freud to seek sanctuary in England, where he, his wife, and his daughter Anna found refuge in early June. He was still working, most notably on *An Outline of Psychoanalysis,* which he did not live to complete. Anything but a simplistic introduction, it shows Freud in a flexible mood that few psychoanalysts have followed, or even known about. Writing about the uncertainty of psychoanalytic cures, he notes: "The future may teach us to exercise a direct influence, by means of particular chemical substances, on the amounts of energy and their distribution in the mental apparatus. It may be that there are other, still undreamt-of possibilities of therapy" (Freud, vol. 23, p. 182)—a remarkable statement.

With its vicissitudes, the fate of psychoanalysis remains unpredictable. Its early appeal beyond sympathetic outsiders in Vienna, mainly Central European physicians of Jewish background, slowly grew until it gained medical approval and cultural acceptance. But Jung and his allies in Zurich and Adler in Vienna split off to construct their own schools. By the 1920s, some analytic vocabulary and even analytic ideas became downright fashionable. The assault on European culture by Nazi and Fascist and Communist dictatorships at home and aggression abroad shifted the centers of analytic thinking from Austria and Germany mainly to the United States, where Freudian analysis flourished mightily after the Second World War.

But the prognosis is more tentative in the early twenty-first century. The stunning reputation of Freudian psychoanalysis among the social sciences in the 1950s was too overwhelming to hold. And the success of drugs in affecting moods has raised hopes for cures through medication, which is cheaper and perhaps more effective than Freud's "talking cure." Clashing predictions are normal in the early twenty-first century, but limited evidence strongly suggests that in the end a combined treatment with both medication and psychoanalytic sessions may provide the best answer, giving psychoanalysis a prominent but not exclusive role in the therapeutic process.

See also **Adler, Alfred; Ellis, Havelock; Gender; Homosexuality and Lesbianism; Jung, Carl Gustav; Nietzsche, Friedrich; Psychoanalysis; Psychology; Rank, Otto; Schnitzler, Arthur; Sexuality.**

BIBLIOGRAPHY

Primary Sources

Freud, Sigmund. *The Standard Edition of the Complete Psychological Works of Sigmund Freud.* 24 vols. Edited and translated by James Strachey et al. London, 1953–1974.

Freud, Sigmund, and Wilhelm Fleiss. *The Complete Letters of Sigmund Freud to Wilhelm Fleiss, 1887–1904.* Edited and translated by Jeffrey Moussaieff Masson. Cambridge, Mass., 1985.

Freud, Sigmund, and Ernest Jones. *The Complete Correspondence of Sigmund Freud and Ernest Jones, 1908–1939.* Edited by R. Andrew Paskaus. Cambridge, Mass., 1993.

Freud, Sigmund, and C. G. Jung. *The Freud/Jung Letters: The Correspondence between Sigmund Freud and C. G. Jung.* Edited by William McGuire. Translated by Ralph Manheim and R. F. C. Hull. Princeton, N.J., 1974.

Freud, Sigmund, and Oskar Pfister. *Psychoanalysis and Faith: The Letters of Sigmund Freud and Oskar Pfister.* Translated by Eric Mosbacher. New York, 1963.

Secondary Sources

Amacher, Peter. *Freud's Neurological Education and Its Influence on Psychoanalytic Theory.* New York, 1965.

Clark, Ronald W. *Freud: The Man and the Cause.* London, 1980.

Ellenberger, Henri F. *The Discovery of the Unconscious: The History and Evolution of Dynamic Psychiatry.* New York, 1970.

Gay, Peter. *Freud: A Life for Our Time.* New York, 1988.

Jones, Ernest. *The Life and Work of Sigmund Freud.* 3 vols. New York, 1953–1957.

Rosenblit, Marsha L. *The Jews of Vienna, 1867–1914: Assimilation and Identity.* Albany, N.Y., 1983.

Scull, Andrew, ed. *Madhouses, Mad-Doctors, and Madmen: The Social History of Psychiatry in the Victorian Era.* Philadelphia, 1981.

PETER GAY

FRIEDRICH, CASPAR DAVID (1774–1840), German painter.

Caspar David Friedrich (born 5 September 1774 in Greifswald, died 7 May 1840 in Dresden) is the outstanding painter of German Romanticism. His importance for German art is comparable to that of Eugène Delacroix for Romanticism in France or that of J. M. W. Turner in Great Britain. At most, Philipp Otto Runge's (1777–1810) influence may be said to rival Friedrich's.

Greifswald in New Western Pomerania, Friedrich's birthplace, had been under Swedish rule from 1648 to 1814, and only the Congress of Vienna (1814–1815) brought its cession to Prussia. Friedrich was the sixth of ten children in an artisan's family. His father was a soap boiler and chandler. At the age of sixteen, Friedrich first received lessons from an art teacher at the University of Greifswald. From 1794 to 1798, he studied at the outstanding Copenhagen Art Academy. Among his mentors were Nikolai Abraham Abildgaard (1743–1809) and Jens Juel (1745–1802), who made a name for himself as a portraitist and landscape painter. By autumn of 1798, Friedrich was active in Dresden, where he led a largely uneventful life. Only relatively late in life, at age forty-four, he married and had three children with his wife, a simple girl from the neighborhood.

Six times between 1801 and 1826 Friedrich undertook the journey to his home, Greifswald, and to the nearby island of Rügen, where he found many subjects for his paintings. Other trips, also on foot and accompanied by artist friends, took him to the Silesian Riesengebirge in 1810 and to the Harz Mountains in 1811; quite frequently he traveled the Elbe Sandstone Mountains and northern Bohemia—always with paintbrush or pen in hand. In his later years, he took cures several times at the health resort of Teplice (Bohemia). He never journeyed to Italy—in contrast to many southern German Romantics, who settled in Rome, taking the collective label of the "Nazarenes."

CAREER

Initially, Friedrich attempted to make a living by doing sepia landscapes. His first success came in 1805. At a contest organized by the "Weimarer Kunstfreunde," his two drawings—submitted on the initiative of the poet Johann Wolfgang von Goethe (1749–1832), who subsequently became increasingly critical of Friedrich's art—shared first prize with another entry.

At Christmas of 1808 Friedrich exhibited the painting *Cross in the Mountains* in his Dresden studio. With this work, he created a pure depiction of landscape—the rays of the setting evening sun playing around a rock overgrown with firs, from which rises a small cross with the crucified Christ—as an altarpiece, thus endowing the landscape with sacred dignity. The chamberlain Basilius von Ramdohr took offense at it and published a polemic stating that "indeed it is true impudence when landscape painting sets about sneaking into the churches and onto the altars." Even though the painting never served its originally intended purpose as an altarpiece, a public controversy soon erupted, and various of Friedrich's friends defended his work vehemently. In the end, the artist's name became generally known—even if in a controversial way.

More lasting was the response to the *Monk by the Sea,* a painting Friedrich created a short time afterward, and probably the most radical he ever executed in all his life. In the fall of 1810, Friedrich sent it, together with its companion piece (in the same format), the *Abbey in an Oakwood,* to an exhibition at the Berlin Akademie, where the two paintings were hung one above the other. Famous in this context is the essay "Empfindungen vor Friedrichs Seelandschaft" (Emotions on beholding Friedrich's sea scenery), published by the poet Heinrich von Kleist on 13 October 1810 in the *Berliner Abendblätter,* which Kleist edited: "With its two or three mysterious objects, the painting lies there like the apocalypse, as if it pondered Edward Young's *Night Thoughts*. And since in all its uniformity and boundlessness, it has nothing but the picture frame as a foreground, when looking at the painting it appears as if one's eyelids had been cut off." In this almost abstract work, the observer discerns on the bottom a narrow, bright, sandy stripe—the seashore; above it an equally dark narrow stripe—the sea; and then, covering four-fifths of the canvas, the sky pervaded with clouds. The small figure of a monk represents the only vertical. On the crown prince's urging, the king of Prussia purchased the two paintings displayed in Berlin.

In 1824 the king of Saxony granted Friedrich the honorary title of "extraordinary professor" as well as a modest annual salary. However, Friedrich was not allowed to teach drawing classes at the Art Academy in Dresden—he was regarded as too much of a loner and outsider. If until the mid-1810s, Friedrich was at the zenith of his brief artistic fame, thereafter the "death-yearning emptiness" of his art was considered as outdated. Toward the end of his life, Friedrich seemed to have fallen into oblivion. Yet since the so-called *Jahrhundertausstellung* at the Berlin National-galerie in 1906, where thirty-six of his paintings were shown, his fame has steadily grown.

Wanderer above a Sea of Fog. Painting by Caspar David Friedrich c. 1817. BILDARCHIV PREUSSISCHER KULTURBESITZ/ ART RESOURCE, NY

THE INFINITE LANDSCAPE

Since his rediscovery around 1900, Friedrich has come to be considered the painter of the "infinite landscape." We view his landscapes as a "mirror of the soul" and comprehend Friedrich as an artist who—thoroughly a product of Romanticism—has directed "the gaze inward," along the lines of his motto: "The painter ought not merely to paint what he discerns in front of him but also what he sees inside of him. If he does not see anything in himself, though, he ought to refrain altogether from painting what he perceives in front of him."

Time after time Friedrich juxtaposed pairs of opposites such as morning and evening, youth and old age, birth and death, becoming and expiring. In the depiction of nature, particularly in its cyclical changes, he sought to encompass human existence and to capture at least to some extent the meaning of transitory existence. In his works he associates human fate with the cycle of seasons. In group after group of new paintings he followed the hours of the day, the yearly cycle, the stages of life, the courses of rivers, the rhythm of departure and return of ships, the alternation of high and low tide, of sowing and harvesting. Friedrich's characters seek the view and experience of nature; seen from behind, they draw the observer's gaze into nature. The viewer is encouraged to perceive nature as do these figures and become meditatively engrossed in it.

Yet Friedrich did not complete his paintings in a natural setting. All of his works took shape in the studio. He created them from memory, with the aid of numerous graphic studies of nature. Before his "inner eye" the countless details—rock formations and river mouths, fishing nets and sailboats, the stones at the seashore and the trees with their massive branches—came together to form the composition. In all this, Friedrich was concerned with the meaningful correlation between the details, not with the reproduction of a particular scenic feature. In nature he perceived the hieroglyphics of a spiritual script, the ciphers of an unknown alphabet. By means of their balanced and well-calculated composition, his paintings were intended to convey an idea of a hidden allegory, without spelling things out too clearly.

When Friedrich died in 1840 after a protracted illness, he did not leave behind any disciples or epigones of any standing. Instead of a Romantic striving for a symbolic interpretation of nature, the Düsseldorf School of landscape painting, more decidedly oriented toward realism, gained the upper hand. Only belatedly, the isolated figure of Friedrich in the sphere of graphic arts came to be recognized as a significant counterpart to the poets and writers of early German Romanticism such as Novalis (Friedrich Leopold von Hardenberg; 1772–1801), August Wilhelm von Schlegel (1767–1845), and Ludwig Tieck (1773–1853).

See also **Delacroix, Eugène; Novalis (Hardenberg, Friedrich von); Romanticism; Schlegel, August Wilhelm von; Turner, J. M. W.**

BIBLIOGRAPHY

Börsch-Supan, Helmut. *Caspar David Friedrich.* Munich, 2005.

Börsch-Supan, Helmut, and Karl Wilhelm Jähnig. *C.D.F. Gemälde, Druckgraphik und bildmäßige Zeichnungen.* Munich, 1973. Catalogue raisonné.

Hofmann, Werner. *Caspar David Friedrich: Naturwirklichkeit und Kunstwahrheit.* Munich, 2005.

Koerner, Joseph Leo. *Caspar David Friedrich and the Subject of Landscape.* London, 1990.

Schmied, Wieland. "Faces of Romanticism: Friedrich, Delacroix, Turner, Constable." In *The Romantic Spirit in German Art, 1790–1990,* edited by Keith Hartley. Edinburgh and London, 1994. Exhibition catalog.

———. *Caspar David Friedrich.* Translated from the German by Russell Stockman. New York, 1995.

———. *Caspar David Friedrich: Zyklus, Zeit, und Ewigkeit.* Munich, 1999.

WIELAND SCHMIED

FURNITURE. Furniture framed the everyday domestic lives of Europeans throughout the long nineteenth century. Accumulating enough savings so as to be able to furnish one's home was the dream of the urban working class, whereas the wealthy expended great time and energy on the acquisition of furnishings appropriate to their station. New institutions of distribution arose to supply rich and poor; in addition to the small custom shops and open-air markets of the early modern world, consumers could now also purchase their furniture from distributors ranging from stores selling poor-quality furniture on credit to the most luxurious of specialized and department stores. The work of these new retailers was seconded by that of advertisers and commentators.

By the nineteenth century both specialized and department stores were heavily advertising their wares, providing potential consumers with a vision of what they could acquire. Those advertisements were often bullying in tone, promising social and marital success as well as psychological fulfillment to those who purchased wisely and great ills and troubles to those who did not acquire what was recommended for them. The style in which the homes of the poor, the petite bourgeoisie, and the wealthy were furnished also became a major preoccupation of both government officials and cultural critics. Competitions were held across Europe to encourage designers to imagine affordable, healthy, and appropriate furnishings for each social class. Taste professionals further argued that working-class households that dwelt in homes

Table from Hardwicke Hall, Derbyshire, England. Created in the 1830s and called the "Sea Dog" table because of its zoomorphic decoration, this piece reflects the influence of the French Empire style. ©HISTORICAL PICTURE ARCHIVE/CORBIS

furnished with styles originally designed for the palaces of kings would be dissatisfied with their lot and inclined toward revolution. Decorating magazines included long articles on how the country houses of the wealthy should differ from their apartments in town. City dwellers living with furniture designed for rural homes would be ill-adapted for the particular rigors of urban life. Carved furnishings filled with hard-to-clean crevices and too heavy to move would encourage the spread of disease. Furniture, like architecture, was also the site of polemics between nationalists and regionalists, each arguing that from the style of the home emanated a sense of solidarity. Those who sought to reinforce regional identifications argued that people should live in the traditional styles of their region. Nationalists, sought, rather, to create a single style that would undercut those local affiliations and enable those who lived in the same polity to share an aesthetic every day.

PEOPLE'S RELATIONS TO FURNITURE

This profusion of new institutions, advertisements, and prescriptive commentaries necessarily shaped people's relations to the furniture they acquired, or sought to acquire. While this was not yet a mass consumer society, more people had more choice concerning the appearance of their homes than ever before. With that choice came a new sense of responsibility and possibility.

Europeans in this period used their homes for two, sometimes conflicting, purposes. The first was simply to provide the physical context for domestic life, the second to represent, and even constitute, the social and psychological self. A fundamental goal for all—young and old, single and married, rich and poor, urban and rural—was to create a comfortable and aesthetically pleasing context for their domestic everyday lives. Furnishings provided the props needed for sleeping, eating, dressing, socializing, and often working. There was, then, a functional role for furnishings. Equally crucial, however, was the role they played in the daily reconstitution of the self. Furnishings, like clothing and other elements of material culture, located individuals socially, temporally, and even politically. Throughout this period, for example, domestic interiors were markedly national in inflection. Thus, while German households were quite internationalist, containing goods of German, French, Italian, and English origin, French imports were limited to the British, and English and Italian households also tended to favor national styles (although French furnishings did travel throughout Europe).

Differences in national taste were equaled by differences among social classes. The gap in living standards in this period was vast. Until the second half of the twentieth century most urban dwellers lived in extremely cramped quarters, which often served as the site of labor as well as living. Single room dwellings housing multigenerational families and a workshop were far from uncommon. Those living in the country sometimes had more space, but very rarely the disposable income, or perhaps perceived need, to furnish their homes elaborately. Even those who had little space or disposable income, however, had some access to the posters and leaflets advertising the kind of interiors available to some and every major and most small cities had retailers that specialized in selling furniture on credit. The commercial, industrial, and professional classes, by contrast, came in this period to live in spacious apartments or single-family dwellings. They furnished these homes with great care and great concern for the appropriateness of that decoration to the household's professional and social position and often replaced furnishings as their social situation improved or declined. Tensions arose among these representational tasks. Cherished remnants of a past moment of life could sit uneasily with objects chosen in a later present with an eye toward the future. A subcultural identification—of class, region, or religion—could lead taste in a direction different from that of the national community.

Further complicating this dynamic was the fact that people, even if they lived alone, were also part of families. The families and family homes, however modest or luxurious, in which people passed their childhoods shaped their expectations of domesticity and the domestic environment. Whether they sought to emulate, modify, or escape those settings, they were influenced by them. Homes were often also more literally shaped by previous generations through inheritance. Even if inherited goods were discarded, they maintained a ghostly presence in the home. New families created by marriage or cohabitation were just as complex as those of birth. Husbands and wives came into their joint home with different pasts, and perhaps, different visions for the future. Those differences were often made dramatically tangible in the context of the home.

CRISIS OF STYLE

Due in part to this symbolic and representational weight being carried by furnishings and in part to changing dynamics within the world of production, by the end of the nineteenth century there was a general sense of crisis: no style appropriate to the modern era was understood to have emerged. The stylistic innovations of the end of the nineteenth century known as *style moderne*, *jugendstil*, or *liberty* were most often condemned by commentators as being both in poor taste and, because of their minimal use of machinery, inappropriate styles for the modern age. The British Arts and Crafts movement with its medieval referents and emphasis on hand labor, most famously represented by the English poet and artist William Morris (1834–1896), was also understood to be nostalgic and hopelessly ill-suited to modernity. Consumers were not much more enthusiastic than the critics about these styles, which were, in any case, too expensive for the majority to imagine acquiring. To the horror of design professionals most Europeans on the eve of World War I were still living in homes filled with either second-hand or antique furniture on the one hand or contemporary interpretations of historical styles on the other. The persistent dominance of historicism and eclecticism was understood to pose a threat in three domains: the economic, the political, and the social.

It was not only the perceived aesthetic archaism that worried commentators, however, but a particularly pernicious mode of production that they argued it enabled. Historicist furniture styles, because of their extensive use of carving, turning, caning, inlay, and veneer were very labor intensive. In their efforts to produce inexpensive versions of these intrinsically luxurious styles, furniture distributors (like their colleagues in the clothing industries) turned to outwork and sweated labor. Rather than create large factories, distributors built on the already existing network of small artisans, sometimes advancing materials, sometimes simply buying completed work at a low price. Workers driven

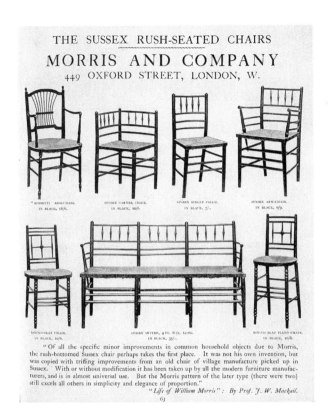

THE SUSSEX RUSH-SEATED CHAIRS

MORRIS AND COMPANY
449 OXFORD STREET, LONDON, W.

"ROSSETTI" ARM-CHAIR, IN BLACK, 16/6.   SUSSEX CORNER CHAIR, IN BLACK, 10/6.   SUSSEX SINGLE CHAIR, IN BLACK, 7/-.   SUSSEX ARM-CHAIR, IN BLACK, 9/9.

ROUND-SEAT CHAIR, IN BLACK, 10/6.   SUSSEX SETTEE, 4 FT. 6 IN. LONG, IN BLACK, 35/-.   ROUND SEAT PIANO CHAIR, IN BLACK, 10/6.

"Of all the specific minor improvements in common household objects due to Morris, the rush-bottomed Sussex chair perhaps takes the first place. It was not his own invention, but was copied with trifling improvements from an old chair of village manufacture picked up in Sussex. With or without modification it has been taken up by all the modern furniture manufacturers, and is in almost universal use. But the Morris pattern of the later type (there were two) still excels all others in simplicity and elegance of proportion."
"Life of William Morris": By Prof. J. W. Mackail.
63

Advertisement for Sussex chairs made by Morris and Company, nineteenth century. The Sussex rush-seat chair was typical of the kind of simple, well-crafted furniture manufactured by William Morris and his partners. PRIVATE COLLECTION/THE BRIDGEMAN ART LIBRARY

to produce more and more quickly necessarily turned out poor quality items while living in abject poverty. New, modern styles that could be efficiently produced in factories, it was argued, would enable employers to pay decent wages while also providing consumers with durable (and appropriate) furnishings. The immiseration of furniture workers was further feared because of their concentration in particular neighborhoods, like Paris's Faubourg St. Antoine or London's East End, and their history of labor organization and political radicalism.

The industry's continued production of historicist styles was also understood to weaken it on the international market. Since the working drawings and models for these styles were freely available, international competition turned exclusively on a combination of economies and efficiencies in the production process and access to cheap raw materials. Each European nation-state worried about the others' supposed advantages in the domain of production and all were worried about competition

from the United States. French and English commentators worried about the greater efficiency of the Germans and the Americans while the Germans thought the British school system and the French craft traditions would enable both to outsell them. Efforts to mandate a new style or to encourage innovation through improved school curricula, access to museums and libraries, or competitions, all proved of limited effect, largely because consumers preferred historicist pastiche to the modernist styles invented for them. However engaged in modernity they were in other domains of their lives, even other aesthetic domains such as the fine arts, music, or literature, the vast majority of European consumers in the long nineteenth century looked to their homes for reassuring links to their familial and national pasts.

See also **Housing; Popular and Elite Culture.**

BIBLIOGRAPHY

Auslander, Leora. *Taste and Power: Furnishing Modern France.* Berkeley, Calif., 1996.

Gere, Charlotte, and Michael Whiteway. *Nineteenth-Century Design from Pugin to Mackintosh.* New York, 1994.

Hunter-Stiebel, Penelope. *Of Knights and Spires: Gothic Revival in France and Germany.* New York, 1989.

Siebel, Ernst. *Der grossbürgerliche Salon, 1850–1918: Geselligkeit und Wohnkultur.* Berlin, 1999.

Stansky, Peter. *Redesigning the World: William Morris, the 1880s and the Arts and Crafts.* Princeton, N.J., 1985.

Troy, Nancy J. *Modernism and the Decorative Arts in France: Art Nouveau to Le Corbusier.* New Haven, Conn., 1991.

LEORA AUSLANDER

FUTURISM. The futurist art movement was founded in 1909 by the Italian poet, journalist, critic, and publisher Filippo Tommaso Marinetti (1876–1944). It was the first expression of the avant-garde in the fields of art and literature and sought to overturn aesthetic traditions and conventions; to bridge the gap between art and life; and to institute a program of political, intellectual, and moral regeneration. The futurist project of innovation attempted to obliterate the contemplative, intellectual concept of culture and aimed at a total

EXCERPT FROM THE FUTURIST MANIFESTO

1. We want to sing about the love of danger, about the use of energy and recklessness as common, daily practice.
2. Courage, boldness, and rebellion will be essential elements in our poetry.
3. Up to now, literature has extolled a contemplative stillness, rapture, and rêverie. We intend to glorify aggressive action, a restive wakefulness, life at the double, the slap, and the punching fist.
4. We believe that this wonderful world has been further enriched by a new beauty, the beauty of speed. A racing car, its bonnet decked-out with exhaust pipes like serpents with galvanic breath ... a roaring motorcar, which seems to race on like machine-gun fire, is more beautiful than the *Winged Victory of Samothrace.*
5. We wish to sing the praises of the man behind the steering wheel, whose sleek shaft traverses the Earth, hurtling at breakneck speed, it too, along the race-track of its orbit.
6. The poet will have to do all in his power, passionately, flamboyantly, and with generosity of spirit, to increase the delirious fervor of the primordial elements.
7. There is no longer any beauty except the struggle. Any work of art that lacks a sense of aggression can never be a masterpiece. Poetry must be thought of as a violent assault upon the forces of the unknown with the intention of making them prostrate themselves at the feet of mankind.
8. We stand upon the furthest promontory of the ages! ... Why should we be looking back over our shoulders, if what we desire is to smash down the mysterious doors of the Impossible? Time and Space died yesterday. We are already living in the realms of the Absolute, for we have already created infinite, omnipresent speed.
9. We wish to glorify war—the only cleanser of the world—militarism, patriotism, the destructive act of the libertarian, beautiful ideas worth dying for, and scorn for women.
10. We wish to destroy museums, libraries, academies of any sort, and fight against moralism, feminism, and every kind of materialistic, self-serving cowardice.
11. We shall sing of the great multitudes who are roused up by work, by pleasure or by rebellion; of the many-hued, many-voiced tides of revolution in our modern capitals; of the pulsating, nightly ardor of arsenals and ship-yards, ablaze with their violent electric moons; of railway stations, voraciously devouring smoke-belching serpents; of workshops hanging from the clouds by their twisted threads of smoke; of bridges which, like giant gymnasts, bestride the rivers, flashing in the sunlight like gleaming knives; of intrepid steamships that sniff out the horizon; of broad-breasted locomotives, champing on their wheels like enormous steel horses, bridled with pipes; and of the lissom flight of the airplane, whose propeller flutters like a flag in the wind, seeming to applaud, like a crowd excited.

It is from Italy that we hurl at the whole world this utterly violent, inflammatory manifesto of ours, with which today we are founding "Futurism," because we wish to free our country from the stinking canker of its professors, archaeologists, tour-guides, and antiquarians.

For far too long has Italy been a market-place for junk dealers. We want to free our country from the endless number of museums that everywhere cover her like countless graveyards.

Museums, graveyards! – – – They're the same thing, really, because of their grim profusion of corpses that no one remembers. Museums. They're just public doss-houses, where things sleep on forever, alongside other loathsome or nameless things! Museums; ridiculous abattoirs for painters and sculptors, who are furiously stabbing each other to death with colors and lines, all along the walls where they vie for space.

Source: F. T. Marinetti, *Critical Writings*. Edited by Günter Berghaus; translated by Doug Thomson. New York, 2006.

and permanent revolution in all spheres of human existence. What was later called the "Futurist Refashioning of the Universe" (the title of a manifesto published by Giacomo Balla and Fortunato Depero in 1915) was aimed at a transformation of humankind in all its physiological, psychological, and social aspects.

Many of the ideas synthesized in the *Foundation and Manifesto of Futurism* (1909) can already be detected in the decade preceding futurism, when Marinetti gained influence on the cultural climate of his country. His studies of law (1895–1899) had provided him with a sound knowledge of modern political theories. He also took a lively interest in the practical politics of his country, particularly those pursued by radical and subversive groups. Therefore, his aesthetic program of renewal was always complemented by political engagement. Marinetti's literary works and theoretical essays of the years 1900 to 1909 were a testament to his ideological development and prefigure many of the aesthetic concepts expressed in his manifestos of 1909–1914.

Marinetti had grown up in Alexandria, Egypt, and had experienced the great advances of modern civilization during his first visit to Paris in 1894. At the turn of the century, Italy also began to catch up with the economic developments in other major European countries. The agrarian character of the young nation underwent a rapid and profound transformation and gave way to industrial capitalism, especially in the North, where around the turn of the century a modern urban lifestyle began to take shape. Milan, Genoa, and Turin were the first to introduce a modern transport system; streets were illuminated with powerful arc lamps; houses were fitted with sanitary services unknown anywhere else in the peninsula.

THE FOUNDATION AND INITIAL MANIFESTO OF FUTURISM

However, despite this "Arrival of the Future," Italy's cultural identity remained firmly rooted in the past. The great achievements of the Renaissance weighed heavily on the modern generation. Instead of reflecting a country transformed by steam engines, automobiles, airplanes, electricity, and telephones, artists remained in their ivory towers and stood aloof from the experience of the

industrial age. Marinetti and a group of bohemian artists and writers who used to congregate at Milan's Caffè del Centro declared war on the establishment and sought to resuscitate the dormant cultural life of their country, which, in their view, was steeped in traditionalism and ignored the great advances of the modern world.

In 1908 Marinetti attempted to set up a new artistic school, which he intended to name *Elettricismo* or *Dinamismo*. As the editor of a successful international poetry magazine, *Poesia*, he possessed excellent connections in Italy and abroad. With the help of a business friend of his late father he managed to place a foundation manifesto, which he had previously circulated as a broadsheet and issued in several Italian newspapers, on the front page of *Le Figaro* (20 February 1909). In the following months, this foundation and manifesto of futurism caused a tremendous stir. It rung in a new era in the history of modernist culture and set the tone for the operational tactics adopted by other avant-garde art movements in the early twentieth century.

Marinetti claimed to have received nine thousand five hundred letters of affiliation in response to his foundation manifesto, predominantly from young men between twenty and thirty. Whatever the true figure may have been, the publication certainly generated a lively debate on futurism in France as well as in Italy. Marinetti fuelled this controversy by engineering major theater scandals with productions of his plays, *Le Roi Bombance* (King Guzzle) and *Poupées électriques* (Electric dolls), by carrying out a variety of street actions, and by organizing a series of some twenty soirées, which counted among the most controversial theater events in living memory. The futurist *serate* contained a mixture of poetry readings, declamations of manifestos, presentations of paintings, and music. But their main aim was, as Marinetti said, "to introduce the fist into the artistic battle" and to enable "the violent entry of life into art." They always ended in a pandemonium of fisticuffs and heated verbal exchanges between stage and auditorium.

In 1909–1914 Marinetti and his followers published no fewer than forty-five manifestos that outlined their artistic concepts and ideas. As to the form and content of these pronouncements, Marinetti developed a specifically futurist "art of writing manifestos" that assimilated the persuasive methods of political propaganda and commercial advertising. The futurist manifestos became an essential ingredient of Marinetti's publicity machine. They were an effective medium for propagating the politics and aesthetics of his movement; they were cheap and quick to produce; they could reach a wide audience by being distributed as flyers or by being recited from the stage. They were also mailed to journalists, press agents, and the editors of national and international newspapers, thus finding their way into a large number of periodical publications (without incurring the cost of advertising fees).

Preparing, organizing, and, finally, carrying out such a campaign was a task that demanded immense energy and considerable funds. Marinetti possessed both. The first Italian edition of the *Foundation and Manifesto of Futurism* boasted an editorial caption: "Direzione del movimento futurista: Corso Venezia, 61—Milano," giving the impression that futurism was a large-scale enterprise directed by a proper board of management. Reality, however, was much more modest: right through the year 1909, the "movimento futurista" was a one-man band, supported by a group of writers (Paolo Buzzi, Enrico Cavacchioli, Corrado Govoni, Libero Altomare, Federico de Maria) and two secretaries (Decio Cinti and Lisa Spada). It was only in 1910 that the new *literary* school expanded into other fields of artistic expression and developed into a *movement* proper.

Although Marinetti entertained amicable contacts with nonconformist painters and draftsmen in the Lombardy region, it took nearly a year before the first of them began to join the futurist movement. In January or February 1910 they held a number of meetings to write a manifesto specifically concerned with the state of the fine arts in Italy. The text was issued on 11 February 1910, followed, on 11 April 1910, by a technical manifesto and, on 5 February 1912, by a theoretical declaration in the catalog of their first group exhibition at the Galerie Bernheim-Jeune in Paris. In its early phase, futurist painting remained attached to the styles and painterly manners of impressionism, symbolism, and divisionism. It was only when Gino Severini (1883–1966) and Ardengo Soffici (1879–1964) informed the group about the artistic revolution unleashed by cubism that Umberto Boccioni (1882–1916), Carlo Carrà (1881–1966),

and Luigi Russolo (1885–1947) set off for Paris to bring themselves up to date with the latest developments in northern European painting. The experience, largely financed by Marinetti, led to a feverish refashioning of futurist painting and a subsequent tour of more than thirty-five works executed in the new style to Paris (February 1912), London (March 1912), Berlin (April 1912), Brussels (June 1912), Amsterdam (September 1912), Chicago (March 1913), and Rotterdam (May 1913).

Futurist painting took as its subject matter "the multi-colored, polyphonic tides of revolution in the modern capitals"—the hustle and bustle of street life in the metropolis, the pulsating dynamism of trade and commerce, the machine as a civilizing power, the social and political tensions in industrialized countries, and so on. To render these experiences in a novel and up-to-date fashion, the painters studied the science of optics, the physiology and psychology of vision, and the analysis of movement in chronophotography and cinematography. From this they arrived at the conclusion that the life force and the dynamic flux of movement links matter with its surrounding space, that the atmosphere dissolves the borders of independent objects, and that sense impressions should be depicted as a unified whole. However, the futurists did not restrict themselves to the scientific analysis of the world and a rational organization of the constituent elements of painting; they also absorbed Henri Bergson's (1895–1941) reflections on the new experience of time and space, and took into account how the artist's subjective experiences of reality affects his or her state of mind. For example, when emotive reactions to a train ride or to the view of a busy boulevard were made a central concern of a painting, the image was turned into a sum total of the artist's impressions and sensations, both past and present. Increasingly, the futurists shook off the remnants of mimetic realism and developed an aesthetic that in their manifestos they summed up under the headings simultaneity, interpenetration, synthesis, multiple viewpoints, and universal dynamism. Painting as a complex network of forms, colors, and force-lines was meant to connect not only the depicted objects and their surrounding space, but also to draw in the viewer until in the end she or he becomes "the center of the picture." Thus, futurist painting revolutionized both the production and the reception process of a work of art.

Plastic Dynamism: Horse and Houses. Pen and ink drawing by Umberto Boccioni, 1914. ©ESOTRICK COLLECTION, LONDON, UK/THE BRIDGEMAN ART LIBRARY

A similar concern was pursued by Boccioni in his sculpture. He sought to represent matter in terms of movement and duration, lines of force and interpenetration of planes, using a variety of materials for expressing an essentialist reality hidden beneath the surface of observable phenomena. The object depicted was shown to exist not as an autonomous body but as a dynamic relationship between weight and expansion. Boccioni's sculptures grew beyond their physical limits into the surrounding space, where in a dynamic fashion they fused with the environment and shaped its atmosphere. Movement was synthesized as "unique forms of continuity in space" that take hold of the viewer and force him or her to a similarly dynamic relationship with the sculpture exhibited.

Another field with far-reaching influence was futurist music. In August 1910 the composer Francesco Balilla Pratella (1880–1955) joined the futurist circle and subsequently published three manifestos that criticized the traditionalist outlook and the obstructive commercialism of the Italian musical world. More radical in outlook were the ideas of Russolo, who experimented with an idea of replacing traditional music with music based on a wide range of sounds related to, but not simply imitative of, the noises of everyday life. Since conventional musical instruments were far too limited in their sound spectrum, Russolo invented a new type of noise machine, the *intonarumori*, the first of which made explosive sounds like an automobile engine, a crackling sound like rifle fire, a humming sound like a dynamo, or different kinds of stamping noises. The instruments looked like sound boxes with large funnels attached and could be tuned and rhythmically regulated by means of mechanical manipulation. A stretched diaphragm produced, by variations in tension, a scale of tones, different timbres, and variations in pitch. Russolo explained his inventions in a manifesto of 11 March 1913, *The Art of Noise,* and demonstrated them on 2 June 1913 at the Teatro Storchi in Modena. A full orchestra of noise intoners was presented on 21 April 1914 at the Teatro dal Verme in Milan and on 20 May 1914 at the Politeama in Genoa. Russolo then started a tour abroad and presented his instruments in London, Liverpool, Dublin, Glasgow, Edinburgh, Vienna, Moscow, St. Petersburg, Berlin, and Paris.

Initially, Italian futurism was centered on Milan and had two important offshoots in Rome and Florence. In the course of the next five years, local branches sprung up in dozens of towns and cities, all linked in some way to the futurist headquarters, but often acting independently and in quite a few cases in opposition to Marinetti and his closest circle of collaborators. This led to a number of desertions, such as the Florentine Lacerba group, who insisted that futurism ought not to be confused with "Marinettism." There also existed artists who shared many of the futurists' concerns without ever formally joining the movement. For example, in Rome, the brothers Anton Giulio Bragaglia (1890–1960) and Arturo Bragaglia (1893–1962) set up an art circle and organized a range of public events that ran parallel to the activities of the "official" group headed by Giacomo Balla (1871–1958). A profusion of theoretical statements caused the term *futurism* to assume quite a definite meaning, but it could also be used in a wider sense to signify "antitraditionalism," "modernism," or "radical art." Particularly in the popular press one could find artists and groups being called "futurist" although they were not directly linked to Marinetti's movement. And since Marinetti was keen to document the fundamental significance of his movement and its international appeal, he did not protest when artists such as Alexander Archipenko (1887–1964), Paul Klee (1879–1940), Wassily Kandinsky (1866–1944), and Pablo Picasso (1881–1973) were referred to as "futurist."

In the decade before the inception of the futurist movement, Marinetti had made a considerable impact in France through the publication of three collections of poetry, two plays, and a large number of essays in literary journals and cultural magazines. The publication of the *Foundation and Manifesto of Futurism* in a French newspaper indicated that Marinetti did not intend to limit his radius of influence to Italy alone. He published most of his early manifestos both in Italian and French versions and had them translated into various other (including some non-European) languages. Consequently, futurism became an international movement that exercised a profound influence on the arts and cultural attitudes in other countries. There was hardly a modernist movement that did not in some way or other receive inspiration and stimulation from futurism. However, as the ideas that had originated in Italy interacted with the specific traditions of the receiving cultures, they fomented a process of assimilation and gave rise to a number of futurisms, which developed an increasingly independent and original character. Marinetti welcomed this development and refused to treat his movement as a narrow school or "church." In 1909–1914 response to his ideas was most strongly felt in France, Russia, and Germany. But also in Japan and Latin America one can find futurism encouraging artists to develop their own brands of modernism.

POLITICAL FUTURISM

When Marinetti published his *Foundation and Manifesto of Futurism,* he presented a far-reaching program of renewal that linked aesthetic innovation with a radical transformation of the real world. As he was fully aware that literary manifestos and works of art were not a sufficient means to set ablaze the somnolent and stultified cultural scene in Italy, he made politics a significant component of the futurist movement from the very beginning. He extended the radius of his activities beyond the traditional intellectual elites and sought to find allies on the political battlefield. He undertook numerous attempts to gather the support of the anarchosyndicalists of northern Italy. He planned to stand in the local elections in Piedmont, with an anarchosyndicalist program of a nationalistic bent. During the 1913 elections he published a political manifesto and had a hundred thousand copies distributed, thus giving rise to the suspicion that he intended to stand against the reformist Socialist Leonida Bissolati (1857–1920). Although this was not the case, in an interview with *Giornale d'Italia,* of 30 October 1913, Marinetti announced that in the near future he intended to enter the political arena on a list for a really important constituency. This idea came to fruition when, in 1918, he founded the Futurist Political Party, formed an alliance with Benito Mussolini's (1883–1945) Fasci di Combattimento, and stood as a candidate in the national elections of November 1919.

Although Marinetti had a decidedly international upbringing and launched his career through a series of French-language publications, his engagement in radical, left-wing politics was always combined with a passionate nationalism. Like many intellectuals of his generation, he felt that the unification process of Italy (the Risorgimento) would only be brought to completion when the "still unredeemed territories" (*terra irredenta*) had been liberated from Austrian domination. This largely determined his ardent support for Italy's intervention in World War I. However, given his political leanings, his attitude toward solving conflicts by militant means was also rooted in other, more philosophical concepts.

Marinetti made little distinction between revolution and war. Both were seen to be two sides of the same coin: regenerative violence. When a French magazine questioned Marinetti on the militant character of his artistic program, he stated that the equation "futurism = revolution = war" was for him "a question of health." In Marinetti's political ideology, war was a purifying and revitalizing medication for the Italian race, a leaven for the dough of humanity, and an antidote to traditionalism. He repeatedly emphasized that war, as he understood it, was not a return to barbarity, but an expression of the life force that could restore health to a body politic in a state of dissolution. This mystical view, largely based on Friedrich Wilhelm Nietzsche (1844–1900), Bergson, and Georges-Eugène Sorel (1847–1922), was aptly captured in his formula, "war, the ultimate purgative of the world." Marinetti supported the use of violence as a means of achieving political objectives and praised it as a vital ingredient of the "military railroad into the future," the long path toward a better society. He repeatedly quoted the examples of the French Revolution and the Risorgimento to show that war was intimately linked to the struggle for freedom, equality, and justice. Therefore, he exalted violence as "a gay manner of fertilizing the Earth! Because the Earth, believe me, will soon be pregnant. She will grow big—until she bursts!"

With Italy's entry into World War I, a number of futurists lined up for voluntary service. Consequently, futurism lost much of its artistic significance, only to resurface again after the war as a political movement. After 1922 it experienced a revival as an aesthetic force, especially in the applied arts, that lasted well into the 1930s.

See also **Avant-Garde; Italy; Modernism.**

BIBLIOGRAPHY

Primary Sources

Apollonio, Umbro, ed. *Futurist Manifestos.* London, 1973.

Caruso, Luciano, ed. *Manifesti, proclami, interventi e documenti teorici del futurismo, 1909–1944.* 4 vols. Florence, 1980.

Marinetti, Filippo Tommaso. *Teoria e invenzione futurista.* 2nd ed. Edited by Luciano De Maria. Milan, 1983.

———. *Critical Writings.* Edited by Günter Berghaus. Translated by Doug Thompson. New York, 2006.

Scrivo, Luigi, ed. *Sintesi del futurismo: Storia e documenti.* Rome, 1968.

Secondary Sources

Berghaus, Günter. *Futurism and Politics: Between Anarchist Rebellion and Fascist Reaction, 1909–1944.* Oxford, U.K., 1996.

Berghaus, Günter, ed. *International Futurism in Arts and Literature: Interdisciplinary Studies on Futurism as an International Phenomenon.* Berlin and New York, 2000.

Crispolti, Enrico. *Storia e critica del futurismo.* Rome, 1986.

Salaris, Claudia. *Storia del futurismo: Libri, giornali, manifesti.* Rome, 1985. Rev., enlarged ed., 1992.

GÜNTER BERGHAUS

GAGERN, HEINRICH VON (1799–1880), German politician.

Heinrich von Gagern's life and career mirror the fortunes of German liberalism and nationalism during the crucial period from the end of the Napoleonic Wars in 1815 to the final unification of Germany in the 1870s. Gagern draws most attention (sometimes admiring, sometimes critical) for his central role in the liberal-nationalist revolution of 1848, but he was also a significant figure in the decades before and after.

Born August 20, 1799 into the German imperial nobility, Gagern came from a noted political family. Already in 1815 he upheld the strong family commitment to German nationalism as a volunteer at the Battle of Waterloo (16–18 June 1815). Gagern became even more deeply involved in the German nationalist movement during his university years and by 1818 had assumed a leadership position within the new nationalist *Burschenschaft* or student fraternity movement. Forced into exile in the reactionary year 1819, Gagern was still able to enter the service of the Grand Duke of Hessen-Darmstadt two years later.

In the wake of the revolutions of 1830, Gagern was elected to the Diet of the Grand Duchy. His position as a vocal member of the opposition cost him his government post in 1833, but he continued in the parliament for three more years. Having retired to his estate, Gagern returned to the Darmstadt Diet as opposition leader in 1847.

It was during the revolution of 1848, however, that Gagern reached the summit of his political influence. First he was named to lead a new liberal government in the Grand Duchy. Already at this state level Gagern displayed his moderate liberal tendencies, supporting a catalog of liberal rights and reforms while trying to steer between the potential dangers of a radical popular revolution and an unreconciled reactionary regime. Many historians have criticized Gagern and other liberals for not going far enough during the revolution and leaving the door open for the eventual return to power of the old order.

Gagern's commitment to national unification, his parliamentary experience, and his relatively rare ability to command respect on both the left and right wings of the political spectrum led to his election to the presidency of the German National Assembly when it met in Frankfurt beginning in May 1848. In June, Gagern gave a demonstration of his perhaps unique political position when he broke a deadlock over the question of forming a temporary executive for the new German state by forging a centrist compromise solution.

Gagern became head of the national government in December as the result of yet another deadlock, this time over the question of whether to draw up a constitution that would allow the Austrian monarchy to participate in the new German nation-state (the so-called *Grossdeutsch* or Greater Germany solution). Before 1848, Gagern had favored the idea of a Prussian-led German state (the *Kleindeutsch* or Little German solution). Even then, however, Heinrich had wanted to prevent Austria's complete exclusion by forging a "wider union" with it. In this he was motivated in part by his nationalist and imperialist desire to maintain an outlet for German emigration and goods in southeastern Europe. During the revolution Gagern continued to pursue this policy, and in March of 1849 it was another of Gagern's compromise solutions that produced a narrow majority in favor of a Prussian hereditary emperor coupled with universal manhood suffrage. The Prussian king's notorious refusal to accept the offer so associated with Gagern's policies effectively ended the latter's power.

Gagern hung on for two more months on a caretaker basis before he and many other moderate liberals finally left the parliament. During the 1850s Gagern occasionally let his voice be heard in various liberal and nationalist causes. By the early 1860s, when competing versions of German unification were once again on the political table, Gagern this time surprised and alienated many former allies when he put his weight behind a Germany including Austria rather than backing the new Prussian-led unification being engineered by Otto von Bismarck (1815–1898). He did come out in guarded support of the new German Reich in 1870–1871, but was mistrusted by both political parties and failed in his bid to secure election to the new German Reichstag. Gagern died on 22 May 1880.

By the 1870s, Gagern had clearly become a marginal if controversial figure, facts that probably go some way toward explaining the strange lack of later scholarly attention to such a central figure of nineteenth-century German liberal and nationalist politics. If neglected, he was nonetheless one of the most prominent and important political actors of the period.

See also **Germany; Liberalism; Nationalism; Revolutions of 1848.**

BIBLIOGRAPHY

Eyck, Frank. *The Frankfurt Parliament 1848–1849.* London, 1968.

Vick, Brian E. *Defining Germany: The 1848 Frankfurt Parliamentarians and National Identity.* Cambridge, Mass., 2002.

Wentzcke, Paul. *Heinrich von Gagern: Vorkämpfer für deutsche Einheit und Volksvertretung.* Göttingen, 1957.

BRIAN VICK

GAJ, LJUDEVIT (1809–1872), Croatian nationalist leader.

Ljudevit Gaj helped lead the first Croatian national movement in modern times, the Illyrian movement. That movement dominated Croatian political and cultural life from 1832 to 1841. From the latter date, the Illyrians remained influential but were forced to compete with other visions of a Croatian future. Gaj's legacy is mixed: he was a talented organizer with a novel vision, but he is often accused of having appropriated the ideas of others. His public career ended in scandal in 1848.

Gaj was born in Krapina, Croatia, in 1809. Like other national revivalists of his era, he was not born of Croatian parents; he was of German/Slovak background. He was intelligent and talented and wished to study Croatia's history. Gaj came of age as the Hungarian national movement gained force, so it is logical that he was motivated to a great degree by the desire to establish a Croatian counterforce to the Hungarian movement, which he believed threatened the integrity of Croatia and Croatian culture.

From 1826 to 1829, he studied in Austria (first Vienna, then Graz); he then went to Budapest, where he came into contact with Jan Kollár, the Slovak language reformer. Kollár's belief in the unity (reciprocity) of the Slavic languages undoubtedly influenced Gaj's own ideas. While in Budapest, Gaj published the *Short Outline of a Croatian-Slavic Orthography,* which eliminated foreign (non-Slavic) influences and introduced a phonetic alphabet. This alphabet, Gaj believed, could be used by others who spoke similar languages (Croatian, but also other Slavic tongues). While in Budapest, he also wrote the poem "Croatia Has Yet to Perish," which later became a patriotic Croatian song.

Gaj returned to Zagreb in 1832 with a law degree and novel ideas about the language of the South Slavs. Along with a coterie of other cultural figures, he created what came to be called the Illyrian movement. First, he applied to be allowed to publish a newspaper called *The Morning Star of Croatia, Slavonia, and Dalmatia*. This proposal would only be approved in 1835, when the Habsburg emperor deemed it useful as a counterpoint to the much more threatening Hungarian national movement. That newspaper was published at first in the kajkavian dialect of Croatian, which was the dialect dominant in Zagreb. However, within a year, Gaj began to publish the paper in the štokavian dialect, which was spoken by Croats in Bosnia and much of Dalmatia and Croatia. This decision, rooted in his belief that only the most "reciprocal," broad-based language could fuel a national movement, went against the grain in Zagreb, but built on the work of other Illyrians, primarily Count Janko Drašković, whose 1832 *Dissertation or Discourse . . .* had proposed both the Illyrian name for a future South Slavic state and the use of štokavian as a literary vehicle for nation-building.

The choice of štokavian was, of course, Gaj's most notable practical contribution to the national movements of the South Slavs. It signified his desire to reach out to otherwise fragmented peoples, including Serbs, who uniformly spoke the štokavian dialect. Štokavian was also the language of Dubrovnik, which all Croats had come to idealize over the centuries. The Serbian response to this act of Croatian self-sacrifice was not particularly positive. Vuk Karadžić, Gaj's Serbian counterpart, declared in a famous 1842 article that speakers of štokavian were Serbs—"all and everywhere," as he put it.

Nevertheless, the Illyrians formed a political party (the National Party), which dominated Croatian politics until 1841. The National Party had no allies among the traditional Croatian political strata. The party did have support in Vienna, however, at least until the emperor no longer found it a valuable counterforce to Hungarian nationalism. In 1841 Croatian conservatives finally got their act together, creating a Unionist Party, commonly referred to as the "magyarone" party, for its desire for close ties to Hungary. For the next seven years, the Illyrians were out of favor in Vienna and Zagreb. In 1848, however, they had a chance to recapture some of their lost glory. The Croatian Sabor (diet), provoked by the hostile words of the Hungarian nationalist leader Lajos Kossuth, passed

much of the old Illyrian political agenda. The Illyrian choice for Ban of Croatia, Josip Jelačić, was accepted by the emperor, whose fear of Hungary once again spurred him to support Croatia. Gaj, however, did not benefit from this revival of Illyrian prestige. In 1848, he was accused (accurately) of accepting money for using his influence in the name of the Serbian government. Thereafter, he retired from public life.

See also **Austria-Hungary; Jelačić, Josip; Metternich, Clemens von; Nationalism.**

BIBLIOGRAPHY

Despalatovic, Elinor Murray. *Ljudevit Gaj and the Illyrian Movement.* Boulder, Colo., 1975.

NICHOLAS MILLER

GALL, FRANZ JOSEPH (1758–1828),
inventor of phrenology.

Franz Joseph Gall was born in the Swabian village of Tiefenbronn, in the German grand duchy of Baden, where his father, a wealthy Roman Catholic wool merchant, was mayor. Gall's parents intended him for the church, but in 1777, the same year he married a young Alsatian girl, he began medical studies at Strasbourg. In 1781 he moved to Vienna, where he received his medical degree in 1785. Thereafter, until his death in Paris in August 1828, he carried on a highly successful conventional medical practice.

Gall's first publication, *Philosophisch-Medicinische* (1791), was largely a diatribe against metaphysics and idealist and romantic speculations. Gall regarded himself as an empiricist revealing "Nature's truths" and took as his particular mission the integration of scientific problems of mind and brain with those of life and society. From the mid-1790s he began collecting and studying human and animal skulls, as well as conducting extensive anatomical dissections of the brain. He developed his ideas in public lectures and demonstrations in Vienna from 1796 until 1801, when the emperor of Austria forbade them on grounds of being conducive to materialism, immorality, and atheism. In 1805, with his assistant, the medical student Johann Gaspar Spurzheim (1776–1832), he undertook a lecture tour of Germany, Denmark, The Netherlands,

Switzerland, and France, which lasted until October 1807 when he settled in Paris. The tour was a huge success, earning him fame and fortune, but at the same time raising considerable controversy, especially from fellow medical professionals.

Gall's skull doctrine (*Schädellehre*) or "Organologie" as he preferred to call what others were to denominate craniology and (after 1815) phrenology, was based on six propositions, none of which was strictly original. The first was that humans and animals were born with innate faculties or aptitudes. Although this was a commonsensical observation, it flew in the face of the French *idéologues* who emphasized the importance of environment and learning over innate endowment. Gall's second proposition was that the brain was the organ of the mind, that is, in opposition to the mind-body dualism posited by René Descartes, that the mind (as brain) was part of the organization of the body as a whole, rather than something separate from it. Third, Gall proposed that the brain was not a homogeneous unity, but an aggregate of cerebral organs ("faculties") with discrete functions. Hitherto, within philosophies of mind, "mental faculties" indicated nonspecific functional parameters; in Gall's system, however, they were physical operational vectors in self-contained compartments of brain-matter. From the point of view of the history of psychology, this assignment of specific mental functions to specific anatomical organs was the most revolutionary aspect of Gall's system. Fourth, he maintained that these cerebral organs were topographically localized, and, fifth, that, other factors being equal, the relative size of any one of them could be taken as an index to its power of manifestation. Finally, Gall proposed that since the skull ossified over the brain during infant development, external craniological means could be used to diagnose the internal state of the mental faculties. Here Gall's theory intersected with contemporary interest in physiognomy, especially as rekindled in the late eighteenth century by the Reverend Johann Caspar Lavater (1741–1801). Significantly, the first full account of Gall's doctrine (which was written by Spurzheim) was not entitled a craniological system or brain organology, but rather, *The Physiognomical System of Drs. Gall and Spurzheim* (1815). Gall's physiognomy was profoundly different from that delineated by Lavater, however. Not only did it give no scope to immaterial and occult forces, but, crucially, it related external signs of character to internal neurophysiological functions. Although Gall saw himself simply as recasting psychology from a branch of philosophy to one of biology, his physiognomy also fitted with a broader and more fundamental contemporary European project: the perception of the self in terms of psychological interiority.

Since the turn of the twentieth century the mention of phrenology has conjured only the craniological aspect of Gall's doctrine. For most of the nineteenth century, however, Gall's ideas were perceived as pivotal to reconceptualizing psychology, neuroanatomy, and philosophy. Opponents and advocates alike appreciated that his reduction of questions of mind and brain to the single domain of dynamic physiology was a grandiose means to sweep away centuries of metaphysical speculations and reflections. Later pioneers in brain function acknowledged and built upon Gall's researches, while positivist social scientists, such as Auguste Comte, regarded Gall as crucial to a major shift in the conceptualization and analysis of man's place in nature.

See also **Comte, Auguste; Phrenology; Psychology.**

BIBLIOGRAPHY

Primary Sources

Gall, F. J. *Anatomie et physiologie du système nerveux en général, et du Cerveau en particular.* 4 vols. Paris, 1810–1819. Includes an atlas of one thousand plates. The first 2 volumes were coauthored by J. G. Spurzheim.

———. *Sur les functions du cerveau et sur celles de chacune de ses parties.* 6 vols. Paris, 1822–1825. English translation by W. Lewis, Jr. Boston, 1835.

Spurzheim, J. G. *The Physiognomical System of Drs. Gall and Spurzheim.* London, 1815.

Secondary Sources

Heintel, Helmut. *Leben und Werk von Franz Joseph Gall: Eine Chronik.* Würzburg, Germany, 1986.

Wyhe, John van. "The Authority of Human Nature: The *Schädellehre* of Franz Joseph Gall." *British Journal for the History of Science* 35 (2002): 17–42.

Young, Robert M. "Gall." In *Dictionary of Scientific Biography*, vol. 5, edited by Charles Coulston Gillespie, 250–256. New York, 1972.

ROGER COOTER

GALTON, FRANCIS (1822–1911), English scientist and originator of the eugenics movement.

Francis Galton is best known for his origination of the eugenics movement, but he was also a versatile scientist who made diverse contributions to the fields of geography, meteorology, genetics, statistics, psychology, and criminology. Galton was born on 16 February 1822 into a wealthy family in Birmingham, England—his father a banker descended from the Quaker Barclay family (of banking fame) and his mother the daughter of the celebrated physician and poet Erasmus Darwin (1731–1802) by his second wife. Galton was a half-cousin to Charles Darwin (1809–1882), whose father, Robert, was Erasmus Darwin's son by his first wife.

Although young Galton showed some signs of being a prodigy, his formal academic career was undistinguished; he started but did not complete medical training, and he failed to win honors in mathematics at Cambridge. After several years of idle drifting, he finally found purpose in active, outdoorsy pursuits and came to public prominence in the early 1850s as an African explorer. His map and geographical descriptions of present-day Namibia won him the Royal Geographical Society's Gold Medal for 1853, and his book *Tropical South Africa* (1853) provided a more popularized account and gained him a name as a travel writer. Galton subsequently became a central figure in the Royal Geographic Society and helped plan many of the epic African exploring expeditions of the 1860s and 1870s. In 1855 Galton wrote *The Art of Travel,* the first extensive "how-to" book for explorers and travelers in the wild. In the late 1850s Galton had the idea to plot simultaneous barometer readings from many different European locations on a single map—thus inventing the now ubiquitous weather map.

Galton's socially most momentous work was stimulated by Charles Darwin's evolutionary theory as introduced in 1859 in *On the Origin of Species.* Whereas Darwin at that point emphasized the evolution of physical characteristics in animals and plants, Galton was convinced that the most important intellectual and psychological variations in humans are also inheritable, and thus constitute the main basis of future human evolution. In an extrapolation that his cousin did not completely accept, Galton argued in *Hereditary Genius* (1869) and *Inquiries into Human Faculty and Its Development* (1883) that human evolution could be deliberately facilitated by exercising selective breeding practices—a program that he first called "viriculture" and then, more effectively, "eugenics." This project became Galton's obsession and consuming passion for the rest of his long life.

In his efforts to place eugenics on a scientific footing, Galton originated several techniques and theories that continue to be actively used today in many different fields. One was the idea for the modern intelligence test, which Galton hoped would be a scientific measure of hereditary mental ability in young adults, so the most able could be identified and encouraged to intermarry and have many offspring. Galton's own tests measured neurophysiological functions, such as reaction time and sensory acuity, and met with little practical success. Nevertheless, his general eugenic idea remained alive and, following the development of a more effective testing approach by Alfred Binet and Théodore Simon in 1905, helped produce the continuing controversy regarding the hereditary or environmental determination of intelligence.

To measure the relative influences of "nature and nurture"—a catchphrase that Galton introduced in 1874—Galton had the idea of comparing similarities and differences between genetically identical, monozygotic twins, and nonidentical, dizygotic twins. His own, relatively simplistic study stimulated several more ambitious and sophisticated (although still somewhat inconclusive) investigations, including surveys of "separated" identical twins that continue to receive much fascinated attention. In an effort to express mathematically the relative strengths of hereditary relationships such as the similarities in height between fathers and sons, uncles and nephews, and other kinship pairs, Galton devised the basic techniques for calculating "coefficients of correlation"—a momentous statistical invention later perfected by Galton's disciple and biographer Karl Pearson (1857–1936). While searching for hereditary marks of personal individuality, Galton became interested in the subject of fingerprints and developed the first practical system of fingerprint classification according to "whorls," "loops," and "arches" that remains in general use.

And at a time when most evolutionary biologists believed in the existence of at least a degree of "Lamarckian" inheritance, that is, of acquired characteristics, Galton denied that possibility in a speculative genetic theory that correctly anticipated much of the early twenty-first century's accepted wisdom about the mechanisms of inheritance.

Although he acknowledged a role for environmental influences and nurture, Galton was more interested in, and believed in the greater relative importance of, nature. His own work primarily stressed "positive" eugenics—the encouragement of a high rate of propagation by highly intelligent and able parents. Some others who followed him, however, emphasized the darker, negative side of eugenics—the discouragement or forced prevention of breeding by those deemed unfit or the products of degeneration. Thus the dark and unintended side of Galton's multifaceted legacy includes the involuntary sterilization of the retarded, restrictive immigration laws, and—at least indirectly—the enormities of Nazi genocide.

See also **Degeneration; Eugenics; Lamarck, Jean-Baptiste; Science and Technology.**

BIBLIOGRAPHY

Primary Sources

Galton, Francis. "Co-relations and Their Measurement." *Proceedings of the Royal Society* 45 (1888): 135–145. Famous paper introducing the method of statistical correlation.

———. *Memories of My Life*. London, 1908. Galton's vividly written autobiography.

Secondary Sources

Cowan, Ruth. S. "Nature and Nurture: The Interplay of Biology and Politics in the Work of Francis Galton." In *Studies in the History of Biology*, edited by W. Coleman and C. Limoges, vol. 1, 133–208. Baltimore, Md., 1977. A critical analysis of Galton's theories, arguing that they were strongly influenced by his conservative political inclinations.

Fancher, Raymond E. "The Measurement of Mind: Francis Galton and the Psychology of Individual Differences." In *Pioneers of Psychology*, by Raymond E. Fancher. 3rd ed., 216–245. New York, 1996. A summary of Galton's life and his influence on psychology.

Gillham, Nicholas Wright. *A Life of Sir Francis Galton: From African Exploration to the Birth of Eugenics*. Oxford, U.K., 2001.

Pearson, Karl. *The Life, Letters, and Labours of Francis Galton*. 3 vols. Cambridge, U.K., 1914, 1924, 1930. A massive biography written from the standpoint of Galton's major disciple, but invaluable for its detail.

RAYMOND E. FANCHER

GAMBETTA, LÉON-MICHEL (1838–1882), French statesman and founder of the French Third Republic (1870–1940).

Léon Gambetta was born 2 April 1838 at Cahors (Lot), in southwestern France. His French mother and Italian-born father ran a grocery. Gambetta studied law in Paris (1857–1859) and soon displayed his talents as an orator. His impassioned defense plea in the "Baudin Trial" (November 1868), attacking the legitimacy of the Second Empire, brought him to national prominence. He was elected to the Chamber of Deputies in May 1869. His election manifesto, the "Belleville Programme," defined the republican agenda into the twentieth century: "universal" (that is, male) suffrage; freedom of speech and association; separation of church and state; and free, compulsory, secular education. Together, he and the politician and historian Adolphe Thiers were the founders of the French Third Republic (1870–1940) and thus of modern republicanism in France.

Emperor Napoleon III's capture at Sedan during the Franco-Prussian War (1870–1871) saw the empire overthrown and a republic proclaimed (4 September 1870). As minister of the interior in the Government of National Defense, Gambetta escaped the besieged capital by balloon, crossed enemy lines, and raised an army of 110,000. In the elections of February 1871, he was returned in ten departments. As a patriotic statement, he chose to represent Bas-Rhin in Alsace. Refusing to ratify the peace treaty that gave Alsace to Germany, Gambetta resigned on 1 March 1871.

Gambetta spent several months in the country recovering his health and was not involved in politics during the Paris Commune of 1871. He was again elected to the Chamber in July 1871 and chose to represent Paris. France was now nominally a republic, but monarchists had a majority in the Chamber and sought a restoration. Gambetta set out to create broad support for the republic. In November 1871 he established a newspaper, *La république française* (The French republic). During the 1870s he toured the provinces preaching republicanism to the "new social strata": the petty bourgeoisie and peasantry, whose growing political importance he predicted.

Gambetta developed "opportunism," a gradual implementation of the republican program. He toned down the revolutionary image of republicanism, presenting it as a viable system of government in which all political adversaries could operate. He persuaded republicans to accept the compromises required to pass the Constitution of 1875: a president to name prime ministers (instead of total parliamentary control) and a conservative, rurally based senate to balance the lower house (instead of a unicameral legislature).

Gambetta's republicanism rested on his reverence for the Revolution of 1789, his commitment to the "rights of man" (he said nothing about the "rights of women"), and his anticlericalism. He made "Clericalism, that is the enemy!" the catchphrase of republicans for generations. He did not oppose religious belief (though, like many republicans, he was a freethinker), but he attacked the secular power of the Catholic Church and especially church control of education, which had greatly increased under the Second Empire. He proposed a secular, national system of elementary education for both sexes, recognizing the importance of girls' education for the future of republicanism.

Despite his attachment to Alsace-Lorraine, Gambetta came to believe that revanchism (the politics of revenge) was futile and dangerous. He considered meeting with the German chancellor Otto von Bismarck, to improve relations with Germany, but this was unacceptable in 1870s France. He supported modernizing the French army and developing colonialism as a way to restore French greatness.

Many expected Gambetta to become prime minister in 1879, as leader of the majority grouping in the Chamber of Deputies, but President Jules Grévy (a republican) bypassed him. He was instead elected president (speaker) of the Chamber (1879–1881). When he was finally appointed prime minister on 14 November 1881, his support among republicans had dwindled. Rather than establishing a "Great Ministry" of leading republicans, as anticipated, he had to appoint unknown figures. His government survived only until 26 January 1882. At the end of that year he suffered an attack of appendicitis while recovering from an accidental, self-inflicted gunshot wound. Doctors feared to operate on such a prominent figure and he died from peritonitis on 31 December 1882, aged forty-four. Jules Ferry, premier of France (1880–1881, 1883–1885), implemented Gambetta's republican program of education, infrastructure development, and colonial expansion.

In his own time, Gambetta was revered as the father of the republic. The fall of the Third Republic (1940) reduced his standing, but in the 1960s and 1970s the work of J. P. T. Bury and Jacques Chastenet reestablished his significance. He made republicanism a practical form of government and helped end eighty years of instability that began with the Revolution of 1789.

See also **Anticlericalism; Education; Ferry, Jules; France; Franco-Prussian War; Thiers, Louis-Adolphe.**

BIBLIOGRAPHY

Primary Sources

Halévy, Daniel, and Émile Pillias, eds. *Lettres de Gambetta, 1868–1882.* Paris, 1938.

Reinach, Joseph, ed. *Discours et plaidoyers politiques de M. Gambetta.* Paris, 1880–1885.

Secondary Sources

Amson, Daniel. *Gambetta; ou, Le rêve brisé.* Paris, 1994.

Antonmattei, Pierre. *Léon Gambetta: Héraut de la République.* Paris, 1999. The best modern biography.

Bury, John Patrick Tuer. *Gambetta and the Making of the Third Republic.* London, 1973.

———. *Gambetta and the National Defence: A Republican Dictatorship in France.* Westport, Conn., 1971.

———. *Gambetta's Final Years: "The Era of Difficulties," 1877–1882.* London and New York, 1982. Bury's trilogy is the most scholarly account of Gambetta's political career.

Chastenet, Jacques. *Gambetta.* Paris, 1968.

Elwitt, Sanford. *The Making of the Third Republic: Class and Politics in France, 1868–1884.* Baton Rouge, La.,

1975. Elwitt's interpretation of Gambetta's role in the founding of the Republic remains central.

Grévy, Jérôme. *La république des opportunistes, 1870–1885.* Paris, 1998. Grévy provides the most scholarly modern interpretation of Gambetta's role.

SUSAN K. FOLEY, CHARLES SOWERWINE

GARIBALDI, GIUSEPPE (1807–1882),
Italian military and nationalist leader.

The life of Giuseppe Garibaldi is fascinating, the English historian George Macaulay Trevelyan noted in 1909, because it contains all the ingredients of a novel. This observation is prescient. What is perhaps the most diffuse political myth of nineteenth-century Europe was indeed constructed by means of a biographical account strikingly similar to a fictional work, which Garibaldi himself, at little more than fifty years of age, had set out to make known to a vast public. This was in 1859, when his precocious *Memoirs* (*Memorie*) were published in New York by A. S. Barnes & Burr, and then in London, Paris (translated and tinkered with by Alexandre Dumas), Brussels, Hamburg, and elsewhere. Great public acclaim came immediately, because the story unfolded amid romantic passions and gallant adventures and exuded the exoticism of the wild lands of Latin America and the ancient fascination of the Mediterranean. It was a winning plot, breathtaking, sometimes incredible, and always played out along the lines of a fiction. The myth, moreover, called out to be separated from reality; the hero had to be distinct from the common man, and the story had to become a place where fantasies were fulfilled.

In Italy the situation was different. Already sensitive to the Romantic vein of Sir Walter Scott, Lord Byron, and Victor Hugo, the youthful Italian nationalist movement had attracted a group of writers, such as Silvio Pellico, the marchese d'Azeglio, Francesco Guerrazzi, and Alessandro Manzoni, who in their works took up remote themes in Italian history and used them as parables of the battle in progress for the independence of the country. These works included examples of physical courage, martial virtue, and national pride. Yet by their very nature, they were sunk in a remote past, and by the early nineteenth century, one needed a

good dose of optimism to believe that times were ripe for the country to erase a centuries-long tradition of political fragmentation, military defeats, and foreign domination. It is for this reason that the myth of Garibaldi was so effective among the cultured elites, students, soldiers, and politicians, and could become a sort of popular faith—centered around the icon of a Christ with red shirt, long flowing hair, blond beard, and flashing eyes. At the moment in which it sought to enter into the club of European powers, Italy needed military glory. And Garibaldi was a warrior. "War is the true life of a man!" he would write in the preface to the 1872 edition of his *Memoirs.*

EARLY LIFE AND EXILE

That life, which would enter precociously into legend, began on 4 July 1807 in Nice. The son of a sea captain who had intended for him a career as a professional, Garibaldi very early betrayed his father's aspirations and, at the age of sixteen, began to traverse the length and breadth of the Mediterranean and the Black Sea, as far as Smyrna, Istanbul, Odessa, and Taganrog. In 1832, far from Italy, the young sailor first heard of Henri de Saint-Simon and Giuseppe Mazzini, of socialism and nationalism, and he was smitten. Two years later, when the partisans of Mazzini organized an insurrection at Genoa, Garibaldi, who was serving on a ship anchored in the harbor, debarked and attempted to participate in the escapade. The revolt, however, came to naught, and Garibaldi, never having returned to his ship, ended up being accused, tried in absentia, and condemned to death. He thus became an exile and a martyr in the cause of liberty, and the following year, after joining Giovine Italia (Young Italy, a revolutionary organization founded by Mazzini in 1831), he departed for Latin America.

He arrived at Rio de Janeiro at the end of 1835, welcomed by Mazzini's supporters as the "hero of Genoa," and two years later joined the republicans of the Rio Grande do Sul, a province of the empire of Brazil that was struggling for its independence. Employed by the rebels to command the small separatist fleet, at the head of a crew of adventurers and buccaneers, Garibaldi conducted forays against Brazilian ships, laid daring ambushes, suffered reprisals, conquered cities, endured arduous retreats, and was wounded, impri-

Caricature of Garibaldi by Theobald Chartran, 1878.
©BETTMANN/CORBIS

soned, and tortured. And he met the eighteen-year-old Creole Anita, who became his companion and whom he later married. In 1840, when the Brazilians looked to have bested the rebels, he left the Rio Grande province and arrived at Monte-video in the following year, after an adventure-filled march of five months. There, he promptly threw himself into the bitter civil war that had broken out in Uruguay in the wake of independence, a war intertwined with the conflict between Argentina and the liberal powers of Europe. In Montevideo, the adventure recommenced. Having taken command of the naval squadron of the progressives of José Fructuosa Rivera, Garibaldi took up the fight against the Argentine fleet, together

with English and French contingents. He was brash, daring, and capable. He attacked the enemy and quickly retreated, requisitioned civil and military vessels, hid in the great fluvial network of the Paraná, organized impossible forced marches through the forest, occupied cities and villages, and was accused by the Argentine press of theft and violence against the civil population. Hero or brigand, his fame in Montevideo grew by the day, and his name appeared ever more frequently in the European and North American press.

ITALIAN CAMPAIGNS

Finally, in 1848, Garibaldi left South America, attracted by events in Italy and strengthened by an experience that had taught him the art of war and guerilla tactics; tempered him in the command of men; accustomed him to dangerous situations, unequal contests of force, and public violence; and, not least, made him suspicious of the complex games of the political arena. He returned from South America with a concept of military dictatorship that he hoped would provide an antidote to those games but that, even though ennobled by appeals to classicism, would be difficult to transplant from its Latin American context to a European milieu.

In Italy, in 1849, Garibaldi was a protagonist in the desperate struggle of the Roman Republic against the French, Neapolitans, and Austrians. His deeds were on the lips of all, and even his flight from Rome became legendary: the perilous journey north, the death of his wife, Anita, along the way, and his long wandering through Tuscany, Liguria, and the North African coast. As always, there was no repose for Garibaldi. In 1850 he went to New York, then to Peru, and from there to China. Yet in 1854 he was again in Europe, and in the following year he bought part of the island of Caprera, a refuge from the delusions of public activity and, obviously, a classic site of pilgrimage for the devout of the whole globe, aiming to see and meet their hero. Meanwhile, giving testament to his realism and entering on a collision course with Mazzini, he decided to support the nationalist project of the Savoyard monarchy. In 1859, having been named a general, he led his Cacciatori delle Alpi (Alpine Hunters) to war against the Austrians. Shortly thereafter, on 11 May 1860, Garibaldi landed with a thousand volunteers (the Redshirts) on a Sicily in

The Last Attack on Rome by the French. Engraving from the *Illustrated London News,* 1849. Garibaldi and his Italian volunteers were unsuccessful in protecting Rome against the French assault in 1849. ©CORBIS

the throes of revolution. In the span of two months, thanks to a rapid series of military successes that laid low the far more numerous Bourbon army, Garibaldi conquered Palermo and the entire island. He then went to Calabria, rapidly traversed the south of Italy, and on 7 September entered triumphantly into Naples, capital of the Bourbon king, Francis II.

The conquest of the Kingdom of the Two Sicilies was stunning, on a military level, because of the disparity of the forces in the field and the blinding speed of events. On a political level, the situation was more complex because Garibaldi was operating on a razor's edge. Though he was a democrat, Mazzini was deeply suspicious of him. Garibaldi was supported by the newly proclaimed king of Italy, Victor Emmanuel II, but failed to prevail over the subtle political and diplomatic maneuverings of Count Cavour, who while interested in the success of the undertaking had to repudiate it officially in front of his French allies, and who had no intention of granting any leeway to the democrats. Little wonder, then, that after 1861—the year of Italian unification—Garibaldi became both a national hero and a source of grave embarrassment for Italy's right-wing government. His priority was to liberate Rome from papal rule, an unrealistic objective in light of existing Italian

alliances. Yet the general moved of his own accord, and in the summer of 1862 he assembled a small army of volunteers and attempted a surprise attack. He landed in Sicily and then moved to Calabria, where he prepared to set out for the north, but was intercepted by regular Italian troops in Aspromonte, who opened fire, wounded him, and arrested him. Five years later, in 1867, he again planned to use force to regain Rome. To prevent this he was arrested, but made a theatrical escape only to flee in improbable fashion and be defeated by the French at Mentana.

FINAL YEARS AND LEGACY

The military undertaking of 1867 was Garibaldi's last, other than his participation on the French side in the Franco-Prussian War (1870–1871). But the last twenty years of his life, from 1862 to 1882, took an increasingly schizophrenic form, between the already worldwide scale of his myth and the great difficulties of integrating a charismatic leader of his ilk into Italian political life. In the words of the American ambassador in Turin, he had become "a great power." London welcomed him in 1864 with the largest crowd ever seen in the British capital; Abraham Lincoln sought, unsuccessfully, Garibaldi's participation in the battle against slavery; Poles fighting for independence sought his aid. And his *Memoirs* were translated into eleven languages. Meanwhile in Italy, everyone adopted his iconic image, but neither democrats nor moderates were disposed to follow him in his initiatives or in his strident denunciations of parliamentary government. To make matter worse he described Cavour in exceptionally harsh terms after 1860 and called Mazzini a "coward" and a "rogue" after 1867. The truth is that the life of this pirate who became a general, the republican who supported the Savoyard monarchy, the Freemason and populist, internationalist and individualist, does not fit any neat categories of party politics or even class struggle.

Even after his death on Caprera on 2 June 1882, the icon of Garibaldi continued to be invoked in very different political contexts. It was the banner of those who pressed for Italy's intervention in World War I in 1915, of Fascists preaching dictatorship, and of the Socialists and Communists who in 1948 vied for control of the government with the Christian Democrats of Alcide De Gasperi. In the late twentieth century, the story of the general would be reprised by Bettino Craxi, another controversial and innovative leader. Yet the changing and often contradictory uses to which his image has been put illustrates, if not the ambiguity, then certainly the political fragility of Garibaldi.

See also **Cavour, Count (Camillo Benso); Italy; Kingdom of the Two Sicilies; Mazzini, Giuseppe; Nationalism; Risorgimento (Italian Unification); Rome; Victor Emmanuel II; Young Italy.**

BIBLIOGRAPHY

Primary Sources

Garibaldi, Giuseppe. *Autobiography of Giuseppe Garibaldi.* 3 vols. Translated by A. Werner. London, 1889. Reprint, with a new introduction, New York, 1971.

Secondary Sources

Banti, Alberto Mario. *La nazione del Risorgimento: Parentela, santità e onore alle origini dell'Italia unita.* Turin, 2000.

Calabrese, Omar. *Garibaldi: Tra Ivanhoe e Sandokan.* Milan, 1982.

Ridley, Jasper. *Garibaldi.* London, 1974. Reprint, London, 1991.

Scirocco, Alfonso. *Garibaldi: Battaglie, amori, ideali di un cittadino del mondo.* Rome, 2001.

Smith, Denis Mack. *Garibaldi: A Great Life in Brief.* New York, 1956. Reprint, Westport, Conn., 1982.

Trevelyan, George Macaulay. *Garibaldi and the Thousand.* London, 1909. Reprint, New York, 1979.

Ugolini, Romano. *Garibaldi: Genesi di un mito.* Rome, 1982.

PAOLO MACRY

GASKELL, ELIZABETH (1810–1865), English author.

Elizabeth Gaskell is remembered for realistic novels and short stories of dramatic power and psychological depth, and for her biography of fellow novelist Charlotte Brontë (1816–1855). She produced six full-length novels and at least ten novellas, many short stories and essays, and a major literary biography. She depicted the "condition of England" in "industrial novels" recognized for their verisimilitude, portrayed the conflicts, behaviors, and achievements of her young female protagonists, and consistently upheld the values of honesty and reconciliation in human relationships.

Elizabeth Cleghorn Stevenson Gaskell was born into a Unitarian family on 29 September 1810, in Chelsea, London, the second surviving child of William and Elizabeth Holland Stevenson. When her mother died soon after, her father sent her to be raised by an aunt in Knutsford, Cheshire. After nearly five years at a private boarding school in Warwickshire, she lived variously in Knutsford, London, Newcastle, Edinburgh, Wales, Liverpool, and Manchester. On 30 August 1832, she married William Gaskell, a Unitarian minister attached to the Cross Street Chapel in Manchester. Henceforth her home was in Manchester, although her zest for travel and later her literary success enabled her to travel frequently around Britain and to Germany, France, and Italy.

Elizabeth and William Gaskell had at least seven children, of whom four daughters lived to survive their mother: Marianne, born in 1834; Margaret Emily, called Meta, 1837; Florence Elizabeth, 1842; and Julia Bradford, 1846. In 1850 the family moved to their largest and most permanent home at 84 Plymouth Grove, now a Manchester Historic Buildings Trust site.

Gaskell's life was full of family responsibilities, social events, and philanthropy, yet she had already published a few short pieces when she sold her first novel, *Mary Barton*, in 1848. Depicting the lives of industrial workers in Manchester with substantial realistic detail and sympathy for both worker and mill owner in hard economic times, the novel met with criticism and success. Gaskell followed this with other short pieces and in 1853 another socially conscious novel, *Ruth*, about a "fallen woman" who redeems herself by virtuous self-sacrifice. About the same time she published sections of *Cranford* (complete edition 1853), an amusing and perceptive novel about women's lives in a town closely based on Knutsford. Her fourth novel *North and South*, serialized in 1854–1855 (complete edition 1855), shows its female protagonist's personal growth and achievement in both pastoral and industrial settings.

Gaskell's friends and acquaintances included Charles Dickens (1812–1870), Harriet Beecher Stowe (1811–1896), John Ruskin (1819–1900), Harriet Martineau (1802–1876), Florence Nightingale (1820–1910), and other writers, artists, educators, philanthropists, and publishers. After her friend Charlotte Brontë's untimely death, Gaskell was asked to write her biography. The resulting *Life of Charlotte Brontë* (1857) attracted much interest and threats of lawsuits for Gaskell's depiction of certain individuals. In the next six years, Gaskell continued to publish short stories and major short novels, including *My Lady Ludlow, Lois the Witch,* and *Cousin Phillis*. In 1863 she published her full-length historical novel, *Sylvia's Lovers,* set in a North Sea whaling port in the 1790s.

Around 1865 she decided to purchase a home for her husband's retirement. Without his knowledge, she chose and furnished a house in Hampshire, while writing perhaps her most graceful and mature novel, *Wives and Daughters*. On 12 November 1865, while at tea with her daughters in the new house, she suddenly died. Her final novel is read today with its publisher's comment about how she would have ended it.

In her lifetime, Gaskell enjoyed popular success but suffered criticism of her socioeconomic

Elizabeth Gaskell. THE LIBRARY OF CONGRESS

analyses, especially for her sympathy for workers in *Mary Barton* and *North and South*. *Ruth* was judged immoral by some. *Cranford* was always popular, but for decades she was remembered either for the "industrial novels" (rediscovered by twentieth-century Marxists) or for the charm of her "pastoral" settings. In the later twentieth century, however, critics looked again at her writing as a whole; the new critical attention, encouraged by feminism and new historicism, stimulated the publication of new editions, making her works readily available. In 1985 the Gaskell Society formed in England; members can now be found worldwide. The Society publishes a scholarly *Journal* and newsletters; an extensive Internet website is maintained in Japan. Readers and scholars today recognize the complexity of Gaskell's psychological and material realism in addition to her skill and delight in storytelling.

See also **Brontë, Charlotte and Emily; Dickens, Charles; Eliot, George; Martineau, Harriet; Nightingale, Florence.**

BIBLIOGRAPHY

Primary Sources

Gaskell, Elizabeth. *The Letters of Mrs. Gaskell.* Edited by J. A. V. Chapple and Arthur Pollard. Manchester, U.K., 1966.

———. *Further Letters of Mrs. Gaskell.* Edited by John Chapple and Alan Shelston. Manchester, U.K., 2000.

Secondary Sources

Chapple, John. *Elizabeth Gaskell: The Early Years.* Manchester, U.K., 1997.

Easson, Angus, ed. *Elizabeth Gaskell: The Critical Heritage.* London: 1991.

Foster, Shirley. *Elizabeth Gaskell: A Literary Life.* Houndsmills, U.K., 2002.

Gaskell Society Journal. Issued yearly beginning in 1987.

The Gaskell Web. Available at http://www.lang.nagoya-u.ac.jp/~matsuoka/Gaskell.html.

Hughes, Linda K., and Michael Lund. *Victorian Publishing and Mrs. Gaskell's Work.* Charlottesville, Va., 1999.

Schor, Hilary M. *Scheherezade in the Marketplace: Elizabeth Gaskell and the Victorian Novel.* New York, 1992.

Sharps, John Geoffrey. *Mrs. Gaskell's Observation and Invention: A Study of Her Non-Biographic Works.* London, 1970.

Stoneman, Patsy. *Elizabeth Gaskell.* Bloomington, Ind., 1987.

Uglow, Jenny. *Elizabeth Gaskell: A Habit of Stories.* London, 1993.

Weyant, Nancy S. *Elizabeth Gaskell: An Annotated Bibliography of English Language Sources, 1976–1991.* Metuchen, N.J., 1994.

———. *Elizabeth Gaskell: An Annotated Guide to English Language Sources, 1992–2001.* Lanham, Md., 2004.

Mary Haynes Kuhlman

GAUDÍ, ANTONIO (1852–1926), Catalan architect.

Antonio Gaudí y Cornet was born in southern Catalonia, into a family of coppersmiths and metal workers from whom he claimed to have inherited an intuition for spatial modeling. He studied at the Barcelona School of Architecture, receiving his license to practice in 1878. It was a fine time to be entering the field: the newly laid out streets of the Cerdà plan—the gridded extension ara of the city beyond the medieval walls—were filling with houses, and the Catalan cultural *Renaixensa* (renaissance) was extending its enthusiastic embrace of regional traditions to all areas of artistic production, encouraging an arts and crafts movement that would provide support for the architectural inventions of Gaudí and his contemporaries. The quest for a regional, and eventually a "national," identity embedded in the traditions of the past yet suited to a people with modern aspirations, would have its political outlet in the movement for governmental autonomy known as Catalanisme, particularly the conservative branch of Catalanisme that became increasingly organized and increasingly dominant during Gaudí's lifetime. Gaudí's pride in his Catalan heritage led him to sympathize with the Catalan cause, and his work became increasingly situated within the "search for a national architecture" that engaged a number of the most prominent Barcelona architects of his time.

EARLY CAREER

Gaudí's career in architecture school was less than distinguished. He was independent by nature and learned more from the illustrated books in the library than he did in the classroom. During these years he acquired a deep admiration for the theories of the French architect Eugène-Emmanuel Viollet-le-Duc (1814–1879), particularly with regard to structural rationalism (by which advances in structural technology were seen to determine stylistic transformation) and the expression of national character through architecture. Gifted in drafting and structural calculation, Gaudí easily found work in architectural offices to offset the expenses of his student years. Most important was the work that he did for the neo-gothic architect Joan Martorell, who through his connections with important Catalan religious figures would eventually recommend Gaudí as architect of the Sagrada Familia Temple in 1883. It was possibly Martorell's influence, too, that led Gaudí toward a more pious life, away from the dandyism that is said to have characterized his early years in Barcelona. The Sagrada Familia project would occupy his entire career, becoming the exclusive focus of his practice after 1914.

Gaudí produced fewer than twenty buildings, some incomplete, over the course of his career. Nevertheless, because of his novel approach to architectural design, fusing structure and form to produce inclined columns and ruled surfaces of multiple curvature, often cloaked in colorful tile and mosaic revetments, Gaudí is admired as a major, if eccentric, figure in the modernist canon.

In the first two decades of his practice, Gaudí's work rehearses a series of historical styles while avoiding facile imitation. That his first house near Barcelona, the Casa Viçens (1883–1885) was commissioned by a tile manufacturer probably suggested the precedent of Mudéjar architecture—that is, the architecture influenced by Muslims living under post-reconquest Christian rule (twelfth to sixteenth centuries)—in which decorative tiles of Islamic production were fused with Gothic structural systems to produce textured and colorful surfaces of inventive plasticity. In the buildings that he designed for the estate of the shipping and textile magnate Eusebi Güell i Bacigalupi (1884–1887), a similar delight in Arabic texture and polychromy are evident in the impressed terra-cotta wall patterns, the brick openwork, and, for the first time, the broken-tile work (*trencadís*) that would continue to appear thereafter in his work. The dragon that guards the entrance gate is a prodigious work of wrought iron, a craft that he developed to free-form exuberance in the buildings of his mature phase. The interior of the stable introduced a system of stepped diaphragm arches that recall Catalan Gothic structures, particularly those of the Cistercian monastery at Poblet, for which Gaudí in his childhood had developed an elaborate restoration plan.

The Güell estate constructions were especially important in that they marked the beginning of the close relationship between Gaudí and the patron who would subsequently commission some of his most important works: the Güell Palace in the medieval sector of the old city (1886–1889), the chapel for the Colònia Güell, a factory town just south of Barcelona, and the Park Güell (1900–1914), a failed real estate venture, which, with its serpentine bench of vivid *trencadís* collages and its gingerbread gatehouses, has become one of the most successful and fanciful of Barcelona's city parks.

In the Güell Palace, which evokes a familial Venetian heritage, the parabolic arches that form the entranceways into the building predict the central paraboloid dome that rises spectacularly above the central hall, piercing through the roof to allow light into the heart of the building. Parabolic arcades and galleries here create a layered spatial progression that Gaudí would develop with ever-greater subtlety throughout his practice. More obviously Gothic in structure and typology is the Casa Figueres, or "Bellesguard" (1900–1904), built on the site of the palace of King Martin the Humanist, with crenellation, a watchtower, and a very elaborate series of flat brick Catalan vaults and diaphragm arches, most strikingly visible in the attic room.

The undulating twin crests and balconies of the Casa Calvet (1899–1900) indicate a flirtation with the baroque, as do the solomonic columns of the exuberant and colorful entranceway. But it is in the organic fluidity of the specifically designed furniture of the family apartment that Gaudí here announced a new design sensibility based on the curvatures of nature and of the human body.

LATER WORKS: ORGANICISM

After 1900 Gaudí's work, while evincing a certain affinity with the contemporary art nouveau, projects a unique character that can best be classified as "Gaudínian." Continuing the polychromatic effects and complex geometries of the earlier works, his mature architecture introduces far greater plasticity, exploiting ruled surfaces of interlocking curvatures to produce mathematically derived forms of fluid volume and profile. Rather than the capricious forms of pure fantasy, this organicism responds to a rigorous geometry and is facilitated by the creative exploitation of traditional Catalan brickwork vaulting techniques as well as a desire to contain physical stresses within the bodies of the structures themselves. The inclined columns that appear, for example, in the galleries or arcades throughout the Park Güell, directly receive the loads and thrusts incumbent on these elements, while the continuous curves of the window openings in the Casa Batlló (1904–1906) or the Casa Milà (1906–1910), illustrate the architect's concept that, within a given architectural organism, there are no supporting or supported parts, but rather a dynamic continuum where every part plays both roles.

It is from this later period in his practice that most of the written record of Gaudí's thoughts on architecture comes, primarily in the form of

Casa Milà, designed by Gaudí in 1906. ©James Sparshatt/
Corbis

aphoristic teachings recorded by young disciples who would visit the master in his workshop at the Sagrada Família: "To be original is to return to the origin [i.e., nature]," "the straight line is man's line, the curved line is God's," "color is life; pallor is death."

In the Casa Batlló (1904–1906), Gaudí cloaked an undistinguished earlier house in a glittering, watery blue mosaic facade with bone-like columns supporting the flowing stonework of the continuous first-floor balcony. Farther up the fashionable Pasco de Gràcia, Gaudí erected the Casa Milà (1906–1910), a gigantic apartment house that occupies two full building lots and wraps the corner in sinusoidal waves of carved stone that is often confused, in its fluidity, with concrete. The free-plan, framed-iron building with virtually no right angles, organically winds around two elliptical patios and the central courtyard of the urban block, bringing light directly into almost every room of

the four apartments that share each floor. The roof terrace is a landscape of sculptural forms that cap chimneys, air vents, and stairwells, these helmeted forms were originally intended by Gaudí to accompany an oversized statue of the Virgin Mary at the crest of the highly visible facade.

SAGRADA FAMILIA

Gaudí took greatest pleasure in his work on religious buildings, especially the Expiatory Temple of the Sagrada Família, which occupied him throughout his career. Earlier church projects provided the opportunity to try out, on a reduced scale, ideas he was considering for this building he considered his masterwork. For the Güell Colony chapel (1898–1916), his search for ever more efficient structural resolution led him to invent a remarkable hanging model of cords weighted with small sacks of birdshot representing the loads that the building would withstand once built. The resultant catenary profiles, when photographically inverted, served as guides for the parabolic arcs and towers of the church. The crypt, the only part of the chapel that was built, is the most dramatic and daring of his structural experiments.

The Sagrada Família was originally conceived in the 1880s as the "mother church" of a fundamentalist Catholic association devoted to Saint Joseph with an antimodernist and antisocialist mission. In the first decade of the twentieth century it was, with Gaudí's blessing, taken up as a symbol of an increasingly religious and conservative Catalanism. Taking on the project after the crypt and apse had been set in place by another architect, Gaudí expanded the scale of the project to an entire city block, and decided to build only the Nativity facade, to serve as an indication, for those who would follow him, of the scope of his architectural and symbolic vision. The building process was often extremely slow, depending as it did on expiatory donations, but by 1926, when Gaudí was run over by a trolley on his way to mass, the four parabolic towers were almost complete. He left behind a series of plaster models and drawings that indicated that he was still refining his ideas for the interior and had only roughly considered the other three facades. In 1936, at the outbreak of the Spanish civil war, Gaudí's workshop and studio were burned and most of this material was destroyed.

El Templo Expiatorio de la Sagrada Familia. Gaudí spent most of his professional life working on the Sagrada Familia, an expiatory temple intended to revitalize spirituality in an increasingly secularized and industrialized Catalonia. The church remains under construction. ©ROGER ANTROBUS/CORBIS

Passion) was complete and much of the interior forest of branching columns and starburst vaults was standing. Meanwhile, in the year 2003, the Vatican opened the formal process for the beatification of Antonio Gaudí, responding to the case presented by clerics close to the Sagrada Familia project and focusing further attention on his person and his beliefs.

Aesthetically, Gaudí's work found an enthusiastic following among European expressionist and surrealist artists in the early twentieth century. His ornate facades tended to repel the functionalist architects of the modern movement, though Le Corbusier (Charles-Édouard Jeanneret; 1887–1965) was struck by the apt simplicity of his structural strategies. More recently, postmodern interest in architectural expression and ornamentation, as well as deconstructivist explorations of freer formal solutions have given revived relevance to Gaudí's work and vision.

See also **Barcelona; Spain; Viollet-le-Duc, Eugène.**

BIBLIOGRAPHY

Bassegoda Nonell, Juan. *El gran Gaudí.* Sabadell, Spain, 1989.

Bergós, Joan. *Gaudí: The Man and His Work.* Translated by Gerardo Denis. Boston, 1999.

Bonet, Jordi. *The Essential Gaudí: The Geometric Modulation of the Church of the Sagrada Familia.* Translated by Mark Burry. Barcelona, 2000.

Burry, Mark. *The Expiatory Church of the Sagrada Familia.* London, 1993.

Collins, George. *Antonio Gaudí.* New York, 1960

Collins, George, and Juan Bassegoda Nonell. *The Designs and Drawings of Antonio Gaudí.* Princeton, N.J., 1983.

Giralt-Miracle, Daniel, ed. *Gaudí 2002: Miscellany.* Barcelona, 2002.

Kent, Conrad, and Dennis Prindle. *Park Güell.* New York, 1993.

Lahuerta, Juan José. *Antoni Gaudí, 1852–1926: Architecture, Ideology, and Politics.* Translated by Graham Thompson. Milan, 2003.

Martinell, César. *Gaudí: His Life, His Theories, His Work.* Translated by Judith Rohrer; edited by George R. Collins. Cambridge, Mass., 1975.

Van Hensbergen, Gijs. *Gaudí.* New York, 2001.

JUDITH ROHRER

Much of the controversy surrounding Gaudí since his death has tended to center on the Sagrada Familia project and whether it should be continued or left as a monument to the architect's vision. The politics of the temple have been as much a part of this debate as the aesthetics: too reactionary for the avant-garde, too Catalan during the dictatorship of Francisco Franco (r. 1936–1975). Since the late twentieth century a devoted team of architects, sculptors, and engineers has been working, to mixed reviews, to complete the temple "as Gaudí would have wanted it," piecing together shards of the plaster models, and using computerized projections to discover the geometric "laws" that generated the architect's structural solutions. As of 2005, a second transept portal (that of Christ's

GAUGUIN, PAUL (1848–1903), French artist renowned for his development of symbolism in painting.

Paul Gauguin traveled the globe under the French flag. In his youth he was a sailor in the merchant marine, traveling from Paris to India to Peru; in his maturity, he was a stockbroker, an insurance executive, a tarpaulin salesman, and then, finally, a professional artist, moving from Paris to Copenhagen to Brittany to Martinique before finally traveling to French Polynesia. In his worldwide reach, he was an instrument of imperial France, seeking out the exotic and carrying with him the banner of *la mission civilisatrice* (the civilizing mission). Yet in his actual rejection of bourgeois norms of behavior, and in his embrace of one exotic art style and then of another, he was an antagonist of nationalism and imperialism.

Gauguin was born in Paris in 1848 but lived the first seven years of his life in Lima, Peru. The artist's parents, Clovis Gauguin and Aline Chazal, were committed republicans (she was the daughter of the great feminist-socialist, Flora Tristan [1803–1844]) and fled France in anticipation of the coming Empire. Gauguin's early years in Peru, although spent in the confines of family and local elites, nevertheless allowed the adult artist to claim an exotic identity.

After a period of education in Orléans and Paris, Gauguin entered the merchant marines in 1865. Two years later, upon the death of his mother, he came under the influence of his wealthy guardian, Gustave Arosa, a collector of modern French painting, especially the work of Eugene Delacroix (1798–1863) and the Barbizon School. By 1874, Gauguin—now married to the Danish Mette Gad and working as a stockbroker—was an amateur painter. He visited the first impressionist exhibition held that year in the former studios of the photographer Felix Nadar (1820–1910), and met Camille Pissarro (1830–1903). By 1878, Gauguin was a professional artist. He exhibited with the impressionists in 1880, and attracted the attention of no less than Joris-Karl Huysmans (1848–1907) in 1881 for his unidealized, nude portrait of *Suzanne Sewing* (1880).

In 1882, Gauguin's fortunes fell. A stock market crash led to the artist's firing from the brokerage firm for which he worked. Seeking an inexpensive place to live as well as the company of fellow artists, Gauguin traveled to Pont Aven, in Brittany, in the summer of 1886. There he developed—partly in collaboration with Emile Bernard (1868–1941)—a style of painting that critics would label "cloisonnism," so called because it recalled medieval, cloisonné enamel. Gauguin's first cloissonnist painting is *Vision After the Sermon: Jacob Wrestling with the Angel* (1888), a work that was singled out in 1891 by the critic Albert Aurier. In his article "Symbolism in Painting: Paul Gauguin," the young critic heralded the arrival of a new art that paralleled the idealist school of poetry associated with Paul Verlaine (1844–1896), Arthur Rimbaud (1854–1891), and Stephane Mallarmé (1842–1898). The non-naturalist colors and the dream-like character of the scene (the Breton women in the foreground imagine the biblical scene visible at right) combine to convey an abstraction far removed from Impressionist norms. After a short but turbulent stay with Vincent van Gogh (1853–1890) in Arles in late 1888 (ending with the self-mutilation of the younger Dutch painter), Gauguin returned to Brittany. His fortunes, however, could not be reversed, and by 1890 he was resolved to leave the metropolis for the distant colony of Tahiti.

Gauguin departed from Paris without his wife or children in May 1891 in order to establish what he called a "Studio of the Tropics . . . where material life can be lived without money." There he would occupy a hut, he said, in a state of "primitiveness and savagery." Yet the circumstances of his departure from France and arrival in Papeete were not primitive. His second-class passage was paid by the Colonial Ministry, and he possessed official letters of introduction. At first, he was well received by the Governor of Tahiti, but his hopes to secure lucrative portrait commissions were quickly dashed. Soon thereafter, he retreated to Mataiea, a small town some thirty kilometers to the south, where he rented a little house that faced the bay. There he remained for nearly two years, devoting himself to representing the faces and bodies of native women.

Gauguin's paintings of women constitute the core of his Tahitian work. In *Mana'o Tupapa'u*

The Vision after the Sermon (Jacob Wrestling with the Angel). Painting by Paul Gaugin, 1888. NATIONAL GALLERY OF SCOTLAND, EDINBURGH, SCOTLAND/ BRIDGEMAN ART LIBRARY

(*The Specter Watches Over Her*) from 1892, Gauguin painted a young native woman lying on her stomach on a bed, her feet crossed and her face directed at the spectator. She lies on yellow-white sheets shaded in green, blue, and pink; below that is a bedspread or opened pareu with orange blossoms and leaves on an indigo field. Above and to the left is seen an ominous, hooded woman, a *tupapa'u* or ancestor figure in profile. Though the subject and composition of *Mana'o Tupapa'u* may be compared with popular and sexist nudes painted by the popular Salon artists Jean-Leon Gerome (1824–1904), Adolphe-William Bouguereau (1825–1905), and Alexandre Cabanel (1823–1889), it also challenges that tradition. It is indebted both to the notorious *Olympia* of Edouard Manet (1832–

1883) and the antique marble *Hermaphrodite* in the Louvre. That uncanonical Hellenistic sculpture was the subject in 1863 of a poetic homage of the same title by Charles Algernon Swinburne (1837–1909) that helped launch a school of "decadent" poets and artists whose psychologically intense and formally vivid works undermined the established hierarchies of lyric poetry, and helped lead to the Symbolism of Verlaine and Mallarmé. In the summer of 1893, Gauguin returned to France in the hope of renewing ties to his friends and estranged family. He quickly arranged with the dealer Paul Durand-Ruel to exhibit his Tahitian works, but was disappointed that only eleven of forty-four works found buyers. The following year, he returned to the Pacific, never to come back to France.

Gauguin's ambitions at this time are summarized in his large *Where do we come from? What are we? Where are we going?*, completed in 1897. Here Gauguin jettisoned academic procedures; nearly every figure or group of figures occupies a different pictorial space and time. The picture invokes Byzantine mosaics, the pan-Athenaic frieze from the Parthenon, *The Seven Acts of Mercy* of Caravaggio (1573–1610) and *A Sunday Afternoon on the Island of the Grande Jatte* by Georges Seurat (1859–1891). Its iconography is derived from Tahitian cosmogony, the Book of Genesis, and Thomas Carlyle's *Sartor Resartus* (1833–1834).

In 1901, Gauguin sailed for Atuona in the Marquesas Islands. There he built and decorated a native-style house—which he called "the House of Pleasure"—just a stone's throw from a police station, a Catholic church, and a Protestant mission. The house no longer exists, but its lintel, doorjambs, and base survive in the Musée d'Orsay in Paris; these are boldly carved in shallow relief and represent a female nude, and a number of heads whose style suggests Marquesan *tiki* figures.

In the Marquesas, Gauguin invited scandal: he displayed pornographic prints, pursued liaisons with native women, and spread rumors. He was personally flamboyant, wearing a pareu around his waist and carrying a walking stick shaped like a dildo. He wrote letters of protest to administrators in Tahiti and Paris, sometimes deploring police brutality toward native people, and at other times pitching invectives at colonial officials. Although in poor health, he undertook to assist Marquesan men and women in their efforts to resist the forced internment of native children in convent schools.

On 30 May 1903, Joseph Martin, vicar of the Marquesas, issued the following bulletin: "The only recent noteworthy event has been the death of a contemptible individual named Gauguin, a reputed artist, but an enemy of God and everything that is decent." Gauguin had died of syphilis three weeks earlier and was buried in the grounds of Calvary cemetery—represented in the background of *The White Horse* (1902)—overlooking Atuona. Thus concluded the life of an artist celebrated in the early twenty-first century for his sophistication and independence, and yet derided for his sexism

and colonialism. In its almost relentless focus upon the vulnerable, nude bodies of Maohi women, his art conforms to the widespread racism of an age of imperialism; yet in its rejection of Salon tradition and openness to indigenous forms, it represents a rebuke to that very order.

See also **France; Huysmans, Joris-Karl; Modernism; Painting; Pissarro, Camille; Primitivism; Tristan, Flora; Van Gogh, Vincent.**

BIBLIOGRAPHY

Brettell, Richard, et al. *The Art of Paul Gauguin.* Washington, D.C., 1988.

Druick, Douglas W., and Peter Kort Zegers, with Britt Salvesen. *Van Gogh and Gauguin—The Studio of the South.* Chicago, 2001.

Eisenman, Stephen F. *Gauguin's Skirt.* New York, 1997.

Pollock, Griselda. *Avant-Garde Gambits—1888–1893: Gender and the Color of Art History.* New York, 1993.

STEPHEN F. EISENMAN

GENDER. Gender as the idea and practices of differences between men and women functioned on a number of cultural levels and in social practice. The French Revolution of 1789 brought to the fore ideas of gender that had been echoing during the Enlightenment, though the trends in thinking and behavior were often contradictory. A slogan of the Revolution was "liberty, equality, fraternity," and this emphasized the brotherhood behind the ideas of citizenship in the Declaration of the Rights of Man and of the Citizen. The French Revolution attacked the authority of an absolutist monarch and substituted for him the rule of citizens, who had metamorphosed from the king's subjects. Women during the Revolution asked that they receive the same rights as men, most notably in Olympe de Gouges's celebrated *Declaration of the Rights of Woman and of the Female Citizen* (1791). When the Revolution declared the absolute power of fathers to have ended, there was a simultaneous move to reduce the power of husbands. Both of these tendencies worked to reduce the hierarchy of gender in order to bring a commitment to equality into practice. When France entered into war with Austria and Prussia in 1792, women demanded to

RESISTING GENDER ROLES

The Norwegian playwright Henrik Ibsen's *A Doll's House* (1879) was an international sensation because it showed gender being contested by a wife, Nora, who senses her ignorance and inferiority and wants to correct the situation. This scene occurs at the end of the play when Nora decides she will leave her husband and children. Her husband's reaction is to try to enforce gender order and codes.

HELMER: Nora, how can you be so unreasonable and ungrateful? Haven't you been happy here?

NORA: No; never. I used to think I was; but I haven't ever been happy.

HELMER: Not—not happy?

NORA: No. I've just had fun. You've always been very kind to me. But our home has never been anything but a playroom. I've been your doll-wife, just as I used to be Papa's doll-child. And the children have been my dolls. I used to think it was fun when you came in and played with me, just as they think it's fun when I go in and play games with them. That's all our marriage has been, Torvald.

HELMER: There may be a little truth in what you say, though you exaggerate and romanticize.

But from now on it'll be different. Playtime is over. Now the time has come for education.

NORA: Whose education? Mine or the children's?

HELMER: Both yours and the children's, my dearest Nora.

NORA: Oh, Torvald, you're not the man to educate me into being the right wife for you.

HELMER: How can you say that?

NORA: And what about me? Am I fit to educate the children?

HELMER: Nora!

NORA: Didn't you say yourself a few minutes ago that you dare not leave them in my charge?

HELMER: In a moment of excitement. Surely you don't think I meant it seriously?

NORA: Yes. You were perfectly right. I'm not fitted to educate them. There's something else I must do first. I must educate myself. And you can't help me with that. It's something I must do by myself. That's why I'm leaving you.

HELMER (*jumps up*): What did you say?

NORA: I must stand on my own feet if I am to find out the truth about myself and about life. So I can't go on living here with you any longer.

HELMER: Nora, Nora!

NORA: I'm leaving you now, at once. Christine will put me up for tonight—

HELMER: You're out of your mind! You can't do this! I forbid you!

Source: Henrik Ibsen, *A Doll's House* (New York, 1966), 96–97.

enter the army so that they too could perform their civic duty. Again, they emphasized equality rather than gender difference.

GENDER IN THE NAPOLEONIC CODE AND THEREAFTER

Aside from this sense of equality, there was a countermove toward gender dimorphism that made men and women more distant in social roles. This appeared in the growing popularity of Jean-Jacques Rousseau's work. Many revolutionaries on the left believed, following the sense of Rousseau's *Émile* and the *New Héloïse*, that women should not be active in public life. Instead, they should raise their children to be honest and virtuous citizens. No

longer were women simply breeding to perpetuate the family lineage, their role as mother became cultural, and this pivotal duty was called republican motherhood. With the writing of the Napoleonic Code in 1803 and 1804 and its spread to other European countries, equality among men and women received a blow, with gender hierarchy emphasized—not equality. Although Napoleon's code of laws allowed brothers and sisters to receive equal inheritances, other parts of the code forbade married women from owning property, including their own wages. Women were not allowed to work or run a business without written permission from their husbands, and a woman could not serve as a witness in court or be a guardian to her own children should her husband die. A woman was required to live wherever her husband determined. Should she commit adultery, she was to be imprisoned and fined. The only time a man could be punished for a similar offense was if he brought a concubine to live in the conjugal household. The Napoleonic Code established the gender framework for the nineteenth century, and that framework highlighted and enforced gender difference.

The framework by which gender was constructed around male privilege and female inferiority affected all classes and walks of life, making gender into a category that was acted out in everyday tasks and behavior. In this largely agrarian society women often worked as hard as men but had less stature and fewer rights—even when it came to food. Their portions were simply smaller and the esteem in which they were held, lower. Gender also determined the jobs one performed, with men mostly working in the fields and caring for the large animals and with women tending vegetable gardens, the smaller animals, and the dairy. Gender shaped the disparagement of women in rural life. Many a proverb talked about women in the same breath with animals: "A good horse and a bad horse need the spur; a good wife and a bad wife need the rod," common wisdom held. It was not uncommon for there to be sexual assault and battering of women, both of these sanctioned because of the woman's perceived lesser status within the hierarchy of gender. Nonetheless, in multigenerational agrarian households such as those in eastern Europe, senior women determined the assignment of tasks to younger women and had more stature than daughters, daughters-in-law, and younger sisters-in-law. Here, age and status hierarchy coexisted alongside and within gender hierarchy.

Ideas of gender determined the operation of the middle-class home in the nineteenth century. As contact with South Asia, the Middle East, and China grew, an ideology of "separate spheres" for men and women had also developed in the eighteenth century, from which Rousseau's ideology of gender developed. In this theory, which also was a centerpiece of developing republican ideas, men were meant to direct public life and women should be confined to the home—à la the harem or zenana. Great paeans to separate spheres filled volumes of poetry, fiction, and song. "The family

is the kingdom of woman—her life," wrote one Russian author at midcentury of the feminized household. In a celebrated novel in verse from the mid-1850s, Coventry Patmore praised women as the "Angel in the House," while John Ruskin's *Sesame and Lilies* (1865) enthused about the delicate women who sweetened life for other family members—particularly the hard-working husband and father. For these reasons, men of letters announced, women should not be educated, work, or participate in public life. Such ideas filtered down to affect the lives of working women, who became virtual pariahs—as the French reformer Flora Tristan (1803–1844) saw it—because they needed to support their families. So while women worked, workingwomen were somewhat disgraced in the larger public eye because of their gendered beliefs. Furthermore, the delicacy imputed to middle-class women by these men of letters contributed to labor-force segmentation. Women, it was said, could do only "delicate" and intricate jobs, with the further thought that the heavy, muscular work of men was more valuable. Yet, gender's hierarchies in the home shaped domestic and working life in tandem. Whereas once there had been more male household servants than female ones, by the end of the nineteenth century domestic service, because it was situated in the feminized home, was predominantly female. It was as poorly paid and as arduous a job as existed because of the long hours—stretching to almost twenty hours per day—and the heavy nature of the work in the days before the invention of household conveniences.

Even dress resonated gender dimorphism, as women's fashions became incredibly elaborate and simultaneously constricting—even dangerous. In the eighteenth century men and women alike in the aristocracy and upper classes had worn wigs, makeup, high heels, corsets, and lacy and luxurious fabrics. Both wore clothing that emphasized sexual characteristics. But this changed along with the changes in gender ideology. Women continued to don increasingly tight corsets, petticoats, and dainty slippers, each of which in its own way was a health hazard. While the hypersexualized shape of these clothes emphasized the sexuality of women's bodies, men, in contrast, abandoned the corsets, high heels, and makeup they had worn earlier in favor of the somber and streamlined black suit.

Men's sexuality was more masked as women's was emphasized—both of these in line with the gendered roles that women's place was reproducing in the home while men's was in the public dealing with somber and weighty issues. Middle-class men's appearance testified to their responsibilities, while women's announced their procreativity. As mass armies and imperial power developed in the Europe of the nineteenth century, common men sported sailor's and soldier's uniforms and the elite donned hunting and tropical clothes—all of these associated with the authority and power of masculinity.

INDUSTRIALIZATION, URBANIZATION, AND GENDER

As Europe industrialized during the nineteenth century, both young men and young women found opportunity in cities. In a society bifurcated at its base by gender, men were paid higher wages than women, who often received wages below subsistence level. Women increasingly found it difficult to find well-paying jobs allowing them to work outside the home. From midcentury on, trade legislation, called "protective," kept women from actually working in a variety of jobs and regulated their hours though not men's. In Britain this legislation was said to protect the unborn fetus, the beginning of governmental concern for embryos, and to keep women out of jobs that would hurt women's health. The irony behind this was that men were actually at greater risk and had higher rates of illness. The regulations thus showed that gender ideology was more important than scientific fact.

Most women had to have income to support their families, but gender ideology affected their ability to gain it. In the face of the variety of gendered proscriptions blocking them from well-paid industrial jobs, many did casual work at home such as making toys, doing piecework in sewing, painting buttons, plaiting straw, and similar outwork. This was usually very low paid work, although in some cases women could enlist the entire household to work alongside them. Those women who could not make ends meet on below subsistence pay turned to casual or full-time prostitution to support themselves. Many lived in common-law unions, producing illegitimate children who were disadvantaged, along with their

The Kiss. Early twentieth-century French postcard. PRIVATE COLLECTION/BRIDGEMAN ART LIBRARY/GIRAUDON

mothers, by this illegitimacy. Ill health was not uncommon in these conditions, and plays, novels, and operas abounded that testified to the plight of disadvantaged women. Nevertheless, the tears and sentiment these works produced validated the situation rather than leading to its eradication. Charitable groups also arose to aid women in distress.

As trade unions grew in the second half of the nineteenth century, they came to be gendered male. Because so many women toiled in outwork, their participation in union activity was far lower than men's. In addition to dues that low-paid women could not afford, men did not want women in unions because of the workings of gender. Women in jobs, it was said, would drag down men's confidence, and most would not attack the gender privilege on which this labor segmentation rested. Some men in craft unions, stressing the independent and noble masculinity of the artisan, actually endorsed women working in factories. In France, for instance, shoemakers and independent weavers found it unproblematic to send their wives and daughters to work in factories in order to support their own craft existence and gendered dignity as an autonomous worker. Within neighborhoods, however, women's gendered segregation in the domestic sphere promoted the success of unions as they built solidarity around shared tasks, daily crisis management of everyday life concerns, and information sharing while doing work such as laundering together. While men often dominated in the public activity of strikes, gendered divisions called on women to provide behind-the-scenes support—and they did.

In addition to ordinary jobs in factories and work in agriculture, professional and creative jobs were gendered male. Laws kept women from the legal and medical professions and from financial fields such as stockbroking. Women in most countries could not receive professional training or degrees, which made countries such as Switzerland, which did allow women in medical school, magnets for women seeking higher education. When women were allowed into universities in Greece, England, and Germany, riots broke out or women were not allowed to receive degrees. Even when they surpassed men in exams, Oxford and Cambridge Universities did not grant women degrees until well into the twentieth century. In Germany women were often made to sit behind curtains when attending lectures or they were cordoned off behind ropes. Nor were they always allowed into libraries or other repositories. Knowledge was gendered male to such an extent that German men protested women teaching in the new kindergartens that were springing up. As with union opposition to women in factories, these protests came for good reason. When women entered such professions as nursing, librarianship, and teaching, these jobs became degraded according to the hierarchy in the workings of gender. Salaries, status, and the general prestige accorded the job fell once it became categorized as female. The situation was powerfully endorsed in the works of the British naturalist Charles Darwin, who, in his many writings on natural selection and evolution during the 1850s, 1860s, and 1870s, concluded that women and people of color were far less evolved than white European men.

If science and knowledge were for men, Christianity was increasingly for women as part of the unfolding of gender. In much of eastern Europe in contrast, Jewish men spent great amounts of time studying the Torah and engaging in devotional activities. While both men and women attended Christian churches, as the century wore on men defected to clubs, sports, and other forms of sociability. This pertained to both working- and middle-class men. Women increased their religious commitment through church attendance, religiously based charities including those committed to conversion, and the training of their children in their religious duties. The number of women in religious orders increased far more than did the number of men. The dimorphism was so great that people spoke and worried about the "feminization of religion." There was even more to the gendering of religion in this century to the extent that the authority in Christian churches, whether Protestant or Catholic, remained male. Despite the defection of male parishioners, churches remained a bastion of gender hierarchy because of the small number of men in positions of great authority over increasing numbers of women faithful.

THE ATTACK ON MALE PRIVILEGE

Women and men alike attacked these unequal conditions based on gender from the beginning, when Rousseauian ideas of gender gained currency. The French Revolution itself sparked brilliant tracts such as Mary Wollstonecraft's *Vindication of the Rights of Woman* (1792)—a work that resonates down to the present day. In this work, Wollstonecraft equated male privilege with aristocratic privilege, advocating the solution of equal education and equal opportunity for men and women alike. Women attempted to overcome gender inequality, Wollstonecraft maintained, by simpering ways and sexual plots—none of this allowing for the development of rational skills. Wollstonecraft was a child of the Enlightenment, and others simultaneously pushed for a greater recognition of women's superior feelings and the love that women brought to society. These ideas were found in Wollstonecraft's own daughter's work. Mary Shelley's *Frankenstein* (1818) fit this Romantic mold, while other writers such as Germaine de Staël and George Sand celebrated women's goodness, finer feelings, and more highly developed sense of culture—a position

A Girl of Chioggia Dreaming of Her Loves. Photograph
by Carlo Naya (1816–1882). COLLEZIONE NAYA-BOHM, VENICE, ITALY/
BRIDGEMAN ART LIBRARY

that validated women's inequality by praising their subordinate skills, some believed. To others, women's superior sensibility was the ground on which their claims to equality were based. Major social thinkers such as Henri de Saint-Simon and Auguste Comte held similarly Romantic views, and like early feminists they hoped that greater place given to women would make society better—as long as these societies were led by men's great capacities for engineering, technology, and science.

Socialist ideas of gender also gained currency after midcentury. As developed in the work of Karl Marx and the Manchester factory owner Friedrich Engels, the inequality of women stemmed from the institution of private property. Private property caused the subordination of women because property owners, especially those in the middle and upper classes, needed a guarantee of paternity so that their property would pass to legitimate heirs. Engels outlined the theory in great detail in his germinal work, *The Origin of the Family, Private*

Property, and the State (1884). Gender inequality would disappear, Engels maintained, once socialism had been realized in society and accomplished its main goal of abolishing private property. After that, there would be no need for the repression of women. This theory influenced socialist parties across Europe in the late nineteenth and early twentieth centuries. Although women were active in socialism because of the promised gender equality, some women, such as Clara Zetkin (1857–1933), the major German activist, attacked feminism as an ideology for gender equality that would benefit only the middle classes. Socialism, these women maintained, would help everyone economically as well as politically.

Gender increasingly shaped political imagery and political issues, especially with the rise of organized feminism after midcentury. Although Queen Victoria (r. 1837–1901) served as Britain's monarch despite the guarantee of male privilege in the common law, the royal family simultaneously played the role of middle-class couple in which a wife obeyed and worshipped male authority. In their carefully staged photographs, they abandoned royal garb for those of the gendered social elite: the queen looked adoringly at Prince Albert, while he struck commanding poses—thus aligning themselves with gender expectations. In other cases, the queen's rule had real and palpable consequences, as Parliament used the fact of a female monarch to continue to drain the monarchy of power. Some members of the middle class, however, drew inspiration from Victoria's rule to contest the gender order. Women activists saw Victoria radiating the force of womanhood, and they worked all the more for more egalitarian laws about marriage, property ownership, and work. Barbara Smith Bodichon (1827–1891) and Bessie Parkes (1829–1925) were but two who claimed that gender hierarchy needed to be reversed in all of these spheres, and the cause of gender equality was advanced by Harriet Taylor Mill and John Stuart Mill's *The Subjection of Women* (1869)—a book translated into the major European languages and read around the world. In England in 1882, the Married Women's Property Act consolidated women's ownership of property, including their wages, and later in the century women gained the right to divorce and to guardianship of their children. These reforms ended some of the economic and social prerogatives awarded men because of their privileged status in gender theory.

The final stage in the prewar struggle against the ideas and practices of gender hierarchy came with the creation of organized national and international suffrage movements. National suffrage societies were strongest in Great Britain, though the feminist movement had hundreds of thousands of adherents in France, Germany, and most of the rest of Europe. But in countries such as France and Germany feminists took different approaches to ending the lack of esteem and rights for women and the concomitant privilege of men. In Germany women fought for the right to *Bildung*—that is the acquisition of general humanistic self-development through education and cultivation of the mind. In France, while the majority of women eschewed suffrage, they worked for gender equality across the board, for example through legal, educational, and institutional reform. The end result of the feminist and suffrage movements was not only legal change and eventually the vote (the first occurred in Finland in 1906), but also a louder, more widely heard voice on behalf of gender equality, although there were those, such as Francesco Crispi, prime minister of Italy late in the nineteenth century, who maintained that instead of filling out ballots "women's hands were meant for kissing."

BLOWS AGAINST GENDER INEQUALITY AT THE TURN OF THE CENTURY

By the end of the nineteenth century a "new woman" had appeared in the middle and lower-middle classes to challenge by her very way of life strict gender roles. These women held jobs, sometimes lived in boardinghouses apart from the supervision of their families, and led independent lives and often maintained their single status. In some countries there was seen to be a "surplus women" problem, so large was the number of single women. There were other eye-catching aspects to the new woman: some smoked, wore slim and more practical clothing, and ventured forth in cities doing philanthropic work on their own. Some played sports such as soccer. The new woman was a phenomenon that disturbed the gender order, although it would not be until after World War I with the advent of the "flapper" or *garçonne* (in France) that new

womanhood was seen as having spread to the working class.

What many of these independent or new women did was increasingly bold by the gender norm stressing female chastity and male sexual adventurism. Women such as Maria Montessori not only went to medical school to develop their professional capacities, they also had children out of wedlock, often refusing to be cramped in the confines of inegalitarian marriage. Novels abounded describing, usually sympathetically, the decisions single women made to flaunt the conventions of gender. Journalists were often less understanding, as they denounced the more public appearance of prominent homosexuals. Heterosexuality mirrored the gendered norm of male control of and superiority to women. The increasing publicity given to single-sex couples—both male and female—brought down the wrath of the press in its role as one of the guardians of gender. Not surprisingly, however, members of the homosexual entourage of the German kaiser sent letters to one another maintaining their superiority to heterosexuals because they needed no contact whatsoever with inferior beings—that is, women. This was a time when, simultaneous to the endorsement of gender equality by some, political and intellectual leaders such as those in the kaiser's entourage equated the lowness of the Jew with that of women. Anti-Semitism and misogyny in gender norms went hand in hand as the twentieth century opened.

Gender norms were affected as birth control became more available to men and women alike by the end of the nineteenth century with the appearance of rubber condoms and the diaphragm. Knowledge of women's ovulatory cycle was more widespread, and this too affected gender. These innovations brought fatherhood and motherhood—key components of gender definitions—under attack. For one thing, between 1880 and 1930 fertility dropped drastically in most of Europe, lessening women's role as reproducers. Simultaneously, obligatory public schooling began to take hold, removing children from parental care for extended periods of time. Schools came to teach children the skills once taught by parents of both sexes. Boys followed in their father's footsteps less often than before, especially as many agricultural and artisanal jobs were industrialized and the attendant skills were no longer required. The role of father as paterfamilias and mother as nurturer for perhaps her entire life weakened ideas of gender, especially since the time of Rousseau. Before World War I, many spoke of a "crisis of masculinity" in the face of the new woman and her place in a growing service sector, legal reforms that reduced some male privileges such as the right to take a wife's property to keep her economically impoverished, and the expansion of state power. The decline of small agriculture during this period reduced the number of men who could have control over an extended domain.

Gender resonated both at home and abroad through imperialism. The image of the virile hunter, adventurer, and conqueror filled the media and found its way into popular novels and stories. Although he had much criticism to offer, Rudyard Kipling memorialized rugged soldiers, wise administrators, and the rough and ready European common man who braved the seas in a variety of capacities. Many European men kept concubines from local peoples and lived outside the standard European family when working abroad. These situations were seen in novels such as Joseph Conrad's *Heart of Darkness* (1902), which portrayed many tough-minded male characters, an equally forceful African woman, and a clueless white woman back in Belgium. When governments began allowing or even insisting that men take their families to the colonies, it used to be maintained that women were the worst imperialists and they were the ones who turned imperialism into a nasty business—again a highly gendered interpretation based on the wisdom of the imperialist male and the stupidity of the imperialist female. Moreover, men, it was said, lived lovingly among the local folk, although scholarship now shows the exploitation behind the concubinal relationship. Colonial societies often urged women to go to the colonies, first, to do their gendered duty of civilizing the European man living on his own, and, second, to help build the white presence in the colonies by breeding with men there the superior Caucasian race. In an unexpected turn of events, imperialism was another of those situations that offered opportunities for gendered resistance. Men often did not have to behave as responsible breadwinners, and they could and did flaunt the norms of Western heterosexuality by engaging in sexual relationships with men when they were beyond the purview of European scrutiny. Women found sexual

Après l'Emancipation. Cartoon on female emancipation by Luc Leguey from the French magazine *Le Pêle-Mêle* 3 March 1901. PRIVATE COLLECTION/BRIDGEMAN ART LIBRARY/ARCHIVES CHARMET

freedom: the case of the English lepidopterist Margaret Fontaine (1862–1940), who traveled the world quite alone before World War I, reveals a life of adventure—including sexual adventure—and escape from the gendered confines of domesticity. Fontaine was one of many hundreds—male and female—for whom the colonies offered freedom from gendered proscriptions.

At the turn of the century intellectuals and scientists joined those who contested gender in their daily lives. Theories such as those of the physicians Havelock Ellis and Sigmund Freud came to maintain that sexual and gender behavior were not sanctioned by a divinity. Ellis in his pioneering work *Sexual Inversion* (1896) claimed that homosexuality was not a moral issue but rather a natural act and even a part of personality. Freud wrote many works addressing gender issues, but his theories in general suggested that there was no one pattern for being male and female. Before World War I, then, there were changing practices and theories about gender. Some hoped that the war would clarify the transitional situation, restoring men's masculinity and God-given privilege and reasserting women's natural inferiority and domestic role. The gendered results of the war are still being debated.

See also **Bourgeoisie; Comte, Auguste; Conrad, Joseph; Darwin, Charles; Ellis, Havelock; Engels, Friedrich; French Revolution; Freud, Sigmund; Gouges, Olympe de; Ibsen, Henrik; Kipling, Rudyard; Labor Movements; Marx, Karl; Mill, John Stuart; Montessori, Maria; Napoleonic Code; Saint-Simon, Henri de; Sand, George; Shelley, Mary; Staël, Germaine de; Suffragism; Victoria, Queen; Wollstonecraft, Mary; Working Class.**

BIBLIOGRAPHY

Clark, Anna. *The Struggle for the Breeches: Gender and the Making of the British Working Class.* Berkeley, Calif., 1995.

Duberman, Martin Bauml, Martha Vicinus, and George Chauncey Jr. *Hidden from History: Reclaiming the Gay and Lesbian Past.* New York, 1989.

Engel, Barbara Alpern. *Women in Russia, 1700–2000.* Cambridge, U.K., 2004.

Frevert, Ute. *Women in German History: From Bourgeois Emancipation to Sexual Liberation.* Translated by Stuart McKinnon-Evans in association with Terry Bond and Barbara Norden. New York, 1989.

Haan, Francisca de. *Gender and the Politics of Office Work: The Netherlands, 1860–1940.* Amsterdam, 1998.

Herzog, Dagmar. *Intimacy and Exclusion: Religious Politics in Pre-Revolutionary Baden.* Princeton, N.J., 1996.

Kaufman, Suzanne K. *Consuming Visions: Mass Culture and the Lourdes Shrine.* Ithaca, N.Y., 2005.

Kent, Susan Kingsley. *Gender and Power in Britain, 1640–1990.* London, 1999.

Malone, Carolyn. *Women's Bodies and Dangerous Trades in England, 1880–1914.* Woodbridge, Suffolk, U.K., 2003.

Merrick, Jeffrey, and Bryant T. Ragan Jr., eds. *Homosexuality in Modern France.* New York, 1996.

Nye, Robert A. *Masculinity and Male Codes of Honor in Modern France.* New York, 1993.

Scott, Joan Wallach. *Gender and the Politics of History.* New York, 1988.

Smith, Bonnie G. *Changing Lives: Women in European History since 1700.* Lexington, Mass., 1989.

Wildenthal, Lora. *German Women for Empire, 1884–1945.* Durham, N.C., 2001.

BONNIE G. SMITH

GENERATION OF 1898. In Spain, as 1898 was drawing near, a national social, economic, and political crisis intensified. Movements favoring Catalan and Basque autonomy gained momentum with the formation of labor unions headed by anarchists and socialists. In 1868 the Spanish throne became vacant with the expulsion of Queen Isabella II of the Bourbon line. Following a number of failed provisional governments, the Bourbon line to the Spanish throne was reinstated in 1874, in the person of Isabella's son, Alfonso XII. The return of the Bourbon dynasty to the Spanish throne is known as the Restoration period. Alfonso XII was succeeded by his son, Alfonso XIII, who was born a few months after his father's death. Until 1902, the year when Alfonso XIII came of age, Spain was ruled by the regent Maria Christina. The rule of Alfonso XIII ended in 1923, when he was overthrown by a coup d'état led by Primo de Rivera. Between the 1870s and the turn of the century the infrastructure of cities such as Madrid and Barcelona changed. Clashes between labor and capitalists fragmented the Spanish bourgeoisie, a class held partly responsible for the national crisis. In the political arena, the key descriptor for this period is instability. The continuum of ill-fated governments made Spaniards weary and dispirited. These feelings were further fueled when Spain lost the Spanish-American War in 1898 and consequently lost Cuba, Puerto Rico, and the Philippines, the last of its colonies.

REGENERATION OF SPAIN

Spanish thinkers sought to solve the nation's ills by calling for a regeneration of Spain, questioning what constituted "lo español," that is, what was purely Spanish. They questioned the spiritual and moral values of Spain, and believed that a reevaluation of the Spanish national character would lift the country from its prostration.

A group of literary, cultural, and political male writers attempted to redefine the concept of "lo español." Their writings encompassed all genres of Spanish national literature. Collectively, these writers are known as the Generation of 1898, and their works are key to understanding the process leading to the development of modern Spain. The characteristics of this group are: writings that reflect an intellectual search for truth instead of for aesthetic pleasure; a reverence for the region of Castile turning it into a symbol of what is purely Spanish; an individualistic stance; a new approach to the study of Spanish history; a reestablishment of both medieval and golden age authors as literary models; a fierce criticism of the Restoration period; and the use as philosophical anchors of the ideas of Friedrich Wilhelm Nietzsche (1844–1900), Arthur Schopenhauer (1788–1860), and Søren Kierkegaard (1813–1855).

Most of the Generation of 1898 were young Spanish intellectuals who were literary writers whose paths crossed with journalism: the novelists Miguel de Unamuno y Jugo (1864–1936); Pío Baroja (1872–1956); José Martínez Ruíz, known as "Azorín" (1873–1967); Ramiro de Maetzu y Whitney (1875–1936); Ángel Ganivet (1865–1898); and Ramón María del Valle-Inclán (1866–1936); the dramatist Jacinto Benavente y Martínez (1866–1954); the poet Antonio Machado y Ruiz (1875–1939); and other intellectuals, such as the social historian Joaquín Costa y Martínez (1846–1911), regarded today as a precursor of the Generation. In their manifesto of 1901, Baroja, Azorín, and Maetzu call on science to find solutions for a new social regeneration of Spain "aplicar todos los conocimientos de la ciencia en general a todas las llagas sociales" (apply all scientific knowledge in general to every social ill). This regeneration would begin with the Spanish intellectuals and trickle down to the masses and would be accomplished by studying Spanish history from another perspective, that is, from its "intra-historia," as Unamuno states. This "intra-historia" (intrahistory), would be palpable in the ordinary deeds of common folk, and is important because it carries within itself a connectedness and continuity not found in the Spanish history books. Writers could find this "intra-historia" in the central countryside of Spain, such as Castile, as well as in the works of Spanish medieval writers, including Gonzalo de Berceo and Jorge Manrique. While there were some members of the Generation who looked toward the future (Costa), others saw that revisiting Spain's past history was the way to regenerate Spain because it was in the past that true Spanish character could be found (Ganivet and Unamuno).

LITERARY WORKS

Joaquín Costa focused on the economic and social ills of Spain. His response to "el problema de España" was to modernize the country and eliminate the oligarchic system. Costa believed that Spain needed to "ponerle doble llave al sepulcro de Cid" (put double locks on El Cid's grave), meaning that it was time to stop living in Spain's past. Some of these preoccupations are reflected in Costa's writings. Ganivet's essay *Idearium español* (1897; Spanish idearium) defines certain aspects of the Spanish character: individualism, a constant preoccupation with a military past, and a disorganization in Spain's political and social life that precluded Spain from being on par with its European neighbors. What was needed, according to Ganivet, was to awaken Spain from its "abulia" (paralyzed will). For Ganivet, Spain had to look inward. Considered the eccentric of the group, the novelist, dramatist, and poet Valle-Inclán in his four *Sonatas* rewrites the myth of Don Juan for fin-de-siècle Spain. For Valle-Inclán, the novel became a canvas for linguistic experimentation producing what is now considered the best Spanish prose since Miguel de Cervantes Saavedra. Furthermore, these experimentations make Valle-Inclán one of the most innovative writers of the Generation of 1898. He entitled his dramatic works "esperpentos" (grotesque and deformed caricatures), very much in the same vein as paintings that Goya produced during his dark period. Valle-Inclán's "esperpentos" depict what he considered to be the tragic reality of his homeland: a decadent Spain.

The novelist Pío Baroja presented his characters in a constant struggle against hierarchy in a world full of pessimism. He shared with the other members of the Generation of 1898 a fierce criticism of the Restoration period. The essayist, novelist, dramatist, and poet Miguel de Unamuno is considered today to be the philosopher of the group. In his essay *En torno al casticismo* (1895; Concerning what is purely Spanish), Unamuno takes a new look at Spanish history and the role of Castile in Spanish history. In his novels, Unamuno exposes the contradictions of his life: a tension between the inevitability of death, and the struggle to live the present in a country in need of change.

José Martínez Ruíz "Azorín," regarded as the group's master of style, describes with melancholy an almost frozen-in-time Castilian landscape. For Azorín, the quality of timelessness in the Castilian landscape has yet to be discovered. Yet he realizes that time cannot be stopped, and that Spain has not moved forward in time. Azorín's style uses considerable repetition and this repetition also gives a continuity to his prose. On the other hand, his prose reflects the monotony of Spanish village life, which, as an avid traveler, he experienced first-hand. Azorín's style of repetition also gives continuity to his views on both medieval and golden age Spanish literature. His writings include sequels to masterworks of Spanish literature: the anonymous *Lazarillo de Tormes* (1554) and *La Celestina* (1519), and José Zorrilla's *Don Juan Tenorio* (1844).

The poet Antonio Machado also expresses his love for Castile with a deep introspection. In Machado's hands, Castile becomes a symbol that inspires change and action. In his autobiographical poems, the reader sees another side of Castile, a side that is inevitably tied in with the poet's happy and sad existence. The novelist and essayist Ramiro de Maetzu shares with the other members of the Generation of 1898 a preoccupation for the future of Spain. In his essay *Hacia otra España* (Looking toward another Spain) (1899), in which he strongly criticizes the culture of Restoration Spain, he advocates the need for a new Spain, one that helps itself by looking toward the rest of Europe. The Nobel prize winner in literature (1922) Jacinto Benavente censured Spanish society in his brand of satirical comedy. He effectively modernized the Spanish drama by distancing it from the Romantic excesses of his own century. His modern comedies are on par with those of Henrik Ibsen (1828–1906), Gerhart Hauptmann (1862–1946), Oscar Wilde (1854–1900), and Gabriele D'Annunzio (1863–1938), the masters of modern European theater.

Although these writers identified some of the reasons for the fin-de-siècle crisis in Spain, their approach for solving this crisis was escapist and therefore ineffective. They advocated looking toward Spain's past and returning to life as it existed in Castile, a region they revered. The members of the 1898 Generation were reactionary voices against realism and the values of the middle class. Theirs was a quest for regenerating Spain by adopting a set of elitist intellectual and spiritual values that disregarded pressing economic, labor, gender, and education issues. In this sense, the Generation of 1898 failed to follow Costa's advice to throw away the key of El Cid's grave and focus on Spain's present ills. Only one of the members of the Generation of 1898 moved in Costa's direction (Maetzu). Maetzu went into public life well into the twentieth century, and by then he had already changed many of his past ideological positions.

CRITICAL RESPONSE

Some critics today credit the Generation of 1898 with having produced a body of work comparable to the golden age of Spanish literature (that is, the sixteenth and seventeenth centuries). From the standpoint of Spanish history, through their intellectual influence, this generation succeeded in giving Spaniards another way to interpret Spanish history: By revisiting the political history of Spain. Their body of work is on par with that of Cervantes de Saavedra, Luis de Góngora y Argote (1561–1627), Garcilaso de la Vega (1503–1536), and Francisco Gómez de Quevedo y Villegas (1580–1645).

The members of the 1898 Generation raised intellectual concerns over traditional Spanish values and the character of Spaniards and for this they deserve credit. On the other hand they did not address the socioeconomic problems plaguing the nation's middle class. Hence, conspicuously absent from their writings are topics such as gender, despite the fact that this was one of the topics of the day in Spain during the late nineteenth and early twentieth centuries. Also lacking is the literary canon's inclusion of Spanish female writers as part of the Generation of 1898. This gives the impression that no female literary production related to Spanish regeneration existed during the Restoration period. Modern critics highlight the importance of Carmen de Burgos Seguí, Concepción Gimeno de Flaquer, and Emilia Pardo Bazán, just to name a few women writers of this period. Contrary to the Generation of 1898, these women writers did offer practical solutions for the political, economic, educational, and social issues needing resolution during the Spanish fin de siècle.

See also **Barcelona; Intellectuals; Madrid; Spain.**

BIBLIOGRAPHY

Blanco Aguinaga, Carlos. *Juventud del 98.* Madrid, 1970.

Carr, Raymond. *Modern Spain, 1875–1980.* New York, 1980.

Caws, Mary Ann. *Manifesto: A Century of -Isms.* Lincoln, Neb., 2001.

Costa, Joaquín. *Oligarquía y caciquismo: Colectivismo agrario y otros escritos.* Madrid, 1973.

Machado, Antonio. *Obras: Poesía y Teatro.* Buenos Aires, 1964.

Maetzu, Ramiro de. *Obra literaria olvidada, 1897–1910.* Edited by Emilio Palacios Fernández. Madrid, 2000.

Ramsden, Herbert. *The 1898 Movement in Spain: Towards a Reinterpretation: With Special Reference to En torno al Casticismo and Idearium español.* Totowa, N.J., 1974.

Shaw, Donald Leslie. *The Generation of 1898 in Spain.* New York, 1975.

Ugarte, Michael. *Madrid 1900: The Capital as Cradle of Civilization and Culture.* University Park, Pa., 1996.

LESLIE ANNE MERCED

GENEVA CONVENTION.

In the seventeenth and eighteenth centuries bilateral treaties between belligerents had sometimes provided for the reciprocal treatment of the sick and the wounded. But nationalist aggressiveness and the use of popular armies since the Napoleonic Wars (1803–1815) tended to do away with such restraint. In the Crimean War (1854–1856), for instance, nearly 60 percent of the wounded died as a result of lack of treatment. The popular success of Jean-Henri Dunant's *Un souvenir de Solférino* (1862; A memoir of Solférino) reflected something of the humanitarian mood of the Victorian mid-century. The book vividly recounts Dunant's experience at the battlefield of Solférino, during the Franco-Austrian campaign of 1859, where nearly forty thousand wounded and dying soldiers had been left unattended in conditions of untold horror. Something needed to be done. Together with the Swiss lawyer and philanthropist Gustave Moynier (1826–1910), Dunant organized an international meeting in Geneva in the fall of 1863—at which the participants, including representatives of nearly all European states, agreed unofficially to set up national associations—and sent observers to monitor the battles in the Schleswig-Holstein War waged in 1864 by Prussia and Austria against Denmark.

At the initiative of the Swiss government, directed to twenty-five states, a diplomatic conference opened on 8 August 1864 at the town hall in Geneva. Representatives of sixteen states attended. On 22 August the Convention for the Amelioration of the Condition of the Wounded in Armies in the Field—the Geneva Convention—was adopted. In ten articles the Convention provided for the neutrality of the medical services, including the wounded, the ambulances, the hospitals, and the medical personnel, as well as civilians treating the wounded. Authorized personnel were to be recognized by an arm band with a red cross on a white surface—the reverse of the colors of the Swiss flag.

Although the Geneva Convention was soon ratified by most European states, including the Great Powers (the United States joined in 1882), its rules were ignored or often misused in the Franco-Prussian War of 1870–1871. Suggestions for the strengthening of the Geneva rules and extending their scope to include maritime warfare were debated in conferences in Geneva and Brussels in 1868 and 1874. Following the 1863 example of the Union armies in the American Civil War, most European countries adopted military manuals that regulated behavior in warfare. The Institut de Droit International, an unofficial but influential association, codified many of the existing rules in an 1880 declaration.

It was only at the peace conference held at The Hague in 1899 that further significant progress was reached. As disarmament talks did not progress, the delegations turned their attention to the further development of the humanitarian laws of war. In addition to agreeing on the establishment of the Permanent Court of Arbitration, the Conference agreed on two important instruments: Convention

(IV) Respecting the Laws and Customs of War on Land, and Convention (X) on the Adaptation to Maritime Warfare of the Principles of the Geneva Convention. The former dealt with the conditions of occupation of enemy territory and the treatment of prisoners of war. The latter extended the Geneva provisions to the protection of hospital ships and the treatment of the wounded, the sick, and the shipwrecked who fell in the hands of the adversary. In addition, three declarations were adopted on the prohibition of exploding (dumdum) bullets, the launching of projectiles from balloons, and projectiles diffusing chemical weapons. The Geneva Convention itself was amended in 1906 by provisions regarding national Red Cross organizations, exchange of information concerning protected persons, and the punishment of nations that violated the provisions.

A Second Peace Conference was held at The Hague in 1907. Altogether it adopted thirteen instruments, most of which were of lesser significance than those of 1899. Some of them (for example, on the establishment of an International Prize Court) were never implemented. Others (such as those regarding the position of neutrals) were unrealistic and were never followed in practice. The main contribution of the 1907 conference was to amend aspects of the 1899 conventions, but it did not bring great changes. On the basis of the experiences of World War I, two more conventions were adopted in 1929 on the treatment of the wounded and the sick and on prisoners of war. These were updated and considerably extended by the four 1949 Geneva Conventions that integrated provisions on the status and role of the Red Cross. In 1977 these were further extended by two protocols, one of which (Protocol II) applied to internal armed conflicts.

The actual effects of the 1864 Red Cross Convention and subsequent developments have been unclear. The ratio between civilian and military casualties was one to three in World War I, in World War II one civilian was killed or injured for every military casualty, and in the civil wars of the late twentieth century there were three civilian casualties for every military death or injury. Already in his 1795 essay *Zum ewigen Frieden* (Toward perpetual peace), Immanuel Kant indicted representatives of the old natural law, the humanist lawyers Hugo Grotius, Emmerich von Vattel, and Samuel von Pufendorf as "miserable comforters" who had failed to understand that only entry into a pacific federation would provide exit from the "state of barbarism," as he characterized the diplomatic-military system of his time. Yet, the Geneva Convention and the further agreements have undoubtedly ameliorated the condition of many victims of armed conflict. Moreover, the activities of the Red Cross have been invaluable. The question remains, however, whether humanitarian law may also have contributed to the astonishing toleration of the endemic wars of the twentieth century.

See also **International Law.**

BIBLIOGRAPHY

Best, Geoffrey. *Humanity in Warfare: The Modern History of the International Law of Armed Conflicts.* London, 1980.

Moorehead, Caroline. *Dunant's Dream: War, Switzerland, and the History of the Red Cross.* London, 1998.

Nussbaum, Arthur. *A Concise History of the Law of Nations.* New York, 1954. See pp. 224–230.

Martti Koskenniemi

GEORGE IV (1762–1830; regent 1811–1821; ruled 1821–1830), one of the most controversial and loathed monarchs in British history.

Born on 12 August 1762, George Augustus Frederick, 21st Prince of Wales, was notorious as a young man for drinking, gambling, and other acts of indiscretion and his failures as a politicians and a leader began quite early in his political life. He allied himself with the opposition leader Charles James Fox (1749–1806) in 1781, no doubt as part of the Hanoverian tradition of sons rebelling against fathers' political appointees. This alliance hardened the government's dislike and distrust of the Prince of Wales, clearly exhibited during the first bout of insanity George III (1738–1820) experienced from 1788 to 1789.

Furthering poor relations with his father's government, George secretly married a Catholic widow, Maria Anne Fitzherbert (1756–1837) in

1785, but the marriage was dissolved as required by the Royal Marriages Act of 1772, since the king and Privy Council had not granted permission for the marriage to take place. In 1795, the prince then married his cousin, Caroline of Brunswick (1768–1821), a disaster from the outset. The birth of their only child, Charlotte Augusta, followed in 1796 even as the couple had already separated. George III refused to allow the two to divorce and they would live apart for the rest of Caroline's life.

The Prince of Wales was, after 1811, regent for his father until the latter's death. He soon broke ties with Fox, appointing William Wyndham Grenville (1759–1834) to form a ministry, but differences arose between the two almost immediately and he kept his father's government in power. With the 1812 resignation of Richard Colley Wellesley (1760–1842), the regent was forced to reconfigure his government and he invited several Whigs to join the Tories in forming a government. Most Whigs refused, as they hoped they could negotiate a Catholic emancipation measure in exchange for their support and participation in his new government. The regent, furious over this tactic, maintained a Tory government and in 1812, the 2nd Earl of Liverpool (1770–1828) began his long political career heading the government of the regent and future king. However, George IV's few attempts to be taken seriously as a leader were dashed by his well-known self-indulgence in mistresses, parties, and building projects at a time when the country was embroiled in the Napoleonic Wars and the economic crises that followed. Lord Liverpool was forced to address growing hostility toward the monarch. In 1817, crowds broke the windows of the regent's carriage on this way to open Parliament. His government was forced to suspend habeas corpus and reinstate several laws concerning seditious behavior in order to quell anti-monarchical sentiment.

The next crisis to embroil George's political life was his effort to exclude Caroline from being crowned queen. He ordered his government to initiate legal proceedings against Caroline that would ultimately end the marriage before any question of coronation could become a matter of public debate. The very public trial lasted eleven weeks with the House of Lords, leaders of the Anglican

George IV. Portrait by Sir Thomas Lawrence and Studio. ©CHRISTIE'S IMAGES/CORBIS

Church, and the heads of the judicial system in attendance. But with little evidence of any just cause to divorce Caroline and deny her right to be queen, combined with widespread and vocal public support behind her, the government's bill was withdrawn at the last minute rather than risk a full debate in the House of Commons upon its final reading. Refused admission to the 1821 coronation ceremony, Caroline lost much of her public support even as her husband gained nothing but contempt among his subjects.

Relationships with his ministers only became more strained as George IV's alcohol and laudanum addiction clouded his judgment further and he grew more and more distant from the workings of his government throughout the 1820s. While he approved of George Canning (1770–1827), who became prime minister in 1827, his influence over the Tory and Whig Parties was already negligible, even as he tried to interfere with issues of political importance such as the growing popular sentiment to eliminate restrictions on Dissenters and Catholics, and more widely, to reform Parliament. His last Tory prime minister, Arthur Wellesley, the 1st Duke of Wellington (1769–1852), described George IV as "the most extraordinary compound of talent, wit, buffoonery, obstinacy, and good feelings, in short, a medley of the most opposite qualities…that I ever saw in any character in my life."

George IV died on 26 June 1830 after a series of strokes. The public celebrated, rather than mourned, the loss of their monarch whose time as regent and reign as king were marked by selfishness, scandal, and very poor political judgment.

See also **Fox, Charles James; Great Britain; Wellington, Duke of (Arthur Wellesley).**

BIBLIOGRAPHY

David, Saul. *Prince of Pleasure: The Prince of Wales and the Making of the Regency.* New York, 1998.

Fulford, Roger. *George the Fourth.* Rev. ed. London, 1949.

Hibbert, Christopher. *George IV: Prince of Wales, 1762–1811.* New York, 1974.

Huish, Robert. *Memoirs of George the Fourth.* London, 1831.

Lacquer, Thomas. "The Queen Caroline Affair: Politics in the Reign of George IV." *Journal of Modern History* 54 (1982): 153–182.

Parissien, Steven. *George IV. Inspiration of the Regency.* New York, 2002.

Richardson, Joanna. *George IV: A Portrait.* London, 1966.

Smith, E. A. *George IV.* New Haven, Conn., 1999.

NANCY LOPATIN-LUMMIS

GÉRICAULT, THÉODORE (1791–1824), French painter, draftsman, lithographer, and sculptor.

Théodore-Jean-Louis-André Géricault was born into a recently enriched bourgeois family that moved from Rouen to Paris in 1796. After his mother's death in 1808 he received an annuity that allowed him to pursue an artistic career in relative financial independence despite his father's reservations. After a brief period in the studio of Carle Vernet, he began a rigorous academic training with Pierre-Narcisse Guérin, but attended classes for only six months or so. His early training was marked by irregular application to the expected routine and independent efforts to educate himself by copying the established masters and drawing from life.

He sought precocious success at the Salon (a major public exhibition normally held every two years in the Louvre) in 1812 with his *Charging Chasseur.* The work received favorable notice from critics and garnered Géricault a gold medal. In 1814 he exhibited his *Wounded Cuirassier* to less favorable attention. Both paintings were prepared at the last minute and contain faults of execution that reveal the artist's erratic education, yet they also exhibit a stunning and, for the period, unexpected painterly verve and colorism. Both also show Géricault's early attraction to modern military subjects handled in the manner of Antoine-Jean Gros (1771–1835). The focus of the paintings on single, anonymous figures engaged in action is unusual: they are neither conventional portraits nor full-blown history paintings. Together they formed an allegory of France's recent history, the first referring to the embattled Empire of 1812 and the second to the defeated France of 1814.

Indirection and belated attempts to acquire the accepted training of a classical history painter characterized Géricault's career in the years after 1814. He competed for the Rome Prize in 1816 and, failing to win, financed his own trip to Italy. His drawings from this period reveal a fascination with sadistic violence, lust, and victimization. He was also attracted to popular life on the peninsula and sought to depict it in his newly acquired classical manner, particularly in a series of paintings devoted to the Barbieri horse race in Rome.

Upon returning to France in late 1817, Géricault began searching for a subject from contemporary life to treat in the grand manner of history painting. He eventually settled on a recent shipwreck off the West African coast that resulted from the incompetence of an aristocratic French naval officer who owed his appointment to favoritism of the restored Bourbon monarchy. After the wreck, 150 passengers and crew members were set adrift on a makeshift raft, while the officers and privileged commandeered the lifeboats. Mutiny, murder, and cannibalism quickly decimated the castaways, of whom only ten survived. Géricault pictured the moment when the survivors

The Madwoman. Painting by Thédore Géricault, 1822. SCALA/
ART RESOURCE, NY

on the raft attempted to attract the attention of a
rescue vessel, after thirteen days adrift at sea. Like
other subjects he considered, the narrative combined bizarre violence with a political scandal that
reflected poorly on the Restoration government.
The painting has been interpreted allegorically in a
variety of ways: as about the need for humanity to
join forces to save itself, about race relations
(some of the figures are black) in an age of expanding colonialism, and about the state of the French
social body in post-Revolutionary France. The
painting plays a transitional role in the history of
French painting insofar as Géricault attempted to
combine the heroic nudity of classical history
painting with an event drawn from contemporary
life.

Though admired by many, the *Raft of the
Medusa* (1819) did not have the public success for
which Géricault had hoped. A period of deep
depression ensued. Profiting from an opportunity
to exhibit the *Raft* at William Bullock's Egyptian
Hall in London, he departed for an extended stay in
England. There he completed a series of lithographs

focusing on common life and particularly the plight
of the indigent poor.

Sometime in his later career, probably after his
return to Paris in 1821, Géricault executed a series
of portraits of insane people, about which very little
is known for certain. Possibly ten were completed;
five are known today. Each appears to portray a
different form of mental illness, and they were
possibly done to aid the research of a medical
doctor. They are remarkable for the care with
which the artist considers his humble subjects,
and the incisiveness of their realism.

Géricault's behavior throughout his life was
self-destructive, and in 1822 he lost a substantial
part of his fortune, forcing him to paint for money
for the first time in his life. In his final year, as he
was slowly wasting away from the degenerative
disease that killed him, Géricault expressed the
belief that he had wasted his talents. He executed
sketches for history paintings protesting the
Inquisition and the African slave trade, part of his
lifelong ambition to reinvest large-scale painting
with the moral import and relevance to public
debate it had had at the end of the eighteenth
century, but he was unable to paint the canvases.
Though little known to the general public at the
time of his death, his life and work quickly became
legendary within the nascent Romantic movement.
Today he is revered as one of the greatest painters
in the French tradition.

See also **Delacroix, Eugène; France; Painting; Romanticism.**

BIBLIOGRAPHY

Bazin, Germain. *Théodore Géricault: Étude critique, documents, et catalogue raisonné.* Paris, 1987–1997.

École nationale supérieure des beaux-arts. *Géricault: Dessins
et estampes des collections de l'École des beaux-arts.* Paris,
1997. Catalogue of a major show of Géricault's prints
and drawings with important essays.

Michel, Régis, ed. *Géricault.* 2 vols. Paris, 1996. Major
scholars address various aspects of Géricault's life, art,
and legacy.

Réunion des musées nationaux. *Géricault.* Paris, 1991.
Catalogue from the major retrospective exhibition in
1991 with important essays.

DAVID O'BRIEN

GERMANY. Germany was little more than a "geographical expression" on the eve of the French Revolution. A loose confederation of 314 sovereign territorial states, 1,400 independent imperial knights, and 51 "free" cities had existed since 1512 as the Holy Roman Empire of the German Nation. For most of this period, the Catholic house of Habsburg at Vienna wore the crown of Charlemagne. Polycentrism characterized the Holy Roman Empire: there existed no cultural, economic, or political center comparable to London or Paris. The British historian James Bryce (1838–1922), citing Voltaire, stated that it was neither holy, nor Roman, nor an empire. Its primary purpose was to leave undisturbed the territorial sovereignty and social order of its roughly three hundred rulers. The empire's army existed mainly on paper—a motley collection of superannuated warriors whose various uniforms reflected the quilting of the German map. Its twenty million people had little contact with the empire's agencies.

REVOLUTION AND RESTORATION, 1789–1847

The greatest threat to the empire came from beyond its borders in 1789, when the French Constituent Assembly voted to abolish the nobility, nationalize church property, strike down feudal dues, ban guilds, introduce a land tax, secularize education, and promulgate a constitution as well as a bill of rights. The small German middle class—mainly university-educated civil servants—initially embraced these "French ideas." But as the Revolution in Paris took a radical turn with the creation of a republic in September 1792, the beheading of King Louis XVI in January 1793, and the Reign of Terror by September 1793, its German supporters recoiled. Still, neither Berlin nor Vienna introduced a single reform program to meet the challenges of the National Convention in Paris.

German rulers, under the leadership of Kaiser Francis II at Vienna, ignored the potential threat from French internal developments and instead measured that threat mainly in terms of its effect on the European concert. They half-heartedly mounted no fewer than three coalition wars against France between 1792 and 1806. They symbolically crowned the last Holy Roman Emperor, Francis II, on 14 July 1792—the third anniversary of the storming of the Bastille prison in Paris. And Austria

"Our aim is very simple to define: nothing more and nothing less than the preservation of the world as we know it." (Prince Klemens von Metternich, 1820)

"This war [between France and Germany] represents the German revolution, a greater political event than the French revolution.... You have a new world, new influences at work, new and unknown objects and dangers with which to cope.... The balance of power has been entirely destroyed." (Benjamin Disraeli, 1871)

"The earlier errors of a Turkish policy against Russia, a Moroccan against France, fleet against England, irritating everyone, blocking everyone's way and yet not really weakening anyone. Basic cause: lack of planning, craving for petty prestige victories." (Kurt Riezler, July 1914)

and Prussia eagerly turned east to join Russia in the Partitions of Poland, with Prussia doing so in 1793 and both Prussia and Austria participating in 1795.

Napoleon Bonaparte rudely ended their insouciance in 1799 when he seized power in Paris and began more than a decade of warfare in a relentless drive for hegemony in Europe. In short order, "the world spirit on horseback," as the German philosopher Georg Wilhelm Friedrich Hegel called Bonaparte, on the bayonets of his armies reformed the empire. First, he conquered and annexed the left bank of the Rhine. Then, in 1806 he bundled sixteen German minor states, including Bavaria, Saxony, Westphalia, Württemberg, and Baden, into a satrapy, the Confederation of the Rhine. Next, he placed his brother Jérôme on the throne of a newly created Kingdom of Westphalia. And finally he introduced the Napoleonic Civil Code in these German states and ruthlessly secularized church lands. Napoleon defeated the old regime armies one by one—most notably that of Austria at Austerlitz in December 1805 and that of Prussia at the twin battles of Jena and Auerstädt in October 1806. Few observers even noticed that Francis II, spurred into action by Napoleon, formally abolished the Holy Roman Empire on 6 August 1806 in favor of a new

"Austrian Empire." Ironically, by eliminating some three hundred states, Napoleon took the first steps toward creating a more manageable "German" state.

The French incursions into central Europe crystallized political ideologies. Liberals embraced British notions of civil liberty and parliamentary government. Specifically, the majority rallied around a broad program of freedom of the press, freedom of trade, separation of church and state, habeas corpus, creation of a civilian militia, and a written constitution. Only a minority continued to look across the Rhine at republican/imperial France. Conservatives rallied under the slogan of "throne and altar" to deny the French Revolution and Bonaparte's reforms. They opposed free trade, secularization, constitutionalism, and militia, and instead upheld the principles of church, monarchy, and nobility. Finally, the French incursions also brought a third "ism," that of nationalism. Beginning with the notion of cultural nationalism, its proponents quickly moved forward to political nationalism—to the idea that all Germans should be united into a sovereign nation to defend the national culture.

Defeat often drives reform. Thoroughly humiliated by Napoleon, Prussia took the lead under King Frederick William III (r. 1797–1840). A group of reformers such as Karl vom Stein, Karl August von Hardenberg, and Hermann von Boyen led the royal bureaucracy to reform the state of Frederick II (r. 1740–1786). Stein's Reform Edict of 1807 abolished feudalism by decreeing that "there shall exist only free people." The following year, Stein's Municipal Ordinance gave self-government to cities. In 1810 Prussia abolished the medieval guild structure in the Freedom of Trade and Occupations Acts. Two years later, it emancipated its Jews. Under Gerhard von Scharnhorst and August Neithardt von Gneisenau, Prussia reformed its armed forces to better reflect the "nation in arms." And under Wilhelm von Humboldt it transformed the old Academy of Sciences into the modern secularized University of Berlin (now Humboldt University of Berlin).

While Prussia reformed, Napoleon in June 1812 sought to defeat the last Continental power, Russia. His Grand Army of 700,000 men (including 34,000 Austrians, 20,000 Prussians, and another 25,000 from his German satellites) was defeated by a combination of Russian resistance, partisan warfare, and harsh winter. As the army disintegrated and Napoleon fled to Paris, his German creations crumbled. The resulting "wars of liberation" against the Corsican were a mixture of monarchism and antiforeign feeling, vaguely nationalistic and quasi religious. The new motto, "With God for King and Fatherland," and the freshly minted Iron Cross reflected this unusual symbiosis. In October 1813 a multinational Austrian, Prussian, Russian, and Swedish army defeated Napoleon at Leipzig in the so-called Battle of the Nations. Exiled to Elba, Napoleon returned to France, only to be defeated again, this time by British and Prussian armies at Waterloo in June 1815.

More than three hundred emperors, kings, princes, and diplomats met at Vienna to restore a broken world. Under the leadership of Prince Klemens von Metternich, Hardenberg, Tsar Alexander I of Russia, and Viscount Castlereagh of Britain, the Congress of Vienna (1814–1815) struggled to find a compromise between revolution and restoration. It met only once—to sign the final accords. In secret sessions, the leaders rearranged the map of Europe: Austria obtained Tirol, Salzburg, Trieste, Istria, Dalmatia, Lombardy, and Venice, thus shifting its center of gravity to southeastern Europe. Prussia took two-fifths of Saxony, much of the former Kingdom of Westphalia, and most of the west bank of the Rhine River. Russia annexed Napoleon's Grand Duchy of Warsaw; Britain took overseas bases at the Cape, Ceylon, and Malta.

With regard to the future organizational form of the German states, the congress (by the Final Act of 1815) established a loose German Confederation (or Deutsche Bund) of thirty-five sovereign states and four "free" cities. The diet of the confederation convened at Frankfurt under permanent Austrian headship. Its mandate was "to preserve Germany's external and internal security and the independence and integrity of the several German states." Austria was the confederation's largest state with ten million inhabitants; Prussia came next with eight million; and within what was now referred to as the "Third Germany," Bavaria was the largest state with more than three million. All

German signatories promised to promulgate constitutions for their lands, and eventually a number of them kept that promise, including Baden, Bavaria, Brunswick, Hanover, Hesse-Kassel, Mecklenburg-Schwerin, Nassau, and Württemberg. The larger issues of "liberalism" and "nationalism" remained unresolved.

The period between the Congress of Vienna and the revolutions of 1848–1849 was pregnant with choice. Borders had to be redrawn. New states and a new German Confederation needed to be digested. Secularization of former church and imperial lands demanded time to heal. "French ideas" largely had been discredited, but there remained high expectations—of a constitution, of liberalization of press and assembly, of economic liberalization, and of national unity. Not surprisingly, the thirty years following the Congress of Vienna constituted a continuous tug of war between the forces of reform and restoration.

Metternich saw the confederation as his "own child," as a vehicle to maintain the "principle of political-social immobilization" in central Europe. To this end, he joined Alexander I in 1815 to concoct the Holy Alliance—through which they hoped to "provide succor and support in any place" against liberal and national activities. What Prussian historian Heinrich von Treitschke (1834–1896) would later call the "international fire brigade" did in fact intervene between 1821 and 1831 to crush liberal uprisings in Naples and Piedmont, Greece, Spain, and Poland. By striking the adjectives "of peoples" and "of citizens" from the preamble of the Holy Alliance in favor of the term "of monarchs," Metternich and Alexander I had made their positions clear.

But the genie released by the French Revolution could not so easily be put back into the bottle. On 18 October 1817, the fourth anniversary of the Battle of the Nations and the tercentenary of Martin Luther's Reformation, radical university students organized into fraternities (*Burschenschaften*) gathered at the Wartburg Castle (where Luther had translated the New Testament into German) under the national colors black, red, and gold and burned lists of reactionaries (notably Metternich and Alexander I). They demanded what already had become the classic liberal reform platform as well as a "German national state based on freedom and unity." When Karl Sand, a theology student at Mannheim, in March 1819 assassinated the playwright and Russian councilor August von Kotzebue as a tsarist "spy," Metternich was outraged. His response was encapsulated in the so-called Carlsbad Decrees drafted between 6 and 31 August 1819. Three stand out. The University Decree banned the *Burschenschaften* and instituted a system of "supervising" university lecturers; the Press Decree reinstituted censorship of all journals, papers, and books; and the Search Decree established a special Central Office of Investigation to root out "revolutionary intrigues." As well, the national colors were banned in public, and parliaments were closed as being "un-German."

External events once more stirred passions in the German states. The French Revolution of July 1830, the Belgian independence movement of that same year, and the Polish uprising of 1830–1831 agitated liberals and nationalists alike. In May 1832 roughly twenty-five thousand liberals waving the black, red, and gold colors gathered at Hambach Castle in the Rhine Palatinate to demand political reform and national unity. The gathering was important because it included middle-class intellectuals, civil servants, students, Polish refugees, and (for the first time) women. Metternich's reaction was hardly surprising: on 28 June 1832 he crafted the "Six Articles" that strengthened the Carlsbad Decrees in rigor of enforcement and length of incarceration.

The next round in the struggle struck close to home, when a group of University of Heidelberg students stormed the main Frankfurt police station in 1833, killing six gendarmes. Prussian troops eventually restored order and sentenced two hundred students to long terms of hard labor and prison; Metternich drafted another sixty articles to again tighten existing restrictions on freedom of assembly, speech, and the press.

The most dramatic round in the battle between reform and restoration came in 1837 over the so-called Göttingen Seven. The University of Göttingen (in Hanover) had been the main center of "British ideas" on constitutionalism in Germany for decades. In 1837 Victoria of Hanover ascended the British throne and Ernst August, the Duke of Cumberland, took over that of Hanover. The king celebrated his coronation by dissolving parliament and by abolishing the constitution of 1833. Seven prominent academics (including the historian F. C. Dahlmann and the philologist Jacob Grimm) protested this political coup d'état—and were first dismissed from their posts and then exiled from Hanover. While the German Confederation did nothing to restore the constitution, Göttingen Seven societies sprang up in Great Britain, Switzerland, and the United States. Ernst August dismissed the brouhaha with the terse comment, "One can always get professors, actors and whores."

The political arena was not the only place where liberalism made a determined showing. In 1818 Prussia took the lead in abolishing internal tariffs and duties, encouraging free trade within the German Confederation. Its finance minister, Friedrich von Motz, even envisioned "a free Germany under the protection and umbrella of Prussia"—a notion that did not go down well in Vienna, but was realized by Prussia in 1834 through the founding of the Zollverein, a customs union that excluded Austria. Motz received backing from Friedrich List, a German-American economist, who spoke out not only for free trade within the confederation but also for protective tariffs against cheaper foreign-produced—read British—goods as well. Most ominously, List came up with the notion of a German-dominated central Europe (*Mitteleuropa*), which would play a prominent role in German war aims in 1914.

In the area of religion, the return of orthodoxy, whether Catholic or Protestant, evinced strong reactions. In central and eastern Germany, theological rationalists, offended by the authoritarian church government of their states, founded the movement of the so-called friends of light or *Lichterfreunde* in 1841. In time, their religious rebellion took on common political ideals. Their Catholic reform-minded brethren, enraged when the "holy coat" of Jesus Christ in 1844 became the object of a pilgrimage of nearly one million faithful to Trier, broke away from Rome and instead called for a "German" national church and the abolition of confession, fasting, pilgrimages, indulgences, and celibacy of the clergy.

By the 1840s, the very face of Germany was beginning to change. Figures are notoriously imprecise for the early nineteenth century, but of the confederation's thirty million people in 1816,

about 60 percent were engaged in some form of agriculture—as yeoman farmers, smallholders, and landless laborers. By 1848 that population (excluding the Habsburg lands) had swelled by roughly ten million; it would reach forty-five million by 1864. There had developed in the three decades after 1816 a modest shift of about 5 percent of the population from the countryside to the emerging preindustrial centers; that shift would grow steadily after 1850. More dramatic was a simultaneous movement overseas. If one takes as a yardstick the territories of the German Empire of 1871, emigration rose from 50,000 in the 1820s to 210,000 in the 1830s to 480,000 in the 1840s. Nine out of ten migrated to the United States. Numerous German states subsidized emigration in an effort to elude a perceived Malthusian nightmare of overpopulation.

Behind this population explosion lay the triple revolutions in agriculture, industry, and banking. The three-crop rotation system, the development of a fertilizer industry, the importation of Swiss and Dutch cows, the rapid expansion of potato and sugar beet planting, and the regular use of fodder crops doubled the use of arable land in Prussia, doubled its milk output, and grew by half its grain yields. A founding generation of lower-middle-class industrialists such as August Borsig, Georg Henschel, Leopold Hoesch, Friedrich Krupp, Mathias Stinnes, and Karl von Stumm accumulated wealth and spurred urban growth. Much of this was fueled in the 1830s by new annuity banks, then after the years 1846 and 1847 by Friedrich Wilhelm Raiffeisen's communal credit and savings banks, and finally by urban commercial and investment banks—joint-stock institutions able to mobilize venture capital. According to one estimate, the number of artisans, craftsmen, and textile and metal workers in German cities rose from 1.64 million in 1800 to 2.93 million by around 1847.

Finally, the 1840s saw a turn toward a vague but virulent nationalism. Professors of German language and literature met at special conferences (*Germanistentage*) to pursue the "national question" at an academic level. More popularly, songs such as "Die Wacht am Rhein" (The watch on the Rhine) and "Deutschland über alles" (Germany above all) not only became clarion calls for nationhood but even defined the physical parameters of that future state. And under King Frederick William IV (r. 1840–1861), Prussia welcomed into its territories former nationalist "demagogues" such as Ernst Moritz Arndt and Ludwig Jahn—who in 1847 founded a national gymnastics club (*Turnerbund*) as the first step toward a citizens' militia—as well as many of the Göttingen Seven. Grimm joined the Prussian Academy of Sciences and Dahlmann became a professor at University of Bonn. All seemed forgiven.

REVOLUTION AND REACTION, 1848–1849

For the third time since 1789, foreign events again stirred the German pot: between 22 and 24 February 1848 revolts broke out in Paris against the July Monarchy of Louis-Philippe. Throughout the German states, liberals took to the streets by mid-March to press their reform demands. Vienna erupted into violence on 13 March when students, workers, apprentices, and lower-middle-class burghers, fired up by the Hungarian Lajos Kossuth's liberal and nationalist speeches in Budapest, poured into the streets. Artisans and guildsmen destroyed factories to protest industrialization. Peasants stormed manor houses to burn feudal records. Initial street clashes caused sixty deaths; the Habsburgs moved to pastoral Innsbruck. Five days later, a similar crowd took to the streets in Berlin, only to be confronted by royal troops who shot 230 protestors; the Hohenzollerns fled to Potsdam.

There existed no central leadership to direct the liberals' efforts. Rather, the German revolts varied, colored largely by regional politics. In central and north Germany, they were carried out by a middle-class political elite. In southwest Germany, under Gustav von Struve and Friedrich Hecker, they had a radical, democratic slant. In Saxony, they turned comic-opera in 1849 because of the involvement of the Russian anarchist Mikhail Bakunin and the composer Richard Wagner. In Bavaria, they revolved around King Louis I (Ludwig I) and his colorful mistress, Lola Montez. Throughout central Europe, the revolutions followed a similar pattern. Initial demonstrations met with limited armed force, whereupon rulers generally panicked and agreed to the rebels' demands. After a frenetic pace of radical legislation, the liberals ran out of steam and finances. Counterrevolutionary forces—the military,

bureaucracy, nobility, and crown—thereupon seized the initiative and regained control.

In the end, reaction triumphed. In Austria, senior army officers and royal bureaucrats placed the eighteen-year-old Francis Joseph I (r. 1848–1916) on the throne and reconquered the revolt-torn provinces one by one: Count Joseph Radetzky, a Czech, defeated rebellious Italian forces at Custoza; Prince Alfred zu Windischgrätz, a German, smashed the Czech revolt at Prague; and Josip Jelačić, the ban (provincial governor) of Croatia, joined Windischgrätz to storm Vienna. At Berlin, General Friedrich von Wrangel was disappointed when Berliners allowed his troops to retake the city without firing a shot. At Munich, Louis I abdicated; Montez fled to London. At Dresden, both Bakunin and Wagner yielded to advancing Prussian troops. Everywhere, reinstalled governments instituted martial law, revoked recently enacted liberal and national reforms, banned parliaments, and meted out harsh sentences especially to student leaders.

As the regional revolutions ran their course, the Frankfurt National Assembly convened at St. Paul's Church on 18 May 1848 amid the ringing of church bells and the thunder of cannon fire to draft a constitution and to bring about unification. Dominated by civil servants, lawyers, educators, and judges, the gathering constituted the first freely elected assembly in German history. It quickly enacted a host of legislation pertaining to individual freedoms, secular education, sanctity of private property, a national supreme court, the creation of a German navy, and a bicameral system of constitutional monarchical government. But it soon divided over the issue of nationalism. What constituted the "German nation"? Was it to be defined by language, by culture, or by "ancient" ancestral rights of possession? In the end, most delegates voted for the latter, that is, to include in the new Germany the Polish lands of Posen (Poznań) and West Prussia, the Czech kingdoms of Bohemia and Moravia, and even the "German harbor" of Trieste.

The final act of the Frankfurt parliament came on 27 March 1849 when, after long debate, by a vote of 290 for and 248 abstentions it offered the imperial crown to King Frederick William IV of Prussia. Once more accompanied by the pealing of church bells and the thunder of cannon fire, the assembly sent its offer out over Europe's first electric telegraph. But Frederick William IV, now firmly back in power at Berlin on the bayonets of his army, refused to accept what he termed a "crown from the gutter," that is, one offered by parliamentary hands. British historian A. J. P. Taylor discerningly called Germany's failure to embark upon a parliamentary constitutional course in 1848–1849 the "hinge of fate" at which Germany "failed to turn."

Reaction ruled after 1849. The Frankfurt parliament simply crumbled. Frederick William IV dissolved a freshly elected Prussian parliament. Francis Joseph I of Austria renounced his predecessor's promise of a constitution. Terms such as *democrat* and *liberal* were deemed to be subversive. Many of those who had fought for change and had lost turned their back on Germany. Popularly known as "Forty-Eighters," they quickly came to dominate the German communities of the American Midwest. Many joined the Republican Party of Abraham Lincoln under the slogan "For Unity, For Freedom, Against Slavery." Former German liberals such as Hecker, Struve, and Carl Schurz, well before Lincoln's Emancipation Proclamation of 1863, made abolition of slavery a central goal. Led by the Forty-Eighters, 6,000 Germans in New York, 6,000 in Illinois, and 4,000 in Pennsylvania answered President Lincoln's call of April 1861 for volunteers.

Still, the twin issues of constitutional reform and national unity refused to disappear from the stage. They simply moved from the streets and parliaments to national associations such as the Congress of German Economists (founded 1858), the National Union (1859), the German Jurists (1860), and the National Chamber of Commerce (1861). Ironically, Frederick William IV, having contemptuously rejected the imperial crown, now lusted after it. Beginning in the spring of 1850, he appealed to fellow kings and princes to convene as an imperial Reichstag and to underwrite his dream of German unity by royal fiat. This transparent stratagem was quickly spied by the Austrian prime minister, Prince Felix zu Schwarzenberg. On 29 November 1850 he ordered the Prussian prime minister, Baron Otto von Manteuffel, to Olmütz in Moravia, and there forced him to renounce all union plans and to reaffirm Austrian leadership within the German Confederation. The so-called Punctation of Olmütz was widely regarded as a public humiliation for Prussia.

UNIFICATION UNDER PRUSSIA, 1864–1890

Otto von Bismarck was one of the few Prussians delighted by Olmütz. The king's union plan smelled to him too much of liberalism and Romanticism. He firmly believed that unification could be achieved only through a clash of arms between the two main contenders, Austria and Prussia. "There is no room for both," he wrote a friend, "thus we cannot get along over the long haul. We steal each other's breath." The only legitimate Prussian state policy, he wrote, was one based on "egoism rather than Romanticism." But this was wishful thinking by a radical outsider. The king had earlier summarized Bismarck with the comment, "red reactionary, smells of blood, to be used only when the bayonet reigns."

Frederick William IV rendered his state one last service: he stayed out of the Crimean War (1853–1856), thus earning Russia's gratitude, while Francis Joseph I repaid Russian help against Hungarian rebels in 1849 by joining Britain and France in an alliance in December 1854. In 1857 Frederick William IV suffered a series of strokes, and the following year his brother William replaced him as regent. William's one love was the army, and when Sardinia, aided by Emperor Napoleon III of France, in 1859 tried to wrest the provinces of Lombardy and Venetia from Austria, the regent ordered mobilization of his army. It was a disaster. Units were grossly understaffed, ill trained, and badly led. Infuriated, William appointed General Albrecht von Roon as war minister to reform the army. This would cost money and likely lead to a clash with the liberals and their fondness for militias, for two- rather than three-year military service, and for control over "the power of the purse." When the moderate Prussian liberals in May 1861 agreed to fund the reforms "provisionally," the left wing of the moderate liberals reconstituted itself in June as the German Progressive Party. Roon pushed for unconditional passage of his army bill. And he had a close friend, one he knew would not shy away from confrontation: Bismarck.

Caricature of Bismarck and King William I. The relationship between the aging William and his powerful prime minister is lampooned in this French cartoon, published c. 1870, as tensions between France and Germany escalated. Musée de la Ville de Paris, Musée Carnavalet, Paris, France/ Bridgeman Art Library/Lauors/Giraudon

William I, king since 1861, appointed Bismarck prime minister in September 1862 as a last, desperate effort to end a constitutional crisis that had developed over the liberals' refusal to pass Roon's army budget. In his first speech to the budget commission of the Prussian parliament, Bismarck took up the challenge—and more. The "great issues of the day," he informed a startled gathering, would be decided not by speeches and majority votes as at Frankfurt in 1848–1849, but rather by "iron and blood," that is, on the field of battle. To that end, Prussia needed to reform its military. He resolved the budgetary impasse by a piece of constitutional chicanery. Because the House of Lords and the House of Deputies had failed to hammer out a firm military budget, a "gap" existed in the constitution, one that left king and government with no recourse other than to run the affairs of state in lieu of consent. An angry parliament adamantly refused to ratify the army budget; a determined Bismarck simply collected taxes; and a delighted Roon thoroughly reformed the military.

"Prussian I am, and Prussian I want to remain." These words succinctly encapsulate Bismarck's views on German unification. The Austro-Prussian antagonism unleashed by Frederick the Great's invasion of Silesia in 1740 could be resolved only by a test of strength. He desired no merger of Prussia with other states, no constitutional convention to unify the German states. Instead, Prussia was to wrest primacy in Germany from Austria. Above all, it needed to pursue only policies that lay within its "own interest," the concept of realpolitik being hereafter closely associated with Bismarck.

In his memoirs, Bismarck wrote the story of German unification as the piece-by-piece unraveling of a great score that he had orchestrated. Reality was different. He was a pragmatist. To be sure, he had a clear conception of Prussia's role in future German affairs and an iron will to execute that policy. Yet, he could be flexible in his methods, and he appreciated the concerns that motivated the other players on the European chessboard. He, unlike his successors, practiced the "art of the possible." He was perfectly willing to react to the ebb and flow of European affairs, to pounce on opportunities as they presented themselves.

He did not have long to wait. In November 1863 the Danish king, Christian IX, announced that he would annex the province of Schleswig and promulgate a constitution for Holstein, both of which Denmark administered under the Treaty of London (1852). Bismarck cared little for the Germans in the provinces—"It is no concern of ours whether the Germans of Holstein are happy"—but he spied an opportunity to revoke a constitution, preempt the national issue, and draw Austria into an untenable situation. Vienna rose to the bait, and in January 1864 joined Prussia in a war against Denmark. By the end of that month, Christian IX conceded defeat; Austria and Prussia assumed separate administrations of the two provinces.

There is no question that Bismarck set out to make the Austrian position in Holstein as difficult as possible. "The clock of German dualism," he informed an associate, "has to be put right by war." Prussian forces invaded Bohemia in June 1866, launching the Austro-Prussian (or Seven Weeks') War. An alliance with Italy threatened Austria's southern front; Russia maintained benevolent neutrality toward Prussia as reward for its noninvolvement in the Crimean War. Most of the states of the "Third Germany" sided with Austria. On 3 July Roon's reformed army under Helmuth von Moltke, chief of the General Staff, routed the Austrians at the battle of Königgrätz (now Hradec Králové, Czech Republic; also called battle of Sadowa). Austria surrendered its primacy in Germany and was forced to accept a "compromise" (Ausgleich) with the Magyars of Hungary.

Bismarck revealed his mettle as a statesman in victory. He rejected the generals' demands to continue the war and their desire for a victory parade through Vienna. He had achieved his political goals. Prussia was free to reconstitute central Europe. He now instituted his "lesser German" (Kleindeutsch) solution to national unity, one that did not include Austria. Prussia annexed Schleswig-Holstein, Hanover, Hesse-Kassel, Nassau, and Frankfurt, and it engineered military conventions with the three southern German states of Baden, Bavaria, and Württemberg. At home, the Prussian parliament by a vote of 230 to 75 passed an indemnity bill, forgiving Bismarck for having ruled illegally since 1862.

The German Confederation at Frankfurt ceased to exist. In its place, Bismarck created the North German Confederation. He crafted a constitution with a bicameral system. The Bundesrat was a federal council of the forty-three ambassadors of the confederation; Prussia, with the votes of the recently annexed states, had seventeen votes, sufficient for a veto. The Bundesrat exercised control over foreign and defense policy, fiscal matters, and communications and commercial law. The Reichstag, the lower house, was elected by universal, secret, manhood suffrage—the most progressive in Europe. Its members enjoyed immunity from prosecution and the power annually to accept or to reject the budget. Bismarck set the size of the standing army at 1 percent of the population, automatically funded at the rate of 225 thaler per recruit.

The third war of German unification—the Franco-Prussian War—remains hotly debated. In February 1870 the Spanish parliament (Cortes) chose Prince Leopold, a member of the Catholic (Sigmaringen) branch of the House of Hohenzollern, as their king. France, for centuries paranoid about Austro-Spanish Habsburg "encirclement,"

now feared Prusso-Spanish Hohenzollern "encirclement." On 19 July 1870 Napoleon III declared war on Prussia after Bismarck "edited" William I's charitable telegram from Bad Ems on a conversation with a French envoy by excising from it all conciliatory phrases.

Where does the responsibility for the war lie? With Napoleon III's "bellicosity"? With Bismarck's "duplicity"? Bismarck's biographers by and large agree that there is no incontestable proof that he forced war with France. Rather, they argue that once the candidate for the Spanish throne emerged, Bismarck seized the moment either to humiliate France diplomatically or to provoke a war with Paris—both aimed at completing national unity. The war against Napoleon III was settled with a stunning Prussian victory at Sedan on 2 September; that against a hastily constituted provisional government of national defense dragged on until January 1871. This was no ordinary "cabinet war." National passions were aroused. Casualties escalated demands. While the generals again desired a complete victory, Bismarck opted to conclude peace with France for fear of European involvement. On 18 January 1871 the German Empire—including the three southern German states—under Kaiser William I, was proclaimed in the Hall of Mirrors at the Palace of Versailles. The historian Otto Pflanze has argued that it was a union of three powerful forces: Hohenzollern authoritarianism, Prussian militarism, and German nationalism. The annexation of Alsace and part of Lorraine was the result of the latter of those three forces.

Bismarck's "German revolution," in the words of the British Conservative leader Benjamin Disraeli, had "entirely destroyed" the European balance of power. What to do? Initially, Bismarck sought to avoid "entangling alliances." But recurring squabbles in the Balkans and a Russo-Turkish War in 1877 aroused in him the "nightmare of coalitions." Thus, he used his annual "cure" to assess Germany's future. The resulting Bad Kissingen memorandum of June 1877 is a model of clarity. Bismarck set up two cardinal axioms: no conflicts among the major powers in central Europe, and German security without German hegemony. He ruled out further territorial aggrandizement. Germany was "satiated" and required no more Danes, French, or Poles; it

Proclaiming the German Empire. Engraving from *Harper's Weekly Magazine,* 1871. Following his defeat of the French in the Franco-Prussian War, Prussian king William I is declared German emperor in a ceremony at the Palace of Versailles, the traditional home of French kings. ©Corbis

had to be content with its position of "semi-hegemony" in Europe. France was to be isolated and the other major Continental powers brought into a diplomatic web radiating out from Berlin. And as long as Germany did not build a fleet and pursue a policy of imperialism, British vital interests would not be threatened.

Bismarck quickly enacted his alliance plans. In October 1879 he concluded the Dual Alliance with Austria-Hungary; in 1882 he expanded it to include Italy (forming the Triple Alliance); and in 1883, Romania. The capstone of his alliance policy was the Reinsurance Treaty with Russia in 1887. Historians later spoke of a *pax Germanica.* Berlin had become the diplomatic capital of Europe. Paris had been isolated. Vienna, Rome, and St. Petersburg had been reined in with regard to their ambitions in the Balkans—a region the "Iron Chancellor" deemed not worth "the bones of a single Pomeranian grenadier." Historians have argued that Bismarck, through his alliance system, forced four decades of peace on Europe.

Bismarck's domestic policies were less successful. To be sure, he extended the North German Confederation's bicameral constitutional system to the new empire. For the first decade as chancellor, he worked with liberal deputies and government bureaucrats to promulgate a uniform civil and criminal legal code (1873), to nationalize the Prussian state railroads under the Imperial Railroad Office (1875), to create a national postal system (1876), to found a central treasury and bank (1876), and to establish a High Court of Appeals at Leipzig (1879). As well, he introduced a national currency and the metric system. And for the first decade of his rule, he encouraged liberal free-trade policies.

Yet, two forces bedeviled him: political Catholicism in the Rhine, Silesia, Baden, and Bavaria as well as the new Marxist labor movement in the rapidly industrializing urban centers. A third force, liberalism, he would abandon once it had served his purposes. Catholics made up 40 percent of the German population and after 1871 were organized in the Center Party under Ludwig Windthorst. The party's program principally was to safeguard Catholic rights in a Protestant empire. The Center Party was emotionally allied with the Catholic states Prussia had defeated: Austria and France. With a regular 30 percent of the national vote, it played a pivotal role in parliament. Bismarck deeply disliked Windthorst. "I have my wife to love," he famously stated, "and Windthorst to hate." When the Vatican Council pronounced the dogma of papal infallibility during Prussia's war with France, Bismarck took this as a call to battle. In 1873 he had Adalbert Falk, the Prussian minister of ecclesiastical affairs and education, pass a series of laws that established state supervision of schools, withdrew state support from the Catholic Church, instituted obligatory state marriage, and made state examinations mandatory for all candidates for church office.

The so-called Kulturkampf ("struggle of cultures") was aimed not so much at Rome but at the Center Party in general and at its French and Polish voters in Germany in particular. Bismarck hoped to strangle the party in the cradle. But proscription often breeds success: during the Kulturkampf, the Center's share of votes rose by a third. The sordid affair was laid to rest in 1887 by Pope Leo XIII, who saw not Protestant Prussia but secular Italy as the Vatican's real enemy. Its legacy was one of internal divisiveness, bitterness, and dissension. It would cast its long shadow down to the Center Party's votes for Adolf Hitler's Enabling Act in 1933.

The year 1878 also saw Bismarck's turn away from liberalism. He had put in place much of the National Liberals' economic program, and the start in 1873 of what is sometimes called the Great Depression (which extended to 1896) alarmed him sufficiently to embrace protectionism—against cheap Russian and American grains and British manufactured goods. In the so-called rye and iron alliance, he forged an uneasy bond between industry and agriculture. He used two assassination attempts by anarchists against William I in 1878 to "refound" the Reich along conservative, protec-

tionist lines—and to split the liberals into two competing factions. A small group continued as the National Liberals while a majority faction organized itself as the Progressive Liberal Party. Again, the legacy was one of divisiveness and bitterness. Social historians would later suggest that the lack of a liberal revolution to sweep away the Reich's premodern social structure constituted a divergence (*Sonderweg*) from Western "normative" societies.

Bismarck's assault on liberalism was closely tied to his attack on socialism. He became alarmed at the physical transformation of the Reich: in the two decades after unification, 75 percent of the growth of Germany's population—some ten million—took place in urban centers. The Social Democratic Party (SPD), founded in 1875, quickly captured the votes of this human infusion. Bismarck disliked the party's revolutionary Marxist domestic program and its pacifist, internationalist foreign policy. In 1878 he decided to strangle the socialist movement in the crib, as he had tried earlier with the Center Party. A host of antisocialist laws outlawed the SPD's nonparliamentary organizations, banned its public meetings, and proscribed its printed materials. Conversely, the Iron Chancellor sought to woo the rank and file away from the party through state-sponsored social security legislation, most notably national health insurance in 1883, accident insurance in 1884, and both disability and old-age insurance in 1889. But the antisocialist laws suffered the same fate as the Falk laws: by 1890, trade-union membership rose fivefold, to 278,000, and the SPD's share of the national vote to 1.43 million. Rebuffed by the state, the SPD turned to what sociologists have termed "negative integration," creating organizations and programs parallel to official state ones and in spirit and body turning inward and rejecting the state.

William I died in 1888. His terminally ill successor, Frederick III, served for only ninety-nine days. He was succeeded by his twenty-nine-year-old son, William II. Bismarck, alarmed by so-called enemies of state, such as liberals, Catholics, and socialists, turned to reaction. He toyed with notions of overthrowing the constitution, of replacing the Reichstag with an economic council, of reviving the infamous "gap" theory of 1862, and even of launching a military coup. In March 1890 William II dismissed the Reich's founder. The bitter titan disappeared into retirement at Friedrichsruh near Hamburg.

IMPERIAL INTERLUDE, 1890–1914

"Dropping the Pilot," as a cartoon in the English weekly magazine *Punch* put the dismissal of Bismarck in March 1890, was well received in many German quarters. A generation had reached maturity since unification, one tired of hearing of the great deeds of 1866 and 1870, the "satiated" Reich, and "semi-hegemony." It thirsted for action and deeds of its own. Unification, the sociologist Max Weber argued in 1895, would have been little more than "a youthful spree" and a "costly extravaganza," had it been anything less than "the starting point of German power-politics on a global scale." Bismarck's self-imposed bonds of restraint were soon broken in favor of an ill-defined but virulent policy of "world politics" (*Weltpolitik*).

At first, William II, influenced by the Christian Social Workers movement, founded by Adolf Stoecker, a court chaplain, set out to rule as the self-styled "king of the beggars." William allowed the antisocialist laws to lapse in 1890. That same year, he canceled the hated Reinsurance Treaty with despotic Russia. His government extended social legislation to prohibit Sunday work, set up courts of arbitration to deal with wage disputes, and outlawed the employment of children under the age of thirteen. The new chancellor, General Leo von Caprivi, rescinded Bismarck's protectionist policies and replaced them with a liberal Russo-German trade treaty in 1894.

It proved to be a brief reforming interlude. Within two years, William II had swung back to a conservative, protectionist course. Bismarck's levies against foreign iron and grains were reintroduced. Johannes von Miquel, the Prussian finance minister, revived Bismarck's "rye-and-iron" alliance under the guise of an aggressive union of agrarians and industrialists (*Sammlungspolitik*)—against Social Democrats, National Liberals, and Progressives. Under the "politics of concentration," industrialists voted for high tariffs against Russian and American grains, while agrarians voted for expenditures on what they termed "the ugly, ghastly fleet."

Indeed, the creation of a battle fleet under Admiral Alfred von Tirpitz beginning in 1898 marked the official launching of a policy of "world politics." Wealth was no longer concentrated in land but rather in industry and commerce. In the four decades after unification, German coal production rose from 38 to 179 million tons; steel production of 13 million tons in 1913 was second only to that of the United States. Giant cartels dominated the burgeoning chemical, electrical, coal, and steel industries. Stock companies grew to more than five thousand, with aggregate holdings of about $3.4 billion. The Reich's share of global trade climbed to 13 percent, just behind Britain's 15 percent. Its population grew by 60 percent, to 67 million by 1914. Emigration fell to less than 200,000 people per annum. The flow from country to city became a flood; urban industrial centers tripled in population under William II. Historians have depicted Imperial Germany as an anthill, constantly on the move and constantly working. The SPD's share of the popular vote rose in proportion to urbanization: from 27 percent in 1898 to almost 35 percent (4.5 million votes) in 1912.

Not surprisingly, this economic explosion created demands for what Weber had called "power-politics on a global scale." Middle-class pressure groups such as the German Navy League, German Colonial League, Pan-German League, and even the Women's League endorsed Chancellor Bernhard von Bülow's demand for "a place in the sun." Hand in hand with Tirpitz, the unctuous Bülow after 1898 vigorously pursued *Weltpolitik*. Berlin expanded and added on to a colonial empire initially established by Bismarck—in the words of historian A. J. P. Taylor, as "the accidental by-product of an abortive Franco-German entente"— the island of Nauru, Palau, the Carolines and Marianas, German Southwest and East Africa, Togoland, the Cameroons, and Jiao Xian. It mattered little that these colonies were economic drains or that few Germans invested in them (3.8 percent of total overseas investments) or colonized them (only one out of every thousand emigrants went there). Prestige dominated the drive overseas. No island was too rocky, no plot in Africa too barren to escape attention. Kurt Riezler, senior consultant at the chancellor's office, in 1914 summarized *Weltpolitik* simply as "craving for petty prestige victories."

The Imperial German Navy became the most obvious manifestation of "world politics." Its architect, Tirpitz, saw it as both a domestic and a foreign political instrument. At home, it would rally the parties of Miquel's *Sammlungspolitik* by way of state building contracts and global trade (social imperialism), and thus serve as a "strong palliative against Social Democrats." Overseas, it would catapult Germany into the ranks of global powers, eventually able to challenge a declining Britain's "heritage." Tirpitz saw only two alternatives: Germany either became a prosperous world power or it would remain forever a "poor farming country." By way of two major navy bills in 1898 and 1900—augmented by supplementary bills in 1906, 1908, and 1912—he strove to create a mighty battle fleet of sixty capital ships by the mid-1920s, one capable of confronting "perfidious Albion" (i.e., Britain) in the North Sea.

It was not to be. Britain met Tirpitz's unilateral challenge financially and materially—the former by way of its vastly superior capital markets and the latter by way of a technological breakthrough with HMS *Dreadnought* in 1906. The Reich government, unable under the Bismarckian constitution to levy direct taxes, fell ever deeper into debt. By 1914, it had exhausted domestic capital markets by borrowing 5,000 million gold marks. As well, *Weltpolitik* had alienated not only the established colonial powers but also newcomers such as Japan and the United States. The German challenge was so direct that Britain abandoned "splendid isolation" and concluded agreements with rivals old and new: Japan in 1902, France in 1904, and Russia in 1907. After a serious diplomatic defeat during the first Moroccan crisis of 1905–1906, German leaders spoke of "encirclement." William II likened the Reich's position after 1907 as being akin to that of Frederick II after the Austro-French-Russian "diplomatic revolution" of 1756.

Domestically, politics took place less and less in the Reichstag; instead, it became dominated by extraparliamentary mass movements through public meetings and rallies as well as lobbying of deputies. The Kaiser's maladroit handling of political crises such as the 1907 homosexual scandal uncovered by the journalist Maximilian Harden, the 1908 *Daily Telegraph* interview in which he told the

British that his fleet was being built not against them but against America and Japan, and the 1913–1914 civil-military confrontation in Zabern (Saverne), Alsace, eroded the crown's prestige. Most dramatically, the elections of 1912 brought a crushing victory by what Bismarck had once termed "enemies of the Reich": the Social Democrats, Guelphs, Poles, Alsatians, and a new Jewish party received more than 50 percent of the popular vote. Twelve of the deputies elected were Jewish. Nationalists were outraged. Anti-Semitism became more pronounced. The net result was a vulgarization of politics and a brutalization of debate. Visions of *Weltpolitik* receded from view.

The upshot was a return to Continental politics. In 1905 Count Alfred von Schlieffen, chief of the German General Staff, completed his desperate plan to fight a two-front war against France and Russia. The army again received primacy in defense outlays. Foreign policy was scaled back from "world politics" to "Balkan politics." The German flag would have to "fly over the fortifications on the Bosphorus," the Kaiser decreed, "or I shall suffer the sad fate of the great exile on St. Helena," Napoleon I. Even the political vocabulary had changed by 1914. William II, Schlieffen, and Chancellor Theobald von Bethmann Hollweg spoke ever more frequently in racial and social Darwinistic terms—of a coming "struggle for survival" that would pit the "Germans in Europe" against both the "Latins (Gauls)" and the "Slavs (Russia)." The assassination of the Austro-Hungarian heir apparent, Archduke Francis Ferdinand, at Sarajevo on 28 June 1914—the trigger for World War I—took place against a backdrop of pessimism and despair.

Literally thousands of books have been written about the "July crisis" of 1914. After decades of acrimonious debate, historians are now largely agreed on several conclusions. First, the decision for war was not a German "grab for world power," as the historian Fritz Fischer provocatively termed it, but rather one to secure (and if possible enhance) the position of "semi-hegemony" created in 1871. Second, Vienna, and not Berlin, seized the initiative after Sarajevo and made the first decision to risk a European war to uphold its position as a Great Power. Third, Berlin reacted to Vienna's call for help by issuing the infamous "black check" of 5 July, assuring full German

JULIUS KLINGER

Ausstellung moderner Verkehrsmittel

Ausstellungshallen am Zoo • Berlin 1909 • 23. Oktober bis 6. November.

Poster announcing the Exhibition of Modern Consumer Goods, Berlin, 1909. The prosperity and industrial development of the imperial period resulted in a plenitude of consumer goods. ©CORBIS

support even if, in the Kaiser's words, "some serious European complications" (read war) should arise. Helmuth von Moltke (the younger), chief of the General Staff, likewise counseled war, "and the sooner the better." Chancellor von Bethmann Hollweg was prepared to take what he called a "calculated risk": if Russia backed down and did not support Serbia, then Berlin would have "outmaneuvered" the Anglo-French-Russian Entente, that is, scored a diplomatic victory; and if Russia opted for war and Germany entered it simply to preserve Austria-Hungary, "then we have the prospect of winning it." In the end, he was prepared to take what his confidant Riezler called "a leap in the dark." Bismarckian realpolitik was the first casualty of war in 1914.

See also **Austro-Prussian War; Bebel, August; Bismarck, Otto von; Congress of Vienna; Franco-Prussian War; Frederick William III; Frederick William IV; Gagern, Heinrich von; Hardenberg, Karl August von; Napoleonic Empire; Prussia; Restoration; Stein, Heinrich Friedrich Karl vom und zum; William I; William II; Windthorst, Ludwig.**

BIBLIOGRAPHY

Berghahn, Volker R. *Germany and the Approach of War in 1914.* 2nd ed. New York, 1993. The first and still most useful survey of why Germany opted for war in July 1914.

———. *Imperial Germany, 1871–1914: Economy, Society, Culture, and Politics.* Providence, R.I., 1994. A highly detailed analysis of German internal politics.

Bucholz, Arden. *Moltke, Schlieffen, and Prussian War Planning.* New York, 1991. A solid comparison of the strategic thoughts of Imperial Germany's most famous chiefs of the General Staff.

———. *Moltke and the German Wars, 1864–1871.* New York, 2001. A well-presented study of the general who fought Bismarck's three wars.

Carr, William. *The Origins of the Wars of German Unification*. London, 1991. Good analysis of Bismarck's three wars by a senior scholar.

Cecil, Lamar. *Wilhelm II*. 2 vols. Chapel Hill, N.C., 1989–1996. A superbly crafted biography of the last of the Hohenzollerns.

Craig, Gordon A. *Germany, 1866–1945*. Oxford, U.K., 1978. An encyclopedic history of Germany since unification; a sequel to James Sheehan (below).

Epstein, Klaus. *The Genesis of German Conservatism*. Princeton, N.J., 1966. The first volume of what was to have become the standard work on German conservatism.

Eyck, Frank. *The Frankfurt Parliament, 1848–1849*. London, 1968. Essential analysis of the delegates and their actions at Frankfurt.

Farrar, L. L., Jr. *Arrogance and Anxiety: The Ambivalence of German Power, 1848–1914*. Iowa City, 1981. Good analysis of the major strains of German foreign policy from Bismarck to Wilhelm II.

Fischer, Fritz. *War of Illusions: German Policies from 1911 to 1914*. Translated by Marian Jackson. New York, 1975. Translation of *Krieg der Illusionen: Die deutsche Politik von 1911 bis 1914* (1969). An unfortunately truncated version of Fischer's classic indictment of German *Weltpolitik* up to the July crisis of 1914.

Gall, Lothar. *Bismarck: The White Revolutionary*. 2 vols. Translated by J. A. Underwood. London, 1986. Translation of *Bismarck: Der weisse Revolutionär* (1980). Solid, well-organized biography of Bismarck focusing on his politics.

Geiss, Imanuel. *German Foreign Policy, 1871–1914*. London, 1976. A brief but useful survey of German foreign policy from unification to World War I.

Geiss, Imanuel, ed. *July 1914: The Outbreak of the First World War: Selected Documents*. New York, 1968. A radically shortened version of Geiss's two-volume *Julikrise und Kreisgausbruch 1914: Eine Dokumentensammlung* (1963–1964). Provides some of the most important documents pertaining to Germany's "leap in the dark" of July 1914.

Gooch, G. P. *Germany and the French Revolution*. London, 1920. Still the standard account of the topic.

Hamerow, Theodore S. *Restoration, Revolution, Reaction: Economics and Politics in Germany, 1815–1871*. Princeton, N.J., 1958. A solid analysis of German politics from the Congress of Vienna to unification; follows the arguments of Rudolf Stadelmann (below).

———. *The Social Foundations of German Unification, 1858–1871*. 2 vols. Princeton, N.J., 1969–1972. Classic analysis of the Iron Chancellor's domestic policies.

Herwig, Holger H. *"Luxury" Fleet: The Imperial German Navy, 1888–1918*. Rev. ed. London, 1987. By now the standard analysis of German naval building under Tirpitz and William II.

———. *Hammer or Anvil? Modern Germany, 1648–Present*. Lexington, Mass., 1994. A manageable paperback history of Germany since the Peace of Westphalia.

Kissinger, Henry. *A World Restored: Metternich, Castlereagh, and the Problems of Peace, 1812–1822*. Boston, 1957. A political science analysis of balance of power and "satisfaction" theories.

Kraehe, Enno E. *Metternich's German Policy*. Vol. 2: *The Congress of Vienna, 1814–1815*. Princeton, N.J., 1983. A balanced, masterful analysis of Metternich's German polices.

Meinecke, Friedrich. *The Age of German Liberation, 1795–1815*. Translated by Peter Paret and Helmuth Fischer. Berkeley, Calif., 1977. Translation of *Das Zeitalter der deutschen Erhebung, 1795–1815* (1957). A classic analysis of the wars of liberation in their political and intellectual context.

Mommsen, Wolfgang J. *Imperial Germany, 1867–1918: Politics, Culture, and Society in an Authoritarian State*. Translated by Richard Deveson. London, 1995. Translation of *Der autoritäre Nationalstaat: Verfassung, Gesellschaft, und Kultur des deutschen Kaiserreiches* (1990). A brilliant synthesis of German society and politics from unification to defeat.

Pflanze, Otto. *Bismarck and the Development of Germany*. 2nd ed. 3 vols. Princeton, N.J., 1990. The standard English-language treatment of Bismarck's domestic and foreign policies.

Sheehan, James J. *German Liberalism in the Nineteenth Century*. Chicago, 1978. A dated but still informative survey of classic nineteenth-century German liberalism.

———. *German History, 1770–1866*. Oxford, U.K., 1989. An encyclopedic history of the German states from Frederick II to Bismarck; followed by Gordon Craig (above).

Simon, Walter M. *The Failure of the Prussian Reform Movement, 1807–1819*. Ithaca, N.Y., 1955. A useful overview of the Prussian reformers after 1806.

Stadelmann, Rudolf. *Social and Political History of the German 1848 Revolution*. Translated by James G. Chastain. Athens, Ohio, 1975. Translation of *Soziale und politische Geschichte der Revolution von 1848* (1948). Brilliant, brief, unrivaled analysis of the German revolutions.

Taylor, A. J. P. *The Struggle for Mastery in Europe, 1848–1919*. Oxford, U.K., 1954. A solid, well-reasoned work that sets the background to the "German question."

Wehler, Hans Ulrich. *The German Empire, 1871–1918*. Translated by Kim Traynor. Leamington Spa, U.K., 1985. Translation of *Das deutsche Kaiserreich, 1871–1918* (1973). A monument to the argument for the "primacy of domestic politics."

HOLGER H. HERWIG

GIOLITTI, GIOVANNI (1842–1928),
Italy's greatest prime minister after Count Cavour, the architect of Italian unity.

Giovanni Giolitti defined the Italian liberal state in its heyday from 1901 until 1914. His long career can be divided into two very different parts. After graduating in law from the University of Turin in 1860, he entered the civil service, where he became expert in financial questions in the Finance Ministry and later in the Corte dei Conti, Italy's highest administrative oversight body. During this first period Giolitti seemed the perfect technocrat. The second and longest part of his career began in 1882, when Giolitti entered Parliament. He was elected uninterruptedly from 1882 until the final election under fascism in 1924. Once in Parliament he gravitated to the liberal left and became noted as a critic of government waste, financial mismanagement, excessive taxation, and costly colonial ventures in Africa. Thus his first appointment as a government minister in the government of the imperialist Francesco Crispi was bound to end unhappily. Giolitti headed the Treasury Ministry and eventually that of finance, with oversight of Crispi's aggressive foreign policy ventures.

THE POLITICAL CRISIS OF THE 1890S
Giolitti formed his first government in 1892. It lasted barely a year and was marked by a growing scandal around the Banca Romana, a politically well-connected financial institution. In the wake of this crisis, Giolitti began the process of banking reform, which was completed by the Crispi government of 1894–1896.

On leaving office, Giolitti found himself under relentless attack by Crispi and his allies. The danger of criminal prosecution lasted almost until Crispi's government fell in March 1896 on news of the Italian defeat at Adwa in Ethiopia. Between 1896 and 1900 Giolitti's career gradually recovered. These were difficult years of economic crisis and social turmoil that reached a climax with the imposition of martial law in the aftermath of the food riots of May 1898. Although he hesitated a bit too long, Giolitti joined the liberal democratic opposition to the Pelloux-Sonnino government's effort to shift the constitutional balance of power from Parliament to the crown and the executive. His alliance in 1899 and 1900 with the veteran leader of the liberal left, Giuseppe Zanardelli, prepared the ground for the reformist Zanardelli government of 1901 to 1903, in which Giolitti served as interior minister and initiated the "new course" in domestic policy. Giolitti had for some time argued in favor of toleration for trade union activity. He wanted to draw organized labor and reformist Socialists like Filippo Turati and Leonida Bissolati into the institutional framework of the state. At the same time, Giolitti also abandoned the old anticlerical biases of the liberal political class and sought a reconciliation with the Vatican. Thus he deliberately stood aside when divorce legislation was introduced in 1902 and 1903.

THE GIOLITTIAN ERA, 1903–1914
Already during his first government of 1892–1893 and especially from 1903 to 1914, Giolitti revealed a mastery of the art of running elections. He also understood how bureaucracy operated down to the most minute details. These skills proved to be both an asset and a liability. Giolitti made the liberal parliamentary system operate on a high level of efficiency, but in the process he acquired a reputation as a corrupt manipulator of the democratic process. In fact, Giolitti was exceptionally honest and did nothing more than his predecessors in using the power of the state to control elections—only he did it better and more successfully. Giolitti's fundamental limitation as a statesman lay elsewhere. He was a state builder but he had no sweeping vision of fundamental reform. He believed that the Italian state was a fragile construction that needed decades to catch up to the more advanced countries of Europe. Consequently, his vision of reform was structural and incremental. He nationalized the rail system, the telephone and telegraph lines, and the life insurance companies and attempted to bring the major shipping lines under state control. In 1903 and 1904 he and the treasury minister, Luigi Luzzatti, refunded the Italian public debt at substantially lower interest rates, but the surpluses were used to defer major tax and fiscal reform. He did not build a modern political party structure, nor did he prepare Italy for the age of mass politics.

Giolitti was a consummate man of the center. He governed from the center-left in 1892–1893 and from 1901 to 1903. Giolitti offered a position in his 1903 government to Turati and to the leaders of the left-wing Radical Party. When the opening to the left was rejected by the Socialists, who feared that the masses would not understand such a radical departure from socialist tradition, Giolitti comfortably shifted to the center-right in 1904 and 1905 and stayed there during his long government from 1906 to 1909. In 1911 he moved again to the left with a program of reform that included universal manhood suffrage and the nationalization of the life insurance companies to help fund worker pensions. With the onset of the Libyan war in September 1911, Giolitti moved once again to the center-right.

The introduction of almost universal manhood suffrage in 1912 changed the political rules in a fundamental way. Not only did the Italian Socialist Party move to take advantage of the new opportunities, but organized Catholics did as well. The Vatican, which had forbidden Catholic participation in national elections after the seizure of Rome by the new Italian state in 1870, began to relax this veto starting with the elections of 1904, when faced with the rising power of socialism. Responding to Giolitti's abandonment of anticlericalism and his description of church-state relations as two parallels that should never touch, Pope Pius X allowed Catholics to support liberal candidates where the danger of a Socialist victory existed. Catholic influence in the elections of 1909 increased, but during the elections of 1913 it became clear that liberals needed substantial Catholic assistance to maintain their positions in the major centers of northern Italy. During the elections of 1913, the head of the Catholic Electoral Union, Count Vincenzo Gentiloni, set out a number of conditions for candidates to obtain Catholic backing. The Gentiloni Pact, as it came to be known, made a large number of liberal deputies dependent on clerical backing and weakened Giolitti's control over the new parliamentary majority that resulted from the 1913 elections.

THE WAR AND THE CRISIS OF THE GIOLITTIAN POLITICAL SYSTEM

Faced with mounting opposition, Giolitti resigned in March 1914. He was succeeded by the conservative Antonio Salandra. Inexplicably, with the outbreak of World War I in August 1914, Giolitti refused to take advantage of his parliamentary majority to topple Salandra and resume power, even when it was clear in early 1915 that Salandra was moving Italy into war on the side of the British and French. From the outbreak of war in August 1914, Giolitti supported Italian neutrality between the contending parties on grounds that Italy was too weak and fragile to endure a war that Giolitti correctly believed would be long and difficult. When the Piedmontese statesman finally acted against Salandra in late April and May 1915, it was too late to reverse Italy's commitment to the side of the Entente. Faced with royal opposition to any new Giolitti government, he withdrew and spent much of the war in his political district of Cavour.

With the end of the war, Giolitti, now in his late seventies, put forward a sweeping and ambitious set of reforms for the postwar era and took advantage of the ineptitude of the governments of Vittorio Emanuele Orlando (1917–1919) and Francesco Nitti (1919–1920) to reclaim power in the summer of 1920 as the last hope to restore political and economic stability to the liberal state. Giolitti succeeded in ending Gabriele D'Annunzio's occupation of the disputed city of Fiume and began to work toward a final resolution of the city's status with Yugoslavia. His government also peacefully mediated the withdrawal of workers who occupied the automobile factories in Milan in September 1920. But when Giolitti was unable to win any support for his policies from the Socialist Party, he shifted to the right. His government watched passively as the Fascist squads began their campaign of violence against Socialist and Catholic labor and peasant organizations. Giolitti also unwisely called elections in the spring of 1921 that allowed the Fascists, including Benito Mussolini, to enter Parliament.

Giolitti left office for the last time in July 1921. In October 1922, most observers expected him to form a government that included the Fascists, but King Victor Emmanuel III, his old enemy Antonio Salandra, and Mussolini outmaneuvered the old statesman. On 29 October 1922 the king appointed Mussolini to form the next government and Giolitti's career effectively ended. He supported the new Fascist government until the assassination of the Socialist leader Giacomo Matteotti by the Fascists. Giolitti passed into opposition and from 1925 to his death in 1928 was a lonely voice in defense of the old liberal parliamentary state.

Giolitti's historic merit was to have recognized the need to bring the organized forces of the Italian working classes within the framework of the liberal state. He greatly strengthened the parliamentary institutions of liberal Italy. In 1914 he understood that Italy could not withstand the shock of World War I and would have kept the country out of the war or have brought it in under much more favorable circumstances, but he showed a tragic inability to act before the decision for war was irrevocable. Over the long term, Giolitti failed to reach a stable accommodation with the Italian Socialist Party, but the Socialists were partly at fault, especially in 1920. The years after 1918 were difficult ones for Giolitti. He neither understood nor sympathized with mass democratic politics, and he totally misjudged the danger posed by fascism to the liberal state that he identified with and defended.

See also **Cavour, Count (Camillo Benso): Crispi, Francesco; D'Annunzio, Gabriele; Italy; Liberalism; Turati, Filippo.**

BIBLIOGRAPHY

Coppa, Frank. *Planning, Protectionism, and Politics in Liberal Italy.* Washington, D.C., 1971.

De Grand, Alexander. *The Hunchback's Tailor: Giovanni Giolitti and Liberal Italy from the Challenge of Mass Politics to the Rise of Fascism, 1882–1922.* Westport, Conn., 2001.

ALEXANDER DE GRAND

GIRONDINS. The Girondins were one of the two principal factions that emerged in the National Convention during the radical phase of the French Revolution. Their opponents were known as the Montagnards, or the Mountain. These factions cannot be properly called political parties—they lacked the parliamentary discipline or cohesion to justify that label—but they did coalesce into loose groupings, and the struggle between Girondins and Montagnards came to dominate the proceedings of the National Convention from the fall of 1792 until late May 1793, when twenty-nine Girondin deputies were proscribed from that body.

The Girondins first emerged as a recognizable group in the Legislative Assembly, which sat from late 1791 until September 1792, and were known then as Brissotins, due to the prominent leadership role played by Jacques-Pierre Brissot de Warville (1754–1793). The group included the deputies Jean-François Ducos (1765–1793), Pierre-Victurnien Vergniaud (1753–1793), Armand Gensonné (1758–1793), and Marguerite-Elie Guadet (1758–1794), all of whom came from Bordeaux in the department of the Gironde, which gave the faction its later name. Outside of the Legislative Assembly, the Brissotins enjoyed the support of such prominent figures as Marie-Jean Caritat, marquis de Condorcet (1743–1794), Nicolas de Bonneville (1760–1828), Claude Fauchet (1744–1793), Jean-Marie Roland de la Platière (1734–1793) and his wife, Manon Roland (1754–1793), whose home functioned as a kind of salon for the Girondins under the National Convention.

Virtually all of the Brissotins were reelected to the National Convention, where they were joined by Condorcet, Fauchet, Charles-Jean-Marie Barbaroux (1767–1794), Jean-Baptiste Louvet de Couvray (1760–1797), Jérome Pétion de Villeneuve (1756–1794), and Antoine-Joseph Gorsas (1752–1793). The deputies from the Gironde, all eloquent orators, quickly emerged as the leaders of the group. The first critical issue to confront them was the September Massacres of 1792, a wave of killings that claimed the lives of more than one thousand alleged counterrevolutionaries in the prisons of Paris. Although initially silent, the Girondin leaders eventually condemned the leaders of the Montagnards—most notably Maximilien Robespierre (1758–1794), Georges-Jacques Danton (1759–1794), and Jean-Paul Marat (1743–1793)—as the instigators of the killings, demanding that they and others be brought to justice. Radicals in Paris soon branded this campaign as anti-Parisian hostility.

It was the trial of Louis XVI (1754–1793), deposed from his throne in the uprising of 10 August 1792, that crystallized opposition between Girondins and Montagnards. While leading Girondins had supported the end of the monarchy, they were reluctant to see the king executed. They favored the *appel au peuple,* a sort of national referendum, denounced by the Montagnards as an effort to deny the will of the people, which in their view had already been expressed in the streets of Paris. Girondins dominated the constitutional committee, chaired by Condorcet, but could not muster the necessary votes to secure passage of a new constitution. They also favored free trade, but failed in their efforts to prevent adoption of price controls, known as the grain maximum. The Girondins favored the declaration of war in 1792, but setbacks in that war not only led to the downfall of the king but also would eventually harm the political fortunes of the Girondins, most notably when General Charles-François du Perier Dumouriez (1739–1823), who had personal ties to several of the deputies, defected to the Austrians in April 1793.

Other events contributed to the growing tensions between Girondins and Montagnards in the National Convention in the winter and spring of 1793. Girondin deputies complained frequently that their lives were endangered by threats from anarchists and assassins in Paris, and those fears seemed substantiated in March by the pillaging of Gorsas's printing press. In April the Girondins filed impeachment charges against Marat, who regularly defended popular violence in the pages of his newspaper and called for the dismissal of all deputies who had voted for the *appel au peuple.* Marat was acquitted by a Parisian jury, however, which elevated his reputation and increased the hostility of Parisian radicals toward the Girondins. Girondin deputies responded by convening a Commission of Twelve to investigate allegations that the section assemblies of Paris were plotting an insurrection against the National Convention. That initiative also backfired. The arrests of Jacques-René Hébert (1757–1794) and Jean Varlet (1764–1832) incited Paris militants rather than cowing them, and the insurrection that the Girondins feared began on 31 May 1793.

The insurrection of 31 May, although it threatened violence, was remarkably peaceful, but three days of confrontation and demonstrations did result in the proscription of twenty-nine Girondin deputies from the National Convention. A number of the proscribed deputies fled Paris for Caen, where they tried to rally their provincial supporters

against the Montagnards. Those who remained in Paris were placed under house arrest and were brought to trial in October, after the federalist revolt had been suppressed. They died on the guillotine on 31 October 1793. Others, including Barbaroux, Pétion, and Guadet, were eventually tracked down in the provinces and either committed suicide or were executed. Among the leading Girondins, only Louvet survived the Terror and after 9 Thermidor Year II (27 July 1794) resumed his place in the National Convention, as did most of the seventy-six deputies who had been expelled from the Convention for having protested the proscription of their leaders. While the Revolution now embraced the moderate republicanism that the Girondins had championed, the Girondin deputies themselves cannot be said to have reasserted themselves as a group after Thermidor.

See also **Federalist Revolt; French Revolution; Jacobins; Robespierre, Maximilien.**

BIBLIOGRAPHY

Jordan, David P. *The King's Trial: Louis XVI vs. the French Revolution.* Berkeley, Calif., 1979.

Patrick, Alison. *The Men of the First French Republic: Political Alignments in the National Convention of 1792.* Baltimore, Md., 1972.

Slavin, Morris. *The Making of an Insurrection: Parisian Sections and the Gironde.* Cambridge, Mass., 1986.

Sydenham, Michael J. *The Girondins.* London, 1961.

PAUL R. HANSON

GISSING, GEORGE (1857–1903), British novelist and man of letters.

George Robert Gissing was born in Wakefield, Yorkshire, in 1857. A brilliant classics student, he seemed destined for an academic career but his prospects were ruined when, at the age of eighteen, he was imprisoned for stealing money to support a young prostitute whom he later married.

After a brief exile in America, Gissing returned to London in 1877 and scraped a living as a tutor while completing his first novel, *Workers in the Dawn* (1880), an ambitious "socialistic" novel that drew little attention. Undeterred, he produced in rapid succession several more novels set in the poorest levels of late-Victorian London life. Gissing's stance toward the slums—a strange mixture of loathing and compassion—was molded by his experiences as an educated, cultured man forced to cohabit entirely with those he viewed as irremediably ignorant and vulgar. His *Demos* (1886) investigates and condemns the horrors of rampant industrialism, but also descants on the futility of most philanthropic endeavor. For Gissing, democracy meant, in effect, mob rule and, worse, the end of all art, which flourishes in the soil of inequality. Other of his slum fictions, *Thyrza* (1887) and *The Nether World* (1889), offer a rather more balanced and sympathetic, but no less grim, picture.

In his short career Gissing wrote twenty-two novels, many short stories, a travel book, and some criticism. Turning aside from the slums as his prospects improved, the novels of his middle period deal with the lower levels of middle-class life and social problems of the day, or at least those where issues of class, money, and sexuality are uppermost. *The Emancipated* (1890) denounces Puritanism from the perspective of a self-assured, independent, misanthropic artist—a recurring fantasy self-image of the author's. *In the Year of Jubilee* (1894) is a panoramic novel that attacks conventional marriage and the vulgar pretensions of those he called "the vile lower middle class." As Gissing told Morley Roberts in a letter, "my books deal with people of many social strata . . . [but] the most characteristic, the most important, part of my work is that which deals with a class of young men distinctive of our time—well-educated, fairly bred, but *without money*" (italics added). Godwin Peake, hero of *Born in Exile* (1892), is characteristic of this type: he is an intelligent, poor man who tries to penetrate the life of an upper-class cultured family by simulating religious views that he really despises. After the publication of *The Whirlpool* (1897), a wide-ranging study of corruption among the artistic moneyed classes, Gissing's creative energy flagged somewhat. The most distinctive product of his last phase was *The Private Papers of Henry Ryecroft* (1902), the curious part-fictional, part-autobiographical memoir of a retired writer.

At the turn of the century Gissing's precarious health deteriorated quickly, and in 1903 he died of emphysema in France, where he had gone to live with a third partner. His private life had been miserable. He had contracted two wretched marriages: one wife was an alcoholic, the other mentally unstable. His impracticality and unwillingness to compromise with the literary marketplace kept him fairly poor, even though some of his books sold quite well. He refused, for example, to serialize much of his work, or to engage in journalism, and he sold most of his manuscripts for cash down. His sensitivity about having an unavowable guilty secret kept him aloof and limited his friendships. Yet misery seemed to feed rather than to inhibit his genius.

At the turn of the twenty-first century, Gissing was firmly placed as one of the best late Victorian authors of the second rank. Some readers are repelled by his gloom, cultural conservatism, and extended passages of psychological analysis; but many more find his saturnine sense of humor, his lively dialogue, and his distinctively confiding, melancholy, occasionally exalted style challenging and insightful. His novels are not technically ambitious. All of them lie within the scope of the naturalistic and documentary tradition, and he has more in common with European masters such as Émile Zola (1840–1902) and Ivan Turgenev (1818–1883) than with most of his English contemporaries. He is remembered best for his masterpiece *New Grub Street* (1891), which deals with struggling authors and their creative, financial, and marital difficulties. Also highly regarded is *The Odd Women* (1893), one of the best novels of emergent feminism, which deals from several different angles, not all of them equally sympathetic, with the plight—economic and marital—of the genteel, well-educated, single woman. Most agree that Gissing's work offers a most accessible pathway into urban alienation and rootlessness, as Victorian certainties started to disintegrate under the impact of modernism.

See also **Modernism; Realism and Naturalism; Turgenev, Ivan; Zola, Émile.**

BIBLIOGRAPHY

Primary Sources

Gissing, George. *The Collected Letters of George Gissing.* Edited by Paul Mattheisen, Arthur C. Young, and Pierre Coustillas. 9 vols. Athens, Ohio, 1990–1997.

This superbly edited collection has reshaped current understanding of Gissing's career, and the long biographical essays preceding each volume are masterly.

———. *The Nether World.* Edited by Stephen Gill. Oxford, U.K., 1992.

———. *New Grub Street.* Edited by John Goode. Oxford, U.K., 1993.

———. *The Whirlpool.* Edited by William Greenslade. London, 1997.

———. *The Odd Women.* Edited by Patricia Ingham. Oxford, U.K., 2000.

Secondary Sources

Halperin, John. *Gissing: A Life in Books.* Oxford, U.K., 1982.

Tindall, Gillian. *The Born Exile: George Gissing.* London, 1974.

PETER MORTON

GLADSTONE, WILLIAM (1809–1898), British politician.

Born in Liverpool on 29 December 1809, William Ewart Gladstone was one of the most influential statesmen and political leaders in nineteenth-century Britain. A member of Parliament (MP) for sixty-two years (1832–1895), he served as a cabinet minister many times after 1841, and as prime minister four times (1868–1874, 1880–1885, 1886, and 1892–1894). Often regarded as a quintessential Victorian, in many ways his influence set standards for later generations of politicians, including both Margaret Thatcher and Tony Blair.

RELIGION AND POLITICS

Gladstone hailed from a family of wealthy Liverpool merchants of Scottish origin. His father, Sir John (1764–1851), was originally a Presbyterian, but his mother, Anne Mackenzie Robertson (1772–1835) belonged to the Scottish Episcopalian tradition. It was in an Anglican evangelical environment that William had his first and most influential religious experiences, most revealingly expressed in the diaries, which he kept on a daily basis from 1825 to 1896. "'Truth, justice, order, peace, honour, duty, liberty, piety,' these are the objects before me in my daily prayers with reference to my public function, which for the present commands (& I fear damages) every other: but this is the best part of me. All the rest is summed up in 'miserere.'" This was Gladstone's self-perception in 1872 on approaching the zenith of his career. His intense religiosity was frequently satirized by both hostile contemporaries (quick to denounce inconsistencies in his behavior as evidence of hypocrisy), and twentieth-century historians, who operated in a much more skeptical and secular environment and had no time for piety in politics. Historians at the turn of the twenty-first century tend to take a more sympathetic view. However, there is no question that he fell short of his own (incredibly demanding) moral and political standards. Furthermore, his religious views changed over the years. During his student days at Eton and Oxford, he abandoned evangelicalism for the high church, with its tractarian emphasis on the sacraments and the apostolic succession. Later, although he remained firmly committed to the Anglican orthodoxy, he adopted many of the attitudes associated with the more liberal broad church and, for example, saw no contradiction between creation and evolution.

In politics his views changed even more radically: he started as a reactionary Tory and ended his career as the idol of left-wing Liberals and Irish nationalists. By contrast, in the field of economics and public finance, Gladstone remained a lifelong devotee of the government tradition established by Sir Robert Peel (1788–1850), who presided over a largely successful but very divisive Conservative government in 1841–1846. Peel and his foreign secretary, Lord Aberdeen (George Hamilton-Gordon; 1784–1860), were Gladstone's mentors at a crucial stage of his career. It was Peel who directed Gladstone's attention and energies away from the explosive Irish question, to which he would have wished to devote himself, to the apparently dry and technical demands of the board of trade. It was an inspired choice. The academically distinguished young minister (he shared with Peel the unusual distinction of having achieved a "double" first at Oxford, in both mathematics and classics) relished the challenge and soon mastered the intricacies of British commercial legislation better than most contemporaries.

Like Peel, Gladstone became a convert to free trade and the repeal of the Corn Laws, which protected British farming from international competition and which the bulk of the Conservative Party regarded as an article of political faith. When Peel pushed repeal through Parliament (with the help of the opposition), the party split and Gladstone followed his mentor into the wilderness. However, in 1853, after a memorable parliamentary duel with Benjamin Disraeli (1804–1881) over the latter's proposed budget (which was defeated), Gladstone accepted to serve as chancellor of the Exchequer in a free-trade coalition government led by Lord Aberdeen. His achievements at the treasury created what historians regard as the "social contract" of mid-Victorian Britain. Balancing direct with indi-rect taxation (each targeting different social classes, so that all would contribute and none would feel unfairly exploited), Gladstone reduced duties on hundreds of items of mass consumption, thus stimulating output, domestic demand, foreign trade, and employment. The systematic reduction of state expenditure (retrenchment) enabled him to cut taxation, again a policy that appealed to all classes, especially in view of the fact that central government expenditure was dominated by the servicing of the national debt and the armed forces (social expenditure was funded through local rates raised by municipal authorities and the Poor Law boards). The fortunate coincidence between his tenure at the treasury and the economic boom of 1850 to 1873 further strengthened Gladstone's reputation.

Free trade had caused Gladstone's first clash with contemporary mainstream conservatism, but the final break came over foreign policy in the 1850s. A classicist, Gladstone had always loved Italy, spending holidays in Rome and Naples whenever possible. It was in Naples in 1853 that he first became interested in the plight of Italian patriots, many of whom had been imprisoned after the failed liberal revolution of 1848. While the Conservative Party was not prepared to criticize the Italian status quo, the Liberal leader Lord Palmerston (Henry John Temple; 1784–1865) welcomed Gladstone's pleas for reforms on the peninsula. In 1859 Gladstone finally accepted that his views on both free trade and Italy precluded any reconciliation with his old party. As chancellor of the Exchequer in the last Palmerston government (1859–1865), Gladstone came to support electoral reform in 1864, when he realized that the artisans

were enthusiastic about his cherished policies of free trade and "retrenchment." After Palmerston's death, Gladstone served in the short-lived reform ministry (1865–1866) of Lord Russell (John Russell; 1792–1878) before becoming party leader and eventually prime minister in 1868.

GLADSTONE'S GOVERNMENTS

By then the electoral franchise had been greatly extended by Disraeli and Lord Derby (Edward George Geoffrey Smith Stanley; 1799–1869), who presided over a minority Tory government in 1866–1868. However, Gladstone was able to secure the immediate electoral benefits of the second reform act when the Liberals achieved a large majority at the general election of 1868. His first government (1868–1874) had a mandate for further radical changes. These included the local franchise for women (1869), the separation between church and state in Ireland (1869), followed by land reform (1870), the creation of a public system of primary schools in Britain (1870), the reform of trade union laws (1871), and the introduction of the secret ballot for elections (1872). Eventually the government was defeated on Gladstone's proposal to reform Irish university education in 1873, and the Liberals lost the ensuing general election (1874), when the prime minister proposed to abolish the income tax in a further campaign to cut central government expenditure. In 1875 Gladstone resigned the party leadership and considered complete retirement from public life.

However, he was catapulted back into the limelight by the popular response to the so-called Bulgarian Atrocities (1876). Press reports of large-scale "ethnic cleansing" in Bulgaria (where Ottoman forces massacred some twelve thousand Orthodox Christians in the attempt to repress a nationalist insurrection) generated a wave of protest, which Gladstone exploited to embarrass the Conservative government. However, the latter stuck to their pro-Ottoman policy to the extent of threatening war against Russia, who had intervened on behalf of Bulgarian nationalism. Although Disraeli (from 1876 Lord Beaconsfield) managed to avoid war in Europe, he allowed his colonial proconsuls to start ill-starred and expensive wars in Afghanistan and South Africa. In 1879

Gladstone Addresses the House of Commons upon the Irish Land, 1881. Undated engraving. ©HULTON-DEUTSCH COLLECTION/CORBIS

and 1880 Gladstone attacked the foreign and financial policy of the government in the first of his "Midlothian campaigns." Ostensibly electoral campaigns to wrestle the parliamentary seat of Midlothian (Scotland) from the Tories, the campaign became highly publicized, national whistle-stop speaking tours that introduced Britain to electoral techniques hitherto associated with U.S. presidential primaries. The Liberals achieved a large majority at the 1880 election and Queen Victoria (who disliked Gladstone's political preaching and feared his radicalism) had no alternative but to appoint him as her prime minister.

Gladstone's second government was plagued by continuous external emergencies, especially in Egypt (which Gladstone invaded in 1882 in flagrant violation of his previous advocacy of a peaceful and multilateral foreign policy) and in Ireland (where he tried to repress rural unrest). The two crises haunted his ministry and eventually brought about its downfall in 1885. Meanwhile, however, he implemented an impressive series of reforms that targeted Irish land tenure (1881–1883) and elec-

toral corruption (1883) and that introduced a more democratic parliamentary franchise and a more equitable distribution of seats (1884 and 1885).

In 1886 Gladstone's adoption of Home Rule (parliamentary self-government) for Ireland opened a new phase in British politics, but split the Liberal Party, a section of which crossed the floor to support a Conservative administration and preserve the Union. During the following six years Gladstone campaigned vigorously for Home Rule. His efforts might have resulted in a substantial Liberal majority at the ensuing election, had it not been for the 1890 divorce scandal that destroyed the career of Charles Stewart Parnell (1846–1891), the leader of the Irish National Party, and undermined the credibility of the Liberal-Nationalist alliance. Nevertheless Gladstone managed to win the 1892 election, but his comparatively small majority was not enough to force the recalcitrant and overwhelmingly Unionist House of Lords to accept the Second Home Rule Bill (1893).

In 1894 Gladstone resigned and retired from politics. Yet, his ideas remained very influential in the party, which eventually was brought back to office in 1906, under Sir Henry Campbell-Bannerman (1836–1908), on a largely Gladstonian program. He spent his last years at Hawarden Castle, the country house in Wales that he had acquired through his wife, Catherine Glynne (1812–1900), whom he had married in 1839. They formed a happy and mutually supportive couple for nearly sixty years. Gladstone died at Hawarden on 19 May 1898.

See also **Disraeli, Benjamin; Great Britain; Liberalism; Victoria, Queen.**

BIBLIOGRAPHY

Bebbington, David William. *The Mind of Gladstone: Religion, Homer, and Politics.* Oxford, U.K., and New York, 2004.

Biagini, Eugenio F. *Liberty, Retrenchment, and Reform: Popular Liberalism in the Age of Gladstone, 1860–1880.* Cambridge, U.K., and New York, 1992 and 2004.

Boyce, D. George. "In the Front Rank of the Nation: Gladstone and the Unionists of Ireland, 1868–1893." In *Gladstone Centenary Essays,* edited by David Bebbington and Roger Swift, 184–201. Liverpool, 2000.

Hammond, John Lawrence. J. *Gladstone and the Irish Nation.* New York, 1938.

Matthew, Henry Colin Gray. *Gladstone 1809–1898.* 2 vols. Oxford, U.K., and New York, 1997.

O'Day, Alan. "Gladstone and Irish Nationalism: Achievement and Reputation." In *Gladstone Centenary Essays,* edited by David Bebbington and Roger Swift, 163–183. Liverpool, 2000.

Parry, Jonathan Philip. *Democracy and Religion: Gladstone and the Liberal Party, 1867–1875.* Cambridge, U.K., and New York, 1986.

Vincent, John. "Gladstone and Ireland." *Proceedings of the British Academy* (1977): 193–238.

EUGENIO F. BIAGINI

GLINKA, MIKHAIL (1804–1857), the first of the Russian national composers.

One characteristic of nineteenth century European music was the formation of national schools that combined the ideas of the "great" music nations (Italy, France, and Germany had been style setters since the eighteenth century) with typical national elements. In this context, Mikhail Glinka is regarded as the father of Russian music. His two main works, the operas *A Life for the Tsar* and *Ruslan and Lyudmila,* marked the beginning of a genuinely Russian music culture that after Glinka's death was to become highly significant in Europe.

Glinka was born in Novospasskoye (now Glinka) in 1804 as a son of a landowner. Church services, the folk songs of his nanny, and his uncle's orchestra of serfs provided the young Glinka with his first musical experiences. Soon he began taking piano and violin lessons, which he continued after moving to St. Petersburg in 1817. Having concluded his general education at a boarding school for noble students, he worked as a civil servant in the Russian capital to support his material existence. The real interest of the musically gifted Glinka, however, was the salons of the intellectuals, where he became acquainted with poets such as Alexander Pushkin, Vasily Zhukovsky, and Alexander Griboyedov, among others. Decisive for his creative career was a stay of several years in Germany and Italy, where he intensively absorbed European music life and personally came to know the composers Vincenzo Bellini, Gaetano Donizetti, Felix Mendelssohn-Bartholdy, and Hector Berlioz. In 1833, Glinka, whose musical training until then had not progressed beyond refined dilettantism, studied compositional theory in Berlin with Siegfried Dehn, an authority in this field.

Back in St. Petersburg in the following year, Glinka, who had previously tried his hand at only minor pieces, began to work on an opera about the Russian folk hero Ivan Susanin. The first performance of the opera, dedicated to Tsar Nicholas I with the title *A Life for the Tsar,* on 27 November 1836 was a sensational success. The story of a Russian peasant who in the "time of troubles" at the beginning of the seventeenth century sacrificed his life for the Russian tsar and so contributed to the defeat of the Polish occupiers met the ideological demands of Nicholas I's era, which was characterized by the patriotic trinity of "autocracy, orthodoxy, and nationality." In spite of a certain stylistic conservatism that could not deny the western European influence, the importance of the work as a genuine Russian opera in the context of an Italian-dominated music theater was immediately recognized by his contemporaries. The achievement of Glinka, who had received only semi-professional training at best, was remarkable.

Less successful, although perhaps even more creative, was Glinka's second opera, *Ruslan and Lyudmila* (based on Pushkin's poem), first performed in 1842. The unbalance and lack of dramaturgical stringency of the libretto, which was taken from a Russian fairy tale, were regarded as problematic. Nevertheless, *Ruslan and Lyudmila* was to become the second foundation of Russian classical music. Whereas *A Life for the Tsar* began the tradition of Russian historical opera, *Ruslan and Lyudmila* established the genre of the Russian fairy-tale opera, and introduced orientalism into Russian music. But the lukewarm reception of his second opera and the unbroken enthusiasm of Russians for Italian music theater embittered Glinka deeply. He sought refuge in extensive travels abroad, composed some smaller orchestral works (among others, the fantasy *Kamarinskaya* and the two *Spanish Overtures*), and renewed his studies with Dehn. Glinka's desire to dedicate himself to church music was left unfulfilled: the musician, who was in poor health throughout his life, died prematurely in Berlin in 1857.

Glinka soon became known as a spiritual father to all of his "successors"—the nationally oriented circle of Mily Balakirev, Modest Mussorgsky, and Nikolai Rimsky-Korsakov, as well as Peter Tchaikovsky, who had the reputation of being a musical westerner. Although Glinka also composed smaller orchestral works, chamber and piano music, and numerous songs, it was his two operas that were decisive for the development of Russian music culture.

With the genres of the historical and fairy-tale opera, Glinka established a framework for a series of master works of Russian music theater. His combination of basic components of European music culture with a specific Russian melos, drawing on folk motives and oriental influences referring to the Asian and Caucasian aspects of the Russian Empire, became a model for future generations of composers. In western Europe especially, open-minded progressionists such as Franz Liszt and Berlioz recognized Glinka's importance as a pioneer of Russian musical expression. After the fall of the tsarist reign, Glinka's influence lasted in the Soviet Union. Soviet patriotic culture, based on Russian nationalism and Soviet discourse, turned the composer into a national hero. *A Life for the Tsar* was renamed *Ivan Susanin*—the title originally conceived by the composer—and Glinka's works maintained their canonical validity as the first milestones of Russian classical music.

See also **Mussorgsky, Modest; Nicholas I; Rimsky-Korsakov, Nikolai; Westernizers.**

BIBLIOGRAPHY

Brown, David. *Mikhail Glinka: A Biographical and Critical Study.* London, 1974.

Glinka, Mikhail Ivanovich. *Memoirs.* Translated by Richard B. Mudge. Westport, Conn., 1963. Translation of *Zapiski* (1854–1855).

Taruskin, Richard. *Defining Russia Musically: Historical and Hermeneutical Essays.* Princeton, N.J., 1997.

MATTHIAS STADELMANN

GODWIN, WILLIAM (1756–1836), British writer and philosopher.

A major philosopher, powerful novelist, and innovative historian, William Godwin was born to a Calvinist family in Cambridgeshire. His thorough education was completed by five years at Hoxton College with intensive studies in Latin, Greek, Hebrew, mathematics, natural sciences, divinity, philosophy, rhetoric, French, German, and Italian. A passionate reading of the French philosophes led him to reject the ministry for the intellectually exciting London of the 1780s.

He became a professional writer, publishing sermons, biographies, novels—whatever his teeming brain furnished. By the late 1780s he attained distinction as writer on current events. In the revolutionary 1790s, Godwin exploded into prominence with his *Enquiry Concerning Political Justice* (1793), a work of political and social philosophy advocating an egalitarian society of responsible individuals. Incited by Edmund Burke's *Reflections on the Revolution in France* (1790), Godwin assessed Burke's political structures for their success at serving basic human nature and exposed monarchy, aristocracy, and the church as institutions for perpetuating property inequalities and limiting free enquiry. *Political Justice* advocates and exemplifies the courage to challenge the establishment.

Godwin followed *Political Justice* with his most influential novel, *Things As They Are; or the Adventures of Caleb Williams* (1794). *Caleb Williams* is at once a detective, psychological, political, and Gothic novel. This diversity is unified by a coherent philosophy that dramatizes the nature and power of ideology and the workings of domestic tyranny.

Other works of the 1790s express vigorous resistance to Britain's decline into intolerance and repression in response to the French Revolution. When the attorney general indicted the executive officers of two reform societies, Godwin's "Cursory Strictures on the Charge Delivered by Lord Chief Justice Eyre to the Grand Jury" (October 1794) demonstrated the indictment's distortion of existing statutes on treason. Its arguments, adopted by the defense, saved those officers' lives. In 1795 the government of William Pitt (called Pitt the Younger, 1759–1806) introduced two bills to curb protest and dissent. Godwin responded with *Considerations on Lord Grenville's and Mr Pitt's Bills Concerning Treasonable and Seditious Practices, and Unlawful Assemblies*, arguing that both bills exceed precedents: Grenville's bill, an "atrocious" extension of the definition of treason; Pitt's, functioning to license and silence meetings, Godwin called "despotic" and "disgraceful." The bills passed and restricted traditional liberties of speech, assembly, and the press.

In this atmosphere of fear and reprisal, Godwin continued principled writing. In 1797 his *The Enquirer* raised hackles with a censure of Christianity for promoting bigotry. In 1798 he published a tender memorial to his wife who died in childbirth, *Memoirs of Mary Wollstonecraft*. His next work, the Gothic novel, *St. Leon* (1799), examines the alienating effects of limitless wealth and eternal youth.

Godwin's next work is a bitter reflection of the times and his role in them. In *Thoughts occasioned by the perusal of Dr. Parr's Spital Sermon . . . being a reply to Dr. Parr, Mr. Mackintosh, the Author of an Essay on Population, and others* (1800), Godwin responds to two erstwhile friends, James Mackintosh (1765–1832) and Samuel Parr (1747–1825), who turned on Godwin for not repudiating his radicalism. He also answers *An Essay on the Principle of Population* by Thomas Robert Malthus (1766–1834), which rejects Godwin's social vision of justice and benevolence as a beautiful fiction but contrary to the "fixed . . . laws of human nature" and offers a mathematical demonstration that population growth must inevitably outstrip food supply and produce chaos. Eventually "rapine and murder must reign at large. . . ." Godwin replied that the earth's productive capacities are far from fully employed and rational people will practice restraint and limit their offspring to what the land can support. Malthus's fearful and divisive vision harmonized with the fraught atmosphere of 1800.

With his second wife, Mary Jane Clairmont, Godwin published *The Juvenile Library*, books for children, small books for little hands, written with clarity and simplicity. For adult readers, his *Life of Chaucer* (2 vols., 1803) offers a full account of the manners, habits, and influences of Chaucer's age. *Fleetwood* (1805) is perhaps the first fictional scrutiny of domestic unhappiness. *The Lives of Edward and John Philips* (1815) examines the period following the death of Oliver Cromwell (1599–1658) as a calamity from which the nation never recovered its "independence, strong thinking, and generosity." *Mandeville* (1817), a breathtakingly original study of paranoia, is told by a Protestant bigot and captures the manic side of contemporary evangelicalism. *Letter of Advice to a Young American* (1818) advocates the development of the imagination through reading. Reviewers, by necessity friendly to a coercive government, generally sought reasons to attack his writings.

Meanwhile, Malthus's *Essay on the Principle of Population* grew in influence through multiple editions. Measures to assist the poor were opposed for encouraging population growth. Appalled, Godwin published *Of Population* (1820), a withering attack on the logic, data, and assumptions behind Malthus's arguments. With the weight of the establishment behind them, Malthus's arguments continued to be heard while Godwin's sunk into obscurity.

Godwin's four-volume *History of the Commonwealth of England* (1824–1828) fulfilled a long-held ambition to write a comprehensive history of the period of the English Civil War and the Commonwealth. His account of civil war, rule by Parliament, execution of Charles I (r. 1625–1649), and reign of Cromwell conveys a perspective sympathetic to the proud, pious, and principled Commonwealthmen who accomplished a successful revolution.

Godwin, at seventy-four, published *Cloudesley* (1830), a complex study of character and feeling. In 1831 came *Thoughts on Man*, essays on free will, necessity, and human perfectibility, arguing for education that rejects mimicry and embraces an intellectual independence. *Deloraine* (1833), Godwin's last novel, a story of passion, murder, and flight, celebrates love between a father and daughter that honors Godwin's feelings for his own daughter, the widowed Mary Shelley (1797–1851). His last work, *Lives of the Necromancers* (1834), draws from a lifetime of learning to list occult events.

Godwin's lifelong campaign alerted individuals to conditionings that impair their development as free and perceptive citizens. He represents a rare example of a creative writer whose thinking has the rigor of a philosopher and a philosophical writer with a creative imagination and a feeling for language. His life is an extended story of resilience and tenacity in a society unfairly prejudiced against him, a society often terrified by his ideas. He died in 1836.

See also **Shelley, Mary; Wollstonecraft, Mary.**

BIBLIOGRAPHY

Primary Sources

Godwin, William. *Collected Novels and Memoirs of William Godwin.* 8 vols. Edited by Mark Philp. London, 1992.

———. *Political and Philosophical Writings of William Godwin.* 7 vols. Edited by Mark Philp. London, 1993.

Secondary Sources

Marshall, Peter H. *William Godwin.* New Haven, Conn., 1984. Contains rich accounts of Godwin's philosophical writings.

St. Clair, William. *The Godwins and the Shelleys.* London, 1989. Best biography of Godwin.

KENNETH W. GRAHAM

GOETHE, JOHANN WOLFGANG VON

(1749–1832), German poet, novelist, dramatist, natural scientist, and philosopher.

Johann Wolfgang von Goethe is perhaps the last universal genius known to the West. He is best known as the writer of *Faust: A Tragedy*, one of the greatest contributions to the Western canon of epic poetry, and as the perfecter, if not originator, of the genre of the bildungsroman (the novel of education).

YOUTH AND EARLY LITERARY FAME

Goethe was born in Frankfurt am Main on 28 August 1749, the son of Johann Kaspar Goethe (1710–1782), who, though trained as a lawyer, was frustrated in his hopes of entering the civil administration of his native Frankfurt. As a result, he lived a life of quiet retirement, dedicating himself to the education of his children. Goethe's mother, Katharina Elisabeth Textor (1731–1808), was the daughter of a former mayor of Frankfurt.

In his autobiography *Dichtung und Wahrheit* (Poetry and truth), Goethe writes of these early years as well as his formation as a poet until the time of his leaving for Weimar in November 1775. Even in the early twenty-first century this autobiography remains the highest example of the genre. Within it, Goethe interweaves an account of growing up in his parental home with the expanding mental horizon of the child, boy, and youth as he comes to know the complex social structure of the imperial city of Frankfurt with its rich medieval and imperial, Christian and Jewish traditions.

Although early signs of literary ability emerged in his youth, these talents fully emerged only during Goethe's student years at the University of Leipzig. Conforming to his father's wishes, he followed in his father's footsteps to Leipzig in order to prepare for a career in the law and public administration. Under the influence of the older, genial, yet often acerbic Ernst Wolfgang Behrisch, the young student began to write light, Anacreontic (convivial) lyrics, which meshed with the rococo tastes of the "Little Paris" of eighteenth-century Leipzig. Always living at full tilt, he eventually succumbed to a series of physical and mental illnesses. Goethe returned to his familial home in Frankfurt, considering himself a failure both as a student and a poet. This was a period of deep introspection, marked by a turn to the study of alchemy and astrology—esoteric sciences that later served him well in the composition of *Faust*.

Upon recovery, Goethe resolved to continue his law studies at the University of Strasbourg. From his first entry into the Alsatian capital to his love affair with Friederike Brion, he underwent a series of life-changing experiences. Goethe's description of this phase of his life in *Dichtung und Wahrheit*—what he called the "Sesenheim Idyll," named after Brion's hometown—represents the complex lyrical narrative structure that characterized his novelistic and historical writings. Organized around the image of the uncompleted towers of the Strasbourg Minster (cathedral), the Sesenheim Idyll depicts a world of an older and more integrated German culture. As Goethe came to see in his mind's eye the original design of the cathedral so he comes to see the inner organization and even the ideal structure of this culture. Both viewing the architectural whole of the Gothic cathedral and seeing a totality of this culture are the result of *Anschauung*. This central Goethean concept consists of training the eye to see the interrelation of parts to whole and whole to parts through a repeated process of intense viewing. *Anschauung* also provided the bridge from Goethe's literary works to his scientific research of nature.

Anschauung formed the core of another central Goethean concept, *Bildung*. As education in the broad sense, of self-formation based on the development of the individual's unique characteristics, *Bildung* is an education in seeing. The individual comes to see the interconnected wholes both in and between nature and culture as she comes to see the observer in relationship to what is observed. In the early 1770s, the young Goethe incorporated these insights into a larger philosophy, which with only slight alterations he continued to believe in for the rest of his life. From the Dutch philosopher Baruch Spinoza (1632–1677) Goethe learned to look upon nature as the "living garment of God," and from the German philosopher Johann Georg Hamann (1730–1788) he came to understand that the world consists of individualities, one-of-a-kind entities. Applied to human life, individuality becomes a guiding value and revealed a new human type for Goethe. From it he derived the value that it is incumbent upon each individual to realize as far as possible what makes him or her unique.

This growing sense of himself as a participant within a common culture was heightened and further developed through Goethe's contact with the philosopher Johann Gottfried von Herder (1744–1803). Herder showed Goethe the beautiful simplicity of nature, the power of the early German *Volksliede* (folk songs), and the profundities of Shakespearean drama. Under his tutelage, the young Goethe came to see how a culture formed not just an inner totality but also a specific way of viewing and experiencing the world. He awakened in him an appreciation of German culture, which appeared to be so provincial and thus quaint in comparison to the dominant neoclassical taste and universalizing reason of the Enlightenment. Under Herder's influence Goethe also pursued the study of "German" architecture and came to see in the Strasbourg Minster a new aesthetic principle. With Herder's help he published the groundbreaking essay "Von deutscher Baukunst" (1773; On German architecture), which contributed to the greater understanding of the principles of Gothic architecture. Furthermore, Goethe learned from Herder not just to appreciate the early German *Volksliede* but to imitate them. His ballads of these years along with the lyrics inspired by Brion—"Kleine Blumen, kleine Blätter" (Small flowers, small leaves) and "Wie herrlich leuchtet mir die Natur" (How marvelously does nature shine for me!)—brought about a new epoch of German poetry. To the Strasbourg years also belong his first important dramas, *Götz von Berlichingen* (1773) and *Clavigo* (1774).

In Wetzlar and then back in Frankfurt, Goethe became the center of a talented and eccentric group of young writers that became identified as the Sturm und Drang. Although not published until 1788, *Egmont* belongs to this highly creative period. Compared to his earlier efforts, this drama exhibits a marked maturation of his powers as a dramatic poet. Many of Goethe's projects of the mid-1770s, however, remained unfinished. The first version of *Faust* (discovered only in 1887) also belongs to this period. But it was the work that went against the dominant type of this literature that brought its twenty-five-year-old author European-wide fame. *Die Leiden des jungen Werthers* (The sorrows of young Werther) is an epistolary novel that is stylistically beautiful and engulfingly sentimental. Published in 1774, this novel derived its story line from Goethe's own experience in Wetzlar. His love affair with Charlotte Buff, the daughter of the town's *Amtmann* (senior civil servant), brought him to the brink of suicide when it abruptly ended.

Goethe in the Roman Campagna. Portrait by Johann Heinrich Tischbein the Elder, 1787. KAVALER/ART RESOURCE, NY

THE WEIMAR YEARS AND THE
ITALIAN JOURNEY

Upon receiving several invitations from its young duke, Goethe eventually decided to move to the Thuringian duchy of Saxe-Weimar-Eisenach in November 1775. Weimar would prove to be his home for the rest of his life. Assuming a position in the government, he interested himself in agriculture, horticulture, and mining, which were paramount to the economic and social welfare of the duchy. Goethe not only took these responsibilities seriously in an administrative sense, he also engaged in them with the eyes of a scientist. They in fact became the basis for his interest in the wide range of research into nature that was to occupy him for the rest of his life. The literary output of this period was limited in number but remark-able in quality. The lyrics "Wanders Nachtlieder" (Wanderer's night songs), "An den Mond" (To the moon), and "Gesang der Geister über den Wassern" (Singing of the spirits over the water) and the ballad "Der Erlkönig" (King of the elves) belong to this period, as does the original prose version (1779) of the drama *Iphigenie auf Tauris.* Goethe also wrote the first draft of his novel of theatrical life titled *Wilhelm Meisters theatralische Sendung* (1777; Wilhelm Meister's theatrical mission), which like *Iphigenie* would be reworked to its final form in Italy.

In September 1786 Goethe left Weimar for Italy, a journey he had planned at least since 1775 and in a certain way ever since as a child he viewed the "Piranesi-like prints" in his father's collection.

Italy proved more than he even dreamed of. Carefully recorded in the *Italienische Reise* (1816–1817; Italian journey), these experiences opened Goethe to a new aesthetic. No longer viewed against the neoclassicism from which he revolted in his youth and not even perceived in terms of the creativity of the Renaissance, the artworks of ancient Greece and Rome had an overwhelming and long-lasting impact upon him. Although the move to Weimar had weakened his ties to former friends and to the Sturm und Drang movement as a whole, the experience of Italy brought a complete break and a new understanding of and a creative dedication to the principles of classical art. The resulting German classicism was based not on the rigid laws of French neoclassicism but on a broader and more organic understanding of both nature and art. On a personal level, Italy represented a time of completion of a number of unfinished works and more importantly of new plans for the future.

This new understanding of classical principles resulted in a new iambic version of *Iphigenie auf Tauris* (1787); a new series of lyrics, the *Römische Elegien* (1795; Roman elegies) and the *Venezianische Epigramme* (Venetian epigrams; the product of a second visit to Italy in 1790); and a drama on the Renaissance revival of the classical ideal, *Torquato Tasso* (1790). Classicism also influenced Goethe's continuing work on *Faust,* which appeared as a *Fragment* in 1790, as well as the reformulation of the Wilhelm Meister story as a novel of education, *Wilhelm Meisters Lehrjahre* (1795–1796). This exemplary bildungsroman was no longer the account of a young dreamer, a purposeless youth overwhelmed by the demands of life in general and of art in particular. Rather, it is the story of the misadventures and wrong decisions of a talented but misdirected young man. Meister gradually comes to a new understanding of himself as he reflects on his past actions. Action and reflection in fact become the poles of the novel. The process of this education, however, does not just evolve through self-knowledge; for Meister comes to know himself only as he comes to know the culture in which he lives and through which he interacts. Goethe's concept of *Bildung* is thus an integrated process of knowing the world in the self and the self in the world. Stylistically, *Wilhelm Meisters Lehrjahre* marks Goethe's maturation as a novelist.

This style is capable of including direct forms of realistic description, highly figurative moments, rich in poetic episodes, and some of Goethe's best-known lyric poems. Goethe further extended these stylistic innovations in the sequel to the *Lehrjahre* titled *Wilhelm Meisters Wanderjahre* (1821–1829; Wilhelm Meister's journeyman years).

The return to Weimar witnessed a change in Goethe's life. No longer involved with the day-to-day administration of the duchy in any official way, he lived a life of genial retirement, away from the ducal court and its intrigues. He shared this life with his companion, Christiane Vulpius (1765–1816), who bore him a son, August, in 1789 and to whom he was finally married in 1806. The only public function he served in these years was as director of the ducal theater. Appointed in 1791, Goethe occupied this post for the next twenty-two years. This directorship also gave him the opportunity of staging the numerous plays he wrote during this period. These include the dramas *Der Gross-Cophta* (1792; The Great Cophta) and *Der Bürgergeneral* (1793; The citizen general) as well as a number of works of lesser quality.

The years of classicism for Goethe found their focus in his relationship with the Johann Christoph Friedrich von Schiller (1759–1805). Beginning in June 1794, this friendship led Goethe to take up again his interest in poetry and drama. A whole series of poetry belongs to this period: "Der Zauberlehrling" (The sorcerer's apprentice), "Der Gott und die Bayadere" (The God and the bayadere), "Alexis und Dora," and "Der neue Pausias" (The new pausias). Perhaps his most innovative poem, however, was the epic of middle-class life, *Hermann und Dorothea* (1798). Schiller also inspired Goethe to return to *Faust. Faust, Part One* appeared in 1808, while Goethe continued to work on what would become *Part Two* for the rest of his life. The literary journal *Athenäum,* which was founded in 1798 by August Wilhelm and Friedrich von Schlegel and became the organ of German Romanticism, praised *Faust: Part One* (as it had other works of Goethe) and declared it one of the greatest examples of Romantic literature. Though they thought of Goethe as their inspiration, the poets and critics of the early Romantic movement increasingly found themselves the target of Goethe's and Schiller's negative criticism.

GOETHE'S SCIENTIFIC STUDIES

These years also saw the first culmination of Goethe's studies of nature. Of all the changes in the evaluations of Goethe's contributions to diverse fields of endeavor, his studies of nature have been the subject of the most radical reinterpretation at the turn of the twenty-first century. These studies are no longer seen as merely unenlightened by the reigning mechanistic model of nature or simply as the extension of his literary interests. They are now understood as inaugurating a new and powerful understanding of nature and humankind's relationship to nature that are foundational for the study of the environment and of the phenomenological approach to nature in general.

Highly critical of the mechanistic model and mathematical abstractions that define modern science, Goethe invented his own "method" of research based on training in the observation of individual phenomena. His was an empirically based study that aimed not at abstract and causal models but at the development of *Anschauung* and the perception of repeated patterns, the typical, or what he called the *Urphänomene*. Understanding resulted not so much in an explanatory process as in a moment of seeing, an insight, an aperçu. In this way Goethe denied the rational view that came to dominance in the seventeenth and eighteenth centuries, which resulted in the exploitation of nature for human purposes. For him the human being is realizable only within a common nature, and human perception is itself a part of this nature. The moral (*sittlich*), therefore, did not mark a break from lawful nature but was a further intensification of it.

Goethe's first published scientific studies were in comparative osteology (the scientific study of bones). In fact these studies were only a part of a larger research project in comparative animal morphology; in many ways he created both this field and comparative plant morphology as well. In 1784 Goethe announced the discovery of the fusion of the intermaxillary bone in the upper jaw, supposed to be found only in apes, into the human jawbone. Goethe thus presented a persuasive argument for evolution; but, unlike Darwinian versions of this theory, he emphasized that the human being was an "intensified" (*gesteigert*) form of animal that at once marked a continuation of nature

and a spiritual break from nature. Goethe also studied plants through a similar comparative morphology. His botanical interests began before the trip to Italy but definitely flourished during his journey to southern Italy and Sicily. The vast variety of flora growing under diverse conditions stimulated in him the search for the unifying principle or archetype of all plants. In *Versuch, die Metamorphose der Pflanzen zu erklären* (1790; An attempt to explain the metamorphosis of plants), he demonstrated through a series of graduated leaf formations that the primal leaf formed the prototype of all the other organs of the plant.

Within his scientific writings, Goethe is perhaps best recognized for his study of color. Between 1791 and 1792, he published the two parts of his *Beiträge zur Optik* (Essays on optics), and in 1810 he produced his monumental *Farbenlehre* (Theory of color). Rather than impose a theoretical structure on experience, Goethe sought to allow light and darkness to phenomenalize themselves in such a way that all observers could see. In opposition to Isaac Newton's theory that all colors are part of pure light as is exemplified by refraction through a prism, Goethe understood color as a dialectic between light and darkness. Darkness is not a negative condition of light as Newton argued but rather produced in the eye an inclination to light. Conversely, light produced an inclination toward darkness. What the eye sees as color, therefore, is the result of a dialectical interrelationship of light and darkness. Against the experience of light, the eye compensates by producing darkness as the colors of blue, indigo, and violet. Against darkness, the eye sees the lighter colors of yellow, orange, and red. Goethe also expanded this phenomenological method into the fields of mineralogy, geology, and meteorology.

FINAL YEARS

What is generally considered to be the third and last phase of Goethe's literary career transcends the "romanticism" of his youth and the classicism of his middle years. In the last thirty years of his life Goethe came to an appreciation of the great diversity of individuals and the multiplicity of cultures within an image of cosmic harmony open to human comprehension through the "basic phenomena" of humankind and nature. This last period can be said to have begun with the death of Schiller (1805). In 1809 he published *Die Wahlverwandtschaften* (Elective affinities). Just as with the *Lehrjahre,* this psychological novel inspired other novelists throughout the nineteenth century. During the 1820s he worked on and published the sequel to the *Lehrjahre,* in which he addressed such contemporary social problems brought on by early industrialization. Goethe also expanded his notion of literature to what he termed "world literature" as the background against which all evaluations should be made. He found additional inspiration in non-German and even non-Western literary works. Suggested by a German edition of the works of the Persian poet Hafez, Goethe composed his last and most concise and most profound lyrics for the *West-östlicher Diwan* (1819; West-Eastern divan).

Goethe will perhaps always be remembered as the poet of *Faust.* This monumental epic is a compendium of human knowledge, a reconnection of modernity's relationship to the classical heritage, and a redefinition of the human. Yet following the decades he had devoted to its completion, Goethe, perhaps sensing the limitations of the epic form for comprehending modern life, turned to autobiographic writings in the final years of his life. In general Goethe considered the French Revolution of 1789 and the world it introduced across Europe as culturally cruder and less supportive of individual development than the one the revolution replaced. In addition to *Dichtung und Wahrheit,* the four parts of which appeared between 1811 and 1833 (the year after the poet's death), he edited the diary of his trip to Italy and published it as the *Italienische Reise;* published accounts of his experiences with Duke Charles Augustus in the wars against France, in *Campagne in Frankreich, 1792* (Campaign in France) and *Die Belagerung von Mainz, 1793* (The siege of Mainz), both issued in 1822; and wrote a collection of notes dealing with his life after 1775 (published as *Tag- und Jahreshefte* [1830; Day and year papers]). All of these works he considered parts of a single grand confession "from my life" (*Aus meinem Leben*), the title he gave to the collection of these diverse autobiographical writings.

To this list of autobiographical writings could be added the *Gespäche mit Eckermann in den Letzten Jahren seines Lebens* (*Conversations with Geothe in the Last Years of His Life*). These conversations with his secretary Johann Peter Eckermann ranged widely over such topics as German, French, Italian, and British literature, ancient and modern history, and contemporary political and social problems. In themselves, the *Conversations* exhibit the power and subtlety of Geothe's mind. Geothe died in Weimar on 22 March 1832.

See also **Germany.**

BIBLIOGRAPHY

Primary Sources

Goethe, Johann Wolfgang von. *Goethes Werke.* 14 vols. Edited by Lieselotte Blumenthal and Erich Trunz. Hamburg, Germany, 1949–1960. The standard German edition of Goethe's works.

———. *Goethe's Collected Works.* 12 vols. Edited by Victor Lange, Eric Blackall, and Cyrus Hamlin. New York, 1983–1989. Reprint, Princeton, N.J., 1994–1995. The leading translation of Goethe into English.

———. *Scientific Studies.* Edited and translated by Douglas Miller. New York, 1988. Reprint, Princeton, N.J., 1995. The most complete set of Goethe's scientific writings in English.

Secondary Sources

Amrine, Frederick, ed. *Goethe in the History of Science.* 2 vols. New York, 1996.

Atkins, Stuart. *Goethe's "Faust": A Literary Analysis.* Cambridge, Mass., 1958.

Bortoft, Henri. *The Wholeness of Nature: Goethe's Way toward a Science of Conscious Participation in Nature.* Hudson, N.Y., 1996.

Boyle, Nicholas. *Goethe: The Poet and the Age.* Vol. 1: *The Poetry of Desire (1749–1790).* Oxford, U.K., 1991.

———. *Goethe: The Poet and the Age.* Vol. 2: *Revolution and Renunciation (1790–1803).* Oxford, U.K., 2000.

Brown, Jane K. *Goethe's "Faust": The German Tragedy.* Ithaca, N.Y., 1986.

Emrich, Wilhelm. *Die Symbolik von "Faust II": Sinn und Vorformen.* 3rd ed. Frankfurt am Main, Germany, 1964.

Gearey, John. *Goethe's "Faust": The Making of Part I.* New Haven, Conn., 1981.

Matthaei, Rupprecht, ed. *Goethe's Color Theory.* New York, 1971.

Nisbet, H. B. *Goethe and the Scientific Tradition.* London, 1972.

BENJAMIN C. SAX

GOGOL, NIKOLAI (1809–1852), Russian short-story writer, novelist, and playwright.

Nikolai Vasilyevich Gogol was born on 31 March (19 March, old style) 1809 in the Poltava district of Ukraine, to a minor landowning family representative of the Ukrainian gentry's cultural hybridity: their official name was Gogol-Janowski, with Janowski signaling their partly Polish heritage (which Gogol later denied); they generally spoke Russian at home but Ukrainian at times; they corresponded in Russian but read in Russian, Ukrainian, and Polish. They were loyal subjects of the Russian Empire; only after Gogol arrived in the imperial capital of St. Petersburg in 1828 did he begin to perceive a tension between Ukrainian and Russian identities. Noting the St. Petersburg craze for all things "Little Russian" ("Little Russia" being a slightly patronizing "Great Russian" name for Ukraine), Gogol exploited this fad in his first major publication, *Evenings on a Farm near Dikanka* (two volumes, 1831–1832). The *Dikanka* tales, all set in a traditional Ukrainian milieu, are introduced by an invented narrator (a naive beekeeper) who claims to have collected them from his fellow villagers. This figure serves in part to shield the author from critical attack, evidence of Gogol's acute and persistent anxiety about his works' reception. The tales themselves reveal tensions between traditional (oral, Ukrainian, local) cultural forms and the standards (written, Russian, imperial) of high literature.

Dikanka's success established Gogol's reputation, although his provincial origins and his deeply eccentric personality kept him from full participation in the capital's sophisticated literary salons. In the story cycle *Mirgorod* (1835), chatty village narrators are replaced by a single and more authoritative voice. The swashbuckling tale "Taras Bulba" draws on Cossack history to imagine an epic past. The story "Old-World Landowners" evokes the old-time Ukrainian gentry in terms both warmly nostalgic and permeated by complex irony. This elusive irony, which makes it all but impossible to pin down the author's point of view, anticipates the stories known as the Petersburg tales: "Nevsky Prospect," "The Portrait," "Diary of a Madman" (published together in the 1835 collection *Arabesques,* which also included essays on history and art), "The Nose" (published in a journal in 1836), and "The Overcoat" (published in Gogol's 1842 *Collected Works*). In these tales the slightness and absurdity of the plots often serve to draw attention to the narrators' virtuoso performances: in "The Nose" when a bureaucrat's body part runs off and impersonates a government official, the narrator's commentary intensifies readers' bewilderment: "how was it that Kovaliov did not understand that he couldn't advertise for his nose in a newspaper office? Not that I would think it too expensive to advertise:...I am certainly not a mercenary person: but it's improper, awkward, not nice!"

In Gogol's comedy *The Inspector General* (1836), provincial town officials mistake a dim-witted young visitor for a government inspector. The townspeople's energetic lying, fawning, and bribing inspire the visitor to improvise his own fantastically comic lies about himself and life in the capital. The play was well received but Gogol felt that it was not fully appreciated. His dissatisfaction with the public's response helped convince him to leave for Rome, where he spent much of the rest of his life. Here Gogol wrote *Dead Souls* (1842), a novel about a confidence man pursuing a scheme that involves buying dead serfs. The title evokes not only these serfs but also the grotesque puppetlike landowners who populate the novel and the grim stasis of its provincial Russian setting. The narrative's interest derives less from plot or psychology than from linguistic and stylistic play, as well as from mysterious hints that readers should seek in it a profound hidden message about Russia. *Dead Souls* provoked much controversy; readers eagerly awaited the second volume, which would, the author promised, clarify all the ambiguities of the first. Gogol labored for years over this sequel, but he succumbed to a psychological and religious mania that finally led him to burn the manuscript. His last published work, *Selected Passages from Correspondence with Friends* (1847), provoked outrage with its bizarre mix of religious homily and reactionary diatribe. Gogol wrote little in his final years, dedicating himself to a regimen of spiritual purification and fasting that led to his death in Moscow on 4 March (21 February, old style) 1852.

Nineteenth-century criticism generally represented Gogol as a realist who exposed social injustice;

early-twentieth-century critics began to emphasize instead his work's surreal and grotesque qualities. Soviet critics attempted to categorize Gogol as a realist, although this required them to play down his spirituality and his conservative politics. While contemporary critics have accorded new attention to Gogol's religious thought, overall the modernists' emphasis on Gogol's stylistic innovation still informs most readings of his work.

See also **Chekhov, Anton; Dostoyevsky, Fyodor; Pushkin, Alexander; Tolstoy, Leo.**

BIBLIOGRAPHY

Primary Sources

Gogol, Nikolai. *Polnoe sobranie sochinenii.* 14 vols. Moscow, 1937–1952. Authoritative Russian text.

———. *Letters of Nikolai Gogol.* Edited by Carl R. Proffer. Translated by Carl R. Proffer and Vera Krivoshein. Ann Arbor, Mich., 1967.

———. *Selected Passages from Correspondence with Friends.* Translated by Jesse Zeldin. Nashville, Tenn., 1969.

———. *The Theater of Nikolay Gogol.* Edited by Milton Ehre. Translated by Milton Ehre and Fruma Gottschalk. Chicago, 1980. Reprint, as *Gogol: Plays and Selected Writings,* Evanston, Ill., 1994.

———. *Arabesques.* Translated by Alexander Tulloch. Ann Arbor, Mich., 1982.

———. *The Complete Tales of Nikolai Gogol.* Edited by Leonard J. Kent. 2 vols. Chicago, 1985.

———. *Dead Souls.* Translated by Bernard Guilbert Guerney. Edited by Susanne Fusso. New Haven, Conn., 1996.

———. *The Collected Tales of Nikolai Gogol.* Translated by Richard Pevear and Larissa Volokhonsky. New York, 1998.

Secondary Sources

Fanger, Donald. *The Creation of Nikolai Gogol.* Cambridge, Mass., 1979.

Gippius, V. V. *Gogol.* Edited and translated by Robert A. Maguire. Ann Arbor, Mich., 1981. Reprint, Durham, N.C., 1989. Originally published, 1924.

Maguire, Robert A. *Exploring Gogol.* Stanford, Calif., 1994.

Maguire, Robert A., ed. and trans. *Gogol from the Twentieth Century: Eleven Essays.* Princeton, N.J., 1974.

Nabokov, Vladimir. *Nikolai Gogol.* Norfolk, Conn., 1944.

ANNE LOUNSBERY

GONCHAROV, IVAN (1812–1891), Russian realist novelist.

Ivan Goncharov's *An Ordinary Story* (1847) is frequently acknowledged as the first Russian realist novel, but it was his second novel, *Oblomov* (1859), that established his literary legacy both in Russia and abroad. Its main hero, the novel's namesake, was first perceived as a symbol of the lethargic and parochial society of Russian serfdom, but has since come to symbolize the warm-hearted, dreamy, and apathetic qualities of the Russian national character. The novel as a whole, at once a compassionate and ironic study of the rich ambiguity of the human condition, anticipates the sensibility of modernist fiction by writers such as Marcel Proust and Virginia Woolf. Oblomov, both the character and the novel, inspired the life and work of Samuel Beckett. In Russia, Goncharov's first two novels had particular influence on Ivan Turgenev, Leo Tolstoy, and Anton Chekhov. Goncharov's last novel, *The Precipice* (1869), was seen as inferior to his earlier work. In addition to the three novels, Goncharov wrote a travelogue, *The Frigate Pallada* (1858), and several pieces of minor fiction, poetry, and criticism, which have received relatively little attention.

Goncharov was born into a wealthy family of provincial merchants in 1812. Following his father's death when Goncharov was seven, his childhood passed under the exceedingly protective influence of his mother and intellectually stimulating guardianship of a godfather, a retired navy officer. After eight oppressive years at the School of Commerce in Moscow, Goncharov, a voracious reader since an early age, enrolled in the Department of Philology at Moscow University. After graduating in 1835, he entered government service in St. Petersburg for a lengthy and moderately successful career, first as translator at the Ministry of Finance, then in 1852–1855 as secretary on a diplomatic mission to Japan (the trip that gave him material for his travelogue), and after 1856 as a government censor. In a generation dominated by the ideologically engaged and socially critical members of the gentry, Goncharov, a bureaucrat of merchant origin, remained an outsider. At the university, he avoided the student circles that produced revolutionary-minded men such as Alexander

Herzen and Mikhail Bakunin; in the 1840s, he was less intensely involved in the literary world than writers such as Turgenev and Fyodor Dostoyevsky; and during the social change at the turn of the 1860s, he, unlike his contemporaries, did not develop a strong ideological position. In his politics, he was a moderate Westernizer, believing that, in addition to the abolition of serfdom and corporal punishment, what Russians needed was to observe existing laws rather than introduce new ones. Fellow literati disliked Goncharov, considering him an apathetic, ironic, and comfort-seeking person.

Goncharov's first novel, *An Ordinary Story,* is a coming-of-age narrative that tapped into the European tradition of the bildungsroman (novel of formation). The personal growth of the hero, Alexander Aduev, recapitulates the cultural developments of the 1840s: Alexander overcomes the Romantic affectations of his youth and embarks on a realistically practical path toward "a fortune and a career." However, Alexander's alter ego, his uncle Peter, has already traveled this path, achieving both—only to recognize that he has been stifling the emotional lives of both himself and his wife. This pattern of ambiguous circularity, with neither side of the apparently clear opposition between spiritual and pragmatic values receiving a preference from the author, is characteristic of Goncharov's best work. The novel's early reviewers focused on its objectivity and its rejection of the Romantic idiom as exemplary of realism in literature.

Goncharov's next novel, *Oblomov,* published during a time of social reforms and seen as an indictment of moral corruption in society, solidified his literary fame. Although he did not challenge the prevalent readings of his first two novels, Goncharov was puzzled by them, for he thought of himself as an intuitive and self-absorbed writer whose art was averse to ideology. *Oblomov* tells the story of a person who takes dozens of pages to get out of bed and more than a hundred to leave his room. His childhood friend succeeds in forcing him out of his apathy for a brief period of time before he finally recedes to his original state of dreamy inactivity, culminating in an easy death. Unlike its early critics, the novel's aesthetically minded readers have come to appreciate it for its mastery in the portrayal of a life devoid of narrative,

for its skill in revealing the frequent absurdity of dialogue, for its skepticism about the value of teleological aspirations in human experience, and for its evocations of poetry and symbolism contained in the objects of everyday life.

See also **Chekhov, Anton; Dostoyevsky, Fyodor; Gogol, Nikolai; Tolstoy, Leo; Turgenev, Ivan.**

BIBLIOGRAPHY

Primary Sources

Goncharov, Ivan Aleksandrovich. *The Frigate Pallada.* Translated by Klaus Goetze. New York, 1987. Translation of *Fregat Pallada.*

——. *Oblomov.* Translated by Natalie Duddington. New York, 1992.

——. *An Ordinary Story.* Translated by Marjorie L. Hoover. Ann Arbor, Mich., 1994. Translation of *Obyknovennaia istoriia.* Also translated as *A Common Story* and *The Same Old Story.*

——. *The Precipice.* Translated by Laury Magnus and Boris Jakim. Ann Arbor, Mich., 1994. Translation of *Obryv.*

Secondary Sources

Ehre, Milton. *Oblomov and His Creator: The Life and Art of Ivan Goncharov.* Princeton, N.J., 1973.

Diment, Galya. *The Autobiographical Novel of Co-Consciousness: Goncharov, Woolf, and Joyce.* Gainesville, Fla., 1994.

Peace, Richard. *Oblomov: A Critical Examination of Goncharov's Novel.* Birmingham, U.K, 1991.

Setchkarev, Vsevolod. *Ivan Goncharov: His Life and His Works.* Wurzburg, Germany, 1974.

KONSTANTINE KLIOUTCHKINE

GONCOURT, EDMOND AND JULES DE. Edmond (1822–1896) and Jules (1830–1870) de Goncourt, known to literary history as the Goncourt brothers, wrote and published jointly, signing their works with both their names, until Jules's death in 1870 at the age of forty, after which Edmond continued to write singly. While their importance lies chiefly in their work as novelists and diarists, their writings include journalistic pieces, theater criticism, art criticism, social history, biography, and drama. They contri-buted significantly to the promotion

of Japanese art in France and to the renewal of interest in eighteenth-century French culture.

The most popular of their novels during their lifetime was *Renée Mauperin* (1864), the narrative of a young middle-class woman who inadvertently causes the death of her brother. Their most influential book, *Germinie Lacerteux* (1865), inspired by their discovery that their recently deceased maid had led a debauched existence, narrated the double life of a domestic servant. The book's concentration on the working class and its audacious depiction of a sexual pathology was seen as a provocation by the literary establishment, but the novel met with Victor Hugo's approval and strongly influenced the young Émile Zola. One of the novels, planned jointly but written by Edmond after his brother's death, *La Fille Élisa* (1877), continued their exploration of the seamy side of French society by focusing on prostitution and prison life, depicting a harlot starkly different from the idealized hooker of Romantic literature or the patriotic prostitute that Guy de Maupassant would depict three years later in "Boule de suif." Edmond's *Les Frères Zemganno* (1879) transposes his relationship with his brother into the world of circus entertainers while attempting to explore the psychology of that relationship.

The Goncourt brothers are usually seen as major participants in the development of realism in France, along with Gustave Flaubert and Zola. Like their two better-known contemporaries, the Goncourts conducted extensive research for each of their novels and, like Zola, frequently featured characters from the lower rungs of the economic ladder. Like most nineteenth-century realist writers, they accorded the milieu a determining role in the fate of their characters. The strongest example occurs in *Madame Gervaisais* (1869), perhaps their best novel, in which a well-read, freethinking bourgeois lady converts to Catholicism while in Rome under the influence of a milieu rich in religious sensations. The climate, the baroque churches, as well as the pageantry, the music, and the incense of Catholic Rome, lead the protagonist to a neurotic mysticism that culminates in her death. In this novel and others, the Goncourts depreciate the mental stability of women, whose lives end in insanity, death, or both. However, in their questioning of the reality of a unified, independent self

that accompanies their study of the pathologies of the mind, the Goncourts subscribed to a psychological outlook that nurtured many subsequent novelists.

The Goncourts' novels are marked by an aestheticism not found in other writers deemed realist during this period. Rejecting the notion that everyday reality should be represented by a neutral style, the Goncourts developed a mode of writing known as *écriture artiste,* which departed from normative French syntax by prepositioning adjectives that normally belong in postposition, preferring abstract nouns to adjectives (*whiteness* rather than *white*), nominal constructions relying on weak verbs, and paratactic constructions in which series of qualifiers or nouns are juxtaposed without connecting conjunctions. In their writing, qualities and colors frequently precede the objects in which they inhere, giving an impressionistic quality to their prose. The prevalence of visual and olfactory sensations effectively promotes the importance of milieu, especially in a novel such as *Madame Gervaisais.*

In addition to their novels, some of which are still in print in the early twenty-first century in paperback editions in France, considerable attention has been given since the 1960s to their *Journal,* a multivolume work that began appearing in 1885 and which is a mine of information on Parisian literary culture from 1851 to 1896, while including broader descriptions, such as those on life in Paris during the Franco-Prussian War (1870–1871) and the Paris Commune that followed. Biased, eccentric, misogynist, self-serving, and sometimes unfair, this record of their daily observations and thoughts nonetheless allows the reader to penetrate into the important artistic and intellectual circles of the time.

France's most prestigious literary prize—the Prix Goncourt—is the result of a legacy from Edmond that established an Académie Goncourt which, since 1903 has given itself the task of annually selecting the best French novel.

See also **Flaubert, Gustave; France; Franco-Prussian War; Hugo, Victor; Zola, Émile.**

BIBLIOGRAPHY

Caramaschi, Enzo. *Réalisme et Impressionisme dans l'œuvre des Frères Goncourt.* Pisa, 1971.

Grant, Richard B. *The Goncourt Brothers*. New York, 1972.

Ricatte, Robert. *La création Romanesque chez les Goncourt, 1851–1870*. Paris, 1953.

Vouilloux, Bernard. *L'art des Goncourt: Une esthétique du style*. Paris, 1997.

EMILE J. TALBOT

GORKY, MAXIM (pseudonym of Alexei Maximovich Peshkov; 1868–1936), Russian writer.

Maxim Gorky was one of the most influential public voices in pre–World War I Russia, as a result of his stories of ordinary but restless individuals struggling against humiliation and suffering, and his own persona as a "writer from the people." Gorky was born on 28 March (16 March, old style) 1868 in the Volga River town of Nizhny Novgorod into a lower-middle-class family. His father's death forced him to live with his maternal grandparents, who raised him in an atmosphere of petty-merchant narrow-mindedness, family violence, deep religiosity, and growing poverty. His formal education lasted only from 1877 to 1878, but he had learned to read from his grandfather, and his grandmother inspired him with folktales. Gorky soon became a voracious reader.

In 1878 poverty forced ten-year-old Gorky to begin his formative years of wandering and labor. He worked as a helper in a shoe store, an apprentice and errand-boy in a drafting workshop, a cook's helper on a Volga steamboat (where the cook was a self-educated folk philosopher), an apprentice in an icon studio, a construction worker, and a sales assistant at the public market. In 1884 he moved to Kazan hoping to enter the university but was not admitted. Here he was introduced into illegal student "self-education" circles, where he encountered populist socialism. Hardship, uncertainty, and personal doubt continued to torment him. In 1887 he shot himself in an attempted suicide. After recovering, he took part in efforts to educate peasants in the ideas of socialism—an experience that helped convince him of peasant backwardness. In 1888 he returned to Nizhny Novgorod, where, the following year, government authorities briefly imprisoned him for associating with radicals. In 1891 he resumed "tramping" around Russia, not "for the sake of wandering itself but from a desire to see where I am living and what sort of people are around me" (from a 1910 letter).

In 1892 Gorky began writing. He published his first story under the pseudonym Maxim Gorky, or "Maxim the Bitter," a name reflecting his simmering anger about life in Russia and a determination to speak the bitter truth. He wrote incessantly, publishing in local newspapers. He viewed literature less as an aesthetic practice (though he worked hard on style and form) than as a moral and political act that could change the world. He described the lives of people in the lowest strata and on the margins of society, revealing their hardships, humiliations, and brutalization, but also their inward spark of humanity. From 1895 to 1896, he worked as a journalist for a newspaper in Samara, writing daily columns and sketches that exposed moral and social abuses. He later worked for other newspapers and magazines, while continuing to publish stories and the occasional poem, which were beginning to attract a national audience.

Gorky's reputation as a unique literary voice from the lower depths of society and as a fervent advocate of Russia's social, political, and cultural transformation (by 1899, he was openly associating with the emerging Marxist social-democratic movement) helped make him a celebrity among both the intelligentsia and the growing numbers of "conscious" workers. At the heart of all his work was a belief in the inherent worth and potential of the human person (*lichnost*). He counterposed vital individuals, aware of their natural dignity, and inspired by energy and will, to people who succumb to the degrading conditions of life around them. Still, both his writings and his letters reveal a "restless man" (a frequent self-description) struggling to resolve contradictory feelings of faith and skepticism—of love of life and disgust at the vulgarity and pettiness of the human world.

The years 1900 to 1905 saw growing optimism in Gorky's writings and growing participation in the opposition movement, for which he was again briefly imprisoned in 1901. Now a financially successful author, editor, and playwright, he gave needed financial support to the Russian Social Democratic Labor Party, though he also supported

liberal appeals to the government for civil rights and social reform. The brutal shooting of workers marching to the tsar with a petition for reform on 22 January (9 January, old style) 1905 ("Bloody Sunday"), which set in motion the Revolution of 1905, seems to have pushed Gorky more decisively toward radical solutions. He now became closely associated with Vladimir Lenin's Bolshevik wing of the party—though it is not clear whether he ever formally joined, and his relations with Lenin and the Bolsheviks would always be rocky. His most influential writings in these years were a series of political plays, most famously *The Lower Depths* (1902). In 1906 the Bolshevik Party organized a fund-raising trip to the United States, where Gorky wrote his famous novel of revolutionary conversion and struggle, *Mat* (*Mother*, 1907). His experiences there—which included a scandal over his traveling with his lover rather than his wife—deepened his contempt for the "bourgeois soul" but also his admiration for the boldness of the American spirit.

From 1906 to 1913, Gorky lived on the island of Capri, partly for health reasons and partly to escape the increasingly repressive atmosphere in Russia. He continued to support the work of Russian social democracy, especially the Bolsheviks, and to write fiction and cultural essays. Most controversially, he articulated, along with a few other maverick Bolsheviks, a philosophy he called "god-building," which sought to recapture the power of myth for the revolution and to create a religious atheism that placed collective humanity where God had been and that was imbued with passion, wonderment, moral certainty, and the promise of deliverance from evil, suffering, and even death. Though god-building was suppressed by Lenin, Gorky retained his belief that "culture"—the moral and spiritual awareness of the value and potential of the human self—would be more critical to the revolution's success than political or economic arrangements.

An amnesty granted for the three hundredth anniversary of the Romanov dynasty in 1913 allowed Gorky to return to Russia, where he continued his social criticism, mentored other writers from the common people, and wrote a series of important cultural memoirs, including the first part of his autobiography. On his return, he wrote that his main impression was that "everyone is so crushed and devoid of God's image." The only solution, he repeatedly declared, was "culture." His later years were marked by ambivalence about the Bolshevik Revolution—he continued to insist on the need for culture and morality even while supporting the cause of socialist transformation in Russia.

In Soviet times, all the complexities in Gorky's life and outlook were reduced to an iconic image (echoed in heroic pictures and statues still seen throughout the former Soviet Union): Gorky as a great Russian writer who emerged from the common people, a loyal friend of the Bolsheviks, and the founder of the increasingly canonical "socialist realism." In turn, dissident intellectuals dismissed Gorky as a tendentious ideological writer, though some Western writers noted Gorky's doubts and criticisms. In the early twenty-first century greater balance is to be found in work on Gorky, where one finds a growing appreciation of the complex moral perspective on modern Russian life expressed in his writings. Some historians have begun to view Gorky as one of the most insightful observers of both the promises and moral dangers of revolution in Russia.

See also **Bolsheviks; Intellectuals; Lenin, Vladimir; Tolstoy, Leo.**

BIBLIOGRAPHY

Gorky, Maxim. *Autobiography of Maxim Gorky.* New York, 1962. Also published in three separate volumes: *My Childhood, My Apprenticeship* (or *In the World*), and *My Universities.*

Kaun, Alexander. *Maxim Gorky and His Russia.* New York, 1931.

Scherr, Barry P. *Maxim Gorky.* Boston, 1988.

Yedlin, Tovah. *Maxim Gorky: A Political Biography.* Westport, Conn., 1999.

MARK D. STEINBERG

GOUGES, OLYMPE DE (1748–1793),
playwright, political pamphleteer, and founding figure of the modern French feminist movement.

Olympe de Gouges was born Marie Gouze on 7 May 1748 in Montauban, France. Her mother, Anne-Olympe Mouisset, came from a family of drapers and her father, Pierre Gouze, was a butcher. There is, however, some doubt about her legitimacy, and it is possible, as she claimed, that her natural father was Jean-Jacques Lefranc, the marquis de Pompignan (1709–1784), president of the Cour des aides (financial court) of Languedoc and a poet-playwright of some note. She was married in 1765, at the age of seventeen, to Louis-Yves Aubry, a supplier and caterer to the intendant of Languedoc. She gave birth to a son, Pierre Aubry, in 1766, and in that same year Louis-Yves Aubry perished in the great flood in Montauban. At nineteen, the widow Aubry took up the name Olympe de Gouges—which she used henceforth on all but notarial documents—and formed a liaison with a well-to-do businessman-bachelor from Lyon, Jacques Biétrix de Rozières. In 1768 Biétrix installed her permanently in Paris with a comfortable income and considerable independence.

EARLY CAREER

Noted for her Mediterranean beauty, her lively wit, her passion for theater, and her love of exotic domestic pets, Gouges rapidly established herself at the heart of fashionable libertine and literary society in the 1770s. She developed connections with the coterie of Philippe d'Orléans (1747–1793), who repaid her attentions with a military commission for her son. Sometime after 1778, perhaps at the encouragement of her two closest literary friends, the marquis de Cubières (a fellow Languedocian) and the Parisian writer Louis-Sébastien Mercier, Gouges began writing novellas and theatrical works. Though she dedicated the first two volumes of her *Oeuvres* to d'Orléans in 1788, she later distanced herself publicly from his entourage.

Little is known about her early education except that she was able to sign her marriage certificate and therefore likely to have received the rudiments of literacy in youth. She was largely self-educated and preferred to compose orally with the use of a secretary. Whether through reading or social osmosis in the 1770s and 1780s Gouges absorbed the major ideas of the Enlightenment—especially those of Jean-Jacques Rousseau and the Baron de Montesquieu—and became familiar with

the feminine literary tradition that descended from Madame de Sévigné (1626–1696) and Antoinette de Deshoulières (1638–1694). A Rousseauian faith in natural sympathy as a basis for moral reform, as well as a suspicion of courtly refinement, shaped her worldview throughout her lifetime. By 1784 she was reputed to be the author of two novellas and about thirty plays in the fashionable genre of the *drame bourgeois*. Her first publications appeared in 1788—a novella, the *Memoire de Mme de Valmont,* and a play, *Zamore et Mirza; ou, L'heureux naufrage* (Zamore and Mirza, or the happy shipwreck)—the latter work, however, was widely known before it appeared in print.

Political controversy marked Gouges's public career from its beginnings. A stridently abolitionist drama, *Zamore et Mirza* was submitted, anonymously, for a reading by the review committee of the Comédie-Française in 1785, and accepted by majority vote for adoption into the Comédie's repertoire. The play, however, was repeatedly passed over for production in the next several years. The Comédiens met solicitations and protests by the author and her supporters with misogynist invective against women of letters and accusations of feminine impertinence. This misogynist rhetoric was in reality a smokescreen for powerful political opposition to the play's abolitionist message among the king's courtiers, who cynically used sexist stereotypes to discredit the author and thereby avoid provoking a public debate about slavery.

Gouges came to the cause against slavery remarkably early—well before the formation of the Société des Amis des Noirs (Society of the Friends of Blacks) in 1788. Little is known about the sources of Gouges's interest in abolitionism. Perhaps, as she later recalls, it was her horror at having witnessed the abuse of a black woman slave in her early youth. By the late 1780s she was frequenting the circles of liberal reformers such as Jacques-Pierre Brissot de Warville and the marquis de Condorcet, as well as the group that came to be known as the Société des Amis de la Constitution (the Jacobin Club), and later, the Cercle Social.

REVOLUTIONARY ACTIVISM

With the outbreak of revolution in 1789 she threw herself fully into the political fray as a prolific

Madame Aubry, Called Olympe de Gouges. Aquatint, 1784. BRIDGEMAN-GIRAUDON/ART RESOURCE, NY

pamphleteer. Though a champion of constitutional monarchy, Gouges was less interested in legal and constitutional reform than in the causes of social welfare and civil rights on behalf of the disenfranchised and underprivileged: slaves, children, the poor, the unemployed, and, not least, women. In a flurry of pamphlets, journal articles, and broadsides, published from 1789 to 1792, she offered proposals for a voluntary patriotic contribution to rescue the nation from bankruptcy, a luxury tax to fund national workshops for the poor and unemployed, and houses of refuge for women and children at risk. And she advocated the legitimation of children born out of wedlock; equality of inheritance; the regulation of prostitution; the opening of public and private professions to all on the basis of talent rather than birth, color, or sex; and the legalization of divorce.

The sources of Gouges's feminism were multiple. From an early age she was acutely aware of the civil and economic inequalities of women: Her possible illegitimacy and consequent disinheritance, her mother's financial suffering and dependency as a widow, her own arranged and unhappy marriage, and her financial vulnerability as a young widowed mother, all no doubt marked her. The cynical misogyny of the Comédie-Française was likely to have sharpened her awareness of the degraded situation of women, even in the highest stations. Finally, it is likely that she was exposed to systematic analyses of how to improve the civil and political situation of women through her association with the Condorcets and the Jacobin Club. By 1788 she was already beginning to formulate her views about the situation of women and the means of its improvement and to address her views to women directly, most elaborately in her novella *Le prince philosophe, conte orientale* (1789; The philosopher prince, an Oriental tale).

The exclusion of women from active citizenship in the French Constitution of 1791 crystallized her ideas and precipitated the composition of her greatest political pamphlet, *La déclaration des droits de la femme et de la citoyenne* (The declaration of the rights of woman and of the female citizen), published in September 1791. In an act of rhetorical genius Gouges added or substituted "woman" for "man" in each article of the famous Declaration of the Rights of Man and of the Citizen of 1789. Thus Article I announced "Woman is born free and remains equal to men in her rights. Social distinctions may be based only upon public utility." Pursuing the same strategy with the ensuing sixteen articles of the declaration, she succinctly re-envisioned civil and political society along sexually egalitarian lines and exposed the contradictions and exclusions concealed by the purportedly universalist claims of the original document. At the end of her *Declaration* she sketched the outlines for a new "social contract" between men and women that would be the basis for the moral regeneration of society as a whole through a mutually chosen and egalitarian association of the sexes. Along with Mary Wollstonecraft's *Vindication of the Rights of Women* (1792), Gouges's *Declaration of the Rights of Woman* remains, to this day, one of the most powerful and concise expressions of the modern feminist movement worldwide: women's right to political representation, to equality before the law, to equal property and inheritance rights and to freedom of expression and self-determination in public and private life.

Gouges dedicated her *Declaration* to the queen, Marie-Antoinette, and in the preface appealed to the queen to join in the cause of improving woman's lot by rallying to the movement for revolutionary reform. While often sharply critical of the king and queen, Gouges held the view that constitutional monarchy was the most suitable form of government for France, even after the declaration of the republic in September 1792. During the king's trial she remained allied with the Girondist faction, advocating a reprieve for the king and a national referendum on his fate; she had an intense dislike for Maximilien Robespierre, leader of the radical Jacobins. As the revolutionary crisis deepened in 1793 and the radical Jacobins tightened their grip upon a nation in civil war, Gouges repeatedly denounced the Terror and was finally arrested and guillotined on 3 November 1793 for publishing a seditious broadside (*Les trois urnes* [The three urns]) in which she championed the federalist cause.

FEMINIST LEGACY

Gouges's *Declaration of the Rights of Woman* received little attention upon its initial publication in 1791, and throughout the first half of the nineteenth century she was remembered as a minor playwright and an unruly revolutionary woman who had paid for her unruliness with her head. The French historian Jules Michelet remarked briefly upon her precocious feminism in his *Femmes de la Révolution* (1854). For the French feminists of 1848 and beyond she came to seen as a visionary and a martyr to the feminist cause: her searing assertion in the *Declaration* that "Woman has the right to mount the scaffold; she ought equally to have the right to mount to the tribune" seemed to prophesy not only her own end but also the fate of women in postrevolutionary French politics. It is only since the 1970s, with the renewal of the feminist movement in France, that Gouges has begun to receive scholarly and public recognition as one of the political founders of modern France.

See also **Federalist Revolt; Feminism; French Revolution; Reign of Terror; Robespierre, Maximilien; Wollstonecraft, Mary.**

BIBLIOGRAPHY

Primary Sources

Gouges, Olympe de. *Oeuvres.* Edited by Benoîte Groult. Paris, 1986.

Hunt, Lynn, ed. and trans. *The French Revolution and Human Rights: A Brief Documentary History.* Boston, 1996.

Levy, Darline Gay, Harriet Branson Applewhite, and Mary Durham Johnson, eds. and trans. *Women in Revolutionary Paris, 1789–1795.* Urbana, Ill., 1979.

Secondary Sources

Blanc, Olivier. *Olympe de Gouges.* Paris, 1981.

Godineau, Dominque. *Women of Paris and Their French Revolution.* Translated by Katherine Streip. Berkeley and Los Angeles, 1998.

Scott, Joan Wallach. *Only Paradoxes to Offer: French Feminists and the Rights of Man.* Cambridge, Mass., 1996.

CARLA HESSE

GOYA, FRANCISCO (1746–1828), Spanish painter.

Like Henri Matisse and Pablo Picasso, Francisco José de Goya y Lucientes is an artist whose stylistic evolution builds on traditions that are eventually surpassed in the creation of a new and revolutionary idiom. His career opens with several religious commissions—altarpieces and frescos—executed in a derivative late Baroque idiom. Yet, in the decade before his death he would push beyond known limits of oil painting and print making in such works as his well-known "Black" paintings and in the lithographic series *The Bulls of Bordeaux*.

Born on 30 March 1746 in the village of Fuendetodos, Goya received his earliest artistic training in the Aragonese capital of Saragossa, under the Neapolitan-trained painter José Luzán y Martínez (1710–1785). He was probably in Madrid by 1766, when he competed unsuccessfully in a drawing competition at the Royal Academy of San Fernando. Five years later, he was in Italy, entering in another academic competition in Parma. He received an honorable mention for his submission, *Hannibal Crossing the Alps* (1771).

Upon his returning to Saragossa in 1772, Goya mainly painted religious commissions. Some of these were for private patrons, such as *The Burial of Christ* (1772), others for religious organizations, such as the fresco illustrating *The Adoration of the*

Name of God (1772) and a series of murals for the Charterhouse of Aula Dei, outside Saragossa (1773–1774). In 1773, Goya married María Josefa Bayeu (1752–1812), sister of the court painter Francisco Bayeu y Subiás (1734–1795).

It was probably through Bayeu's influence that the artist was invited to the court of Madrid in 1774 to paint designs (also known as cartoons) for the Royal Tapestry Factory. Goya's ability was apparently recognized, and he was given permission to paint tapestry cartoons "of his own invention"—that is, he was allowed to develop original subjects for these images. He painted three series of tapestry cartoons for rooms in the royal residences before the tapestry factory cut back production in 1780, due to a financial crisis brought on by Spain's war with England.

The decade of the 1780s was nevertheless one of great advancement for the artist, beginning with his election to the Royal Academy of Fine Arts of San Fernando in 1780. His fame for painting portraits and religious paintings—more prestigious than tapestry cartoons—grew as he won patronage from the grandest families in Spain, including the Duke and Duchess of Osuna. Works painted for these patrons include a family portrait (1788) and two scenes from the life of Saint Francis Borja (1788). Goya's appointment as court painter in April 1789, four months after Charles IV (r. 1788–1808) had acceded to the throne, cemented his fortunes.

In spite of his professional success, documents and paintings of the early 1790s suggest the artist's growing unease with the limitations imposed on painters by traditions and patronage. Themes from his final series of cartoons, such as *The Straw Mannikin* and *The Wedding* (1792), betray an increasing irony. As one of several academicians whose opinion on the institutional curriculum was requested in 1792, Goya's submitted his own report, in which he stated: "there are no rules in painting." Thus, although the turn in Goya's art to new subject matter is often credited to a serious illness suffered in 1792–1793, this change may in fact have been part of a more gradual evolution. From 1793 onward, in addition to his continuing work as a painter of commissioned portraits and religious paintings, Goya explored experimental subjects—ranging from shipwrecks to scenes of everyday life in Madrid—in uncommissioned paintings, prints, and drawings.

The experimentation of the 1790s culminated in the publication in 1799 of *Los Caprichos*, a series of eighty aquatint etchings. Goya began developing the series no later than 1797, and it appears that his first objective was to satirize customs and types of Madrid. The scope of the project seems to have expanded as Goya invented images of increasing whimsy, culminating in scenes of goblins and spirits. It is often thought that these etchings jeopardized Goya's relationship with his patrons: that this is not the case is proven by Goya's promotion to first court painter eight months after their publication. In 1803, in exchange for a stipend that would allow his son Javier to study painting, Goya turned the plates for *Los Caprichos* over to the government printing establishment, the Calcografía (Madrid), where they can be seen today.

As first court painter, Goya painted *The Family of Charles IV*. He produced sketches for each individual's face before creating the full-size portrait of fourteen almost life-size figures. The realism of the faces has led to interpretation of the portrait as satire, but this is highly unlikely given the patrons' approval of their representation. Moreover, the portrait is a virtuoso performance by an artist for his most important patron, as freely handled paint sparkles over the surface to suggest the royal finery of brocades, silks, and fine gauzes. During these years, Goya's role as first court painter probably also included painting works for the king and queen's close confidant, Manuel de Godoy (1767–1851). These include such portraits as *Manuel Godoy as Commander in the War of the Oranges* (c. 1801) and probably *The Naked Maja* and *The Clothed Maja* (c. 1797 and c. 1805, respectively).

THE NAPOLEONIC WAR AND ITS AFTERMATH

The career to which Goya had so long aspired—as first court painter to the old regime monarchy—would come to an end in 1808 when Napoleonic forces invaded Spain. The royal family left the country and abdicated in agreement with Napoleon I (r. 1804–1814/15), whose brother, Joseph Bonaparte (r. 1808–1813), assumed the Spanish throne. During the five-year rule of Joseph Bonaparte, Goya continued to paint portraits, sometimes for supporters of the French regime (see, for example, *General Nicolas Guye* [1810]). Upon the restoration of the Spanish king

The Disasters of War: And There Is No Remedy. Engraving by Francisco José de Goya y Lucientes c. 1808–1820. Horrified by the French invasion of Spain in 1808 and the ensuing violence, Goya created a series of etchings denouncing the pointless savagery of warfare. © Archivo Iconografico, S.A./Corbis

Ferdinand VII (r. 1808–1833, the son of Charles IV and Maria Luisa) in 1814, Goya was one of several palace employees whose possible involvement with the French regime was investigated: however, he was found innocent of any wrongdoing, and his salary was restored.

The war inspired one of Goya's most famous and perhaps his most often reproduced series of etchings, *The Disasters of War*. Like *Los Caprichos*, this series evolved over time. The earliest etchings, three of which bear the date 1810, show scenes of war and its immediate effects. The series would then expand to encompass scenes of Madrid during the war, and specifically the famine that ravaged

Madrid in 1811–1812. Even after the Spanish government of Ferdinand VII was restored in 1814, Goya probably continued work on these etchings creating fantastic caricatures (known as the *caprichos enfáticos*) that seem to satirize the repressive restored regime. Curiously, *The Disasters of War* was never published by Goya, perhaps because of its controversial subject matter: the first edition of eighty plates was published in 1863, thirty-five years after his death.

On 24 February 1814, as Madrid was awaiting the return of its restored monarch, Goya wrote to the interim government offering to "perpetuate with his brush the most notable and historical actions or scenes of our glorious insurrection against the tyrant of Europe." That offer was accepted on 9 March 1814. The result of this commission was the well-known paintings *The Second of May, 1808* and *The Third of May, 1808* (1813–1814). Although these two paintings are among Goya's most famous works, little is known of their original function, placement, or early reception: one hypothesis is that they were painted to decorate a triumphal arch (or perhaps some other architectural setting) upon the triumphant return of Ferdinand VII to Madrid in May 1814. To date, their first known documentation is a record of 1834, which lists them in storage in the Prado museum.

Another effect of the war involves the famous paintings of the naked and clothed *majas*. After Godoy had left the country with Charles IV and Maria Luisa in 1808, his collection was dispersed: many paintings (including the *Rokeby Venus* by Diego Rodríguez de Silva Velázquez [1599–1660], which ended up in the National Gallery, London) found their way out of the country. The paintings that remained in 1814, including the two *majas*, were sequestered by the Inquisition. Inquiry led to the finding that these works were by Goya, who was ordered to explain himself. His testimony does not survive, but it seems possible that he was protected by his status and possibly age.

Goya continued in his position as first court painter under the restored monarch, who nevertheless preferred the neoclassical style of the younger Vicente López (1772–1850). In 1819, Goya purchased a villa on the outskirts of Madrid, and painted on the walls of its two main rooms images of witchcraft, religious ceremonies, and mythical subjects today known as the "black" paintings (1819–1823). These enigmatic paintings were transferred to canvas during the 1870s, exhibited at the Exposition Universelle in 1878, and returned to the Spanish governments in 1881 by their French owner, who perhaps had failed to find a more lucrative sale.

In 1824, Goya left Spain and after a brief trip to Paris settled in Bordeaux among a colony of Spanish exiles. Here he continued to paint and draw, and also to experiment with the new technique of lithography—leading to the publication of the *Bulls of Bordeaux* (1825–1828), a masterpiece in that medium. He died in Bordeaux on 26 April 1828.

See also **French Revolutionary Wars and Napoleonic Wars; Painting; Spain.**

BIBLIOGRAPHY

Bareau, Juliet Wilson. *Goya: Drawings from his Private Albums.* London, 2001.

Gassier, Pierre, and Juliet Wilson. *The Life and Complete Works of Francisco Goya.* New York, 1971.

Sayre, Eleanor A. *The Changing Image: Prints by Francisco Goya.* Boston, 1974.

Tomlinson, Janis A. *Goya in the Twilight of Enlightenment.* New Haven, Conn., 1992.

Tomlinson, Janis A. *Francisco Goya y Lucientes 1746–1828.* 2nd ed. London, 1999.

JANIS A. TOMLINSON

GREAT BRITAIN. The United Kingdom was formally created with the 1800 Act of Union, which merged the Irish Parliament (1690–1800) with the Parliament of Great Britain. The latter had already incorporated the Scottish Parliament with the 1707 Union (Wales had been under the English crown since 1536). In both cases the relevant legislation had to be approved by each of the two Parliaments, and, although there were well- supported claims that the Scottish Parliament in 1707 and its Irish counterpart in 1800 were bribed and coerced into accepting the union, there is also plenty of evidence that in each case there was genuine support for the move. By 1800 it was clear that the Scottish Union was a success, which had enhanced both stability in domestic affairs and security against foreign invasion. A further important result had been the creation of a "common market"—with the abolition of tariffs and trade barriers between England and Scotland—that provided the context for spectacular economic growth throughout the century. By the same token, the Scots were able to participate in the exploitation of the overseas empire that British colonists and trading companies were creating in America and India.

EIGHTEENTH CENTURY

In 1800 it was hoped that the Irish Act of Union would have similar beneficial results for both parties. In particular, the British, who had been fighting revolutionary France since 1793, were eager to consolidate their control over Ireland. The latter was then a populous and unstable country. With about eight million inhabitants, it accounted for nearly one third of the entire population of the British Isles—a much larger proportion than ever since. The country's instability was largely due to the economic and political crisis that accompanied the loss of the American colonies in the period from 1776 to 1789. While Irish trade was slow to recover from the shock, republican ideas spread among both the Protestant and the Catholic middle classes, especially in Belfast and Dublin. These ideas were sponsored by the Society of the United Irishmen and were given a sharper edge by the French Revolution. Once France started to invade the rest of Europe, the possibility that Ireland too could be "liberated" by sans-culottes armies electrified patriot opinion and encouraged revolutionary plots. However, many of the leaders of the United Irishmen were arrested before the rebellion started in May 1798. The main areas of revolutionary activity were the Presbyterian northeast, the counties around Dublin, and County Wexford in the southeast, where the rebellion acquired a violent sectarian dimension.

The rebellion has been celebrated by some historians as "the year of liberty" and was unquestionably widely supported by both Protestants and Catholics. It could have succeeded only with adequate and timely French help, which, however, failed to materialize. Had the rising succeeded, the course of Irish history would have been different, especially in view of the virulent anti-Christian agenda of the French government (which had fiercely persecuted the church in various parts of Europe and had imprisoned the pope himself). So here is a paradox: although the Catholic peasantry and some of the parish clergy supported the rebellion, the church hierarchy feared the prospect of a Jacobin republic in Dublin. Over the eighteenth century, despite the Penal Laws, the Catholic Church had quietly enjoyed effective toleration under the Hanoverian monarchy, whose government sponsored the establishment of the Maynooth seminary in 1795, after the Jacobin Revolution made it impossible for Irish priests to continue to be educated in France. In this context, many Catholics regarded the proposal of a Union as the lesser of two evils, especially if accompanied by full political rights ("emancipation").

Although nineteenth-century Irish nationalists celebrated the old Dublin Parliament as the last bulwark of Irish freedom, in the eighteenth century the perception had been different. For one thing, for most of the century this exclusively Protestant assembly had lacked power—its deliberations requiring London's sanctions to become effective. It was only in 1782 that the parliamentary leader Henry Grattan (1746–1820) secured a degree of independence under the British crown. "Grattan Parliament" became a milestone in Irish constitutional history, but did not solve Ireland's problems. It was only in 1793 that Catholics were granted the vote, but not the right to stand for Parliament. By then Britain and Ireland were already at war against revolutionary France, whose radical democracy and secularism added a further ideological edge to the conflict.

WILLIAM PITT

In proposing a parliamentary union with Ireland, the British prime minister William Pitt the Younger (1759–1806) had hoped that the two countries could stand together against godless Jacobinism on a Christian liberal platform. Moreover, the union, he hoped, would help to modernize the Irish economy and at the same time resolve insular sectarian conflicts through Catholic emancipation. However, George III (r. 1760–1820) vetoed emancipation, believing that it would be inconsistent with his coronation oath to defend the confessional, Anglican constitution of the kingdom. The situation was very delicate: the king's mental health was unstable; the country faced Napoleonic France; but also, among the artisans and lower-middle classes in Britain, Thomas Paine's *Rights of Man* (1791) had become a best-seller and had been followed by the publication of other important radical works, including Mary Wollstonecraft's *A Vindication of the Rights of Woman* (1792) and William Godwin's *Enquiry Concerning Political Injustice* (1793). Rather than face a constitutional conflict with the king, Pitt, who was also in poor

Portrait of a Victorian family c. 1865. ©Hulton-Deutsch Collection/Corbis

health, preferred to resign. A new and more docile prime minister implemented a union without Catholic emancipation. It was a fatal mistake that would have disastrous consequences for both countries.

Meanwhile the questions that inflamed both Europe and America—liberty, the rights of man, representative government and its relationship with the sovereign—had long been discussed also within the British Parliament. In the 1780s the American War of Independence and the stubborn behavior of the British government had generated a wide debate as to the extent to which the king's influence on the outcome of parliamentary elections was compatible with national interest. The advocates of constitutional reform found their most energetic spokesman in Charles James Fox (1749–1806), who demanded electoral reform and effective parliamentary control over the executive. The last twenty years of the century were dominated by Fox's relentless critique of both the king and of

Pitt, his faithful servant. However, it must be remembered that Pitt too wanted moderate reform, but was determined to work *with* the king, rather than *against* him. With the king's help, he was able to check Fox's radical agenda from 1783. Although both Pitt and Fox belonged to the Whig tradition—which had triumphed in the "Glorious Revolution" of 1688 to 1690—the two men differed in temperament, outlook, and ultimate goals. In the nineteenth century the Conservative Party regarded Pitt as one of their founding fathers, while Fox became the great hero of the Liberals. However, the two eighteenth-century statesmen operated in a context within which "parties" were at best temporary alliances between gentlemen "sharing the same prejudice about the common good," to paraphrase the British political philosopher Edmund Burke's famous definition. At worst, they were rather corrupt networks of clients and friends hoping to benefit from government or private patronage and bidding for power in a context in which commercial growth and imperial expansion created enormous opportunities for enterprising individuals.

During his tenure as prime minister (1783–1801, 1804–1806), Pitt set new standards of ministerial professionalism. After the beginning of the French wars he displayed unparalleled energy in the pursuit of military victory. His greatest achievement was to consolidate the political and economic situation at home through a mixture of repression and reform. While civil liberties were drastically restricted from 1794, he mobilized the country's financial resources as no other minister had ever done before. The efficiency of the British "fiscal-military" state was perfected in 1799, when the newly introduced income tax increased the revenue to the extent that the previously spiraling national debt was brought under control. Simultaneously, because the fiscal burden was now more broadly spread across all social classes, the income tax helped to assuage popular discontent about taxation, and further strengthened national unity.

Military victory in a series of naval battles culminated with the Battle of Trafalgar in 1805, when Admiral Horatio Nelson (1758–1805) destroyed the joint French-Spanish fleet together with Napoleon's dream of invading the United Kingdom. From then on, Britain was able to sustain a more aggressive strategy, particularly by sending an army to fight the French in the Iberian Peninsula under the command of Arthur Wellesley (later duke of Wellington, 1769–1852). However, it was only in June 1815 that Wellington was able to inflict the final blow on Napoleon and his army when he faced them on the Belgian battlefield of Waterloo.

1815–1851

Britain played a leading role in the postwar European settlement, defined by the Vienna Treaty in 1815. In central Europe, Russia, Austria, and Prussia became the pillars of the conservative Holy Alliance system, which aimed at preventing the repetition of the wars and related blood bath of the period from 1792 to 1815. In diplomatic terms, the system relied on the idea of the Concert of Europe, which depended on the plenipotentiaries of the Great Powers meeting at periodical congresses and conferences in order to debate and peacefully

resolve their differences before the latter degenerated into open conflict. Britain supported the Concert, but remained skeptical about the Holy Alliance. Instead, London sponsored liberal nationalism whenever the latter was consistent with British interests: thus the rebellions of the Spanish colonies in Latin America, the Greek patriots struggling against the Ottoman Empire, and the Belgian insurgents in 1830 were all directly or indirectly supported by the British government.

Meanwhile the country began to recover from the Napoleonic wars under the skilled leadership of Lord Liverpool (Robert Banks; 1770–1828), who developed the Pittite tradition of government in a distinctly Tory direction. In the years 1812 to 1827 he became one of the longest-serving prime ministers in British history. His policy was to support economic growth through commercial liberalism and a stable currency based on gold, but to resist demands for constitutional change. The latter focused on two issues: Catholic emancipation and the extension of the parliamentary franchise. In Parliament, reform was advocated by Fox's disciples, led by the Earl Grey (Charles Grey; 1764–1845) and Lord John Russell (1792–1878), who belonged to two of the most illustrious Whig families. In the country, the alliance between the radical artisans and predominantly middle-class Nonconformists provided the cause of reform with an important constituency.

The Nonconformists, or Dissenters, comprised all the Protestant groups who had refused to accept the Act of Uniformity of 1862, which restored the Episcopalian nature of the Church of England. In the early nineteenth century they included Congregationalists, Baptists, Quakers, and Unitarians. The Presbyterians were regarded as Nonconformists in England, Wales, and Ireland, but were the established church in Scotland. Moreover, during the eighteenth century a new and important dissenting body had emerged from the revivalist preaching of John (1708–1791) and Charles (1707–1788) Wesley: the Methodists. Their work was increasingly effective among the working poor, especially in industrializing England and Wales. It was an age of general religious revival that transformed the spiritual landscape of the United Kingdom, with profound political implications on the country's traditional constitution.

The cause of Catholic emancipation was mainly an Irish cause and found a powerful champion in Daniel O'Connell (1775–1847). He was in many ways unusual: he had a native fluency in Gaelic, and yet he was steeped in the cosmopolitan, liberal culture of France. His aim was to stimulate a national (nonsectarian) revival, but he relied increasingly on the support of the Catholic Association and the parish priests. As a Catholic he was debarred from taking a seat in Parliament, but he could stand for election: he did so and won a seat in County Clare in 1828. By then Lord Liverpool had been replaced by the Duke of Wellington. Faced with the difficult choice between enforcing the law (at the cost of widespread unrest in Ireland) or changing it, Wellington opted for the latter option. After all, Pitt himself had damned religious disqualifications as early as 1800, and there was much to be said for incorporating the Catholics into the kingdom's constitutional framework. However, the government did not survive such a concession, which staunch Tory traditionalists regarded as anathema. At the election of 1830, occasioned by the death of the king George IV (r. 1820–1830), the Tories lost control of the House of Commons, and the new sovereign William IV (r. 1830–1837) called for the leader of the opposition, Earl Grey, to form a government. The new prime minister pressed for a full-scale reform bill. The "Great" Reform Bill was passed in 1832 and included new electoral franchises to empower the urban middle class and the better-off farmers, replacing ancient, capricious, and often corrupt hereditary franchises with a system consistently based on residence, property, and achievement of what contemporaries called "independence." Moreover, the Reform Act enacted a drastic redistribution of seats: many "rotten boroughs"—where, on the basis of medieval charters, few individuals enjoyed the privilege of the vote—were abolished. Seats were reallocated to both the counties and to the hitherto unrepresented industrial towns (including Manchester). Scotland and Wales, whose prereform electorates had been miniscule, were effectively enfranchised for the first time. Grateful, Scotland responded by electing a majority of Reform (later Liberal) members of Parliament (MPs).

The reform zeal of the new ministry was further displayed in a series of important measures over the next few years. In 1833 slavery was abolished in the British Empire (although the full implementation of the measure was effectively delayed until 1838): planters were paid a compensation and the slaves were gradually turned into tenant farmers. In 1834 the Poor Law Amendment Act reformed the system of rate-supported poor relief and established local representative bodies to administer it. In 1835 the Municipal Corporations Act created elective municipalities with wide-ranging powers. Meanwhile a good system of rate-supported primary schools was organized in Ireland. Finally, the government introduced more effective regulations of the conditions of work in the factories.

The latter was in partial response to the workers' agitation. This took two main forms. On the one hand, the new trade unions (legalized in 1824–1825) and radical groups demanded a shortening of working hours, the introduction of restrictions on child labor, and a more humane implementation of the notoriously punitive Poor Law. On the other, from 1839 a large number of artisan and working men and women joined a movement that proposed a comprehensive program of political democracy, summarized in the six points of their Charter: universal (male) suffrage, vote by secret ballot, payment of MPs, the abolition of property qualifications for parliamentary candidates, annual Parliaments, and equal electoral districts. At its peak Chartism involved millions of people under the leadership of fiery demagogues such as the barrister Feargus Edward O'Connor (c. 1796–1855). This was unprecedented for a democratic movement in Europe. On the other hand, support for Chartism was not exclusive of popular participation in the existing electoral process. Although the electorate was small and deference to one's "betters" was the rule, riots, bribery, and drunken celebrations were commonplace and involved both electors and nonelectors. Moreover, support for the Charter was not constant over the years 1839 to 1848: instead it followed the ups and downs of the economy to the extent that the movement was sometimes described as embodying "the politics of hunger."

There is no doubt that there was hunger. In Britain, trade fluctuations periodically resulted in phases of acute unemployment, which in turn affected local taxation (the Poor Law rates went up) and the government's central revenue (the income from duties on items of popular consumption

Manhood Suffrage Riots in Hyde Park. Painting by Nathan Hughes, 1866. In July of 1866, London officials attempted to prevent a public meeting of the Reform League, which advocated expansion of the franchise beyond the parameters established in 1832. The confrontation quickly escalated to violence and a number of reform advocates were beaten by police. PRIVATE COLLECTION/ BRIDGEMAN ART LIBRARY

declined). This produced not only discontent, but also budget deficits, which the Whigs were unable to deal with. At the election of 1841 they were defeated by the reinvigorated Tories, or (as they now preferred to call themselves) Conservatives. Their new leader, Sir Robert Peel (1788–1850), refined Liverpool's fiscal and financial policies and emulated Pitt when he decided to reintroduce the income tax in 1842. The income tax had previously been regarded as a "war tax." After Waterloo, Liverpool had wanted to keep it on to pay off the national debt, but Parliament had forced him to drop it. The resulting fiscal system was perceived as grossly inequitable, not only because it relied on highly regressive indirect taxes on popular consumption, but also because it preserved the Corn Laws, which protected British farming against international competition, and were supposed to keep the price of bread artificially high.

Thus Peel faced a difficult situation. Consistent with the Liverpool tradition, he tried to reform the economy without touching the constitution. Thus, while the Chartists were ruthlessly put down, new Mines and Factory Acts improved working conditions, conveying the impression that social amelioration would be possible without a democratic revolution. The additional revenue from the income tax helped to balance the budget. Moreover, it allowed Peel to relieve working-class consumers of some of the most bitterly resented taxes on the necessities of life.

Peel and his cabinet, including William Ewart Gladstone (1809–1898), had by now become converts to the idea that only complete free trade would relieve the British economy from its periodical crises. This involved repealing the Corn Laws, which the Conservative Party regarded as sacrosanct and indeed a part of the "constitution" that the Peel government had been elected to defend. The position of the government was not improved by the vigorous campaign of the Anti–Corn Law League. Under the leadership of the radical free trader Richard Cobden (1804–1865), the League argued that free trade would bring about global prosperity through interdependence between Britain's manufacturing economy and the economies of the other countries, which were eager to export raw materials in exchange for industrial products. By 1846 the League had won the economic argument. In an act of almost suicidal self-denial, Peel and his cabinet pushed the repeal of the Corn Laws through the Commons, where the measure was supported by the Whigs (now calling themselves Liberals) and opposed by the Conservatives. In the Lords the duke of Wellington loyally supported Peel, again with the help of the Liberal peers. The Conservative Party split with the protectionist majority, now led by Lord George Bentinck (1802–1848) and Benjamin Disraeli (1804–1881), rejecting Peel and his supporters, who formed a third party between the Tories and the Liberals.

In insisting on the immediate repeal of the Corn Laws, Peel had been motivated—among other things—by the impending collapse of the Irish economy. In the western counties, a large and growing population depended almost exclusively on potato crops for food. In 1845 an unprecedented combination of bad weather and a particularly devastating fungus destroyed the crops. This would have been enough to cause famine and emigration, but the recurrence of the potato blight in 1846 and 1848 brought about a demographic catastrophe. Although Ireland would not directly benefit from the repeal of the Corn Laws, Peel and his cabinet took the view that the famine was something like a warning from the Almighty that legislation should not interfere with the free circulation of food. However, they did not limit themselves to this negative and (as far as Ireland was concerned) symbolic measure. They staged a major relief operation, buying and importing Indian meal to feed the starving peasants in Ireland. Given the lack of railways and navigable rivers, it is questionable whether the limited amount of food that the government could actually distribute would have been adequate to avoid the catastrophe. However, for as long as Peel was prime minister the government was at least *perceived* to be doing something serious about the famine. When Peel was replaced by Lord John Russell in 1846, the partial (and short-lived) recovery of Irish farming in 1847, "donor fatigue," and dogmatic free-market advisers persuaded the Liberal government to discontinue the relief operation and rely instead on the Irish Poor Law. It was a disastrous decision. Irish landowners, already in debt, were unable to shoulder the additional fiscal burden of the greatly increased poor rates. Many went bankrupt. Worse, a million peasants died and another million emigrated, especially to the United States. By the same token, many, predominantly Catholic, farmers who managed to escape disaster actually profited from the tragedy when they were able to buy the lands that bankrupt Protestant landowners were forced to sell.

The potato blight also devastated other parts of northern Europe, including Finland and the Netherlands, and crop failures and bad harvests contributed to the Europe-wide revolutions of 1848. But in no other part of Europe was the famine as devastating as in Ireland, because nowhere else was there the same combination of a large population, a single-crop subsistence economy, and lack of alternative forms of employment. The Scottish Highlands are a good example of how the situation was dealt with elsewhere. In the first instance, Scottish overpopulation had already been partly reduced by means of the enclosures and related evictions, which forced a large number of crofters to emigrate. The industrial belt in central Scotland and in the Glasgow area attracted many of them, while others shipped across to Canada. By the time the potato blight struck, the population at risk was much smaller than in Ireland, and could be more easily relieved by private and public charity before donor fatigue and liberal economics set in. Moreover, the geography of the Highlands facilitated the relief operations: unlike Ireland, which forms a solid mass of land without navigable rivers, the tormented coastline of the Scottish Highlands, with its deep bays linked to long lochs, facilitated the distribution of relief by food ships. The different outcomes of the famine in Ireland and Scotland may perhaps be reflected in the fact that, while the large Irish American community in the United States has traditionally been pronationalist and deeply resentful of the British connection, the equally large Scottish community in Canada has always been strongly loyalist. Even in the twenty-first century, Canada is a monarchy, nominally under the British crown.

While the economy of the Highlands was devastated by the famine, the country's religious landscape was transformed by the so-called Great Disruption of the Church of Scotland (1843). The established Presbyterian Church enjoyed unparalleled influence and prestige in Scotland. Its General Assembly—consisting of ecclesiastical and lay representatives—operated as a sort of unofficial parliament for the country as a whole. The church managed the Scottish Poor Law system and the parish primary schools. Its theological seminaries were the four ancient universities (Edinburgh, St. Andrews, Aberdeen, and Glasgow). Under the 1707 Act of Union the church enjoyed greater autonomy than the Church of England, and the Evangelical Party within the Assembly was particularly jealous about preserving such autonomy. In particular, the Evangelicals, who by 1843 represented a majority of the delegates to the General Assembly, resented the practice of lay patronage in the appointment of parish ministers, according to which the local squire could impose his choice on the congregation, despite the fact that the latter had the right to elect its minister. The Evangelicals voted to discontinue the practice, but the decision of the Assembly needed the endorsement of the British government—who retained ultimate control on matters pertaining to the established churches. Peel, then the prime minister, refused to act not because of his views of the specific question under discussion, but because he was afraid of setting a precedent that the Tractarians in the Church of England could then appeal to in the attempt to "Romanize" Episcopalianism. Thus, ironically, the Evangelical Party in Scotland was snubbed because the government opposed the Anglo-Catholic Party in England. The Evangelicals did not like it: they claimed that the government had actually breached the Act of Union and—refusing to accept Peel's decision—moved out of the established church under the guidance of the leading theologian of the age, Thomas Chalmers (1780–1847). Nearly one half of the ministers and their congregations nationwide left the Auld Kirk to establish the Free Church of Scotland. The latter—which accounted for the overwhelming majority of the worshippers in the Highlands and the Isles—embodied Scottish opposition to Anglocentric

parliamentary rule to such an extent that it became what historians have described as a form of "surrogate nationalism." In theological terms it was strictly Calvinistic. In political terms it was close to the Liberal Party, as the latter was generally sympathetic to the claims of religious freedom and even separation between state and church (a cause that was enthusiastically supported by radicals and Nonconformists in both England and Wales).

Not only was Evangelicalism strong in Scotland. It was also transforming the religious landscape of the rest of the British Isles. A series of revivals resulted in a dramatic increase of the total number of members of Nonconformist denominations in England and Wales: as early as 1851, census returns indicated that about 50 percent of churchgoers were Dissenters. The latter dominated religious life in Northern Ireland, the industrial North of England, the Midlands, and Wales, where a remarkable national awakening began around the politically powerful Welsh-speaking Dissenting chapels.

1851–1901

The first thirteen years of Queen Victoria's reign (r. 1837–1901) had thus been characterized by political unrest, social conflict, and economic tragedy. However, from 1851 the situation improved considerably. Indeed, the 1850s were a decade of great economic expansion—with Britain as "the workshop of the world"—and social consolidation. As Chartism petered out, friendly societies, cooperatives, and trade unions absorbed the energy and attention of a growing proportion of the working classes. Despite the prophecies of Karl Marx (1818–1883) and Friedrich Engels (1820–1895), far from challenging capitalism, the working men and their associations were eager to adapt to market expectations. Their ideological inspiration came from Samuel Smiles's best-seller *Self-Help* (1859), which honored the genius and enterprise of the self-made man, and from the writings of liberal economists and political thinkers such as John Stuart Mill (1806–1873), the author of the *Principles of Political Economy* (1848) and *On Liberty* (1859). The Crystal Palace international exhibition of 1851 was a celebration of British achievement in the fields of industrial production, manufacturing, and design. It set standards for the rest of the world—which was quick to catch up. In these boom years, even Ireland started to recover from the famine: as farmers were

A London chimney sweep, 1884. The ubiquitous figure of the sweep was an obvious reminder of the difficult nature of labor in Victorian England. ©CORBIS

eager to make the most of the new economic climate, nationalism faded into insignificance or American exile and the traditional two-party system appeared adequate to represent the wishes and the needs of the Irish electors.

In domestic politics the leading figures were the Liberals Lord Palmerston (Henry John Temple; 1784–1865) and Lord John Russell and the Peelite Gladstone, who became chancellor of the exchequer in the 1853–1855 coalition government under the earl of Aberdeen (George Hamilton-Gordon; 1784–1860). As chancellor, Gladstone proceeded to implement free trade, reducing import duties and aiming at balancing direct and indirect taxation. His policies appealed to consumer pressure groups (such as the cooperatives) as well as to middle-class reformers and radicals, such as Cobden and the great Quaker leader John

Bright (1811–1889). From then until 1929 free trade remained a sort of secular religion in popular politics, the creed on which the success of the Liberal Party was secured and retained.

The major challenges to mid-Victorian self-confidence came from abroad. In 1853 the country joined France in a war to prevent Russia from undermining the Ottoman Empire in eastern Europe. London was worried about Russian colonial expansion in central Asia and felt that the Ottoman Empire was the best barrier against such designs. The war (1853–1856) was fought in Crimea, on the Black Sea, where Sevastopol was the main naval base of the Russian fleet. Although Britain and France, and their junior ally the Italian Kingdom of Sardinia, managed to defeat the Russians, the war highlighted the inefficiency of the British army (especially the medical and supply services) and the civil service—both of which underwent substantial modernization over the next twenty years. In 1857 Britain faced a major rebellion in India, where the sepoys (Indian troops) of the East India Company massacred their officers and seized a number of cities. Britain's response was facilitated by the fact that the country had been sending troops to China, which Palmerston was successfully trying to force to accept Anglo-Indian imports (primarily opium, hence the name of the conflict). These troops were rapidly redeployed in India and managed to crush the numerically stronger insurgents. The Indian Mutiny prompted the Palmerston government to transfer the powers hitherto exercised by the East India Company to a secretary of state directly accountable to Parliament.

The Palmerston era came to an end only with the prime minister's death in 1865. His successors Lord John Russell (now elevated to the House of Lords as the earl Russell) and Gladstone were determined to satisfy the popular demand for franchise reform. They agreed with John Bright that the time had come when it was safer to enfranchise the working man than to keep him out of the constitution. Mill would have wanted to see the vote extended to women as well, and his campaign elicited substantial support in Parliament, but not enough to bring about the desired amendment to the Reform Bill. Later he further elaborated his case in *The Subjection of Women* (1869), which became immediately a classic of feminist thought. Even the vote for the working men was quite contentious and split the Liberals. Eventually Lord Derby (Edward George Geoffrey Smith Stanley; 1799–1869) and Disraeli persuaded a minority Conservative government to support an alternative Reform Bill, which—drastically amended by the pro-reform Liberals—was passed in 1867. This Second Reform Act conferred the vote on borough householders on a residential qualification, but did not extend the same provision to county constituencies or to Ireland, and avoided any drastic redistribution of seats. The result was, however, much more radical than Disraeli would have wanted. The working men were now a majority in many borough constituencies, and were rabidly Liberal in politics.

The first election under the reformed system resulted in a landslide Liberal victory. Gladstone, the new prime minister, had a precise reform agenda, which he immediately proceeded to implement. The disestablishment of the Protestant Church of Ireland created religious equality before the law between all denominations in Ireland. The 1870 Irish Land Act tried (unsuccessfully) to satisfy the tenant farmers' aspirations to stability of tenure. The 1870 Education Act created a system of rate-supported primary schools under elected school boards, inspired by the Massachusetts school system. For the first time women could both vote and stand for election for local authorities. The Married Women's Property Act (1870) was an important move toward equality in property rights (it was further strengthened by the second Gladstone government in 1882). In 1871 trade unions received full legal protection for their funds, and a separate law defined the conditions under which peaceful strikes could be conducted. Both laws had been prepared in consultation with the newly organized Trades Union Congress (TUC), which from 1868 met annually to define the labor movement's policy aims.

One guiding principle of Gladstonian liberalism was meritocracy, irrespective of differences of creed or social standing: thus the ancient universities of Oxford and Cambridge ceased to be the preserve of members of the Church of England, while the army was reformed and professionalized with the abolition of the system under which commissions could be purchased rather than earned through proven competence, merit, and military valor. In foreign affairs Gladstone pursued British aims through multilateral negotiations and the Concert of Europe, and advocated international arbitration wherever possible, as in the Anglo-American dispute over the losses inflicted on U.S. shipping by British-built confederate cruisers during the American civil war. This was the famous *Alabama* case, named after one of these privateering warships. Eventually a specially convened international court ruled that the British government owed reparations to Washington, and Gladstone promptly agreed to pay. The government ran out of steam in 1873, when a bill to reform Irish university education was rejected in the Commons, and in 1874 Gladstone lost the general election.

Disraeli was then able to form a Conservative government with a working majority—the first since 1846. Although his victory came as a surprise, he presided over a series of important reforms that rivaled Gladstone's achievements. Between 1875 and 1878 trade union laws were further reformed to the full satisfaction of the labor movement, city councils were empowered to clear slums, the school system was expanded, and factory legislation was consolidated. Important laws were passed to improve public health and reduce river pollution. Yet Disraeli, who became the earl of Beaconsfield in 1876, found foreign affairs much more interesting than domestic reform. His unilateralist approach to the eastern question (the Ottoman Empire and the Russians were again at war with one another, this time over Bulgaria) generated both support and opposition at home. Gladstone led a Liberal campaign over the Bulgarian Atrocities in 1876, after press revelations about the massacre of some twelve thousand Christian peasants by Ottoman troops. On the other hand, Tory nationalist fervor reached a peak in 1878, when Britain seemed ready to go to war on behalf of the Ottomans to stop the Russians. Eventually, Beaconsfield and his foreign secretary, Lord Salisbury (Robert Arthur Talbot Gascoyne-Cecil; 1830–1903), managed to find a peaceful and satisfactory way out of the eastern crisis with the 1878 Berlin Congress. However, the Conservative eagerness to wave the flag resulted in two embarrassing colonial wars in Afghanistan and Zululand in 1879, in both of which the British were initially defeated.

In the election of 1880 Gladstone exploited popular disappointment about these defeats, as well as the general concern about trade depression and budget deficits. The outcome was another Liberal victory, which returned him to 10 Downing Street, the official residence of the prime minister. Despite his earlier criticism of Tory imperialism, the Liberal prime minister found himself pursuing similar policies, especially in Egypt. Britain decided to invade that country in 1882 in order to secure the control of the Suez Canal Zone when it was felt that a nationalist military government was threatening western interests.

Although Gladstone's second government has often been unfavorably compared with his first administration, its achievements were substantial: in particular, the system of parliamentary representation was drastically reformed. In 1883 a Corrupt Practices Act dealt effectively with the question of electoral expenses and corruption. In 1884 the Third Reform Act adopted a uniform residential household franchise for both counties and boroughs throughout the United Kingdom, including Ireland. As a result, a majority of the electorate (about 70 percent of the total) consisted of working men. Finally, in 1885 a radical redistribution of seats brought about the Chartist dream of "equal electoral districts." One of the first results of the act was the return of a larger number of working-class representatives to Parliament, where they sat as members of the Liberal Party (the so-called Lib-Labs).

The other major area of government reform was Ireland. From 1874 the decline in agricultural prices had severely affected the Irish farmers and landowners. Unable to pay the old rents, tenants were evicted. The problem became political when Michael Davitt (1846–1906) organized the farmers in the Irish Land League, with the aim to resist eviction and enforce lower rents. In Parliament the League was supported by Charles Stewart Parnell (1846–1891), an Irish Protestant landowner who had adopted the cause of Irish nationalism and demanded Home Rule (Parliamentary self-government) for his country. Parnell's nationalist rhetoric was calculated to attract the support of the Irish Republican Brotherhood or Fenians, a militant society particularly strong in the United States. The Fenians advocated violent insurrections and resorted to terrorism to achieve Irish independence. However, Parnell's actual program was neither republican nor independentist. Ireland had too much to gain from the British Empire—which was also an *Irish* empire, as scholarship at the turn of the twenty-first century has demonstrated—for Parnell to consider full separation. What he wanted was the restoration of something like the old "Grattan Parliament," which, he hoped, would enable the Irish to look after their own domestic affairs more effectively than they were able to do through Westminster. This program was supported by the Catholic hierarchy (who abhorred republicanism) and by many parish priests. Thus Parnell squared the circle of establishing a movement that was comprehensive of all shades of nationalism and truly popular, and yet conservative enough to obtain the blessings and support of the church and, potentially, even of the British government. Where he failed was in Ulster, whose Protestant

The Unemployed of London: Inscription on the Gates, West India Docks. Engraving from the *Illustrated London News*, 20 February 1886. The London docks were a locus of the labor unrest that culminated in the West End Riots of 8 February 1886. PRIVATE COLLECTION/BRIDGEMAN ART LIBRARY

majority was appalled by the prospect of "Rome Rule" in a predominantly Catholic Ireland. At first, the British government's response was to try to make the Union work better for Ireland: the Second Land Act of 1881 granted the tenant farmers what they had been demanding for years—fair rents, fixity of tenure, and free sale ("the Three F's"). Under this law specially appointed land courts were empowered to set rents below the market rate, and the law protected tenants from eviction for as long as they paid the rent. However, as the worldwide crisis of agricultural prices worsened, within a few years even the judicially settled rents proved too high to be payable. The Irish responded by voting for Parnell, whose party secured most seats outside northeast Ulster in 1885. Gladstone interpreted the outcome of this election as a referendum for Home Rule, and decided to act accordingly.

He then proposed a bill granting Ireland a status similar to that of Canada. This came with a third land bill, which proposed to use treasury loans to enable Irish tenants to purchase their farms (the loans would then be repayable in terminable annuities through the Irish government). The two bills were very controversial and caused the Liberal Party to split between Unionists and Home Rulers. The Liberal Unionists were led by the Whig Lord Hartington (Spencer Compton; 1833–1908) and the radical Joseph Chamberlain (1836–1914). At the ensuing election (June 1886) Gladstone and Parnell were defeated by the coalition between Liberal Unionists and Conservatives, who formed the next government under Lord Salisbury.

Salisbury's government (1886–1892) sought consolidation at home and abroad. The creation of county councils (1888) proved an important step in the reform of local government in Britain, and in 1891 primary education became free. In Ireland they introduced sweeping land acts—de facto moving toward Gladstone's idea of using treasury money for land purchase—and created a Congested Districts Board with wide-ranging powers and generous resources to develop the economy of the west of Ireland. Salisbury and his nephew Arthur James Balfour (1848–1930; Irish chief secretary, 1887–1891) hoped that these reforms would "kill Home Rule by kindness." However, as nationalism continued to inflame rural unrest, the government curtailed civil liberty through special police powers.

Meanwhile unemployment and recurrent trade crises generated social unrest in England as well. In 1887 the police clashed with a demonstration in London. In 1889–1891 a series of strikes mobilized previously unorganized sectors of the working classes, including the dockers, the matchmakers, and the gas workers. These strikes saw socialist agitators involved for the first time in the organization of the unskilled workers. Socialism had been surprisingly weak in British politics until then. The labor movement had been politically divided between Conservatives and Liberals, with a majority of the trade union members solidly aligned with Gladstone's party. The situation did not change at the end of the century, and the few socialist societies that had been established from 1882 remained small and marginal, despite the demonstrations and strikes in the years from 1887 to 1891. The principal of them were the Social Democratic Federation (Marxist), the Fabian Society (pursuing the socialist "permeation" of existing political parties), and the Independent Labour Party (ILP) founded in Bradford in 1893. Three ILP candidates were in Parliament until 1895, when they lost their seats in the general Conservative reaction.

The election of 1892 brought Gladstone back to power, but with a comparatively small majority that proved inadequate to the task of forcing Home Rule through the predominantly Unionist House of Lords. The Liberal–Irish Nationalist alliance had been weakened by the Parnell divorce scandal in 1890, and the resulting loss of credibility proved fatal to the Second Home Rule Bill (1893), after whose rejection Gladstone resigned and retired from Parliament. His ideas remained very influential in the party, which, however, was defeated at the election of 1895.

Salisbury was then back in government with Joseph Chamberlain as his colonial secretary. Despite the government's ambitious program of social reforms, an unwillingness to increase the income tax, and the increased demands of the military services prevented serious progress in the field of welfare legislation. In particular the Boer War (1899–1902) proved long and expensive. It resulted in the British annexation of the former Boer republics and the creation of modern South Africa, but the scandals associated with the importation of Chinese indentured laborers and the use of concentration camps for Boer civilians created considerable embarrassment for the government. In 1902 Salisbury was replaced by Balfour, whose government effectively solved the land problem in Ireland by completing the transfer of property from the old landowners to the farmers (1903 Wyndham Act). However, Balfour was unable to stop the disintegration of the coalition's electoral support, now threatened by Chamberlain's revived radicalism. Chamberlain proposed the adoption of import tariffs to sustain employment and pay for social reforms without increasing the income tax. While his proposal divided both Conservatives and Unionists, it gave new unity and enthusiasm to the Liberals, who fought a vigorous campaign to retain free trade, which was popularly regarded as the cause of "the big loaf" (i.e., cheap bread and foodstuff in general). This resulted in the Liberal electoral victory of 1906, when Henry Campbell-Bannerman (1836–1908) formed a government. The new government was supported by the Labour Representation Committee (or LRC, which changed its name to Labour Party in 1906), and by the Irish Nationalist Party, which continued to demand Home Rule.

1901–1914

It was the beginning of a new era. The change had already been prepared by the passing of Queen Victoria, who had died in 1901. The new sovereign, Edward VII, reigned for only nine years, but, like his mother, he too defined an age, which was one of emancipation, liberalism, social and scientific innovation, and confidence in the future. He was succeeded in 1910 by his son George V (r. 1910–1936).

Social reform was sponsored both by Labour and, especially, by the radical "New Liberalism" that dominated post-1908 government policy. The Labour Party had been established as the Labour Representation Committee (LRC) in

A Diamond Jubilee portrait of Queen Victoria, 1897. The 75th anniversary of the popular queen's ascension to the throne was marked by massive celebrations throughout England. ©BETTMANN/CORBIS

1900. Originally it was created by the TUC in response to changes in trade union legislation that threatened the very right to strike in the years 1899 to 1902, when the Liberal opposition was weak and unable to help. Thus the LRC was set up primarily to advocate trade union interests. Although socialist societies were affiliated to it, neither the LRC nor the early Labour Party had a socialist program or ideology, and most of their members were essentially liberal in their ideological outlook. In 1903 the chairman of the LRC, James Ramsey MacDonald (1866–1937), struck a secret electoral pact with the Liberal Party in order to coordinate the strategies of the two anti-Conservative parties at the forthcoming election. Although the pact worked well, in terms of results the 1906 election was a resounding Liberal success, and, as the socialist playwright George Bernard Shaw

(1856–1950) remarked at the time, Labour seemed little more than "a cork" floating on the Gladstonian tide.

In some respects, the governments of Henry Campbell-Bannerman (1905–1908) and Herbert Henry Asquith (1908–1916) were indeed "Gladstonian." In particular, their opposition to the women's suffrage campaign—opposition that was stiffened by their revulsion at the militant methods adopted by the suffragettes—was indeed consistent with Gladstone's old Liberalism. On the other hand, there was also a "New Liberalism" that went well beyond mere Gladstonianism. The Liberal politicians who came to the forefront of party politics from the 1890s argued that the state should accept responsibility for the creation of conditions under which citizens would enjoy a degree of liberty from the anxieties of old age, unemployment, and sickness. Pensions and national insurance would sustain domestic demand and indirectly stimulate economic growth and living standards. Radical economists such as John Atkinson Hobson (1858–1940) insisted that the benefits of Gladstonian free trade should be shored up by decisive government action to secure "positive liberty." Ministers such as Asquith (1852–1928), David Lloyd George (1863–1945, prime minister 1916–1922), and Winston Churchill (1874–1965)—who had recently abandoned Conservatism for Liberalism over the issue of free trade—proceeded to legislate along these lines from 1908. By 1910 the new reforms required the government to increase taxation, which Lloyd George proposed to do by raising the income tax. Outraged at what they regarded as an attack on private property, the House of Lords broke constitutional convention by rejecting a money bill. In response, Asquith dissolved Parliament twice in 1910: the first election (in January) was about forcing the Lords to accept "the People's Budget"; the second election (December) was about reducing the power of the Lords. The Liberals won both elections, and in 1911 the Parliament Act reduced the Lords to the status of a revising chamber with suspensory veto of two years, after which a bill that they opposed would become law automatically. This paved the way for further reforms, including the disestablishment of the Episcopalian Church in Wales and the Irish Home Rule Act. Both were passed in 1912, both were suspended by the Lords for two years, and were due to be enacted in 1914. Then, however, the outbreak of World War I caused the government to suspend all controversial legislation (and both acts were very controversial) for the duration of the war, in order to maximize national unity.

The Asquith government's inability to avoid the war could be seen as its greatest failure. However, it is unlikely that the government could have done much to either prevent the war or avoid Britain's involvement in it. In the 1890s under Salisbury, Britain had cultivated Germany as a potential ally against France, whose colonial expansionism in Africa London regarded with alarm. Later, Germany's ambitious program of naval rearmament and her unpredictable kaiser brought about a complete change of mind in London. By 1904 France was Britain's informal ally. Moreover, Britain now regarded Russia—another old enemy—as a barrier against German expansionism. This Anglo-German rivalry was a disaster for both countries, but no amount of good will on either side was able to compensate for the combined effects of Germany's erratic foreign policy and the perverse operation of the system of countervailing alliances, which involved countries going to war on behalf of their friends irrespective of any threats to their own national interests. The year 1914 marked the end of an era not only for the United Kingdom, but also for the rest of Europe.

See also **Alliance System; Boer War; Chartism; Concert of Europe; Conservatism; Corn Laws, Repeal of; Crimean War; Crystal Palace; East India Company; Emigration; French Revolutionary Wars and Napoleonic Wars; Imperialism; India; Ireland; Labour Party; Scotland; Sepoy Mutiny; Tories; Waterloo; Whigs.**

BIBLIOGRAPHY

Bayly, Christopher Alan. *Imperial Meridian: The British Empire and the World, 1780–1830.* London and New York, 1989.

Bebbington, David William. *The Nonconformist Conscience: Chapel and Politics, 1870–1914.* Oxford, U.K., 1982.

Bew, Paul. *Charles Stewart Parnell.* Dublin, 1991.

Biagini, Eugenio F. *Gladstone.* London and New York, 2000.

Briggs, Asa. *The Age of Improvement, 1783–1867.* London, 1959.

Daunton, Martin J. *Progress and Poverty: An Economic and Social History of Britain, 1700–1850.* Oxford, U.K., and New York, 1995.

———. *Trusting Leviathan: The Politics of Taxation in Britain, 1799–1914.* Cambridge, U.K., and New York, 2001.

———. *Wealth and Welfare: An Economic and Social History of Britain, 1851–1951.* Oxford, U.K., and New York, 2005.

Davies, John. *A History of Wales.* London and New York, 1993.

Devine, Thomas Martin. *The Scottish Nation, 1700–2000.* London and New York, 1999.

Eccleshall, Robert, and Graham Walker, eds. *Biographical Dictionary of British Prime Ministers.* London and New York, 1998.

Foster, Robert Fitzroy. *Modern Ireland, 1600–1972.* London and New York, 1988.

Hempton, David. *Religion and Political Culture in Britain and Ireland: From the Glorious Revolution to the Decline of Empire.* Cambridge, U.K., and New York, 1996.

Hilton, Boyd. *The Age of Atonement: The Influence of Evangelicalism on Social and Economic Thought, 1795–1865.* Oxford, U.K., and New York, 1988.

———. "Lord Liverpool: The Art of Politics and the Practice of Government." *Transactions of the Royal Historical Society* 5th series, 38 (1988): 147–170.

Hoppen, K. Theodore. *The Mid-Victorian Generation, 1846–1886.* Oxford, U.K., and New York, 1998.

Hutchison, I. G. C. *A Political History of Scotland, 1832–1924: Parties, Elections and Issues.* Edinburgh, 1986.

Jackson, Alvin. *Ireland, 1798–1998: Politics and War.* Oxford, U.K., 1999.

Jenkins, Terence Andrew. *Disraeli and Victorian Conservatism.* London and New York, 1996.

———. *Sir Robert Peel.* London and New York, 1999.

Longford, Elizabeth. *Wellington.* London, 2002.

MacDonagh, Oliver. *The Emancipist: Daniel O'Connell, 1830–47.* London, 1989.

Mandler, Peter. *Aristocratic Government in the Age of Reform: Whigs and Liberals, 1830–1852.* Oxford, U.K., and New York, 1990.

Mitchell, Leslie George. *Charles James Fox.* London, 1992.

ó Gráda, Cormac. *Ireland: A New Economic History, 1780–1939.* Oxford, U.K., and New York, 1994.

Packer, Ian. *Lloyd George.* London and New York, 1998.

Parry, J. P. "Disraeli and England." *The Historical Journal* 43, no. 3 (2000): 699–728.

Porter, Bernard. *The Lion's Share: A Short History of British Imperialism, 1850–1983.* London and New York, 1984.

Pugh, Martin. *The Making of Modern British Politics, 1867–1945.* Oxford, U.K., 2002.

Reid, Alastair J. *United We Stand: A History of Britain's Trade Unions.* London and New York, 2004.

Steele, David. *Lord Salisbury: A Political Biography.* Cambridge, U.K., and New York, 1999.

Turner, Michael J. *Pitt the Younger: A Life.* London and New York, 2003.

EUGENIO BIAGINI

GREAT REFORMS TIMELINE

1855: Alexander II becomes tsar of the Russian Empire
1856: Russia concedes defeat in the Crimean War
1861: Emancipation of proprietary/seigniorial serfs and establishment of *volost* courts
1862: State Treasury created; state budget henceforth published
1863: Emancipation of appanage peasants; university statute; abolition of dehumanizing corporal punishments in military
1864: Zemstvo statute; judicial reform
1865: Temporary regulations on censorship
1866: Emancipation of state peasants; creation of State Bank
1874: Universal military service statute

GREAT REFORMS (RUSSIA). Between 1861 and 1874, Alexander II, tsar of Russia (r. 1855–1881), decreed major reforms of Russia's social, judicial, educational, financial, administrative, and military systems. His program came to be known as the Great Reforms. These acts liberated roughly 40 percent of the population from bondage, created an independent judicial system, introduced self-governing councils in towns and rural areas, eased censorship, transformed military service, strengthened banking, and granted more autonomy to universities. Alexander II accomplished this program in a mere thirteen years with the assistance of his brother Grand Duke Konstantin Nikolayevich, reform-minded bureaucrats, and conservative state servitors who placed loyalty to the tsar above their policy preferences.

The Great Reforms introduced a period of rapid social and economic development that was unrivaled in Russian history, save for the rule of Peter the Great (r. 1682–1725). Several key principles shaped the reforms: liberation of peasants from centuries of personal bondage, legality as an antidote to arbitrariness and caprice in judicial and administrative systems, greater openness (*glasnost*) in official and civil affairs, and civic engagement of all members of society. The overall goals were to accelerate economic development and restore Russia's military dominance as a Great Power after its sobering defeat in the Crimean War (1853–

1856). That defeat forced recognition that Russia's bonded and illiterate soldiers, with their outdated weapons and tactics, were no match for the soldiers western European powers put in the field with the benefits of the Industrial Revolution behind them.

CAUSES

Historians have long debated the causes for the Great Reforms. Marxist historians of the former Soviet Union identified economic crisis in the serf economy and increasing peasant disorders before 1861 as proofs of the "crisis of feudalism" and the rising political consciousness of the working masses. Other late Soviet historians, such as Peter A. Zaionchkovsky and V. A. Fedorov, and most Western scholars argued that the serf economy was not in decline, although it had little potential for dynamic growth, and that the "rebellions" were rarely mass actions, but often individual acts of passive resistance. Intellectual historians have pointed to the rise of abolitionist and reform sentiments among critics of serfdom and state corruption. The first criticisms dated to the late eighteenth century, when such works as Alexander Radishchev's *A Journey from St. Petersburg to Moscow* (1790) appeared, pointing not only to serfdom's abuses but also judicial and administrative corruption. Such writers as Ivan Turgenev (1818–1883) and painters as Alexei Venetsianov (1780–1847) also depicted Russia's bonded peasants in a sympathetic light, stressing their human dignity. Defeat in the Crimean War, however, proved decisive in moving Alexander II and such leading figures as Peter Valuev, minister of the interior, to initiate fundamental changes.

EMANCIPATION OF THE SERFS

The cornerstone of the Great Reforms was the emancipation of Russia's peasants. They fell into three groups. The proprietary or seigniorial serfs were the property of individual landowners and lived in conditions of virtual slavery; Alexander II proclaimed their liberation from personal bondage on 3 March (19 February, old style) 1861. The appanage peasants lived on the personal properties of the Romanov family; Alexander II granted them personal freedom in 1863. They received land allotments in 1863 and were placed on forty-nine-year redemption payments in 1865. The state peasants lived on state lands under state administrators; they received freedom in 1866.

The core "freedom" the peasants received was the elimination of the personal, arbitrary, and capricious power of their noble and state masters. Members of the noble landowning estate and the tsar's agents could no longer buy and sell peasants, mortgage them for cash, order their daily labors, determine whom and when they married, move them from one estate to another, break up families, beat them, claim sexual rights over them, exile them to Siberia, impose both police and judicial authority over them, demand that they gather forest products such as berries for their masters' larders, or decide who would enter military service for virtually their entire adult lives.

The emancipation legislation involved a land reform that transferred as much as half of the nobility's land to the peasants. The reformers tried to design this transfer so that it would not cause dangerous instability in the countryside. They also tried to soften the economic blows to the nobility and to guarantee that peasants would continue to produce crops and pay their taxes. These aims led to restrictions on the peasants and opportunities for economic coercion for the gentry; the peasants' freedom was thus ambiguous.

Except for household serfs and those peasants who chose to accept a free "pauper's allotment" of one-quarter the size of other allotments, emancipated peasants received land for which they had to pay the state redemption payments scheduled for forty-nine years. Land went not to individual peasants, but to officially constituted communes, whose peasant leaders oversaw land distribution and took on some of the functions (e.g., collecting taxes) that serf owners had formerly executed. The legislation prohibited emancipated peasants from leaving their designated communes for nine years; after 1870, they could leave, but only with the approval of the commune's leadership.

Many peasants were disappointed not to receive land freely, and most former serfs received less land than they had cultivated before the emancipation. Their land usually did not include critical forest, meadows, or access to waterways. Most land transfer settlements inflated land prices, and thus redemption payments. Former state peasants generally received more land than they had previously cultivated. Many former serfs subsequently had to enter into extortionate agreements with their former masters, rendering labor in exchange for access to the lord's forest, to water sources, and to meadows.

Despite peasants' frustrations and protests, land shortages, and failures to meet their tax and redemption payment obligations, two facts point to the emancipation's positive impact: the population of the Russian Empire, which was more than 80 percent peasant, exploded in the post-emancipation years in demographic testimony to the improving health of the liberated peasantry, especially children; and peasants began to buy more land from the nobility in the succeeding decades. By 1905 peasants had purchased over 25 million hectares (62 million acres) of land.

The reformers included a specifically peasant court (the *volost* or township court) in the emancipation legislation to free peasants from their former masters' judicial tyranny, while providing a hybrid judicial institution that instructed peasants in the law. The courts had peasant judges who decided petty civil disputes according to customary law, while referring to the state code of laws (with the assistance of a literate clerk) to ensure that their decisions did not violate statutory law. The township courts underwent reform and expansion in 1889 and survived until the end of the imperial era. By 1900, hundreds of thousands of peasants were taking their disputes to these courts each year, making knowledgeable use of the court's procedures.

OTHER GREAT REFORMS

Progress toward the rule of law, publicity or transparency of judicial proceedings, and civic engagement also characterized the judicial reform of 1864. This reform established an independent judiciary, introduced trial by jury for criminal cases, opened court sessions to the public, and established justices of the peace. Peasants were included among those eligible to serve as jurors, and the publicity of court sessions enabled journalists to report on cases. Court records reveal that most juries had peasant majorities, because members of the nobility tried to avoid burdensome jury duty. Justices of the peace existed in rural areas until 1889 and in cities until 1917. They also attracted hundreds of thousands of cases by the turn of the century.

The zemstvo reform of 1864 addressed the need for new systems of local administration. Serf owners and state administrators had been largely responsible for overseeing public works and welfare. True to the reform principle of public engagement, the reformers designed local district and provincial councils, the zemstvos, with locally elected delegates from peasant communes, the ranks of landowners, and towns. The councils were made responsible for economic and social welfare of their region. These organs of local self-governance proved successful in public health programs, elementary education, fire insurance, and statistical bureaus. They also became a crucible of Russian liberalism, because zemstvo employees developed confidence in their living knowledge of rural Russia's needs. The zemstvos ultimately proved fertile ground for opposition to the tsarist regime. A municipal reform of 1870 established town councils, similar to the zemstvos, which were even more successful.

Two additional reforms of the 1860s supported higher education and expanded freedom of the press: the University Statute of 1863 and new "temporary" regulations on censorship in 1865. The guiding figure in the university reform was A. V. Golovnin, the minister of education from 1861 to 1866. The new statute took shape against the backdrop of increasing student activism. Despite their refusal to grant students more rights, the reformers granted university professors considerable autonomy over curriculum, hiring and promotion, and internal university judicial proceedings. The state also increased the universities' budgets and provided scholarships for graduate students and scholars to study abroad. Other educational reforms opened secondary education to any student who could pass the entrance exams, regardless of social estate. The University Statute did not open universities to matriculation by female students.

The increasing numbers of educated Russians had more to read after the government eased censorship in 1865. A rapidly expanding number of journals and newspapers resulted, from serious political and literary endeavors to sensationalist papers that specialized in gruesome crimes and scandal. The "temporary" regulations lasted into the twentieth century.

The Great Reforms also addressed economic development and the military directly through banking measures and the military reform of 1874. Under the leadership of Mikhail Reitern, the minister of finance, the state established the State Bank. During the 1860s it also began to publish the annual budget (a further embodiment of the principle of transparency), centralized state finances in the newly formed State Treasury, and supported commercial banking through subsidies to encourage investment. The policy worked: sixty commercial banks opened in Russia between 1864 and 1874; they helped finance Russia's subsequent industrial development.

The military reform of 1874 was the last Great Reform. Dmitri Milyutin, the minister of war from 1861 to 1881, spearheaded reforms in the army, while Grand Duke Konstantin Nikolayevich did so for the navy. Milyutin oversaw the elimination of class-based service (peasants serving under noble officers), overcentralized military administration, antiquated weapons, and tactics that favored parade-ground precision over agile fighting skills. In 1863 he persuaded Alexander II to abolish dehumanizing corporal punishments that had characterized military service. Over the next ten years, Milyutin reduced service from twenty-five years to fifteen, revised officers' education, brought military judicial procedures into line with the 1864 judicial reform, improved provisions for soldiers, created military districts in the empire to decentralize administration, sponsored open debate through military journals, and developed programs to provide basic literacy to peasant soldiers. The percentage of literate soldiers rose from under 10 percent to 50 percent by the end of the 1860s. On 13 January (1 January, old style) 1874 Alexander II announced Milyutin's most dramatic reform: a universal military service statute, which required every male citizen to serve for up to fifteen years on active and reserve duty in what thus became a citizen army, rather than one based on class. The higher the recruit's education, the lower was his term of active service.

CONSEQUENCES/IMPACT

As a consequence of the Great Reforms, the nobility lost two key defining features of their status: ownership of other human beings who provided them free labor and freedom from military service. As the zemstvos and reformed courts took root, landowning gentry also lost their dominant roles in rural life, even finding that their former serfs could sit in judgment over them in jury trials. Emancipated peasants, however frustrated by the terms of the land reform, took advantage of the courts and zemstvos to pursue their interests and engage in public life. Many became landowners themselves. Expanded educational opportunities through zemstvo schools, universities and institutes, and military service increased literacy among the peasantry and stimulated the growth of professions among the other social estates. The Russian Empire continued to be a predominantly agricultural, illiterate, and rural society (over 80 percent of the population still lived in the countryside in 1897), but state-sponsored industrialization and urbanization provided opportunities for all layers of society. By 1913 the Russian Empire was in the top tier of world economies.

The Great Reforms, however, did not alter the political structure of the empire. The Russian tsar remained an autocrat, above the law and without any formal constraints on his personal will. The tension between the social and economic transformations the Great Reforms introduced and the persistent patriarchal paternalism of the autocratic system worsened after 1881 when radical populists

assassinated Alexander II, the "Tsar Liberator." Ultimately, Russian citizens as heirs to the Great Reforms would reject their tsar's continued treatment of them as dependent children in need of paternal direction.

See also **Alexander II; Russia; Serfs, Emancipation of.**

BIBLIOGRAPHY

Primary Sources

Frierson, Cathy A., ed. and trans. *Aleksandr Nikolaevich Engelgardt's Letters from the Country, 1872–1887.* New York and Oxford, U.K., 1993. Most influential eyewitness account of rural relations in the countryside in the first two decades after emancipation.

Secondary Sources

Burbank, Jane. *Russian Peasants Go to Court: Legal Culture in the Countryside, 1905–1917.* Bloomington, Ind., 2004. Definitive study of township courts in late imperial era.

Eklof, Ben. *Russian Peasant Schools: Officialdom, Village Culture, and Popular Pedagogy, 1861–1914.* Berkeley and Los Angeles, 1986. Definitive account of zemstvo educational programs.

Eklof, Ben, John Bushnell, and Larissa Zakharova, eds. *Russia's Great Reforms, 1855–1881.* Bloomington, Ind., 1994. Anthology of articles by Russian, American, and British scholars.

Emmons, Terence. *The Russian Landed Gentry and the Peasant Emancipation of 1861.* London, 1968.

Emmons, Terence, and Wayne S. Vucinich, eds. *The Zemstvo in Russia: An Experiment in Local Self-Government.* Cambridge, U.K., 1982. Anthology of articles on various zemstvo programs.

Field, Daniel. *The End of Serfdom: Nobility and Bureaucracy in Russia, 1855–1861.* Cambridge, Mass., 1976.

Frieden, Nancy Mandelker. *Russian Physicians in an Era of Reform and Revolution, 1856–1905.* Princeton, N.J., 1981. Definitive study of zemstvo public health programs.

Frierson, Cathy A. *"All Russia Is Burning!" A Cultural History of Fire and Arson in Late Imperial Russia.* Seattle, Wash., 2002. Includes chapters on zemstvo fire insurance and village planning programs.

Hoch, Steven L. "On Good Numbers and Bad: Malthus, Population Trends, and Peasant Standard of Living in Late Imperial Russia." *Slavic Review* 53, no. 1 (1994): 41–75.

Kucherov, Samuel. *Courts, Lawyers, and Trials under the Last Three Tsars.* New York, 1953.

Lincoln, W. Bruce. *The Great Reforms: Autocracy, Bureaucracy, and the Politics of Change in Imperial Russia.*

DeKalb, Ill., 1990. Excellent study of origins, details, and impact of the reforms.

Moon, David. *The Abolition of Serfdom in Russia, 1762–1907.* London, 2001.

Worobec, Christine D. *Peasant Russia: Family and Community in the Post-emancipation Period.* Princeton, N.J., 1991.

Wortman, Richard S. *The Development of a Russian Legal Consciousness.* Chicago, 1976.

Zaionchkovsky, Peter A. *The Abolition of Serfdom in Russia.* Edited and translated by Susan Wobst. Gulf Breeze, Fla., 1978. The premier late Soviet study of emancipation.

CATHY A. FRIERSON

GREECE. The Greeks were the first of the subject peoples of the Ottoman Empire to achieve independence, thereby setting in motion the process of the gradual breakup of the Ottoman Empire. The Greek example was to be followed during the nineteenth and early twentieth centuries by the Serbs (who had secured a qualified autonomy in 1815), Romanians, Bulgarians, and Albanians. The Greek national movement is also significant in that it was the first nationalist movement to develop within a non-Christian polity. Although the Greeks were in their overwhelming majority Orthodox Christians, their Ottoman overlords were Muslims and Muslims were the largest element in the Ottoman Empire.

The Ottoman was a multi-ethnic, multi-religious empire. That the Greeks were the first of its subject peoples to establish an independent state is due to a number of factors. The armed insurrection that broke out in 1821 would have had no chance of success had the Ottoman Empire not been in manifest decline, under threat from external enemies and with its authority challenged by warlords and ill-disciplined janissaries from within. Geography also played a role. The very large seaboard of the Greek lands, and the fact that the Ionian Islands, to the northwest of present-day Greece, were not under Ottoman rule, made the Greeks more open to influences from the west than their neighbors to the north.

Moreover, while they were always second-class citizens as Christians, Greeks enjoyed a privileged position within the Ottoman state structure. Greeks controlled the affairs of the Orthodox Church, whose head, the Ecumenical Patriarch, and higher clergy were always Greek. The hierarchy of the Orthodox Church exercised a considerable measure of authority, civil as well as religious, over the Orthodox Christian flock, including the large numbers of Orthodox Christians who were not Greek-speakers or of Greek ethnic origin. From the early eighteenth century, Greek notables of Constantinople (called Phanariot Greeks) played an important role in the conduct of imperial foreign policy.

Much of the seaborne commerce of the empire was conducted in Greek ships, while Greek or Hellenized Orthodox merchants came to control much of the commerce of the Balkan Peninsula. These merchants generated the wealth that was indispensable to the intellectual revival that was so significant a development both in the Greek world and in the mercantile diaspora communities that were coming into existence in the late eighteenth and early nineteenth centuries. Well-to-do merchants founded or subsidized schools and colleges and underwrote the cost of printing the increasing number of books that began to be published in Greek for a Greek audience. Most importantly, merchants subsidized the studies of young Greeks in the universities of western and central Europe.

During the early centuries of Ottoman rule in the Greek lands, there had been little awareness among the Greeks of the heritage of ancient Greece. Now, however, Greek students became aware of the extraordinary reverence for the language and civilization of classical Greece that existed among educated Europeans. They returned from Europe to the Greek lands determined to share their enthusiasm, at times amounting to an obsession, for Greek antiquity with their compatriots. It was during the early years of the nineteenth century that Greek nationalists, to the chagrin of the Orthodox Church (which equated antiquity with paganism) began to name their children (and their ships) after worthies of ancient Greece, such as Leonidas, Pericles, Aspasia, and Miltiades. Adamantios Korais (1748–1833) played a leading role in the attempt, by no means always successful, to instill in the Greeks the notion that they were the lineal descendants of the ancient Greeks so widely regarded as the progenitors of European civilization. A native of Smyrna (Izmir), he spent most of his adult life in France and was one of the foremost classical scholars of his age. He essentially saw education as the means of emancipating the Greeks from what he perceived as the yoke of the Ottoman Turks.

Others, however, placed their hopes of freedom in armed struggle. Foremost among these was Rigas Velestinlis (also known as Rigas Pheraios, 1758–1798). Under the influence of the French Revolution, Rigas elaborated an ambitious scheme for a Balkan-wide uprising against the Turks, and seems to have won the support of a small group of like-minded revolutionaries. He envisaged a revived Byzantine Empire, but with republican in place of monarchical institutions. Although he advocated equality for all the many peoples of the Ottoman Empire, including the Turks, the new state was to be Greek in language and culture. When, however, he arrived in Trieste on his way to launch his insurrection in December 1797, he was betrayed by a fellow Greek and handed over, with a number of his fellow conspirators, to the Ottoman authorities. The Ottomans strangled Rigas in Belgrade in June 1798.

Rigas's revolutionary project thus came to nothing, although his example remained an inspiration to future generations of Greek nationalists. These included the three young Greeks, Athanasios Tsakalof, Emmanuel Xanthos, and Nikolaos Skoufas. In 1814 in Odessa in southern Russia, these men founded the Philiki Etairia, or "Friendly Society," a secret revolutionary society whose purpose was to free the Greek motherland from the Ottoman yoke. With an elaborate hierarchical structure and initiation rituals influenced by freemasonry, attempts were made to recruit adherents throughout the Greek world and the communities of the diaspora. A failed effort was made to recruit Count Ioannis Capodistrias, a Greek from Corfu, as leader of the conspiracy; Capodistrias had served as the joint foreign minister of the Russian Tsar Alexander I (1777–1825) from 1816. The conspirators then turned for leadership to General Alexander Ypsilantis, a Phanariot Greek in the Russian service, and put it about that the enterprise enjoyed Russian support. This claim was without foundation, but gained credence among the Greeks as Russia was the sole Orthodox Christian power and, at a popular level, there was widespread belief in prophecies that, with Russian help, Orthodox Christians would once again rule in Constantinople, the former capital of the Byzantine Empire.

THE WAR OF INDEPENDENCE

The long-planned insurgency was launched in early 1821. The timing was intended to take advantage of the efforts of the Ottoman sultan Mahmud II (1785–1839) to crush the power of Ali Pasha (1741–1822), a Muslim Albanian warlord, who had carved out a fiefdom in what is now southern Albania and northwestern Greece that was effectively independent of Ottoman control. A force under the command of General Ypsilantis crossed the river Pruth into the Ottoman province of Moldavia, but was soon defeated. The insurgents in the Peloponnese met with greater success. Furious fighting, in which atrocities were committed on both sides, led the Turks to withdraw to their coastal fortresses. When news of the revolt reached the Ottoman capital, the Ecumenical Patriarch Gregory V was executed; this was not, as is still sometimes maintained, because he could not bring himself to condemn the insurgents. He and the Holy Synod did that in robust fashion. He was executed because, in Ottoman eyes, he had failed in his primary duty: that of ensuring the loyalty of his Orthodox flock to the Ottoman sultan.

On the Greek side, much of the burden of fighting was borne by the *klefts*, essentially bandits skilled in guerrilla warfare who had preyed on the Ottoman authorities and on rich Greeks, and who had acquired a scarcely justified reputation as defenders of the oppressed Greeks against Ottoman tyranny. The Greek cause was also much assisted by the strong nautical tradition that had developed in the islands of the Aegean. Greek mariners made effective use of small-fire ships to wreak havoc among the cumbersome Ottoman men-of-war.

The threat to the established order posed by the insurgency found little support among the conservative powers of Europe. Nonetheless, volunteer philhellenes (supporters of the Greek cause), nurtured on an idealized vision of ancient Greece and who in many instances were somewhat shocked by their encounter with Greek reality, journeyed from the countries of Europe and the United States to help the cause of Greek freedom. Their practical contribution to the war effort was limited, but pro-Greek agitation did serve to sustain sympathy for the Greek cause in the West.

Constitutional government was established in the areas of the Peloponnese and what is now southern mainland Greece at an early stage of the war for independence, a constitution being adopted early in 1822. But dissension soon manifested itself among the insurgents. Their politics were complicated, but in essence they reflected antagonism between two broad groupings. The first consisted of the Peloponnesian notables, the ship-owners of the islands, and the small number of Phanariot grandees who had rallied to the insurgent cause. These comprised what came to be known as the "civilian" or "aristocratic" party. The second group, the "military" or "democratic" party, by contrast, reflected the interests of the *kleft* leaders who had borne the brunt of the fighting; the most important of these leaders was Theodore Kolokotronis (1770–1843). The internal conflict can be seen as a contest between modernizers and traditional elites. The modernizers were inspired by nationalist rhetoric. Besides ridding the Greek lands of their Turkish overlords, they sought to fashion a liberal, constitutional state on the European model. Such a state would entail curtailing the extensive privileges of the church, whose support for the nationalist cause had been ambiguous, and the creation of a regular army—again after European models—to replace the irregular bands favored by the *klefts*. The traditional elites tended to look on the war as a religious crusade against the Muslim Turks rather than as a struggle for constitutional government and democracy. Their overriding concern was the retention of the privileges that they had enjoyed under Ottoman rule.

In 1824 these tensions erupted in internecine strife, which inevitably had serious consequences for the conduct of the war. Moreover, a new threat to the insurgents emerged in the form of Mehmet Ali, the ruler of Egypt, and of his son Ibrahim

Pasha, who had been offered lavish territorial compensation by Sultan Mahmud II in return for their assistance in crushing the revolt. For a time, the ruthless tactics employed by Ibrahim Pasha appeared to place the success of the Greek insurgency in doubt.

Help for the Greeks was at hand from an unlikely quarter, however, in the shape of the Great Powers (Britain, France, Austria, Russia, and Prussia), who were becoming increasingly concerned at the continuing instability and the consequent damage to their commercial interests in the region. Moreover, Britain and France were fearful that the ongoing conflict might strengthen Russian influence in the region. In 1826, Britain and Russia proposed joint mediation in the conflict through the Protocol of St. Petersburg. By the Treaty of London of 1827, France aligned itself with Britain and Russia. Thus was initiated the policy ambiguously termed "peaceful interference" by the British Foreign Secretary, George Canning (1770–1827). This resulted in the destruction in October 1827 of the Turkish-Egyptian fleet by a combined British, French, and Russian fleet at the Battle of Navarino.

INDEPENDENT GREECE

This naval victory ensured that some form of independent Greek state would come into existence, although its frontiers took some time to establish. Greek independence was formally recognized in 1832 by the three "Protecting Powers," Britain, France, and Russia. These Powers insisted that Greece be ruled by a king chosen from a royal house other than their own. Thus it was that Otto of Wittelsbach (1815–1867), second son of King Louis I of Bavaria, ascended the throne of Greece in 1833. His inheritance was not a promising one. Years of fighting had devastated the country economically. The structures of a functioning state had to be created where none had existed before. Moreover, the newly independent state contained fewer than a third of the Greeks that had been under Ottoman rule at the outbreak of the revolt.

Although the Protecting Powers had envisaged that Otto would introduce constitutional rule to Greece, it was not until 1844 that a reluctant Otto conceded a constitution and then only after a military coup, the earliest manifestation of a pattern of military intervention in the political system that was to characterize the politics of the new state. By the standards of the day, the 1844 constitution was a relatively liberal document (it granted virtually universal manhood suffrage, although women had to wait for over a century for the vote). Transplanting the institutions of parliamentary democracy to a society whose historical experience and values were very different from those of western Europe, however, proved difficult. Moreover, Greek politicians showed themselves adept at manipulating the country's fledgling democratic institutions and keeping themselves in power through the dispensation of patronage. *Rouspheti,* the dispensation of favors, and *mesa,* having the right connections, were key elements in the political system.

Otto's affection for his adopted country (he frequently wore the traditional dress of the *foustanella* or kilt) was not reciprocated by many of his subjects. They resented the fact that he remained a Catholic in a country whose Orthodox religious tradition manifested strong undercurrents of anti-Catholicism and, indeed, of anti-Westernism. In 1862 there was an attempt against the life of his wife, Amalia, and Otto was driven into exile in his native Bavaria following a putsch by the army.

Otto's successor was a member of the Danish Glucksberg dynasty who ascended the throne in 1863 as King George I, beginning a fifty-year reign that was ended by his assassination by a madman in 1913. A new constitution amplified the democratic rights granted in 1844, although the sovereign retained considerable, albeit vaguely defined, powers in matters of foreign policy. An important stage in the country's constitutional evolution was reached when, in 1875, King George conceded the principle that he would only call upon a politician to form a government if he enjoyed the "declared" support of a majority of members of parliament. The adoption of this principle brought an end to continual changes of government and ushered in a more or less functioning two-party political system, with the modernizing Harilaos Trikoupis alternating in power with his more demagogic rival, Theodore Deliyannis during the last quarter of the nineteenth century.

Greek irregular volunteers. Photographed at Thessaly during the Greco-Turkish War, 1897. ©CORBIS

TERRITORIAL EXPANSION

The slow and uneven process of consolidating the country's democratic institutions took place against a background of continued agitation for the implementation of the *Megali Idea,* the "Great Idea" of bringing about the incorporation within the Greek kingdom of the large Greek populations that had remained under Ottoman rule when Greece had achieved its independence in the 1830s. Politicians across the political spectrum shared in these aspirations. Where they differed was in how best they could be achieved. Politicians such as Trikoupis believed that territorial expansion was best essayed by a strong and economically developed state. By contrast, his rival Deliyannis believed that Greece could only become a truly viable state when the large, and in many cases prosperous, Greek populations that remained under Ottoman rule were incorporated into the Greek state.

A basic problem confronting Greece in the nineteenth century was that while the Ottoman Empire may have been "the sick man of Europe," it was nonetheless a great deal more powerful than Greece, whose territorial aspirations ran far ahead of its military potential. Hence, during the nineteenth century, the incorporation of areas of Greek

Greek troops during the Balkan War, 1912. ©BETTMANN/CORBIS

settlement into the new state came about as a result of great-power diplomacy and not by military action. The first accession of territory was Britain's 1863 cession of the Ionian Islands, which had been a British protectorate since 1815, as a kind of dowry for King George I. The second great accession of territory, that of the agriculturally rich province of Thessaly and a part of Epirus, came about in 1881 as a result of negotiations at the Congress of Berlin of 1878, which brought an end to the great Eastern crisis of 1875–1878. When Greece tried to go it alone in armed confrontation with the Ottoman Empire, as in the ill-fated Greco-Turkish War of 1897 (also known as the Thirty Days' War), the results were disastrous. It was during the Balkan Wars of 1912–1913 that Greece learned the lesson that it could hope to confront the Ottoman Empire militarily only in alliance with the other Balkan states that had gained their independence during the nineteenth century. The Balkan Wars

resulted in a massive increase in the territory of the Greek kingdom and broadly established the country's present-day frontiers.

See also **Nationalism; Ottoman Empire.**

BIBLIOGRAPHY

Campbell, John, and Philip Sherrard. *Modern Greece.* London, 1968.

Clogg, Richard. *A Concise History of Greece.* 2nd ed. Cambridge, U.K., 2002.

Clogg, Richard, ed. and trans. *The Movement for Greek Independence 1770–1821: A Collection of Documents.* London, 1976.

Dakin, Douglas. *The Unification of Greece 1770–1923.* London, 1972.

———. *The Greek Struggle for Independence, 1821–1833.* London, 1973.

Gallant, Thomas. *Modern Greece.* London, 2001.

Henderson, G. P. *The Revival of Greek Thought 1620–1821.* Edinburgh, 1971.

Koliopoulos, John S. *Brigands with a Cause: Brigandage and Irredentism in Modern Greece. 1821–1912.* Oxford, U.K., 1987.

Petropulos, John Anthony. *Politics and Statecraft in the Kingdom of Greece, 1833–1843.* Princeton, N.J., 1968.

Woodhouse, C. M. *Capodistria: The Founder of Greek Independence.* London, 1973.

RICHARD CLOGG

GRIMM BROTHERS. Jacob Ludwig Carl Grimm (1785–1863) and Wilhelm Carl Grimm (1786–1859), the two oldest surviving children of Philipp Wilhelm Grimm and Dorothea Zimmer Grimm, may be unique in the history of letters both for the breadth of their scholarly achievements and for the length of their scholarly collaboration. Away from home to attend school in Cassel and, later, at the University of Marburg, they shared lodgings and the study of law. As adults, they held complementary positions as librarians in Cassel, librarians and professors at the University of Göttingen, and professors at the University of Berlin; they also shared a home, a circumstance unchanged by Wilhelm's marriage to Henriette Dorothea Wild in 1825. Whether working together or independently, the Grimm brothers made unparalleled contributions to the disciplines of folklore and linguistics, inventing both fields of study and methodologies appropriate to those fields.

FOLKLORE AND LITERATURE

Much of the Grimms' popular reputation rests upon their collection of fairy tales, *Children's and Household Tales (Kinder- und Hausmärchen)*. This work may have been inspired by Clemens Brentano and Achim von Arnim, writers who published an early collection of German folk songs, *The Boy's Magic Horn (Des Knaben Wunderhorn,* 1805). In any case, letters that Wilhelm and Jacob exchanged in 1805, while Jacob was working for Friedrich Carl von Savigny in Paris, show both brothers developing an interest in literature, oral and written, of earlier times. Their collecting resulted in one volume of fairy tales in 1812, which was dedicated to the wife and infant son of Achim von Arnim; a second volume followed in 1815, and a third in 1822. Editions published in 1819, 1837, 1840, 1843, 1850, and 1857 revised texts, added new tales and, occasionally, omitted old ones for a total of more than two hundred tales. Ludwig Grimm, a younger brother, illustrated the 1819 second edition and Wilhelm's son, Herman, published an eighth edition in 1864. The second and subsequent editions, which were largely Wilhelm's work, expanded, edited, and polished the tales, creating in the process a paradigm for the literary fairy tale and making them more acceptable for a child audience. In the years before and during World War II, the tales were sometimes used to support a Nazi agenda; more recently, feminist, psychological, mythic, allegorical, Marxist, and other critics have variously interpreted the tales. *Kinder- und Hausmärchen* was first translated into English by Edgar Taylor (*German Popular Stories,* 1823). His translation, illustrated by George Cruikshank, has been followed by numerous others, among which are notable translations by Margaret Hunt (1884), Ralph Manheim (1977), Jack Zipes (1987), and Maria Tatar (2004). The fairy tales also live on in translations into more than one hundred languages as well as in films, sound recordings, musicals, poems, and Web sites.

Together, the brothers also published *German Legends* in two volumes (1816, 1818); in the foreword they defined the differences among legend, history, and fairy tale. Either together or separately, the brothers eventually published a number of Irish, Icelandic, Spanish, Danish, Latin, and additional German texts dating from the eighth to the sixteenth century. Jacob alone published *Teutonic Mythology* in two volumes (*Deutsche Mythologie,* 1835), in which he supplemented the all too slim extant material with parallels in folk tales and Norse myth. Wilhelm's two early studies of runes (1821, 1828), an alphabet used by German peoples early in the first millennium, anticipated subsequent interest in that field, and Jacob's critical edition of *Reynard the Fox (Reinhart Fuchs,* 1834), including variants of this trickster tale in Latin, Flemish, and multiple dialects of German, remains a model of early textual criticism.

Jacob (right) and Wilhelm Grimm. Portrait by Anna Maria Elisabeth Jerichau-Baumann, 1855. BILDARCHIV PREUSSISCHER KULTURBESITZ/ART RESOURCE, NY

LINGUISTICS

Jacob Grimm advanced the methodology of historical and comparative linguistics. In the process he both codified important phonological changes and also created the vocabulary to describe them. The most famous of these, the First Germanic Sound Shift, is often called Grimm's Law, although the Danish scholar Rasmus Rask had noted the phenomenon earlier. This theory posits nine original Indo-European consonants, all of which underwent changes in Germanic languages. Thus, for example, Germanic languages like English and German have the consonant *f* in words where all other Indo-European languages have the consonant *p* (English *father*, Latin *pater*). In the last two decades of the twentieth century Grimm's Law was challenged, most directly by the glottalic theory of Thomas V. Gamkrelidze and Vjačeslav V. Ivanov, a theory that would require changing previously held views of the consonant patterns of Indo-European, the location of the Indo-European homeland, the migratory patterns of these people, and the identity of those modern languages that most closely resemble Indo-European. Regardless of the eventual outcome of this debate, Jacob Grimm's theoretical method remains sound. So do his contributions in describing other early phonological shifts and the vocabulary to name them, for example, *umlaut*, the vowel shifts that produce noun inflections such as *mouse-mice*, and *ablaut*, the vowel shifts that produce verb inflections such as *write-wrote-written*. Jacob describes these and other matters in the monumental *German Grammar* (*Deutsche Grammatik*, 1819–1837); he continued this work in a two-volume *History of the German Language* (*Geschichte der deutschen Sprache*, 1848).

The last large project the brothers undertook together was the *German Dictionary*. They began this project after they had been expelled from the University of Göttingen for refusing to swear an oath of allegiance to Ernst August, the new king of Hanover who had unilaterally revoked the country's constitution. The *German Dictionary*, originally conceived to include all German words from the time of Martin Luther to Johann Wolfgang von Goethe, eventually expanded to include words both earlier and later, along with etymologies and illustrative quotations. This work anticipated the modern practices of describing rather than prescribing usage and of including all varieties of words. Jacob did most of the work on volume 1 (*A-Biermolke*, 1854), Wilhelm most of the work on volume 2, which was published posthumously (1860). Jacob had completed volume 3 through the word *frucht* at the time of his death in 1863. The thirty-third and final volume of the dictionary was finally published a century later, an example of the broad and lasting legacy of the Grimm brothers in the field of linguistics.

See also **Cruikshank, George; Germany.**

BIBLIOGRAPHY

Primary Sources

Grimm, Jacob. *Reinhart Fuchs.* Berlin, 1835.

———. *Deutsche Grammatik.* 4 vols. Göttingen, 1819–1837.

———. *Geschichte der deutschen Sprache.* 2 vols. Leipzig, 1848; 2nd ed., 1853.

———. *Teutonic Mythology.* Translated by James Steven Stallybrass. Reprint. New York, 2004. Translation of *Deutsche Mythologie* (1835; 4th ed., 1855).

Grimm, Jacob, and Wilhelm Grimm. *The German Legends of the Brothers Grimm.* Translated and edited by

Donald Ward. Philadelphia, 1981. Translation of *Deutsche Sagen* (Vol. 1, 1816, Vol. 2, 1818.).

———. *Deutsches Wörterbuch*. Vols. 1–3. Leipzig, 1854–1864. Reprint. Munich, 1999 (33 vols.). CD-ROM: Trier, 2000.

———. *The Complete Fairy Tales of the Brothers Grimm*. Translated by Jack Zipes. 3rd ed., illustrated by Johnny B. Grulle. New York, 2003. Translation of *Kinder- und Hausmärchen* (Vol. 1, 1812; Vol. 2, 1815; Vol. 3, 1822; 7th ed., 1857).

———. *The Annotated Brothers Grimm*. Edited and translated by Maria Tatar. Introduction by A. S. Byatt. New York, 2004. Translations of forty-six tales and two prefaces.

Grimm, Wilhelm. *Über deutsche Runen*. Göttingen, 1821.

———. *Zur Literatur der Runen: Nebst Mittheilung runischer Alphabete und gothischer Fragmente aus Handschriften*. Vienna, 1828.

———. *Die deutsche Heldensage*. Göttingen, 1829. Reprint. Darmstadt, 1957.

Secondary Sources

Gamkrelidze, Thomas V., and Vjačeslav V. Ivanov. *Indo-European and the Indo-Europeans: A Reconstruction and Historical Analysis of a Proto-Language and a Proto-Culture*. 2nd ed. Translated by Johanna Nichols. Edited by Werner Winter. Berlin and New York, 2000.

Hettinga, Donald R. *The Brothers Grimm: Two Lives, One Legacy*. New York, 2001.

Michaelis-Jena, Ruth. *The Brothers Grimm*. New York and London, 1970.

Peppard, Murray B. *Paths through the Forest: A Biography of the Brothers Grimm*. New York, 1971.

ELIZABETH L. HOLTZE

GUESDE, JULES (1845–1922), French socialist.

Few figures better embody the force and the frailties of the Second International's "classical" Marxism than Jules Guesde, its French apostle. In historical memory, however, the frailties loom largest. The neoliberals and neoconservatives of the early twenty-first century, if they remember Guesde at all, recall a purveyor of ideological illusion. Even Guesde's heirs have dismissed him. Communists have written him off as a revolutionary who opposed their revolution, while Social Democrats have indicted him for antireformist rigidity. Yet, for some scholars, his creative force has been well worth remembering. Guesde, after all, animated Marxist socialism's rise from inchoate sect in the 1880s to political centrality during the French twentieth century.

Mathieu Basile (he adopted his mother's maiden name as a *nom de plume*) was born in Paris, on 11 November 1845. Scion of the teaching profession, rebelling against maternal Catholicism and paternal politics (while always retaining his family's traditions of learning and austerity), the youthful Guesde launched himself into the journalistic milieu of the late Second Empire, soon becoming caught up in the time's incendiary republicanism.

The Franco-Prussian War and the Paris Commune found him editing a radical newspaper in Montpellier, and his enthusiastic support for the Parisian revolutionaries earned him a prison term, which he escaped by fleeing to Switzerland. There, infuriated by the bloody repression of the Commune, he moved beyond radical republicanism toward social revolution, ironically in favor of the anti-Marxist "Bakuninist" faction of the disintegrating First International. Soon, however, Guesde turned toward political socialism, and, upon returning to France in 1876, he threw himself into the creation of a "labor party." He was to be a central figure in the resultant birth of the Parti Ouvrier—from which today's French Socialist and Communist Parties trace their origins. By 1882, with support from Karl Marx (1818–1883) and Friedrich Engels (1820–1895) themselves, Guesde had hardened his faction of the movement (the "Guesdists," as they came to be known) into what was to become the Parti Ouvrier Français (POF), the embodiment of Marxist socialism in France.

Then followed Guesde's ascendancy in the French political culture, as he preached a schematic but potent version of Marxism—limning the ubiquity of class conflict, indicting capitalist exploitation, prophesying inevitable socialist revolution. His charismatic persona (he was often compared in style and appearance to an Old Testament prophet), his tireless speaking tours throughout France's provincial industrial towns, his spectacular campaign in favor of the international May Day celebrations, his role in the founding of the Second International, his incessant organizational work (Guesde's tiny Parisian apartment was long the real Secretariat of the POF)—all contributed to forging France's most aggressive ideological movement. With Guesde's triumphant election to the Chamber of Deputies in 1893, Marxist socialism had blasted its way into the heart of French politics.

Yet Guesde's victories during the 1890s concealed debilitating contradictions. The great advocate of labor solidarity was dubious about trade unions, viewing them as vitally necessary to workers' class-consciousness, yet distrusting them as inherently "reformist." His internationalism could lapse into an abstract and antinational cosmopolitanism. And he signally failed to reconcile his revolutionary principles with his electoral practices. The moment of truth came in 1899, with the entry of his one-time ally Alexandre Millerand (1859–1943) into the "bourgeois" government of Pierre-Marie-René Waldeck-Rousseau (1846–1904), to Guesde's frustrated fury. For a time, it seemed as if "reformists" led by Millerand and Jean Jaurès (1859–1914) would triumph over the POF's intransigent Marxists.

Mobilizing all his enormous reserves of passion and intelligence, Guesde campaigned ferociously against Jaurès's "ministerialist" socialism, and by 1905 had prevailed. That year's merger of French socialist factions took place on terms dictated by Guesde, and his Marxist ideals suffused the newly unified Socialist Party. Yet the aging Guesde spent his last years defending principles reviled as anachronistic by his own party's radical left and reformist right. His final decade was tragic. The outbreak of World War I witnessed Guesde, that firm internationalist and militant class warrior, joining an all-party (and all-class) government of national defense, and he was to denounce the Bolshevik seizure of power in 1917, despite its apparent realization of his life-long revolutionary aspirations. Classical Marxism seemingly had little to offer a world characterized by total war and a "revolution against *Capital*" (as Antonio Gramsci [1891–1937] cleverly described the Bolshevik heresy). When Guesde died on 28 July 1922, the times had passed him by—in favor of Benito Mussolini (1883–1945) and Vladimir Lenin (1870–1924).

See also **Bakunin, Mikhail; Jaurès, Jean; Marx, Karl; Paris Commune; Second International; Waldeck-Rousseau, René.**

BIBLIOGRAPHY

Stuart, Robert. *Marxism at Work: Ideology, Class and French Socialism during the Third Republic.* Cambridge, U.K., 1992. A study of the Parti Ouvrier's ideology focused on Guesde's thought.

Willard, Claude. *Le Mouvement Socialiste en France (1893–1905): Les Guesdistes.* Paris, 1965. The definitive political and social history of the POF, with much information on Guesde's militancy.

———. *Jules Guesde, L'Apôtre et la Loi.* Paris, 1991. The most recent, and the best, biography.

ROB STUART

GUIMARD, HECTOR (1867–1942), French architect and designer.

While Hector Guimard's architectural and design works were often scorned during his lifetime and even destroyed in the generations following his death and until the 1960s, he now has become the central emblematic figure for the entire art nouveau movement (a late-nineteenth-century design style characterized by sinuous lines, foliate forms, and a strong influence from the art of Japan), the representative who best characterizes the fleeting era at the end of the nineteenth and the beginning of the twentieth centuries. However, during his lifetime, Guimard was also very sensitive to differentiate his own work, which was often called *le style Guimard*, from that of the broader implications of art nouveau. In this way, Guimard forged his own identity based upon deeply ingrained principles of what a house or a chair should look like and where all parts in a building could be designed to create an integrated effect.

As Guimard's career as an architect and designer evolved during the 1890s, he was well aware—through his traditional training at the École des Beaux-Arts and through initiatives of the period—that French planners and critics were dedicated to redesigning public and private interior spaces. There was a decided interest in new materials—metal and glass, organic plant motifs—and a growing initiative to move away from the historical styles of past periods. Art and industry were recognized as working together; by the time of the Exposition Universelle of 1900 French government and private initiatives were on display. One point was continually reiterated: architects and designers had to create a "modern style" that did not remain rooted in the past.

As one of the younger architects of the art nouveau era, Guimard focused on a series of issues that were linked to middle-class living. He improved apartments and designed homes that were neither excessively costly nor overly extravagant in terms of a visual impression; he opened up interior spaces so that more light could penetrate, and he utilized new forms that were often standardized through prefabrication, such as the entranceways to the Paris Métro system. Guimard's first fundamentally radical design, the building that established his name and career in the eyes of the public, was the apartment house known as the Castel-Béranger (1894–1898). Here, Guimard achieved some of his goals. He used variegated color effects on sections of the building's facade while the interior courtyard let more light into the individual apartments. But it was Guimard's fusion of various materials throughout the building that demonstrated new ways for architects to work with industry; the effect was to generate considerable discussion in the design community. He soon was recognized as both an architect who advanced practical solutions for housing problems and as an inventor of ornamental designs that were, in effect, more iconoclastic than his architecture. This was especially noticeable in the iron doorway to the Castel-Béranger where by molding the material into a series of whiplash curvilinear motifs he provided a hallmark design for the *style Guimard* as it stressed abstraction from nature that had not been visualized earlier.

With the construction of buildings, many of which are now destroyed, and the public exhibition of his models and drawings, Guimard soon found himself at the center of critical debate. Those who were linked to the traditions of the academy rejected his ideas; others, those interested in working independently to invent new shapes or to use materials freely, saw Guimard as a visionary. In examining the critical reception of his era, during

the 1890s, and just after 1900, Guimard established himself in a new role: he became, in the eyes of many, emblematic of the typical architect-designer. Working alone, Guimard was able to advance a new formalistic language. The Castel-Béranger became a heroic statement where Guimard effectively demonstrated how architecture and the industrial arts could be united in one monument to create a "modern" effect.

Even though Guimard did not participate in the 1900 Exposition Universelle in Paris, his presence was evident in the design of the Métro system, especially through the creation of a wide range of Métro entrances. Paris was somewhat late in building an urban inner-city railroad network—London, Vienna, New York were in advance—but by 1900, with the support of Adrien Benard, and the city of Paris, the Métro system was constructed. Benard, a passionate supporter of art nouveau, was totally dedicated to the idea of having a modern style define the new Paris. By giving Guimard, the new architect-designer, the official responsibility to create entranceways to the Métro system, Benard made him the provocative architect who became the representative of the new era itself. As several variations of Guimard's Métro system were constructed, critics began to dub this so-called new approach *le style Métro* suggesting that Guimard, in yet another way, was responsible for naming an entire movement that had an immediate, visual impact on the public.

The great variety of Métro entranceways was innovative. Whether Guimard used bulbous vegetal forms open to the sky that supported electric lights or emphasized covered stairways or complete pavilions that used frosted glass or other modern materials the designs were like nothing that had been seen before. A sense of mystery permeated these sites as passengers emerged from the darkness of the underground to be surrounded by vegetal shapes or by shimmering light effects reinforced by reflections off the surface of glass or metal. With so many of these entranceways appearing throughout the city it was clear that "newness" was on everyone's mind. The sad reality is that so few of these entranceways survived a wave of hatred against what was perceived as the art nouveau style.

Porte Dauphine metro station, Paris. Designed by Hector Guimard in 1900. Guimard's design of the metro entrances was so influential that French art nouveau is often called the Style Métro. ©PAUL ALMASY/CORBIS

Although his name was linked with the creation of a truly modern style in 1900, it was not until several years later, when Guimard exhibited his designs at the Exposition Internationale de l'Habitation at the Grand Palais, that the term *le style Guimard* was first used. It became another name given to those adventurous aspects of architecture and design that were part of art nouveau. At the exposition, Guimard used postcards as a form of self-promotion; he was now becoming a master of self-advancement, presenting himself as the principal architect-designer of the new. He saw himself as an entrepreneurial overseer who directed the work of numerous artisans and craftsmen creating harmonious ensembles of furniture or decorative designs for home interiors. Guimard supported the creation of profoundly original shapes that emphasized the intimate relationship between art industries. By working in so many areas, including the development of new designs for ceramics, Guimard remained a viable member of the modern style until after 1910. Since there were few architects who could follow Guimard's innovations, and many members of the public disliked the style, the art nouveau aesthetic was short lived. It was supplanted by a cleaner, linear style more in keeping with the burgeoning machine age.

See also **Art Nouveau; Degeneration; Fin de Siècle; France; Paris.**

BIBLIOGRAPHY

Grady, James. "Hector Guimard: An Overlooked Master of Art Nouveau." *Apollo* 89, no. 2 (1969): 284–295.

Guimard. Exhibition catalog. Paris, 1992.

Lynonnet, Jean-Pierre, Bruno Dupont, and Laurent Sully Jaulmes. *Guimard Perdu, Histoire d'une Méprise*. Paris, 2003.

Vigne, Georges. *Hector Guimard, Architect Designer, 1867–1942*. Translated by Blake Ferris. New York, 2003.

GABRIEL P. WEISBERG

GUIZOT, FRANÇOIS (1787–1874),

French politician and historian. François Guizot was a leading politician during the July Monarchy (1830–1848). His father was an influential Protestant lawyer in Nímes, guillotined for his federalist sympathies during the Terror. The family moved to Geneva where Guizot was educated. In Paris from 1805 he inserted himself into intellectual circles around the philosopher and academic Pierre-Paul Royer-Collard. He became professor of modern history at the University of Paris (1812). In 1814 he supported the Bourbon Restoration, secured a post in the ministry of the interior, and followed Louis XVIII (r. 1814–1815; 1815–1824) into exile during the Hundred Days. He was rewarded with a ministerial post at the Second Restoration and made a councillor of state. Along with a tiny number of liberals dubbed *doctrinaire* because of the limited nature of their liberalism, he had some impact in moderating the royalist reaction after the Hundred Days.

In the ultra-royalist backlash that followed the murder of the heir to the throne in 1820, Guizot lost all but his university chair, and between 1822 and 1828 his university course was suspended. He survived by turning his university lectures into books at a time when history was very popular, publishing *Histoire de la révolution de l'Angleterre* (1826–1827), *Histoire de la civilisation en Europe* (1828), and *Histoire de la civilisation en France* (1830–1832). His history is still a pleasure to read. He also wrote for *Le Globe*, a leading liberal journal, and in 1827 was a founder (later chairman) of *Aide-toi, le ciel t'aidera* (Help yourself and Heaven will help you), which promoted the creation of liberal electoral committees to combat official electoral corruption. Like other liberals, Guizot revered the constitutional Charter of 1814 because it balanced royal and parliamentary authority. The latter, modeled on the British parliament, he admired, being a lifelong Anglophile (although British foreign ministers must have found it hard to believe). He was convinced that the old monarchy could be harmonized with aspects of 1789, including both new centralized institutions of government and the electoral principle, producing his ideal, a *juste milieu*, or middle way. Like other liberals, he became critical of the Restored Bourbons only when legislation such as the law of the double vote ate away at the Charter. He was no revolutionary.

In 1830 Guizot was elected to the Chamber of Deputies and voted with the majority of 221 deputies who protested at Charles X's speech opening the parliamentary session. He took a leading role in organizing the appointment of Louis-Philippe (r. 1830–1848) as king in August 1830 and became his first minister of the interior. He was a minister for all but five years for the July Monarchy. As minister of public instruction from 1832 to 1835 he introduced legislation in 1833 that directed all communes of more than five hundred inhabitants to set up a primary school for boys. Every town of six thousand inhabitants was to run a higher primary school, while every department had to create an *école normale*, a college to train young men to teach. The new teachers earned two hundred francs annually. The law also created a body of school inspectors. In 1836, following protests, communes were encouraged to admit girls if there was enough space. These laws did not make primary schooling free, secular, or obligatory. Places were only free for the children of poor parents, and each religious group had a say in the running of the school, but Guizot's legislation was a first step. By 1845 the schools had three million pupils.

In 1840, a few months after his appointment as ambassador to London, Guizot became minister of foreign affairs in a government headed by Marshal Soult, which Guizot effectively ran until 1848. His surprisingly disputatious foreign policy with Britain brought the two close to war over trifling rivalries and jealousies. Guizot resisted all proposals for extending the suffrage and became a much-criticized symbol for bourgeois indifference to social problems. In successive elections, 1842 and 1846, his government increased its majority.

Dismissed by Louis Philippe during the 1848 revolution, he followed the king into exile in England, returning a year later to stand unsuccessfully for the Legislative Assembly. His subsequent total retirement to his Norman home, Val Richer, to a quarter century of private life is in sharp contrast to contemporaries such as Louis-Adolphe Thiers. He completed *Mémoires pour server à l'histoire de mon temps* (1858–1867; Memoirs to serve as a history of my time) and *Histoire parlementaire de la France* (1863–1864).

In his lectures at the Sorbonne and in his writing, much of which was translated into English, Guizot applauded the early, more moderate period of the 1789 Revolution, defining it as a successful takeover of power by the bourgeoisie. Like many, he presented the 1789 Revolution as the climax of a long struggle for liberty, democracy, and national sovereignty, but his definitions of the last two of these differed from those in customary use by 1848. By democracy he did not mean the attempt to create political democracy in 1792 and 1793, which he saw as leading inexorably to the Terror of 1793–1794. Instead he praised the quest for social democracy, by which he meant personal freedom and equality. Guizot also applauded national sovereignty, which he always asserted the July monarchy represented. What he cherished was what he called the sovereignty of reason, not popular sovereignty. He remained convinced, even after the adoption of male suffrage in 1848, that representative government should be in the hands of those with *capacité*, the financial as well as the intellectual clout to make independent judgments in the name of the whole community. He was happy with the July monarchy electorate of 250,000, arguing that this tiny minority (in a population of thirty-six million) would grow slowly as vital education programs civilized the whole population. After 1848 such elitist arguments were unsustainable, although disappointment with the results of universal male suffrage was widespread, even among radicals. Alexis de Tocqueville, who attended Guizot's Sorbonne lectures, acknowledged him as a formative influence on his own thinking.

See also **Charles X; France; Napoleon III; Restoration; Revolutions of 1830; Revolutions of 1848; Thiers, Louis-Adolphe.**

BIBLIOGRAPHY

Alexander, Robert. *Re-writing the French Revolutionary Tradition: Liberal Opposition and the Fall of the Bourbon Monarchy.* Cambridge, U.K., and New York, 2003.

Craiutu, Aurelian. *Liberalism under Siege: The Political Thought of the French Doctrinaires.* Lanham, Md., 2003.

Johnson, Douglas. *Guizot: Aspects of French History, 1787–1874.* London and Toronto, 1963.

Pilbeam, Pamela. *The Constitutional Monarchy in France, 1814–48.* Harlow, U.K., 2000.

PAMELA PILBEAM

GYPSIES. *See* **Romanies (Gypsies).**

HAECKEL, ERNST HEINRICH

(1834–1919), German physician, zoologist, evolutionary biologist.

Ernst Heinrich Haeckel, known during his lifetime as "the German Darwin," was born on 16 February 1834 in Potsdam, Prussia, and died in Jena, Germany, on 9 August 1919. Haeckel died in his beloved home, Villa Medusa, after having lived in Jena for the last fifty-eight years of his life. For most of that time he was a professor of zoology at the University of Jena.

Haeckel's scientific perspective on the origins and development of organisms was based on an uneasy syncretism of the archetypal Romantic biology of Johann Wolfgang von Goethe and the evolutionary theory of Charles Darwin. Haeckel was one of the earliest proponents of Darwinian theory in Germany. The two men met three times during their lives and corresponded. Haeckel is credited for being the first to explicitly state in print, in his *Generelle Morphologie der Organismen* (1866; General morphology of organisms), that "Man has evolved from apes just as these have evolved from lower animals"—an explosive admission that Darwin deliberately avoided in his *On the Origin of Species* (1859). It is also in his *Generelle Morphologie der Organismen* that Haeckel introduced the idea—now considered incorrect—for which he is most famous, the "biogenetic law": ontogeny recapitulates phylogeny. His famous illustrations of a developing human embryo replicating the analogous sequence of stages of the evolution of life on earth still appear in college textbooks (although there is a lingering controversy over whether they were falsified by Haeckel).

Haeckel was also the first to use the drawing of the "phylogenetic tree" to visually represent the Darwinian view of advanced forms of life emerging from more primitive species. An accomplished visual artist who celebrated the truth and beauty of nature in drawings, watercolors, and oil paintings, Haeckel reproduced his throbbing, almost psychedelic vision of sea microorganisms as observed through his microscope in an influential volume of illustrations, *Kunstformen der Natur* (1899; Art forms in nature). The spiny, mandala-like images in his book were borrowed by many art nouveau (*Jugendstil*) artists, including the Parisian architect René Binet (1826–1911), who used the form of one of these microbes as the inspiration for a pavilion built for the 1900 Universal Exhibition in Paris. Dancer Isadora Duncan (1877–1927) was an ardent admirer of Haeckel, and during her tour of Germany in 1903–1904 she based some variations of her "dance of the future" on Haeckel's evolutionary ideals. In science, art, and culture, Haeckel was unquestionably one of the most famous and influential men of the nineteenth century.

By 1904, the year of his seventieth birthday, Haeckel had achieved enormous international acclaim as a populizer of science rivaled, perhaps, only by late-twentieth-century scientists such as Carl Sagan and E. O. Wilson. His rapid rise to fame followed the publication in Germany in 1899 of

Die Weltraetsel (1900; *The Riddle of the Universe*). Within five years of publication, each of these editions had sold more than one hundred thousand copies. The unprecedented success of this book was due to its vivid and apparently convincing philosophy of life based on Haeckel's concept of monism, "the connecting link between religion and science." Although Haeckel had first proposed his scientific religion of monism in a lecture he gave in Altenburg, Germany, on 9 October 1892, these ideas did not catch fire in the general public, with the exception of Roman Catholic priests enraged by his anti-Christian (and especially antipapist) polemics. *The Riddle of the Universe* changed all that. Monism was to replace dualisms in science (vitalism, a form of materialistic dualism) and religion (distinctions between psyche and body, natural and supernatural, nature and God). More importantly, an explicitly pantheistic and atheistic "monistic religion" based on "the good, the true, and the beautiful" in nature would replace Christianity. There would be no chapels or cathedrals in this new science-based faith, for nature itself would be worshipped through a new aesthetic vision in science. All scientists would develop the skills and sensitivities of artists, and artists would sing, paint, and dance the eternal flame of life as reflected through the prismatic truth of evolution.

Due to the overwhelming popularity of monism among "free thinkers," artists, scientists, and pantheists—particularly those in the German youth movement who were already practicing sun worship, nudism, vegetarianism, and Aryan mysticism—in January 1906 disciples of Haeckel in Jena formed an organization to promote the scientific religion of monism. The German *Monistenbund,* as it was called, grew by 1915 to six thousand members in forty-five cities. Membership fell during World War I and again after Haeckel's death in 1919. As they did with many other competing organizations and political parties, the Nazis banned the *Monistenbund* in 1933.

Perhaps Haeckel's most detailed statement of his pantheism and his contempt for Christianity can be found in his short 1914 book, *Gott-Natur (Theophysis): Studien uber monistische Religion* (God-nature [theophysics]: studies in monistic religion). In it, he proposed that his universal God be named the "All-God" (*Allgott*), "Pantheos," or

"*Deus intramundanus.*" The revered prophets of the new monistic religion were to be Giordano Bruno, Benedict de Spinoza, and Goethe instead of Jehovah, Christ, and Allah. According to the seven principles of theophysics, (1) God is nature itself, eternal and imperishable; (2) God is the laws of nature itself, impersonal, unconscious, unyielding; (3) God possesses no free will; (4) God does not perform supernatural miracles or wonders; (5) God as a universal substance is a trinity of attributes (matter, energy, and the psychom—a word Haeckel coined for the unity of psyche and body); (6) God is blind fate; and (7) God is no judge and knows no difference between good and evil.

Haeckel's last major work was *Kristallseelen: Studien über des anorganische Leben* (1917; The souls of crystals: studies of inorganic life). In it, Haeckel argues that life sprang from nonlife, and that the fact that crystals grow, move, transform, and have a symmetric internal structure like biological beings suggests that they, too, have a soul or psyche and are probably the inorganic source of life on this planet. This is an extension of an idea Haeckel had proposed as early as 1877 about living cells and microbes known as protozoa, that each cell or protozoa had its own psyche and that the totality of organic matter was "ensouled" (*beseelt*). Haeckel may have been prescient when he speculated about the origins of life from nonlife, for current scientific speculation also points to crystals as the form of inorganic matter from which life sprang almost four billion years ago.

Haeckel's international reputation as a prophet of science evaporated after World War I due to his very public support of the German war effort. In the last year of his life he was a member of the *Thule-Gesellschaft,* the underground organization that would later produce many members of the Nazi party, an act consistent with his lifelong support of Otto von Bismarck, the kaisers, and German nationalism.

See also **Darwin, Charles; Evolution; Germany; Goethe, Johann Wolfgang von; Nationalism; Romanticism.**

BIBLIOGRAPHY

Breidbach, Olaf. "The Former Synthesis—Some Remarks on the Typological Background of Haeckel's Ideas about Evolution." *Theory in Biosciences* 121 (2000), 280–296.

Gasman, Daniel. "Haeckel's Religious Monism: Its Cultural Impact." *Acts of the XVIIth International Congress for the History of Science* 1, session 16.3 (1985).

Haeckel, Ernst. *The Riddle of the Universe.* Translated by Joseph McCabe. New York, 1900.

———. *The Wonders of Life: A Popular Study of Biological Philosophy.* Translated by Joseph McCabe. London, 1905.

———. *Gott-Natur (Theophysis): Studien über monistischen Religion.* Leipzig, 1914.

———. *Kristallseelen: Studien über des anorganische Leben.* Leipzig, 1917.

Kockerbeck, Carl. *Ernst Haeckels "Kunstformen der Natur" und ihr Einfluss auf die deutsche bildende Kunst der Jahrhundertwende.* Frankfurt-am-Main, 1985.

Mattern, Wolfgang. "*Grundung und erste Entwicklung des deutschen Monistenbundes, 1906–1918.*" Ph.D. diss., The Medical Faculty of the Free University of Berlin, 1983.

Sandmann, Jürgen. *Der Bruch mit der humanitären Tradition: Die Biologisierung der Ethik bei Ernst Haeckel und anderen Darwinsiten seiner Zeit.* Stuttgart, 1990.

Schloegel, Judy Johns, and Henning Schmidgen. "General Physiology, Experimental Psychology, and Evolutionism: Unicellular Organisms as Objects of Psychophysiological Research, 1877–1918." *Isis* 93 (2002), 614–645.

Weber, Heiko. *Monistische und antimonistische Weltanschauung: Eine Auswahlbibliographie.* Berlin, 2000.

RICHARD NOLL

HAGUE CONFERENCES.

The Hague conferences of 1899 and 1907 were the product of a paradox. On the surface the nineteenth century seemed to have addressed successfully the escalation of war in the Revolutionary/Napoleonic Era. The reconstructed Europe that emerged from the Congress of Vienna (1814–1815) did not seek the utopian solution of ending war altogether. Instead it addressed warmaking in contexts of limitation and projection. Domestically, the midcentury conflicts from the Crimea in 1853–1856 to the Russo-Turkish War of 1877–1878 could be legitimately characterized as "cabinet wars" in the traditional style. Fought for definable, understandable purposes, interfacing force and negotiation, they were ultimately settled on terms acceptable not only to the participants, but the other Great Powers as well.

THE WAR MATRIX

To limitation, the European states increasingly added projection: directing aggressive impulses outward in an emerging age of imperialism. The British historian and journalist A. J. P. Taylor's comment that World War I might have been averted had Austria-Hungary possessed an extra-European empire has aged better than most historical one-liners. Great-power rivalry was more often defused than exacerbated by frictions generated by territory disputes involving unfamiliar places.

Imperialism's stakes might be high, but even the most belligerent governments did not perceive them as mortal. In disagreements over such geographically remote flecks on the map as Penjdeh, which engaged British and Russian diplomats in 1887; and Fashoda, which took Britain and France to the brink in 1898, there was always room for negotiation. The Great Game remained a game.

Imperialism's wars also directed public belligerence and military aggressiveness beyond Europe's frontiers. The remote locations provided an aura of glamour to what was usually a hard and bloody slog. The enemies were usually sufficiently alien in culture and appearance to make their annihilation a matter for scorekeeping rather than regret. The disparities of force made the final outcomes comfortably certain. In an era when mass spectator sports were just beginning to emerge, imperialism's conflicts provided an opportunity for readers of newspapers with headlines such as "Boers sabered by moonlight" to support their chosen "team."

Beneath this relatively comfortable surface, however, stress points multiplied as the century progressed. Arguably beginning with the writings of Carl von Clausewitz (1780–1831), visibly developing in the aftermath of the Franco-Prussian War (1870–1871), was an increasing tendency in Europe's armies to abstract the nature of conflict. War was projected as existential, embodying no limits and tending to develop unchecked its capacities for violence and destruction. This process of reification was enhanced by the rise of general staffs, whose self-defined reason for being was to diminish war's apocalyptic impact by systematic planning. The synergistic development of military technology after 1871, in particular a network of increasingly effective weapons from magazine rifles to heavy artillery, further encouraged projections of mutually destructive total war. Finally, the spiraling expenses of keeping pace with Europe's escalating arms race were increasingly understood as mere harbingers of the costs, human and material, a general European war would incur.

INITIATIVES

Imperialism's conflicts were also showing uncomfortable aspects, suggesting the transition from the state wars of the nineteenth century to the total wars of the twentieth. Civilian infrastructures were increasingly targeted as part of military operations. "Pacification" increasingly denied distinctions between combatants and civilian populations. Violence acquired an ideological dimension, with European troops and their local auxiliaries indiscriminately smiting enemies understood as symbolizing not merely the "other," but the alien, set apart by unbridgeable chasms of culture and race.

Across Europe, developing grassroots peace movements called attention to these manifestations, but they were handicapped by their identification with intellectuals, radicals, and women. The first concrete step toward addressing the upward spiral of violence in warmaking came from the unlikely source of Imperial Russia. On 24 August 1898, Tsar Nicholas II (r. 1894–1918) issued an imperial rescript (decree) calling for an international peace conference. On a pragmatic level, the Russian government sought international recognition for its recent commercial and political gains in China. Nicholas and his advisors, however, were also concerned with recent Western technical advances Russia could match only at disproportionate expense. A Polish banker, Jan Bloch, published *The Future of War* (1899), which predicted a mutual attrition that would ultimately destroy the old European order. Nicholas had met with Bloch personally and was sufficiently concerned to raise the argument that something must be done at the highest levels.

No state could afford to ignore the Russian initiative in the context of growing public anxiety about the risks of future war. Just what was to be done, however, remained obscure. Other governments—including the United States, making its debut on the great-power stage in the aftermath of the Spanish-American War, pressed for clarification. The Russians replied with an eight-point list. The specifics of its first half proposed a freeze on the size and budgets of armed forces with a view to eventual force reductions, and the banning of weapons and technologies more advanced than the ones in use. The second half called for codifying and revising the laws of war—or more accurately, the laws governing the conduct of war.

It was the second half that dominated discussion when the conference finally met at The Hague in 1899. The participants—Russia included—showed from the beginning a general unwillingness to take any concrete initiatives on arms limitation, let alone arms reduction. War remained the last resort of states, as it had been the final argument of kings. If the peace movement could not be ignored nationally or internationally, cultures of belligerence were no less widespread and no less influential in the Western world. Considered as a disarmament conference, The Hague was a failure. The meeting did, on the other hand, produce a spectrum of statements addressing behavior in war and binding on the "high contracting parties": a Convention on the Law and Customs of War on Land, another on maritime war, and separate declarations prohibiting the discharge of explosives from balloons, the use of projectiles diffusing asphyxiating gas, and the use of expanding bullets, more commonly known as dumdums.

Little of the material in these formulations was new. Prior to the middle of the nineteenth century, the "laws of war" existed as custom, as principle, as national laws and military regulations, and not least in religious teachings. In a culture whose defining passion was classification, this was unacceptably vague. In 1856 the Declaration of Paris codified maritime law. In 1868 an international conference at St. Petersburg banned weapons that unnecessarily aggravated suffering. The Brussels Conference of 1874 denied belligerents unlimited power to injure an enemy.

INTENTIONS AND RESULTS

The Hague's documents had a common intention: to collate and rationalize the laws and customs of war, defining them more precisely and mitigating their severity as far as possible. Article 1 of the annex to the Convention on Land Warfare, for example, defined belligerent status as requiring a chain of command, a distinctive emblem recognizable at a distance, arms carried openly, and operations conducted "in accordance with the laws and customs of war." Articles 5 through 20 establish the rights and responsibilities of prisoners of war—including a clause stating "any act of insubordination" warrants adopting "such measures of severity as may be necessary." Article 22 reiterates that the right to injure an enemy is not unlimited. Article 23 prohibits, among other things, refusing to take prisoners, and destroying enemy property unnecessarily. Articles 25–28 forbid bombarding undefended towns and require taking "all necessary steps" to spare public buildings in a bombardment zone—unless they are being used for military purposes.

The Convention recognized the right of spontaneous armed resistance to invasion, and granted such resisters belligerent status if they observed the laws and customs of war. It required occupiers to respect, "unless absolutely prevented," the laws of the occupied territory. Like all international law, however, that of The Hague was weighted heavily in favor of sovereign states. Punishment for violations was vague and limited: a few references to responsibility and a few more to compensation. The Conventions' mitigating aspects were nevertheless sharply challenged by armies and governments masking fears of weakness beneath assertion of state sovereignty. Germany in particular took a lead in that criticism, prefiguring its behavior in 1914–1918. In 1907 a second Hague Conference clarified a spectrum of disputed issues, most of them involving naval war. A third conference was intended for within eight years of the second.

World War I intervened. For four years the assumptions and principles of the Hague negotiators were tested to the point of destruction. Yet despite being honored as much in the breach as in the observance, despite being regularly challenged on pragmatic and principled grounds, the Law of the Hague has shaped the conduct of two world wars and dozens of lesser conflicts, extending into the twenty-first century. The robust common sense of its fundamental principles may be anything but utopian. When acted upon, the Hague Conven-

tions provide correspondingly workable ground rules that even the most ideologically motivated combatants in practice find sufficiently welcome to denounce their absence.

See also **Armies; International Law; Pacifism; Science and Technology.**

BIBLIOGRAPHY

Best, Geoffrey. *Humanity in Warfare*. New York, 1980.

Roberts, Adam. "Land Warfare: From Hague to Nuremberg." In *The Laws of War. Constraints on War in the Western World*, edited by Michael Howard, George J. Andreopoulos, and Mark R. Shulman, pp. 116–139. New Haven, Conn., and London, 1994.

DENNIS SHOWALTER

HAITI. Haiti has the paradoxical history of having gone from being, in 1789, the most profitable colony in the Americas to suffering, in the early twenty-first century, as the poorest nation in the Western Hemisphere. To understand how and why this has come to pass it is necessary to understand the central role Haiti—in its prior existence as the French colony of Saint Domingue—played in the broader history of the French Empire and the Atlantic world of the eighteenth century. And it is necessary to understand the forces that during the nineteenth century sapped the radical possibilities augured in by Haitian independence in 1804. The complicated economic, political, and social history of Haiti's struggles in the nineteenth century help explain the devastating conflicts that wracked the country during a twentieth century in which its history was dominated by the actions of the United States.

FROM EUROPEAN SETTLEMENT TO INDEPENDENCE

In 1492 Christopher Columbus created the first European settlement in the Americas on the north coast of Española, the island that is today divided into Haiti and the Dominican Republic (and that is known as Hispaniola in the Anglophone world). The Spanish were the first to settle, and they introduced both slavery and sugar plantations to their colony of Santo Domingo. The Spanish, however, focused most of their energy in the sixteenth and seventeenth centuries on the colonization of mainland Latin America, and they abandoned the western portion of Española, which was eventually settled, at first illegally and then, after 1697, with Spanish approval, by the French. Over the course of the eighteenth century, Saint Domingue moved from the margins of the colonial system to its very center, and became the richest colony in the area through an economy based on the production of sugar and coffee for export to Europe.

The economy depended on the brutal exploitation of nearly half a million slaves, who died so quickly that they had to be replaced by constant arrivals from Africa. By 1789, approximately two-thirds of the enslaved people on the island—who made up 90 percent of the population—had been born in Africa. From this enslaved population there emerged, in 1791, a brilliantly organized uprising that overwhelmed the planters and established itself as a military and political force to be reckoned with. By 1793 the French administrators had decreed the abolition of slavery in the colony in a bid to win the insurgents to their side in the midst of an imperial war against Britain and Spain. The decision was ratified in 1794 in Paris, and during the next eight years a complicated and conflictual process of emancipation was instituted on the island. While the governors of the colony, at first French administrators and then local leaders such as Toussaint-Louverture, remained committed to a plantation economy, most of the former slaves had other ideas. They sought the autonomy of land ownership, and pursued social mobility through military service and in the colony's towns. Administrators responded with often draconian laws seeking to compel workers to stay on plantations, where, though they were paid a small amount for their labor, their opportunities were of course quite limited.

Despite the limits placed on their freedom, the former slaves were haunted by the idea that they might be returned to slavery. In the early 1800s, shortly after coming to power in France, Napoleon Bonaparte took a series of decisions that led to a disastrous and brutal war in Saint Domingue. Seeking to reassert metropolitan control over the boldly autonomous regime of Toussaint, he also allowed his colonial policies to be shaped by the advice of colonial planters who argued for a containment and ultimately a reversal of emancipation. By the middle of 1802 it had become clear to the people of Saint Domingue that France intended to return them to slavery. Although Toussaint had surrendered and then been deported off the island, and his major generals had also gone over to the French side, small groups of insurgents, often led by African-born leaders, fought a war they understood quite literally as one of "liberty or death." In time, the insurrection grew, swelled by defections from the French side, and by 1803 it was clear that France, despite a massive commitment of troops to the colony, was facing a huge military loss. They withdrew in late 1803 and Jean-Jacques Dessalines, the general then leading the insurrection, declared the birth of a new nation called Haiti on 1 January 1804. The name of the nation was derived from the original indigenous name that had been erased by Columbus. The choice was rich with symbolism: Haiti was meant to be a response not just to the brutality and inequality of slavery but also to the larger history of European colonization and oppression in the Americas.

THE CHALLENGES OF INDEPENDENCE

The challenges faced by the people of Haiti after independence were enormous. The colony had been constructed entirely to serve the economic needs of France for sugar and coffee. Its environment had already been devastated by the late eighteenth century—commentators at the time already complained of the problems of deforestation—and the colony had been artificially populated through a slave trade aimed at sustaining a highly industrialized plantation system. The economic niches that were available to Haiti—the production of sugar and coffee—depended on a labor system that, understandably enough, was anathema to many former slaves. Instead, they successfully created a world that was the antithesis of the plantation by taking ownership of small plots of land and producing for themselves and for local markets. Out of slavery was born a culture of independence and subsistence in which the religious practices that came to be known as Vodou took root and thrived.

In the early nineteenth century, Haiti was relatively isolated from the European empires that had once dominated its political life. Although

Thomas Jefferson, the U.S. president, set a policy of isolation, refusing to extend recognition to the new nation, trade continued with the United States. The new nation's leaders, meanwhile, cultivated connections with other parts of the Americas, notably when Alexandre Pétion welcomed a beleaguered Simon Bolívar to take refuge in Haiti. Relations with France, meanwhile, were unsurprisingly strained. France also refused to extend diplomatic recognition to the new state, a refusal that essentially blocked recognition by any of the other European powers. Planters hoping to recover their fortune regularly put forth plans for reconquest. During the first decades of the nineteenth century, a series of negotiations took place between France and Haiti. For the Haitian leadership, gaining French acknowledgment of their independence was crucial, because other European powers would not openly trade with Haiti until France had officially accepted the new nation. Haiti successfully rebuffed some of France's more absurd attempts to actually regain control of the colony. But, under President Jean-Pierre Boyer, the Haitian government eventually agreed to an 1825 deal by which their old colonizers would acknowledge their existence as a sovereign state and reopen diplomatic and trade negotiations.

The cost, however, was quite steep: Haiti agreed to pay 150 million francs (later reduced to 60 million), which was to be distributed to planters as an indemnity for the losses they had suffered during the revolution. It was, in a sense, a fine for Haiti's successful revolution, paid to the individuals who had overseen and profited from the brutal system of slavery in the colony. And it had far-reaching effects. Haiti took out loans from French banks and began a process of paying them off, one that lasted into the twentieth century. Haiti did have economic successes during this period: over the course of the nineteenth century, elites successfully sustained and expanded the nation's coffee economy. But the possibilities for reinvestment of the money made through the export of coffee were undermined, in part by the heavy taxation that was necessary to pay off the debt to France. The profits of the rural population were also diminished by practices of local merchants in Haiti's ports who used their near-monopoly on exports to their advantage. There were also ongoing political conflicts in the country, some of which pitted peasant movements seeking a greater say in the nation's governance against often-authoritarian rulers based in Port-au-Prince. Haiti's nineteenth century, however, was more complicated than is usually acknowledged, and included periods of relative political stability and economic growth alongside periods of instability.

Haiti's elite, meanwhile, continued to confront an extremely hostile world. In an era of rising "scientific" racism and imperialism, the presence of a proud and independent nation founded by slave revolution was a major challenge to the reigning order. While African Americans and abolitionists wrote admiringly of Haiti's history, deeply racist portrayals of Haiti and its people dominated in the United States and Europe. The vision of Haiti as a backward and barbaric nation populated by poor, superstitious people helped justify the 1915 occupation of the island by the United States, which was to have dramatic consequences on the twentieth-century history of the nation. In many ways, more than two hundred years after gaining independence from France, and more than seventy years after the "Second Independence" that came with U.S. withdrawal in 1934, Haiti is still seeking a true and fruitful independence on its own terms.

See also **Caribbean; Colonialism; French Revolution; Napoleon; Toussaint Louverture.**

BIBLIOGRAPHY

Ardouin, Beaubrun. *Études sur l'histoire d'Haïti suivies de la vie du général J.-M. Borgella.* 1853–1865. 11 vols. Reprint, Port-au-Prince, Haiti, 1958.

Dubois, Laurent. *Avengers of the New World: The Story of the Haitian Revolution.* Cambridge, Mass., 2004.

Gaillard, Gusti-Klara. *L'expérience haïtienne de la dette extérieure; ou, Une production caféière pillée, 1875–1915.* Port-au-Prince, Haiti, 1990.

Nicholls, David. *From Dessalines to Duvalier: Race, Colour, and National Independence in Haiti.* Cambridge, U.K., 1979.

Sheller, Mimi. *Democracy after Slavery: Black Publics and Peasant Radicalism in Haiti and Jamaica.* Gainesville, Fla., 2000.

Trouillot, Michel-Rolph. *Haiti, State against Nation: The Origins and Legacy of Duvalierism.* New York, 1990.

LAURENT DUBOIS

HAMBURG. Hamburg, a seaport of Germany, is located where two smaller tributaries flow into the Elbe, approximately fifty miles from the North Sea. For most of its long-standing history, Hamburg has been not only a city but also an independent state with its own government, postal system, flag, and mint. Hamburg merchants, acting as intermediaries for Scandinavian, East European, and Atlantic trade, conducted their own foreign policy, mainly with bilateral commercial treaties. Through politics of strict neutrality, they managed to maintain Hamburg's independence against the pressures of its powerful neighbors, Denmark and Prussia.

HAMBURG AND NAPOLEON

During the early stages of the French Revolution, leading Hamburg circles—in accordance with their city's cosmopolitan, republican, and free-press tradition—openly sympathized with Enlightenment ideals of education, religious tolerance, rational administration, and citizen-based government. Their social clubs, reading circles, pamphlets, and newspapers created a lasting basis for enlightened civic engagement. Initially, Hamburg profited from the French Revolutionary wars, filling the vacuum created by Napoleon's imposition of the anti-English Continental Blockade on conquered territories. Hamburg merchants fought hard (and paid belligerents large sums) to preserve the city's neutrality during the subsequent Prussian-Austrian wars against France, a neutrality often condemned by adherents to the German patriotic movement born in the battle against Napoleonic forces.

This prosperity did not last. In 1806, after Prussia's disastrous defeat at Jena, Hamburg was occupied by French troops and incorporated into the Napoleonic Empire. Trade and manufacture slumped sharply with Hamburg's inclusion in the blockade. Hundreds of ships lay idle; thousands of workers lost their jobs. The French also confiscated English goods, conducted house-searches, conscripted inhabitants into the French army, exacted monetary contributions and bribes, and—when the poor protested—executed rioters. Nonetheless, French rule brought one improvement: the French constitution. For the first time, Hamburg inhabitants were granted uniform civil and economic rights, executive and judiciary powers were separated, and the city administration was rationalized. Thus, for instance, Hamburg's 6,500 Jews—Germany's largest Jewish community—were granted civil rights and government representation. Nonetheless, when French troops withdrew after Napoleon's Russian defeat, city inhabitants greeted Lieutenant Friedrich Karl von Tettenborn (1778–1845) and his Russian cavalry with jubilation and quickly restored their own constitution. This was premature. Tettenborn, no stranger to monetary exactions himself, did little to prepare the city for the next French offensive; he departed soon after the French lay siege to Hamburg in May 1813. This marked the beginning of the city's real suffering.

Now under French martial law, Hamburg was forcibly rebuilt—by means of heavy punitive contributions, massive forced labor, and extensive destruction of housing—into a fortress. The resumption of war worsened conditions further. The French confiscated the silver of Hamburg's bank, turned many churches into stables, and collected troops for a last-ditch defense. In December 1813, all inhabitants without supplies of food to last a six months' siege were expelled from the city. Approximately twenty thousand people were left to wander the winter countryside; many died. In early 1814, Allied troops surrounded a city whose population was disease-ridden and starving. The French refused to surrender the city until April 1814—a full month after Paris itself had fallen to the Allies. Hamburg had suffered more in the war than most other European cities; its population, about 130,000 in 1800, was reduced by almost one-fourth.

It took decades for the city to recover, but its strategic location stood it in good stead. The Vienna Congress guaranteed the city's sovereignty; in 1815, Hamburg became one of the Free Cities of the German Confederation. When the war ended, returning merchants could exploit the expansion of Atlantic trade that had followed the independence of North and then South and Central American countries. Hamburg became the major transit port for grain shipments from eastern Europe and for Britain's increasing production of cheap industrial goods; its merchants participated in the growing trade with Asia, Africa, and the East Indies. The harbor was enlarged and modernized. Between 1820 and 1860, the size of the Hamburg merchant fleet doubled; its

Houses along a canal in Hamburg c. 1900. ©Sean Sexton Collection/Corbis

tonnage increased more than six-fold. In 1841, the Hamburg Stock Exchange was established. The city's first railways were built shortly thereafter. The Hamburg-American line HAPAG, which was to assume a dominant position in transatlantic shipping, was founded in 1847. The city was badly hit by a fire in 1842, which destroyed 1,749 houses, 102 warehouses, and rendered over one-tenth of the population homeless. The economic prestige of its merchants—one of whom pledged his family fortune as security for loans—helped raise money to rebuild. By 1850, with a population of 170,000, Hamburg was again a preeminent European port.

CITIZENSHIP AND POLITICS

Hamburg's government, however, remained antiquated. Its city charter, which dated from 1712, was based on corporate privileges—the bulk of which were reserved for merchants and property-owning "burghers." To become a burgher, one had to meet strict religious, income, property, and residence criteria, as well as pay a hefty entrance

fee. This restricted burghers to a small, exclusive minority with special voting, employment, marriage, and property-holding privileges. Most other inhabitants, being non-burghers, had fewer rights (Jews did not regain equal rights until the 1850s) and no power over city government. This government was divided between a self-recruiting *Rat* or senate of prominent merchants and lawyers, and ordinary burghers. The former held the highest executive, administrative, and judiciary powers, and ran foreign affairs. Their power was inadequately balanced by Hamburg's burghers. These were organized in various parish-based administrative bodies; they also met in large assemblies. In 1860, these assemblies were transformed into a *Bürgerschaft* or City Council, elected by intricate combinations of ordinary, property-owning, and Senate-appointed administrative burghers. This was Hamburg's only representative body.

Political influence was thus the purview of a small minority. Although the Hamburg constitution of 1860 abolished burghers' economic-corporatist privileges and abrogated the judicial power of the senate, both retained their political monopoly. The result was strongly elitist: in 1879, for instance, 22,000 burghers—out of an adult male population of 103,000 and a total population of 450,000—could vote for and participate in the city-state's government.

This mercantile-burgher oligarchy had its challengers. An anti-elite, guild-friendly burgher group had long sought to curtail the power of Hamburg's free-trading merchants. This division within Hamburg's government helped fuel the (brief and unsuccessful) 1848–1849 revolution. The protectionists were defeated in the 1850s, as industrialization and favorable trade conditions promoted the abolition of guilds and tariffs throughout German states. A liberal, professional intelligentsia with a large following among educational and artisans' organizations then raised the banner of democratization. By the 1870s, their leadership had been usurped by Hamburg's social democrats, whose further development of artisans' and workers' organizations soon made them the largest oppositional group in Hamburg. During the 1890s, socialists' democratic challenge to Hamburg's oligarchy was unattractively echoed by petty-bourgeois and white-collar nationalists within the anti-Semitic German-Social Reform Party.

All these sought to broaden the Hamburg franchise, break the government oligarchy, and, not least, gain insight and power over the Hamburg administration. For Hamburg was also administered by burghers—amateurs appointed by the senate or by various parish and neighborhood burgher associations. The resultant unsupervised multitude of administrative mini-jurisdictions was a byword for sluggishness and opacity. Some reforms had been undertaken after the 1842 fire. But both administration and government ignored Hamburg's recurrent and deadly cholera epidemics (which primarily hit the poor) until, in 1892, 17,000 people sickened and 8,600 died. The appalling housing and sanitary conditions exposed by subsequent investigations promoted reconsideration of government scope and responsibility. It was decided to ease burgher entrance requirements. In 1894, around 14 percent of the adult male population could vote in city elections. By 1904, the figure had risen to 23 percent.

HAMBURG AS GERMANY'S PORT

These changes reflected Hamburg's new position as a self-administering city within the new German Empire (formed in 1871). The loss of Free City status had been less painful than anticipated. Victories over Austria and France, increased German patriotism, and the security of belonging to a major power outweighed the suspicion that cosmopolitan, republican Hamburg merchants felt toward the Prussian aristocrat Otto von Bismarck (1815–1898). Hamburg's increasing importance as a trading center and the city's acceptance, in 1888, of the Zollverein or German Customs Union (encouraged by imperial co-finance of a massive, modern Free Harbor) soon reconciled it to the empire. By the 1890s, imperial plans for both colonies and a vastly expanded navy gained enthusiastic support from leading Hamburg circles.

Incorporation into the empire gave Hamburg three seats in the German parliament, which was elected by an all-male suffrage. The experience of national elections proved traumatic, as Hamburg's social democrats quickly conquered the city's three parliamentary districts (the third was taken in 1890). The fact that Hamburg was thus represented, at the national level, by elements regarded as foreign to the burgher population, reinforced antisocialist sentiment at home.

The powerful Hamburg socialist vote reflected the city's economic modernization. Incorporation into the empire had stimulated both trade and industry. Shipbuilding expanded dramatically; by 1900, Hamburg's more than eighty shipyards were dominated by three giants, building, among other things, warships for an increasingly expansionist Germany. The Hamburg steamship fleet increased more than five-fold between 1880 and 1907. Great shipping concerns (among them HAPAG, now the world's largest) transported both goods and people; between 1870 and 1914, over 2.3 million emigrants passed through Hamburg. In 1914, Hamburg placed third—after London and New York—among the harbors of the world.

Hamburg was also industrializing. In 1866, 600 factories had employed 18,000 workers; by 1914, 5,000 plants employed 150,000. Hamburg's food, alcohol, and tobacco-processing industries, always important to the city's economy, had expanded in scope and variety, and were complemented by industries processing jute, rubber, oil, and other raw materials, often for re-export within the Free Harbor itself. By the 1880s, chemical, electrical, metal, and machinery factories further diversified Hamburg's economy. This expansion was fueled by massive work-force immigration. In 1860, 250,000 people lived in Hamburg; by 1890, 620,000. In 1905, the population exceeded 800,000; on the eve of World War I, Hamburg had more than a million inhabitants. Hamburg's inefficient and narrow government made it difficult to adjust police, housing, educational, or welfare institutions to this rapid expansion. Workers turned to self-help, establishing a self-contained subculture of "red" cooperatives, insurance associations, and leisure and educational organizations that reinforced Hamburg's social divides.

The depth of this division was evident in 1906. By then, both social democrats and populist anti-Semites had entered city council elections. The still-narrow franchise severely limited their chances of success. The anti-Semites peaked in 1901 at three representatives (out of a council of 160). The social democrats did better, gaining thirteen seats in 1904. Despite these low numbers, many Hamburg burghers were appalled at the "introduction of race-hate and class-hate" into the city council. In 1906, Hamburg's municipal electorate was, therefore, again narrowed: the votes of poorer burghers were devalued. This "suffrage robbery" was not soon forgotten by Hamburg's working classes. The continuing division between Hamburg workers and burghers would, in fact, stamp Hamburg's postwar history.

See also **Berlin; Cities and Towns; Denmark; Germany; Prussia; Trade and Economic Growth; Zollverein.**

BIBLIOGRAPHY

Baasch, Ernst. *Geschichte Hamburgs 1814–1918.* 2 volumes. Gotha, 1924–1925.

Evans, Richard J. *Death in Hamburg: Society and Politics in the Cholera Years 1830–1910.* London, 1990.

Herzig, Arno, Dieter Langewiesche, and Arnold Sywottek. *Arbeiter in Hamburg: Unterschichten, Arbeiter, und Arbeiterbewegung seit dem ausgehenden 18. Jahrhundert.* Hamburg, 1983.

Hurd, Madeleine. *Public Spheres, Public Mores, and Democracy: Hamburg and Stockholm, 1870–1914.* Ann Arbor, Mich., 2000.

Jochmann, Werner, ed. *Hamburg: Geschichte der Stadt und ihrer Bewohner.* Volume 2: *Vom Kaiserreich bis zur Gegenwart.* Hamburg, 1986.

Kleßmann, Eckart. *Geschichte der Stadt Hamburg.* Hamburg, 1981.

Liedtke, Rainer. "Germany's Door to the World: A Haven for Jews? Hamburg, 1590–1933." *Jewish Culture and History* 4, no. 2 (2001): 75–86.

Lindemann, Mary. *Patriots and Paupers: Hamburg, 1712–1830.* New York, 1990.

Loose, Hans-Dieter, ed. *Hamburg: Geschichte der Stadt und ihrer Bewohner.* Volume 1: *Vom den Anfängen bis zur Reichsgründung.* Hamburg, 1982.

Lüth, Erich. *Hamburg: 1870–1910.* Frankfurt, 1979.

Morris, Jonathan. "Hamburg, Health, and Bourgeois Liberalism." *Journal of Urban History* 21, no. 2 (1995): 256–264.

Pelc, Ortwin, ed. *Hamburg: die Stadt im 20. Jahrhundert.* Hamburg, 2002.

Schmidt, Burghart. *Hamburg im Zeitalter der Französischen Revolution und Napoleons.* Hamburg, 1998.

Schramm, Percy Ernst. *Neun Generationen: Dreihundert Jahre deutscher "Kulturgeschichte" im Lichte der Schicksale einer Hamburger Bürgerfamilie (1648–1948).* 2 volumes. Göttingen, 1963–1964.

———. "Liberalismus in Hamburg und Bremen zwischen Restauration und Reichsgründung (1830–1870)." *Historische Zeitschrift,* supplement 19 (1995): 135–160.

Schulz, Andreas. "Weltbürger und Geldaristokraten: Hanseatisches Bürgertum im 19. Jahrhundert." *Historische Zeitschrift* 259 no. 3 (1994): 637–670.

Sommer, Theo. *Hamburg: Weltstadt im Wellengang der Zeiten.* Hamburg, 2004.

Stammer, Wilhelm Chr. K. *Hamburgs Werften 1635–1993.* Hamburg, 1994.

Teuteberg, Hans J. "Die Entstehung des Modernen Hamburger Haffens (1866–1896)." *Tradition* 17, nos. 5–6 (1972): 256–291.

Trautmann, Günter. "Liberalismus, Arbeiterbewegung und Staat in Hamburg und Schleswig-Holstein 1862–1869." *Archiv für Sozialgeschichte* 15 (1975): 51–110.

MADELEINE HURD

HARDENBERG, KARL AUGUST VON (1750–1822), Prussian reformer.

As chancellor of Prussia from 1810 to 1822, Karl August von Hardenberg was one of the two leading figures, along with Karl Freiherr vom Stein, in the Reform Movement (1807–1815), which produced profound legal and socioeconomic changes in Prussia. Hardenberg's principal legislative accomplishments included two economic decrees of 1810, which moved Prussia toward a free-market economy, and which many historians credit with unleashing powerful long-term economic growth. He also succeeded in keeping the Prussian state intact in the face of political and financial pressure from Napoleon, and he navigated the state from its alliance with Napoleon through the successful War of Liberation against France in 1813–1814. But after Napoleon's defeat, Hardenberg encountered a backlash against his proposals for further political reforms, and he died without having realized his dream for the adoption of a parliamentary constitution in Prussia.

Hardenberg was born on 31 May 1750 in Essenrode, Hanover, to a wealthy noble landowning family. He studied at the University of Göttingen, and served as an official in Hanover and Brunswick before accepting an appointment in the Prussian civil service, where he made his reputation as the administrator of Prussia's new territories in Ansbach-Bayreuth, and as a member of the general directory in Berlin after 1798.

From 1804 to 1806, Hardenberg served as Prussian foreign minister. In this capacity he played a pivotal role in formulating Prussia's foreign policy—initially supporting rapprochement with France, and then advocating war. Hardenberg's effectiveness as foreign minister was limited by bitter infighting with his rival, Christian von Haugwitz, one of the king's cabinet councillors. Six months before the outbreak of hostilities with France, Frederick William III (r. 1797–1840) dismissed Hardenberg from office, under pressure from French officials who were upset by Hardenberg's support for an alliance with Britain. In January 1807 Hardenberg returned to office as the king's chief adviser, but Napoleon forced the king to dismiss him again in October of the same year.

In May 1810 Frederick William III named Hardenberg chancellor of Prussia, following Stein's thirteen-month ministry of 1807–1808 and the subsequent eighteen-month "interim"

ministry led by Karl vom Stein zum Altenstein and Friedrich Ferdinand Alexander Dohna. As chancellor, Hardenberg sought to fulfill the bold plan for rebuilding Prussia that he had articulated in his Riga Memorandum of September 1807, shortly after Prussia's capitulation to Napoleon in the disastrous Treaty of Tilsit. Hardenberg had argued that Prussia needed to imitate its conqueror by undergoing "a revolution . . . leading to the ennoblement of mankind," which would transform the subjects of the Prussian king into *Staatsbürger* (citizens of the state). This revolution, however, would "be made not through violent impulses from below or outside, but through the wisdom of the government," and it would culminate in a political system combining "democratic principles in a monarchical government" (quoted in Levinger, p. 46).

Hardenberg successfully promoted several major economic reforms, along with social reforms including the Jewish Emancipation decree of 1812. Although he was forced to retreat from certain controversial proposals, such as a universal income tax, his decrees went a long way toward abolishing the remnants of aristocratic privilege in Prussia, and liberalized the economies of the towns as well. The Finance Edict of 27 October 1810 declared the state's intention to equalize tax burdens, reform the tariff and toll system, create freedom of enterprise, and secularize church lands. The *Gewerbesteueredikt* (enterprise tax edict) of 2 November 1810 eliminated the guilds' monopolies over the practice of trades. Anyone, whether a resident of the countryside or the towns, could now begin practicing a trade simply by paying an annual "tax on enterprises"—though a certificate of competence was required for certain occupations. The *Gewerbesteueredikt* constituted a significant step toward the creation of a fully free labor market in Prussia.

Hardenberg's ambitions for political reform, by contrast, remained largely unfulfilled—in part because of the inherent difficulties in harmonizing democratic and monarchical forms of government. He sought to achieve this goal by rationalizing the Prussian administration and by educating the citizenry for responsible and enlightened political participation. But his program for administrative rationalization met with considerable resistance, although a watered-down version of his plan for a new Prussian council of state was adopted in 1817. Hardenberg had even less luck with several experimental representative institutions that he created between 1811 and 1815. Rather than rallying the "nation" around its king, these assemblies frequently challenged the government's authority. Although Hardenberg persuaded Frederick William III on three successive occasions to promise the establishment of a Prussian constitution, these negative experiences with representative politics ultimately convinced the king to renege on his pledges—so that Prussia remained without a constitution until the Revolution of 1848.

In 1815 Frederick William elevated Hardenberg to the title of prince, in gratitude for his leadership during the French occupation and the War of Liberation. Hardenberg remained in office as chancellor until his death in November 1822. Confronting an increasingly vocal opposition at court, he acquiesced to certain conservative measures such as the draconian Carlsbad Decrees of 1819. Until the final months of his life, however, he continued to lobby unsuccessfully for a Prussian constitution.

See also **Congress of Vienna; Frederick William III; Germany; Liberalism; Metternich, Clemens von; Napoleonic Empire; Prussia; Restoration; Stein, Heinrich Friedrich Karl vom und zum.**

BIBLIOGRAPHY

Hofmeister-Hunger, Andrea. *Pressepolitik und Staatsreform: die Institutionalisierung staatlicher Öffentlichkeitsarbeit bei Karl August von Hardenberg (1792–1822).* Göttingen, 1994.

Levinger, Matthew. *Enlightened Nationalism: The Transformation of Prussian Political Culture, 1806–1848.* New York, 2000.

Meinecke, Friedrich. *The Age of German Liberation, 1795–1815.* Edited by Peter Paret. Translated by Peter Paret and Helmuth Fischer. Berkeley, Calif., 1977.

Thielen, Peter. *Karl August von Hardenberg, 1750–1822: Eine Biographie.* Cologne, 1967.

Vogel, Barbara. *Allgemeine Gewerbefreiheit: die Reformpolitik des preussischen Staatskanzlers Hardenberg (1810–1820).* Göttingen, 1983.

MATTHEW LEVINGER

HARDIE, JAMES KEIR (1856–1915),
Scottish politician and labor organizer.

James Keir Hardie was a leading political figure in the Independent Labour Party and the Labour Party, and his career was a representation of independent Labour politics. His trade union activities thrust him to fame and led to his parliamentary success as the first independent Labour member of Parliament (MP) in 1892.

Hardie was born in Legbrannock, Lanarkshire, in Scotland, on 15 August 1856 the illegitimate son of David Hardie, a ship's carpenter, and Mary Keir, a domestic farm servant. He became a messenger boy at the age of seven, and worked in a shipyard and became a baker's errand boy before working in the coal mines between 1867 and 1878. However, there he was victimized for his trade union activities. He opened a stationer's shop at Low Waters in 1878 and became a correspondent for the *Glasgow Weekly Mail,* becoming a full-time journalist in 1882. He was editor of the *Cumnock News* between 1882 to 1886. He also acted as a trade-union organizer and was secretary of the Lanarkshire miners in 1879, of the Ayrshire miners in 1880, and of the Scottish Miners' Federation in 1886. In 1880 he married Lillie Wilson, by whom he had two daughters and two sons.

In his early years Hardie was a staunch Liberal, but a number of events, including a failure to strengthen Scottish miners' trade unionism radicalized his politics to the extent that *The Miner,* his new newspaper formed in January 1887, established links with socialists. In April 1888 he fought a parliamentary by-election at Mid-Lanark as an Independent Labour candidate but was defeated after obtaining only 617 votes, 8.2 percent of those cast. However, in 1892 he was returned to Parliament as MP for West Ham South, presenting himself as the MP for the unemployed. His success projected him forward in independent Labour politics and he chaired the foundation conference of the Independent Labour Party (ILP) held at Bradford in January 1893. His position as leader of the new movement was strengthened by the fact that he formed the *Labour Leader,* as the successor to *The Miner,* in 1889 and made it a weekly publication from March 1894.

Hardie lost his West Ham South seat in the 1895 general election and despite contesting other seats, most notably Bradford East in November 1896, was not returned to Parliament until 1900, when he became MP for Merthyr Tydfil, a seat that he held until his death. In his pursuit of a broader alliance, he objected to the fusion of the ILP with other socialist groups such as the quasi-Marxist Social Democratic Federation, and his strategy came to fruition on 27 February 1900 when the trade unions and the ILP formed the Labour Representation Committee. This was a small party but it gained increasing trade union support and made a political breakthrough in the January 1906 general election in which it secured thirty seats. At that point it became the Labour Party, and Hardie acted as Chairman of the Parliamentary Labour Party between 1906 and 1908 and 1909–1910, although he was traveling the empire and the world in 1907–1908.

In reality, Hardie was an excellent propagandist but not a particularly accomplished organizer of the Labour Party, and his period in office was marred by controversy. He was a great advocate of women's suffrage but favored the approach of Emmeline Pankhurst (1858–1928) and her Women's Social and Political Union, which emphasized that women should be first given the parliamentary franchise on the same terms as men, which was rejected by many in the Labour movement who wanted the full enfranchisement of men and women and not simply a measure that would only give some middle-class women the vote. This led Hardie to threaten to leave the ILP and the Labour Party. He also faced criticism from the Left over his ambivalent attitude toward the White Australia policy although his antiracist attitude in South Africa and his condemnation of British rule in India, which provoked a storm in Britain, restored his credibility with independent Labour.

From 1910 until his death Hardie was effectively Labour's elder statesman who would take up the vital issues of the day. He supported the industrial struggles of the immediate prewar period but was consumed by the threat of war in Europe. He hoped that the Second International, of the socialist movement, would prevent war and was faced with a difficult encounter with patriotism in his constituency on 6 August 1914, just after the war broke out. He died, a rather disillusioned man, on 26 September 1915.

The Times obituary of Hardie, which appeared the day after his death, was grudging of his achievements and suggested that he was "an ineffective leader of the independent group which owed its existence in great measure to his unflagging energy." In 1917 A. G. Gardiner added that "he was the one man in the parliamentary Labour Party who was unqualified to lead it." Nevertheless, he fought for the right of workers and for the preservation of peace in the face of war, and the *Merthyr Pioneer* of the 2 October 1915 rightly suggested that with his death the "member for Humanity has resigned his seat."

See also **Asquith, Herbert Henry; Great Britain; Labor Movements; Labour Party; Lloyd George, David; Pankhurst, Emmeline, Christabel, and Sylvia; Second International; Socialism.**

BIBLIOGRAPHY

Benn, Caroline. *Keir Hardie.* London, 1992.

Hughes, Emrys. *Keir Hardie.* London, 1956.

Morgan, Kenneth O. *Keir Hardie: Radical and Socialist.* London, 1975.

KEITH LAYBOURN

HARDY, THOMAS (1840–1928), English novelist and poet.

The son of a stonemason and former house servant, Thomas Hardy was born on 2 June 1840, in Higher Bockhampton, a hamlet on the edge of a heath near the county town of Dorchester, in the western shire of Dorset. His early education at home and in different schools ended with his apprenticeship to a local architect at the age of sixteen. When he was twenty-two, Hardy took employment in London with an architect, a large part of whose business was in restoring ancient Anglican churches, an activity that Hardy in later years regretted (because of the accompanying destruction of original stone and wood tracery and fabrics).

In his spare time Hardy wrote poetry, without attaining publication. He turned to prose and had some success with his second published novel,

Under the Greenwood Tree (1872). The acclaim for his fourth novel, *Far from the Madding Crowd* (1874), led him not only to leave architecture in order to write full-time but also to marry Emma Lavinia Gifford, who for several years assisted him by recopying his draft manuscripts, but who by the time of her death in 1912 had developed religious and social obsessions that seriously strained the marriage. A succession of novels and short stories from 1870 to 1896 earned him fame and financial security. Some of the novels before and after *The Return of the Native* (1878) were unsuccessful experiments in form and subject; but beginning in 1886 with *The Mayor of Casterbridge,* and continuing with *The Woodlanders* (1886) and *Tess of the d'Urbervilles* (1891) and culminating with *Jude the Obscure* (1895), Hardy's increasingly biting irony, painful denouements of his characters' lives, and eloquent critiques of conventional social, sexual, and religious beliefs made him controversial even as the sales of his books grew.

Partly in resentment at the denunciations by some of his critics (and in spite of his fame and the admiration of many distinguished readers and critics), he finally declared his intention to write no more fiction and returned to poetry, publishing his first book of poems, *Wessex Poems and Other Verses,* in 1898, and his second, *Poems of the Past and the Present,* in 1901. In his own judgment his chef d'oeuvre was *The Dynasts* (published in three volumes, 1903–1908), a verse-drama in nineteen acts (130 scenes), consisting of a melange of prose stage directions intermixed with extensive verse passages. This work, influenced by the German philosopher Eduard von Hartmann (1842–1906), interprets the events of the Napoleonic Wars as determined by Spirits of the Age, much in the manner of classical Greek and Roman myths. As the product of a famous novelist, Hardy's verse was initially greeted with skepticism and impatience, but by the publication of the third volume of *The Dynasts* he was one of Britain's most respected poets, and the subsequent six volumes of verse he published solidified his stature. The poems written in regret and mourning for Emma after her death in November 1912 (twenty-one of which were published under the blanket name "Poems of 1912–13") are generally admired as some of the finest, most poignant love poems in the English language. In early 1914 Hardy married Florence Dugdale, who had been informally working as his secretary. Hardy died 11 January 1928.

The attacks on convention that had caused conservative reviewers and readers of the nineteenth century to scorn Hardy's novels did not have a comparable effect on the reception of his verse (although there was tongue-clucking over such poems as "Hap"). Some of his most effective poems lament the pointlessness of war, as in "Drummer Hodge," regarding the Boer War (1899–1902), and "Channel Firing," written just before World War I (1914–1918). For Hardy, in both his fiction and his poetry, it is the human life that continues to go on during national crises and economic conundrums that merits respect and attention ("In Time of 'The Breaking of Nations'").

This priority is true for his fiction as well as for his poetry. Early in his career he realized that by concentrating on a single section of Britain (which he called Wessex, comprising Dorset and parts of five other southwestern counties of England) he could find ample material to demonstrate general truths and in effect to interrelate all of his writings. This decision also in time came to inspire a large tourist industry that continues to the twenty-first century, as admirers search for the actual locales in which Hardy imagined his stories and poems taking place. Even after he ceased writing new novels he continued to revise old ones for new editions. One of his principal concerns was to adjust Wessex settings, others were to clarify personalities and to bring sexual dilemmas into sharper relief. The reasons for, and the aesthetic effects of, these revisions constitute still unresolved controversies in Hardy scholarship, which are extremely well surveyed by Simon Gatrell.

Numerous other controversies about Hardy exist. Biographically, basic questions about Hardy may never be "solved," such as whether his affection for his cousin Tryphena Sparks was erotic, and whether his tendency to be infatuated with such society women as Florence Henniker resulted from the unsatisfactoriness of his marriage to Emma or the marriage became emotionally bland because of this tendency. The most reliable authority on biographical issues is Michael Millgate, but among others Robert Gittings offers interesting alternative views and information.

Still of substantive interest are Hardy's views of gender and his presentation of women: although he is accused by some of condescension toward women, others admire him for a deep empathy with women in a patriarchal society that in effect condoned rape and exploitation. Marxism and its assorted poststructuralist and political variants have offered some of the more provocative avenues into this area of Hardy's work and continue to attempt to place Hardy within both Victorian and modern culture.

Hardy remains an extraordinarily approachable touchstone for an understanding of nineteenth-century life and writings. Eschewing the phantasm of Charles Dickens (1812–1870) and the constricted social range of Jane Austen (1775–1817), along with these two writers he is the most widely read (by nonacademicians) of the plethora of fiction writers of the nineteenth century. Most of his poetry was written in the twentieth century, and suitably he has been one of the chief models for British poets since his time; but he also stands not much lower than Robert Browning (1812–1889) and Alfred Lord Tennyson (1809–1892) as widely read poets who can be classed as Victorian.

See also **Dickens, Charles; Eliot, George; Gaskell, Elizabeth; Great Britain; Tennyson, Alfred.**

BIBLIOGRAPHY

Boumelha, Penny. *Thomas Hardy and Women: Sexual Ideology and Narrative Form.* Sussex, U.K., 1982.

Gatrell, Simon. *Hardy the Creator: A Textual Biography.* Oxford, U.K., 1988.

———. *Thomas Hardy's Vision of Wessex.* Houndmills, Basingstoke, U.K., 2003.

Gittings, Robert. *Young Thomas Hardy.* Harmondsworth, U.K., 1975.

———. *The Older Hardy.* London, 1978.

Millgate, Michael. *Thomas Hardy: A Biography Revisited.* Oxford, U.K., 2004.

Taylor, Dennis. *Hardy's Poetry, 1860–1928.* Rev. ed. Basingstoke, U.K., 1989.

Widdowson, Peter. *Hardy in History: A Study in Literary Sociology.* London and New York, 1989.

DALE KRAMER

HAUSSMANN, GEORGES-EUGÈNE
(1809–1891), creator of modern Paris.

Georges-Eugène Haussmann was not an architect, an engineer, a city planner, a hydrologist, or a landscape designer. He was a lawyer by education, a career administrator by choice, and the man who created modern Paris (where he was born and where he died).

He pompously (and illegitimately) called himself a baron. His maternal grandfather, a revolutionary and Napoleonic general, Georges-Frédéric Dentzel (1755–1828), had been ennobled during the First Empire, but French titles are not heritable through the female line. His paternal grandfather, Nicolas Haussmann, also had a revolutionary past. The grandson's administrative career is a classic example of the breach forced by the bourgeoisie into government service during the French Revolution, which was widened by Napoleon's reforms of the state.

Haussmann was educated at the Lycée Henri IV, the best school in Paris, where he made an important friendship with the duc de Chartres, the eldest son of the duc d'Orléans who would become King Louis-Philippe (r. 1830–1848). He studied law at the Sorbonne during one of the golden ages of French university life, and not only heard some of the most powerful minds of the day lecture, he also met and knew those who would create the brilliant culture of the July Monarchy: the poet Alfred de Musset (1810–1857) and the composer Hector Berlioz (1803–1869), among others.

The Revolution of 1830 was Haussmann's big break, as it was for his generation of "frustrated careerists" with some tincture of idealism. Haussmann fought in the Trois Glorieuses—the three "glorious days" of revolution, was slightly wounded carrying a message to the Hôtel de Ville, and when Louis-Philippe was chosen king, Haussmann was able to ask the heir apparent for an appointment; he was named secretary general in the department of Vienne. He slowly climbed the provincial administrative pole. Advancement in the July Monarchy was sluggish and Haussmann spent at least as much time advertising his abilities and frustration as he did performing undemanding administrative tasks.

Things were not made easy by his abrasive personality, and he was sent to cool his heels as sub-prefect in St. Girons, in the Pyrenees. He often traveled to Bordeaux to escape boredom, and there he met and married Louise-Octavie de Laharpe, a *bordelaise* who brought a comfortable if not extravagant dowry to the marriage. They would have two daughters: Henriette-Marie and Fanny-Valentine. Soon after his marriage he was posted to the sub-prefecture of Blaye, about twenty-five miles down river from Bordeaux. Unfortunately, his patron, now the duc d'Orléans, died in a carriage accident in 1842. Haussmann's career was stalled. Another revolution, in 1848, intervened, and Haussmann, not closely identified with the July Monarchy because of his insignificance, played his cards brilliantly. His early Bonapartism was cautious, quiet, and probably sincere. When Louis-Napoleon Bonaparte (later Napoleon III, r. 1852–1871) was elected president of the Second Republic, Haussmann intrigued for a promotion. It came on 24 January 1849, as prefect of the Var. His charge was to browbeat and intimidate the republicans and manipulate the election. He accomplished both and enjoyed the work. His reward was the prefecture of the Yonne (11 May 1850), another turbulent department to be cowed. Again success as a tough and competent prefect brought rewards. He was named prefect of the Gironde, had an interview with Louis-Napoleon on 1 December 1851, the eve of his coup d'état, and left Paris for Bordeaux. He brought the Orleanist city (and department) into the Bonapartist fold.

Haussmann's combination of exceptional competence and authoritarianism, bordering on bullying, succeeded. Napoleon III made a triumphal visit to Bordeaux, orchestrated by Haussmann, and there proclaimed his famous formula: "The Empire is Peace!" The following year (1853) Haussmann was appointed prefect of the Seine, the most important post in the administration. This time he was not charged with intimidating republicans and Orleanists: he was to transform Paris, the most ambitious, successful, and enduring legacy of the Second Empire.

At their first interview since his appointment, the emperor gave Haussmann a map with a series of new streets indicated in three colors to signify their order of importance. He also told his new prefect that there would be no special funds for the gigantic task of urban renewal. These sketchy proposals—the original map has vanished, only a copy made in 1868 survives—were the only concrete plans Haussmann got from his master. He met sometimes daily with the emperor to discuss the rebuilding of the capital, but according to Haussmann, Napoleon III was vague about what he wanted. He was a dreamer, a man with grand, even extravagant, ideas about transforming the city—many of them directly borrowed from his uncle, Napoleon I (r. 1804–1814/15)—who depended upon others to realize them. Haussmann could not have done his work without the support of Napoleon III: the imperial will and authority was fundamental. But it is the servant and not the master who determined the look, the shape, and the infrastructure of Paris. This last, the sewer system and the water supply, was not even mentioned by the emperor.

Haussmann began by making the first accurate topographical map of Paris. The earliest projects, which came to be known as the first of three *réseaux* (street systems) into which Haussmann divided the work, concentrated on the historic core of Paris. The Louvre-Tuileries palace was the first project. Napoleon III wanted to establish himself as a reformer, put men to work, and set his mark on one of the most prestigious monuments in Paris. He linked the Louvre to the Tuileries, the logical conclusion to centuries of expansions and additions. The first streets he built formed the so-called *grande croisée* that cut through the city north-south (boulevard Sébastapol on the Right Bank, boulevard St. Michel on the Left Bank) and east-west (rue de Rivoli). The latter had been left unfinished by Napoleon I. It was now extended into the unruly and politically volatile eastern quadrant of Paris.

Barricades, easily thrown up in the narrow, twisting streets of Old Paris, had been the chief weapon of urban insurrection in 1830 and 1848. In 1848, it had taken the army a week to cross the city and clear the barricades. One of Haussmann's first projects was not only to extend the rue de Rivoli but to cut a new street (boulevard Voltaire) so that eastern Paris could be attacked, if necessary, from front and rear. This was the only strategic system of streets built in Paris until 1868. The cliché that Haussmann's broad streets were to

Building the Avenue de l'Opera. Photograph by Charles Marville. MUSÉE DE LA VILLE DE PARIS, MUSÉ CARNAVALET, PARIS, FRANCE/BRIDGEMAN ART LIBRARY/LAUROS/GIRAUDON

make urban insurrection impossible does not explain his urban transformations. The new boulevards were not primarily built to facilitate cavalry charges and provide a clear field for cannon fire. Only two strategic networks, of the hundreds of new streets cut in Paris, were built, one of them fifteen years after the boulevard Voltaire. This relaxed response to urban insurrection casts doubt on the thesis: the fact that barricades were built during the Commune uprising, in 1871, invalidates the hypothesis.

What drove Haussmann's transformation were his thorough, indeed obsessive, interpretation of the aesthetic principles of the day, his belief in urban hygiene, his devotion to transportation above other concerns, his focus on control of the city achieved by regularity and order, and the unrelenting application of his beliefs. The convergence of these ideas in so authoritarian, arrogant, and

bureaucratic-minded a personality had important consequences for Paris. Haussmann had little respect for the past and only contempt for the Middle Ages. He did not hesitate to demolish some of Paris's precious medieval inheritance. In the name of slum clearance he turned the Ile de la Cité, the cradle of Paris and one of the most densely populated neighborhoods in the city, into a virtually uninhabited urban museum. He attempted to give the city a new center at the Place du Châtelet: a failed project. He was devoted to the rectilinear and lopped off a part of the Luxembourg gardens to preserve this urban principle and demolished whatever lay in the path of his straight streets. He created a number of urban optical illusions to give the impression of order, regularity, and rectilinearity. He set the dome of a new building (the cour de Commerce) off-center so it would visually bisect the boulevard Sébastopol. He angled the pont

Sully at the eastern end of the Ile St. Louis—all the other Seine bridges are parallel—in order to create the illusion that the Place de la Bastille (Right Bank) was in line with the dome of the Panthéon (Left Bank). He insisted that every urban perspective down one of his boulevards be closed by a monument or important public building. Where none existed he built what was required. Nowhere is the rigidity of bureaucratic thinking so well expressed as in these pedantic urbanscapes.

There are also grand and admirable examples of *haussmannisme* (a contemporary coinage). The twelve streets that debouch into the Arc de Triomphe form a stunning urban star pattern. The many parks built to satisfy Napoleon III's wishes—most importantly the parcs Monceau, Batignolles, Montsouris, and Buttes-Chaumont—are beautiful and useful, a welcome relief from the otherwise stone city. They were designed by Haussmann's assistant, Jean-Charles Alphand (1817–1891), as were the Bois de Boulogne on the western side of Paris and the Bois de Vincennes on the east. The iron and glass sheds at Les Halles, the Paris markets, designed by Victor Baltard (1805-1874), became one of the marvels of modern architecture and the new city. Charles Garnier (1825–1898) designed the Opéra, the most expensive and luxurious building of the age; although not opened until 1875, the Opéra was an empire project, and the Avenue de l'Opéra that leads to the ornate building is thought to be the quintessential street of Haussmann's Paris.

The serried rows of similar apartment buildings lining the new boulevards, all in the Beaux-Arts style that dominated architectural training and public taste, were of uniform height, building materials, and their ornamentation (such as balconies) were constrained by building codes. They give Paris the homogenous appearance that is one of its beauties.

Haussmann's most visionary work was the incorporation of the *banlieue*, the suburbs surrounding Paris. By imperial decree in 1860, he doubled the landmass of Paris and added 200,000 inhabitants. His most successful work was underground, where he did not have to cut into the dense fabric of a historic city. His new sewer system was a mirror image of the streets of Paris. The city's water supply had been drawn from the Seine (where waste was also dumped) and the Ourcq Canal. Despite public protest by those who appreciated the taste of the river, Haussmann brought well water to Paris by aqueduct, from more than 100 miles away. This was the work of Marie-François-Eugène Belgrand (1810–1878), another talented collaborator.

Although he built extensively, Haussmann built predominately for the bourgeoisie. The poor, driven from the center of Paris, sought refuge in the *banlieue* where housing was cheaper. Paris became what it has remained, a city with a wealthy core surrounded—especially on the east, north, northeast, and southeast—by poor neighborhoods. Only at the turn of the twenty-first century has eastern Paris been subject to gentrification.

It was Haussmann's unconventional and dubiously legal expedients for raising money that brought him down. He received support from the National Assembly for each of the three *réseaux*, but this was never enough. As years went by and the work appeared endless (and endlessly expensive), the politicians were less willing to grant funds. He was entitled to the *octroi*, a tax on all building materials and wine that came into the city. Some say he built in expensive materials because they were more highly taxed. The *octroi* went up as Paris built and grew. This, too, was not enough money. The city borrowed hugely, interest rates went up, and the debt was not retired until 1929.

At the beginning of the work, Haussmann regularly condemned for public use more property than he needed to cut new streets. What was not used he later sold at a profit because of improvements in the infrastructure. The juries of landowners who had to approve condemnations soon put an end to this practice. They made themselves the beneficiaries of Haussmann's improvements. He increasingly turned to deficit spending, a radical and distrusted process of urban finance at the time.

Haussmann had always counted on enhanced property values that would increase future property taxes, but now he began borrowing against the future. Contractors were required to front the cost of the project. They would be paid, with interest, upon completion. Until then Haussmann used the money to finance and leverage other projects.

Avenue de l'Opera, Paris, photographed in the late nineteenth century. ©BETTMANN/CORBIS

Those who wanted to work for the city were forced to lend Haussmann money, and only the biggest contractors could participate. He then devised an even more dubious scheme. The city began issuing proxy bonds (*bons de délégation*) based on the amounts owed by contractors. These bonds were soon traded on the market and interest rates were driven up to 10 percent, which in turn drove up the cost of building.

Haussmann's financial legerdemain became the target for opponents of the imperial regime, including conservative financial interests who were shut out of the lucrative gambling in urban finance. He was attacked in a witty and pointed pamphlet, *Les Comptes fantastiques d'Haussmann* (1868), written by Jules Ferry (1832–1893). Haussmann, secure in the support of the emperor, disdained the attack. But he had become a lightening rod for discontent, and on 2 January 1870 the emperor reluctantly withdrew his support.

The debacle of the empire at the Battle of Sedan several months later sent Haussmann running for cover and eventually out of France for a time. He briefly entertained an offer to haussmannize Rome, but the deal fell through. He was elected to the senate of the Third Republic in 1875, but retired from politics soon afterward. In his last years, he wrote his *Mémoires* in three dense, self-serving volumes (1890) and died in his Paris apartment the next year, some months after his wife. He is buried in Père Lachaise cemetery, not far from Alfred de Vigny (1797–1863), his schoolmate.

See also Cities and Towns; France; Napoleon III; Revolutions of 1830.

BIBLIOGRAPHY

Gaillard, Jeanne. *Paris, la ville, 1852–1870.* Paris, 1976.

Haussmann, Georges-Eugène. *Mémoires du baron Haussmann.* 3 vols. Paris, 1890–1893.

Jordan, David P. *Transforming Paris: The Life and Labors of Baron Haussmann.* New York, 1995.

Zola, Émile. *The Kill.* Translated by Arthur Goldhammer. New York, 2004.

DAVID P. JORDAN

HEGEL, GEORG WILHELM FRIEDRICH (1770–1831), German philosopher.

Georg Wilhelm Friedrich ("Wilhelm" to friends and family) Hegel was born in Stuttgart, Germany, the city of residence of the Duke of Württemberg, in 1770.

Hegel's father was a minor functionary in the revenue office of the court, and Hegel's mother came from a long line of distinguished Protestant reformers. The Hegel household put a premium on learning and education; they subscribed to the leading journals of the time, and they encouraged their obviously gifted son in his education. When Hegel was thirteen, his mother died of a disease that he also had at the time, and it was decided shortly thereafter that, following his mother's wishes, he would study to become a Protestant minister at the famous seminary in Tübingen. Nonetheless, he was not sent off to a Protestant cloister school, as was typical at the time, but to a more-or-less Enlightenment-oriented *Gymnasium* in Stuttgart.

In 1788, when Hegel entered the seminary at Tübingen, he was ranked first in class, a distinction he soon lost, as he found the intellectual atmosphere stifling and his broad educational background to be cramped by the narrowness of his studies there. While at the seminary, however, he befriended and roomed with two other seminarians who were equally dissatisfied with life there: Friedrich Hölderlin, later to become one of Germany's greatest poets, and Friedrich Schelling, later to become one of Germany's leading philosophers.

Under the influence of one of the disaffected preceptors at the seminary, Carl Immanuel Diez, the three friends began to study the recently published works of Immanuel Kant. With the coming of the French Revolution in 1789, the three linked their studies of Kant's devastating critique of all prior metaphysics and his emphasis on human spontaneity and freedom to the political events playing out in France, mixing a love of ancient Greece and the philosophy of Benedict de Spinoza into the blend. They all resolved not to become pastors and to use their learning to further the "new" revolution in Germany.

After completing his studies in 1793, Hegel took the usual route for young intellectuals at the time and became a house tutor for a wealthy family in Bern. Although miserable and depressed in his existence there, he managed to further his studies of Kant and acquire knowledge of both the Scottish Enlightenment and the writings of Edward Gibbon. He also stayed in touch with Schelling and Hölderlin; Schelling had staged a meteoric rise in German philosophy, becoming Johann Gottlieb Fichte's successor at Jena, and Hölderlin had become a house tutor in Frankfurt, perfecting his poetic talents. Hölderlin managed to get Hegel a job as a house tutor in Frankfurt as well, and in 1797 Hegel moved there. He formed a close bond with a group of other young Swabians there, who, like himself and Hölderlin, shared an enthusiasm for Kant, Fichte, and the French Revolution. He continued to work on several manuscripts, none of which were ever published in his lifetime (but which were published at the beginning of the twentieth century under the title of *Hegel's Early Theological Writings*). His main concern at this point was the shape that a modern religion might take as a leading contributor to the revolutionary movements sweeping Europe. After his father died in 1799, he came into a small inheritance that he used (after writing Schelling and winning his backing) to support himself in Jena as an unsalaried private lecturer at the university there.

In January 1801 Hegel moved to Jena, where he took up teaching and co-editing a journal with Schelling. When Schelling left in 1803 for Würzburg, Hegel was left on his own; he had no salaried job, only a few publications, and a dim future. During that period, he managed to stage

Georg Wilhelm Friedrich Hegel. Portrait by Johann Jakob Schlesinger. BILDARCHIV PREUSSISCHER KULTURBESITZ/ART RESOURCE, NY

one of the most remarkable self-realizations in history, finally composing in 1805 and 1806 his masterwork, *The Phenomenology of Spirit.* In that work (published in 1807), Hegel argued that all philosophy, religion, and art were attempts by human beings collectively (what Hegel called in his term of art, "spirit," *Geist*) to determine the meaning of what it is to be human, and that one could grasp these attempts at "spirit's" self-definition only by attending to the history of the ways in which different communities had organized themselves around what was for them authoritative conceptions of knowledge, law, politics, divinity, ethical life, and art. However, each of those collective efforts at achieving a final, or absolute, knowledge of "spirit" had until the present age broken down under the weight of the contradictions hidden deep within those shared conceptions. These contradictions were so powerful that attempts to realize those conceptions in practice had over historical time foundered under the weight of the incompatible demands they put on

the members of the community. Their successors, as new collective forms of life (new "shapes of spirit"), were, given the historical consciousness that had begun with the Greeks, bound to see themselves as the successors to those ways of life only to find that they too broke down under the weight of their own contradictions. Only in the modern period, Hegel argued, did we realize, after Kant, why that had to be so: Each of them attempted to secure some kind of authority for themselves that was independent of human activity (such as the gods, God, nature, tradition, and utility) only to find that what had looked authoritative eventually turned out to be only an exercise in individual power or based on a false myth. Only in the modern period have we come to see that the "absolute" is merely collective human sense-making activity over time, and thus the moderns began the construction of their "post-revolutionary" world with the self-consciousness that the only norms that can be binding on them are those that they collectively author for themselves. Hegel also controversially claimed that religion is to be understood as part of this development, so that the historical development of *Geist* is in fact equivalent to God's becoming conscious of himself. Hegel's historicizing of all philosophical, religious, and artistic movements, along with his bold claim that after the *Phenomenology,* such movements had culminated in a consciousness of the "absolute" as human freedom, proved to be immensely influential in European thought, but many thought at the time (and still do so today) that in saying that this historical process is the path through which God becomes conscious of himself in and through the human community developing an understanding of its own freedom, Hegel had to be endorsing atheism. Some thought he was a kind of pantheist, and others thought (and still do think) that he was an orthodox Christian theist. Hegel's views on religion were controversial in his own day and remain controversial in our own.

Despite the success of his book, Hegel was unable to procure a job at any German university, and thus near the end of 1807 he moved to Bamberg, where he edited a pro-Napoleonic newspaper (at nearly the height of the Napoleonic Wars in Germany), socialized quite a bit, and continued his philosophical work. In 1808 a friend procured for him a position as the director of a famous *Gymnasium* in Nuremberg. Hegel was immensely successful at reconstituting the once great school (by then in sad decline), and he became a prominent figure in Nuremberg society. In 1811 he married the daughter of a high-ranking member of the Nuremberg patriciate who was more than twenty years his junior. In 1812 and 1816 Hegel brought out his *Science of Logic,* in which he argued that thought was unconstrained by anything other than self-legislated norms in defining its own conditions of intelligibility, and that such a conception involved working through the contradictions seemingly inherent in such a view until one attained, at the end, a view of "thought thinking itself" as the absolute (a mix of Aristotle, Kant, Spinoza, and Christianity). In 1816 Hegel's fondest wish was answered: he was offered a professorship at Heidelberg University, where he moved with his wife and two young sons. They also took into the house Hegel's illegitimate son, whom he had fathered by his landlady while working on the *Phenomenology* in Jena, an arrangement that proved to have sad consequences for both Hegel and the boy later in Berlin.

In 1818 the powerful Berlin University offered Hegel a professorship. Despite the mild protestations of his wife (overcome by getting his mother-in-law to intercede for him), he moved himself and his family to Berlin, where he was to remain for the rest of his life. About two years after his arrival, the Prussian government, using the assassination of a conservative playwright by a deranged student as a pretext, began a repressive crackdown on those they viewed as subversives ("demagogues," as they were called at the time). Hegel's first two choices for teaching assistants were arrested and interrogated by the authorities for such subversive activities; the first was found guilty and barred for life from teaching at any German university, and the second was arrested but ultimately freed (although on penalty of teaching without pay for a year). During the student's arrest, Hegel visited him late at night on a skiff with some other students, speaking Latin to him through his jailhouse window so his conversation could not be understood by the guards. Hegel also continued to drink toasts each 14 July to the storming of the Bastille, an act that endeared him to his devoted cadre of admiring students.

In 1820 Hegel's reputation went through a particularly rough patch when he published his major work on political philosophy, *The Philosophy of Right.* In the preface, he rather nastily settled some scores with old opponents, such as J. F. Fries, a German liberal philosopher who was also a virulent anti-Semite and who had lost his job because of his anti-Semitic writings (which the Prussian authorities found subversive). Seemingly most damning, though, was Hegel's statement in the preface that the ground rule of modern philosophy had to be the proposition that what is rational is actual, and what is actual is rational. Almost everybody at the time took that to mean that what is, is right, and it is right because it is. Hegel thus acquired a reputation for being an apologist for the existing repressive Prussian government, and his work came to be seen by many as little more than an apology for repressive tyranny. Hegel, surprised by this reaction, apparently even supplied information for an 1824 *Brockhaus Enzyklopädie* entry on him, which stated that his works were in no way a defense of the ruling order. However, the damage had been done. The misunderstanding had to do with Hegel's rather technical use of the term "actual" (*wirklich*) to make his point; he wanted to argue that in the modern world, reason is "actual" in the sense that it is what is "at work" in the world; he did not mean that it is completely instantiated or that the existing order of things itself should be taken to be completely rational. In fact, the book defended a version of the kind of political and social order that the Prussian reformers had tried to put into practice. In Hegel's conception, the kind of freedom "at work" in modern life could be secured only by a universal commitment to the very general human rights of life, liberty, and property, and by a commitment to the practices involved in a universalistic morality that nonetheless made room for an appeal to personal conscience. Those two linchpins of modern life themselves, however, could be secured only in an institutional order that consisted of nuclear families based on love and free consent to marry, market societies ordered by the idea of careers open to talent but nonetheless tempered by all kinds of mediating institutions (such as professional associations), and a state based on a constitutional monarch and a set of representative institutions. Despite that last claim, however, Hegel remained resolutely anti-democratic, holding that representation was best secured by updating the older notion of the estates (a notion by then already virtually dead in Germany). This put Hegel irremediably at odds with the "liberal" reformers in Prussia, who sensed in Hegel's anti-democratic sentiments a taste instead for Prussian authoritarianism.

Despite all this, Hegel became an intellectual celebrity of the first order. Hundreds of students and Berliners of all stripes came to hear his lectures on the philosophy of history, philosophy of art, philosophy of religion, and history of philosophy. In all these lectures, Hegel continued the pattern he laid out in the *Phenomenology*, arguing that each of these topics had to be understood in terms of the "spirit" in which each was created and carried out; this meant that certain forms of religion (such as Greek religion), which were essentially bound to the ways of life they attempted to interpret and express, had to experience their demise as those ways of life themselves fell apart. In the case of art, it meant the loss of centrality of art for modern civilization. In Hegel's immensely controversial formulation, in Greek life art and religion existed in harmony with each other. In medieval times, however, art had become subservient to religion (in that there could be no "aesthetic truth" that had the authority to contradict the truth of the revealed religion), and in modern times, both art and religion had become subservient to philosophy, in that no "aesthetic truth" nor any "religious truth" had the authority to contradict the universal truths of morality, the claims of justice in a modern state, or the truths discovered by modern science.

Hegel took trips to Holland, the most "commercial" of all countries (except for Britain), in 1822; to Vienna, a German power but which was Catholic, which Hegel thought must condemn it to some kind of backwardness, in 1824; and to Paris, the home of the Revolution itself, in 1827. In all cases, he went to see for himself how modernity was playing itself out. In 1824 he played a courageous part in the freeing of Victor Cousin, a French liberal who had been arrested on trumped-up charges in Germany on the instigation of the French police (who wanted him quietly disposed of). Hegel's role in freeing Cousin led in fact to the invitation to visit him in Paris in 1827. At home, Hegel continued to quarrel with the liberals, and he and Friedrich Schleiermacher (the great theologian) engaged in a long-running series of petty and frivolous disputes, each one upping the ante. Hegel continued, though, until near the end of his life to be known as a happy figure on the social scene in Berlin and a person of immense intellectual authority. Hegel's gregarious nature was muted in the last year of his life, during which he was chronically ill with a stomach ailment; his sudden and unexpected death in 1831 was ruled due to cholera, but it was almost certainly connected with the stomach ailment, which had plagued him for some time.

Within only a few years after his death, the authority of Hegelianism, once so dominant, had fairly well evaporated. The younger crowd of Hegelians quickly split into various camps; one of them, David Friedrich Strauss, joked that, like the Jacobins and Girondins of the French Revolution, they had become "left" and "right" Hegelians. The Prussian government, worried about the "left" Hegelians in particular, became suspicious of all forms of Hegelianism. When Karl Marx claimed to have brought "left" Hegelianism to its logical conclusion in his doctrines of historical materialism and communism, that seemed to seal Hegel's fate for the Prussians. Hegel was revived again only much later in the twentieth century as a thinker in his own right, although his historical influence has never been doubted.

See also **Berlin; Fichte, Johann Gottlieb; Germany; Marx, Karl; Schelling, Friedrich von.**

BIBLIOGRAPHY

Primary Sources

Hegel, G. W. F. *Philosophy of History.* Translated by J. Sibree. New York, 1956.

———. *Hegel's Political Writings.* Translated by T. M. Knox. Oxford, U.K., 1964.

———. *Gesammelte Werke.* Edited by Rheinisch-Westfälische Akademie der Wissenschaften. Hamburg, 1968–. This is the critical edition of Hegel's works, but it is still in progress, and it is also somewhat expensive.

———. *Hegel's Philosophy of Nature: Part Two of the Encyclopedia of the Philosophical Sciences.* Translated by A. V. Miller. Oxford, U.K., 1970.

———. *Hegel's Philosophy of Mind: Part Three of the Encyclopedia of the Philosophical Sciences.* Translated by William Wallace and A. V. Miller. Oxford, U.K., 1971.

———. *Werke in zwanzig Bänden.* Edited by Eva Moldenhauer and Karl Markus Michel. Frankfurt am Main, 1971. Although not the critical edition of Hegel's works, this is the most often used and most widely accessible of all the collections.

———. *Aesthetics: Lectures on Fine Art.* Vols. 1–2. Translated by T. M. Knox. Oxford, U.K., 1975.

———. *Early Theological Writings.* Translated by T. M. Knox and Richard Kroner. Philadelphia, 1975.

———. *Lectures on the Philosophy of World History: Introduction: Reason in History.* Translated by H. B. Nisbet. Cambridge, U.K., 1975.

———. *Phenomenology of Spirit.* Translated by A. V. Miller. Oxford, U.K., 1977.

———. *System of Ethical Life (1802/3) and First Philosophy of Spirit (Part III of the System of Speculative Philosophy 1803/4).* Translated by H. S. Harris and T. M. Knox. Albany, N.Y., 1979.

———. *Lectures on the Philosophy of Religion.* Vols. 1–3. Edited by Peter Hodgson. Translated by R. F. Brown, P. C. Hodgson, and J. M. Stewart. Berkeley, Calif., 1984.

———. *Three Essays, 1793–1795.* Edited and translated by Peter Fuss and John Dobbins. Notre Dame, Ind., 1984.

———. *Introduction to the Lectures on the History of Philosophy.* Translated by T. M. Knox and A. V. Miller. Oxford, U.K., 1985.

———. *Elements of the Philosophy of Right.* Edited by Allen W. Wood. Translated by H. B. Nisbet. Cambridge, U.K., 1991.

———. *The Encyclopedia Logic: Part One of the Encyclopedia of the Philosophical Sciences.* Translated by T. F. Geraets, W. A. Suchting, and H. S. Harris. Indianapolis, Ind., 1991.

———. *Phenomenology of Spirit.* Translated by Terry Pinkard. Cambridge, U.K., forthcoming.

Secondary Sources

Findlay, J. N. *Hegel: A Reexamination.* New York, 1958. The first great reinterpretation of Hegel for the English-speaking world after World War II.

Kaufmann, Walter. *Hegel: A Reinterpretation.* Garden City, N.Y., 1966. This was one of the first postwar works to reinterpret Hegel and played a crucial role in demolishing the myth of Hegel as a Prussian militarist or a proto-Nazi.

Pinkard, Terry. *Hegel: A Biography.* Cambridge, U.K., 2000. The first major biography of Hegel in English with short discussions of all of Hegel's works.

Pippin, Robert. *Hegel's Idealism: The Satisfactions of Self-Consciousness.* Cambridge, U.K., 1989. One of the major landmarks in Hegel scholarship.

Taylor, Charles. *Hegel.* Cambridge, U.K., 1975. A monumental study by one of the leading philosophers of the twentieth century and a landmark in Hegel studies.

TERRY PINKARD

HEINE, HEINRICH (1797–1856), German poet and political writer.

Heinrich Heine was born in Düsseldorf into a family of Jewish businessmen, of whom his father was the least effectual; his Uncle Salomon may have been the richest commoner in Germany and came to govern his nephew, who was vexed for the greater part of his life by a fortune unjustly in the hands of the investment banker rather than of the poet. Efforts to prepare Heine for a commercial career having proved unavailing, he was sent to study law, although his main interests were history and literature. As Jewish disabilities were restored after the fall of Napoleon I (r. 1804–1814/15), Heine had himself baptized in 1825 before taking his degree in Göttingen. He had been accumulating a body of poetry, published as *Buch der Lieder* (1827; Book of songs), mostly about unrequited love, loosely inspired by infatuations with Uncle Salomon's two daughters (and heiresses). The poems urbanize and ironize conventions of Romantic verse with dexterity in meter and rhythm, ingenious rhymes, and outrageous puns. Many were to go out into the world in thousands of musical settings. But at first the public was more interested in his prose works, beginning with *Die Harzreise* (1826; The Harz journey), included in the first of four volumes of *Reisebilder* (1826–1831; Travel pictures), amalgams of essay and imagination, fictionalized autobiography, and coded political resistance.

After briefly editing a Munich political journal and traveling in Italy, Heine's attention was riveted by the Revolutions of 1830 as an indication that the torpid world of the Metternichian restoration was turning again. In May 1831, he went to Paris to see for himself and was to remain there for the rest of

Heinrich Heine. ©CORBIS

his life. With critical sympathy, Heine weighed the stability, revolutionary threats, and class stresses of the July monarchy in pungent newspaper articles on the painting salon of 1831, published as *Französische Maler* (1834; French painters); on political events during 1832, collected as *Französische Zustände* (1833; Conditions in France); and on politics and culture from 1840 to 1844, retrospectively revised as *Lutezia* (1851; Lutetia). He then tried to explain Germany in *Zur Geschichte der Religion und Philosophie in Deutschland* (1835; On the history of religion and philosophy in Germany) and *Die romantische Schule* (1836; The Romantic school). These two works were combined for the French as *De l'Allemagne* (1835; On Germany), in opposition to the book of that name by Anne-Louise-Germaine de Staël (1766–1817), which Heine believed had given a false picture of a poetic, quietistic land; instead he declared Germany to be the true revolutionary nation, its philosophy potentially overthrowing God and Christianity, opening the possibility for this-worldly comfort and pleasure for all people. The central issue of Heine's politics, partly

influenced by a temporary allegiance to the French Saint-Simonian movement, was the propagation of a neo-pagan sensualism or Hellenism against repressive, Judeo-Christian spiritualism or "Nazarenism."

During the mid-1840s, Heine associated for some months with Karl Marx (1818–1883) and published ferocious political verse in a second volume of poetry, *Neue Gedichte* (1844; New poems), as well as the mock-epics *Deutschland: Ein Wintermärchen* (1844; Germany: A winter's tale), a bitter verse commentary on a clandestine visit home in 1843, and *Atta Troll: Ein Sommernachtstraum* (1847; Atta Troll: A midsummer night's dream), a spoof of the competing political poets. But Heine's hopes were dashed by the Revolutions of 1848, which coincided with the breakdown of his long-threatened health, confining him in paralysis and pain to his "mattress-grave." He believed his disease to be venereal, but modern observers suspect a neural condition such as multiple sclerosis. Remaining alert and creative almost to his last hour, Heine revised some of his views, announcing a return to God on his own terms in his third volume of poetry, *Romanzero* (1851; Romancero).

Heine has been the most controversial figure in the history of German literature. His life and career were a series of quarrels and scandals, some the result of his own poor judgment. Insisting upon the superiority of his revolutionary vision, he fought tyranny and oppression while refusing common cause with the dissident liberals or with the Jewish emancipation movement. He was regarded by some as a Frenchified aesthete, lascivious and immoral, politically unreliable, contemptuous of the values of the nation. His poetry remained popular—nearly forty editions of collected works had appeared by the end of the Weimar Republic in 1933—but the opposition to him became stridently anti-Semitic, dramatized by tumults over monuments to him, the most elaborate of which, the Loreley Fountain, intended for Düsseldorf, wound up in the South Bronx, New York City. The modernist sensibility contributed to a devaluation of his poetry around 1900. But the 1960s witnessed a vigorous revival of Heine as a visionary uniting revolutionary purpose with gratification and plenitude, an intermediary link between Georg Wilhelm Friedrich Hegel (1770–1831) and Marx, a steadfast cosmopolitan democrat, a courageous opponent of capitalism and superstition, a deep philosopher and prophet. Editions, studies, and public demonstrations proliferated. This enthusiasm has been receding into a more analytic critical practice, but Heine remains for many a world-historical figure.

See also **Germany; Marx, Karl; Revolutions of 1830; Revolutions of 1848.**

BIBLIOGRAPHY

Cook, Roger F., ed. *A Companion to the Works of Heinrich Heine.* Rochester, N.Y., 2002.

Höhn, Gerhard. *Heine-Handbuch: Zeit, Person, Werk.* 3rd rev. ed. Stuttgart, 2004.

Kruse, Joseph A. *Heinrich Heine: Leben und Werk in Daten und Bildern.* Frankfurt am Main, 1983.

Liedtke, Christian. *Heinrich Heine.* Reinbek bei Hamburg, 1997.

Mende, Fritz. *Heinrich Heine: Chronik seines Lebens und Werkes.* 2nd rev. ed. Berlin, 1981.

Peters, George F. *The Poet as Provocateur: Heinrich Heine and His Critics.* Rochester, N.Y., 2000.

Sammons, Jeffrey L. *Heinrich Heine: A Modern Biography.* Princeton, N.J., 1979.

Sternberger, Dolf. *Heinrich Heine und die Abschaffung der Sünde.* Hamburg, 1972.

Windfuhr, Manfred. *Rätsel Heine: Autorprofil—Werk—Wirkung.* Heidelberg, 1997.

JEFFREY L. SAMMONS

HELMHOLTZ, HERMANN VON

(1821–1894), German scientist.

Hermann Ludwig Ferdinand von Helmholtz was one of the most versatile scientists of the nineteenth century, endowed with a keen theoretical understanding of physical phenomena, with an unusual ability for putting them into a mathematical form, and with a rare intuition for instrumentation and experimental exploration. Above all, he was able to connect remote scientific fields with each other. During the last decades of his life, he held an outstanding position in European science.

LIFE

Helmholtz was born in Potsdam, near Berlin, on 31 August 1821. Unable to afford a university education, he entered the Prussian military medical school, which was connected with the university. After taking his doctorate degree with the physiologist Johannes Müller in 1842, Helmholtz served a one-year internship in Berlin's Charité Hospital and then worked as a military surgeon in Potsdam until 1848. Many of Müller's students later came to play important roles in physiology and related subjects, and in 1845 some of them took part in founding the Physical Society, which remains the official German organization of physicists. In July 1847, Helmholtz read his memoir *On the Conservation of Force* to this group, announcing what was later called the energy conservation principle.

After serving as an anatomy instructor at the Berlin Academy and as an assistant to Müller for a year, Helmholtz began his academic career as a professor of physiology at the University of Königsberg in 1849. There he measured the velocity at which frog muscles conducted nerve impulses and devoted himself to sensory physiology. In 1850 he became famous for inventing the ophthalmoscope, which opened up vast possibilities for ophthalmology. Five years later, Helmholtz moved to the University of Bonn as a professor of anatomy and physiology, and three years later he taught physiology at the University of Heidelberg. During his Heidelberg years, he finished two treatises on sensory physiology, the *Handbook of Physiological Optics* (1856–1867) and *On the Sensation of Tone as a Physiological Basis for the Theory of Music* (1863)—presentations that still carry authority in their field and remain standard references in many respects.

The height of Helmholtz's career and fame began when he took up the Berlin chair of physics in 1871. The new German Reich had found in Helmholtz the "Reich's chancellor of science," as he was sometimes called. He began to devote himself almost exclusively to physics, mainly electrodynamics.

Helmholtz was made a noble by the German emperor in 1883 and four years later became the founding president of the Physikalisch-Technische Reichsanstalt, a nonacademic government institute of physics and technology in Berlin-Charlottenburg. Helmholtz died in Berlin on 8 September 1894. After his death, the rapid development of modern physics away from its mechanistic foundations soon made Helmholtz's worldview outdated but did not overshadow his individual contributions.

WORK

The unifying idea of Helmholtz's scientific work can be found in his mechanistic interpretation of nature—that is, in the view that all physical phenomena can be explained in terms of mechanics. This idea served also as a background to Helmholtz's energy conservation principle, to which he was led by asking whether the mechanical equivalent of muscular heat and work could be accounted for solely by the metabolic process. If this were the case, the assumption that a separate life force existed would become obsolete. Helmholtz's energy conservation principle thus marked the beginning of organic physics, which sought to reduce all organic processes to the laws of physics and chemistry, and ultimately to mechanics.

To many contemporaries, Helmholtz's reductionism appeared to be downright materialism, and it is true that at the beginning of his career Helmholtz had strong sympathies with the materialist inclinations of the revolutionary movement of 1848. Helmholtz never claimed, however, that mental phenomena could be reduced to or identified with biological (and thus ultimately with mechanical) processes, as the materialists did. On the contrary, in the famous controversy with the physiologist Ewald Hering (1834–1918) on space perception, Helmholtz argued that visual perception requires a mind that has learned from movements in space and draws unconscious inferences from them. Hering, on the other hand, claimed that perception depends on an innate physiological mechanism that does not require a judging consciousness to turn incoming sensations into perceptions.

Other problems of visual physiology that Helmholtz dealt with included the accommodation of the eye, color vision, contrast phenomena, optical illusions, and eye movements. In physiological acoustics, he developed the resonance theory of hearing, in which the sensations produced by the resonating endings of the acoustic nerves are perceived as a tone. He also solved the problem of consonance and dissonance, which made it possible to explain musical harmony.

From his work with organ pipes, which he needed for his experiments on the physiology of hearing, Helmholtz was led to questions of hydrodynamics. In 1858 he demonstrated the invariance of vortices in ideal fluids and developed the notion of the vortex sheet, which foreshadowed the notion of the boundary layer, which is central to modern fluid mechanics.

In his work on electrodynamics, Helmholtz tried to mediate between James Clark Maxwell's field theory and the Continental approaches, which were based on action at a distance, merging them into a compromise version. The experimental work of his student Heinrich Hertz, which culminated in his detection of electromagnetic waves in 1887–1888, had originally emerged from attempts to confirm Helmholtz's rendering of Maxwell's theory.

Helmholtz is also known as the author of some twenty-five popular and philosophical essays. His interest in philosophy was roused by his father, who was an enthusiast of German idealism, and it gained momentum from his work on perception. In 1855 Helmholtz joined and stimulated the rising neo-Kantian movement with a lecture, "Human Vision," in which he propagated a new epistemology as a cure for speculation in the manner of Hegelian philosophy. He developed an empiricist theory of perception, called the theory of signs, which started from the skeptical claim that human sensations cannot be taken as images of reality, but only as signs, without any similarity to the objects signified. The order humans give to those sensations, however, originates with the outer objects, and this order can be taken as a true image of the world's causal order. One can never know for certain that a sensation is caused by an object, but all human perceptions are hypotheses to this effect and are constantly tested through voluntary manipulation of the world.

From his philosophy of perception, Helmholtz was led to the foundations of geometry, where he defended an empiricist interpretation of the axioms. Space has to be taken as the epitome of the movability of rigid bodies or, equivalently, of the congruence of relations between bodies and surfaces. He found that such movements and relations were possible not only in Euclidean space but also in non-Euclidean space. He concluded that non-Euclidean spaces are conceivable and that the Euclidean axioms are not necessarily true of space as claimed by Kant.

See also **Einstein, Albert; Hertz, Heinrich; Maxwell, James Clerk; Physics; Science and Technology.**

BIBLIOGRAPHY

Primary Sources

Helmholtz, Hermann von. *Wissenschaftliche Abhandlungen.* 3 vols. Leipzig, Germany, 1882–1895. An almost complete collection of Helmholtz's scientific papers.

———. *Vorlesungen über theoretische Physik.* 6 vols. Leipzig, Germany, 1897–1907. Lectures on theoretical physics, given during his time as president of the Physikalisch-Technische Reichsanstalt.

———. *Epistemological Writings: The Paul Hertz/Moritz Schlick Centenary Edition of 1921.* Edited by Robert S. Cohen and Yehuda Elkana. Translated by Malcolm F. Lowe. Dordrecht, Netherlands, and Boston, 1977. This edition has become famous for its extensive and congenial annotation in the context of rising logical empiricism.

———. *Helmholtz's Treatise on Physiological Optics.* Edited by James P. C. Southall. 3 vols. Rochester, N.Y., 1924–1925. Reprint, Mineola, N.Y., 2005. Translation of *Handbuch der physiologischen Optik.*

———. *Science and Culture: Popular and Philosophical Essays.* Edited by David Cahan. Chicago, 1995. Selected popular and philosophical writings.

Secondary Sources

Cahan, David, ed. *Hermann von Helmholtz and the Foundations of Nineteenth-Century Science.* Berkeley, Calif., 1993. An excellent collection, written by historians and philosophers of science and covering virtually all areas of Helmholtz's work. Includes a fairly complete bibliography of secondary works.

Cranefield, Paul F. "The Organic Physics of 1847 and the Biophysics of Today." *Journal of the History of Medicine and Allied Sciences* 12 (1957): 407–423. Vivid account of the program of organic physics, its context, and its limitations.

Darrigol, Olivier. "From Organ Pipes to Atmospheric Motions: Helmholtz on Fluid Mechanics." *Historical Studies in the Physical and Biological Sciences* 29 (1998): 1–51. Profound account of Helmholtz's contributions to fluid mechanics, exemplifying Helmholtz's unity of thought across many disciplines.

Hatfield, Gary. *The Natural and the Normative: Theories of Spatial Perception from Kant to Helmholtz.* Cambridge, Mass., 1990. Profound history of spatial perception in the nineteenth century, concentrating on the philosophical context.

Heidelberger, Michael. "Hermann von Helmholtz (1821–1894)." In *Die großen Physiker.* Vol. 1: *Von Aristoteles bis Kelvin,* edited by Karl von Meyenn, 396–415, 474–475, and 528–531. Munich, Germany, 1997. Attempt at a short general account of Helmholtz's life and work.

Koenigsberger, Leo. *Hermann von Helmholtz.* 3 vols. Translated by Francis Welby. Oxford, U.K., 1906. Rich and authoritative, yet hagiographic and somewhat Whiggish account of Helmholtz's work and life by one of his students.

Rechenberg, Helmut. *Hermann von Helmholtz: Bilder seines Lebens und Wirkens.* Weinheim, Germany, 1994. Heavily illustrated, very readable scientific biography.

Richards, Joan L. "The Evolution of Empiricism: Hermann von Helmholtz and the Foundations of Geometry." *British Journal for the Philosophy of Science* 28 (1977): 235–253. Account of Helmholtz's foundational work on geometry and its later impact; still valid.

Schiemann, Gregor. *Wahrheitsgewißheitsverlust: Hermann von Helmholtz' Mechanismus im Anbruch der Moderne.* Darmstadt, Germany, 1997. Thorough exploration of Helmholtz's mechanical interpretation of nature and its contemporary context in philosophy, science and society.

MICHAEL HEIDELBERGER

HERDER, JOHANN GOTTFRIED

(1744–1803), German philosopher and critic.

With the turn of the seventeenth to the eighteenth century, German culture, both intellectual and artistic, entered a period of exceptionally rapid growth and development. By the end of the eighteenth century, German philosophy, literature, music, historiography, philology, classical studies, linguistics, theology, educational theory, and jurisprudence had all emerged from relative obscurity to occupy positions in which they represented international standards of excellence or would do so in the early decades of the nineteenth century. (In the course of the nineteenth century the list would expand to include such fields as mathematics, chemistry, biology, medicine, physics, and engineering.) As important as any of the names commonly associated with this remarkable eighteenth- and early-nineteenth-century trajectory is that of Johann Gottfried Herder.

Herder's great aim was to solve the historical, cultural, and anthropological problem of uniting the one and the many, while at the same time preserving the difference between them: to grasp

Eighteenth-century thought was fed into the nineteenth century through two channels: Kant and Herder. Its idealism sprang from going beyond Kant, in directions pointed out (but warned against) by him. Its naturalism, historicism, nationalism, monism, and near mysticism … were developments from Herder's ideas. If the Romantic philosophers can say, with Faust, that two souls dwell in their breast, … one was Kantian, the other was Herderian.

Lewis White Beck, *Early German Philosophy*, pp. 367–368.

the entire range of human experience and activity as *both* a unified pattern of development, *and,* at the same time, a manifold pageant of irreducibly distinct phenomena. The early essay "Über den Fleiß in Mehreren Gelehrten Sprachen" (1764; On diligence in several learned languages) presents a capsule formulation of the philosophical program that would occupy him throughout his career. In it, Herder asserts that the nature of every human being is at once a product and a reflection of that person's embeddedness in a particular national community (*Volk*). Every people, in accordance with its distinctive environmental conditions and historical circumstances, has developed a unique national character. This is manifested in its particular "mode of thought" (*Denkungsart*), which is embodied above all in its national language.

The cognitive structure implicit in the syntax and semantics of each language, its repertoire of communicative and expressive resources, as well as its distinctive sensory qualities—in particular, its auditory and rhythmic register—combine to constitute a nationally and culturally specific way of being in the world. Yet, at the same time, humankind is not (or not merely) a collection of isolated monads but is in some sense (at least in prospect) one. Thus from the outset the task of what Herder would call his "human philosophy" (*menschliche Philosophie*) is framed: to articulate a vision of humanity in all its manifes-

tations and on all its levels, from the individual to the communal to that of the race at large, as a vast, historically self-actualizing process of unity-in-difference. It is in the nature of the case, moreover, as Herder conceives it—such is the linkage of theory and practice in his outlook—that the pursuit of this goal must itself contribute decisively to realizing the very state of affairs that it seeks to describe.

LANGUAGE

Herder's *Abhandlung über den Ursprung der Sprache* (*Treatise on the Origin of Language*) won the prize set by the Berlin Academy for 1770 for the best account of how human beings had invented language. His solution was, in effect, to deny the premise of the question: there neither is nor could be any human invention (or other acquisition) of language, because instinctively *human* nature and the capacity for language are strictly co-original. Language and thought are inseparable, because language and reflective self-consciousness—the capacity that distinguishes us from the lower animals—emerge in tandem out of the basic constitution of our nature. Language is thus the defining mark of what it means to be human at all.

HUMAN NATURE

For Herder, languages (and therefore modes of thought) are many and various; linguistic capacity (and therefore the structure of consciousness) is universal. Nor is this the only example of Herder's predilection for thinking simultaneously in terms of oppositions and syntheses. For him, the mind is both continuous with the senses and yet not reducible to them. He denies that the mind can be understood (as many in the eighteenth century had proposed) as a collection of discrete "faculties" (such as reason, will, imagination, and the like). Herder's conception of the thinking-feeling-acting human being is determinedly holistic. Yet it is also a differentiated holism, in which now one, now another aspect of our overall psychological-physiological being is from time to time singled out for emphasis. This occurs with particular frequency in Herder's reflections on aesthetics, in which he characteristically seeks to ground the essential qualities of different types of art by reference to the different modes of sense perception that predominate in our apprehension of them. Discussions of these topics are scattered throughout Herder's writings. Especially important in this regard are *Von Erkennen und Empfinden der Menschlichen Seele* (1778; On cognition and sensation in the human soul) and, for aesthetics, the first and fourth of the *Kritische Wälder* (1769; Critical forests) and the essay "Plastik" (1778; Plastic arts).

LITERATURE

Herder made his mark initially in his early twenties with the collections *Über die Neuere Deutsche Literatur. Fragmente* (1766–1767; *Fragments on Recent German Literature*). As language is the defining capacity of human beings generally, so poetry is the form in which language is quintessentially realized. And as language is culture-specific, so the national literature of a people is the form above all in which its distinctive character finds expression. Literature at its most genuine is folk poetry. It is the natural outgrowth of the *Volk*, simple, direct, and powerful in articulation, as close as possible in its animating sensibility to the primitive roots of the native culture, and so uncontaminated by the refinements and affectations of later, all-too-sophisticated stages of civilization. Yet, as Herder could not fail to recognize, precisely the latter was the hallmark of his own, excessively cultivated and rational-to-a-fault, age of Enlightenment. A significant portion of his work is dedicated to overcoming the dilemma implicit in this state of affairs: how to reinvigorate the cultural life of his own nation at a point in history at which the energy and vitality necessary for doing so seem to belong to an irrecoverably distant past. Among the important efforts in this vein are (in addition to the *Fragments*) the essays on Shakespeare and Ossian in the anthology *Von Deutscher Art un Kunst* (1773; Of German character and art), the two-volume collection of *Volkslieder* (1778–1779; Folk songs), and his myriad engagements as both translator and commentator with the literature—very broadly conceived—of other peoples, including in particular, in several works, the Hebrew Scriptures.

HISTORY

The view of history and historical development sketched in "On Diligence in Several Learned

[Herder's] writings radically transformed the notion of relations of men to each other.... His vision of society has dominated Western thought; the extent of its influence has not always been recognized because it has entered too deeply into the texture of ordinary thinking. His immense impact ... is due principally to his central thesis—his account of what it is to live and act together.... This idea ... has entered every subsequent attempt to arrive at truth about society.

Isaiah Berlin, *Vico and Herder,* p. 199.

Languages" is expanded and elaborated, and at the same time the prospects of carrying out the agenda implicit in this view rendered still more problematic, in 1774 with *Auch Eine Philosophie der Geschichte zur Bildung der Menschheit* (*Another Philosophy of History for the Cultivation of the Human Race*). Herder's final attempt to achieve his goal came with his projected but (like almost all his major projects) uncompleted magnum opus, the multivolume *Ideen zur Philosophie de Geschichte der Menschheit* (1784–1791; *Ideas on the Philosophy of the Human Race*). (Many of the themes of the *Ideas* are carried forward, in a manner somewhat reminiscent of the *Fragments* of the late 1760s, in the several collections of *Briefe zu Beförderung der Humanität* [Letters for the advancement of humanity] between 1793 and 1797.)

Herder's overarching concern, as always, is with the problem of how to do equal justice to the competing claims of the universal and the particular, of humanity considered as a whole on the one hand and individual nations and peoples on the other. For Herder, history is the story of the realization of all the possibilities inherent in the virtually limitless range of human potential. At different historical junctures one culture or another will typically assume the leading role in the overall progression, yet this position is inevitably transitory. Each culture also has its life cycle of birth, growth, and decline, analogous to that of the individual human being.

If Herder's attempt to view each individual, nation, and people (*Volk*) at once from the outside, *sub specie humanitatis,* and from the inside, through an act of empathetic, imaginative identification with it, ultimately falls short—and there can be few more disappointed looking back over their life's work than was Herder—that cannot be held too strongly against him. No one else, neither before nor since (not Giambattista Vico [1668–1744], not Georg Wilhelm Friedrich Hegel [1770–1831]), had solved the problem either. And so it remains as much a live issue today as in Herder's time, equally resistant to attempts to resolve and dismiss it.

Herder was in many respects a difficult figure to classify and assess in his own time and he has remained so ever since. It has not been possible here to do more than suggest some of the principal themes in his large and disparate body of work. There is much in this oeuvre in a wide range of disciplines. The chief obstacle standing in the way of this is that even in the early twenty-first century only a relatively small portion of his writings have been translated into English. Until this state of affairs is remedied, Herder is likely to remain, as Hans-Georg Gadamer noted of him in 1942, a figure of widely acknowledged importance, one of whom many have heard, but whom far fewer have actually read.

See also **Germany; History.**

BIBLIOGRAPHY

Primary Sources

Herder, Johann Gottfried. *Sämmtliche Werke.* 33 vols. Edited by Bernhard Suphan. Berlin, 1877–1913. The most comprehensive edition of Herder's works.

——. *Reflections on the Philosophy of the History of Mankind.* Abridged and with an introduction by Frank E. Manuel. Chicago and London, 1968. English rendering of selections from the *Ideas.* Lucid overview of principal elements in Herder's philosophy of history.

——. *Werke in zehn Bänden.* 10 vols. Edited by Günter Arnold et al. Frankfurt am Main, 1985ff. Selected works edition reflecting current scholarship on Herder.

——. *Selected Early Works, 1764–1767: Addresses, Essays, and Drafts;* Fragments on Recent German Literature. Edited by Ernest A. Menze and Karl Menges. University Park, Pa., 1992. Introduces the early Herder to English-speaking readers, with helpful introductory material and commentary.

——. *Against Pure Reason: Writings on Religion, Language, and History.* Edited by Marcia Bunge. Minneapolis, Minn., 1993. Emphasis on Herder as philosopher and interpreter of religion.

Secondary Sources

Beck, Lewis White. *Early German Philosophy: Kant and His Predecessors.* Cambridge, Mass., 1969. Reprint, Bristol, U.K. 1996. Fundamental source for the German philosophical tradition.

Berlin, Isaiah. *Vico and Herder: Two Studies in the History of Ideas.* New York, 1976. Seminal essays by one of the great intellectual historians.

Koepke, Wulf. *Johann Gottfried Herder.* Boston, 1987. Introductory overview of Herder's life and works.

Morton, Michael. *Herder and the Poetics of Thought: Unity and Diversity in* On Diligence in Several Learned Languages. University Park, Pa., and London, 1989. Detailed analysis of Herder's first philosophical publication, with implications for his subsequent writings.

MICHAEL MORTON

HERTZ, HEINRICH (1857–1894), German scientist.

Heinrich Hertz's name has been given to a unit of frequency, an honor he received because he was the first person to produce electromagnetic waves (radio waves) artificially and to demonstrate that their behavior is similar to that of light (1886–1888). Hertz and most of his contemporaries considered these experiments the final proof that light is nothing but electrical waves, and more generally a decisive corroboration of James Maxwell's field theories and a rejection of theories such as Wilhelm Weber's, which were based on direct actions at a distance. Settling the long-standing question of the nature of light and electromagnetism earned Hertz a name as one of the leading physicists of his time.

Born in 1857 in Hamburg, Heinrich Hertz studied first engineering and then physics at the Dresden and Munich polytechnic schools before moving to Berlin University in 1878. Here Hermann Helmholtz had developed his own version of Maxwell's theory and tried to design experiments that would favor this theory rather than Weber's. Soon Hertz distinguished himself by solving a prize problem showing that if conduction currents are accompanied by mass transport, the mass is extremely small. With an eye to Hertz, Helmholtz subsequently formulated another prize problem calling for the detection of effects of the so-called displacement current that should exist according to Maxwell's theory. However, Hertz estimated that the chances of a successful outcome of such experiments were slim and instead turned to other problems concerning elasticity and hardness, evaporation, the tides, a new dynamometer, floating plates, and cathode rays, which he incorrectly believed, because of one of his experiments, were electrically neutral (they have since been explained as a ray of electrons). Employed from 1880 as Helmholtz's assistant, Hertz wrote eleven papers on these subjects.

In 1883 he was appointed professor of theoretical physics at Kiel University and the following year he gave a public series of lectures, *Modern Ideas on the Constitution of Matter,* which anticipated some of his later ideas concerning natural philosophy and the nature of electromagnetism. According to Albrecht Fölsing, who published Hertz's lecture notes in 1999, these lectures show that by 1884 Hertz had completely adapted a Maxwellian point of view and had thought out the oscillator that he later used to produce electrical waves. Jed Buchwald, on the other hand, has argued that Hertz continued to adhere to Helmholtz's electromagnetic theory until he conducted his crucial experiments; this school of thought questions whether Hertz's laboratory equipment of 1886 to 1888 owes much to his thought experiments of 1884.

Hertz again turned to experimental work after he had moved to a professorship at the polytechnic school in Karlsruhe, in 1885. Having accidentally discovered that he could produce fast electrical oscillations in capacitively loaded wires breached by spark gaps, he returned to the problem Helmholtz had posed: detecting the effects of the displacement current. After two years of intensive experimentation, he was able to detect and produce electromagnetic waves.

Hertz left it to Marconi to pursue the technological potentials of his discovery and instead turned to theoretical clarifications of Maxwell's theory for bodies at rest and bodies in motion. His first paper on these matters offers an almost axiomatic presentation of Maxwell's theory and contains Maxwell's equations in the form they con-

tinue to be presented. The second paper, based on the assumption that a fictive space-filling medium called the "ether" is dragged by moving bodies, was soon rendered obsolete by Hendrick Lorentz's and Albert Einstein's relativity theories.

The theoretical papers were published after Hertz had moved to a professorship in Bonn, in 1889. His axiomatic presentation did not make any assumptions about the nature of the electromagnetic field, and his remarks that Maxwell's theory is nothing other than Maxwell's equations have even led many physicists to conclude that he found such questions either unimportant or unscientific. However, most modern scholars are of the opinion that Hertz believed that the electromagnetic field should eventually be explained as a state in a mechanical ether and that he thought of his last book, *Principles of Mechanics,* as the basis for such a reduction of electromagnetism as well as all other natural phenomena to the laws of mechanics.

The book, which can be considered as the last major foundational work in the classical mechanistic tradition, is interesting for physical, mathematical, and philosophical reasons. In the introduction, Hertz explains physical theories as (mental) images of the world (anticipating later ideas about models) and sets up three conditions that are necessary to judge and compare such images. His own image did not base itself on force as a basic concept but relied on hidden masses (the ether?) to produce the effects usually ascribed to forces. It was presented in a differential geometric form that has been imitated in later treatments of mechanics.

Hertz began his work on mechanics in 1891. The following summer he contracted an infection of his nose. The infection gradually worsened and eventually led to his premature death in 1894, shortly before the publication of his last book.

See also **Electricity; Helmholtz, Hermann; Marconi, Guglielmo; Maxwell, James Clerk; Physics.**

BIBLIOGRAPHY

Baird, Davis, R. I. G. Huges, and Alfred Nordmann, eds. *Heinrich Hertz: Classical Physicist, Modern Philosopher.* Volume 198 of *Boston Studies in Philosophy of Science.* Boston, 1998.

Buchwald, Jed Z. *The Creation of Scientific Effects: Heinrich Hertz and Electric Waves.* Chicago, 1994.

Fölsing, Albrecht. *Heinrich Hertz: Eine Biographie.* Hamburg, 1997.

Hertz, Heinrich. *Gesammelte Werke.* Vols. 1–3. Leipzig, 1884.

———. *Die Constitution der Materie: Eine Vorlesung über die Grundlagen der Physik aus dem Jahre 1884.* Edited by Albrecht Fölsing. Berlin, 1999.

Lützen, Jesper. *Mechanistic Images in Geometric Form: Heinrich Hertz's Principles of Mechanics.* Oxford, U.K., 2005.

Nordmann, Alfred. "Heinrich Hertz: Scientific Biography and Experimental Life." *Studies in History and Philosophy of Science* 31 (2000): 537–549.

JESPER LÜTZEN

HERZEN, ALEXANDER (1812–1870),
Russian writer and political thinker.

In the early 1840s Alexander Ivanovich Herzen was a leading member of the Westernizer group, which claimed, against the so-called Slavophiles, that Russia's historical evolution could not be understood apart from western European politics and culture. Among the Westernizers Herzen stood not with the moderate or reformist faction, but with the radicals—Vissarion Belinsky (1811–1848) and Mikhail Bakunin (1814–1876)—who demanded that sweeping social as well as political changes be instituted in Russia for justice's sake. Herzen's impassioned advocacy of the peasant land commune as the foundation of the future society subsequently earned him the reputation as the "father of Russian socialism."

EARLY LIFE AND WORK
Born in Moscow on 6 April (25 March, old style) 1812, the son of a wealthy and culturally sophisticated serf-owner, Herzen was the beneficiary of a superb domestic education. In his memoirs, *My Past and Thoughts* (1852–1868), he attributed his moral awakening at the age of fourteen to the hanging of the Decembrists, the palace conspirators who in 1825 sought to abolish serfdom and introduce Western-style government in Russia. In 1827, with his close friend Nikolai Ogarev (1813–1877), he swore an oath of faithfulness to the Decembrists' cause. By the early 1830s Herzen had become an adept of French socialism, an admirer of Claude-Henri de Saint-Simon's socialist feminism, and a believer in the imminent dawning of a new age of history, a "new Christianity." For his views Herzen was arrested in 1834. He served two years of exile in Vyatka province and three years in Vladimir province. For subversive remarks made in his correspondence he was rearrested and sent to Novgorod for 1841 and 1842. These troubles with the Russian authorities imparted to his views in the Westernizer–Slavophile controversy a certain intransigence.

In two key essays, *Dilettantism in Science* (1843) and *Letters on the Study of Nature* (1845–1846), Herzen laid out his philosophy of history. He argued that the European past may be divided into three stages: antiquity, a period during which people experienced joy and suffering directly, without the intermediacy of an intellectual system that could "explain" those sensations; Christianity, a period during which human life was experienced through the prism of religious and other idealist belief systems; and the contemporary period, during which materialist scholars had finally rejected the twin tyrannies of religion and abstract belief. In *Dilettantism and Scholarship* Herzen warned against the Mandarin contemplativism of Right Hegelians, who had contented themselves with the dictum: "All that is real is rational, and all that is rational is real." In *Letters on the Study of Nature* Herzen's hero was the English philosopher Francis Bacon (1561–1626), who "destroyed in the eyes of thinking people the old metaphysics." Taken together, both works constituted a battle cry against the Slavophiles, who, in Herzen's opinion, wanted to freeze Russian development in the idealist (read: religious) stage. These essays were also a challenge to the moderate Westernizers: in 1846 they precipitated a personal break with the historian Timofei Granovsky (1813–1855), who could not countenance Herzen's atheism.

HERZEN'S BREAK WITH THE WEST
In 1847 Herzen and his young family left Russia for western Europe. He would never return to his native land. Between 1847 and 1851 Herzen reevaluated his views on the relationship between western Europe and Russia; he also articulated the principles of the agrarian socialism that made his name in radical circles.

In his fourteen *Letters from France and Italy* (1847–1852) he attacked German mysticism, the self-satisfaction and meanness of the French bourgeoisie, the lies of French liberals, and the treachery of the French National Assembly and of Louis-Napoleon Bonaparte (later Napoleon III, r. 1852–1871). He now asserted that European civilization itself was rotten, and therefore doomed to be liquidated. He predicted the destruction of the French monarchy, established religion, private property, and family codes. He identified himself not with then-fashionable political republicanism but rather with what he called "social republicanism."

Herzen's most important political book, *From the Other Shore* (1847–1850), developed these ideas with extraordinary force. In it he described Europe as a senile, exhausted world that cannot be saved. He advised his readers to discard all political banners, to forget about liberal promises of progress, and to trust instead the creative powers of nature to renew human life once the old order had disappeared. He excoriated liberals who, in February 1848, heralded democracy but who, in late June that year, urged the French National Guard to mow down demonstrators from the common people. Against these "liberals" whose deeds had proved them "conservatives" and "cannibals," he raised the banner of socialism, of the "new Christianity," of the "new barbarians marching to destroy the old order." He called reason an implacable "executioner," and wrote that the purpose of his generation was "not to be the harvesters but the executioners of the past." Strangely, he refused to idealize the common people on whose behalf he felt a social revolution should be inaugurated. He depicted them as unenlightened "slaves to habit," who "will die of thirst by the well, without suspecting that there is water in it, because their fathers never told them so." In the epilogue, written in December 1849, Herzen announced that his generation filled him with shame and declared: "I am truly horrified by modern man." He lamented the "misfortune" of being born when the old world was dying and depicted himself as one of a handful of isolated prophets doomed to perish in the coming age of barbarism.

From the Other Shore is a brilliant, self-contradictory work. Isaiah Berlin and Aileen M. Kelly have interpreted its rejection of liberal and other political banners as a principled repudiation of all ideological verities. They have seen Herzen as a forerunner of Berlin's value pluralism. Yet *From the Other Shore* is also a powerful endorsement of socialism, a political order that Herzen understood to be a product of nature and that he therefore welcomed, in spite of the "barbarism" that would accompany its foundation.

In "The Russian People and Socialism" (1851) Herzen repeated his claim that European civilization was in its death throes, but he now added that the Slavic tribes were beginning to coalesce around the principle of mutual liberty. Like the anarchist Bakunin, he foresaw a multinational Slavic polity of "autonomous peoples" organized in a loose federalist structure. In Russia society itself would be based on the peasant commune. Herzen insisted that, within the commune, problems were solved without litigation, for peasants "very rarely cheat one another. An almost boundless good faith prevails amongst them." He asserted that strong fraternal ties between members of the commune had enabled Russian peasants to survive the Mongol yoke and the "German" bureaucracy imposed upon them by Peter the Great and his successors. Herzen added that Russia's future "lies with the muzhik [peasant] just as the regeneration of France lies with the worker." Although he praised Russian peasants for their resistance to St. Petersburg, he was fully cognizant of rural Russia's benighted ignorance. He therefore hastened to underscore the importance of Russian intellectuals, whom he portrayed as "the most independent creatures in the world." He uncompromisingly predicted: "Whatever happens, we shall accept nothing from the enemy camp. Russia will never be Protestant. Russia will never be *juste-milieu* [middle of the road]." "The Russian People and Socialism" laid the foundation for future social programs relying on the commune and the critical intelligentsia. Herzen's federalism also had a significant impact on subsequent socialist thinkers, but some, such as Peter Tkachev (1844–1886) and Vladimir Lenin (1870–1924), rejected federalism in favor of a centralized dictatorship of virtue.

HERZEN AS JOURNALIST AND MEMORIST

From the mid-1850s to his death in Paris on 21 January (9 January, old style) 1870, Herzen was undoubtedly the most important Russian journalist abroad. In *The Polar Star* (1855–1868) and *The Bell* (1857–1867) he printed exposés of the history of the Romanov dynasty, criticisms of government policies and officials, and attacks on serfdom and later on the slow pace of implementing the peasant emancipation. These publications, along with the four-volume anthology *Voices from Russia* (1858–1860), were read by intellectuals and occasionally even by government officials, including Tsar Alexander II himself. By virtue of this journalism, some historians have classified Herzen as a contributor to the peasant emancipation of 1861 and to the Great Reforms of the 1860s, but most scholars agree that, after Herzen announced his sympathy for Polish independence in 1863, his influence on official and liberal circles quickly diminished.

Berlin has rightly called Herzen's memoirs, *My Past and Thoughts,* "one of the great monuments to Russian literary and psychological genius, worthy to stand beside the great novels of Turgenev and Tolstoy" (p. 209). The book is also an idiosyncratic portrait of the Russian intelligentsia from the 1820s through the mid-1860s. Herzen's characterizations of Moscow University in the 1830s and 1840s, of the Westernizer–Slavophile debate, and of individuals such as Belinsky and Bakunin left a permanent mark on the way Russians have understood their cultural history. His stylistic innovations profoundly influenced the autobiographical genre, thereby shaping the literary forms through which the Russian past has been encoded to this day.

See also **Bakunin, Mikhail; Belinsky, Vissarion; Slavophiles; Westernizers.**

BIBLIOGRAPHY

Acton, Edward. *Alexander Herzen and the Role of the Intellectual Revolutionary.* Cambridge, U.K., 1979.

Berlin, Isaian. *Russian Thinkers.* New York, 1978.

Herzen, Alexander. *My Past and Thoughts: The Memoirs of Alexander Herzen.* Translated by Constance Garnett and Humphrey Higgens. 4 vols. New York, 1968. A revision of the translation first published 1924–1927.

———. *From the Other Shore; and, "The Russian People and Socialism."* Translated by Moura Budberg and Richard Wollheim. Oxford, U.K., 1979.

Kelly, Aileen M. *Toward Another Shore: Russian Thinkers between Necessity and Chance.* New Haven, Conn., 1998.

———. *Views from the Other Shore: Essays on Herzen, Chekhov, and Bakhtin.* New Haven, Conn., 1999.

Malia, Martin E. *Alexander Herzen and the Birth of Russian Socialism, 1812–1855.* Cambridge, Mass., 1961.

G. M. HAMBURG

HERZL, THEODOR (1860–1904), Hungarian founder of the modern Zionist movement.

Though best known for his role as the primary mobilizer for the eventual creation of the State of Israel in 1948, Theodor Herzl's career trajectory encompassed a great deal more than politics. In fact, his early activities as an influential journalist, playwright, novelist, and essayist proved crucial for fulfilling his later political agenda, while his immersion in the cultural and social worlds of fin-de-siècle central Europe combined with his upbringing in an assimilated Jewish family undeniably helped shape his plan for a Zionist state. Despite a century of scholarly inquiry into his life and times, the central paradox concerning how this thoroughly assimilated Viennese cosmopolitan came to be the most passionate—and successful—advocate for the establishment of a Jewish homeland in Palestine remains under debate.

EARLY YEARS IN BUDAPEST

Born on 2 May 1860 in Budapest, Herzl is often described as having had a childhood typical of many assimilated central European Jews of the time. His father, Jacob Herzl (1833–1902), a businessman, and mother, Jeannette Diamant Herzl (1836–1911), while not particularly religiously observant, belonged to an economically established, assimilated Jewish subculture that remained firmly devoted to fostering German culture and language. Though Herzl received training in Hebrew language and Biblical history in preparation for his bar mitzvah, his family referred to the ceremony as a "*Konfirmation,*" in order to emphasize its parallel to the Christian rite of passage. Due to rising anti-Semitism, Herzl soon transferred to Budapest's Evangelical Gymnasium

Theodor Herzl. Anonymous portrait painting, 1914. ERICH LESSING/ART RESOURCE, NY

where, ironically, most students were Jewish, and where he developed his love for German literature. A careful and elegant dresser, as well as a romantic dreamer with an ironic wit, Herzl fostered his passion for writing with the founding of the student literary group *Wir* (We) in 1874, though the influence of his sister Pauline (1859–1878), an actress who died of illness at an early age, also inspired his later desire to write for the theater.

CAREER DEVELOPMENTS IN VIENNA

Soon after Pauline's death, the family moved to Vienna, where Herzl entered the university to study law. Faced with the rise of violent anti-Semitism and the establishment of nationalist student groups, Herzl indicated his growing desire for the achievement of social status and rank; one of his diary entries notes his longing to become a member of the Prussian nobility. In 1881 he joined Albia, a nationalist *Burschenschaft* (student dueling fraternity), from which he angrily resigned only two

years later after the organization's enthusiastic reception of an anti-Semitic speech by fellow member Hermann Bahr (1863–1934) on the occasion of the death of Richard Wagner (1813–1883). After graduating from the university in 1884 and serving as a law clerk, Herzl soon realized that, due to anti-Semitism, he would never be able to become a judge and focused instead upon his career as a writer. As early as 1882, he wrote diary entries indicating that Jews had been prevented both externally and internally from improvement of their "race" and noted that behind his dandyish exterior he hid mounting doubt and despair for his situation as a Jew.

At that time, early turn-of-the-century Vienna was rapidly becoming a world-class center of arts and culture as well as host to the poets, dramatists, novelists, and essayists of the Jung Wien circle of writers, including Hugo von Hofmannsthal (1874–1929), Bahr, and Richard Beer-Hofmann (1866–1945). Many of these were secular Jews like Herzl, who broke away from their successful professional fathers, rejecting jobs in business and law in favor of pursuing careers in literature and journalism; they tended to spend much of their time congregating in Vienna's now-famous coffeehouses to discuss the latest topics in art, literature, and politics. Herzl, however, actually did not become close to this illustrious coffeehouse set save for a lasting friendship with Arthur Schnitzler (1862–1931). Instead, he remained an aloof cosmopolitan who spoke German, French, Hungarian, Italian, and English, and actually spent more time traveling abroad than anchored in Vienna, casting doubt on the common assumption that both Herzl's background and political goals stemmed from a thoroughly "Viennese" outlook on life, culture, and politics. In fact, it has been argued compellingly that Herzl's time away from Vienna is not only indicative of his overall discomfort with the typical world of assimilated Jewish life in central Europe, but also that it is an important factor in explaining Herzl's rejection of assimilation as a solution to the problems of anti-Semitism and his "conversion" to Zionism.

It is thus from a position of social isolation that Herzl pursued his career as a freelance journalist and playwright, first publishing a series of travel pieces and short essays entitled *Neues von der Venus* (News from Venus) in 1887 and *Das Buch der Narrheit* (The book of folly) in 1888. Already in 1889 Herzl had achieved a long dreamed of success with the performance of one of his plays at Vienna's esteemed Burgtheater. That same year, Herzl married Julie Naschauer, daughter of a Jewish oil magnate; they had three children: Pauline (1890), Hans (1891), and Margarethe (1893); by most accounts, however, his marriage was an unhappy one. During this time, he began to develop stronger Zionist tendencies; however, his political goals at this point remained firmly relegated to the stage. By 1897 he achieved his first theatrical success with *Das Neue Ghetto* (The new ghetto), a politically themed play written three years before in Paris bemoaning the condition of modern Jews who, though emancipated, continued to live in a "new ghetto" without walls.

PARIS AND THE DREYFUS AFFAIR

However, it was as a feuilletonist (writer of magazine-style essays with a personal perspective) that Herzl first achieved significant renown in the Viennese public sphere; he was appointed Paris correspondent for the Viennese newspaper *Neue Freie Presse* in 1891. Herzl remained in Paris until 1895, by which time he had gained much exposure to increasing political anti-Semitism, including the infamous Dreyfus affair of 1894–1900, when French army captain Alfred Dreyfus (1859–1935) was tried on fabricated charges of high treason and sentenced to life imprisonment, though later pardoned. Until the affair, French Jewry had enjoyed the reputation of being the most successfully assimilated and stable Jewish community in western Europe. The reports Herzl sent back to Vienna indicated just how distraught and unsettling he found these anti-Semitic events, particularly as they occurred, to everyone's astonishment, in "republican, modern, civilized France." Yet, despite the common myth that the affair remained the decisive turning point in the solution to the problems of anti-Semitism—indeed, Herzl himself later stated in his diary that the Dreyfus trial made him a Zionist—recent scholarship emphasizes that while certainly a key event, the affair instead represented a moment in which Herzl cemented his goal to find a workable *political* solution. Herzl's previous responses had

been restricted to romantic fantasies: challenging leading anti-Semitic Viennese politicians such as Georg von Schönerer (1842–1921), Karl Lueger (1844–1910), and Prince Alois von Lichtenstein to a duel; or, as a 1893 diary entry suggested, entering into an imaginary "pact" with the Vatican according to which, in exchange for their help battling anti-Semites, Jews would convert to Christianity on the steps of St. Stephen's Cathedral in Vienna. This shift from such theatrical solutions to equally romantic yet increasingly viable political plans indicates how Herzl's early aesthetic sensibilities continued to inform his later plans for the formation of a Jewish homeland.

THE REALIZATION OF A DREAM

In 1895, Herzl completed his outline for the political realization of his Zionist ideals in *The Jewish State: An Attempt at a Modern Solution of the Jewish Question*. Identifying Jews as a community of fate, the tract rejects assimilation as a political solution to anti-Semitism. On 29 August 1897 Herzl delivered the keynote speech to the first Zionist Congress in Basel, Switzerland, cementing the passion for his firm political and ideological goals. Continually drawn to drama and to self-promotion, Herzl enthusiastically proclaimed in his diary, "At Basel I founded the Jewish State." As president of the Zionist organization and founder of *Die Welt,* its weekly newspaper that soon gained a circulation of ten thousand, Herzl committed himself fully to the Zionist cause. Though visits with foreign heads of state such as the German kaiser, William II (r. 1888–1918), and Pope Leo XIII (1878–1903) in far-flung cities such as Constantinople and Jerusalem yielded no immediate political results, his activities raised awareness of Zionism as a cause of serious international importance. At the same time, he continued to function as a writer, completing his utopian novel *Altneuland,* describing in detail how the future state will function, in 1902. By 1903, his meetings with the British government resulted in an offer for an autonomous Jewish colony in Uganda. While this suggestion was never realized, it represented the first substantial step on the path of political recognition for the Zionists.

On 3 July 1904, Herzl died of cardiac sclerosis in Edlach bei Wien. Until the end, his dual commitment to art and politics made possible the advancement of his Zionist plan. It remains debatable to what extent Herzl's transformation from detached bourgeois dandy to ideologically driven Zionist leader stemmed from a deep hatred of his own situation as an assimilated Jew; some twenty-first-century scholars tend to view his acts more positively from the position of Herzl's role as a quintessential modern cosmopolitan Jew. Whatever the case, his passion undeniably stemmed from the complex intertwining of the personal with the political in fin-de-siècle central Europe.

See also **Dreyfus Affair; Fin de Siècle; Jews and Judaism; Schnitzler, Arthur; Vienna; Zionism.**

BIBLIOGRAPHY

Bein, Alex. *Theodore Herzl: A Biography.* Translated by Maurice Samuel. London, 1941.

Beller, Steven. *Herzl.* London, 1991.

Cohen, Israel. *Theodor Herzl, Founder of Political Zionism.* New York, 1959.

Elon, Amos. *Herzl.* New York, 1975.

Fraenkel, Josef. *Theodor Herzl: A Biography.* London, 1946.

Herzl, Theodor. *The Diaries of Theodor Herzl.* Edited and translated with an introduction by Marvin Lowenthal. London, 1956.

Robertson, Ritchie, and Edward Timms, eds. *Theodor Herzl and the Origins of Zionism.* Edinburgh, 1997.

Wistrich, Robert S. *The Jews of Vienna in the Age of Franz Joseph.* Oxford, U.K., 1990.

LISA SILVERMAN

HIRSCHFELD, MAGNUS (1868–1935), German physician, psychiatrist, and sex reformer.

The most prominent spokesman of the homosexual emancipation movement of the late nineteenth and early twentieth centuries, Magnus Hirschfeld founded the world's first homosexual rights organization, the Scientific-Humanitarian Committee (Wissenschaftlich-humanitäres Komitee), in 1897. Attacked for his socialist leanings, his Jewish ancestry, and his homosexual orientation, he left Germany in 1930 and died in French exile.

EARLY ACTIVITIES AND INFLUENCES

Born to the family of a noted Jewish physician in the Pomeranian city of Kolberg on Germany's Baltic coast on 14 May 1868, Hirschfeld affiliated with the Social Democratic Party and began writing newspaper articles as a teenager. He followed the example of his father and his two older brothers by taking up medicine. Hirschfeld enrolled at the universities of Strasbourg, Munich, and Heidelberg before completing his M.D. degree at Berlin in 1892. His studies brought him into contact with a number of distinguished German medical professors of the late nineteenth century, including his fellow Pomeranian Rudolf Virchow (1821–1902), whose career yoked scientific research and involvement in progressive politics in a way that inspired Hirschfeld.

As a university student, Hirschfeld embraced a secularistic worldview informed by Darwinism and consequently ceased describing his religious confession as Jewish. In Germany, it was above all the Jena zoologist Ernst Haeckel (1834–1919) who popularized Charles Darwin's notion of sexual selection as the key that unlocked the riddles of nature. Hirschfeld affiliated with the Monist League, which Haeckel founded to advance popular scientific knowledge and to provide an alternative to conventional church services by organizing Sunday morning gatherings for reverential reflection on nature. In its spiritual dimension, monism repudiated the Judeo-Christian dualism of body and soul, postulating instead a unity down to the level of the individual cell. Monism influenced Hirschfeld's later sexological work, in which he questioned and ultimately repudiated the commonsense understanding of sexual dimorphism, the notion that men and women are polar opposites. The monistic outlook also led Hirschfeld to assert an underlying harmony of physical and psychological traits in homosexuals.

Hirschfeld began the practice of medicine in Magdeburg, where he initially specialized in naturopathy, a holistic form of therapy that aims to fortify the immune system through balanced nutrition, open-air exercise, plenty of water, and avoidance of alcohol and tobacco. Many traditional physicians take a dim view of naturopathy, and practicing it schooled Hirschfeld in defying received wisdom. Monism and naturopathy both contributed to Hirschfeld's ultimate convictions that any affliction linked with homosexuality is not inherent to the orientation per se but instead a stress response to social opprobrium, and that the best therapy is to grasp fully the fundamental naturalness of one's psychological and physical being. From the 1890s onward, Hirschfeld made joint cause with naturists (i.e., nudists), antivaccinationists, and teetotalers who participated in a broad spectrum of voluntaristic activism termed the "life reform movement" in turn-of-the-century German social history. Hirschfeld's early involvement in this movement provided him with practical experience in public speaking and mobilizing support for hygienic and political reform that he would later apply to the cause of homosexual emancipation.

CHAMPION OF HOMOSEXUAL EMANCIPATION

A final impetus that pushed Hirschfeld in the direction of homosexual emancipation was the 1895 trial of Oscar Wilde (1854–1900), which elicited widespread discussion beyond England. To Hirschfeld, the time seemed ripe for public enlightenment on homosexuality, and in 1896 he gave up his naturopathic practice in Magdeburg and moved to Charlottenburg, a suburb of Berlin, where he increasingly specialized in sexology and psychiatry. His first sexological treatise, titled *Sappho and Socrates; or, How Is the Love of Men and Women for Persons of Their Own Sex to Be Explained?* (1896), was released under a pseudonym, but Hirschfeld simultaneously instructed the publisher to reveal his identity to anyone who inquired. The ensuing contacts led in 1897 to the founding of the Scientific-Humanitarian Committee. With the word *scientific*, Hirschfeld invoked a touchstone of modernity that rendered moot the traditional religious category of sinfulness. But the word also pointed to medical and biological research suggesting that homosexuality ought not to be seen as a sickness. With the corollary *humanitarian*, Hirschfeld aimed to suggest a program to ameliorate all the everyday forms of intolerance under which homosexuals suffered needlessly—from social discrimination, in all its multifarious forms, to the psychic cost of internalized oppression, such as heightened susceptibility to alcoholism and suicidal depression.

The Scientific-Humanitarian Committee set as its primary goal the reform of the statute of the German penal code that criminalized sodomy, and to this end it submitted a petition to the Reichstag. Written by Hirschfeld and widely circulated between 1897 and 1930, the petition was eventually endorsed by thousands of prominent Germans. From the outset, August Bebel (1840–1913) and other members of the Social Democratic Party gave strong, if not entirely unanimous, support to Hirschfeld's petition. Aware that his campaign amounted to a posthumous revival of the reform efforts of Karl Heinrich Ulrichs (1825–1895), Hirschfeld prepared a second edition of Ulrichs's *Investigations into the Riddle of Man-Manly Love* and published it in 1898. Unlike Ulrichs, who came out publicly as a homosexual in 1867, Hirschfeld himself never made an issue of his personal sexual identity, no doubt out of concern that it would diminish his authority as an objective, scientific expert. Hirschfeld recognized that eliminating popular prejudice was even more important than law reform, and to this end he gave numerous public addresses and wrote the booklet *What Should People Know about the Third Sex?* (1901), of which fifty thousand copies were in print by 1911 and which was also published in English, Dutch, and Danish translations.

Hirschfeld adopted from Ulrichs the term *third sex* for homosexuals, but in doing so he sacrificed scientific accuracy to political expediency. Hirschfeld followed Darwin in his recognition that no two individuals in a biopopulation, not even identical twins, are actually identical. Variation and diversity among uniquely different individuals are a given of the natural world, whereas such notions as purely male and purely female are essentialist abstractions that do not occur in nature; a "third sex" is likewise a fiction. Physiological bisexuality is evident in every man's nipples, for example, or in the rudimentary spermatic cord of every woman. While essentialist thinking is indispensable in mathematics and the sciences of inanimate matter, such as physics, it is out of place in biology. How novel this concept was became evident when Hirschfeld—like Darwin himself—sometimes slipped back into typological thinking.

Hirschfeld was first and foremost a naturalist, and his favorite method was to make a series of observations and to develop conjectures from this evidence. In 1898 he published the first version of an extensive sexological questionnaire that underwent repeated revisions and expansions up to its seventh and final printing in 1930. Anticipating the later survey work of the American sexologist Alfred Kinsey (1894–1956), Hirschfeld personally interviewed thousands of homosexuals, and he gathered detailed data on the sex lives of thirty thousand individuals. He also explored firsthand the gay bars and other venues of the homosexual subculture in Berlin and other European, American, and North African metropolises prior to publishing a thousand-page monograph titled *The Homosexuality of Men and Women* (1914; English translation, 2000). He coined the term *transvestitism* with his monograph *The Transvestites* (1910; English translation, 1991).

From Hirschfeld's perspective, homosexuals, transvestites, and hermaphrodites were all part of a broad array of "sexual intermediates" whose very existence demonstrated the fallacy of simplistic, binary, male–female thinking. In 1899 the first volume of the *Yearbook for Sexual Intermediate Types* (*Jahrbuch für sexuelle Zwischenstufen*) appeared under Hirschfeld's editorship. Uninterrupted even by World War I, this monumental journal appeared until 1923, and in encyclopedic fashion it surveyed the fields of medicine, law, psychology, anthropology, sociology, religion, history, art, and literature in addition to reporting on current events and the work of the Scientific-Humanitarian Committee and providing sweeping bibliographies of relevant publications.

BACKLASH, WEIMAR REVIVAL, NAZI ERA EXILE

Hirschfeld enjoyed growing support and public recognition until his 1907 appearance in court as a sexological expert in the Eulenburg affair, which turned on allegations of homosexuality within the entourage of Kaiser William II leveled by the journalist Maximilian Harden (1861–1927). Harden's vindication in court, attributable in part to Hirschfeld's testimony, elicited an anti-Semitic and antihomosexual backlash from pro-monarchist conservatives, and the homosexual emancipation movement was forced into quiescence until the kaiser's abdication in 1918.

Hirschfeld revived his campaign on behalf of homosexual rights during the years of the Weimar Republic, and in 1919 he fulfilled a vision he had cherished since the turn of the century by founding the Institute for Sexology (Institut für Sexualwissenschaft), which was a Berlin center for research and education, sexual counseling and therapy, and advocacy on behalf of sexual privacy and reproductive rights. In 1919 he helped script and appeared in the feature film *Different from the Others,* which extended to the cinema his campaign for the reform of German law. Hirschfeld's purview now extended well beyond homosexuality to include, among other things, the legalization of abortion, and this campaign brought him into a productive alliance with the newly founded German Communist Party as well as the Social Democratic Party.

In 1928 Hirschfeld cofounded the World League for Sexual Reform, which lauded the sexual politics of the pre-Stalinist Soviet Union as exemplary. Success appeared within reach when, late in 1929, a Reichstag committee supported reform of the entire penal code, but a new election brought a staggering rise in support for the Nazis. Brutally assaulted by fascists as early as 1920, excoriated in the Nazi press, and challenged by rivals within the homosexual emancipation movement for his medicalizing approach to sexuality, his political leanings, and his Jewishness, Hirschfeld departed in late 1930 for a lecture tour to the United States and Asia, residing upon his return to Europe in Switzerland and France rather than Germany. The Institute for Sexology was closed by the Nazis in February 1933 and the bulk of its library publicly burned on 10 May 1933. Hirschfeld died in exile in Nice, France, on 14 May 1935, his sixty-seventh birthday.

Tirelessly active as an author, researcher, and organizer, Hirschfeld achieved international recognition as Germany's leading authority on sexuality. Within Germany he was both admired and abjured for his advocacy of homosexual rights. Shaped by the Wilhelmine era's unquestioning faith in scientific enlightenment, his reform work advanced during the democracy of the Weimar Republic only to be destroyed by the Nazi regime.

See also **Haeckel, Ernst Heinrich; Homosexuality and Lesbianism; Ulrichs, Karl Heinrich; Wilde, Oscar.**

BIBLIOGRAPHY

Bullough, Vern L. *Science in the Bedroom: A History of Sex Research.* New York, 1994.

Herzer, Manfred. *Leben und Werk eines jüdischen, schwulen un sozialistischen Sexologen.* 2nd ed. Hamburg, Germany, 2001.

Hirschfeld, Magnus. *The Homosexuality of Men and Women.* Translated by Michael A. Lombardi-Nash. Amherst, N.Y., 2000.

LeVay, Simon. *Queer Science: The Use and Abuse of Research into Homosexuality.* Cambridge, Mass., 1996.

Steakley, James D. "Iconography of a Scandal: Political Cartoons and the Eulenburg Affair in Wilhelmine Germany." In *Hidden from History: Reclaiming the Gay and Lesbian Past,* edited by Martin Bauml Duberman, Martha Vicinus, and George Chauncey Jr., 233–263. New York, 1989.

————. "Per scientiam ad justitiam: Magnus Hirschfeld and the Sexual Politics of Innate Homosexuality." In *Science and Homosexualities,* edited by Vernon A. Rosario, 133–154. New York, 1997.

Wolff, Charlotte. *Magnus Hirschfeld: A Portrait of a Pioneer in Sexology.* London, 1986.

JAMES D. STEAKLEY

"History has had assigned to it the office of judging the past and of instructing the present for the benefit of future ages. To such high offices the present work does not presume: it seeks only to show what actually happened [*wie es eigentlich gewesen*]." (Leopold von Ranke, 1824)

"We have gained perhaps in originality, and at least in literary form; but we have lost in scientific utility. Almost all our historians are autodidacts; they have had no masters, and they have raised no pupils. . . . They are commonly *litterateurs* before they are scholars." (Georges Monod, on France, 1876)

"The history of England is emphatically the history of progress." (Thomas Macaulay)

HISTORY. The "creation myth" of academic history focuses upon one man: the German historian Leopold von Ranke (1795–1886). Ranke, it is said, swept aside the inaccurate, romantic historiography of the Enlightenment, and in its stead propounded a "scientific" methodology that placed the subject on a professional footing. Ranke's revolution was founded upon the use of archival sources, which were to be placed in the political and cultural contexts of their own time, and footnoted rigorously so that others could retrace the research. History should be unbiased, objective, methodical, not partisan or philosophical. The aim was "only to show what actually happened," rather than to pass moral or intellectual judgment upon the past. This methodology spread from the University of Berlin, where Ranke worked from 1825 onward, to the rest of Europe.

This brief account, while not wholly inaccurate, is misleading in several respects. Ranke's claim to originality was dubious: the analytical use of original, archival documents long predated his efforts, as did footnotes. Various seventeenth-century scholars, for example, had made extensive and critical use of royal archives, and the idea of contextualizing documents can be traced back still further. Indeed, in Ranke's own work on the Reformation, only about one in ten of his footnotes cited an archival document; the rest referred to sources previously published by earlier generations of German scholars. He was perhaps more programmatic than others in his methodology, but not the originator of academic history.

What established the creation myth was a combination of Ranke's self-promotion and his tactical lionization by those who later claimed him as forebear. Ranke's image gained a particular momentum because he was a great teacher, and his pedagogic model (using seminars to discuss sources) was successfully exported to the rest of Europe in later decades. The sense that Germany led the way in serious history gained weight from the ongoing publication by the *Monumenta Germaniae Historica* of original documentary sources (although itself predated by efforts such as Ludovico Antonio Muratori's [1672–1750] early eighteenth-century *Rerum Italicarum Scriptores*), and the establishment in 1859 of the academic history journal *Historische Zeitschrift.*

For Ranke's inheritors, moreover, the myth had a particularly useful role. The supposed scientism of his method was used to bolster history's claim to be a valid subject for serious study in its own right. The "scientific"—and hence "objective"—nature of Rankean history was held to distinguish it from subjective subjects such as literature and philosophy. However, this rested upon a misunderstanding of what Ranke's method involved. French, English, and American historians saw "science" in opposition to "art," and some even thought that history could employ analytical methods similar to the natural sciences. In fact, the German term *Wissenschaft* meant simply an organized body of knowledge, not "science" in distinction to other subjects. But in a period when the natural sciences were making heroic and public advances, the temptation to claim that history stood among them was great.

One may also argue that Ranke's most famous dictum—"only to say how it really was"—is another mistranslation. It may be better rendered as "only to say how it *essentially* was," the "essence" being the destinies that God had ordained for nations in the past and the present. Rather than asserting a kind of bloodless facticity, Ranke aimed at a more metaphysical truth—something not well understood by those who hailed him as their progenitor.

HISTORY AND PEDAGOGY

Professionalization can also, more bluntly, be seen as the process by which people are paid to do history, train others to do it, and establish an academic apparatus to support their labors. This occurred in most countries late in the nineteenth century. Germany led the way—for several decades, history graduates from Europe and even America travelled to Germany for professional training—but France, England, and Italy hurried along behind. Precise dates can mislead, however: while the *Revue critique d'histoire et de littérature* was founded, in imitation of *Historische Zeitschrift,* in 1866, and similarly the *English Historical Review* in 1886, both journals were initially directed toward the general public as much as the nascent profession, and had a strongly literary bent. Similarly, there were professors in history at Oxford from the middle of the century (and at Cambridge a little later on); but they had little impact upon how history was taught, developed, or researched.

History was taught at Oxford from 1853, but only as a stand-alone subject from 1871 (1873 at Cambridge). The teachers (as opposed to the professors) were not specialists in any particular topic or period and did very little research. There was no graduate school or formal historical training. The situation was similar in France and Italy.

It was not until the last quarter of the nineteenth century that, beyond Germany, academic history became fully professional. In France the foundations were laid by the government minister and historian Victor Duruy (1811–1894). Under his leadership the École Pratique des Haute Etudes began in 1868 to provide new scholars with training in palaeography, diplomatic practices, philology, and the critical analysis of primary sources. Duruy was soon moved from his government post, but in the following decade a new generation took up the reins. Gabriel-Jean-Jacques Monod (1844–1912) began the *Revue Historique* in 1876 with an agenda that hailed the arrival of a new, Rankean methodology. Monod stressed the journal's lack of religious or political affiliations; it would, he said, pursue "disinterested and scientific research." Between 1885 and 1905 the Sorbonne became the center for new historical study, with graduate training at its heart.

England lagged behind: Oxford was locked into a complacent and conservative curriculum that marked it ever after, and while Cambridge debated the intellectual project of history more energetically, its actual teaching and training were little better. The vanguard of change was more to be found in London and Manchester, where around the turn of the twentieth century Albert Frederick Pollard (1869–1948) and Thomas Frederick Tout (1855–1929) respectively imbued new generations of historians with the critical skills necessary for their profession's development. The most radical of this generation was Frederic William Maitland (1850–1906), whose work on the social and cultural impact of law still leaves an imprint upon current debates. But Maitland was appointed as a teacher of law, not history, and his influence was only really felt well after his death. And this was true elsewhere: formal structures for producing the next generation of historian were sparse. In England, doctorates in history appeared only in the 1920s.

HISTORY AND THE STATE

The more rigorous (if not original) methodology that accompanied the professionalization of history was in each country proclaimed as a "scientific history." As noted above, this was based in part upon mistranslation, and in part upon the nineteenth-century romance with the hard sciences. But such claims were also made within a financial context. To establish history as a profession, someone had to be persuaded to fund it. History proclaimed its value and importance to the state by asserting its "scientific" credentials. But what did the state get back from history?

A short answer would be "national legitimation," but the contours of this varied considerably from country to country. The "essence" that German historians, following Ranke, divined in their national history was one of self-confidence, progress, and racial destiny. Monod ascribed the Prussian victory over Napoleon III (r. 1852–1871) in 1870 to the sense of national unity that German historians had forged earlier that century. Shortly thereafter, French schools introduced classes on "civic instruction," based upon the history that Monod's generation were writing, that depicted the revolution of 1789 as the apotheosis of French bourgeois identity. Thus, ironically, at the very moment that French historiography most strongly proclaimed its "objective, independent, scientific" spirit, it was hailed most directly into the cause of the nation state. This nationalist project splintered, however, early in the twentieth century, in the aftermath of the Dreyfus affair. That event revealed the politics of Monod's *Revue Historique* to be firmly republican, and historians were uneasy about the way in which the new Right had co-opted the patriotic utility of history.

Italy and England shared the desire for narratives of the nation-state, but the stories their historians told were rather different (notwithstanding some attempts to write themselves into a "Germanic" medieval history, thus simply borrowing the patriotic clothes of that powerful country). It was quite impossible for Italy to write of its earlier history as politically unified; instead, therefore, it emphasized a unity of culture and intellectual achievement, stretching back to the early Italian Renaissance and the Roman Empire. England, meanwhile, trumpeted political continuity and the

rise of parliamentary democracy; virtues that translated into an imperial self-belief that subject-nations may well have mistaken for arrogant hypocrisy. The history taught by Oxford and Cambridge emphasized positive example and consensus, rather than past conflicts, and history professors saw their pedagogic task as providing a civic education for the future leaders of empire. If, as legend has it, World War I was won on the playing fields of Eton, the British Empire was administered through the complacent narratives of medieval constitutionalism.

HISTORY AND THE PUBLIC

Various factors fed into the professionalization of history, from the opening of national archives early in the nineteenth century, to the states' development of educational structures at all levels of pedagogy, to the philosophical developments (and misrepresentations) within historiography itself. Some things were gained, and some were lost. Among the latter was the beginning of a fissure between professional historian and reading public. The "scientific" and "objective" historiography of the nineteenth century, in contrast to its Enlightenment forebears, tended to disengage from political argument and intervention, and some of the history published by journals and university presses became "academic" in the pejorative sense.

It is ever the case that history is written by the victors—in this case, the employed, university historians who, by the turn of the twentieth century, predominated in almost every country. It should be remembered that one element too easily erased by the narrative or myth of professionalization is the role of the amateur. For much of the nineteenth century, some of the greatest history was written by amateurs—those not employed by the state, although methodologically often stronger than the majority of "professionals": for example the American medievalist Henry Charles Lea (1825–1909), the Frenchman Hippolyte-Adolphe Taine (1828–1893), and the Englishman John Richard Green (1837–1883), to name but three. Moreover, their conception of history was often broader than that envisaged by an academy slavish to Ranke's focus upon high politics. However, by the last years of the nineteenth century, particularly in Italy, the first impact of Marxist thought was being felt upon historical writing; the seeds for a new century's crop of historians—intent on uniting society, academy, and politics—had been sown.

See also Civilization, Concept of; Education; Ranke, Leopold von; Universities.

BIBLIOGRAPHY

Berger, Stefan, Mark Donovan, and Kevin Passmore, eds. *Writing National Histories: Western Europe since 1800.* London, 1999. A comprehensive collection of essays on the topic.

Breisach, Ernst. *Historiography: Ancient, Medieval, and Modern.* Chicago, 1983. Places "professionalization" in broader context.

Grafton, Anthony. *The Footnote: A Curious History.* Revised edition. Cambridge, Mass., 1997. Witty and readable critique of Ranke and his precursors.

Iggers, Georg G., and James M. Powell, eds. *Leopold von Ranke and the Shaping of the Historical Discipline.* Syracuse, N.Y., 1990. A levelheaded collection of essays on the development of modern history.

Kenyon, John. *The History Men.* 2nd ed., rev. London, 1993. Conservative and old-fashioned, but very usefully detailed on historians in (mainly) England.

Keylor, William R. *Academy and Community: The Foundation of the French Historical Profession.* Cambridge, Mass., 1975. A wonderful and detailed study of the nineteenth and early twentieth century.

Slee, Peter. *Learning and a Liberal Education: The Study of Modern History in the Universities of Oxford, Cambridge, and Manchester, 1800–1914.* Manchester, U.K., and Wolfesboro, N.H., 1986. A good starting point for English developments.

Soffer, Reba N. *Discipline and Power: The University, History, and the Making of an English Elite, 1870–1930.* Stanford, Calif., 1994. The best, and most thoughtful, study of the professionalization of history and its political context.

JOHN H. ARNOLD

HOBSON, JOHN A. (1858–1940), English radical economist.

The son of a local newspaper proprietor, Hobson was born in Derby. He attended Oxford University and then taught school in Exeter before coming to London in 1885 to write for his father's newspaper. Originally an orthodox free-market liberal, Hobson began to move in a more radical direction under the influence of Charles Booth's revelations about poverty in the capital. In 1889, together with A. F. Mummery, he published *The Physiology of Industry,* which challenged the conventional notion that full employment of resources was the norm in society, arguing instead that the British economy had a tendency to save too much and invest too little. Over the next twenty years, Hobson strove to put these insights into a more radical context. In *The Industrial System* (1909) and in many other writings, he argued that historic privilege, monopolies, and unequal life chances led to a maldistribution of wealth and income in Britain. The few rich were in possession of surplus, unearned wealth that could be taxed away without affecting economic performance and redistributed to the masses via higher wages, welfare benefits, and better education. Hobson thus became an energetic proponent of progressive taxation and state-led reforms, the ultimate objective being a society based on equality of opportunity. His work became an important component of the "New Liberalism" in Britain and had some influence on Liberal Party welfare reforms after 1906.

In his most famous book, *Imperialism: A Study* (1902), Hobson extended his analysis to investigate recent European imperial expansion. In the early 1890s, he had supported imperial expansion on the grounds that new markets were important in finding employment for the poor. In *Imperialism,* however, he reacted to recent British expansion in China and Africa by arguing passionately that excess saving by the wealthy, the result of badly distributed income, found an outlet in foreign investment and that imperialism was essentially a competitive struggle for new investment markets in which the rich benefited and the masses paid the costs through taxation. He also claimed that economic reform would eliminate most foreign investment and thus remove the pressure for expansion. Hobson described London-based finance as the "governor of the imperial engine," the orchestrator of a complex group of political, military, business, and religious interests who also benefited from imperialism. A large part of the book was taken up with an analysis of the political, economic, and ideological strategies used by governing elites under the guidance of finance to convince the mass of the population that imperial expansion was in their interests. Because it had such a strong influence on Vladimir Lenin, *Imperialism* has often been seen as a proto-Marxist work, but it was essentially an outcome of a long radical tradition wherein imperialism was viewed as a symptom of a diseased capitalism, although one capable of reform and of supporting a peaceful international world.

Just before 1914, Hobson moved away from the stark analysis of *Imperialism* and in *The Economic Interpretation of Investment* (1911) presented imperialism as a stage on the way to the creation of a peaceful world society of interdependent, coequal states. On the outbreak of war in 1914, which he saw as the outcome of imperial rivalry, Hobson first turned his attention to the analytical and practical problems involved in restoring peace and setting up international institutions that could guard peace in future and regulate European imperial activity. His main theoretical effort went into *Towards International Government* (1915), and he gave vigorous support to the League of Nations movement. In *Democracy after the War* (1917) he also reasserted many of the arguments of *Imperialism*. At the end of the war, disgusted by the punitive nature of the peace settlement and the failure to set up an effective League of Nations that could supervise the development of European colonies, he joined the Labour Party and in the early 1920s advised it on trade and colonial issues, arguing for an active colonial economic development policy in the context of indirect rule and free trade.

Hobson lived long enough to see the ideas contained in *The Physiology of Industry* generously hailed by John Maynard Keynes as an important precursor of his own revolutionary thinking in the *General Theory*. His autobiography, *Confessions of an Economic Heretic* (1938), brought his key ideas to a new public; and, in the run-up to World War II, his original stance on imperialism attracted an attention far greater than it had originally received. *Imperialism: A Study* was reprinted in 1938, with a new preface, and hailed as a classic work. Hobson died in 1940.

See also **Economic Growth and Industrialism; Imperialism.**

BIBLIOGRAPHY

Cain, Peter. *Hobson and Imperialism: Radicalism, New Liberalism, and Finance, 1887–1938.* Oxford, U.K., 2002.

Freeden, Michael. *The New Liberalism: An Ideology of Social Reform.* Oxford, U.K., 1978.

Long, David. *Towards a New Liberal Internationalism: The International Theory of J. A. Hobson.* Cambridge, U.K., 1996.

PETER CAIN

HOFMANNSTHAL, HUGO VON

(1874–1929), Austrian poet, playwright, and essayist.

Hugo von Hofmannsthal was one of the great German writers of the twentieth century and a leading figure in Austrian intellectual life from the 1890s until his death at the age of fifty-five. He was important as a lyric poet, a playwright, and an essayist, but also as a librettist and a central figure in the Salzburg Festival during the 1920s. He represents the best of an elite cultural tradition, with concerns that belong to a broadly European modernism from Charles Baudelaire to the English writers and poets of the early twentieth century. But most of his mature work aimed to connect with folk traditions and with popular history and experience, and this was especially evident in his response to World War I. A person of extraordinary grace and sensitivity, Hofmannsthal tried to make creative sense of the crises and catastrophes of the early twentieth century. His heritage was a very Austrian blend of Jewish, Catholic, Italian, bourgeois, and aristocratic. His great-grandfather was a silk manufacturer and an ennobled Jew, whose son married an Italian and converted to Catholicism. Hugo von Hofmannsthal grew up in Vienna, immersed in the high culture his father loved; even as a teenager, he was acknowledged as the epitome of poetic genius by the leading Viennese modernists, most of whom were nearly a generation older. As a young man, his pronounced aestheticism culminated in the crisis of language he described in his fictional "Letter of Lord Chandos" in 1902, after which his work moved strongly in an ethical and social direction.

Hofmannsthal did not produce a particularly massive body of work for a great writer, but he wrote a large number of significant works in a variety of genres over a long period of time. His genius lay in imagination, in giving form, in finding his way into other human experiences and portraying them on stage. For a long time he was regarded simply as an aesthete, or as important mainly for his lyric poetry and verse plays, but his moral and didactic concerns were apparent as early as 1893 in his lyric drama, *Der Tor und der Tod* (Death and the fool). The idea of the total work of art increasingly appealed to him after the turn of the century, when he began to collaborate with the composer Richard Strauss in writing operas such as *Der Rosenkavalier* (1910; The cavalier of the rose). In his collaborations and adaptations with Strauss and others, Hofmannsthal was motivated by his skepticism about language and his desire to blend words and music. His concern with moral themes became more pronounced in plays such as *Jedermann* (1911; Everyman) and *Das Salzburger grosse Welttheater* (1922; The Salzburg great theater of the world) as he aimed to reach a wider audience. Hofmannsthal's emphasis on restoration and adaptation ran the risk of artificiality and loss of connection with contemporary life, and yet in *Der Turm* (1927; The tower) he commented perceptively on the political atmosphere of the 1920s in Central Europe, while two of his most popular plays, *Der Schwierige* (1921; The difficult man) and *Der Unbestechliche* (1923; The incorruptible), achieved a level of comedy that one is not accustomed to expect from the German stage. Hofmannsthal also produced an important body of prose, including not only essays and aphorisms, but also short narrative pieces, an unfinished novel (*Andreas*), and a huge published correspondence. Since World War II, scholars and critics have increasingly emphasized the connections among all his works and the continuity of his development as a writer.

Hofmannsthal increasingly identified with and took responsibility for the fate of Austria during World War I, and he came to understand politics as a part of culture, tradition, and morality. His essays from the last fifteen years of his life are remarkable pieces of writing, as well as important and influential arguments that shaped understandings of "the Austrian idea" and "the conservative revolution" in German culture. He clearly belongs in the tradition of German literature and culture, but his intellectual development was shaped in distinctive ways by his Austrian context. Michael Steinberg's account of Hofmannsthal's relationship to the Salzburg Festival in the 1920s emphasizes his cosmopolitan nationalism and his "conservative drive to reconstitute and render coherent a transcendent Austrian cultural identity and tradition" (p. xi). Hofmannsthal's blend of a mystical sensibility and a conservative attitude brings to mind the British political theorist Edmund Burke in some respects, but for Hofmannsthal the rupture of historical continuity was not the French Revolution but World War I.

See also **Austria-Hungary; Fin de Siècle; Modernism; Vienna.**

BIBLIOGRAPHY

Broch, Hermann. *Hugo von Hofmannsthal and His Time: The European Imagination, 1860–1920.* Edited and translated by Michael P. Steinberg. Chicago, 1984.

Hofmannsthal, Hugo von. *Selected Works.* Vol. 1: *Selected Prose.* Translated by Mary Hottinger, Tania Stern, and James Stern. Introduction by Hermann Broch. New York, 1952.

———. *Selected Works.* Vol. 2: *Poems and Verse Plays* (bilingual edition). Edited by Michael Hamburger. New York, 1961.

———. *Selected Works.* Vol. 3: *Selected Plays and Libretti.* Edited by Michael Hamburger. New York, 1963.

Kern, Peter Christoph. *Zur Gedankenwelt des späten Hofmannsthals: Die Idee einer schöpferischen Restauration.* Heidelberg, Germany, 1969.

Kovach, Thomas A., ed. *A Companion to the Works of Hofmannsthal.* Rochester, N.Y., 2002.

Steinberg, Michael P. *The Meaning of the Salzburg Festival: Austria as Theater and Ideology, 1890–1938.* Ithaca, N.Y., 1990.

Volke, Werner. *Hugo von Hofmannsthal in Selbstzeugnissen und Bilddokumenten.* Reinbek bei Hamburg, Germany, 1967.

Wunberg, Gotthart. *Der frühe Hofmannsthal: Schizophrenie als dichterische Struktur.* Stuttgart, Germany, 1965.

DAVID S. LUFT

HÖLDERLIN, JOHANN CHRISTIAN FRIEDRICH (1770–1843), German poet.

Born in Lauffen (Swabia) in 1770, Friedrich Hölderlin was an exact contemporary of William

Wordsworth, Georg Wilhelm Friedrich Hegel, and Ludwig van Beethoven. Instructed in music and foreign languages, he studied at the Protestant seminary in Tübingen (with Hegel and Friedrich Wilhelm Joseph von Schelling), where he read widely in philosophy. When he graduated in 1793 he had already given up plans for the ministry and begun work on his novel *Hyperion*. He supported himself modestly off and on as a tutor during the next nine years.

Although Hölderlin met some leading German writers of his time—Johann Gottfried von Herder, Johann Wolfgang von Goethe, Novalis (Friedrich Leopold von Hardenberg)—and was encouraged by Johann Christoph Friedrich von Schiller in the beginning, he belonged to neither the classicist nor the Romantic literary circles. By contrast, he studied philosophy with Johann Gottlieb Fichte in Jena in 1794–1795 and maintained his friendship and collaboration with Hegel and Schelling, documented in a fragment from 1795 known as "The First Program for the System of German Idealism." Historians of philosophy continue to debate the significance of Hölderlin's contributions to German idealism in this text and other philosophical fragments from the late 1790s.

WORKS

In 1796 Hölderlin finished his Hellenophilic epistolary novel *Hyperion* (published in two volumes in 1797 and 1799) with its dominant themes of Greek beauty, political freedom, philosophical idealism, and sublimated love, and then until 1800 he worked on an unfinished tragedy, *The Death of Empedocles,* also set in Greece, about a philosopher-king's felt need for self-sacrifice as a form of totalization of experience. If these were all Hölderlin had ever written, he would be remembered at best as a minor writer with a passion for ancient Greece. But during an intense period of seclusion in Homburg near Frankfurt from 1798 to 1800, everything changed: he wrote fragmentary essays on philosophy and theory of literature that are still appreciated for their original insights; undertook his close study and brilliant translations of the Greek poet Pindar (c. 522–c. 438 B.C.E.), believed to be the best translations of Pindar into any language; and began to write the great poems for which he is famous.

Hölderlin's poetry from 1799 to 1805, most of it unpublished at the time, is highly varied, remarkably unique, and thus difficult to characterize. He wrote in many forms, principally elegies, odes, and one form he sometimes called "hymns," sometimes, idiosyncratically, "patriotic songs" (*vaterländische Gesänge*). From Pindar he adopted the long triadic form for his own dialectical manner of argument and counterargument, and also the loosely structured syntax that Pindar's Greek employs. With a style exploiting daring metaphors and frequent ambiguity, Hölderlin treated themes of great complexity. In his elegies ("Bread and Wine," "Homecoming"), longing and despair—for a Hellenized past or a contemporary Germanic homeland—could in the end turn toward a tenuous hope. Some of his hymns are "river poems" ("At the Source of the Danube," "The Migration," "The Rhine," "The Ister") with geographically and historically shaped narratives of the destinies of gods and men. Several of his hymns are detailed accounts of Christ and Christianity ("Celebration of Peace," "The Unique One," "Patmos") with a pronounced but uncertain messianic subtheme; a very late and enigmatic hymn ("Mnemosyne") blends Greek and Christian references with considerable personal pathos. Perhaps his greatest single poem, "Remembrance"—written after an eventful journey on foot to Bordeaux in the years 1801 and 1802, and learning upon his return of the death of his lover—combines an elegiac treatment of love with a mythic handling of the possibilities of human action.

In his last productive years Hölderlin continued to write ambitious poems that exist only as fragments; translated Sophocles' (c. 496–406 B.C.E.) *Oedipus Tyrannus* and *Antigone* into a bizarre German; and appears to have become involved in his friend Isaak von Sinclair's political intrigues. But his mental health declined rapidly and in 1806 he entered a Tübingen clinic. Probably schizophrenic, he remained under care until his death in 1843. During these years he wrote numerous surprisingly but deceptively simple poems, sometimes under the name "Scardanelli."

CONTROVERSIES

Several controversies surround Hölderlin's life and work: political, philosophical, and literary.

While he was first an enthusiast of the French Revolution and then, like many of his generation, disappointed by it, he was not a Jacobin and probably never participated in any serious political conspiracy. Revolutionary themes appear throughout his poetry, but they are neither consistent nor sustained, and he can scarcely be called a "political poet." Hölderlin may have had a decisive influence on early German idealist philosophy, but he was undoubtedly one of the fundamental influences on Martin Heidegger's mature ("ontological") philosophy. Heidegger's many commentaries on Hölderlin's poems argued that they enact an original encounter of men, gods, being, and language, sometimes couching this interpretation in nationalist mythography. However confused and inaccurate Heidegger's commentaries now often appear, they contributed to a more vulgar nationalist mythification of Hölderlin during World War II that was as misrepresentative as it was widespread. More careful philosophic commentary since Heidegger (Maurice Blanchot, Paul de Man) has brought out the seriousness and difficulty of Hölderlin's engagement with problems of language, mediation, and death. Finally, while Hölderlin is probably the most "ancient Greek" of all modern Western writers, he is not a "German classicist" as literary historians understand this term. Rather, he breaks with literary history in anticipating the Dionysiac Friedrich Wilhelm Nietzsche (1844–1900), the German expressionist Georg Trakl (1887–1914), and the postapocalyptic Paul Celan (1920–1970). He has become the most internationally influential German poet of the last two centuries, surpassing even Rainer Maria Rilke (1875–1926), and he is arguably the German language's greatest poet.

See also **Fichte, Johann Gottlieb; Germany; Hegel, Georg Wilhelm Friedrich; Novalis (Hardenberg, Friedrich von).**

BIBLIOGRAPHY

Primary Sources

Hölderlin, Friedrich. *Sämtliche Werke.* Edited by Friedrich Beissner et al. 8 vols. Stuttgart, 1943–1985.

———. *Hymns and Fragments.* Translated by Richard Sieburth. Princeton, N.J., 1984.

———. *Hyperion.* Translated by Willard Trask. New York, 1965.

———. *Poems and Fragments.* Translated by Michael Hamburger. London, 1966.

———. *Sämtliche Werke.* Edited by D. S. Sattler et al. 18 vols. to date. Frankfurt, 1975–present. Complete works.

———. *Essays and Letters on Theory.* Translated and edited by Thomas Pfau. New York, 1988.

Secondary Sources

Fioretos, Aris, ed. *The Solid Letter: Readings of Friedrich Hölderlin.* Stanford, Calif., 1999. A selection of post-Heideggerian interpretations, with an extensive bibliography of Hölderlin scholarship and translations in English.

Heidegger, Martin. *Erläuterungen zu Hölderlins Dichtung.* 4th ed. Frankfurt, 1971. The commentaries.

TIMOTHY BAHTI

HOLY ALLIANCE. The term *Holy Alliance* refers to several related phenomena. In the narrowest sense, the Holy Alliance was a treaty signed in Paris on 26 September 1815 by the emperors Francis I of Austria (also ruled as Francis II, Holy Roman Emperor), Alexander I of Russia, and Prussian king Frederick William III "in the name of the Most Holy and Indivisible Trinity." More broadly, the treaty represented an attempt by its composer, Alexander I, to establish new principles for international and domestic politics in Europe following the Napoleonic Wars. By the early 1820s, the expression came to mean the reactionary policies pursued by the three "eastern" empires against the threats of social and national revolution that persisted after the Napoleonic era. Despite occasional conflicts among the allies, this conservative coalition endured as a bulwark of the international order until 1854, during the Crimean War.

The "Holy Alliance of Sovereigns of Austria, Prussia, and Russia" departed from convention in emphasizing an overarching vision of international relations rather than concrete mutual obligations among the signers. The opening paragraph stated that the three sovereigns had recognized the "necessity" of basing their relations "upon the sublime truths which the Holy Religion of our Saviour teaches." They had reached this recognition during the preceding three years, when "Divine Providence" had showered blessings upon "those States which place their confidence and their hope on it alone." The treaty's only object was to announce that the allies would take guidance from Christianity's "precepts of Justice, Christian Charity, and Peace" in their domestic administration and relations with other states. As the text stated, Christianity must apply not only to "private concerns" but must also exercise "an immediate influence on the councils of Princes" as the only way to consolidate and improve "human institutions."

With these stipulations, the treaty then laid out three articles. The first stated that, following "holy Scriptures," the three rulers would be united by "a true and indissoluble fraternity," regarding one another as compatriots, obligated to help one another "on all occasions and in all places." They also pledged to act as "fathers of families" in relation to their subjects and armies, leading them in a "spirit of fraternity," to defend "Religion, Peace, and Justice." Article II declared that the only principle governing relations among the governments and their subjects "shall be that of doing each other reciprocal service." All rulers and subjects would regard themselves as "members of one and the same Christian nation." Thus, the monarchs would consider themselves as "merely delegated by Providence" to rule "three branches of the One family," since the Christian world had "no other Sovereign than Him to whom alone power really belongs." Additionally, the three rulers would advise their people to strengthen themselves in Christian principles and duties. The third article invited all powers recognizing the "sacred principles which have dictated the present Act" to join "this Holy Alliance."

The treaty had originated in the "great events which have marked the course of the three last years in Europe," a reference to a period in which Alexander had undergone an intense spiritual and political crisis that revolutionized the Russian ruler's understanding of politics and history. Napoleon's invasion of Russia in June 1812 and occupation of Moscow that autumn had confronted the Russian emperor with a mortal threat to his throne. Alexander defied his enemies' expectations by refusing to parley with Napoleon's representatives. By 19 October, events in Spain

obliged Napoleon and his forces to evacuate Moscow and retrace their invasion route, crossing Russia's western border in mid-December, badly depleted by harsh winter weather, partisan detachments, and the following Russian army led by Prince Mikhail Kutuzov and Alexander. Having expelled the usurper from Russia, Alexander defied his advisors and allies by embarking on an all-out campaign to dethrone Napoleon. At the head of a broadening alliance, Alexander liberated the German lands in 1813 and led an international army into Paris at the beginning of April 1814. When the victorious allies—led by Russia, Great Britain, Austria, and Prussia—gathered at the Congress of Vienna in the fall of 1814, Alexander's power and influence had reached their zenith.

The turnabout in Alexander's fortunes reinforced an equally profound shift in his religious views. Previously an Enlightenment freethinker, Alexander had found consolation in Bible reading during the Napoleonic invasion at the prompting of his friend Prince Alexander Golitsyn. Golitsyn and others at court, including Roxandra Sturdza, soon introduced Alexander to a developing vein of Christian mysticism that had arisen in the Germanies among Catholics and Pietist Protestants alike. Such thinkers as Franz von Baader, Jakob Böhme, and Johann Jung-Stilling (whom Alexander visited in July 1814) saw the upheaval of the current age as the precursor to a new epoch of enlightenment and harmony under God's guidance. This new regime would replace the decadent old order destroyed by the French Revolution and the Napoleonic Wars. By the time he reached Vienna for the peace conference, Alexander seemed to believe that God had chosen him as the instrument for the creation of a new order of things. Many attributed this view to Baroness Barbara Juliane von Krüdener, an "awakened" Lutheran from Livonia who figured very visibly in Alexander's entourage.

The Holy Alliance embodied Alexander's vision of the new international order. Its promulgation followed the deliberations of the Vienna congress, where Alexander's efforts to reshape Europe's territorial arrangements—especially in regard to Poland and Germany—had faced strong resistance from Lord Castlereagh, the British ambassador, Austrian chancellor Clemens von

Metternich, and the French representative Charles-Maurice de Talleyrand. The treaty's high-flown language inspired bemusement from Castlereagh, who called it "sublime mysticism and nonsense," while Metternich dismissed it as "a loud-sounding nothing." The latter, however, requiring Alexander's support in other matters, agreed to sign the document alongside Prussia. Britain's prince regent politely declined to adhere, while the Ottoman sultan (ruler of a considerable Christian population in the Balkans) and the pope were not invited to take part. Contemporaries and later historians saw in the Alliance a cover for Russian designs on European dominance, yet Alexander's own correspondence with friends and advisors suggests that he took his transformative mission very seriously.

Alexander's original vision for the Holy Alliance became more concrete after the Vienna congress, especially as unrest continued to challenge the post-Napoleonic settlement in Italy, Spain, and central Europe. In particular, Alexander showed a growing concern for the maintenance of domestic order, within the post-Vienna states (often restored monarchies), in addition to promoting harmony among them. These emphases solidified in the course of a series of international congresses among the leading European powers: at Aix-la-Chapelle in 1818, Troppau in late 1820, and Laibach in early 1821. At Aix, Alexander aroused British and Austrian opposition by urging the victorious allied Great Powers, now joined by Restoration France, to establish concrete terms for joint action in guaranteeing the new status quo. The British objected to the principle of intervention, while Metternich wished to avoid the reappearance of Russian troops in Europe, following their recent evacuation of France. By late 1820, however, Metternich moved closer to Alexander's interventionist position for the maintenance of order in Europe, as unrest broke out across the Continent, including nationalist agitation in Germany and Italy, as well as rebellions in Spain, Portugal, and Greece. Alexander himself moved closer to Metternich's legitimism at this time, following the October mutiny by his beloved Semyonovsky regiment in St. Petersburg, which he saw as a sign of a revived spirit of revolution that he had conquered only six years earlier.

At Troppau and Laibach, the Holy Alliance took on new form as a coalition comprising Russia,

Austria, and Prussia—often opposed by Britain and France—united in their claim that defense of the "monarchical principle" justified intervention against any and all rebellion. Alexander's ideal of a new international order had thus become a reactionary weapon against all apprehended disorder, as Austrian troops suppressed rebellion in Italy while the allies imposed a conservative regime on the German states. This new orientation was reinforced in 1825 when Alexander was succeeded by Nicholas I, who shared his brother's hatred of disorder, if not his mysticism. Until the 1850s, the allies acted whenever they could against threats to the political status quo: against revolution in Poland in 1830–1831, against constitutionalism in the Germanies before 1848, and against revolutionary Hungary in 1849.

Nonetheless, general ideological accord masked deeper-lying and more practical tensions that ultimately broke the alliance in the 1850s. Austro-Prussian contention for dominance in the German lands became particularly acute after the revolutions of 1848, while chronic ferment in the Ottoman Balkans led to Austrian fears of Russia in that arena. These latter concerns compelled the Austrian government to support—with Prussia's assent—Britain, France, and the Ottoman Empire in the Crimean War. This fundamental shift in Austrian policy ended the Holy Alliance and inaugurated an enduring Austro-Russian rivalry that culminated sixty years later in the outbreak of World War I.

See also **Austria-Hungary; Congress of Vienna; Conservatism; Crimean War; French Revolutionary Wars and Napoleonic Wars; Prussia; Russia.**

BIBLIOGRAPHY

Primary Sources

Hertslet, Edward, ed. "Text of the Holy Alliance." In *The Map of Europe by Treaty: Political and Territorial Changes since the General Peace of 1814.* London, 1875.

Secondary Sources

Hartley, Janet. *Alexander I.* London and New York, 1994.

Martin, Alexander. *Romantics, Reformers, Reactionaries: Russian Conservative Thought and Politics in the Reign of Alexander I.* DeKalb, Ill., 1997.

Rich, Norman. *Great Power Diplomacy, 1814–1914.* New York, 1992.

Schroeder, Paul W. *The Transformation of European Politics, 1763–1848.* Oxford, U.K., 1994.

Zorin, Andrei. "Star of the East: The Holy Alliance and European Mysticism." *Kritika* (spring 2003): 314–342.

DAVID MCDONALD

Count Robert de Montesquiou. Portrait by Giovanni Boldini, 1897. The count, who divided his time between the turn-of-the-century homosexual underworld and the high society of Paris, probably served as the model for Marcel Proust's Baron Charlus. MUSÉE D'ORSAY, PARIS, FRANCE/LAUROS/GIRAUDON/BRIDGEMAN ART LIBRARY

HOMOSEXUALITY AND LESBIANISM.

The word *homosexuality* dates from 1868 and 1869 when first used by Karl Maria Kertbeny (1824–1882), a German-speaking writer and journalist of Hungarian descent, in a private letter and two anonymous tracts criticizing the law code of the North German Confederation. It reappeared in print only in 1880 and did not really catch on for another fifteen years. Kertbeny was not alone in wanting to devise a term for same-sex desire that carried no connotation of religious or legal condemnation. For instance, Karl Heinrich Ulrichs (1825–1895) came up with *Uranianism* (mid-1860s), Karl Westphal (1833–1890) with *contrary sexual feeling* (1869), Arrigo Tamassia (1849–1917) with *inversion of the sexual instinct* (1878), and Marc-André Raffalovich (1864–1934) with *unisexuality* (1896). By the century's end, someone of either sex who felt same-sex desire was most commonly called an *invert* or *homosexual.* Earlier terms, such as *sodomite* or *pederast* for a man and *tribade* or *Sapphist* for a woman, faded from use (without entirely disappearing), although *lesbian* has remained current.

Michel Foucault (1926–1984) has famously contended that by the very act of naming the homosexual, science literally created a new being. Social constructionists follow Foucault by theorizing that before the 1870s someone who committed a stigmatized sexual act might be a sinner or a criminal but otherwise had no particular sexual identity. The newly named homosexual, in contrast, was perceived—and came to perceive himself or herself—as a distinct social and psychological type with a specific (generally pathological) personality. Although social constructionism informs much of the research on nineteenth-century homosexuality, the historical record is more subtle, complex, and ambiguous than this approach allows for. There are indications in police, judicial, and medical sources that men and women who felt same-sex desire had already begun to develop an embryonic sense of identity well before 1870.

THE LAW

In legal terms, sodomy included all nonprocreative sexual acts between any two people, but referred most specifically to anal penetration of one man by another (buggery). The usual penalty for sodomy in early modern Europe was death, although executions were rare by the eighteenth century, except in Britain and the Dutch United Provinces. Women almost never faced prosecution for same-sex activity unless they cross-dressed to pass themselves off as men or used a dildo to penetrate their partner. The prosecution of twelve women for "sodomitical filthiness" in a series of Dutch trials in the 1790s was therefore highly unusual and moreover pales in significance compared to the prosecution for sodomy of one thousand or more men in the same United Provinces between 1730 and 1811.

In the late eighteenth and early nineteenth centuries, most European states reduced the penalty for sodomy to a prison term and some decriminalized it altogether. The last execution for the crime on the Continent took place in the United Provinces in 1803. Britain stopped hanging sodomites in 1835, although sodomy remained a capital offense there until 1861, when Parliament lowered the penalty to prison for ten years to life, which was still much higher than anywhere else in Europe. In addition, the Labouchère Amendment to the Criminal Law Amendment Act of 1885 outlawed "any act of gross indecency" between male persons, whether in public or private. Like most other law codes, British law failed to mention sex between women. There is an improbable tale that this was because Queen Victoria herself could not believe women capable of such depravity. In fact, it would seem that Victorian society as a whole had difficulty conceptualizing an autonomous female sexuality that required repression. In Prussia, sex between two females had been covered by the criminal code until 1851, but an attempt in 1909 to extend antihomosexual legislation in the German Empire to women because of "the danger for the life of the family and the youth" posed by lesbianism bogged down over the difficulty of defining what precise sexual acts should be declared illicit.

France was the first country to decriminalize same-sex acts in 1791. Napoleon enshrined this reform in the penal code of 1810 and spread its principles to many of the nations he conquered. Bavaria, under the influence of its own reforming jurists, decriminalized sodomy in 1813, and several German states followed Bavaria's example. Sodomy remained a criminal offense in Prussia, which eventually imposed its criminal law on the North German Confederation in 1869 and the German Empire in 1871. Even where sodomy was a crime, however, prosecutions were relatively few (but reliable statistics are lacking). Conversely, in states with no penalty at all for sodomy, the police still used laws against public indecency to harass those men who solicited sex or engaged in sexual relations in public spaces. Courts often defined public space broadly enough to include places where no actual witness was present or where a third party could not possibly see anything.

THE SUBCULTURE

It is impossible to know the number of male and female homosexuals in nineteenth-century Europe. Contemporary estimates, which ranged from 0.002 to 4.0 percent of the population, were little more than guesses, but observers could not fail to notice a considerable homosexual presence in the biggest cities. Rightly or wrongly, most believed that there were more male than female homosexuals, in part because of their own preconceptions about female purity and in part because the men were simply more publicly visible. Homosexuality and lesbianism were often considered symptomatic of the physical degeneration and mental exhaustion brought on by the hectic pace of urban life. In reality, of course, only in cities, with large populations and the possibility of anonymity, could extensive homosexual and lesbian subcultures flourish (which does not mean that clandestine same-sex activity did not also occur in small towns and rural areas). Networks of friendship based on shared same-sex interests among men and women are hard to reconstruct, but police reports, trial records, and newspaper stories have enabled historians to uncover a great deal about male homosexual subcultures. In London, Paris, Berlin, Munich, and Rome—and many lesser towns and cities as well—male prostitutes openly walked the streets, while men searched for sexual partners in parks, gardens, and squares, and around public urinals. They also frequented specialized bars and cafés, boardinghouses and hotels, and restaurants and bathhouses that served a predominantly or exclusively male homosexual clientele, and they regularly attended private parties and large public drag balls, especially during the carnival season.

While historians of male homosexuality emphasize sexual activities, historians of lesbianism have more usually focused on the strong emotional bonds that united many nineteenth-century women in so-called romantic friendships in which the erotic element was not always explicit, if it even existed at all. For example, most (but not all) contemporaries believed that "the Ladies of Llangollen"—Lady Eleanor Butler (1739–1829) and Sarah Ponsonby

(1755–1831), who lived together in Wales from 1780—led a pure (meaning sexless) life. The poet William Wordsworth celebrated them as "sisters in love." Similarly, the French painter Rosa Bonheur (1822–1899) described herself and her lifelong companion as "two women [who] can feel for each other the charm of a vibrant and passionate friendship, without anything altering its purity." On the other hand, the English gentlewoman Anne Lister (1791–1840) left to posterity a coded diary covering the period from 1817 to 1840, revealing herself as a rather mannish woman who flirted with, seduced, and had sex with numerous women in both England and France. She also had a clear sense of her "oddity" (her own word): "I love and only love the fairer sex and … my heart revolts from any love but theirs."

By the end of the century, lesbianism was far more common than most contemporaries realized. Even in Russia in the 1890s, for instance, the gynecologist Ippolit Tarnovsky (1833–1899) reported cases of same-sex desire in cities and villages among women of all social classes. Fairly open and self-conscious lesbian subcultures flourished in Paris and possibly in other major cities as well. In Paris these ranged from the well-known circle of wealthy intellectual women around Natalie Barney (1876–1972) and her lover Renée Vivien (1877–1909) down to the city's overlooked and often-forgotten working-class lesbians, including (but not limited to) prostitutes and prisoners. Parisian lesbians also frequented their own special venues; indeed, from the 1880s onward certain bars and cabarets in the Montmartre district became notorious for their lesbian clientele.

PUBLIC ATTITUDES

One indicator of prevalent social attitudes toward homosexuality is public reaction when scandals broke. In 1824, for example, after a beating at the hands of some soldiers exposed the homosexuality of the aristocratic French writer Astolphe de Custine (1790–1857), high society turned its back on him. By the 1870s the mass-circulation press was bringing such scandals to the attention of millions. The most notable of these were the trial (and acquittal) of the transvestite prostitutes Ernest Boulton and Frederick Park in London in 1871; the Cleveland Street scandal of 1889 to 1890, involving a male brothel in London that catered to the upper classes; the trial and conviction of Oscar Wilde (1854–1900) for gross indecency in 1895; the conviction of Baron Jacques d'Adelswärd-Fersen (1880–1923) in 1903 for corrupting adolescent boys in Paris; and the Eulenburg affair of 1907 to 1908, which centered on accusations of homosexuality leveled by a journalist against Kaiser William II's friend and advisor, Count Philipp zu Eulenburg (1847–1921).

The increased public awareness of and concern over homosexuality was a reflection of fin-de-siècle anxieties. Elite male privilege faced new challenges from feminism, socialism, and even homosexual visibility, and nationalists everywhere worried about the fatal consequences for their country of the cultural decadence, physical degeneration, and declining virility that they imagined all around them. With feminist demands for education, careers, and political rights seemingly threatening to destabilize the traditional family, some men suspected that feminism was little more than a lesbian plot. Newspapers regularly carried stories implying that same-sex desire endangered society, while satirical reviews published essays and caricatures poking fun at effeminate pretty boys who giggled, minced, and gossiped and at mannish lesbians who dressed in trousers and smoked. The stereotypes of lesbians and homosexual men propagated in this way in the 1890s and early 1900s would endure another hundred years in the popular imagination. Paradoxically, despite the overtly hostile tone, all this press coverage, by presenting homosexuality as just one more aspect of modern urban life, may ultimately have contributed to its normalization. The press also made many isolated homosexuals and lesbians aware that they were not alone, and in this way inadvertently helped forge a stronger sense of identity.

MEDICINE

Medicine, too, shared in the growing preoccupation with homosexuality. Starting in the 1790s, forensic doctors were the first to study same-sex acts, because courts relied on their testimony to prove that sexual relations had occurred between men. They examined the body for physical evidence of sodomy, such as a misshapen penis or a dilated anus. (They paid less attention to women, who rarely committed sex crimes and whose sexual

Lesbians in a restaurant. Illustration by Paul Balluriau in the French journal *Gil Blas*, 14 October 1894. MARY EVANS PICTURE LIBRARY

activities with each other left no discoverable trace on the body.) By the latter half of the century, doctors and especially psychiatrists were going further and trying to understand the personality of the homosexual and the lesbian in order to establish whether same-sex desire constituted an anomaly, a pathology, or a mental disorder. The new concept of "inversion" implied a discrepancy between an individual's physical sex and his or her subjective gender identity. Male homosexuals were held to be essentially feminine in character and comportment; conversely, lesbians were considered masculine.

By the 1870s most psychiatrists and sexologists distinguished between "congenital inverts" who had an inborn gender anomaly and those inverts who "acquired" their condition for various reasons: excessive timidity with the opposite sex; time spent in isolation from the other sex in prison, the army, or the church; seduction by a predatory homosexual or lesbian; or simply the search for new and exotic pleasures to satisfy a jaded appetite.

Most doctors agreed that it was pointless to repress congenital inverts—although the Italian criminologist Cesare Lombroso (1835–1909) urged that they be imprisoned as "a source of contagion"—but many persisted in their efforts to cure acquired inversion. Eventually in the 1890s, however, some sexologists, such as Richard Von Krafft-Ebing (1840–1902) and Albert Moll (1862–1939) in Germany and Havelock Ellis (1859–1939) in England, concluded on the basis of interviews and investigations that homosexuality was not a disease, that homosexuals and lesbians could lead productive and respectable lives, and that the search for a cure should be given up along with all repressive legislation. Sigmund Freud (1856–1939) went even further with his theory of "universal bisexuality" first brought forward in 1905. According to Freud, all human beings are born "polymorphously perverse" and seek pleasure orally, anally, and genitally with sexual objects of either sex; as they mature into adulthood, however, most repress their latent desires and manifest a preference for reproductive genital sexual activity with a partner of the opposite sex. For Freud, homosexuals and lesbians did not constitute a distinctly different *third sex* (to use a common late-nineteenth-century term) but were ordinary men and women who remained stuck in an early stage of development. Defenders of same-sex desire were no longer limited to their traditional evocation of the glories of the homoerotic culture of Ancient Greece; they now had scientific arguments in their arsenal.

IN DEFENSE OF HOMOSEXUALITY

Those who defended homosexuals or lesbians against prejudice and the law always knew that they risked being taken for one themselves. The English philosopher Jeremy Bentham (1748–1832) wrote hundreds of pages over a fifty-year period defending same-sex relations but was never brave enough to publish them. Apart from pornography, the first published defense of homosexuality was by an obscure Swiss milliner, Heinrich Hössli (1784–1864). Hössli's two-volume *Eros: The Male Love of the Greeks* (1836–1838) was a rambling plea for toleration on the grounds that the historical record proved same-sex love to be entirely natural. The German jurist Karl Heinrich Ulrichs (1825–1895) brought out *Vindex: Social and Legal Studies in Man-Manly Love* in 1864 under the pseudonym Numa Numantius. He put forward the theory that male homosexuals had a female soul locked in a male body. Ulrichs also called for the decriminalization of homosexuality in a speech at the Congress of German Jurists in Munich in August 1867. The German sexologist Magnus Hirschfeld (1868–1935) founded the world's first homosexual rights organization, the Scientific-Humanitarian Committee, in Berlin in 1897. He also published (from 1899) the *Yearbook for Sexual Intermediate Types* to educate the public and lobby for the repeal of antihomosexual legislation. Adolf Brand (1874–1945), another German, published *The Special* from 1896 and founded the Community of the Special in 1903 to revive "Hellenic standards after centuries of Christian barbarism." The only other organization of this kind in Europe was the British Society for the Study of Sex Psychology, established in 1913 to work more broadly toward greater sexual freedom and law reform.

On the eve of World War I, then, Europe's semiclandestine homosexual and lesbian subcultures had assumed the shape they would have for the next three generations, until radical gay liberation emerged in the 1970s and openly gay and lesbian lifestyles appeared in the 1980s, bringing into being a very different "gay" world.

See also **Bentham, Jeremy; Ellis, Havelock; Freud, Sigmund; Krafft-Ebing, Richard von; Hirschfeld, Magnus; Lombroso, Cesare; Marriage and Family; Prostitution; Psychology; Public Health; Sexuality; Symonds, John Addington; Ulrichs, Karl Heinrich; Wilde, Oscar.**

BIBLIOGRAPHY

Cocks, H. G. *Nameless Offences: Homosexual Desire in the Nineteenth Century.* London, 2003.

Cook, Matt. *London and the Culture of Homosexuality, 1885–1914.* Cambridge, U.K., 2003.

Faderman, Lillian. *Surpassing the Love of Men: Romantic Friendship and Love between Women from the Renaissance to the Present.* New York, 1981.

Fone, Byrne. *Homophobia: A History.* New York, 2000.

Lauritsen, John, and David Thorstad. *The Early Homosexual Rights Movement (1864–1935).* New York, 1974.

Mosse, George L. *Nationalism and Sexuality: Respectability and Abnormal Sexuality in Modern Europe.* New York, 1985.

Peniston, William A. *Pederasts and Others: Urban Culture and Sexual Identity in Nineteenth-Century Paris.* New York, 2004.

Robb, Graham. *Strangers: Homosexual Love in the Nineteenth Century.* London, 2003.

Steakley, James D. *The Homosexual Emancipation Movement in Germany.* New York, 1975.

van Casselaer, Catherine. *Lot's Wife: Lesbian Paris, 1890–1914.* Liverpool, U.K., 1986.

Vicinus, Martha. *Intimate Friends: Women who Loved Women, 1778–1928.* Chicago and London, 2004.

MICHAEL SIBALIS

HOUSING. Nineteenth-century Europe witnessed remarkable improvements in housing, but the benefits of new building were not equally shared. For Europe's growing middle classes, suburbs offered new possibilities for family life and individual privacy, while the outfitting of homes fueled the new consumer economy. The middle-class home came to exemplify, in theory if not always in practice, a transformation in Europe's physical and moral landscape. For the majority of workers, however, Europe's demographic and industrial revolutions ushered in a century of residential dislocation and difficult living conditions. Indeed, what middle-class reformers referred to as the "housing question" was in fact a housing crisis of immense proportions, brought on by factors beyond the control of individuals or governments. The failure of individuals and governments to meet the persistent demand for housing laid the basis for government intervention in the early decades of following century.

POPULATION GROWTH AND URBANIZATION
Population growth and rapid urbanization were the underlying factors behind Europe's housing shortage in the nineteenth century. With the decline in mortality rates after about 1780, Europe's population began to increase. Between 1800 and 1850 population grew from an estimated 205 million to 275 million. By 1900 Europe's population was more than twice that of 1800, or 414 million. This demographic increase fueled industrialization and urbanization throughout Europe, most notably in Britain. In 1801 the population of England

Tenement houses in the Santa Lucia quarter of Naples, c. 1890. ©ALINARI ARCHIVES/CORBIS

and Wales was 38 percent urban. By 1851 that figure had increased to 54 percent, and by 1881, 70 percent. By 1900 London's population (6.5 million) was nearly twice that of Paris (3.3 million). Berlin (2.4 million) and Vienna (1.7 million) also housed large populations, but Britain commanded the highest urban densities, with Manchester, Birmingham, and Glasgow all reaching above one million by 1900, while France's rural exodus would not occur until well into the twentieth century.

In every major city, urban developments, suburbs, and mass commuter transportation in particular, transformed the social landscape. European cities were no longer what urban historians call "walking cities," in which noble rentiers, bourgeois professionals, artisans, domestics, and unskilled day laborers all lived in the same neighborhoods, and often within the same multistory dwellings. The social diversity of walking cities began to give way when, between 1780 and 1830, a growing number of families, spurred on by developers and a desire for increased living space, built "suburban" villas

on converted farmlands on the urban periphery. With the appearance of general contractors (as early as 1790 in Britain), such developments increasingly involved the subdivision and development of entire tracts of land. Railway construction added to this trend and, after 1850, urban peripheries became full-blown streetcar suburbs, allowing ever-increasing numbers of middle-class (and some skilled artisan) families to flee the city. For most workers, however, the new suburbs remained beyond their reach. Unskilled workers in particular could not afford the cost of daily commuting. Since much employment was irregular or seasonal, most working-class families tended to reside in close proximity to sources of employment.

Rural and urban industrialization, along with significant changes in agricultural production, meant that the working and residential lives of most Europeans were in a constant state of transition. Many workers engaged in both rural and urban occupations on a seasonal basis, often preempting the possibility of owning or even renting their own home in a fixed community. With the expansion of large-scale industrial factories (and later, department stores), the role of cottage industries and sweatshops actually expanded as sources of employment for working men, women, and children. In both rural and urban areas, housing became increasingly scarce for this segment of Europe's working population. In response to this situation, from the early decades of the century, paternalistic employers in the emerging textiles, mining, and iron (and later, steel) industries, and even some department store owners, provided worker housing, in some cases creating veritable "company towns." The minority of workers able to secure these forms of housing fared better than the majority who could not. Whether company housing or urban tenement, it was not at all uncommon for workers to share their living space with extended family, coworkers, or even strangers. Pooling meager resources was one strategy for surviving a high-rent housing market, especially in urban centers.

Scholars interested in the comparative history of suburbanization have often distinguished between an "Anglo-American" model, in which middle-class residents fled the urban center to create new, socially segregated neighborhoods on the urban periphery, and a "Continental" model, in which working-class families were cast to the periphery in order to make way for gentrified (often quite wealthy) neighborhoods in the urban center. Napoleon III's (r. 1852–1871) Paris has provided the most notorious case for the latter. Under the guidance of the prefect Georges-Eugène Haussmann (1809–1891), and in the name of public order and public health, a combination of large government subsidies and speculative lending were used to demolish working-class slums in order to make way for wide avenues (the better to maneuver troops and artillery into the city center, and to connect traffic to nearby rail terminals) and the immense, bourgeois apartment blocks that lined them. Many workers were pushed to the new industrial zones on the northern and eastern edge of the city, where housing was often makeshift, while those remaining in the city found their living quarters increasingly cramped and their rents high. In imitation, Brussels, Vienna, and Budapest each embarked on their own "Haussmannization" policies, as did Lyon, Marseille, and a few other provincial French cities, though on a far more modest scale. These examples aside, suburbanization on the Continent could also resemble the Anglo-American model in many respects, especially by the period 1900–1914. In much of Germany, where professional urban planning was employed more than in any other European country, town extensions were greatly preferred over the rebuilding of urban centers. And on the southern and western periphery of Paris, where only a century earlier aristocratic villas had dotted an agricultural landscape, dense and solidly middle-class suburbs like Coubevoie and Neuilly-sur-Seine emerged in a continuous arc of comfort and privacy.

Most new building, whether in Britain or on the Continent, was the work of private hands, especially land developers and local builders, and relied very little on government-directed planners. The type of housing developers built usually involved a combination of factors, including existing local vernacular forms, property values, the availability and cost of investment capital, municipal regulations and building codes, and the internal dynamics of the local building industry. The luxury apartment buildings that lined the avenues of Haussmann's Paris and Vienna's "Ring" were

exceptions that proved the rule. The same could be said of the Hampstead Garden suburb, outside London, which sought to overcome the monotonous drab of most new building through explicit use of landscape architecture and urban planning. Very little of the new building involved the work of architects and when it did, local reactions were more often circumspect than celebrated.

WORKING-CLASS HOUSING

With the exception of Germany, systematic planning, when employed at all, was most likely to be found in the development of company-sponsored worker housing. It is true that, in many cases, including the industrialist Robert Owen's "cooperative" factory village at New Lanark, Scotland, employers usually sought to impose moral discipline on workers as well as control their movements. But these experiments often improved worker living conditions in measurable ways. In Ireland during the 1840s, the Quaker John Richardson built a picturesque company town for workers at his linen mill. Similarly, at Essen in the 1860s, the Krupp works erected attractive, low-density housing for its workers, in a planned residential zone complete with parks, recreational areas, and shared facilities. While such instances were indeed remarkable and occasionally successful, they were exceedingly rare. Most company housing consisted of cheaply constructed dwellings, often without adequate heating or proper sanitation facilities. Overcrowding was common, as was the tendency of some owners to use a combination of low wages, high rents, and high-priced company stores to bind workers financially to their creditor-employers.

In urban areas, workers were often forced to reside in slumlike conditions. With relatively little new construction or renovation taking place in urban working-class neighborhoods, workers in these areas tended to live in increasingly dilapidated buildings, in which five or six individuals might share a small one- or two-room apartment. In the second half of the century, retailers, commercial interests and especially railroads were—in Haussmannesque fashion—displacing workers through demolition and eviction. In England, some four thousand workers were displaced in this way between 1850 and 1900.

Two women outside a rural cottage, northern Ireland, c. 1903. ©CORBIS

Conditions were somewhat better for skilled workers who could more often afford to rent one of the newer dwellings, which took a variety of forms across Europe. In England and Scotland, new worker housing often took the form of terraces and tenements. But self-contained cottages were also common in England and Wales and on the Continent in Belgium. As at Glasgow, France's major cities (Paris, Lyon, and Marseille) tended to house their workers in tenements. By contrast, workers in provincial cities like Bordeaux, Amiens, and Lille often resided in terraced or detached houses, or two-family flats. Compared to both England and the United States, these French dwellings tended to have fewer rooms and less "private" space. English workers often had their own yards, while kitchens, bedrooms, living rooms, and parlors all were separate. Even the "back-to-backs" of Yorkshire (so called because these units shared a back wall) had by 1900 achieved greater privacy by locating toilet facilities in the basement. With the exception of Bremen, where single-family worker housing was common, the family life of German workers usually revolved around the two or three rooms they inhabited in the ever-present six-flat tenement.

MIDDLE-CLASS HOUSING

The middle-class professionals, white collar workers, and artisans who inhabited the new houses and apartments being built throughout Europe experienced a greater share of comfort, privacy, and functionality in their daily lives. Comfort came through new developments in furniture design, as well as new production and distribution methods that made upholstered furnishings available to a wider range of consumers. Comfort also came through developments in indoor heating, plumbing, and, toward the end of the nineteenth century, electricity. With the decline in fertility among Europe's middle classes, individuals living in newer homes were more likely to have, if not a room of their own, a degree of living space and privacy unimaginable by most Europeans in any previous century. Living spaces within wealthier middle-class homes also became increasingly specialized. Here, separate bedrooms, parlor, game room, boudoir, library, dining room, pantry, and kitchen each served a particular function, with hallways clearly separating public and private activities. This new setting provided an intimate stage on which new modes of family life and ideas about the proper roles of men and women in society were played out or resisted.

By the end of the century, only a modest number of workers (usually skilled) benefited from these new amenities. Demand for new worker housing remained high, but the incentives for investors, in the absence of government intervention, remained low. The key was "regularity of income," which many workers, especially the unskilled, did not enjoy. As one historian has observed, "Suburbs gave access to the cheapest land to those with the greatest security of employment and with leisure to enjoy it." For the unskilled, low wages, inconsistent employment, and the need to reside within walking distance to work (usually no more than 1.5 miles) translated into high rents and high rates of poverty in the most congested housing districts. For example, with the flight of its middle classes, the *Marais* district of Paris, which had long been a bastion of elite living on the right bank of central Paris, changed considerably after 1850. The lack of open sites, restrictive building regulations, and the quickening pace of middle-class desertion brought a dramatic reduction in new construction in the *Marais*—this at a time when the working-class population density of central Paris was twice that of London. As in Britain, where laissez-faire conditions largely drove the housing market, Parisian

investors chose to build upscale housing for bourgeois elites, the middle classes, and skilled workers, all far more likely to meet their rent obligations than the unskilled working poor.

LANDLORD-TENANT CONFLICT

Perpetual overcrowding, high rents, and absentee ownership often resulted in conflict between workers and building managers. Large tenements especially, in which complex layers of ownership created distance between owners and tenants, had a high potential for poor management. Scottish tenements became increasingly associated with social tensions and political conflict. This was largely the result of a rigid system of annual leases that provided no flexibility for workers—in a labor market in which work contracts were often of short duration. Through a law of 1911, Scotland joined most European cities in guaranteeing more flexible leases. Indeed, in much of Britain, landlord-tenant conflict was endemic, and especially so after 1890. This is perhaps no surprise, given that per capita wages in England increased only about 7 percent in the years from 1895 to 1913, as compared to 107 percent for the preceding thirty-five years. To be sure, in tenements where a resident caretaker was employed—in Paris, the *concierge* played this role, as sometimes a husband or wife did, if the tenement was family-owned—the probability of conflict was reduced. In Vienna, however, a city in which half of all tenement owners in 1910 resided on their properties, rent strikes broke out the following year, and worker housing became a major issue for the Social Democratic Party. Throughout Europe, by the turn of the twentieth century, rent strikes were increasingly common, the result of ever-higher rents resulting from chronic housing shortages.

THE "HOUSING QUESTION"

Middle-class reactions to the dramatic rise in urban populations, particularly the squalid conditions many workers faced in the first half of the century, took several directions. As we have seen, a handful of reformers, utopians, and business owners attempted to ameliorate worker housing conditions through the building of experimental, planned communities. More commonly, however, the perceptions of middle-class observers toward the living conditions of European workers were highly colored by increasingly bitter relations between workers and

Tyninghame House, Haddington, Scotland. The mansion, with its extensive grounds, was the home of the Earls of Haddington. ©BETTMANN/CORBIS

employers, and worker struggles to win greater political rights and improved working conditions. In this context, the working classes came to be seen as the dangerous classes. Moreover, bourgeois observers could not help but notice the large numbers of workers who continued to succumb to periodic outbreaks of cholera, such as occurred in 1832, and who were susceptible to other forms of contagious disease. In the early 1880s, the Parisian hygienist Octave Du Mesnil (1832–1898) identified the city's many lodging houses as key sources of smallpox and typhoid epidemics. In France and elsewhere, moral reformers, who were also eager to impose strict moral standards on their fellow bourgeois, joined public health officials in viewing the squalid conditions in which many workers lived as a direct consequence of their supposed lack of moral and religious virtue.

In some circles at least, including a growing number of municipal and state authorities, the tendency to blame the consequences of the housing shortage on

workers changed after 1880, as major critics of laissez-faire economics became more vocal and as it became obvious that privately planned housing schemes were woefully inadequate solutions to the problem. Reformers and government officials increasingly associated the housing problem with the more general one of poverty. In 1880s Paris, an array of socialist groups debated proposals for the financing of "low-rent" housing, but none managed to overcome the municipal council's staunch defense of its own autonomy against state intervention. In Britain, during the 1890s, legislative action opened the way for government intervention in worker housing through town planning, council housing, and transportation. Through the municipalities, a modest degree of control was imposed on the British housing industry. But even in Britain, this was not yet a solution. Indeed, while the "housing question" sparked much debate throughout Europe in the years before World War I, no European country found an adequate solution to the persistent gap between low worker wages and the higher rents necessary to make good housing profitable. Only in the

1920s, in the wake of the war, did municipalities take it upon themselves to fund major housing projects.

The "housing question," as it emerged and evolved in Europe during the long nineteenth century, was the product of and reflected major changes in society—from sweeping demographic change, urbanization, industrialization, and class formation, to changes in health policy, the emergence of new social thinking, and the beginnings of government intervention into the economy. As such, the "housing question" impacted the lives of the vast majority of Europeans in profound ways. Further study of these fundamental changes in housing and housing policy will improve our understanding of the many contexts that led to greater government intervention in housing during the twentieth century, as well as the technocratic impulses that often shaped these efforts. Comparative analysis and a reexamination of old arguments may also shed new light on the processes resulting in today's increasingly "suburbanized" Europe. At the end of the nineteenth century, moreover, European governments faced the daunting problem of how to overcome the persistent shortage of housing for an ever-growing population and, in urban areas especially, how to integrate the continual influx of migrants from the countryside (and other nations) into the social fabric. At the beginning of the twenty-first century, European nations face a similar problem of integration, and once again, the "housing question" presents itself as one closely associated with poverty and integration.

See also Aristocracy; Bourgeoisie; Cities and Towns; Class and Social Relations; Demography; Furniture; Public Health; Working Class.

BIBLIOGRAPHY

Bullock, Nicholas, and James Read. *The Movement for Housing Reform in Germany and France, 1840–1914.* Cambridge, U.K., and New York, 1985.

Daunton, M. J., ed. *Housing the Workers, 1850–1914: A Comparative Perspective.* London and New York, 1990.

Eleb, Monique, and Anne Debarre. *L'invention de l'habitation moderne: Paris, 1880–1914.* Paris, 1995.

Hohenberg, Paul M., and Lynn Hollen Lees. *The Making of Urban Europe, 1000–1994.* Rev. ed. Cambridge, Mass., 1985, 1995.

Perrot, Michelle, ed. *From the Fires of the Revolution to the Great War.* Volume 4 of *A History of Private Life,* general editors Philippe Ariès and Georges Duby. Cambridge, Mass., 1990.

Rodger, Richard. *Housing in Urban Britain, 1780–1914.* Cambridge, U.K., and New York, 1995.

Shapiro, Ann-Louis. *Housing the Poor of Paris, 1850–1902.* Madison, Wis., 1985.

R. DARRELL MEADOWS

HUGO, VICTOR (1802–1885), French novelist, poet, and playwright.

The complete works of Victor Hugo are vast and varied. Hugo wrote in all the major genres—poetry, drama, and prose narrative—and transformed each one of them. He was also an accomplished visual artist and an astute literary critic. Engaging fiercely with the social issues of his day, Hugo held writers to the highest standards of aesthetic force and social responsibility.

Victor-Marie Hugo was born in 1802, two years before Napoleon I (r. 1804–1814/15) named himself emperor, having defended Republican France against the coalition of European armies. By the time Hugo turned sixteen, France once again had a Bourbon king. An aspiring poet without inherited wealth (his father had been a captain in Napoleon's army), Hugo wrote odes to Louis XVIII (r. 1814–1824) and received a royal pension in appreciation. By July 1830, when a revolution established the July Monarchy (putting Louis Philippe [r. 1830–1848] on the throne) Hugo had produced two very successful books of poetry, *Odes et Ballades* (1828; Odes and ballads) and *Les Orientales* (1829; Orientalia), a work devoted to the Romantic themes of nature and exotic beauty.

Hugo had also begun to write for the theater. The preface to his first play, *Cromwell* (1827), stridently proclaimed artistic freedom from the conventions of the classical theater—rules that had been in place for centuries, concerning formal structure, appropriate vocabulary and action, and the separation of tragic and comic genres. On a Shakespearian model, *The Preface of Cromwell* called for a mixture of tragic and comic elements,

Victor Hugo. Photograph by Pierre Petit, after 1860.
Bridgeman-Giraudon/Art Resource, NY

of sublime and grotesque, and of common language and high rhetoric. *Hernani* (1830), which put theory into practice, caused a scandal. Supported by friends in the battle that erupted on opening night, Hugo triumphed, becoming the de facto leader of the young writers known as Romantics.

During the 1830s, Hugo published three major collections of poetry: *Les Feuilles d'automne* (1831; Autumn leaves), *Les Chants du crépuscule* (1835; Songs of the half-light), and *Les Voix intérieures* (1837; Inner voices). *Les Rayons et les Ombres* (Sunlight and shadows) followed in 1840. Fighting censorship and riposting stern critics, he also produced popular plays, among them *Le Roi s'amuse* (1832; The king is amused), *Lucrèce Borgia* (1833), and *Ruy Blas* (1838). The Hugo family hosted elegant parties at their apartment on the fashionable Place Royale (today the Place des Vosges) even receiving the king's son (the Duc d'Orléans), who became a personal friend. Elected

to the Académie Française in 1841, Hugo was named *pair de France* (peer) in 1845. Monarchist, celebrated lyric poet, popular playwright as well as novelist (*Notre Dame de Paris* [*The Hunchback of Notre Dame*] appeared in 1831), Hugo was at his peak during the 1840s, poised for a successful career as a conservative politician.

Two events changed his life. The first was personal: the accidental drowning of his daughter Léopoldine in 1843. Devastated by this loss, Hugo stopped writing for a number of years. The second was political: the Revolution of 1848 put an end to the July Monarchy and established the Second Republic. Hugo backed the successful conservative candidate for president, Louis Napoleon Bonaparte (later Napoleon III, r. 1851–1871), but he aggressively opposed the coup d'état of 2 December 1851, when the newly elected president declared himself emperor as his uncle had done before him. For his opposition Hugo was expelled from France. On the run, he published a violent pamphlet against the emperor, "Napoléon-le-Petit" (Napoleon the Little), thereby sealing the fate of his exile that would last nineteen years. A violent narrative poem, *Les Châtiments* (1853; Punishments), followed, excoriating the emperor, calling upon the French people to revolt against his tyranny, and invoking divine vengeance upon the usurper.

Hugo experienced exile in the Channel Islands (first Jersey, then Guernsey) as a kind of death in life. He saw himself as "not yet a cadaver, already a ghost." To pass the time he experimented with the new medium of photography, created a brilliant oeuvre of drawings, and explored various forms of mysticism, attempting to communicate with the spirit of Léopoldine. He also militated against the death penalty (having already published two important prose works on this theme, *Le dernier jour d'un condamné* [*The Last Day of a Condemned Man*] in 1829 and *Claude Gueux* in 1834). Once a month he and his family served dinner to a group of poor children from Guernsey. The former royalist had become a republican, a thundering voice of freedom and social justice.

Hugo's writing took on new power, reach and depth. *Les Contemplations* (1856; Contemplations), perhaps his greatest collection of poems, presents a memoir of the poet's soul. The work is

Victor Hugo's funeral, Paris, 1885. Hugo's stature in French society was clearly manifested in the magnificent funeral procession mounted in his honor and in the enormous number of French citizens who gathered to pay their respects. ©HULTON-DEUTSCH COLLECTION/CORBIS

divided into two parts, a before and after separated by the date of Léopoldine's death. In the second part, a range of haunting poetic voices explores themes of infinity and cosmic truth in poems of striking formal innovation. In parallel with this work, though even more ambitious, *La Légende des Siècles* (1859; The legend of the ages) presents an epic history of the human soul, tracing the progress of humanity throughout history in verse. *Les Chansons des rues et des bois* (1865; Songs from street and wood), a collection of short poems about love and nature, confirms that the exiled poet had not lost his light touch and his joy at being alive.

The premier writer of France became a property owner for the first time in the land of exile, purchasing Hauteville House with the proceeds from *Les Contemplations*. Here he wrote a major

work of criticism, *William Shakespeare* (a lucid analysis of the value and urgency of art, and of relations between aesthetic value and social utility in the nineteenth-century historical context) and many of his greatest novels. He completed *Les Misérables* (begun much earlier) in 1862. Sentimental tale, allegory of the triumph of good over evil, and searing critical analysis of social conditions during the July Monarchy, this massive novel was a hugely popular success. In *Les Travailleurs de la mer* (1866; *The Toilers of the Sea*), inspired by the rugged coast of Guernsey, Hugo places the heroic Gilliatt in epic conflict with the forces of nature at sea. *L'Homme qui rit* (1869; *The Man Who Laughs*), a brilliant novel set in seventeenth-century England, returns to themes of social injustice. Kidnapped as a child, its hero Gwynplaine has been grotesquely disfigured, an eerie smile cut into his face. Having discovered his aristocratic identity, he speaks before the House of Lords about the suffering of the oppressed; his impassioned plea for social justice, however, meets with laughter, because the smile cut into his face ironically offsets the force of his words and his tears.

In 1859 Hugo refused an offer of amnesty, declaring that he would return to France only when liberty returned. In 1870, upon the departure of Napoleon III (defeated in the Franco-Prussian War), he did so triumphantly. In 1871 Hugo was elected Deputy, on the Left, in the National Assembly of the Third Republic. His last novel, *Quatre-Vingt-Neuf* (*Ninety-Three*), was published in 1874 (the title refers to the year of revolutionary regicide and of counterrevolutionary challenge in the Vendée uprising). The novel tells a story of conflict and reconciliation that carries a contemporary message: amnesty for the Communards, whose rebellion in 1871 was violently suppressed. A poet to the end of his life—*Les Quatre Vents de l'esprit* (The four winds of the spirit) appeared in 1881, *Dieu* (God) and *La Fin de Satan* (The end of Satan), among other works, were published posthumously—Hugo died in 1885. He received a state funeral attended by two million mourning Parisians and was buried in the Panthéon.

Monumental in stature, Hugo fits uneasily into the frames of literary history. Critics who emphasize his early work consider him primarily a Romantic poet who, having introduced sophisticated innovations of tone, vocabulary, rhythm, rhyme, syntax, and theme that left subsequent poets breathless, trying to catch up with him, went out of fashion in the second half of the century. His vast epic novels, symbolic *romans poèmes* (poem novels) whose action is frequently interrupted by lengthy digressions and whose language is sometimes deceptively simple, remain largely unassimilable by critics more at home in the realist tradition. His magnificent late visionary poems are often neglected in favor of more canonically modern works. Finally, critics are often puzzled in the face of the continuous development of Hugo's immense literary talent on the one hand and the radical turn of his political perspective on the other. The fact that Hugo both dramatized his ideological reversal from royalist to republican and claimed to have been a socialist all along only makes matters more confusing. One thing is clear, however:

Hugo believed in the force of the word and the power of ideas. For him, the word is a living being, and form and content are indissolubly linked. His sophisticated conception of language (see "Réponse à un Acte d'Accusation" [Response to an accusation] in *Les Contemplations*) enabled him to fulfill the dream of modern artists: to be at once radically innovative as an artist and a writer fully engaged in the task of transforming the world.

See also **France; Lamartine, Alphonse; Napoleon III; Romanticism.**

BIBLIOGRAPHY

Bénichou, Paul. *Les Mages Romantiques.* Paris, 1988.

Brombert, Victor. *Victor Hugo and the Visionary Novel.* Cambridge, Mass., 1984

Falkayn, David. *Guide to the Life, Times and Works of Victor Hugo.* Honolulu, Hawaii, 2001.

Gaudon, Jean. *Victor Hugo, le temps de la Contemplation.* Paris, 2003.

Petrey, Sandy. *History in the Text: "Quatrevingt-Treize" and the French Revolution.* Amsterdam, 1980.

Robb, Graham. *Victor Hugo.* New York, 1999.

SUZANNE GUERLAC

HUMBOLDT, ALEXANDER AND WILHELM VON.

Wilhelm and Alexander von Humboldt were born in 1767 and 1769, respectively, the sons of a Prussian army officer who died in 1779.

ALEXANDER VON HUMBOLDT

After studying economics and then engineering, Alexander von Humboldt developed a strong interest in botany, geology, and mineralogy and began work in the mining department of the Prussian government in 1792, where he excelled in mine supervision. Soon after he began traveling extensively in Europe, where he learned the techniques of geophysical and astronomical measurement.

In 1796 he inherited sufficient funds to plan extended exploratory travels, and in June 1799 he began a five-year expedition to the Spanish colonies in Central and South America with the French botanist Aimé Bonpland. Covering more than six thousand miles, this epic voyage took Alexander von Humboldt to Peru, Venezuela, Cuba, Colombia, Mexico, Ecuador, the Canary Islands, and the United States (where he became friends with Thomas Jefferson). He finally returned to Europe in August 1804.

On this physically demanding journey, Humboldt studied many natural phenomena, including volcanoes, oceanic currents, meteor showers, indigenous flora and fauna, the length and configuration of large rivers, and variations in Earth's magnetic field. He collected some sixty thousand plant specimens, approximately 10 percent of which were unknown in Europe. He also gathered statistical information on the social and economic situation in Mexico (New Spain) and ascended a number of peaks in the Andes mountain range using only very basic climbing equipment. After returning from this extraordinary voyage, Humboldt began to plan the publication of a work that would synthesize the scientific knowledge he had accumulated, a process that would take more than twenty years and remained unfinished at the time of his death.

Many factors interrupted this enterprise, not the least of which was Humboldt's fame as an explorer. He was frequently summoned by Prussian leaders to take up diplomatic duties in various cities of Europe and was employed as a tutor to the Prussian crown prince. Favoring Paris as a city of residence, Humboldt quickly developed links with scientists and politicians such as Joseph Louis Gay-Lussac and Simón Bolívar, but after 1827 he returned to Berlin as a result of dwindling funds. He also undertook another period of overseas exploration between May and November 1829, this time traveling in the Russian Empire, where on the initiative of the Russian minister of finance he visited precious metal mines in the Urals.

Among Humboldt's practical suggestions was establishing a network of meteorological and geomagnetic stations to record weather-related information. In addition, between 1805 and 1834 he published thirty-four volumes providing an account of his Latin American journey.

Despite these sustained distractions, the first volume of Humboldt's magnum opus, *Kosmos,* was eventually published in 1845, the second in 1847, the next two in 1850 and 1858, with a fifth appearing posthumously in 1862. The aim of

Alexander von Humboldt. Portrait by Friedrich Georg Weitsch, 1806. BILDARCHIV PREUSSISCHER KULTURBESITZ/ART RESOURCE, NY

Kosmos was to provide a general assemblage of all things on Earth that constituted the perceptible world, with generalizations supported by significant factual detail. Humboldt thus attempted to give an account of the overall structure of the physical universe as it was then comprehended, from the outermost nebulae and the celestial spheres to the mosses found growing on granite rocks. He also emphasized the link between the imaginative arts and scientific discovery. *Kosmos* was a great popular success and was subsequently translated into many European languages. It was one of the last great attempts at a general survey of all scientific knowledge in the European intellectual tradition, citing over nine thousand sources in total.

In addition to preparatory work on this wide-ranging survey and the publication of his detailed travel journals, after returning from Latin America in 1804 Humboldt began to lay the foundations for the subjects of physical geography and meteorology, using the research he conducted during his extended journey. He published numerous specialized volumes within the sequence of travel journals, in which specific aspects of the expedition's scientific results were presented. These included an account of meteorological data in terms of isotherms and isobars, an analysis of the relation between physical geography and plant life (including the presentation of concepts such as plateau and the mean height of a summit), and an investigation into the role played by volcanic forces in the development of Earth's crust. He also studied various weather phenomena, including tropical storms and the relation between temperature and elevation above sea level, and discovered important geological features such as the igneous origins of some types of rock and the grouping of volcanoes in relation to subterranean fissures. His fame as an explorer was significant in his own lifetime, and he used this standing to promote scientific investigation in educational establishments and in ruling circles. He died in 1859.

WILHELM VON HUMBOLDT

The intellectual achievements of Wilhelm von Humboldt were significant, although sometimes overshadowed by those of his younger brother. If Alexander was the natural scientist of the Humboldt family, Wilhelm was the social scientist, specializing in the philosophy of language, political theory, and the philosophy of history. The encouragement and analysis of wide-ranging creative activity was a key theme running through much of his work. His most enduring contribution to the social sciences was to pioneer a modern approach to linguistic theory that conceived of language as a rule-governed system of communication, an approach that would receive renewed attention a century later in the work of Noam Chomsky. Humboldt emphasized the notion of language as a creative mental activity.

Wilhelm von Humboldt conducted detailed studies of aspects of particular languages, including Basque and the ancient Kawi language of Java, from which he distilled some insightful general observations. In consequence, he wrote *The Heterogeneity of Language and Its Influence on the Intellectual Development of Mankind* (published posthumously in 1836), in which he articulated the idea that the function of words was to embody meaning conditioned by the beliefs of a community. He treated the search for an "inner form" of languages as an important means of linguistic classification. Humboldt's approach to studying languages had two strands; the first searched for cultural diversity and the second focused on underlying and universal commonalities. Inspired in part by his brother's expedition to Latin America, he studied American Indian languages, seeing language as a key feature marking the emergence of humanity from nature. It was here that his linguistic philosophy connected to his other interests in the social sciences.

Humboldt's political theory emphasized the essential value of the individual and the proportional development of personal capacities to a complete and consistent whole, adopting a humanistic approach to the topic. Through a wide spectrum of experiences, voluntary associations and individual study, Humboldt recommended the activation of all the faculties that were latent within the human mind. In 1791 Humboldt published *On the Limits of State Action*, in which he defended an Enlightenment conception of individual liberty. In some ways, this work anticipated John Stuart Mill's approach to political freedom, emphasizing the limits of state power. In relation to the philosophy of history, Humboldt conceived of the historian's role as demonstrating the process of ideas becoming actualized in historical development, and here his views connected to some extent with the German idealist philosophers of the day. In particular he maintained a lifelong friendship and correspondence with Friedrich Schiller. Maintaining a teleological conception of the historical process, Humboldt saw the goal of history as the fulfillment of the idea through humanity's self-realization. He also published works on the moral character of human subjects as comparative anthropology, analyzed the ideas of specific philosophers on spiritual development and the divine, and translated classical Greek authors, including Aeschylus.

In the practical realm of state affairs, Humboldt served for a short time as Prussian minister of education (from 1809), yet he was generally critical of state control of education. He later served as a diplomat and ambassador in Vienna,

Rome, and London, and at the Congress of Prague in 1813 he was instrumental in convincing Austria to form an alliance with Prussia and Russia against France. However, he eventually became disillusioned with the direction of Prussian government policy and gave up public service in 1819 in order to concentrate on his numerous intellectual pursuits.

Wilhelm's death in 1835 had a profound effect on his brother Alexander, who honored Wilhelm's memory by publishing volumes of his linguistic and aesthetic writings. It is unlikely that any two brothers have before or since contributed so significantly to the development of modern European natural and social sciences.

See also **Darwin, Charles; Germany; Hegel, Georg Wilhelm Friedrich; Science and Technology.**

BIBLIOGRAPHY

De Terra, Helmut. *Humboldt: The Life and Times of Alexander von Humboldt, 1769–1859.* New York, 1955.

Humboldt, Alexander von. *Political Essay on the Kingdom of New Spain.* New York, 1811.

———. *Personal Narrative of Travels to the Equinoctial Regions of the New Continent.* London, 1814.

———. *Cosmos.* London, 1849–1871.

Humboldt, Wilhelm von. *On Language: The Diversity of Human Language-Structure and Its Influence on the Mental Development of Mankind.* Cambridge, U.K., 1988.

Sweet, Paul. *Wilhelm von Humboldt: A Biography.* Columbus, Ohio, 1978–1980.

VINCENT BARNETT

HUNDRED DAYS. After being forced to unconditionally abdicate on 6 April 1814, deposed Emperor Napoleon I left France for exile on the Mediterranean island of Elba. Restoration of the Bourbon regime followed when Austria, Russia, Prussia, and Great Britain placed the exiled Louis XVIII on the French throne. His subjects welcomed the time to recover from the bloody wars of the Revolutionary and Napoleonic eras that had cost millions of lives. The Bourbons offered the peace so desired by the French people, and the victorious powers believed that France's ancient ruling family would show its gratitude by being pliant in matters of foreign affairs. With France tired of war and a submissive ruler on its throne, the Allies believed that a peace based on sound principles could be concluded to restore the European balance.

Unfortunately for the well-intentioned but lackluster king, attempts to bolster his popularity by granting a liberal constitution failed because of deep-rooted popular suspicion of the Bourbons. Louis was despised. Among those groups most disaffected, the peasants feared the redistribution of land to compensate the nobles for land lost during the Revolution. Although the French government did not intend to comply with the resonant demands of this special interest group, the peasantry feared being betrayed by the Bourbons. Always a favorite among the peasants regardless of his crushing taxes and the wars that devoured their young, Napoleon became increasingly viewed as the guarantor of their land and thus of the Revolution.

Learning of the growing discontent in France, Napoleon escaped from Elba on 26 February 1815 in a great gamble to restore his empire. Escorted by one thousand soldiers, he landed in France near Antibes on 1 March. From Paris, Louis issued countless orders for Napoleon's arrest, but increasing numbers of soldiers joined their former emperor. Parisian mobs added to the king's discomfiture by rioting and posting placards calling for the death of the Bourbons. With Napoleon only one march away from the capital, the Bourbon court fled to Belgium. On the following evening, 20 March, Napoleon entered Paris, restored the empire, and began the Hundred Days: 20 March to 22 June 1815.

Napoleon found that the political climate had irrevocably changed, despite the popular support he received in Paris. In his absence, many former disciples had adopted the tenets of liberalism with its premium on constitutional government. Consequently, he failed to establish absolutist control over the government. In fact, a parliamentary system appeared to be the only means of establishing national unity. Yet the new era of political parties made it difficult to avoid alienating the various factions. Thus, when the new constitution formally established a parliamentary government on 23 April 1815, both leftists and conservatives felt slighted.

Napoleon's genius might well have enabled him to navigate these troubled waters had war not disturbed his work. By 1815 he was willing to accept being ruler of France rather than master of Europe. Despite his attempts to secure peace with the Allied powers, the Allies branded him "an Enemy and Disturber of the tranquility of the World." On 25 March, Austria, Russia, Prussia, and Great Britain each agreed to furnish an army of 150,000 men and not lay down arms "until Bonaparte shall have been put absolutely beyond the possibility of exciting disturbances and of renewing his attempts to seize the supreme power in France."

Following his decisive defeat at Waterloo on 18 June, the French legislature demanded his abdication; Napoleon conceded on 22 June. He left the capital and retired to his home of Malmaison as the French legislature carried on the war. As Allied armies converged on Paris, the former emperor offered his services to the French government as a mere general, but was rebuffed. To speed Napoleon out of the country, the French government placed at his disposal a frigate in the port of Rochefort. Hoping to reach the United States, Napoleon arrived in Rochefort on 3 July—the same day that Paris capitulated—only to find the port blockaded by a British fleet. Learning that Louis had returned to Paris on 8 July and issued orders for his arrest, Napoleon sought amnesty with the British, and even thought they might allow him to settle in Great Britain. The British dashed this hope by imprisoning him on the rocky island of St. Helena in the middle of the South Atlantic Ocean. By not executing the former emperor, as the Prussians desired, the British did not create a martyr for anti-Bourbonists to rally around. Far removed from Europe, Napoleon had no chance to repeat his escape from Elba. He died a prisoner on St. Helena on 5 May 1821.

See also **Napoleon; Restoration; Waterloo; Wellington, Duke of (Arthur Wellesley).**

BIBLIOGRAPHY

Primary Sources

Brett-James, A., comp., ed., and trans. *The Hundred Days: Napoleon's Last Campaign from Eyewitness Accounts.* London, 1964.

Secondary Sources

Chandler, David. *Waterloo: The Hundred Days.* London, 1980.

Schom, Alan. *One Hundred Days: Napoleon's Road to Waterloo.* New York, 1992.

MICHAEL V. LEGGIERE

HUSSERL, EDMUND (1859–1938), Austrian philosopher.

One of the most significant and prolific philosophers of the late nineteenth and mid-twentieth centuries, Edmund Gustav Albrecht Husserl is widely known for his development of several forms of phenomenology. As a student, Husserl attended Franz Brentano's (1838–1917) lectures on descriptive psychology or psychognosy at the University of Vienna, which inspired him to undertake his own intensive investigations in the introspective structural analysis of the contents of thought. Throughout his later period, Husserl explored the implications of these findings for a variety of traditional philosophical problems in logic, philosophy of mathematics, philosophical psychology, and philosophy of mind, metaphysics, and theory of knowledge.

Husserl was born in Prossnitz (Prostejov) in Moravia, which now is part of the Czech Republic and was then a garrison town of the Austrian Empire. He studied astronomy, physics, and mathematics at the Universities of Leipzig and Berlin with the famous mathematicians Karl Weierstrass (1815–1887) and Leopold Kronecker (1823–1891). He also attended lectures in philosophy by Wilhelm Wundt (1832–1920) and Tomas Garrigue Masaryk (1850–1937), a student of Brentano's. Husserl wrote his dissertation in mathematics at the University of Vienna with Leo Königsberger (1837–1921), who in turn had studied with Weierstrass, earning a doctorate in 1883 with the thesis *Beiträge zur Theorie der Variationsrechnung* (Contributions toward a theory of the calculus of variations). After 1884, Husserl began attending lectures by Brentano, and decided to devote his continued studies to philosophy. Changing venues again, this time to the University of Halle, Husserl wrote his *Habilitationsschrift* titled *Über den Begriff der Zahl* (On the concept of number) in 1887 with Carl Stumpf

(1848–1936), another former student of Brentano's. This work, reflecting Husserl's developing interests in logic and philosophy of mathematics from an intentionalist point of view, was revised as Husserl's first major publication, *Philosophie der Arithmetik: Psychologische und logische Untersuchungen* (Philosophy of arithmetic: psychological and logical investigations), appearing in 1891.

In this early phase of his philosophy, Husserl was under the influence of Brentano's thesis of the immanent intentionality of all psychological phenomena, according to which every thought intends an object that is literally contained within the thought. Some of his critics at the time misinterpreted his adoption of an intentionalist standpoint with respect to the origin of number concepts, seeing it as an objectionable form of psychologism. Gottlob Frege (1848–1925) in particular complained of Husserl's efforts to construe the nature of objective mathematical entities and relations in terms of subjective psychological factors. Although Husserl had been critical also of Frege's logicism—the effort to reduce all of mathematics to pure logic—as mere empty formalism, Frege's objections seem to have struck home at some deep level, and Husserl soon came to renounce his early efforts to explain mathematical concepts by appeal to Brentano's intentionalist theory of mind. In the foreword to the first edition of his major work, the *Logische Untersuchungen* (Logical investigations, 1900–1901), Husserl speaks of his "disastrous choice of terminology" in referring to the "psychological nature" of the collective combinations that constitute the conceptual foundations of arithmetic in his early theory. By the time of the second revised edition of this two-volume work in 1913, Husserl had undergone what many twenty-first-century thinkers lament while others celebrate as his transcendental turn. His philosophy from this time forward took on a more distinctively Kantian slant, meaning that he began to think of philosophy as directed toward the discovery of the presuppositions of experience that of necessity lie beyond what can be empirically known.

Also in 1913, Husserl published the three volumes of his *Ideen* (Ideas), in which he outlined the main principles of his phenomenology. For Husserl, Brentano first sowed the seed of *Ideen* in his lectures on descriptive psychology, which he also spoke of as *phenomenology*. Husserl explains his project as that of investigating the essential ideal structures of consciousness, which he proposes to do by means of the method of *epoché*. This word in its original Greek meaning signifies a pause or halting in the pursuit of an activity. The ancient Skeptics applied the term to a suspension of belief due to the difficulties of attaining certainty in knowledge. Husserl advances a similar interpretation that he refers to as "bracketing the natural attitude." He requires that phenomenology begin by suspending belief in the existence of objects corresponding to the contents of thoughts in order to investigate their structures independently of the existence or nonexistence of things. In his later Sorbonne lectures, the *Cartesian Meditations*, Husserl describes progressive stages of the *epoché*, leading to an increasingly more penetrating grasp of the underlying intentional structures of consciousness, culminating finally in the transcendental *epoché*. What Husserl claims to discover in the process is an infinitely receding series of time horizons involving the contents of psychological presentations, and concerning the potential for the thinking subject to act in response to what is perceived. As each horizon is attained another presents itself, posing an equally formidable purely descriptive phenomenological challenge. This led Husserl later in life to describe himself always as a beginner in philosophy, faced with a series of infinite tasks, as though nothing substantial had previously been achieved on which to build.

In his final years, Husserl concentrated on the problems of intersubjectivity, trying to understand how it is possible for different thinkers to be conscious of and refer in thought and language to the same object from a phenomenological standpoint. The natural attitude, with its assumption that the contents of consciousness correspond to real external things that are objectively causally interrelated as explained by empirical science and subject to natural scientific law, is once again the focus of Husserl's critical analysis, especially as it applies to psychology and sociology in his unfinished but powerfully insightful later work, *The Crisis of the European Sciences* (1936).

Although Husserl did not directly exert an influence on popular European culture, his pioneering studies in phenomenology were of crucial importance to his student Martin Heidegger (1889–1976) in his existential phenomenology and ontology or theory of being, and to Jean-Paul Sartre (1905–1980) and Maurice Merleau-Ponty (1908–1961) and their followers. Through these later writers, Husserl's impact eventually extended beyond academic philosophy to the modern tradition of existentialism in philosophy and literature.

See also **Brentano, Franz; Frege, Gottlob.**

BIBLIOGRAPHY

Primary Sources

Husserl, Edmund. *Husserliana: Edmund Husserl—Gesammelte Werke.* Dordrecht, 1950–. Definitive ongoing edition of Husserl's collected works in German.

———. *The Crisis of European Sciences and Transcendental Phenomenology.* Translated by David Carr. Evanston, Ill. 1970.

———. *Cartesian Meditations: An Introduction to Phenomenology.* Translated by Dorion Cairns. The Hague, 1977.

———. *Ideas Pertaining to a Pure Phenomenology and to a Phenomenological Philosophy.* Translated by Fred Kersten. The Hague, 1980–1982.

———. *Philosophy of Arithmetic: Psychological and Logical Investigations: With Supplementary Texts from 1887–1901.* Translated by Dallas Willard. Dordrecht, 2003.

Secondary Sources

Bell, David. *Husserl.* London, 1990. An introduction to Husserl's thought intended for beginning readers presupposing minimal prior familiarity with philosophy in the phenomenological tradition.

Carr, David. *Interpreting Husserl: Critical and Comparative Studies.* Dordrecht, 1987. Examination, among other interesting topics, of the concept of the transcendental ego in the later Husserl; explores the transitional periods in Husserl's thought throughout his career.

Rollinger, Robin D. *Husserl's Position in the School of Brentano.* Dordrecht, 1999. Well-documented treatment of Husserl's philosophy in relation to Brentano's empirical psychology, psychologism, and immanent intentionality thesis, within the broader Brentano school in descriptive psychology and intentionalist epistemology.

Smith, Barry, and David Woodruff Smith, eds. *The Cambridge Companion to Husserl.* Cambridge, U.K., 1995. Essays on Husserl's philosophy, including the theory of perception, knowledge, meaning and language, mer-

eology or theory of part-whole relations, and philosophy of mathematics.

Sokolowski, Robert, ed. *Edmund Husserl and the Phenomenological Tradition: Essays in Phenomenology.* Washington, D.C., 1988. Multiple facets of Husserl's phenomenology explored in a collection of essays; clear exposition of Husserl's theory of ideas and idea contents or *noemata.*

Spiegelberg, Herbert. *The Phenomenological Movement: A Historical Introduction.* Third revised and enlarged edition. The Hague, 1982. Classic detailed study of the historical roots of phenomenology; particularly valuable for understanding the dynamic personal and philosophical relation between Brentano and Husserl.

Zahavi, Dan. *Husserl's Phenomenology.* Stanford, Calif., 2003. Comprehensive discussion of Husserl's philosophy, with special emphasis on the topics of the phenomenology of internal time consciousness, body, intersubjectivity, and life-world.

DALE JACQUETTE

HUXLEY, THOMAS HENRY (1825–1895), British zoologist, education reformer.

Dubbed "Darwin's bulldog" for his combative role in the Victorian controversies over evolutionary theory, Thomas Huxley was a leading zoologist, popularizer, and education reformer. His writings, teaching, and administration helped to define the "man of science" as a public figure and to reshape the institutions of British science in the second half of the nineteenth century.

Huxley was born in Ealing, a small village west of London, in 1825. With only two years of formal education, he was apprenticed to general medical practitioners in Coventry and London's East End. At the age of twenty, he completed his first examination for a medical degree at University College. Lacking the financial means to continue his education, he entered the navy, where he gained an appointment as assistant surgeon on a survey ship. Huxley spent the next five years (1846–1851) pursuing natural history alongside his official duties, concentrating on marine invertebrates, such as *physalia*, the Portuguese man-of-war. His research had important implications for prevailing theories of alternation of generations and parthenogenesis, theories that he sought to overturn in part by a redefinition

Thomas Huxley, 1880. HIP/ART RESOURCE, NY

of the "individual" animal as composed of apparently independent parts of a complex life cycle. He also had ambitions that his meticulous comparative anatomy and physiology would lead to a substantial reordering of taxonomic groups.

Shortly after his return to England in 1851, Huxley was elected a fellow of the Royal Society of London and was awarded its royal medal the following year. But despite this high scientific reputation, he was unable to gain a position to sustain his zoological research. In extensive correspondence with his fiancée, who lived in Sydney, Australia, with her family, he expressed increasing dismay and bitterness at the lack of professional positions in science, a reflection, he judged, of a general lack of recognition for scientific work in Britain. Once he gained a foothold in the institutional establishment, Huxley devoted a great portion of his time and energy to the reform of scientific institutions and to increasing the status and authority of science in Britain.

SCIENTIFIC CAREER

In 1854 Huxley obtained a lectureship at the School of Mines, and an appointment as paleontol-

ogist to the Geological Survey, both jobs unexpectedly vacated by his chief mentor, Edward Forbes (1815–1854). These were comparatively new institutions, established by the government in the 1840s, and closely linked to Britain's growing industries and empire. Huxley moved quickly to the inner circles of metropolitan science. In the following year, he became Fullerian professor of the Royal Institution, and lecturer at St. Thomas's Hospital, London. Huxley also established himself in more public domains, giving evening lectures to "working men," and writing a regular column on science for the *Westminster Review*. Within these varied settings, Huxley developed a theory of morphological types, in which every living creature was conceived as a modification of a small number of forms. The theory had been especially well developed in Germany, where it was closely linked with embryological research, and Huxley followed leading German anatomists in arguing that members of a particular animal group each passed through a common series of embryological stages.

Huxley's reputation outside of specialist scientific circles arose through his combative role in the evolution debates of the 1860s. Despite his previous opposition to transmutation, and despite persistent reservations about the role of natural selection in modifying species, Huxley became an outspoken defender of Charles Darwin, and a popularizer of Darwinian theory, almost immediately after the publication of *Origin of Species* in 1859. He presented lively summaries of Darwin's views in a variety of popular forums. In a series of technical papers in paleontology, comparative anatomy, and physical anthropology, he argued for the affinity of humans and apes, engaging in a protracted controversy with the comparative anatomist Richard Owen (1804–1892), who had placed humans in a distinct subclass based on perceived differences in brain anatomy. Sometimes Huxley used these more specialist debates as platforms for his wider campaigns of institutional and cultural reform, as in his famous clash with the bishop of Oxford, Samuel Wilberforce (1805–1873), at the 1860 meeting of the British Association.

INSTITUTIONAL AND CULTURAL REFORMS

The reforms that Huxley initiated as a teacher and administrator were of considerable consequence.

He persistently campaigned for the introduction of scientific subjects to English schools and universities, whose curricula had long been dominated by classical languages. As a member of the London school board, he used his considerable skills as a negotiator and arbitrator in advocating science as a part of nonsectarian religious and moral education. Another arena in which Huxley had particular success was in the establishment of laboratory methods of teaching for the life sciences. Using the resources of the government School of Mines, he initiated teacher training courses in biology, beginning in 1871 at a new facility in South Kensington. In so doing, he helped to shift the emphasis and authority in the life sciences to laboratory-based research, following the pattern already established in universities and institutes on the Continent.

In addition to his efforts to reform establish institutions of teaching and research, Huxley sought to expand the role of science in culture more generally. Through extensive public speaking and journal writing, he pursued a broad agenda as a social critic and authority on matters of politics and general welfare. His rhetorical powers were displayed to great effect in the Metaphysical Society, composed of many of Victorian England's most celebrated men of learning, and which featured short position papers followed by discussion. At the organizational meeting of this society in 1869, Huxley coined the term *agnosticism* to distinguish his own creed from those of others in the group, many of whom were clergymen. The term epitomized liberalist principles of free discussion, as well as the critical, candid, and disinterested manner Huxley sought to identify with scientific inquiry.

Huxley's efforts to pronounce scientifically on social and moral issues continued after his retirement from teaching and administration in 1885. He wrote long articles challenging the Genesis account of creation and the authenticity of miracles. He engaged in a series of highly political controversies over land nationalization, socialism, and Irish Home Rule, bringing aspects of Darwinian theory and racial anthropology, and principles of scientific method to bear on current affairs. That Huxley is far better known in the twenty-first century for his essays on politics, religion, and philosophy than for his vast body of technical papers in

zoology, geology, and anthropology is perhaps indicative of the success of his campaign to increase the prominence of science in general culture.

Huxley died on 29 June 1895, survived by Henrietta, whom he had married in 1855, after an engagement of nearly eight years. The couple had eight children, one of whom died in early childhood.

See also **Darwin, Charles; Evolution; Science and Technology.**

BIBLIOGRAPHY

Primary Sources

Foster, Michael, and E. Ray Lankester, eds. *The Scientific Memoirs of Thomas Henry Huxley.* 4 vols. and supplement. London, 1898–1902.

Huxley, Thomas. *Collected Essays.* 9 vols. London, 1893–1894.

Secondary Sources

Barr, Alan, ed. *Thomas Henry Huxley's Place in Science and Letters: Centenary Essays.* Athens, Ga., 1997.

Desmond, Adrian. *Huxley: From Devil's Disciple to Evolution's High Priest.* London, 1998.

Di Gregorio, Mario. *T. H. Huxley's Place in Natural Science.* New Haven, Conn., 1984.

White, Paul. *Thomas Huxley: Making the "Man of Science."* Cambridge, U.K., 2003.

PAUL WHITE

HUYSMANS, JORIS-KARL (1848–1907), French fin-de-siècle novelist and art critic.

Joris-Karl (Charles-Marie-Georges) Huysmans was the son of a Dutch painter and a French musician. During his life he never ceased to emphasize his parents' joint influence, which he felt was so important to him and that had made him, as he said in his 1885 autobiography, "an inexplicable amalgam of a Parisian aesthete and a Dutch painter." This mixture appeared for the first time in 1874 when Huysmans published a collection of prose poems entitled *Le Drageoir à épices* (A dish of spices), a volume bearing the name of Jorris-Karl Huÿsmans, a name he thought to be the Dutch form of Charles-Georges Huysmans. Although *Le*

Drageoir is a "skillfully cut jewel" as French poet Theodore de Banville described it, the volume aroused hardly any interest.

Huysmans had more success with *Marthe, histoire d'une fille* (1876; *Marthe*), a novel published outside of France, in Brussels, because of its subject matter: the relationship between a young journalist and a prostitute. The naturalist writer Émile Zola, for example, complimented the young writer, saying that he was one of the novelists of the future. With that, a friendship was born. Joris-Karl Huysmans, together with other admirers such as fellow writers Paul Alexis, Henry Céard, Léon Hennique, and Guy de Maupassant, visited Zola every week. But Huysmans never became a true naturalist disciple, his style being, as writer Jean Richepin noted in 1880, far more captivating, idiosyncratic, and colorful than Zola's "pale prose."

Les Soeurs Vatard (1879; The Vatard sisters), *En Ménage* (1881; Living together), and *A Vau-l'eau* (1882; *With the Flow*) already suggest the direction in which Huysmans's style would develop, a style indebted to, but at the same time different from, the one defined in the naturalists' credo. Huysmans's was a pessimistic and misogynistic literature, telling of the misery of life, forcing men to flee fin-de-siècle society and seek refuge from the world.

A Rebours (*Against Nature*), the breviary of the decadent movement that was published in 1884, is often considered to mark a decisive moment in the career of Joris-Karl Huysmans. It was, as Stéphane Mallarmé put it, "the one book that had to be written," a book that scorned conventional aesthetic (naturalist) principles and that became a model for a new generation of decadent writers. However Huysmans sought no disciples and rejected the role as a founder of a literary movement. Thus he described himself in his diary as a "Mère Cigogne n'accouchant que de fausses couches," a fertile child-bearer who produced only miscarriages. But *A Rebours* also continued on the same pessimistic course—in *A Rebours* Huysmans expressed, as he told his friend and fellow writer Léon Bloy, a "haine du siècle" (a hatred for his century)—while adding a more supernatural, spiritual dimension, which he saw as absent from naturalist writings.

En Rade (1887; *Becalmed*), often considered to be an "oeuvre à part" (a separate work), and *Là-Bas* (1891; *The Damned*), also are novels in which Huysmans continued his quest for a more spiritual approach to literature, exploring the world of dreams in *En Rade* and the satanic milieu in *Là-Bas*. It is also at this point that Huysmans's literature and personal life became more and more intertwined. Therefore, Huysmans's conversion to Catholicism in 1892 could be seen as a direct result of his literary research, first into satanism and then into Catholicism. Huysmans's fascination with these topics gradually led to his embrace of religion.

The literary account of Huysmans's conversion is told in *En Route* (1895), which was an immediate sales success and motivated other conversions in and outside the country (although some people found his conversion to be highly suspect). From that moment on religion constituted an exclusive theme in Huysmans's writings as well as his personal life. In 1898, shortly after the publication of *La Cathédrale* (*The Cathedral*), a celebration of the cathedral of Chartres and a commentary on Christian symbolism, Huysmans retired from the civil service, where he had worked for more than thirty years, and retreated to Ligugé, near the Benedictine monastery, to live as an oblate. Huysmans's refuge in this "oasis," as he called it in his diary, lasted only for two and a half years. The expulsion of the monks in 1901 (due to the new Law on Associations) forced him go back to Paris. *L'Oblat* (*The Oblate of Saint Benedict*), published in 1903, is based on Huysmans's experiences in Ligugé, telling the story of a French religious community at the beginning of the century.

Meanwhile, Huysmans had also published the hagiography of a Dutch saint, *Sainte Lydwine de Schiedam* (1900; Saint Lydwine of Schiedam), and had become the first president of the Goncourt Academy. But slowly his health problems took over his life, forcing him to stay indoors and travel less. One of his last trips led him to Lourdes; Huysmans's experiences there are recounted in the last book published during his lifetime, *Les Foules de Lourdes* (1906; The crowds of Lourdes). Shortly after having been promoted to the rank of Officier de la Légion d'honneur, Huysmans died on 12 May 1907 of complications of mouth cancer.

Huysmans may still be known for his celebrated decadent masterpiece, *A Rebours,* yet his reputation continues to grow as readers discover his charting the decline of naturalism and the dramatic development of one man's religious faith.

See also **Fin de Siècle; Realism and Naturalism; Symbolism.**

BIBLIOGRAPHY

Baldick, Robert. *The Life of J.-K. Huysmans.* Oxford, U.K., 1955

Bertrand, Jean-Pierre, Sylvie Duran and Françoise Grauby, eds. *Huysmans, à côté et au-delà.* Louvain and Paris, 2001.

Bonnet, Gilles. *L'Ecriture comique de J.-K. Huysmans.* Paris, 2003.

Borie, Jean. *Huysmans. Le Diable, le célibataire et Dieu.* Paris, 1991.

Buvik, Per. *La luxure et la pureté: essai sur l'œuvre de J.-K. Huysmans.* Oslo and Paris, 1989.

Cogny, Pierre. *J.-K. Huysmans à la recherche de l'unité.* Paris, 1953

Lloyd, Cristopher. *J.-K. Huysmans and the Fin-de-siècle Novel.* Edinburgh, 1991.

Smeets, Marc. *Huysmans l'inchangé. Histoire d'une conversion.* Amsterdam and New York, 2003.

Smeets, Marc, ed. *Joris-Karl Huysmans. CRIN 42.* Amsterdam and New York, 2003.

Ziegler, Robert. *The Mirror of Divinity. The World and Creation in J.-K. Huysmans.* Newark, N.J., 2004.

MARC SMEETS